The **Rough Guide** to

South India

written and researched by

David Abram, Nick Edwards
and Mike Ford

GUIDES

NEW YORK · LONDON · DELHI

www.roughguides.com

Contents

The colonial legacy
colour section following
p.312

Prayers in stone
colour section following
p.600

◄◄ Mosque and fishing boats at Vizhinjam ◄ *Kudamattom* ritual, Kerala

4

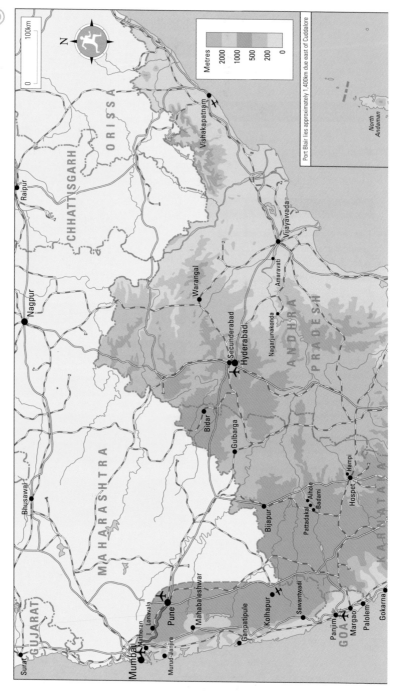

N

0   100km

Metres
2000
1000
500
200
0

Port Blair lies approximately 1,400km due east of Cuddalore

GUJARAT

Surat

Bhusawal

Nagpur

Raipur

CHHATTISGARH

ORISSA

MAHARASHTRA

Mumbai

Matheran

Murud-Janjira

Lonavala

Pune

Mahabaleshwar

Ganpatipule

Kolhapur

Sawantwadi

Panjim

GOA

Margao

Palolem

Gokarna

Hospet

Hampi

Pattadakal

Aihole

Badami

Bijapur

Gulbarga

Bidar

KARNATAKA

Warangal

Secunderabad

Hyderabad

Nagarjunakonda

ANDHRA PRADESH

Amaravati

Vijayawada

Vishakapatnam

North Andaman

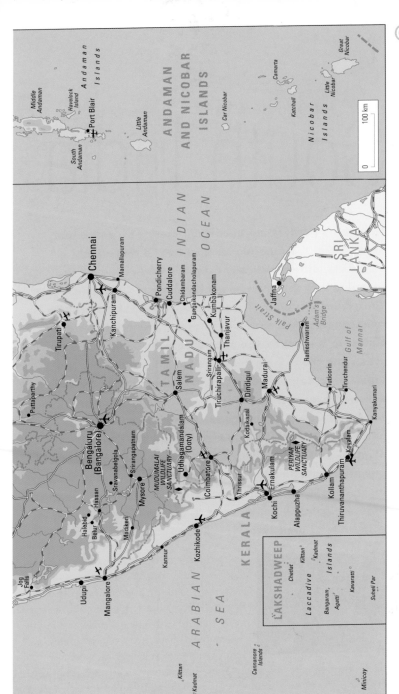

See inset map below for continuation (at same scale)

Introduction to
South India

Though its borders are uncertain, there's no doubt that South India, the tapering tropical half of this mighty peninsula, differs radically from the landlocked North. Stepping into the greenhouse humidity of Chennai or Thiruvananthapuram (Trivandrum), you enter a world far removed from the muted hues of the great Indian river plains. In the South, the coconut groves seem a deeper green and the rice paddies positively luminescent, the faces are a darker brown and the vermilion caste marks smeared over them arrestingly red. The region's heavy rainfall means that lush paddy fields and palm groves patchwork the volcanic soils during all but the hottest months. And under a sun whose rays feel concentrated by a giant magnifying glass, the ubiquitous colours of South India – of silk saris, shimmering classical dance costumes, roadside political posters and frangipani flowers – radiate with a life of their own.

South India's three mightiest rivers – the Godavari, the Krishna and the Cauvery (Kaveri) – and their countless tributaries, flow east across a low, fertile alluvial basin that has been inhabited as long as anywhere in the Subcontinent. Separated from the prehistoric Indus valley civilizations of the northwest by tracts of barren hills, the earliest South Indian societies are thought to have evolved independently of their northern cousins. Periodic attacks left their marks on the territory referred to in some of India's oldest inscriptions as **Dravidadesa**, "Land of the Dravidians". But none of the invading forces – the Mughals, Portuguese, French and British – were ever fully able to subjugate the South. As a result, traditions, languages and ways of life have endured intact here for more than two thousand years – a fact that lends to any journey into the region a unique resonance.

The persistence of a distinctly Dravidian culture in part accounts for the **regionalism** that has increasingly dominated the political and cultural life of the South since Independence in 1947. With the exception of Goa, a former Portuguese colony, and the Andaman and Nicobar Islands, the borders of the states covered in this book – Maharashtra, Karnataka, Kerala, Tamil Nadu and Andhra Pradesh – were drawn along linguistic lines. Each state boasts its own distinctive styles of music, dance, architecture and cuisine, not to mention religious cults and dress. Moreover, attempts by New Delhi to homogenize the country by imposing Hindi, the most widely spoken language in the North, as the medium of education and government, have consistently met with resistance, stimulating support for the regional parties whose larger-than-life leaders beam munificently from giant hoardings in every major town and city.

More pervasive even than the power of politics in South India is the influence of **religion**, which, despite the country's resolutely secular constitution, still permeates every aspect of life. Of the four major faiths, **Hinduism** is by far the most prevalent, practised by around eighty percent of the population. If the sacred peaks of the Himalayas are Hinduism's head, and the Ganges its main artery, then the temple complexes of the South are its spiritual heart and soul. Soaring high above every urban skyline, their colossal towers are emblematic of the awe with which the deities enshrined inside them have

7

▼ Sabhanayaka Nataraja Temple detail, Chidambaram

been held for centuries. Some, like the sea-washed temple at Tiruchendur in Tamil Nadu, are thought to be as old as human speech itself; others, such as the Sabarimala forest shrine in Kerala, are less ancient, but attract greater numbers of pilgrims than even Mecca. For foreign visitors, however, the most extraordinary of all have to be the colossal Chola shrines of Tamil Nadu. Joining the crowds that stream through Chidambaram's Sabhanayaka Nataraja temple or Shri Ramalingeshwara in Rameshwaram will take you to the very taproot of the world's last surviving classical culture, some of whose hymns, prayers and rites predate the Egyptian pyramids.

By comparison, **Islam**, South India's second religion, is a fledgling faith, first introduced by Arab traders along the coast in the twelfth century. Later, offshoots of the Muslim dynasties that ruled the North carved out feudal kingdoms beyond the Godavari, establishing a band of Islamic culture across the middle of the Deccan plateau. Other elements in the great South Indian melting pot include a dozen

> If the sacred peaks of the Himalayas are Hinduism's head... then the temple complexes of the South are its spiritual heart and soul.

or more denominations of **Christianity**, ranging from the ancient Syrian Orthodoxy believed to have been introduced by the apostle St Thomas, to the Roman Catholicism of Old Goa's Portuguese Jesuits. The region also harbours sites sacred to **Jains**, followers of the prophet Mahavira, a contemporary of Buddha, while there are a couple of ancient **Buddhist** sites in Andhra Pradesh and a thriving Tibetan community in southern Karnataka. Finally, in Kochi, Kerala, a vestigial population of **Jews** is all that remains of a once thriving mercantile community.

Since Independence, these diverse groups have coexisted more or less peacefully, rarely succumbing to the waves of communal blood-letting that have often blighted life in the northern cities. The last decade or so has seen a dramatic rise in **caste violence**, however. The age-old hierarchy introduced by the Aryans more than three thousand years ago still forms the backbone of South Indian society, crossing all religious and ethnic divides. But recent political reforms have enabled members of disadvantaged minorities to claim a fairer share of government jobs and university places, as well as political posts, and this has generated widespread resentment, strengthening the very divisions positive discrimination was intended to dissolve.

South India, though, remains one of the most relaxed and congenial parts of Asia to explore. It is also among the easiest. In all

Meals Ready

Many people come to India expecting the rich, meaty cuisine served up in British curry houses, but the reality turns out to be a lot more exciting: vegetarians, in particular, will find southern cooking a delight. Wander into almost any restaurant or canteen displaying a "Meals Ready" sign, and you'll have a tin tray with little cups, or a fresh green banana leaf, spread in front of you. In (or on) to this, legions of busy waiters will spoon a variety of rice, fresh vegetables and bean preparations, dhals, breads, yoghurt, pickles, poppadums and sauces, each flavoured with a different blend of spices, lime juice, coconut milk and sour mango. And, at the first sign that you're making any headway with this bewildering quantity of food, they'll slop another ladleful on.

Each region has its own distinctive style of set leaf or plate meal; the one thing they have in common is that they'll fill you to bursting point and cost next to nothing. For the ultimate "Meals Ready" experience, head for any branch of *Saravana Bhavan* in Chennai (see p.520), *Fry's Village Restaurant* in Kochi (see p.460), or just about anywhere that's doing a brisk trade.

▲ Oyster-shell window, Fontainhas, Panjim

9

Masala movies

Emblematic of modern India at its most highly charged and lurid are the huge, hand-painted hoardings that tower over city intersections. Featuring blood-splattered macho men, curvaceous heroines in various states of distress (and undress), chubby, bulging-eyed bad guys and explosions a-plenty, they give you a pretty good taste of the kind of movies churned out by the record-beating film industries of Mumbai and Chennai. Whether in Hindi, Tamil or another Dravidian language, all follow formulaic hero-gets-the-girl plots, interrupted at frequent intervals by sweeping song-and-dance sequences whose ubiquitous soundtracks crackle out of hi-fis from Pune to Pondicherry (Puducherry). Catch the latest box-office smash at one of the big-city cinema houses, primed by our background accounts on Bollywood (p.143) and the Tamil film industry (p.514).

but the remotest districts, accommodation is plentiful, generally clean and inexpensive by Western standards. Freshly cooked, nutritious food is nearly always available. Getting around is usually straightforward, although the sheer size and problematic geography of the South means journeys can be long. The region's extensive rail network moves vast numbers of people at all times of the day and night, and if a train isn't heading where you want to go, a bus almost certainly will be. Furthermore, the widespread use of English makes communication relatively easy. South Indians are the most garrulous and inquisitive of travellers, and train rides are always enlivened by conversations that invariably begin with the refrain of "Coming from?" or "Your native place?"

The extent to which you enjoy travelling in South India will probably depend less on your luck with hotels, restaurants and transport than your reaction to the country itself. Many people expect some kind of exotic time warp, and are surprised to find a consumer culture that's as unashamedly materialistic as anywhere. It is a credit to the South Indians' legendary capacity for assimilating new ideas, however, that the modern and traditional thrive side by side. Walking through central Bengaluru (formerly Bangalore), you could brush shoulders with a mobile-toting software programmer one moment and a trident-wielding ascetic the next, while rickety bicycles mingle with Japanese luxury cars. There are, of course, the usual travel hassles: interminable queues, packed buses and constant encroachments on your personal space. Yet, just when your nerves feel stretched to breaking point, South India always offers something that makes the effort worthwhile: a glimpse of a wild elephant from a train window; a sumptuous vegetarian meal delicately arranged on a fresh banana leaf; or a hint of fragrant cardamom in your tea after an all-night *kathakali* recital.

Where to go

South India's boundaries vary according to whom you're talking to: while some regard the River Krishna, the upper limit of India's last Hindu empire, as the real north–south divide, others place the Sub-continent's main cultural fault line at the River Godavari or, further north still, at the Vindhya Hills, the barrier of arid table-topped mountains bounding the Ganges Basin. In this guide we've started with **Mumbai**, a hot, congested city which is the arrival point for most international flights. Mumbai gets a pretty bad press, and most people pass straight through, but those who stay find themselves witness to the reality of modern-day India, from the deprivations of the city's slum-dwellings to the glitz and glamour of Bollywood movies. Though it's not culturally or linguistically part of the South, we've also included the southern part of **Maharashtra** state for

▲ Commuters at Churchgate Station, Mumbai

Teyyattam

From late October to May, archaic ritual dances known as *teyyattam* take place in over 400 villages and temples along the north Malabar coast. Performances often last all night, and provide a spectacular way of discovering the traditions that lie at the heart of Kerala. Each community nurtures an allegiance to a popular deity; the body and expression of the dancer, the *theyyam*, becomes a vessel for the deity to connect with their devotees. According to tradition, a *theyyam* must come from a low-caste family, but while they perform, their humble status is eliminated and social equality reigns. The *theyyam* starts to learn the art when he is 9 years old and will, for the next eight years, receive training in dance, martial arts and massage. Some *theyyam* are required to dance deft steps while wearing a headdress (*mudi*) almost twice their size; there are also particularly rare and dangerous *teyyattam* where the dancer dons a headdress the height of a coconut tree. For more on *teyyattam*, and where to track it down, see pp.491 & 791.

those travellers making way overland along the **Konkan Coast** to Goa or Karnataka.

The other major gateway (though there are now several other points of entry) is **Chennai**, capital of **Tamil Nadu**, in the deep South, which is a slightly less stressful place to start your trip. Although it's another major metropolis bursting at the seams, hidden under its surface are artful gems such as regular public performances of classical music and dance. With regular flights and ship departures to Port Blair, Chennai is also the major springboard for the **Andaman Islands**, a remote archipelago ringed by coral reefs and crystal-clear seas, over 1000km east of the mainland in the Bay of Bengal.

The majority of visitors' first stop after Chennai is **Mamallapuram**, an ancient port littered with weatherworn sculpture sites, including the famous Shore temple. To get right off the beaten track you only have to head inland to **Kanchipuram**, whose innumerable Hindu shrines span the golden age of the illustrious Chola kingdom, or to **Tiruvannamalai**, where one of the region's massive temple complexes rises dramatically from the base of a sacred mountain, site of countless ashrams and meditation caves. Back on the coast, the former French colony of **Pondicherry** (now Puducherry) retains a distinctly Gallic feel, particularly in its restaurants, where you can order *coq au vin* and a bottle of Burgundy before a stroll along the promenade. The Cauvery (Kaveri) Delta, further south, harbours astonishing crops of monuments, some of the most impressive of which are around **Thanjavur** (Tanjore), the Cholas' former capital, dominated by the awesome Brihadishwara temple. You could profitably spend days exploring the town's watery hinterland, hunting out bronze-casting villages, crumbling ruins and other forgotten sacred sites among the web of rivers and irrigation canals. Most travellers press on south to **Madurai**, the region's most atmospherically charged city, where the mighty Meenakshi-Sundareshwar temple presides over a quintessentially Tamil swirl of life.

The two other most compelling destinations in Tamil Nadu are the island of **Rameshwaram**, whose main temple features a vast enclosure of pillared corridors, and **Kanyakumari**, the auspicious southernmost tip of India, where the Bay of Bengal, Indian Ocean and Arabian Sea flow together. The dark shadows visible on the horizon from here mark the start of the **southern and western Ghats**, which stretch for more than 1000km in a virtually unbroken chain all the way to Mumbai, forming a sheer barrier between Tamil Nadu and neighbouring Kerala. Covered in immense forests and windswept grasslands, the mountains rise to the highest peaks in peninsular India, with sides sculpted by tea terraces, coffee plantations and cardamom groves. The hill stations of **Udhagamandalam** (Ootacamund, or Ooty as it's still better known) and **Kodaikanal**, established by India's former colonial rulers as retreats from the summer heat of the plains, attract hordes of Indian visitors in the run-up to the rains, but see plenty of foreign tourist traffic during the winter, too.

Heading north, a string of smaller former dynastic capitals punctuate the journey across the eastern edge of the Deccan plateau to **Hyderabad**, capital of **Andhra Pradesh**, whose principal landmarks are the Charminar and

▶ Women on Gokarna beach

Golconda fort. Andhra's other attractions, by contrast, lie much further off the beaten track. Comparatively few Western visitors ever reach them, with the exception of **Puttaparthy**, the ashram of India's most famous living saint, Sai Baba, and **Tirupati**, whose temple

▼ Sravanabelgola

receives more pilgrims than anywhere else on earth and is an essential stop for all Indians, especially followers of Vishnu.

West of Tamil Nadu, neigbouring **Kerala**'s appeal lies less in its religious monuments, many of which remain off-limits to non-Hindus, than its infectiously easy-going, tropical ambience. Covering a long thin coastal strip backed by a steep wall of hills, this is the wettest and most densely populated state in the South. It is also the most distinctive, with a culture that sets it squarely apart. Its ritualized theatre (Kathakali), faintly Southeast Asian architecture and ubiquitous communist graffiti (Kerala was the first place in the world to gain a democratically elected communist government) are perhaps the most visual expressions of this difference. But spend

> **Modern and traditional thrive side by side. Walking through central Bengaluru (formerly Bangalore), you could brush shoulders with a mobile-toting software programmer one moment and a trident-wielding ascetic the next.**

a couple of days exploring the spicy backstreets of old **Kochi** (Cochin), the jungles of the **Cardamom Hills** around the Periyar Wildlife Sanctuary or the hidden aquatic world of the coastal **backwaters**, and you'll see why many travellers end up staying here a lot lon-

ger than they originally intended. If you're not pushed for time and find yourself crossing northern Kerala during the winter, set aside a few days to search for Teyyattam, a spectacular masked dance form unique to the villages around Kannur.

A short ride across the mountains takes you to **Mysore** in **Karnataka**, whose opulent maharaja's palace, colourful markets and comfortable southern California-like climate have made it among South India's most popular tourist destinations. **Bengaluru** (Bangalore), the hectic modern capital, is not one of the highlights of the state, which are for the main part scattered over a vast area of rolling, granite-boulder-strewn uplands. Most of the state's gems, such as the richly carved Hoysala temples of **Belur** and

Halebid, or the extraordinary Jain colossus at **Sravanabelgola**, are religious monuments. Amongst other extraordinary sights are the mausolea, mosques and Persian-style palaces of **Bijapur**, often dubbed the "Agra of the South". Almost unsurpassable, however, is the awesome scale and faded splendour of the Vijayanagar ruins at **Hampi**, on the River Tungabhadra. Until it was ransacked by a confederacy of Muslim sultanates in 1565, this was the magnificent capital of South India's last Hindu empire, which encompassed most of the peninsula.

Only one day's journey to the west, the palm-fringed, white-sand beaches of **Goa** offer a change of scenery from the rocky terrain of the Deccan. Succumbing to the hedonistic pleasures of warm seawater, constant sunshine and cheap drinks, many travellers find it hard to tear themselves away from the coast.

When to go

The relentless tropical sun aside, the source of South India's irrepressible fecundity lies in its high **rainfall**. Unlike the north of the country, which sees only a single deluge in the summer, most of peninsular India receives **two annual monsoons** – one sucked in from the Arabian Sea in the southwest, and the other on stormy northwesterly winds off the Bay of Bengal. The heaviest rains are reserved for the Western Ghats, a chain of mountains running parallel with the southwest coast. Cloaked for the most part in dense forest, these form a curtain that impedes the path of the first summer monsoon, which breaks in June and lasts through October. In a nutshell, you should, when planning a trip to South India, largely avoid the rainy seasons. The novelty of torrential downpours and the general mayhem that attend the annual deluges wears off very quickly. Road blockages, landslides and burst riverbanks can interrupt the best-laid travel

▼ Keralan backwaters

15

plans, and you will soon tire of the discomfort of being wet through for days on end; the widespread flooding is also none too healthy, emptying the sewers and polluting reservoirs. Broadly speaking, rule out the period between April and September, when in turn firstly two months of stifling heat and then the southwest monsoon grip the whole peninsula. From late October until April, the weather is perfect in

Karnataka and Goa, but less reliable in Kerala, where, by November, the "retreating", or northwest monsoon means constant grey skies and showers. Being on the eastern side of the mountains, Tamil Nadu gets even heavier rains at this time, as does coastal Andhra Pradesh. To enjoy the far south and the Andaman Islands at their best, come between January and March, before the heat starts to build up again.

Average temperatures and rainfall

	Jan	Feb	Mar	Apr	May	June	July	Aug	Sept	Oct	Nov	Dec
Bengaluru (Kar)												
Av daily max (°C)	28	31	33	34	33	30	28	29	28	28	27	27
Rainfall (mm)	4	14	6	37	119	65	93	95	129	195	46	16
Chennai (TN)												
Av daily max (°C)	29	31	33	35	38	37	35	35	34	32	29	28
Rainfall (mm)	24	7	15	25	52	53	83	124	118	267	309	139
Hyderabad (AP)												
Av daily max (°C)	29	31	35	37	39	34	30	29	30	30	29	28
Rainfall (mm)	2	11	13	24	30	107	165	147	163	71	25	5
Kochi (Ker)												
Av daily max (°C)	31	31	31	31	31	29	28	28	28	29	30	30
Rainfall (mm)	9	34	50	139	364	756	572	386	235	333	184	37
Madurai (TN)												
Av daily max (°C)	31	31	31	31	31	29	28	28	28	29	30	30
Rainfall (mm)	26	16	21	81	59	31	48	117	123	179	161	143
Mumbai (M)												
Av daily max (°C)	31	32	33	33	33	32	30	29	30	32	33	32
Rainfall (mm)	0	1	0	0	20	647	945	660	309	17	7	1
Panjim (Goa)												
Av daily max (°C)	31	32	32	33	33	31	29	29	29	31	33	33
Rainfall (mm)	2	0	4	17	18	580	892	341	277	122	20	37

28

things not to miss

It's not possible to see everything that South India has to offer in one trip – and we don't suggest you try. What follows is a selective taste of the region's highlights: outstanding buildings, natural wonders, spectacular festivals and unforgettable journeys. They're arranged in five colour-coded categories, which you can browse through to find the very best things to see and experience. All highlights have a page reference to take you straight into the guide, where you can find out more.

01 Hampi Page **335** • The great ruined capital of the Vijayanagar dynasty, its superb monuments scattered over boulder-strewn plains around the Tungabhadra River.

02 Mamallapuram Page **536** •
Popular fishing and stone-carving village, with magnificent boulder friezes and temples cut from solid rock.

04 Keralan ritual theatre
Pages **457** & **787** • Kerala is the place to experience *kathakali*, one among several flamboyant forms of ritual theatre unique to the state.

03 Sravanabelgola Page **298** • This mystical Jain colossus at Sravanabelgola forms the centrepiece of southern Karnataka's most atmospheric pilgrimage town.

05 Venkateshvara Temple, Tirumala Page **674** • The world's most visited religious site, attracting more pilgrims than Mecca

06 Golgumbaz tomb Page **355** • The finest of the many sublime Islamic monuments that litter the Deccan regions of Karnataka.

08 Elephanta Caves Page **136** • These ancient caves, cut from solid rock in Mumbai harbour, offer the perfect escape from the madness of the Maharashtrian capital.

09 Scuba diving Pages **71, 465** & **697** • Some of the richest, clearest sea water in the world lies off the Andaman Islands (in the Bay of Bengal) and Lakshadweep archipelago (in the Arabian Sea), offering wonderful diving opportunities.

07 Meenakshi Temple, Madurai Page **601** • One of South India's greatest temples, surmounted by soaring *gopuras* and home to a range of spectacular festivals.

10 Ayurvedic massage Pages **74** & **386** • Experience holistic Indian healthcare at its most indulgent with a traditional Ayurvedic massage at Kovalam, Varkala or a string of spa resorts in the hills.

12 **Feni** Page **57** • The ultimate tropical cocktail base, Goan *feni*, is distilled from coconut sap collected twice daily by teams of toddy tappers. Sample a drop of the hard stuff yourself at Palolem or Benaulim.

11 **Thanjavur** Page **580** • The mighty Brihadishwara is the behemoth of Tamil Nadu's great Chola shrines, still visited by streams of pilgrims every day.

13 **Chariot festivals** Pages **66** & **585** • Among the great spectacles of southern India are temple chariot (*rath*) festivals, such as this one at Thiruvarur in Tamil Nadu.

14 **Old Goa** Page **197** • Belfries and Baroque church facades loom over trees on the banks of the Mandovi, all that remains of a once-splendid colonial city.

16 **Golconda Fort** Page **659** • This dramatic fort, sitting on a hilltop just outside Hyderabad, was once the capital of the Qutb Shahi dynasty.

17 **Kalarippayattu** Page **377** • Kerala's unique martial art, practised in gyms throughout the state.

15 **The Nilgiri Blue Mountain Railway** Page **633** • The bone-shaking ride up to Ooty on one of Asia's last steam railways is a must for Raj-ophiles, and worth it for the views alone.

19 Elephants Pages **430** & **489** • Spot elephants in the wild in Kerala's Periyar, Muthanga and Tholpetty wildlife sanctuaries.

18 Drum orchestras Pages **369** & **782** • Ear-splitting Keralan drum orchestras are one of the key ingredients of Kerala's uniquely intense temple festivals.

20 Gokarna Page **321** • This temple town offers not just sacred sites but beautiful beaches popular with budget travellers fleeing the commercialism of nearby Goa.

21 Boating on the backwaters Page **416** • Hire a *kettu vallam* (rice barge) or take the local ferryboat through Kerala's Kuttanad backwater region – South India at its most luxuriant.

22 Jog Falls Page **320** • India's highest waterfall offers awesome views and refreshingly wet walks.

24 Sacred art Pages **427** & **762** • Vibrant murals, such as this sixteenth-century mural from Mahadeva temple in Ettumanur, form part of the South's rich repertoire of sacred art.

23 Tamil sculpture Pages **573** & **757** • The great Tamil shrines of the Cauvery (Kaveri) Delta writhe with sensuous stone sculpture, such as this bas-relief of Shiva and Parvati at Gangaikondacholapuram.

25 Seafood curry Pages **51** & **52** • Coastal cuisine has been elevated to an art form in parts of the South, notably in Goa, Mangalore and northern Kerala's Malabar region.

26 Kochi Page **446** • Atmospheric former colonial settlement, suffused with contrasting Portuguese, Dutch, British and Keralan influences.

27 Heritage hotels Page **46** •Sample the refined architecture of Goa and Kerala in homestays and guesthouses converted from ancestral mansions.

28 Palolem beach Page **247** • Far from a secret, but still breathtakingly beautiful despite the hordes who winter here.

Basics

Basics

Getting there

Most visitors to South India fly into either of the major international gateways, Mumbai (Bombay) or Chennai (Madras). Non-stop flights from London reach Mumbai in just nine hours and Chennai in ten hours. Other options include flying to Bengaluru (formerly Bangalore) or Thiruvananthapuram. North America is on the opposite side of the globe and journeys will involve at least one change of plane. There are direct flights with the national carriers of Australia and South Africa, though most travellers from the southern hemisphere change planes en route.

Airfares worldwide always depend on the **season**, with the highest being from roughly November to March, when the weather in South India is best; fares drop during the shoulder seasons – April to May and August to early October – and you'll get the best prices during the low season, June and July. Fares peak in November, around Diwali, as Indian emigrants travelling home for holidays with their families create a surge in demand.

Charter flights may be cheaper than anything available on a scheduled service, though departure dates are fixed and withdrawal penalties are high. For destinations such as Goa and Kerala, you may even find it cheaper to pick up a bargain **package deal** from a travel agent, and then find your own accommodation when you get there. Indian law prohibits the sale of flight-only tickets by charter companies, but operators sometimes get around this by tacking budget accommodation to their tickets, which (if it exists at all) travellers ditch on arrival. Note also that charter tickets to India are not allowed to cover more than 28 days. If you wish to stay in the country for longer than that, you have to take a scheduled flight. Nor is it possible to fly in on a charter and out on a scheduled flight, or vice versa.

Many **tour operators** run trips to India, offering activities such as trekking and safaris, as well as sightseeing and sunbathing. Specialist minority-interest tours range from steam locomotives and textiles to religion, food and wildlife. In addition, many companies will arrange tailor-made tours, and can help you plan your own itinerary. However, sightseeing tours can often isolate you from the country, shutting you off in air-conditioned hotels and buses, and are generally more expensive than organizing everything independently. For a list of operators running tours to India. See p.31.

Finally, if India is only one stop on a longer journey, you might want to consider buying a **Round-the-World** (RTW) ticket: Mumbai, as well as Delhi, features on many "off-the-shelf" itineraries. Figure on £950/US$1850–£1500/US$2900 for a RTW ticket including India, open for one year.

Whatever your route to South India, give some thought to your arrival time. Cheaper flights tend to land in the middle of night and by shelling out a little extra you could get a far more convenient schedule.

Flights from the UK and Ireland

It takes around nine to ten hours to fly **from the UK** direct to South India, with Mumbai being both the nearest and cheapest port of entry. British Airways, Jet Airways and Air India all offer direct services, with Chennai, Bengaluru (Bangalore), Thiruvananthapuram and Kochi alternative points of access. Direct flights start at £410 to Mumbai with BA, rising to £540 in high season. Fares are a little more on Air India or Jet.

Other airlines are likely to route passengers through their hub city on the way, which can double the total travelling time, so by and large you get what you pay for. Qatar Airways are now a major carrier, with a rapidly expanding network and amazingly low fares (from as low as £250 to Mumbai), routed through their hub, Doha. Comfortable, though more expensive, non-direct options include SriLankan Airlines and Emirates. Some Eastern European and Central Asian carriers also offer rock-bottom fares, but you'll usually find this means longer waits for connecting flights and less sociable departure and arrival times – sometimes in the middle of the night.

Charter flights and **package tours** to Goa can be found for as little as £250 during low season but cost a lot more over Christmas and the New Year, when you should expect to pay upwards of £1000. Though it's possible to fly to India from some of the UK's regional airports they tend to involve a stop at Heathrow and the add-ons are very expensive. Emirates fly to Dubai and onwards from Birmingham, Manchester and Glasgow.

There are no direct flights to South India **from Ireland**. However, BA flies direct to Mumbai from London, and several carriers, including Alitalia, Lufthansa and Royal Jordanian, fly there from Dublin, Cork or Shannon via their home capitals. Discounted fares hover at €600–750.

Flights from the US and Canada

Whether you fly **from the US and Canada** via Europe (from the East Coast) or over the Pacific (from the West Coast), it's a long haul, involving one or more intermediate stops. Air India and Jet Airways both fly to Mumbai direct from New York, but you'll arrive fresher and less jet-lagged if you stop over for a few days somewhere en route. Agents will often break the journey into two sections anyway, which allows a wider choice of carriers for the transatlantic (or trans-Pacific) leg

From the East Coast, you'll stop over somewhere in Europe (most often London), the Gulf, or both. Figure on at least eighteen hours' total travel time. Prices are most competitive out of New York, where the cheapest low-season consolidated fares to Mumbai hover around US$1250 (rising to US$1600 in high season). From Washington or Miami, figure on US$1600 in low season, US$1850 in high season; from Chicago, US$1600/2000; and from Dallas/Fort Worth, US$1800/3000.

From the West Coast, it works out slightly quicker to fly west rather than east – a

minimum of 22 hours' total travel time – and there may not be much difference in price. From Los Angeles or San Francisco you're looking at a minimum of US$1300 to fly to Mumbai in low season, and up to US$1700 in high season.

The only direct flight **from Canada** to India is from Vancouver to Delhi on Air Canada, which takes around twenty hours. All other carriers, such as KLM/Northwest Airlines, fly via their home base, which involves a change of plane and longer flight times. Typical discounted low and high season fares to Mumbai from Montreal, Toronto and Vancouver are Can$2000/2600.

Flights from Australia, New Zealand and South Africa

Flying from Australia or New Zealand, the main (and cheapest) South Indian gateway city is Chennai, with Mumbai not far behind. Only Qantas fly direct **from Australia** to India, with flights from both Sydney and Melbourne to Mumbai; expect to pay around Aus$1900. Most travellers however make at least one change of plane in a South or Southeast Asian hub city: flights with carriers such as SriLankan Airlines, Singapore Airlines and Malaysia Airlines are considerably cheaper at around Aus$1500. However, there is a huge choice of airlines flying to the region, and in order to get the best price most agents will combine two or more carriers. Because of higher demand, the best-value tickets are generally from Australia's east coast.

From New Zealand, the cheapest fares to India are in the NZ$2000–2250 range if you depart from Auckland; add on approximately NZ$150 for flights from Wellington or Christchurch. There are no direct flights, and most travellers change in one of the major Australian cities or in Hong Kong.

From South Africa you can fly direct to Mumbai from Johannesburg with South African Airlines from around ZAR4000; flying time is approximately 8 hours 30 minutes. Add another ZAR800 for flights from Cape Town or Durban. You might also consider flying indirect via the Gulf, which will be cheaper.

RTW fares from all three countries can take in India; tickets stopping in Mumbai are

Fly less – stay longer! Travel and climate change

Climate change is the single biggest issue facing our planet. It is caused by a build-up in the atmosphere of carbon dioxide and other greenhouse gases, which are emitted by many sources – including planes. Already, flights account for around three to four percent of human-induced global warming: that figure may sound small, but it is rising year on year and threatens to counteract the progress made by reducing greenhouse emissions in other areas.

Rough Guides regard travel, overall, as a global benefit, and feel strongly that the advantages to developing economies are important, as are the opportunities for greater contact and awareness among peoples. But we all have a responsibility to limit our personal "carbon footprint". That means giving thought to how often we fly and what we can do to redress the harm that our trips create.

Flying and climate change

Pretty much every form of motorized travel generates CO_2, but planes are particularly bad offenders, releasing large volumes of greenhouse gases at altitudes where their impact is far more harmful. Flying also allows us to travel much further than we would contemplate doing by road or rail, so the emissions attributable to each passenger are greater. For example, one person taking a return flight between Europe and California produces the equivalent impact of 2.5 tonnes of CO_2 – similar to the yearly output of the average UK car.

Less harmful planes may evolve but it will be decades before they replace the current fleet – which could be too late for avoiding climate chaos. In the meantime, there are limited options for concerned travellers: to reduce the amount we travel by air (take fewer trips, stay longer!), to avoid night flights (when plane contrails trap heat from Earth but can't reflect sunlight back to space), and to make the trips we do take "climate neutral" via a carbon offset scheme.

Carbon offset schemes

Offset schemes run by ⓦ **climatecare.org**, ⓦ **carbonneutral.com** and others allow you to "neutralize" the greenhouse gases that you are responsible for releasing. Their websites have simple calculators that let you work out the impact of any flight. Once that's done, you can pay to fund projects that will reduce future carbon emissions by an equivalent amount (such the distribution of low-energy lightbulbs and cooking stoves in developing countries). Please take the time to visit our website and make your trip climate neutral.

ⓦ**www.roughguides.com/climatechange**

---

available with Thai Airways, Air New Zealand, Qantas and Malaysia Airlines, starting from around Aus$3500, NZ$4550 or ZAR12,500.

Airlines, agents and operators

Online booking

ⓦwww.expedia.co.uk (in UK), ⓦwww .expedia.com (in US), ⓦwww.expedia.ca (in Canada)
ⓦwww.lastminute.com (in UK)
ⓦwww.opodo.co.uk (in UK)
ⓦwww.orbitz.com (in US)

ⓦwww.travelocity.co.uk (in UK and Ireland), ⓦwww.travelocity.com (in US), ⓦwww .travelocity.ca (in Canada)
ⓦwww.zuji.com.au (in Australia), ⓦwww .zuji.co.nz (in NZ)

Airlines

Aeroflot US ☎1-888-686-4949, Canada ☎1-416/642-1653; ⓦwww.aeroflot.com.
Air Canada Canada ☎1-888-247-2262, ⓦwww .aircanada.com.
Air France UK ☎0870 142 4343, Republic of Ireland ☎01/605 0383, US ☎1-800-237-2747, Canada ☎1-800-667-2747; ⓦwww.airfrance.com.

Air India UK ☎020/8560 9996 or 8745 1000, US ☎1-800-223-7776, Canada ☎416/865-1033, Australia ☎02/9283 4020, New Zealand ☎09/631 5651; ⓦwww.airindia.com.

Air New Zealand Australia ☎13 24 76, New Zealand ☎0800 737000; ⓦwww.airnewzealand.com.

Alitalia UK ☎0870 544 8259, Republic of Ireland ☎01/677 5171, US ☎1-800-223-5730, Canada ☎1-800-361-8336; ⓦwww.alitalia.com.

All Nippon Airways US ☎1-800-235-9262, ⓦwww.anaskyweb.com.

Asiana Airlines US ☎1-800-227-4262, ⓦwww.flyasiana.com.

Biman Bangladesh Airlines UK ☎020/7629 0252, US ☎1-888-702-4626 or 1-212/808-4477; ⓦwww.bimanair.com.

British Airways UK ☎0870 850 9850, Republic of Ireland ☎1890 626 747, US and Canada ☎1-800-247-9297, Australia ☎1300 767 177, New Zealand ☎09/966 9777, South Africa ☎011/441 8600; ⓦwww.ba.com.

Cathay Pacific US ☎1-800-233-2742, Australia ☎131747, New Zealand ☎09/379 0861, South Africa ☎011/700 8930; ⓦwww.cathaypacific.com.

Czech Airlines US ☎1-800-223-2365, Canada ☎416/363-3174; ⓦwww.cza.cz.

Delta Air Lines US and Canada ☎1-800-221-1212, ⓦwww.delta.com.

Emirates UK ☎0870 243 2222, US ☎1-800-777-3999, Australia ☎03/9940 7807, New Zealand ☎09/308 3352, South Africa ☎0861/363 738; ⓦwww.emirates.com.

Etihad UK ☎020 8735 6700, US ☎0212/984 1878, Australia ☎02/9293 2855; South Africa ☎011/343 9140; ⓦwww.etihadaiirways.com.

Gulf Air UK ☎0870 777 1717, Republic of Ireland ☎0818 272 818,   US ☎1-888-359-4853, South Africa ☎011/268 8909; ⓦwww.gulfairco.com.

Jet Airways UK ☎020/8970 1525, US ☎1-800-225-522; ⓦwww.jetairways.com.

KLM Royal Dutch Airlines UK ☎0870 507 4074, Australia ☎1300 303 747, New Zealand ☎09/309 1782, South Africa ☎011/881 9600; ⓦwww.klm.com.

Kuwait Airways US ☎1-201-582-9200, ⓦwww.kuwait-airways.com.

Lufthansa UK ☎0870 837 7747, Republic of Ireland ☎01/844 5544, US ☎1-800-645-3880, Canada ☎1-800-563-5954, Australia ☎1300 655 727, New Zealand ☎09/303 1529, South Africa ☎011/325 1925; ⓦwww.lufthansa.com.

Malaysia Airlines US ☎1-800-552-9264, Australia ☎13 26 27, New Zealand ☎0800 777747; ⓦwww.malaysia-airlines.com.

Northwest/KLM Royal Dutch Airlines US and Canada ☎1-800-225-2525, ⓦwww.nwa.com.

Pakistan International Airlines UK ☎0800 587 1023, US ☎1-800-578-6786 or 1-212-760-8484; ⓦwww.piac.com.pk.

Qantas UK ☎0845 774 7767, Republic of Ireland ☎01/407 3278, US ☎1-800-227-4500, Australia ☎131313, New Zealand ☎09/357 8900, South Africa ☎011/441 8491; ⓦwww.quantas.com.

Qatar Airways UK ☎0870 770 4215, US ☎1-877-777 2827, Canada ☎1-888 366 5666, Australia ☎03/8676 6400, South Africa ☎021/936 3080; ⓦwww.qatarairways.com.

Royal Brunei Airlines UK ☎020/7584 6660, ⓦwww.bruneiair.com.

Royal Jordanian UK ☎020/7878 6300, US ☎1-800-223-0470, Canada ☎1-800-363-0711; ⓦwww.rja.com.jo.

Royal Nepal Airlines US ☎1-800-266-3725, ⓦwww.royalnepal.com.

Sahara Airlines UK ☎0870 127 1000, US ☎1-212/685-5456, Canada ☎1-416/966 4825; ⓦwww.airsahara.net.

Saudi Arabian Airlines UK ☎020/7798 9898, US ☎1-800-472-8342; ⓦwww.saudiairlines.com.

Singapore Airlines US ☎1-800-742-3333, Canada ☎1-800-663-3046, Australia ☎13 10 11 or 02/9350 0262, New Zealand ☎0800 808909; ⓦwww.singaporeair.com.

South African Airways South Africa ☎0861 359 722, ⓦwww.flysaa.com

SriLankan Airlines UK ☎020/8538 2001, US ☎1-877-915-2652, Canada ☎1-416/277-9000, Australia ☎02/9244 2234, New Zealand ☎09/308 3353; ⓦwww.srilankan.aero.

Swiss UK ☎0845 601 0956, US ☎1-877-359-7947, Australia ☎1300 724 666, New Zealand ☎09/977 2238; ⓦwww.swiss.com.

Thai Airways UK ☎0870 606 0911, US ☎1-212/949-8424, Canada ☎1-416/971-5181, Australia ☎1300 651960, New Zealand ☎09/377 3886; ⓦwww.thaiair.com.

United Airlines UK ☎0845 844 4777, US ☎1-800-241-6522; ⓦwww.united.com.

Virgin Atlantic Airways UK ☎0870 380 2007, US ☎1-800-821-5438; ⓦwww.virgin-atlantic.com.

Agents and operators

Abercrombie and Kent UK ☎0845 070 0600, ⓦwww.abercrombiekent.co.uk; Australia ☎1300 851800, New Zealand ☎0800 441638, ⓦwww.abercrombiekent.com.au. Upmarket sightseeing trips covering the main cities of the south, the hill stations including Ooty, and the backwaters.

Adventure Center US ☎1-800-228-8747, ⓦwww.adventurecenter.com. Trekking and cultural tours such as their "South Indian Encounter", a two-week tour which visits the major cities and the shore temples of Mamallapuram. They also offer a spice tour of Kerala which includes a backwater trip.

Andrew Brock/Coromandel UK ☎01572/821330, ⓦwww.coromandelabt.com. Run several tours, including a seven-day diving trip in the Andaman Islands, based on Havelock Island.

Audley Travel UK ☎01869/276222, ⓦwww.audleytravel.com. Privately guided, tailor-made itineraries using alternative accommodation including homestays, tents and heritage properties. The eleven-day "Classic Coromandel" tour visits sacred sites including Madurai, while the sixteen-day "Temple, Spices and Backwater" trip takes in several of Tamil Nadu's finest religious sites.

Bales UK ☎0845 057 1819, ⓦwww.balesworldwide.com. Escorted tours vary in length from 6 to 25 days and feature the main cities, hill stations, spice plantations and the backwaters.

Blazing Trails UK ☎01293/533338, ⓦwww.blazingtrailstours.com. Fifteen-day escorted motorcycle tours of Karnataka's tourist highlights on Enfields, starting and finishing in Goa. Also a fourteen-day Kerala tour.

Butterfield & Robinson US ☎1-800-678-11147 or 1-866-551-9090, ⓦwww.butterfield.com. Bespoke tours, with an emphasis on walking and cycling: they provide their own uniquely designed bicycles. Also run a six-day spice plantation tour in Kerala.

Classic Oriental Tours Australia ☎1300 747400, ⓦwww.classicoriental.com.au. Wide choice of tours encompassing three-day city breaks, a seven-day Kerala tour and a 22-day itinerary which includes Periyar Wildlife Park.

Cox & Kings UK ☎020/7873 5000, ⓦwww.coxandkings.com. Wide range of five- to nine-day tours of South India. Each one has a fairly specific theme, such as hill stations, Kerala, Hyderabad and the Deccan and plantation tours.

Deccan Odyssey ⓦwww.deccan-odyssey-india.com. Luxury eight-day train tour of Maharashtra's highlights starting in Mumbai and visiting Goa, Pune and Aurangabad.

Discovery Initiatives UK ☎01285/643333 ⓦwww.discoveryinitiatives.co.uk. Wildlife specialists offering a twelve-day elephant study tour based around the parks of Mudumalai, Nagarhole and Bandipur.

ebookers UK ☎0800 082 3000, ⓦwww.ebookers.com; Republic of Ireland ☎01/488 3507, ⓦwww.ebookers.ie. Low fares on an extensive selection of scheduled flights and package deals.

Essential India UK ☎01225/868544, ⓦwww.essential-india.co.uk. A range of tours, from nine days to sixteen, covering Tamil Nadu, Kerala, Mumbai and Goa.

Exodus UK ☎0870 240 5550, ⓦwww.exodustravels.co.uk. Experienced specialists in small-group itineraries, treks and overland tours.

First Choice UK ☏ 0870 850 3999 (or ☏ 0870 757 2757 for flights only), ⓦ www.firstchoice.co.uk. Standard resort packages to Goa, at a range of prices.
Geographic Expeditions US ☏ 1-800-777-8183, ⓦ www.geoex.com. Remote mountain treks and unusual tours including sea kayaking in the Andamans.
Hayes & Jarvis UK ☏ 0870 366 1636, ⓦ www .hayesandjarvis.co.uk. Budget two-week sun breaks in Goan resort hotels.
High Places UK ☏ 0845 257 7500, ⓦ www .highplaces.co.uk. Biking and boating in Kerala.
Imaginative Traveller UK ☏ 0800 316 2717, ⓦ www.imaginative-traveller.com. A large range of South Indian tours, the longest of which – the 22-day "South India Adventure" – includes Kovalam, Madurai, Thekkady, Kodagu (Coorg), Hampi and ends in Goa. They also do a week-long tour of Goa, Hampi and Badami.
Jewel in the Crown UK ☏ 01293/533338, ⓦ www.jewelholidays.com. Established Goa and Kerala specialist, offering a wide range of holidays in both states; they also run motorcycle tours on Enfields.
JMC UK ☏ 0870 750 5711, ⓦ www.jmc.com. Owned by Thomas Cook and affiliated to the airline of the same name, this big firm offers a wide range of package holidays to Goa at competitive prices.
Kerala Connections UK ☏ 01892/722440, ⓦ www.keralaconnect.co.uk. South India specialists whose tours cover a wide range of budgets. They offer itineraries in Tamil Nadu, Karnataka and Lakshadweep, as well as Kerala.
Lazy Days in Goa UK ☏ 01202/484257, ⓦ www .lazydays.co.uk. Quality accommodation in north and south Goa, ranging from one-bed apartments to country houses on private estates.
Make My Trip US toll free ☏ 1-800-INDIA-10 or 1-877-845-3596; Australia ☏ 1300 664404; ⓦ www.makemytrip.com. Reliable online India specialist agent offering access to rock-bottom discounted international and domestic fares, with offices in the US and Australia.
Myths and Mountains US ☏ 1-800-675-6984 or 1-775-832-5454, ⓦ www.mythsandmountains .com. Special-interest trips, tailor-made or group, with an emphasis on culture, crafts, religion and traditional medicine. The "Real South India" tour includes heritage properties, Ayurvedic massage and medicine and a stay on a houseboat, while the "Yoga, meditation and Ayurveda" trip (of the same length) visits various ashrams and ends with three days in an Ayurvedic resort.
North South Travel UK ☏ 01245/608291, ⓦ www.northsouthtravel.co.uk. Friendly, competitive travel agency offering discounted fares worldwide – profits are used to support projects in the developing world, especially the promotion of sustainable tourism.
On the Go Tours UK ☏ 020/7371 1113,

ⓦ www.onthegotours.com. Itineraries include an eight-day cooking trip to Goa.
Peregrine Adventures Australia ☏ 1300 854444, ⓦ www.peregrine.net.au. Offer a fourteen-day tour which includes Chennai, Kochi, Periyar Wildlife Park and the backwaters.
Pettitts India UK ☏ 01892/515966, ⓦ www .pettitts.co.uk. Regular tours include a sixteen-day tour of Karnataka, a seventeen-day "Spices and Sandalwood" tour, and a 22-day tour of South India which includes Tamil Nadu, Kerala, and Mysore. Tailor-made trips also available.
SD Enterprises UK ☏ 020/8903 3411, ⓦ www .indiarail.co.uk. Run by Indian rail experts, SD Enterprises put together complex itineraries for independent travellers wanting to explore India by train, as well as budget packages to Goa and Kerala.
Somak Holidays UK ☏ 020/8423 3000, ⓦ www .somak.co.uk. Top-end packages in select Goan hotels, plus optional excursions to Mumbai and Kerala. All clients get a complimentary half-day tour of Panjim and Old Goa.
Soul of India UK ☏ 020/8901 7320, ⓦ www .soulofindia.com. Escorted and tailor-made spiritual journeys/pilgrimages, including a "Hindu and Christian South India" trip and an Ayurveda tour includes a seven-day rejuvenation programme at the *Taj Garden Retreat* in Kumarakom.
STA Travel UK ☏ 0871 230 0040, ⓦ www .statravel.co.uk; US ☏ 1-800-781-4040, ⓦ www .statravel.com; Australia ☏ 13 47 82, ⓦ www .statravel.com.au; New Zealand ☏ 0800 474400, ⓦ www.statravel.co.nz; South Africa ☏ 0861 781781, ⓦ www.statravel.co.za. Worldwide specialists in independent travel; also student IDs, travel insurance, car rental, rail passes, and more. Good discounts for students and under-26s.
Trailfinders UK ☏ 0845 058 5858, Republic of Ireland ☏ 01/677 7888, Australia ☏ 1300 780 212; ⓦ www.trailfinders.com. One of the best-informed and most efficient agents for independent travellers.
Trans Indus Travel UK ☏ 020/8566 2729, ⓦ www .transindus.co.uk. Wide range of South India tours, including a nine-day tour around Kerala, and sixteen-day tours of Hampi and the Deccan, and the Malabar coast.
Voyages Jules Verne UK ☏ 0845 166 7003, ⓦ www.vjv.co.uk. Thirteen classic India-wide heritage tours, but only one in the south. The "Splendours of the South" is a fourteen-day trip which covers wildlife, temples and the backwaters.
Western & Oriental Travel UK ☏ 0870 499 1111, ⓦ www.westernoriental.com. Award-winning upmarket agency with a wide range of itineraries. These include a fourteen-day Karnataka and Goa trip visiting Bengaluru (Bangalore), Mysore, Halebid, Belur and Gokarna, the seventeen-day "Lost Kingdoms of the Deccan" tour which takes in Hyderabad, Bijapur,

Badami and Hampi and a "Mind, Body, Spirit" trip with a focus on yoga and Ayurveda. **Wilderness Travel** US ☎1-800-368-2794, ⓦ www.wildernesstravel.com. Their seventeen-day "Treasures of South India" tour takes in the highlights of Tamil Nadu and coastal Kerala.

Worldwide Quest Adventures US ☎1-800-387-1483, ⓦ www.worldwidequest.com. Frequent departures for their sixteen-day cultural tour, "Glimpses of the South", which takes in Chennai, Kanchipuram and other temple towns, Periyar Wildlife Park, Kochi, Goa and Mumbai.

Getting around

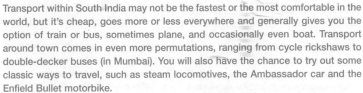

Transport within South India may not be the fastest or the most comfortable in the world, but it's cheap, goes more or less everywhere and generally gives you the option of train or bus, sometimes plane, and occasionally even boat. Transport around town comes in even more permutations, ranging from cycle rickshaws to double-decker buses (in Mumbai). You will also have the chance to try out some classic ways to travel, such as steam locomotives, the Ambassador car and the Enfield Bullet motorbike.

By train

Travelling by **train** is one of the great experiences of South India, and the system works remarkably well given its complexity. Sure, trains are sometimes hours late but more often they show up in timely fashion. They're surprisingly efficient too – the reservation you made several weeks ago half way across the country will (probably) be pasted to the side of the carriage. Ordered meals are usually delivered promptly to your seat, too.

It's worth bearing in mind, with journeys frequently lasting twelve hours or more, that an **overnight** train can save you a day's travelling and a night's hotel bill. While sleeper carriages are often a hive of activity during the day, between 9pm and 6am anyone with a bunk reservation is entitled to exclusive use of their bunk. When travelling overnight, however, it's wise to padlock your bag – metal attachments for chains are invariably provided under the lower bunk.

The network and trains

The **rail network**, run by **Indian Railways** (ⓦwww.indianrail.gov.in), covers almost the whole of South India; only a few places (such as some parts of the Ghats) are inaccessible by train. The fastest trains are the special a/c **"superfast"** type, named Rajdhani or Shatabdi Express, which cover routes between major cities much faster than other services. **Intercity trains**, called "**express**" or "**mail**", vary a lot in the time taken to cover the same route and can take almost twice as long as superfast trains. Chennai to Bengaluru (Bangalore), for example, takes 4 hours 50 minutes on the Shatabdi Express, but as much as 8 hours, or even longer on slower express trains. They are however still much faster than local "**passenger**" trains, which you need only use to get right off the beaten track. Note that express, mail and especially

At the end of each chapter in this book, you'll find a **Travel details** section summarizing major transport connections in the relevant state. In addition, **Moving on** boxes at the end of each major city give details of onward transport from that city.

superfast trains cost a fair amount more than ordinary passenger trains, so if travelling unreserved you must buy the right ticket to avoid being fined.

Most lines are either metre-gauge or broad-gauge (1.676m, or 4ft 6in), the latter being faster; most remaining metre-gauge lines are now being converted to broad-gauge. The only narrow-gauge lines (often referred to as "toy trains") in the South run to Matheran in Maharashtra and Ootacamund (Ooty) in Tamil Nadu, and the steep sections of the latter route see the only steam engines still in use in the region.

Classes of train travel

Indian Railways distinguishes between no fewer than seven **classes of travel**, though they will not all be available on every train. On long overnight journeys, most budget travellers tend to travel in sleeper class (aka second class reserved); an open window keeps you cool enough, and brings you into contact with the world outside, while a/c involves being sealed away behind opaque glass. Doing without a sleeper on an overnight journey is, however, a false economy. Bed rolls (sheet, blanket and pillow) are available in first class and a/c second for that extra bit of comfort. Sleeping accommodation is normally in the form of **tiers**, swing-down sleeping bunks fastened with chains – in a/c and first non-a/c they're padded, whereas in sleeper class they're merely slatted.

Of **non-a/c options, second-class unreserved** is painfully crowded and noisy, with no chance of a berth overnight, but incredibly cheap at Rs188 for a thousand-kilometre journey on an express or mail train. However, the crush and hard wooden seats (if you even get one) make it viable only for short hops or for the extremely hardy. Far more civilized and only around fifty percent more expensive is **second-class sleeper** (Rs301 for 1000km), which must be booked in advance even for daytime journeys. If you have an unreserved ticket and travel in a sleeper carriage, even if it is not full, you will be charged a Rs60 fine as well as the difference in fare. **First-class** non-a/c, in comfortable if ageing compartments of two to four berths costs about 3.5 times as much as sleeper class (Rs986 for 1000km); it is used mainly by English-speaking business travellers. It must also be booked, but this is easier at short notice owing to the higher cost.

Air-conditioned travel, unavailable on "passenger trains", falls into five categories but only one or two will be available on any particular service, except for the Rajdhani, which has three – first class, two-tier and three-tier sleepers. Shatabdi, because it covers shorter daytime routes, comprises exclusively chair cars, which come in two classes – ordinary a/c chair car and, for double the price, the roomier executive a/c chair car; this hardly warrants the extra fare though.

Distance chart (kilometres)

	Bengaluru	Chennai	Hyderabad	Kanyakumari	Kochi
Bengaluru		334	566	674	546
Chennai	334		704	703	669
Hyderabad	566	704		1240	1112
Kanyakumari	674	703	1240		304
Kochi	546	669	1112	304	
Madurai	432	461	998	242	363
Mangalore	347	681	913	716	412
Mumbai	1033	1387	739	1655	1351
Panjim	570	904	712	1073	769
Thiruvananthapuram	761	790	1327	87	217

Sample railway ticket prices

The following prices are for the Chennai to Bengaluru (Bangalore) route (361km), presuming all classes were available. Rajdhani Express does not run this route but tickets in its three classes (denoted by *) for an equivalent distance would cost Rs100–200 above those shown for the Mail/Express trains below.

Shatabdi Express:		Three-tier a/c*	Rs399
Executive a/c chair car	Rs1105	A/c chair car	Rs311
A/c chair car	Rs580	Sleeper class	Rs142
Mail/Express train:		Second class (unreserved)	Rs89
First class a/c*	Rs1019	**Passenger train:**	
Two-tier a/c*	Rs576	First class	Rs364
First class	Rs466	Second class	Rs49

Air-conditioned three-tier sleepers (3AC) cost slightly less than normal first class (Rs845 for 1000km for a mail or express, but more on Rajdhani). Three-tier can feel a bit cramped, especially with loads of luggage, but represents good value; they are, however, not as common as the **a/c two-tier sleepers** (2AC) which cost half as much again – Rs1221 for 1000km, and more again for Rajdhani. Top of the tree is **a/c first class** (1AC), which offers shared compartments for two or four and has a little more luxury with carpeting and more presentable bathrooms, but at Rs2159 for 1000km and more on the Rajdhani, this is not much cheaper than flying. Bed linen is provided free on most a/c services, while meals are also included on Rajdhani and Shatabdi trains.

Ladies' compartments exist on all overnight trains for women travelling on their own or with other women; they are usually small and can be full of noisy kids, but can give untold relief to women travellers who otherwise have to endure incessant staring in the open section of the carriage. Some stations also have ladies-only waiting rooms.

Timetables and tickets

Timetables of all mail, express and superfast trains are available online at Ⓦwww .indianrail.gov.in, though the website is poorly designed and takes some getting used to. You can also check fares and availability online. Alternatively, you can pick up a copy of the biennial *Trains at a Glance*, available from information counters and newsstands at all main stations, and from IR agents abroad (see p.38).

Madurai	Mangalore	Mumbai	Panjim	Thiruvananthapuram
432	347	1033	570	761
461	681	1387	904	790
998	913	739	712	1327
242	716	1655	1073	87
363	412	1351	769	217
	627	1465	984	329
627		939	35	629
1465	939		582	1568
984	357	582		986
329	629	1568	986	

Rail records

Comprising 42,000 miles (over 60,000km) of track and 14,000 locomotives that daily transport an average of 12 million passengers, India's **rail network** is the second largest in the world (after the Russian train network). It's also the biggest employer on the planet, with a workforce of around 1.6 million.

One record the country's transport ministers are somewhat less proud of, however, is the **accident rate**. Four to five hundred crashes occur annually in India, causing between seven and eight hundred fatalities, which makes this also the most dangerous rail network in the world, by a long chalk.

The country's worst rail disaster took place in Ferozabad, near Delhi, in 1995, when a cyclone blew a train off a bridge, killing 800. In August 1999, another 350 passengers died when two trains – carrying a total of 2500 people – collided head on in West Bengal. On both occasions, as in sixty percent of Indian rail accidents, human error was cited as the cause. In reality, lack of adequate training, maintenance and investment at government level are the real roots of the problems facing India's ageing network.

Train passengers, however, can take solace in the fact that travelling by rail in India is considerably safer than using the buses. An average of 233 people die on the country's roads every day (that's 85,000 annually).

All rail **fares** are calculated according to the exact distance travelled. *Trains at a Glance* prints a chart of fares by kilometres, and also gives the distance in kilometres of stations along each route in the timetables, making it possible to calculate what the basic fare will be for any given journey. All much easier online, once you've worked out the peculiarities of the site.

Each individual train has its own **name and number**, prominently displayed in station booking halls. When buying a second-class ticket, it makes sense to pay the tiny extra fee to reserve a seat or sleeper (the fee is already included in the price of the higher classes). To do so, you fill in a form specifying the train you intend to catch, its number, your date of travel, and the stations you are travelling to and from, plus your age and sex (this helps conductors to determine who you are). Most stations have **computerized booking counters** (these are listed in *Trains at a Glance*), and you will be told immediately whether or not seats are available.

Booking tickets

Online ticket reservation is now available across the whole network via the **Indian Railway Catering and Tourism Corporation**, (⊛www.irctc.co.in), and offers by far the simplest way of booking your seat. Until recently there were restrictions on major foreign credit cards but now you can safely book from anywhere in the world and use any major card. The service charge is only Rs40 for second and third classes, and Rs60 for first. You just need to set up an account and password the first time you log on, after which you can access your personal travel record, check your reservations and, if need be, cancel any of them. Again, only a small fee is deducted before the refund is directly credited back to your card.

If you can't book online, you'll need to go to a **reservation office**, often (in main stations) in a separate building and generally open from Monday to Saturday from 8am to 8pm, and on Sunday until 2pm. In larger cities, the major stations have special **tourist sections** to cut the queues for foreigners and Indian citizens resident abroad, with helpful English-speaking staff; however, if you don't pay in pounds sterling or dollars (traveller's cheques or cash), you must produce an encashment certificate to back up your rupees. Elsewhere, buying a ticket in person can often involve a long wait, though women can get round this at ticket counters which have "**ladies' queues**"; travelling in a mixed group or couple, a woman will find it easier to get all the tickets if she queues up on her own. Alternatively, many travel agents will secure tickets for a

Tatkal tickets

Though regarded as something of a rip-off in India, Indian Railways' late-availability reservation system, or **Tatkal**, can be a great help for foreign tourists. A quota of ten percent of places is reserved on most trains under this scheme, which are bookable at any computerized office. Tickets are released five days before the train departs, with an extra charge of Rs150 in sleeper or chair car, and Rs300 in first or a/c sleepers (Rs75/200 during low season, July 15 to Sept 15). The real catch, however, is that you also have to pay for the entire length of the journey from originating to terminating station, however much or little of the ride you do (hence the rip-off), so Tatkal is obviously not worth it if you want to get on, say, the Guwahati–Kanyakumari Express between Trichy and Madurai. If the amount of the route you are planning to cover makes the cost worthwhile, though, you're pretty well guaranteed to find a place, especially if you get in early.

One of the routes on which Tatkal is most likely to be helpful to foreign travellers is **Mumbai–Goa**, on the Konkan Railway, where standard tickets sell out weeks in advance and are thus not available to tourists newly arrived in the country (unless they've booked online).

fairly reasonable fee of Rs25–50. Failure to buy a ticket at the point of departure will result in a stiff penalty if the ticket controller (known as the "TC") finds you.

It is important to plan your train journeys in advance, as demand often makes it impossible to buy a long-distance ticket on the same day that you want to travel (although the **Tatkal** quota system – see the box above – has made life a little easier if you're happy to pay extra). Travellers following tight itineraries tend to buy

Indrail passes

Indrail passes are available for periods ranging from half a day to ninety days. Passes cover all fares and reservation fees and are valid on all trains; they're available only to foreigners and Indians resident abroad. Even if you travel a lot, passes work out considerably more expensive than buying your tickets individually (especially in second class), but they will save you queuing for tickets, allow you to make and cancel reservations without charge, and generally smooth your way in, for example, finding a seat or berth on a "full" train (passholders get priority for tourist quota places). Indrail passes are available, for sterling or US dollars, at main station tourist counters in India, and outside the country at IR agents (see p.38).

	First class a/c a/c first class sleeper, or a/c chair car		First class or a/c		Second class	
	Adult	Child	Adult	Child	Adult	Child
1 day*	$95	$48	$43	$22	$19	$10
4 days*	$220	$110	$110	$55	$50	$25
7 days	$270	$135	$135	$68	$80	$40
15 days	$370	$185	$185	$95	$90	$45
21 days	$396	$198	$198	$100	$100	$50
30 days	$495	$248	$248	$125	$125	$63
60 days	$800	$400	$400	$200	$185	$95
90 days	$1060	$530	$530	$265	$235	$120

Children under 5 travel free
*For sale outside India only; half-day and two-day pass also available.

departure tickets from particular towns the moment they arrive, to avoid having to trek out to the station again – at most large stations, it's possible to reserve tickets for journeys starting elsewhere in the country.

If there are no places available on the train you want, check at the tourist counter (or ask the stationmaster) if any seats or berths have been set aside as a "**tourist quota**". This quota is available in advance but usually only at major or originating stations. As a last resort, if you get on where the train starts its journey, **baksheesh** may persuade a ticket controller to "reserve" you an unreserved seat or, better still, a luggage rack where you can stretch out for the night. You could even fight your way on and grab one yourself, although your chances are slim. As for attempting to **travel unreserved**, for journeys of any length it's too uncomfortable to be worth considering on any major route.

Indian Railways sales agents abroad

Australia Adventure World, ☎ 02/9956 7766, ⓦ www.adventureworld.com.au.
UK SD Enterprises Ltd ☎ 020/8903 3411, ⓦ www .indiarail.co.uk.

Cloakrooms

Most stations in India have **cloakrooms** (sometimes called "parcel offices") for passengers to leave their baggage. These can be extremely handy if you want to go sightseeing in a town and move on the same day. In theory, you need a current train ticket or Indrail pass to deposit luggage, but they don't always ask; they may however refuse to take your bag if you can't lock it. Losing your reclaim ticket causes problems; the clerk will be assumed to have stolen the bag if he can't produce it, so there'll be untold running around to obtain clearance before you can get your bag without it. Make sure, when checking baggage in, that the cloakroom will be open when you need to pick it up. The standard charge is currently Rs10 for the first 24 hours, Rs12 for the next 24 hours and Rs15 per day thereafter.

By air

Though obviously more expensive than going by train or bus, **flying** can save a lot of time: Mumbai–Chennai, for example, can take around thirty hours' hard travelling by train compared to a mere 1 hour 45 minutes by plane. Delays and cancellations can whittle away the time advantage, especially over short distances, but if you're short of time and plan to cover a lot of ground, you should definitely consider flying.

India's national domestic carrier is **Indian Airlines** – IA or just plain "Indian" as it recently re-branded itself (toll free ☎ 1800 180 1407, ⓦ www.indian-airlines.nic.in). It serves over 140 routes countrywide, including all major cities in the South, but is gaining an increasingly poor reputation for sloppy service and an almost total lack of customer care. **Air India** (☎ 022/2279 6666, ⓦ www.airindia.com), the country's international carrier, also runs a few domestic legs as feeder services from across the region to its hub, Mumbai, while "no-frills" subsidiary, **Air India Express** (☎ 022/2279 6330; ⓦ www.airindia.com), operates mainly routes between Kerala and the Gulf. **Jet Airways** (☎ 022/3989 3333; ⓦ www .jetairways.com) flies many of the major routes covered by IA, and generally provides a more efficient and slicker service than the national airline. Among the smaller private airlines, **Air Sahara** (toll free ☎ 1800/223020, ⓦ www .airsahara.net) operates a reliable, expanding network that now reaches most corners of southern India.

The real success story of the past few years, however, has been India's first low-cost airline, **Air Deccan** (☎ m98925 77008, ⓦ www.flyairdeccan.net), which has slashed fares across the board by adopting the "no-frills" approach. They fly to many destinations in South India, often for ludicrously small amounts of money: you can, for example, pick up tickets for Chennai–Mumbai for as little as Rs500 plus taxes, though these special deals tend to be in short supply and sell out well in advance, so you should buy your tickets well ahead of departure.

Hot on the heels of Air Deccan, other private, low-cost carriers have joined the fray, notably **Kingfisher Airlines** (toll free ☎ 1800 233 3131, ⓦ www.flykingfisher.com), launched in 2005 by flamboyant beer tycoon Vijay Mallya. With the slogan "Fly the Good Times", Kingfisher offers a flashier experience than the competition, calling its planes "funliners" and kitting them out with designer white-and-red upholstery and employing exclusively female cabin crews of so-called "flying models". **SpiceJet** (toll free ☎1800 180 3333, ⓦwww.spicejet.com) is more in the mould of Air Deccan, prioritizing low prices over frills. Other more recent newcomers are **IndiGo** (☎m99103 83838, ⓦwww.goindigo.in), **Go Air** (toll free ☎1800 222111, ⓦwww.goair.in) and **Paramount Airways** (toll free ☎1800 180 1234, ⓦwww .paramountairways.com).

These new airlines have increased the number of flights covering the major routes, and added some direct flights to and from the smaller cities. For more, see the Travel details sections at the end of each chapter.

Booking tickets

Airlines have offices or representatives in all the places they fly to, listed in this book in the relevant city sections. IA tickets must be paid for in hard currency or with a **credit card** (not accepted in smaller towns).

The domestic airlines all have a number of **special deals**. IA offers 25 percent discount for under-30s and students, and 50 percent for over-65s, while others offer multi-flight passes and discounts. Deals come and go all the time as companies jostle for custom, but at the time of writing Air Sahara's **Sixer** deal offered good value (six tickets for Rs33,600/£394/$760), as did Kingfisher's **King Saver** (six ticket coupons, valid for six months, for Rs32,400/£380/$733).

One major drawback with flying inside India (particularly with the less efficient Indian Airlines) is that you tend to have to spend a considerable amount of time queuing at the airline office to get a **reservation**; it's often quicker to book through a hotel or travel agent, which is the norm for booking on private carriers.

Theoretically, **lost paper tickets** should no longer be an issue, since all IATA member airlines were supposed to issue only e-tickets as of March 2007. The catch, however, is that some of the smaller airports are not yet geared up to processing them so if you get an e-ticket for a domestic flight added on to an international flight, make sure it will be honoured before you leave home. Otherwise you might find yourself being asked to pay all over again; Indian Airlines are particularly prone to doing this.

Another problem concerns **booking tickets online** direct with the airlines because not all accept foreign credit cards. For the time being, it is best to presume that you will not be able to pay with a foreign card, unless it is proven otherwise, so be prepared to find an airline office or agent.

By bus

Although generally less comfortable than travelling by train, **buses** fill in the gaps in the rail network, and can sometimes be quicker. They go almost everywhere, and more frequently than trains (though mostly in daylight hours).

Services vary somewhat in price and standard. Ramshackle **government-run** affairs, sometimes still packed with livestock as well as people and luggage, cover both short and very long distances; in the latter case, express services are run which have limited stops. In more widely travelled areas there are also usually additional **private** buses offering more leg-room and generally travelling faster – not necessarily a plus point when you consider the dilapidated state of the vehicles.

Some clue as to comfort can be gained from the description given to the bus, although there are fewer top-end vehicles in the south. "**Ordinary**" buses usually have minimally padded fixed upright seats. "**Deluxe**", "**luxury**" and even "**super-deluxe**" are fairly interchangeable terms and when applied to government buses may hardly differ from "ordinary". Usually they refer to private services, though, and should then guarantee a softer, sometimes reclining, individual seat. You can check this out when booking, and it's also worth asking if your bus has a video or music system – if so, the deafening noise will prevent any chance of sleep. Always try to avoid the back seats – they accentuate bumpy roads, launching you into the air several times a minute. Try to sit in the middle of the bus for safety.

Luggage travels in the hatch on private buses, sometimes at a small extra charge. You can usually squeeze it into an unobtrusive corner inside state-run vehicles, although you may occasionally be requested to store it on the roof (passengers travelling on the roof is a rare event these days); check that it's well secured and not liable to get squashed. Baksheesh is in order for whoever puts it up there for you.

Booking tickets

Buying a bus ticket is usually less of an ordeal than buying a train ticket, although at large city bus stations there may be twenty or so counters, each assigned to a different route. When you buy your ticket you'll be given the registration number of the bus and, sometimes, a seat number. As at railway stations, there is usually a separate, quicker, ladies' queue, although it may not be signed in English.

You can always get on ordinary state buses without a ticket, while at bus stands outside major cities you can usually only pay on board, so you have to be sharp to secure a seat. Prior booking is usually available and preferable for express state buses and private services and it is a good idea to check with the agent exactly where the bus will depart from. You can usually pay on board private buses, too, though that reduces your chances of a seat.

By boat

Apart from flat-bottomed river ferries, which are common along the Konkan coast

(particularly in Goa), the **boat services** you're most likely to use in South India are those plying the backwaters of **Kerala**, where the majority of settlements are still most easily reached by water (see pp.416–417). The other region of South India still heavily reliant on ferries is the **Andaman Islands**, where to reach any of the offshore islands you'll have to take a government ferry from the capital, Port Blair; see p.693 for more details. For information on getting to the Andamans by boat, a crossing of three to four days, see p.686.

By car

It's much more usual for tourists in South India to be driven than it is for them to drive; car rental firms operate on the basis of supplying **chauffeur-driven vehicles**.

Chauffeur-driven car rental

Arranged through tourist offices or local car rental firms, a chauffeur-driven car will start from about Rs1200 per day, usually including 200km mileage, with additional kilometers charged at the rate of Rs 6–7km per day. On longer trips, the driver sleeps in the car for which his firm may charge an additional Rs150–200. You should generally give a tip (*batta*) to the driver of Rs100–150. For more advice on renting a car with a driver, see the box below.

Renting a car: some tips

Plenty of potentially expensive, and frustrating, misunderstandings can be avoided when **renting a car** and driver by sticking to the following rules:

- Always shop around first to compare prices, though as a rule of thumb Rs1000–1200 for 200km and Rs6–7/km thereafter is standard.
- You should agree with the rental company in advance your itinerary, the approximate mileage, travelling time, pick-up and drop-off locations, and who is paying for fuel and taxes and driver allowance. Fix the details in a contract if necessary.
- Should a deposit be required (one will sometimes will asked for, but you're entitled to refuse), it's a good idea to wait until the time of departure to pay it – otherwise a different car may turn up from the one you agreed to. The remaining balance should be paid on the last day of the trip. Never pay the full amount in advance; and always insist on a receipt for any money you hand over.
- Never leave your passport or a credit card slip as security.
- Ideally, meet the driver (especially if it is for a long journey) ahead of departure, in order to ensure that his English is up to the task. Refuse any deal without a full written contract (one copy for you).
- Before leaving, check the vehicle (brakes, lights, indicators, steering).

Self-driven car rental

The big international chains, Avis (ⓦwww .avis.com) and Hertz (ⓦwww.hertz.com), usually have their offices in the upmarket hotels of major cities and are the best bet for **self-drive car** rental; contact numbers for them are listed throughout the Guide. In India the charge is much the same as it would be to be driven by a chauffeur, with a Rs1000 deposit against damage, though if you pre-book in your home country it can cost a whole lot more.

Driving in India is not for beginners. If you do drive yourself, expect the unexpected, and count on other drivers taking whatever liberties they can get away with. Traffic circulates on the left, but don't expect road regulations to be obeyed. In the city, it's heavy and particularly undisciplined: vehicles cut in and out without warning, and you have to cope with pedestrians, cyclists and cows wandering nonchalantly down the middle of the road as if you don't exist. In the country the roads are narrow, in terrible repair and hogged by overloaded Tata trucks that move aside for nobody, while something slow-moving like a bullock cart or a herd of goats can easily take up the whole road. To overtake, sound your horn – the driver in front will signal if it is safe to do so; if not, he will wave his hand, palm downwards, up and down. The vast number of potholes doesn't make for a smooth ride either, and during the monsoon, roads can become flooded and dangerous; rivers burst their banks and bridges get washed away. Ask local people before you set off, and proceed with caution, sticking to main highways as much as possible. It is very dangerous to drive at night – not everyone uses lights, and bullock carts don't have any.

You should have an **international driving licence** to drive in India, but this is often overlooked if you have your licence from home (though beware of police in Goa, who are quick to hand out fines). **Insurance** is compulsory, but not expensive. Car seatbelts are not compulsory but very strongly recommended. **Accident** rates are high, and you should be on your guard at all times. If you do have an accident, it might be an idea to leave the scene quickly and go straight to the police to report it; mobs can assemble fast, especially if pedestrians or cows are involved.

Fuel is reasonably cheap, at around Rs44 per litre, but the state of the roads will take its toll, and mechanics are not always very reliable, so a knowledge of **vehicle maintenance** is a help, as is a check-over every so often to see what all those bone-shaking journeys are doing to your car. Luckily, if you get a flat tyre, puncture-wallahs can be found almost everywhere.

The classic Indian automobile is the Hindustan Ambassador (basically a Morris Oxford), nowadays largely superseded by more modern vehicles such as the Japanese-style Maruti Suzuki: these two are likely options if you're renting a car.

By motorbike

Travelling by a **motorbike** or **moped** is a great way of getting around, especially since a motorbike can be taken in the luggage car of a train for the same price as a second-class passenger fare. Although one or two places may **rent** them out for local use, **buying** one is a reasonable proposition, with some classics locally available, and gives you maximum flexibility. You could, of course, bring your own bike all the way **overland** from Europe but remember it is that much further again to the south of India and you will need to consider spares and to bring a *carnet de passage*. Helmets are best brought from home, even if you are planning to get a bike once in India. If you're unsure of negotiating the purchase of your own bike or travelling around on your own you could join a **motorbike tour** (see Agents and operators, p.31), though be prepared for some long days on the pillion.

Buying a motorbike

If it's an old British classic you're after, the **Enfield Bullet** (350 model), sold cheapest in Pondicherry on the coast of Tamil Nadu, leads the field. If low price and practicality are your priorities, however, a smaller model, perhaps even a **moped** or a scooter, might better fit the bill. Many Japanese makes are now made in India, as are Vespas and Lambrettas, and motorbikes of various sorts can easily be bought new or secondhand.

Garages and repair shops are a good place to start to look; Bales Road in Chennai is particularly renowned. Obviously, you will have to **haggle** for the price, but you can expect to pay half to two-thirds the original price for a bike in reasonable condition. Given the right bargaining skills, you can **sell** it again later for a similar price – perhaps to another foreign traveller – by advertising in hotels and restaurants. A certain amount of bureaucracy is involved in transferring vehicle ownership, but a garage should be able to put you on to a broker ("auto consultant") who, for a modest commission (around Rs500–1000), will help you find a seller or a buyer, and do the necessary paperwork.

Some **knowledge of mechanics** is necessary to ensure that you are not being sold a pup so, if you are not too savvy yourself, make sure you take someone with you to give the engine, forks, brakes and suspension the once-over. Bear in mind that experienced overlanders often claim that making sure the seat is comfy is the crucial element to an enjoyable trip.

Renting a motorbike

Motorbike rental is confined to a few tourist spots like Goa, Hampi, Kovalam, Varkala, Mamallapuram, Pondicherry, and the Andamans. Prices range from around Rs150 per day for a moped/scooter to Rs400 for a bigger motorbike. The quality of the bikes can't be relied upon, however, so you should be well versed in maintenance. If you do break down in the middle of nowhere, you may need to flag down an empty truck to transport the bike to the nearest town for repairs.

By bicycle

In many ways the bicycle is the ideal form of transport in South India, offering total independence without any loss of contact with local people. You can camp out, take the bike into your room with you – and, if you get tired of pedalling, you can put it on top of a bus as luggage, or transport it by train (it goes in the luggage van: get a form and pay a small fee at the station luggage office).

Bringing a bike from abroad requires no *carnet* or special paperwork, and most airlines allow you to take cycles at no extra cost – though they may insist on them being flat-packed in cardboard covers (available in good cycle shops). Spare parts and accessories may be of different sizes and standards in India, though, and you may have to improvise. Bring basic spares and tools and a pump. Panniers are the obvious thing for carrying your gear, but fiendishly inconvenient when not attached to your bike, and you might consider sacrificing ideal load-bearing and streamlining technology for a backpack you can lash down on the rear carrier.

Buying a bike in India presents no great difficulty; most towns have cycle shops and even cycle markets. The advantages of a local bike are that spare parts are easy to get, locally produced tools and parts will fit and your vehicle will not draw a crowd every time you park it. Disadvantages are that Indian bikes tend to be heavier and less state-of-the-art than ones from abroad – bikes with gears, let alone mountain bikes, are virtually unheard of. Prices start at around Rs1500. Selling should be quite easy: you won't get a tremendously good deal at a cycle market, but you may well be able to sell privately, or even to a rental shop.

Bicycles can be **rented** in most towns, usually for local use only: this is a good way to find out if your legs and bum can survive the Indian bike before buying one. The going rate is Rs20–50 per day or Rs2–3 per hour, and occasionally more in tourist centres. You may have to leave a deposit, or even your passport, as security.

For more information on cycling abroad, see ⓦwww.ibike.org.

City transport

City transport takes various forms, with **buses** the most obvious. These are usually single-decker, though double-deckers (some articulated) exist in Mumbai and elsewhere. City buses can get unbelievably crowded, so beware of pickpockets, razor-armed pocket-slitters and "Eve-teasers" (see p.77); the same applies to **suburban trains** in Mumbai and Chennai.

To see a variety of places around town, consider hiring a **taxi**, **rickshaw** or **auto-rickshaw** for the day. Find a driver who speaks English reasonably well, and agree a price beforehand. A taxi for a day will cost around Rs800–1000, an auto-rickshaw Rs400–500. The driver will invariably act as a guide and source of local knowledge, and you should give a bit extra if he's done a good job.

Taxis

Taxis are usually rather battered Ambassadors, or in Mumbai old Fiat Padminis, but they are gradually being usurped by more modern vehicles. Blue-painted a/c "cool cabs" are increasingly available, though they cost 40–50 percent more than standard taxis. With any luck, the driver will agree to use the **meter**; in theory you're within your rights to call the police if he doesn't, but the usual compromise is to agree a fare for the journey before you get in. Naturally, it helps to have an idea in advance of what the fare should be, though any figures quoted in this or any other book should be treated as being the broadest of guidelines only. From places such as main stations, you may be able to find other passengers to share a taxi to the town centre; many stations, and certainly most airports, operate **prepaid taxi schemes** with set fares that you pay before departure; more expensive prepaid limousines are also available.

Rickshaws

The **auto-rickshaw**, that most Indian of vehicles, is the front half of a motor-scooter with a double seat mounted on the back. Cheaper than taxis, better at nipping in and out of traffic, and theoretically metered (again, in most places they probably won't use them

and you should agree a fare before setting off), auto-rickshaws are on the downside a little unstable and their drivers often rather reckless, but that's all part of the fun. In major tourist centres rickshaws can, however, hassle you endlessly on the street, often shoving themselves right in your path to prevent you ignoring them, and once they've got you on board, they may try to take you to several shops before reaching your destination. Moreover, agreeing a price before the journey will not necessarily stop your rickshaw-wallah reopening discussion when the trip is under way, or at its end. In general it is better to hail a rickshaw than to take one that's been following you, and to avoid those that hang around outside posh hotels.

Lots of towns and cities in South India also have larger versions of auto-rickshaws known as **tempos**, with six or eight seats behind, which usually ply fixed routes at flat fares. They are for shared use and often only move off when full.

Slower and cheaper still is the **cycle rickshaw** – basically a glorified tricycle with a large raised seat behind. In spite of the fact that this remains the most common form of public taxi in many provincial South Indian towns, foreign visitors often feel uncomfortable being pedalled around by someone half their size for what by Western standards are tiny sums. In the end, though, to deny them your custom on those grounds is spurious logic; cycle rickshaw drivers will earn even less if you don't use them, and there's nothing to stop you from tipping them extra for their pains (even if, as is likely, you'll already have been charged more than the locals' rate). Bear in mind, too, that cycle rickshaws are a far more environmentally sound way of travelling than the alternatives.

Accommodation

There are far more Indians travelling around South India at any one time – whether for holidays, on pilgrimages or for business – than there are foreign tourists, and a vast infrastructure of hotels and guesthouses caters for their needs. On the whole, accommodation for foreign tourists, like so many other things in South India, provides extremely good value for money, though in the major cities and resorts, especially, prices soar for luxury establishments providing Western-style comforts and service.

Hotels and guesthouses

There are a huge variety of hotels, guest-houses and lodges throughout South India, ranging from tiny flea-bitten holes costing under Rs100 to super-luxurious giants that will set you back hundreds of dollars for a night.

Check-out time varies – in some places, such as hill stations or beach resorts, 9–10am is the norm, while in upper-bracket places it is more likely to be noon. Across most of the region, however, at least in the budget to lower mid-range bands, places operate a 24-hour system, under which you are simply obliged to leave by the same time as you arrived.

Unfortunately not all hotels have **single rooms**, so it generally works out more expensive to travel alone; you may be able to negotiate a slight discount though for single occupancy of a double. It's not unusual to find rooms with three or four beds, however – great value for **families** and small groups.

In cheap hotels and hostels, you needn't expect any additions to your basic bill, but as you go up the scale you'll find **taxes** and **service charges** creeping in, sometimes adding as much as a third on top of the original tariff. Taxes vary from state to state, but service is generally ten to fifteen percent. These hidden charges are usually added to your bill.

Officially, all establishments are obliged to provide a printed tariff list and most in fact do. However, like most other things in India, the price of a room may well be open to **negotiation**. If you think the rate is too high, or if all the hotels in town are empty, try

haggling. You may get nowhere – but nothing ventured, nothing gained.

Inexpensive hotels

While accommodation prices in South India are generally on the up, there's still an abundance of **cheap hotels and lodges**, catering for backpacking tourists and less well-off Indians. Most charge Rs150–250 for a double room, and some outside the big cities have rates below Rs100. Even cheaper still are *dharamshalas*, hostels run by religious establishments and pilgrim guest-houses (see p.47).

Budget accommodation tends to be cheaper the further you get off the beaten track; it's most expensive in Mumbai, where prices are at least double those for equivalent accommodation in most other cities.

Cold showers or "bucket baths" are the order of the day – not really a problem in South India for most of the year. It's always wise to check out the state of the bathrooms and toilets before taking a room. Bed bugs and mosquitoes are other things to look for – splotches of blood around the bed and on the walls where people have squashed them are tell-tale signs.

If a taxi driver or rickshaw-wallah tells you that the place you ask for is full, closed or has moved, it's more than likely because he wants to take you to a hotel that pays him commission – added, in some cases, to your bill. **Hotel touts** operate in some major tourist spots, working for commission from the hotels they take you to; this can become annoying, but sometimes paying the little extra may be well worth it, especially if you arrive alone in a new place at night.

Accommodation price codes

All **accommodation prices** in this book have been categorized according to the price **codes** below. The prices given are for a double room; in the case of dorms, we give the per person price in rupees.

Rooms covered under codes ❶ and ❷ are usually very basic but often include attached (en-suite) bathrooms and sometimes even TV; some will have shared bathrooms (non-attached) and not all will have an outside window. You can expect hotels in codes ❸ and ❹ to be attached, most likely with TV, and have a better standard of decor and furnishing and maybe a balcony; some of the cheaper a/c rooms fall into this category or, if non-a/c, will have mosquito nets provided. Hotels in codes ❺ and ❻ are guaranteed to be smart, spacious, more tastefully furnished and more often than not a/c; breakfast may be included too. Hotels in codes ❼ and ❽ become positively luxurious, almost invariably with central a/c, and boast far better facilities (such as swimming pools) and service; most top-end Indian business hotels belong here. Code ❾ is the preserve of the multinational chains and elite home-grown networks of five-stars run by companies such as the Taj Group, as well as upscale heritage or boutique hotels pitched at well-heeled foreign tourists; these provide quality to match anywhere in the world.

In non-touristy parts of the region, and in most major towns and cities, accommodation keeps the same prices throughout the year. But in resorts along the coast, and in wildlife sanctuaries and hill stations, rates fluctuate wildly with demand, inflating two- or three-fold during peak season (mid-Dec to mid-Jan in Goa and Kerala, and April to May for the mountains). We indicate such fluctuations in the Guide where appropriate.

Price code **spans** in the Guide usually indicate the cost of the cheapest non-a/c and cheapest a/c rooms, where applicable. All **taxes** (see opposite) are included in the prices we quote.

❶ up to Rs200	❹ Rs500–1000	❼ Rs2000–3000
❷ Rs200–300	❺ Rs1000–1500	❽ Rs3000–5000
❸ Rs300–500	❻ Rs1500–2000	❾ Rs5000 and upwards

Mid-range hotels

Even if you value your creature comforts, you don't need to pay through the nose for them in South India. A large, clean room, with a freshly made bed, your own spotless bathroom with (often sit-down) toilet, cable TV and hot and cold running water can still cost under Rs400 (£5/$9). Extras that bump up the price include taxes, mosquito nets, a balcony and, above all, **air-conditioning**. Abbreviated in this book and in India itself as **a/c**, air-conditioning is not necessarily the advantage you might expect – in some hotels you can find yourself paying double for a system that is so dust-choked, wheezy and noisy as to preclude any possibility of sleep – but providing it entitles a hotel to consider itself mid-range. Some also offer a halfway-house option known as **air-cooled** – noisy and not as

effective as full-blown a/c, but better than nothing in severe heat. It's only found in drier climes as coolers do not work in areas of extreme humidity, such as along the coast. Many medium-priced hotels also have attached **restaurants**, and even room service.

New hotels tend to be lined inside, on floors and walls, with marble (or some imitation), which can make them feel totally characterless. They are, however, much cleaner than older hotels, where dirt and grime clings to cracks and crevices, and damp quickly devours paint. Some mid-range hotels also feel compelled to furnish their rooms with wall-to-wall carpeting, which often smells due to humidity and damp.

Tourist bungalows

Most state governments run their own **"tourist bungalows"**, similar to mid-range

Low-impact accommodation

South India has had options for the eco-conscious traveller in the shape of ramshackle bamboo **beach huts** without electricity since before eco-tourism was ever heard of. They might have come about more by accident than intent but they still exist and low-budget foreigners often stay in them, creating little impact on the environment, for weeks or months at a time.

What is gradually developing, however, is an infrastructure of more eco-friendly accommodation options that also appeal to tourists who require higher levels of comfort. These mainly fall into two categories: **homestays** where rooms are rented in family houses, bypassing much of the consumption caused by large hotels; and upmarket but green **jungle resorts** in the wildlife sanctuaries, which make every effort to recyle and use natural materials in their construction. Another encouraging development are a new breed of man-powered **houseboats** in Kerala designed to minimize pollution of the water.

hotels, but often also offering pricier a/c rooms and cheaper dorms. They are usually good value, though they vary a lot from state to state and even within states. Tamil Nadu's, for example, tend to be rather run down, whereas Karnataka's are, as a rule, very well kept; Kerala's alternate between positively luxurious and downright grubby; and Goa's are all sited in the most congested locations. We've indicated such places throughout the Guide by including the state acronym in the name – for example, *KTDC Palace*, which stands for *Kerala Tourist Development Corporation Palace*. Bookings for state-run hotels can be made in advance by telephone, or through the state tourist offices throughout the country (see p.94 for websites).

Upmarket hotels

Luxury hotels in India fall into several categories: old-fashioned institutions brimming with class, modern jet-set chain hotels, largely confined to big cities and tourist resorts; a new breed of designer-chic boutique hotels; and classy jungle lodges in wildlife parks.

The faded grandeur of the Raj lingers on in the venerable edifices of British imperial hangouts such as Mumbai and the hill stations of the Nilgiri Hills in the far south. In addition, some former princely palaces or aristocratic seats in the region (notably in Karnataka and Goa) have been converted into **heritage hotels** where you can sample grand period architecture at close quarters.

Kerala has devised its own spin on "heritage tourism", re-locating characteristic

antique wood houses from villages to luxury resort campuses on the coast on backwaters. Well-to-do families with beautiful old country mansions have also started to open their doors to guests, charging five-star tariffs for the privilege. And in the Western Ghats of inland Kerala, Goa and Karnataka you'll find so-called **eco resorts**, often consisting of tree houses or thatched, village-style mud huts equipped with low-impact comforts.

Modern deluxe establishments – slicker, brighter and far more businesslike – tend to belong to chains, including the Indian-owned Taj Group, who run the country's finest hostelry, the *Taj Mahal Palace and Tower* in Mumbai. It's becoming more common for luxury chains to quote tariffs in US dollars (or euros in the case of Kerala), starting at $100 and rising to a hefty $500, sometimes even more for suites. In palaces and heritage hotels, however, you'll still get excellent value for money, with rates only just beginning to approach those of their counterparts back home.

Note that only the standard "rack rates" will be offered to you if you walk into a top hotel direct, though special reductions are available online. You may also find **discounts** through travel agencies (listed in the Guide) offering up to sixty percent off certain luxury hotels, depending on the season.

Railway retiring rooms

At the budget end of the scale, many **railway stations** have **retiring rooms** where passengers can sleep – if they can put up with station noises. These rooms can be particularly handy if you're catching an early morning train, but cannot be booked in advance and tend to fill up quickly. They vary in price (❶ for non-a/c to ❸ for a/c), but generally charge roughly the same as a budget hotel, and have large, clean, if somewhat institutional rooms, occasionally (in major stations) with a/c; dormitories, where you can bank on being woken at the crack of dawn by a morning chorus of throat-clearing, are often available, too.

Homestays

Throughout South India, but especially in those parts of southern Kerala frequented by large numbers of foreign tourists, rooms are sometimes offered in family houses. "**Homestay**" accommodation comes in various forms, from no-frills annexes tacked on to the back of an existing block, to beautifully designed guest wings in period buildings, with antique furniture and private gardens. Home-cooked food is generally available, and you'll find most host families bring a strong sense of vocation to their business, interacting with guests at meal times and showing them around the local area – all of which can make for a very memorable and rewarding experience. Homestays also have the advantage of falling into the low-impact category, of course.

Rates vary according to the quality of the accommodation, and food – but tend to be slightly higher than comparable hotel accommodation. Reviews of homestays appear throughout the Guide; bookings are best made direct by telephone, or online via the homestay's website. Unlike with more formal or luxury hotels, advance payments by credit card are not usually required to secure the reservation: a follow-up confirmation call will suffice.

The international organization **Servas** (⟨W⟩www.indiaservas.org) represents some 558 hosts in India, who can sometimes be a source of **free places to stay**. You must first join the organization before you travel (details on the website), after which you are sent a list of potential hosts. There is no guarantee a bed will be provided – it's up to the individual.

Hostels and camping

YMCAs and **YWCAs**, confined to big cities, are often plusher and pricier than mid-range hotels. They are usually good value, but are frequently full, and some are exclusively single-sex.

Official and non-official **youth hostels**, some run by state governments, are only really found in a handful of the larger cities. They give HI cardholders a discount, but rarely exclude non-members; prices match the cheapest hotels. Where there is a youth hostel, it usually has a dormitory and may well be the best budget accommodation available; this is especially true of those run by the Salvation Army.

It's unusual to **camp** in India, except when on a trek, although many hotels do allow camping on their grounds. The YMCA (⟨W⟩www.ymcaindia.org) run a few sites, as do state governments (Maharashtra in particular), and the Scouts and Guides.

Staying in religious communities

Religious institutions offer accommodation for pilgrims and visitors, and may put up tourists; a donation is often expected, and certainly appreciated, but some of the bigger ones charge a fixed, nominal fee. Pilgrimage sites, especially those far from other accommodation, also have **dharamshalas** where visitors can stay – they're very cheap and very simple, usually with basic, communal washing facilities; some charitable institutions have rooms with simple attached bathrooms. They either operate a donations system or charge a nominal fee, which can be as low as Rs20. **Ashrams** are another source of rooms, especially if you are taking a course at the institution in question; again, some have fixed charges, others simply ask for donations.

Food and drink

India's aromatic and delicious food has a richly deserved reputation throughout the world, and food in the South is some of the finest in the Subcontinent, with a range of cuisines that reflect the region's broad spectrum of cultures. As well as offering wonderful fresh fish, South India can be particularly special if you're a vegetarian, and even the most confirmed meat-eaters will find themselves tucking into delicious veg curries with relish.

The regional variety of Indian cuisine – and the South is no exception – is vast and astonishing. Geographical features, such as climate, soil and aspect, and religious and cultural beliefs all play their part in creating this range of unique flavours, but most crucial is the almost alchemical mix of spices into a **masala**, and the cooking methods then applied.

What Westerners call a curry covers a range of dishes, each made with a different *masala*. The word **curry** probably originates from the *karhi* leaf, a type of laurel, found in much of Indian cooking, especially in the South. Curry powder does not exist in India, the nearest equivalent being the northern *garam masala* ("hot mix"), a combination of dried, ground black pepper and other spices, added to a dish at the last stage of cooking to spice it up. Commonly used **spices**, mostly grown along the lush spice belt of the Western Ghats particularly in Kerala, include pepper, cardamom, cloves, cinnamon, chilli, turmeric, garlic, ginger, coriander – both leaf and seed – cumin and saffron. Some are used whole, so beware of chewing on them.

It's the Indian penchant for **chilli** that alarms many Western visitors, though if you have a fondness for the hotter curries served in Indian restaurants in Britain, you may find those in India mild on the whole. The majority of newcomers develop a tolerance for it, but if you don't, stick to mild dishes and eat rice and plenty of *dahi* (curd), or even sweets such as *barfi* (see p.54) to counter the effects. Fresh lime squeezed onto hot curries also tends to reduce the fire. Curd rice, a typical southern dish, is calming and good for an upset stomach, as is tender-coconut water. Beer is one of the best things for

washing chilli out of your mouth; the essential oils that cause the burning sensation dissolve in alcohol, but not in water. A softer option – a lassi (sweet or salty curd drink) – to accompany your meal can also help cool things down.

Where to eat

Restaurants vary enormously in price and quality. The best places to try genuine South Indian cuisine are **"meals" restaurants**, the equivalent of a North Indian thali restaurant. Found all over the region, usually clustered around major bus stations and busy bazaars, they are a fast, cheap (around Rs25), informal and hygienic way to fill your stomach – and the food, often served on a banana leaf, can be terrific. Many of the best are Udupi-run (see p.52); some are solely vegetarian, but some also serve chicken and fish.

A good way of approaching a "meal" is to order a vegetarian meal, with fish or chicken on the side. Most "meals" restaurants often come with a plain canteen and a more upmarket section, sometimes with a/c, and you may even encounter some that come with separate veg and non-veg sections (see opposite). "Meals" restaurants also serve typical South Indian breakfasts (see p.56) in the morning.

Occasionally found along main highways, though more prevalent in north India, **dhabas** are a Punjabi tradition and cater mainly to truck drivers serving basic but delicious wholesome food, including dhal and *roti* (see Glossary, p.816).

Deluxe restaurants, such as those in five-star hotels, are expensive by Indian standards, costing upwards of Rs400 for a main course, but they offer the chance to sample top-quality classic Indian cuisine at a fraction of the price you'd pay at home – assuming you could find Indian food that good. A wide variety of dishes will be offered – if you're in a group, order a variety of dishes and sample each one.

Cheaper than those in luxury hotels are the restaurants that cater for local Indian families, domestic tourists and businessmen. Clean, and often with an a/c parlour, they serve good Indian food at affordable local prices; expect to pay around Rs60–120 for a typical vegetarian main course, 25 percent more for meat dishes.

An alternative place to eat – catering specifically for foreign travellers with unadventurous tastebuds, or simply a hankering for home – is the **tourist restaurant**, found in beach resorts, hill stations and travellers' centres. Here you can get Western food galore: pancakes and fritters, omelettes and toast, chips, fried prawns, cereal and fruit salad. They tend to be somewhat overpriced (expect to pay around fifty percent more than in locals' restaurants) and the food is under-spiced – they are not of course, authentically Indian. Their popularity is instead based around their social function as meeting places.

Finally, should you be lucky enough to be invited into someone's **home**, you will get to taste the most authentic Indian food of all. Most Indian women are expert cooks, trained from childhood by mothers, grand-mothers and aunties, and aided by daughters and nieces. They can quite easily spend a whole day cooking – grinding and mixing the spices themselves – and using only the freshest ingredients.

Veg vs non-veg

Most religious Hindus, and a large majority of people in the far south, do not eat meat, while some orthodox brahmins will not eat onions and garlic or any food cooked by anyone outside their household. Jains are even stricter and will go as far as shunning tomatoes, which remind them of blood.

Many eating places state whether they are vegetarian or non-vegetarian – "**veg**" and "**non-veg**". Sometimes you will come across restaurants advertising both veg and non-veg, indicating they have two separate kitchens and, often, two distinct parts to the restaurant so as not to contaminate or offend their vegetarian clientele. You'll also see "**pure veg**" advertised, which means that no eggs or alcohol are served.

Veganism as such is not common, however, so if you're vegan you'll need to be fairly vigilant and enquiring. Dairy products for example are prevalent in most Indian sweets, and in many restaurants and homes ghee (unclarified butter) is used for frying.

As a rule, **meat-eaters** should exercise caution in India: even when meat is available, especially in the larger towns, its quality is not assured and you won't get much in a dish anyway – especially in railway canteens where it's mainly there for flavouring. Note that what is called "mutton" is in fact goat. Hindus, of course, do not eat beef, and Muslims shun pork, so you'll only find those in a few Christian enclaves such as the beach areas of Goa, in the few Tibetan communities and among the Kodavas of the Kodagu (Coorg) hill country of Karnataka, who love pork. In Kerala, due to a liberal mix of religions and cultures, attitudes to food can be more relaxed, and both beef and pork appear on the same menu.

Fish is popular throughout the region, particularly in the coastal towns and beach resorts, and fish dishes, whether as steaks or in curries, are often beautifully cooked and very good value, though (especially inland) it can be pre-frozen rather than fresh.

When to eat

It's rarely a problem finding food at any time of day in India. Given the country's massive and somewhat transient population, railway and bus stations have places to eat that open virtually 24/7, although some of the smaller eating dens often look a little

---

In the South – perhaps even more so than elsewhere – **eating with your fingers** is *de rigueur*, and cutlery may not always be available. Wherever you eat, however, remember to use only your right hand (see p.75), and wash your hands before you start. Use the tips of your fingers to avoid getting food on the palm of your hand.

unsavoury. There will always at least be somewhere to get a warming cup of Chai.

Breakfast is often available from 5am onwards around bus and railway stations, and served up to around 11am. The more salubrious restaurants tend to open from 7am or 8am. **Lunch** menus will appear from noon until 3pm, while **evening meals** are usually served from 6 or 7pm until around 11pm. Mid-range and luxury hotels will often stay open as long as there are people eating and drinking, and offer room service for those needing to eat even later.

South Indian food

For the first-time visitor, South India's bewildering range of regional cuisines can challenge all preconceptions of Indian food. Occasionally, a sweeping generalization is made that the cuisine of North India is rich and spicy, while that of the South is plain. With cuisine ranging from the rich northern-style Mughlai cooking, developed within the opulent courts of Muslim Hyderabad, to the more simple vegetarian dishes of Tamil Nadu, it soon becomes clear that this is quite simply not true. The street food and snacks of Mumbai are superb, and the rest of Maharashtra is renowned for its seafood, kebabs, puris and vegetarian fare. Goan cuisine reflects strong Portuguese influences, and Karnataka draws heavily from the plain cooking of its southern neighbours as well as from the rich, aromatic cooking of Hyderabad. Kerala's cuisine is remarkably varied, with a range of delicious fish dishes and a lot of coconut-based recipes. And finally Tamil Nadu has the strongest vegetarian tradition in the south but nevertheless offers pockets of regional variety such as Chettinad – with its memorable chicken dishes – and the cuisine of the small, diminishing Franco-Indian population of Pondicherry, which has its own unique cuisine.

For more detail on many of the dishes covered here, see the Glossary on pp.816–818.

Maharashtrian cooking

Maharashtrians take their food very seriously, or in the words of a local expression "as equal to god". As the state capital, Mumbai, is India's largest and most cosmopolitan city, it's no surprise to find a huge variety of flavours and food styles across the region. Maharashtrian cuisine tends to use a lot of coconut, cashews and peanuts – the oil of the latter is the main cooking medium. Another distinguishing feature is the use of a deep purple berry called *kokum,* which has a sweet and sour taste and acts as a digestif.

The most famous Mumbai dish is **Bombay duck**, a rather misleading name as it is actually a small fish which is either cooked fresh in batter or sun-dried and commonly eaten in curry (see the box on p.122 for more). Another local speciality is dhansak, a lentil-based dish popular amongst Mumbai's Parsi community. Aubergines are widely used, with baby *brinjals* often stuffed with coconut. For dessert, seek out *puran poli – roti* stuffed with a mixture of saffron, cardamom powder, gram (chickpea) and *jaggery*.

Goan cooking

Goan cuisine is often divided into two separate traditions, based loosely on the religious or cultural differences between the Hindu and Catholic populations of the state. While Hindu Goan food has resisted Portuguese influence, the Catholic style of cuisine has borrowed and maintained many colonial traditions. Some interesting fusions have resulted.

The hot-and-sour **vindaloo** curry, found on menus in Indian restaurants worldwide, is possibly the most famous of all Goan dishes. Vindaloo originates from the Portuguese *vinho d'alho*, literally "garlic wine", and consists of either meat or fish seasoned with vinegar, but is most traditionally made with pork. Goan food is particularly distinctive in that it uses palm vinegar, a Portuguese introduction, in many of its preparations. In fact, the **Portuguese influence** spread far beyond the borders of their once colonial enclave, when they introduced vegetables and spices to the rest of India and beyond from the New World. These included green and red chilli peppers, which eventually replaced black pepper as the source of heat in Indian cooking. Another key ingredient of Goan cuisine is ground coconut, which appears in assorted dishes, from fish curries to cakes.

Pork specialities from Goa include: chouriço (red sausages), leitao (suckling pig) and balchao (pork in a rich brown sauce). Essentially a vindaloo, sarpotel (pork with liver and heart, vinegar, chillies, spices and tamarind) combines the best of both Portuguese and Indian influences, as does assado (a spicy, pan-cooked beef preparation, usually served with salad and potatoes).

Although meats like pork and beef feature heavily, Goan cuisine is most famous for its exceptional **fish and seafood**. Best prepared with pomfret, a flat fish found in coastal waters throughout India, the classic Goan fish curry is cooked with spices mixed with coconut and tamarind, and is usually served with plain, boiled rice. Another fish curry, caldeen, is prepared by marinating the fish in vinegar and then cooking it in a spicy coconut and chilli sauce. Clams, lobster and prawns are also dished up in a variety of ways, including in soups such as sopa de camarão, a prawn soup cooked with puréed potatoes, egg yolk and milk, and apa de camarão, a spicy prawn pie with a rice and semolina crust.

Goa is also celebrated for its **cakes and desserts** such as bebinca, a custard made with gram flour, eggs and coconut milk.

Hyderabadi and Andhran cooking

Some connoisseurs may argue, and not without a certain justification, that the haute cuisine originating from Hyderabad in Andhra Pradesh represents the pinnacle of all **Indian Muslim cooking**. Although the grandeur of a once luxurious court has faded, traditions still linger on and if you find yourself in the city, a culinary tour will leave indelible impressions. Many Hyderabadi dishes will already be familiar to visitors. Preparations such as korma (an aromatic but mild and creamy curry), pilau (aromatic fried rice; also known as pulau, pullao and pilaf) and biriyani (aromatic baked rice) feature prominently in India and are recognized worldwide.

During the height of the Nizam's rule (nineteenth/early twentieth century) Hyderabad attracted Muslims from all over India and abroad, bringing with them their favoured recipes and ideas. Some spice combinations are derived from Persian recipes, and these are combined with indigenous ingredients from the spice belts of the nearby Malabar Coast to create a uniquely rich and aromatic cuisine. With the addition of tamarind and local spices, Persian dried lamb with beans became the delicious dalcha, while the fiery til ki chutney, made from sesame seeds, was inspired by Middle Eastern tahini. Common ingredients used in Hyderabadi cuisine include: cassia buds, karhi leaves, chillies, cinnamon, cardamom, tamarind, peanuts, coconut milk and dahi. Mixing these spices is a fine art, best illustrated by potli ka masala, an unusual mixture consisting of khas (vetivert) and dried rose petals, ground and sprinkled onto prepared food, and sometimes present in meat dishes such as nahari (a slow-cooked stew of lamb with tongue and trotters). Other meat dishes include lukmi, which is a kind of deep-fried ravioli, and chippe ka gosht, where lamb, marinated in yoghurt and coconut, is cooked slowly in an earthenware pot, giving it a distinctive earthy flavour.

As with Muslim cooking everywhere, Hyderabadi cuisine is heavily meat-orientated. However, there are also delicious **vegetarian** dishes, such as bagheri (or Hyderabadi) baingan – small aubergines cooked with peanut paste – as well as several rice preparations; like khichari (rice cooked with lentils and ghee), a traditional breakfast.

Outside Hyderabad, and the ubiquitous biriyani, **Andhran cuisine** is generally accepted as the hottest of South India's culinary styles, rather unsurprisingly as the state produces the legendary Guntur chilli, one of the hottest red chilli peppers in the world. There is however just about room for other flavours to seep through the firewall – a typical dish is chicken braised in red chillies, fenugreek, garlic and ginger, then pan roasted with curry leaves and dressed with lemon.

Karnatakan cooking

Sandwiched between the meat-loving Muslim enclaves of Hyderabad and the central Deccan, and the lush coastal region to the south, **Karnataka** enjoys the best of both worlds in terms of food. In Bengaluru's (Bangalore's) restaurants you can find sumptuous chicken biriyanis inspired by Andhra Pradeshi cuisine and traditional vegetarian "meals" with unlimited portions of vegetables, sambar, rice and rasam (pepper water). The state's cuisine is probably the mildest in South India, with mustard seeds used much more frequently than chillies. Palm sugar is added to many dishes to increase sweetness, while tomatoes are used in greater proportions to bring out the flavour of the local sweet tamarinds.

The most famous Karnatakan cuisine comes from the town of **Udupi**, to the north of Mangalore, where the Udupi brahmins have gained a legendary reputation as excellent restaurateurs and hotel-keepers. Their vegetarian cuisine, developed in part through making offerings at their famous Krishna temple, has become synonymous with quality. Throughout the South, restaurants and hotels will often boast that they are "Udupi-run" and they are well worth seeking out, not just because of the legendary food, but also for their excellent value. An Udupi meal is typically presented on a banana leaf and comprises rice and a range of different vegetable curries, which vary from day to day, accompanied by pickles. Udupi restaurants are also good for *iddlis*, *vadai* and *dosas* (see opposite) – it's said that the ubiquitous masala dosa, wrapped around a filling of potatoes and vegetables, was invented by an Udupi brahmin.

Mangalore itself is not without its local specialities. Its coastal location lends itself to a strong seafood diet which includes *gassi* (*gashi*), a ladyfish curry based on chilli and coconut. *Sannas* are a popular Mangalorean version of the ubiquitous *iddli*, fluffed up by the addition of either toddy or yeast.

While Bengaluru (Bangalore) offers the widest choice, a visit to **Mysore** also provides an opportunity to sample a fine selection of Karnatakan cuisine with good Andhra and Udupi restaurants. The city's best-known dish is Mysore *pak*, a sweet made from a rich, crumbly mixture of maize flour and ghee. There is further regional variety within Karnataka in the form of the meat-dominated specialities of the Kodavas (see p.302) and the North Indian-style food of the central Deccan in the north of the state, where spicy curries are accompanied by *joleata roti*, a chapati made from locally grown maize.

Keralan cooking

Kerala has a rich and varied cuisine, heavily influenced by the spice belt along the Western Ghats and its plentiful **fish** supplies along the Malabar Coast and the Kuttinad backwaters. Kerala has always been a key centre for the **spice trade**, and has attracted traders throughout history from all over the world. These different cultures, including Arabs, Phoenicians, Egyptians, Greeks, Romans and Chinese, were all instrumental in the development of Keralan cuisine. Today, Syrian Christians, an ancient Iraqi Jewish community and indigenous Keralan Christians, Hindus and Muslims have combined to create a tolerant and liberal atmosphere that is reflected in the food. Furthermore, the hot, steamy climate and lush mountains combine to make the state a veritable greenhouse, providing a huge range of vegetables, from beans to bitter gourds, and fruits, such as mangoes, bananas and jackfruit, all of which are used in the cuisine of this region.

The main **spices** used in Keralan cuisine are cardamom, cinnamon, cloves, cumin, ginger, coriander, tumeric and peppers. Spices are recognized for their tonic properties, especially on the digestive system and are often used for specific medicinal purposes in accordance with Ayurvedic principles.

One typical Keralan dish is **appam** – rice pancakes mixed with coconut, and cooked in a wok, known as *cheena chatti* (Chinese pot). Also known as *kallappam* or *wellayappam*, *appam* is traditionally served with an *"eshtew"* (stew) of chicken and potatoes in a creamy white mild sauce, flavoured with spices such as pepper and cloves and complemented with coconut milk. While the *eshtew* may or may not have been inspired by European imports, the Malabar pudding – made of sago and topped with liquid *jaggery* and coconut milk instead of sugar and cream – has far more obvious European roots.

The most famous Keralan dish is its wonderful **fish curry**, or *molee*, cooked in a delicious cream of tomatoes, ground coconut and coconut milk. The coastal waters contain a huge variety of seafood including marlin and shark, and the day's catch is proudly displayed on the stands of the seaside tourist restaurants of Kovalam and Varkala. Some of the best fish comes from the backwaters, where the black *karimeen*, a flat sole-like fish that hugs the muddy bottoms, is justifiably prized. Also known as fish tamarind, *kodampoli* (*Garcinia indica*) provides the distinctive flavour in the fiery fish curry, *meen vevichathu*, which is cooked in an earthenware pot. Muslim fishermen of the Mopilah community favour shellfish, as well as beef, while the Christian fishing communities around Kovalam specialize in catching pomfret, mackerel, squid, prawns and other seafood, which they then sell on the beach to the highest bidder.

Rice in various forms features heavily in the Keralan diet. Pilau (see Glossary, p.817) is especially popular among Muslims, and along the coast is usually served with prawns. Occasionally tapioca, known locally as *kappa*, appears an alternative staple, whether accompanying coastal fish curries or served as deep-fried chips.

Tamil cooking

Tamil cuisine is one of the oldest culinary heritages in India, retaining many elements of the ancient Dravidian culture that flourished in the deep south some 4000 years ago. Although meat and fish are widely available, it is also traditionally vegetarian, with a predominance of pure-veg places (see p.49).

Tamil cooking uses a complex masala that includes curry leaves, coriander, cardamom, cumin, cinnamon, cloves, garlic, ginger, nutmeg, tamarind and in some dishes, rosewater. It is also on of the hottest cuisines of the South, with abundant use of chillies. Roadside cafes tend to serve unfathomably hot dishes, and you'll see free bowls of chillies provided for nibbling and delicious tongue-tingling chilli bhajis on offer. Beyond the penchant for red-hot chilli peppers, however, the deep South has an exquisite culinary tradition, most notably in the classic regional style of Chettinad.

Chettinad cuisine originates from the hundred or so villages that make up the Chettiar community, in the Sivaganga and Pudokottai areas of the state. Its cooking style uses a rich, exotic and fairly hot masala, comprising fragrant spices such as star anise (introduced to Tamil Nadu from China during the Chola period), black pepper,

saffron, mace and cloves, as well as ingredients as diverse as cashews and rose petals. Tamarind, ginger and garlic are also used to give Chettinad its distinctive flavour. Although traditionally most dishes are vegetarian, the delicious masala lends itself particularly well to chicken and lamb dishes.

North Indian food

Cuisine from across all of India is widely available, and those with a penchant for North Indian food and tandoori (clay oven) preparations will find dishes such as chicken tikka (boneless cubes of tandoori chicken, marinated with yoghurt, spices and herbs) and other favourites feature on the menus of more upmarket restaurants and five-star hotels, particularly in the evenings.

As well as the many "meals" restaurants, you'll also find more expensive **thali** restaurants, especially in big cities, but in South India these will serve South Indian food, with maybe one or two North Indian style dishes in them. In many thali restaurants, you can eat as much as you want ("unlimited"), with staff circulating with refills of everything, though you will also find "limited" thalis.

Street food and snacks

Finding snacks and light meals should never be a problem. Most quintessential of all South Indian food are *iddlis* (steamed rice cakes), *vadai* (deep-fried lentil cakes) and *dosas* (rice pancakes), which come either with filling (masala) or plain (*sada*) – dished up with *sambar* (lentil soup) and coconut chutney. They are served as breakfast, snacks and frequently as part of "meals" dishes throughout South India.

Street food also includes: *bhel puris*, a Mumbai speciality consisting of puffed rice, finely chopped vegetables and spices and small puris stuffed with tamarind sauce (see p.139), *pani* puris (the same puris dunked in peppery and spicy water – only for the seasoned), *baida roti* (egg *roti* stuffed with minced meat, bhajis (deep-fried cakes of vegetables in chickpea flour), as well as the more familiar samosas (meat or vegetables in a pastry triangle, fried) and pakoras (vegetables or potato dipped in chickpea flour batter and deep-fried). Kebabs are common in the north and around Hyderabad,

Paan

You may be relieved to know that the red stuff people spit out all over the streets of major cities isn't blood, but juice produced by chewing **paan** (also known as paan masala), a digestive, commonly taken after meals, and also a mild stimulant.

A paan consists of chopped or shredded nut (always referred to as betel nut, though in fact it comes from the areca palm), wrapped in a leaf (which *does* come from the betel tree). It may be prepared with ingredients such as *katha* (a red paste), *chuna* (slaked white lime, to activate the betel), *mitha masala* (a mix of fennel seeds, sweet spices and other flavourings) and *zarda* (chewing tobacco, not to be swallowed on any account, especially if made with *chuna*). The triangular package thus formed is wedged inside your cheek and chewed slowly; in the case of *chuna* and *zarda* paans, you spit out the juice as you go. Paan is an acquired taste; novices should start off – and preferably stick – with the sweet and harmless *mitha* variety, which is the most benign form and easier to ingest.

Paan is sold by paan-wallahs, often from tiny stalls squeezed between shops. Paan-wallahs develop big reputations and some of the more extravagant concoctions come wrapped in edible silver and, in some rare cases, even gold foil; these are often produced at weddings.

most frequently *sheekh* kebab (minced lamb grilled on a skewer) but also *shami* kebab (small minced lamb cutlets). With all street snacks, though, remember that food left lying around attracts germs – make sure it's freshly cooked. This said, many veteran travellers to India will argue that street food freshly cooked in front of your eyes is actually safer than a lot of restaurant food.

You won't find anything called "Bombay mix" (or even Mumbai mix) in India, but there's no shortage of dry spicy **snack** mixes, often referred to as *channa chur*. Jackfruit chips, sold in some places as a savoury snack, are rather bland; rather sweeter are fried banana chips, seen across the region in bright yellow piles. Cashew nuts are a real bargain. Peanuts, also known as "monkey nuts", usually come roasted and unshelled. Dry-roasted chickpeas are a high-protein snack but watch your teeth.

Sweets

Indians tend to have rather a sweet tooth and Indian **sweets**, usually made of milk, can be seriously sugar-laden. Although the emphasis on milk products is stronger in the North than in the South, sweets are popular throughout India, and sweet shops thrive in all cities and large towns. Addicts will enjoy hunting down regional specialities.

Barfi, a kind of fudge made by reducing condensed milk, varies from moist and delicious to dry and powdery. It comes in various colours and flavours from plain, creamy white, bright orange carrot to livid green *pista* (pistachio), and is sometimes sold covered with edible silver leaf. Smoother-textured, round *pedha* and thin diamonds of *kaju katri*, plus moist *sandesh* and the harder *paira*, are among many other types of sweet made from boiled-down milk. Numerous types of gelatinous **halwa** are especially popular in Hyderabad, all of them quite different in taste and texture from the Middle Eastern variety. Of the regional varieties, Mysore *pak*, made from a rich crumbly mixture of maize flour and ghee, is available all over India.

At the softer, stickier end of the spectrum, *jalebis*, those circular orange tubes dripping syrup, are made of deep-fried treacle and are just as sickly as they look. *Gulab jamuns*, deep-fried cream cheese sponge balls soaked in syrup, are just as unhealthy but utterly divine. Then there is *ladoo*, knobbly yellow balls usually made from semolina flour, which have a much drier, flakier texture.

Indian **chocolate** has improved significantly in recent years, and there is now a range of decent Cadbury and Amul bars available everywhere. This said, some of the indigenous imitations of Swiss and Belgian chocolates present a curious take on chocolate.

Among the large **ice-cream** vendors, Kwality, Vadilal's, Gaylord and Dollops stand out; you'll see carts of ice cream being pushed around by uniformed men. The bigger companies have many, usually quite obvious, imitators; some have no scruples – stay away from water ices unless you have a seasoned constitution. Throughout southern towns and cities, ice-cream parlours selling elaborate iced concoctions, including sundaes, have really taken off. When travelling, especially around coastal Karnataka and parts of Kerala, look out for a local variation known as *gad-bad* (literally "mix-up"), where layers of ice cream come interspersed with chopped nuts and dried and glacé fruit. Be sure to try kulfi, a traditional frozen-milk preparation flavoured with pistachio, mango or cardamom. *Bhang kulfi*, not available everywhere but popular during the festival of Holi, is laced with cannabis, giving it an interesting kick, but should be approached with caution.

Fruit

What **fruit** is available varies with region and season, but there's always a fine choice. Remember that fruit should always be peeled first. Roadside vendors often sell cut and peeled fruit that is sprinkled with salt and spices but don't buy it if it looks like it's been hanging around for a while.

Mangoes are usually on offer, but not all are sweet enough to eat fresh – some are used for pickles or curries. Indians are picky about their mangoes, the ripeness of which they gauge by feel and smell before buying. Among the varieties appearing at different times in the season – from spring to summer – look out for Alphonso, which is grown in the vicinity of Mumbai, and Langra, which is grown all over South India. Oranges and tangerines are generally easy to come by, as are sweet melons and thirst-quenching watermelons, but the South is most famous for its numerous kinds of **bananas**, which are available all year round. Try the delicious red bananas of Kovalam, or the *Nanjangod* variety grown in the vicinity of Mysore, which are considered by many in the city as the best – and most extravagant (at a bank-breaking Rs5 or so per fruit). While travelling on the buses through southern India,

bananas provide a good fallback in places where safe, nourishing and hygienic food might not otherwise be readily available and they're especially good for upset or sensitive stomachs. Note that certain types, however, such as the *Nendrakai* variety from Kerala, are used only for cooking.

Other **tropical fruits** available year-round include coconuts, papayas (pawpaws) and pineapples, while lychees and pomegranates are very seasonal. Among less familiar fruit, the *chiku*, which looks like a kiwi and tastes a bit like a pear, is well worth trying, as is the watermelon-sized jackfruit (*chakkai* in Malayalam), whose spiny green exterior encloses sweet, slightly rubbery yellow segments each containing a seed. The custard apple, a knobbly green case housing a scented white pulp with large black seeds, is another interesting seasonal fruit, with a sweet, creamy texture that does indeed resemble custard.

Non-Indian food

Chinese food is widely available in towns all over the country but in most cases is cooked by Indian chefs and lacks authenticity. However, India does have a small Chinese population, and there's some very good genuine Chinese cuisine to be found in Mumbai, Bengaluru (Bangalore) and Chennai, which has been adapted to local taste by the addition of a hint of spice.

In cities such as Bengaluru (Bangalore) and Mumbai you'll also find a range of other **international cuisines** on offer, such as Tex-Mex, Thai, Japanese, Italian and French, but these are often only available in the restaurants of luxury hotels. Outside of upmarket hotels, Western food is often dire, and expensive compared with Indian food, although international chains serve their standard fare at much cheaper prices. Branches of *Pizza Hut*, *Domino's*, *KFC* and *McDonald's* can be found in Mumbai, Chennai and Bengaluru (Bangalore) in ever-increasing numbers. *Wimpy's*, home-grown chains such as *Kwality's* and independently owned fast-food cafés like *Pizza Corner* can be found in most cities and large towns. A wider selection of Western food is available in tourist centres such as Goa, Pondicherry and Kovalam, ranging from patisseries serving cakes and croissants to restaurants offering lasagne on candle-lit terraces. Small cheese factories are beginning to emerge, providing an alternative to the dreary processed cheese produced by Amul; cheeses and breads made at Auroville (see p.563) are sold throughout the South.

Many places serve a mix of international dishes (usually Chinese, Western and Indian) – often referred to as **multi-cuisine** in the Guide.

Breakfast

Westerners often get "breakfast blues" as finding fry-ups and hash browns can be a problem. If you're not prepared to greet the day with a local breakfast – *iddli*, *vadai*, *dosa* and *uppma* (semolina and nuts) are the most common breakfast snacks – you might head to the cheap and cheerful *India Coffee House* chain, which can be depended upon for a decent coffee and some toast. In established travellers' hangouts, budget hotels and restaurants, favourites such as banana pancakes, muesli, toast, omelette, porridge (not always oatmeal) and and fruit shakes will be on the menu.

Drinks

South India is home to some of the world's premium **coffee**-growing areas and in many places coffee rivals tea in popularity. South Indian coffee is traditionally prepared with sugar and topped with large quantities of milk; in Kerala there's a whole ritual attached – the coffee is poured in flamboyant sweeping motions between tall glasses to cool it down. One of the best places to get a decent coffee is the *India Coffee House* co-operative chain, which has branches in every southern town. Good vacuum-packed filter coffee, grown in Kodagu (Coorg) in Karnataka, is available but is yet to have an impact in cafés and restaurants.

India's undisputed national drink, however, is **tea** (or **chai**) – grown in Darjeeling and Assam in the north and in the Nilgiri Hills, on the border of Kerala and Tamil Nadu, in the south. The tea gardens of the Nilgiris produce fine, full-flavoured teas and often carry a high price tag to match the altitude. Tea is sold by chai-wallahs on just about

every street corner, and traditionally prepared in a different way to in the West, with lots of milk and sugar (though if you're quick off the mark you can usually get them to hold the sugar – ask for "sugar separate"). Ginger, pepper and/or cardamoms may also often added to make a *masala chai*. English tea it isn't, but many travellers find it an irresistible brew. In tourist spots and upmarket hotels, you can get a pot of European-style "tray" tea, which generally consists of a tea bag in lukewarm water – you'd do better to stick to the pukka Indian variety, unless you are in a traditional tea-growing area.

Soft drinks are widely available throughout India. Global brands like Coca Cola and Pepsi are available alongside locally produced alternatives such as Campa Cola (innocuous), Thums Up (not unpalatable), Gold Spot (fizzy orange) and Limca (rumoured to have dubious connections to Italian companies and to contain additives banned there). All contain a lot of sugar but little else. One famous advert for an Indian soft drink proudly maintained "100% artificial – contains no real fruit." None will quench your thirst for long.

Bottled water is available everywhere in 500ml, one-litre and larger bottles. In some tourist places you can refill your own bottle with treated or boiled water, a popular green initiative which helps reduce street refuse. For more on bottled water, see the box on p.61.

Cartons of Frooti, Jumpin, Réal and similar brands of **fruit juice drinks**, which come in mango, guava, apple and lemon varieties are another alternative to carbonated drinks but avoid cartons which look at all mangled, as they may have been recycled. Tender coconut water from **green coconuts** is delicious, very healthy (good if you have an upset stomach) and often the cheapest drink available. Green coconuts are common in coastal areas and are sold on the roadside by vendors who will hack off the top of the coconut for you with a machete and give you a straw to suck up the coconut water (you then scoop out the flesh and eat it).

India's greatest cold drink, **lassi** – originally from the north but now available throughout India – is made with beaten curd and drunk either salted, sweetened with sugar or mixed with fruit. It varies widely from smooth and delicious to insipid and watery, and is sold at virtually every café, restaurant and canteen in the country. Another popular soft drink, particularly enjoyed along the beaches of Mumbai, is *falooda*, which originated in Persia and was brought to India by the Parsis. It is a mixture of milk, vermicelli, basil seeds, ice cream and often flavoured with rose, saffron, mango and chocolate. Freshly made milkshakes are also commonly available at establishments with blenders, as are **fresh fruit juices**, which usually contain liquidized and strained fruit, water and sugar (or salt); street vendors selling fresh fruit juice in less than hygienic conditions are apt to add salt and *garam masala*. In the central and northern cities of South India, especially Hyderabad, Middle Eastern-inspired *sharbat* – flavoured drinks made with sugar, fruit and, often, rose essence – remain popular, especially among Muslims.

With all such drinks, however appetizing they may seem, exercise great caution in deciding where to drink them, unless you're confident your body has acclimatized; find out where the water is likely to have come from and avoid the ice.

Alcohol

Outside cosmopolitan cities such as Mumbai and Banglore, where there are thriving contemporary bar scenes, **drinking** is often a male preserve only, with dimly lit, seedy bars providing discreet zones away from home for men to gather and get drunk. This has taken a terrible toll on family life, especially among the working classes and peasantry, as a consequence of which politicians searching for votes have from time to time played the **prohibition** card.

Once widespread in India, prohibition is now, however, only partially enforced in a few states, notably Tamil Nadu, which retains some semblance of prohibition in the form of "dry" days, high taxes, restrictive licences and health warnings on labels ("Liquor – ruins country, family and life"). Kerala's licensing laws have also resulted in restrictive licences and prohibitive fees to all except government agencies, such as the Kerala Tourist Development Corporation, who have a virtual monopoly on beer

parlours throughout the state. However, alcohol is generally available throughout the South, luxury hotels will serve (overpriced) drinks and most big towns have alcohol stores where you can purchase your own. Curiously, you'll find many non-veg restaurants offer a drinks menu. However, due to the relatively high price of bottled liquor there is still a flourishing illicit liquor trade and every now and then papers report cases of mass contamination from illicit stills leading to extraordinary numbers of deaths.

Beer

Beer is widely available, if rather expensive by local standards. Prices vary from state to state, but you can usually expect to pay Rs40–80 for a 650ml bottle. Kingfisher is the leading brand but there are other lagers to choose from. Unfortunately most of them contain chemical additives such as glycerine but are usually fairly palatable when served cold.

In certain unlicensed restaurants in Tamil Nadu and Kerala, beer comes in the form of "special tea" – a teapot of beer, which you drink from a teacup to disguise the contents. A cheaper and often delicious alternative to beer in is **toddy** (palm wine).

Spirits and other liquor

Spirits usually take the form of "Indian Made Foreign Liquor" (IMFL), made to different recipes from their Western counterparts, although foreign spirits, such as various brands of Scotch whisky, Smirnoff vodka, Southern Comfort and Bacardi rum are increasingly gaining a foothold. Some types of Indian whisky aren't too bad, and are affordable in comparison. Indian gin and brandy can be pretty rough, though the rum is sweet and distinctive. Goan *feni* is a spirit distilled from coconut or cashew fruit which few develop a taste for, and steer well clear of illegally distilled *arak*, which often contains methanol (wood alcohol) and other poisons. A look through the press, especially at festival times, will soon reveal numerous cases of blindness and death as a result of drinking bad hooch (or "spurious liquor" as it's called). Licensed country liquor, sold in several states under such names as *bangla*, is an acquired taste.

Wine

In addition to spirits, India produces several varieties of **wine**, grown in the temperate uplands of neighbouring Maharashtra and Karnataka. The industry is still in its infancy, but with the help of technologies and expertise imported from overseas, standards are steadily improving. That said, by Indian standards even the cheapest brands, such as Vin Ballet and Riviera, are pricey (around Rs200 in shops), and can easily double your restaurant bills. Still more expensive, and correspondingly easier drinking, are Grover's cabernet and white, and Chantilly. At the top end of the market, costing Rs600–850 in Goan restaurants, are Grover's La Reserve,

Sula Chenin Blanc and wines from India's foremost winery, Chateau Indage. The latter, while the best on offer, are comparable with cheap South American or Bulgarian wines you'd expect to pick up for less than £5 in the UK. For those who really want to push the boat out, high-end restaurants in the state also serve a selection of New World wines, at prices marginally higher than you'd expect to pay back home.

Among **sparkling wines**, you've a choice between Marquise de Pompadour (a crisp, refreshing champagne made from a blend of Chardonnay, Pinot Noir and Ugni Blanc grapes), or Joie-Cuve Clos (a better-structured sparkling wine with a fruit-filled bouquet, not unlike Cava).

Health

A lot of visitors get ill in South India just as in the rest of the country, and some of them get very ill. However, if you are careful, you should be able to get through the region with nothing worse than a mild dose of "Kerala belly". The important thing is to keep your resistance high by having a balanced diet and getting plenty of sleep, and to be very aware of health risks such as poor hygiene, untreated water, mosquito bites and undressed open cuts.

Medical resources for travellers

For up-to-the-minute information, make an appointment at a **travel clinic**. These clinics also sell travel accessories, including mosquito nets and first-aid kits. There is plenty of India-specific **information online**, covering which vaccinations are required, and giving details on specific diseases and conditions, drugs and herbal remedies: check out the websites ⓦ www.fitfortravel.scot.nhs.uk, ⓦ www.travelvax.net and ⓦ www.tripprep .com. You could also consult the *Rough Guide to Travel Health* by Dr Nick Jones.

Travel clinics

In the UK and Ireland

Hospital for Tropical Diseases Travel Clinic UK

ⓣ 020/7387 4411, ⓦ www.thehtd.org.
MASTA (Medical Advisory Service for Travellers Abroad) UK ⓣ 0870 606 2782, ⓦ www.masta-travel-health.com. Forty clinics across the UK.
Nomad Pharmacy UK ⓦ www.nomadtravel.co.uk. Clinics in London, Southampton and Bristol.
Tropical Medical Bureau Republic of Ireland ⓣ 1850 487674, ⓦ www.tmb.ie.

In the US and Canada

CDC 1-877-394-8747, ⓦ www.cdc.gov. Official US government travel health site.
Canadian Society for International Health ⓦ www.csih.org. Extensive list of travel health centres in Canada.
International Society for Travel Medicine ⓦ www.istm.org. A full list of clinics worldwide specializing in travel health.

A travellers' first-aid kit

Below are items you might want to take, especially if you're planning to go trekking – all are available in India itself, for a fraction of the price you might pay at home:

- Antiseptic cream
- Insect repellent and cream such as Anthisan for soothing bites
- Plasters/band aids
- A course of Flagyl antibiotics
- Water sterilization tablets or water purifier
- Lint and sealed bandages
- Knee supports
- Imodium (Lomotil) for emergency diarrhoea treatment
- A mild oral anesthetic such as Bonjela for soothing ulcers or mild toothache
- Paracetamol/aspirin
- Multivitamin and mineral tablets
- Rehydration sachets
- Hypodermic needles and sterilized skin wipes

In Australia, New Zealand and South Africa

Travellers' Medical & Vaccination Centre
Ⓦ www.tmvc.com.au. Website lists travellers' medical and vaccination centres throughout Australia, New Zealand and South Africa.
Netcare Travel Clinics Ⓦ www.travelclinic.co.za. Travel clinics in South Africa.

Precautions

The lack of sanitation in India can be exaggerated; it's not worth getting too worked up about, or you'll never enjoy anything. A few **common-sense precautions**, however, are in order, bearing in mind that things such as bacteria multiply far more quickly in a tropical climate, and your body will have little immunity to Indian germs.

For details on the **water**, see the box on p.61. When it comes to **food**, bear in mind that it's quite likely that tourist restaurants and Western dishes will bring you grief – probably more so than local food. Be particularly wary of prepared dishes that have to be reheated – they may have been on display in the heat and flies for some time. Anything that is boiled or fried (and thus sterilized) in your presence is usually all right, though meat can sometimes be dodgy, especially in towns or cities where the electricity supply (and thus refrigeration) frequently fails. Raw unpeeled fruit and vegetables should always be viewed with suspicion, and you should avoid salads unless you know they have been soaked in purified water. Wiping down a plate before eating is sensible, and avoid straws as they may be dusty or secondhand.

Be vigilant about **personal hygiene**. Wash your hands often, especially before eating. Keep all cuts clean – treat them with iodine or antiseptic – and cover them up to prevent infection. Be fussier than usual about sharing things like drinks and cigarettes, and never share a razor or toothbrush. It is also inadvisable to go around barefoot – and best to wear flip-flop sandals, including in the shower.

Advice on avoiding **mosquitoes** is offered under the section on malaria on p.61. If you do get bites or itches try not to scratch them: it's hard, but infection and tropical ulcers can result if you do. Tiger balm, calamine lotion, antihistamine cream and even dried soap may relieve the itching.

Finally, especially if you are going on a long trip, have a **dental check-up** before you leave home – you don't want to go down with unexpected tooth trouble in India. If you do, and it feels serious, head for Mumbai, Chennai or Bengaluru (Bangalore), and ask a foreign consulate to recommend a dentist.

Vaccinations

No **inoculations** are legally required for entry into India, but meningitis, typhoid and hepatitis A jabs are recommended, and it's worth ensuring that you are up to date with tetanus, polio and other boosters. All vaccinations can

be obtained in Mumbai, Chennai and other major cities if necessary; just make sure the needle is new or provide your own.

The frequency with which **hepatitis A** strikes travellers makes a strong case for immunization. Transmitted through contaminated food and water, or through saliva, it can lay a victim low for several months with exhaustion, fever and diarrhoea – and may cause liver damage. The Havrix vaccine has been shown to be extremely effective; though expensive, it lasts for up to ten years. Symptoms by which you can recognize hepatitis include a yellowing of the whites of the eyes, nausea, general flu-like malaise, orange urine (though dehydration could also cause that) and light-coloured stools. If you think you have it, avoid alcohol, try to avoid passing it on and get lots of rest. More serious is **hepatitis B**, passed on like AIDS through blood or sexual contact. There is a vaccine, but it is only recommended for those planning to work in a medical environment, or in rural areas and not for tourists.

Typhoid, also spread through contaminated food or water, is endemic in India, but rare outside the monsoon. It produces a persistent high fever with malaise, headaches and abdominal pains, followed by diarrhoea. Vaccination can be by injection (two shots are required, or one for a booster), giving three years' cover, or orally – tablets, which are more expensive but easier on the arm.

Most medical authorities now recommend vaccination against **meningitis** too. Spread by airborne bacteria (through coughs and sneezes for example), it attacks the lining of the brain and can be fatal. Symptoms include fever, a severe headache, stiffness in the neck and a rash on the stomach and back. If you think you may have meningitis, seek immediate medical attention.

You should have a **tetanus** booster every ten years whether you travel or not. Tetanus (or lockjaw) is picked up through contaminated open wounds and causes severe muscular spasms; if you cut yourself on something dirty and are not covered, get a booster as soon as you can.

Assuming that you were vaccinated against **polio** in childhood, only one (oral) booster is needed during your adult life. Immunizations against mumps, measles, TB and rubella are a good idea for anyone who

What about the water?

One of the chief concerns of many prospective visitors to India is whether the water is safe to drink. To put it simply, it's not, though it's usually your unfamiliarity with Indian micro-organisms that generally causes the problems rather than any great virulence in the water itself.

As a rule, it is not a good idea to drink **tap water**, although in big cities it is usually chlorinated. However, you'll find it almost impossible to avoid untreated tap water completely: it is used to make ice, which may appear in drinks without being asked for, to wash utensils and so on. Most restaurants these days use the ubiquitous (and usually visible) **Aquaguard** purification system, which removes just about all impurities, rendering the water pretty safe.

Bottled water, available in all but the most remote places these days, may seem like the simplest and most cost-effective solution, but it has some major drawbacks. The first is that the water itself might not always be as safe as it seems. Independent tests carried out in 2003 on major Indian brands revealed levels of **pesticide** concentration up to 104 times higher than EU norms. Top sellers Kinley, Bisleri and Aquaplus were named as the worst offenders. The second downside of bottled water is the **plastic pollution** it causes. Visualize the size of the pile you'd leave behind you after getting through a couple of bottles per day, and imagine that multiplied by 4 million, and you have something along the lines of the amount of non-biodegradable land-fill waste generated each year by tourists alone.

The best solution from the point of view of your health and the environment is to purify your own water. **Chemical sterilization** is the cheapest method: **iodine** isn't recommended for long trips owing to its long-term side effects, but **chlorine** is completely effective, fast and inexpensive, and you can remove the nasty taste it leaves with neutralizing tablets or lemon juice.

Alternatively, invest in some kind of **purifying filter** incorporating chemical sterilization to kill even the smallest viruses. An ever-increasing range of compact, lightweight products are available these days through outdoor shops and large pharmacies, but anyone who's pregnant or suffers from thyroid problems should check that iodine isn't used as the chemical sterilizer.

wasn't vaccinated as a child and hasn't had the diseases.

Rabies is a problem in India. The best advice is to give dogs and monkeys a wide berth, and not to play with animals at all, no matter how cute they might look. A bite, a scratch or even a lick from an infected animal could spread the disease; wash any such wound immediately but gently with soap or detergent, and apply alcohol or iodine if possible. Find out what you can about the animal and swap addresses with the owner (if there is one) just in case. If the animal might be infected, or the wound begins to tingle and fester, act immediately to get treatment – rabies is invariably fatal once symptoms appear. There is a vaccine, recommended if you plan to work in rural areas, but it is expensive and only effective for a maximum of three months.

Malaria and other mosquito-borne diseases

Protection against **malaria** is absolutely essential. The disease, caused by a parasite carried in the saliva of female Anopheles mosquitoes, is endemic everywhere in South India and is nowadays regarded as the big killer in the Subcontinent. It has a variable incubation period of a few days to several weeks, so you can become ill long after being bitten. Programmes to eradicate the disease by spraying mosquito-infested areas and distributing free preventative tablets have proved disastrous; within a short space of time, the Anopheles mosquitoes develop immunities to the insecticides, while the malaria parasite itself constantly mutates into drug-resistant strains, rendering the old cures ineffective.

Prophylaxis

It is vital for travellers to take **preventative tablets** according to a strict routine, and to cover the period before and after your trip. The drug most usually used is **chloroquine** (trade names include Nivaquin, Avloclor and Resochin), and you usually take two tablets weekly, but India has chloroquine-resistant strains, and you'll need to supplement it with daily **proguanil** (Paludrine) or weekly **Maloprim**.

Malarone is the newest addition to the armoury against the deadlier *Plasmodium falciparum* strain, and is increasingly prescribed for people travelling to areas, like Goa, where chloroquine- and other drug-resistant forms of malaria are present. Studies have claimed it to be 98 percent effective and to have relatively few side-effects. The main drawback is that it's expensive and is only licensed for use for 28 days (although in practice it's probably safe for longer). Malarone is taken once daily with food or milk, starting two days before entering a malaria risk area and continuing daily until seven days after leaving the area. Children can also take it. **Mefloquine** (Lariam) is now seldom recommended by doctors owing to its potentially disastrous side effects.

Side effects of other anti-malarial drugs may include itching, rashes, hair loss and sight problems. Chloroquine and quinine are safe during pregnancy, but most other anti-malarials should be avoided. As the malaria parasite can incubate in your system without showing symptoms for more than a month, it is essential that you continue to take preventative tablets for at least four weeks after you return home: the most common way of catching malaria is when travellers forget to do this.

Symptoms

The first **signs of malaria** are remarkably similar to a severe flu – shivering, burning fever and headaches – and come in waves, usually beginning in the early evening. They may take months to appear but if you suspect anything, go to a hospital or clinic immediately for a blood test. Malaria is not infectious, but some strains are dangerous and can prove fatal when not treated promptly, such as the virulent choloquine-resistant strain, **cerebral malaria**.

Preventing mosquito bites

The best way of avoiding malaria, of course, is to **avoid mosquito bites**. Sleep under a **mosquito net** if possible – one which can hang from a single point is best (you can usually find a way to tie a string across your room to hang it from). Burn mosquito **coils**, which are readily available in South India, though you should avoid them if you suffer from asthma. Plug-in **vapour mats or oil evaporators** are increasingly commonly used. When out after dusk, smother yourself in mosquito **repellent**. An Indian brand, Odomos, is widely available, very effective and has a pleasant lemon scent, though most travellers tend to bring a DEET-based spray from home; people with sensitive skin are advised to use the new wrist and ankle bands instead, as they are equally as effective as spray. A more natural alternative for those with sensitive skin is **citronella** or Mosi-guard Natural, made in the UK from a blend of **eucalyptus oils**. In India, the New-Age centre, Auroville, produces its own herbal coils, incense and spray, available in all traveller ghettos.

Although they are active from dusk till dawn, female Anopheles mosquitoes prefer to bite in the **evening**, so be especially careful at that time. Wear long sleeves, skirts or trousers, avoid dark colours, which attract mosquitoes, and ensure you have repellent on exposed skin.

Dengue fever, Japanese encephalitis and Chikungunya

Another illness spread by mosquito bites is **dengue fever**, whose symptoms are similar to those of malaria, with the additional symptom of aching bones. There is no vaccine available and the only treatment is complete rest, with drugs to assuage the fever. Occurrences are pretty rare but tend to go in mini-epidemics. **Japanese encephalitis**, yet another mosquito-borne viral infection causing fever, muscle pains and headaches, has been on the increase in recent years in rural rice-growing areas during and just after monsoon, though there have been no reports of travellers catching the disease and you shouldn't need the vaccine. The same is true of the African disease **Chikungunya**, a relatively rare form of viral fever that has afflicted most parts south India over the past few years, notably Alappuzha (Alleppey) in southern Kerala, where it casued at least 125 deaths in 2006. The name is derived from the Makonde word meaning "to bend" referring to the doubled-up posture that's a common symptom of Chikungunya.

Intestinal troubles

Diarrhoea is the most common bane of travellers. When mild and not accompanied by other major symptoms, it may just be your stomach reacting to unfamiliar food. Accompanied by cramps and vomiting, it could well be food poisoning. In either case, it will probably pass of its own accord in 24–48 hours without treatment. In the meantime, it's essential to replace the fluids and salts you're losing, so take lots of water with oral **rehydration salts** (commonly referred to as ORS, or called Electrolyte in India). If you can't get ORS, use half a teaspoon of salt and eight of sugar in a litre of water. Travel clinics and pharmacies sell double-ended moulded plastic spoons with the exact ratio of sugar to salt. If you are too ill to drink, seek medical help immediately.

While you are suffering, it's a good idea to avoid greasy food, heavy spices, caffeine and most fruit and dairy products. Some say bananas and pawpaws are good, as are *kitchri* (a simple dhal and rice preparation), rice soup and coconut water. Curd or a soup made from Marmite or Vegemite (if you happen to have some with you) are forms of protein that can be easily absorbed by your body when you have the runs. Drugs like Lomotil or Immodium simply plug you up – undermining the body's efforts to rid itself of infection – though they can be useful if you have to travel. If symptoms persist for more than a few days, a course of antibiotics may be necessary; this should be seen as a last resort, and only used following medical advice.

It's a good idea to look at what comes out when you go to the toilet. If your diarrhoea contains blood or mucus, the cause may be dysentery or giardia. With a fever, it could well be caused by **bacillic dysentery**, and may clear up without treatment. If you're sure you need it, a course of antibiotics such as tetra-cycline should sort you out, but they also destroy gut flora in your intestines, which help protect you (curd can replenish them to some extent). If you start a course, be sure to finish it, even after the symptoms have gone.

Similar symptoms, without fever, indicate **amoebic dysentery**, which is much more serious, and can damage your gut if untreated. The usual cure is a course of Metronidazole (Flagyl) or Fasigyn, both antibiotics which may themselves make you feel ill, and must not be taken with alcohol; avoid caffeine, too. Symptoms of **giardia** are similar – including frothy stools, nausea and constant fatigue – for which the treatment again is Metronidazole. If you suspect that you have any of these, seek medical help, and only start on the Metronidazole if there is blood in your diarrhoea and it is impossible to see a doctor.

Finally, bear in mind that oral drugs, such as malaria pills and the contraceptive pill, are likely to be largely ineffective if taken while suffering from diarrhoea.

Bites and creepy-crawlies

Biting insects and similar animals other than mosquitoes may also aggravate you. The obvious ones are **bed bugs** – look for signs of squashed ones around cheap hotel beds. An infested mattress can be left in the hot sun all day to get rid of them, but they often live in the frame or even in walls or floors. Other notorious culprits, particularly bother-some in parts of the Andaman Islands, are **sandflies**, whose bites can become unbear-ably itchy. Head and body **lice** can also be a nuisance, but medicated soap and shampoo (foreign brands are normally more effective) usually see them off. Avoid scratching bites, which can lead to infection, sometimes in dangerous forms such as **septicemia** or **tropical ulcers**. Bites from ticks and lice can spread **typhus**, characterized by fever, muscle aches, headaches and, later, red eyes and a measles-like rash. If you think you have it, seek treatment.

Worms may enter your body through skin (especially the soles of your feet) or food. An itchy anus is a common symptom, and you may even see them in your stools. They are easy to treat: if you suspect you have them, get some worming tablets such as Mebendazole (Vermox) from any pharmacy.

Snakes are unlikely to bite unless accidentally disturbed, and most are harmless in any case. The best way to avoid them is to walk heavily, and never poke around holes or crevices in the ground. It's also a good idea to wear sturdy shoes rather than flip-flops at night. It's rare to get bitten but if you do, try to identify the snake and seek immediate medical help: antivenoms are available in most hospitals, A few **spiders** have poisonous bites too, as do scorpions and some centipedes, but they hardly ever prove fatal. **Leeches** may attach themselves to you in jungle areas. Remove them with salt or a lit cigarette; never just pull them off.

Heat trouble

The sun and the heat can cause a few unexpected problems. Many people get a bout of **prickly heat** rash before they've acclimatized – an infection of the sweat ducts caused by excessive perspiration that doesn't dry off. A cool shower, zinc oxide powder (sold in India) or talcum powder, and loose cotton clothes should help. **Dehydration** is another possible problem, so make sure you're drinking enough liquid, and drink rehydration salts when hot and/or tired. The main danger sign is irregular urination (only once a day for instance). Dark urine probably means you should drink more.

Don't underestimate the power of the **sun**. A high-factor sunblock is vital on exposed skin, especially when you first arrive, and on areas newly exposed by haircuts or changes of clothes. A light hat is also a very good idea, especially if you're doing a lot of walking around.

Finally, be aware that overheating can cause **heatstroke**, which is potentially fatal. Signs are a very high body temperature without a feeling of fever, headaches and disorientation. Lowering body temperature (a tepid shower for example) and resting in an air-conditioned room is the first step in treatment.

HIV and AIDS

The increasing presence of **AIDS** has only recently been acknowledged by the Indian government as a national problem. Should you need an injection or a transfusion in India, make sure that new, sterile equipment is used; any blood you receive should be from voluntary rather than commercial donor banks. Try to bring needles from home in your first-aid kit. If you have a shave from a barber, make sure he uses a clean blade, and don't submit to processes such as ear-piercing, acupuncture or tattooing unless you can be sure that the equipment is sterile.

Getting medical help

Pharmacies can usually advise on minor medical problems, and most **doctors** in India speak English. Many hotels also have a doctor on call. Basic medicaments are made to Indian Pharmacopoea (IP) standards, and most medicines are available without prescription – although always check the sell-by date.

Hospitals vary in standard; those in the big cities are generally pretty good, and university and medical-school hospitals are best of all. **Private clinics** and misson hospitals are often better than state-run ones, but may require patients (even emergency cases) to buy necessities such as medicines, plaster casts and vaccines and to pay for X-rays before procedures can be carried out. Costs are a fraction of private health care in the West, though (be sure to keep all original documents and receipts to claim money back on insurance if need be). **Government hospitals** provide all surgical and aftercare services free of charge, and in most other state medical institutions, charges are usually so low that for minor treatment the expense may well be lower than the initial "excess" on your insurance. You will need a companion to stay, or you'll have to come to an arrangement with one of the hospital cleaners, to help you out in hospital – relatives are expected to wash, feed and generally take care of the patient.

Addresses of foreign consulates (who will advise in an emergency), and of clinics and hospitals can be found in the Listings sections for major towns in this book.

The media

With over one billion people and a literacy rate of around fifty percent, India produces a staggering 4700 daily papers in over 300 languages and another 39,000 journals and weeklies. Furthermore, with the advent of satellite and cable, dozens of new TV channels have sprung up, both in English and Indian languages. Radio has a similarly wide range of channels, though it tends to be more localized and there is less programming in English. India's press is among the freest in Asia, and attacks on the government can be quite outspoken. That said, most papers and other forms of media are an active part of the political establishment and are unlikely to print anything that might upset the "national consensus" – particularly when it comes to Pakistan, the Kashmir conflict and foreign affairs generally.

Newspapers and magazines

There are a large number of English-language **daily newspapers**, both national and regional. The most prominent of the nationals are *The Hindu*, *The Statesman*, *The Times of India*, *The Economic Times* and *The Indian Express* (usually the most critical of the government), each of which have regional pages and inserts and are widely read in the South; *The Deccan Herald* is a southern paper, though widely read across India. All are pretty dry and sober, and concentrate on Indian news, though their flowery prose can be entertaining. *Asian Age*, published simultaneously in India, London and New York, is a conservative tabloid that sports a motley collection of colourful stories. All the major Indian newspapers have **websites** (see p.66), with the *Times of India*, *The Hindu* and the *Hindustan Times* providing the most up-to-date and detailed news services.

In recent years, a number of *Time/Newsweek*-style **news magazines** have hit the market, with a strong emphasis on politics. The best of these are *India Today*, published independently, and *Frontline*, published by *The Hindu*. Others include *Outlook*, which is easily readable and covered the widest range of subjects, *Sunday* and *The Week*. These often give a clearer picture of Indian politics than the dailies and also cover more international news. *Business India* is more financially orientated, and the *India Magazine* more cultural. Film fanzines and gossip mags are very popular; *Screen* and *Filmfare* are the best, though you'll have to be reasonably *au fait* with Indian movies to follow a lot of the coverage. Magazines and periodicals in English cover all sorts of popular and minority interests, and there are plenty of sports publications, especially on cricket. The one visitors to South India are most likely to find of interest is the Mumbai edition of *Time Out*, modelled on the popular London and New York listings magazines, which covers the same mix of previews and city-specific features.

Two- to three-day-old editions of **foreign publications** such as the *International Herald Tribune*, *Time*, *Newsweek*, *The Economist* and the international edition of the British *Guardian* are all available from major bookshops in the main cities, the most upmarket hotels, and some other outlets in a few tourist centres, but they're rather expensive (particularly considering that you can now read most of them online for free). Expat-orientated bookstalls stock slightly out-of-date and expensive copies of magazines like *Vogue* and *NME*.

Indian news online

Ⓦ**www.guardian.co.uk/india** High-quality news features are the meat of this "Special Report" section of the *Guardian*'s award-winning website, which also has links to its archived India articles and an excellent dossier on Kashmir. Access is free.

ⓦ www.samachar.com One of the best news gateway sites, featuring the headlines of and links to leading Indian newspapers.

ⓦ www.tehelka.com Alternative news magazine (in)famous for exposing corruption scandals in government.

ⓦ timesofindia.indiatimes.com; ⓦ www .hinduonline.com; ⓦ www.hindustantimes .com; ⓦ www.deccanherald.com The websites of some of India's leading daily papers, with detailed national coverage. *The Deccan Herald* site has a fast-loading text-only format.

Radio

BBC World Service radio can be picked up on short wave, although reception quality is highly variable. The wavelength also changes at different times of day. In the early morning, try 5970Khz; during much of the day 15310Khz or 17790Khz; and in the evening, 9740Khz or 11955. A full list of the World Service's many frequencies appears on the BBC website (ⓦ www.bbc.co.uk /worldservice). **Government** radio also has some broadcasts in English.

Television

The **government-run TV** company, Doordarshan, which broadcasts a sober diet of edifying programmes, has tried to compete with the onslaught of mass access to cable and **satellite TV** but is losing ground fast. The main broadcaster in English is Rupert Murdoch's **Star TV** network, which incorporates BBC World and otherwise dominates the schedules. Zee TV (with Z News) presents a progressive blend of Hindi-orientated chat, film, news and music programmes. Star Sports and ESPN churn out a mind-boggling amount of cricket with occasional forays into other sports – both broadcast Premier and Champions League football, for example. Others include CNN, the Discovery Channel, National Geographic, MTV, the immensely popular Channel V, hosted by scantily clad Mumbai models and DJs, and an increasing number of reasonable film channels like Star Movies, HBO, Zee Studio and AXN. Most hotels from the top end of the budget range upwards have cable TV these days, but exactly how many channels you will get in any particular location is rather hit and miss.

Festivals

Virtually every temple in every town or village across the country has its own festival. While mostly religious in nature, merrymaking rather than solemnity are generally the order of the day, and onlookers are usually welcome. Indeed, if you are lucky enough to coincide your trip with a local festival, it may well prove to be the highlight. Music and dance, originally nurtured within the temple environment, are often key features of temple festivals and, in winter, multi-day music festivals known as "conferences" spring up in most major southern cities where you can hear the cream of Carnatic classical music.

Festivals are invariably dedicated to a particular deity, whether celebrated throughout the region or more localized. The biggest and most splendid of festivals, such as Madurai's three annual festivals (see box, p.600) and Mysore's celebrated

Dussehra festival (see box, p.200), are major attractions. In Karnataka and Tamil Nadu, the focus of a temple festival is usually a **rath** (chariot) in which the deities are borne aloft in procession through the streets. However, in Kerala, instead of a

India has only four national **public holidays:** January 26 (Republic Day); August 15 (Independence Day); October 2 (Gandhi's birthday); and December 25 (Christmas Day). Each state, however, has its own calendar of public holidays, too numerous to list here. Most businesses close on the public holidays and major holidays of their own religion; these are marked with an asterisk below. The Hindu calendar months are given in brackets below, as most of the festivals listed are Hindu.

Key: B=Buddhist; **C**=Christian; **H**=Hindu; **J**=Jain; **M**=Muslim; **N**=non-religious; **P**=Parsi;

January to Feburary (Magha)

(H) Pongal (1 Magha) Tamil harvest festival celebrated with decorated cows, processions and *rangolis* (a colourful design made near the entrance of a house, traditionally painted or created out of coloured rice powder). *Pongal*, a sweet porridge made from newly harvested rice, is eaten by all, including the cows. In the South, the festival, also known as Makar Sankranti, is celebrated in Karnataka and Andhra Pradesh.

(H) Vasant Panchami (5 Magha) One-day spring festival in honour of Saraswati, the goddess of learning, celebrated by kite-flying, wearing yellow saris and the blessing of schoolchildren's books and pens by the goddess.

(N) Republic Day (Jan 26)*

(H) Floating Festival (16 Magha) at Madurai. See p.600.

(N) Elephanta Music and Dance Festival near Mumbai. See p.108.

Feburary to March (Phalguna)

(B) Losar (1 Phalguna) Tibetan New Year celebrations among Tibetan communities throughout India including Karnataka.

(H) Shivratri (10 Phalguna) Anniversary of Shiva's *tandav* (creation) dance and his wedding anniversary. Popular family festival, but also a *sadhu* festival of pilgrimage and fasting, especially at important Shiva temples.

(H) Holi (15 Phalguna)* Festival of colours held during *Dol Purnima* (full moon) to celebrate the beginning of spring, most popular in North India but heartily celebrated in Mumbai and parts of northern Karnataka, where you can expect to be bombarded with water, paint, coloured powder and other mixtures.

(C) Carnival Goa's own Mardi Gras features float processions and *feni*-induced mayhem in the state capital, Panjim. See p.182.

(H) Ulsavam, Guruvayur in Kerala. Although the temple here is off-limits to non-Hindus, the elephant procession with over forty elephants and the elephant race are well worth the visit. See p.476.

March to April (Chaitra)

(H) Ramanavami (9 Chaitra)* Birthday of Rama, the hero of the Ramayana, celebrated with readings of the epic and discourses on Rama's life and teachings.

(C) Easter* Good Friday is a particularly observed day.

(P) Pateti Parsi new year, also known as Nowroz, celebrating the creation of fire. Feasting, services and present-giving.

(P) Khorvad Sal (a week after Pateti) Birthday of Zarathustra (aka Zoroaster).

(H) Chittirai, Madurai Elephant-led procession. See p.600.

(H) Arattu Festival, Thiruvananthapuram Held again during Oct/Nov, this festival celebrates the deities of the rajas of Travancore, who are led to the sea in a procession of elephants. See p.376.

Principal South Indian festivals

April to May (Vaisakha)

(H) Baisakhi (1 Vaisakha) The solar new year, celebrated with music and dancing;

(J) Mahavir Jayanti (13 Vaisakha)* Birthday of Mahavira, the founder of Jainism. The main Jain festival of the year.

(H) Puram Festival, Thrissur in Kerala. Frenzied drumming and elephant parades. See p.470.

(B) Buddha Jayanti (16 Vaisakha)* Buddha's birthday. He was born, attained nirvana and died on the same date.

July to August (Shravana)

(H) Raksha Bandhan/Narial Purnima (16 Shravana) Festival to honour the sea god Varuna. Brothers and sisters exchange gifts, the sister tying a thread known as a *rakhi* to her brother's wrist. Brahmins, after a day's fasting, change the sacred thread they wear.

(N) Independence Day (Aug 15)* India's biggest secular celebration, on the anniversary of its Independence from Britain, celebrated with parades and fireworks.

August to September (Bhadraparda)

(H) Ganesh Chaturthi (4 Bhadraparda) Festival dedicated to Ganesh, especially celebrated in Maharashtra. In Mumbai, huge processions carry images of the god to immerse in the sea. See p.108.

(H) Onam Keralan harvest festival, celebrated with snake-boat races. The Nehru Trophy snake-boat race at Alappuzha (held on the second Saturday of August) is the most spectacular, with long boats each crewed by 150 rowers. See p.376.

(H) Janmashtami (23 Bhadraparda)* Krishna's birthday, an occasion for feasting and celebration, especially in Vaishnava centres like Udupi and in Mumbai.

(H) Avani Mula Festival, Madurai Celebration of the coronation of Shiva. See p.600.

September to October (Ashvina)

(H) Dussehra (1–10 Ashvina)* Ten-day festival (usually two days' public holiday) associated with vanquishing demons, in particular Rama's victory over Ravana in the Ramayana, and Durga's over the buffalo-headed Mahishasura. Dussehra celebrations include performances of the *Ram Lila* (life of Rama). Best seen in the South in Mysore. See p.282.

(N) Mahatma Gandhi's Birthday (Oct 2)* Rather solemn commemoration of Independent India's founding father.

October to November (Kartika)

(H) Diwali (Deepavali) (15 Kartika)* Festival of lights, especially popular in the North

rath, the deity is carried on a pageant of elephants. A few festivals feature elephant races while others, especially along the coast of Kerala, host spectacular boat races and regattas.

A list of the main national and regional celebrations is given in the box on pp.67–69. **Hindu**, **Buddhist** and **Jain** festivals follow the Indian **lunar calendar** and their dates therefore vary from year to year. Determining but celebrated everywhere, to mark Rama and Sita's homecoming in the Ramayana. Festivities include the lighting of oil lamps and firecrackers and the giving and receiving of sweets.

(J) Jain New Year (15 Kartika) Coincides with Diwali, so Jains celebrate alongside Hindus.

(C) Feast of Mar Thoma (Nov 21) A colourful procession of decorated carts leads to this ancient site where St Thomas first landed, at Kodungallur in Kerala. See p.475.

(N) Hampi Festival Government-sponsored music and dance festival. See p.339.

December to January (Pausa)

(C) Christmas (Dec 25)* Popular in Christian areas of Goa and Kerala, and in big cities.

(N) Carnatic Music Festivals, Chennai For around a month every year, the city hosts thirteen or so large music programmes called "conferences", each lasting several days. See p.522.

(N) Mamallapuram Dance Festival Colourful dance and music festival which runs at weekends for several weeks on a stage in front of the Arjuna's Penance bas-relief. See p.541.

(N) Kerala Kalamandalam Festival, Cheruthuruthy The annual festival of music and dance serves as a showcase for this leading arts institution, featuring the best Keralan performers and attracting musicians and dancers from all over the country. See p.477.

Moveable

(M) Ramadan (first day: Sept 2, 2008; Aug 22, 2009) The start of a month during which Muslims may not eat, drink or smoke from sunrise to sunset, and should abstain from sex. Towards the end of the month it takes its toll, so be gentle with Muslims you meet at this time.

(M) Id ul-Fitr (Oct 1, 2008; Sep 21, 2009)*: Feast to celebrate the end of Ramadan, after the lunar month is complete.

(M) Id ul-Zuha (Bakr-Id; Dec 21, 2007; Dec 9, 2008; Nov 28, 2009) Pilgrimage festival coinciding with the end of the Haj to commemorate Abraham's preparedness to sacrifice his son Ismail. Celebrated with the slaughtering and consumption of sheep.

(M) Muharram (first day Jan 10, 2008; Dec 29, 2008; Dec 18, 2009) Commemorates the martyrdom of the (Shi'ite) Imam, the Prophet's grandson and popular saint, Hussain.

them more than a year in advance is a highly complicated business best left to astrologers. **Muslim** festivals follow the Islamic calendar, whose year is shorter and which thus loses about eleven days per annum against the Gregorian calendar. **Christianity** is especially strong in Goa and Kerala where the feasts of saints are celebrated and carols are sung in churches packed to the brim during Christmas.

Sports and outdoor activities

India is not perhaps a place that most people associate with sports. However, cricket is a national obsession and football (soccer) has its place in certain regions. The most popular adventure activities with foreign visitors are trekking and scuba diving.

Sports

Far and away the most popular sport in the South, as in the rest of India, is **cricket**, both from a spectating and participatory point of view. **Football** also has a decent following in some states, especially Goa and Kerala. Other legacies of British rule include **horseracing** and **polo**, while **traditional Indian sports** can also be found in certain places. The best website to find out about sport in India is: Ⓦsify.com/sports.

Cricket

Travellers to India will find it hard to get away from **cricket** – it's everywhere and enjoys extensive coverage on television. Cricketing heroes such as the maestro batsman Sachin Tendulkar are held in the highest esteem and live under the constant scrutiny of the media and public. Matches are played during the winter months, mainly November to March. The three first-class grounds in South India where you are most likely to catch an international game are Mumbai's Wankhede Stadium, Bengaluru's (Bangalore's) Chinnaswamy Stadium and Chennai's MA Chidambaram Stadium, though internationals have also been played at Hyderabad, Kochi, Trivandrum, Pune and Goa. Tickets for One-Day Internationals (ODIs) are in far shorter supply than for Test Matches. Check the press for availability and sale dates; prices range from Rs100 to Rs1000. Inter-state cricket is easy to catch – the most prestigious competition is the Ranji Trophy; tickets are much cheaper and you can invariably pay to go in on the day.

Besides spectator cricket, you'll see games being played on open spaces all around the country. Occasionally, you may even be asked to join in, if it's not too serious a game.

Football

Football (soccer) has a large fan base in Mumbai, Goa and Kerala. The top division of the national championship (NFL) consists of ten teams, mostly belonging to large national organizations, and at the time of writing 2006 champions Mahindra United from Mumbai were again challenging for honours alongside Goa's Dempo Sports Club. Other renowned southern teams include the Sporting Clube de Goa, Mumbai's Air India and Bengaluru's (Bangalore's) Hindustan Aeronautics Ltd; the last two teams are particularly strong in the air. The NFL season runs from January to May, with the Federations Cup acting as a pre-season warm-up in the second half of December. Check the local press or Ⓦindianfootball.com for fixtures; you can usually get in on the day for Rs50–500.

Horseracing and polo

Horseracing can be a good day out, especially if you enjoy a flutter. There are several racecourses around the South, mostly in larger cities such as Mumbai, Hyderabad, Mysore and Bengaluru (Bangalore) but also in some smaller spots such as Ooty. Look in local newspapers, such as *Bangalore Today*, and any local listings magazine to find out when race meetings are being held; season dates vary from city to city but run roughly from November to April.

Polo, originally from upper Kashmir, was taken up by the British to become one of the symbols of the Raj, though the tradition has declined. Today, it's mainly played by the army, so you may catch a game near a major southern cantonment.

Traditional Indian sports

Among the contact sports unique to India, **kushti**, an ancient form of Indian mud-wrestling, has a small but dedicated following and is a favourite of devotees of the monkey god, Hanuman, from whom the wrestlers are believed to descend. The mud the competitors smear themselves in is blended with ghee, rose petals and medicinal herbs. Another form of wrestling, which developed out of training exercises, is **mallakhamb**, which involves complicated postures and a great deal of agility; check out Ⓦmallakhamb.org. However, the most dramatic and ferocious of all is the popular Keralan martial art of **kalarippayattu** (see p.377 and Ⓦkalarippayat.com), which involves both hand-to-hand combat and the use of weapons.

Kabadi, where two teams of seven try to "tag" each other in an enclosed court, to continuous cries of "kabadikabadikabadi", is another traditional Indian pastime. Although still an amateur sport, kabadi is taken very seriously, with state and national championships and a slot in the Asian Games – however, it's not as widely played in South India as it is further north. A similar game of tag, only with nine players and different rules, is **kho kho**, which is particularly popular in its native Maharashtra. If you want to see any of these sports, it's best to ask at local tourist offices or keep an eye on the local press.

Outdoor activities

Though not the prime reason for most people to visit South India, there are a number of outdoor pursuits to be enjoyed. The most common is **trekking**, though **snorkelling** and **scuba diving** are also becoming increasingly popular, and a few other watersports are beginning to make an appearance. For information on South India's **wildlife sanctuaries and national parks**, see the box in Contexts, p.774.

Trekking

Although there are far more **trekking** possibilities in the mountainous north, low-level treks are available in the Western Ghats and Nilgiri Hills (see p.625 & p.639). Popular trekking hubs are: Madikeri in the Kodagu (Coorg) region; Periyar and Munnar in Kerala's Cardamom Hills; Matheran on the outskirts of Mumbai also offers plenty of good short treks

The best time to trek is between November and March, when it's not too hot or wet, especially after New Year in the case of the Nilgiris, which can see rain from the northeast monsoon in November and December.

It isn't necessary to have any specialized gear but it is a good idea to have the following equipment: clothes to wear in layers, sturdy shoes or boots, a waterproof jacket, backpack, compass and map, pocket knife, sleeping bag, sunblock, toiletries and toilet paper, torch, water bottle, basic medical kit and some emergency provisions. It's usually best to take a guide if you are planning to get off the beaten track. They usually only cost around Rs50–100 per person per hour; suggestions on finding guides and on specific routes are given in the relevant chapters.

Scuba diving and snorkelling

The most promising destination for both scuba diving and snorkelling is the **Andaman Islands**, which are ringed by crystal-clear waters containing gigantic coral reefs teeming with tropical fish and other marine life: they are the equal of anywhere in Asia. The diving centres here are well-equipped and reputable, though don't come here expecting rock-bottom prices: dive courses charge around Rs15,000 (£176/$339) for a four-day PADI-approved open-water course. Make sure you book ahead as places can be in short supply during the peak season, between December and February.

The other group of Indian islands offering world-class diving is **Lakshadweep**, a classic coconut-palm-covered atoll, some 400km west of Kerala in the Arabian Sea. The shallow lagoons, extensive coral reefs and exceptionally good visibility make this a perfect option for both first-timers and more experienced divers. The catch is that permit restrictions mean foreigners are only allowed to visit a couple of islands and must stay in phenomenally expensive five-star resorts.

See the box on pp.464–465 for more details.

For anyone on a limited budget, a better option is **Goa**. Visibility is not so great along this stretch of coast, though you can escape the worst of the silt by heading further out to sea by boat, where a handful of islands and two wrecks shelter prolific marine life. Most of the dive sites are shallow (between 10m and 20m), and thus ideal for beginners.

As with other countries, qualified divers should take their current certification card and/or log book; if you haven't used it for one year or more, you may have to take a short test costing around Rs300.

Other watersports

With the increase in package tourism at the beaches, a number of watersports popular around the world are becoming available, particularly in Goa. These include surfing, windsurfing, bodysurfing, jet-skiing and parasailing. Equipment rental and instruction prices are in the Rs50–500 per hour range for the board sports, Rs800–1500 for more expensive gear, as in the last two activities mentioned.

Yoga, meditation and Ayurveda

Yoga is taught all over the South, and there are several internationally known yoga centres where you can train to become a teacher. Meditation is similarly widely practised and specific courses are available in temples, meditation centres and monasteries. South India also has innumerable ashrams — communities where people work, live and study together, drawn by a common (usually spiritual) goal.

Details of yoga and meditation courses and ashrams are provided throughout the Guide. Most centres offer courses that you can enrol on at short notice but many of the more popular ones listed below need to be booked well in advance.

Yoga and meditation

The word "**yoga**" literally means "union", the aim of the discipline being to help the practitioner unite his or her individual consciousness with the Divine. This is achieved by raising awareness of the true nature of self through spiritual, mental and physical discipline.

Many texts and manuscripts have been written describing the practice and philosophy of yoga, but probably the best known are the Yoga Sutras of Patanjali, written by the sage Maharishi Patanjali in either the second century BC or the second or third century AD. He believed the path to realization of the self

consisted of eight spiritual practices which he called the "eight limbs": these were *yama* (moral codes); *niyama* (self-purification through study); *asana* (posture); *pranayama* (breath control); *pratyahara* (sense control); *dharana* (concentration); *dhyana* (contemplation); and *samadhi* (meditative absorption). Of these eight limbs the first four are "external" in nature while the last four are "internal".

Today it is **asanas**, or the physical postures, that are most commonly identified as yoga, but these are just one element of what to many practitioners is a complete transcendental philosophy.

Types of yoga

A multitude of paths and practices exist to help the individual attain the ultimate goal of union with the Divine. Hatha yoga is the term most commonly used for the physical and spiritual practices described above, and there are innumerable approaches to teaching it. Broadly speaking they all focus on a series of *asanas*, which stretch, relax and tone the muscular system of the body and also massage the internal organs. Each *asana* has a beneficial effect on a particular muscle group or organ, and although they vary widely in difficulty, consistent practice will lead to improved suppleness and health benefits.

Iyengar yoga is one of the most famous approaches studied today, named after its founder, BKS Iyengar, a student of the great yoga teacher Sri Tirumalai Krishnamacharya. His style is based upon precise physical alignment during each posture. With much practice, and the aid of props such as blocks, straps and chairs, the student can attain perfect physical balance and, the theory goes, perfect balance of mind will follow. Iyengar yoga has a strong therapeutic element and has been used successfully for treating a wide variety of structural and internal problems. The main Iyengar centre, the Ramamani Iyengar Memorial Yoga Institute, is in Pune (see p.166).

Ashtanga yoga is an approach developed by Pattabhi Jois, who also studied under Krishnamacharya. Unlike Iyengar yoga, which centres around a collection of separate *asanas*, Ashtanga links various postures into a series of flowing moves called *vinyasa*, with the aim of developing strength and agility. The perfect synchronization of movement with breath is a key objective throughout these sequences. Although a powerful form it can be frustrating for beginners as each move has to be perfected before moving on to the next one. See below for contact details.

The son of Krishnamacharya, TKV Desikachar, established a third major branch in the modern yoga tree, emphasizing a more versatile and adaptive approach to teaching, focused on the situation of the individual practitioner. This style became known as **Viniyoga**, although Desikachar has long tried to distance himself from the term. In the mid-1970s, he co-founded the Krishnamacharya Yoga Mandiram (KYM), now a flagship institute in Chennai and, in 2006, an off-shoot now steered by his son Kausthub, called the Krishnamacharya Healing and Yoga Foundation (KHYF).

The other most influential Indian yoga teacher of the modern era has been Swami Vishnu Devananda, an acolyte of the famous sage Swami Sivanda, who established the International Sivananda Yoga Vedanta Center, with more than twenty branches in India and abroad. **Sivananda**-style yoga tends to introduce elements in a different order from its counterparts – teaching practices regarded by others as advanced to relative beginners. This fast-forward approach has proved particularly popular with Westerners, who flock in their thousands to intensive introductory courses staged at centres all over India – the most renowned of them at Neyyar Dam, in the hills east of the Keralan capital, Thiruvananthapuram.

For specific advice on recommended **yoga schools**, see our accounts of Anjuna (p.220), Morjim (p.230) and Arambol (p.237) in the Goa chapter, and Neyyar Dam (p.397) and Varkala (p.402) in Kerala.

Meditation

Meditation is an essential part of both Hinduism and Buddhism and ideally should be practised immediately after performing yoga *asanas*, when the energy of the body has been awakened. Through meditation the practitioner may realize the true nature of mind and self, an essential step on the path to enlightenment.

Courses and ashrams

Ashrams range in size, some taking several thousand people, others just a handful, and their rules, regulations and restrictions vary enormously. While some offer on-site accommodation, and have set programmes, others will require you to stay in the nearest town or village, and only offer guidance and teaching as and when requested. How much you pay also varies enormously – you might be charged Western prices at one, or simply make a donation.

The following well-known establishments routinely welcome foreign visitors:

Ashtanga Yoga Nilayam Mysore ⓦ www.ayri .org. Run by Pattabhi Jois, one of India's great yoga innovators. Courses in ashtanga yoga affiliated with martial arts last at least a month and need to be booked in advance. See also **above**.

Mata Amritanandamayi Math Amritapuri, Vallikkavu, Kerala ⓦwww.amritapuri.org. The ashram of the famous "Hugging Saint", Amma, is a sugar-pink, multistorey affair looming out of the Keralan backwaters between Kollam and Alappuzha. Hundreds of thousands pass through annually for *darshan* and a hug from the smiley guru, whose charitable works have earned for her near-divine status in the south. See p.410 for a biography.

Osho Commune International Pune ☎020/612 6655, ⓦwww.osho.com. Established by the enigmatic Osho, who generated a huge following of both Western and Indian devotees, this centre is set in 31 acres of beautifully landscaped gardens and offers a variety of courses in personal therapy, healing and meditation. For full details, **see p.171**. There are numerous other Indian and international centres dedicated to Osho's teachings.

Prasanthi Nilayam Puttaparthy ☎08555/287236, ⓦwww.saionline.org. The ashram of Satya Sai Baba, one of India's most revered and popular gurus, who has a worldwide following of millions despite the deaths of four followers at the ashram in mysterious circumstances in 2000. **See p.676** for more details. Sai Baba also has a smaller ashram in Bengaluru (Bangalore) and one in Kodaikanal.

Ramamani Iyengar Memorial Yoga Institute Pune ☎020/2565 6134, ⓦwww.iyengar-yoga .com. The main Iyengar Institute dedicated to founder BKS Iyengar, author of 14 yoga books including the classic Light on Yoga. Teacher training courses and yoga classes are offered (book well in advance); there are also centres in Goa (☎098/2301 6995) and Bengaluru (Bangalore) (☎080/2671 3478).

Saccidananda Ashram Kullithalai, near Tiruchirapalli ☎04323/222260, ⓦwww .bedegriffiths.com. Also known as Shantivanam (Sanskrit for Peace Forest), the ashram is situated on the banks of the sacred River Cauvery. Founded by Father Bede Griffiths, a visionary Benedictine monk, it presents a curious but sympathetic fusion of Christianity and Hinduism. Accommodation is in simple huts dotted around the grounds, meals are communal and visitors can join in the services and rituals or just relax. It's very busy during the major Christian festivals.

Sivananda Yoga Vedanta Dhanwantari Ashram Thiruvananthapuram ☎0471/229 0493, ⓦwww.sivananda.org. An offshoot of the original Divine Life Society, a yoga-based ashram where asanas, breathing techniques (pranayama) and meditation are taught. They also run month-long yoga teacher-training programmes, but book well in advance. For more on the ashram and on Sivananda, see p.397.

Sri Aurobindo Ashram Pondicherry, Tamil Nadu ⓦwww.sriaurobindosociety.org.in. Founded in 1968 by "The Mother", spiritual successor to Sri Aurobindo, this commune is surely India's New Age centre. Its stated aim is to live in harmony through spiritual discipline in a sustainable way . It's a popular destination for day-trippers but long-term guests and settlers are welcome. See also p.562.

Vipassana International Academy Hyderabad ☎040/2424 0290, Chennai ☎044/2478 3311, Bengaluru (Bangalore) ☎080/2222 4330, ⓦwww .dhamma.org. Vipassana meditation is a technique originally taught by the Buddha, which helps practitioners develop a deeper awareness of both physical sensations and mental processes. Courses last a minimum of ten days and are fairly austere – 4am starts, ten hours of meditation a day, no solid food after noon, segregation of the sexes and no talking for the duration, other than with the leaders of the course. They are free for all first-time students, offering everyone an opportunity to learn and benefit from this powerful technique. Vipassana is taught in more than 25 centres throughout India, with three regional centres in South India.

Ayurveda

Ayurveda, a Sanskrit word meaning the "knowledge for prolonging life", is a five-thousand-year-old holistic medical system which is widely practised in India and especially popular in the South, where Kerala is a particular stronghold. Ayurvedic doctors and clinics in large towns deal with foreigners as well as their usual patients, and some pharmacies specialize in Ayurvedic prepara-tions, including toiletries such as soaps, shampoos and toothpaste.

Ayurveda stems from the same period of Vedic philosophy as yoga, and places great importance on the **harmony** of mind, body and spirit, acknowledging the psychosomatic causes behind many diseases. The skin is seen as a mirror of our inner health and the body manifests everything that happens internally. Unlike the allopathic medicines of the West, which depend on finding out what's ailing you and then killing it, Ayurveda looks at the whole patient: disease is regarded as a symptom of imbalance, so it's the imbalance that's treated, not the disease.

Ayurvedic theory holds that the body is controlled by three **doshas** (forces), themselves made up of the basic elements of space, fire, water, earth and air, which

Ayurvedic treatments

The deep south, especially Kerala, remains the heartland of Ayurvedic treatment in India. The only centres worth approaching are either well-known and long-established family-run **hospitals** and clinics which offer inexpensive treatments and are not normally targeted at foreigners, or **wellness spas**, normally attached to upscale resorts. In addition, you will find a number of small-time operators around resorts in Goa and southern Kerala, though their credentials may or may not be legitimate. For more advice on the kinds of treatment available, see p.388.

reflect the forces within the self. The three *doshas* are: *pitta*, the force of the sun, which is hot and rules the digestive processes and metabolism; *kapha*, likened to the moon, the creator of tides and rhythms, which has a cooling effect, and governs the body's organs and bone structure; and *vata*, wind, which relates to movement, circulation and the nervous system. People are classified according to which *dosha* or combination of them is predominant. The healthy body is one that has the three forces in the correct balance for its type.

To **diagnose** an imbalance, the Ayurvedic doctor not only goes into the physical complaint but also into family background, daily habits and emotional traits. Once a problem is diagnosed it is then treated with a combination of strict diets (vegetarianism is advised for long-term benefits), massage with essential oils, spiritual practice and ancient herbal medicine. In addition, the doctor may prescribe various forms of yogic cleansing to rid the body of waste substances. Popular **treatments** include *abhyanga* (full body massage), *shirodhara* (head and neck massage followed by a gentle stream of warm medicated oil dripping onto the forehead), *shiro abhyanga* (head massage) and *sarvanghadhara*, a full Ayurvedic oil massage followed by a selection of other treatments.

Culture and etiquette

Cultural differences extend to all sorts of little things, and while allowances will usually be made for foreigners, visitors unacquainted with Indian customs may need a little preparation to avoid causing offence or making fools of themselves. The list of dos and don'ts here is hardly exhaustive: when in doubt, watch what the Indian people around you are doing.

Eating and the right-hand rule

The biggest minefield of potential faux pas has to do with **eating**. This is usually done with the fingers (outside tourist resorts and hotel restaurants), and requires practice to get absolutely right. Rule one is: eat with your **right hand only**. In India, as right across Asia, traditon states that the left hand is for wiping your bottom, cleaning your feet and other unsavoury functions (you also put on and take off your shoes with your left hand), while the right hand is for eating, shaking hands, and so on. While you can hold a cup or utensil in your left hand, and you can use it to help tear your chapati, you shouldn't use it to pass food or wipe your mouth. The rule extends beyond food too: you should also accept things given you with your right hand, for example.

The other rule to beware of when eating or drinking is that your lips should not touch other people's food – *jhutha* or sullied food is strictly taboo. Don't, for example, take a bite out of a chapati and pass it on. When drinking out of a cup or bottle to be shared with others, don't let it touch your lips, but rather pour it directly into your mouth. This custom also protects you from things like hepatitis. It is customary to wash your hands before and after eating.

Temples and religion

Religion is taken very seriously in South India; it's important always to show due respect to religious buildings, shrines, images and people at prayer. Most importantly, you should **dress conservatively** (see below), and try not to be obtrusive. When entering a temple or mosque, remove your shoes and leave them at the door (socks are acceptable). Some temples – Jain ones in particular – do not allow you to enter wearing or carrying leather articles. If you're visiting a *dargah* (Sufi shrine) or Sikh *gurudwara* cover your head with a cap or cloth. Mosques will not normally allow you in at prayer time, and women are sometimes not let in at all. In a Hindu temple, you are sometimes not allowed into the inner sanctum. At a Buddhist stupa or monument, you should always walk round clockwise (with the stupa on your right).

Lastly, Hindus are very superstitious about taking **photographs** of images of deities and inside temples; if in doubt, resist. Do not take photos of funerals or cremations.

Dress

Indian people are very conservative about **dress**. Women are expected to dress modestly, with legs and shoulders covered. Trousers are acceptable, but shorts and short skirts are offensive to many. Men should not walk around bare-chested and should avoid wearing shorts (a sign of low caste), except around the obvious beach resorts. These rules are doubly important in temples and mosques.

Never mind sky-clad Jains or *naga sadhus*, **nudity** is not acceptable in India. The mild-mannered people of Goa may not say anything about nude bathing (though it is in theory prohibited), but you can be sure they don't like it.

In general, Indians find it hard to understand why rich Western sahibs should wander round in ragged clothes or imitate the lowest ranks of Indian society, who would love to have something more decent to wear. Staying well groomed and dressing "respectably" vastly improves the impression you make on local people, and reduces sexual harassment too.

Other possible gaffes

Kissing and **embracing** are regarded in India as part of sex: do not do them in public. It is increasingly common to see young couples holding hands and Indian men often do so as a sign of "brotherliness". Be aware of your **feet**. When entering a private home, you should normally remove your shoes (follow your host's example); when sitting, avoid pointing the soles of your feet at anyone. Accidental contact with someone's foot is always followed by an apology.

Dealing with hassle

Although there is nothing like the same amount of aggressive **touting** on the streets of South India as there is in the North, you will undoubtedly find yourself being offered unwanted services or goods, from guides, rickshaws and rooms to garlands, toys and illegal substances, on a fairly regular basis. Then, of course, there are **beggars** and mendicants just asking for baksheesh (see p.78). The wisest approach is not to get dragged into a dispute and certainly not to display anger, which is often not understood and encourages people to bait you further. It is better to say a single, firm "No thanks", avoid eye contact and walk on briskly. Most touts will not follow you but, if they do, ignore them by remaining silent; they will soon get bored and give up.

Meeting people

As a traveller, you will constantly come across people who want to strike up a **conversation**. English not being their first language, they may not be familiar with the conventional ways of doing this, and thus their line of questioning may seem abrupt if at the same time very formal. "Excuse me, gentleman, what is your mother country?" typically starts an exchange, followed by such questions as "What is your qualification?" and "Are you in service?". Questions about your family, job, even income, are not considered "personal" subjects in India, and it is completely normal to ask people about them. Being curious does not have the "nosy" stigma in India that it has in the West.

Things that Indian people are likely to find strange about you are: lack of religion (you could adopt one), travelling alone, leaving your family to come to India, being an unmarried couple (letting people think you are married can make life easier) and travelling second class or staying in cheap hotels when, as a tourist, you are relatively rich. You will probably end up having to explain the same things many times to many different people.

Asking questions back will not be taken amiss – far from it – so you could take it as an opportunity to ask things you want to know about India. English-speaking Indians are usually extremely well informed and well educated and often far more *au fait* with world affairs than Westerners, so you may be drawn into conversations in which you find yourself way out of your depth.

You should be aware that in the same way as Indian English can seem very formal, your English may seem rude to them. In particular, **swearing** is taken rather seriously in India, and casual use of the F-word is likely to shock.

Women travellers

South India doesn't offer any huge obstacles to women travellers – petty annoyances are more the order of the day. However, few women get through their trip without any hassle, and it's good to prepare yourself to be a little thick-skinned.

You can get round potential hassles to a certain extent by joining women in public places, but you'll find your path easiest if you join up with a male travelling companion. In this case, however, expect Indian men to approach him (assumed, of course, to be your husband – an assumption it is sometimes advantageous to go along with) and talk to him about you quite happily as if you were not there. Beware, however, if you are (or look) Indian with a non-Indian male companion: this may well cause you grief and harassment, as you will be seen to have brought shame on your family by adopting loose Western morals. Even if you're not travelling with a male companion, it's still worth pretending you are married to avoid unwanted attention – it's not a bad idea to wear a wedding ring in any case.

There are however some **advantages** to being a lone female traveller. Women sometimes get preference at bus and train stations where they can join a separate "ladies' queue", and use ladies' waiting rooms. On some overnight trains you can aim for the enclosed ladies' compartments, which are peaceful havens – unless filled with noisy children – or share a berth section with a family so as to draw you into the security of the group.

Lastly, bring your own supply of tampons, not widely available outside Indian cities.

Annoyances

South Indian streets are almost without exception male-dominated, annoying when you find yourself subjected to incessant **staring**. This can usually be stopped by ignoring the gaze and quickly moving on, or by firmly telling the offender to stop looking at you. Most of your fellow travellers on trains and buses will be men, and some may start up unwelcome **conversations** about sex, divorce and the freedom of relationships in the West. These cannot often be avoided, but demonstrating too much enthusiasm to discuss such topics can lure men into thinking that you are easy about sex, and the situation could possibly become threatening. At its worst, in larger cities, all this can become very tiring.

In addition to staring and suggestive comments and looks, outright sexual harassment, or "**Eve teasing**" as it is bizarrely known, is likely to be a nuisance, but not generally a threat. Expect to get groped in crowds, and to have men "accidentally" squeeze past you at any opportunity. This tends to be worse in cities than in small towns and villages but, wherever you are, being followed can be a real problem.

In time you'll learn to gauge a situation – sometimes wandering around on your own may attract so much unwanted attention that you may prefer to stay in one place until you've recharged your batteries or your male fan club has moved on. It's always best to **dress modestly** whenever in public – a *salwar kamise* is perfect, or baggy clothing – and refrain from smoking and drinking in public, which only reinforces suspicions that Western women are "loose" and "easy".

Returning an unwanted touch with a punch or slap is perfectly in order (Indian women often become aggressive when offended), and does serve to vent a little frustration. It should also attract attention and urge someone to help you, or at least deal with the offending man – a man transgressing social norms is always out of line, and any passer-by will want to let him know it. If you feel someone getting too close in a crowd or on a bus, brandishing your left shoe in his face can be very effective.

Finally, in hotels watch out for "peep-holes" in your door (and in the common bathrooms), be sure to cover your window when changing and when sleeping, and avoid the sleazy bars of the southern cities.

Rape

Violent sexual assaults on tourists are extremely rare, but unfortunately the number of reported cases of rape is rising. Though no assault can be predicted, you can take **precautions**: at night avoid quiet, dimly lit streets and alleys; if you find a trustworthy rickshaw/taxi driver in the day keep him for the night journey; and try to get someone to accompany you to your hotel whenever possible. Indian women are still quite timid about reporting rape – it is considered as much a disgrace to the victim as to the perpetrator – but you should always report it to the police, and before leaving the area try to let other tourists, or locals, know, in the hope that pressure from the community may uncover the offender and see him brought to

justice. At present there's nowhere for tourists who've suffered sexual violence to go for sanctuary; most victims seek support from other travellers, or go home.

Tipping and baksheesh

As a presumed-rich sahib or memsahib, you will, like wealthy Indians, be expected to be liberal with the **baksheesh**, which takes three main forms. The most common is **tipping**: a small reward for a small service, which can encompass anyone from a waiter or porter to someone who lifts your bags onto the roof of a bus or keeps an eye on your vehicle for you. Large amounts are not expected – ten rupees should satisfy all the aforementioned. Taxi drivers and staff at cheaper hotels and restaurants do not necessarily expect tips, but always appreciate them, of course, and they can keep people sweet for the next time you call. Some may take liberties in demanding baksheesh, but it's often better just to acquiesce rather than spoil your mood and cause offence over trifling sums.

More expensive than plain tipping is paying people to **bend the rules**, many of which seem to have been invented for precisely that purpose. Examples might include letting you into a historical site after hours, finding you a seat or a sleeper on a train that is "full", or speeding up some bureaucratic process. This should not be confused with bribery, a more serious business with its own risks and etiquette, which is best not entered into.

The last kind of baksheesh is **alms giving**. In a country without a welfare system, this is an important social custom. People with disabilities and mutilations are the traditional recipients, and it seems right to join local people in giving out small change to them. Kids demanding money, pens, sweets or the like are a different case, pressing their demands only on tourists. In return for a service it is fair enough, but to yield to any request encourages them to go and pester others.

Public toilets

There are precious few **public toilets** in the cities other than in railway stations and bus stands and those in the latter, especially, often leave much to be desired. This explains why most Indian men happily urinate on just about any available wall or patch of ground, with little care as to who might be watching. Male travellers may, therefore, feel inclined to follow suite. It's not so easy for women, of course, so they, and the more demure men, have little alternative than to go into a restaurant or hotel and ask nicely to use their facilities, a request unlikely to be refused.

Smoking

Even though a high proportion of Indians, almost exclusively males except for some very Westernized young women in the big cities, still smoke, **no-smoking areas** are on the increase: you can no longer smoke on buses or trains, for example. It is, however, still allowed in just about all hotel rooms, restaurants and bars. The only state to impose a complete ban on smoking in public so far is Kerala (see p.370); this includes streets and beaches too.

The good news for smokers is that **cigarettes** are phenomenally cheap (around Rs20–40 a pack) and *beedis*, the traditional Indian cigarette made from a single low-grade tobacco leaf, are even cheaper. Rizlas are not that widely available or of very high quality, so if you smoke roll-ups, take a good stock with you.

Shopping

So many beautiful and exotic souvenirs are on sale in South India, and at such low prices, that it's sometimes hard to know where to start. On top of that, all sorts of things (such as made-to-measure clothes) that would be vastly expensive at home are much more reasonably priced. Even if you lose weight during your trip, your baggage might well put on quite a bit – unless of course you post some of it home.

Where to shop

Quite a few items sold in tourist areas are made elsewhere and, needless to say, it's more fun (and cheaper) to pick them up at source. The best local buys are noted in the relevant sections of the Guide, along with a few specialities that can't be found outside their regions. South India is awash with street and beach **hawkers**, often very young kids. Although they can be annoying and should be dealt with firmly if you are not interested, do not write them off completely as they sometimes have decent souvenirs at lower than shop prices and are open to hard bargaining.

Virtually all the state governments in India run handicraft "**emporia**". There is also the exceptionally well-stocked Central Cottage Industries Emporium in Mumbai. Goods in these places are generally of a high quality, even if their fixed prices are a little high, they are worth a visit to get an idea of what crafts are available and how much they should cost.

Other famous places to shop in South India include the weekly flea market in **Anjuna**, Goa, where goods from all over the country are sold alongside the latest fluoro rave gear and techno tapes, and **Kovalam**, in southern Kerala, where vendors import handicrafts from northern states such as Rajasthan and Gujarat. For sheer variety, however, **Mumbai** is hard to beat, with its tourist-oriented streetside boutiques, swish CD and fashion shops, antique markets and huge *khadi* store.

Bargaining

You will be expected to **haggle** over the price of almost all goods, with the exception of food, household items and cigarettes. Bargaining is very much a matter of personal style, but should always be light-hearted, never acrimonious. There are no hard and fast rules – it's really a question of how much something is worth to you. It's a good plan, however, to have an idea of how much you want, or ought, to pay. "Green" tourists are easily spotted, so try and look as if you know what you are up to, even on your first day, or put off purchases till later.

Don't take too much notice of initial prices. Some guidebooks suggest paying a third of the opening price, but it's a flexible guideline depending on the shop, the goods and the shopkeeper's impression of you. You may not be able to get the seller much below the first quote; on the other hand, you may end up paying as little as a tenth of it. If you bid too low, you may be hustled out of the shop for offering an "insulting" price, but this is all part of the game, and you'll no doubt be welcomed as an old friend if you return the next day.

Don't start haggling for something if you know you don't want it, and never let any figure pass your lips that you are not prepared to pay. It's like bidding at an auction. Having mentioned a price, you are obliged to pay it. If the seller asks you how much you would pay for something, and you don't want it, say so.

What to buy

South India is a paradise for **souvenir shopping**, as well as a great place to pick up clothes, jewellery and other items. In addition to the items listed below, souvenirs might include toys and puppets, kitchen implements like tiffin boxes, film posters, *ganjifa* cards (see p.177), tea (especially Orange Pekoe from the plantations of the Nilgiri mountains), essential oils (such as eucalyptus, citronella or sandalwood) from Kodaikanal in Tamil Nadu, spices and peacock feather fans (though these are considered unlucky).

Things not to bring home include ivory or anything else made from a rare or protected species, including snakeskin and turtle products. As for drugs – don't even think about it. When it comes to **antiques**, if they really are genuine – and, frankly, that is unlikely – you'll need a licence to export them, which is virtually impossible to get.

Metalware and jewellery

South Indian artisans have been casting **bronze statues** of Hindu deities for over two thousand years – notably in the Cauvery (Kaveri) Delta of Tamil Nadu, where the Chola dynasty took the form to heights never since surpassed. Since medieval times, they have used the "lost-wax" process (see p.761). Top-quality images will have finely detailed fingers and eyes, and the metal should not have pits or spots. Still the best place to watch bronze casters in action is the village of **Swamimalai**, near Kumbakonam (see p.577), where showrooms display awesome dancing Shivas and other Chola-style bronzes. Some Chola bronzes are priceless, such as those in the temples of Tamil Nadu, but affordable miniatures are available direct from the artisans.

Brass and **copperware** can be exquisitely worked, with trays, plates, ashtrays, cups and bowls among the products available. **Bidri** work (see p.359), can be an excellent buy, with jewellery boxes, dishes, bracelets and hookah pipes, among other things, widely sold, particularly in Karnataka and Andhra Pradesh. **Stainless steel** is less decorative and more workaday: thali sets, tiffin and spice tins are all possible buys, available throughout the region.

Among precious metals, **silver** is generally a better buy than **gold** – though the latter is usually 22 carat and very yellow, it's relatively expensive due to high taxes. Silver varies in quality, but is usually reasonably priced, with silver jewellery generally heavier and rather more folksy than gold. There is a bewildering array of silver earrings, necklaces, pendants and bracelets on sale, usually in shops run by exiled Kashmiris. Gold and silver are usually sold by weight, the workmanship costing very little. While silversmiths are ubiquitous in South India, goldsmiths are thinner on the ground, with the largest single concentration around the Kapalishvara temple in the Mylapore district of Chennai (see p.524) and in Kozikhode in northern Kerala.

Gemstones can be something of a minefield; scams abound, and you would be most unwise even to consider buying gems for resale or as an investment without a basic knowledge of the trade. That said, some precious and semi-precious stones can be a good buy in Mumbai, particularly those that are indigenous, such as garnets, black star sapphires and moonstones.

Woodwork and stone carving

Ornate carvings of gods and goddesses are a speciality of Mysore, where members of the *gudigar* caste work with fragrant **sandalwood**, their preferred medium for a thousand years or more. At one time, deities could only be carved from this rare wood, but dwindling forests have forced the price up, and these days fake sandalwood – cheaper soft wood that's been rubbed with essential oil – is almost as common as the real thing. In Kerala, deep-red **rosewood**, inlaid with lighter coloured woods to create geometric patterns, is used for carving elephants and heavy furniture, samples of which are to be found at most state-run emporia. For more authentic Kathakali masks and old wooden jewellery boxes, however, the bric-a-brac and antiques market in the former Jewish quarter of Kochi (Fort Cochin) is the best place to look. Embossed with brass, these traditionally contained a woman's dowry goods. Metal trunks have largely superseded them, but Keralan cabinet-makers still turn out reproductions for the tourist market.

The fishing village of Mamallapuram, just south of Chennai, is renowned as India's **stone-carving** capital. Pieces range from larger-than-life-size icons for temples to pocket-size gods sold to the many tourists who pour through every day. Whatever their size, though, the figures are always precisely carved according to measurements meticulously set out in ancient canonical texts, which explains why little innovation has taken place over the centuries. The only recent developments in Mamallapuram's stone carving has been in the design of chillums, and small pendants, bought wholesale for export to the summer festival hippy market back in Europe.

Textiles and clothing

Homespun, handloom-woven, hand-printed cloth is called **khadi**, and is sold all over South India in government shops called Khadi Gramodyog. Methods of dying and printing this and other cloth vary from the tie-dying (*bandhini*) of Rajasthan to block printing and screen printing of calico (from Kozhikode, Kerala), cotton and silk.

Saris for everyday use are normally made of cotton, although **silk** is used more frequently in the South than in the rest of India. It takes years of practice to carry wearing one off properly, but silk is usually a good buy in India, provided you're sure it is the real thing. The best silk in India comes from **Kanchipuram** (see p.547), in northern Tamil Nadu, whose hallmarks are contrasting borders (known as Ganga–Jamuna borders after India's two most sacred rivers) and ornate designs featuring *gopurams*). Kanchi's weavers are also famous for **brocade** – top-quality silk hand-woven with expensive gold or silver thread.

In Andhra Pradesh, cloth is more likely to be patterned using the **ikat** technique, where yarn is resist- or tie-dyed before being woven. The geometric images of flowers, animals and birds that result have attractive blurred, or "flame", edges that conjure up Southeast Asia, to where *ikat* was exported in the medieval era.

Less expensive cloth to look out for, especially in Goa, includes that touted by the **Lamanis** – the semi-nomadic low-caste minority from northern Karnataka who traditionally lived by transporting salt across the Deccan Plateau. These days, the women and girls make most of the family money through the sale of textiles carefully tailored for the tourist trade. Their rainbow cloth, woven with geometric designs and inlaid with cowrie shells or fragments of mirror and mica, is fashioned into shoulder bags, caps and money belts. If you haggle hard and can put up with all the shouting and tugging that inevitably accompanies each purchase, you can usually pick stuff up at bargain prices.

From Tamil Nadu, an authentic souvenir to take home is the kind of **Madras-check lunghis** worn by most of the men (at least in the countryside); Keralans tend to prefer jazzier varieties, with day-glo colours rendered on polyester. Particularly beautiful and high-quality *lunghis* of creamy cotton or calico are to be found in **Kozhikode**, Kerala (see p.482). Indeed the town's former name of Calicut came about because of its trade in the material. For women, **salwar kamise**, the elegant pyjama suits worn by Muslims, unmarried girls and middle-class students, make ideal travel outfits, although in the sticky heat of the far South you may find them too heavy. Long loose shirts – preferably made of *khadi* and known as *kurta* or *panjabi* – are more practical. Tourist shops sell versions in various fabrics and colours. Block-printed bedsheets, as well as being useful, make good wall-hangings. You will find every region has its own fabrics, its own methods of colouring them and making them up – the choice is endless.

On top of this, with **tailoring** so cheap in India, you can choose the fabric you want, take it to a tailor, and have it made into whatever you fancy. For formal Western-style clothes, you'll want to see quite a posh tailor in a big city, but tailors in almost every village in the country can run you up a shirt or a pair of pyjama-type trousers in next to no time. Many tailors will also copy a garment you already have.

Carpets and rugs

South India is generally less renowned for its **carpets** than the north, but the former Muslim kingdoms of the Deccan, notably around Eluru and Warangal in Andhra Pradesh, have retained weaving traditions dating from the seventeenth century, when Moghul artisans drifted south in the wake of their conquering armies. They brought with them techniques and designs from medieval Persia, and these still feature prominently in today's flat-weave dhurries. The colours tend to be pale pastels, with floral motifs overlaid on cameo backgrounds. In accordance with an old Persian tradition, each design is named after a patron of the weaving industry. The carpets themselves are hard to come by – they are only produced in small numbers by a few families – but you can usually track some down in the Muslim bazaars of Hyderabad. A little-visited spot which has a lively handloom and weaving industry is the Tasara Creative Weaving Centre, near Kozhikode (Calicut) in Kerala (see p.482). For everyday domestic use, **rag rugs**, made from recycled clothing, are good buys. Available just about everywhere, they cost little enough in Europe and North America, but in India are fantastically cheap; many

visitors buy large ones and post them home by surface mail.

Of course, you don't have to go all the way north to buy a **Kashmiri** rug or carpet. Many Kashmiris have set up shop in the main tourist centres of the South and you can find high-quality goods, though not all the dealers are known for their scruples and it is best to learn something about what you are trying to buy before you lay out a lot of cash. A pukka Kashmiri carpet should have a label on the back stating that it is made in Kashmir, what it is made of (wool, silk or "silk touch", the latter being wool combined with a little cotton and silk to give it a sheen), its size, density of knots per square inch (the more the better) and the name of the design. To tell if it really is silk, scrape the carpet with a knife and burn the fluff – real silk shrivels to nothing and has a distinctive smell. Even producing a knife should cause the seller of a bogus silk carpet to demur.

Paintings

The former Chola capital of Thanjavur (Tanjore), in the Cauvery (Kaveri) Delta area of Tamil Nadu, is famous throughout the south for its school of religious painting, which emerged in the nineteenth century under patronage from the local maharaja. "**Painting**" is actually something of a misnomer, as the images are partly raised in low plaster relief, and inlaid with precious stones, glass pieces, pearls, mica and ivory. The Tanjore school's preferred subject is Balakrishna (Krishna as a crawling baby stealing butter balls), and depictions of Vishnu's other incarnations. You'll come across these all over the region, but only in **Thanjavur** itself (see p.578) are you likely to see the artists in action. Prices range from Rs500 to Rs100,000 depending on the age, the size, the quality of the painting and the value of the inlays and gold leaf.

Books and music

Of course, not everything typically Indian is old or traditional. **CDs and audio cassettes** of Hindustani classical, Carnatic, bhangra, *filmi* and Western music are available in most major towns and cities for a fraction of what you'd pay back home. By far the best-stocked stores are in Mumbai, Bengaluru (Bangalore) and Chennai.

Books are also excellent buys in India, whether by Indian writers (see Contexts, p.792) or writers from the rest of the English-speaking world. Once again, they are usually much cheaper than at home, if not always so well printed or bound. Hardback volumes of Indian sacred literature are particularly good value.

Bamboo flutes are incredibly cheap, while other **musical instruments** such as tabla, sitar and *sarod* are sold in music shops in the larger cities. The quality is crucial; there's no point going home with a sitar that is virtually untunable, even if it does look nice. A good place to start looking is Chennai (see p.524), where you can pick up quality Carnatic instruments. For more on Carnatic music, see Contexts, p.775.

Travelling with children

Indians tend to adore kids and you'll be welcomed all the more warmly if you bring yours. The majority of tourists are either unmarried or of middle to retiring age, so the appearance of Western children always generates lots of interest and contact with local parents, especially if you stay in a small, family-run hotel or guesthouse.

The main problem with children, especially small ones, is their vulnerability. The most obvious thing to watch out for is the Indian **sun**, which can roast young, sensitive skin at any time of the day or year. Come armed with sun hats and plenty of maximum-factor block, and keep skin covered as much as possible. Generally, the beaches are safe for kids to splash about in, but always be wary of a strong undertow, which can arise at certain phases of the tide even in relatively shallow water.

Even more than their parents, children need protecting from unsafe drinking water, heat and unfamiliar food. All that chilli in particular may be a problem, even with older kids, if they're not used to it. Remember too, that **diarrhoea**, perhaps just a nuisance to you, could be dangerous for a child: rehydration salts (see p.63) are vital if your child goes down with it.

Make sure too, if possible, that your child is aware of the dangers of rabies; keep children away from **animals**, and consider a rabies jab. Bites and stings are, however, less of a problem than mosquitoes and the concomitant risk of malaria. Always ensure your kids are well protected by prophylactic tablets, or at the very least DEET-based repellent in the evenings, and that they're well covered by a net throughout the night. Special small nets for babies' cots are sold at local markets and may be available through your hotel or guesthouse.

Formula milk and jars of **baby food** are available at supermarkets in the main cities, but are not easy to get hold of elsewhere, and they will taste different from what your baby is used to. Therefore, dried baby food could be worth taking; mix it with hot (boiled) water – any café or chai-wallah should be able to supply you with some. You'll find international brands of **nappies** such as Pampers and Huggies fairly widely available but if you're getting off the beaten track you may want to consider going over to cotton ones – disposing of "disposables" can present major difficulties, even in the resorts, as there is no formal waste provision in most areas. A changing mat is another necessity.

For touring, hiking or walking, **child-carrier backpacks** are ideal; they start at around £40 ($70) and can weigh less than 2kg. If the child is small enough, a fold-up buggy is also well worth packing – especially if they will sleep in it (while you have a meal or a drink). If you want to cut down on long journeys by flying, remember that under 2s travel for ten percent of the adult fare (or less in some cases), and under-12s for half price.

Most **hotels and guesthouses** will provide an extra bed for a small additional charge (usually less than 25 percent of the room rate). Bigger hotels are also likely to be able to provide cots, but check first (through your tour operator if you're on a package holiday).

 # Travel essentials

Costs

For visitors, India is still one of the least expensive countries in the world, and a little foreign currency goes a long way. You can be confident of getting good value for your money, whether you're setting out to keep your budget to a minimum or to enjoy the opportunities that spending a bit more brings. As a foreigner in India, however, you will find yourself penalized by **double-tier entry** prices to museums and historic sites (see box opposite) as well as in upmarket hotels and on airfares, both of which are levied at a higher rate and in dollars. For information on baksheesh and tipping, see Culture and etiquette, p.78.

What you spend depends on you: where you go, where you stay, how you get around, what you eat and what you buy. You can manage on a **budget** of as little Rs500 (£6/$11.50/€9) per day if you stay in the cheaper lodges, eat in local *dhabas* and don't move about too much; double that, and you'll be able to afford comfortable mid-range hotels, as well as meals in smarter restaurants, regular rickshaw or taxi rides and entrance fees to monuments. If you're happy spending up to Rs1500–2000 (£17.50–23.50/$34–45) per day, however, you can really pamper yourself; to spend much more than that, you'd have to be doing a lot of air-conditioned travelling, consistently staying in swish hotels and eating in the top restaurants. Five-star luxury in India is cheap by Western standards but, particularly with all the extra government taxes it incurs, can soon send your budget spiralling.

Accommodation ranges from as little as £2/$3 per night upwards (see p.44), while a no-frills vegetarian **meal** in an ordinary restaurant will typically cost under a quarter of that. Long-distance **transport** can work out to be phenomenally good value if you stick to state buses and standard second-class non-a/c trains, but soon starts to add up if you opt for air-conditioned carriages on the superfast intercity services. See Getting around on pp.33–43 for some guidelines on prices.

Where you are also makes a difference: Mumbai is notoriously pricey, especially for accommodation, while tourist enclaves like the Goa beaches are more expensive for things like food, and will tempt you to buy souvenirs. Out in the sticks, on the other hand, and particularly away from your fellow tourists, you'll find things incredibly cheap, though your choice will obviously be more limited.

Some independent travellers tend to indulge in wild and highly competitive **penny-pinching**, which Indian people find rather pathetic – they know how much an air ticket from your home country to Mumbai costs, and they have a fair idea of what you can earn. Bargain where appropriate, but don't begrudge a few rupees to someone who's worked hard for them: consider what their services would cost at home, and how much more valuable the money is to them than it is to you. Even if you get a bad deal on every rickshaw journey you make, it will only add a minuscule fraction to the cost of your trip. Remember, too, that every pound or dollar you spend in India goes that much further,

Entrance fees

The **Archeological Survey of India (ASI)** operates a double-tiered entry system, with foreign visitors (including non-resident Indians) charged a rate up to 25 times higher than that levied to domestic visitors. Ticket prices for all archeological sites fall into two price categories – $2 or $5, or their rupee equivalents – according to the sites' importance. Although foreigners can theoretically pay in dollars, unless you are carrying a wad of small-denomination greenbacks, you will find yourself paying at the rounded-up rate of Rs50 to $1 – so you will pay either Rs100 or Rs250, as opposed to Rs5/Rs10 for Indians. Throughout the text we list the fee for foreigners in rupees, followed by the price for Indians in square brackets.

With a few exceptions that charge more for foreigners, all other **non-ASI** sites and museums cost very little to get into, usually Rs2–10 and rarely more than Rs25.

Temples are almost always free to enter, when foreigners are allowed into them, that is, though sometimes there will be a nominal fee of a few rupees for access to the inner sanctum or for the whole temple out of puja hours; this fee is the same for everybody. In very busy temples there is sometimes a fast-track entry system into the inner sanctum that typically costs Rs20–50.

and luxuries you can't afford at home become possible here. At the same time, don't pay well over the odds for something if you know what the going rate is. Thoughtless extravagance can, particularly in remote areas that see a disproportionate number of tourists, contribute to inflation, putting even basic goods and services beyond the reach of local people.

Crime and personal Safety

Crime levels in India are a long way below those of Western countries, and violent crime against tourists is extremely rare. Virtually none of the people who approach you on the street intend any harm: many want to sell you something, some want to practise their English, others (if you're a woman) to chat you up. As a tourist, however, you are an obvious target for the tiny number of thieves (who may include some of your fellow travellers), and so it makes sense to take a few precautions.

Most tourists carry valuables in a **money belt**, though most hotels will also have a safe-deposit facility where you can store them. Budget travellers would do well to carry a **padlock**, useful both for securing the doors of cheap hotel rooms and for locking your bag to seats or racks in trains. The prime time for theft on buses and trains is just before you leave, so keep a particular

eye on your gear then. Remember that routes popular with tourists tend to be popular with thieves too.

It's not a bad idea to keep an amount such as $50 or $100 separately from the rest of your money; it's also worth keeping a separate note of your travellers' cheque receipts, insurance policy number and phone number, and a photocopy of the pages in your passport containing personal data and your Indian visa. This will cover you in case you do lose all your valuables. When making a **credit-card** purchase, insist that the transaction is done in front of you, in order to prevent fraud.

If the worst happens and you get robbed, the first thing to do is **report the theft** as soon as possible to the local police. They are very unlikely to recover your belongings, but you need a report from them in order to claim on your travel insurance. If you **lose your passport**, the police will issue you with the all-important "complaint form" you'll need to travel around and check into hotels. Dress smartly and expect an uphill battle; city cops in particular tend to be jaded from too many insurance and travellers' cheque scams. Some even demand baksheesh to cooperate.

Illegal drugs

It is a well-known fact that one of the attractions of India for many travellers is the easy availability and low cost of **drugs**, especially marijuana and hashish. Anybody who is tempted, however, should be aware that all substances illegal at home are illegal in India too. Although the drug laws (and the extent to which they are enforced) differ from state to state, and are in a chronic state of flux, remember that drug offences generally carry much higher penalties than they would at home. In Goa, for example, a recent change in the law has downgraded possession of under 2g of any drug to an offence punishable by an on-the-spot Rs10,000 fine. Get caught with any more than 2g, however, and you'll be considered a dealer and liable to a ten-year prison sentence.

Should you find yourself arrested under the 1985 Narcotics Substances Act, the first thing you should try to do is bribe your way out of the situation as quickly and discreetly as possible. Don't underestimate the seriousness of your predicament. Indian police routinely accept backhanders, but for drugs offences the amount will probably run into thousands of dollars. Should the situation escalate and you find yourself being formally charged in a police station, contact your nearest consul or high commission at the first possible opportunity.

Disabled travellers

For the **disabled traveller**, there is the advantage of social acceptance sometimes lacking in the West, as there are so many disabled Indians. On the other hand, you'll be lucky to see a state-of-the-art wheelchair or a loo for the disabled and the streets are full of all sorts of obstacles that would be hard for a blind or wheelchair-bound tourist to negotiate independently. Kerbs are often high, pavements uneven and littered, and ramps non-existent. There are potholes all over the place and open sewers. Some of the more expensive hotels have ramps for the movement of luggage and equipment, making them accessible to wheelchairs, though this is more by accident than design.

Then again, Indian people are likely to be very helpful if, for example, you need their help getting on and off buses or up stairs. Taxis and rickshaws are easily affordable and very adaptable; if you rent one for a day, the driver is certain to help you on and off, and

perhaps even around the sites you visit. If you employ a guide, they may also be prepared to help you with steps and obstacles.

For further information in India, contact the India Rehabilitation Co-ordination (☏040/2402 2143), a Mumbai-based support group.

Electricity

Voltage is generally 220V 50Hz AC, though direct current supplies also exist, so check before plugging in. Most sockets are triple round-pin but accepting European-size double round-pin **plugs**. British, Irish and Australasian plugs will need an adaptor, preferably universal; American and Canadian appliances will need a transformer, too, unless they are multi-voltage. Power cuts and voltage variations are very common, so voltage stabilizers should be used to run sensitive appliances such as laptops.

Entry requirements

Today, everyone except citizens of Nepal and Bhutan needs a **visa**. If you're going to India on business or to study, you'll need to apply for a special student or business visa; otherwise, a standard tourist visa will suffice. These are valid for six months from the date of issue (not of departure from your home country or entry into India), and cost £30/US$60/Can$62/Aus$55/NZ$90.

Much the best place to get a visa is in your country of residence, from the embassies and high commissions listed on p.87; you should be able to download forms from the embassy and consulate websites. As a rule, visas are issued in a matter of hours; in the US, postal applications take a month as opposed to a same-day service if you do it in person – check with your nearest embassy, high commission or consulate.

In many countries it's also possible to pay a **visa agency** (or "visa expediter") to process the visa on your behalf, which in the UK costs £40–45 (plus the price of the visa). In Britain, try The Visa Service (☏0870 890 0185, ⊛www.visaservice.co.uk); or Visa Express (☏020/7251 4822, ⊛www .visaexpress.com). In North America, where you can expect to pay anywhere between US$150–280 to obtain a visa within two

Indian public holidays: a warning

Wherever you intend to get your visa from, bear in mind that your nearest high commission, embassy or consulate will observe **Indian public holidays** (as well as most of the local ones), and that it might therefore be closed. Always check opening hours in advance by phone, or via the website, beforehand.

weeks, reliable expediters include Travel Document Systems (☎1-202-638 3800, ⓦwww.traveldocs.com) and Visa Connection (ⓦwww.visaconnection.com) – the latter has offices in Vancouver, Calgary, Ottawa and Toronto, as well as in the US.

It is no longer possible to **extend a visa** in India, though exceptions may be made in special circumstances, such as illness. Most people whose standard six-month tourist visas are about to expire head for Bangkok or neighbouring capitals such as Colombo in Sri Lanka or Kathmandu in Nepal; however, in recent years this has been something of a hit-and-miss business, with some tourists having their requests turned down for no apparent reason. The Indian High Commission in Kathmandu is particularly notorious for this.

If you do stay more than 120 days you are supposed to get a **tax clearance certificate** before you leave the country, available at the foreigners' section of the income-tax department in every major city. They are free, but you should take bank receipts to show you have changed your money legally. In practice, tax clearance certificates are rarely demanded, but you never know.

For details of other kinds of visas – five-year visas can be obtained by foreigners of Indian origin, business travellers and even students of yoga – contact your nearest Indian embassy. Finally, in addition to a visa, **special permits** are required for travel to the Andaman Islands and Lakshadweep, though in the case of the Andamans these are now issued on arrival (see p.686). For information on visiting Lakshadweep, see p.464.

For lists of **foreign consulates** in Mumbai and Chennai, see the Listings sections of those chapters.

Indian high commissions, embassies and consulates abroad

Australia High Commission: 3–5 Moonah Place, Yarralumla, Canberra, ACT 2600 ☎02/6273 3999, ⓔhcicouns@bigpond.com. Consulates: Level 27, 25 Bligh St, Sydney, NSW 2000 ☎02/9223 9500, ⓦwww.indianconsulatesydney.org; 15 Munro St, Coburg, Melbourne, Vic 3058 ☎03/9384 0141; ⓦwww.cgindiamel-au.org. Honorary Consulates: Level 1, Terrace Hotel, 195 Adelaide Terrace, East Perth, WA 6004, Australia (mailing address: PO Box 6118, East Perth, WA 6892, Australia) ☎08/9221 1485, ⓔindia@vianet.net.au.

Canada High Commission: 10 Springfield Rd, Ottawa, ON K1M 1C9 ☎1-613/744 3751, ⓦwww.hciottawa.ca. Consulates: 2 Bloor St W, #500, Toronto, ON M4W 3E2 ☎1-416/960 0751, ⓦwww.cgitoronto.ca; 325 Howe St, 2nd floor, Vancouver, BC V6C 1Z7 ☎1-604/662 8811, ⓦwww.cgivancouver.com.

The Netherlands Embassy: Buitenrustweg-2, 2517 KD, The Hague ☎070/346 9771, ⓦwww.indianembassy.nl.

New Zealand High Commission: 180 Molesworth St, Wellington ☎04/473 6390, ⓦwww.hicomind.org.nz.

Republic of Ireland Embassy: 6 Leeson Park, Dublin 6 ☎01/497 0843, ⓔeoidubin@indigo.ie.

South Africa High Commission: The Terraces, 9th Floor, 34 Bree St, Cape Town ☎021/419 8110, ⓦwww.india.org.za. Consulates: 1 Eton Rd, Parktown, Johannesburg ☎011/482 8492, ⓦwww.indconjoburg.co.za; The Old Station Building, 4th Floor, 160 Pine St, Durban ☎031/304 7020, ⓦwww.indcondurban.co.za.

Sri Lanka High Commission: 36–38 Galle Rd, Colombo 3 ☎011/232 7587, ⓦwww.hcicolombo.org. Consulate: 31 Rajapihilla Mawatha, PO Box 47, Kandy ☎08/224563.

Thailand Embassy: 46 Soi 23 (Prasarn Mitr), Sukhumvit Rd, Bangkok 10110 ☎02/258 0300, ⓦwww.embassyofindia-bangkok.org. Consulate: 113 Bumruangrat Rd, Chiang Mai 50000 ☎053/243066, ⓦwww.indcon-chiangmai.com.

UK High Commission: India House, Aldwych, London WC2B 4NA ☎020/7836 8484, ⓦwww.hcilondon.net. Consulates: 20 Augusta St, Jewellery Quarter, Hockley, Birmingham B18 6GL ☎0121/212 2782, ⓦwww.cgibirmingham.org; 17 Rutland Square, Edinburgh EH1 2BB ☎0131/229 2144, ⓦwww.cgiedinburgh.org.

USA Embassy of India (Consular Services): 2107 Massachusetts Ave NW, Washington DC 20008 ☏1-202/939-7000, ⓦwww.indianembassy .org. Consulates: 3 East 64th St, New York, NY 10021 ☏1-212/774-0600, ⓦwww.indiacgny .org; 540 Arguello Blvd, San Francisco, CA 94118 ☏1-415/668-0683, ⓦwww.indianconsulate-sf.org; 455 North Cityfront Plaza Drive, Suite 850, Chicago Il 60611 ☏1-312/595 0405 (ext 22 for visas), ⓦchicago.indianconsulate.com; 201 St Charles Ave, New Orleans, LA 70170 ☏1-504/582-8106; 2051 Young St, Honolulu, HI 96826 ☏1-808/947-2618.

Gay and lesbian travellers

Homosexuality is not generally open or accepted in India, and anal intercourse is a ten-year offence under article 377 of the penal code. Laws against "obscene behaviour" are used to arrest gay men for cruising or liaising anywhere that could be considered a public place.

This said, there are meeting places for **gay men** and gay bars are cropping up in the more Westernized cities such as Mumbai and Bengaluru (Bangalore). Contact the organizations listed given below for information about gay events and parties. For **lesbians**, making contacts is rather more difficult; even the Indian Women's Movement does not readily promote lesbianism as an issue that needs confronting. The only public faces of a hidden scene are the organizations listed below.

Gay and lesbian contacts

Bombay Dost ⓦbombay-dost.pbwiki.com. Wiki page of the (now defunct) Mumbai-based Gay magazine *Bombay Dost*, featuring information

on its popular "Sunday High" club nights in the Maharashtrian capital.
Gay Bombay ⓦwww.gaybombay.org.
Humsafar Trust ⓦwww.humsafar.org. Website set up to promote "a holistic approach to the rights and health of sexual minorities".

Insurance

In the light of the potential health risks involved in a trip to South India – see pp.58–64 – travel insurance is too important to ignore. In addition to covering medical expenses and emergency flights, it also insures your money and belongings against loss or theft. Before paying for a new policy, however, it's worth checking to see whether you are already covered: some all-risks home insurance policies may cover your possessions when overseas, and many private medical schemes include cover when abroad. In Canada, provincial health plans usually provide partial medical cover for mishaps overseas, while holders of official student/teacher/youth cards in Canada and the US are entitled to – albeit meagre – accident coverage and hospital in-patient benefits. Students will often find that their student health coverage extends during the vacations and for one term beyond the date of last enrolment.

After exhausting the possibilities above, you might want to contact a specialist **travel insurance company**, or consider the travel insurance deal offered by Rough Guides (see box below). A typical travel insurance policy usually provides cover for the loss of baggage, tickets and – up to a certain limit – cash or cheques, as well as cancellation or curtailment of your journey. Most of them

---

Rough Guides travel insurance

Rough Guides has teamed up with Columbus Direct to offer you **travel insurance** that can be tailored to suit your needs. Products include a low-cost **backpacker** option for long stays; a **short break** option for city getaways; a typical **holiday package** option; and others. There are also annual **multi-trip** policies for those who travel regularly. Different sports and activities (trekking, skiing, etc) can be usually be covered if required.

See our website (ⓦwww.roughguides.com/website/shop) for eligibility and purchasing options. Alternatively, UK residents should call ☏08700 339988; US citizens should call ☏1-800-749-4922; Australians should call ☏1300 669999. All other nationalities should call ☏+44 8708 902843.

exclude so-called dangerous sports unless an extra premium is paid: in India this can mean scuba-diving, whitewater rafting, windsurfing and trekking with ropes, though probably not Jeep safaris. Many policies can be chopped and changed to exclude coverage you don't need – for example, sickness and accident benefits can often be excluded or included at will. If you do take medical coverage, ascertain whether benefits will be paid as treatment proceeds or only after return home, and whether there is a 24-hour medical emergency number. When securing baggage cover, make sure that the per-article limit – typically under £500 – will cover your most valuable possession. If you need to make a claim, you should keep receipts for medicines and medical treatment, and in the event you have anything stolen, you must obtain an official statement from the police.

Internet

All large cities and many tourist towns have places offering **Internet** and **email** access – these are usually cybercafés, but also include many hotels and some STD (standard trunk dialling) booths. Charges start at around Rs10 per hour, and can go up to as much as Rs120, but are most commonly Rs20–40 for reading mail and browsing, and extra for printing; most cybercafés offer membership deals which can cut costs if you'll be around for a while. In the main cities and resorts faster ISDN/broadband connections are now common, though slow dial-up connections are still the norm in more remote spots. Most places with a decent broadband connection also have webcams and microphones, allowing for VoIP chats via systems such as Skype.

Laundry

In India, no one goes to self-service laundries: if they don't do their own, they send it out to a **dhobi**. Wherever you are staying, there will either be an in-house *dhobi* or one very close by to call on. The *dhobi* will take your dirty washing to a *dhobi ghat*, a public clothes-washing area (the bank of a river for example), where it is shown some old-fashioned discipline: separated, soaped and given a damn good

thrashing to beat the dirt out of it. Then it's hung out to dry in the sun and, once dried, taken to the ironing sheds where every garment is endowed with razor-sharp creases and then matched to its rightful owner by hidden cryptic markings. Your clothes will come back from the *dhobi* absolutely spotless, though this kind of violent treatment does take it out of them: buttons get lost and eventually the cloth starts to fray.

If you'd rather not entrust your Saville Row made-to-measure to their tender mercies, there are **dry-cleaners** in cities and large towns.

Living in India

While in India, you may consider doing some voluntary charitable work. Several charities welcome volunteers on a medium-term commitment for a couple of months or so. If you do want to spend your time working for an **NGO** (**non-government organization**), you should make arrangements well before you arrive by contacting the body in question, rather than on spec. Special visas are generally not required unless you intend to work for longer than six months.

Voluntary work resources

Basic Needs India Trust India ☎080/2545 9235, ⓦwww.basicneeds.org. Bengaluru (Bangalore)-based charity working with the mentally ill in their communities, reaching a large number of people in a way that conventional institutional-based care cannot.
Charities Aid Foundation (CAF) UK ☎01732/520000, ⓦwww.cafonline.org/cafindia. Can provide the contact details and aims of 2350 voluntary organizations in India.
India Development Information Network India ☎011/2371 1401, ⓦwww.infodev.org. INDEV is another huge databank, accessed through their website, with over 2500 Indian NGOs.
Voluntary Service Overseas (VSO) UK ☎020/8780 7200, ⓦwww.vso.org.uk; Canada ☎1-888-VSO-2911, ⓦwww.vsocanada.org. A British government-funded organization (with a Canadian affiliation) that places volunteers on various projects around the world, including India.

Other work and study options

The only other really viable ways of living in India beyond the normal six-month tourist visa are if you get a work visa through being employed by an overseas company – hi-tech is the most likely area – or if you get accepted to study at an Indian university, in which case you will need a student visa. The following websites contain some useful tips and leads:

Ⓦ **www.india.studyabroad.com**
Ⓦ **www.gapguru.com**

Mail

Mail can take anything from three days to four weeks or even more to get to or from India, depending largely on where exactly you are; ten days to a fortnight is about the norm. Most **post offices** are open Monday to Friday 10am to 5pm and Saturday 10am till noon, but big city GPOs, where the poste restante is usually located, keep longer hours (Mon–Fri 9.30am–6pm, Sat 9.30am–1pm). Stamps aren't expensive, and aerogrammes and postcards cost the same to anywhere in the world. You can also buy stamps at big hotels. Ideally, you should have mail franked in front of you.

Having parcels sent out to you in India is not such a good idea – chances are they'll go astray. If you do have a parcel sent, have it registered. **Sending a parcel** out of India can be quite a performance. First you have to get it cleared by customs at the post office (they often don't bother, but check), then you take it to a tailor and agree a price to have it wrapped in cheap cotton cloth (which you may have to go and buy yourself), stitched up and sealed with wax. In big city GPOs, people offering this service will be at hand. Next, take it to the post office, fill in and attach the relevant customs forms (it's best to tick the box marked "gift" and give its value as less than Rs1000 or "no commercial value" to avoid bureaucratic entanglements), buy your stamps, see them franked, and dispatch it. Parcels shouldn't be more than a metre long or weigh more than 20kg. Surface mail is incredibly cheap, and takes an average of three months to arrive – although delivery times vary wildly, and it may take anything from six weeks or a year. It's a good way to dump excess baggage and souvenirs, but don't send anything fragile.

As in Britain, North America and Australasia, books and magazines can be sent more cheaply, unsealed or wrapped around the middle, as printed papers ("book post"). Alternatively, there are numerous **courier** services, although they're not as reliable as they should be, and there have been complaints of packages going astray – it's safest to stick to known international companies such as DHL or Fedex, which have offices in all the state capitals. Packages sent by air are expensive. Remember that all packages from India are likely to be suspect at home, and searched or X-rayed: don't send anything dodgy.

Maps

Even allowing for a bit of bias here, we think you'll find the Rough Guide's **South India map** to be the most user friendly on the market. Drawn at a scale of 1:1,200,000, it features clear modern mapping and bang up-to-date research, and is printed on plastic paper so it won't tear (and should even survive a dip in the Arabian Sea). It's also been tested and proofed on the road by the authors of this guide. Another excellent map of South India is the Nelles' India 4 (South) 1:1,500,000, which shows colour contours, road distances, inset city plans and all but the tiniest places.

Ttk, a Chennai-based company, publishes basic **state maps**, which are widely available in India and in some specialized travel and map shops in the UK. Regional Automobile Associations based in Mumbai and Chennai produce books of **road maps** which are useful for those planning overland routes across India. For basic state-by-state and city road maps try Ⓦmapsofindia .com/maps.

If you need larger-scale **city maps** than the ones we provide in this book – which are keyed to show recommended hotels and restaurants – try Eicher's excellent City Map series (Ⓦmaps.eicherworld.com), featuring Mumbai, Bengaluru (Bangalore), Chennai and Coimbatore.

On the Internet, and much to the displeasure of the Indian government, **Google Earth**'s satellite coverage of the south of the country at Ⓦmaps.google.com is impressive. Though its street mapping remains rudimentary, you can use the satellite images for superb bird's-eye explorations of backwaters and beaches not covered on most published maps.

Money

India's unit of currency is the **rupee**, usually abbreviated "Rs" and divided into a hundred **paise** (pronounced *pi*-suh). Almost all money is paper, with notes of 10, 20, 50, 100, 500 and, more rarely, 1000 rupees; a few 5 rupee notes are still in circulation. Coins in practice start at 25 and 50 paise, and 1, 2 and 5 rupees, though you might still see the odd beaten-up 10 or 20 paise piece. At the time of writing, the **exchange rate** was approximately Rs85 to £1 and Rs44 to $1.

Banknotes, especially lower denominations, can get into a terrible state. Don't accept **torn banknotes**, since no one else will be prepared to take them and you'll be left saddled with the things unless you can be bothered to change them at the Reserve Bank of India or large branches of other big banks. Don't pass them on to beggars; they can't use them either, so it amounts to an insult.

Large denominations can also be a problem, as **change** is usually in short supply. Many Indian people cannot afford to keep much lying around, and you shouldn't necessarily expect shopkeepers or rickshaw-wallahs to have it (and they may – as may you – try to hold onto it if they do). Larger notes – like the Rs500 note – are good for travelling with and can be changed for smaller denominations at hotels and other suitable establishments.

It is worth noting that certain numbers are referred to differently in India to anywhere else in the world: a hundred thousand is a *lakh* (written 1,00,000); ten million is a *crore* (1,00,00,000). The words "million", and "billion" are not in common use, being replaced by ten lakh or ten crore, respectively.

It is illegal to carry rupees (besides spending money of Rs5000) into India, and you won't get them at a particularly good rate in the West anyhow (though you might in Thailand, Malaysia or Singapore). It is also illegal to take over Rs5000 out of the country.

ATMs, cards and traveller's cheques

By far the easiest and simultaneously secure method of exchange is to make withdrawals from the increasingly ubiquitous **ATMs** in India using your **debit card**; the flat transaction fee is usually quite small (typically 1.5 percent). Make sure you have a personal identification number (PIN) that's designed to work overseas. Not all ATMs are geared towards accepting Cirrus, though these are becoming increasingly rare. Most are open 24 hours.

A **credit card** is a handy backup, as an increasing number of hotels, restaurants, large shops and tourist emporia now take them. If you have a selection of cards, take them all in case one gets lost, stolen or chewed in a machine.

In addition to cash and card(s), carry some **traveller's cheques** to cover all eventualities, with a few small denominations for the end of your trip, and for the odd foreign-currency purchase such as tourist-quota rail tickets. US dollars are the easiest currency to convert, with pounds sterling a close second and euros third. Other hard currencies can be changed easily in tourist areas and big cities, but less so elsewhere. If you enter the country with more than $10,000 or the equivalent, you are supposed to fill in a currency declaration form.

Traveller's cheques aren't as liquid as cash, or straightforward to use as cards, but are obviously more secure and you get a slightly better exchange rate for them at banks. Not all banks, however, accept them, and those that do can be quirky about exactly which ones they will change. Well-known brands such as Thomas Cook and American Express are your best bet, but in some places even American Express is only accepted in US dollars and not as pounds sterling. Branches of both companies have offices in the major

At the time of writing, the **exchange rates** were: Rs85.5 to GB£1; Rs45 to US$1; Rs39 to Can$1; Rs34.5 to Aus$1; Rs30 to NZ$1; Rs6 to ZAR1. Check ⓦ www.xe .com for up-to-the-minute exchange rates.

cities of South India; see the relevant accounts in the Guide and collect a full list when you purchase your traveller's cheques.

A compromise between traveller's cheques and plastic is **Visa TravelMoney**, a disposable pre-paid debit card with a PIN which works in all ATMs that take Visa cards. You load up your account with funds before leaving home, and when they run out, you simply throw the card away. Up to nine cards can be purchased to access the same funds – useful for couples or families travelling together – and it's a good idea to buy at least one extra as a backup in case of loss or theft. The card is available in most countries from branches of Thomas Cook and Citicorp. For more information, check the Visa website, ⓦwww.usa.visa.com.

Changing money

Changing money in regular **banks**, especially government-run banks such as the State Bank of India (SBI), can be a time-consuming business, involving lots of form-filling and queuing at different counters, so change substantial amounts at any one time. You'll have no such problems, however, with **private companies** such as Thomas Cook or American Express. Major cities and main tourist centres usually have several **licensed currency exchange bureaux**; rates usually aren't as good as at a bank, but transactions are generally a lot quicker and there's less paperwork to complete.

Outside **banking hours** (Mon–Fri 10am till 2 or 4pm, Sat 10am–noon), large hotels may change money, probably at a lower rate, and exchange bureaux have longer opening hours. Banks at Mumbai and Chennai airports stay open 24 hours, but neither is very conveniently located.

Wherever you change money, hold on to **exchange receipts** ("encashment certificates"); they will be required if you want to change back any excess rupees when you leave the country, and to buy air tickets and reserve train berths with rupees at special counters for foreigners. The State Bank of India now charges for tax clearance forms (see p.87 to find out if you'll need one).

Opening hours

Standard **shop** opening hours in India are Monday to Saturday 9.30am to 6pm. Smaller shops vary from town to town, religion to religion and one to another, but usually keep longer hours. **India Tourism** offices are open in principle Monday to Friday 9.30am to 5pm, Saturday 9.30am to 1pm, though these may vary slightly; **state tourist offices** are likely to be open Monday to Friday 10am to 5pm, but sometimes operate much longer hours.

For opening hours of post offices, see Mail, p.90; for opening hours of banks, see Changing money, opposite. For dates of **public holidays**, see box, p.67.

Phones

Privately run phone services with **international direct dialling** facilities are very widespread. Advertising themselves with the acronyms **STD/ISD** (standard trunk dialling/international subscriber dialling), they are extremely quick and easy to use, and some stay open 24 hours; some booths have fax machines too. Both national and international calls are dialled direct. Your bill, which you can see ticking over on the booth's meter, is calculated in seconds and usually rounded up to the nearest rupee.

Almost all such booths **charge** according to official government rates, which are around Rs10 per minute to most Western countries. "Call back" (or "back call", as it's often known) is possible at most phone booths, although check before you call and be aware that, in the case of booths, this facility rarely comes without a charge of Rs3–5 per minute.

Calling from hotel room phones is often not possible and is always more expensive when it is. Having somebody call you at your hotel, on the other hand, should present no problems (except the odd linguistic issue) and is never charged for. Internet joints in India's big metropolitan cities and tourist centres have started to offer **Net2Phone (or NetPhone)** services, which allow you to make telephone calls over the web for incredibly low rates: typically Rs2–3 for calls to the UK and US. At the time of writing, services were limited to international calls. We've listed where you can access Net2phone in

International dialling codes

	From India	To India
UK	☎00 44	☎00 91
Irish Republic	☎00 353	☎00 91
US and Canada	☎00 1	☎011 91
Australia	☎00 61	☎0011 91
New Zealand	☎00 64	☎00 91
South Africa	☎00 27	☎09091 91

the Guide, but more providers are popping up each month, so keep your eyes peeled for the logo. The widespread iWay cybercafé franchise invariably has the facility.

Home country direct services are also available from any STD/ISD phone to the UK, the US, Canada, Ireland, Australia, New Zealand, South Africa and a growing number of other countries. These allow you to make a collect or telephone credit card call to that country via an operator there. If you can't find a phone with home country direct buttons, you can use any phone toll free, by dialling 000, your country code and 17 (except Canada which is 000-127).

Mobile phones

Call charges to and from **mobile phones** are far lower in India than in Western countries, which is why lots of foreign tourists opt to sign up to a local network while they're travelling. To do this you'll need to buy an Indian SIM card from a mobile phone shop; these cost around Rs300, plus the price of a top-up card (varying from Rs200–500). Your retailer will help you get connected. They'll also advise you on which company to use. Different states tend to be dominated by one or other of the main providers – Airtel, VSNL, Touchtel, Hutch or Idea (formerly AT&T). If you intend to stay inside their designated coverage area, usually one state, charges for texts and calls are cheap (Rs1–2 per min within India). However, once you leave the local coverage area you'll automatically be paying roaming charges (Rs3–5 per min). Note that when roaming, you also pay for incoming calls.

We list mobile numbers in the Guide using the convention ☎m91234 56789. Indian mobile numbers are ten-digit, starting with a 9. However, if you are calling from outside the state where the mobile is based (but not from abroad), you will need to add a zero in front of that.

Photography

Beware of pointing your camera at anything that might be considered "strategic", including airports, anything military and even bridges, train stations and main roads. Remember too that some people prefer not to be photographed, so it is wise to ask before you take a snapshot of them. On the other hand, you'll get people, especially kids, volunteering to pose.

Most photo shops can now transfer **digital** images onto a CD – useful in order to free up memory space. **Camera film**, sold at average Western prices, is widely available in India (but check the date on the box, and note that false boxes containing outdated film are often sold). It's fairly easy to get films developed, though they don't always come out as well as they might at home. Konica studios through South India have hi-tech equipment and process film in one hour (Rs200–250). If you're after **slide film**, buy it in the big cities, and don't expect to find specialist brands such as Velvia.

Time

India is all in one time zone: GMT plus 5 hours 30 minutes. This makes it 5 hours 30 minutes ahead of London, 10 hours 30 minutes ahead of New York, 13 hours 30 minutes ahead of LA, 3 hours 30 minutes ahead of Johannesburg, 4 hours 30 minutes behind Sydney and 6 hours 30 minutes behind New Zealand; however, summer time in those places will vary the difference by an hour.

Tourist information

The Indian government maintains a number of **tourist offices** abroad, whose staff are usually helpful and knowledgeable. Other sources of information include the websites of Indian embassies and consulates (see p.87), travel agents (though their advice may not always be totally unbiased), and the Indian Railways representatives listed on p.38.

Inside India, both national and local governments run **tourist information offices**, providing general travel advice and handing out an array of printed material, from city maps to glossy leaflets on specific destinations. The Indian government's tourist department, India Tourism (Ⓦ www.incredibleindia.org), has branches in most regional capitals. These, however, operate independently of the **state government information counters** and their commercial bureaux run by the state tourism development corporations, usually referred to by their initials (eg KSTDC in Karnataka and TTDC in Tamil Nadu), which offer a wide range of travel facilities, including guided tours, car rental and their own hotels (identified with the relevant acronyms throughout this book).

Just to confuse things further, the Indian government's tourist office has a go-ahead corporate wing too. The **Indian Tourism Development Corporation** (**ITDC**) is responsible for the Ashok chain of hotels and operates tour and travel services, frequently competing with its state counterparts.

Finally, besides our own extensive site on India (Ⓦ www.roughguides.com), these are some useful websites on South Indian **cities** and states, some with search engines, listings and news.

Travel advice

Australian Department of Foreign Affairs Ⓦ www.smartraveller.gov.au.
British Foreign & Commonwealth Office Ⓦ www.fco.gov.uk.
Canadian Department of Foreign Affairs Ⓦ www.voyage.gc.ca.
Irish Department of Foreign Affairs Ⓦ www.foreignaffairs.gov.ie.
New Zealand Ministry of Foreign Affairs Ⓦ www.safetravel.govt.nz.
South African Department of Foreign Affairs Ⓦ www.dfa.gov.za
US State Department Ⓦ www.travel.state.gov.

India Tourism offices overseas

Australia Level 2, Piccadilly, 210 Pitt St, Sydney

NSW ☎ 02/9264 4855, Ⓔ info@indiatourism.com.au.
Canada 60 Bloor St (West), #1003, Toronto, ON M4W 3B8 ☎ 1-416/962-3787, Ⓔ indiatourism@bellnet.ca.
South Africa Hyde Lane, Lancaster Gate, Johannesburg 2000 ☎ 011/325 0880, Ⓔ goito@global.co.za.
UK 7 Cork St, London W1X 2LN ☎ 020/7437 3677, Ⓔ info@indiatouristoffice.org.
USA 3550 Wilshire Blvd, Suite #204, Los Angeles, CA 90010 ☎ 1-213/380-8855, Ⓔ indiatourismla@aol .com; Suite 1808, 1270 Ave of Americas, New York NY 10020 ☎ 1-212/586 4901, Ⓔ rd@itonyc.com.

Indian State Tourist Office websites

Andaman & Nicobar Islands Ⓦ www.and.nic.in
Andhra Pradesh Ⓦ www.aptourism.com
Goa Ⓦ www.goatourism.org
Karnataka Ⓦ www.kstdc.nic.in
Kerala Ⓦ www.keralatourism.org
Lakshadweep Ⓦ www.lakshadweeptourism.com
Maharashtra Ⓦ www.maharashtratourism.gov.in
Tamil Nadu Ⓦ www.tamilnadutourism.org

South Indian cities

Ⓦ **www.explocity.com** Comprehensive city listings for Chennai, Bengaluru (Bangalore), Hyderabad and Mumbai, among other places.
Ⓦ **www.bangalorebest.com**
Ⓦ **www.chennaidirectory.com**
Ⓦ **www.hyderabad.co.uk**
Ⓦ **www.mangalore.com**
Ⓦ **www.mumbai-central.com**
Ⓦ **www.tourism.pon.nic.in**
Ⓦ **www.aponline.gov.in**
Ⓦ **www.goacom.com**
Ⓦ **www.karnataka.com**
Ⓦ **www.kerala.com**
Ⓦ **www.cs.utk.edu/~siddhart/tamilnadu**
Ⓦ **www.anislands.com**

Other useful websites

Ⓦ **www.indiamike.com** Popular travel forum run out of a bedroom in New Jersey by inveterate India-phile Mike Szewczyk. Lively chat rooms, bulletin boards, photo archives and banks of members' travel articles, as well as a daily news feed.
Ⓦ **www.rediff.com** Another leading India-specific portal with great search facilities and a site plan that stretches from news to travel.
Ⓦ **www.travelintelligence.net/wsd/articles/ artbyplce_143.html** A huge selection of top-quality, inspiring travelogues by India experts including William Dalrymple, Sue Carpenter, Justine Hardy and Rupert Isaacson.

Guide

Guide

Mumbai and southern Maharashtra

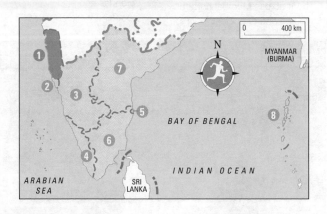

CHAPTER 1 # Highlights

* **The Gateway of India**
Mumbai's defining landmark,
and a favourite spot for an
evening stroll. See p.118

* **Chhatrapati Shivaji
Museum** A fine collection
of priceless Indian art, from
ancient temple sculpture to
Mughal armour. See p.122

* **CS (Victoria) Terminus** A
fantastically eccentric pile,
perhaps the greatest railway
station ever built by the
British. See p.127

* **Elephanta Island** Catch a
boat across Mumbai harbour
to see one of ancient India's
most wonderful rock-cut
Shiva temples. See p.136

* **Bollywood blockbusters**
Check out the latest Hindi
mega movie in one of the city
centre's gigantic Art-Deco
cinemas. See p.143

* **Janjira Fort** An island fortress
rising sheer from the Arabian
Sea – the only stronghold not
conquered by the Marathas.
See p.157

* **Matheran** Ramshackle old
British-era hill station, where
you can laze on shady colonial
verandas and enjoy leisurely
woodland walks. See p.158

△ Chhatrapati Shivaji Terminus (Victoria Terminus)

Mumbai and southern Maharashtra

Ever since the opening of the Suez Canal in 1869, the principal gateway to the Indian Subcontinent has been **MUMBAI (Bombay)**, the city Aldous Huxley famously described as "the most appalling . . .of either hemisphere". Travellers tend to regard time spent here as a rite of passage to be survived rather than savoured. But as the powerhouse of Indian business, industry and trade, and the source of its most seductive media images, the Maharashtrian capital can be a compelling place to kill time. Whether or nor you find the experience enjoyable, however, will depend largely on how well you handle the heat, humidity, hassle, traffic fumes, relentless crowds and appalling poverty of India's most dynamic, Westernized city.

First impressions of Mumbai tend to be dominated by its chronic **shortage of space**. Crammed onto a narrow spit of land that curls from the swamp-ridden coast into the Arabian Sea, the city has, in less than five hundred years since its "discovery" by the Portuguese, metamorphosed from an aboriginal fishing settlement into a sprawling megalopolis of over sixteen million people. Being swept along broad boulevards by endless streams of commuters, or jostled by coolies and hand-cart pullers in the teeming bazaars, you'll continually feel as if Mumbai is about to burst at the seams.

The roots of the population problem and attendant poverty lie, paradoxically, in the city's enduring ability to create **wealth**. Mumbai alone generates nearly forty percent of India's GNP and tax income, its port handles half the country's foreign trade, and its movie industry is the biggest in the world. Symbols of prosperity are everywhere: from the phalanx of office blocks clustered on Nariman Point, Maharashtra's Manhattan, to the expensively dressed teenagers posing in Colaba's trendiest nightspots.

The flip side to the success story is the city's much chronicled **poverty**. Each day, hundreds of economic refugees pour into Mumbai from the Maharashtrian hinterland. Some find jobs and secure accommodation; many more end up living on the already overcrowded streets, or amid the squalor of Asia's largest slums, reduced to rag-picking and begging from cars at traffic lights.

However, while it would definitely be misleading to downplay its difficulties, Mumbai is far from the ordeal some travellers make it out to be. Once you've

Mumbai or Bombay?

In 1996 Bombay was renamed **Mumbai**, as part of a wider policy instigated by the right-wing Maharashtrian nationalist Shiv Sena Municipality to replace names of any places, roads and features in the city that had connotations of the Raj. The Shiv Sena asserted that the British term "Bombay" derived from the Marathi title of a local deity, the mouthless "Maha-amba-aiee" (Mumba Devi for short; see p.129). In fact, historians are unanimously agreed that the Portuguese, who dubbed the harbour "Bom Bahia" ("Good Bay") when they first came across it, were responsible for christening the site and that the later British moniker had nothing to do with the aboriginal Hindu earth goddess.

The name change was widely unpopular when it was first imposed, especially among the upper and middle classes, and non-Maharashtrian immigrant communities, who doggedly stuck to Bombay. More than a decade on, however, "Mumbai" seems to have definitively taken root with the dotcom generation and even outgrown the narrow agenda of its nationalist originators – just as "Bombay" outlived the Raj.

overcome the major hurdle of finding somewhere to stay, you may begin to enjoy its frenzied pace and crowded, cosmopolitan feel.

Most tourists heading south from Mumbai skip **southern Maharashtra** altogether. If you have a little time, however, it's worth breaking the journey up, either by following the little-frequented route south down the **Konkan Coast** via the island fortress of **Janjira** and pilgrimage town of **Ganpatipule**, or else by climbing through the Sahayadri Hills to **Pune**. Connected to Mumbai by a hi-spec six-lane expressway, the former capital of the Maratha Peshwars is nowadays a major commercial centre, although it's best known abroad as the home of the much-derided Osho ashram. Amid the narrow streets of its old quarter, **the city** retains plenty of old-world Maratha character, and also boasts a unique and idiosyncratic museum. En route to it from the coast, you could do worse than spend a night or two at **Matheran**, this region's most beautiful hill station, and at **Lonavala**, whose hotels serve as a convenient base from which to visit some of the earliest Buddhist rock-cut art in the western Deccan, at **Karla**, **Bhaja** and **Bedsa Caves**. Another long day's journey south of Pune, **Mahabaleshwar** is Maharashtra's busiest hill station, providing coolness, wooded walks and fine views. The last major towns before reaching the Goan border, in the far south of the state, are **Kolhapur**, which holds a more traditional atmosphere than most as well as some striking Raj-era architecture, and **Sawantwadi**, renowned as a centre for the painting of traditional Indian playing cards, or *ganjifa*.

Some history

Mumbai originally consisted of seven **islands**, inhabited by small Koli fishing communities. The town of Gherapuri on **Elephanta** is thought to have been the major settlement in the region until the early fourteenth century, when the Yadava ruler, King Bhima, founded a new capital at nearby Mahim after the old one in north India had been threatened by the Khilji sultans of Delhi. In 1534, Sultan Bahadur of Ahmedabad ceded the land to the **Portuguese**, who felt it to be of little importance and concentrated development in the areas further north at Vasai, which they would rechristen Baçaim (modern-day Bassein). They handed over the largest island to the English in 1661, as part of the dowry when the Portuguese Infanta Catherine of Braganza married Charles II; four years later Charles received the remaining islands and the port, and the town took on

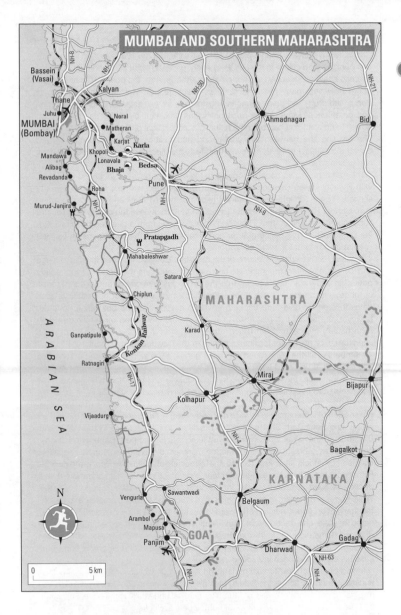

MUMBAI AND SOUTHERN MAHARASHTRA

the anglicized name of Bombay (see box opposite). This was the first part of India that could properly be termed a colony; elsewhere on the Subcontinent the English had merely been granted the right to set up "factories", or trading posts. Because of its natural safe harbour and strategic position for commerce, the **East India Company**, based at Surat, wanted to buy the land; in 1668 a deal was struck, and Charles leased Mumbai to them for a pittance.

The dons

Criminals have always been a part of Mumbai's life, but the 1980s saw an intensification of **organized crime** in the city. Previously, gangsters had confined their activities to small-scale racketeering in poor neighbourhoods. After the post-1970s real-estate boom however, many petty "landsharks" became powerful godfather figures, or **dons**, with drug- and gold-smuggling businesses as well as involvement in extortion and prostitution. Moreover, corrupt politicians who employed the gangs' muscle-power to rig elections had become highly placed political puppets with debts to pay. The dividing line between the underworld and politics grew increasingly blurred during the 1990s – in 1992, no fewer than forty candidates in the municipal elections had criminal records.

The gangs have also become integral to the dirty war between India and **Pakistan**, with Karachi-based Dawood Ibrahim heavily implicated with the Pakistani security services – he is thought to be behind the bombings of 1993 – and Mumbai's leading don, Chhota Rajan, with the Indian forces. In fact, many see the bungling of Rajan's subsequent extradition from Thailand and his escape from a guarded hospital room (he drugged his Thai police guards and climbed out of the window using his bed sheets) as payment for services rendered.

The late 1980s saw the entrance of the dons into **Bollywood**, when the rise of video and TV made regular film financiers nervous of investing in the industry. Mob money poured in and it's an open secret that the film industry is one of the favoured forms of money-laundering with the dons – rival films mysteriously put back their release dates in order to give mob-backed movies a clear run at the box office. In 2000, however, the authorities began to take action, and Bollywood mogul Bharat Shah (who usually has around ten billion rupees invested in films at any one time) was imprisoned for two years for financial links to the Dawood Ibrahim gang.

Mumbai is still the playground for mafia gangs, each with their own personalities and legends. If you read any newspapers while you're in the city you won't escape this phenomenon; the media revels in the shocking and bloodthirsty exploits of the gangsters, and the unfolding sagas run like a Bollywood blockbuster.

None has proved quite as riveting as the arrest and subsequent trial for illegal possession of firearms of Bollywood megastar **Sanjay Dutt**, son of cinema megastars Nargis and Sunil Dutt. Shortly after his breakthrough appearance in the 1993 Hindi blockbuster *Khalnayak*, police raided Dutt junior's luxury home in Bandra and discovered a hidden cache of automatic weapons, grenades and ammunition. His accusers claimed the stockpile linked him to the atrocities of 1993–94. Dutt protested his innocence, but still had to endure eighteen months of incarceration and more than a decade of court appearances before his case finally came to a close in late 2006. While some of the charges made against him stuck, the verdict ultimately exonerated the star. Indian public opinion afterwards held that the macho Hindu action hero had acted less like a hardened villain than a victim of his own tough screen image – Dutt's dignified demeanour in court and images of his repentant visits to Ganpati temples in the run-up to his trial played well in the popular media, and since the end of the case his career has been in ascendance again.

A vivid portrait of the Mumbai underworld and its connections with the city's politics and movie industry appears in Suketu Mehta's award-winning book, *Maximum City*. You also gain a gutsy insider's view of Mumbai's criminal underbelly in the novel *Shantaram* by Gregory David Roberts. Reviews of both appear in Books on pp.792–800.

The English set about an ambitious programme of fortifying their outpost, living in the area known today as Fort. However, life was not easy. Malaria, "Chinese Death" (cholera), beri beri and "fluxes" (dysentery) culled many of

Record rains

On July 26, 2005, Mumbai sustained the **heaviest rainfall** ever to have been recorded in a city over a 24-hour period: a staggering 942mm. The storm caused havoc – landslides and flooding killed an estimated 100 people in the city and stranded 150,000 more. It also provoked a downpour of criticism for the Mumbai Municipality, whose corrupt management was blamed for the failure of the city's infrastructure to cope with the crisis.

the first settlers, prompting from the colony's chaplain the declaration that "two monsoons are the age of a man". **Gerald Aungier**, the fourth governor (1672–77), began planning what he stated was "the city which by God's assistance is intended to be built", and by the start of the eighteenth century the town was the capital of the East India Company. Aungier is credited with encouraging the mix that still contributes to the city's success, welcoming Hindu traders from Gujarat, Goans, Muslim weavers and, most visibly, the business-minded Zoroastrian **Parsis**.

Much of the British settlement in the old Fort area was destroyed by a devastating fire in 1803, prompting substantial rebuilding. The arrival of the **Great Indian Peninsular Railway** half a century or so later improved communications, encouraging yet more immigration from elsewhere in India. This crucial artery, coupled with the cotton crisis in America following the Civil War, gave impetus to the great Bombay cotton boom and established the city as a major industrial and commercial centre. With the opening of the Suez Canal in 1869, and the construction of enormous docks, Bombay's access to European markets improved further. **Sir Bartle Frere**, governor from 1862 to 1867, oversaw the construction of the city's distinctive colonial-Gothic buildings; the most extravagant of all, **Victoria Terminus** railway station – now officially Chhatrapati Shivaji Terminus or CST – is a fitting testimony to this extraordinary age of expansion.

As the most prosperous city in the nation, Bombay was at the forefront of the **Independence** struggle; Mahatma Gandhi used a house here, now a museum, to coordinate the struggle through three decades. Fittingly, the first British colony took pleasure in waving the final goodbye to the Raj, when the last contingent of British troops passed through the Gateway of India in February 1948. Since Independence, Mumbai has prospered as India's commercial and cultural capital and this period has seen the population grow tenfold to more than sixteen million.

However, the resultant overcrowding has done little to foster relations between the city's various minorities and the past two decades have seen repeated outbursts of **communal tensions** among the poorer classes. Strikes and riots paralysed the metropolis throughout the 1980s and early 1990s as more and more immigrants from other regions of the country poured in. The mounting discontent fuelled the rise of the extreme right-wing Maharashtrian party, the **Shiv Sena**, founded in 1966 by the former cartoonist, Bal "the Saheb" Thackery, a self-confessed admirer of Hitler. Many people blamed Sena cadres for orchestrating the attacks on Muslims that followed in the wake of the Babri Masjid destruction in Ayodhya in 1992–93, when thousands were murdered by mobs as the city descended into anarchy for ten days.

Only a few months later, on March 12, 1993, ten massive **bomb blasts** killed 260 people and damaged several landmark buildings. The involvement of

Muslim godfather Dawood Ibrahim (see box, p.102) and the Pakistani secret service was suspected – as, indeed, it was a decade or so later in the wake of two other bloody bomb attacks that brought the city to a standstill: the first, in August 2003, killed 107 tourists right outside the **Gateway of India** itself; the second, on July 7, 2006, simultaneously blew apart seven packed commuter trains at points across the city.

After each of these terrible blows, however, the city bounced back with amazing ebullience, and in the popular imagination it continues to be identified less with terrorist outrages than with the **glamour** purveyed by its movie and satellite-TV industries. Bollywood starlets, VJs and playboy heirs to industrial fortunes provide the staple for the gossip columns and fanzines lapped up across the country, while hundreds of Hindi blockbusters are shot in its streets and suburban studios each year.

Rajiv Gandhi's reforms of the early 1990s paved the way for a consumer boom across India, but nowhere has **economic liberalization** been more passionately embraced than in Mumbai. Following decades of stagnation, the textiles industry has been supplanted by rapidly growing IT, finance, health-care and back-office support sectors. Whole suburbs have sprung up to accommodate the affluent new middle-class workforce, with shiny shopping malls, multiplex cinemas and car showrooms to relieve them of their income.

Far from keeping up with the boom, however, the city's infrastructure continues to deteriorate – as the chaos that ensued after the 2005 floods vividly demonstrated (see box, p.103). Corruption in politics and business has drained away investment from socially deprived areas. Luxury appartments in Bandra may change hands for half-a-million dollars or more, but an estimated 7–8 million people (just under fifty percent of Mumbai's population) live in slums with no toilets, on just six percent of the land.

Arrival

Unless you arrive in Mumbai by train at **Chhatrapati Shivaji Terminus** (formerly Victoria Terminus), be prepared for a long slog into the centre. The international and domestic **airports** are way north of the city, and ninety minutes or more by road from the main hotel areas, while from **Mumbai Central** railway or **bus station**, you face a laborious trip across town.

In transit

If you're only passing through Mumbai between flights and need to sit out half the night, it's worth knowing that the *Leela Kempinski* and *Royal Meridien* five-stars are both a short, complimentary transfer bus ride from the international terminal at CST. Their air-conditioned restaurants, coffee shops and bars make much more comfortable places to kill time than the departure lounge at the grungy airport – and their toilets are in a different league.

The domestic airport is being gradually upgraded and its new **retiring rooms** are an option worth considering if you'd like to get some shut-eye between planes – though they're rarely available at short notice. Check at the information desk on the Arrivals concourses in terminals 1 or 2.

By air

Mumbai's busy **international airport**, **Chhatrapati Shivaji** (30km north), is divided into two "modules", one for Air India flights and the other for foreign airlines. Once through customs and the lengthy immigration formalities, you'll find a 24-hour State Bank of India exchange facility and ATM, government (ITDC) and state (MTDC) tourist information counters, car rental kiosks, cafés and a prepaid taxi stand in the arrivals concourse. There's also – very usefully – an **Indian Railways booking office** which you should make use of if you know your next destination; it'll save you a long wait at the reservation offices downtown. If you're on one of the few flights to land in the afternoon or early evening – by which time most hotels tend to be full – it can be worth paying on the spot for a room at the **accommodation booking desk** in the arrivals hall. All of the domestic airlines also have offices outside the main entrance, and there's a handy 24-hour **left luggage** "cloakroom" in the car park nearby (Rs60 per day, or part thereof; maximum duration 90 days).

Many of the more upmarket hotels, particularly those near the airport, send out **courtesy coaches** to pick up their guests. **Taxis** are not too extravagant. To avoid haggling over the fare or being duped by the private taxi companies outside the airport, go to the "Pre-Paid" taxi desk in the arrivals hall. The price on the receipt, which you hand to the driver on arrival at your destination, is slightly more than the normal meter rate (around Rs380 to Colaba or Nariman Point, or Rs175 to Juhu), but at least you can be sure you'll be taken by the most direct route. Taxi-wallahs sometimes try to persuade you to stay at a different hotel from the one you ask for. Don't agree to this; their commission will be added onto the price of your room.

Internal flights land at Mumbai's **domestic airport** (26km to the north of downtown and 2km west of the international airport), officially also called Chhatrapati Shivaji, but still, somewhat confusingly, referred to by many Mumbaikars by its old name, "Santa Cruz". It is divided into separate terminals: the cream-coloured one (Module 1A) for the government-run Indian Airlines, and the blue-and-white (Module 1B) for private carriers. If you're transferring directly from here to an international flight take the free "fly-bus" that shuttles every fifteen minutes between the two; look for the transfer counter in your transit lounge.

The ITDC and MTDC both have 24-hour **information counters** in the arrivals hall, and there's a foreign exchange counter and accommodation desk tucked away near the first-floor exit. The official "Pre-Paid" taxi counter on the arrivals concourse charges around Rs400 to Colaba. Don't be tempted by the cheaper fares offered by touts outside, and avoid **auto-rickshaws** altogether, as they're not allowed downtown and will leave you at the mercy of unscrupulous taxi drivers on the edge of vile-smelling Mahim Creek, the southernmost limit of their permitted area.

Malaria warning

Due to the massive slum encampments and bodies of stagnant water around the **airports**, both the international and domestic terminals are major **malaria** black spots. Clouds of mosquitoes await your arrival in the car park, so don't forget to smother yourself with strong insect repellent before leaving the terminal.

By train

Trains to Mumbai from most central, southern and eastern regions arrive at **Chhatrapati Shivaji Terminus or CST** (formerly **Victoria Terminus**, or VT), the main railway station at the end of the Central Railway line. From here it's a ten- or fifteen-minute ride to Colaba; taxis queue at the busy rank outside the south exit, opposite the new reservation hall.

Mumbai Central, the terminus for Western Railway trains from northern India, is a half-hour ride from Colaba; take a taxi from the forecourt, or flag one down on the main road – it should cost around Rs175.

Some trains from South India arrive at more obscure stations. If you find yourself at **Dadar**, way up in the industrial suburbs, and don't want to shell out on a taxi (Rs600), cross the Tilak Marg road bridge onto the Western Railway and catch a suburban train into town (remembering to purchase a ticket at the hatch on platform 1 beforehand). **Kurla** station, where a few Bengaluru (Bangalore) trains pull in, is even further out, just south of the domestic airport; taking a suburban train for Churchgate is the only reasonable alternative to a taxi (Rs400). From either, it's worth asking at the station when you arrive if there is another long-distance train going to Churchgate or CST (Victoria Terminus) shortly after – it's far preferable to trying to cram into either a suburban train or bus.

By bus

Nearly all interstate **buses** arrive at **Mumbai Central** bus stand, a stone's throw from the railway station of the same name. Government services use the main **Maharashtra State Road Transport Corporation (MSRTC)** stand itself; private ones operate from the roadside next to Mumbai Central railway station, two minutes' walk west on the opposite side of busy Dr AN Marg (Lamington Road). To get downtown, either catch a suburban train from Mumbai Central's local platform, over the footbridge from the mainline or jump in a cab at the rank in front of the station.

Note that while most MSRTC buses terminate at Mumbai Central, those from **Pune** (and surrounding areas) end up at the **ASIAD** bus stand, a glorified parking lot near the **Dadar** railway station, further north. Again, you can travel onwards by suburban train or taxi.

Information

The best source of **information** in Mumbai is the excellent **India Tourism** (Mon–Fri 8.30am–6pm, Sat 8.30am–2pm; ⓣ022/2203 3144, ⓔindiatourism@vsnl.com) at 123 M Karve Rd, opposite Churchgate station's east exit. The staff here are exceptionally helpful and hand out a wide range of leaflets, maps and brochures on both Mumbai and the rest of the country. There are also 24-hour tourist **information counters** at Chhatrapati Shivaji International (ⓣ022/2682 9248) and domestic (ⓣ022/2615 6920) **airports**.

The **Maharashtra State Tourism Development Corporation (MTDC) office**, on Madam Cama Road opposite the LIC Building in Nariman Point (Mon–Sat 8.30am–7pm; ⓣ022/202 6731, ⓦwww.maharashtratourism.com), can reserve rooms in MTDC resorts and also sells tickets for city sightseeing tours (see p.112).

For detailed **listings**, the most complete source is Mumbai's *Time Out*, which carries full details of what's on and where, just like its London and New York

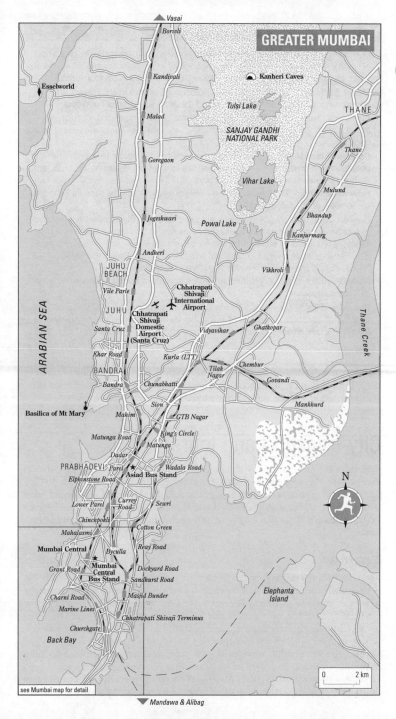

GREATER MUMBAI

Vasai

Borivli

Kandivali

Esselworld

Malad

Kanheri Caves

Tulsi Lake

SANJAY GANDHI
NATIONAL PARK

THANE

Goregaon

Thane

Vihar Lake

Mulund

Jogeshwari

Bhandup

Powai Lake

Kanjurmarg

Andheri

Vikhroli

JUHU
BEACH

Vile Parle

Chhatrapati
Shivaji
International
Airport

JUHU

Chhatrapati
Shivaji
Domestic
Airport
(Santa Cruz)

Santa Cruz

Vidyavihar

Ghatkopar

ARABIAN SEA

Khar Road

Kurla (LTT)

Chembur

Thane Creek

BANDRA

Bandra

Chunabhatti

Tilak
Nagar

Govandi

Basilica of Mt Mary

Mahim

Sion

Mankhurd

GTB Nagar

Matunga Road

King's Circle

Matunga

Dadar

PRABHADEVI

Parel

Wadala Road

Elphinstone Road

Asiad Bus Stand

Lower Parel

Currey
Road

Sewri

Chinchpokli

Mahalaxmi

Cotton Green

N

Mumbai Central

Reay Road

Byculla

Grant Road

Mumbai
Central
Bus Stand

Dockyard Road

Sandhurst Road

Charni Road

Masjid Bunder

Elephanta
Island

Marine Lines

Chhatrapati Shivaji Terminus

Churchgate

Back Bay

0   2 km

see Mumbai map for detail

Mandawa & Alibag

Festivals in Mumbai

Mumbai has its own versions of all the major Hindu and Muslim **festivals**, plus a host of smaller neighbourhood celebrations imported by its immigrant communities. Exact dates vary from year to year; check in advance at the government tourist office.

Makar Sankranti (Jan). A celebration of prosperity, when sweets, flowers and fruit are exchanged by all, and kites are flown in the parks as a sign of happiness.

Elephanta Music and Dance Festival (Feb). MTDC-organized cultural event including floodlit performances by classical artists with the Shiva cave temple as a backdrop.

Gokhulashtami (July/Aug). Riotous commemoration of Krishna's birthday; terracotta pots filled with curd, milk-sweets and cash are strung from tenement balconies and grabbed by human pyramids of young boys.

Nowroz (July/Aug). The Parsi New Year is celebrated with special ceremonies in the fire temples and feasting at home.

Ganesh Chathurthi (Aug/Sept). Huge effigies of Ganesh, the elephant-headed god of prosperity and wisdom, are immersed in the sea at Chowpatty Beach in a ritual originally promoted by freedom-fighters to circumvent British anti-assembly legislation. Recently it has seemed in danger of being hijacked by Hindu extremists such as the Shiv Sena, tingeing it more with chauvinism than celebration.

Nariel Purnima (Sept). Koli fishermen launch brightly decorated boats to note the end of the monsoon.

Ramadan (Sept to early Nov). The annual Muslim fast is marked in Mumbai with the opening of a vibrant all-night food market in the narrow lanes around the Minara Masjid mosque, where you can dine alfresco on flame-grilled kebabs and mint tea.

counterparts. Alternatively, check out the "Metro" page in the *Indian Express* or the "Bombay Times" section of the *Times of India*. All are available from street vendors around Colaba and the downtown area.

City transport and tours

Transport congestion has eased slightly since the opening of the huge flyover that now scythes straight through the heart of the city from just north of CST station. During peak hours, however, gridlock is the norm and you should brace yourself for long waits at junctions if you take to the roads by taxi, bus or auto. Local **trains** get there faster, but can be a real endurance test even outside rush hours.

Trains

Mumbai's local **trains** carry an estimated 6.1 million commuters each day between downtown and the sprawling suburbs in the north – half the entire passenger capacity of Indian Railways (see box opposite). One line begins at CST (VT), running up the east side of the city as far as Thane. The other leaves Churchgate, hugging the curve of Back Bay as far as Chowpatty Beach, where it veers north through Mumbai Central, Dadar, Santa Cruz and Vasai, beyond the city limits. Services depart every few minutes from 5am until midnight, stopping at dozens of small stations. Carriages remain packed solid virtually the whole time, with passengers dangling precariously out of open doors to escape the crush, so start to make your way to the exit at least three

A "Super-dense" Crush

The suburban rail network in Mumbai is officially the busiest on the planet. No other line carries as many passengers, nor crams them into such confined spaces. At peak times, as many as 4700 people may be jammed into a nine-carriage train designed to carry 1700, resulting in what the rail company, in typically jaunty Mumbai style, refers to as "Super-dense Crush Load" of 14–16 standing passengers per square metre. Not all of these actually occupy floor space, of course: ten percent will be dangling precariously out of the doors.

The busiest stretch, a sixty-kilometre segment between Churchgate Terminus and Virar in north Mumbai, transports nearly 900 million people each year, the highest of any rail network in the world. **Fatalities** are all too frequent: on average, 3500 die on the rail network annually, from falling out of the doors, crossing the tracks or because they're hit by overhead cables while riding on the roof.

The daily ordeal of commuting has its own distinct culture, with regulars forming life-long friendships that might never extend beyond the carriage. People look out for each other, sharing newspapers and saving seats for their "train friends" in the comfiest spots out of the sun. In *Maximum City*, Suketu Mehta describes how latecomers who are forced to sprint up the platform to catch their train will always find helping hands extended from the open doors, and space miraculously made where none existed before:

And at the moment of contact, they do not know if the hand that is reaching for theirs belongs to a Hindu or Muslim or Christian or Brahmin or Untouchable or whether you were born in this city or arrived this morning or whether you live in Malabar Hill or Jogeshwari; whether you're from Bombay or Mumbai or New York. All they know is that you're trying to get to the city of gold, and that's enough. "Come on board", they say. "We'll adjust."

stops before your destination. Peak hours (approximately 8.30–10am & 4–7pm) are the worst of all. Women are marginally better off in the "ladies carriages"; look for the crowd of colourful saris and *salwar kamises* grouped at the end of the platform.

Buses

BEST (Brihanmumbai Electric Supply and Transport; ☎022/2285 6262, ⓦwww.bestundertaking.com) operates a **bus** network of labyrinthine complexity, extending to the furthest-flung corners of the city. We've listed bus numbers for Mumbai's sights in our accounts, but you can easily check all the routes on the BEST website, which has an excellent "point-to-point" facility (from drop down menus you specify your starting and finishing points, and it will generate the bus numbers). Recognizing the bus numbers in the street, however, can be more problematic, as the numerals are written in Marathi (although in English on the sides). Aim, wherever possible, for the "Limited" ("Ltd") services, which stop less frequently, and avoid rush hours at all costs. Tickets should be bought from the conductor on the bus.

Taxis and car rental

With rickshaws banished to the suburbs, Mumbai's ubiquitous black-and-yellow **taxis** are the quickest and most convenient way to nip around the city centre. In theory, all should have meters and a current "tariff card" (to convert the amount shown on the meter to the correct fare); in practice, particularly at

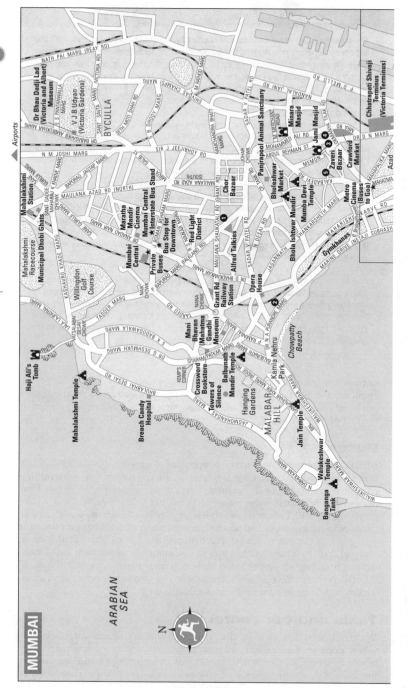

MUMBAI

ARABIAN SEA

N

Airports

Dr Bhau Daji Lad
(Victoria and Albert)
Museum

V J B Udyan
(Victoria Gardens)

BYCULLA

Panjrapool Animal Sanctuary

Minara Masjid

Jami Masjid

Chhatrapati Shivaji
Terminus
(Victoria Terminus)

Mahalakshmi
Station

Chor
Bazaar

Bhuleshwar
Market

Zaveri
Bazaar

Crawford
Market

Maratha
Mandir
Cinema

Mumba Devi
Temple

Metro
Cinema
(Buses
to Goa)

Mahalakshmi
Racecourse
Municipal Dhobi Ghats

Mumbai Central
Interstate Bus Stand

Bus Stop for
Downtown

Red Light
District

Bhola Ishtwar Mandir

Willingdon
Golf
Course

Mumbai
Central

Private
Buses

Alfred Talkies

Grant Rd
Railway
Station

Opera
House

Gymkhanas

Haji Ali's
Tomb

Mani
Bhavan
(Mahatma
Gandhi
Museum)

Chowpatty
Beach

Mahalakshmi Temple

Breach Candy
Hospital

Crossword
Bookstore

Balbunath
Mandir Temple

Towers
of Silence

Hanging
Gardens

Kamla Nehru
Park

MALABAR
HILL

Jain Temple

Walukeshwar
Temple

Banganga
Tank

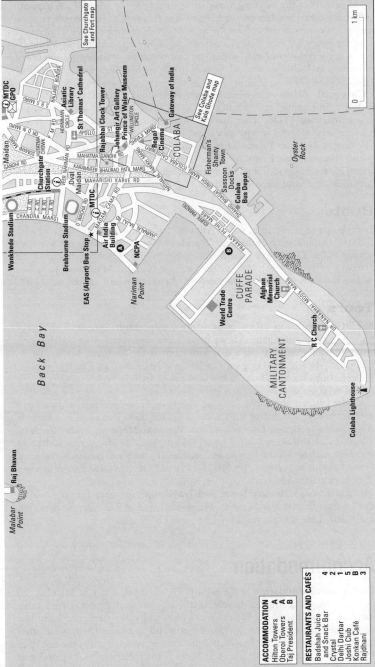

Elephanta Island

Mandawa & Alibag

See Churchgate
and Fort map

0   1 km

Back Bay

Malabar Point

Raj Bhavan

Wankhede Stadium

Brabourne Stadium

CHANDRA MARG

EAS (Airport) Bus Stop

Churchgate Station

Maidan

Oval Maidan

Maidan

MTDC GPO

Asiatic Library

St Thomas' Cathedral

HORNIMAN CIRCLE

BALLARD BUNDER

S B S MARG

P M RD

P M RD

HUTATMA CHOWK

APOLLO

MAHATMA GANDHI RD

VEER NARIMAN RD

GANDHI RD

Rajabhai Clock Tower

Jehangir Art Gallery

Prince of Wales Museum

WELLINGTON CIRCLE

Gateway of India

See Colaba and
Kala Ghoda map

COLABA

Regal Cinema

D WACHA RD

MTDC

MADAM CAMA RD

Air India Building

A

NCPA

Nariman Point

KARAMVEER BHAURAO PATIL MARG

MAHARISHI KARVE RD

JAMNALAL BAJAJ RD

NATHALAL PAREKH MARG

SHIVAJI MARG

MADAME CAMA RD (COLABA CAUSEWAY)

SHAHID BHAGAT SINGH MARG

Fisherman's Shanty Town

Sassoon Docks

Colaba Bus Depot

DUFF PARADE

PRAKASH PETHE MARG

B

World Trade Centre

CUFFE PARADE

Afghan Memorial Church

R C Church

DR MANOHAR MHATRE MARG

DR NANABHAI MOOS MARG

MILITARY CANTONMENT

Colaba Lighthouse

Oyster Rock

ACCOMMODATION	
Hilton Towers	A
Oberoi Towers	A
Taj President	B

RESTAURANTS AND CAFÉS	
Badshah Juice and Snack Bar	4
Crystal	2
Delhi Darbar	1
Joshi Club	5
Konkan Café	B
Rajdhani	3

night or early in the morning, many drivers refuse to use them. If this happens, either flag down another or haggle out a fare. As a rule of thumb, expect to be charged Rs9 per kilometre after the minimum fare of around Rs20, plus a small sum for heavy luggage (Rs5–10 per article). The latest addition to Mumbai's hectic roads is the **cool cab**, a blue taxi that boasts air conditioning and tinted windows, and charges around forty percent higher rates for the privilege (☎022/2824 6216).

Cars with drivers can be rented per eight-hour day (Rs1000–1300 for a non-a/c Ambassador, upwards of Rs1500 for more luxurious a/c cars), or per kilometre, from ITDC. They have an (occasionally) staffed counter at the Government of India tourist office and on the eleventh floor of the Nirmal Building at Nariman Point. Otherwise, go through any good travel agent (see p.151). Ramniranjan Kedia Tours and Travels (☎022/2437 1112, ⓦwww.rnk.com) are recommended if you want to book a vehicle on arrival at Chhatrapati Shivaji international airport.

Boats

Ferryboats regularly chug out of Mumbai harbour, connecting the city with the far shore and some of the larger islands in between. The most popular with visitors is the **Elephanta Island** launch (see p.136), which departs from the Gateway of India (see p.118), as do frequent boats to **Mandawa Jetty**, for Alibag, the transport hub for the rarely used **coastal route south** (see p.118).

Tours

MTDC's whistlestop "City" tour (daily except Mon 2–6pm; Rs100, not including admission charges) is an inexpensive way to cram south Mumbai's touristic highlights into half a day, with stops at the Museum, Marine Drive, Chowpatty Beach, the Hanging Gardens and Mani Bhavan. The trip starts at the company's booth in front of the Gateway of India, where you can purchase tickets in advance.

A more leisurely alternative, focusing mainly on period buildings and the city's colonial history, is to follow the excellent guided walks organized by architects Abha Bahl and Brinda Gaitonde of the **Mumbai Heritage Walks Society**. The tours are run every Sunday (except during the monsoons), cost Rs100 (or Rs50 for students on production of a student ID card) and last ninety minutes. Further details are available on ☎022/2281 0123 or 2834 4622, or at ⓦwww.bombayheritagewalks.com.

Finally, the outfit **Reality Tours and Travels** operate compelling trips out to the Dharavi shantytown in north Mumbai, classed as Asia's largest slum. For more details, see the box on p.135.

Accommodation

Finding **accommodation** at the right price when you arrive in Mumbai can be a real problem. Budget travellers, in particular, can expect a hard time: standards at the bottom of the range are grim and room rates exorbitant. The best of the relatively inexpensive places tend to fill up by noon, which can often mean a long trudge in the heat with only an overpriced fleapit at the end of it, so you should really phone ahead as soon as (or preferably well before) you arrive. Prices in upmarket places are further inflated by the state-imposed "**luxury tax**" (between four and thirty percent depending on how expensive the room is), and "**service charges**" levied by the hotel itself; both add-ons are included in the price symbols used in the following reviews.

Colaba, down in the far southern end of the city, is where the majority of foreign visitors head first. A short way across the city centre, **Marine Drive**'s accommodation is generally a little more expensive, but more salubrious, with Back Bay and the promenade right on the doorstep. If you're arriving by train and plan to make a quick getaway, a room closer to **CST** (VT) station is worth considering. Alternatively, **Juhu**, way to the north near the airports, hosts a string of flashy four- and five-stars, with a handful of less expensive places behind the beach. For those who just want to crawl off the plane and straight into bed, a handful of overpriced options are also available in the suburbs around the **airports**, a short taxi ride from the main terminal buildings.

Colaba and Kala Ghoda

A short ride from the city's main commercial districts, railway stations and tourist office, **Colaba** makes a handy base. It also offers more in the way of food and entertainment than neighbouring districts, especially along its busy main thoroughfare, "**Colaba Causeway**" (Shahid Bhagat Singh – SBS – Marg). The streets immediately south and west of the Gateway of India are chock-full of accommodation, ranging from grungy guesthouses to India's most famous five-star hotel, the *Taj Mahal Palace & Tower*. Avoid at all costs the nameless lodges lurking on the top storeys of wooden-fronted houses along **Arthur Bunder Road** – the haunts of touts who depend on commission to finance their heroin habits.

The hotels below are marked on the map of Colaba and Kala Ghoda on p.119, except for the *Taj President*, which is on the main Mumbai map (pp.110–111).

Budget

Aga Bheg's & Hotel Kishan Ground, 2nd & 3rd floor, Shirin Manzil, Walton Rd ☎022/2284 2227 or 022/2202 1534. Muslim-run pair of budget guesthouses on different floors of the same building. Both are a bit noisy and rough looking, but acceptably clean, and among the cheapest options in Colaba. ❹

Lawrence 3rd floor, 33 Sri Sai Baba Marg (Rope Walk Lane), off K Dubash Marg, behind *TGI's* ☎022/2284 3618 or 5633 6107. Strictly speaking in the arty Kala Ghoda district rather than Colaba proper, close to the Jehangir Art Gallery, this is arguably south Mumbai's best rock-bottom choice. Six well-scrubbed doubles (one single) with fans, and not-so-clean shared shower-toilet; breakfast included in the price. Advance booking is essential. ❹

Red Shield Red Shield House, 30 Boram Behram (Mereweather) Rd, near the *Taj* ☎022/2284 1824 or 2282 4613, ✉redshield@vsnl.net. Ultra-basic bunk beds (Rs150) in cramped, stuffy dorms (lockers available), or larger good-value doubles (Rs600 without a/c, Rs900), fully en suite. Rates include three meals, served in a sociable travellers' canteen. Priority is given to women, and your stay is limited to one week or less. ❶–❹

Sea Shore 4th floor, 1-49 Kamal Mansion, Arthur Bunder Rd ☎022/2287 4237. Among the best budget deals in Colaba. The sea-facing rooms with windows (Rs550) are much nicer than the airless cells on the other side. Friendly management and free, safe baggage store. Common baths only, though some rooms have a/c. If it's full try the wooden-partitioned rooms at the less salubrious *India* (☎022/2283 3769; ❹–❺) or the grubby but bearable *Sea Lord* (☎022/2284 5392; ❹–❺) in the same building. ❹–❺

Mid-range

Ascot 38 Garden Rd ☎022/6638 5566, ⓦwww.ascothotel.com. One of the oldest and most comfortable small hotels in Mumbai, dating from the 1930s but with state-of-the-art glass-and-marble designer interiors. The rooms are centrally air-conditioned and very spacious for the price, plus they're fitted with CD players. ❼

Bentley's 17 Oliver Rd ☎022/2284 1474, ⓦwww.bentleyshotel.com. Dependable old Parsi-owned favourite in four different colonial tenements, all on leafy backstreets. The rooms are quiet, secure and spacious, if – since they've scarcely been upgraded since the departure of the

British – a little worn. Some have a/c and small balconies overlooking rear gardens, but the overall shabbiness isn't compensated for by the rates, which are higher than you'd expect for the level of comfort. ⑥–⑦

Godwin Jasmine Building, 41 Garden Rd ☎022/2287 2050, ⓦwww.mumbainet.com/hotels /godwin. Top-class three-star with large, international-standard rooms and great views from upper floors (ask for 804, 805 or 806 when you book). The *Garden* (☎022/2283 1330, ⓦwww.fhrai.com) next door is similar but slightly inferior. Both ⑦

Moti International 10 Best Marg ☎022/2202 1654. British-era building with original painted stucco and woodwork. It's quiet and clean with friendly management, though frayed around the edges. The rooms range from non-attached doubles (Rs1200) to deluxe with a/c, fridges and TVs. ⑤–⑥

Regent 8 Best Marg ☎022/2287 1854, ⓔhotelregent@vsnl.com. Smart, international-standard hotel on a small scale, popular mainly with Gulf Arabs; the rooms aren't large, but good value in this bracket, with large cable TVs, fridges and Internet access. ⑧

Sea Palace Kerawalla Chambers, 26 PJ Ramchandani Marg ☎022/2284 1828, ⓦwww .seapalacehotel.com. Comfortable, well-maintained hotel at the quiet end of the harbour front. All rooms are a/c but sea views cost extra. Breakfast and light meals are served on a sunny terrace at the front. ⑧

🏊 **Strand** Apollo Bunder (PJ Ramachandani Marg) ☎022/2288 2222, ⓦwww .hotelstrand.com. Deservedly popular mid-scale option on the seafront that's nicely situated, respectable and efficiently run. The rooms are plain, but well aired, with higher ceilings than usual, and a few surviving Art-Deco features add character. Their "Super-Deluxe" frontside rooms have the best harbour views. ⑦–⑧

🏊 **YWCA** 18 Madam Cama Rd ☎022/2202 5053, ⓦwww.ywcaic.info. Relaxing, secure and quiet hostel with spotless attached rooms (recently renovated and with windows and TVs) from Rs1800 and same-day laundry service. Rates include membership, breakfast and generous buffet dinner – a bargain for south Mumbai. Advance booking (by money draft) obligatory. ⑥

Luxury

Fariyas 25 Arthur Rd ☎022/2204 2911, ⓦwww .fariyas.com. Compact luxury hotel, overlooking the Koli fishing *basti* on one side, with all the trimmings of a five-star but none of the grandeur. Doubles from $220. ⑨

Gorden House 5 Battery St ☎022/2287 1122, ⓦwww.ghhotel.com. Ultra-chic designer boutique place behind the Regal cinema. Each floor is differently themed: "Scandinavian" (the easiest to live with), "Mediterranean" and "American Country"; CD players in every room, but no pool. Doubles from $220. ⑨

🏊 **Taj Mahal Palace & Tower** PJ Ramchandani Marg ☎022/5665 3366, ⓦwww .tajhotels.com. The stately home among India's top hotels (see p.120), and the haunt of Mumbai's *beau monde*, with 546 luxury rooms, shopping arcades, a huge outdoor pool, nine bars and restaurants, plus one of the city's favourite nightclubs (*Insomnia*, see p.144). Prices vary according to view: if your budget can stretch to it, go for a sea-facing suite in the old wing, where rates range from $500 to $1000; in the *Tower*, count on half that. ⑨

Taj President 90 Cuffe Parade ☎022/5665 0808, ⓦwww.tajhotels.com. Modern, business-oriented five-star occupying an eighteen-floor skyscraper just south of Colaba. A much more competitively priced option than its sister concern, the *Taj Mahal Palace & Tower*, though lacking old-world style and atmosphere. The pool is outdoors and large, with a multi-gym and steam room adjacent. Rates start at around $250–300. ⑨

Marine Drive and Nariman Point

At the western edge of the downtown area, Netaji Subhash Chandra Marg, or **Marine Drive**, sweeps from the skyscrapers of Nariman Point in the south to Chowpatty Beach in the north. Along the way, four- and five-star hotels take advantage of the panoramic views over Back Bay and the easy access to the city's commercial heart, while a couple of inexpensive guesthouses are worth trying if Colaba's cheap lodges don't appeal.

The hotels below are marked on the Churchgate and Fort map on p.126, apart from the *Hilton Towers* and the *Oberoi*, which are marked on pp.110–111.

Ambassador VN Rd ☎022/2204 1131, ⓦwww .ambassadorindia.com. Ageing four-star whose scruffy concrete exterior and slightly worn furnishings are redeemed by its choice location, close to the sea and main shopping and café strip. Even if you're not staying, pop up to the revolving *Pearl of the Orient* restaurant (see p.141) for the matchless city views. ⑨

Astoria Jamshedji Tata ☎022/6654 1234, ✉astoria@hathway.com. Smart business hotel in refurbished 1930s Art-Deco building near the Eros cinema. The rooms are nowhere near as ritzy as the lobby but offer good value this close to the centre. ⑨

Bentley 3rd floor, Krishna Mahal, Marine Drive ☎022/2281 5244. Not to be confused with *Bentley's* in Colaba (see p.113), this small, friendly guesthouse is across town on the corner of D Rd/Marine Drive, near the cricket stadium. It had a major face-lift in 2004 and the marble-lined rooms are clean and comfortable for the price, though most share shower-toilets. Rates (from Rs780) include breakfast. ⑤

🏃 **Chateau Windsor** 5th floor, 86 VN Rd ☎022/2204 4455, ⓦwww.chateauwindsor .com. Impeccably neat and central, with unfailingly polite staff and a choice of differently priced, 1950s-style rooms, squeezed onto three floors and accessed via an old cage lift and narrow landings. Very popular, so reserve well in advance. ⑥–⑦

Hilton Towers Nariman Point ☎022/6632 4343, ⓦwww.hilton.com. This north wing of the former *Oberoi* was recently acquired by the Hilton Group and serves, along with its former sibling next door (see opposite), as the city's premier business hotel. It offers all the facilities and trimmings you'd expect of an international five-star, including a gigantic lobby and sea views from its pool. From around $300. ⑨

🏃 **Intercontinental** 135 Marine Drive ☎022/3987 9999, ⓦwww.mumbai .intercontinental.com. This ultra-chic boutique hotel is currently one of India's most stylishly modern addresses. The rooms have huge sea-facing windows and state-of-the-art gadgets (such as 42 inch plasma screens, DVD players, safes with laptop rechargers and broadband connections), while the rooftop pool, bars and restaurants (including the famous *Dome* – see p.144) rank among Mumbai's most fashionable. Doubles from $350. ⑨

Marine Plaza 29 Marine Drive ☎022/2285 1212, ⓦwww.hotelmarineplaza.com. Ritzy but small luxury hotel on the seafront, with (pseudo-) Art-Deco atrium lobby, glass-bottomed rooftop pool and the usual five-star facilities. Rooms $330–475. ⑨

Oberoi Towers Nariman Point ☎022/2232 5757, ⓦwww.oberoihotels.com. India's tallest hotel enjoys a prime spot overlooking Back Bay (the views from the 35th-floor conference room are stupendous). Glitteringly opulent throughout, and – together with its northern wing, now managed by the Hilton Group – the first choice of business travellers, though lacking the heritage character of the *Taj*. Rooms $350–2500 per night. ⑨

Sea Green/Sea Green South 145 Marine Drive ☎022/6633 6525, ⓦwww.seagreenhotel.com & 145A Marine Drive 022/2282 1613, ⓦwww .seagreensouth.com. Jointly owned and enduringly popular pair of green-and-white-painted hotels on the seafront. Rates are quite high for the rooms, which are fitted with threadbare coir carpets and thirty-year-old furniture, but on the plus side, they do both have great views of the bay and retain a period feel lacking in most mid-range places. ⑥–⑦

Around Chhatrapati Shivaji (Victoria) Terminus

Arriving in Mumbai at **CST** (VT) after a long train journey, you may not feel like embarking on a room hunt around Colaba. Unfortunately, the area around the station and the nearby GPO, though fairly central, has little to recommend it. The majority of places worth trying are mid-range hotels grouped around the crossroads of P. D'Mello (Frere) Road, St George's Road and Shahid Bhagat Singh (SBS) Marg, immediately southeast of the post office (5min on foot from the station). CST (VT) itself also has **retiring rooms** (Rs250), although these are always booked up by noon, or even days in advance. The following are all marked on the Churchgate and Fort map on p.126.

City Palace 121 City Terrace ☎022/2261 5515, ⓦwww.hotelcitypalace.net. Large and popular hotel bang opposite the station. "Ordinary" rooms are tiny and windowless, but have a/c and are perfectly clean. The pricier ones higher up the building have bird's-eye views over Nagar Chowk. And there's a reliable left-luggage facility for guests. ⑤–⑥

Grand 17 Shri SR Marg, Ballard Estate ☎022/5658 0500, ⓦwww.grandhotelbombay.com. British-era place out near the old docks and former financial district. It was closed for extensive renovation work at the time of our last visit in Feb 2007, but should be open by the winter 2007–08. ⑨

Oasis 276 SBS Marg ☎022/2269 7887, ⓦwww.hoteloasisindia.com. Very well placed for

CST station, this is the best-value budget option in this area: non-a/c attached doubles from under Rs780 with good beds, clean linen and TVs. It's worth splashing out on a top-floor "deluxe" room as they offer better views. ④—⑤

Prince 34 Walchand Hirachand Rd ☎022/2261 2809, ⓔ mumbaiprince@hotmail.com. The best fallback if *Oasis* is full: nothing special, but neat and respectable. Avoid the airless partition rooms upstairs. ④—⑤

Railway 249 P. D'Mello Rd ☎022/3022 2300 or 5602 2222, ⓦ www.hotelrailway.com. Popular mid-range place near CST (VT) with some a/c rooms,

though it's recently hiked its prices and is a touch claustrophobic for the money, with few windows on offer. ⑦

🏃 **Residency** 26 Rustom Sidhwa Marg DN Rd ☎022/6667 0555, ⓔ residencyhotel@vsnl .com.com. This is a great little mid-priced hotel, and one of the few commendable options in the bustling Fort district, close to the best shopping areas and only a short taxi ride from Colaba. Its variously priced rooms (all with safes and Internet points) offer unbeatable value, especially the no-frills "standard" options, though you'll have to book a couple of weeks ahead to get one. ⑥—⑦

Juhu and around the airports

Hotels in the congested area around the international and domestic **airports** cater predominantly for transit passengers, business executives and flight crews, at premium rates. If you can face the thirty-minute drive across town and afford the first-world room tariffs, head for **Juhu**, one of the city's swisher suburbs, which faces the sea and is a lot less hectic. Nearly all the hotels below have courtesy buses to and from the terminal building, or at worst can arrange for a car and driver to meet you.

Holiday Inn Balraj Sahani Marg, Juhu ☎022/2693 4444, ⓦ www.holidayinnbombay.com. Formulaic five-star – exactly what you'd expect from a *Holiday Inn* – and slap on the beach, with a decent-sized swimming pool. Rooms from around $200. ⑨

Hyatt Regency Airport Rd, Andheri (East) ☎022/6696 1234, ⓦ www.mumbai.regency.hyatt .com. Ancient Hindu precepts on architecture and design were incorporated into the plans for this ultra-luxurious five-star, right next to the airport. The results are impressive, and a notch more stylish than the competition, with extensive use of Malaysian teak, floor-to-ceiling windows, step-down rain showers and polished dark marble floors. From $300. ⑨

🏃 **ISKCON** Juhu Church Rd, Juhu ☎022/2620 6860, ⓦ www.iskconmumbai .com. Idiosyncratic hotel run by the International Society for Krishna Consiousness. The building itself is a hotch-potch of mock Mughal, Gujarati and Western styles, and the rooms are very large for the price, though certain restrictions apply (no alcohol, meat or caffeine may be consumed on the premises). Forty days advance booking recommended. ⑥—⑦

JW Marriott Juhu Tara Rd, Juhu ☎022/6693 3000, ⓦ www.marriott.com. Palatial five-star complex, hemmed in by high walls and a tighter-than-average security cordon. Inside lie five opulent restaurants, three pools (one of them filled with treated salt water) and blocks of luxury rooms looking through landscaped grounds and rustling palms to the beach. From around $400. ⑨

Lotus Suites Andheri Kurla Rd, International Airport Zone, Andheri (East) ☎022/2827 0707, ⓦ www.lotussuites.com. An "Eco-Four-Star at Three-Star prices" is how this environment-friendly hotel describes itself. Designed with energy-saving building materials, a/c and fittings, it features "green" trimmings such as pot plants instead of cut flowers, jute slippers and recycling bins in the rooms. A very comfortable option for under $200 if you book online. ⑨

Midland Jawaharlal Nehru Rd, Santa Cruz (East) ☎022/2611 0414, ⓦ www.hotelmidland.com. Dependable two-star with well-furnished twin-bedded rooms. Rates (from Rs3000) include courtesy bus and breakfast. ⑧

Orchid 70-C Nehru Rd, Vile Parle (East) ☎022/2616 4040, ⓦ www.orchidhotel.com. Award-winning "Eco-Five-Star", built with organic or recycled materials and using low-toxin paints. Every effort is made to minimize waste of natural resources, with a water-recycling plant and "zero garbage" policy. As with sister concern *Lotus Suites* (see above), even the coat hangers are "green" – they're made of compressed sawdust. Rooms from around $330. ⑨

Sea Princess Juhu Tara Rd, Juhu ☎022/2661 1111, ⓦ www.seaprincess.com. The homeliest of the five-stars overlooking Juhu beach. A couple of decades old now, but with cosy, recently refitted rooms (some boasting sweeping sea views) and a swish restaurant, in addition to a pool from which you can walk straight onto the sands. Doubles from $275. ⑨

The City

Nowhere reinforces your sense of having arrived in Mumbai quite as emphatically as the **Gateway of India**, which, alongside its grandly gabled and domed neighbour, the *Taj Mahal Palace & Tower*, stands as the city's defining landmark. Crowds of trippers congregate here on evenings and weekends, though you'll want to be here in the early morning if you're planning a trip from the adjacent boat jetty across the harbour to the ancient rock-cut Shiva temple on **Elephanta Island**. Only a five-minute walk north, the **Prince of Wales Museum** (or the Chhatrapati Shivaji Maharaj Vastu Sangrahalaya as it was recently renamed) should be next on your list of sightseeing priorities, as much for its flamboyantly eclectic architecture as for the art treasures inside. The museum provides a foretaste of what lies in store just up the road, where the cream of Bartle Frere's Bombay – the University and High Court – line up with the open *maidans* on one side, and the boulevards of **Fort** on the other. The commercial hub of the city, Fort is a great area for aimless wandering, with plenty of old-fashioned cafés, department stores and street stalls crammed between the pompous Victorian piles. The innumerable banks and other financial institutions at the east end of Fort around **Horniman Circle** – site of the British era's oldest buildings, **St Thomas' Cathedral** and the old **town hall** – stand as reminders of the cotton-boom prosperity of the late nineteenth century. But for the fullest sense of why the city's founding fathers declared it Urbs Prima in Indis, you should visit the **Chhatrapati Shivaji Terminus**, formerely the **Victoria Terminus**, the high watermark of India's Raj architecture.

Few visitors venture much further north from here than they have to, but teeming **central Mumbai** certainly has its appeal. Beginning at **Crawford Market**, a quirky British structure crammed with fresh produce, you can press north into the thick of the intense **bazaar** district to visit the Mumba Devi temple, from which the city takes its new name. Beyond lie the Muslim neighbourhoods, which encompass some of Mumbai's most interesting backstreet bazaars, as well as a serene little **Jain animal sanctuary**.

When the crush of city's central districts gets too much, an evening stroll along **Marine Drive**, bounding the western edge of the downtown area, is the ideal antidote. From there you can skirt Mumbai's most affluent enclave, Malabar Hill, to reach two important religious sites, the Hindu **Mahalakshmi temple** and Muslim **tomb of Haji Ali**.

Apart from **Elephanta**, a rock-cut cave on an island in Mumbai harbour containing a wealth of ancient art, the other incentive to break out of Mumbai altogether is the thousand-year-old **Kanheri Cave** complex, carved from a forested hillside, to which you can get within striking distance by train.

Colaba

At the end of the seventeenth century, **Colaba** was little more than the last in a straggling line of rocky islands extending to the lighthouse that stood on Mumbai's southernmost point. Today, the original outlines of the promontory (whose name derives from the Koli who first lived here) have been submerged under a mass of dilapidated colonial tenements, hotels, bars, restaurants and handicraft emporia. If you never venture beyond the district, you'll get a very

For a rundown of **guided tours** of Mumbai, see p.112.

distorted picture of Mumbai; even though it's the main tourist enclave and a trendy hangout for the city's rich young things, Colaba has retained the sleazy feel of the port it used to be, with touts, dealers and pimps hissing at passers-by from the kerbsides.

The Gateway of India

Commemorating the visit of King George V and Queen Mary in 1911, India's own honey-coloured Arc de Triomphe, the **Gateway of India**, was built in 1924 by George Wittet, the architect responsible for many of the city's grandest constructions. Blending indigenous Gujarati motifs with high Victorian pomp, it

△ The Gateway of India

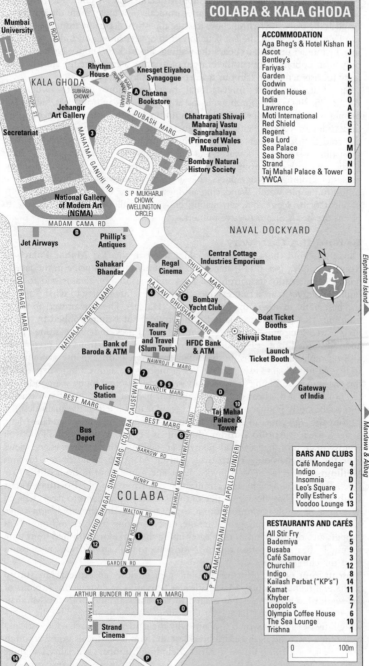

COLABA & KALA GHODA

ACCOMMODATION

Aga Bheg's & Hotel Kishan	H
Ascot	J
Bentley's	I
Fariyas	P
Garden	L
Godwin	K
Gorden House	C
India	O
Lawrence	A
Moti International	E
Red Shield	G
Regent	F
Sea Lord	O
Sea Palace	M
Sea Shore	O
Strand	N
Taj Mahal Palace & Tower	D
YWCA	B

Mumbai University

Rhythm House

Knesget Eliyahoo Synagogue

KALA GHODA

SUBHASH CHOWK

A Chetana Bookstore

Jehangir Art Gallery

Secretariat

Chhatrapati Shivaji Maharaj Vastu Sangrahalaya (Prince of Wales Museum)

Bombay Natural History Society

S P MUKHARJI CHOWK (WELLINGTON CIRCLE)

National Gallery of Modern Art (NGMA)

MADAM CAMA RD

B

Jet Airways

Phillip's Antiques

NAVAL DOCKYARD

Sahakari Bhandar

Regal Cinema

Central Cottage Industries Emporium

C Bombay Yacht Club

Boat Ticket Booths

Reality Tours and Travel (Slum Tours)

HFDC Bank & ATM

Shivaji Statue

Bank of Baroda & ATM

Launch Ticket Booth

NAWROJI F MARG

D

Police Station

MANDLIK MARG

Gateway of India

BEST MARG

Taj Mahal Palace & Tower

Bus Depot

BARROW RD

HENRY RD

COLABA

WALTON RD

H

OLIVER ROAD

GARDEN RD

J K L

ARTHUR BUNDER RD (H N A A MARG)

Strand Cinema

M G ROAD

HOPE ST

MAHATMA GANDHI RD

COOPERAGE MARG

NATHALAL PAREKH MARG

SHIVAJI MARG

RAJKAVI GHUSHAN MARG

TULLOCH RD

COLABA CAUSEWAY

SHAHID BHAGAT SINGH MARG

B BEHRAM MARG

MEREWEATHER ROAD

P J RAMCHANDANI MARG / APOLLO BUNDER

STRAND RD

N

Elephanta Island

Mandawa & Alibag

BARS AND CLUBS

Café Mondegar	4
Indigo	8
Insomnia	D
Leo's Square	7
Polly Esther's	C
Voodoo Lounge	13

RESTAURANTS AND CAFÉS

All Stir Fry	C
Bademiya	5
Busaba	9
Café Samovar	3
Churchill	12
Indigo	8
Kailash Parbat ("KP's")	14
Kamat	11
Khyber	2
Leopold's	7
Olympia Coffee House	6
The Sea Lounge	10
Trishna	1

0   100m

was originally envisaged as a ceremonial disembarkation point for passengers alighting from the P&O steamers, but – ironically – is today more often remembered as the place the British chose to stage their final departure from the country. On February 28, 1948, the last battalion of troops remaining on Indian soil slow-marched under the arch to board the waiting ship back to Tilbury. Nowadays, the only boats bobbing about at the bottom of its stone staircase are the launches that ferry tourists across the harbour to Elephanta Island (see p.136).

The Gateway made international headlines more recently when, on August 25, 2003, a car bomb exploded at the taxi rank in front of it, killing 107 people. As a consequence, armed guards routinely patrol the area, inspecting the undersides of parked vehicles. The increased security doesn't seem to have deterred the day-trippers who pour in year round for a glimpse of Mumbai's most filmed landmark, however, and on evenings and weekends crowds gather in the paved plaza in front of the arch to feed the pigeons, be snapped by the posses of strolling photographers, ride silver horse-drawn *gaddis* around the *Taj*, or just to people-watch. Wandering amongst them are another perennial feature of the Colaba scene: hawkers selling enormous balloons, which they use to bump the heads of prospective punters.

Behind the Gateway

Directly behind the Gateway, the older hotel in the **Taj Mahal Palace & Tower** complex (see p.114) stands as a monument to local pride in the face of colonial oppression. Its patron, the Parsi industrialist J.N. Tata, is said to have built the old *Taj* as an act of revenge after he was refused entry to what was then the best hotel in town, the "whites only" *Watson's*. The ban proved to be its undoing. *Watson's*, where Mark Twain wrote about being mobbed by crows, disappeared long ago, but the *Taj*, with its grand grey-and-white-stone facade and red-domed roof, still presides imperiously over the seafront, the preserve of visiting diplomats, sheikhs, businessmen and aircrew on expense accounts, as well as Mumbai's air-kissing jet set. Lesser mortals are allowed in to experience the tea lounge, shopping arcades and vast air-conditioned lobby – a good place to cool down if the heat of the harbourfront has got the better of you (there's also a fabulously luxurious loo off the corridor to the left of the main desk).

From the *Taj*, you can head down the promenade, PJ Ramchandani Marg, better known as **Apollo Bunder** (the name is a colonial corruption of the Koli words for a local fish, *palav*, and quay, *bunda*), taking in the sea breezes and views over the busy harbour. Alternatively, Shivaji Marg heads northwest towards **Wellington Circle** (SPM Chowk), the hectic roundabout in front of the Art-Deco Regal cinema. The latter route takes you past the old **Bombay Yacht Club**, another idiosyncratic vestige of the Raj. Very little seems to have changed here since its smoky common rooms were a bolt-hole for the city's *burra-sahibs*. Behind its half-timbered, gabled facade, dusty sporting trophies and models of clippers and dhows stand in glass cases lining the corridors, polished from time to time by bearers in cotton tunics. If you want to look around, seek permission from the club secretary.

Just in front of the *Taj*, a small public park encloses an **equestrian statue** of the eighteenth-century Maratha leader **Shivaji**. The courageous exploits of the warlord, whose dynasty managed to run rings around both the Mughals and the British in India, have led to his adoption as a figurehead by the right-wing Shiv Sena party, which explains why the garden is so uncharacteristically well tended. Come here before breakfast and you'll see locals going through bizarre early-morning fitness routines, including Mumbai's speciality, Laughter Yoga (see box, p.147).

Southwards along Colaba Causeway

Reclaimed in the late nineteenth century from the sea, the district's main thoroughfare, **Colaba Causeway** (this stretch of Shahid Bhagat Singh Marg), leads south towards the military cantonment. Few tourists stray much further down it than the claustrophobic hawker zone at the top of the street, but it's well worth doing so, if only to see the neighbourhood's earthy **fresh produce market**, a couple of blocks south of the Strand cinema, which provides an unexpected splash of rustic colour amid the urban surroundings. From here, return to the main road and turn left to reach the gates of Mumbai's wholesale seafood market, **Sassoon Docks**. Photographed to powerful effect by Sebastião Salgado in his book, *Work*, the docks are at their most vigorous in the hours immediately before and after sunrise, when coolies haul the night's catch in crates of crushed ice over gangplanks to the quayside, while Koli women, their saris hitched up *dhoti*-style, cluster around the auctioneers on the quaysides. The stench, as overpowering as the noise, comes mostly from bundles of one of the city's traditional exports, **Bombay duck** (see box, p.122), drying on the trawlers' rigging. Note that **photography** is strictly forbidden, as the docks are adjacent to a sensitive navy area.

Hop on any bus heading south down Colaba Causeway (#3, #11, #47, #103, #123 or #125) through the cantonment to reach the **Afghan Memorial Church of St John the Baptist**, built in 1847–54 as a memorial to the British victims of the First Afghan War. With its tall steeple and tower, the pale yellow church wouldn't look out of place in Worcester or Suffolk. If the door is unlocked, take a peep inside at the battle-scarred military colours on the wall

△ Sassoon Docks

Bombay duck

Its name suggests some kind of fowl curry, but **Bombay duck** is actually a fish – to be precise, the marine lizard fish (*Harpalon nehereus*), known in the local dialect of Marathi as *bummalo*. How this long, ribbon-like sea creature acquired its English name no one is exactly sure, but the most plausible theory holds that the Raj-era culinary term derives from the Hindustani for mail train, *dak*. The nasty odour of the dried fish is said to have reminded the British of the less salubrious carriages of the Calcutta–Bombay *dak* when it pulled into VT after three days and nights on the rails, its wooden carriages covered in the stinking mould that flourished in the monsoonal humidity.

and marble memorial plaques to officers who died in various campaigns on the Northwest Frontier.

Downtown Mumbai

The critic and travel writer Robert Byron (of *Road to Oxiana* fame), although a wholehearted fan of New Delhi, was unenthusiastic about the architecture of **downtown Mumbai**, which he described as "that architectural Sodom".Today, the massive monuments of Empire and Indian free enterprise appear not so much ugly as intriguing. Between them, you'll occasionally come across still more curious buildings, with facades flanked by what appear to be Mesopotamian griffins. These are old Zoroastrian (Parsi) **fire temples** – or *agiaries* – erected by wealthy worthies in the late nineteenth century. Few attract more than a trickle of ageing worshippers, and as a non-Parsi you won't be allowed inside, but they're a definitive Mumbai spectacle.

The area immediately north of Colaba, centred on the crescent of MG Road and Subhash Chowk, is known as **Kala Ghoda** ("Black Statue"), after the large equestrian statue of King Edward VII that formerly stood in its main square. Flanked by the city's principal museum and art galleries, the district has in recent years been re-launched as a "cultural enclave" – as much in an attempt to preserve its many historic buildings as to promote the contemporary visual arts that have thrived here since the 1950s. Fancy stainless-steel interpretative panels now punctuate the district's walkways, and on Sundays in December and January, the **Kala Ghoda Fair** sees portrait artists, potters and *mehendi* painters plying their trade in the car park fronting the Jehangir Art Gallery.

Chhatrapati Shivaji Museum (Prince of Wales Museum)

Set back from Mahatma Gandhi (MG) Road in its own grounds, the **Prince of Wales Museum of Western India** (daily except Tues 10.15am–6pm; Rs300 [Rs6 for students and Indian nationals], camera Rs30 – no tripods or flash), recently renamed as the tongue-twisting **Chhatrapati Shivaji Maharaj Vastu Sangrahalaya**, ranks among the city's most distinctive Raj-era constructions. Crowned by a massive white Mughal-style dome, it houses a superb collection of paintings and sculpture that you'll need several hours, or a couple of visits, to get the most out of. The building was designed by George Wittet, of Gateway of India fame, and is the epitome of the hybrid **Indo-Saracenic** style – regarded in its day as an "educated" interpretation of fifteenth- and sixteenth-century Gujarati architecture, mixing Islamic touches with typically English municipal brickwork.

To justify the hefty entrance fee demanded from foreigners, the museum's curators recently introduced an **audio tour** (included in the ticket price), which you collect at the admissions kiosk inside. Given the haphazard nature of the exhibitions and absence of contextual information, this would have been a welcome initiative if the commentary were up to scratch, but you'll probably find it does little to enhance your visit. The heat and humidity inside the building can also be a trial. For breaks, the institutional tea-coffee kiosk in the ground-floor garden is a much less congenial option than the *Café Samovar* outside (see p.140), but to exit the museum and re-enter (which you're entitled to do) you'll have to get your ticket stamped in the admissions lobby first.

The ground floor
The **Key Gallery** in the central hall of the **ground floor** provides a snapshot of the collection's treasures. Highlights here include the richly bejewelled Rewa dagger, a few choice Mughal paintings, an exquisitely enamelled Lucknowi hookah and – to the right of the entrance – stucco Buddhist figures dating from the fifth century AD. These were unearthed by the archeologist Henry Cousens in 1909 at Mirapur Khas, an early Gupta stupa that was bricked over soon after construction, which explains why the pieces remain so well preserved: traces of black and red paint are still visible on some of them. The standing figure, thought to represent a donor disciple, is the most recognizable of the group, his high rank denoted by non-matching earrings and a gracefully held lotus flower.

The main **sculpture room** on the **ground floor** displays some fine fourth- and fifth-century heads and figures from the Buddhist state of Gandhara, a former colony of Alexander the Great (hence the Greek-style features). Important Hindu sculptures include a seventh-century Chalukyan bas-relief from Aihole depicting Brahma seated on a lotus, and a sensuously carved torso of Mahisasuramardini, the goddess Durga, with tripod raised ready to skewer the demon buffalo.

The first and second floors
Once past a missable mezzanine gallery dominated by facsimiles of prehistoric artefacts and Assyrian bas-reliefs, the main attraction on the **first floor** has to be the famous collection of **Indian painting**. Most of it was amassed by the Peshwa diplomat, Nana Phadnis (1741–1800), from distress sales of aristocratic heirlooms during the breakup of the Mughal Empire. Featured here are pages of the Mughal emperor Akbar's own lavish edition of the *Panchatantra* – the Indian equivalent of Aesop's fables – and an equally well-known portrait of Shah Jahan in old age. More fine medieval miniatures are housed in the recently inaugurated **Karl & Meherbai Khandalavala Gallery**, on the renovated east wing of this floor. Around a contemporary mock-courtyard made of rubber and wood, objects collected by a wealthy Parsi lawyer and his wife, former curators of the museum, are displayed to great effect. They include priceless pieces of Ghandaram sculpture, a splendid devotional wall hanging from Nathdwara in Rajasthan, Chola bronzes and some of the country's finest surviving examples of medieval Gujarati woodcarving.

Indian **coins** are the subject of the spanking new **House of Laxmi gallery**, also in the east wing. Starting from punch-marked copper nuggets from the sixth century BC to the silver rupees of the Raj, the collection traces the evolution of metal money in the Subcontinent up until the end of the British era. Its curators claim it will be the most comprehensive numismatic exhibition in the country.

Himalayan *thangkas*, deities and ritual objects dating from the thirteenth century onwards form the backbone of the **Buddhist gallery**, also on the first floor. The **second floor** showcases a vast array of Oriental ceramics and glassware, and some European art gifted by wealthy Parsi benefactors, including a minor Titian and a Constable. Finally, among the grizzly **weapons** and pieces of armour stored in a small side gallery at the top of the building are a cuirass, helmet and jade dagger which the museum only recently discovered belonged to Akbar – the Persian inscription on the breast-plate hinted at its provenance, but wasn't translated until a few years ago.

Kala Ghoda Art Galleries

Technically in the same compound as the Prince of Wales Museum, though approached from further up MG Road, the **Jehangir Art Gallery** (daily 11am–7pm; free) is Mumbai's longest-established venue for contemporary art, with five small halls specializing in twentieth-century arts and crafts from around the world. You never know what you're going to find – most exhibitions last only a week and exhibits are often for sale.

On the opposite side of MG Road, facing the museum and Mukharji Chowk, stands the larger **National Gallery of Modern Art** (NGMA; daily except Mon 11am–5pm; Rs150 [Rs20]), housed in a converted concert hall. It holds a mix of permanent and temporary exhibitions on three storeys, charting the development of modern Indian art from its beginnings in the 1950s to the present day. The installations, in particular, tend to be a lot more adventurous than those you'll find in the Jehangir across the road.

Around Oval Maidan

Some of Mumbai's most important Victorian buildings flank the eastern side of the vast green **Oval Maidan**, where impromptu cricket matches are held almost every day (foreign enthusiasts are welcome to take part, but should beware the *maidan*'s demon bowlers and less-than-even pitches). The dull yellow old **Secretariat** now serves as the City Civil and Sessions Court. Indian civil servant G.W. Forrest described it in 1903 as "a massive pile whose main features have been brought from Venice, but all the beauty has vanished in transhipment". Inside, you can only imagine the originally highly polished interior, which no longer shines. The court buzzes with activity: lawyers in black gowns, striped trousers and white tabs bustle up and down the staircases, whose corners are emblazoned with expectorated paan juice, and offices with perforated swing-doors give glimpses of textbook images of Indian bureaucracy – peons at desks piled high with dusty, beribboned document bundles.

Across AS D'Mello Road from the Old Secretariat are two major buildings belonging to **Mumbai University** (established 1857), which were designed in England by Sir Gilbert Scott, architect of the Gothic extravaganza that is London's St Pancras railway station. Access through the main gates is monitored by caretakers who only allow you in if you say you're visiting the library. Funded by the Parsi philanthropist Cowasjee "Readymoney" Jehangir, the **Convocation Hall** greatly resembles a church. The **library** (daily 10am–10pm) is beneath the 79.2-metre-high **Rajabhai Clock Tower**, which is said to have been modelled on Giotto's campanile in Florence. Until 1931, it chimed tunes such as *Rule Britannia* and *Home Sweet Home*. You can scale the grand staircase from the lobby to enter the magnificent vaulted reading room, whose high Gothic windows and stained glass still evoke a reverential approach to learning.

Dabawallahs

Mumbai's size and inconvenient shape create all kind of hassles for its working population – not least having to stew for over four hours each day in slow municipal transport. One thing the daily tidal wave of commuters does not have to worry about, however, is where to find an inexpensive and wholesome home-cooked lunch. In a city with a wallah for everything, it will find them. The members of the **Nutan Mumbai Tiffin Box Suppliers Charity Trust**, known colloquially, and with no little affection, as "**dabawallahs**", see to that. Every day, around a thousand *dabawallahs* deliver freshly cooked food from 160,000 suburban kitchens to offices in the downtown area. Each lunch is prepared early in the morning by a devoted wife or mother while her husband or son is enduring the crush on the train. She arranges the rice, dhal, *subzi*, curd and *parathas* into cylindrical aluminium trays, stacks them on top of one another and clips them together with a neat little handle. This **tiffin box**, not unlike a slim paint tin, is the lynchpin of the whole operation. When the runner calls to collect it in the morning, he uses a special colour code on the lid to tell him where the lunch has to go. At the end of his round, he carries all the boxes to the nearest railway station and hands them over to other *dabawallahs* for the trip into town. Between leaving the wife and reaching its final destination, the tiffin box will pass through at least half a dozen different pairs of hands, carried on heads, shoulder-poles, bicycle handlebars and in the brightly decorated handcarts that plough with such insouciance through the midday traffic. Tins are rarely, if ever, lost – a fact recently reinforced by the American business magazine, *Forbes*, which awarded Mumbai's *dabawallahs* a 6-Sigma performance rating, the score reserved for companies who attain a 99.9 percentage of correctness. This means that only one tiffin box in 6 million goes astray, in efficiency terms putting the illiterate *dabawallahs* on a par with bluechip firms such as Motorola.

To catch them in action, head for **CST (VT)** or **Churchgate** stations around late morning, when the tiffin boxes arrive in the city centre. The event is accompanied by a chorus of "*lafka! lafka!*" – "hurry! hurry!" – as the *dabawallahs*, recognizable in their white Nehru caps and baggy pyjama trousers, rush to make their lunch-hour deadlines. Nearly all come from the same small village near Pune and are related to one another. They collect Rs150–200 from each customer, or around Rs5000–6000 per month in total – not a bad income by Indian standards. One of the reasons the system survives in the face of competition from trendy fast-food outlets is that *daba* lunches still work out a good deal cheaper, saving precious paise for the middle-income workers who use the system.

Hutatma Chowk (Flora Fountain)

A busy five-point intersection in the heart of the Fort area, the roundabout formerly known as **Flora Fountain** has been renamed **Hutatma Chowk** ("Martyr's Square") to commemorate the freedom fighters who died to establish the state of Maharashtra in the Indian Union. The chowk centres on a statue of the Roman goddess **Flora**, erected in 1869 to commemorate Sir Bartle Frere. It's hard to see quite why they bothered – the Raj architecture expert, Philip Davies, was not being unkind when he said, "The fountain was designed by a committee, and it shows."

Horniman Circle and the Town Hall

Horniman Circle, formerly Elphinstone Circle, is named after a pro-Independence newspaper editor. It was conceived in 1860 as a centrepiece of a newly planned Bombay by the then Municipal Commissioner, Charles Forjett, on the site of Bombay "Green". Forjett, a Eurasian, had something of a peculiar reputation; he was fond of disguising himself in "native" dress and

CHURCHGATE AND FORT

ACCOMMODATION

Ambassador	I
Astoria	L
Bentley	D
Chateau Windsor	J
City Palace	C
Grand	F
Intercontinental	H
Marine Plaza	M
Oasis	E
Prince	B
Residency	A
Railway	G
Sea Green/	
Sea Green South	K

RESTAURANTS, CAFÉS AND BARS

Apoorva	7
Britannia & Co	4
Cha Bar	11
Czar Bar	H
The Dome	9
Gaylord's	3
Ideal Corner	10
Jimmy Boy	
Kyani's "House of Cakes" Bakery	5
Mocha Bar	I
The Pearl of the Orient	8
The Pizzeria	6
The Tea Centre	2
Vithal Bhelwala	

0   200m

prowling about certain districts of the city to listen out for seditious talk. In 1857, at the time of the Uprising (known to the British as the Indian Mutiny), Forjett fired on two suspected revolutionaries from a cannon on the Esplanade (roughly the site of the modern *maidans*). Later, the space served as a cotton market and parade ground.

Flanking the east side of the circle, the impressive **Town Hall** on SBS Marg was among the few buildings in Mumbai that pleased Aldous Huxley; "(Among) so many architectural cads and pretentious bounders," he wrote in 1948, "it is almost the only gentleman." The Doric edifice, dating from 1833, was originally built to house the vast collection of the **Asiatic Society Library**, still open to the general public (Mon–Sat 10am–7pm). Save for the addition of electricity, little has changed here since the institution was founded. Inside the reading rooms, lined with wrought-iron loggias and teak bookcases, scholars pour over mouldering tomes dating from the Raj. Among the ten thousand rare and valuable manuscripts stored here is a fourteenth-century first edition of Dante's *Divine Comedy*, said to be worth around US$3 million, which the Society famously refused to sell to Mussolini. Visitors are welcome but should sign in at the Head Librarian's desk on the ground floor.

St Thomas' Cathedral

The small, simple **St Thomas' Cathedral** (daily 6.30am–6pm) on Tamarind Street is reckoned to be the oldest British building in Mumbai, blending classical and Gothic styles. After the death of its founding father, Governor Aungier, the project was abandoned; the walls stood 5m high for forty-odd years until enthusiasm was rekindled by a chaplain to the East India Company in the second decade of the eighteenth century. It was finally opened on Christmas Day, 1718, complete with the essential "cannon-ball-proof roof". In those days, the seating was divided into useful sections for those who should know their place, including one for "Inferior Women".

St Thomas' whitewashed and polished brass-and-wood interior looks much the same as when the staff of the East India Company worshipped here in the eighteenth century. Lining the walls are memorial tablets to British parishioners, many of whom died young, either from disease or in battle.

The General Post Office

Widely acclaimed as one of the more successful British attempts to fuse Victorian-Municipal and Indian sacred architecture, the stately **General Post Office** on Walchand Hirachand Marg (Fort Street), just east of VT, took its cue from the Golgumbaz mausoleum in Bijapur. A huge dome forms its centrepiece and defining feature, and is most dramatic when viewed from inside the building. Scale the stairs to the right of the entrance to reach a whispering gallery on the first floor – the perfect vantage point from which to survey the comings and goings around the grand circular postal counter at ground level. Above you, pigeons fly terrifying trajectories through the wonky paddle fans, and corridors lead to offices full of undelivered parcels and sleepy clerks – a scene little changed in sixty or more years.

Chhatrapati Shivaji Terminus (Victoria Terminus)

Inspired by St Pancras station in London, F.W. Stevens designed **Victoria Terminus**, the most barmy of Mumbai's buildings, as a paean to "progress". Built in 1887 as the largest British edifice in India, it's an extraordinary amalgam of domes, spires, Corinthian columns and minarets that was succinctly defined by the journalist James Cameron as "Victorian-Gothic-Saracenic-Italianate-Oriental-St Pancras-Baroque". In keeping with the current re-Indianization of the city's roads and buildings, this icon of British imperial architecture has been renamed **Chhatrapati Shivaji Terminus**, in honour of a Maratha warlord. However, the new name is a bit of a mouthful and the locals mostly still use **VT** (pronounced "vitee" or "wee-tee") when referring to it.

Few of the two million or so passengers who fill almost a thousand trains every day notice the mass of decorative detail. A "British" lion and Indian tiger stand guard at the entrance, and the exterior is festooned with sculptures executed at the Bombay Art School by the Indian students of John Lockwood Kipling, Rudyard's father. Among them are grotesque mythical beasts, monkeys and plants and medallions of important personages. To minimize the sun's impact, stained glass was employed, decorated with locomotives and elephant images. Above it all, "Progress" stands atop the massive central dome.

An endless frenzy of activity goes on inside: hundreds of porters in red with impossibly oversize headloads; TTEs (Travelling Ticket Examiners) in black jackets and white trousers clasping clipboards detailing reservations; spitting checkers busy handing out fines to those caught in the act; chai-wallahs with trays of tea; trundling magazine stands; crowds of bored soldiers smoking *beedis*; and the inexorable progress across the station of sweepers bent double. Amid it all, whole families spread out on the floor, eating, sleeping or just waiting and waiting.

The central bazaars

A kilometre or so north of CST (VT) station, lining the anarchic jumble of streets beyond Lokmanya Tilak Road, Mumbai's teeming **central bazaars** are India at its most intense. You could wander around here for days without seeing the same shop front twice. In practice, most visitors find a couple of hours mingling with the crowds in the heat and din quite enough. Nevertheless, the market districts form a fascinating counterpoint to the wide and Westernized streets of downtown, even if you're not buying.

In keeping with traditional divisions of guild, caste and religion, most streets specialize in one or two types of merchandise. If you lose your bearings, the best way out is to ask someone to wave you in the direction of **Mohammed Ali Road**, the busy road through the heart of the district (now surmounted by a gigantic flyover), from where you can hail a cab.

Crawford Market

Crawford (aka Mahatma Phule) **Market**, ten minutes' walk north of CST, is an old British-style covered market dealing in just about every kind of fresh food and domestic animal imaginable. Thanks to its pompous Norman-Gothic tower and prominent position at the corner of Lokmanya Tilak Road and Dr DN Marg, the Crawford Market is also a useful landmark and a good place to begin a foray into the bazaars.

Before venturing inside, stop to admire the **friezes** wrapped around its exterior – a Victorian vision of sturdy-limbed peasants toiling in the fields designed by Rudyard Kipling's father, Lockwood, as principal of the Bombay School of Art in 1865. The **main hall** is still divided into different sections: pyramids of polished fruit and vegetables down one aisle, sacks of nuts or oil-tins full of herbs and spices down another. Around the back of the market, in the atmospheric wholesale wing, the pace of life is more hectic. Here, noisy crowds of coolies mill about with large reed-baskets held high in the air (if they are looking for work) or on their heads (if they've found some).

One place animal-lovers should definitely steer clear of is Crawford Market's **pet and poultry** section, on the east side of the building. You never quite know what creatures will turn up here, cringing in rank-smelling, undersized cages.

North of Crawford Market

The streets immediately **north of Crawford Market** and west of **Mohammed Ali Road** form one vast bazaar area. Ranged along both sides of narrow **Mangaldas Lane**, the cloth bazaar, are small shops draped with lengths of bright silk and cotton. Low doorways on the left open onto a colourful **covered market** area, packed with tiny stalls.

Eastwards along Mangaldas Lane from Lokmanya Tilak, the pale green-washed domes, arches and minarets of the **Jami Masjid**, or "Friday Mosque" (c.1800), mark the start of the Muslim neighbourhoods. **Memon Street**, cutting north from the mosque, is the site of the **Zaveri Bazaar**, the jewellery market where Mumbaikars come to shop for dowries and wedding attire.

By the time the gleaming golden spire that crowns the **Mumba Devi temple**'s cream-and-turquoise tower appears at the end of the street, you're deep in a maze of twisting lanes hemmed in by tall, wooden-balconied buildings. One of the most important centres of Devi worship in India, the temple was built early in the nineteenth century, when the deity was relocated from her former home to make way for CST (VT) station. Mumba Devi's other claim to fame is that her name is the original root of the city's modern name.

Bear left at the temple and keep heading along the main bazaar for ten or fifteen minutes and you'll arrive at another important Hindu enclave, **Bhuleshwar**. The district is famous throughout the city for its colourful **phool galli** (flower lane), where temple-goers buy luxurious garlands, lotus bundles and marigolds heaped in huge baskets. Of the 85 shrines said to be crammed into its lanes the most important is the **Bhola Ishtwar Mandir**, the ancient Shiva temple around which this district is believed to have first grown up in the eighteenth century. Its odd mix of Gujarati, Rajasthani and Konkan architectural styles reflects the origins of the neighbourhood's first immigrants. Jain merchants also settled here from the northwest, erecting a pair of finely carved white marble temples – **Shantinath** and **Parshavanath** – tucked away down a narrow lane just off the next crossroads, Jayamber Chowk. Animal lovers should ask the way here to the nearby **Panjarapool animal sanctuary**, where around four hundred beautiful brown *gir* cows are cared for, along with a menagerie of pigeons, rabbits, chickens and ducks. You can purchase donatory bowls of grain and *ladoo* balls to feed them at reception, where stern-faced Jain attendants enforce the strict no-photography rule.

Chor Bazaar, Mutton Road and the red-light district

Jump in a taxi at the junction just down the lane from the Mumba Devi temple for the two-kilometre trip north to the other concentration of markets around **Johar Chowk**, just north of SP Patel Road. The most famous of these, **Chor Bazaar** (literally "thieves' bazaar", though vendors peevishly insist the name is a corruption of the Urdu *shor*, meaning "noisy"), is the city's largest **antiques**-cum-flea market. Friday, the Muslim holy day, is the best day to be here: from 9am onwards, the neighbourhood is cluttered with hawkers and hand-carts piled high with bric-a-brac and assorted junk. At other times, the antique shops down on **Mutton Road** are the main attraction. Once, you could hope to unearth real gems in these dark, fusty stores, but your chances of finding a genuine bargain nowadays are minimal. Most of the stuff is pricey Victoriana – old gramophones, chamber pots, chipped china – salvaged from the homes of Parsi families on the decline. The place is also awash with **fakes**, mainly small bronze votive statues, which make good souvenirs if you can knock the price down.

Press on north through Chor Bazaar and you'll eventually come out onto **Grant Road** (Maulana Shaukatali Road). Further north and west, in the warren of lanes below JB Behram Marg, lies the city's infamous **red-light district**. **Kamathipura**'s rows of luridly lit, barred shop fronts, from where an estimated 25,000 prostitutes ply their trade, are one of Mumbai's more degrading and unpleasant spectacles. Many of these so-called "**cage girls**" are young teenagers from poor tribal areas, and from across the border in Nepal, who have been sold by desperate parents into **bonded slavery** until they can earn the money to pay off family debts.

Marine Drive and Chowpatty Beach

Netaji Subhash Chandra Marg, better known as **Marine Drive**, is Mumbai's seaside prom, an eight-lane highway with a wide pavement built in the 1920s on reclaimed land. Sweeping in an arc from the skyscrapers at Nariman Point

△ Marine Drive

in the south, the route ends at the foot of Malabar Hill and Chowpatty Beach. The whole three-kilometre stretch – still often referred to by Mumbaikars as the "Queen's Necklace", after the row of lights which illuminate its spectacular curve at night – is a favourite place for a stroll; the promenade next to the sea has uninterrupted views virtually the whole way along, while the peeling, mildew-streaked Art-Deco apartment blocks on the land side remain some of the most desirable addresses in the city.

Just beyond the huge flyover at its northern end are a series of cricket pitches known as **gymkhanas**, where there's a good chance of catching a match any day of the week. A number are exclusive to particular religious communities. The first pitch doubles as a swanky outdoor wedding venue for Parsi marriages; others include the Catholic, Islamic and Hindu pitches, the last of which has a classic colonial-style pavilion.

Chowpatty Beach

Chowpatty Beach is a Mumbai institution, which really comes to life at night and on Saturday. People do not come here to swim (the sea is foul) but to wander, sit on the beach, let the kids ride a pony or a rusty Ferris wheel, have a massage, get ears cleaned or picnic on *bhel puri* (see box, p.139) and cups of kulfi. For the last century or so, Gupta Bhelwallas's *bhel puri* stall has satisfied the discerning Mumbai palate with a secret concoction of the sunset snack; you'll find it amid the newly constructed "shacks" to which the *bhel*-wallahs were recently moved as part of the Municipality's bid to clean up the beach.

Once a year in September the **Ganesh Chathurthi** festival (see box, p.108) draws gigantic crowds to participate in the immersion of idols, both huge and small, of the elephant-headed god Ganesh.

Mani Bhavan (Mahatma Gandhi Museum)

A ten-minute walk north from the middle of Chowpatty Beach (along P Ramabai Marg), **Mani Bhavan**, at 19 Laburnum Rd (daily 9.30am–6pm), was Gandhi's Bombay base between 1917 and 1934. Throughout the campaign for Independence, the Mahatma spent long spells here, organizing strikes among the city's textile workers, addressing mass rallies and negotiating with British officials. This was where he issued his famous call for a boycott of the Prince of Wales' state visit in 1921 – a protest which, much to Gandhi's dismay, resulted in the death of 58 (mainly Parsi) dissenters who chose to attend the festivities. The Congress Party's triumphant "Quit India" movement was also launched from the house in 1942.

Set in a leafy upper-middle-class road, Mani Bhavan has now been converted into a permanent memorial to the Mahatma with an extensive research library. Within the lovingly maintained polished-wood interior, the walls are covered with photos of historic events and artefacts from the man's extraordinary life – the most disarming of which is a friendly letter to Hitler suggesting world peace. Gandhi's predictably simple sitting room-cum-bedroom is preserved behind glass. Laburnum Road is a few streets along from the Bharatiya Vidya Bhavan music venue on KM Munshi Marg – if coming by taxi ask for the nearby Gamdevi Police Station.

Malabar Hill

Its shirt-tails swathed in greenery and brow bristling with gigantic skyscrapers, the long promontory enfolding Chowpatty Beach at the north end of Back Bay

The Towers of Silence

High on Malabar Hill, screened from prying eyes by a high wall and dense curtain of vegetation, stand the seven **Towers of Silence**, where the city's dwindling Zoroastrian community (better known as Parsis) dispose of their dead. Pollution of the four sacred elements (air, water, earth and, holiest of all, fire) contradicts the most fundamental precepts of the 2500-year-old Parsi faith, first imported to India when Zoroastrians fled from Sassanid Persia to escape Arab persecution in the seventh century. So instead of being buried or cremated, the bodies are laid out on top of open-topped, cylindrical towers, called *dokhmas*, for their bones to be cleaned by **vultures** and the weather. The remains are then placed in an ossuary at the centre of the tower.

Recent decades have seen a sharp decline in the number Parsis choosing this traditional funerary rite, one reason for which is the disappearance of India's vultures – a result of their exposure to the anti-inflammatory drug, Diclofenac, which is fed to cattle and therefore found in the carcasses on which the birds more commonly feed. Solar panels have instead been installed in the towers, to use the sun's rays to dispose of the corpses; captive vultures are being considered as another solution. The Towers of Silence are strictly closed to visitors.

has been south Mumbai's most desirable neighbourhood almost since the city was founded. The British were quick to see the potential of its salubrious breezes and sweeping sea views, constructing bungalows at the tip of what was then a separate island – the grandest of them the Government House, originally erected by Mountstuart Elphinstone in the 1820s and now the seat of the serving Governor of Maharashtra, **Raj Bhavan**. In early colonial times, Malabar pirates plagued the Konkan coast, and a lookout tower was erected on the hilltop here to act as an early warning system – whence the promontory's name. It now holds some of the most expensive real estate in Asia, with prices approaching US$1500 per square metre.

City tours invariably take in Malabar Hill's principal landmarks. Although none might be classed as unmissable, the temples and surviving colonial-era residences, many of them overgrown and covered in mildew, form an interesting counterpoint to the modernity towering on all sides. From the **Balbunath temple**, one of the Mumbai's most popular Hindu shrines, located off the busy roundabout at the far north end of Chowpatty, you can follow a tangle of paths through the woods above, crossing the **Hanging Gardens**, a public park much appreciated by generations of courting couples, and **Kamala Nehru Children's Park**, with its popular "Old Woman's Shoe". The parks are edged by Malabar Hill's main artery, BG Kher Marg (formerly Ridge Road), which leads after a kilometre to a **Jain Temple**. Inside, mirrors and colourful paintings line halls that lead to marble image of Adinath, the first of the twenty-four Jain *tirthankaras*.

The hill tapers off beyond here to a narrow spit, shelving steeply down to Back Bay on one side and the rocky seashore on the other. The famous **Walukeshwar temple**, the oldest Hindu shrine surviving *in situ* in Mumbai, can be reached via a lane turning right off the main road. According to the Ramayana, Rama paused here during his journey south to rescue Sita from the clutches of the evil Ravana, and fashioned a *lingam* out of sand to worship Shiva. Over time, the Walukeshwar, or "Sand Lord" shrine, became one of the Konkan's most important relgious centres, venerated even by the Malabari pirates who menaced the islands.

Today's temple, erected in 1715 after the original had been destroyed by the Portuguese, is of less note than the **Banganga tank** below it. The spring that feeds the greenish body of water, encircled by a wall of multistorey apartment blocks, is believed to have been created by an arrow fired from Rama's own bow. Today, it's a minor pilgrimage site, busiest on "white" (full-) and "black" (no-) moon days of the month. At other times, Banganga's stone *ghats*, numerous crumbling shrines and murky waters see little more than a trickle of bathers, drawn mostly from the slums encrusting the broken land along the nearby shore. A path picks its way past the shacks, and the washing lines of the *dhobis* who live in them, to a small cremation *ghat*.

Central Mumbai: Mahalakshmi to Byculla

The centre of Mumbai, beyond Malabar Hill, is mostly made up of working-class neighbourhoods: a huge mosaic of dilapidated tenements, markets and industrial eyesores left over from the Victorian cotton boom. For relief from the urban cauldron, residents travel west to the seashore to worship at the **Mahalakshmi Temple** (if they're Hindus) or the island **tomb of Haji Ali** (if they're Muslims). Both make great excursions from south Mumbai, and can be combined with a foray across town to the recently revamped **Dr Bhau Dadji Lad Museum** in Byculla, calling en route at the **Mahalakshmi dhobi ghats** – one of the city's more offbeat sights.

Buses #83, #132 or #133 will take you from Colaba to Haji Ali's, within a stone's throw of the Mahalakshmi Temple. To continue east from here to Byculla, your best option would be to catch a cab, though bus #124 will take you as far as the *dhobi ghats*. These are also easily accessible from south Mumbai by train or bus (see p.134).

Mahalakshmi Temple

Mahalakshmi Temple is joined to the nearest main artery, Bhulabhai Desai Road, by an alley lined with stalls selling spectacular floral offerings and devotional pictures. Mumbai's favourite *devi*, **Lakshmi**, goddess of beauty and prosperity – the city's most sought-after attributes – is here propitiated with coconuts, sweets, lengths of shimmering silk and giant lotus blooms. Gifts pile so high that the temple *pujaris* run a money-spinning sideline reselling them. Their little shop, to the left of the entrance, is a good place to buy cut-price saris and brocades infused with lucky Lakshmi energy. While you're here, find out what your future holds by joining the huddle of devotees pressing rupees onto the rear wall of the shrine room. If your coin sticks, you'll be rich.

Haji Ali's Tomb

Occupying a small islet in the bay just north of the Mahalakshmi is the mausoleum of the Muslim saint, Afghan mystic **Haji Ali Bukhari**. The tomb is connected to the mainland by a narrow concrete **causeway**, only passable at low tide. When not immersed in water, its entire length is lined with beggars; the prime sites – closer to the snack bars that flank the main entrance, near the small mosque, and the gateway to the **tomb** itself – are allocated in a strict pecking order. If you want to make a donation, spare a thought for the unfortunates in the middle. The white Mughal domes and minarets of the tomb itself look a lot less exotic close up than when viewed from the shore, silhouetted against the sun as it drops into the Arabian Sea. But the site is a great place to head for on Thursday and Friday evenings, when large crowds gather around the headland to watch the sunset and listen to live **qawwali** music. Non-Muslims are welcome, but you'll need to keep well covered up (a headscarf should be worn by women).

The traditional way to round off a trip to the mausoleum is a glass or two of fresh fruit juice at the legendary **Haji Ali Juice Centre**, just to the right of the entrance to the causeway. Customers either cram into the tiny dining hall or else order from their cars.

Mahalakshmi dhobi ghats

On the face of it, the idea of going out of your way to ogle Mumbai's dirty washing sounds like a very perverse pastime. If you're passing, however, the **municipal dhobi ghats**, near Mahalakshmi suburban railway station, are a sufficiently impressive spectacle to break a trip across town to see. The huge open-air laundry is the centre of one of those miraculous Indian institutions which, like the *dabawallahs'* operation (see p.125), is usually regarded by Westerners with disbelief. Each morning, washing from all over Mumbai is brought here to be thrown into soapy piles, soaked in concrete vats of caustic soda and thumped by the resident *dhobis* at the countless flogging stones, barrels and shanty shacks inside the compound. The next day, after being hung out to dry in colourful rows, pressed with charcoal irons, folded in newspaper and bound with cotton thread, the bundles are returned whence they came. One of Mumbai's more curious photo opportunities, the bird's-eye view over the V-shaped rows of *dhobi ghats* from Mahalakshmi road bridge attracts a trickle of curious foreign tourists throughout the day (Bill Clinton even found time to slot in a visit in 2005), though the earlier in the day you get here, the more *dhobi* action you'll see.

Much the easiest way to get to Mahalakshmi is to jump on a suburban train from Churchgate. Emerging from the station, turn left and follow the road over the rail tracks – the *ghats* will be below you on your left (the hawkers from the nearby slums who work the spot will show you the way). Bus #124 from Colaba and Haji Ali will also drop you there.

Byculla and the Dr Bhau Dadji Lad Museum

During the cotton boom of the late nineteenth century, Bombay expanded rapidly on to newly reclaimed land further north, engulfing the city in a swathe of brick mills and chimney stacks. These were left to moulder when the bottom later fell out of the textile business and today, despite the revitalization schemes periodically dreamed up by the Municipality, form one India's most spectral post-industrial wastelands.

The only reason you might wish to venture into it would be to visit the **Dr Bhau Dadji Lad Museum** (daily except Wed 10.30am–4.30pm; admission Rs20) in Byculla-East. When it opened in 1872, the **Victoria and Albert Museum**, as it was then, was hailed as "one of the greatest boons the British have conferred on India". Set in a classically planned botanical garden (which these days accommodates a rather depressing zoo), the splendid Palladian-style edifice was in its day the most stylish building in the city – elegant, fashionable and daintily decorated. A century or more of neglect took its toll, but the building was recently restored it to its former glory and definitely warrants a detour. Its collection of lithographs, prints, documents, uniforms and models relating to the development of Bombay don't perhaps quite live up to the promise of their sumptuous Victorian surroundings, but will interest aficionados of colonial history. In the adjacent garden, the carved stone pachyderm after which the Portuguese are said to have named Elephanta Island presides over a collection of forlorn British statues, moved here during Independence beyond the reach of angry mobs.

North Mumbai

A jarring mix of modern high-rise apartment blocks and vast shantytowns, the urban sprawl of north Mumbai epitomizes the contrasting facets of the Maharashtrian capital. On the northern shore of Mahim Creek, **Bandra** and, to a lesser extent, **Juhu**, near the airports, are where the upwardly mobile classes aspire to work and live. Cleaner and greener, they're less crowded than downtown and offer twenty-first-century shopping and dining – convenient if you're only passing through Mumbai between flights and don't want to engage in the mayhem further south.

Bandra

If south Mumbai is synonymous with old money and conservative attitudes, **Bandra** – the "Queen of Suburbs" – typifies the fast bucks and liberal mores of yuppy north Mumbai. Some of the city's most desirable real estate encrusts the low, sea-facing ridge of Bandra's **Pali Hill**, the first enclave in the area to be colonized by the rich and famous after a causeway was built to it in the mid-nineteenth century. The district is now home to a glittering mix of

Dharavi: the £700 million slum

Flying into Mumbai airport, your plane's undercarriage will almost skim the corrugated-iron rooftops of the vast shantytown spread across the middle of Mumbai known to be officially **Asia's largest slum**. Sprawling over 175 hectares, **Dharavi's** maze of dilapidated shacks and narrow, stinking alleyways is home to more than a million people. An average of 15,000 of them share a single toilet. Infectious diseases such as dysentery, malaria and hepatitis are rife; and there aren't any hospitals. Yet Dharavi was recently described by the UK's *Observer* newspaper as "one of the most inspiring economic models in Asia": hidden amid the warren of ramshackle huts and squalid open sewers are an estimated 15,000 single-room factories, employing around a quarter of a million people and turning over a staggering £700 million (US1.4 billion) annually.

The majority of small businesses in Dharavi are based on **waste recycling** of one kind or another. Slum residents young and old scavenge materials from across the city and haul them back in huge bundles to be re-processed. Aluminium cans are smelted down, soap scraps salvaged from schools and hotels and reduced in huge vats, leather reworked, disused oil drums restored and discarded plastic reshaped and re-moulded. An estimated 10,000 workers are employed in the plastics sector alone. Ranging from Rs3000–15,000 per month, wages are well above the national average, and though Dharavi may not have any health centres, it does hold a couple of banks, and even ATMs.

You can see the economic miracle for yourself by joining one of the **"Slum Tours"** run by Reality Tours and Travels out of Colaba. Tickets for these engaging guided trips cost Rs300 (which includes transport), or you can also opt for a longer and more comfortable version with an a/c car. For more details, contact Krishna Pujari on ☎022/2283 3872, or ☎m98208 22253, check out ⓦwww.realitytoursandtravel .com, or just drop in to their booking office (Mon–Fri 10.15am–8.35pm, Sat 10.15am–3.45pm) off Colaba Causeway (SBS Marg), on the first floor of Akbar Hose Nawroji Fardonji Marg, opposite the *Laxmi Vilas Hotel* (see map, p.119 – but note that to find the place you'll need further directions by phone or their website as it's hidden behind a shop).

Bollywood stars, millionaire industrialists, sports celebs and media moguls, whose favourite pastime seems to be swooshing in imported luxury cars along Bandra's seafront, **Carter Road**. Hip young things descend here en masse from across the city on weekends to spend their call-centre bonuses in the thoroughfare's numerous designer clothes boutiques, air-conditioned malls and trendy cafés. If you've had your fill of workaday India for a while, this is where to come to escape.

Droves of Roman Catholic pilgrims, meanwhile, press on south to the famous **Basilica of Mount Mary**, on the spit at the southern end of Bandra called Land's End. Erected in the twentieth century after a fire destroyed the original Portuguese-era chapel sited here, the modern church houses a revered miracle-working Madonna, at whose feet petitioners leave wax effigies of body parts, babies and other symbols of either affliction or wishes to be fulfilled.

Juhu

Chances are, if a Bollywood flick from the 1980s featured a song-and-dance sequence filmed against a backdrop of glamorous beachside hotels and palm-fringed swimming pools, it will have been shot in **Juhu**. In the northwest of the city near the airports, this smart suburb used to be where the city's jet set lived, shopped and threw wild parties. When model and feminist icon Protima Bedi decided to streak as a protest to "male chauvinist attitudes to the female body" in 1974, it was along Juhu's golden sands that she sprinted for the cameras.

The area's rise as a playground for the wealthy began in the 1930s, after the playboy Parsi industrialist, Jamshetji Tata, built a bungalow overlooking the beach. Later, he landed here at low tide in his Gypsy Moth after flying all the way from Karachi – the historic flight that would eventually kick-start the construction of Bombay airport. A rash of five-stars and luxury apartment blocks soon followed in his wake.

Subsumed by the sprawl of Greater Mumbai, Juhu is these days far from the relaxing, exclusive neighbourhood it used to be in Tata's day, but still holds great fascination for ordinary Mumbaikars, who flock here in their thousands on weekends for a sunset stroll and a paddle, to play beach cricket, ride camels, watch the dancing *hijras* (eunuchs) and chomp through paper wraps of *bhel puri*. For a few weeks in the monsoon of 2005, their ranks were swelled by tens of thousands of gem prospectors after rumours circulated that diamonds had been washed up on the beach. No pukka diamonds, however, were found – the original stones that sparked the great "**Gem Rush**" turned out to be the glass eyes of Ganpati idols dunked in the sea here during the Ganesh Chathurthi festival.

Elephanta

An hour's boat ride northeast across Mumbai Harbour from Colaba, the island of **Elephanta** offers the best escape from the seething claustrophobia of the city – as long as you time your visit to avoid the weekend deluge of noisy day-trippers. Populated only by a small fishing community, it was originally known as **Gherapura**, the "city of Ghara priests", until the island was renamed in the sixteenth century by the Portuguese in honour of the carved elephant they found at the port (now on display outside the Dr Bhau Dadji Lad – formerly Victoria and Albert – Museum in Byculla). Its chief attraction is its unique **cave temple**, whose massive **Trimurti** (three-faced)

Shiva sculpture is as fine an example of Hindu architecture as you'll find anywhere.

"**Deluxe**" **boats** set off from the Gateway of India (daily except Mon: Oct–May hourly 9am–2.30pm; Rs120 return including government guide; book through the kiosks near the Gateway of India). Ask for your guide at the cave's ticket office on arrival – tours last thirty minutes. **Ordinary ferries** (daily except Mon: Oct–May hourly 9am–3pm; Rs100 return), also from the Gateway of India, don't include guides and are usually more packed. Cool drinks and souvenir stalls line the way up the hill, and, at the top, the MTDC *Chalukya* restaurant offers substandard food and warm beer, served on a terrace with good views out to sea, Note that you cannot stay overnight on the island and that the caves are closed on Mondays.

The Cave

Elephanta's impressive excavated eighth-century **cave** (daily except Mon 9.30am–5pm; $5 [Rs10]), covering an area of approximately 5000 square metres, is reached by climbing more than one hundred steps to the top of the hill, lined by souvenir and knick-knack stalls. Inside, the massive columns, carved from solid rock, give the deceptive impression of being structural. To the right as you enter, note the panel of **Nataraj**, Shiva as the cosmic dancer. Though spoiled by the Portuguese who, it is said, used it for target practice, the panel remains magnificent: Shiva's face is rapt, and in one of his left hands he removes the veil of ignorance. Opposite is a badly damaged panel of Lakulisha, Shiva with a club (*lakula*).

Each of the four entrances to the simple square main **shrine** – unusually, it has one on each side – is flanked by a pair of huge fanged *dvarpala* guardians (only those to the back have survived undamaged), while inside a large *lingam* is surrounded by coins and smouldering joss left by devotees. Facing the northern wall of the shrine, another panel shows Shiva impaling the demon

△ Cave 1, Elephanta

Andhaka, who wandered around as though blind, symbolizing his spiritual blindness.

The panel behind the shrine on the back wall portrays the marriage of Shiva and Parvati, but the cave's outstanding centrepiece is its powerful six-metre bust of **Trimurti**, the three-faced Shiva, whose profile has become almost as familiar to Indians as that of the Taj Mahal. To the left as you face it, the god is shown in his angry form (Bhairava), with a hooked nose, thick moustache and headdress writhing with cobras. To the right, Vamadeva – Shiva as the Creator – has a gentle, more feminine appearance, wearing flowers in his hair. The central figure shows Shiva as the Supreme Preserver, Mahadeva: note the splendid headdress, coiled dreadlocks and calm expression, intended to convey the stillness of eternity.

Other noteworthy sculptures in Cave 1 include one presenting Shiva as **Ardhanarishvara**, half-male and half-female. Near the second entrance on the east, Shiva and Parvati are depicted on **Mount Kailasha** with Ravana about to lift the mountain. His curved spine shows the strain.

From Cave 1 you can follow a paved path around the north flank of the hillside past a string of other, unfinished excavations, which exemplify how the caves were originally dug out and carved. If you've the stamina, follow the dirt path that leads from the end of the paved trail beyond these to the summit of Elephanta Hill, a stiff hike of fifteen minutes. At the top you'll be rewarded with an encounter with a couple of rusting Portuguese cannons and a magnificent view back over Mumbai harbour to the distant city beyond.

The outskirts: Kanheri Caves

Overlooking the suburb of Borivli, 42km out at the northern limits of Mumbai's sprawl, are the Buddhist **Kanheri Caves** (daily 9am–5.30pm; $2 [Rs10]), ranged over the hills in virtually unspoilt forest. It's an interminable journey by road, so catch one of the many **trains** (50min) on the suburban line from Churchgate (marked "BO" on the departure boards; "limited stop" trains are 15min faster) to Borivli East. When you arrive, take the Borivli East exit, where a **bus** (for Kanheri Caves via SG Parles; Rs17), **auto-rickshaw** (about Rs100) or **taxi** (about Rs130) will take you the last 15km. Bring water and food as the stalls here only sell warm soft drinks.

Kanheri may not be as spectacular as other cave sites, but some of its sculpture is superb – though to enjoy the blissful peace and quiet that attracted its original occupants you should **avoid the weekends**. Most of the caves, which date from the second to the ninth century AD, were used simply by monks for accommodation and meditation during the four months of the monsoon, when an itinerant life was impractical. They are connected by steep winding paths and steps; engage one of the friendly local guides at the entrance to find your way about, but don't expect any sort of lecture as their English is limited. The risk of muggings in some of the remoter caves means it is not advisable to venture off the beaten track alone.

In **Cave 1**, an incomplete *chaitya* hall (a hall with a stupa at one end, an aisle and row of columns at either side), you can see where the rock was left cut, but unfinished. Two stupas stand in **Cave 2**; one was vandalized by a certain N. Christian, whose carefully incised Times Roman graffiti bear the date 1810. A panel shows seated Buddhas, portrayed as teachers. Behind, and to the side, is the *bodhisattva* of compassion, Padmapani, while to the right the *viharas* feature rock-cut beds.

Huge Buddhas, with serenely joyful expressions and unfeasibly large shoulders, stand on either side of the porch to the spectacular **Cave 3**. Between them, you'll see the panels of "donor couples", thought to have been foreigners that patronized the community.

The sixth-century **Cave 11** is a large assembly hall, where two long "tables" of rock were used for the study of manuscripts. Seated at the back, in the centre, is a figure of the Buddha as teacher, an image repeated in the entrance, to the left, with a wonderful flight of accompanying celestials. Just before the entrance to a small cell in **Cave 34**, flanked by two standing Buddhas, an unfinished ceiling painting shows the Buddha touching the earth. There must be at least a hundred more Buddha images on panels in **Cave 67**, a large hall. On the left side, and outside in the entrance, these figures are supported by *nagas* (snakes representing *kundalini*, yogic power).

Eating

Mirroring its cosmopolitan makeup, Mumbai is crammed with interesting **eating places**, whether you fancy splashing out on a buffet lunch-with-a-view from a starred hotel restaurant, or simply tucking into piping-hot *roti* kebab by gaslight in the street. In south Mumbai, Colaba's cafés, bars and restaurants encompass just about the full gamut of the city's gastronomic possibilities. The majority – among them the popular travellers' haunts, *Leopold's* and the *Café Mondegar* (see p.140 & p.144) – are up at the north end of the Causeway. However, don't be discouraged by the heat and traffic from venturing outside Colaba for a meal. A short walk or taxi ride north to **Kala Ghoda** and into **Fort** are some of the best cafés and restaurants in the city, among them Mumbai's last surviving traditional Parsi diners, whose menus and decor have changed little over three or four generations.

Restaurants and cafés are listed by district. Phone numbers have been given where we recommend you reserve a table for dinner. Beware of service charges levied on your bill by some of the more expensive places. Except where noted, places listed under Colaba and Kala Ghoda can be found on the map on p.119, and those under Churchgate and Fort on p.126; the rest are found on the map on pp.110–111.

Colaba and Kala Ghoda

All Stir Fry *Gorden House Hotel.* Build-your-own wok meal from a selection of fresh veg, meat, fish, noodles and sauces, flash-cooked in front of you (Rs250–350 per bowl). The satay and dim sum are particularly good. Trendy minimalist decor, glacial a/c and snappy service.

Bademiya Behind the *Taj* on Tulloch Rd. Legendary Colaba kebab-wallah serving delicious flame-grilled chicken, mutton and fish

---

Street food

Mumbai is renowned for distinctive street foods – and especially **bhel puri**, a quintessentially Mumbai masala mixture of puffed rice, deep-fried vermicelli, potato, crunchy puri pieces, chilli paste, tamarind water, chopped onions and coriander. More hygienic, but no less ubiquitous, is **pao bhaji**, a round Portuguese-style bread roll served on a tin plate with griddle-fried, spicy lentil stew, and **kanji vada**, savoury doughnuts soaked in fermented mustard and chilli sauce. And if all that doesn't appeal, a pit-stop at one of the city's hundreds of **juice bars** probably will. There's no better way to beat the sticky heat than with a glass of cool milk shaken with fresh pineapple, mango, banana, *chikoo* (small brown fruit that tastes like a sweet pear) or custard apple. Just make sure they hold on the ice – made, of course, with untreated water.

steaks, as well as veg alternatives, wrapped in paper-thin, piping hot *rotis*, from benches on the sidewalk. Rich families from uptown drive here on weekends, eating on their car bonnets, but there are also little tables and chairs if you don't fancy a takeaway.

Busaba 4 Mandlik Marg ☎022/2204 3779. Sophisticated bar-restaurant specializing in Far-Eastern cuisine – Thai, Korean, Burmese, Vietnamese and Tibetan staples, with exotic salads (green mango and glass noodle). One of *the* places to be seen (if you can't quite afford to eat at *Indigo* next door). Count on Rs750–1000 per head for the works.

Café Samovar Jehangir Art Gallery, MG Rd ☎022/2284 8000. Very pleasant, peaceful semi-alfresco café opening onto the museum gardens, with a good-value lunch menu (Rs65) featuring pilau, stuffed *parathas* and biriyanis, as well as plenty of à la carte choices (prawn curry, *roti* kebabs and fresh salads and dhansak. They also served delicious chilled guava juice and beer (Rs100), but note no drinks served 1–3pm.

Churchill 103 Colaba Causeway. Tiny 26-seater Parsi diner, with a bewildering choice of dishes, including salads, pastas and burgers, mostly meat-based and served in mild sauces alongside a blob of mash and boiled veg – ideal if you've had your fill of spicy food. No alcohol. Main courses around Rs150–200.

Indigo 4 Mandlik Marg ☎022/2236 8999. One of the city's most fashionable restaurants, and for once deserving of the hype. The Italian-based cooking has a Konkan-Keralan twist (Kochi oysters with saffron ravioli, for example). House flambée is extremely popular, as much for its head-turning potential as anything else. Count on Rs1000-plus for three courses. Reservations essential.

Kailash Parbat ("KP's") 1 Pasta Lane, near the Strand cinema. Uninspiring on the outside, but the breakfast *aloo parathas*, and pure veg nibbles, hot snacks and sweets (across the road) are worth the walk. A Colaba institution – try their famous *makai-ka* (corn) *rotis*.

Kamat Colaba Causeway. Friendly little eatery serving unquestionably the best South Indian breakfasts in the area, as well as the usual range of southern snacks (*iddli*, *vada*, *sambar*), delicious spring *dosas* and (limited) thalis for Rs40–100. The best option in the area for budget travellers with big appetites.

Khyber opposite Jehangir Art Gallery ☎022/2267 3227. Opulent Arabian Nights interior and uncompromisingly rich "Northwest Frontier" cuisine, served by black-tie waiters. The chicken tikka is legendary, but their tandoori dishes and kebab platter are superb too. Count on Rs850–1000.

Konkan Café *Taj President Hotel*, Cuffe Parade (see map, p.110–111) ☎022/5665 0808. This is *the* place to push the boat out: a sophisticated five-star hotel restaurant serving fine regional cuisine from coastal Maharashtra, Goa, Karnataka and Kerala – all at reasonable prices. You can choose from their thali platters (Rs400–500) or go à la carte: the crab in butter pepper garlic is to die for, as is the tiger prawn in *kokum* garlic and *meen pollichattu* (red snappers steamed Keralan-style in banana leaves). Quite simply some of the most mouthwatering South Indian food you'll ever eat.

Leopold's Colaba Causeway. A Mumbai institution for decades, Leopold's is the number-one hangout for India-weary Western travellers, who cram onto its small tables for overpriced, largely uninteresting food. Among the white faces you might spot are Gregory David "Shantaram" Roberts, who immortalized the place in his best-selling biog-novel and still drops in from time to time. Three hundred items feature on the menu from scrambled eggs to "chilly chicken"; cold beers cost Rs150. There's also a gloomy a/c bar upstairs (not recommended for women).

Olympia Coffee House Colaba Causeway. *Fin-de-siècle* Irani café with marble tabletops, wooden wall panels, fancy mirrors and a mezzanine floor for women. Waiters in Peshwari caps and *salwar kamises* serve melt-in-the-mouth kebabs, flavoured with subtle spices and delicious curd-based dips. It gets packed out at breakfast time for cholesterol-packed "mutton mince and fried eggs", which regulars wash down with bright orange chai. For dessert, go for their trademark "custard". A quintessential (and inexpensive) Bombay experience.

The Sea Lounge *Taj Mahal Hotel*. Spacious 1930s-style lounge café on the first floor of the *Taj* with a backdrop of the Gateway and harbour. Come for afternoon tea or a late breakfast – it's worth splashing out on for the atmosphere. Opens at 7am for breakfast; closes at midnight. Pastries Rs300–350; coffees and teas Rs150–225; breakfast Rs710.

Trishna 7 Sai Baba Marg (Ropewalk Lane), Kala Ghoda ☎022/2261 4991 or 2270 3213. Visiting dignitaries and local celebs, from the President of Greece and Imran Khan to Bollywood stars, have eaten in this dimly lit Mangalorean, tucked away down a narrow sidestreet on the south edge of Fort. It serves wonderful fish dishes in every sauce going, with prices to match the clientele (main courses from Rs450). Butter pepper garlic crab (sold by weight, average cost around Rs550) is their signature dish, but the pomfret stuffed with green masala is great too. Very small, so book in advance.

Churchgate and Fort

Apoorva Vasta House (Noble Chambers), SA Brelvi Rd ☎022/2287 0335. Currently the city's busiest Mangalorean, hidden up a side street off Horniman Circle (look for the tree trunk wrapped with fairy lights). The cooking's completely authentic and the seafood – simmered in spicy coconut-based gravies – fresh off the boats each day. Try their definitive Bombay duck, *surmai* (kingfish) in coconut gravy or sublime prawn *gassi*, served with perfect *sanna* and *appams*. Beers and spirits served on the ground floor.

Britannia & Co Opposite the GPO, Sprott Rd, Ballard Estate. Quirky little Parsi restaurant, famous as much for its quaint period atmosphere as its wholesome Irani food. Most people come for the sublime "berry pulao" (chicken, mutton or vegetable), made with deliciously tart dried berries imported from Tehran (Rs165, but portions are gigantic). For afters, there's the house "caramel custard". One of the city's unmissable eating experiences. Open 11.30am–3.30pm.

Cha Bar Oxford Bookstore, 3 Dinsha Wacha Rd, Churchgate. Chic a/c café accessed via the downtown's top bookshop, popular mainly with well-heeled students. They serve an exhaustive range of single-estate regional teas and coffees, from high-fired Darjeeling to Kashmiri *kawa* and Ladhaki butter tea, as well as trendy Ayurvedic brews and house "tea cocktails"; and there's a tempting menu of (pricey) light snacks and toasties.

Gaylord's VN Rd. The covered terrace at *Gaylord's* makes a great place to break for a drink, snack or light meal, with a tempting array of freshly baked savouries and cakes sold through the adjacent pastry shop (you elbow your way in, order and pay for what you want at the counter and then take it to your table yourself, while the uniformed waiters look blankly on). Good, strong *kona* coffee is served from bubbling glass pots. It's all a bit chaotic but fun and a prime spot for crowd-watching.

Ideal Corner 12 F/G Hornby View, Gunbow St ☎022/2262 1930. Another Parsi café with a cult following, but more in the thick of things than *Britannia* and less old world since its recent facelift. Go for one of their delicious homemade Parsi specialities: *kchchidi* prawn, lamb dhansak or chicken *farcha*, rounded off with the legendary *lagan* custard (a nutty crème caramel served chilled in little foil tubs). Most mains Rs50–75. Closed eves and Sun.

Jimmy Boy 11 Bank St, Vikas Bldg, off Horniman Circle ☎022/2270 0880. Among the few places left in Mumbai where you can sample pukka Parsi wedding food (albeit in rather inauthentic a/c surroundings, to a Shania Twain soundtrack). Go for the Rs265 fixed menu (pomfret and green chilli sauce steamed in a banana leaf, mutton pilau with dhansak dhal and dessert).

Joshi Club 31-A Narottamwadi, Kalbadevi Rd (see map, p.110–111) ☎022/2205 8089. Also known as *The Friends Union Joshi Club*, this eccentric thali canteen serves what many aficionados regard as the most genuine and tasty Gujarati-Marwari meals in the city, dished up on unpromising Formica tables against a backdrop of grubby walls. Rs85 buys you unlimited portions of four vegetable dishes, dhals and up to four different kinds of bread, with all the trimmings (and banana custard). Extra *farsan* (similar to Bombay mix) and sweets cost Rs25. Finding it requires some effort: walk or catch a cab to the bottom of Kalbadevi Rd (opposite the Metro cinema, see map, p.126); head north across Vardhaman Chowk, and continue up Kalbadevi Rd for 5min until you see a signboard on your right for "Bhojanalaya", below a first-floor window. The locals will know where it is.

Kyani's "House of Cakes" Bakery opposite Metro cinema. The most old-fashioned and authentic Parsi joint in the city, worth a visit more for the atmosphere than for the food – neither of which has altered in over ninety years since the café first opened. They serve freshly baked biscuits and cakes, "bun-maska" (basically warm buttered rolls) and good strong chai in china cups.

Mocha Bar VN Rd. Chilled terrace café where swarms of north Mumbai bratpackers order American-style coffees, Mediterranean mezes and outrageously expensive New World wines, crashed out on bolster cushions and smoking fruit-flavoured tobacco on hookah pipes: very much the zeitgeist.

The Pearl of the Orient *Ambassador Hotel*, VN Rd ☎022/229 1131. Revolving Oriental restaurant in this faded four-star hotel. The cooking's nothing special (and expensive at around Rs750–1000 for three courses), but the views over the city are extraordinary.

The Pizzeria corner of VN Rd and Marine Drive. Delicious, freshly baked pizzas served on newly renovated terrace overlooking Back Bay (or to take away). Plenty of choice, and moderate prices (Rs200–325 per pizza).

The Tea Centre Resham Bhavan, 78 VN Rd. Another vestige of colonial days which, despite a lavish refit, has retained its Raj-era charm, with paddle fans, comfy furniture and waiters wearing old-style "ice-cream-wafer" *pugris*. Fine tea is its *raison d'être* (see p.145), but they also serve delicious Continental snacks (try the fluffy cheese omlettes) and cakes, as well as a good-value "Executive Lunch" (Rs225).

Vithal Bhelwala 5 AK Naik Marg (Baston Rd), close to CST (VT). Mumbai's favourite *bhel puri* outlet, open since 1875 and still doing a roaring trade. No fewer than 25 kinds of *bhel* are on offer, including one pitched at British palates, with "boiled veg and cornflakes". They also do delicious potato cutlets, served with crunchy puri and yoghurt. Handy for the movie houses and the station.

Crawford Market and the central bazaars

Badshah Juice and Snack Bar Opposite Crawford Market, Lokmanya Tilak Rd. Mumbai's most acclaimed *falooda* joint also serves delicious kulfi, ice creams and dozens of freshly squeezed fruit juices. The ideal place to round off a trip to the market, though expect to have to queue for a table.

Delhi Darbar Corner of Maulana Shaukatali Rd (Grant Rd) and PB Marg (Falkland Rd), opposite Alfred Talkies. On the fringes of the red-light district, but a must for lovers of authentic Mughlai cuisine: waiters in Peshawari caps serve up superb flame-grilled chicken and mutton *sheekh* kebabs, biriyanis, pilaus and the house speciality, chicken tikka, rounded off with the creamiest lassis in Mumbai. Most dishes only cost Rs50–150.

Rajdhani Mangaldas Rd (in the silk bazaar opposite Crawford Market). Outstanding, eat-till-you-burst Gujarati thalis. Very cramped and more expensive than usual (Rs175 on weekdays, or Rs225 for the "Special" Sunday lunch), but they don't stint on quality. Closed Sun eves.

Chowpatty Beach

Crystal 19 Chowpatty Seaface, near Wilson College. Chowpatty is crammed with snack joints and cheap restaurants, but this one stands out – not that you'd ever know it from the grimy decor. Homesick Punjabis and lovers of authentic North Indian home cooking travel here from across the city to eat the wholesome dhal *makhini, alu jeera* and other spicy vegetarian dishes, served from a soot-blackened kitchen. Most mains under Rs50. And don't miss the lightly chilled *kir* (rice pudding with nuts, flavoured with cardamom) for dessert.

Bars and nightlife

Mumbaikars have an unusually easy-going attitude to alcohol; popping into a **bar** for a beer is very much accepted (for men at least), even at lunchtime. Colaba Causeway, where you'll find *Leopold's* (see p.140) and *Café Mondegar*, forms the focus of the travellers' social scene but if you want to sample the pulse of the city's nightlife, venture up to Bandra and Juhu.

In 2005, the killjoy Mumbai Municipality, in a bid to crack down on what its Shiv Sena mandarins perceived as out-of-control Western decadence, slapped a 1.30am **curfew** on the city's nightlife. The local cops were warned that if they accepted bribes to circumvent the shutdown they'd face dismissal. The effect was instant and a catastrophe for smaller, niche venues playing more experimental music, few of which could make ends meet with such limited opening hours. The law, however, proved a boon for the bigger clubs hosted by Mumbai's five-star hotels, which are allowed to stay open until 3am.

Performing arts in Mumbai

Mumbai is a major centre for traditional performing arts, attracting the finest **Indian classical musicians** and **dancers** from all over the country. Frequent concerts and recitals are staged at venues such as: Bharatiya Vidya Bhavan, KM Munshi Marg (☎022/2363 0224), the headquarters of the international cultural (Hindu) organization; and the National Centre for the Performing Arts, Nariman Point (NCPA; ⓦwww .ncpamumbai.com).

Despite the 2005 curfew, Mumbai's **nightclub** scene remains the most full-on in India. Tiny, skin-tight outfits that show off razor-sharp abs and pumped-up pecs are very much the order of the day, especially in venues

Bollywood

For anyone brought up on TV, it's hard to imagine the power that **movies** continue to wield in India. Every village has a cinema within walking distance and, with a potential audience in the hundreds of millions, the Indian film industry is the largest in the world, producing around 1000 full-length features each year. Regional cinema, catering for different language groups (in particular the Tamil cinema of Chennai), though popular locally, has little national impact. Only Hindi film – which accounts for a half of all the films made in India – has crossed regional boundaries to great effect, most particularly in the north. The home of the Hindi blockbuster, the "all-India film", is Mumbai, famously known as **Bollywood**.

To overcome differences of language and religion, the Bollywood movie follows rigid conventions and genres; as in myth, its characters have predetermined actions and destinies. Knowing a plot need not detract from the drama, and indeed it is not uncommon for Indian audiences to watch films numerous times. Unlike the Hollywood formula, which tends to classify each film under one genre, the Hindi film follows what is known as a "**masala format**", and includes during its luxurious three hours a little bit of everything, especially romance, violence and comedy. Frequently the stories feature dispossessed male heroes fighting evil against all odds, with a love interest thrown in. The sexual element has tended to be repressed, with numerous wet sari scenes and dance routines featuring the tensest pelvic thrusts, but strictly no kissing, though this is beginning to change. Other typical **themes** include male bonding and betrayal, family melodrama, separation and reunion, and religious piety. Dream sequences are almost obligatory, too, along with a festival or celebration scene – typically Holi, when people shower each other with paint – a comic character passing through, and a depraved, alcoholic and mostly Western-style nightclub scene, filled with strutting villains and lewd dancing.

Recent blockbusters have also seen the introduction of a new stock character, the returning emigrant, or "NRI" (Non-Resident Indian). This is one element in a more general trend sweeping Bollywood at the moment, as the big studios seek to pull in Hindi-speaking audiences in the UK, US and Canada. Overseas tickets typically cost ten times the admission to even the flashiest of Mumbai's cinemas, and together with videos and DVD sales now account for forty percent of the industry's revenues. Budgets, production standards and on-screen sauciness have all been on the rise as a result, with more and more films using foreign locations, smaller spangly miniskirts and MTV-style choreography.

Visitors to the city should have ample opportunity to sample the delights of a Hindi movie, traditional or otherwise. To make an educated choice, buy *Time Out Mumbai* magazine, which contains extensive **listings** and reviews. Alternatively, look for the biggest, brightest hoarding, and join the queue. Seats in a comfortable air-conditioned cinema cost Rs75–150, or less if you sit in the stalls (not advisable for women).

Of the two hundred or so **cinemas**, only a dozen or so regularly screen **English-language** films. The most central and convenient are the gloriously Art-Deco halls dating from the twilight of the Raj: the Regal in Colaba; the Eros opposite Churchgate station, and the Metro (@ www.adlabscinemas.com), at Dhobi Talao junction – the latter was recently converted into a state-of-the-art multiplex. Down on Nariman Point, near Express Towers, the Inox (@ www.inoxmovies.com) is another big multi-screen venue, built only a few years ago in retro Mumbai-Art-Deco style.

frequented by Bollywood's movers and shakers – and the pretty young things desperate to break into the industry. Dominated by *filmi* pop mixes, the music is far from cutting edge by the standards of London or New York, but no one seems to mind. The dance floors get as rammed as a suburban commuter train and the cover charges are astronomical. Door policies and dress codes tend to be strict ("no ballcaps, no shorts, no sandals"), and, in theory, most clubs have a "couples-only" policy – they charge per couple on the door (with a portion of the entrance cost redeemable at the bar). In practice, if you're in a mixed group or don't appear sleazy you shouldn't have any problems. At the five-star hotels, entry can be restricted to hotel guests and members.

Bars

Café Mondegar Colaba Causeway (see map, p.119). Draught beer by the glass or pitcher (both imported and Indian) and deliciously fruity cocktails are served in this small café-bar. The atmosphere is very relaxed, the music tends towards cheesy rock classics and the clientele is a mix of Westerners and students; murals by a famous Goan cartoonist give the place a cheerful ambience.

Czar Bar *Hotel Intercontinental*, 135 Marine Drive (see map, p.126). Trendy vodka bar with chic, minimalist decor, clever lighting and 24 brands on offer (from Rs250/shot), plus a full range of other drinks and cocktails. Music is lounge until around 11pm, then picks up. Quiet on weekday nights, but popular on weekends.

The Dome *Hotel Intercontinental*, 135 Marine Drive (see map, p.126). Easily south Mumbai's most alluring spot for a sundowner, on the rooftop of this smart boutique hotel. Plush white sofas and armchairs line up alongside the candle-lit tables, spread in front of the eponymous domed rotunda and a very sexy raised pool. The views over Back Bay can occasionally make the sky-high drink prices (Rs350 for beer; Rs450 for a shot and mixer) feel worth it. Popular mainly with overpaid expats.

Indigo 4 Mandlik Rd, Colaba (see map, p.119). The coolest hangout in Colaba, frequented by young media types and would-be wine buffs. Its funky, stripped-bare decor set a new trend in the city. See also p.140.

Leo's Square 1st floor, *Leopold's*, Colaba Causeway (see map, p.119). Pretty much the same drinks menu and prices as *Leopold's* downstairs, but here you can enjoy a/c, a back-lit bar and quality sound system.

Olive 4 Union Park Rd, Pali Hill. Nowhere pulls in Bollywood's A-list like *Olive*. If you want to rub shoulders with Hrithik, Abhishek and Aishwarya, Preity and Shilpa, this is your best bet, though dress to kill – and come armed with a flexible wallet. Although basically just a pretext to crowd-watch, the food is fine gourmet Mediterranean.

Nightclubs

Enigma *JW Marriott Hotel*, Juhu Tara Rd. If you want to see what Hindi film stars and hip young Indian millionaires do for kicks, this is the place to come: the sexiest outfits, the latest Bolly-bhangra mixes, most gorgeous decor and stiffest entrance cost (from Rs1500 per couple).

Insomnia *Taj Mahal Palace & Tower* (see map, p.119). Well-heeled yuppies and their NRI (non-resident Indian) relatives strut their stuff in this warren of illuminated bars, hardwood dance floors and chill-out spaces beneath the *Taj*, featuring one of the city's heftiest sound systems. Open to non-members, but you'll have to look your best. Cover Rs1000–1500 per couple. Punters start arriving at 11pm and it usually stays open until 3am.

Polly Esther's *Gorden House Hotel*, Battery St, Colaba (see map, p.119). Retro club with brightly coloured Seventies/Eighties decor, leather upholstery and a Nineties night on Thurs, where the waiters wear ludicrous fluoro-coloured Afro wigs; pop, rock, disco and Motown on the weekend. Rs750–1000 per couple.

Squeeze 5th Rd, Khar. Bandra's funkiest nightspot is aptly named: it's packed seven nights a week, and bursting at the seams on weekends, when the music's less dominated by Hindi pop than elsewhere. Fridays hosts Submerge – the city's original and best House night (they usually throw in plenty of hip-hop and R&B for good measure). Admission Rs1000–1500 per couple.

Voodoo Lounge Arthur Bunder Rd, Colaba (see map, p.119). This cavernous, but delightfully louche, little dive off Colaba Causeway plays host to Mumbai's one and only gay club, from 9pm on Sat (it's dead and depressing the rest of the week). The atmosphere's restrained by Western standards, but welcoming and sociable for both gay and straight men and women, though most of the punters do come to cruise. Admission Rs250/head.

Shopping

Mumbai is a great place to shop, whether for last-minute souvenirs or essentials for the long journeys ahead. Locally produced **textiles** and export-surplus clothing are among the best buys, as are **handicrafts** from far-flung corners of the country. With the exception of the swish arcades in the five-star hotels, prices compare surprisingly well with other Indian cities. In the larger shops, rates are fixed and **credit cards** are often accepted; elsewhere, particularly dealing with street vendors, it pays to haggle. Uptown, the **central bazaars** – see p.128 – are better for spectating than serious shopping, although the **antiques** and Friday **flea market** in the Chor, or "thieves" bazaar, can sometimes yield the odd bargain. The **Zaveri** (goldsmiths') **bazaar** opposite Crawford Market is the place to head for new gold and silver **jewellery**. **Tea** lovers should check out the *Tea Centre* on VN Road (see p.141), which sells a wide range of quality tea, including the outrageously expensive "fine tippy golden Orange Pekoe" (Rs1200 per 250g).

Opening hours in the city centre are Monday to Saturday, 10am to 7pm. The Muslim bazaars, quiet on Friday, are otherwise open until around 9pm (or through the night during Ramadan).

Antiques

The **Chor Bazaar** area, and Mutton Street in particular, is the centre of Mumbai's **antique trade** (for a full account, see p.129). Another good, if much more expensive, place is **Phillip's** famous antique shop, on the corner of Madam Cama Road, facing SP Mukharji Circle, and opposite the Regal cinema in Colaba, which was in the middle of a major re-fit on our last visit. Brass, bronze and wood Hindu sculpture, silver jewellery, old prints and aquatints form the mainstay of its collection. Most of the stuff on sale dates from the twilight of the Raj – a result of the Indian government's ban on the export by foreigners of items more than a century old.

In the **Jehangir Art Gallery** basement, a branch of the antiques chain Natesan's Antiqarts offers a tempting selection of antique (and reproduction) sculpture, furniture, paintings and bronzes.

Clothes, textiles and household goods

Mumbai produces the bulk of India's **clothes**, mostly the lightweight, light-coloured "shirtings and suitings" favoured by droves of uniformly attired office-wallahs. For cheaper Western clothing, you can't beat the long row of stalls on the pavement of MG Road, opposite the Mumbai Gymkhana. "**Fashion Street**" specializes in reject and export-surplus goods ditched by big manufacturers, selling off T-shirts, jeans, summer dresses and sweatshirts. Better-quality cotton clothes (often stylish designer-label rip-offs) are available in shops along **Colaba Causeway**, such as Cotton World, down Mandlik Marg.

If you're looking for **traditional Indian clothes**, head for the Khadi Village Industries Emporium at 286 Dr DN Marg, near the Thomas Cook office. As Whiteaway & Laidlaw, this rambling Victorian department store used to kit all the newly arrived *burra-sahibs* out with pith helmets, khaki shorts and quinine tablets. These days, its old wooden counters and shirt and sock drawers stock dozens of different hand-spun cottons and silks, sold by the metre or made up as vests, *kurtas* or block-printed *salwar kamises*. Other items include the ubiquitous white Nehru caps, *dhotis*, Madras-check *lunghis* and fine brocaded silk saris.

Fab India, whose flagship branch is at 137 MG Rd in Kala Ghoda, sells a huge range of contemporary Indian cotton clothes, made with traditional block-printed and mirror-inlayed fabrics. They also stock a great range of **soft furnishings** and **household goods**. For tablecloths, cotton and silk quilts, rattan blinds and upholstery fabric, another place worth trying is Chunilal Mulchand & Co, at the Indian Mercantile Mansion on Madam Cama Road, close to the Prince of Wales Museum. They'll copy **loose covers** for sofas and lounge chairs in a week. Malabar, at the *Taj Mahal Palace & Tower*, is much pricier, but stocks some exquisite beaded cushion covers and throws in traditional Indian **textiles**. For other designer home furnishings – everything from cutlery to curtain panels – Contemporary Arts & Crafts at 19 Jagmohandas Marg (Napean Sea Road) up in the exclusive Malabar Hill area, is a must.

Handicrafts

Regionally produced **handicrafts** are marketed in assorted state-run emporia at the World Trade Centre, down on Cuffe Parade, and along Sir PM Road, Fort. The quality is consistently high – as are the prices, if you miss out on the periodic holiday discounts. The same goes for the **Central Cottage Industries Emporium**, 34 Shivaji Marg, near the Gateway of India in Colaba, whose size and central location make it the single best all-round place to hunt for souvenirs. Downstairs you'll find inlaid furniture, wood- and metalwork, miniature paintings and jewellery, while upstairs specializes in toys, clothing and textiles – Gujarati appliqué bedspreads, hand-painted pillowcases and Rajasthani mirror-work, plus silk ties and Noel Coward dressing gowns. **Mereweather Road** (now officially B Behram Marg), directly behind the *Taj*, is awash with Kashmiri handicraft stores stocking overpriced papier-mâché pots and bowls, silver jewellery, woollen shawls and rugs. Avoid them if you find it hard to shrug off aggressive sales pitches.

Perfume is essentially a Muslim preserve in Mumbai. Down at the south end of Colaba Causeway, around Arthur Bunder Road, shops with mirrored walls and shelves are stacked with cut-glass carafes full of syrupy, fragrant essential oils. **Incense** is hawked in sticks, cones and slabs of sticky *dhoop* on the pavement nearby (check that the boxes haven't already been opened and their contents sold off piecemeal). For bulk buying, the hand-rolled, cottage-made bundles of incense sold in the Khadi Village Industries Emporium on Dr DN Marg (see p.145) are a better deal; it also has a handicraft department where, in addition to furniture, paintings and ornaments, you can pick up glass bangles, block-printed and calico bedspreads and wooden votive statues produced in Maharashtrian craft villages.

Books

Mumbai's excellent English-language **bookshops** and bookstalls are well stocked with everything to do with India, and a good selection of general classics, pulp fiction and travel writing. Indian editions of popular titles cost a fraction of what they do abroad and in addition there are often lots of interesting works by lesser-known local authors. If you don't mind picking through dozens of trigonometry textbooks, back issues of *National Geographic* and salacious 1960s paperbacks, the **street stalls** between Flora Fountain and Churchgate station can also be good places to hunt for secondhand books.

Chetana 34 K Dubash Rd (Rampart Row), Colaba. Exclusively religion and philosophy.

Crossword Bookstore Mohammed Bhai Mansion, Huges Rd, Kemp's Corner, a ten-minute walk north of Chowpatty Beach ☏ 022/2384 2001. Mumbai's largest retailer, in smart new a/c premises, complete with its own coffee bar. Open Mon–Fri 10am–8pm, Sat & Sun 10am–9pm.

Nalanda Ground floor, *Taj Mahal Palace & Tower*. An exhaustive range of coffee-table tomes and paperback literature, though at top prices.

Oxford Bookstore Apeejay House, 3 Dinsha Vacha Rd, Churchgate. Not quite as large as Crossword, but almost, and much more easily accessible if you're staying downtown or in Colaba. It also has a very cool a/c café, the *Cha Bar* (see p.141).

Search Word SBS Marg (Colaba Causeway). The best bookstore in Colaba, with shelves full of guides and a great range of Indian fiction – at discounts only rivalled by the Strand in Fort.

Gregory David "Shantaram" Roberts numbers among the regulars.

Shankar Book Stand Outside the *Café Mondegar*, SBS Marg (Colaba Causeway). Piles of easy-reads, guidebooks, classic fiction, and most of the old favourites on India, at competitive rates.

Strand Next door to the Canara Bank, off PM Rd, Fort. The best-value bookshop in the city centre, with the full gamut of Penguins and Indian literature, sold at amazing discounts.

Music

The most famous of Mumbai's many **musical instrument shops** are near the Moti cinema along SV Patel Road, in the central bazaar district. Haribhai Vishwanath, Ram Singh and RS Mayeka are all government-approved retailers, stocking sitars, sarods, tablas and flutes. For guaranteed top quality, however, it's advisable to make the trek north to Bhargava's Musik, at 4/5 Imperial Plaza, 30th Rd in Bandra, which numbers among its clients some of India's top classical performers.

For **cassettes and CDs** a good first stop if you're based down in Colaba is Rhythm House, on Subhash Chowk opposite the Jehangir Art Gallery. This is a veritable Aladdin's cave of classical, devotional and popular music from all over India, with a reasonable selection of Western rock, pop and jazz, as well as DVDs of classic and contemporary Hindi movies. A ten-minute walk further north along Dr DN Rd in Fort, Planet M is a Virgin/HMV-style megastore stocking an array of music CDs and computer games to rival any in the country.

Sports

In common with most Indians, Mumbaikars are crazy about **cricket**. Few other spectactor sports get much of a look-in, although the **horse racing** at Mahalakshmi draws large crowds on Derby days. Further down the social scale, more

---

Laughter Yoga

On the principle that laughter is the best medicine, Mumbai doctor Madan Kataria and his wife Madhuri – aka "the Giggling Gurus" – have created a new kind of therapy: *hasya* (laughter) yoga. There are now over 300 **Laughter Clubs** in India and many more worldwide; around 50,000 people join the Laughter Day celebrations in Mumbai on the first Sunday of May each year, with tens of thousands more participating worlwide.

Fifteen-minute sessions start with adherents doing yogic breathing whilst chanting "Ho ho ha ha", which develops into spontaneous "hearty laughter" (raising both hands in the air with the head tilting backwards), "milkshake laughter" (everyone laughs while making a gesture as if they are drinking milkshake), and "swinging laughter" (standing in a circle saying "aaee-oo-eee-uuu") before the rather fearsome "lion laughter" (extruding the tongue fully with eyes wide open and hands stretched out like claws, and laughing from the tummy). The session then winds up with holding hands and the chanting of slogans ("We are the laughter club member (sic) . . . Y . . . E . . .S!").

Laughter clubs take place between 6am and 7am (so you'll have to get up at the crack of dawn to catch one) at various venues around the city, including Colaba Woods in Cuffe Parade and Juhu Beach. For the full story, go to ⓦ www.laughteryoga.org.

traditional **Maharashtrian games**, such as kabadi and *kho kho*, form the focus of weekend activities at Shivaji Park in central Mumbai. Previews of all forth-coming events are posted on the back pages of the *Times of India*, and in *Time Out Mumbai*.

Cricket

Cricket provides almost as much of a distraction as movies in the Maharashtrian capital, and you'll see games in progress everywhere, from impromptu sunset knockabouts on Chowpatty Beach to more formal club matches in full whites at the gymkhanas lined up along Marine Drive. In south Mumbai, **Oval Maidan** is the place to watch local talent in action, set against a wonderfully apt backdrop of imperial-era buildings. Something of a pecking order applies here: the further from the path cutting across the centre of the park you go, the better the wickets and the classier the games become.

Pitches like these are where Mumbai's favourite son, **Sachin Tendulkar**, cut his cricketing teeth. The world's most prolific batsman (in one-day cricket) still lives in the city and plays regularly for its league-winning club side at the **Brabourne Stadium**, off Marine Drive. A kilometre or so further north, 45,000-capacity **Wankhede Stadium** is where major test matches are hosted, amid an atmosphere as intense, raucous and intimidating for visiting teams as any in India.

The Indian cricket season runs from October through February. Tickets for big games are almost as hard to come by as seats on commuter trains, but foreign visitors can sometimes gain preferential access to quotas through the Mumbai Cricket Association's offices on the first floor of Wankhede.

Horse racing and horse riding

The **Mahalakshmi Racecourse**, near the Mahalakshmi Temple just north of Malabar Hill, is the home of the **Royal Western India Turf Club** – a

△ Cricket on Oval Maidan

throwback to British times that still serves as a prime stomping ground for the city's upper classes. Race meets are held twice weekly, on Wednesdays and Saturdays between November and March, and big days such as the 2000 Guineas and Derby attract crowds of 25,000. Entrance to the public ground is by ticket on the day. Seats for the colonial-era stand, with its posh lawns and exclusive *Gallops Restaurant*, are alas allocated to members only. Race cards are posted in the sports section of the *Times of India*, and can be downloaded (along with form guides) from Ⓦwww.rwitc.com.

On non-race days, the Mahalakshmi ground doubles as a riding track. Temporary membership of the **Amateur Riding Club of Mumbai**, another bastion of elite Mumbai, entitles you to use the club's thoroughbreds for classes. Full details on how to do this, along with previews of forthcoming club **polo** matches, are posted at Ⓦwww.arcmumbai.com.

Maharashtrian sports

Shivaji Park, an enormous public playing field in the central district of **Dadar**, teems throughout the weekend with intense matches of **kabadi**, a tag game in which "raiders" from one team try to "capture" defenders from the other while holding their breath and chanting (see p.71). This is also where you can catch the more rarely played **kho kho**, another tag game where one team squat down and the other dart around them, and, weirdest of all, **mallakham**, a kind of gymnastic-yogic workout involving spins, leaps and turns around rows of poles. Games are orchestrated by the **Shree Samartha Vyayam Mandir** (Ⓦwww.shivajipark.com/inshivajipark /samarth.html), an organization which promotes traditional sports in the city among young people. Shivaji Park is most easily reached from Churchgate via Dadar suburban railway station.

The other game particularly popular in Maharashtra that you might wish to track down while you're here is **kushti** (wrestling). Stocky lads, dressed in old-school loin cloths and smothered in coconut oil, attempt to floor each other in dark, red-sand pits called *akharas* – a memorable photo opportunity. Several *akharas* survive in Mumbai; the India Government Tourist Office in Churchgate can help arrange visits.

Children

There's little in the way of dedicated children's entertainment in Mumbai, though any small kids travelling with you will undoubtedly enjoy the busking acrobats, balloon sellers, camel rides and other gimcrackery on display daily at Chowpatty and Juhu beaches (covered on p.131 & p.136 respectively). **Kamla Nehru Park** on Malabar Hill also holds a perennially popular playground featuring the famous "Old Woman's Shoe", which has fascinated generations of Mumbaikars and is still going strong.

With a full day to spare, you might contemplate a longer trip, 60km north of the city centre, to **Esselworld** (daily 9am–5.30pm; adults Rs350/450, children Rs250/350 on weekdays/weekends; Ⓦwww.esselworld.com), India's largest amusement park, on Gorai Island. And if that doesn't appeal, a ferry ride away lies the heat-beating **Water Kingdom** aquatic theme park (admission with ticket for Esselworld; same website), complete with huge wave pool, log flow, slides and slippery big dippers.

Listings

Airlines, domestic *Air Deccan* ☎ 3900 8888, ⓦ www.airdeccan.net; *Go Air* ☎ 1800 222111, airport ☎ 022/6577 1178, ⓦ www.goair.in; *Indian Airlines*, Air India Building, Nariman Point ☎ 022/2202 3031, counter at the airport ☎ 022/2682 9328, ⓦ www.indian-airlines.nic.in; *IndiGo Airlines* 17 Jolly Maker Chambers II, 255 Nariman Point ☎ 099/1038 3838 or toll free ☎ 1800 180 3838, ⓦ www.goindigo.in; *Jet Airways*, Amarchand Mansion, Madam Cama Rd ☎ 022/2285 5788, ⓦ www.jetairways.com; *Kingfisher* First Floor, Arrivals Hall, Terminal 1-A, domestic airport ☎ 022/6649 9393, or toll free ☎ 1800 1800 101, ⓦ www.flykingfisher.com; *Sahara Airlines*, Unit 7, ground floor, Tulsiani Chambers, Nariman Point ☎ 022/2283 6000, Airport Terminal 1-B toll free ☎ 1800 223020, ⓦ www.airsahara.net; *SpiceJet* c/o Akbar Travels, Terminus View, 169 D.N.Road, opp CST Station, toll free ☎ 1800 180 3333, ⓦ www.spicejet.com.

Airlines, international See pp.29–30 for airlines' website addresses. *Aeroflot*, ground floor, 14 Tulsiani Chambers, Free Press Journal Rd, Nariman Point ☎ 022/2285 6648; *Air France*, 201/B Sarjan Plaza, 100 Dr Annie Besant Rd, Worli, North Mumbai ☎ 022/2346 6276; *Air India*, 1st Floor, Air India Building, Nariman Point ☎ 022/2548 9999 or toll free ☎ 1800 227722; *Alitalia*, 5th Floor, CG House, Annie Besant Rd, Prabhadevi, Worli, North Mumbai ☎ 022/5663 0800; *British Airways*, 4th Floor, CG House, Annie Besant Rd, Prabhadevi, Worli, North Mumbai ☎ m98925 77470; *Cathay Pacific*, Bajaj Bhavan, 3rd floor, 226 Nariman Point ☎ 022/5657 2222; *Delta*, Interglobe Enterprises Limited, 12th Floor, Bajaj Bhavan, Nariman Point ☎ 022/2826 7007; *Egypt Air*, Oriental House, 7 J Tata Rd, Churchgate ☎ 022/2283 3798; *Emirates*, 228 Mittal Chambers, Nariman Point ☎ 022/2879 7979; *Gulf Air*, Ground Floor, Maker Chamber V, Nariman Point ☎ 022/2202 1626; *Japan Airlines*, 9th Floor, 911 Raheja Centre, Nariman Point ☎ 022/2283 3136; *KLM*, 201-B Sarjan Plaza, 100 Annie Besant Rd, Worli, North Mumbai toll free ☎ 1800 114777; *Kuwait Airways*, 901 Nariman Bhavan, 9th Floor Nariman Point ☎ 022/6655 5655; *Lufthansa*, 3rd floor, Express Towers, Nariman Point ☎ 022/6630 1940; *Qantas Airways*, 2nd floor, Godrej Bhavan, Home St ☎ 022/2200 7440; *Qatar Airways*, Bajaj Bhavan, Nariman Point ☎ 0124/456 6000; *Saudi Air*, 3rd floor, Express Towers, Nariman Point ☎ 022/2202 0199; *Singapore Airlines*, Taj Mahal Palace & Tower, Apollo Bunder (PJ Ramachandani Marg), Colaba ☎ 022/2202 8316; *South African Airways*, Podar House, 10 Marine Drive, Churchgate ☎ 022/282 3450; *Sri Lankan Airlines*, 2nd Floor Vaswani Mansion, 12 Dinshaw Vachha Rd, Churchgate ☎ 022/282 3288; *Thai Airways*, Ground Floor, Maker Chamber IV, Nariman Point ☎ 022/5637 3737.

Airport enquiries Chhatrapati Shivaji international airport ☎ 022/2682 9000, Chhatrapati Shivaji (Santa Cruz) domestic airport ☎ 022/2615 6600; ⓦ www.mumbaiairport.com.

Ambulance ☎ 101 for general emergencies; but you're nearly always better off taking a taxi. See also Hospitals, see opposite.

Banks and currency exchange The most convenient place to change money when you arrive in Mumbai is at the State Bank of India's 24hr counter in Chhatrapati Shivaji international airport. Rates here are standard but you may have to pay for an encashment certificate – essential if you intend to buy tourist-quota train tickets or an Indrail pass at the special counters in Churchgate or CST (VT) stations. All the major state banks downtown change foreign currency (Mon–Fri 10.30am–2.30pm, Sat 10.30am–12.30pm); some (eg the Bank of Baroda) also handle credit cards and cash advances. Most now have 24hr ATMs that can handle international transactions, usually Visa, Delta and Mastercard. It's worth noting that there's sometimes a limit on how much you can take out in one day: it can be as low as Rs5000. For the location of large branch ATM machines downtown, see our maps; the closest to home if you're staying in Colaba is the Bank of Baroda's at the north end of SBS Marg (Colaba Causeway). Thomas Cook's big Dr DN Marg branch (Mon–Sat 9.30am–7pm; ☎ 022/2204 8556), between the Khadi shop and Hutatma Chowk, can also arrange money transfers from overseas.

Consulates and high commissions Although the many consulates and high commissions in Mumbai can be useful for replacing lost travel documents or obtaining visas, most of India's neighbouring states, including Bangladesh, Bhutan, Burma, Nepal and Pakistan, only have embassies in New Delhi and/or Kolkata (Calcutta). All of the following are open Mon–Fri only: *Australia*, 16th Floor, 36 Maker Tower V, Nariman Point (9am–5pm; ☎ 022/5669 2000); *Canada*, 41/42 Maker Chambers VI, Nariman Point (9am–5.30pm; ☎ 022/2287 6027); *China*, 1st floor, 11 ML Dahanukar Marg (10am–4.30pm; ☎ 022/2282 2662); *France*, 2nd floor, Datta Prasad, N Gamadia Cross Rd (9am–1pm & 2.30–5.30pm; ☎ 022/2495 0918); *Germany*, 10th floor, Hoechst House, Nariman Point (8–11am; ☎ 022/2283 2422); *Indonesia*, 19 Altamount Rd, Cumbala Hill

(10am–4.30pm; ☎022/2351 1678); *Republic of Ireland*, 38 Western Indian House, Sir PM Rd (9.30am–1pm; ☎022/2287 1931); *Netherlands*, 1st Floor, Forbes Building, Chiranjit Rai Marg, Fort (9am–5pm; ☎022/2201 6750); *Poland*, 2nd Floor Manavi Apt, 36 BG Kher Marg, Malabar Hill (☎022/2363 3863); *Singapore*, 10th floor, Maker Chamber IV, 222 Jamnal Bajaj Marg, Nariman Point (9am–noon; ☎022/2204 3205); *South Africa*, Gandhi Mansion, 20 Altamount Rd (9am–noon; ☎022/2389 3725); *Sri Lanka*, Sri Lanka House, 34 Homi Modi St, Fort (9.30am–11.30am; ☎022/2204 5861); *Sweden*, 85 Sayani Rd, Subash Gupta Bhawan, Prabhadevi (10am–12.30pm; ☎022/2436 0493); *Thailand*, Malabar View, 4th floor, Dr Purandure Marg, Chowpatty Sea Face (9–11.30am; ☎022/2363 1404); *United Kingdom*, 2nd floor, Maker Chamber IV, Nariman Point (8am–11.30am; ☎022/2283 0517); *USA*, Lincoln House, 78 Bhulabhai Desai Rd (8.30am–11am; ☎022/2363 3611).

Hospitals The best hospital in the centre is the private Bombay Hospital (☎022/2206 7676, ⓦwww.bombayhospital.com), New Marine Lines, just north of the government tourist office on M Karve Rd. Breach Candy Hospital (☎022/2367 1888, ⓦwww.breachcandyhospital.org) on Bhulabhai Desai Rd, near the swimming pool, is also recommended by foreign embassies.

Internet access A couple of cramped 24hr places (Rs40/hr) can be found in Colaba, just round the corner from *Leopold's* on Nawroji F Marg, though it's worth paying the Rs5 extra at Access Infotech, located down a small alley further along Colaba Causeway on the left, which is faster and more comfortable.

Left luggage If your hotel won't let you store bags with them, try the cloakrooms at the airports (see p.105), or the one in CST (VT) station (Rs10/day). Anything left here, even rucksacks, must be securely fastened with a padlock and can be left for a maximum of one month.

Libraries Asiatic Society (see p.127), SBS Marg, Horniman Circle, Ballard Estate (Mon–Sat 10.30am–7pm); British Council (for British

newspapers and magazines), A Wing, 1st floor, Mittal Tower, Nariman Point (Tues–Sat 10am–6pm); Mumbai Natural History Society, Hornbill House (Mon–Fri 10am–5pm, Sat 10am–1pm, closed 1st & 3rd Sat of the month), has an international reputation for the study of wildlife in India. Visitors may obtain temporary membership, which allows them access to the library, natural history collection, occasional talks and the opportunity to join organized walks and field trips.

Pharmacies Bombay Chemist, 39–40 Kakad Arcade, opposite Bombay Hospital, New Marine Lines (☎022/2207 6171) opens daily 8am–11pm. Kemps in the *Taj Mahal* also opens late.

Photographic studios and equipment The Javeri Colour Lab, opposite the Regal cinema in Colaba, stocks colour-print and slide film, and can burn files from your memory cards onto disc. A small boutique behind the florists in the Sahakari Bhandar covered market does instant Polaroid passport photos.

Police The main police station in Colaba (☎022/2285 6817) is on the west side of Colaba Causeway, near the crossroads with Best Marg.

Postal services The GPO (Mon–Sat 9am–8pm, Sun 9am–4pm) is around the corner from CST (VT) Station, off Nagar Chowk. Its poste restante counter (Mon–Sat 9am–6pm, Sun 9am–3pm) is among the most reliable in India, although they trash the letters after four weeks. The much less efficient parcel office (10am–4.30pm) is behind the main building on the first floor. Packing-wallahs hang around on the pavement outside. DHL (☎022/2850 5050) has eleven offices in Mumbai, the most convenient being the 24hr one under the *Sea Green Hotel* at the bottom of Marine Drive.

Travel agents The following travel agents are recommended for booking domestic and international flights, and long-distance private buses where specified: Cox and Kings India, 271/272 Dr DN Marg ☎022/2207 3065, ⓦwww.coxandkings.com; Sita World Travels, 8 Atlanta Building, Nariman Point ☎022/2286 0684, ⓔbom@sitaincoming.com; Thomas Cook, 324 Dr DN Rd, Fort ☎022/2204 8556, ⓦwww.thomascook.co.in.

Moving on from Mumbai

Most visitors aim to escape Mumbai as soon as possible, and the city is equipped with "super-fast" services to make **onward travel** speedy and painless (by Indian standards). All the major international and domestic **airlines** have offices in the city, the **railway** networks operate special tourist counters in the main reservation halls, and dozens of **travel agents** and road transport companies are eager to help you on your way by **bus**. In addition to the information here, see Travel details, p.178.

By air

Indian Airlines and other **domestic carriers** fly out of Chhatrapati Shivaji domestic airport (aka Santa Cruz; ⓦ www.mumbaiairport.com) to destinations all over India. Availability on popular routes should never be taken for granted – check with the airlines as soon as you arrive. **Tickets** can be bought directly from airline offices (see p.150), via the Internet (though not always – see below), or through any reputable travel agent.

Booking **flights online** may not always be as straightforward as it is back home, especially when it comes to **low-cost airlines** – such as Air Deccan, IndiGo, Go Air and SpiceJet – which only accept payments by credit or debit cards registered in India. The same applies to Indian Airlines who, although they do issue E-tickets for domestic flights, won't honour them if you've booked as part of a multi-leg route through another international airline from abroad. The easiest solution is to pay in cash in person at the airline's office (even the rockiest of rock-bottom budget carriers have counters at the airport).

By train

The quickest and most convenient place for foreign nationals to make reservations is at the efficient tourist counter (no. 28) on the first floor of the **Western Railway's booking hall**, next door to the Government of India tourist office in **Churchgate** (Mon–Fri 9.30am–4.30pm, Sat 9.30am–2.30pm; ☎ 022/2209 7577). This counter, at the far (bottom) end of the booking hall, has access to special "tourist quotas", which are released the day before departure if the train leaves during the day, or the morning of the departure if the train leaves after 5pm. If the quota is "closed" or already used up, and you can't access the "Emergency quota" (always worth a try), you will have to join the regular queue. As elsewhere in the country, periods before major national holidays (notably **Diwali**, when half of India is on the move) should be avoided at all costs. But if you do find yourself having to travel when there don't seem to be any tickets left, bear in mind you can pay extra for a special Tatkal seat (see p.155 for full details on these) – an option well worth considering, for example, if you want to get to Goa on the oversubscribed Konkan Railway route.

Mumbai's other "Tourist Ticketing Facility" is in the snazzy air-conditioned **Central Railway booking office** to the rear of **CST** (VT; Mon–Sat 8am–1.30pm & 2–3pm, Sun 8am–2pm; ☎ 022/2262 2859), the departure point for most trains heading east and south. Indrail passes can also be bought here, and there's an MTDC tourist information kiosk in the main concourse if you need help filling in your reservation slips.

Tickets for seats on the **Konkan Railway** can be booked at either Churchgate or CST booking halls; for more information on getting to Goa by rail, see the box on pp.154–155. Just to complicate matters, some **Central Railway** trains to **South India** – notably those running via the Konkan Railway to **Kerala** – do not depart from CST at all, but from **Kurla station** (aka Lokmanya Tilak Terminus, or **LTT**), up near the airports. Others leave from **Dadar**, also way north of the centre. Getting to either on public transport can be a major struggle, though many long-distance trains from CST (VT) or Churchgate stop there and aren't as crowded.

Wherever you're heading, a good investment for anyone planning to do much rail travel is Indian Railways' indispensable *Trains at a Glance*, available from most station bookstalls for Rs30. You can also access **timetables** via the Indian Railways website at ⓦ www.indianrail.gov.in, and even **book tickets** online.

The services listed below are the most direct and/or the fastest. This list is by no means exhaustive and there are numerous slower trains that are often more convenient for smaller destinations. All the details listed below were correct at the time of writing, but departure times, in particular, should be checked when you purchase your ticket, or in advance via the Indian Railways website: ⓦ www.indianrail.gov.in.

Destination	Name	No.	From	Departs	Journey time
Chennai	Mumbai–Chennai Express	#6011	CST	Daily 2pm	26hr 45min
Goa (Margao)	Mumbai–Madgaon Express	#KR0111	CST	Daily 11pm	11hr 45min
Hyderabad	Hussain-sagar Express	#2701	CST	Daily 9.50pm	14hr 20min
Kochi (Cochin)	Netravati Express	#6345	LTT (Kurla)	Daily 11.40am	26hr 25min
Kolhapur	Sahyadri Express	#1023	CST	Daily 5.50pm	12hr 15min
Lonavala	Udyan Express	#6529	CST	Daily 8.40am	2hr 50min
Mysore	Sharavathi Express	#1035	Dadar	Tues 9.30pm	23hr 40min
Pune	Udyan Express	#6529	CST	Daily 8.40am	3hr 35min
Thiruvanan-thapuram (Trivandrum)	Netravati Express	#6345	LTT (Kurla)	Daily 11.40am	31hr

By bus

The main departure point for long-distance **government buses** leaving Mumbai is the frenetic **Central bus stand** on JB Behram Marg, opposite Mumbai Central railway station. States with bus company counters here (daily 8am–8pm) include Maharashtra, Karnataka and Goa. Few of their services compare favourably with train travel on the same routes. Reliable timetable information can be difficult to obtain, reservations are not available on standard buses, and most long-haul journeys are gruelling overnighters. Among the exceptions are the deluxe buses run by MSRTC to Pune and Kolhapur; the small extra cost buys you more leg-room, fewer stops and the option of advance booking. The only problem is that most leave from the ASIAD bus stand in Dadar, thirty minutes or so by road or rail north of Mumbai Central.

Private buses cover most of the same routes. They tend to be faster, more comfortable and easier to book in advance – though again, long distance services invariably depart at night. Tickets are sold from a row of booths on busy Dr Anadao Nair Marg, just outside Mumbai Central railway station, on the opposite side of the main (north–south) road from the Central bus stand (see map pp.110–111). Note that fares on services to popular tourist destinations such as Goa and Mahabaleshwar increase by as much as 75 percent during peak season.

Since the advent of low-cost airlines, easily the best-value way to travel the 500km from Mumbai to Goa has been by **plane**. Rock-bottom fares for the hour-long flight down the coast tend to be in short supply, however, and are difficult to obtain online from abroad (see p.152). The same applies to tickets for the Konkan Railway, which are routinely sold out weeks in advance. Faced with a prolonged stay in Mumbai, or the prospect of a hellish overnight bus journey, most travellers pay their way out of trouble by opting for a pricier flight with Jet Airways, Indian Airlines or Sahara Air, or stumping up for a premium Tatkal rail ticket (see opposite). Alternatively, consider heading south in stages, via Pune or the beautiful, rarely travelled Konkan Coast of southern Maharashtra.

By air

Between 15 and 21 flights leave daily from Chhatrapati Shivaji (aka Santa Cruz) domestic airport, 30km north of the city, for Goa's Dabolim airport. The cheapest fares are offered by Air Deccan (Wwww.airdeccan.net), IndiGo (Wwww.goindigo.in), and Go Air (Wwww.goair.in), who sell tickets on their websites from as low as Rs550, though the normal rate is more like US$60. Low-cost rivals SpiceJet (Wwww.spicejet.com) and Kingfisher Airlines (Wwww.flykingfisher.com) also offer competitive tickets. Flying with Indian Airlines (Wwww.indian-airlines.nic.in) will set you back $105, or it will cost $100 with Sahara (Wwww.airsahara.net) or Jet (Wwww.jetairways.com). In addition, Air India (Wwww.airindia.com) operate a service from Mumbai (also for $100) which few people seem to know about, so you can nearly always get a seat (the one drawback is that you have to check in three hours before departure as Air India is an international carrier).

Demand for seats can be fierce around Diwali and Christmas/New Year, when you're unlikely to get a ticket at short notice. At other times, one or other of the carriers should be able to offer a seat on the day you wish to travel – though perhaps not at the lowest fares. If you didn't pre-book when you purchased your international ticket, check availability with the airlines as soon as you arrive; tickets can be bought directly from their offices (see Listings on p.150), through any reputable travel agent in Mumbai (bearing in mind that an agent may charge you the dollar fare at a poorer rate of exchange than that offered by the airline company), by phone or direct via the Internet (though note that few of the low-cost airlines accept payments by credit or debit cards not registered in India; for more on this, see Basics, p.39).

All Goa flights leave from Chhatrapati Shivaji (aka Santa Cruz) domestic airport, 30km north of the city centre.

By train

The **Konkan Railway** line runs daily express trains from Mumbai to Goa. **Fares** for the twelve-hour journey from CST start at Rs293 for standard sleeper class,

By boat

Three companies operate boat services from the Gateway of India to **Mandawa jetty**, on the far side of Mumbai harbour, from where buses shuttle to nearby **Alibag**, transport hub for the route southwards down the Konkan coast. Ranging from comfortable air-conditioned catamarans (Rs100) to bog-standard launches (Rs55), the ferries leave roughly every hour; tickets should be purchased in advance from the PNP, Ajanta or Maldar company booths, on the north side of Shivaji Marg, near the MTDC Information counter.

rising to Rs1242 for second class a/c or Rs2345 for luxurious first class a/c. However, these services are not always available at short notice from the booking halls at CST and Churchgate. If you're certain of your travel dates in advance (ie if you're flying into Mumbai and want to catch the train to Goa soon after arriving), consider **booking online** at ⓦ www.konkanrailway.com. There are downsides to this: you're only entitled to relatively expensive three-tier a/c fares (Rs1242 one-way) and must make your booking between seven and two days before your date of departure – but all in all, online reservation is a much more convenient way to secure a seat than leaving it until you arrive in Mumbai. You could also make the reservation through an Indian Railways agent in your home country, see Basics, p.38.

The other alternative is to shell out a for a **Tatkal ticket**. A quota of ten percent of places on most trains is reserved under this scheme, bookable at the computerized offices in CST or Churchgate. Tickets are released five days before the train departs, and there's an extra charge of Rs150 in the sleeper or chair car, Rs300 in first or a/c sleepers. The catch is that travellers also have to pay for the entire length of the journey from originating to terminating station, but as several of the express services down the southern Maharashtrian coast start and finish in Mumbai and Goa respectively, this isn't generally an issue.

Don't, whatever you do, be tempted to travel "unreserved" class on any Konkan service, as the journey as far as Ratnagiri (roughly midway) is overwhelmingly crushed. The most convenient of the Konkan services is the overnight Mumbai–Madgaon Express (see box, p.153). The other, only slightly faster, train is the Mandovi Express (#KR0103), leaving at 7am from CST.

By bus

The Mumbai–Goa bus journey ranks among the very worst in India. Don't believe travel agents who assure you it takes thirteen hours. Depending on the type of bus you get, appalling road surfaces along the sinuous coastal route make sixteen to eighteen hours a more realistic estimate.

Fares start at around Rs300 for a push-back seat on a beaten-up Kadamba (Goan government) or MSRTC coach. Tickets for these services are in great demand in season with domestic tourists, so book in advance at Mumbai Central or Kadamba's kiosks on the north side of Azad Maidan, near St Xavier's College (just up from CST station). Quite a few **private overnight buses** (around a dozen daily) also run to Goa, costing from around Rs275/450 (low/high season) for no-frills buses to Rs750/850 for swisher a/c Volvo coaches with berths (which bizarrely you may have to share). Tickets should be booked at least a day in advance through a reputable travel agent (see p.151), or direct through the bus company. The largest operator for Goa is Paulo Travels (ⓦ www.paulotravels.com).

Southern Maharashtra

The southern part of **Maharashtra**, dividing Mumbai and Goa, ranks among the areas of the country least explored by outsiders. Yet its scattered towns and cities hold plenty of traditional Maharashtrian character, and the landscape – a mix of rugged, table-top hills and palm-fringed coast, cut by countless rivers and estuaries – is as diverse as any in South India.

Until the mid-nineteenth century, this was the homeland of the **Maratha** warlords, who at the peak of their power in the 1700s ruled over a vast swath of the Subcontinent – from the foothills of the Himalayas to the southernmost fringes of the Deccan Plateau – and were a thorn in the southern flank of successive Mughal emperors. It wasn't until the British subjugated them in the Battle of Khadki in 1817 that the rich volcanic soils of the Deccan could be opened up and a railway line built through the Sahyadri Hills, supplying the world with cotton when its main source was interrupted by the American Civil War.

Another dimension to the Pax Britannica peace dividend was that Bombay's overheated *burra-* and *memsahibs* could finally, after decades in fear of Maratha attacks, retreat to the relative comfort of the hills around the port, where the resort of **Matheran** was established on top of a 900-metre plateau. Connected to the main line via a wonderful **narrow-gauge railway,** the hill station and its toy trains still function in much the same gentle fashion as they have for over a century: road traffic is banned and the main attractions remain the fresh air, fragrant woodland and panoramic views.

The same route used to transport cotton though the Sahyadri Hills was recently upgraded with an eight-lane expressway and super-fast electrified railway line. But the corridor has served as a key trade artery since ancient times. Dating from the first century BC, a string of magnificent **rock-cut caves** attest to its former prominence, and these archeological sites – dotted around the hill town of **Lonavala** – provide the main incentive to break the journey to **Pune**, the former Maratha capital and a booming, modern industrial centre. Some of the region's most awesome **forts** crown hilltops around the city, but its principal visitor attractions – a well-stocked museum and Peshwa palace – lie amid the streets of its atmospheric old town.

Maratha citadels also punctuate the journey south via the **Konkan Coast**, the most striking of them at **Murud-Janjira**, which rises seamlessly from the waves. Further south, **Ganpatipule** is the region's chief pilgrimage centre, where you can walk on miles of virtually deserted, palm-fringed beaches. By the time you reach **Kolhapur**, the main town in the far south of the state, famous for its temple and Raj-era maharaja's palace, Mumbai feels a world away. Pressing on from there to Goa, another recommended stop is the market town of **Sawantwadi**, where traditional Indian playing cards – *ganjifa* – are still painted by hand.

South via the Konkan Coast

Despite the recent appearance of a string of upscale resorts pitched at wealthy urbanites, the coast stretching south from Mumbai, known as the **Konkan**, remains relatively unspoilt. Empty beaches, backed by casuarina and areca trees and coconut plantations, regularly slip in and out of view, framed by the distant Ghats, while little fortified towns preserve a distinct coastal culture, with its own dialect of Marathi and fiery cuisine. The number of rivers and estuaries slicing the coast meant that for years this little-explored area was difficult to navigate, but the Konkan railway, which winds inland between Mumbai and Kerala via Goa, now renders it easily accessible.

Murud-Janjira

The first place to warrant a break in the journey south down the Konkan is the quiet port of **MURUD-JANJIRA**, 165km from Mumbai. A traditional trade centre formerly belonging to the Siddis of Janjira, the region's ruling dynasty, it still retains plenty of attractive wood-built houses, some brightly painted and fronted by pillared verandas. The gently shelving beach is wide and safe for swimming, though the sand is cleaner and softer 3km north in **Kashid**.

Five kilometres south of Murud, an imposing sixteenth-century **fort**, built on an island in the river at **Janjira**, was one of the few the Marathas failed to penetrate. You can get to it by local *hodka* boat (around Rs15 return) from **Rajpuri jetty** (reachable by auto-rickshaw); boats run throughout the day, but will only depart once they're full – which rarely takes long on weekends, but can involve frustrating waits if you're here during the week. Although most of its interior is overgrown and derelict, the fort is ringed by impressive battlements that can be still be encircled on foot, giving fine views of the bay and surrounding countryside.

Practicalities

The nearest railhead to Murud is Roha, a two-hour bus ride away, which is why most travellers still reach the town by jumping on one of the hydrofoil catamarans or regular diesel launches from the Gateway of India in Mumbai to **Mandawa**, on the southern side of the harbour. Buses meet the boats and shuttle passengers straight to **Alibag**, from where you can catch regular government buses to Murud. Most direct services from Mumbai Central take six hours; there are also two faster ASIAD services (5.45am & 11am; 4hr 30min), which must be booked in advance. Don't jump out prematurely at the inland bus stand but continue to Murud's main street, Durbar Road, parallel to the coast, where you'll find the tiny post office, covered market and a handful of basic restaurants.

The best of the **accommodation** is also lined up along Durbar Road. Slap on the sands, the *Golden Swan Resort* (T02144/274078, W www.goldenswan .com; 6–9) sits on the edge of town and is the most comfortable option, with smart a/c chalets and less appealing non-a/c rooms in an older colonial-style block, all with TVs, plus a restaurant serving local Malvani cuisine. Opposite is the newer *Club Leisure Shoreline* (T02144/274640; 5–7), which has more recently fitted rooms and lower tariffs. Further north up Durbar Road, the *Mirage Holiday Homes* (T02144/276744; 5–6) occupies an attractive period building, with more character than the competition. The *Nest Bamboo House* (T02144/276144; 4), which has simple palm-thatch and bamboo huts fitted with beds, lights and fans, is the only commendable budget option.

All of these places serve food, but there is no shortage of regular, clean and inexpensive local **eating options** on Durbar Road, including the *Anand Vatika*, south of the chowk, which serves South Indian veg snacks and fuller North Indian meals in a shady garden, and the *Hotel Vinayak*, whose menu is more extensive in theory than practice. In addition, a row of seafront stalls south of the chowk dish up tasty seafood and veg snacks.

Ganpatipule

Some 215km south of Marud-Janjira lies the Konkan coast's other worthwhile stopover, **GANPATIPULE**, a tiny village with a long, golden sandy beach and a very fine **Ganpati temple**. Although attracting thousands of Indian pilgrims each year, this sleepy place sees relatively few foreign visitors, with most of the tourists being honeymooners from Mumbai. The temple is built around a Ganapati *omnar*, a naturally formed – though not strictly accurate – "image" of the elephant god.

Accommodation is available at the lacklustre MTDC *Resort* (☎02357/235248, ⓕ235328; ④–⑤), which offers a choice between standard non-a/c rooms in its main block and pricier a/c cottages; there are also cheaper beds under canvas in its *Tent Resort* (same phone; ③) – all a stone's throw from the beach. Two cheaper options, both on the approach road to the beach and offering good discounts out of season, are the *Shri Ganesh Kripa* (☎02357/235229; ③–④), with basic attached rooms, and the *Shreesagar* (☎02357/235145; ④), which has clean, compact doubles with TV. For **food**, there's decent Nepalese cooking at the MTDC *Resort*, a Punjabi menu at the *Shri Ganesh Kripa*, or *dhabas* at the bottom of the village towards the main road.

To get to Ganpatipule, either make your way to Ratnagiri (on the Konkan railway and well connected by state and private buses) and take a local bus (10 daily; 1hr–1hr 30min) the last 32km, or take one of the direct MSRTC services from Mumbai, Pune or Kolhapur. All the buses stop outside the MTDC *Resort*.

Matheran

The little hill station of **MATHERAN**, 108km east of Mumbai, is set on a narrow north–south ridge, at an altitude of 800m in the Sahyadri Range. From viewpoints with such names as Porcupine, Monkey and Echo, at the edge of sheer cliffs that plunge into deep ravines, you can see way across the hazy plains – on a good day, so they say, as far as Mumbai. The town itself, shrouded in thick mist for much of the year, has, for the moment, one unique attribute: all motorized vehicles are prohibited. That, added to the journey up, on a **miniature train** that chugs its way through spectacular scenery to the crest of the hill, gives the town an agreeably quaint, time-warped feel.

Matheran (literally "mother forest") has been a popular retreat from the heat of Mumbai since the nineteenth century. These days, however, few foreign visitors venture up here, and those that do only hang around for a couple of days, to kill time before a flight or to sample some of India's most charming colonial-style hotels. There's really nothing much to do other than relax, explore the woods on foot or horseback, and enjoy the fresh air and views.

The tourist season lasts from mid-September to mid-June (at other times it's raining or misty), and is at its most hectic between November and January, in April and May, and on most weekends, when droves of young couples pour in from the city. After consuming huge quantities of sugar, in many and various forms, most spend the afternoons careering wildly around town on horseback, more often than not in peculiar headgear and shouting at the tops of their voices.

As the crow flies, Matheran is only 6.5km from Neral on the plain below, but the train climbs up on 21km of track with no fewer than 281 curves, said to be among the sharpest on any railway in the world. After 1907, the demanding haul was handled by four complex steam engines, but sadly they puffed their last in 1980 and were replaced by cast-off diesels from Darjeeling, Shimla and Ooty. The two-hour train ride is a treat, especially if you get a window seat, but be prepared for a squash and hard benches.

In 1974, the All India Rail Strike cut Matheran off. To combat the situation, the track from Neral was made passable for Jeeps and finally in 1984 was sealed up to **Dasturi Naka**, 2.5km from the town, though any attempts to extend it through the town have been thwarted by the encouragingly eco-friendly local

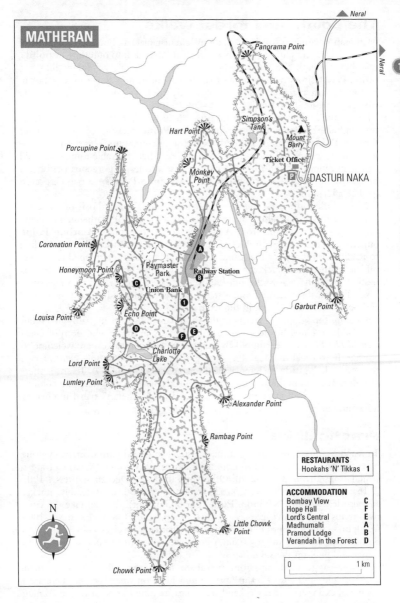

MATHERAN

Neral

Panorama Point

Simpson's Tank

Hart Point

Mount Barry

Ticket Office

Porcupine Point

Monkey Point

DASTURI NAKA

Coronation Point

Paymaster Park

Railway Station

Honeymoon Point

Union Bank

Garbut Point

Louisa Point

Echo Point

Lord Point

Charlotte Lake

Lumley Point

Alexander Point

Rambag Point

RESTAURANTS
Hookahs 'N' Tikkas   1

ACCOMMODATION
Bombay View	C
Hope Hall	F
Lord's Central	E
Madhumalti	A
Pramod Lodge	B
Verandah in the Forest	D

N

Little Chowk Point

0   1 km

Chowk Point

authorities. At the time of our last research trip, with the railway line closed pending repair work after much of it had been destroyed by a particularly heavy monsoon, Dasturi Naka was as far as you could travel by motorized transport. Work on resurrecting the line has proceeded at a fast pace, and it should be up and running again by the winter of 2007–08, but you'd do well to check beforehand.

The points and forest walks

Matheran occupies a long, narrow, semi-circular plateau, bounded for most of its extent by sheer cliffs. These taper at regular intervals into outcrops, or **points**, revealing through the tree canopy wonderful panoramas of distant hills and plains. Few visitors manage more than half a dozen in a single outing, but in midwinter when temperatures are pleasantly cool, it's possible to tick off the majority in a long day's trek.

For a quick taster, head south from the main bazaar past *Lord's Central Hotel* on Matheran's eastern flank to **Alexander Point**, pressing on beyond it to **Chowk Point** – the most southerly of the mountain's spurs. This shouldn't take more than a couple of hours there and back. Another enjoyable route on an old cart track winds around the western rim, past a series of gorgeous British-era bungalows to **Louisa**, **Coronation** and **Porcupine Points** – a trip best saved for late afternoon.

With a little more time and energy – and a reasonably solid pair of trainers – you could also wander along the spectacular eastern spur of Matheran mountain, visible across the ravine from Alexander Point, to exposed **Garbut Point**. Superb views extend in all directions from the length of the ridge top leading to it; allow a full day for the round trip. In addition, steeper, stepped paths peel off the main orbital track at various junctions to the red-tiled **tribal villages** nestled on bluffs below the hill station, and these too make enjoyable short hikes. The most frequented routes start just beyond Alexander Point in the east and near Coronation Point in the west.

Accurate topographical **maps** of the mountain and its many paths are all but impossible to come by, although hanging proudly in the dining room of *Lord's Central Hotel* is a wonderful old British-era one, which walkers are welcome to consult. If you feel the need for more guidance than our simple plan offers, a recommended **guide** is Terence de Lima (☏m94233 67739). Terence offers customized walks in the area showcasing the cream of local scenery and colonial architecture, as well as engaging background on Matheran's tribal minorities, flora and fauna.

Practicalities

To reach Matheran by **train**, you must first get to **Neral Junction**, easily done by taking the hourly suburban train from **Mumbai** (CST or Dadar) to Kargat, which stops there (2hr 15min). Otherwise, the daily Deccan Express #1007 (7.15am) or Sahyadri Express #1023 (5.50pm) are both considerably quicker and also leave from CST. From **Pune** (2hr 30min–3hr), you can take the same two trains – Sahyadri Express #1024 (7am) and Deccan Express #1008 (3.30pm) – in the opposite direction. Note that later services going both ways do not connect with the toy train. A good alternative from Pune is to travel to Karjat and pick up the suburban service to Mumbai.

Narrow-gauge trains up from **Neral** to **Matheran** (2hr) depart at 9am, 10.45am and 5pm (also 7.30am April to mid-June) on weekdays and there are a couple of extra services at weekends. All trains are timed to tie in with incoming mainline services, so don't worry about missing a connection if the train you're on is delayed – the toy train service should wait. Matheran **station** is in the centre of town on MG Road, which runs roughly north–south. Leaving town, there is a little halt on the miniature railway near the Dasturi Naka taxi stand, but, unless you've already booked a seat, you won't be allowed on.

All **motor transport**, including shared taxis and minibuses from Neral (Rs50 per person, Rs250 for car), parks at the taxi stand next to the MTDC

Holiday Camp at **Dasturi Naka**. From here you can walk with a porter (Rs50–60), be led by horse (Rs80–100), or take a hand-pulled rickshaw (Rs120–150) – now the only place left in India where such rickshaws are officially permitted. If you're happy to carry your own bags, follow the rail tracks, which cut straight to the middle of Matheran, rather than the more convoluted dirt road. However you arrive, you must pay a **toll** (Rs25) to enter the town, valid for your entire stay.

To **change money**, the Union Bank near the station can cash traveller's cheques only but the rates are poor; the larger hotels accept credit cards.

Accommodation and eating

Matheran has plenty of **hotels**, though few could be termed cheap. Most are close to the railway station on MG Road and on the road behind it, Kasturba Bhavan. Reduced rates of up to fifty percent often apply to midweek or long stays, and during the rainy off-season (when many places close down). Note that 10am or 11am checkouts are standard. Virtually all the hotels provide **full** or **half board** at reasonable rates, but if you want to eat out, or are on a tight budget, try one of the numerous thali joints around the station or tasty kebab and tikka dishes at *Hookahs' N' Tikkas*, also on MG Road.

Bombay View north Matheran, southwest of Paymaster Park ☎ 95 2148 230453. Housed in a huge converted colonial-era mansion, this place is the best budget option in town; it's a notch pricier than the more basic places down by the station, but well worth the extra. Most of its rooms are enormous, with high ceilings, sit-outs and forest or garden views. Veg meals are served in an atmospheric old dining hall, complete with original vaulted stone arches, to the rear, and the staff are friendly and helpful. Advance booking recommended on weekends. ❸–❹

Hope Hall MG Rd ☎ 95 2148 230253, opposite *Lord's Central*. Decent-sized, clean, attached rooms arranged around a secluded yard with badminton and table tennis, at the quiet end of town. Run by friendly brother–sister duo. Among the few commendable budget options this close to the station. ❹

Lord's Central MG Rd ☎ 95 2148 230228, ⓦ www.matheran.com. With its verandas, brown-painted woodwork, plaid blankets and friendly spaniel, *Lord's* is the kind of place you imagine the Famous Five might have spent their

△ *The Verandah in the Forest*, Matheran

holidays in the 1930s – locked in a dowdy pre-Independence time-warp, it'll appeal to Rajophiles and homesick Brits. Though it does boast spectacular views from its lovely garden (where they've recently installed a pool), it definitely lacks the elegance of the *Verandah in the Forest*. Full-board only (Rs1400–2000 per night; thirty percent discounts for stays of two nights or more); booking recommended. **❻**

Madhumalti Just north of railway station ☎95 2148 230144. Basic lodge close to the station with attached rooms among the enclave just below the tracks. Nothing special, but acceptably clean and handy if you're lugging your baggage around. **❸**

Pramod Lodge Just south of the railway station ☎95 2148 230144. This is where all the porters and touts will try to take you, because it hands out commission. The rooms aren't as well maintained

as the *Madhumalti's*, but would do as a fallback option for a night. **❸**

🏃 **The Verandah in the Forest** 2km southwest of station ☎95 2148 230296, ⓦwww.neemranahotels.com. Set in woods a short way above Charlotte Lake, this sumptuously restored nineteenth-century bungalow, part of the marvellous Neemrana heritage chain, is reason enough to come to Matheran. Apart from the evocative period decor and furnishings, its greatest asset is a huge west-facing veranda smothered in foliage – one of the most perfect spots in India for afternoon tea and biscuits (though if you eat here beware of the pilfering monkeys). Rooms are reasonably priced (Rs2000–4500/2500–5000 weekdays/weekends). The one catch is they're not officially allowed to serve food. **❽–❾**

Lonavala and around

Just thirty years ago, the town of **LONAVALA**, 110km southeast of Mumbai and 62km northwest of Pune, was a quiet retreat in the Sahyadri Hills. Since then, the place has mushroomed to cope with hordes of holiday-makers and second-home owners from the state capital, and is now only of interest as a base for the magnificent **Buddhist caves** of **Karla**, **Bhaja** and **Bedsa**, some of which date from the Satavahana period (second century BC).

Frequent buses arrive at Lonavala's central **bus stand**, just off the old Mumbai–Pune Road, but the train is infinitely preferable. Lonavala is on the main railway line between Mumbai (3hr) and Pune (1hr 30min), and most express trains stop here. The **railway station** is on the south side of town, a ten-minute walk from the bus stand area; take the path right at the end of platform 1 to get there. With a car, or by taking an early train, it's just about possible to take in the caves as a day-trip from Mumbai, but it's better to allow yourself a full day to get around.

Several of the banks around town have **ATMs**, though none have foreign exchange facilities. There's a small Internet café, Balaji's, on the road running south from the railway station (Rs40/hr).

Accommodation

With a couple of exceptions, Lonavala's limited **accommodation** offers poor value, mainly because demand well outstrips supply for much of the year. Rates drop between October and March, and for longer stays, and you can expect reductions on weekdays. But this isn't somewhere you're likely to want to unpack your bags.

Adarsh Behind the bus stand on Shivaji Rd ☎02114/272353. Clean a/c and non-a/c rooms, some overlooking a central courtyard. Best fallback in this bracket if the *Chandralok* has no vacancies. **❻–❼**

Chandralok Opposite the bus stand on Shivaji Rd ☎02114/272294, ⓦwww.hotelchandralok.net. Set

back from the market street, this well-run mid-range place has good-sized, well-aired, modern rooms with shiny ceramic tiled floors, plus a quality thali restaurant at ground level. **❺**

🏃 **Ferreira Resort** D Shahani Rd, Ward C, near Telephone Exchange, a 5min rickshaw ride from the train and bus stands

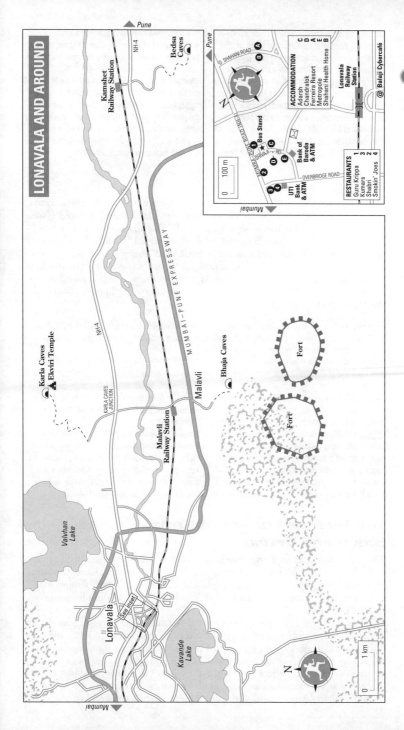

LONAVALA AND AROUND

Pune
Bedsa Caves
Kamshet Railway Station
NH-4
Karla Caves
Ekviri Temple
KARLA CAVES JUNCTION
NH-4
Valvhan Lake
Lonavala
See inset
Kavande Lake
MUMBAI–PUNE EXPRESSWAY
Malavli
Malavli Railway Station
Bhaja Caves
Fort
Fort
Mumbai
N
0   1 km

Inset

Pune
D. SHAHANI ROAD
B
A
N
Bus Stand
D
C
E
RD
Bank of Baroda & ATM
UTI Bank & ATM
OVERBRIDGE ROAD
Lonavala Railway Station
Mumbai
0   100 m
@ Balaji Cybercafé

ACCOMMODATION
Adarsh   C
Chandralok   D
Ferreira Resort   A
Metropole   E
Shahani Health Home   B

RESTAURANTS
Guru Krippa   1
Kumars   3
Shabri   2
Smokin' Joes   4

☎02114/272689. The one budget place worthy of mention: a pleasantly old-fashioned place, in homely cream colours with flaking blue-plaster ceilings, run by a hospitable Goan lady. Located down a quiet suburban backstreet, its rooms are all attached, peaceful and clean, and have little balconies opening onto a leafy rear plot. A much more appealing option than the fancier places in the centre of town, and it usually has vacancies. **❹**
The Metropole Close to the bus stand on Shivaji Rd ☎02114/273808, ⓦwww.hotelthemetropole.com.

This smart new four-star is Lonavala's most comfortable option, boasting central a/c and modern furnishings, as well as a rooftop pool and ersatz "Punjabi-dhaba" restaurant. **❼–❽**
Shahani Health Home D Shahani Rd, 5min rickshaw ride east of the railway station ☎02114/272784, ⓜm93260 28440. A quirky not-for-profit place offering 62 large rooms in a worn, rather institutional block on the quiet edge of town; worth trying if the *Ferreira Resort* opposite is full, but not nearly as congenial. **❸–❹**

Eating

Most of Lonavala's hotels lay on full board or have serviceable **restaurants**, but you'll eat fresher food in places along the main Mumbai–Pune Road, which cater more for the brisk through trade. The town also holds a bewildering number of shops selling the local sweet speciality, **chikki** – a moreish amalgam of dried fruit and nuts set in rock-solid honey toffee. *Super Chikki* on the main street allows you to sample the many varieties before you buy. Their main competitor, *National Chikki*, further down, is also recommended; this is also the best place to stock up on delicious deep-fried nibbles (*namkeen*), the other local speciality.

Guru Krippa Mumbai–Pune Rd. Sparkling, clean pure veg joint on the main street: piping-hot South Indian snacks, cheese toasties, and inexpensive thalis with Chinese and Punjabi main meals. Also a good selection of ice creams, kulfi and full-on *faloodas*.

🏃 Kumars Mumbai–Pune Rd. A big, bustling place with surreal English-country-house-theme murals that gets packed on weekends for its great Mughlai and tandoori specialities: try the delicious *murg handi* (boneless chicken pieces slow cooked in a traditional, spicy, creamy gravies, mopped up with hot naan bread. Most dishes come in shiny copper *karahis*, snappily served by waiters in black ties and baggy tartan waistcoats. They

also do cold beers, and terrific mixed dry-fruit and rose-flavoured lassis. Count on Rs200–250 per head.
Shabri *Hotel Rama Krishna*, Mumbai–Pune Rd. Along with *Kumars*, this is the well-heeled Mumbaikars' favourite, serving a wide range of North and South Indian dishes, and chilled beer, in a large, busy ground-floor dining hall. Most mains under Rs150.
Smokin' Joes Overbridge Rd, just off the main Mumbai–Pune Rd. A huge range of freshly baked pizzas, from Rs85 to Rs300 (depending on size and toppings), served up on modern wood tables in a snug a/c restaurant with big glass windows. They also do take-outs: ☎02114/277744.

The Buddhist caves of Karla, Bhaja and Bedsa

The three cave sites of **Karla**, **Bhaja** and **Bedsa** comprise some of the finest rock-cut architecture in the northwest of the Deccan region. Though not on nearly such an impressive scale as Ajanta and Ellora, India's most famous rock-cut sites in the north of Maharashtra, they harbour some beautifully preserved ancient sculpture.

The three sites lie some way from each other, all to the east of Lonavala. As Karla contains the most spectacular sculpture, it's best left until last. Covering Karla and Bhaja under your own steam by bus and/or train is manageable in a day, if you are prepared for a good walk, but if you want to get out to Bedsa, too, the easiest option is to rent an **auto–rickshaw** (around Rs300–400) or **car** (Rs600–700 for 4hr) for the tour, both of which can usually be found at Lonavala railway station. Finally, it's a good idea to **avoid weekends** if you want to enjoy the caves in peace and quiet; Karla, in particular, gets swamped with noisy day-trippers.

Bhaja

The eighteen **caves** (daily 8.30am–6pm; $2 [Rs10]) at **BHAJA** lie 1.5km from the village of Malavli, to which hourly passenger trains run from Lonavala, 9km west. To reach the caves, follow a path up from the village square near the railway station.

The excavations are among the oldest in India, dating from the late second to early first century BC, during the earliest, Hinayana, phase of Buddhism. Most consist of simple halls – *viharas* – with adjoining cells that contain plain shelf-like beds; many are fronted by rough verandas. Bhaja's apsidal *chaitya* hall, **Cave 12**, which contains a stupa but no figures, has 27 plain bevelled pillars which lean inwards, mimicking the style of wooden buildings. Sockets in the stone of the exterior arch reveal that it once contained a wooden gate or facade. Further south, the last cave, **Cave 19**, a *vihara*, is decorated with superb carvings. Mysteriously, scholars identify the figures as the Hindu gods, **Surya** and **Indra**, who figure prominently in the Rig Veda (c. 1000 BC).

Karla

KARLA (also Karli) is 11km from Lonavala and 3km north of **Karla Caves Junction** on the Mumbai–Pune Road. Take any bus or tempo (six- or eight-seat rickshaws) to the junction (from where it's a Rs30 rickshaw ride), or there are five daily direct **buses** (6am, 9am, 12.30pm, 3pm & 6.30pm) from Lonavala, with the last bus returning from Karla at 6.30pm.

The rock-cut Buddhist **chaitya** hall at Karla (daily 8.30am–6pm; $2 [Rs10]), reached by steep steps that climb 110m, is the largest and best preserved in India, dating from the first century AD. As you approach across a large courtyard, itself hewn from the rock, the enormous fourteen-metre-high facade of the hall towers above, topped by a horseshoe-shaped window and with three entrances below, one for the priest and the others for devotees. To the left of the entrance stands a *simhas stambha*, a tall column capped with four lions. On the right is a Hindu shrine to **Ekviri**, a goddess-oracle revered by Koli fishing communities, for whom Karla is a popular weekend day-trip destination (which explains the number of puja offering stalls and opportunistic political posters lining the steps).

In the porch of the cave, dividing the three doorways, are panels of figures in six couples, presumed to have been the wealthy patrons of the hall. With their expressive faces and sensuous bodies, it's hard to believe these figures were carved around 2000 years ago. Two rows of octagonal columns with pot-shaped bases divide the interior into three, forming a wide central aisle and, on the outside, a hall that allowed devotees to circumambulate the monolithic stupa at the back. Above each pillar's fluted capital kneels a finely carved elephant mounted by two riders, one with arms draped over the other's shoulders. Amazingly, perishable remnants survive from the time when the hall was in use.

Bedsa

It's quite possible that you won't encounter anyone else when visiting the caves at **BEDSA** (daily 8.30am–6pm; $2 [Rs10]), which is one of its great attractions. Once you reach the village, 12km beyond Bhaja on the NH-4, or a three-kilometre bus ride from Kamshet, the nearest railway station, you'll have to ask the way to the unsigned path. The village kids hanging around might scramble up the steep hillside with you, for a fee.

Bedsa's *chaitya* hall, excavated later than that at Karla, is far less sophisticated. The entrance is extremely narrow, leading from a porch that appears to be supported, though of course it is not, by four octagonal pillars more than 7m high, with pot-shaped bases and bell capitals; bulls, horses and elephants rest on inverted, stepped slabs on top. Inside, 26 plain octagonal columns lead to an unadorned monolithic stupa.

Pune (Poona)

At an altitude of 598m, **PUNE**, Maharashtra's second largest city, lies close to the Western Ghat mountains (known here as the Sahyadri Hills), on the edge of the Deccan plains as they stretch away to the east. Capital of the Marathas' sovereign state in the sixteenth century, Pune was – thanks to its cool, dry climate – chosen by the British in 1820 as an alternative headquarters for the Bombay Presidency. Their military cantonment in the northwest of town is still used by the Indian army, and a number of British buildings, such as the Council

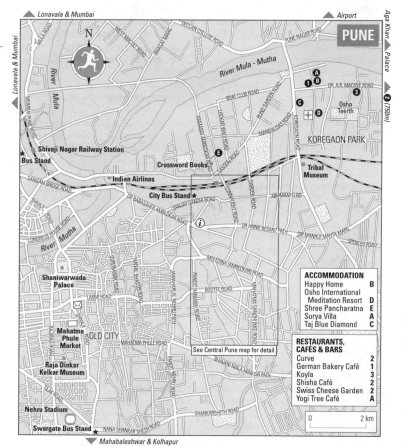

Hall and Deccan College, survive. Since colonial days, Pune has continued to develop as a major industrial city and now ranks along with Hyderabad, Bengaluru (Bangalore) and Chennai as one of South India's fastest growing business centres, with booming software, back-office and call-centre sectors. Signs of the new prosperity abound, from huge hoardings advertising multistorey executive apartment blocks and gated estates, to cappuccino bars, air-conditioned malls and hip clothes stores.

The full-on traffic and ultra-Westernized city centre may come as a shock if all you know about Pune is its connection with India's famously laid-back, New Age guru, Bhagwan Rajneesh, or **Osho** (1931–90). The spiritual teacher founded his ashram in the leafy suburb of Koregaon Park in 1974 and, although its activities nowadays generate a lot less publicity than they did during Rajneesh's lifetime, the centre continues to attract followers from all over the world.

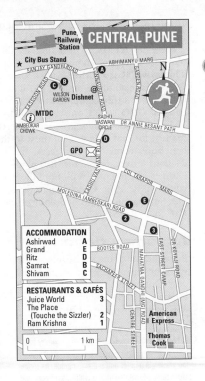

Pune's other main claim to spiritual fame is the presence on its outskirts of *yogacharya* **BKS Iyengar**'s illustrious yoga centre – a far more sober and serious institution than the Osho ashram (see Basics, p.74).

Arrival and information

From Pune's Lohagaon **airport**, 10km northeast of the centre, prepaid taxis (around Rs200) and auto-rickshaws (Rs100–150) take between fifteen and thirty minutes to reach the centre, depending on the traffic. Pune is an important staging point on southern express-train routes from Mumbai (3hr 30min–4hr 30min); the main **railway station** is in the centre of town, south of the river.

There are three main **bus stands**: the **City** bus stand, next to the railway station, is split into two sections, one serving Pune itself (with signs and timetables only in Marathi), the other for destinations south and west, including Goa, Lonavala and Mumbai. **Swargate Bus Stand**, about 5km south, close to Nehru Stadium, services Karnataka and some of the same destinations as City, while the stand next to **Shivaji Nagar** railway station, 3km west of the centre, runs buses to towns in the north. To establish which station you require for your destination, ask at the enquiries hatch of the City bus stand.

Another source of travel information is the **MTDC Tourist Office** (Mon–Sat 10am–5.30pm; ☎0212/2612 6867, ℻2611 9434), inside "I" block of Central Building (enter between Ambedkar Chowk and Sadhu Vaswani Circle). They also have an **information counter** (allegedly Mon–Fri 10am–6pm, Sat

10am–1pm; closed second & fourth Sat of month) opposite the railway station's first-class booking office.

There are **ATMs** all over the city these days. For **changing currency** or traveller's cheques, Thomas Cook is at 13 Thacker House, just off General Thimmaya Road (Mon–Sat 9.30am–6pm; ☎0212/613 8188); American Express have an office on MG Road next to the prominent *Aurora Towers* hotel (Mon–Fri 9.30am–6.30pm, Sat 9.30am–2.30pm; ☎0212/2605 5337). The very efficient **GPO** is on Connaught Road.

Manney's Booksellers, at 7 Moledina Rd, Clover Centre, and Crossword, on the first floor of Sohrab Hall (next to the *Hotel Shree Panchratna*), are the city's best **bookstores**. You can access the **Internet** in many places, including a 24-hour cybercafé on the first floor of the railway station (Rs30/hr), and Dishnet, five minutes' walk from the station on Connaught Road (Rs30/hr). If you're up near the Osho Ashram in Koregaon Park, the best option is Zorba Net Surfing, on the ground floor of the *Hotel Surya Villa*, next to the *Yogi Tree Café* (only Rs15/hr).

Accommodation

Pune is short of decent **hotels** across the scale, which explains why, in keeping with most big cities, prices are high for what you get and vacancies like gold dust. Options are especially limited at the bottom of the range, where advance booking is all but essential. For information on staying at the *Osho International Meditation Resort*, see p.170.

Ashirwad 16 Connaught Rd ☎020/2612 8585, ✉hotelashir@vsnl.com. Despite its proximity to a busy main road, this newish business hotel near the station is a quiet and relaxing choice. Its rooms are well aired, with sparkling white tiled floors and good-sized bathrooms. Ask for one to the rear, which will be less prone to traffic noise. There's a popular veg restaurant on the ground floor, and exchange and travel desks. ❻

Grand near Dr Ambedkar statue at the top of MG Rd ☎020/2636 0728. This colonial-era building, set behind a dimly lit beer garden, used to be most budget travellers' first choice, but it's gone drastically downhill in recent years. Despite the decrepit plumbing and overall shabbiness, the doubles in the rear annexe are bearable for a night or two, but forget the stinky wood-partitioned, bathroom-less singles off reception. ❹

🏃 **Happy Home** 294 Koregaon Park ☎020/2612 2933, ✉happyhomehostel @yahoo.co.im. Pune's nicest budget guest house: far more salubrious, better scrubbed, friendlier and more pleasant than anywhere else in its price bracket, *Happy Home* occupies a modern tenement in a surburban backstreet near the ashram – an area dominated by foreign Osho-ites. The rooms are all clean, have attached bathrooms and small balconies. Discounts for stays of more than two days. ❸–❹

Ritz Connaught Rd ☎020/2612 2995, ✉ritzinternationalhotel@vsnl.com. British-era

place, insensitively revamped with swish marble motel interiors and prices to match – a far cry from the "Heritage Hotel" it claims to be and way overpriced, but comfortable enough. Tariffs include full board – plus they run a renowned Gujarati thali restaurant in the rear courtyard. ❽

🏃 **Samrat** 17 Wilson Garden ☎020/2613 7964, ✉thesamrathotel@vsnl.com. Smart, centrally air-conditioned tower block, with large, spotless rooms in galleries opening onto a central atrium. It's tucked away down a hidden backstreet a stone's throw from the railway station, but easy to find and offers superb value by Pune standards. Complimentary pick up from the airport or railway station with advance warning. Room rates include buffet breakfast. ❼

Shivam 12 Wilson Garden ☎020/2613 7593, ⓕ2605 3472. Opposite the railway station, a lot less appealing inside that its spruce exterior suggests, but clean enough for a short stay, and the beds have good thick mattresses. Some a/c available. ❺–❻

Shree Panchratna 7 Tadiwala Rd ☎020/2605 9999, ⓦwww.hotelshreepanchratna.in. Plain but well-maintained and efficient business hotel close to the railway station, down a quiet side street. The rooms are all a/c, bright, fresh and simply furnished, with shining tiled floors, small balconies and WiFi-enabled desks. ❻

Surya Villa 284/1 Koregaon Park ☎020/2612 4501. Good-sized, attractively furnished rooms spread over four floors in a peaceful suburban block close to the Osho ashram. It's popular mainly with long-staying, foreign ashram-ites. Not such a good deal as the nearby *Happy Home*, but one of the city's most pleasant mid-scale guesthouses. ⑤–⑥

Taj Blue Diamond 11 Koregaon Rd ☏020/2612 5555, ⓦwww.tajhotels.com. 2km northeast of the railway station near the Osho ashram. Pune's top business hotel offering the usual five-star facilities, including Indian and Thai restaurants, 24hr coffee shop, swimming pool, and shops. ⑨

The City

Pune's centre is bordered to the north by the **River Mula** and to the west by the **River Mutha** – the two join in the northwest to form the Mutha-Mula, at Sangam Bridge. The principal shopping area, and the greatest concentration of restaurants and hotels, is in the streets south of the railway station, particularly Connaught and, further south, **MG Road**. The old Peshwa part of town, by far the most interesting to explore, is towards the west between the fortified **Shaniwarwada Palace** and fascinating **Raja Dinkar Kelkar Museum**; old wooden *wadas* – palatial city homes – survive on these narrow, busy streets, and the Victorian, circular **Mahatma Phule Market** is always a hive of activity.

Raja Dinkar Kelkar Museum

Dinkar Gangadhar Kelkar (1896–1990), aside from being a celebrated Marathi poet published under the name Adnyatwass, spent much of his life travelling and collecting arts and crafts from all over the country. In 1975, he donated his collection to the Maharashtrian government for the creation of a museum dedicated to the memory of his son, Raja, who had died at the age of 12. Housed in a huge old-town mansion, the **Raja Dinkar Kelkar Museum** (daily 9.30am–6pm; Rs150 [Rs20]) on 1378 Shukrawar Peth (buses #72 or #74 from the railway station to Mahatma Phule Market), is a wonderful pot-pourri in which beauty and interest is found in both artistic and everyday objects. Paraphernalia associated with paan, the Indian passion, includes containers in every conceivable design, made from silk, wood, brass and silver: some mimic animals or fish, or are egg-shaped and in delicate filigree; others are solid, heavy-duty boxes built to withstand constant use. Also on show are musical instruments, superb Marathi textiles and costumes, toys, domestic shrines and furniture, beauty accessories and a model of Shaniwarwada Palace.

Shaniwarwada Palace

In the centre of the oldest part of town, only the imposing high walls of the **Shaniwarwada Palace** (daily 8am–noon & 2–6pm; $2 [Rs10]) survived three fires in the eighteenth and nineteenth centuries. Founded by the Peshwa ruler Bajrao I in 1730 and the chief residence of the Peshwas until the British arrived in 1817, the building has little to excite interest today, though there's a daily **sound and light** show in English (7pm; Rs100). The entrance is through the Delhi gate on the north side, one of five set into the perimeter wall, whose huge teak doors come complete with nasty elephant-proof spikes. The interior of the palace is now grassed over, the seven-storey building entirely absent. Only one of the guides, usually available in the afternoons, speaks English. Bus #3 runs the 2km southwest from the railway station to the palace.

Aga Khan Palace and Gandhi Memorial

In 1942, Mahatma Gandhi, his wife Kasturba and other key figures of the freedom movement were interned at the **Aga Khan Palace** (daily 9am–5.30pm; Rs100 [Rs5]), which is set in quiet leafy gardens across the River Mula, 5km northeast of the centre (buses #1, #158 & #156). The Aga Khan donated the palace to the state in 1969, and it is now a small Gandhi museum, typical of many all over India, with captioned photos and simple rooms unchanged since they were occupied by the freedom fighters. A **memorial** behind the house commemorates Kasturba, who died during their imprisonment. A small *khadi* shop sells hand-loomed cloth and products made by village cooperatives.

Tribal Museum

The Tribal Research and Training Institute, which runs the **Tribal Museum** on Koregaon Road (Mon–Sat 10am–5pm; free), 2km east of the railway station, is dedicated to the protection and documentation of Maharashtra's numerous tribal groups, such as the Wagdheo, Bahiram, Danteshwari and Marai, who number more than five million. The museum's faded photos, costumes and artefacts serve as an excellent introduction to this little-known world, but the highlights are the wonderful collections of dance masks and Worli wedding paintings. Talk to the director of the museum if you're interested in guided (but culturally sensitive) **tours** to tribal areas.

Osho International Meditation Resort

Pune is the headquarters of Bhagwan Rajneesh's avowedly nonreligious **Osho International Meditation Resort**, 17 Koregaon Park Rd (☎0212/2401 9999, ⓦwww.osho.com; see also box opposite), 2km east of the railway station. With a considerable daily income during peak season (Dec–March) and years of dedicated help from volunteers, the ashram has transformed its forty acres into a dreamy playground of cafés, marble walkways, swimming pools, saunas and clinics, with a shop selling Osho's enormous list of books, DVDs and CDs. The faithful have erected space-age, air-conditioned buildings, landscaped the gardens, bored tube wells for water, and planted trees, organic vegetable plots and groves of giant bamboo to improve air quality. Courses at its **Multiversity**, mostly one to three days in duration ($74–93 per day), are offered in a variety of New Age and traditional techniques. Forty-five-minute lunchtime demos are also available if you just want to dip your toe in. Osho's own brand of jargon still prevails; tennis, for example, is here played as Zennis, which helps you "get out of your body's way, bring the outer and the inner together" in "a unique synthesis of tennis and meditation". There are a host of other courses ranging from primal screaming to meditation techniques and more offbeat workshops with titles such "Zen For Billionaires", "Chakra Magic" and "A Taste of Inner Chocolate".

This ecofriendly bubble follows a strict door policy: visitors who wish to spend longer than the short **guided tours** (daily 9.15am & 2pm; book the day before 9.30am–1pm & 2–4pm; Rs10) must produce two passport photos and an HIV-negative certificate no less than thirty days old. If you don't have one and still want to stay there, you'll have to take an on-the-spot HIV test at the ashram clinic as part of your induction – the registration, HIV test and initial day-pass package costs Rs1280 for foreigners, after which it's Rs450 per day. You'll also need two robes (maroon for daywear, white for evenings), which cost Rs350 inside the ashram or Rs200 from stalls outside. If you want to actually stay inside the ashram, the smart *Osho Guest House* (☎020/6601 9900; ❽) offers stylish, minimalist, Zen rooms for Rs4200 a night – though be warned that the accommodation is situated above the main auditorium, which, as the ashram likes to put it, "can make the 6am Dynamic Meditation hard to resist".

The beautiful **gardens** laid out to the east of the main Osho complex, known as **Osho Teerth**, are open to the public (daily 6–9am & 3–6pm; admission free; no photography), and make a serene place for a stroll, with

Osho

It is nearly forty years since followers began to congregate around **Bhagwan Rajneesh**, the self-proclaimed New Age Guru better known to his tens of thousands of acolytes worldwide as simply **Osho.** Underpinned by a philosophical mishmash of Buddhism, Sufism, sexual liberationism, Tantric practices, Zen, yoga, hypnosis, Tibetan pulsing, disco and unabashed materialism, the first Rajneesh ashram was founded in Pune in 1974. It rapidly attracted droves of Westerners, and some Indians, who adopted new Sanskrit names and a uniform of orange or maroon cottons and a bead necklace (*mala*) with an attached photo of the enlightened guru, in classic style, sporting long greying hair and beard. This immediately identified the wearer as a *sannyasin* (borrowing from Shaivistic tradition, a renunciating mendicant who has attained a state of holiness).

Few early adherents denied that much of the attraction lay in Rajneesh's novel approach to fulfilment. His dismissal of Christianity ("Crosstianity") as a miserably oppressive obsession with guilt struck a chord with many, as did the espousal of liberation through sex. Rajneesh assured his devotees that material comfort was not to be shunned. Within a few years, satellite ashrams were popping up throughout Western Europe, and by 1980 an estimated 200,000 devotees had liberated themselves in six hundred meditation centres across eighty countries.

To protect itself from pollution, nuclear war and the AIDS virus, the organization poured money into a utopian project, **Rajneeshpuram**, on 64,000 acres of agricultural land in Oregon, USA. It was at this point that the tabloids and TV documentary teams really got interested in Rajneesh, now a multimillionaire. Infiltrators leaked stories of strange goings-on at Rajneeshpuram and before long its high-powered female executives became subject to police interest. Charges of tax evasion, drugs, fraud, arson and a conspiracy to poison several people in a neighbouring town to sway the vote in local elections provoked further sensation. Although he claimed to know nothing of this, Rajneesh pleaded guilty to breaches of US immigration laws and was deported in 1985. Following protracted attempts to resettle in 21 different countries, and now suffering complications of the chronic fatigue, ME, the Valium-addicted Rajneesh returned home to Pune, where he died in 1990, aged 59.

The ashram went through a period of internal squabbles and financial trouble in the 1990s. At his death, Rajneesh appointed an inner circle to manage the group, though several departed and the Osho "brand" – which sells around 4 million books each year, supplemented by CDs, DVDs, paintings and photos – is now controlled from Zurich and New York. The Pune ashram wasn't seeing enough of this to meet its costs and consequently has had to re-launch and re-style itself, changing both its name (from Osho Commune International to **Osho International Meditation Resort**) and the pattern of life inside its walls; whereas in its heyday an average stay was three to six months, today people typically stay no more than two weeks and few followers live on site. This has led to a labour shortage, with non-Osho locals brought in to keep the place afloat and, many long-standing devotees maintain, a dismantling of the sense of community that was the source of its attraction.

babbling streams, stands of giant bamboo, mature trees and Zen sculpture artfully placed amid the greenery.

Eating and drinking

Pune's affluent young things have money to burn these days, and new, innovative places to eat and drink open up every month to relieve them of their info-tech salaries. The largest concentration is up in Koregaon Park, where **ABC Farms**, a ten-minute rickshaw ride from the *Taj Blue Diamond*, encompasses

Moving on from Pune

Pune's prominence as a business capital means that it's well connected to towns and cities in southern India. However, demand for seats on planes, trains and buses far exceeds demand and you'd do well to book onward transport as soon as possible.

By air

Regular **flights** depart from Pune's Lohagaon airport for Mumbai, Bengaluru (Bangalore), Chennai, Goa and Hyderabad. A full rundown of destinations, and which carriers fly to them, appears in Travel details at the end of this chapter.

By train

As Pune is one of the last stops for around twenty long-distance **trains** to and from Mumbai, rail services are excellent. Many depart early morning, however, and some terminate at Dadar or (worse still) Kurla, so always check first online at ⓦwww .indianrail.gov.in, or at the station.

The following trains are recommended as the fastest and/or most convenient. Reservations for all trains should be made as far in advance as possible at the **Reservation Centre** next to the main station (Mon–Sat 8am–8pm, Sun 8am–2pm).

Destination	Name	No.	Departs	Journey time
Bengaluru (Bangalore)	Udyan Express	#6529	Daily 11.45pm	9hr
Chennai	Chennai Express	#2163	Daily 12.10am	22hr
Ernakulam (Kochi)/ **Thiruvananthapuram** (Trivandrum)	Udyan Express	#6529	Daily 7.25pm	33hr/39hr
Goa	Goa Express	#2780	Daily 4.40pm	13hr
Hyderabad	Hyderabad Express	#7031	Daily 4.40pm	13hr 5min
Kolhapur	Sahyadri Express	#1023 CST	Daily 10.05pm	8hr
Mumbai	Mumbai Express	#6012	Daily 9.45am	4hr

By bus and taxi

Seek advice from the MTDC tourist information counter at the railway station for information on **state bus** services, as the bus stands display none in English. Services from the long-distance section of the City stand (next to Pune railway station) head south and west, to Mahabaleshwar, Kolhapur, Goa and Lonavala. ASIAD buses to Mumbai also leave here every fifteen minutes between 5.30am and 11.30pm. Additional services in these directions work out of the Swargate stand 5km south. Literally dozens of **private buses** also operate on most popular routes, including to Goa and Mahabaleshwar; you'll find their agents lined up opposite the railway and bus stations. If you book onto one, be sure to check the departure point.

For Mumbai, 24-hour **taxis** leave from agencies at the taxi stand in front of Pune railway station, charging around Rs275 per passenger – though note that they'll only get you as far as Dadar. Pricier a/c "cool cabs" operate from the same place (Rs345 per passenger).

See Travel details at the end of this chapter for a roundup of routes, journey frequencies and durations.

seven or eight of the hippest cafés, bars and restaurants, grouped in a single enclave. The best of them are reviewed below, along with Pune's more established eateries. As with most Indian boom cities, everywhere of note gets jam packed on weekends, when you'll need to book well in advance to be sure of a table.

Restaurants and cafés

German Bakery 291 Koregaon Park. One of the oldest branches of this chain of faded hippy cafés, providing light meals and heavy pastry snacks and breads to a mixed clientele of cellphone-wielding, cigarette-smoking students and clean-living ashram-ites.

Juice World 2436/B East Street Camp. Freshly squeezed fruit juices (Rs20–30) and shakes (try the fabulous dried fruit and *badam*) are the mainstay of this central Mumbai-style place just east of the top of MG Rd. They also serve piping hot snacks such as *aloo paratha* and, throughout the afternoon and evening, tangy Bombay-style *pao bhaji* (street food), which bubbles away on a huge counter griddle.

Koyla Mira Nagar Corner, North Main Rd, Koregaon Park ☎020/2612 0102. Pune's most extravagantly decorated restaurant, featuring twinkling, mirror-inlaid Arabian Nights murals on a Golconda theme (see p.659). The waiters sport long Muslim djellabas and fez caps, and serve Hyderabadi cuisine as sumptuous as the surroundings: complicated, creamy curries and huge, slow-baked biriyanis, rounded off with traditional saffron, cardamom and pistachio-accented desserts. Count on Rs750–900 for three courses. Reservation recommended on weekends.

The Place (Touche the Sizzler) 7 Moledina Rd ☎020/2613 4632. Succulent sizzlers (veg, fish, pork or beef) and door-stopper steaks, dished up with huge piles of perfect fries and salad, are the house specialities of this enduringly popular Parsi-run restaurant in the city centre. For dessert, there's old-school crème caramel or fancier "parfait excelsior" – a self-indulgent pile of ice cream and nuts. Mains Rs200–300.

Ram Krishna 6 Moledina Rd, opposite West End Theatre ☎020/2633 0724. Top-notch North and South Indian veg food, including some fantastic Punjabi tandooris, dished up in a high-ceilinged dining hall with black-tie service, but at restrained prices (most mains Rs60–150). Open 9am–11.15pm.

Swiss Cheese Garden ABC Farms, Koregaon Park ☎020/2681 7413. From Friday to Sunday you'll be lucky to get a table at this quirky Swiss-themed place. Against a backdrop of warm red brickwork and pretty glass mosaic lanterns, or out in a garden wrapped in fairy lights, you can enjoy scrumptious rösti potatoes, fondues (Rs400–550 depending on ingredients), raclettes (Rs400) and wood-baked pizzas (Rs110–200).

Yogi Tree Ground floor, *Hotel Surya Villa*, 284/1 Koregaon Park. This is the favourite hangout of health conscious ashram-ites, serving pure, hygienic juices, grilled sandwiches, tofu steaks (Rs120) and delicious koftas (Rs90), in addition to a very popular stir-fried pak-choi (Rs120). And their deserts are great too.

Bars

Curve ABC Farms, Koregaon Park. Candle-lit outdoor pub, famous for its funky architecture of interconnected raised terraces and trademark curved bar, decorated with mosaics and rope. It has a friendly vibe, but the atmosphere is often compromised by cheesy Western pop. Cocktails Rs200; shorts Rs50; they also do grilled meats and kebabs to order.

Shisha Café ABC Farms, Koregaon Park. Currently Pune's trendiest watering hole: a cavernous gastro-bar on stilts, capped with a huge thatched roof. The interior is lined with Turkish rugs and funky low platforms strewn with cushions to lounge on. Iranian food dominates the menu, but the music's Cuban and BeeBop. They also serve beer and shorts, and hookahs with strawberry-flavoured tobacco.

Mahabaleshwar and around

MAHABALESHWAR, 250km southeast of Mumbai and rivalling Matheran as the most visited hill resort in Maharashtra, is easily reached from Pune, 120km northeast. The highest point in the Western Ghats (1372m), it is subject to extraordinarily extreme **weather** conditions. The start of June brings heavy mists and a dramatic drop in temperature, followed by a deluge of biblical proportions: up to seven metres of rain can fall in the hundred days up to the end of September. As a result, tourists only come here between November and May; during April and May, at the height of summer, the place is packed. There is a Rs10 per head entry fee for visitors, collected at toll booths at each end of town.

The town and around

For most foreign visitors, Mahabaleshwar's prime appeal is its location mid-way between Mumbai and Goa, but it holds enough good **hiking trails** to keep walkers here for a few days, with tracks through the woods to waterfalls and assorted vantage points overlooking the peaks and plains. You can also take **boats** out on the central **Yenna Lake**, and **shop** for strawberries, raspberries, locally made jams and honey in the lively market.

One commendable short route is the walk to **Wilson's Point**, the highest spot on the ridge, which you should aim to reach well before dusk. To pick up the (driveable) trail, head south through the bazaar (away from the bus stand) and straight over the crossroads at the end past the *Mayfair* hotel; ten minutes further up the hill, you reach a red-and-white sign pointing left off the road. Wilson's Point lies another stiff ten minutes up, crowned by a gigantic radio transmitter that is visible for miles. The sunset **panoramas** from here can be breathtaking.

Practicalities

The central **State bus stand** at the northwest end of the bazaar serves Pune (hourly; 3hr 30min), the most convenient railhead, as well as Kolhapur (7 daily; 7hr) and Satara (every two hours; 1hr), which is 17km from Satara Road railway station, connected to Mumbai via Pune and Goa via Miraj. There are five daily buses from Mumbai, the best option being the MSRTC semi-luxury bus which departs from the Mumbai Central bus stand at 7am (7hr). The single daily direct service to Panjim in Goa departs at 9am (12hr). For information on **tours** to Pratapgardh (see opposite), ask at the MSRTC tourist office at the MTDC *Holiday Camp*. There are a couple of unreliable **Internet** joints in the bazaar, and **ATMs** at the Bank of Maharashtra on Main Road (Dr Sabne Rd) and the State Bank of India on Masjid Street.

As in many hill stations, despite an abundance of hotels, prices in Mahabaleshwar are well above average. The cheapest **places to stay** are on the Main Road and the road parallel to it, Murray Peth; with a little haggling, you can pick up rooms for under Rs400 midweek or off season. Accommodation is scarce during the monsoon (mid-June to mid-Sept), when most hotels close, and during peak times like Diwali and over Christmas and New Year, when tariffs double. Apart from the hotel restaurants and ubiquitous thali joints, two worthwhile **eateries** on the Main Road are *Dragon Chinese Den* and *Tinklers-The Taste Bud*, which does excellent, if slightly pricey, South Indian and other snacks.

Hotels

Blue Star 114 Dr Sabne Rd ☎02168/260678. Plenty of peeling plaster but adequate; offers as good off-peak deals as you'll find for a basic attached room with TV. **4**

Deluxe Dr Sabne Rd ☎02168/260202. Clean modern lodge above a fabrics shop. One of the better budget deals. **3–5**

Dreamland Directly below the State bus stand ☎02168/260228, ⓦwww.hoteldreamland.com. Large, established resort hotel in extensive gardens. Rooms range from simple chalets ("cottages") to new a/c poolside apartments with stupendous views. The congenial garden café serves decent espresso and the restaurant fine Indian, Continental, Mexican and Chinese cooking. **6–8**

MTDC Holiday Camp 2km southwest of the centre ☎02168/260318, ⓕ 260300 or Mumbai ☎022/2202 6713. Wide range of good-value, no-frills accommodation, including cottages to sleep four, doubles and group accommodation. Better than average restaurant and beer bar. ❸–❹

Paradise International Main Rd, near bus stand ☎02168/260084. Ramshackle but acceptable mid-range lodge whose saving grace is a pleasant courtyard. ❹–❺

Pratapgadh

An hour's bus ride away from Mahabaleshwar, or a hike of 24km, the seventeenth-century **fort** of **PRATAPGADH** (daily dawn–dusk; free) stretches the full length of a high ridge. Reached by five hundred steps, it is famously associated with the Maratha chieftain, **Shivaji**, who lured the Mughal general Afzal Khan here from Bijapur to discuss a possible truce. Neither, it would seem, intended to keep to the condition that they should come unarmed. Khan attempted to knife Shivaji, who responded by killing him with the gruesome *wagnakh*, a set of metal claws worn on the hand. Modern visitors can see Afzal Khan's tomb, a memorial to Shivaji, and views of the surrounding hills. The easiest way to reach the fort is on MSRTC's daily half-day tour (9.30am–1.30pm; Rs60).

Kolhapur

KOLHAPUR, on the banks of the River Panchaganga 225km south of Pune, is thought to have been an important centre of the Tantric cult associated with Shakti worship since ancient times. The town probably grew around the sacred site of the present-day **Mahalakshmi temple**, still central to the life of the city, although there are said to be up to 250 other temples in the area. With a population of more than half a million, Kolhapur has become a major industrial centre, but the city has retained enough Maharashtrian character to make it worthy of a stopover.

Former capital of the Chhatrapatis (descendants of Shivaji, who made this their capital in 1708), Kolhapur later played an important role in the development of the so-called **Indo-Saracenic** style of British colonial architecture. The architect Major Charles Mant, under the auspices of the maharaja, blended Western styles with Islamic, Jain and Hindu ones, resulting in buildings that would prove profoundly influential. Mant's work, which can be seen all over the city, includes: the High School and Town Hall; the General Library; the Albert Edward Hospital; and the New Palace, now a museum.

The City

The **Mahalakshmi temple**, whose cream-painted sanctuary towers embellish the western end of the city, is thought to have been founded in the seventh century by the Chalukyan king Karnadeva, though what you see today probably dates from the early eighteenth century. It is built from bluish-black basalt on the plan of a cross, with the image of the goddess Mahalakshmi beneath the eastern and largest of five domed towers. Presiding over the square just up the road from the Mahalakshmi temple, the **Rajwada**, or Old Palace, is still occupied by members of the Chhatrapati family. Visitors can see the entrance hall (daily 10am–6pm; free) by passing under a pillared porch which extends out into the town square.

Kolhapur is famous as a centre for traditional wrestling, or *kushti*. On leaving the palace gates, turn right and head through the low doorway in front of you, from where a path picks its way past a couple of derelict buildings to the sunken *motibaug*, or **wrestling ground**. Come here between 5.30am and 5.30pm, and you can watch the wrestlers training. The main season is between June and September, the coolest time of year, but you may see them active at other times. Hindus and Muslims train together, and it's fine to take photographs.

The maharaja's **New Palace** (Tues–Sun 9.30am–1pm & 2.30–6pm; Rs20), 2km north of the centre, was built in 1884, following a fire at the Rajwada. Designed by Major Mant, its style fuses Jain and Hindu influences from Gujarat and Rajasthan and local touches from the Rajwada while remaining indomitably Victorian, with a prominent clock tower. The present maharaja lives on the first floor, while the ground floor holds an absorbing collection of costumes, weapons, games, jewellery, embroidery and paraphernalia such as silver elephant saddles.

Practicalities

Kolhapur **airport**, served by daily Air Deccan flights from Mumbai, lies 8km southeast of the town centre. Two direct express **trains** leave Mumbai CST for Kolhapur via Pune each evening: the Mahalaxmi Express #1011 (8.20pm; 11hr) and the Sahyadri Express #1023 (5.50pm; 12hr 15min). Heading in the other direction, the Mahalaxmi Express, bound for Pune and Mumbai, leaves Kolhapur at 7.35pm. The **railway station** is 500m from the **bus stand** on Station Road, near the centre of town. A five-minute walk from here (turn right) brings you to the **MTDC tourist office**, in the Kedar Complex on Station Road (Mon–Sat 8.30am–6.30pm; ☎0231/269 2935), where you can sign up for a guided **tour** of Kolhapur (Mon–Sat 10am–5.30pm; Rs75). The only place in town to **exchange** traveller's cheques is at the State Bank of India at Dasara Chowk Bridge, near Shahamahar railway station, which also has an ATM; other cash machines can be found at most of the major banks, including the dependable UTI, on Station Road. If you need to get online, Balaji Net Café (Rs20/hr), on Station Road between the bus stand and railway station, is reliable.

There's no shortage of decent, reasonably priced **accommodation** in Kolhapur, most within easy reach of the bus stand along Station Road. The *Maharaja*, at 514 Station Rd (☎0231/265 0829; ❸), is a basic lodge, directly opposite the bus stand, with dozens of good-value, no-frills, clean rooms, and a veg restaurant. If it's full, try the *Sony* (☎0231/265 8585; ❷–❸), diagonally across the square inside the Mahalaxmi Chambers complex. A more comfortable option in a peaceful suburb a five-minute rickshaw drive away is the *Hotel Woodlands*, at 204E Tarabai Park (☎0231/265 0941, ℻263 3378; ❺–❻), which has a range of a/c and non-a/c rooms with TV, plus a 24-hour coffee shop, multi-cuisine restaurant, garden and bar. On the outskirts of town, overlooking the shores of Rankala Lake, the *Shalini Palace* (☎0231/263 0401; ❻) was once the Maharaja's summer residence. Fitted with enormous four-poster beds and upholstered furniture, its suites are an uneasy mish-mash of period and modern features, but are far and away the most luxurious options in Kolhapur, and the grounds have acres of green space for evening strolls. Even if you don't stay here, it's worth considering a trip out to the *Shalini* to eat in its enormous restaurant, located in the former Durbar Hall.

Outside the hotels, the best **food** is to be had in *Subraya* at the top of Station Square, a comfortable a/c restaurant with a varied menu including good

Maharashtrian thalis, breakfast and cheaper South Indian-style snacks such as tasty *dosas*, *vada pao* and filling *pani* puris.

Sawantwadi

SAWANTWADI, 20km north of the Goan border, was the former capital of the Bhonasle dynasty, who ruled this remote corner of Maharashtra for more than three hundred years before the dissolution of their princely privileges by the Indian government in the 1950s and 1960s. Surrounded by forest, it's now a bustling market town with a population of 40,000, many of whom trade coconuts, cashews and betel produced in the surrounding woods.

The Town

Aside from the lively bazaar in the town centre, the main incentive to pause in Sawantwadi is to visit the Bhonasles' nineteenth-century **palace**, still inhabited by the local rani, and famous as a centre for the manufacture of traditional Indian playing cards, or **ganjifa** (see box below). A British-style pile built of local stone, it stands in the centre of town, next to a circular lake.

The *ganjifa* workshop (daily except public holidays 10.30am–12.30pm & 1.30–5.30pm; Rs50) is in the old **Durbar Hall** to the rear of the building. Surrounded by old weapons, hunting trophies, a bust of Queen Victoria and the silver throne made for the last raja's coronation in 1947, a workforce of half a dozen men and women are all that survive of the town's once thriving *ganjifa* industry. Up until the last century, several families were employed manufacturing cards, but by 1959, when the maharaja decided to revive the art form, only one man could be found who still made *ganjifa* (at a rate of two packs per year). Most of what is made here today is exported for sale in other parts of the country or abroad; the sheer amount of time needed to paint a full pack puts the cards beyond the pocket of most Indians.

A small **gallery** on the ground floor of the palace outlines the history of Sawantwadi *ganjifa* and their revival, with a collection of old photographs that vividly evoke the last days of the Raj. Upstairs, you can browse a wide selection of expertly made painted wooden objects and other affordable souvenirs.

Ganjifa

Unlike their counterparts in Western countries, different types of **ganjifa** packs come in suits of varying numbers of cards: eight (known as "Mughal", or *Changkanchan* in Konkani); nine (*Navagraha*, after the "nine planets" frequently enshrined in Hindu temples); ten (*Dasavatara*, after the God Vishnu's "ten incarnations"); twelve (*Rashi*, after the signs of the zodiac); and even sixteen or 24 in the eastern Indian state of Orissa. The mythological and astrological themes also provide the subject matter for the *ganjifa's* rich decoration, meticulously hand-painted according to designs that have been passed down through generations.

For foreign tourists, a set of *ganjifa* makes a beautiful, and affordable, souvenir. Painted in vibrant reds, saffrons and blues, the cards feature ocean-churning tortoises, man-lions, sacred boars, dwarves, axe-wielding or elephant-headed gods, princes and winged griffons, to name but a few of the designs drawn from Hinduism's weird pantheon. In Sawantwadi, sets start at Rs1400.

Spurred by the success of the palace's efforts, other local artisans have followed suit, and the Chitarli Gully bazaar running uphill from the opposite shore of the lake is crammed with the brightly painted toys, wooden fruit and other knick-knacks traditionally given as presents in this area.

Practicalities

Sawantwadi **railway station**, 8km from town, lies on the **Konkan Railway**, only thirty minutes by rail from Goa and reachable on any of KRC's slower passenger services. With the resort of Arambol just down the coast, there's no reason you'd want to try any of the substandard accommodation around the bazaar, but you might want to **eat**. The best option is the vegetarian thali restaurant in the modern, multistorey building at the bottom of Chitarli Gully bazaar (its sign is in Marathi, but as it's virtually the only restaurant in the area, it's easy to locate).

Travel details

Trains

Mumbai to: Bengaluru (Bangalore) (3 daily; 24hr–26hr 10min); Chennai (3 daily; 24–29hr); Hyderabad (2 daily; 14hr 20min–17hr); Kolhapur (3 daily; 11–12hr 15min); Pune (25 daily; 3hr 25min–5hr); Thiruvananthapuram (2 daily; 31hr).
Pune to: Bengaluru (Bangalore) (3–4 daily; 9hr); Chennai (3 daily; 20hr–25hr 45min); Goa (Margao; 1 daily; 13hr); Hyderabad (3–5 daily; 13hr); Kolhapur (4 daily; 8hr); Mumbai (20–23 daily; 3hr 25min–5hr 10min).

Buses

Only state bus services are listed here.
Mahabaleshwar to: Kolhapur (7 daily; 7hr); Mumbai (5 daily; 7–8hr); Panjim (1 daily; 12hr); Pune (hourly; 3hr 30min–4hr); Satara (every 2hr; 1hr).
Mumbai (ASIAD Dadar) to: Kolhapur (4 daily; 10–12hr); Murud-Janjira (2 daily; 4hr 30min); Pune (every 15–30min; 4hr).
Mumbai (Mumbai Central) to: Bengaluru (Bangalore) (3 daily; 24hr); Bijapur (3 daily; 12hr); Goa (2 daily; 16–18); Murud-Janjira (6 daily; 6hr).
Pune to: Bijapur (1 daily; 11–12hr); Goa (4 daily; 15–16hr); Kolhapur (4 daily; 6–7hr); Mahabaleshwar (hourly; 3hr 30min–4hr); Mumbai (every 15–30min; 4hr).

Flights

For a list of airline addresses and websites see p.150; for travel agents, see p.151. In the listings below IA is Indian Airlines, AI Air India, JA Jet Airways, KF Kingfisher, SA Sahara Airlines, AD Air Deccan, GO Go Air, IG IndiGo Airlines, and SJ SpiceJet.
Mumbai (Chhatrapati Shivaji domestic airport) to: Bengaluru (Bangalore) (AI, IA, JA, SA, AD, KF & SJ 24–27 daily; 1hr 30min); Chennai (AI, IA, JA, SA, SJ, AD, KF, GO & IG 19–22 daily; 1hr 45min); Cochin, see Kochi; Coimbatore (GO, JA, IA, AD & SA 5 daily; 1hr 45min–2hr 50min); Goa (AI, IA, JA, SA, KF, GO, IG, AD 16–18 daily; 45min–1hr); Hubli (AD & KF 2 daily; 1hr 35min–2hr 10min); Hyderabad (IA, JA, SA, GO, SJ, KF & AD 17 daily; 1hr 15min–2hr 10min); Kochi (GO, JA, AI, IA, AD & SA 8–10 daily; 1hr 55min); Kolhapur (AD 1 daily; 55min); Madurai (JA & IA 2 daily; 3hr 20min–4hr 20min); Mangalore (IA, KF & AD 3 daily; 1hr 15min); Pune (JA 2 daily; 35min); Thiruvananthapuram (AI, IA, JA & AD 4 daily; 2hr).
Pune to: Bengaluru (Bangalore) (GO, JA, IA, AD & KF 7–9 daily; 1hr 25min–2hr 25min); Chennai (GO & JA 1–2 daily; 1hr 35min–2hr 45min); Goa (IA 1 daily; 50min); Hyderabad (IA & AD 2–3 daily; 1hr–1hr 30min); Mumbai (JA 2 daily; 35min).

2

Goa

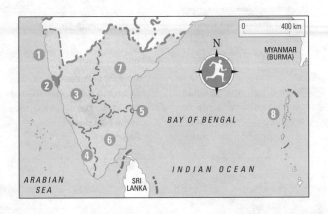

CHAPTER 2 # Highlights

✳ **Old Goa** The belfries and Baroque church facades looming over the trees on the banks of the Mandovi are all that remains of this once splendid colonial city. See p.197

✳ **Beach shacks** Tuck into a fresh kingfish, tandoori pomfret or lobster, washed down with a *feni* cocktail or an ice-cold Kingfisher beer. See p.208

✳ **Ingo's Night Bazaar, Arpora** Cooler and less frenetic than the flea market, with better quality goods on sale and heaps more atmosphere. See p.214

✳ **Flea market, Anjuna** Goa's famous tourist bazaar is the place to pick up the latest party gear, shop for souvenirs, and watch the crowds go by. See p.218

✳ **Nine Bar, Vagator** The epicentre of hip Goa, where trance music accompanies the sunsets over the beach. See p.225

✳ **Arambol** An alternative resort with exquisite beaches and some of Asia's best budget restaurants. See p.233

✳ **Braganza-Perreira house, Chandor** The region's most extravagant colonial-era mansion, crammed with period furniture and fittings. See p.241

✳ **Sunset stroll, Palolem** Tropical sunsets don't come much more romantic than at this idyllic palm-fringed cove in the hilly deep south. See p.247

△ Arambol beach

2

Goa

I f one word could be said to encapsulate the essence of **GOA**, it would have to be the Portuguese *sossegarde*, meaning "carefree". The pace of life in this former colonial enclave, midway down India's southwest coast, has picked up over the past twenty years, but in spite of the increasing chaos of its capital, beach resorts and market towns, Goa has retained the laid-back feel that has traditionally set it apart from the rest of the country. Its 1.4 million inhabitants are unequivocal about the roots of their distinctiveness; while most of the Subcontinent was colonized by the stiff-upper-lipped British, Goa's European overlords were the **Portuguese**, a people far more inclined to enjoy the good things in life than their Anglo-Saxon counterparts.

Goa was Portugal's first toe-hold in Asia, and served as the linchpin for a vast trade network for over 450 years. However, when the Lusitanian empire began to founder in the seventeenth century, so too did the fortunes of its capital. Cut off from the rest of India by a wall of mountains and hundreds of miles of unnavigable alluvial plain, it remained resolutely aloof from the wider Subcontinent – while India was tearing itself to pieces in the run-up to Independence in 1947, the only machetes wielded here were cutting coconuts. Not until 1961, after exasperated Prime Minister Jawaharlal Nehru gave up trying to negotiate with the Portuguese dictator Salazar and sent in the army, was Goa finally absorbed into India.

Those who visited in the late 1960s and 1970s, when the overland travellers' trail wriggled its way south from Bombay, found a way of life little changed in centuries: Portuguese was still very much the lingua franca of the well-educated elite, and the coastal settlements were mere fishing and coconut cultivation villages. Relieved to have found somewhere inexpensive and culturally undemanding to recover from the travails of Indian travel, the "freaks" got stoned, watched the mesmeric sunsets over the Arabian Sea and partied madly on full-moon nights, giving rise to a holiday culture that soon made Goa synonymous with hedonistic **hippies**.

Since then, the state has largely shaken off its reputation as a drop-out zone, but hundreds of thousands of visitors still flock here each winter, the vast majority to relax on Goa's beautiful **beaches**. Around two dozen stretches of soft white sand indent the region's coast, from spectacular 25-kilometre sweeps to secluded palm-backed coves. The level of development varies wildly; while some are lined by ritzy Western-style resorts, the most sophisticated structures on others are palm-leaf shacks and old wooden outriggers that are heaved into the sea each afternoon.

Wherever you travel in Goa, vestiges of former Portuguese domination are ubiquitous, creating an ambience that is at once exotic and strangely familiar.

The festivals of Goa

Some of Goa's **festivals** are on fixed dates each year; ask at a tourist office for the dates of the others. The biggest celebrations take place at Panjim and Margao.

Festa dos Reis (Jan 6). Epiphany celebrations include a procession of young boys decked out as the Three Kings to the Franciscan chapel of Reis Magos, near Panjim on the north bank of the Mandovi, 3km east of Fort Aguada. Other processions are held at Cansaulim and Chandor.

Carnival (Feb/March). Three days of *feni*-induced mayhem, centering on Panjim, to mark the run-up to Lent.

Shigmo (Feb/March). The Goan version of Holi is celebrated with big parades and crowds; drum and dance groups compete and huge floats, which threaten to bring down telegraph wires, trundle through the streets.

All Saints (March). On the fifth Monday in Lent, 26 effigies of saints, martyrs, popes, kings, queens and cardinals are paraded around the village of Velha Goa, near Panjim. A fair also takes place.

Igitun Chalne (May). *Dhoti*-clad devotees of the goddess Lairya enter trances and walk over hot coals at the village of Sirigao, Bichloim.

Sanjuan (June 24). The festival of St John is celebrated all over Goa, but is especially important in the coastal villages of Arambol and Terekol. Youngsters torch straw dummies (representing St John's baptism, and thus the death of sin), while revellers in striped pants dive into wells after drinking bottles of *feni*.

International Film Festival of India (late Nov to early Dec). Panjim was recently nominated as the permanent venue for this Bollywood bash, in which hundreds of movies – both foreign and Indian – are shown over a fortnight, on huge beachside screens and in Panjim's two major venues, the Innox multiplex and Kala Academy.

Christmas (Dec 24–25). Celebrated everywhere in Goa. Late-night Mass is usually followed by music, dancing and fireworks.

Siolim Zagor (first Sun after Christmas). Processions, dance dramas and satirical songs mark this unusual festival at Siolim, in northern Goa near Chapora, which is ostensibly Christian but celebrated with equal enthusiasm by local Hindus.

This is particularly true of Goan **food** which, blending the Latin love of meat and fish with India's predilection for spices, is quite unlike any other regional cuisine in Asia. Equally unique is the prevalence of **alcohol**. Beer is cheap, and six thousand or more bars around the state are licensed to serve it, along with the more traditional tipple, *feni*, a rocket-fuel spirit distilled from cashew fruit or coconut sap.

Travelling around the Christian heartland of central Goa, with its white-washed churches and wayside shrines, it's all too easy to forget that **Hinduism** remains the religion of more than two-thirds of the state's population. Unlike in many parts of the country, however, religious intolerance is rare here, and traditional practices mingle easily with more recently implanted ones. Faced by the threat of merger with neighbouring states, Goans have always put regional cohesion before communal differences at the ballot box. A potent stimulus for regional identity was the campaign through the 1980s to have **Konkani**, the language spoken by the vast majority of Goans, recognized as an official state language, which it eventually was in 1992. Since then, the **immigration** issue has come to dominate the political agenda. Considerably more prosperous than neighbouring states, Goa has been deluged over the past couple of decades with economic refugees, stirring up fears that the region's cultural distinctiveness will

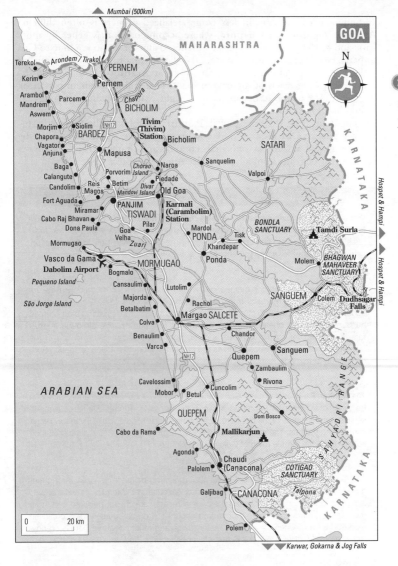

disappear. Among the main employers of migrant labour in recent years has been the **Konkan Railway**, completed in 1997 to form a super-fast land link with Mumbai – another conduit of economic prosperity that has brought lasting changes.

Which beach you opt for when you arrive largely depends on what sort of holiday you have in mind. More developed resorts such as **Calangute** and **Baga** in the north, and **Colva** and **Benaulim** in the south, offer more "walk-in" accommodation and tourist facilities than elsewhere. Even if you're looking for a less touristy scene, it can be worth heading for these centres first, as finding places to stay in less commercialized corners is often difficult. **Anjuna**, **Vagator** and **Chapora**, where accommodation is generally more basic and harder to come by, are the beaches to aim for if you've come to Goa to party. However, the bulk of budget travellers taking time out from tours of India end up in **Palolem**, in the far south, or **Arambol**, both beyond the increasingly long reach of the charter buses. That said, Palolem, in particular, has become a major resort in its own right, with thousands of long-stay visitors in peak season.

Some 10km from the state capital, **Panjim**, the ruins of the former Portuguese capital at **Old Goa** are foremost among the attractions away from the coast – a sprawl of Catholic cathedrals, convents and churches that draw crowds of Christian pilgrims from all over India. Another popular day excursion is to

Getting around

White Maruti van **taxis** serve as the main means of travelling between resorts. You'll find them lined up outside most charter hotels, where a board invariably displays "fixed rates" to destinations in and around the region. These fares only apply to peak season, however, and at other times you should be able to negotiate a hefty reduction.

By ferry
Although gradually being superseded by road bridges, flat-bottomed **ferries** are Goa's quintessential mode of transport. Crammed with cars, buses, commuters on scooters, fisherwomen and clumps of overheated tourists, these rusting blue-painted hulks are incredibly cheap. They're also free for foot passengers (although a small fare is charged for motor vehicles) and run from the crack of dawn to late in the evening. A couple of services, such as the one in the far north of Goa to Terekol Fort, do not run at low tide.

By train
The **Konkan Railway** serves as Goa's principal long-distance transport artery, although it's rarely convenient for shorter journeys within the state. The relative infrequency of services and distance of the line from most of the resorts means you're invariably better off catching the bus. The one trip it really is worth catching the train for is the hour-long ride south to the temple town of Gokarna, in neighbouring Karnataka.

By bus
The Goan transport corporation, Kadamba, runs long-distance services throughout the state from their main stands at Panjim, Mapusa and Margao. Private buses, serving everywhere else (including the coastal resorts) are cheap, frequent and more relaxed than many in India, although you should still brace yourself for a crush on market days and when travelling to major towns and tourist centres. Details on how to get around by bus are listed in the relevant accounts, and on p.189.

By motorcycle taxi
Goa's unique pillion-passenger **motorcycle taxis**, known locally as "**pilots**", are ideal for nipping between beaches or into town from the resorts. Bona fide operators ride black bikes with yellow mudguards and white number plates. Fares, which should be settled in advance, are comparable with auto-rickshaw rates: roughly Rs7 per kilometre.

By rented motorcycle
Renting a motorcycle in Goa gives a lot of freedom but can be perilous. Every season, an average of one person a day dies on the roads; many are tourists

Anjuna's Wednesday **flea market**, a sociable place to shop for souvenirs and dance wear. Further inland, the thickly wooded countryside around **Ponda** harbours numerous temples, where you can experience Goa's peculiar brand of Hindu architecture. The district of Salcete, and its main market town, **Margao**, is also littered with Portuguese mansions, churches and seminaries. Finally, wildlife enthusiasts may be tempted into the interior to visit the nature reserve at **Cotigao** in the far south.

The **best time to come** to Goa is during the dry, relatively cool winter months between mid–November and mid–March. At other times, either the sun is too hot for comfort, or the monsoon rains and clouds make life miserable. During peak season, from mid–December to the end of January, the weather is perfect, with temperatures rarely nudging above 32°C. Finding a room or a

on two-wheelers. Make sure, therefore, that the lights and brakes are in good shape, and be especially vigilant at night: Goan roads can be appallingly pot-holed and unlit, and stray cows, dogs and bullock carts can appear from nowhere.

Officially, you need an **international driver's licence** to rent and ride anything, but in practise a standard licence will suffice if you're stopped and asked to produce your papers by the local police. In 2006, a new law was introduced in Goa requiring that all rented motorcycles carry special **yellow-and-black licence plates**, for which the vehicle's owners pay a couple of thousand rupees extra. This slightly increases the cost of the bike (typically by around Rs50 per day), but the new plates ensure you can ride free from harassment by Goa's notoriously corrupt traffic cops. Go for a cheaper bike with regular black and white plates, on the other hand, and you'll be pulled over with frustrating regularity.

Helmets are also compulsory these days while riding on the highways. The owner of your rented motorbike should provide an Indian-made one, but it may not fit and isn't likely to be of the best quality. **Rates** for motorbikes vary according to season, duration of rental and vehicle; most owners also insist on a deposit and/or passport as security. The cheapest bike, a scooter-style Honda Activa 100cc, which has automatic gears, costs Rs200 per day (with yellow plates). Other options include the perennially stylish Enfield Bullet 350cc, although these are heavy, unwieldy and – at upwards of Rs300 per day – the most expensive bike to rent. For all-round performance and manoeuvrability, you can't beat the fast and light Honda Splendours and Baja Pulsars, which go for Rs250–300, depending on what kind of shape the vehicle is in and how long you rent it for.

Fuel is sold at service stations (known locally as "petrol pumps") in Panjim, Mapusa, Vagator/Anjuna, Margao, Chaudi, and at Arambol in the far north. In smaller settlements, including the resorts, it's sold in mineral water bottles at general stores or through backstreet suppliers – but you should avoid these as some bulk out their petrol with low-grade kerosene or industrial solvent, which makes engines misfire and smoke badly.

Tours

On paper, guided **tours** (daily; Rs200) run by the local tourism authority **GTDC** (⌾www.goa-tourism.com) from Panjim, Margao, Calangute and Colva seem like a good way of getting around Goa's highlights in a short time. However, they're far too rushed for most foreign tourists, appealing essentially to Indian families wishing to combine a peek at the resorts with a whistle-stop puja tour of the temples around Ponda. Most also include a string of places inland that you wouldn't otherwise consider visiting. Leaflets giving full itineraries are available at any GTDC office.

house to rent at that time, however – particularly over Christmas and New Year when tariffs double, or triple – can be a real hassle.

Some history

Goa's sheer inaccessibility by land has always kept it out of the mainstream of Indian history; on the other hand, its control of the seas and the lucrative spice trade made it a much-coveted prize for rival colonial powers. Until a century before the arrival of the Portuguese, Goa had belonged for over a thousand years to the kingdom of **Kadamba**. They, in turn, were overthrown by the Karnatakan Vijayanagars, the Muslim Bahmanis, and Yusuf Adil Shah of Bijapur, but the capture of the fort at Panjim by **Afonso de Albuquerque** in 1510 signalled the start of a Portuguese occupation that was to last 451 years.

As Goa expanded, its splendid capital (now Old Goa) came to hold a larger population than Paris or London. Though Ismail Adil Shah laid siege for ten months in 1570, and the Marathas under Shivaji and later chiefs came nail-bitingly close to seizing the region, the greatest threat was from other European maritime nations, principally Holland and France. Meanwhile, conversions to **Christianity**, started by the Franciscans, gathered pace when St Francis Xavier founded the **Jesuit** mission in 1542. With the advent of the **Inquisition** soon afterwards, laws were introduced censoring literature and banning any faith other than Catholicism. Hindu temples were destroyed, and converted Hindus adopted Portuguese names, such as da Silva, Correa and de Sousa, which remain common in the region. Thereafter, the colony, whose trade monopoly had been broken by its European rivals, went into gradual decline, hastened by the unhealthy, disease-ridden environment of its capital.

Despite certain liberalization, such as the restoration of Hindus' right to worship and the final banishment of the dreaded Inquisition in 1820, the nineteenth century saw widespread civil unrest. During the British Raj many Goans moved to Bombay, and elsewhere in British India, to find work.

The success of the post-Independence Goan struggle for freedom owed as much to the efforts of the Indian government, which cut off diplomatic ties with Portugal, as to the work of freedom fighters such as **Menezes Braganza** and **Dr Cunha**. After a "liberation march" in 1955 resulted in a number of deaths, the state was blockaded. Trade with Bombay ceased, and the railway was cut off, so Goa set out to forge international links, particularly with Pakistan and Sri Lanka: that led to the building of Dabolim airport, and a determination to improve local agricultural output. In 1961, Prime Minister Jawaharlal Nehru finally ran out of patience with his opposite number in Lisbon, the right-wing dictator Salazar, and sent in the armed forces. Mounted in defiance of a United Nations resolution, "**Operation Vijay**" met only token resistance, and the Indian army overran Goa in two days. Thereafter, Goa (along with Portugal's other two enclaves, Daman and Diu) became part of India as a self-governing **Union Territory**, with minimum interference from Delhi.

Since Independence, Goa has continued to prosper, bolstered by iron-ore exports and a booming tourist industry. Dominated by issues of statehood, the status of Konkani and the ever-rising levels of immigration, its political life has been dogged by chronic **instability**. In the 1990s, no fewer than twelve chief ministers held power over a succession of shaky, opportunistic coalitions, and in May 2004, after a spate of chaotic political sackings and failed confidence votes rendered the state ungovernable, New Delhi stepped in to declare **President's Rule,** effectively suspending the State Legislature. The deadlock between the BJP and Congress dominated national headlines for months, until fresh elections could be organized. These eventually returned Congress to power, with **Pratapsingh Rane** as Chief Minister, and since 2005 an uneasy peace has reigned.

In the interior, however, the spectre of communal violence, virtually unheard of in Goa, raised its head from March 2006, when **anti-Muslim riots** erupted in the mining town of Sanvordem. The unrest was sparked by renovation work being carried out against the wishes of local Hindus on a mosque, the **Guddemol Masjid**. Muslim cars and motorcycles were set on fire, houses were attacked, shops looted and people beaten by hard-line nationalists (most of them, it seems, immigrants from neighbouring Karnataka).

At the start of the twenty-first century, as ever-improving infrastructural links with the rest of India render Goa's borders more porous, the survival of the state as a culturally distinct region hinges on the extent to which its government is able to resist the drift towards communal politics, and establish coherent, democratic policies. If the past decade is anything to go by, the chances of this happening seem remote, although the embarrassment of President's Rule does seem to have galvanized the state's leaders.

Panjim and central Goa

Stacked around the sides of a lush terraced hillside at the mouth of the River Mandovi, **PANJIM** (also known by its Marathi name, **Panaji** – "land that does not flood") was for centuries little more than a minor landing stage and customs house, protected by a hilltop fort and surrounded by stagnant swampland. It only became state capital in 1843, after the port at Old Goa had silted up and its rulers

Dabolim airport

Goa only has **one civil airport**: **Dabolim**, on top of a rocky plateau in the south of the state. It recently acquired a new terminal building, but is essentially still a rundown navy aerodrome, with the shells of old Russian military aircraft rotting outside camouflaged hangars, and construction workers and civilian ground traffic moving freely across the runway between flights. Less interesting are the **immigration formalities** for foreigners, which generally take upwards of one hour as ranks of khaki-clad officials scrutinize, stamp and recheck passports, disembarkation slips and customs forms. Be sure to hang on to every piece of paper you're given or you might be delayed.

In the **arrivals hall,** the State Bank of India has a painfully slow **foreign-exchange desk**, which opens to meet flights but isn't entirely dependable. If you use it, ask for an encashment certificate and carefully check the exchange rate (which is likely to be very poor), the condition of notes you receive and the exchange calculation. Better still, use the **ATM** immediately outside the main exit on the arrivals concourse.

Porters pester new arrivals from baggage reclaim onwards; you're entitled to use a trolley without their help, but may have to fight for the privilege. Coaches wait outside to whisk package tourists to their hotels, while other travellers head for the pre-paid **taxi counter,** which you'll find directly opposite the main exit doors of the terminal. Fixed fares to virtually everywhere in the state are displayed behind the desk; pay here and give the slip to the driver when you arrive at your destination.

Anyone **visiting** the airport or **meeting arrivals** should note that a Rs20 visitor ticket (on sale at a hatch next to the ground-floor exit) will buy you entrance to the foyer of the a/c arrivals hall – worth paying to escape the heat and crowds outside.

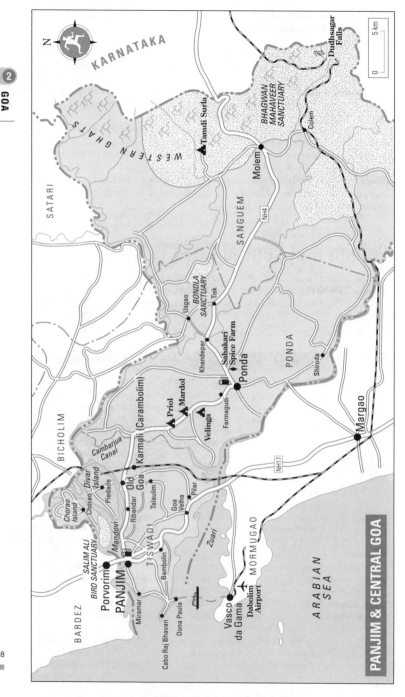

PANJIM & CENTRAL GOA

and impoverished inhabitants had fled the plague. Although the last Portuguese viceroy managed to drain many of Panjim's marshes, and erected imposing public buildings on the new site, the town never emulated the grandeur of its predecessor upriver – a result, in part, of the Portuguese nobles' predilection for constructing their mansions in the countryside rather than the city. Panjim expanded rapidly in the 1960s and 1970s, without reaching the unmanageable proportions of other Indian capitals. After Mumbai, or even Bengaluru (Bangalore), its uncongested streets seem easy-going and pleasantly parochial. Sights are thin on the ground, but the backstreets of the old quarter, **Fontainhas**, have retained a faded Portuguese atmosphere, with colour-washed houses, Catholic churches and shopfronts sporting names such as De Souza and Pinto.

Some travellers see no more of Panjim than its noisy bus terminal – which is a pity. Although you can completely bypass the town when you arrive in Goa, either by jumping off the train or coach at Margao (for the south), or Mapusa (for the northern resorts), or by heading straight off on a local bus, it's definitely worth spending time here – if only a couple of hours en route to the ruined former capital at **Old Goa**.

The area **around Panjim** attracts far fewer visitors than the coastal resorts, yet its paddy fields and wooded valleys harbour several attractions worth a day or two's break from the beach. **Old Goa** is just a bus ride away, as are the unique temples around **Ponda**, an hour or so southeast, to where Hindus smuggled their deities during the Inquisition. Further inland still, the forested lower slopes of the Western Ghats, cut through by the main Panjim–Bengaluru (Bangalore) highway, shelter the impressive **Dudhsagar falls**, reachable only by four-wheel-drive Jeep.

Arrival, information and local transport

European charter planes and domestic flights arrive at **Dabolim airport** (℡0832/254 0788), 29km south of Panjim on the outskirts of Vasco da Gama, Goa's second city. Prepaid taxis into town (45min; Rs475), booked at the counter in the forecourt, can be shared by up to four people.

There's no **train** station in town itself; the nearest one, on the Konkan Railway, is at **Karmali** (11km east of Panjim at Old Goa). State buses to central Panjim await arrivals.

Long-distance and local **buses** pull into Panjim's busy Kadamba bus stand, 1km east of the centre in the district of Pato. Ten minutes' walk, across Ourem Creek to Fontainhas, brings you to several budget hotels. For the more modern west end of town, flag down a motorcycle taxi or jump into an auto-rickshaw at the rank outside the station concourse (Rs25–40).

GTDC's **information** counter, inside the concourse at the main Kadamba bus stand (daily 9.30am–1pm & 2–5pm; ℡0832/222 5620, ⓦwww .goa-tourism.com) is useful for checking train and bus timings, but little else. The more efficient **India Tourism office** is across town on Church Square (Mon–Fri 9.30am–6pm, Sat 9.30am–1pm; ℡0832/222 3412, ⓦwww .tourismofindia.com).

Auto-rickshaws are the most convenient way of **getting around** Panjim; flag one down at the roadside or head for one of the ranks around the city.

Accommodation

The majority of Goa's Indian visitors prefer to stay in Panjim rather than the coastal resorts, which explains the huge number of **hotels** and **lodges** crammed into the town centre, especially its noisy, more modern west end. Foreigners

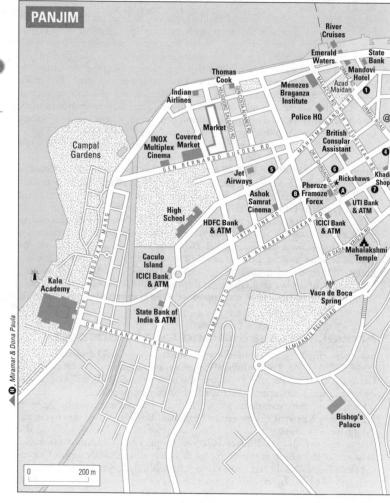

PANJIM

Betim

River Cruises

Emerald Waters

State Bank

Mandovi Hotel

Thomas Cook

Azad Maidan

Menezes Braganza Institute

Indian Airlines

Police HQ

Market

British Consular Assistant

INOX Multiplex Cinema

Covered Market

GEN COSTA ALVARES RD

HEUDORFO SALGADO RD

MALACCA RD

DR ORLANDO RIBEIRO

MAHATMA GANDHI RD

ORMUZ ROAD

DR PISSURLEKAR RD

Campal Gardens

GEN BERNARDO GUEDES RD

Jet Airways

Pheroze Framoze Forex

Rickshaws

Khadi Shop

Ashok Samrat Cinema

DR SHIRODKAR RD

High School

HDFC Bank & ATM

18TH JUNE RD

UTI Bank & ATM

ICICI Bank & ATM

DR ATMARAM BORKAR RD

DR DADA VAIDYA RD

Mahalakshmi Temple

Caculo Island

ICICI Bank & ATM

Kala Academy

DR DHANDDKAR MARG

State Bank of India & ATM

GAMA PINTO RD

Vaca de Boca Spring

DR BRAGANZA PEREIRA RD

ALMIRANTE REIS ROAD

Miramar & Dona Paula

Bishop's Palace

0   200 m

spending the night here instead of on the coast, on the other hand, tend to do so primarily to sample the atmosphere of the old quarter, Fontainhas. Finding a room is only a problem during the festival of St Francis (Nov 24–Dec 3), Dussehra (Sept/Oct) and during peak season (mid-Dec to mid-Jan); the codes below apply to October through March, excluding the above periods, when prices can double or triple. Note that **checkout times** vary wildly.

Afonso St Sebastian Chapel Square, Fontainhas ☏0832/222 2359. This refurbished colonial-era house in a picturesque backstreet is your best bet if you can't afford the *Panjim Inn* down the road. Spotless en-suite rooms, friendly owners and rooftop terrace with views and cool ceramic mosaic

floors – though the rate, which soar to well over Rs1000 for a simple double at Christmas, are a bit over the top. Single occupancy available. ❹
Fidalgo 18th June Rd ☏0832/222 6291, ⓦwww .hotelfidalgo-goa.com. Affordable business-oriented four-star hotel in the bustling commercial end of

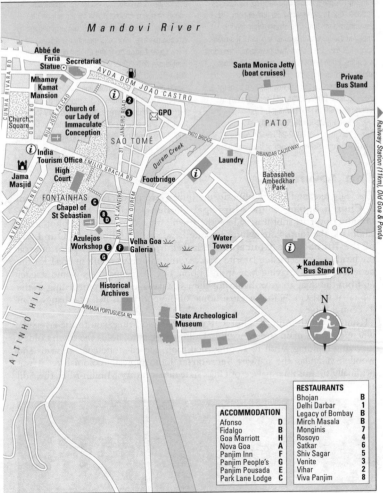

Mapusa, Houses of Goa Museum & Xavier Centre ▲

Mandovi River

Abbé de
Faria
Statue
Secretariat
CUNHA RIVARA RD
DR JOSE
Mhamay
Kamat
Mansion
Church
Square
AVDA DOM JOAO CASTRO
Santa Monica Jetty
(boat cruises)
Private
Bus Stand

RUA JOSE FALCAO
Church of
our Lady of
Immaculate
Conception
JANEIRO ROAD
GPO
PATO
SAO TOMÉ
PATO BRIDGE
India
Tourism Office
EMILIO GRACIA RD
High
Court
Jama
Masjid
FONTAINHAS
Chapel of
St Sebastian
Footbridge
Ourem Creek
RIBANDAR CAUSEWAY
Laundry
Babasaheb
Ambedkar
Park

AVDA PE ANSELO
RUA 31 DE JANEIRO
RUA DA OUREM
Azulejos
Workshop
Velha Goa
Galeria
Water
Tower
Kadamba
Bus Stand (KTC)

ALTINHO HILL
Historical
Archives
ARMADA PORTUGUESA RD
State Archeological
Museum
N

ACCOMMODATION

Afonso	D
Fidalgo	B
Goa Marriott	H
Nova Goa	A
Panjim Inn	F
Panjim People's	G
Panjim Pousada	E
Park Lane Lodge	C

RESTAURANTS

Bhojan	B
Delhi Darbar	1
Legacy of Bombay	B
Mirch Masala	B
Monginis	7
Rosoyo	4
Satkar	6
Shiv Sagar	5
Venite	3
Vihar	2
Viva Panjim	8

▼ Bambolim (hospital), Vasco Da Gama, Dabolim Airport (29km) & Margao

town. It's a comfortable option for the price, with central a/c, a good sized open-air pool, ayurvedic spa, bookshop and popular six-outlet "Food Enclave" on the ground floor (see "Eating" p.195). ⑦–⑧

Goa Marriott Miramar beach ☎0832/243 7001, ⓦwww.marriott.com. Huge five-star out on the edge of town, facing the mouth of the Mandovi. Predictably formulaic, and not a great location for a package holiday (despite what the brochures might suggest), but large and luxurious, with all the mod cons you'd expect. ⑨

Nova Goa Dr Atmaram Borkar Rd ☎0832/222 6231, ⓦwww.hotelnovagoa.com. Classy, centrally

a/c business hotel in the heart of the shopping area and with the usual comforts, plus baths in all rooms and a pool. Popular mainly with visiting Portuguese and corporate clients. ⑦

Panjim Inn E-212, Rua 31 de Janeiro, Fontainhas ☎0832/243 5628, ⓦwww.panjiminn.com. Grand three-hundred-year-old townhouse, now managed as a homely Heritage Hotel, with period furniture, sepia photos, balconies and a veranda, where meals and drinks are served to guests. A new three-storey wing overlooking the river promises to be of a similarly high standard, with better views. ⑥

Panjim People's Rua 31 de Janeiro, Fontainhas ☎0832/222 1122, ⓦwww.panjiminn.com. Part of the *Panjim's Inn* line, in a former high school opposite the original house (see p.191). It's more upmarket than their other two buildings: the rooms are huge, fitted with antique rosewood furniture, gilded pelmets and lace curtains, and the bathrooms feature the Sukhija family's trademark crazy-mosaic tiling. Tariffs mid-season start at around Rs5000 ($110) per night. ❾

Panjim Pousada Rua 31 de Janeiro, Fontainhas ☎0832/243 5628, ⓦwww .panjiminn.com. Sister concern of the *Panjim Inn*

across the road. Within an old Hindu house with oodles of period character. Ask for a room on the first floor, where a lovely wooden balcony, shaded by a breadfruit tree, overlooks the inner courtyard. ❻

Park Lane Lodge Near the Chapel of St Sebastian, Fontainhas ☎0832/222 7154, ⓔpklaldg @sancharnet.in. Cramped but clean and friendly family guesthouse in a rambling 1930s home. Pepper and coffee plants add atmosphere to the narrow communal terrace, and there's a TV lounge upstairs; also safe deposit facilities, Internet access and laundry service. Rates are high in season, but discounts are available at other times. ❺

The Town

The leafy rectangular park opposite the India Government tourist office, known as **Church Square** or the **Municipal Gardens**, forms the heart of Panjim. Presiding over its southeast side is the town's most distinctive and photogenic landmark, the toothpaste-white Baroque facade of the **Church of Our Lady of the Immaculate Conception**. Flanked by rows of slender palm trees, at the head of a crisscrossing laterite walkway, the church was built in 1541 for the benefit of sailors arriving here from Lisbon. The weary mariners would stagger up from the quay to give thanks for their safe passage before proceeding to the capital at Old Goa – the original home of the enormous bell that hangs from its central gable.

Running north from the church, Rua José Falcao brings you to the riverside, where Panjim's main street, Avenida Dom Joao Castro, holds the town's oldest surviving building. With its sloping tiled roofs, carved-stone coats of arms and wooden verandas, the stalwart **Secretariat** looks typically colonial. Yet it was originally the summer palace of Goa's sixteenth-century Muslim ruler, the Adil

△ Church of Our Lady of the Immaculate Conception

Shah. Later, the Portuguese converted it into a temporary rest house for the territory's governors (who used to overnight here en route to and from Lisbon) and then a residence for the viceroy. Today, it accommodates the Goan State Legislature – hence shiny chauffeur-driven Ambassador cars outside and the armed guards at the door.

A hundred metres east, a peculiar statue of a man holding his hands over the body of an entranced reclining woman represents **Abbé de Faria** (1755–1819), a Goan priest who emigrated to France to become one of the world's first professional hypnotists.

Just behind the esplanade, 500m west of the Abbé de Faria statue, stands another grand vestige of the colonial era, the **Menezes Braganza Institute**. Now the town's Central Library (Mon–Fri 9.30am–1pm & 2–5.30pm), this Neoclassical building was erected as part of the civic makeover initiated by the Marquis of Pombal and Dom Manuel de Portugal e Castro in the early nineteenth century. Its entrance lobby on Malacca Road is lined with panels of blue-and-yellow-painted ceramic tiles, known as **azulejos**, depicting scenes from Luis Vaz Camões' epic poem, *Os Luisiades*.

Fontainhas

Panjim's oldest and most interesting district, **Fontainhas**, spreads from the banks of Pato creek opposite the bus stand – a dozen or so blocks of Neoclassical houses rising up the sides of leafy Altinho Hill. Many have retained their traditional coat of ochre, pale yellow, green or blue – a legacy of the Portuguese insistence that every Goan building (except churches, which had to be white) should be colour-washed after the monsoons. While some (notably the Portuguese **Fundacão Oriente** building at the south end of the neighbourhood, and the three wings of the *Panjim Inn*) have been restored, most remain in a state of charismatic decay.

The whitewashed **Chapel of St Sebastian**, still holding to the old colonial decree, stands at the centre of Fontainhas, at the head of a small square where the Portuguese-speaking locals hold a lively annual street *festa* to celebrate their patron saint's day in mid-November. The eerily lifelike crucifix inside the chapel, brought here in 1812, formerly hung in the Palace of the Inquisition in Old Goa. Unusually, Christ's eyes are open – allegedly to inspire fear in those being interrogated by the Inquisitors.

Just off the bottom of the square is a small workshop where you can watch traditional Goan *azulejos* being made. The main sales room, **Galeria Velha Goa**, is a couple of blocks away, next door to the *Panjim Inn*.

Grand colonial-era buildings are to be found up on **Altinho Hill**, which can be reached via the flight of steps beginning alongside the *Park Lane Lodge*. The first one you come to at the top of the steps is the High Court of Goa, a splendid example of late-nineteenth-century Portuguese municipal architecture. Ten minutes' walk further south, occupying the highest point in Panjim, the **Archishop's Palace**, a long, white, double-storeyed building with an imposing facade, is still occupied by Goa's highest ranking prelate, hence the whitewash.

The State Archeological Museum

The most noteworthy feature of Panjim's **State Archeological Museum** (Mon–Fri 9.30am–1.15pm & 2–5.30pm; Rs20; ⓦwww.goamuseum.nic.in) is its impressive size, which stands in glaringly inverse proportion to the collections inside. In their bid to erect a structure befitting a state capital, Goa's bureaucrats ignored the fact that there was precious little to put in it. The only rarities to be found amid the lame array of temple sculpture, hero stones and

Goan food and drink

Not unnaturally, after 450 years of colonization, Goan **cooking** has absorbed a strong Portuguese influence – palm vinegar (unknown elsewhere in India), copious amounts of coconut, tangy tamarind and fierce local chillies also play their part. Goa is the home of the famous **vindaloo** (from the Portuguese *vinho d'alho*, literally "garlic wine"), originally an extra-hot and sour pork curry, but now made with a variety of meat and fish. Other **pork** specialities include *chouriço* red sausages, *sorpotel*, a hot curry made from pickled pig's liver and heart, *leitao*, suckling pig and *balchao*, pork in a rich brown sauce. Delicious alternatives include mutton *xacutti*, made with a sauce of lemon juice, peanuts, coconut, chillies and spices. The choice of **seafood**, often cooked in fragrant masalas, is excellent – clams, mussels, crab, lobster, giant prawns – while **fish**, depending on the type, is either cooked in wet curries, grilled, or baked in tandoori clay ovens. *Sanna*, like the South Indian *iddli*, is a steamed cake of fermented rice flour, but here made with palm toddy. Sweet tooths will adore *bebinca*, a rich, delicious solid egg custard with coconut.

As for **drinks**, locally produced wine, spirits and beer are cheaper than anywhere in the country, thanks to lower rates of tax. The most famous and widespread **beer** is Kingfisher, which tastes less of glycerine preservative than it does elsewhere in India, but you'll also come across pricier Fosters, brewed in Mumbai and nothing like the original. Goan **port**, a sweeter, inferior version of its Portuguese namesake, is ubiquitous, served chilled in large wine glasses with a slice of lemon. Local **spirits** – whiskies, brandies, rums, gins and vodkas – come in a variety of brand names for less than Rs30 a shot, but, at half the price, local speciality **feni**, made from distilled cashew or from the sap of coconut palms, offers strong competition. Cashew *feni* is usually drunk after the first distillation, but you can also find it double-distilled, flavoured with ginger or cumin to produce a smooth liqueur.

dowdy colonial-era artefacts are a couple of beautiful Jain bronzes rescued by Customs and Excise officials from smugglers and, on the first floor, the infamous Italian-style table used by Goa's Grand Inquisitors, complete with its original, ornately carved tall-backed chairs.

The Houses of Goa Museum

Across the river, near the new hilltop suburb of **Porvorim**, renowned local architect Gerard de Cunha and colleagues set up the quirky **Houses of Goa Museum** (Tues–Sun 10am–7.30pm; Rs25; ⓦwww.archgoa.org), 5km from Panjim. Its general aim is to showcase the region's way of life as it used to be before the protective shield of Portuguese rule was lifted in 1961.

The triangular building itself resembles a modern ark, with themed displays divided between four levels interconnected by spiral staircases. After a whistle-stop graphic resumé of Goan history, the exhibitions are largely given over to domestic houses, described as "the prime expression of Goan identity". Pieces of traditional colonial-era houses – from wonderful old doors and oyster-shell windows, to carved railings, ceramic tiles, furniture and masonry – are assembled to explain construction processes and changes in decor and style. Architectural features that were adapted in a uniquely Goan way, such as colour schemes, ornamental gateposts, verandas and false ceilings, are also highlighted, and interactive computer exhibits enable you to delve more deeply into the subjects covered.

The Houses of Goa museum is most easily reached by taxi or auto-rickshaw. With your own transport, head north over the Mandovi bridge and keep going until you reach the big Alto-Porvorim Circle roundabout. Take a right here and follow the road until it forks, then bear left and head straight on for 750m or so, until you reach a second fork, where you bear left again: the museum is next to Nisha's Play School. By bus, you can travel as far as the Alto-Porvorim circle on any Panjim–Mapusa service from the Kadamba stand: get down at *O Coqueiro* restaurant (infamous as the place where international jewel thief and suspected serial killer **Charles Sobhraj** was captured by police in 1987), which is just north of the roundabout, then walk the remaining 2km, or jump into an auto if there's one hanging around.

Eating and drinking

Catering for the droves of tourists who come here from other Indian states, as well as fussy, more price-conscious locals, Panjim is packed with good **places to eat**. Most are connected to a hotel, but there are also plenty of other independently run establishments offering quality food for far less than you pay in the coastal resorts. Vegetarians are particularly well catered for at the numerous Udupi restaurants that have sprung up. Beer, *feni* and other spirits are available in all but the purest "pure veg" places.

If you're unsure about which regional cooking style to go for, head for *The Fidalgo Food Enclave*, in the *Hotel Fidalgo* on 18th June Road, which hosts six different outlets, from Goan to Gujarati, with a great general Indian joint (*Mirch Masala*).

Bhojan *Hotel Fidalgo*, 18th June Rd. Authentic, pure-veg Gujarati thali joint, in the ground-floor restaurant complex of a popular upscale hotel. You won't eat finer Indian vegetarian cuisine anywhere in Goa. Rs120 for the works: five or six different vegetables, dhals, *papad*, rice and various traditional breads, plus fragrant milk sweets for dessert.

Delhi Darbar Mahatma Gandhi Rd, behind the *Hotel Mandovi*. A provincial branch of the famous Mumbai restaurant, and the best place in Panjim – if not all Goa – to sample traditional Mughlai cuisine of mainly meat steeped in rich, spicy sauces (try their superb *rogan ghosh* or melt-in-the-mouth chicken tikka). For vegetarians, there's a generous choice of fresh veg dishes, including a delicious *malai kofta*. Beer and spirits available. Most main dishes are around Rs175–250.

Legacy of Bombay *Hotel Fidalgo*, 18th June Rd. Basically an upmarket Udupi, only with black bow ties instead of grubby cotton tunics. Their menu features the usual *dosas*, South Indian snacks, *pao bhaji* and tasty spring rolls, as well as spiced teas and delicious lassis, but what sets this place apart is its stylish designer decor: the walls are lined with intriguing photographic montages of Mumbai.

Monginis Dr Atmaram Borkar Rd. A highly a/c pastry shop that does great choc-chip cake, date-and-walnut cup sponges and English-style home-made biscuits. Take away, or eat in at the marble mezzanine area.

Rosoyo 18th June Rd. Run by *Megson's*, this busy little fast-food joint is the place to sample tasty,

hygienic Mumbai-style street food: crunchy *bhel puri* (crispy fried noodles served cold with lime, coriander and chopped onion) or delicious *pao bhaji* (spicy tomato and potato-based mush dished up with a blob of butter and a fluffy Portuguese bread roll). They also serve wonderful Gujarati snacks such as *thepla* – chapatis griddle-cooked with curry leaves and cumin, and served with South Indian *chatni* – plus a full range of shakes and ice creams. You'll be hard pushed to spend Rs60 here.

Satkar 18th June Rd. Popular South Indian snack and juice joint. There's a huge range of dishes, including Chinese and North Indian, but most people go for their fantastic masala dosas and piping hot, crunchy samosas – the best in town.

Shiv Sagar Mahatma Gandhi Rd. Smarter than average Udupi café that does a brisk trade with Panjim's middle classes for its consistently fresh, delicious pan-Indian food and fresh fruit juices. The northern dishes aren't so great, but their Udupi menu is superb (try the delicious *palak dosa*, made with spinach), and their fiery *pao bhaji* is a real crowd puller on weekends. A/c child-friendly mezzanine upstairs. No alcohol.

Venite Rua 31 de Janeiro. With its wooden floors and romantic, candle-lit balcony seats, this tourist-oriented place is one of the most atmospheric places to eat in Panjim, with Continental and Goan seafood dishes dominating the menu. Most mains are Rs100–125.

Vihar Around the corner from *Venite*, on Avenida Dom Joao Castro. One of the best South Indian snack cafés in Panjim, and more conveniently situated than its competitors if you're staying in Fontainhas. Try their tasty *rawa* masala dosas or cheese *uttapams*. The only drawback is the traffic noise, so avoid it during rush hours.

 Viva Panjim 178 Rua 31 de Janeiro, behind Mary Immaculate High School, Fontainhas.

Traditional Goan home cooking – *xacutis*, vindaloo, prawn *balchao*, *cafreal*, *amotik* and fantastic freshly grilled fish – served by a charming local lady in an atmospheric colonial-era backstreet. This place should be your first choice for dinner if you're staying in Fontainhas.

Listings

Airlines *Air France*, *Air Seychelles*, *American Airlines*, *Biman Bangladesh*, *Cathay Pacific*, *Gulf Air*, *Kenyan Airways*, *Royal Jordanian*, *Sri Lankan Airlines*, all c/o Jet Air, 102 Rizvi Chambers, 1st floor, H Salgado Rd ☏0832/223172; *Air India*, Colvacar Centaur, Campal ☏0832/243 1100; *British Airways*, DKI Airlines Service, DKI Travel Services Pvt Ltd 102, Shiv Towers, Plot 14, Patto Plaza ☏0832/243 8055; *Alitalia*, Globe Trotters International, G-7 Shankar Parvati Building, 18th June Rd ☏0832/223 0940; *Indian Airlines*, Dempo House, Dr D Bandodkar Rd ☏0832/242 8787 or 223 7826; *Jet Airways*, Sesa Ghor, Patto Plaza, next to GTDC *Panjim Residency*, Pato ☏0832/243 8792; *Sahara Airlines*, Magnum Chambers, 1st floor, Shop No. 9/12, opposite Delhi Darbar, M G Road ☏0832/223 0237.

Banks and ATMs The most efficient places to change money are: Thomas Cook, near the Indian Airlines office at 8 Alcon Chambers, Dr Bandodkar Rd (Mon–Sat 9am–6pm, Oct–March also Sun 10am–5pm); and the Pheroze Framroze Exchange Bureau on Dr P Shirgaonkar Rd (Mon–Sat 9.30am–7pm, Sun 9.30am–1pm). The latter's rates are competitive and they don't charge commission on either currency or traveller's cheques. Nearly all the banks in town nowadays have ATMs, where you can make withdrawals using Visa or Mastercard; several are marked on the map on pp.190–191. Changing money in the regular, government-run banks tends to take a lot longer: the Bank of Baroda (where you can draw money on Visa cards at their Bobcard counter), is on Azad Maidan.

Bookshops The bookshops in the *Hotel Fidalgo* and the *Hotel Mandovi* stock English-language titles, including paperback pulp fiction and guides, but the best selection of Goa-related books is at the Broadway Book Centre on 18th June Rd, near the Caculo Island intersection. It sells a great range of old texts in facsimile editions and lots of architecture and photographic tomes in hardback at discounted prices.

British Consular Assistant The British High Commission of Mumbai has a Tourist Assistance Office in Panjim – a useful contact for British nationals who've lost passports, get into trouble with the law or need help dealing with a death. It's

over near the Kadamba bus stand at 13/14 Dempo Towers, Patto Plaza ☏0832/243 8734 or 8897, ☏664 1297, ✉assistance@goaukconsular.org, ☏www.ukinindia.com. Office opening hours are Mon–Fri 9am–1pm & 2.30–3.30pm. Outside these times, you should contact the main British Consulate in Mumbai ☏022/6650 2222, which in theory has a duty officer on call 24/7.

Cinema Panjim's swanky new multiplex, the 1272-seater Inox, is in the northwest of town on the site of the old Goa Medical College, Dayanand Bandodkar (DB) Marg (☏0832/242 0999, ☏www .inoxmovies.com). Opened for the 2004 International Film Festival of India, the Kiwi-designed complex screens all the latest Hindi blockbusters, and some English-language Hollywood movies; see the local press or their website for listings and booking details.

Hospital The state's main medical facility is the new Goa Medical College, aka GMC (☏0832/245 8700–07), 7km south on NH-17 at Bambolim, where there's also a 24hr pharmacy. Ambulances (☏102) are likely to get you there a lot less quickly than a standard taxi. Conditions are grim by Western standards; relatives sleep on the wards to provide food for patients. Less serious cases can receive attention at the Vintage Hospital, next to the fire brigade headquarters in Panjim's St Inez district (☏0832/564 4401–05).

Internet access Hotels and guesthouses, including the *Park Lane Lodge* and *Panjim Inn* (see pp.191–192), offer Internet access to guests. Otherwise, Cozy Nook Travels, at No.6 Municipal Bldg, 18th June Rd, has a fast ADSL connection.

Music and dance Regular recitals of classical Indian music and dance are held at Panjim's school for the performing arts, the Kala Academy in Campal (☏www.kalaacademy.org), at the far west end of town on Dr Devanand Bandodkar Rd. The building, originally designed by award-winning Goan architect Charles Correa, provides a permanent venue for the event. For details of forthcoming concerts, consult the boards in front of the auditorium or the listings page of local newspapers.

Petrol The main petrol pump in Panjim is on Avda Dom Joao Castro (the main drag along the riverside), just east of the Secretariat building; the fuel sold here is dependably clean. There's also a good pump across the river in Betim – riders without international licences are advised to park up there and catch the ferry over the Mandovi to avoid Panjim's ubiquitous traffic police.

Pharmacies Hindu Pharma, near the tourist office on Church Square (☎0832/222 3176), stocks a phenomenal range of Ayurvedic, homeopathic and allopathic medicines.

Police The Police Headquarters is on Malacca Rd, central Panjim. In an emergency, call ☎100.

Poste restante Panjim's reliable poste restante counter (Mon–Sat 9.30am–1pm & 2–5.30pm) is at the Head Post Office, 200m west of Pato Bridge. Note that to get your stamps franked (the only way to ensure they won't get peeled off and resold by some unscrupulous clerk), you have to walk around the back of the building and ask at the office behind the second door on the right. Indian postal regulations insist that parcels have to be stitched in cotton and sealed; this can be done at the Deepak store, on the corner of the next block north from the post office.

Travel agent AERO Mundial, ground floor, *Hotel Mandovi*, Dr Devanand Bandodkar Rd ☎0832/222 3773.

Old Goa

A one-time byword for splendour with a population of several hundred thousand, Goa's erstwhile former capital, **OLD GOA**, was virtually abandoned following malaria and cholera epidemics from the seventeenth century onwards. Today you need considerable imagination to picture the once-great capital as it used to be. The maze of twisting streets, piazzas and ochre-washed villas has gone, and all that remains is a score of cream-painted churches and convents. Granted World Heritage Status by UNESCO, Old Goa today attracts busloads of foreign tourists from the coast, and as many Christian pilgrims from around India. While the former come to admire the gigantic facades and gilt altars of the beautifully preserved churches, the main attraction for the latter is the tomb of **St Francis Xavier** (see p.200), the legendary sixteenth-century missionary, whose remains are enshrined in the **Basilica of Bom Jesus**. If you're staying on the coast and contemplating a day-trip inland, this is the most obvious and accessible option.

Just thirty minutes by road from the state capital, Old Goa is served by buses every fifteen minutes from Panjim's Kadamba bus stand; alternatively, hop into an auto-rickshaw (Rs75–100), or rent a taxi (Rs250–300). There is nowhere commendable to eat in Old Goa; for a snack or coffee, head a couple of kilometres back along the road to Panjim, where the lifestyle store **Casa de Goa**, housed in a beautifully converted late-sixteenth-century *palacio*, has an excellent **café**.

The Viceroy's Archway and the Church of St Cajetan

On arriving at the river landing stage to the north, seventeenth-century visitors passed through the **Viceroy's Archway** (1597), constructed to commemorate Vasco da Gama's arrival in India and built from the same porous red laterite as virtually all Old Goa's buildings. Above it a Bible-toting figure rests his foot on the cringing figure of a "native", while its granite facade, facing the river, holds a statue of da Gama himself. It's hard to imagine today that these overgrown fields and simple streets with a few cold-drinks stands were once the focus of a lively market, with silk and gem merchants, horse dealers and carpet weavers. The one surviving monument, known as **Adil Shah's Doorway**, predates the Portuguese and possibly even the Muslim period. Hindu in style, it consists simply of a lintel supported by two columns in black basalt, to which are attached the remains of perforated screens. You can find it by turning left at the crossroads immediately above the Arch of the Viceroys.

A short way up the lane from the Gate, the distinctive domed **Church of St Cajetan** (1651) was modelled on St Peter's in Rome by monks from the Theatine Order. While it boasts a Corinthian exterior, you can also spot certain

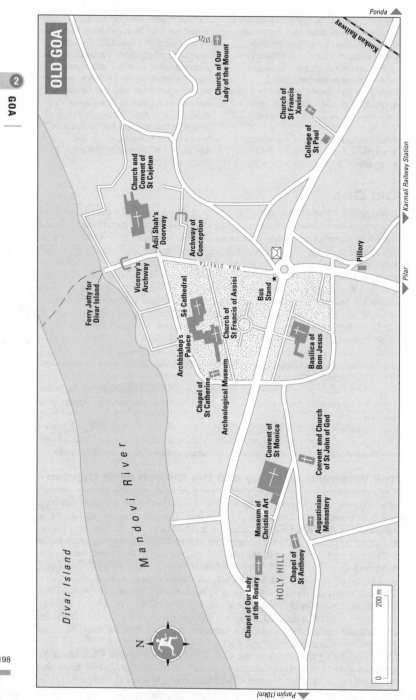

OLD GOA

Church of Our Lady of the Mount

Konkan Railway

Ponda

Church of St Francis Xavier

College of St Paul

Karmali Railway Station

Church and Convent of St Cajetan

Adil Shah's Doorway

Archway of Conception

Viceroy's Archway

RUA DIREITA

Pillory

Pilar

Ferry Jetty for Divar Island

Sé Cathedral

Archbishop's Palace

Chapel of St Catherine

Archeological Museum

Church of St Francis of Assisi

Bus Stand

Basilica of Bom Jesus

M a n d o v i   R i v e r

Convent of St Monica

Convent and Church of St John of God

Divar Island

Museum of Christian Art

Augustinian Monastery

Chapel of Our Lady of the Rosary

HOLY HILL

Chapel of St Anthony

N

200 m

0

Panjim (10km)

non-European elements in the decoration, such as the cashew-nut designs in the carving of the pulpit. Hidden beneath the church is a crypt where the embalmed bodies of Portuguese governors were once kept in lead coffins before they were shipped back to Lisbon. Forgotten for over thirty years, the last batch (of three) was only removed in 1992 on the eve of the state visit to Goa of Portuguese president Mario Soares.

The Sé (St Catherine's Cathedral)

The Portuguese viceroy Redondo (1561–64) commissioned the **Sé**, or **St Catherine's Cathedral**, southwest of St Cajetan's, to be "a grandiose church worthy of the wealth, power and fame of the Portuguese who dominated the seas from the Atlantic to the Pacific". Today it stands larger than any church in Portugal, although it was beset by problems, not least a lack of funds and Portugal's temporary loss of independence to Spain. It took eighty years to build and was not consecrated until 1640.

On the Tuscan-style exterior, the one surviving tower houses the **Golden Bell**, cast in Cuncolim (south Goa) in the seventeenth century. During the Inquisition, its tolling announced the start of the gruesome *auto da fés* that were held in the square outside, when suspected heretics were subjected to public torture and burned at the stake. The scale and detail of the Corinthian-style interior is overwhelming; no fewer than fifteen altars are arranged around the walls, dedicated among others to Our Ladies of Hope, Anguish and Three Needs. An altar to St Anne treasures the relics of the **Blessed Martyrs of Cuncolim**, whose failed mission to convert the Mughal emperor Akbar culminated in their murder, while a chapel behind a highly detailed screen holds the **Miraculous Cross**, which stood in a Goan village until a vision of Christ appeared on it. Said to heal the sick, it is kept in a box; a small opening on the side allows devotees to touch it. The staggeringly ornate gilded main **altar** comprises nine carved frames and a splendid crucifix. Panels depict episodes from the life of St Catherine of Alexandria (died 307 AD), including an interchange of ideas with the pagan Roman emperor Maxim, who wished to marry her, and her subsequent flogging and martyrdom.

The Archbishop's Palace

Adjoining the Sé Cathedral – an exact contemporary – the **Archbishop's Palace** is unique as the last surviving civil building of colonial Goa's golden era. Though in a lamentable state of disrepair, its steeply inclined roofs and white facade still perfectly embody the solidity and imposing strength of the so-called "chã" style of architecture, derived from military constructions of the day, of which the most extreme example was the Viceroy's Fortress Palace (Palacio da Fortaleza) – since vanished without trace. Presenting their most austere aspect to the river, these two fortified palaces formerly dominated the skyline of the waterfront, appropriately enough for a city perennially under threat of attack. These days, the Archbishop's Palace, sandwiched between two of Old Goa's great churches, houses a missable collection of contemporary Christian art in the recently inaugurated Kristu Kala Mandir Art Gallery (daily 10am–6pm; free) – not to be confused with the similar gallery at the Santa Monica Convent (see p.201).

Nineteenth-century photos show that the city-facing side of the building was originally enfolded by a low wall, which surrounded a garden. This has long been dismantled, but the two grand **entrance porches** remain intact. The one on the right (as you look at the building) is original, complete with red decorative frescoes lining the side walls, among the last remaining paintings of their kind left in Goa. During the Portuguese heyday, guards in blue livery would have stood on its steps, as they did in the viceroy's palace and most *hidalgo* (noble) houses.

The Church of St Francis of Assisi and Archeological Museum

Southwest of the cathedral is the ruined **Palace of the Inquisition**, in operation up until 1774, while to the west stands the **Convent of St Francis of Assisi**, built by Franciscan monks in 1517 and restored in the mid-eighteenth century. Today, the core of its **Archeological Museum** (daily except Fri 10am–5pm; Rs5) is a gallery of **portraits** of Portuguese viceroys, painted by local artists under Italian supervision. Other exhibits include coins, domestic Christian wooden sculpture, and downstairs in the cloister, pre-Portuguese Hindu sculpture. Next door, the **Church of St Francis** (1521) features fine

St Francis Xavier

Francis Xavier, the "Apostle of the Indies", was born in 1506 in the old kingdom of Navarre, now part of Spain. After taking a masters' degree in philosophy and theology at the University of Paris, where he studied for the priesthood until 1535, he was ordained two years later in Venice. He was then recruited by (Saint) **Ignatius Loyola** (1491–1556) along with five other priests into the new "Society of Jesus", which later became known as the **Jesuits**.

When the Portuguese king, Dom Joao III (1521–57), received reports of corruption and dissolute behaviour among the Portuguese in Goa, he asked Ignatius Loyola to dispatch a priest who could influence the moral climate for the better. In 1541 Xavier was sent to work in the diocese of Goa, constituted seven years earlier, and comprising all regions east of the Cape of Good Hope. Arriving after a year-long journey, he embarked on a busy programme throughout southern India. Despite frequent obstruction from Portuguese officials, he founded numerous churches, and is credited with converting 30,000 people and performing such miracles as raising the dead and curing the sick with a touch of his beads. Subsequently he took his mission further afield to Sri Lanka, Malacca (Malaysia), China and Japan, where he was less successful.

When Xavier left Goa for the last time, it was with the ambition of evangelizing in China; however, he contracted dysentery aboard ship and died on the island of San Chuan (Sancian), off the Chinese coast, where he was buried. On hearing of his death, a group of Christians from Malacca exhumed his body – which, although the grave had been filled with lime to hasten its decomposition, they found to be in a perfect state of preservation. Reburied in Malacca, his body was later removed and taken to Old Goa, where it has remained ever since, enshrined in the Basilica of Bom Jesus.

However, Saint Francis' incorruptible corpse has never rested entirely in peace. Chunks of it have been removed over the years by relic hunters and curious clerics: in 1614, the right arm was dispatched to the Pope in Rome (where it allegedly wrote its name on paper), a hand was sent to Japan, and parts of the intestines to Southeast Asia. One Portuguese woman, Dona Isabel de Caron, even bit off the little toe of the cadaver in 1534; apparently, so much blood spurted into her mouth, it left a trail to her house and she was discovered.

Every ten years, the saint's body is carried in a three-hour ceremony from the Basilica of Bom Jesus to the Sé Cathedral, where visitors file past, touch and photograph it. During the 2004–05 "**exposition**", around 256,000 pilgrims flocked for *darshan* or ritual viewing of the corpse, these days a shrivelled and somewhat unsavoury spectacle.

decorative frescoes, *hidalgos'* tombstones in the floor paving, and paintings on wood showing the life of St Francis of Assisi.

Basilica of Bom Jesus

Close to the Convent of St Francis, the 1605 church of **Bom Jesus**, "Good" or "Menino Jesus" (Mon–Sat 9am–6.30pm, Sun 10am–6.30pm), is known principally for the **tomb of St Francis Xavier**. In 1946, it became the first church in India to be elevated to the status of Minor Basilica. On the west, the three-storey Renaissance facade encompasses Corinthian, Doric, Ionic and Composite styles.

The interior is entered beneath the choir, supported by columns. On the northern wall, in the centre of the nave, is a cenotaph in gilded bronze to **Dom Jeronimo Mascarenhas**, the Captain of Cochin and benefactor of the church. The main altar, extravagantly decorated in gold, depicts the infant Jesus under the protection of St Ignatius Loyola (founder of the Jesuit Order); to each side are subsidiary altars to Our Lady of Hope and St Michael. In the southern transept, lavishly decorated with twisted gilded columns and floriate carvings, stands the **Chapel and Tomb of St Francis Xavier**. Constructed of marble and jasper in 1696, it was the gift of the Medici, Cosimo III, the Grand Duke of Tuscany; the middle tier contains panels detailing the saint's life. An ornate domed reliquary in silver contains his remains; for a week around his feast day, December 3, tens of thousands of pilgrims – Hindus as well as Christians – queue for *darshan* (ritual viewing) of the casket before attending open-air Mass in the square outside.

Holy Hill

A number of other important religious buildings and a museum stand opposite Bom Jesus on **Holy Hill**. The **Convent of St Monica**, constructed in 1627, destroyed by fire in 1636 and rebuilt the following year, was the only Goan convent at the time and the largest in Asia. It housed around a hundred nuns, the Daughters of St Monica, and also offered accommodation to women whose husbands were called away to other parts of the empire. The **church** adjoins the convent on the south. As they had to remain away from the public gaze, the nuns attended mass in the choir loft and looked down upon the congregation. Inside, a **Miraculous Cross** rises above the figure of St Monica at the altar. In 1636, it was reported that the figure of Christ had opened his eyes, motioned as if to speak, and blood had flowed from the wounds made by his crown of thorns. The last Daughter of St Monica died in 1885, and since 1964 the convent has been occupied by the Mater Dei Institute for nuns.

Next door to the Chapel of the Miraculous Cross stands Goa's foremost **Museum of Christian Art** (daily 9.30am–5pm; Rs15). Exhibits include processional crosses, ivory ornaments, damask silk clerical robes and some finely sculpted wooden icons dating from the sixteenth and seventeenth centuries, among them an unusual statue of John the Baptist wearing a tiger-skin wrap (in the style of the Hindu god Shiva).

Nearby, the **Convent of St John of God**, built in 1685 by the Order of Hospitallers of St John of God to tend to the sick, was rebuilt in 1953. At the top of the hill, the **Chapel of Our Lady of the Rosary**, constructed in 1526 in the Manueline style (after the Portuguese king Manuel I, 1495–1521), features Ionic plasterwork with a double-storey portico, cylindrical turrets and a tower that commands fine views across the river from the terrace where Albuquerque surveyed the decisive battle of 1510. Its cruciform interior is unremarkable, except for the marble tomb of **Catarina a Piró**, believed to have been the first European woman to set foot in the colony. A commoner, she eloped here to escape the scandal surrounding her romance with Portuguese nobleman Garcia de Sá, who later rose to be governor of Goa. Under pressure from no less than Francis Xavier, Garcia eventually married her, but only *in articulo mortis* as she lay on her deathbed. Her finely carved tomb, set in the wall beside the high altar, incorporates a band of intricate Gujarati-style ornamentation, probably imported from the Portuguese trading post of Diu.

Ponda and around

PONDA, 28km southeast of Panjim and 17km northeast of Margao, is Ponda district's administrative headquarters and main market town. Straddling the busy Panjim–Bengaluru (Bangalore) highway (NH-4), it's not a place to spend any time. However, scattered among the lush valleys and forests **around Ponda** are a dozen or so **Hindu temples** founded during the seventeenth and eighteenth centuries, when this hilly region was a Christian-free haven for Hindus fleeing persecution by the Portuguese. Although the temples are fairly modern by Indian standards, their deities are ancient and held in high esteem by both local people and thousands of pilgrims from Maharashtra and Karnataka.

The temples are concentrated in two main clusters: the first to the north of Ponda, on the NH-4, and the second deep in the countryside, around 5km west of the town. Most people only manage the **Shri Manguesh** and **Shri Mahalsa** (Ⓦ www.mahalsa.org), between the villages of **Mardol** and **Priol**. Among the most interesting temples in the state, they lie just a stone's throw from the main highway and are passed by regular **buses** between Panjim and Margao via Ponda. The others are farther off the beaten track, although they are not hard to find on motorbikes; locals will wave you in the right direction if you get lost.

Mardol and Priol

Although the **Sri Manguesh** temple originally stood in a secret location in Cortalim, and was moved to its present site between **MARDOL** and **PRIOL** during the sixteenth century, the structure visitors see today dates from the 1700s. A gateway at the roadside leads to a paved path and courtyard that gives onto a water tank, overlooked by the white temple building, raised on a plinth. Also in the courtyard is a seven-storey *deepmal*, a tower for oil lamps. Inside, the floor is paved with marble, and bands of decorative tiles emblazon the white walls. Flanked by large *dvarpala* guardians, embossed silver doorways with floriate designs lead to the sanctum, which houses a *shivalingam*.

Two kilometres south, the **Mahalsa Marayani** temple was also transferred from its original site, in this case Salcete *taluka* further south, in the seventeenth century. Here, the *deepmal* is exceptionally tall, with 21 tiers rising from a figure of Kurma, the tortoise incarnation of Vishnu. Original features include a marble-floored wooden *mandapa* (assembly hall) with carved pillars, ceiling panels of parakeets and, in the eaves, sculptures of the incarnations of Vishnu.

Dudhsagar waterfalls

Measuring a mighty 600m from head to foot, the famous **Dudhsagar water-falls**, on the Goa–Karnataka border, are some of the highest in India, and a spectacular enough sight to entice a steady stream of visitors from the coast into the rugged Western Ghats. After pouring across the Deccan plateau, the headwaters of the Mandovi River form a foaming torrent that fans into three streams, then cascades down a near-vertical cliff face into a deep green pool. The

Konkani name for the falls, which literally translated means "sea of milk", derives from clouds of foam kicked up at the bottom when the water levels are at their highest. Overlooking a steep, crescent-shaped head of a valley carpeted with pristine tropical forest, Dudhsagar is set amid breathtaking **scenery** that is only accessible on foot or by Jeep; the recently upgraded Margao–Castle Rock railway actually passes over the falls on an old stone viaduct, but services along it are infrequent.

One you've reached Dudhsagar, there's little to do beyond enjoying the views and clambering over the rocks below the falls in search of pools to swim in. The **best time to visit** is immediately after the monsoons, from October until mid-December, when water levels are highest, although the falls flow well into April. Unfortunately, the train line only sees two services per week in each direction, neither of them returning the same day. As a result, the only practicable way to get there and back is by four-wheel-drive **Jeep** from **Colem** (reachable by train from Vasco, Margao and Chandor, or by taxi from the north coast resorts for around Rs1250). The cost of the onward thirty- to forty-minute trip from Colem to the falls, which takes you across rough forest tracks and two or three river fords, is Rs650 per person; the drive ends with an enjoyable ten-minute hike, for which you'll need a sturdy pair of shoes. Finding a Jeep-wallah is easy; just turn up in Colem and look for the "Controller of Jeeps" near the station. However, if you're travelling alone or in a couple, you may have to wait around until the vehicle fills up, or else fork out to cover the cost of hiring the whole Jeep yourself. Alternatively, if you've travelled here **by motorcycle** you may – water levels permitting – ride to within easy reach of the falls: Enfields and Pulsars have enough clearance to ford the streams en route, but not Honda Activas and other small-wheeled scooters. Anyone who's ridden all the way to Colem on these bikes, and is determined not to stump up the Jeep fare, should follow the dirt track that runs alongside the main railway line for approximately 8km until it meets the Jeep route, thus bypassing the stream crossings – the way local stallholders make the journey each day.

North Goa

Beyond the mouth of the Mandovi estuary, the Goan coast sweeps **north** in a near-continuous string of beaches, broken only by the odd saltwater inlet, rocky headland, and three tidal rivers – the most northerly of which, the Arondem, still has to be crossed by ferry. Development is concentrated mainly behind the seven-kilometre strip of white sand that stretches from the foot of **Fort Aguada**, crowning the peninsula east of Panjim, to Baga creek in the north. Encompassing the resorts of **Candolim**, **Calangute** and **Baga**, this is Goa's prime charter belt and an area most independent travellers steer clear of.

Since the advent of mass tourism in the 1980s, the alternative "scene" has drifted progressively north away from the sunbed strip to **Anjuna** and **Vagator** – now predominantly Israeli rave enclaves boasting some of the region's loveliest beaches – and scruffier **Chapora**, a workaday fishing village which has in the last few seasons been colonized by Russians. Further north still, **Arambol** has thus far escaped any large-scale development, despite the completion of the new road bridge across the Chapora River. What little extra traffic there is since the new road link tends to focus on the low-key resorts just south of Arambol, namely **Aswem** and **Mandrem**, where facilities remain basic by modern standards.

North Goa's market town, **Mapusa**, is this area's main jumping-off place, with bus connections to most resorts on the coast. If you're travelling here by train via the **Konkan Railway**, get off the train at **Tivim** (☎0832/229 8682), 19km west of Margao, from where you'll have to jump in a bus or taxi for the remaining leg.

Mapusa

MAPUSA (pronounced "Mapsa") is the district headquarters of Bardez *taluka*. A dusty collection of dilapidated, mostly modern buildings ranged around a busy central square, the town is of little more than passing interest, although it does host a lively **market** on Friday mornings. Anjuna's market may be a better place to shop for souvenirs, but Mapusa's is much more authentic. Local specialities include strings of spicy Goan sausages (*chouriço*), bottles of toddy (fermented palm sap) and large green plantains from nearby Moira.

Practicalities

Tivim (Thivim), the nearest railway station to Mapusa, is 12km east in the neighbouring Bicholim district. Buses should be on hand to transport passengers into town, from where you can pick up local services to Calangute, Baga, Anjuna, Vagator, Chapora and Arambol. These leave from the **Kadamba bus stand**, five minutes' walk west of the main square, where all state-run services from Panjim also pull in. **Motorcycle taxis** hang around the square to whisk lightly laden shoppers and travellers to the coast for around Rs50–65. **Taxis** charge considerably more (around Rs150), but you can split the fare with up to five people.

The Konkan Railway's Konkan–Kanya Express (#KR0111) arrives in Tivim at around 9.30am, leaving plenty of time to find **accommodation** in the coastal resorts west of Mapusa. Avoid staying in the town if possible, but if you can't, try GTDC's *Mapusa Residency* (☎0832/226 2794, ⓦwww.goa-tourism .com; ❹–❺), on the roundabout below the square, which has spacious and clean rooms and a Goa **tourist information** counter. Best of the **eating** options on or around the main square are the *Ruchira*, within the *Hotel Satyaheera* on the north side of the main square, which serves a standard multi-cuisine menu and cold beer. For quick, authentically Goan food, you won't do better than the *FR Xavier* café over in the Municipal Market, which has been here (and changed little) since the Portuguese era. The waiters leave heaped baskets of fresh veg patties and beef samosas on your table, billing you for what you eat at the end.

Candolim and Fort Aguada

Compared with Calangute, 3km north along the beach, **CANDOLIM** (from the Konkani *kandoli*, meaning "dykes", in reference to the system of sluices that the area's first farmers used to reclaim land from nearby marshes) is a surprisingly relaxed resort, attracting mainly middle-aged package tourists from the UK and Scandinavia. Over the past few years, however, its ribbon development of hotels and restaurants has sprouted a string of holiday complexes, and during peak season the few vestiges of authentically Goan culture that remain here are drowned in a deluge of Kashmiri handicraft stalls, luridly lit terrace cafés and shopping arcades. On the plus side, Candolim has lots of pleasant places to stay, many of them tucked away down quiet sandy lanes and better value than comparable guesthouses in nearby Calangute, making this a good first stop if you've just arrived in Goa and are planning to head further north after finding your feet.

△ Fort Aguada

Immediately south, **Fort Aguada** crowns the rocky flattened headland at the end of the beach. Built in 1612 to protect the northern shores of the Mandovi estuary from Dutch and Maratha raiders, the bastion encloses several natural springs, the first source of drinking water available to ships arriving in Goa after the long sea voyage from Lisbon. The ruins of the fort can be reached by road; follow the main drag south from Candolim as it bears left, past the turning for the *Taj Holiday Village*, and keep going for around 1km until you see a right turn, which runs uphill to a small car park. Nowadays, much of the site serves as a prison, and is therefore closed to visitors. It's worth a visit, though, if only for the superb views from the top of the hill where a four-storey Portuguese **lighthouse**, erected in 1864 and the oldest of its kind in Asia, looks down over the vast expanse of sea, sand and palm trees.

From the base of Fort Aguada on the northern flank of the headland, a rampart of red-brown laterite juts into the bay at the bottom of picturesque **Sinquerim Beach** (in effect the southernmost reach of Calangute beach). This was among the first places in Goa to be singled out for upmarket tourism. Taj Group's *Fort Aguada* resorts, among the most expensive hotels in India, lord over the sands from the slopes below the battlements.

Warning

Candolim Beach has seen a spate of **drownings** over the past few years. The undertow here has always been strong at certain phases of the tide, but the currents rarely proved treacherous until June 6, 2000, when the 61,000-tonne bulk carrier MV *River Princess* ran aground just off Sinquerim. Since then, the ship's owners, its insurers and the Goan government have been embroiled in a dispute over who should foot the bill for salvaging the vessel. Work finally started after the monsoons in 2006, and was still advancing a year later – making the waters around the ship, with whipped-up eddies and whirlpools, even more dangerous.

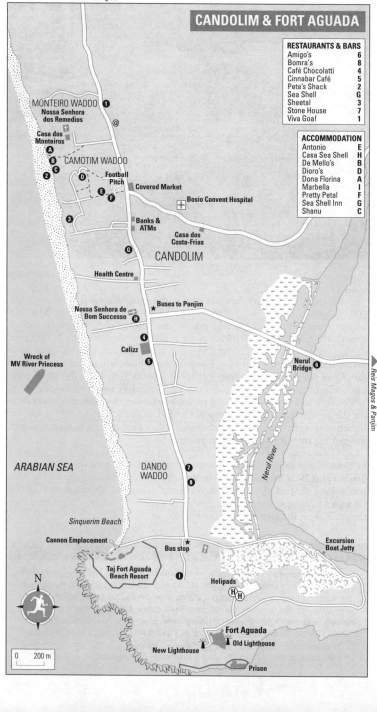

▲ Calangute

CANDOLIM & FORT AGUADA

RESTAURANTS & BARS

Amigo's	6
Bomra's	8
Café Chocolatti	4
Cinnabar Café	5
Pete's Shack	2
Sea Shell	G
Sheetal	3
Stone House	7
Viva Goa!	1

ACCOMMODATION

Antonio	E
Casa Sea Shell	H
De Mello's	B
Dioro's	D
Dona Florina	A
Marbella	I
Pretty Petal	F
Sea Shell Inn	G
Shanu	C

MONTEIRO WADDO
Nossa Senhora dos Remedios

Casa dos Monteiros

CAMOTIM WADDO

Football Pitch

Covered Market

Bosio Convent Hospital

Banks & ATMs

Casa dos Costa-Frias

CANDOLIM

Health Centre

Buses to Panjim

Nossa Senhora de Bom Successo

Calizz

Wreck of MV River Princess

Nerul Bridge

Nerul River

Reis Magos & Panjim

ARABIAN SEA

DANDO WADDO

Sinquerim Beach

Cannon Emplacement

Bus stop

Excursion Boat Jetty

Taj Fort Aguada Beach Resort

Helipads

N

Fort Aguada
Old Lighthouse

New Lighthouse

Prison

0   200 m

GOA

2

In addition to its nearby fort, Candolim also harbours a bumper crop of wonderful **old mansions** and typically Goan houses, some of the best of them in an excellent folk and architectural museum called **Calizz** (daily 10.30am–11.30pm; admission Rs1200, includes meal; Ⓦ www.calizz.com) on the south side of the village near Acron Arcade. Comprising half a dozen beautifully restored period buildings spread over a site of several acres, the complex showcases various styles of traditional Goan houses – both Christian and Hindu – from humble mud structures dating from pre-colonial times to sumptuous Portuguese palacios with chapels attached. On display inside them is a superb array of antiques, furniture, religious icons and daily artefacts. Visits kick off with an engaging 90-minute guided tour, after which you're served a traditional Indo-Portuguese-Goan feast, comprising dishes that would have been prepared in the houses you've looked at.

Practicalities

Buses to and from Panjim stop every ten minutes or so at the stand opposite the *Casa Sea Shell*, in the middle of Candolim. A few continue south to the *Fort Aguada Beach Resort* terminus, from where services depart every thirty minutes for the capital via Nerul village; you can also flag down buses from anywhere along the main drag to Calangute. **Taxis** are ubiquitous. During the season, however, there is often a shortage of **motorcycles for rent** here, and you may find yourself having to search for a bike in Calangute.

There are several ATMs dotted along the main drag (see map opposite) and you can **change money** at any number of private exchange places dotted around Candolim, although their rates are unlikely to be as competitive as those on offer in Calangute. For **Internet** access, Sify-I-Way, at the north end of the village on the main road, offers a fast broadband connection.

Accommodation

Candolim is charter-holiday land, so **accommodation** tends to be expensive for most of the season. That said, if bookings are down you can find some great bargains here.

Antonio Camotim Waddo ☏0832/248 9735, ☏m98223 381214. Spacious and comfortable chalet-style rooms, some with kitchenettes, all with good-sized balconies, in a two-storey block between the road and the beach. It's situated in a quiet, traffic-free neighbourhood well away from the strip, and it's efficiently run by the Pires family. ❹

Casa Sea Shell Fort Aguada Rd, near *Bom Successo* ☏0832/247 9879. A modern block with its own pool, picturesquely situated beside a small chapel. The rooms are large, with spacious tiled bathrooms, and the staff and management unfailingly welcoming and courteous. If they're full, ask for a room in the identical and slightly cheaper (but pool-less) *Sea Shell Inn* (☏0832/248 9131) up the road. ❺

De Mello's Sequeira Waddo ☏0832/248 9650. Pink and orange place in the dunes that takes the overspill from the (pricier) *Dona Florina* next door. Smallish rooms with not so private balconies, but only a stone's throw from the beach and very quiet. ❹

Dioro's Camotim Waddo ☏0832/329 0713 or ☏m98232 69376, ✉ diorosgoa@yahoo.com. Very large, tiled, spotless rooms with huge balconies and fridges, in a quiet residential area well back from the main road and close to the beach. Great value for money, considering the space and comfort, even at Christmas; and there's a well kept garden. ❹

Dona Florina Monteiro's road, Sequeira Waddo ☏0832/248 9051, Ⓦ www .donaflorina.com. Large guesthouse in a superb location, overlooking the beach in the most secluded corner of the village. Its friendly owner, Jessica D'Souza, recently added a breezy rooftop terrace with ceramic mosaic floors for guests to practise yoga on (*sanyasins* from the Rashneesh *ashram* from Pune have long been its mainstay). Well worth paying a little extra for if you want idyllic sea views. No car access. ❹–❺

Marbella Sinquerim ☏0832/247 9551, Ⓦ www .marbella.com. Individually styled suites and spacious rooms (from Rs1750) in a beautiful house built to resemble a traditional Goan mansion. The decor, fittings and furniture are gorgeous, especially in the top-floor "Penthouse" (Rs3150), and the whole place is screened by a giant mango tree. Unashamedly romantic and definitely worth splashing out on. ⑥–⑧

Pretty Petal Camotim Waddo ☎ 0832/348 9184, ⓦ www.prettypetalsgoa.com. Not as twee as it sounds: very large, modern rooms, all with fridges and balconies, and relaxing, marble-floored

communal areas overlooking lawns. Their top-floor apartment, with windows on four sides and a huge balcony, is the best choice, though more expensive. ⑤–⑥

Shanu Escrivao Waddo ☎ 0832/248 9899. Good-sized, well-furnished rooms with narrow balconies right on the dunes, some of them with uninterrupted views of the sea (a real rarity). Ask the hospitable owners for #120 (or failing that #118, #111, #110 or #107). Breakfast is served in your room. ④

Eating and drinking

Candolim's numerous beach **cafés** are a cut above your average seafood shacks, with pot plants, high-tech sound systems and prices to match. The further from the *Taj* complex you venture, the lower the prices become.

Amigo's 3km east of Candolim at Nerul bridge ☎ 0832/240 1123 or ☎ m98221 04920. Though well off the beaten track, this rough-and-ready riverside shack, tucked away under the bridge that Jason Bourne's girlfriend sped off in *The Bourne Supremacy*, is famed locally for its superb fresh seafood, served straight off the boats. *Tamoso* (red snapper) is their speciality, but they also do stuffed pomfret, calamari chilli-fry, barramundi and, best of all, Jurassic-sized crabs in butter-garlic sauce (order the day before). Count on Rs250–350 for the works, with drinks. You can phone your order in advance. The owners also run enjoyable crab-catching trips.

Bomra's Souza Waddo, Fort Aguada Rd, south Candolim ☎ m98221 49633 or 98221 306236. Understated, relaxed place, on a dimly lit gravel terrace by the roadside. From the outside you'd never know this was one of Goa's gastro-nomic highlights, but the food – contemporary Burmese and Kachin cuisine – is superb. Try their spinach wraps in fragrant tahini sauce for starters, or the beef in peanut curry.

Café Chocolatti near Acron Arcade. Goa's answer to Juliette Binoche's "Vianne Rocher" in the movie *Chocolat*, the British-raised owner of this delightful café in south Candolim, Nazneen, has conjured up a Mecca for choco-holics. Over a perfect cup of freshly ground coffee in the garden, you can indulge in gourmet Belgian-style truffles, tinged with chilli, mocca and orange, and crunchy almond-flavoured Italian biscuits.

Cinnabar Café Acron Arcade, Fort Aguada Rd. Hip new café, with Italian-style glass- and wood-panelled interior, stone vases and Indian curios, serving what we reckon is Goa's best cappuccino. Occasional DJs add to the ambience. Opens at 8am for cooked breakfasts.

Pete's Shack Sequeira Waddo. One beach shack that deserves singling out because it's always professional and serves great healthy salads (Rs70–200), with real olive oil, mozzarella and balsamic vinegar. All the veg is carefully washed in chlorinated water first, so the food is safe and fresh. The same applies to their seafood sizzler and tandoori main courses. For dessert, try the wonderful chocolate mousse or cooling mint lassis. Their real pride and joy, however, is the loo – which must be the grandest on any Goan beach.

Sea Shell *Sea Shell Inn*, Fort Aguada Rd. A congenial terrace restaurant in front of an old colonial-era *palacio* decked with green fairy lights. Sizzlers, spaghetti bolognese and beef steaks are their speci-alities, but they do a range of seafood, Indian and Chinese dishes, as well as delicious cocktails. Not as pricey as it looks, either (most mains Rs175–300).

Sheetal Murrod Waddo. One of the few restaurants in Goa specializing in authentic Mughlai cuisine. Served in copper *karais* with braziers by a team of snappy waiters dressed in traditional *salwars*, the menu features a long list of chicken, mutton and vegetarian dishes steeped in rich sauces. Count on Rs300–375 per head, plus drinks.

Stone House Fort Aguada Rd. Blues-nut Chris D'Souza hosts this lively, low-lit bar-restaurant, spread in front of a gorgeous bare-laterite Goan house. Prime cuts of beef and kingfish served with scrumptious baked potatoes are their most popular dishes. Blues enthusiasts should come just for the CD collection. Most mains under Rs225.

Viva Goa! Fort Aguada Rd. Succulent, no-nonsense Goan food fresh from the market – mussel fry, barramundi (*chonok*), lemonfish (*modso*) and sharkfish steaks fried *rechado* style in chili paste or in millet (*rawa*) – served on a roadside terrace. Tourists are welcome, but it's essentially local food at local prices.

Calangute

A 45-minute bus ride up the coast from Panjim, **CALANGUTE** was, in Portuguese times, where well-to-do Goans would come for their annual *mudança*, or change of air in May and June, when the pre-monsoonal heat made life in the towns insufferable. It remains the state's busiest resort, but has changed beyond recognition since the days when straw-hatted musicians in the beachfront bandstand would regale smartly dressed strollers with Lisbon *fados* and Konkani *dulpods*.

Beach parties of a less genteel nature first started to become a regular feature of life here in the late 1960s. Stoned out of their brains on local *feni* and cheap *charas*, the tribes of long-haired Westerners lying naked on the vast white sandy beach soon became tourist attractions in their own right, pulling in bus-loads of visitors from Mumbai, Bengaluru (Bangalore) and beyond. Calangute's flower-power period, however, is decidedly long gone.

Nowadays, the owners of swish resort hotels look back on the hippy era with a mixture of amusement and nostalgia. They and their fellow Colongutis have paid a high price for the recent prosperity. Mass package tourism, combined with a huge increase in the number of Indian visitors (for whom this is Goa's number one beach resort), has placed an impossible burden on the town's rudimentary infrastructure. Each year, as another crop of construction sites blossoms into holiday complexes, what vestigal charm the village has retained gets steadily more submerged under ferro-concrete and heaps of garbage. Hemmed in by four-storey buildings and swarming with traffic, the market area, in particular, has now taken on the aspect of a typical makeshift Indian town of precisely the kind that most travellers used to come to Goa to get away from.

In short, this is somewhere to avoid, although most people pass through here at some stage, to change money or shop for essentials. The only other reason to endure the chaos is to eat: Calangute boasts some of the best **restaurants** in the whole state.

Practicalities

Buses from Mapusa and Panjim pull in at the small bus stand-cum-market square in the centre of Calangute. Some continue to Baga, stopping at the crossroads behind the beach en route.

For **changing money**, Thomas Cook have a branch in the main market area (Mon–Sat 9.30am–6pm), where there's also an efficient ICICI Bank with 24-hr ATM. Private currency changers on the same street include Wall Street Finances (Mon–Sat 9.30am–6pm), opposite the petrol pump and in the shopping complex on the beachfront, who exchange both cash and traveller's cheques at bank rates. At the Bank of Baroda (Mon–Fri 9.30am–2.15pm, Sat 9.30am–noon, Sun 9.30am–2pm), just north of the market on the Anjuna road, you can make encashments against Visa cards; commission is one percent of the amount changed, plus Rs125 for the authorization phone call.

Petrol pumps in north Goa

The main Calangute **petrol pump** was closed down in 2000 when it was found to be bulking out its supply with solvents. As a result, you'll either have to travel up to the one **between Anjuna and Vagator** to refill, or else head into **Mapusa**. There's also a station just **north of Arambol** on the Kerim–Terekol road, but the locals claim it laces its petrol too. As ever, ensure the attendants reset the pumps to zero before serving you – they often don't, in order to overcharge and pocket the extra.

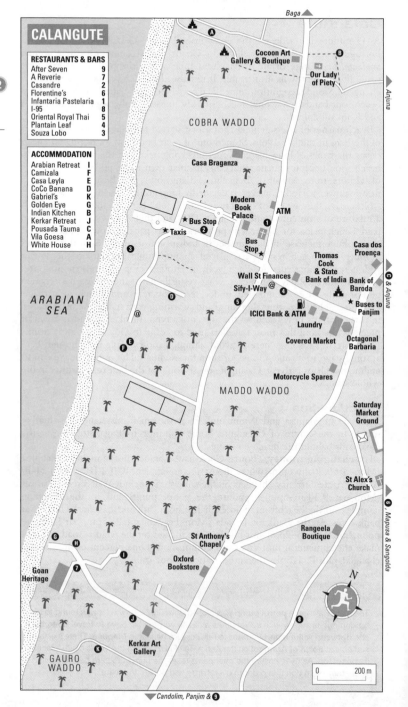

CALANGUTE

RESTAURANTS & BARS
After Seven	9
A Reverie	7
Casandre	2
Florentine's	6
Infantaria Pastelaria	1
I-95	8
Oriental Royal Thai	5
Plantain Leaf	4
Souza Lobo	3

ACCOMMODATION
Arabian Retreat	I
Camizala	F
Casa Leyla	E
CoCo Banana	D
Gabriel's	K
Golden Eye	G
Indian Kitchen	B
Kerkar Retreat	J
Pousada Tauma	C
Vila Goesa	A
White House	H

Baga

Anjuna

Cocoon Art Gallery & Boutique

Our Lady of Piety

COBRA WADDO

Casa Braganza

Modern Book Palace

ATM

★ Bus Stop
★ Taxis

Bus Stop ★

Casa dos Proença

Thomas Cook & State Bank of India

Bank of Baroda

& Anjuna

Wall St Finances

Sify-I-Way @

★ Buses to Panjim

ICICI Bank & ATM

Laundry

Covered Market

Octagonal Barbaria

ARABIAN SEA

Motorcycle Spares

MADDO WADDO

Saturday Market Ground

St Alex's Church

Mapusa & Sangolda

St Anthony's Chapel

Rangeela Boutique

Oxford Bookstore

N

Goan Heritage

Kerkar Art Gallery

GAURO WADDO

0   200 m

Candolim, Panjim &

There are innumerable cafés scattered around town offering broadband **Internet** access, notably Sify-I-Way: Rs60/hr for drop-ins, or Rs30/hr for members. One of Goa's best bookshops, The Oxford Bookstore, stands on the south side of town, directly opposite St Anthony's Chapel on the main Candolim road. Modern Book Palace, just off the beach road, stocks mainly titles on India and Goa, including a particularly good selection of bird field guides. Down in Gauro Waddo near *Gabriel's*, on the edge of Candolim, Café Literrati (10am–7pm; closed Wed) has a more off-beat, bibliophile feel about it, with a great collection of paper- and hard-backs shelved in a converted Portuguese-era house.

Accommodation

In spite of the encroaching mayhem, plenty of budget travellers return to Calangute year after year, staying in little family guesthouses in the fishing *waddo* where the pace of life remains remarkably unchanged.

Inexpensive

Camizala 5-33B Maddo Waddo ☎0832/227 9530 or ☎m98229 86544. Lovely, breezy place with only four rooms, common verandas and sea views. About as close to the beach as you can get, and the *waddo* is very quiet. Cheap considering the location. ❸–❹

Gabriel's Gauro Waddo ☎0832/227 9486, ✉fele@rediffmail.com. A congenial guesthouse very close to the beach, midway between Calangute and Candolim, run by a gorgeous family who go out of their way to help guests. The rooms are large, with quiet fans, lockable steel cupboards and decent mattresses; the rear side ones have balconies looking across the toddy groves and dunes. ❹

Indian Kitchen Behind Our Lady of Piety Church ☎0832/227 7555, ✉ikitchen2602@yahoo.co.in. Jazzily decorated guesthouse with crazy mosaic tiling, brightly patterned walls and lanterns. The rooms, all en suite, have fridges and music systems. ❸–❹

Mid-range

Arabian Retreat Gauro Waddo ☎0832/227 9053, ⓦwww.nivalink.com/arabianretreat. Swathed in greenery and shaded by areca palms, this new block has large rooms with balconies on both sides (those on the first floor are best), and some have a/c. Much loved by frequent returnees are Simba the cat and Foxy the dog. Only Rs800 per double, but rising to Rs1400 from Dec to mid-Jan. ❹

Casa Leyla Maddo Waddo ☎0832/227 6478 or 227 9068, ⓦwww.cocobananagoa.com. This is a great place if you're a family looking for somewhere with plenty of space for a longish let, say of at least one week. The rooms are huge and well furnished, with fridges, kid-friendly beds and chairs, and basic self-catering facilities,

while the house itself, whose upper storey sits in the palm canopy, is set deep in the secluded fishing ward, behind the quietest stretch of the beach. ❹–❻

CoCo Banana 1195 Umta Waddo ☎0832/227 6478 or 227 9068, ⓦwww.cocobanana.com. Very comfortable, spacious chalets, all with bathrooms, fridges, mosquito nets, extra-long mattresses and verandas, around a central garden – but no a/c. Down the lane past *Meena Lobo's* restaurant, it's run by a very sorted Swiss-Goan couple, Walter and Marina Lobo, who have been here for nearly twenty years. Rates double at Christmas. ❺

Golden Eye Gaura Waddo ☎0832/227 7308, ⓦwww.hotelgoldeneye.com. Situated on the sand, the rooms are attractively done out, with spacious tiled bathrooms and toilets, and some have views from their balconies. No pool. ❹–❼

White House 185/B Gauro Waddo, near *Goan Heritage* hotel ☎0832/227 7938, ☎ 227 6509. Immaculate, large rooms in a modern block close to the beach, with balconies, bathrooms and some views. They also offer spacious apartments for Rs1200 per night. If full, try the slightly shabbier *Dona Cristalina* along the lane (☎0832/229 7012). ❺

Expensive

Kerkar Retreat Gauro Waddo ☎0832/227 6017, ⓦwww.subodhkerkar.com. Colour-themed "boutique hotel", artfully decorated with original paintings (by local artist and owner, Subodh Kerkar), Goan *azulejos* and designer furniture creating an effect that's modern, but definably Goan. The only downside is the roadside location. ❼

Pousada Tauma Porba Waddo ☎0832/227 9061, ⓦwww.pousada-tauma.com. Small luxury resort complex, comprising double-storey laterite villas ranged around a pool. It's near the middle of Calangute, but screened from the din by lots of vegetation. Understated decor and repro-antique furnishings, and a very exclusive atmos-phere, preserved by five-star prices. Their big draw is a first-rate Keralan Ayurvedic health centre (open to non-residents). From $340–490 per night (including taxes). ❾

Vila Goesa Cobra Waddo ☎0832/227 7535, ⓦwww.vilagoesa.com. A stone's throw from the beach and very swish, set around a lush garden of young palms and lawns. Rooms are on the small side for the price, and the bathrooms are ceilinged closets, so a little stuffy. Occasional live music and a cocktail bar. All rooms have balconies. ❻–❼

Eating and drinking

Ever since *Souza Lobo* opened on the beachfront to cater for Goan day-trippers in the 1930s, Calangute has been somewhere people come as much to eat as for a stroll on the beach, and even if you stay in resorts elsewhere you'll doubtless be tempted down here for a meal.

After Seven Gauro Waddo, midway between Calangute and Candolim, down a lane leading west off the main road, between the Lifeline Pharmacy and a small chapel, ☎92261 88288. Smart little restaurant in a quiet garden setting; it recently had to change its name from *After Eight* following threats of legal action from Nestlé (they've had to start opening an hour earlier too). The menu offers mainly sophisticated Continental dishes, such as camembert soufflé (Rs175) and grilled fish drizzled with pistachio emulsion (Rs295). They also claim to offer Goa's longest wine list. Reservation recommended.

🏃 A Reverie Near *Hotel Goan Heritage*, Gauro Waddo ☎98231 74927 or ☎93261 14661. Unashamedly over-the-top gourmet place on the south side of Calangute, centered on a grand terracotta-tiled canopy. Both the gastronomic menu and ambience are as about extravagant as Goa gets, but the prices remain within reach of most budgets (around Rs750 per head, plus drinks – very reasonable given the quality of the food). Try the smoked French duck with truffles and spiced berry sorbet. Reservation recommended.

Casandre Beach Rd ⓦwww.casandre.com. Housed in a smartly renovated Portuguese-era home, with a deep veranda fronting the main drag, this popular roadside restaurant is run by three enthusiastic Goan brothers and their Swiss/British wives. The menu is gigantic, but the seafood, s'eak and sizzler specials listed on a blackboard tend to be the best bets.

🏃 Florentine's 4km inland from Calangute church at Saligao, next door to the Ayurvedic Natural Health Centre. Well worth the trip inland to taste Florence D'Costa's legendary chicken *cafreal*, made to a jealously guarded family recipe that pulls in crowds of locals and tourists from across north Goa. The restaurant is a down-to-earth place, with prices to match, serving only chicken, some seafood and vegetarian snacks.

Infantaria Pastelaria Next to St John's Chapel, Baga road. Roadside terrace café run by *Souza Lobo's* that gets packed out for its stodgy crois-sants, freshly baked apple pie and traditional Goan sweets (such as *dodol* and home-made *bebinca*). Top of the savoury list, though, are the prawn and veg patties, which locals buy by the boxload.

I-95 Behind the Art Chamber, Castello Vermelho, 1.115 A Gauro Waddo. Alfresco fine dining devised by a team of go-ahead young chefs: meat and seafood grilled on smoky lava stones; chicken breast in sesame seed and ginger (Rs350); grilled Atlantic salmon escalopes on a bed of Swiss-style rösti potatoes with fresh basil cream sauce. For veggies there's baked goat's cheese with roast beetroot and walnut dressing. Classy, but not pretentiously so. Count on the best part of Rs1000 per head for three courses, plus drinks.

🏃 Oriental Royal Thai Two minutes' walk south off the main crossroads on the beach road, at the *Hotel Mira* ☎0832/3292809 or ☎98221 21549. Sumptuous Thai cuisine prepared by master chef Chawee, who turns out eighteen house sauces to accompany choice cuts of seafood, meat and poultry, as well as plenty of vegetarian options. Be sure to try their signature dish, *soom tham* (papaya salad). At around Rs700–800 for three courses, it's good value for cooking of this standard.

Plantain Leaf Market area. The best Udupi restau-rant outside Panjim, if not all Goa, where waiters in matching shirts serve the usual range of delicious *dosas* and other spicy snacks in a clean, cool marble-lined canteen, with relentless background *filmi* music. Try their definitive *iddli*-vada break-fasts, delicious masala *dosas* or the cheap and filling set thalis (Rs55).

Souza Lobo Beachfront. A Calangute institution, even though the food – served on gingham tablecloths by legions of fast-moving waiters in

Madras-checked shirts – isn't always what it used to be. Stuffed crab, full baby kingfish and crepe Souza are the house specialities. Most main dishes Rs175–275.

Nightlife

Calangute's **nightlife** is surprisingly tame for a resort of its size. All but a handful of the bars wind up by midnight, leaving punters to prolong the short evenings back at their hotels, find a shack that's open late, or else head up to Baga (see p.214).

Down on the south edge of Calangute in Gauro Waddo, the **Kerkar Art Gallery** (T 0832/227 6017, W www.subodhkerkar.com) hosts evenings of **classical music and dance** (Tues 6.45pm; Rs300), held in the back garden on a sumptuously decorated stage, complete with incense and candlelight. The

Dead lucky?

Bob's Inn, midway between Calangute and Candolim, is not somewhere you'd associate with quickening heartbeats (quite the opposite in fact). But pulses must have raced in the bar the day photographs of its most notorious, recently deceased regular, "**Jungle Barry**", popped up on newspaper front pages all over the world. What at first seemed like a surreal joke turned out to be one of the most improbable scenarios imaginable: that hard-drinking, guitar-strumming Jungle Barry, with his tatty khaki shorts, long grey hair and beard, and catatonic appearance, had in fact been none other than the aristocratic fugitive "Lucky" **Lord Lucan**.

First published in the UK's *Sunday Telegraph* in September 2003, the revelations were based on extracts from a book written by a retired Scotland Yard detective, Duncan MacLaughlin. Obsessed for years with tracking down the fast-living peer, who'd vanished in 1974 after his children's nanny had been found bludgeoned to death, MacLaughlin had been led to Goa by pictures he'd been shown of a boozy old hippy who ran "bush tours" out of *Bob's Inn*.

Many theories as to Lucan's whereabouts had been posited over the years. Some believed he'd been kidnapped by the IRA; others that he'd shot himself and had had a friend feed his remains to the lions in London Zoo. He'd variously been spotted in Melbourne, Mozambique, Dublin and San Francisco, and many other places besides, but no one had ever managed to provide incontestable proof of his fate.

The photographs shown to MacLaughlin did indeed suggest some resemblance in the distinctively arched eyebrows, hairline and lack of earlobes. But when the ex-policeman started to dig for more evidence, other coincidences started to pile up, such as Barry's reputedly posh English accent and his encyclopedic knowledge of vintage cars.

However, the *Sunday Telegraph*, who snapped up rights to MacLaughlin's subsequent book, was to rue its rush to print. No sooner had Jungle Barry's blurry mugshot appeared in the paper than a flood of people emerged claiming they recognized the man in the photos as one Barry Halpin, a well-known performer from the pubs and folk scene of northern England in the 1960s. Among them was the singer and comic Mike Harding, who reportedly laughed until he cried when he saw Halpin's face in the newspapers.

The whole episode still raises smirks in *Bob's Inn*, where it is regarded as a fitting coda to a life spent spinning long and unlikely yarns. Jungle Barry never lived long enough to witness his "outing" by the over zealous former drug-squad officer, but would doubtless have enjoyed the notoriety if he had. His picture still hangs in the bar, where he is fondly remembered.

recitals, performed by students and teachers from Panjim's Kala Academy, are kept comfortably short for the benefit of Western visitors, and are preceded by a short introductory talk.

Baga

BAGA, 10km west of Mapusa, is basically an extension of Calangute; not even the locals agree where one ends and the other begins. Lying in the lee of a rocky, wooded headland, the only difference between this far northern end of the beach and its more congested centre is that the scenery here is marginally more varied and picturesque. Overlooked by a rocky headland draped in vegetation, a small tidal river flows into the sea at the top of the village, past a spur of soft white sand where ranks of brightly coloured fishing boats are moored.

Since the package boom, Baga has developed more rapidly than anywhere else in the state and today looks less like the Goan fishing village it still was in the early 1990s and more like a small-scale resort on the Spanish Costas, with a predominantly young, charter-tourist clientele to match. If you can steer clear of the lager louts, Baga boasts distinct advantages over its neighbours: a crop of excellent **restaurants** and a **nightlife** that's consistently more full-on than anywhere else in the state, if not all India.

Accommodation

Accommodation is harder to arrange in Baga than in Calangute, as most of the hotels have been carved up by the charter companies; even rooms in smaller guesthouses tend to be booked up well before the season gets under way. The majority of family-run places lie around the north end of the beach, where night-times have been a lot more peaceful since Goa's premier club, *Tito's*, acquired soundproofing.

Saturday night bazaars

One of the few genuinely positive improvements to the north Goa resort strip in recent times has been the **Saturday Night Bazaar**, held on a plot midway between Baga and Anjuna. The brainchild of an expat German called Ingo, it's run with great efficiency and a sense of fun that's palpably lacking these days from the Anjuna Flea Market. The balmy evening temperatures and pretty lights are also a lot more conducive to relaxed browsing than the broiling heat of mid-afternoon on Anjuna beach; moreover, the laid-back ambience is preserved with a "three-strikes-and-out" ban on hassling customers, which means you can even walk past the normally full-on Lamani women from Karnataka unmolested.

Although far more commercial than its predecessor in Anjuna, many old Goa hands regard this as far truer to the original spirit of the flea market. A significant proportion of the stalls are taken up by foreigners selling their own stuff, from reproduction Indian pop art to antique photos, the latest trance party wear, hand-polished coconut shell art and techno DJ demos. There's also a mouthwatering array of ethnic food concessions to choose from and a stage featuring live music from around 7pm until midnight, when the market winds up. Admission is free.

Somewhat confusingly, a **rival** in much the same mould, called **Macy's**, has opened nearby, closer to Baga by the riverside. Spurned by the expatriate designers and stallholders, this one's not quite as lively as its rival, though in recent years has made an effort to close the gap, with better live acts and more foreign stallholders.

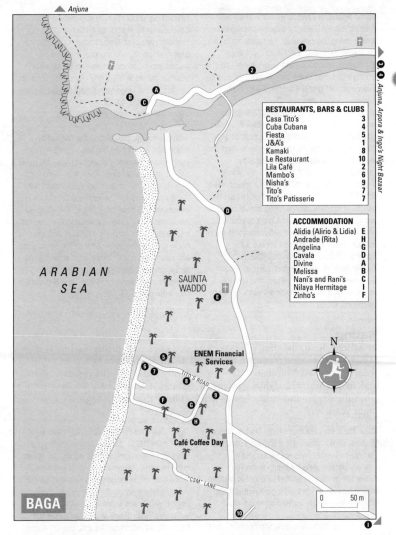

RESTAURANTS, BARS & CLUBS

Casa Tito's	3
Cuba Cubana	4
Fiesta	5
J&A's	1
Kamaki	8
Le Restaurant	10
Lila Café	2
Mambo's	6
Nisha's	9
Tito's	7
Tito's Patisserie	7

ACCOMMODATION

Alidia (Alirio & Lidia)	E
Andrade (Rita)	H
Angelina	G
Cavala	D
Divine	A
Melissa	B
Nani's and Rani's	C
Nilaya Hermitage	I
Zinho's	F

ARABIAN
SEA

SAUNTA
WADDO

ENEM Financial
Services

TITO'S ROAD

Café Coffee Day

"CSM" LANE

BAGA

N

0   50 m

Anjuna

Anjuna, Arpora & Ingo's Night Bazaar

Inexpensive

Alidia (Alirio & Lidia) Baga Rd, Saunta Waddo
☎0832/227 6835, ✉alidia@rediffmail.com.
Attractive modern chalet-style rooms with particularly comfy beds and good-sized verandas looking
on to the dunes. Most go for Rs1000–1500, but
there are a handful of cheaper options on the
ground floor (Rs800) for budget travellers. Plus
they've recently added a pool. ④–⑤

Andrade (Rita) Just south of *Tito's* Lane
☎0832/227 9087. Half a dozen sea-facing rooms.
Those on the lower floor are smaller, but with
larger verandas than the much nicer top-storey
ones. Friendly management, and close to the
liveliest stretch of beach. ④

Angelina Saunta Waddo ☎0832/227 9145,
✉angelinabeachresort@rediffmail.com.
Spacious, well-maintained rooms with large,
gleaming tiled bathrooms and big balconies, in the
thick of things off Tito's Lane. The best rooms are
on the top storey of the newest of the three blocks.
Owners Stanley and Preciosa D'Sa are perfect
hosts. A/c available. Unbeatable value for money in
this enclave. ③

Divine Near *Nani's and Rani's*, north of the river ☎0832/227 9546. Run by a couple of hospitable, animal-loving Gulf returnees, the rooms are on the small side, but impeccably clean; some have attached shower-toilets, and there's lovely upper terrace with sunbeds and shades, presided over by a menagerie of animal finials on the rooftops. Advance booking essential. ❹

Melissa 620 Anjuna Rd ☎0832/227 9583 or ☎m98221 80095. Four modern rooms in a clean, quiet block on the north side of the river, all with attached shower-toilets. Good off-season discounts, too, offered by hosts Magdeline and Seby Fernandes. ❷

Nani's and Rani's North of the river (House #164) ☎0832/227 6313, @jeshuafern@yahoo.com. A handful of red-tiled, whitewashed budget cottages in a secluded garden behind a huge colonial-era house. Fans, some attached bathrooms, well-water, outdoor showers and Internet access. ❹

Zinho's 7/3 Saunta Waddo ☎0832/227 7383. Tucked away off the main road, close to *Tito's*. Seventeen modest-sized, clean rooms above a family home; those in the new a/c block are a bit overpriced. ❹–❺

Moderate to expensive

Cavala Baga Rd ☎0832/227 7587 or 227 6090, ⓦwww.cavala.com. Modern hotel in tastefully traditional laterite, with a pool surrounded by banana groves; spacious twin-bedded rooms and separate balconies, but a little close to the road for comfort. Rooms range from simple non-a/c doubles to luxurious suites. ❹–❽

Nilaya Hermitage Arpora Bhati ☎0832/227 6793, ⓦwww .nilayahermitage.com. Set on the crest of a hilltop 6km inland from the beach, with matchless views over the coastal plain, this ranks among India's most exclusive hotels, patronized by a very rich international jet set (Richard Gere, Giorgio Armani, Sean Connery and Kate Moss are all rumoured to have stayed here). The complex is a fantasy of rich Indian colours, fiddly ironwork and gilded pillars, opening onto a dreamy pool. Room tariffs include use of the steam room, gym and clay tennis court. Rooms from around $375 for two (or $580 over Christmas–New Year), including meals and airport transfers. Minimum stay three nights. ❾

Eating

Nowhere else in the state offers such a good choice of quality **eating** as Baga. Restaurateurs – increasing numbers of them European expats or refugees from upper-class Mumbai – vie with each other to lay on the trendiest menus and most romantic, stylish gardens or terraces. It's all a very far cry indeed from the rough-and-ready beach-shack culture that held sway only seven or eight years ago.

Casa Tito's Opposite Ingo's Night Market, Arpora. Boutique-style restaurant in a stylishly renovated Portuguese *palacio*, filled with wonderfully evocative memorabilia belonging to the Tito's family. The menu's dominated by gourmet Mediterranean cuisine, served from a garden grill; it also functions as a lounge bar (see opposite). Most dishes Rs225–275.

Fiesta Tito's Lane ☎0832/227 9894, ⓦwww.fiestagoa.com. Run by the glamorous but improbably named Yellow and Maneck Contractor, Baga's most extravagantly decorated restaurant enjoys a perfect spot at the top of a long dune, with sea views from the veranda of a 1930s house. Giant paper lanterns and an old fishing boat filled with scatter cushions set the tone. The contemporary Mediterranean food is as delectable as the décor: try their carpaccio of beef for starters, followed by lasagne, ravioli or the succulent wood-baked pizzas (Rs200). Most starters and mains Rs250–300. Reservations recommended.

J&A's Anjuna Rd ☎0832/227 5274 or ☎m098231 39488, ⓦwww.littleitalygoa .com. Mouthwatering, authentic Italian food (down to the imported Parmesan, sun-dried tomatoes and olive oil) served in the gorgeous candle-lit garden of an old fisherman's cottage. There's an innovative range of salads and antipasti, a choice of sumptuous pasta dishes, wood-fired pizzas and tender steaks (with rosemary potatoes) for mains. For dessert, go for the melt-in-the-mouth hot chocolate soufflé. Count on at least Rs750 per head for three courses, plus drinks.

Le Restaurant Baga Rd ☎m98221 21712. Stylish French gastronomy served against a chic, fun backdrop of contemporary art, white-painted Goan furniture and fairy lights. The three Gallic partners have ingeniously concocted their elaborate menu from local ingredients. Go for the prawns with filo-wrapped mushrooms or crispy sardines with mint coulis and vanilla-scented mashed potato. But be warned: portions are stylishly minimalist/meagre depending on your point of view. Rs750–1000 per head, plus drinks. Reservation recommended. Closed Sat.

Lila Café Baga Creek. Laid-back bakery-cum-snack-bar, run by a German couple who've been here for decades. Their healthy home-made breads and cakes are great, and there's an adventurous lunch menu featuring spinach à la crème, aubergine pâté and smoked water-buffalo ham. Open 8am–8pm.

Nisha's Tito's Lane ⌾0832/227 7588. This little restaurant, occupying a sandy terrace just down from *Tito's*, can't be beaten for simply prepared seafood – snapper, kingfish, tiger prawns and lobster – flame-grilled or tandoori-baked to perfection in front of you by chef Frankie Almon and his crew. Freshness counts more here than fancy sauces. For starters, try calamari in chilli oil with lemon. Most mains are a reasonable Rs250–325.

Tito's Patisserie *Tito's*, Tito's Lane. Relaxed little a/c café that couldn't be further away from the headlong atmosphere of *Tito's* by night. Their chilled pastries – including toffee and apple tart, banoffee pie and lemon cheesecake – are delicious, as is the freshly ground espresso and cappuccino; and it's only a skip from the beach.

Nightlife

That Baga's **nightlife** has become legendary in India is largely attributable to one club, *Tito's*. Lured by TV images of sexy dancewear and a thumping sound-and-light system, hundreds of revellers descend on its long narrow terrace each night to drink, shuffle about and watch the action, the majority of them men from other states who've come to Goa as an escape from the moral confines of life at home. For Western women, in particular, this can sometimes make for an uncomfortably loaded atmosphere, although since a facelift (and a hike in door charges), *Tito's* seems to have put the era of Kingfisher-fuelled brawls behind it. New theme bars and clubs are also popping up each year, offering increasingly sophisticated alternatives.

For anyone who's been travelling around the rest of the country, Baga by night – complete with drunken karaoke, toga parties and all the garishness of a Saturday in British clubland – can come as an unpleasant shock. So, too, can the traffic congestion on Fridays and Saturdays; if you venture down here by motorbike on the weekend, park well away from Tito's Lane or you might find yourself jammed in until the small hours.

For more on the area's nightlife, see the accounts of Calangute (p.209) and Anjuna (p.218).

Bars and clubs

Casa Tito's Arpora, opposite Ingo's Night Market. Chic Italian gastro-lounge bar in an old Portuguese-era house, with traditional furniture, family memorabilia, resident DJs, cocktails and gourmet food. Perfect post-Ingo's chillout spot.

Cuba Cubana 82 Xim Waddo, Arpora Hill, ⌾www.clubcubana.net. Glam nightclub on a forested hilltop inland from Baga, spread around an underlit open-air pool. Its high entrance charge – Rs600 for single/accompanied men; Rs400 for women (except Wed, "Ladies Night" when girls get in free) buys you unlimited drinks from a well-stocked bar – a policy intended to keep out the low-spending riff-raff from down on the strip. R&B, hip hop and garage (they purposely stay well away from techno) played on a twin-storey dance floor. Fri, Sat & Sun 9.30pm–5am.

Kamaki Tito's Lane, Saunta Waddo. Big-screen sports and a state-of-the-art karaoke machine account for the appeal of this a/c, Brit-dominated bar just up the lane from *Tito's*. Rs100 cover charge sometimes applies.

Mambo's Tito's Lane, Saunta Waddo. Large, semi-open air pub with wooden decor and a big circular bar that gets packed out most nights in season with a lively, mixed crowd. Once again, karaoke is the big draw, though drinks cost well above average, and they slap on a Rs300–400 cover charge after 11pm, or when there's live entertainment. "Ladies Night", on Wednesday, means free entry and free drinks for women.

Tito's Tito's Lane, Saunta Waddo ⌾www.titosgoa.com. Occasional cabarets, fashion shows and guest DJs feature throughout the season at India's most famous nightclub. Red upholstery and uniformed waiters set the tone; music policy is lounge grooves till 11pm, and hip hop, house, salsa and trance thereafter. See the noticeboard for retro and other theme nights. Admission prices are

Rs600 for men, which includes free drinks, and free for women (who also get free drinks). At Christmas, prices can soar to Rs1000 or more depending on the attraction. Open 8pm–late Nov–Dec; and until 11pm out of season. Tuesdays and Saturdays are busiest.

Anjuna

ANJUNA, the next sizeable village up the coast from Baga, was until a few years back the last bastion of alternative chic in Goa – where the state's legendary full-moon parties were staged each season, and where the Beautiful Set would rent pretty red-tiled houses for six months at a time, make trance mixes and groovy dance clothes, paint the palm trees in their gardens with fluoro colours and spend months lazing on the beach. A small contingent of fashionably attired, middle-aged hippies still turn up, but thanks to a combination of the Y2K music ban (see p.224) and overwhelming growth in popularity of the flea market, Anjuna has seriously fallen out of fashion. Even the young Israeli hellraisers who inundated the village during the late 1990s – and were largely responsible for the government's crackdown on parties – come in much reduced numbers these days.

As a consequence, the scattered settlement stately of old Portuguese houses and whitewashed churches, nestled amid a labyrinth of leafy lanes behind a long golden sandy beach, nowadays more closely resembles the place it was before the party scene snowballed than it has for decades. With the airport only an hour's drive away, full-scale tourism development must eventually creep around the headland from neighbouring Baga, but for the time being the village is enjoying a well earned break from noisy crowds.

The one day of the week when the relative peace and quiet is completely shattered is on Wednesdays, when Anjuna hosts the famous **flea market**, held under a coconut plantation backing the south side of the beach. The big gatherings that used to happen at the Shore Bar afterwards are a thing of the past, but the perfect hippy sunset can still be had at *Zoori's* (see p.222), overlooking the north end of the beach, while the *Nine Bar* in Vagator continues to pumps out definitive, 120-beats/min Goa Trance each evening from its huge sound system (see p.225).

The flea market

Anjuna's Wednesday **flea market**, held in the coconut plantation behind the southern end of the beach is, along with Ingo's Night Market at Arpora, *the* place to indulge in a spot of souvenir shopping. Two decades ago, the weekly event was the exclusive preserve of backpackers and the area's seasonal residents, who gathered here to smoke chillums and to buy and sell party clothes and jewellery: something like a small pop festival without the stage. These days, however, everything is more organized and mainstream. Pitches are rented out by the metre, drugs are banned and the approach roads to the village are choked solid all day with a/c buses and Maruti taxis ferrying in tourists from resorts further down the coast. Even the beggars have to pay *baksheesh* to be here.

The range of goods on sale has broadened, too, thanks to the high profile of migrant hawkers and stallholders from other parts of India. Each region or culture is allotted its own corner. At one end, ever diminishing ranks of alternative Westerners congregate around racks of fluoro party gear and designer beachwear, while in the heart of the site, Tibetan jewellery sellers preside over orderly rows of turquoise bracelets and Himalayan curios. Most distinctive of all are the Lamani women from Karnataka, decked from head to toe in traditional tribal garb and selling elaborately woven multicoloured cloth, which they

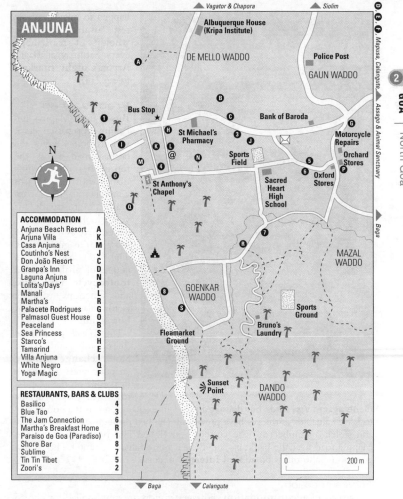

ANJUNA

Vagator & Chapora   Siolim

Albuquerque House
(Kripa Institute)

DE MELLO WADDO

Police Post

GAUN WADDO

Bus Stop

Bank of Baroda

St Michael's
Pharmacy

Motorcycle
Repairs

Orchard
Stores

N

Sports
Field

Oxford
Stores

St Anthony's
Chapel

Sacred
Heart
High
School

MAZAL
WADDO

GOENKAR
WADDO

Sports
Ground

Fleamarket
Ground

Bruno's
Laundry

Sunset
Point

DANDO
WADDO

0   200 m

Baga   Calangute

ACCOMMODATION

Anjuna Beach Resort	A
Arjuna Villa	K
Casa Anjuna	M
Coutinho's Nest	J
Don João Resort	C
Granpa's Inn	D
Laguna Anjuna	N
Lolita's/Days'	P
Manali	L
Martha's	R
Palacete Rodrigues	G
Palmasol Guest House	O
Peaceland	B
Sea Princess	S
Starco's	H
Tamarind	E
Villa Anjuna	I
White Negro	Q
Yoga Magic	F

RESTAURANTS, BARS & CLUBS

Basilico	4
Blue Tao	3
The Jam Connection	6
Martha's Breakfast Home	R
Paraiso de Goa (Paradiso)	1
Shore Bar	8
Sublime	7
Tin Tin Tibet	5
Zoori's	2

fashion into everything from jackets to money belts, and which makes even the Westerners' party gear look positively funereal. Elsewhere, you'll come across dazzling Rajasthani mirrorwork and block-printed bedspreads, Keralan woodcarvings, Gujarati appliqué, Orissan palm-leaf manuscripts, pyramids of colourful spices and incense, "export-surplus" jeans and tops, spangly miniskirts, sequined shoes and Ayurvedic cures for every conceivable ailment.

What you end up paying for this exotic merchandise largely depends on your ability to **haggle**. Prices are sky-high by Indian standards, as tourists not used to dealing in rupees will part with almost anything. Be persistent, though, and cautious, and you can usually pick things up for a reasonable rate.

Even if you're not spending, the flea market is a great place just to sit and watch the world go by. Mingling with the suntanned masses are bands of strolling musicians, mendicant *sadhus* and fortune-telling bulls. And if you

△ Anjuna flea market

happen to miss the show, rest assured that the whole cast reassembles every Saturday at Baga/ Arpora's **night markets** (see p.214).

Practicalities

Buses from Mapusa and Panjim drop passengers at various points along the tarmac road across the top of the village, which turns north towards Chapora at the main Starco's crossroads. If you're looking for a room, get off here as it's close to most of the guesthouses. The crossroads has a couple of small **stores**, a **motorcycle taxi** rank, and functions as a de facto village square and **bus stand**.

The *Manali* guesthouse (see opposite) and Oxford Stores **change money** (at poor rates). The Bank of Baroda on the Mapusa road will make encash- ments against Visa cards, but doesn't do foreign exchange, nor is it a good place to leave valuables, as thieves have previously climbed through an open window and stolen a number of "safe custody" envelopes. The **post office**, on the Mapusa road near the bank, has an efficient poste restante counter. The *Manali* guesthouse also offers broadband **Internet access** (Rs40/hr).

Accommodation

After years of **accommodation** shortages, visitors are now spoiled for choice in Anjuna, especially those on more flexible budgets.

Yoga in Anjuna

The **Brahmani Centre** (ⓦwww.brahmaniyoga.com; ☏m93705 68639) offers drop-in Ashtanga yoga classes by expert teachers at their studio in the garden of the *Granpa's Inn* (*Hotel Bougainvillea*); all levels of ability are catered for. If you're looking for a fully fledged retreat or course, you won't do better than the **Purple Valley** centre, 10mins' ride away in Assagao (ⓦwww.yogagoa.com), which has accommo- dation for up to 40 guests and what must be one of the loveliest yoga *shalas* (practice areas) in India. Their top-drawer teachers include Manju Jois and Sharath Rangas- wamy, the eldest son and grandson of the illustrious Ashtanga Guru, Shri K.Pattabhi Jois. See also box on "Yoga in Morjim", p.230.

Inexpensive

Arjuna Villa #681/1 De Mello Waddo, 4th Lane ☎0832/227 4590 or 227 4591, ✉godfreymathia @hotmail.com. Pleasant budget rooms (Rs500– 600) with tiled floors and high ceilings, opening on to a deep common veranda (again, those on the upper storey are much nicer). You can play floodlit badminton. **④**

Coutinho's Nest Soronto Waddo ☎0832/227 4386. Small, very respectable family guesthouse on the main road, in the centre of Anjuna. Their immaculate rooms are among the village's best budget deals. Shared shower-toilets only. **②–③**

Lolita's/Days' Behind Orchard Stores ☎0832/227 4526 or 227 3289. A handful of simple, large rooms with high tiled roofs and attached shower-toilets, run by the affable Darryl Days. The pricier one has an air cooler, fridge and cable TV. Peaceful, despite its proximity to the road. Bookable through Joel's Mini Store next door.

Manali South of Starco's crossroads ☎0832/227 4421. Anjuna's most popular all-round budget guesthouse has simple rooms opening onto a yard, with shared toilets and fans. There's a safe deposit, money-changing, library, Internet connection and sociable terrace-restaurant. Good value, so book in advance. **①–②**

Martha's 907 Montero Waddo ☎0832/227 4194, ✉mpd8650@hotmail.com. Eleven immaculate en-suite rooms run by a friendly family. Amenities include kitchen space, fans and running solar-heated water. Two pleasant houses also available. **④**

Palmasol Guest House Praia de St Anthony ☎0832/227 3258. Huge, comfortable rooms in an immaculately kept old house very near the beach. The larger ones have running water, verandas, cooking space and a relaxing garden; cheaper alternatives are in the back yard. **②–③**

🏃 **Peaceland** Soronto Waddo ☎0832/227 3700. Simple en-suite rooms in two blocks (Rs400–500), run by a charming local couple with the help of a pair of friendly dogs. All have high, clay-tiled roofs, mosquito nets, rucksack racks, hammocks, clothes hangers and other nice homely touches that make this easily the best-value place in its class. **③**

Starco's On the crossroads. No phone. Some of the cheapest rooms in Anjuna: simple, but well-maintained, clean and screened from the road outside. Good value if you're happy with bare-bones amenities. Its unique selling points are pebble-lined bathroom walls and Goa's only surviving Morris Minor (kept in mint condition in the yard). **③**

Mid-range

Anjuna Beach Resort De Mello Waddo

☎0832/227 4499, ✉fabjoe@sancharnet.com. 32 spacious, comfortable rooms with balconies, fridges, attached bathrooms and solar hot water in a new concrete building ranged around a well-kept pool. Those on the upper floors are best. There's also a block of apartments for long stayers; both are very good value. **⑤–⑥**

Don João Resort Soronto Waddo ☎0832/227 4325 or 222 2147, ⊛www.goacom.org/hotels /donjoao. Large former charter hotel, slap in the middle of the village, with a pool. A bit shabby around the edges, but comfortable enough and a good deal in this bracket. **⑥**

🏃 **Granpa's Inn** Gaun Waddo ☎0832/227 3270, ⊛www.granpasinn.com. Formerly known as *Bougainvillea*, a lovely 200-year-old house set in half an acre of lush gardens, with a kidney-shaped pool and shady breakfast terrace. They offer three categories of rooms, all fully en-suite: non-a/c standards; suites in the main house; and poolside (in a recently built chalet block built in traditional style, but with modern furnishings and private outdoor showers). Ashtanga yoga on site; and there's a billiards table. Very popular, so book well ahead. **⑤–⑦**

Palacete Rodrigues Near Oxford Stores, Mazal Waddo ☎0832/227 3358. Two-hundred-year-old residence converted into a midscale guesthouse, with carved wood furniture and a relaxed, traditional-Goan feel. Single occupancy available. The three economy options in a separate block around the back are particularly good value. **⑤**

Sea Princess House #649 Goenkar Waddo, Dando ☎m98904 49090. Simple guesthouse in a prime position in the middle of the beach, near the *Shore Bar*. The rooms are spacious, and all have bathrooms with dependable plumbing, but aren't as well maintained as they might be and suffer from mosquitoes. Its main selling point is the location, right on in the dunes. **④**

Tamarind Kumar Waddo ☎0832/561 2399 or 227 4319, ⊛www.thetamarind.com. Pleasant stone-lined rooms with relaxing sit-outs opening onto a small pool. Some way inland, but they lay on complimentary transfer buses to the beaches. Other noteworthy attributes include a full-size billiards table and Goa's largest doberman (friendly). Mostly booked by charter companies, but worth trying for a vacancy. **⑥–⑦**

Villa Anjuna Near Anjuna beachfront ☎0832/227 3443, ⊛www.anjunavilla.com. Modern, efficient resort hotel close to the beach, on the main road through the village. Amenities include a fair sized pool and Jacuzzi. Popular with clubbers, as it's a short stagger from *Paradiso* (so sometimes a little noisy at night). **⑥**

White Negro 719 Praia de St Anthony, south of the village, near St Anthony's Chapel ☎0832/227 3326, ⓔdsouzawhitenegro@rediffmail.com. A row of twelve spotless back-to-back chalets catching the sea breeze, all with attached bathrooms, tiled floors, safe lockers and mozzie nets. Quiet, efficient and good value. ❹

Expensive

Casa Anjuna D'Mello Waddo 66 ☎0832/227 4123–25, ⓦwww.casaboutiquehotelsgoa.com. Set in a converted 200-year-old colonial mansion, this exclusive small hotel has 19 rooms, all of them fitted with handsome Indo-Portuguese-style four-posters, tapestries and textiles. The verandas are also gorgeous, as are the large pool and garden – a riot of frangipani, bougainvillea and alamanda flowers. Meals are served on what must be one of the loveliest roof terraces in India. Rs6000–8000 (rising to Rs15,000 and 18,000 over Christmas). ❾

Laguna Anjuna De Mello Waddo ☎0832/227 4305, ⓦwww.lagunaanjuna.com. Alternative "boutique resort" comprising 25 colourfully decorated, domed laterite cottages with wooden rafters and terracotta tiles, grouped behind a convoluted pool. Restaurant, pool tables and bar. A bit shabby round the edges these days, but popular nonetheless. Doubles from $130 mid-season, rising to $180 for Christmas–New Year. ❽

Yoga Magic ⓦwww.yogamagic.net. Innovative "Canvas Ecotel", offering low-impact luxury on the edge of Anjuna in Rajasthani hunting tents. The structures are all decorated with block-printed cotton, furnished with cushions, silk drapes, coir carpets and solar halogen lights, and are colour-themed to correspond with the Yogic chakras. They also have an even more luxurious (but only slightly more expensive) "Maharani Suite" in a wing of an adjacent stone house. Open mid-Nov to March. ❽

Eating and drinking

Responding to the tastes of its alternative visitors, Anjuna boasts a good crop of quality **cafés** and **restaurants**, many of which serve healthy vegetarian dishes and juices. If you're hankering for a taste of home, call in at the **Orchard Stores** on the eastern side of the village, which, along with its rival **Oxford Stores**, directly opposite, serves the expatriate community with as vast range of pricey imported delights such as Digestive biscuits, Marmite and extra-virgin olive oil. They also offer delicious coffee and fresh croissants.

Basilico De Mello Waddo ☎0832/227 3721. Cool, Italian-run garden restaurant hidden away down one of the village's quieter lanes. The pizzas and pasta dishes are authentic, service is efficient and the atmosphere relaxed. Most mains Rs175–225.

Blue Tao On the main road through the village. Another Italian-run place, this time an "alternative health restaurant" that offers some of Goa's most delicious breakfasts (sourdough and wholemeal breads, herbal teas, tahini and spirulina spreads). In addition to a full menu of main courses (Rs125–175), they also do a tempting range of juices, including wheatgrass, ginseng and Ayurvedic concoctions. Non-smoking and kid-friendly.

The Jam Connection Near Oxford Stores. Fresh, interesting salads (with real organic rocket and garden herbs), mocha and espresso coffee, home-made ice cream and all-day breakfasts, served in a lovely garden. You can lounge on bamboo easy chairs or on tree platforms. Daily except Wed 11am–7pm.

Martha's Breakfast Home *Martha's* guesthouse, 907 Montero Waddo. Secluded, very friendly breakfast garden serving fresh Indian coffee,

crepes, healthy juices (including a delicious ABC – apple, beetroot and carrot juice), apple and cinnamon porridge, fruit salads with curd and – the house speciality – melt-in-the-mouth waffles with real maple syrup.

Sublime near *Martha's* guesthouse, Montero Waddo ☎m93261 12006. Great little "gastro-bistro" where the food really lives up to the name: Indian-American chef Chris rustles up superb steaks, seafood, chicken and stir-fried vegetable dishes from an open-counter kitchen. For starters, opt the squid in ginger sauce (Rs140). Mains include balsamic beefsteak stuffed with mushroom and blue cheese on a bed of baby potatoes and fresh asparagus. Easily Anjuna's best restaurant, though it's still refreshingly informal and affordable.

Tin Tin Tibet Near Oxford Stores. Well-established budget café, serving the usual budget-travellers grub, plus Tibetan specialities (*momos* and *thukpa*), and some Israeli dishes. For dessert, try their fried banana with cashew nuts.

Zoori's North end of the beach. Chilled Israeli-run café-restaurant occupying a perfect spot on the clifftops – one of the most beautiful places in Goa for sunset. Screened from the brouhaha of the nearby car park, its terraces step down the hillside, strewn with lounging platforms, beds and big cushions. And the food's as delicious as the views: big, juicy fillet steaks are the house speciality, but they also do tasty Mexican enchilladas, tortillas, pasta and fresh hoummus, as well as chocolate soufflé and biscuit cake that regulars drive from far away for. Open 10am–midnight.

Nightlife

Anjuna no longer deserves the reputation it gained through the early 1990s as a legendary rave venue, but at least one big **party** is still held in the area around the Christmas–New Year full-moon period.

For the rest of the season, techno heads have to make do with the rather shabby, mainstream *Paraiso de Goa*, aka *Paradiso*, overlooking the far north end of Anjuna beach. Part owned by the government, this place epitomizes the new, more above-board face of Goa Trance. Presiding over a dance space surrounded by spacey statues of Hindu gods and Tantric symbols, visiting DJs spin text-book trance for a mainly Indian and Russian crowd. It's all a bit commercial, but even the now legendary Goa Gill, one of the leading free-party hosts of the 1980s and 1990s, has given the club his seal of approval by playing here. *Paradiso* keeps to a sporadic timetable, but should be open most nights from around 10pm; admission charges are Rs250–600, depending on the night.

Along similar lines, but with free admission, is the *Nine Bar* (see p.225), above Vagator beach. Down on the beach proper, the *Shore Bar* used to be *the* place to hang out after the flea market, attracting hundreds of people for sunset, but it has fallen out of favour over the past few years and now lacks the atmosphere of the *Nine Bar*.

Vagator

Barely a couple of kilometres of clifftops and parched grassland separate Anjuna from the southern fringes of its nearest neighbour, **VAGATOR**. Spread around a tangle of winding backlanes, this is a more chilled, undeveloped resort that appeals, in the main, to Israeli and southern European beach bums who've been coming back for years.

With the red ramparts of Chapora fort looming above it, Vagator's broad sandy **beach** – known as "**Big Vagator**" – is undeniably beautiful. However, a peaceful swim or lie on the sand is out of the question here as it's a prime stop for bus parties of domestic tourists. A much better option, though one that still sees more than its fair share of daytrippers, is the next beach south. Backed by a steep wall of crumbling palm-fringed laterite, **Ozran** (or "Little") **Vagator beach** is actually a string of three contiguous coves. To reach them you have to walk from where the bus parks above Big Vagator, or drive to the end of the lane running off the main Chapora–Anjuna road (towards the *Nine Bar*), from where footpaths drop sharply down to a wide stretch of level white sand (look for the mopeds and bikes parked at the top of the cliff). The Israeli- and Italian-dominated scene in the prettiest, southernmost cove here revolves around a string of large, well established shacks, at the end of which a face carved out of the rocks – staring serenely skywards – is the most prominent landmark. Relentless racquetball, trance sound systems and a particularly sizeable herd of stray cows are the other defining features.

Practicalities

Buses from Panjim and Mapusa, 9km east, pull in every fifteen minutes or so at the crossroads on the far northeastern edge of Vagator, near where the main

The dark side of the moon

Lots of visitors come to Goa expecting to be able to party on the beach every night, and are dismayed when the only places to dance turn out to be **mainstream clubs** they probably wouldn't look twice at back home. But the truth is that the full-on, elbows-in-the-air beach party of old, when tens of thousands of revellers would space out to huge techno sound systems under fluoro-painted palm trees, chilling out afterwards in the surf under massive full moons, is well and truly a thing of the past in Goa – thanks largely to the kill-joy attitude of the local government.

Goa's coastal villages saw their first big raves back in 1960s with the influx of hippies to Calangute and Baga. Much to the amazement of the locals, the preferred pastime of these wannabe *sadhus* was to cavort naked on the sands together on full-moon nights, amid a haze of chillum smoke and loud rock music blaring from makeshift PAs. The villagers took little notice of these bizarre gatherings at first, but with each season the scene became better established, and by the late 1970s the **Christmas and New Year** parties, in particular, had become huge events, attracting travellers from all over the country.

In the late 1980s, the local party scene received a dramatic shot in the arm with the coming of Acid House and techno. Ecstasy became the preferred dance drug as the dub-reggae scene gave way to rave culture, with ever-greater numbers of young clubbers pouring in for the season on charter flights. Goa soon spawned its own distinctive brand of psychedelic music, known as **Goa Trance**. Distinguished by its multilayered synth lines and sub-bass rhythms, the hypnotic style combines the darkness of hard techno with a brighter ambient edge. Cultivated by artists such as Goa Gill, Juno Reactor and Hallucinogen, the new sound was given wider exposure when big-name DJs Danny Rampling and Paul Oakenfold started mixing Goa Trance in clubs and on national radio back in the UK, generating a following among music lovers who previously knew nothing of the place which had inspired it.

The **golden era** for Goa's party scene, and Goa Trance, was in the early 1990s, when big raves were held two or three times a week in beautiful locations around Anjuna and Vagator. For a few years the authorities turned a blind eye to the growing scene. Then, quite suddenly, the plug was pulled. For years, drug busts and bribes had provided the notoriously corrupt Goan cops with a lucrative source of *baksheesh*. But after a couple of drug-related deaths, a series of sensational articles in the local press and a decision by Goa Tourism to promote upmarket over backpacker tourism, the police began to demand impossibly large bribes – sums that the organizers (many of them drug dealers) could not hope to recoup. Although the big New Year and Christmas events continued unabated, smaller parties, hitherto held in off-track venues such as "Disco Valley" behind Middle Vagator beach and the "Bamboo Grove" in south Anjuna, started to peter out, to the dismay of those local people who'd become financially dependent on the raves and the punters they pulled into the villages.

Against this backdrop, the imposition during the run up to the Y2K celebrations of an **amplified-music ban** between 10pm and 7am sounded the death knell for Goa's party scene. Seven or so years on, it has virtually disappeared without trace, limited to a couple of established, above-board clubs – notably the *Nine Bar* in Vagator (see p.225) and *Paradiso* in Anjuna (see p.223). The occasional hush-hush house party does from time to time escape the notice of the local police, but don't come to Goa expecting Ko Pha Ngan or Ibiza-on-the-Arabian Sea, or you'll be sorely disappointed.

road peels away towards Chapora. From here, it's a one-kilometre walk over the hill and down the other side to the beach. *Bethany Inn*, on the north side of the village, has a **foreign exchange** licence (for cash and traveller's cheques), and efficient **travel agency** in the office on the ground floor. If you need medical attention, contact Dr Jawarhalal Henriques at Zorin, near the petrol pump in Chapora (☎0832/227 4308).

Accommodation

Accommodation in Vagator comprises of a couple of pricey resort hotels, family-run budget guesthouses and dozens of small private properties rented out for long periods. **Water** is in very short supply here, and you'll be doing the villagers a favour if you use it frugally at all times. Tariffs typically double here at Christmas–New Year.

Bethany Inn Just south of the main road ☎0832/227 3731, ⓦwww.bethanyinn.com. Seven clean, self-contained rooms with minibar fridges, balconies and attached bathrooms (Rs600); plus four additional a/c options in a new block, with big flat-screen TVs, larger balconies and more spacious tiled bathrooms (Rs1200). Tastefully furnished throughout, and efficiently managed by a pair of young brothers from Pune. ❹–❺

Boon's Ark Near *Bethany Inn* ☎0832/227 4045. Pleasant, clean and well run place offering modern rooms that open onto small verandas and a well tended little garden. Room service, money changing and bikes to rent. ❹–❺

Dolrina Vagator Beach Rd ☎0832/227 3382, ⓔdolrina@hotmail.com. Nestled under a lush canopy of trees near the beach, Vagator's largest budget guesthouse is run by a friendly Goan couple and features attached or shared bathrooms, a sociable garden café, individual safe deposits and roof space. Single occupancy rates, and breakfasts available. ❸–❹

Jolly Jolly Lester Vagator Beach Rd ☎0832/227 3620, ☎m98224 88536, ⓦwww.hoteljollygoa .com. Eleven pleasant doubles with tiled

bathrooms, lockers and fresh towels provided, set in shady woodland and a garden lovingly protected by owners Lazarus and Remy from marauding monkeys. Small restaurant on site; single occupancy is possible. ❸

Jolly Jolly Roma Vagator Beach Rd ☎0832/227 3005 or ☎m98224 88536. Very smart, good-sized chalet-style rooms with high ceilings, nice furniture and private Verandas, again surrounded by a well tended garden; they also offer laundry, exchange facilities and a small library. ❹

Julie Jolly South side of the village ☎0832/227 3357. One of the most pleasant places in Vagator, set on the edge of a leafy belt and within easy reach of Ozran beach. All rooms are tiled and well aired; self-caterers can stay in larger suites with sitting rooms and kitchenettes. ❹–❺

Leoney Resort On the road to Disco Valley ☎0832/227 3634, ⓦwww.leoneyresort.com. Comfortable option, with swish "mock Portuguese" chalets and pricier (but more spacious) octagonal "cottages" on the sleepy side of the village, ranged around a very nice little pool. Restaurant, laundry, lockers, foreign exchange facilities and cyber café on site. No advance bookings Dec–Jan. ❼–❽

Eating, drinking and nightlife

Vagator boasts an eclectic batch of **restaurants**, with wildly varying menus and prices, and an equally dramatic turnover of chefs. Western tourists tend to stick to the pricier ones lining the road through the village, while Indian visitors frequent the more impersonal, cheaper places down on the beach itself. For a sundown drink, head to *Nine Bar*, encircled by a fortress-style laterite wall that opens onto a great chill-out terrace and the sea on one side. Big trance sounds attract a fair-sized crowd for sunset, especially on Wednesdays after the flea market; the dancing starts after dark and keeps going until the bar closes around 10pm.

Bean Me Up near the petrol pump. India's one and only American-run tofu joint – the last word in Goan gourmet healthy eating. Main courses (around Rs175–225) come with steamed spinach, brown bread and hygienically washed salads; try their delicious Thai-style tempeh in spicy cashew sauce. There's also a tempting range of vegan desserts – the banana pudding with soya whip is a winner.

China Town Chapora Crossroads, next to *Bethany Inn*. This small roadside restaurant, tucked away just south of the main drag, is the village's most popular budget eating place, serving particularly seafood dishes in addition to a large Chinese selection, as well as all the usual Goa-style travellers' grub.

Nine Bar above Ozran beach. Boasting a crystal trance sound system, this clifftop café enjoys a

225

prime location, with fine sea views from its terrace through the palm canopy, where Nepali waiters serve up cold beer and the usual range of budget travellers' grub. Entrance is free, but drink prices are stiff (Rs150 for a beer); you'll have your bags searched on the way in for drugs and explosives. Strictly no photography.

Chapora

Huddled in the shadow of a Portuguese fort on the opposite, northern side of the headland from Vagator, **CHAPORA**, 10km from Mapusa, is a lot busier than most north coast villages. Dependent on fishing and boat-building, it has, to an extent, retained a life of its own independent of tourism. That said, the recent relaxation of Goa's drug laws have made a significant impact here over

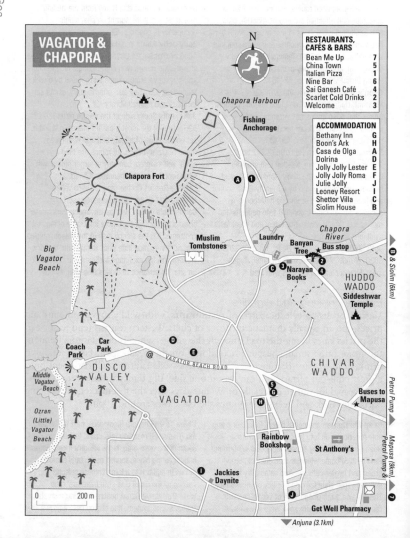

VAGATOR & CHAPORA

N

Chapora Harbour

RESTAURANTS, CAFÉS & BARS
Bean Me Up   7
China Town   5
Italian Pizza   1
Nine Bar   6
Sai Ganesh Café   4
Scarlet Cold Drinks 2
Welcome   3

Fishing Anchorage

ACCOMMODATION
Bethany Inn   G
Boon's Ark   H
Casa de Olga   A
Dolrina   D
Jolly Jolly Lester E
Jolly Jolly Roma   F
Julie Jolly   J
Leoney Resort   I
Shettor Villa   C
Siolim House   B

Chapora Fort

Muslim Tombstones

Laundry

Chapora River

Banyan Tree

Bus stop

B & Siolim (6km)

Big Vagator Beach

Narayan Books

HUDDO WADDO

Siddeshwar Temple

Coach Park

Car Park

DISCO VALLEY

VAGATOR BEACH ROAD

CHIVAR WADDO

Petrol Pump

Middle Vagator Beach

VAGATOR

Buses to Mapusa

Ozran (Little) Vagator Beach

Rainbow Bookshop

St Anthony's

Mapusa (9km), Petrol Pump &

Jackies Daynite

Get Well Pharmacy

0   200 m

Anjuna (3.1km)

Siolim Zagor

While much of India has had to learn to live with the spectre of religious violence, Goa's Christians and Hindus, despite the sabre-rattling of their respective right-wing politicians, manage to coexist peacefully and in a spirit of mutual respect unsurpassed on the Subcontinent. Emblematic of this communal harmony, and indeed the richness of Goa's melting-pot culture in general, is the extraordinary **Zagor festival**, held in Siolim, just east of Chapora, on the first Sunday after Christmas.

Although ostensibly a Christian celebration, coinciding with the feast day of Nossa Senhora de Guia, the night-long event blends together elements from both religions. It centres on a small Hindu shrine, housed under peepal tree down a lane near the ferry ramp. This sacred spot is associated with an important local deity called **Zagoryo**, believed to be the guardian of the village dams (*bunds*) that hold the river off the rice paddy. During the festival, each household makes offerings to Zagor to give thanks and ensure the village is protected from flooding over the coming year: Christians give candles, Hindus give oil and both offer cakes of pressed rice called *pohe*.

The festivities start with a sombre candle-lit **procession** through Siolim, in which an effigy of Zagor is carried around the various *waddos* of the village, stopping at wayside crosses and shrines along the way to receive offerings. Everyone then gathers at a *mand*, or sacred arena, in a Catholic house for a **dance drama**. The actors in this ancient ritual, assuming hereditarily assigned roles, are always drawn from two old Siolim families: the Shirodkars (Hindus) and D'Souzas (Catholics); it enacts stories from the legend of the Zagor deities. At dawn, when the play is complete and the priests have recited mantras and Christian scriptures to invoke the god's protection, Zagor is carried amid much pomp back to his shrine, where offerings of roasted maize, *feni* and fermented rice pikelets (called *sanna*) are placed before his small domed shrine.

Traditionally, local satirists used to take over at this point, performing **zupatteos**: songs poking fun at politicians, priests and anyone else who deserved to be taken down a peg or two. These days, however, the culmination of Zagor tends to be Konkani *tiatr* play, followed by a set of crowd-pleasing Konkani classics from local rock star, Remo Fernandes, who was born and still lives in Siolim.

Aside from being a model of religious tolerance, Zagor is a great spectacle and enormous fun. Surprisingly few tourists participate, but foreigners are welcomed enthusiastically, both to the religious dance drama and resolutely secular, *feni*-fuelled party that succeeds it.

the past three or four years. Whereas the main street used to retain a workaday indifference to the annual invasion of foreigners, now it's largely given over to budget travellers' cafés, with everyone spliffing up in public at sunset time. Even so, it's unlikely Chapora will ever develop into a major resort; tucked away under a dense canopy of trees on the muddy southern shore of a river estuary, it lacks both the space and the white sand that have pulled crowds to Calangute and Colva. The main drawback to staying here is the general grubbiness of the accommodation on offer, which tends to be booked for long periods to hard-drinking, heavy-smoking hippies.

Chapora's chief landmark is its venerable old **fort**, most easily reached from the Vagator side of the hill. At low tide, you can also walk around the bottom of the headland, via the anchorage and the secluded coves beyond it to Big Vagator, then head up the hill from there. The red-laterite bastion, crowning the rocky bluff, was built by the Portuguese in 1617 on the site of an earlier Muslim structure (thus the village's name – from *Shahpura*, "town of the Shah"). Deserted in the nineteenth century, it lies in ruins today, although the **views** up and down the coast from the weed-infested ramparts are still superb. Also worth a visit is the village's busy little **fishing anchorage**, where you can buy delicious calamari fresh off the boats most evenings.

Practicalities

Direct **buses** arrive at Chapora three times daily from Panjim, and every fifteen minutes from Mapusa, with departures until 7pm from various points along the main road. **Motorcycle taxis** hang around the old banyan tree at the far end of the main street, near where the buses pull in. Air, train and bus **tickets** may be booked or reconfirmed at Soniya Tours and Travels, next to the bus stand.

Much the most congenial place to stay in Chapora is the *Casa de Olga* (☎0832/227 4355, ☎m98221 57145; ❸–❹), an immaculate, red-and-white-painted little guesthouse near the fishing anchorage. It's run with great efficiency and enthusiasm by a young couple called Edmund and Elifa. Their nicest rooms are the five in a new block to the rear, which are all en suite and have good sized balconies. Cheaper and more basic is *Shettor Villa* (☎0832/227 3766, ☎m98221 58154; ❷), off the west side of the main street. Half a dozen of its rooms, ranged around a sheltered backyard, come with fans and attached bathrooms; the other eighteen share shower-toilets. The above appear on the map on p.226.

The only luxury place is an elegantly converted *palacio* called ⚑ *Siolim House* (☎0832/227 2138, ⓦwww.siolimhouse.com; ❺) in nearby Siolim (5km east along the estuary from Chapora). The three-hundred-year-old building numbers among the few hotels in the state that manage to recapture the period feel of the Portuguese era. Romantic, beautifully furnished rooms and suites are ranged around a central pillared courtyard, with bathtubs, gorgeous oyster-shell windows, four-poster beds and a twelve-metre pool in the garden.

Out on the road leading towards the fishing anchorage, *Italian Pizza* is Chapora's best **restaurant**, in a small courtyard next to a martial arts gym. Aside from its delicious home-baked pizzas (Rs60–220), house specialties include Mediterranean standards such as filets of local fish in garlic and olive oil, and squid marinated in lemon sauce. They also do daily specials that include minestrone, ravioli and proper gnocchi. Otherwise, take your pick from the crop of inexpensive little cafés and restaurants lining the main street. The popular *Welcome*, halfway down, offers a reasonable selection of cheap and filling seafood, Western and veg dishes, plus relentless reggae and techno music and backgammon sets. *Scarlet Cold Drinks* and the *Sai Ganesh Café*, both a short way east beyond the banyan tree, knock up fresh-fruit juices and milkshakes. All of the above appear on the map on p.226.

The far north

Bounded by the Chapora and Arondem (aka "Terekol") rivers, **Pernem** is Goa's northernmost district. Apart from the fishing village of **Arambol**, which, during the winter, plays host to a large contingent of hippy travellers seeking a less pretentious alternative to Anjuna and Vagator, the beautiful Pernem coastline remains the quietest stretch of shoreline in the state. Catch the tide right, and it is possible to walk in a couple of hours all the way from the sandy spit at **Morjim**, on the opposite side of the river mouth from Chapora, to Arambol, via the villages of **Aswem** and **Mandrem**, where facilities for visitors are limited to a handful of shacks and small hut camps. In the far north, **Terekol fort**, on the Maharashtrian border, makes a good target for a day-trip by motorbike or taxi.

Travelling north from **Siolim**, on the south bank of the River Chapora, the entry point to Pernem proper is the far side of the new road bridge at **Chopdem**. Head straight on for 200m or so until you arrive at a T-junction. A right turn here will take you along the quick route to Arambol; bear left, and you'll head along one of the few stretches of undeveloped coastline remaining in Goa – an area that looks, since the completion of the bridge, to be living on borrowed time.

Morjim

Viewed from Chapora fort, **MORJIM** (or **Morji**) appears as a dramatic expanse of empty sand sweeping north from a spoon-shaped spit to the river mouth – one of Goa's last remaining nesting sites for Olive Ridley turles (see box, p231). Behind it, broken dunes are backed by a dense patch of palms and casuarina trees, sheltering a mixed Hindu-Christian village whose inhabitants still live predominantly from fishing and rice farming. Bypassed completely by the main road north, their settlement has remained a relative backwater. Only in the past three or four years, since the completion of the Siolim bridge, has it started to see many tourists, the majority of them young Russians (whose early-morning fitness routines on the beach are still regarded with puzzled amusement by the straw-hatted handnet fishers working the foreshore).

Arrival, information and eating

Half a dozen **buses** per day connect Morjim with Panjim, from 7am; heading the other way, you can pick up a direct bus from Panjim at 5pm, and there are frequent services from Mapusa via Siolim. They'll drop you on the main road, five minutes' walk from the beachfront area at **Vithaldas Waddo**. If you're planning to stay anywhere else, keep your eyes peeled for the roadside signboards or you could be in for a long walk – rickshaws are few and far between this far north.

The main turning for Vithaldas Waddo, 1km back from the beach, is where you'll find Morjim's **Internet café**, *Amigo's*; access (on a slow connection) costs Rs40/hour. They also have telephone and fax facilities, and are licensed to **change money**.

△ Fishing at Morjim

Yoga in Morjim

Tucked away in a fold of the wooded hill just inland from Morjim beach is the secluded **Yoga Village** (☎0832/224 4546, ⓦwww.yogavillage.org), where you can study yoga techniques and philosophy under the guidance of **Yogi Manmoyanand**, an upcoming teacher who mastered his art during a seven-year stint in a Himalayan cave. Fourteen-day retreats cover a wide range of yogic techniques, from *pranayama* to *mudras*, *bandhas* and the full range of poses (*asanas*). Vedic discourse (under an old banyan tree) and relaxing Ayurvedic massages are also included in the cost of the course that, aside from tuition, also includes meals and accommodation (in well set-up cane and palm-leaf huts). For full details, check the website.

For **food**, you won't do better than *Britto's*, a small, family-run shack five minutes' walk down the beach, where millet-fried mussels, clams in spicy coconut sauce, vegetable fried rice and Chapora calamari in lime are the specialities; they also serve stupendously good lassis and fresh fruit juices.

Accommodation

Most of the **accommodation** in Morjim is in private houses which get snapped up early in the season, or even the previous one by entrepreneurial Muscovites who then sublet them at inflated rates. But you can usually find vacant rooms in one or other of the small guesthouses that have opened close to the beach, and a couple of higher-end places have recently sprung up.

Camp 69 Vithaldas Waddo ☎0832/224 4458. The oldest established place on the beachfront, now boasting large, well-spaced "log cabins", fitted with beds, sofas, fans and en-suite bathrooms. They also run a relaxing little terrace restaurant shaded by palms and flowering trees. ➍

Hard Rock ("Gilbert's") Temb Waddo ☎m98225 81928, Ⓔbobmarley_gilbert@hotmail.com. Local lad Gilbert Fernandes has converted a wing of his family home, behind the southernmost part of the beach, with very stylish oxide floors and ochre-washed walls. Comfortable, secluded and retaining plenty of Goan atmosphere. ➍

Montego Bay Vithaldas Waddo ☎0832/224 4222, ⓦwww.montegobaygoa.com. A dozen or so plush Rajasthani tents, stylishly equipped with driftwood beds, fans, coir mats and bathrooms with running water, at a breezy spot in the dunes under coconut trees. The most relaxing option bang on the beach, though overpriced. Breakfast included. ➐

Morjim Beach Resort Temb Waddo ☎m08326 52 1994, Ⓔrahul_goa@hotmail.com. This guesthouse is a long plod south down the beach, midway between the village centre and sandy spit at the end: you'll need at least a bicycle to stay here. But it is perfectly situated in the centre of the beach and well set up, with proper rooms and suites as well as leaf huts and "cottages". All have quiet fans, quality mattresses, fridges and sliding glass windows. ➎–➑

Naga Cottages Rasal-Vithaldas Waddo ☎m98225 83240, ⓦwww.nagacottages.com. Spacious suites with large semi-circular balconies on both sides, overlooking open fields and palm groves. Gleaming tiled floors, kitchenettes, flat-screen TVs and cane swings make this a luxurious option by local standards. ➏–➐

Papa Jolly's House #749/A-B, Morjim–Aswem Road, Mardi Waddo ☎0832/224 4113–4 or ☎m98221 03780, ⓦwww.papajollysgoa.com. A self-styled "Spiritual Holiday Resort", complete with a lovely curved pool. The new laterite building is pleasant enough, as is the location, but the tariffs – sweetened with lots of soothing New Age blurb on their website – are ludicrous: Rs4600 ($107) for a double room, rising to Rs7770 ($180) at Christmas. ➑

Tequila Sunset Hideout Vithaldas Waddo ☎m98225 88003. Large, new rooms, with attached bathrooms (closets) and big tiled balconies overlooking a beachfront plot. There's also a first-floor café-restaurant offering great sea views. ➍

White Feather House #694/A Morjim–Aswem Rd ☎m98502 42011 or ☎m94226 35465, Ⓔwhitefeather_gh1@yahoo.co.in. Comfortable, midrange place just back from the road. Its rates are way over the top, but the rooms are large, breezy and pleasant, and nearly always full. From the roof terrace you get a view across the dunes to the sea. ➍

The turtle wind

When a strong and steady on-shore breeze blows through the night in early November at Morjim – the long, empty beach west of the ferry ramp at Chopdem – the locals call it a **turtle wind** because such weather normally heralds the arrival of Goa's rarest migrant visitors: the **Olive Ridley marine turtles** (*Lepidochelys olivacea*).

For as long as anyone can remember, the spoon-shaped spit of soft white sand at **Temb**, the far southern end of the beach, has been the nesting ground of these beautiful sea reptiles. Each winter, a succession of females emerges from the surf during the night and, using their distinctive flippers, crawls to the edge of the dunes to lay their annual clutch of 105–115 eggs. Just over two months later, the fresh hatchlings clamber out and crawl blinking over their siblings to begin the perilous trek back to the water, guided into the sea by reflected moonlight. Little more is known about how these enigmatic creatures spend the rest of their long lives (turtles frequently live for over a century), but it is thought that the females return to the beaches where they were born to lay their own eggs. Some have been known to travel as far as 4500km to do this.

Once a thriving species, with huge populations spread across the Pacific, Atlantic and Indian oceans, the Olive Ridley is nowadays **endangered**. Aside from a wealth of traditional predators (such as crows, ospreys, gulls and buzzards, who pick off the hatchlings during their dash for the sea), the newborns and their parents are vulnerable to a host of man-made threats. In Morjim, as in most of Asia, the eggs are traditionally considered a delicacy and local villagers collect them to sell in Mapusa market. Many (perhaps as many as 35,000 worldwide) are killed accidentally by fishermen, caught up in fine shrimp nets or attracted by squid bait used to catch tuna. Floating litter, which the hapless turtles mistake for jellyfish, has also taken its toll over the past two decades, as have tar balls from oil spills, which coat the animals' digestive tracks and hamper the absorption of food. The growth of tourism poses an additional danger: electric lights behind the beaches throw the hatchlings off course as they scuttle towards the sea, and sand compressed by sunbathers' trampling feet damages nests, preventing the babies from digging their way out at the crucial time. On average, only two out of a typical clutch of more than one hundred survive into adulthood to reproduce. In Goa, the resulting decline has been dramatic. Of the 150 nesting females that used to return each year to Morjim, for example, only six showed up in 2006–07.

However, under the auspices of the Forest Department, a scheme has been launched to revive turtle populations. Locals are employed to watch out for the females' arrival in November, and guard the nests after the eggs have been laid until they hatch. You'll see them camped under palm-leaf shades on the beach, with the nests fenced in and marked by Forest Department signs. One of the main reasons the fishing families at Temb have so enthusiastically espoused the initiative is that its success promises to bring about the creation of an official **nature sanctuary** at Morjim, forever blocking plans to build unwanted tourist resorts on their beach.

So far, the government-led conservation attempt has not proved all that effective. After an initial leap in hatchling figures, recent results have shown a marked dip, which the Forest Department ascribes to an increase in tourist activity.

Watching the nesting turtles is an unforgettable experience, although one requiring a certain amount of dedication, or luck. No one knows for sure when an Olive Ridley female will turn up, but with a strong turtle wind blowing at the right time, the chances are good. Much more predictable are the appearances of the hatchlings, who emerge exactly 54 days after their mothers laid the eggs. If you ask one of the wardens looking after the nests, they can tell you when this will be.

For more on international attempts to save marine turtles, including the massive synchronized *arribida* (arrival) of around 200,000 at the Bhita Kanika Sanctuary, Orissa, on the east coast of India, visit the website of the World Wildlife Fund (Ⓦwww.wwf.org).

Aswem

A solitary whitewashed crucifix rises from the rocks dividing Morjim from **ASWEM**, the next village north. Aside from the odd German nudist or two, you should have the sands pretty much to yourself until you arrive at the burgeoning cluster of shacks and hut camps midway along the beach. Huddled under the canopy of a beautiful coconut *mand*, this ad hoc tourist settlement started to snowball after a couple of French restaurateurs from Baga opened a chic beach café here (*La Plage* – see below).

La Plage excepted, amenities remain basic (leaf huts are the norm as the local council has vigorously enforced the Coastal Protection Zone building ban), but the beach is all the more appealing for that. It's clean, quiet for most of the season and, outside the full-moon period, safe for kids to swim off. Only at the far northern end, where a tidal creek periodically prevents you from continuing north towards Arambol, has package tourism made any discernable inroads: Maruti vans deposit punters here to overnight in purpose-built hut camps on the shoreline, but the setup is very low-key.

Practicalities

Sporadic **buses** from Panjim and Mapusa cover the quiet stretch of road running parallel to the beach inland, from where a five-minute walk across the paddy fields brings you to the shacks (signboards indicate the paths). Other than the cafés, there are no facilities whatsoever here. Nearly everyone who stays rents a scooter from somewhere else to get to and around Aswem. The nearest Internet access and shops are at Morjim, an idyllic half-hour plod south.

For **food**, head to 🍴 *La Plage* (☎m98502 58543; closed evenings), where light Gallic–Mediterranean, heat-beating snacks and drinks (chilled asparagus soup, mint lassis, Moroccan salads, fresh strawberries and cream), along with sumptuous chargrilled seafood and barbequed main courses, are dished up by Nepalis in black *lunghis* against a diaphanous backdrop of floaty white muslin. It's a surreal counterpoint to the fishing *waddo* down the beach, but a very pleasant breakfast or lunch venue nonetheless.

Accommodation

Change Your Mind ☎0832/561 3716 or ☎m98223 89290. Basic huts and treehouses behind a lively shack. ❷–❸

Gopal ☎0832/224 4431, ✉gopal@ingoa.com. In much the same mould as *Change Your Mind*, at identical rates. ❷–❸

Palm Grove ☎0832/224 7440. Pick of the hut camps: further up the beach from the others, and with large treehouses that are not only well spaced but also have sea views. Owners Ratnagar and Nali accept telephone bookings. ❹

🏃 **Yab Yum** ☎0832/651 0392, ⓦwww.yabyumresorts.com. A campus of beautiful domed structures made from palm thatch, mango wood and laterite, with curvy moulded concrete floors and walls, painted pale purple. They're very large and attractively furnished inside, featuring beds on platforms and comfy mattresses, glitter balls, paper lanterns and muslin drapes – though such alt-chic comes at quite a high price (Rs3300 per double or Rs4400 for suites). They also offer a handful of similarly stylish faux-Portuguese-era cottages, and wooden deck for yoga and play tipi for the kids. Rates include breakfast. ❹

Mandrem

A magnificent, and largely empty, beach stretches north of Aswem towards Arambol, uninterrupted save for a couple of large-scale hut camps and a single package hotel. Whether or not **MANDREM** can continue to hold out against the rising tide of tourism remains to be seen, but for the time being, nature still has the upper hand. Olive Ridley marine turtles nest on the quietest stretch, and you're more than likely to catch a glimpse of one of the white-bellied fish eagles that live in the casuarina trees – their last stronghold in Pernem. If you can afford it, the best spot from which to savour this last unspoilt strip of the Goan coast is Denzil Sequeira's exclusive beachhouse *Elsewhere* (see below), nestled in the dunes just north of the creek and unquestionably the most beautiful hideaway hereabouts. The rest of this area's accommodation is tucked away inland at **Junasa Waddo**, where a handful of small guesthouses and hotels have sprung up.

Practicalities

Public transport is thin on the ground. Visitors walk or rent scooters for the five-minute ride to **Madlamaz-Mandrem**, a typically north Goan market village straddling the main road inland. Parsekar Stores holds an Anjuna-style stock of tourist-oriented food and drink – including muesli, olive oil and Nilgiri cheese – and natural cosmetics; and there's a tiny **laundry** above a jeweller's shop in the small courtyard just to the east of the main road.

Accommodation

Dunes ☎0832/224 7219 or 224 7071, ⓦwww .dunesgoa.com. Huge "holiday village" of twin-bedded, yellow-painted leaf huts. They're a notch too close together for comfort and are brightly lit, so spoiling the aspect of the beach at night, but this is an efficiently run outfit that fills up in peak season. Pricier en-suite available. ④–⑤

Elsewhere ☎022/2373 8757 or ☎m98200 37387, ⓦwww.aseascape.com. Goan fashion photographer Denzil Sequeira converted his grandfather's hot-season retreat into a dream getaway, retaining its colonial-era character with a gorgeous sea-facing veranda and traditional wood furniture, yet incorporating modern elements (a fridge, two cobalt-blue bathrooms and luminous white cotton drapes that catch the breezes). Flanked by the beach on one side and a creek on the other, it's romantic and exclusive, but affordable if you get a group together (the three bedrooms sleep six). He's recently renovated four more little villas further towards the sand spit south of the main house – all of them beautifully situated. From US$306 per night in season. ⑨

Otter Creek ☎022/2373 8757 or ☎m98200 37387, ⓦwww.aseascape.com.

Three stylish luxury tents, each with their own bamboo four-posters, bathroom, colour-washed sit-out and jetty on the river; you have to cross a rickety foot bridge to get there, or walk over the dunes from the beach. Rs3320 ($86) per night in season. ⑨

Riva Resort ☎0832/224 7088 or 224 7612, ⓦwww.rivaresorts.com. The other big hut camp, next to *Dunes*. This one's more upmarket, with swisher huts and higher rates (Rs500–2000 depending on the level of comfort, rising to a hefty Rs2000–10,000 at Christmas). The site centres on a huge bar-restaurant that hosts DJ nights and has big-screen video. ③–⑤

Villa River Cat ☎0822/224 7928 or ☎m98901 57060, ⓦwww.villarivercat.com. Quirky riverside hotel, screened from the beach by the dunes, with distinctive hippy-influenced decor and furniture. The sixteen rooms are all individually designed: mosaics, shells, devotional sculpture and hammocks set the tone. Some have balconies, and there's a great sunset roof terrace and rear garden for lounging in. Host Rinoo Seghal is an animal lover, so brace yourself for a menagerie of cats and dogs. Artists and musicians receive a ten percent discount. ⑤–⑧

Arambol (Harmal)

The largest coastal village in Pernem district is **ARAMBOL** (sometimes called **Harmal**), 32km northwest of Mapusa. If you're happy with basic amenities but want to stay somewhere lively, this might be your best bet. The village's two beaches are beautiful and still relatively unexploited – thanks to the locals, who a few years back managed to block proposals put forward by a local landowner to site a sprawling five-star resort here. The majority of foreigners who stay in Arambol tend to do so for the season, and over time a close-knit expat community (of mostly ageing hippies who've been coming here for years) has

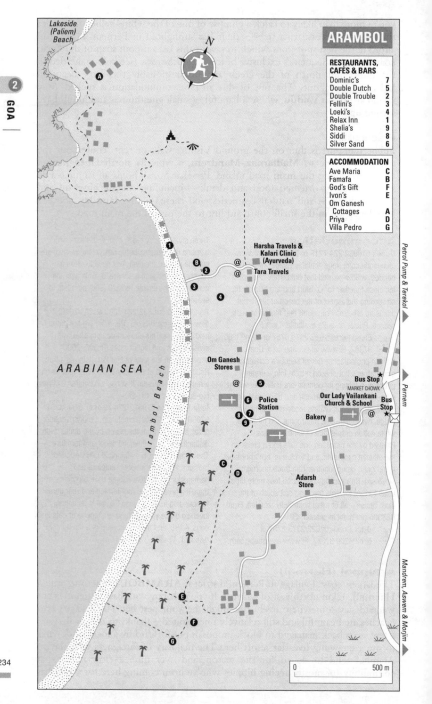

ARAMBOL

RESTAURANTS, CAFES & BARS

Dominic's	7
Double Dutch	5
Double Trouble	2
Fellini's	3
Loeki's	4
Relax Inn	1
Shelia's	9
Siddi	8
Silver Sand	6

ACCOMMODATION

Ave Maria	C
Famafa	B
God's Gift	F
Ivon's	E
Om Ganesh Cottages	A
Priya	D
Villa Pedro	G

Lakeside (Paliem) Beach

N

Harsha Travels & Kalari Clinic (Ayurveda)

Tara Travels

ARABIAN SEA

Arambol Beach

Om Ganesh Stores

Police Station

Bus Stop

MARKET CHOWK

Our Lady Vailankani Church & School

Bakery

Bus Stop

Adarsh Store

Petrol Pump & Terekol

Pernem

Mandrem, Aswem & Morjim

0   500 m

grown up, with its own alternative health facilities, paragliding school, yoga gurus and wholefood cafés.

Modern Arambol is scattered around an area of high ground west of the main coast road. From here, a bumpy lane runs downhill to the more traditional fishing quarter, clustered under a canopy of widely spaced palm trees. The main **beach** lies 200m further along a lane that the predominantly British, festival-going tourist population call Glastonbury Street. Strewn with dozens of old wooden boats and a line of tourist café-bars, the gently curving bay is good for bathing, but much less picturesque than its neighbour around the corner, **Paliem** or "**Lakeside**" **beach**. To reach this, follow the track over the headland to the north; beyond a rather insalubrious-smelling, rocky-bottomed cove, the trail emerges to a broad strip of soft white sand hemmed in on both sides by steep cliffs. Behind it, a small **freshwater lake** extends along the bottom of the valley into a thick jungle. Hang around the banks of this murky green pond for long enough, and you'll probably see a fluorescent-yellow human figure or two appear from the bushes at its far end. Fed by boiling hot springs, the lake is lined with sulphurous mud, which, when smeared over the body, dries to form a surreal, butter-coloured shell. The resident hippies swear it's good for you and spend much of the day tiptoeing naked around the shallows like refugees from some obscure tribal initiation ceremony – much to the amusement of Arambol's Indian visitors –but in recent years, the banks have been annexed by a local entrepreneur, and you now have to pay for a scraping of what little mud remains.

Arrival and information

Buses to and from Panjim (via Mapusa) pull into Arambol every half-hour until noon, and every 90 minutes thereafter, at the small bus stop on the main road. A faster private **minibus** service from Panjim arrives daily opposite the chai stalls at the beach end of the village. There are plenty of places offering broadband **Internet access**, motorcycle rental and money changing.

Accommodation

Standards of tourist accommodation in Arambol lag well behind the rest of the state, although there are signs of improvement, with a crop of new, family guest-houses beginning to appear on the south side of the village in **Modlo** and **Girkar Waddos**. This area is much more peaceful, but you have to walk down the beach to get there – not such a great idea at night if you're female. The warren of narrow sandy lanes behind the north end of the beach, known as **Khalcha Waddo**, is busier, but – with the exception of those listed below – its guesthouses are uniformly cramped and grotty.

Ave Maria House #22, Modlo Waddo ☎0832/224 2974. Arambol's largest guesthouse offers good-value rooms, with or without bathrooms, and a sociable rooftop restaurant in a three-storey modern building. Tricky to find: turn left on to a *kutcha* track where the main road through the south side of the village makes a sharp right bend. ❸

Famafa Khalcha Waddo ☎0832/229 2516, ⓦwww.travelingoa.com/famafa. Large, ugly concrete place just off "Glastonbury Street"; popular with Israelis, and correspondingly rowdy, but it usually has vacancies and is very close to the beach. ❸

God's Gift House #411, Girkar Waddo ☎0832/224 2318. Variously priced, sizeable rooms, all tiled and with comfortable verandas; some also have living rooms and kitchens. Rates are good and the proprietors friendly. ❷

Ivon's Girkar Waddo ☎0832/224 2672 or ☎m98221 27398. The pick of the bunch: clean, tiled rooms, all with attached bathroom and fronted by good-sized tiled balconies opening onto a well-groomed family compound or the dunes. ❹

Om Ganesh Cottages ☎0832/224 2957. In the cove between the village and Lakeside beach; book at the Om Ganesh stores on the main drag

(☎0832/224 2957). Nicest of the "cottages" stacked up the cliffside just south of Lakeside beach. The sea views from their verandas are superb, but some may find the Israeli chillum scene in the nearby cafés a disincentive. Rates vary wildly according to demand, and advance booking (with a deposit) is all but essential by mid-season. ④—⑤

Priya Modlo Waddo ☎0832/224 2661. Welcoming

ten-room guesthouse that's the best fallback if nearby *Ave Maria* is full. ③

Villa Pedro Girkar Waddo ☎0832/224 7689. Small family place amid the *toddy* grove just in from the beach – well placed if you want to be near the sea, but a fair way away from the village. The rooms are clean and pleasant, and some have sea views. Good value. ②

Eating

Thanks to its annually replenished pool of expatriate gastronomic talent, Arambol harbours a handful of unexpectedly good **restaurants** – not that you'd ever guess from their generally lacklustre exteriors. The village's discerning hippy contingent cares more about flavours than fancy decor, and prices reflect the fact that most of them eke out savings to stay here all winter. If you're on a really rock-bottom budget, stick to the "rice-plate" shacks at the bottom of the village. Tasty thalis at *Sheila's* and *Siddi* come with *puris*, and both have a good travellers' breakfast menu of pancakes, eggs and curd. *Dominic's*, also at the bottom of the village (near where the road makes a ninety-degree bend), is renowned for its fruit juices and milkshakes.

Double Dutch Main Street, halfway down on the right (look for the yellow signboard). Spread under a palm canopy in the thick of the village, this laid-back café is the hub of alternative Arambol. Renowned for its melt-in-the-mouth apple pie, it also does a tempting range of home-baked buttery biscuits, cakes (Buddha's Dream's a winner), healthy salads and sumptuous main meals (from Rs120), including fresh buffalo steaks and the perennially popular "mixed stuff" (stuffed mushrooms and capsicums with sesame pesto).

Double Trouble "Glastonbury Street". Spin-off of *Double Dutch*, offering classy Italian and French-style seafood dishes from around Rs150.

Fellini's "Glastonbury Street". Italian-run place serving delicious wood-fired pizzas (Rs80–140), and authentic pasta or gnocchi with a choice of

over twenty sauces. It gets horrendously busy in season, so be here early if you want snappy service.

Relax Inn Arambol beach. Top-quality seafood straight off the boats and unbelievably authentic pasta (you get even more expat Italians in here than at *Fellini's*). Try the *vongole* (clam) sauce. Inexpensive, but expect a wait as they cook to order.

Silver Sand Opposite Arambol chapel. At the south side of the village, this is another deceptively ordinary streetside café specializing in fresh seafood (including Chapora calamari), home-made pasta, ratatouille for vegans and popular chocolate cake, baked daily. The espresso's top-notch, too, and there can be queues at breakfast for the home-made pineapple jam.

Nightlife and entertainment

Evenings in Arambol tend to revolve around the café–restaurants and whichever bar is hosting **live music**. There are free jam sessions at *Loeki's*, just off "Glastonbury Street", on Sunday and Thursday evenings. Standards vary with whoever happens to blow in, but there have been some memorable impromptu gigs held here over the past few seasons.

Sports and holistic therapies

Posters pinned to palm trees and café noticeboards around Arambol advertise an amazing array of **activities**, from kite surfing to reiki. A good place to get a fix on what's happening is the *Double Dutch* "Bullshit Info" corner, which displays email addresses and meeting details for just about everyone who does anything.

For the adventurous, there's **paragliding** from the clifftops above Lakeside beach, run by a couple of German and British outfits who've been here for the

Getting to Terekol at Low Tide

Access to Terekol is difficult at **low tide**, when the river ferry is suspended for a few hours. To check tide times, phone the *Fort Tiracol* (see below). If you're booked to stay in the hotel, they'll lay on a launch to get you across. Alternatively, pay a local boatman to shuttle you over; or, as a last resort, catch the other ferry that leaves from the jetty 4km further upriver – once on the far bank, follow the lane to the first village, turn left at the crossroads there and keep going for 10km via a winding route that takes you through USHAC the iron ore mines).

best part of a decade, alternating between Goa and Manali. The cost of the flight includes all the equipment you'll need and full instruction. At the south end of Arambol Beach, ask at the *Surf Shack* for details of **kite surfing** courses and equipment rental.

Each season, an army of holistic therapists also offer their services and run courses in Arambol, making this a great place to learn new skills. Look out for Iyengar-qualified **yoga** teacher Sharat (@www.hiyogacentre.com), who holds five-day classes on the beach (Rs1000), as well as two-week intensives. Prospective students usually have to sign up by Wednesday lunchtime.

Terekol

North of Arambol, the sinuous coast road climbs to the top of a rocky, undulating plateau, then winds down through a swathe of thick woodland to join the River Arondem (or Terekol), which it then follows for 4km through a landscape of vivid paddy fields, coconut plantations and temple towers protruding from scruffy red-brick villages. The tiny enclave of **TEREKOL**, the northernmost tip of Goa, is reached via a clapped-out car ferry (every 30min; 5min) from the hamlet of Querim, 42km from Panjim. If the tide is out and the water levels are too low for the ferry to run, you can either backtrack 5km, where there's another one, or arrange for the boatman at the jetty to run you across (for a negotiable fee).

Set against the backdrop of a filthy iron-ore complex, the old **fort** that dominates the estuary from the north – an ochre-painted building with turreted ramparts that wouldn't look out of place in coastal Portugal – was built by the Marathas at the start of the eighteenth century, but taken soon after by the Portuguese. These days, it serves as a low-key luxury **Heritage Hotel**, *The Fort Tiracol* (☎0832/227 6793 or ☎02366 227631, @www.nilayahermitage.com; ⑨), created by the owners of the swish *Nilaya Hermitage* at Arpora (see p.216). The seven rooms are all decorated in traditional ochre and white, with black-oxide floors, black-tiled drench showers and rustic wood and wrought-iron furniture; tariffs start at $135 per night. Non-residents are welcome to visit the restaurant and stylish lounge bar, where you can eat authentic Goan cooking while enjoying what must rank among the finest seascapes in southern India.

South Goa

Beyond the unattractive port city of Vasco da Gama and the nearby Dabolim airport, Goa's southern reaches are fringed by some of the region's finest **beaches**, backed by a lush band of coconut plantations, and green hills scattered with attractive villages. An ideal first base if you've just arrived in the region is

Benaulim, 6km west of Goa's second city, **Margao**. The most traveller-friendly resort in the area, Benaulim stands slap in the middle of a spectacular 25-kilometre stretch of pure white sand. Although increasingly carved up by Mumbai time-share companies, low-cost accommodation here is plentiful and of a consistently high standard. Nearby Colva, by contrast, has degenerated over the past decade into an insalubrious charter resort. Frequented by huge numbers of day-trippers, and boasting few discernible charms, it's best avoided.

With the gradual spread of package tourism down the coast, **Palolem**, a couple of hours' south of Margao down the main highway, has emerged as the budget travellers' preferred resort, despite its relative inaccessibility. Set against a backdrop of forest-cloaked hills, its beach is spectacular and development restrained, although the numbers of visitors can feel overwhelming in high season.

Margao and around

The capital of prosperous Salcete *taluka*, **MARGAO** – referred to in railway timetables and on some maps by its official government title, **Madgaon** – is Goa's second city. Surrounded by fertile farmland, the town has always been an important agricultural market, and was once a major religious centre, with dozens of wealthy temples and *dharamshalas* – however, most of these were destroyed when the Portuguese absorbed the area into their Novas Conquistas ("New Conquests") during the seventeenth century. Today, Catholic churches still outnumber Hindu shrines, but Margao has retained a cosmopolitan feel due to a huge influx of migrant labour from neighbouring Karnataka and Maharashtra.

If you're arriving in Goa on the Konkan Railway from Mumbai or South India, you'll almost certainly have to pause in Margao to pick up onward transport by road. The other reason to come here is to shop at the town's **market**. Stretching from the south edge of the main square to within a stone's throw of the old railway station, the bazaar centres on a labyrinthine covered area where you'll find everything from betel leaves and sacks of lime paste to baby clothes and cheap Taiwanese toys. When the syrupy air gets too stifling, explore the streets around the market, among which is one given over to cloth merchants and tailors. Also worth checking is the excellent little government-run **Khadi Gramodyog** shop, on the main square (near the *Kamat*), which sells quality hand-spun cottons and raw silk by the metre, as well as ready-made traditional Indian garments.

A rickshaw ride north, the **Church of the Holy Spirit** is the main landmark in Margoa's dishevelled colonial enclave, next to the serene **Largo de Igreja** square. Built by the Portuguese in 1675, it ranks among the finest examples of late-Baroque architecture in Goa, its interior dominated by a huge gilt reredos dedicated to the Virgin. Just northeast of it, overlooking the main Ponda road, stands one of the state's grandest eighteenth-century *palacios*, **Sat Banzam Ghor** ("Seven Gables house"). Only three of its original seven high-pitched roof gables remain, but the mansion is still an impressive sight, its facade decorated with fancy scroll work and huge oyster-shell windows.

For more of Goa's wonderful vernacular colonial architecture, you'll have to head **inland from Margao**, where villages such as **Lutolim**, **Racaim** and **Rachol** are littered with decaying old Portuguese houses, most of them empty – the region's traditional inheritance laws ensure that old family homes tend to be owned by literally dozens of descendants, none of whom are willing or can afford to maintain them.

Another reason to head into Margao is to catch a movie in South Goa's principal **cinema**, the Osia Multiplex (℗0832/270 1717), out in the north of

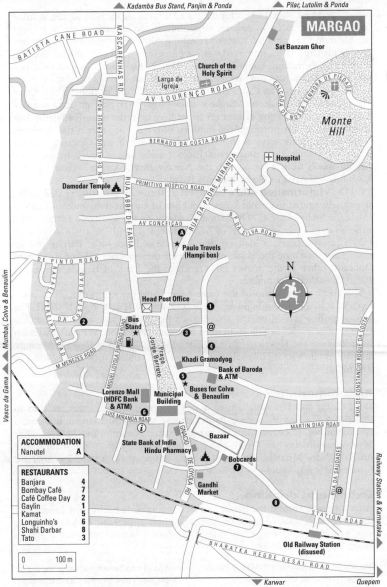

MARGAO

BATISTA CANE ROAD

MASCARENHAS RD

▲ Kadamba Bus Stand, Panjim & Ponda   ▲ Pilar, Lutolim & Ponda

Sat Banzam Ghor

Largo de Igreja

Church of the Holy Spirit

CALÇADA DE NOSSA SENHORA DE PIEDADE

AV. LOURENÇO ROAD

Monte Hill

RUA DE ALBUQUERQUE ROAD

BERNADO DA COSTA ROAD

+ Hospital

RUA ABBE DE FARIA

Damodar Temple ▲

PRIMITIVO HOSPICIO ROAD

RUA DA PADRE MIRANDA

B P DA SILVA ROAD

AV. CONCEIÇÃO

DE PINTO ROAD

A ★ Paulo Travels (Hampi bus)

N

RUA DE RAFAEL PEREIRA ROAD

DA COSTA ROAD

Head Post Office ⊠

❶

Mumbai, Colva & Benaulim ◀

Vasco da Gama ◀   Mumbai, Colva & Benaulim ◀

❷

@

Bus Stand ★

❸

❹

M. MENEZES ROAD

Khadi Gramodyog

MIGUEL LOYOLA FURTADO ROAD

Praça Jorge Barreto

❺

Bank of Baroda & ATM

★ Buses for Colva & Benaulim

Lorenzo Mall (HDFC Bank & ATM)

Municipal Building

❻

LUIS MIRANDA ROAD

ⓘ

RUA DE CONSTANCIO ROQUE DA COSTA

MARTIN DIAS ROAD

State Bank of India

Hindu Pharmacy

J. IGNACIO DE LOYOLA RD

Bazaar

Bobcards ❼

RUA DA SAUDADES

ACCOMMODATION
Nanutel   A

Gandhi Market

❽

@

STATION ROAD

Railway Station & Karnataka ▶

RESTAURANTS

Banjara	4
Bombay Café	7
Café Coffee Day	2
Gaylin	1
Kamat	5
Longuinho's	6
Shahi Darbar	8
Tato	3

0   100 m

BHARATKA HEGDE DESAI ROAD

Old Railway Station (disused)

▼ Karwar   Quepem ▼

town near the Kadamba bus stand. It screens Hollywood as well as Bollywood releases; tickets cost Rs70–100.

Arrival and information

Margao's new **railway station** lies 3km south of the centre, its reservation office (Mon–Sat 8am–4.30pm, Sun 8am–2pm; ☎0832/271 2940) divided between the ground and first floor. Tickets for trains to Mumbai are in short supply, so make your reservation as far in advance as possible. If you're catching the four times weekly train to Hospet (en route to Hampi) get here early to avoid long queues. Several principal trains stop in Margao at unsociable times of night, but there's a 24-hour information counter (☎0832/271 2790), and a round-the-clock prepaid auto-rickshaw and taxi stand outside the exit.

Local private buses to Colva and Benaulim leave from in front of the *Kamat Hotel*, on the east side of Margao's main square. Arriving on long-distance government services you can get off either here or at the main **Kadamba bus stand**, 3km further north, on the outskirts of town. The latter is the departure point for interstate services to Mangalore, via Chaudi and Gokarna, and for services to Panjim and north Goa. Paulo Travel's deluxe coach to and from Hampi works from a lot next to the *Nanutel Hotel*, 1km or so south of the Kadamba bus stand on Padre Miranda Road.

GTDC's **information office** (Mon–Fri 9.30am–5.30pm; ☎0832/222 5528), which sells tourist maps and keeps useful lists of current train and bus times, is inside the lobby of the *GTDC Margao Residency*, on the southwest corner of the main square. There are plenty of ATMs dotted around the town centre: try HFDC, in the Lorenzo Mall, on the west side of Praça Jorge Barreto just up from *Longuinho's*; or the Bank of Baroda on the opposite side of the square. Bobcards office in the market sub-branch of the Bank of Baroda, on Station Road, does Visa encashments.

The GPO is at the top of the central municipal gardens, although its poste restante is in a different building, 200m west on the Rua Diogo da Costa. The central **police** station on the west side of the main square near the GPO is ☎0832/270 5095. For visitors in need of medical attention, Margao's two main **hospitals** are: the Hospicio (☎0832/270 5664 or 270 5754), Rua De Miranda, and the Apollo Victor Hospital, in the suburb of Malbhat (☎0832/272 8888 or 272 6272).

Accommodation

With Colva and Benaulim a mere twenty-minute bus ride away, it's hard to think of a reason why anyone should choose to **stay** in Margao: however, a commendable place in town is the three-star *Nanutel* (☎0832/270 0900, ⓦwww.nanuindia.com; ❺–❻), a multi-storey block north of the main square on Rua Padre Miranda. Pitched at visiting businessmen, it has 55 central a/c rooms and a small pool.

Eating and drinking

After a browse around the bazaar, most visitors make a beeline for *Longuinho's*, the long-established hangout of Margao's English-speaking middle classes. If you are on a tight budget, try one of the South Indian-style pure-veg cafés along Station Road.

Banjara De Souza Chambers ☎0832/272 2088. This swish basement restaurant is Goa's classiest North Indian joint outside Panjim, specializing in rich Mughlai and tandoori dishes. Tasteful wood and oil-painting decor, unobtrusive *ghazaal* background music, imported liquors and slick service. Most main courses around Rs150–200.
Bombay Café Station Rd. Popular with office workers and shoppers for its cheap veg snacks,

served on tin trays by young lads in grubby cotton uniforms. Handy pitstop for the market, and open early for breakfast.
Café Coffee Day Shop 18/19 Vasanth Arcade, near Popular High School. Goa's answer to *Starbucks* has a super-cool a/c branch tucked away off the Municipal Gardens square, popular with local college kids. Aside from a perfect latte, it serves spicy savouries (such as mini-pizzas and salad wraps) and, most memorably, a very sinful "sizzling

brownie" (Rs75), which will have chocoholics begging for loyalty cards.

Gaylin Behind Grace Church. A/c Chinese restaurant serving a good selection of Cantonese and Szechuan dishes (mostly steeped in hot red Goan chilli paste). Count on Rs1750–250 for three courses; extra for drinks.

Kamat Praça Jorge Barreto, next to the Colva/Benaulim bus stop. The town's busiest Udupi canteen, serving the usual South Indian selection, as well as hot and cold drinks. More hygienic than it looks, but *Tato* up the road is cleaner.

Longuinho's Luis Miranda Rd. Relaxing, old-fashioned café serving a selection of meat, fish and veg mains, freshly baked savoury snacks, cakes and drinks. The food isn't up to much these days, and the 1950s Goan atmosphere has been marred

by the arrival of satellite TV, but it's a pleasant enough place to catch your breath over a beer.

Shahi Darbar Station Rd. As its name implies, this is the place to come for meaty Muslim food. The traditional chicken biriyanis (Rs75–100), scooped up with piping hot *rotis*, are fantastic.

Tato Tucked away up an alley off the east side of Praça Jorge Barreto. The town's brightest and best South Indian café serves the usual range of hot snacks (including especially good samosas at breakfast time, and masala dosas from midday on). A bit cramped downstairs, but well worth the effort to find. For a proper meal, climb the stairs to their cool a/c floor, where you can order wonderful thalis (for Rs40) and a range of North Indian dishes, as well as all the Udupi nibbles dished up on the ground floor.

Chandor

Thirteen kilometres east of Margao across Salcete district's fertile rice fields lies sleepy **CHANDOR** village, a scattering of tumbledown villas and farmhouses ranged along shady tree-lined lanes. The main reason to venture out here is the splendid **Braganza-Perreira/Menezes-Braganza house** (daily except holidays, no set hours; recommended donation Rs100), regarded as the grandest of Goa's colonial mansions. Dominating the dusty village square, the house, built in the 1500s by the wealthy Braganza family for their two sons, has a huge double-storey facade, with 28 windows flanking its entrance. Braganza de Perreira, the great-grandfather of the present owner, was the last knight of the king of Portugal; more recently, Menezes Braganza (1879–1938), a journalist and freedom fighter, was one of the few Goan aristocrats actively to oppose Portuguese rule. Forced to flee Chandor in 1950, the family returned in 1962 to find their house, amazingly, untouched. The airy tiled interiors of both wings contain a veritable feast of **antiques**.

The house is divided into two separate wings, owned by different branches of the old family. Both are open to the public, though there are no set hours as such – just turn up between 10am and noon or 3 and 5pm, go through the main entrance, up the stairs and knock at either of the doors. You'll be expected to leave a donation of at least Rs100. Furniture enthusiasts, and lovers of rare Chinese porcelain, in particular, will find plenty to drool over in the Menezes-Braganza wing (to the right as you face the building), which has preserved the famous journalist's library. Next door in the **Braganza-Perreira** portion, an ornate oratory enshrines St Francis Xavier's diamond-encrusted toenail, recently retrieved from a local bank vault. The house's most famous feature, however, is its ostentatiously grand ballroom, or **Great Salon**, where a pair of matching high-backed chairs, presented to the Braganza-Perreiras by King Dom Luís of Portugal, occupy pride of place.

Colva

A hot-season retreat for Margao's moneyed middle classes since long before Independence, **COLVA** is the oldest and largest – but least appealing – of south Goa's resorts. Its outlying *waddos* are pleasant enough, dotted with colonial-style villas and ramshackle fishing huts, but the beachfront is dismal: a lacklustre collection of concrete hotels, souvenir stalls and fly-blown snack bars strewn around a bleak central roundabout. The atmosphere is not improved by heaps of rubbish dumped in a rank-smelling ditch that runs behind the beach, nor by the stench of drying fish wafting from the nearby village. Benaulim, only a five-minute drive further south, has a far better choice of accommodation and range of facilities, and is altogether more salubrious.

Benaulim

According to Hindu mythology, Goa was created when the sage Shri Parasurama, Vishnu's sixth incarnation, fired an arrow into the sea from the top of the Western Ghats and ordered the waters to recede. The spot where the shaft fell to earth, known in Sanskrit as Banali ("place where the arrow landed") and later corrupted by the Portuguese to **BENAULIM**, lies in the dead centre of Colva Beach, 7km west of Margao. Twenty years ago, this atmospheric fishing and rice-farming village, scattered around the coconut groves and paddy fields between the main Colva–Mobor road and the dunes, had barely made it onto the backpackers' map. Since the completion of the nearby Konkan railway, however, big-spending middle-class Indians have started to holiday here, in the luxury resorts and time-share apartment complexes that have mushroomed in the rice fields. As a result, the village has lost some of its famously *sossegarde* feel. Even so, if you time your visit well (avoiding Diwali and the Christmas peak season), Benaulim is still hard to beat as a place to unwind. Its tourist scene is neither particularly "alternative" nor alcohol-driven. The seafood is superb, accommodation and motorbikes cheaper than anywhere else in the state, and the beach breathtaking, particularly around sunset, when its brilliant white sand and churning surf reflect the changing colours to magical effect. Shelving away almost to Cabo da Rama on the horizon, the beach is also lined with Goa's largest, and most colourfully decorated, fleet of wooden outriggers, and these provide welcome shade during the heat of the day.

Practicalities

Buses from Margao and Colva roll through Benaulim every fifteen minutes or so, dropping passengers at the Maria Hall crossroads. Ranged around this busy junction are two well-stocked general stores, a couple of café-bars, a bank, pharmacy, laundry and the taxi and auto-rickshaw rank, from where you can pick up **transport** to the beach, 1.5km west.

Signs offering **motorbikes** for rent are dotted along the lane leading to the sea: rates are standard, descending in proportion to the length of time you keep the vehicle. Worth bearing in mind if you're planning to continue further south is that motorbikes are much cheaper to rent (and generally in better condition) here than Palolem, where there's a relative shortage of vehicles. **Petrol** is sold by the litre from a table at the roadside, two minutes' walk south down the road leading to *Royal Palm Beach Resort*, but tends to be laced with solvent and smokes badly. Local boys will try to get you to pay them to fill your bike up in Margao, but invariably pocket half of the money in the process, so if you've a valid licence and find a bike with yellow plates do it yourself (Margao's main petrol pump is on the west side of the Praça Jorge Barreto – see map on p.239). **Bicycles** cost around Rs75–100 per day to rent. If you're intending to stay for a long time, it might be worth buying one. Several cycle shops in Margao sell standard Indian-style Hero models for Rs2000–2500; you can expect to resell it again for half the original price.

For **changing money**, the Bank of Baroda on Maria Hall has a (temperamental) ATM. Currency and travellers cheques, may be changed at GK Tourist Centre, at the crossroads in the village centre, and New Horizons, diagonally opposite. It's often worth comparing rates at the two.

For **Internet access**, GK Tourist Centre and New Horizons have broadband connections (Rs40/hr).

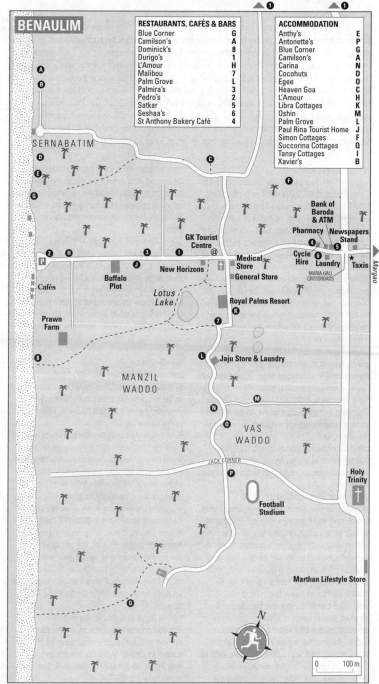

BENAULIM

RESTAURANTS, CAFÉS & BARS

Blue Corner	G
Camilson's	A
Dominick's	8
Durigo's	1
L'Amour	H
Malibou	7
Palm Grove	L
Palmira's	3
Pedro's	2
Satkar	5
Seshaa's	6
St Anthony Bakery Café	4

ACCOMMODATION

Anthy's	E
Antonette's	P
Blue Corner	G
Camilson's	A
Carina	N
Cocohuts	D
Egee	O
Heaven Goa	C
L'Amour	H
Libra Cottages	K
Oshin	M
Palm Grove	L
Paul Rina Tourist Home	J
Simon Cottages	F
Succorina Cottages	Q
Tansy Cottages	I
Xavier's	B

2

GOA

SERNABATIM

Bank of Baroda & ATM

Pharmacy   Newspapers Stand

GK Tourist Centre @

Cycle Hire   Laundry   Taxis

Medical Store

Margao

New Horizons

General Store

MARIA HALL CROSSROADS

Buffalo Plot

Cafés

Lotus Lake

Royal Palms Resort

Prawn Farm

Jaju Store & Laundry

MANZIL WADDO

VAS WADDO

JACK CORNER

Holy Trinity

Football Stadium

Marthan Lifestyle Store

N

0   100 m

Varca Cavelossim, Mobor & Palolem

Accommodation

Aside from the unsightly time-share complexes and five-stars that loom in the fields around the village, most of Benaulim's **accommodation** consists of small budget guesthouses, scattered around the lanes a kilometre or so back from the beach. The majority are featureless annexes of spartan tiled rooms with fans and, usually, attached shower-toilets; the only significant difference between them is their location. The best way to find a vacancy is to hunt around on foot or by bicycle, although if you wait at the Maria Hall crossroads or the beachfront with luggage, someone is bound to ask if you need a room. Of the more comfortable mid-range places, the most desirable are tucked away north of the village in Sernabatim (technically in Colva, but within easy cycling distance).

Inexpensive

Antonette's Jack Corner, House #1695 Vas Waddo ☎0832/277 0358 or ☎m99223 12984. Next to a crossroads where all the local fishermen and lads hang out, but in an otherwise peaceful corner of the village, with very large, well furnished rooms for the price, the best of them to the rear of the building looking over the fields. Well stocked fridges with beers and bottled water on the upstairs landing. Owner Geraldo Rodrigues is exceptionally friendly and helpful. ①–②

Cocohuts Sernabatim ☎m98221 01398. Among the few bona fide budget options this far north of the village, a stone's throw from the beach. Its eight leaf huts have tiled floors and attached bathrooms, but heat up in the day and the beds are a bit grubby. An only slightly more appealing prospect are the six rooms in an adjacent block, which have high clay-tiled roofs and partition toilets. ③

Egee Vas Waddo ☎0832/277 0422. Half a dozen nicer-than-average budget rooms, on the first floor above a family house in the quiet southern half of the village. ②

Libra Cottages Vas Waddo ☎0832/277 0598. Spartan but clean budget rooms, all with fans, attached bathrooms, sound plumbing and Western toilets. ③

Oshin Mazil Waddo ☎0832/277 0069, ⓔinaciooshin@rediffmail.com. Large, triple-storey complex set well back from the road. Opening on to leafy terraces, its rooms are spacious and clean, with en-suite bathrooms and balconies; those on the top floor afford views over the tree tops. A notch above most places in this area, and good value, but quite a walk from the beach. ③–④

Paul Rina Tourist Home Beach Rd ☎0832/277 0591. Nice big rooms, secluded balconies and attached shower-toilets in a modern house next to the beach road. A little better than the standard budget places. If full, try the cheaper *Caroline Guest House* (☎0832/277 0590) opposite. Both ②

Simon Cottages Sernabatim Ambeaxir ☎0832/277 1839. Currently among the best budget deals in Benaulim, in a quiet spot at the unspoilt north side of the village and with huge rooms on three storeys, all with shower-toilets and verandas, opening onto a sandy courtyard. Owner Tina offers fridges and kitchen utensils for Rs100 extra.

Succorina Cottages 1711/A Vas Waddo ☎0832/277 0365. Small but immaculate rooms in a newish, pink-coloured house, 1km south of the crossroads in the fishing village, offering glimpses of the sea across the fields from large first-floor sit-outs. A perfect place to get away from the tourist scene, and a 5min walk from the quietest stretch of beach. Telephone bookings accepted. ①–②

Mid-range

Anthy's Sernabatim ☎0832/277 1680, ⓔanthysguesthouse@rediffmail.com. Rooms right on the sea, with tiny bathrooms and breezy verandas; there's a Keralan Ayurvedic massage centre on site too. ⑤

Blue Corner Ambeaxir Sernabatim. Popular new hut camp right on the beach, run by an enthusiastic young crew led by hospitable owner, Raj. Large palm leaf structures with fans, mosquito nets, attached shower-toilets and plywood sitouts. Quiet and secure, and the bar-restaurant is one of the most happening places on the beach in the evenings. ⑤

Camilson's Sernabatim ☎0832/277 1582, ⓦwww.camilsons.com. Small resort of good sized rooms with private terraces, set very close to the beach amid a manicured garden, well away from the village. The rooms have private terraces and comfy cane chairs; and there are some larger ones set aside for families. Telephone bookings accepted. ④–⑤

Carina Tamdi-Mati, Vas Waddo ☎0832/277 0413, ⓦwww.carinabeachresort.com. Good-value – if somewhat lackadaisical – midscale hotel in a tranquil location on the south side of Benaulim, with a pool, garden and bar-restaurant. Some rooms have a/c. ⑤

Heaven Goa 1 Ambeaxir Sernabatim, ☏0832/277 0365, ⓦwww.heavengoa.co.in. Run by a welcoming Swiss-Keralan couple, this new block of a dozen or so rooms occupies a plum spot, 10min back from the sea beside a lily pond alive with frogs, egrets and water buffalo. The rooms are spacious and well set up (with wood shelves, mosquito nets, shiny tiled floors and balconies overlooking the water). Expert Ayurvedic massages are offered; and they've started baking fresh pizzas in a wood oven, too. Excellent value for money in this bracket. ❹

L'Amour Beach Rd ☏0832/277 0404, ⓦwww .lamourbeachresort.com. Benaulim's oldest hotel comprises a comfortable thirty-room cottage complex, with terrace restaurant, travel agent, money-changing and some a/c rooms: No single occupancy. Reasonable rates. ❹

Palm Grove Tamdi-Mati, 149 Vas Waddo ☏0832/277 0059, ⓦwww.palmgrovegoa.com. Secluded hotel surrounded by beautiful gardens, offering two classes of room, some of them a/c; plus there's one of Benaulim's better restaurants on site. A bike ride back from the beachfront, but very pleasant, and the management is helpful. ❹–❺

Tansy Cottages Beach Rd ☏0832/277 0574, ⓔtansycottages@yahoo.in. Variously sized apartments, from rooms with self-catering kitchenettes (painted shocking purple; Rs500) to one- and two-bedroom flats in a two-storey block (lurid green colour; Rs700–1000). The balconies could be more private, but you get lots of space indoors for your money, plus fridges and cooking utensils.

Xavier's Sernabatim ☏0832/277 1489, ⓔjovek @sanchar.net. Next door to *Camilson's*, and very similar, with well maintained, large rooms ranged around a lovely garden, virtually on the beach. All rooms have private terraces and low-slung cane chairs to lounge on. ❸–❺

Eating and drinking

Benaulim's proximity to Margao market, along with the presence of a large Christian fishing community, means its **restaurants** serve some of the tastiest, competitively priced seafood in Goa. The best shacks flank the beachfront area, where *Johncy's* catches most of the passing custom. However, you'll find better food at lower prices at places further along the beach, which seem to change chefs annually; the only way to find out which ones offer the best value for money is to wander past and see who has the most customers. An enduring favourite is *Dominick's*, whose garrulous owner hosts bonfire parties one night per week (traditionally on Thursdays), featuring a live band; prices here are on the high side. *Pedro's* on the beachfront is marginally better value and also puts on gigs, mostly on Saturday nights.

Blue Corner Ambeaxir Sernabatim. Great little beachside joint specializing in seafood and authentic Chinese. House favourites include "fish tomato eggdrop soup", scrumptious "dragon potatoes" and, best of all, their "super special steak". Also featured on an eclectic menu are tasty Italian dishes, sizzlers and, for homesick veggies, a pretty good cauliflower cheese. Most mains are Rs100–250.

Camilson's Ambeaxirr Sernabatim. Host Jovek's mum, Maria, does most of the masala preparation, so the Goan dishes – prawn vindaloo, fish *caldin* and *balcao* – are top notch. Less spicy alternatives include a particularly tasty lemon rice. Facing one of the most tranquil stretches of the beach, the terrace is most atmospheric at night, with the waves crashing in only a few feet away.

Durigo's Sernabatim, 2km north of Maria Hall on the outskirts of Colva. This is the locals' favourite place to eat, serving traditional Goan seafood of a kind and quality you rarely find in the shacks: try their tasty mussels, lemonfish (*modso*) or barramundi (*chonok*), marinated in spicy, sour *rechead* sauce and pan-fried in millet. They also serve delicious local coconut *feni*, as well as the usual range of bottled beers. Some may find the atmosphere a bit rough and ready (though the service is unfailingly polite), in which case follow the example of the village's middle classes and order a takeout.

L'Amour *L'Amour* hotel. One of Benaulim's slicker restaurants, serving an exhaustive multi-cuisine dinner menu (mains Rs125–175), as well as drinks. With background noise limited to chinking china and hushed voices, it's also a relaxing place for breakfast: fresh fruit, muesli, yoghurt and pancakes.

Malibou Vas Waddo, near *Palm Grove*. Cosy little corner café-restaurant that's also a popular late-night drinking spot. Attentive service, fresh seafood, and a tandoor to bake pomfret, kebabs and spicy chicken. Mains from Rs125.

Palm Grove *Palm Grove* hotel. Mostly Goan seafood, with some Indian and Continental options, served in a smart new garden pagoda, against a backdrop of illuminated trees. Main courses Rs150–200.

Palmira's Beach Rd. Benaulim's best tourist breakfasts: wonderfully creamy and fresh set curd, copious fruit salads with coconut, real espresso coffee, warm local bread (*bajri*) and the morning paper.

Satkar Maria Hall Crossroads. No-frills locals' Udupi canteen that's the only place in the village where you can order regular Indian snacks –

samosas, masala dosas, hot pakoras and spicy chickpea stew (*channa*) – at regular Indian prices. And the *pao bhaji* breakfast here is a must.

Seshaa's/St Anthony Bakery Café Maria Hall Crossroads. A local institution, *Sesha's* is a gloomy and rather cramped lads' café that's great for pukka Goan *channa bhaji* and, best of all, deliciously flaky veg or beef patties. On the opposite side of the road, *St Anthony Bakery* is equally popular (especially in the mornings) serving the same local grub, but is less male-dominated – and its patties come straight out of the ovens.

The far south: Canacona

Ceded to the Portuguese by the Raja of Sund in the Treaty of 1791, Goa's **far south** – **Canacona** district – was among the last parts of the territory to be absorbed into the Novas Conquistas, and has retained a distinctly Hindu feel. The area also boasts some of the state's most outstanding scenery. Set against a backdrop of the jungle-covered Sahyadri hills (an extension of the Western Ghat range), a string of pearl-white coves and sweeping beaches scoop its indented coastline, enfolded by laterite headlands and colossal piles of black boulders.

With the exception of the village of **Palolem**, whose near-perfect beach attracts a deluge of travellers during high season, coastal settlements such as **Agonda**, a short way north, remain rooted in a traditional fishing and toddy-tapping economy. However, the red gash of the **Konkan Railway** threatens to bring its days as a tranquil rural backwater to an end. For the last few years, it has been possible to reach Canacona by direct "super-fast" express trains from Mumbai, Panjim and Mangalore: the developers' bulldozers and concrete mixers are sure to follow.

The region's main transport artery is the NH-17, which crawls across the Sahyadri and Karmali ghats towards Karnataka via the district headquarters, **Chaudi**; travellers jump off here for Palolem, a few kilometres across the fields, and the small market at this point is useful for essentials. Bus services to and from Margao are frequent; off the highway, however, bullock carts and bicycles still outnumber motor vehicles. The only way to do the area justice is by motorcycle, although it's advisable to rent one further north (Benaulim's your best bet for this) and drive it down here, as few are available in situ.

Agonda

AGONDA, 10km north of Chaudi, can only be reached along the sinuous coast road connecting Cabo da Rama with NH-17 at Chaudi. No signposts mark the turning, and few of the tourists that whizz past en route to Palolem pull off here, but the beach is superb – albeit with a strong undertow that weak swimmers should be very wary of (head for the safer cove at the far southern end of the beach, where the fishing boats are moored).

Facilities for visitors are basic, but adequate, and well spaced apart: Agonda never gets too congested, even in peak season. **Places to stay and eat** are dotted along the road behind the beach, and over the past couple of seasons a handful of small guesthouses and treehouse camps have also opened up at the northern end, beyond the church.

For **food**, *Dercy's* is the most enduringly popular option, though it's definitely been exploiting its own success in recent years, serving frozen fish rather than local stuff as it used to. A little further up the road, *La Dolce Vita* is a more sophisticated alternative – an infectiously fun terrace restaurant run by an energetic Italian couple. Decked out in pretty pastel blue furniture with matching awnings, it serves authentic wood-baked pizzas, delicious house pasta and pesto, and proper chocolate pudding and tiramisu for dessert. For a sundowner, the *Sun Set Bar*, up on a bluff just south of *Dercy's* surveying the bay, is hard to beat.

Accommodation

Common Home South side of beach ☎ 0832/264 7890. Chic, Brit-owned place with pretensions as a boutique hotel (repro antique wood doors, interesting furniture and floaty mosquito nets). Not at all the kind of place you'd expect to find here, but efficiently run and comfortable, if a touch overpriced. ⑥

Dercy's South end of the beach, on the roadside ☎ 0832/264 7503. Exceptionally clean and relaxing rooms, with tiled floors and good sized bathrooms. Those on the first floor (front side) have a common sea-facing Veranda that catches the breezes; you can lie in bed and hear the waves crashing only 100m away. They also run a couple of rows of (rather overpriced) beach huts on the opposite side of the lane.

Dunhill Beach Resort A short way down the lane beyond *Dercy's* ☎ 0832/264 7328, ⓔ dunhill-resort@rediffmail.com. All the rooms here are en-suite with small Verandas opening onto a sandy enclosure, where you can eat locally caught fish (the pan-fried *rawa* mackerel is delicious). Internet access (for guests only). ❸

Fatima South side of beach, next to *La Dolce Vita* ☎ 0832/264 7477, ☎ m94233 32888. Very good value budget guesthouse offering spacious, squeaky clean en-suite rooms for Rs400: shiny tiled floors, bucket hot water, and sea views from the upper floor, plus there's a friendly Great Dane the size of a horse. Best of the cheapies. ❸

Jelicia North end of the beach, 100m before *Sea View*. No phone. A couple of simple budget rooms, with coconut-wood rafters and clay-tile roofs, plus three huts on the beach. ❶–❷

Palm Beach Lifestyle Resort Behind *Dercy's* ☎ 0832/264 7783, ⓦ www.palmbeachgoa.com. Simple but very pleasant chalets that have painted wood floors, comfy foam mattresses, relaxing decks and uninterrupted sea views. The most restful option in Agonda, and good value. ❺

Maria Paul Just north of *Dercy's* towards the church ☎ 0832/264 7606. This modern pink building on the roadside – look for the "Welcome Aboard" life ring – is a bigger and slightly more anonymous guesthouse than the others in the village, which some might prefer. Six large, cool marble-floored rooms. ❹

Sami Near the church ☎ m98504 53805. Most appealing of the village's small hut camps, right on the beach. The larger-than-average huts are far enough apart, with painted balconies; bikes are available to rent. Also worth trying is the similar nearby *Madhu* (☎ 0832/264 7116). Both ❷–❸

Sea View At the far north end of the beach ☎ 0832/264 7548. The quietest option: three lovely mud-and-thatch huts with cow-dung floors (a lot more fragrant than they may sound) and decent beds, run by Mrs Fatima Fernandes. They're ultra basic, but clean and secluded, and slap on the sand. ❷–❸

Palolem

Nowhere else in peninsula India conforms so closely to the archetypal image of a paradise beach as **PALOLEM**, 35km south of Margao. Lined with a swaying curtain of coconut palms, the bay forms a perfect curve of golden sand, arcing north from a giant pile of boulders at the spur of Sahyadri Ghat, which tapers into the sea draped in thick forest. For those foreigners who found their way here before the mid-1990s, however, Palolem is most definitely a paradise lost these days. With the rest of Goa largely carved up by package tourism, this is the first-choice destination of most independent travellers, and the numbers can feel overwhelming in peak season, when literally thousands of people spill across the beach. Behind them, an unbroken line of shacks and Thai-style bamboo- and palm-leaf huts provide food and shelter that grows more sophisticated (and

Water shortages in Palolem

The vast increase in Palolem's visitor numbers has led, in part, to the severe water shortages that have afflicted Canacona district over the past three years. The municipality seems unwilling or unable to do anything about the problem, so the onus falls on tourists to **use as little water as possible** during their stay. One of the most effective ways you can do this is to **avoid water toilets**, which dump a colossal quantity of untreated sewage into often poorly manufactured septic tanks below the ground. Traditional pig loos, still common in the village, are a far cleaner, greener option.

less Goan) with each season – not least because many of the businesses here are now run, if not owned, by expatriates. Thanks to a local law forbidding the construction of permanent buildings close to the beach (enforced by periodic bulldozing of the entire resort), development has been restrained, but it's still a far cry from the idyll of only a few years ago.

Palolem in full swing is the kind of place you'll either love at first sight or want to get away from as quickly as possible. If you're in the latter category, try smaller, less-frequented **Patnem** beach, a short walk south, where the shack scene is more subdued and the sand emptier. Further south still, **Rajbag**, around half-an-hour's walk from Palolem, used to be one of Goa's last deserted beaches until a vast, seven-star luxury resort was recently built slap behind it.

Arrival and information

Frequent **buses** run between Margao and Karwar (in Karnataka) via Chaudi

△ Palolem beach

(every 30min; 2hr), from where you can pick up an **auto-rickshaw** (Rs50–75) or **taxi** (Rs100–150) for the 2km journey west to Palolem. Alternatively, get off the bus at the Char Rastay ("Four-Way") crossroads, 1.5km before Chaudi, and walk the remaining kilometre or so to the village. Hourly buses also go all the way to Palolem from Margao; these stop at the end of the lane leading from the main street to the beachfront. The last bus from Palolem to Chaudi/Margao leaves at around 4.30pm; check with the locals for the precise times, as these change seasonally. **Bicycles** may be rented from a stall halfway along the main street for the princely sum of Rs10 per hour (with discounts for longer periods). The village has a dozen or more STD/ISD **telephones**; avoid the one in

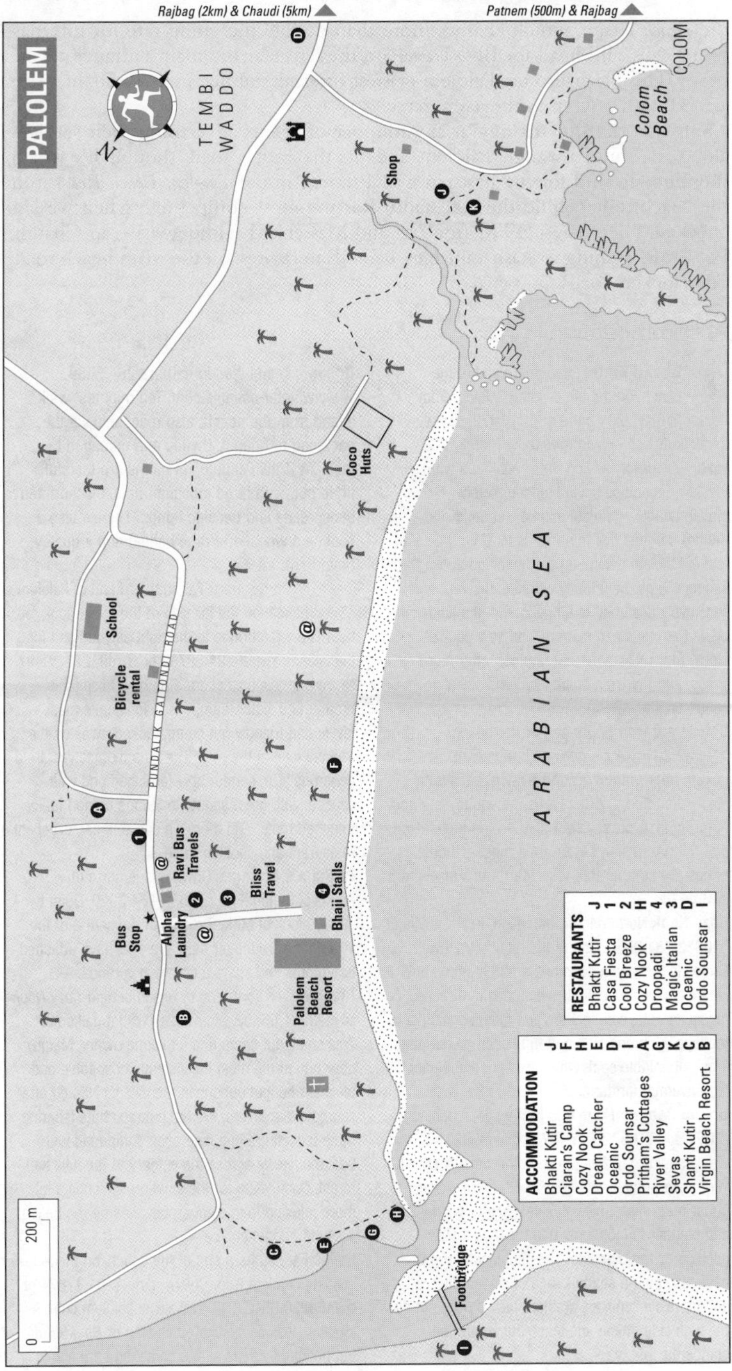

PALOLEM

Rajbag (2km) & Chaudi (5km) ▲

Patnem (500m) & Rajbag ▲

Chaudi (4km) ▲

N

TEMBI WADDO

COLOM

Colom Beach

ARABIAN SEA

Shop

Coco Huts

School

Bicycle rental

PUNDALIK GAITONDE ROAD

Ravi Bus Travels

Bliss Travel

Bhaji Stalls

Bus Stop

Alpha Laundry

Palolem Beach Resort

Footbridge

ACCOMMODATION

Bhakti Kutir	J
Ciaran's Camp	F
Cozy Nook	H
Dream Catcher	D
Oceanic	E
Ordo Sounsar	I
Pritham's Cottages	A
River Valley	G
Sevas	K
Shanti Kutir	C
Virgin Beach Resort	B

RESTAURANTS

Bhakti Kutir	J
Casa Fiesta	1
Cool Breeze	2
Cozy Nook	H
Droopadi	4
Magic Italian	3
Oceanic	D
Ordo Sounsar	I

0   200 m

the *Beach Resort*, which charges more than double the going rate for international calls, and head for Bliss Travel, on the left near the main entrance to the beach. This place also has Palolem's fastest Internet connections (Rs50/hr) – go armed with a wrap as the a/c's fierce.

You can **change money** at any number of agents advertising their services along the lanes through Palolem and on the beach road, though it's worth shopping around for the best rates; LKP Forex in the *Palolem Beach Resort* (on the beachfront behind the taxi stand) was the most competitive when we last checked. The nearest **ATM** (for Visa and Mastercard withdrawls) is in Chaudi. For those wishing to stash valuables, Lalita Enterprises, on the main beach road, offer lockers for Rs30 per day.

Accommodation

Bhakti Kutir Far southern end of the beach, on the hill dividing Palolem from Colom ☏0832/264 3469 or 264 3472, ⓦwww.bhaktikutir.com. Environmentally-friendly, Indian-village-style "Eco Huts" equipped with Western amenities (including completely biodegradable chemical toilets), set amid mature gardens five minutes' walk from the south end of Palolem beach, on the headland above the fishing village. Beautifully situated, discreet and sensitively designed to blend in with the landscape by its German-Goan owners. The new double-storey units (❽), aimed at families, offer more space, and there's a quality Ayurvedic healing centre on site. ❻–❽

Ciaran's Camp South end of the beach ☏0832/264 3477, ⓦwww.ciarans.com. Luxury huts ranged around a lawn, each with stone-tiled floors, Artex walls, mosquito nets and bathrooms. A breezy spot slap on the beachfront, and a more stylish set up than most – though prices are comparable with star hotels elsewhere in Goa. ❽

Cozy Nook North end of the beach, near the island ☏0832/264 3550. One of the most attractive setups in the village, comprising 25 bamboo huts (sharing seven toilets, but with good mattresses, mosquito nets, safe lockers and fans) opening onto the lagoon on one side and the beach on the other – an unbeatable spot, which explains the higher than average tariffs. ❻

Dream Catcher North end of the beach behind *Cozy Nook* ☏0832/264 4873 or ☏m98221 37446, ⓔlalalandjackie7@yahoo.com. Individually styled, very glam Keralan-style huts, with more space, better mattresses, nicer textiles, bigger windows and sturdier foundations than most, in a plum position by the riverside. The couple who run it have also built a shaded yoga *shala* for classes, and there's a "chillout-ambient bar". Prices are on the high side, to say the least, but so are the standards. ❼–❽

Oceanic Tembi Waddo ☏0832/264 3059, ⓦwww.hotel-oceanic.com. Ten minutes' walk inland from the beach; also reachable via the backroad to Chaudi. Owned and managed by a resident British couple, its rooms are tastefully fitted out, with large mosquito nets, blockprinted bedspreads and bedside lamps. There's also a pool on a wooded terrace behind and a quality restaurant. ❼–❽

Ordo Sounsar Far southern end of Palolem beach, on the far side of the creek (look for the rickety footbridge to the right as you head for the island) ☏m98224 88769 or ☏m94226 39497, ⓦwww.ordosounsar.com. Run by a hospitable brother and sister team, this is Palolem's most idyllic and friendly hut camp, tucked away on the tranquil side of the river. The huts themselves are a generous size, comfortably furnished and well spaced, with great sitouts to lounge on and funky thatched roofs; and there's a sociable bar, excellent restaurant and snooker table. ❹

Pritham's Cottages Down a lane north of Pundalik Gaitondi Rd ☏0832/264 3320. Quiet two-storey block of budget rooms in the centre of the village: they're bigger than average, have attached bathrooms and share a common veranda. ❸

River Valley North end of beach behind *Cozy Nook* ☏m98221 55502, ⓔsrmh2141@hotmail.com. This small hut camp and its young owner, Manju, offer one of the most consistently hospitable and pleasant budget options in the village. Named after sacred Indian rivers, the ten bamboo huts (sharing three toilets) are in a nice open compound with beautiful views across the estuary to the hills and forest. Good value for the location, which is a lot more relaxing than comparable sites on the beach. A sound budget choice. ❹

Sevas Far southern end of the beach, on the hill dividing Palolem from Colom ☏m93261 17674 or ☏m94220 65437, ⓦwww.sevaspalolem.com. A cheaper, less sophisticated version of *Bhakti Kutir*, but beautifully done all the same, and the site is peaceful. The "ethnic" cabañas have traditional rice-straw roofs, mud-and-dung floors, hygienic squat-style loos and bucket baths. They also offer massages and yoga classes, and there's a pleasant restaurant serving very good thalis for Rs90. **④**

Shanti Kutir North end of beach behind *River Valley* and *Dream Catcher* ✆m94224 50392 or ✆m99609 17150. Keralan-run hut camp of 30 huts (some en suite) on stilts; pleasantly secluded and with an appealing location on the river. Rates vary according to proximity to the water. **③–④**

Virgin Beach Resort Palolem village ✆0832/264 3451. New tiled rooms in a modern three-storey block near the lane running from the main junction in the village to the far north end of the beach. Not exactly the kind of architecture that enhances the village's natural feel, but it's an out-of-the-way spot and some may consider the comfort and security a good trade-off, and it offers good value. **③–④**

Eating and drinking

Palolem's **restaurants** and **bars** reflect the cosmopolitan make-up of its visitors. Each year, a fresh batch of innovative, ever more stylish places open, most of them managed by expats – and both standards, and prices, have increased greatly as a consequence. For those on tight budgets, there are a couple of cheap and cheerful **bhaji stalls** outside the landmark *Palolem Beach Resort*, and a pair of local cafés along the road running parallel with the beach that serve filling breakfasts of *pao bhaji*, fluffy bread rolls, omelettes and chai for next to nothing, and equally inexpensive fish-curry-rice meals and samosas from lunchtime. Again, you'll find several good options in the *waddo* of Colom, just south of Palolem.

Bhakti Kutir Far southern end of the beach, on the hill dividing Palolem from Colom. Laid-back terrace café-restaurant with rustic wooden tables and an Indo-European fusion menu: sunny tomato and mozzarella salad (with fresh basil), fish from the bay and North Indian vegetarian dishes, all made with local and organically produced ingredients.

Casa Fiesta Pundalik Gaitondi Rd. Funky expat-run place on the main drag, offering an eclectic menu of world cuisine: hoummus, Greek salad, Mexican specialities and fish *pollichatu*; mains (mostly under Rs200) come with delicious roast potatoes.

Cool Breeze Beach Rd. This is one of the classiest restaurants in the village. Their steaks, tandoori chicken and seafood, in particular, have set new standards for Palolem, and the prices are reasonable. Come early, or you could face a long wait for a table – and leave room for the banoffee pie dessert. Most mains are around Rs200–250.

Cozy Nook Far north end of the beach. Wholesome Goan-style cooking served on a small terrace that occupies a prime position opposite the island at the end of the bay. The filling four-course set dinners (7–9pm; Rs150–200) are deservedly popular, offering imaginative and carefully prepared dishes such as pan-fried fish, aubergine with shrimps and fresh beans. They also do a tasty veg equivalent (Rs130), as well as a full seafood and North Indian curry menu, and in high season there's a great (and hygienic) salad bar (eat all you like for Rs120).

Droopadi Beachfront. This place enjoys both a top location and Palolem's best Indian chef, who specializes in rich, creamy Mughlai dishes and tandoori fish. Go for the superb *murg makhini* or crab masala with spinach. With most main courses Rs125–400, prices are low considering the quality of the cooking.

Magic Italian Beach Rd. On the busy approach to the seafront, this is south Goa's number-one Italian restaurant, serving home-made ravioli and tagliatelle, along with scrumptious wood-fired pizzas (Rs150–225).

Oceanic Tembi Waddo. Chilled terrace restaurant, set well back from the beach but worth the walk for the better-than-average food and background music (the owner is an ex-Womad sound man). North and South Indian dishes are the chef's forte (especially *dum aloo* Kashmiri and butter chicken), but there are also great red and green Thai curries, tempting desserts (including lemon-and-ginger cheesecake and banoffee pie) and coffee liqueur. Check the specials board for dishes of the day. Occasional live music.

Ordo Sounsar Far southern end of Palolem beach (for directions see "Accommodation" opposite). With most places using previously frozen fish instead of fresh these days, this laid-back restaurant, on a terrace in a hut camp of the same name, is something special. Seasonal Goan seafood and vegetarian are their their specialities: pomfret stuffed with green chilli; papaya curry in coconut juice; green-pea *xacutti*; prawn balchao; shark *ambotik*; white cabbage in lime dressing – all made with the choicest ingredients brought fresh each day. Count on Rs300–400 for two courses. Advance booking advisable.

South of Palolem: Colom, Patnem and Rajbag

Once across the creek and boulder-covered spur bounding the south end of Palolem beach, you arrive at **COLOM**, a largely Hindu fishing village scattered around a series of rocky coves. Dozens of long-stay rooms, leaf huts and houses are tucked away under the palm groves and on the picturesque headland running seawards. This is the best place in the village to start an accommodation hunt – the lads will know of any vacant places; but be warned that most of the rooms here are very basic indeed and may not have running water, let alone toilets. Alternatively, there are several good guesthouses reviewed along with Palolem's accommodation (see p.250).

A string of small hut camps and shacks line the next beach south, **PATNEM**, but the scene is altogether more subdued here than in Palolem. The beach, curving for roughly a kilometre to a steep bluff, is broad, with little shade, and shelves quite steeply at certain phases of the tide, though the undertow rarely gets dangerously strong.

There are plenty of good **accommodation** and **eating** options here, though be warned that room rates have gone through the roof over the past few seasons. At the top of the range is *Goyam* (☏m94238 21181, ⓦwww .goyam.net; ⑥–⑦), towards the north end of the beach, which has luxury, double-storeyed wooden bungalows painted pretty pastel colours, slap on the sand. Partly screened by casuarina trees, each is smartly furnished and fitted with bathrooms, mosquito nets and swings on sea-facing balconies. The restaurant, an off-shoot of the popular *Droopadi* in Palolem, does superb seafood prepared in rich North Indian style: crab *makhini* and tandoori sea bass (Rs350–400) are their signature dishes. A bit further along, *Home* (☏0832/264 3916, ⓔhomeispatnem@yahoo.com; ⑤), is a chic little Swiss-British-run guesthouse, comprising an annexe of en-suite rooms attractively decked out with textiles, lampshades and other cosy touches. They also run Patnem's best beach café, serving mezes, freshly baked bread, Swiss röstis, fresh salads (from around Rs100), proper Lavazza espresso and wonderful desserts (banoffee pie, warm apple tart with fresh cream, chocolate and walnut cake). It's a particularly pleasant option for breakfast, with Chopin playing over the sound system and sparrows chirping in the palms. Another comfortable place worth singling out here is *Papaya* (no phone; ③), which has wood and thatch rooms comparable in comforts to *Goaym*, but for a fraction of the price – plus it remains in the shade all day.

Among the string of **camps** behind the beach shacks, *Namaste* (☏m98504 77189; ④–⑤), is a dependable, fun budget option, run by the amiable Satay, most of whose clientele come back season after season. Rates range from Rs600–1000 depending on size of room and time of year; all have shower-toilets attached. In the same bracket, *Casa Fiesta* nearby (☏0832/647 0367; ④–⑤) has a selection of good-sized huts with unobstructed sea views. *Shiva* (no phone; ①–③) is the cheapest choice on Patnem, with huts from as low as Rs200, or less depending on demand.

Among the many shacks lining the beach, *Tantra* does particularly generous evening meals of jumbo prawns, lobster and fresh local fish. Vegetarians on a budget should try the monster biriyanis served by at the *Sealands* for around Rs50.

At low tide, you can walk around the bottom of the steep-sided headland dividing Patnem from neighbouring **RAJBAG**, another kilometre-long sweep of white sand. Sadly, its remote feel has been entirely submerged by the massive five-star *Goa Grand Intercontinental* (ⓦwww.intercontinental.com; ⑨), recently erected on the land behind it – much to the annoyance of the locals, who campaigned for four years to stop the project.

It's possible to press on even further **south from Rajbag**, by crossing the Talpona River via a hand-paddled ferry, which usually has to be summoned from the far bank (fix a return price in advance and only pay once you've completed both legs of the trip, as the boatmen are rumoured to have been holding wealthy tourists from the *Goa Grand* to ransom by refusing to paddle them back unless they hand over huge "tips"). Once across, a short walk brings you to **Talpona Beach**, backed by low dunes and a line of straggly palms. From there, you can cross the headland at the end of the beach to reach **Galjibag**, a remote white-sand bay that's a protected nesting site for Olive Ridley marine **turtles**. A strong undertow means swimming isn't safe here.

Cotigao Wildlife Sanctuary

The **Cotigao Wildlife Sanctuary**, 12km southeast of Palolem, was established in 1969 to protect an isolated and vulnerable area of forest lining the Goa–Karnataka border. Best visited between October and March, Cotigao is a peaceful and scenic park that makes a pleasant day-trip from Palolem. Encompassing 86 square kilometres of mixed deciduous woodland, the reserve is certain to inspire tree lovers, but less likely to yield many wildlife sightings: its tigers and leopards were hunted out long ago, while the gazelles, sloth bears, porcupines, panthers and hyenas that allegedly lurk in the woods rarely appear. You do, however, stand a good chance of spotting at least two species of monkey, a couple of wild boar and the odd gaur (the primeval-looking Indian bison), as well as plenty of exotic birdlife, including hornbills. Any of the buses running south on the NH-14 to Karwar via Chaudi will drop you within 2km of the gates. However, to explore the inner reaches of the sanctuary, you really need your own transport. The wardens at the reserve's small **Interpretative Centre** at the main gate, where you have to pay your entry fees (Rs15, plus Rs75 for a car, Rs20 for motorbike, Rs40 for camera permit) will show you how to get to a 25-metre-high tree-top watchtower, overlooking a **waterhole** that attracts a handful of animals around dawn and dusk. You can also **stay** in a rather unprepossessing little room (❷) in the compound behind the main reserve gates; it's rented out on a first-come first-served basis. Food and drink may be available by prior arrangement, and there's a **shop** at the nearest village, 2km inside the park.

More inspiring accommodation is to be found at a secluded riverside location on the edge of Cotigao. Hidden away in a working spice plantation, ⚑ *Pepper Valley* (☎0832/264 2370 or ☎m98504 51714, ⓦwww.peppervalley .com ❸–❹) comprises a row of a dozen simple huts and cottages (half of them with attached bathrooms) on the riverbank, shaded by a canopy of areca palms, with cashew bushes, banana, pineapple and yam plants growing around. There's a bar and restaurant serving authentic local and Western food, and a stage area that hosts yoga and tai chi classes through the season. You can also sign up for expert guided walking tours of the Cotigao Sanctuary. Full details of these and their holistic therapy courses are posted on their website (see above). To find *Pepper Valley*, turn left at the Cotigao Interpretative Centre, then follow the road for 500m until you see a signboard indicating a motorable track off to the right.

Seats on planes from Goa can be in short supply at certain times of year, especially around Diwali and Christmas. Try and book flights directly through the **airline**, as private agents charge the dollar fare at poor rates of exchange; addresses of airline offices in Panjim are listed on p.196. Tickets for all **Konkan Railway** services can be booked at the KRC reservation office on the first floor of Panjim's Kadamba bus stand (Mon–Sat 8am–8pm, Sun 8am–2pm) or at KRC's main reservation hall in Margao station (Mon–Sat 8am–4.30pm, Sun 8am–2pm; ☎0834/271 2780). Make your reservations as far in advance as possible, and try to get to the offices soon after opening time – the queues can be horrendous. Seats on the Konkan Railway from Goa to Mumbai are in notoriously short supply as the lion's share of the quotas goes to longer-distance travellers from Kerala, with the result that peak periods tend to be reserved up to two months in advance. One way around this is to **book online** (ⓦ www.konkanrailway.com), though bear in mind if you do you'll only be eligible for the relatively expensive three-tier a/c fares (Rs1250 one-way) and must make your booking between seven and two days before your date of departure.

Kadamba **bus tickets** can be bought in advance at their offices in Panjim and Mapusa bus stands (daily 9–11am & 2–5pm); private companies sell through the many travel agents immediately outside the bus stand in Panjim, and at the bottom of the square in Mapusa. **Information** on all departures and fares is available from Goa Tourism's counter inside Panjim's bus stand (see p.189).

For a full rundown of destinations reachable from Goa by bus, train and plane, see Travel details at the end of this chapter.

To Mumbai

Between fifteen and twenty-one **flights** leave Goa's Dabolim airport daily. The cheapest fares are offered by Air Deccan (ⓦ www.airdeccan.net), who can sell tickets from as low as Rs550. Low-cost rivals SpiceJet (ⓦ www.spicejet.com) and Kingfisher Airlines (ⓦ www.flykingfisher.com) also offer competitive tickets. Flying with Indian Airlines (ⓦ www.indian-airlines.nic.in) will set you back $105, or $100 with Sahara (ⓦ www.airsahara.net) and $100 with Jet (ⓦ www.jetairways.com). Air India (ⓦ www .airindia.com) operates a service to Mumbai (also for $100) that few people seem to know about, so you can nearly always get a seat (the one drawback is that you have to check in three hours before departure as Air India is an international carrier).

Four to five services run daily on the **Konkan Railway**, the most convenient being the overnight Konkankanya Express (#0112), which departs from Margao at 6pm (or Karmali, near Old Goa, 11km west of Panjim, at 6.30pm), arriving at CST (commonly known as "Victoria Terminus", or "VT") at 5.50am the following day. The other fast train from Goa to Mumbai CST is the Mandvi Express (#0104), departing Margao at 10.10am (or Karmali at 10.37am) and arriving at 9.45pm the same evening.

The cheapest, though far from most comfortable, way to get to Mumbai is by **night bus**, which takes fourteen to eighteen hours, covering 500km of rough road at often terrifying speeds. Fares vary according to levels of comfort, and luxury buses arrive two or three hours sooner. The most popular private services to Mumbai are those run by a company called Paulo Travels, who lay on a range of different services, from no-frills buses for Rs275/450 low/high season to swisher a/c Volvo coaches with berths (which you may have to share) costing Rs750/850. It's worth pointing out, however, that women travellers have complained of harassment during the journey. For tickets, contact Paulo Travels: at their desk in the *Hotel Fidalgo* on 18th June Rd, or at the main office just outside the Kadamba bus stand, Panjim (☎0832/222 3736 ⓦ www.paulotravels.com,). In south Goa, their main outlet is at the *Hotel Nanutel*, opposite *Club Harmonia*, in Margao (☎0834/272 1516). Information on all departures and fares is available online.

To Pune

Pune is connected to Goa's Dabolim airport by Indian Airlines' daily **flight**. You can also get there by train on the #2779 Goa Express, departing at 3.40pm and arriving early the following morning at 4.15am, and on any number of private night buses from Panjim (tickets for which should be purchased in advance from the companies' offices outside the Kadamba bus stand).

To Hampi

The most stress-free and economical way to reach Hospet from Goa is the four-times-weekly **train** service from **Margao**. The Vasco–Howrah Express (#2848) departs every Tuesday, Thursday, Friday and Sunday at 8.15am, arriving six hours later. Fares range from Rs190 for sleeper class to Rs650 for second-class a/c.

The **bus** journey covering the same route is no cheaper than the train (sleeper class) and is far more gruelling. Two or three clapped-out government services leave Panjim's Kadamba stand (platform 9) each morning for Hospet, the last one at 10.30am. Brace yourself for a long, hard slog; all being well, it should take nine or ten hours, but delays and breakdowns are frustratingly frequent. **Tickets** for Kadamba and KSRTC (Karnatakan State Road Transport Corporation) services should be booked at least one day in advance at the hatches in the bus stand. From Margao, you can also travel to Hampi on a swish **night bus**, complete with pneumatic suspension and berths. The service, operated by Paulo Travels (⊛ www.paulotravels.com), leaves at 8pm from a lot next to the Nanutel Hotel on Margao's Rua da Padre Miranda, arriving in Hampi early the next morning at 7am. Tickets cost Rs500–700 and can be bought from most reputable travel agents around the state. Although the coach is comfortable enough, the coffin-like berths can get very hot and stuffy, making sleep very difficult; moreover, there have been complaints from women of harassment during the night on this service.

To Gokarna, Jog Falls, Mangalore and southern Karnataka

From Goa, the fastest and most convenient way to travel down the coast to Gokarna is via the **Konkan Railway**. At 2.25pm, the Verna–Mangalore Passenger (KR1 DN) leaves Margao, passing through Chaudi at 2.58pm en route to Gokarna Road, the town's railhead, where it arrives at around 4pm. The station lies 9km east of Gokarna itself, but a minibus is on hand to shuttle passengers the rest of the way. As this is classed as a passenger service, you don't have to buy tickets in advance; just turn up at the station 30min before the departure time and pay at the regular ticket counter. As ever, it is a good idea to **check timings** in advance, through any tourist office or travel agent, or via the KRC's website (⊛ www .konkanrailway.com).

Buses take as much as two-and-a-half hours longer to cover the same route. A direct service leaves Margao's interstate stand in the north of town daily at 1pm. You can also get there by catching any of the services that run between Goa and Mangalore, and jumping off either at **Ankola**, or at the Gokarna junction on the main highway, from where frequent private minibuses and tempos run into town.

The Konkan highway is straightforward by **motorcycle**, with a better-than-average road surface, and frequent fuel stops along the way. Travelling on a rented bike also gives you the option of heading down sandy side lanes to explore some of the gorgeous beaches glimpsed from the road. Aside from the obvious dangers involved in motorcycling on Indian highways, the main drawback is crossing the border, which can involve a *baksheesh* transaction. For Jog Falls, the easiest route is to catch a **train** on the Konkan Railway to Honavar (two stations south of Gokarna Road; 2hr 15min), from where seven daily buses run up the *ghats* to Jog.

Travel details

Trains

Margao (Madgaon) to: Chaudi (3 daily; 30–50min); Colem (4 weekly; 55min); Gokarna (2 daily; 1hr 50min); Hospet (4 weekly; 6hr); Hubli (4 weekly; 4hr); Mangalore/Kanakadi (5 daily; 4–6hr); Mumbai (4–5 daily; 9hr 30min–11hr 30min); Pune (1 daily; 13hr).

Buses

Benaulim to: Cavelossim (hourly; 20min); Colva (every 30min; 20min); Margao (every 30min; 15min); Mobor (hourly; 25min).
Chaudi to: Gokarna (2 daily; 3hr); Karwar (every 30min; 1hr); Margao (every 30min; 1hr 40min); Palolem (2 daily; 15min); Panjim (hourly; 2hr 15min).
Mapusa to: Anjuna (hourly; 30min); Arambol (12 daily; 1hr 45min); Baga (hourly; 30min); Calangute (hourly; 45min); Chapora (every 30min; 30–40min); Mumbai (6 daily; 13–17hr); Panjim (every 15min; 25min); Vagator (every 30min; 25–35min).
Margao to: Agonda (4 daily; 2hr); Benaulim (every 30min; 15min); Cavelossim (8 daily; 30min); Chandor (hourly; 45min); Chaudi (every 30min; 1hr 40min); Colva (every 15min; 20–30min); Gokarna (2 daily; 4hr 30min); Hampi (1 nightly; 10hr); Karwar (every 30min; 2hr); Mangalore (5 daily; 7hr); Mapusa (10 daily; 2hr 30min);

Mobor (8 daily; 35min); Mumbai (2 daily; 16–18hr); Panjim (every 30min; 50min); Pune (1 daily; 12hr).
Panjim to: Arambol (12 daily; 1hr 45min); Baga (every 30min; 45min); Bijapur (7 daily; 10hr); Calangute (every 30min; 40min); Candolim (every 30min; 30min); Chaudi (hourly; 2hr 15min); Gokarna (2 daily; 5hr 30min); Hampi (2 daily; 9–10hr); Hospet (3 daily; 9hr); Hubli (hourly; 6hr); Hyderabad (1 daily; 18hr); Kolhapur (hourly; 8hr); Mahabaleshwar (1 daily; 12hr); Mangalore (4 daily; 10hr); Mapusa (every 15min; 25min); Margao (every 15min; 55min); Morjim (6 daily; 1hr 30min–2hr); Mumbai (6 daily; 14–18hr); Mysore (2 daily; 17hr); Old Goa (every 15min; 20min); Ponda (hourly; 50min); Pune (7 daily; 12hr).

Flights

For a list of airline websites, see p.38. In the listings below IA is Indian Airlines, AI Air India, JA Jet Airways, SA Sahara Airlines, AD Air Deccan, KF Kingfisher, IG IndiGo, SJ SpiceJet.
Dabolim airport (near Vasco da Gama) to: Bengaluru (Bangalore) (DA, IA, JA, KA 5–6 daily; 1hr–4hr 20min); Chennai (IA, JA, SA 2–4 daily; 3hr 15min–4hr 30min); Kochi (Cochin) (IA 2 weekly; 1hr 10min); Kozhikode (Calicut) (IA, 3 weekly; 1hr); Mumbai (IA, AI, JA, SA & AD 8–10 daily; 40–50min); Pune (IA; daily; 50min).

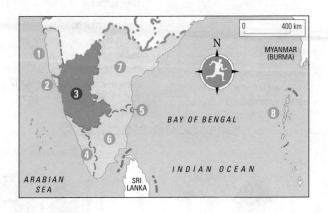

3

Karnataka

CHAPTER 3   # Highlights

* **Mysore** The sandalwood city has bundles of old-fashioned charm and lots to see, including the opulent Maharaja's Palace. See p.277

* **Halebid and Belur** Two wonderfully ornate Hoysala temples, set in the slow-paced Karnataka country-side. See p.295 & p.297

* **Jog Falls** India's highest waterfalls offer fresh air, superb views and the chance to take a dip after the downhill hike. See p.320

* **Gokarna** A quiet Hindu holy town, blessed with a series of exquisite crescent beaches – ideal relaxation for mind, body and spirit. See p.321

* **Hampi** Home to the remains of the Vijayanagar kingdom, scattered among fertile plantations punctu-ated by extraordinary rock formations. See p.335

* **Bijapur** Known as the "Agra of the South" for its splendid Islamic architecture including the huge, domed Golgumbaz. See p.352

* **Bidar** Rarely visited Muslim outpost in the remote northeast of the state, famed for its *bidri* metalwork and magnif-icent medieval monuments. See p.359

△ Ibrahim Rauza, Bijapur

3

Karnataka

Created in 1956 from the princely state of Mysore, **KARNATAKA** – the name is a derivation of the name of the local language, Kannada, spoken by virtually all of its 53 million inhabitants – marks a transition zone between northern India and the Dravidian deep south. Along its border with Maharashtra and Andhra Pradesh, a string of medieval walled towns, studded with domed mausoleums and minarets, recalls the era when this part of the Deccan was a Muslim stronghold, while the coastal and hill districts that dovetail with Kerala are quintessential Hindu South India, profuse with tropical vegetation and soaring temple *gopuras*. Between the two are scattered some of the peninsula's most extraordinary historic sites, notably the ruined Vijayanagar city at Hampi, whose lost temples and derelict palaces stand amid an arid landscape of surreal beauty.

Karnataka is one of the wettest regions in India, its **climate** dominated by the seasonal monsoon, which sweeps in from the southwest in June, dumping an average 4m of rain on the coast before it peters out in late September. Running in an unbroken line along the state's palm-fringed coast, the **Western Ghats**, draped in dense deciduous forests, impede the path of the rain clouds east. As a result, the landscape of the interior – comprising the southern apex of the triangular Deccan trap, known here as the **Mysore Plateau** – is considerably drier, with dark volcanic soils in the north, and poor quartzite-granite country to the south. Two of India's most sacred rivers, the Tungabhadra and Krishna, flow across this sun-baked terrain, draining east to the Bay of Bengal.

Broadly speaking, Karnataka's principal attractions are concentrated at opposite ends of the state, with a handful of lesser-visited places dotted along the coast between Goa and Kerala. Road and rail routes dictate that most itineraries take in the brash state capital, **Bangalore**, rechristened **Bengaluru** in 2006, a go-ahead, modern city, which epitomizes the aspirations of the country's new middle classes with glittering malls, fast-food outlets and a nightlife unrivalled outside Mumbai. The state's other major city, **Mysore**, appeals more for its old-fashioned ambience, nineteenth-century palaces and vibrant produce and incense markets. It also lies within easy reach of several important historical monuments. Close to the city, the fortified island of **Srirangapatnam** was the site of the bloody battle of 1799 that finally put Mysore State into British hands, with the defeat of the Muslim military genius **Tipu Sultan**; parts of the fort, a mausoleum and Tipu's summer palace survive.

A cluster of other unmissable sights lies further northwest, dotted around the dull railway town of **Hassan**. Around nine centuries ago, the Hoysala kings sited their grand dynastic capitals here, at the now middle-of-nowhere villages of **Belur** and **Halebid**, where several superbly crafted temples survive intact. More impressive still, and one of India's most extraordinary sacred sites, is the

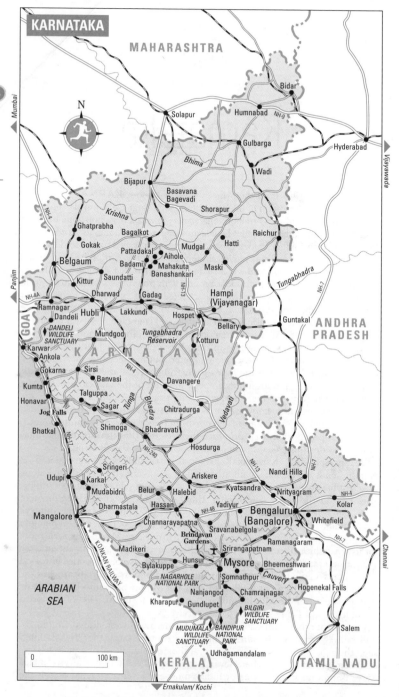

18-metre Jain colossus at **Sravanabelgola**, which stares serenely over idyllic Deccan countryside.

West of Mysore, the Ghats rise in a wall of thick jungle cut by deep ravines and isolated valleys. You can either traverse the range by rail, via Hassan, or explore some of its scenic backwaters by road. Among these, the rarely visited coffee- and spice-growing region of **Kodagu** (**Coorg**) has to be the most entrancing, with its unique culture and lush vistas of misty wooded hills and valleys. Most Coorgi agricultural produce is shipped out of **Mangalore**, the nearest large town, of little interest except as a transport hub. Situated midway between Goa and Kerala, it's also a convenient place to pause before embarking on the journey along Karnataka's beautiful **Karavali coast**. Interrupted by countless mangrove-lined estuaries, the state's 320-kilometre-long red-laterite coast has always been difficult to navigate by land, and traffic along the recently revamped highway remains relatively light. Although there are plenty of superb beaches, facilities are, with rare exceptions, nonexistent, and locals often react with astonishment at the sight of a foreigner. Few Western tourists visit the famous Krishna temple at **Udupi**, an important Vaishnavite pilgrimage centre, and fewer still venture into the mountains to see India's highest waterfalls at **Jog Falls**, set amid some of the region's most spectacular scenery. However, atmospheric **Gokarna**, further north up the coast, is an increasingly popular beach hideaway for budget travellers. Harbouring one of India's most famous *shivalinga*, this seventeenth-century Hindu pilgrimage town enjoys a stunning location, with a high headland dividing it from a string of exquisite beaches.

Winding inland from the mountainous Goan border, NH-4A and the rail line comprise sparsely populated **northern Karnataka**'s main transport arteries, linking a succession of grim industrial centres. This region's undisputed highlight is the ghost city of Vijayanagar, better known as **Hampi**, scattered around boulder-strewn hills on the south banks of the Tungabhadra River. The ruins of this once splendid capital occupy a magical site, while the ancient bazaar is a great spot to hole up for a spell. The jumping-off place for Hampi is **Hospet**, from where buses leave for the bumpy journey north across the rolling Deccan plains to **Badami**, **Aihole** and **Pattadakal**. Now lost in countryside, these tiny villages were once capitals of the Chalukya dynasty (sixth to eighth centuries), and the whole area is littered with ancient rock-cut caves and finely carved stone temples.

Further north still, in one of Karnataka's most remote and poorest districts, craggy hilltop citadels and crumbling wayside tombs herald the formerly troubled buffer zone between the Muslim-dominated northern Deccan and the Dravidian-Hindu south. The bustling, walled market town of **Bijapur**, capital of the Bahmanis, the Muslim dynasty responsible for the eventual downfall of Vijayanagar, harbours South India's finest collection of Islamic architecture, including the world's second-largest freestanding dome, the Golgumbaz. The first Bahmani capital, **Gulbarga**, site of a famous Muslim shrine and theological college, has retained little of its former splendour, but more isolated **Bidar**, to which the Bahmanis moved from Gulbarga in the sixteenth century, definitely deserves a detour en route to or from Hyderabad, four hours to the east by bus. Perched on a rocky escarpment, its crumbling red ramparts harbour Persian-style mosaic-fronted mosques, mausoleums and a sprawling fort complex evocative of Samarkand and the great Silk Route.

Some history

Like much of southern India, Karnataka has been ruled by successive Buddhist, Hindu and Muslim dynasties. The influence of Jainism has also been marked;

India's very first emperor, **Chandragupta Maurya**, is believed to have converted to Jainism in the fourth century BC, renounced his throne, and fasted to death at Sravanabelgola, now one of the most visited Jain pilgrimage centres in the country.

During the first millennium AD, this whole region was dominated by power struggles between the various kingdoms, such as Vakatakas and the Guptas, who controlled the western Deccan and at times extended their authority as far east as the Coromandel coast in modern-day Tamil Nadu. From the sixth to the eighth centuries, briefly interrupted by thirteen years of Pallava rule, the **Chalukya** kingdom encompassed Maharashtra, the Konkan coast on the west, and the whole of Karnataka. The **Cholas** were powerful in the east of the region from about 870 until the thirteenth century, when the Deccan kingdoms were overwhelmed by General Malik Kafur, a convert to Islam.

By the medieval era, Muslim incursions from the north had forced the hitherto warring and fractured Hindu states of the south into close alliance, with the mighty **Vijayanagars** emerging as overlords. Founded by the brothers Harihara and Bukka, their lavish capital, named Vijayanagar, ruled an empire stretching from the Bay of Bengal to the Arabian Sea, and south to Cape Comorin. The Muslims' superior military strength, however, triumphed in 1565 at the Battle of Talikota, when the **Bahmanis** laid siege to Vijayanagar, reducing it to rubble and plundering its opulent palaces and temples.

Thereafter, a succession of Muslim sultans held sway over the north, while in the south of the state the independent **Wadiyar Rajas** of Mysore, whose territory was comparatively small, successfully fought off the Marathas from the north. In 1761, the brilliant Muslim campaigner Haider Ali, with French support, seized the throne. Haider Ali and his son, Tipu Sultan, turned Mysore into a major force in the south, before Tipu was killed by the British at the **Battle of Srirangapatnam** in 1799.

Following Tipu's defeat, the **British** restored the Wadiyar family to the throne, which they kept until riots in 1830 led them to appoint a commission to rule in their place. Fifty years later, the throne was once more returned to the Wadiyars, who remained governors until Karnataka was created by the merging of the states of Mysore and the Madras Presidencies in 1956. In the years since its creation, the state has been spared the excesses of communal and political unrest, although the scene can be volatile. Following Independence the political scene was largely dominated by the Congress party until it was routed in the 1990s – first by a reunited Janata Dal, and subsequently by a fundamentalist BJP alliance. The most recent state elections failed to produce a clear winner, and an uneasy alliance exists, this time between the BJP and Congress.

Bengaluru (Bangalore) and around

Once across the Western Ghats, the cloying air of Kerala and the Konkan coast gradually gives way to the crisp skies and dry heat of the dusty **Mysore Plateau**. The setting for E.M. Forster's acclaimed Raj novel, *A Passage to India*, this southern tip of the Deccan – a vast, open expanse of gently undulating plains dotted with wheat fields and dramatic granite boulders – formed the heartland of the region's once powerful princely state. Today it remains the political hub of the region, largely due to the economic importance of Karnataka's capital, **Bangalore**, which is November 2006, adopted its local Kannada-language name, **BENGALURU**. With a population of now over eight

The silicon rush

Many visitors are surprised to learn that India is the second-largest exporter of computer software after the US, generating sales of a billion dollars per year. And while in recent years, fellow southern cities Hyderabad and Chennai have joined the hi-tech boom, Bengaluru (Bangalore) remains the heart of this triumvirate of technology, home to giants such as Infosys and Wipro. Having established itself as India's hi-tech capital – dubbed **Silicon Valley** by the Indian press – the city reinvented itself a second time in the early twenty-first century, becoming the call capital of India, if not the world. Construction of modern IT and Communications complexes continues on a massive scale on the city's eastern outskirts, and such is the scale and impact of Bangalore's call-centre industry that the city's old name has become enshrined as a verb in "Hinglish" – to "bangalore" now meaning "to send overseas", as in "I'm just popping out to bangalore this parcel to London, auntie."

Bangalore's meteoric industrial rise began in the early 1980s. Fleeing the crippling costs of Mumbai and Delhi, a group of hi-tech Indian companies relocated here, lured by the comparatively cool climate and an untapped pool of highly skilled, English-speaking labour (a consequence of the Indian government's decision to concentrate its telecommunications and defence research here in the 1960s). Within a decade, Bangalore had become a major player in the software market, and a magnet for multinationals such as Motorola and Texas Instruments (who have their own satellite link with their head offices in Dallas).

For a while, the city revelled in a spending frenzy that saw its centre sprout gleaming skyscrapers, swish stores and shopping malls. Soon, however, the price of prosperity became apparent. At the height of the boom, millions of immigrants poured in, eager for a slice of the action, creating a population explosion from which the city is still reeling. In ten years the population trebled, and now stands at well over eight million. Increased demand had a catastrophic effect on the city's infrastructure – and, in turn, business and industry, leading to the decision of several multinationals to decamp to Hyderabad. And while regular power cuts are now a thing of the past, Bangalore's **traffic congestion** is ever-worsening, with heavy traffic during two rush hours – first in the early morning, and then again in the afternoons to coincide with working hours in the UK and Europe. Add to this rapidly increasing levels of air and noise pollution, the loss of the city's landmarks and slow progress in promised measures to ease congestion, and many Bangaloreans are left wondering what happened to their beloved "Garden City".

million, it's one of the fastest-growing cities in Asia. A major scientific research centre at the cutting edge of India's technological revolution, and home to the burgeoning call-centre industry, Bengaluru has a trendy, high-speed self-image, quite unlike anywhere else in South India.

Up until well after Independence, Bangalore was regarded as something of an urban idyll, and nicknamed the "Garden City" thanks to its gentle climate, broad streets and green public spaces. Senior figures, film stars and VIPs flocked to the city to buy or build dream homes, attracted by its theatres, cinemas and lack of restriction on alcohol. These days the wide avenues, dominated by tower blocks, are increasingly choked with traffic, and pollution has become a real problem, but the city retains a very real appeal for many Indians, with its relaxed, cosmopolitan atmosphere, shopping plazas and the South's most dedicated bar and club culture. For well-heeled visitors, the glut of luxurious five-star hotels, primarily geared towards the large international business fraternity passing through, makes the city an attractive proposition as a base from which to make day-trips. In addition, there are restaurants and cafés dishing up cuisine from all over the region and further afield, and a handful of sights in the city itself, including India's tallest Shiva statue and the vast ISKCON temple.

Some history

In the local Kannada language, the city's original name, Bengaluru translates as the "village of the half-baked *gram*", and to this day *gram* (beans) remains an important local product. In 1537, Magadi **Kempe Gowda**, a devout Hindu and feudatory chief of the Vijayanagar empire, built a mud fort and erected four watchtowers outside the village, predicting that it would, one day, extend as far as each; the city now, of course, stretches way beyond. During the first half of the seventeenth century, Bangalore fell to the Muslim sultanate of Bijapur and changed hands several times before being returned to Hindu rule under the Wadiyar rajas of Mysore. In 1758, Chikka Krishnaraja Wadiyar II was deposed by the military genius Haider Ali, who set up arsenals here to produce muskets, rockets and other weapons for his formidable anti-British campaigns. Haider Ali, together with his son, **Tipu Sultan**, greatly extended and fortified Bangalore, but Tipu was overthrown by the British in 1799. The British set up a cantonment, which made the city an important military station, and then passed the administration over to the Maharaja of Mysore in 1881. After Independence, the erstwhile maharaja became governor of Mysore state. Bangalore was designated capital in 1956, and retained that status when Karnataka state was created in 1973. Following the example of Chennai and Mumbai, in 2006 the Government of Karnataka agreed to revert to the city's pre-colonial name, Bengaluru.

Arrival, information and city transport

Recently expanded and revamped to accommodate increased traffic and international flights, **Bengaluru airport** is 13km north of the city centre; for details of departures, see the box on p.276. The 24-hour **KSTDC desk** in the arrivals hall (☏080/2526 8012) stocks leaflets on Karnataka and can book hotel rooms. Branches of the State Bank of Mysore (daily 8am–7pm) and Vijaya Bank (daily 8.30am–12.30pm) **change money**; there are also **ATMs** that accept foreign cards. You can get into the city by **taxi** (Rs170–200; book at the prepaid desk), on one of the **auto-rickshaws** (Rs90–100) that gather outside, or by **bus** – numerous local services run along the main road a few hundred metres from the terminal.

Most trains arrive at **Bengaluru City railway station**, west of the centre, near Kempe Gowda Circle, and across the road from the main bus stands. As you come into the entrance hall from the platforms, the far left-hand corner holds an **ITDC booth** (daily 8am–4pm; ☏080/6533 0138), where you can rent cars and book tours; they will book you a hotel for a fee of ten percent of the day's room rate. You'll find a rank of metered taxis outside; alternatively, prepaid auto-rickshaws charge Rs35–40 for the trip to MG Road, depending on the time of day. All services from Goa, and some from Mumbai, Chennai and Secunderabad terminate at **Yeshwanthpur railway station** in the north of the city, 5km from the main railway station (about Rs40 in an auto-rickshaw) and 9km from MG Road.

Long-distance buses arrive at the huge, bustling **Central (KSRTC) Bus Stand** (also known – something of a misnomer – as the Majestic Bus Stand) opposite Bengaluru City railway station; there's a comprehensive timetable in English in the centre of the stand. A maze of pedestrian flyovers links it with the adjacent **City Bus Stand**, used by local services.

Information

For information on Bengaluru, Karnataka and neighbouring states, go to the excellent **India Tourism office** (Mon–Fri 9.30am–6pm, Sat 9am–1pm;

BENGALURU (BANGALORE)

Whitefield Ashram (25km)

Shiva Mandir, Chennai & Airport (13km)

Ulsoor Lake

ULSOOR ROAD

MCKENZON STREET

COMMERCIAL STREET

CAVALRY ROAD

RICHMOND ROAD

VICTORIA ROAD

BRUNTON ROAD

BRIGADE ROAD

See MG Road & Around map

M GANDHI ROAD

CHURCH STREET

HOSPITAL ROAD

INFANTRY ROAD

CUBBON ROAD

MUSEUM RD

ST MARK'S RD

RESIDENCY ROAD

SHIVAJI NAGAR

Shivaji Nagar Bus Stand ★

Cricket Stadium

GPO

St Mark's Cathedral

Cubbon Park

Government Aquarium

Technological Museum

British Council

Govt Museum

Venkatappa Art Gallery

KASTURBA ROAD

GRANT ROAD

Cash Pharmacy

RICHMOND ROAD

LAVELLE ROAD

RICHMOND CIRCLE

LANGFORD ROAD

Vidhana Soudha

DR AMBEDKAR VEED

Indoor Sports Arena

FORT ROAD

MISSION ROAD

Lalbagh Botanical Gardens

KASTURBA ROAD

NIRUPATHUNGA RD

N

RESTAURANTS, BARS & CLUBS

Aromas of China	6
Casa del Sol	5
Casa Piccolo	5
Colonnade	E
Indraprastha	1
Jockey Club	M
Narthaki	3
Polo Club	L
Rice Bowl	4
Volga	2

ISKCON Temple & B

Railway Station, A & Malleswaram

Yeswanthpur

KSTDC

Racecourse

RACE COURSE ROAD

PALACE ROAD

SESHADRI ROAD

DISTRICT OFFICE ROAD

CUBBONPET ROAD

KSTDC Badami House

J C ROAD

GANDHINAGAR

KEMPE GOWDA RD

KEMPE GOWDA CIRCLE

CHICKPET ROAD

NAGARTHPET ROAD

SUBEDAR CHATRAM ROAD

DHANAVANTRI (TANK BUND) ROAD

City Bus Stand ★

Central Bus Stand ★

Train Reservation Office

City Railway Station

NARASIMHARAJA ROAD

City Market Bus Stand ★

AVENUE RD

S J PARK ROAD

City Market ★

Tipu's Summer Palace

Gavipuram Cave Temple & Bull Temple

Mysore

ACCOMMODATION

Ajantha	N
Goldfinch	D
Janardhana	C
Oberoi	L
Pavana Residency	I
Prashanth	J
Royal Lodge	H
Taj Residency	M
Taj West End	E
Tourist	F
Vellara	O
Vijay Residency	K
Villa Pottipati	A
Vybhav Lodge	G
Windsor Sheraton & Towers	B

0	500 m

265

Guided tours

KSTDC operates a number of guided **tours** from Bengaluru. Though rushed, these can be handy if you're short of time. The twice-daily **city tour** (7.30am–1.30pm or 2–7.30pm; Rs140 or Rs160 a/c bus) calls at Tipu's Summer Palace, the Bull Temple, Lalbagh Gardens, the Government Museum, Vidhana Soudha and Gavi Gangad-hareshwara Temple and winds up with a long stop at Cauvery handicrafts emporium. The **New Bengaluru tour** (Wed–Sun 7.15am–8pm; Rs240) gets you to the "seven new wonders" of the city, including the ISKCON temple, planetarium and musical fountain. "**Outstation**" tours include a long day-trip to Srirangapatnam/Mysore (7.15am–11pm Rs435 or Rs 560 a/c) and another to Belur/Halebid/Sravanabelgola (7.15am–10pm Rs 525 or Rs 600 a/c), but they aren't recommended unless you're happy to spend at least eight hours on the bus.

☎080/2558 5417), in the KFC Building, 48 Church St. You can pick up a free city map here and the staff are helpful in putting together tour itineraries. In addition to the desk at the airport (see p.264), **Karnataka State Tourist Development Corporation** (KSTDC; ⓦwww.kstdc.nic.in) has two city offices. One is at Badami House, NR Square (daily 6.30am–10pm; ☎080/2227 5883), where you can book tours (see box above); the other is their head office on the second floor of Khanija Bhavan, Race Course Road (Mon–Sat 10am–5.30pm, closed second Sat of month; ☎080/2235 2901). These smart new offices are shared with **Karnataka Tourism**, who aren't great at providing face-to-face information for visitors but do have a decent website (ⓦwww.karnatakatourism.com). For up-to-the-minute information about **what's on**, plus details about local restaurants and shops, check the fortnightly ad-sponsored listings magazine *City Info* (ⓦwww.explocity.com), or the monthly *City Information*, both free and available at the larger hotels, India Tourism and magazine stalls.

If you're planning to visit any of Karnataka's **national parks**, call in at the Wildlife Office, Forest Department, Aranya Bhavan, Malleswaram (☎080/2334 1993), 3km north of the main railway station, or approach Jungle Lodges & Resorts, Floor 2, Shrungar Shopping Centre, off MG Road (Mon–Sat 10am–5pm; ☎080/2559 7021, ⓦwww.junglelodges.com). A quasi-government body, Jungle Lodges promotes ecotourism in the state through several upmarket forest lodges, camps and resorts, including the much-lauded *Kabini River Lodge* near Nagarhole (see p.292).

City transport

The easiest way of getting around Bengaluru is by metered **auto-rickshaw**; fares start at Rs12 for the first kilometre and Rs6 per kilometre thereafter. Most meters do work and drivers are usually willing to use them, although you'll occasionally be asked for a flat fare, especially during rush hours.

Bengaluru's extensive **bus** system, run by the Bengaluru Metropolitan Transport Corporation (BMTC), radiates from the City (Kempe Gowda) Bus Stand (☎080/2287 3377), near the railway station. Most buses from platform 17 travel past MG Road. Along with regular buses, BMTC also operates a deluxe express service, Pushpak, on a number of set routes as well as a handful of night buses. Other important city bus stands include the City Market bus stand (☎080/2670 2177), to the south of the railway station, and Shivaji Nagar (☎080/2286 5332), to the north of Cubbon Park – the #P2 Jayanagar service from here is handy for the Lalbagh Botanical Gardens.

You can book **local taxis and chauffeur-driven cars** through several agencies including Suhalaya Travels (℡080/6568 3566, Ⓦwww.suhalayatravels .com) and Cabs India (℡080/4124 8855). Typical rates for car rental are around Rs160 per hour, Rs450 for four hours (which includes 40km), and Rs600 for eight hours (including 80km); the extra mileage charge is around Rs5 per kilometre. Note that most taxi companies start calculating their time and distances from when the car leaves their depot. If you need a taxi for a one-way journey, be prepared to pay for the return fare as well. A metered taxi system is planned for the future, which will make hiring a cab simpler. See Listings on p.274 for details of self-drive car rental.

For **long-distance car rental** and **tailor-made itineraries**, try: Gullivers Tours & Travels (℡080/2558 0818, Ⓔgulliver@satyam.net.in); JK Travels (℡080/2671 7716); SGL Tours & Travels (℡080/2238 3361, Ⓦwww.sgltours .biz); or any KSTDC office or the ITDC booth at the railway station.

Accommodation

Important both as a domestic tourist destination and as a staging post, Bengaluru has plenty of rooms available in all budgets, but they tend to fill up quickly, especially in the smart and mid-range places. Although the 24-hour checkout system operated by most hotels means that openings always crop up, it's well worth phoning ahead. **Budget accommodation** is concentrated around the railway station (which itself has good-value, but often full, retiring rooms; ❶–❸) and Central Bus Stand, though you'd be better off walking ten minutes east to Subedar Chatram Road, where standards improve. In addition to the budget places listed below, it's worth checking out the *YMCA*, midway between the Central Bus Stand and MG Road on Nirupathunga Road in Cubbon Park (℡080/2221 1848, Ⓔymca_bangalore@vsnl.com), which was closed for renovation on our last visit. **Mid-range** and **expensive hotels** are more scattered; some are located around the racecourse, a short rickshaw trip northeast of the station; others are in the MG Road area.

Around Bengaluru City railway station and Central Bus Stand

The following places are marked on the map on p.265:

Pavana Residency 88 RBDGT Charities Building ℡080/2228 6681, Ⓔhotelpavana@hotmail.com. Sizeable rooms of varying standards, some with a/c. It's rather overpriced, but as close to the railway station as you can be, yet quiet. ❹–❺

Prashanth 21 Tank Bund Rd ℡080/2287 4041, Ⓦwww.prashanth-hotel.com. Among the better hotels opposite Central Bus Stand, and all rooms are well lit, with shower-toilets. The *Mayura* nearby is the best fallback. ❹

Royal Lodge 251 Subedar Chatram Rd ℡080/2226 3740. Large, clean and efficient lodge. Most rooms are compact en-suite doubles with cable TV. ❷–❸

Tourist Ananda Rao Circle, Race Course Rd ℡080/2226 2381. This is one of Bangalore's best all-round budget lodges, with long verandas and friendly family management, though the rooms are small. No reservations are accepted, however, and it fills up quickly. ❷

Vijay Residency 18 3rd Cross, Main Road ℡080/2220 3024, Ⓦwww.vijayresidency.net. A few minutes' walk beyond Kempe Gowda Circle, this Comfort Inn franchise is plush and comfortable, with central a/c, foreign currency exchange and two quality restaurants. ❻

Vybhav Lodge 60 Subedar Chatram Rd ℡080/2287 3997. Good, clean budget lodge offering small en-suite rooms with TV, dotted around a little courtyard. Decent value, especially for singles. ❸

Around the Racecourse and Cubbon Park

The following places are marked on the map on p.265:

Goldfinch 32/3 Crescent Rd ℡080/4129 1300, Ⓦwww.goldfinchhotels.com. Luxury hotel with boutique credentials: the 50 rooms are individually and tastefully decorated, and the best have plasma-screen TVs and Jacuzzis. There's also a rooftop barbecue (*Kebab Studio*), a specialist seafood restaurant, and another serving multi-cuisine – and a gym in which to work it all off afterwards. ❾

Janardhana Kumara Krupa Rd ☎080/2225 4444, ☎2225 8708. Neat, clean and spacious rooms with balconies and baths. Well away from the chaos, and good value at this price (despite hefty service charges). ❹–❻

Taj West End Race Course Rd ☎080/6660 5600, ⓦwww.tajhotels.com. Dating back to 1887, with fabulous gardens and long colonnaded walkways. The old wing rooms (from $425), with deep verandas overlooking acres of grounds, have more character. There is also a range of suites ($650–1250). ❾

Villa Pottipati 142 8th Cross, 4th Main Rd, Malleswaram ☎080/2336 0777, ⓦwww .neemranahotels.com. A recently converted 125-year-old villa located in a northern suburb 3km from the centre. The seven doubles (two with bathtubs) and one single room have plenty of character, and there is French and Indian cuisine available. ❽–❾

Windsor Sheraton & Towers 25 Golf Course Rd ☎080/2226 9898, ⓦwww.itcwelcomgroup.in. Ersatz palace run by Welcom/Starwood as a luxurious five-star and catering mainly to business visitors from overseas, Rates start at $475. The hotel boasts 5 restaurants, a gym, Jacuzzis and a pool. ❾

MG Road and around

The following places are marked on the map on p.269, except where noted:

🏃 **Ajantha** 22-A MG Rd (100m down a lane opposite HSBC Bank) ☎080/2558 5858. See map on p.265. Quiet but central hotel in a leafy courtyard, with good-sized doubles and excellent-value single rooms. The *Ajantha* also has a restaurant selling reasonably priced South Indian meals and lunchtime thalis, and a small Internet place at the gate. ❹–❺

Brindavan 108 MG Rd ☎080/2558 4000. Old-style mid-range hotel, 100m off the main road, with some a/c rooms and a travel agent in the grounds. Good value, especially for singles, though often full. ❹–❼

Empire International 36 Church St ☎080/2559 3743, ⓦwww.hotelempireinternational.com. Smart, newish hotel with very comfortable rooms, modern decor and good facilities, including a rooftop restaurant. ❻–❼

Gautam 17 Museum Rd ☎080/2558 8475. Large, characterless concrete block of standard rooms with small balconies, but there's lots of space so it's a good fallback if other places are full. It also has a renowned pure veg restaurant – *Swarna* – on the ground floor. ❹

Oberoi 39 MG Rd ☎080/2558 5858. ⓦwww .oberoihotels.com. See map on p.265. Luxurious rooms, all with balconies, overlooking beautiful gardens with a swimming pool. There's also a health club, plus multi-cuisine and specialist Thai restaurants. ❾

Shangrila 181 Brigade Rd ☎080/4112 1622. Welcoming Tibetan-run lodge right in the thick of things; the comfy standard rooms are as good value as anywhere in the area. ❹

Taj Residency 41/43 MG Rd ☎080/6660 4444, ⓦwww.tajhotels.com. See map on p.265. Luxuries including swimming pool, health club, 24hr café and restaurants. ❾

Vellara 126 Brigade Rd ☎080/2536 9116. See map on p.265. Average but clean hotel within striking distance of MG Rd. Slightly high tariff reflects its location. ❹–❺

The City

The **centre** of modern Bengaluru lies around **MG Road**, about 4km east of Kempe Gowda Circle and the principal train and bus stations. On MG Road you'll find much of the mid-range accommodation, plus restaurants, shops, tourist information and banks. Leafy **Cubbon Park**, with its less-than-exciting museums, lies to the west, while the oldest, most "Indian" part of the city extends south from Bengaluru City railway station, a warren of winding streets at their most dynamic in the hubbub of the **City market**, with its fruit and vegetable vendors, spices and tailor shops. Bengaluru's tourist attractions are spread out; monuments such as **Tipu's Summer Palace** and the **Bull Temple** are some way south of the centre. Most, if not all, can be seen on a half-day tour, but if you plan to explore on foot, be warned that Bengaluru has some of the worst pavements in India.

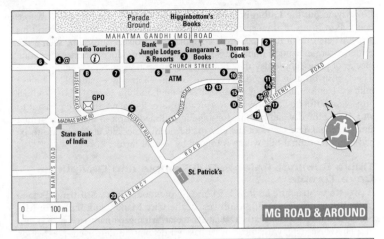

ACCOMMODATION		RESTAURANTS & CAFÉS				BARS & CLUBS			
Brindavan	A	Amaravati	14	Indian Coffee House	1	Bunker	11	Nasa	9
Empire International	B	Bheema's	7	KC Das	4	Coco Grove	5	Oasis	9
Gautam	C	Coconut Grove	5	Koshy's	6	Cohiba Club	3	Pecos	10
Shangrila	D	Dahlia	8	Pizza Corner	15	Down Town	16	Pub World	17
		Gateway	18	Ullas	2	Fusion Lounge	12	Purple Haze	20
		Green Onion	14			Guzzlers Inn	13	Spinn	19

Cubbon Park and around

A welcome green space in the heart of the city, shaded by massive clumps of bamboo, **Cubbon Park** can be accessed from the western end of MG Road. A statue of Queen Victoria presides over the entrance. On Kasturba Road, which runs along its southern edge, the poorly labelled and maintained **Government Museum** (Tues–Sun 10am–5pm; Rs4) features prehistoric artefacts, Vijayanagar, Hoysala and Chalukya sculpture, musical instruments, Thanjavur paintings and Deccani and Rajasthani miniatures. It also includes the adjacent **Venkatappa Art Gallery**, which exhibits twentieth-century landscapes, portraits, abstract art, wood sculpture and occasional temporary art shows. Next door, the **Technological and Industrial Museum** (daily 10am–6pm; Rs15) is geared towards kids. Further towards the junction with MG Road, the octagonal **Government Aquarium** (Tues–Sun except 2nd Tues of month 10am–5.30pm; Rs5) contains a few murky tanks downstairs and some more visible tropical fish upstairs.

Northwest of Cubbon Park, Bengaluru's vast State Secretariat, **Vidhana Soudha**, built in 1956, is the largest civic structure of its kind in the country. K. Hanumanthaiah, chief minister at the time, wanted a "people's palace" which, following the transfer of power from the royal Wadiyar dynasty to a legislature, would "reflect the power and dignity of the people". In theory, its design is entirely Indian, combining local models from Bengaluru, Mysore and Somnathpur with features from Rajasthan and the rest of India. Its overall effect, however, is not unlike bombastic colonial architecture, built in the so-called Indo-Saracenic style – incorporating onion-domes and Oriental features.

Lalbagh Botanical Gardens

Inspired by the splendid gardens of the Mughals and the French botanical gardens at Pondicherry (Puducherry) in Tamil Nadu, Sultan Haider Ali set to work in

1760 laying out the **Lalbagh Botanical Gardens** (daily 9am–7pm; Rs7 before 6pm), 4km south of the centre. Originally covering forty acres, just beyond his fort – where one of Kempe Gowda's original watchtowers can still be seen – the gardens were expanded under Ali's son Tipu, who introduced numerous exotic species of plants, and today they house an extensive horticultural seedling centre. The British brought in gardeners from Kew in 1856 and – naturally – built a military bandstand and a glasshouse, based on London's Crystal Palace, which hosts wonderful flower shows. Now spreading over 240 acres, they are pleasant to visit during the day, and popular for jogging and meditation in the early morning and evening. Great views of the city to the north, especially at sunset, are to be had from the central hill, which is topped by a small shrine.

Tipu's Summer Palace, Bull Temple and Gavipuram Cave Temple

A two-storey structure built in 1791, mostly of wood, **Tipu's Summer Palace** (daily 9am–5pm; $2 [Rs5]), southwest of the City Market and 3km from MG Road, is similar to the Daria Daulat Palace at Srirangapatnam (see p.287), but in a far worse state, with most of its painted decoration destroyed. Next door, the **Venkataramanaswamy temple**, dating from the early eighteenth century, was built by the Wadiyar rajas. The *gopura* entranceway was erected in 1978.

Continuing south from the summer palace, about 6km south of the City Bus Stand (bus #34 & #37) in the Basavanagudi area, Kempe Gowda's sixteenth-century **Bull Temple** (open to non-Hindus; daily 7.30am–1.30pm & 2.30–8.30pm) houses a massive monolithic Nandi bull, its grey granite made black by the application of charcoal and oil. The temple is approached along a path lined with mendicants and snake charmers; inside, for a few rupees, the priest will offer you a string of fragrant jasmine flowers.

Further south, in the suburb of Chamrajpet, the rock-cut **Sri Gavi Gangadhareshwara Temple** (or Gavipuram Cave Temple) has a unique astrological feature. On one January day each year – the holy day of Makara Sankranthi – the sun's alignment causes rays of light to pass between the horns of the Nandi bull statue at the cave entrance and bathe the Shiva *lingam* in the inner sanctum. Candles provide enough light to perform *parikrama* but you'll need to be fairly supple to negotiate the low roof of the cave.

ISKCON temple

A hybrid of ultra-modern glass and vernacular South Indian temple architecture, the gleaming new temple of the ISKCON (International Society of Krishna Consciousness), the **Sri Radha Krishna Mandir**, Hare Krishna Hill, Chord Road (daily 7am–1pm & 4.15pm–8.30pm; ⓦwww.iskconbangalore.org), 8km from the centre, is a fantastic and lavish showpiece crowned by a gold-plated dome. Barriers, designed with huge crowds in mind, guide visitors on a one-way journey through the huge well-organized complex to the inner sanctum, where images of the god Krishna and his consort Radha are displayed.

A **fast-track ticket** (Rs150) is available at the entrance for visitors to bypass the long queues, but this also means missing out on much of the atmosphere, including Krishna chanting. Delicious snacks from the temple's kitchen are available at reasonable prices and a small parting gift of *prasad* is given to all visitors, though donation points throughout and in-your-face merchandizing are evidence of ISKCON's highly successful commercialization. If you wish to stay for longer, the temple offers weekend **yoga** retreats (Sat 4pm–Sun 8pm; Rs200; Ⓣm93419 72259, ⓔretreat@iskconbangalore.org) and one-day spiritual retreats (Sun 9.15am–5.30pm; Rs100; same number)

Regular buses (80A, 80B, 80C and 76) to the temple depart for the complex from the City Bus Stand and also from the Shivaji Nagar bus stand.

Shiva Mandir

The **Shiva Mandir**, behind Kemp Kids Shopping Plaza on Airport Road, 10km from the centre (open 24hr; main complex free, inner sanctum Rs10; ⓦ www.shivmandir.org.in), boasts India's tallest Shiva statue, standing some 20m high and representing Shiva in his Kailash mountain abode. The temple has a certain theme park feel to it, with delightfully tacky miniature representations of the thirteen most important Shiva *lingams* in India, featuring moving *nagas* and an impressive model, cold to the touch, of the Amarnath *lingam* in Kashmir. Kitsch though it may be, it has a practical advantage for devotees – with thirteen opportunities for *darshan*, one visit imbues pilgrims with an entire India-wide pilgrimage. A small Navagraha shrine near the exit with nine statues representing the nine planets is also worth checking out, not least for its interesting acoustics. Shiva *bhajans* blast out 24/7 and all donations and shop proceeds go to the temple's charitable fund.

Eating

With unmissable sights thin on the ground, but tempting cafés and restaurants on every corner, you could easily spend most of your time in Bengaluru **eating**. Nowhere else in South India will you find such gastronomic variety. Around **MG Road**, pizzerias (including *Pizza Hut*), ritzy ice-cream parlours and gourmet French restaurants stand cheek by jowl with regional cuisine from Andhra Pradesh and Kerala, Mumbai *chaat* cafés and snack bars where, in true Bangalorean style, humble thalis from as little as Rs30 masquerade as "executive mini-lunches". Subedar Chatram Road, near the station, has several places for cheap, filling meals, while if you're in the mood to splash out, head to one of the three restaurants at the *Goldfinch Hotel* (around Rs700 per head).

Restaurants and cafés

Amaravati Residency Cross Rd. Excellent Andhran cooking with "meals" served on banana leaves and specialities including biriyanis and fried fish. Hectic at lunchtime, but well worth any wait.

Aromas of China G3–4 Shiva Shankar Plaza, Richmond Circle. One of the city's top Chinese restaurants. Delicacies include quality dim sum and a fine seafood platter (Rs 700) as well as above-average versions of all the usual Chinese favourites, albeit at above-average prices.

Bheema's Asha Building, 31 Church St. Brand-new place specializing in Andhran cuisine. There's an a/c pure veg room on the first floor, while the ground-floor restaurant serves non-veg, including chicken biriyani. Main courses Rs50–100.

Casa del Sol 3rd Floor, Devata Plaza, 131 Residency Rd. Spacious restaurant with a rooftop terrace, specializing in Mediterranean food. There's an all-you-can-eat-and-drink Sunday brunch (noon–4pm) for Rs585, and regular salsa and disco nights.

Casa Piccolo Devata Plaza, 131 Residency Rd. A dozen different tasty pizzas and big portions of Wiener Schnitzel, steaks, fried chicken and ice cream, but no alcohol. Tables outside on the basement patio and flower baskets give the place a European ambience.

Coconut Grove Church St. Mouthwatering and moderately priced gourmet Keralan, Chettinad and Coorg cuisine. Vegetarian, fish and meat preparations are served in traditional copper thalis on a leafy terrace, and there's a wide range of seafood dishes. Try their *meen pappas*, a delicious creamy fish curry, washed down with a "coconock" – the house speciality tender-coconut juice cocktail – though don't attempt the dressed crab without a Black-and-Decker .

Dahlia Brigade Gardens, Church St. Japanese café, tucked in a modern business complex, serving authentic dishes at reasonable prices (Rs250–450).

Gateway 66 Residency Rd ☎080/2558 4545. Two restaurants in one complex: the *Northern Gate* serves a fairly undistinguished selection of Mughlai and other North Indian dishes, while the *Karavalli* specializes in west coast dishes from Goa to Kerala, including seafood and veg, and has a very attractive setting in traditional southern style; there are also tables outside under an old tamarind tree. Reservations essential. Expensive.

Green Onion Next door to the *Amaravati*, this small, modern triangular-shaped establishment offers Chinese food and sweets in an informal café-style atmosphere.

Indian Coffee House MG Rd. The usual cheap South Indian snacks, egg dishes and good filter coffee (at a fraction of the price of the trendy coffee franchises) served by waiters in turbans and cummerbunds. Best for breakfast.

Indraprastha Subedar Chatram Rd. Excellent cheap South Indian snacks, including wonderful special masala dosa, and other veg dishes. Main courses around Rs50. One of the best options around the train and bus stations.

KC Das 38 Church St (corner with St Mark's Rd). Part of the legendary chain of Bengali sweet shops serving traditional steam-cooked sweets, many soaked in syrup and rosewater: try their definitive *rasgullas* and *gulab jamuns*. Eat in or take away.

Koshy's St Mark's Rd. Bengaluru's most congenial meeting place, this spacious, old-style café with cane blinds, pewter teapots and cotton-clad waiters serves full meals, snacks and alcohol, and also has a more expensive modern a/c wing with meals for Rs100–200. The vegetarian options are a bit overpriced, though, and tax is added to the menu prices.

Narthaki Just off Subedar Chatram Rd. The best non-veg restaurant in the station/bus stand area: filling Andhran meals are served on the first floor, while the second-floor restaurant-bar has a full menu of Indian and Chinese dishes. The chicken chilli is a belter.

Pizza Corner Brigade Rd. The most central location of this popular chain. A wide range of quality pizzas (with curry toppings available of course) and other fast-food.

Rice Bowl 40/2 Lavelle Rd. Plush a/c Chinese restaurant; try the chop suey, followed by lychees and ice cream. Evenings only.

Ullas Above cinema, MG Rd. Superb pure-veg restaurant, with a terrace and indoor section. Excellent lunchtime thalis (Rs30–90), a good choice of veg curries (around Rs50), and a reasonable range of breads.

Volga 41/2 Subedar Chatram Rd. Revamped restaurant with a breezy roof garden and a plasticky indoor dining room. Serves good portions of the usual Indian and Chinese fare.

Bars, nightlife and entertainment

The big boom may be over, but Bengaluru's bright young things still have money to spend, and **nightlife** in the city is thriving. A night on the town generally kicks off with a bar crawl along **Brigade Road**, **Residency Road** or **Church Street**, where there are scores of swish **bars**, complete with MTV, lasers and thumping sound systems. Drinking alcohol does not have the seedy connotations here as it does elsewhere in India, and you'll even see young Indian women enjoying a beer with their mates. Pubs close at 11pm but, once in, you generally get served till later. For quiet, elegant drinking head for the bars of five-star **hotels** such as the *Jockey Club* at the *Taj Residency*, the *Polo Club* at the *Oberoi* or, for a taste of colonial grandeur, the *Colonnade* at the *Taj West End*.

Local listings magazines (see p.266) carry details of Bengaluru's small but steady stream of **live music** and **theatre**, some of which is homegrown; there are also a handful of **discos**, though these usually follow a couples-only policy. Bengaluru is also a major centre for **cinema**, with a booming industry and dozens of theatres showing the latest releases from India and abroad. Check the listings page of the daily *Deccan Herald* paper or the free listings magazines to find out what's showing. Western movies are often dubbed into Hindi, although their titles may be written in English; check at the box office. Cinema fans should head for **Kempe Gowda Circle**, where you'll find the Majestic and Triveni cinemas along with posters, hoardings and larger-than-life-size cardboard cut-outs of the latest stars, strewn with spangly garlands. To arrange a visit to a local movie studio, phone Shree Kanteerava Studio (☎080/2337 0603) or Ramoji Film City (☎080/2235 2230).

Bars and clubs

Bunker Residency Cross Rd. This sprawling, smoky, subterranean bunker club with low lights and psychedelic art caters to the needs of hard rock fans every night. Thurs and Sun afternoons feature hip-hop and house respectively.

Coco Grove Church St. Below *Coconut Grove* (see p.271). Small, open-sided street-level bar, good for people-watching. Beer, cocktails, mocktails and bar snacks are available.

Cohiba Club The Pavilion, Church St. New theme bar and restaurant where you can enjoy a selection of big fat cigars, Latin and Cuban music, Spanish tapas and mojitos. Black-and-white posters of cigar-touting celebrities adorn the walls.

Down Town Residency Rd. Large basement pub that also has a reasonable multi-cuisine menu, though the decor is not particularly inspiring. There are a couple of pool tables at the back.

Fusion Lounge Rest House Rd. Trendy new place with futuristic decor featuring red lighting and silver cushions. Cocktails and beers are served, and there are regular DJs. Hefty cover charge at the weekends, though this does include a drink.

Guzzlers Inn 48 Rest House Rd, off Brigade Rd. Popular and established pub showing MTV and Star Sport, and offering snooker, pool and draught beer.

Closed for renovation at time of research but should reopen by the time you read this.

Nasa 1/4 Church St. Cosy, wacky little pub with sci-fi decor resembling the interior of a space shuttle. Gay-friendly, good happy hour deals, TV screens and in-your-face music.

Oasis Church St, next to *Nasa*. Ground-floor restaurant (eves only) and all-day first-floor bar-cum-restaurant with low light and an unobtrusive sound-system.

Pecos Rest House Rd, off Brigade Rd. Small and relaxed pub on three floors with 1960s and 1970s music and posters; popular with a mixed arty set.

Pub World Residency Rd. Pleasant and fairly authentic British-style pub with a long bar, family area and tables. The usual high-volume music and sports on TV. Popular with trendy young professionals.

Purple Haze Residency Rd. Downtown pub, with Hendrix-themed graphics, in a smart and lively upstairs bar. More chance of decent rock here than most places.

Spinn 80 3rd Cross, Residency Rd. Nightclub located in an old colonial house with lounge decor. Funk, house and hip-hop. No shorts. Open late; cover charge at weekends.

Shopping

Bengaluru has many fine shops, particularly if you're after **silk**. A wide range is available at Karnataka Silk Industries Corporation and Vijayalakshmi Silk Kendra, both on Gupte Market, Kempe Gowda Road, and at Deepam Silk Emporium on MG Road. **Handicrafts** such as soapstone sculpture, brass, carved sandalwood and rosewood are also good value. Emporia include: Central Cottage Industries Emporium, 144 MG Rd; the expensive Cottage Industries Exposition Ltd, 3 Cunningham Rd; Gulshan Crafts, 12 Safina Plaza, Infantry Rd; and Karnataka's own state emporium, Cauvery, at the MG Road and Brigade Road crossing. For **silver**, try looking on and around Commercial Street (north of MG Road) and at KR Market on Residency Road, as well as at Jewels de Paragon between MG Road and Kasturba Road. The long-established Natesan's Antiqarts, 64 MG Rd, sells **antiques** and beautifully made reproduction sculpture, furniture and paintings at international art-house prices. If you want to take a look at expensive Indian *haute couture* try Folio at Embassy Chamber, Vittal Mallya Road, which features the work of several well-known Indian designers.

Bengaluru is a great place for English-language **bookshops** (see below), while the best **music** shops in the city centre, selling Indian, Western and World music, are Music World and Planet M, both on Brigade Road, and Rhythms, at 14 St Mark's Rd, beneath the *Nahar Heritage* hotel.

Bookshops

Bookworm off MG Rd. A good place to swap secondhand books, tucked away down a side street near the Jungle Lodges office. They also have some new paperbacks.

Gangaram's 66 MG Rd. Wide selection on India (coffee-table art books and academic), plus the latest paperback fiction and a great selection of Indian greetings cards.

Motilal Banarsidas 16 St Mark's Rd, close to the junction with MG Rd. Shop belonging to an established publishers, offering a superb selection of heavyweight Indology and philosophy titles. Sankars 15/2 Madras Bank Rd. Airy shop with a very good range of fiction, art, educational and religious books. They also have branches in the *Taj Residency* and at Bangalore airport – a great place to spend your last rupees. Sapna Book House 3rd Cross Main Rd, opposite *Vijay Residency*. A massive 32,000-square-foot bibliophile's paradise.

Listings

Airlines, domestic *Air Deccan*, 214/22 7th Cross, Cunningham Rd ☏m98457 77008; *Indian Airlines*, Cauvery Bhavan, Kempe Gowda Rd ☏080/2297 8427, airport ☏2522 6233, enquiries ☏1407; *Jet Airways*, 1–4 M Block, Unity Building, JC Rd ☏080/3989 9999; *Kingfisher* ☏080/4197 9797; *Sahara Airlines*, 39 St Marks Rd ☏080/2210 2777, airport ☏2522 0065.

Airlines, international *Air France*, Sunrise Chambers, 22 Ulsoor Rd ☏080/2555 9360; *Air India*, Unity Building, JC Rd ☏080/2227 7747; *Alitalia*, G-17 Gem Plaza, 66 Infantry Rd ☏080/2559 1936; *Biman Bangladesh*, 22 Sunrise Chambers, Ulsoor Rd ☏080/2559 4240; *British Airways*, 7 St Mark's Rd ☏080/2227 4034; *Cathay Pacific*, Taj West End, Race Course Rd ☏080/2220 2713; *Delta*, 103 Richards Towers, 12 Richard Rd ☏080/2224 4625; *Emirates*, 3 Prestige Sigma, Vittal Mallaya Rd, ☏080/5529 4400; *Gulf Air*, Sunrise Chambers, 22 Ulsoor Rd ☏080/2558 4702; *KLM/Northwest Airlines, Taj West End*, Race Course Rd ☏080/2228 4320; *Lufthansa*, 44/2 Dickenson Rd ☏080/2506 0800; *Malaysia Airlines*, Richmond Circle ☏080/2522 6730; *Pakistan International Airlines*, 108 Commerce House, 911 Cunningham Rd ☏080/2226 0667; *Qantas*, 109A Westminster, Cunningham Rd ☏080/2226 4719; *Royal Nepal Airlines*, 205 Barton Centre, 84 MG Rd ☏080/2559 7878; *Singapore Airlines*, 17 Park View Rd, Tasker Town ☏080/2286 7868; *South African*, 19/20 Richmond Towers, 12 Richmond Rd ☏080/2224 4623; *Swiss*, 51 Richmond Rd ☏080/2221 1983; *Thai Airways*, 100/1 UB Anchorage Bldg, Richmond Rd ☏080/4112 4333.

Ambulance ☏102 (24hr); Hosmat ☏080/2559 3796.

Banks and currency exchange Reliable places to change money include: Thomas Cook, 70 MG Rd, on the corner of Brigade Rd; KHA, 55A Prestige Block, Church St; and American Express, 137 Richmond Circle. There are plenty of ATMs on and around MG Rd including at: State Bank of India, 66 St Marks Rd, and on MG Rd near HSBC; Canara Bank, MG Rd; ING Vysya Bank, Church St; HSBC, MG Rd, opp. *Ajantha Hotel*. In addition, all the major hotels and most of the emporia (see p.273) have exchange facilities.

Car rental You can find self-drive car rental at Avis, *Oberoi*, 37–39 MG Rd (☏080/2558 5858) and Hertz, Unit 12, Raheja Plaza, 17 Commissariat Rd (☏080/5537 5404); both also have offices at the airport. Of local firms, try: Deccan, 30 Sriranga Apts, 1st Temple Rd, Malleswaram (☏080/4128 0600); and Suhalaya Travels, 16B 1st floor, Ulsoor Rd (☏080/5768 3566, ⓦwww.suhalayatravels. com). Charges from Rs1000 per day.

Hospitals Bengaluru, 202 RV Rd (☏080/4118 7600); Hosmat, 45 Magrath Rd (☏080/2559 3796), is the most central; Mallya, Vittal Mallya Rd (☏080/2227 7990), is one of the best.

Internet access Bengaluru has a huge number of Internet bureaus, although connection speed can be surprisingly slow at times. Rates vary slightly but are generally around Rs20/hr. Most places are open around 9am–10pm with a few operating 24 hours a day. Cyberia on Residency Rd (opp. *Pub World*) and the Cyber Café, 13–15 Brigade Rd, are both popular but you're spoiled for choice in the MG/Brigade Rd area. There are a couple of small places along Subedar Chatram Rd at the bus stand side of town and a superfast DSL service in the forecourt of Bangalore City railway station. A number of Internet joints also have Net2Phone facilities, such as the one outside *Hotel Brindavan*, off MG Rd.

Libraries The British Council (English-language) library, 29 Kasturba Rd Cross (Mon–Sat 10.30am–6.30pm; ☏080/2221 3485), has newspapers and magazines which visitors are welcome to peruse in a/c comfort, as does the Alliance Française (French), 16 GMT Rd (☏080/2225 8762), and Max Mueller Bhavan (German), 3 Lavelle Rd (☏080/2221 4964). The Theosophical Society library is on KR Rd, Basavangudi ☏080/2661 6440.

Pharmacies 24hr pharmacy services at the Al-Siddique Pharma Centre, opposite Jami Masjid near City Market, plus Hosmat, Mallya, Manipal and Victoria hospitals.

Photographic services and equipment EKG & Son, Church St, and Foto Circle, 2KV Temple St

(☎080/2287 4356), are digital specialists. Kodak India is at 16 Whitefield Rd (☎080/2809 9800). Adlabs, Mission Rd, Subbaiah Circle, stocks transparency film. GG Welling, 113 MG Rd, and GK Vale, 89 MG Rd, sell transparency and Polaroid film.

Police ☎100.

Postal services The main GPO is on the corner of Raj Bhavan Rd and Cubbon Rd, at the northern tip of Cubbon Park, about ten minutes' walk from MG Rd (Mon–Sat 10am–7pm, Sun 10.30am–1.30pm). There's a more convenient branch on Museum Rd (Mon–Sat 9.30am–1.30pm & 2–5pm).

Travel agents For flight booking and reconfirmation and other travel necessities, try: Gullivers Tours & Travels (see p.267); Marco Polo Tours, Janardhan Towers, 2 Residency Rd (☎080/2227 0167, ℱ2223 6671; or Sita Travels, 1 St Mark's Rd (☎080/2558 6579).

Around Bengaluru

Bengaluru is surrounded by some very pleasant countryside, which includes good walking country in the Nandi Hills to the north and the Bannerghatta National Park to the south. Twenty-five kilometres east of the city centre, **Whitefield** is home to Sai Baba's second ashram. To the west, the **Janapada Loka Folk Arts Museum**, between Bengaluru and Mysore, gives a fascinating insight into Karnatakan culture, while anyone wishing to see or study classical dance in a rural environment should check out the **Nrityagram Dance Village**.

Whitefield

Between the months of March and May each year, India's most famous holy man, Sai Baba, makes his annual pilgrimage from his home in Puttaparthy (see p.676) to **Whitefield** (ⓦwww.saibabaofindia.com/whitefieldashraminfo.html), his ashram on the outskirts of Bengaluru. During his stay, the usually quiet town becomes a hive of activity with thousands of devotees moving to be close to him. Even if you come here out of season, you will still feel Sai Baba's presence – the main road outside the ashram is lined with shops selling Sai paraphernalia – though little happens in the ashram other than the regular Sunday *bhajans* (9–10.30am; free). Located in the heart of the Sala Puria Tech Park, just off the main Bengaluru–Whitefield road on the route into town, the impressive Sri Sathya Sai Heart Hospital, one of his many charitable hospitals offering free treatment, is worth a quick visit.

Buses for Whitefield (#319C, 333E, 335A and 335E) leave Bengaluru every 10–15 minutes, and there are also direct services from Bengaluru airport. **ATMs** can be found at the State Bank of India, 100m down the road from the ashram entrance, and at Canara Bank at the railway crossing. **Internet** access is also available on the main road near the ashram entrance. Demand for **accommodation** in the ashram (☎080/2845 2681) soars when Sai Baba is in residence but is strictly on a first-come basis; rooms can only be booked out of season, though even then just for one night. Alternatively, try the private *Sai Renaissance Hotel* (☎080/2845 6266, ⓦwww.sairenaissance.com; ⑤–⑥), opposite the State Bank of India, which is a pleasant mid-range hotel with clean rooms and a small restaurant.

Janapada Loka Folk Arts Museum

The **Janapada Loka Folk Arts Museum** (daily 9am–6pm; free), 53km southwest of Bengaluru on the Mysore road, includes an amazing array of Karnatakan agricultural, hunting and fishing implements, weapons, ingenious household gadgets, masks, dolls and shadow puppets, carved wooden *bhuta* (spirit-worship) sculptures and larger-than-life temple procession figures, manuscripts, musical instruments and *Yakshagana* theatre costumes. In addition, an incredible 1600 hours of **audio and video recordings** of musicians, dancers and rituals from the state are available for viewing on request.

275

Moving on from Bengaluru

Bengaluru is South India's principal transport hub. Fast and efficient computerized booking facilities make **moving on** relatively hassle-free, although the availability of seats should never be taken for granted; book as far in advance as possible. For an overview of travel services to and from Bengaluru, including flights, see Travel details on p.362.

By air

Bengaluru's modern **airport** is the busiest in South India, with domestic and international connections. There are more than a dozen daily flights to each of **Mumbai**, **Chennai** and **Hyderabad**, plus services to numerous other destinations (see Travel details for more information). Airline offices and recommended travel agents appear in Listings on p.274.

By bus

Most of the wide range of long-distance **buses** from Central Bus Stand can be booked in advance at the computerized counters near Bay 13 (7.30am–7.30pm). As well as Karnataka's state bus corporation (KSRTC), government-run services from Andhra Pradesh, Kerala, Maharashtra, Tamil Nadu and Goa (Kadamba) also operate from Bengaluru. Timings and ticket availability for the forthcoming week are posted on a large board left of the main entrance. For general enquiries, call ☏080/2287 3377.

Several **private bus companies** run luxury coaches to destinations such as Mysore, Bijapur, Ooty, Chennai, Kochi/Ernakulam, Thrissur, Kollam and Thiruvananthapuram. Tickets can be bought from the agencies on Tank Bund Road, opposite the bus stand; operators include Sharma (☏080/2670 2447), National (☏080/2660 3112) and Shama (☏080/2670 5855), each of which advertise overnight deluxe buses to **Goa** and sleeper coaches and services to **Mumbai** and **Chennai**. The most reliable of the private bus companies is Vijayanand Travels (☏080/2297 1257), who also have an office on Tank Bund Road; their distinctive yellow-and-black luxury coaches run to destinations such as Mangalore and Hospet for Hampi.

By train

While Southern Railways complete the conversion to broad gauge, the line from Hassan to Mangalore remains closed – check the situation when you arrive.

To get to the museum, take one of the many slow Mysore buses (not the non-stop ones) from Bengaluru; after the town of Ramanagaram, alight at the 53-kilometre stone by the side of the road. The museum complex has a small restaurant serving simple food, and dorm accommodation. For more details, contact the Karnataka Janapada Trust, 7 Subramanyaswami Temple Road, 5th Cross, 4th Block, Kumara Park West, Bengaluru.

Nrityagram Dance Village

Nrityagram Dance Village (Tues–Sat 10.30am–5pm, Sun 10.30am–3pm; Rs20) is a delightful purpose-built model village, 30km west of Bengaluru, designed by the award-winning architect Gerard de Cunha and founded by the late Protima Gauri. The school attracts pupils from all over the world and hosts regular performances and lectures on Indian mythology and art, as well as offering courses in different forms of Indian dance. **Guided tours** of the complex cost Rs1250 per person (minimum 8), including lunch and a demonstration. **Accommodation** (❼) for longer stays promises "oxygen, home-grown vegetables and fruits, no TV, telephones, newspapers or noise". Contact their Bengaluru office (☏080/2846 6313, ⓦwww.nrityagram.org).

Bengaluru City railway station's reservations office (Mon–Sat 8am–2pm & 2.15–8pm, Sun 8am–2pm; reservations ☎132) is in a separate building, east of the main station (to the left as you approach). Counter 14 is for foreigners. If you have an Indrail Pass, go to the Chief Reservations Supervisor's Office on the first floor (turn left at the top of the stairs), where "reservations are guaranteed". There are two 24hr telephone information lines; one handles timetable enquiries (☎131), the other reels off a recorded list of arrivals and departures (☎133). Trains to Goa and a handful of trains to other destinations depart from Yeshwanthpur railway station (☎080/2337 7161) in the north of the city (see p.264).

The following trains are recommended as the fastest and/or most convenient from Bengaluru.

Destination	Name	No.	Departs	Total time
Chennai	Shatabdi Express*	#2008	daily except Tues 4.25pm	5hr 5min
	Lalbagh Express	#2608	daily 6.30am	5hr 30min
Ernakulam (for Kochi)	Kanniyakumari Express	#6526	daily 9.45pm	12hr 15min
Hospet (for Hampi)	Hampi Express	#6592	daily 10.20pm	9hr 30min
Mumbai	Udyan Express	#6530	daily 8.05pm	23hr 50min
Mysore	Shatabdi Express*	#2007	daily except Tues 11am	2hr
	Tipu Express	#2614	daily 2.15pm	2hr 30min
	Chamundi Express	#6216	daily 6.15pm	3hr
Secunderabad (Hyderabad)	Rajdhani Express*	#2429	4 weekly 8.20pm	10hr 50min
Thiruvanan-thapuram	Kanniyakumari Express	#6526	daily 9.45pm	17hr 20min

*= a/c only

Mysore

A centre of sandalwood-carving, silk and incense production, 159km southwest of Bengaluru (Bangalore), **MYSORE**, the erstwhile capital of the Wadiyar Rajas, is one of South India's most-visited places. Considering the clichés that have been heaped upon the town, however, first impressions can be disappointing. Like anywhere else in the region, visitors stumbling off the bus or train aren't greeted by the scent of jasmine blossom or gentle wafts of sandalwood but by the usual cacophony of careering auto-rickshaws and noisy buses, bullock carts and tongas (horse-drawn carriages). Nevertheless, Mysore is a charming, old-fashioned and undaunting town, dominated by the spectacular **Maharaja's Palace**, around which the boulevards of the city radiate.

Some history

In the tenth century, Mysore was known as "Mahishur" – "the town where the demon buffalo was slain" (by the goddess Durga). Presiding over a district of many villages, the city was ruled from about 1400 until Independence by the

△ Market, Mysore

Hindu **Wadiyars**, and its fortunes were inextricably linked with those of Srirangapatnam, which became the Wadiyar headquarters from 1616 (see p.286). Their rule was unbroken until 1761, when the Muslim Haider Ali and his son Tipu Sultan took over. Two years later, the new rulers demolished the labyrinthine old city to replace it with the elegant grid of sweeping, leafy streets and public gardens that survives today. However, following Tipu Sultan's defeat in 1799 by the British colonel Arthur Wellesley (later the Duke of Wellington), Wadiyar power was restored. As the capital of Mysore state, the city thereafter dominated a major part of southern India. In 1956, when Bangalore became capital of newly formed Karnataka, its maharaja was appointed governor.

Arrival and information

Six or seven daily trains from the state capital arrive at the **railway station**, 1.5km northwest of the centre. Mysore has three **bus** stands. Major long-distance KSRTC services pull in to **Central**, near the heart of the city, where there's a friendly KSTDC booking counter (☎0821/244 4997) for tours (see below); it's also helpful for information regarding bus times. The **Private** stand is on Sayaji Rao Road, about 1km northwest. Local buses, including services for Chamundi Hill and Srirangaptnam, stop at the **City** stand, next to the north-western corner of the Maharaja's Palace.

Five minutes' walk east of the railway station, on Irwin Road in the Old Exhibition Building, is the helpful **tourist reception centre** (daily 10am–5.30pm; ☎0821/242 2096), whose staff do their best to answer queries and can arrange transport, as well as give out brochures and maps. The **KSTDC office** (daily 6.30am–8.30pm; ☎0821/242 3652), at the *Hotel Mayura Hoysala*, 2 Jhansi Lakshmi Bai Rd, is of little use except to book one of their **tours**. The whistle-stop city tour (8.30am; Rs125) makes for a long day, covering Jaganmohan Palace Art Gallery, the Maharaja's Palace, St Philo-mena's Church, the Zoo, Chamundi Hill, Srirangapatnam and Brindavan Gardens. They also run daily tours to Belur, Halebid and Sravanabelgola

MYSORE

St. Philomena's Church ▲

Private Bus Stand ▲

▲ **O & R**

Wesley Cathedral ✝

BANGALORE-MYSORE ROAD

NAZARBAD MAIN ROAD

GUEST HOUSE ROAD

BANGALORE–NILGIRI (BN) ROAD

Central Bus Stand

Sangam Theatre

Clocktower

CHANDRAGUPTA ROAD

ASHOKA ROAD

GPO ✉

UMA TALKIES ROAD

ST STREET

KT STREET

KH HOSPITAL ROAD

Gandhi Square

Cauvery Arts & Crafts Emporium

Bank

SARDAR PATEL ROAD

Devaraja Market

SAYAJI RAO ROAD

Town Hall

City Bus Stand ★

KR CIRCLE

New Statue Circle

Maharajah's Palace

Entrance

VICTORIA ALBERT ROAD

SRI HARSHA ROAD

HARDING CIRCLE

▼ **O & Chamundi Hill**

SAVAJI RAO ROAD

DEVARAJ URS ROAD

VINOBA ROAD

RAMA ROAD

Jaganmohan Palace & Art Gallery

DHANAVANTRI ROAD

Hospital

Tourist Reception Centre ⓘ

TRWIN ROAD

NARAYANA SHASTRI ROAD

KR STREET

DIWAN'S ROAD

Recreation Fields

Railway Booking Office

Railway Station

Railway Museum

JHANSI LAKSHMI BAI ROAD

▲ **K & Kodagu**

N

100 m
0

3

KARNATAKA

ACCOMMODATION
Dasaprakash	B
Gitanjali Farm	Q
Govardhan	L
Green	K
Indra Bhavan	A
KSTDC Mayura Hoysala	E
KSTDC Yatri Niwas	R
Lalitha Mahal Palace	D
Manmars Lodge	H
Metropole	C
Parklane	J
Rajabhadra	F
Regalis	P
Ritz	G
Roopa	I
Sandesh The Prince	O
Sangeeth	M
S.C.V.D.S.	
Viceroy	

RESTAURANTS
Bombay Indra Bhavan	4 & A
Dynasty	5
Lalitha Mahal Palace	R
Le Olive Garden	8
Parklane	N
Pizza Corner	7
RRR	1
Shanghai	3
Shilpashri	2
Siddharth	6

279

(7.30am; Rs325) and Ooty (7am; Rs350). Both are very full days and involve a lot of travelling though. If you want to put together your own itinerary, their **car rental** rate of Rs5.50 per kilometre (for up to 250km per day) is very reasonable. The private Tourist Corporation of India office, inside the *Rajabhadra* on Gandhi Square (☎0821/526 0294), is a KSTDC agent and can also arrange tours and car rental.

The main **post office** (which handles poste restante) is on the corner of Ashoka and Irwin roads (Mon–Sat 10am–7pm, Sun 10.30am–1.30pm). If you need to **change money**, there's a State Bank of Mysore on the corner of Sayaji Rao and Sardar Patel Road, and an Indian Overseas Bank, Gandhi Square, opposite *Dasaprakash Hotel*. There are a couple of **ATMs** around KR Circle and another at the Oriental Bank at the station. For **Internet access**, try Netzone opposite the *Sangeeth Hotel*, Cyberspace on Nazarbad Main Road near the *Ritz*, or on Bangalore–Nilgiri (BN) Road between *Hotel Roopa* and *Pizza Corner*. All currently charge Rs30/hr.

Accommodation

The city has plenty of **hotels** to suit all budgets, and finding a room is only a problem during Dussehra (see p.282), when popular places are booked up weeks in advance. Most foreigners stay near the Maharaja's Palace, on or around **Sri Harsha Road**, which has a range of accommodation to suit all budgets. Other pricier hotels are more spread out, but a good place to start is **Jhansi Lakshmi Bai Road**, which runs south from the railway station. If you're looking for total opulence, then head straight for the *Lalitha Mahal Palace*.

Inexpensive

Dasaprakash Gandhi Square ☎0821/244 2444, ⓦwww.mysoredasaprakashgroup.com. Large, slightly faded hotel complex arranged around a spacious courtyard. It's busy, clean and efficient, though lacking character, and has some a/c rooms, cheap singles and a veg restaurant. ❸–❹

Govardhan Down a lane next to the Opera cinema, Sri Harsha Rd ☎0821/243 4118, ⓦwww .hotelgovardhan.com. Basic budget rooms (some a/c) close to the palace. Frayed around the edges, but clean enough. ❸–❹

Indra Bhavan Dhanavantri Rd ☎0821/242 3933, ⓔhotelindrabhavan@rediffmail.com. This large hotel is a bit dilapidated but has character. En-suite singles and doubles are available; the "deluxe" rooms are the best value, with clean, tiled floors, opening onto a wide, common veranda with a tree-lined vista. Popular with Tibetans. ❷–❸

KSTDC Yatri Niwas 2 Jhansi Lakshmi Bai Rd ☎0821/242 3492, ⓦwww.kstdc.nic.in. The government-run *Mayura Hoysala*'s economy wing offers simple rooms around a central garden, plus dorm beds for Rs75. ❸

Mannars Lodge Chandragupta Rd ☎0821/244 8060. Deservedly popular backpackers' hotel near the bus stand and Gandhi Square. No frills, but some rooms have TV. ❷–❸

Rajabhadra Gandhi Square ☎0821/426 0152. This small, cheap and very basic lodge is just about the best of several look-alikes on the square. The front rooms have good views of the mayhem below, and there are some singles. ❶–❷

Ritz BN Rd ☎0821/242 2668, ⓔhotelritz @rediffmail.com. Slightly run-down but atmospheric colonial-era hotel a few minutes' walk from the clocktower and Harding Circle. Although quite a large building, there are only four rooms, so book ahead. ❸

Sangeeth 1966 Narayana Shastri Rd, near the Udupi Krishna temple ☎0821/242 4693. One of Mysore's best all-round budget deals: small rooms, but clean, friendly and good value. There's also a rooftop sitting area and basement restaurant. ❸

S.C.V.D.S. Sri Harsha Rd ☎0821/242 1379, ⓕ242 7580. Friendly lodge with some a/c rooms and cable TV in most. Some doubles have nice balconies overlooking the palace. ❸–❹

Moderate to expensive

Gitanjali Farm Near *Lalitha Mahal Palace*, Siddar-thanagar ☎0821/247 3779, ⓣm94483 53779, ⓦwww.gitanjalifarm.com. Four light, airy, modern cottages in peaceful grounds 6km from the centre of town. Room-only basis or you can enjoy the home-cooked Coorg style food at an inclusive rate. Advance bookings only. ❾

Green Chittaranjan Palace, 2270 Vinoba Rd, Jayalakshmipuram ☎0821/251 2536, ⓦwww.greenhotelindia.com. An elegant, eco-conscious two-star set in a former royal palace with large gardens on the western outskirts of the city. There are spacious rooms, lounges, verandas, a croquet lawn and well-stocked library, and all profits go to charities and environmental projects. Their auto-rickshaw will pick you up with prior arrangement. They can also be contacted through the Charities Advisory Trust in London (☎+44 (0) 207/794 9835). ❼–❾

KSTDC Mayura Hoysala 2 Jhansi Lakshmi Bai Rd ☎0821/242 5349, ⓦwww.kstdc.nic.in. Reasonably priced rooms and suites in a colonial-era mansion with a terrace restaurant and beer garden. Good value, but the food is uninspiring. ❹–❺

Lalitha Mahal Palace T Narasipur Rd ☎0821/247 0470, ⓦwww.lalithamahalpalace.com. On a slope overlooking the city and visible for miles around, this white, Neoclassical palace was built in 1931 to accommodate the maharaja's foreign guests. It's now a Raj-style fantasy, popular with tour groups. Tariffs are astronomical by Indian standards, ranging from $190 per night turret rooms to $895 for the Viceroy Suite. The tea lounge, restaurant and pool (Rs175) are open to non-residents, and there's a free snooker table in the bar. ❾

Metropole 5 Jhansi Lakshmi Bai Rd ☎0821/425 5566, ⓦwww.royalorchidhotels.com. Luxurious heritage hotel, set in pleasant gardens, built in 1920 by the Maharaja of Mysore. Rooms have high ceilings and a sense of grandeur. There's also a small outdoor pool and gym, plus the *Tiger Trail* multi-cuisine restaurant. ❾

Parklane 2720 Sri Harsha Rd ☎0821/243 0400, ⓦwww.parklanemysore.com. Previously a popular budget place undergoing massive renovation at time of writing, and reopening during 2007. It also features a popular restaurant below and rooftop swimming pool. ❺

Regalis 13/14 Vinobha Rd ☎0821/242 6426, ⓦwww.ushalexushotels.com. Modern and comfortable monolithic hotel with all facilities, including two restaurants, a bar and a swimming pool. Golf can be arranged on request. ❾

Roopa 2724/C Bengaluru–Nilgiri Rd ☎0821/244 3770, ⓦwww.hotelroopa.com. Hotel block with compact but comfy rooms at reasonable prices. ❹–❼

Sandesh The Prince 3 Nazarbad Main Rd ☎0821/243 6777, ⓦwww.sandeshtheprince.com. Smart 4-star with comfortable carpeted and well-furnished rooms and an impressive foyer. Facilities include travel desk, foreign exchange, swimming pool, poolside BBQ, gym, and an excellent ayurvedic centre and beauty parlour, Nandita's Beauty Zone (ⓔnanditanil@yahoo.co.in). ❽–❾

Viceroy Sri Harsha Rd ☎0821/242 4001, ⓦwww.theviceroygroup.com. Business-oriented hotel, with most mod cons and two good restaurants. Rooms are mostly a/c, and the front ones have views over the park to the palace from the front rooms, but generally rather overpriced. ❻–❼

The City

In addition to its official tourist attractions, chief amongst them the **Maharaja's Palace**, Mysore is a great city simply to stroll around. The characterful, if dilapidated, pre-Independence buildings lining market areas such as **Ashoka Road** and **Sayaji Rao Road** lend an air of faded grandeur to the busy centre, which teems with vibrant street life. The best place to get a sense of what's on offer is the Government Cauvery Arts and Crafts Emporium, Sayaji Rao Road (closed Thurs), which stocks a wide range of local crafts, which can be shipped overseas. Elsewhere, souvenir stores spill over with the famous **sandalwood** (see Basics, p.81). The city's famous **Devaraja Market**, on Sayaji Rao Road, is one of South India's most atmospheric produce markets: a giant complex of covered stalls bursting with bananas (the delicious *Nanjangod* variety), luscious mangoes, blocks of sticky jaggery and conical heaps of lurid *kumkum* powder.

Maharaja's Palace ✓

Mysore centre is dominated by the walled **Maharaja's Palace** (daily 10am–5.30pm; Rs20), a fairy-tale spectacle, topped with a shining brass-plated dome surmounting a single tower; it's especially magnificent on Sunday nights and during festivals, when it is illuminated by no fewer than five thousand light bulbs. Designed in the hybrid Indo-Saracenic style by Henry Irwin, the British consultant architect of Madras state, it was completed in 1912 for the 24th

Wadiyar raja, on the site of the old wooden palace that had been destroyed by fire in 1897. Twelve temples surround the palace, some of them of much earlier origin. Although there are six gates in the perimeter wall, entry is on the south side only. Shoes and cameras must be left at the cloakroom inside.

An extraordinary amalgam of styles from India and around the world crowds the lavish **interior**. Entry is through the Gombe Thotti, or **Dolls' Pavilion**, once a showcase for the figures featured in the city's lively Dussehra celebrations (see box below) and now a gallery of European and Indian sculpture and ceremonial objects. Halfway along the pavilion, the brass **Elephant Gate** forms the main entrance to the centre of the palace, through which the maharaja would drive to his car park. Decorated with floriate designs, it bears the Mysore royal symbol of a double-headed eagle, now the state emblem. To the north, past the gate, are dolls dating from the late nineteenth-century, a wooden *mandapa* glinting with mirrorwork and, at the end, a ceremonial wooden elephant *howdah* (frame to carry passengers). Elaborately decorated with 84kg of 24-carat gold, it appears to be inlaid with red and green gems – in fact, the twinkling lights are battery-powered signals to let the *mahout* know when the maharaja wished to stop or go.

Walls leading into the octagonal **Kalyana Mandapa**, the royal wedding hall, are lined with a meticulously detailed frieze of oil paintings illustrating the great Mysore Dussehra festival of 1930, executed over fifteen years by four Indian artists. The hall itself is magnificent, a cavernous space featuring cast-iron pillars from Glasgow, Bohemian chandeliers and multicoloured Belgian stained glass arranged in peacock designs in the domed ceiling. A mosaic of English floor tiles repeats the peacock motif. Beyond here lie small rooms cluttered with grandiose furniture, including a pair of silver chairs and others of Belgian cut-crystal made for the maharaja and Lord Mountbatten, the last Viceroy of India. One of the rooms has a fine ceiling of Burma teak carved by local craftsmen.

Climbing a staircase with Italian marble balustrades, past an unnervingly realistic life-size plaster-of-Paris figure of Krishnaraja Wadiyar IV, lounging comfortably with his bejewelled feet on a stool, you come into the **Public Durbar Hall**, an Orientalist fantasy often compared to a setting from *A Thousand and One Nights*. A vision of brightly painted and gilded colonnades, open on one side, the massive hall affords views out across the parade ground and gardens to Chamundi Hill. The maharaja gave audience from here, seated on a throne made from 280kg of solid Karnatakan gold. These days, the hall is only used during the Dussehra festival, when it hosts classical concerts. Paintings

Mysore Dussehra festival

Following the tradition set by the Vijayanagar kings, the ten-day festival of **Dussehra** (Sept/Oct), commemorating the goddess Durga's slaying of the demon buffalo, Mahishasura, is celebrated in grand style at Mysore. Scores of cultural events occur, including concerts of South Indian classical (Carnatic) music and dance performances, in the great Durbar Hall of the Maharaja's Palace. On Vijayadasmi, the tenth and last day of the festival, a magnificent procession of mounted guardsmen on horseback and caparisoned elephants – one of which carries the palace deity, Chamundeshwari, on a gold *howdah* – marches 5km from the palace to Banni Mantap. There's also a floating festival in the temple tank at the foot of Chamundi Hill and a procession of chariots around the temple at the top. A torchlight parade takes place in the evening, followed by a massive firework display and much jubilation in the streets.

by the celebrated artists Shilpi Siddalingaswamy and Raja Rama Varma, from the Travancore (Kerala) royal family, adorn the walls. The whole is crowned by white marble, inlaid with delicate floral scrolls of jasper, amber and lapis lazuli in the Mughal style. Somewhat out of sync with the opulence are a series of ceiling panels of Vishnu, painted on fire-proof asbestos, dating from the 1930s. The smaller **Private Durbar Hall** features especially beautiful stained glass and gold-leaf painting. Before leaving you pass two embossed silver doors – all that remains of the old palace.

Nearby, behind the main palace building but within the same compound, a line of tacky souvenir shops leads to a small **museum** (same hours; Rs20) run by the royal family which shows paintings from the Thanjavur and Mysore schools, some inlaid with precious stones and gold leaf.

Jaganmohan Palace: Jayachamarajendra Art Gallery

Built in 1861, the **Jaganmohan Palace** (daily 8am–5pm; Rs10; no cameras), 300m west of the Maharaja's Palace, was used as a royal residence until it was turned into a **picture gallery** and museum in 1915 by Maharaja Krishnaraja Wadiyar IV. Most of the "contemporary" art on show dates from the 1930s, when a revival of Indian painting was spearheaded by E.B. Havell and the Tagore brothers Rabrindrath and Gaganendranath in Bengal.

On the ground floor, a series of faded black-and-white photos of ceremonial occasions shares space with elaborate imported clocks. Nineteenth- and twentieth-century paintings dominate the first floor; among them is the work of the pioneering oil painter Raja Ravi Varma who, although not everyone's cup of tea, has been credited with introducing modern techniques to Indian art. Inspired by European masters, Varma gained a reputation in portraiture and also depicted epic Indian themes from the classics, such as the demon king Ravana absconding with Rama's wife Sita. Games on the upper floor include circular *ganjeeb* playing cards illustrated with portraits of royalty or deities and board games delicately inlaid with ivory. There's also a cluster of musical instruments, among them a brass *jaltarang* set and glass xylophone, and harmonicas and clarinet played by Krishnaraja Wadiyar IV himself. Another gallery, centring on a large wooden Ganesh seated on a tortoise, is lined with paintings, including Krishnaraja Wadiyar sporting with the "inmates" of his *zenana* (women's quarter of the palace) during Holi.

St Philomena's Church

Located on the Bengaluru highway 1km north of the Maharaja's Palace, **St Philomena's Church** (daily 5am–6pm; free) is perhaps the most beautiful church in Karnataka and one of the finest in India as a whole. Built in 1840 in Gothic style, it features two magnificent 55-metre-high towers, reminiscent of Cologne Cathedral in Germany. A series of beautiful stained-glass windows show the birth of Christ, his baptism by John, the Last Supper and the Cruci-fixion. The altar bears a statue of St Philomena, a third-century saint from Greece; a reclining statue of her can be seen in the crypt.

Chamundi Hill

Chamundi Hill, 3km southeast of the city, is topped with a temple to the chosen deity of the Mysore Rajas: the goddess Chamundi, or Durga, who slew the demon buffalo Mahishasura. It's a pleasant, easy bus trip (#201 from the City Bus Stand) to the top: sit on the left side for the best views; the walk down, past a huge Nandi – Shiva's bull – takes about thirty minutes. Pilgrims, of course, make the trip in reverse order. The walk isn't very demanding, but by

Silk weaving in Mysore

As an important centre of silk production, Mysore has several silk factories, the most prestigious of which is the Karnataka Silk Industries Corporation's **Silk Weaving Factory** (Mon–Sat 10am–noon & 2–4pm) on HD Kote Road, 4km from the centre. Visitors are welcome and the showroom offers silk – mostly saris – at fixed but competitive prices. You will need a chit from the office to enter the complex; there are no conducted tours. The large factory, founded in the 1920s by the Maharaja of Mysore, runs in shifts signalled by wailing sirens, and consists of huge workshops filled with automated machines. You can see the silk being loomed, some batches with pure gold thread, before it goes into the dyeing process. The machine tenders are happy to explain the operation to you but, with the machines working flat out, you'll be lucky if you can hear a word over the deafening din. They also have a showroom at *KSTDC Yatri Niwas* hotel.

the end of it, after more than a thousand steps, your legs are likely to be a bit wobbly. Take plenty of drinking water, especially if you're walking in the middle of the day.

Don't be surprised if, at the top of the hill, which is dominated by the temple's forty-metre *gopura*, you're struck by a feeling of *déjà vu*: as one of the displays at the **Godly Museum** at the summit states, "5000 years ago at this time you had visited this place in the same way you are visiting now. Because world drama repeats itself identically every 5000 years." Another exhibit goes to the heart of our "problematic world: filthy films, lack of true education, blind faith, irreligiousness, bad habits and selfishness". Suitably edified, proceed along a path from the bus stand, past trinket and tea stalls, to the temple square. Immediately to the right, at the end of this path, are four bollards painted with a red stripe; return here after visiting the temples, when you want to take the path back down the hill.

Non-Hindus can visit the twelfth-century **temple** (daily 7am–2pm, 3.30–6pm & 7–9pm), staffed by friendly priests who will plaster your forehead in vermilion paste. The Chamundi figure inside is solid gold; outside, in the courtyard, stands a fearsome if gaily coloured statue of the demon Mahishasura. On leaving, if you continue by the path instead of retracing your steps, you can return to the square via two other temples and various buildings storing ceremonial paraphernalia and animal figures used during Dussehra. You'll also come across loads of scampering monkeys and the odd dreadlocked *sadhu*, who will willingly pose for your holiday snaps – for a consideration. The magnificent five-metre **Nandi**, carved from a single piece of black granite in 1659, is an object of worship himself, adorned with bells and garlands and tended by his own priest. Minor shrines, dedicated to Chamundi and the monkey god Hanuman among others, line the side of the path and, at the bottom, a little shrine to Ganesh lies near a chai-shop. From here it's usually possible to pick up an auto-rickshaw or bus, back into the city, but at weekends the latter are often full. If you walk on towards the city, passing a temple on the left, with a big water tank (the site of the floating festival during Dussehra), you come after ten minutes to the main road between the *Lalitha Mahal Palace* and the city; there's a bus stop, and often auto-rickshaws, at the junction.

Eating

Mysore has scores of **places to eat**, from numerous South Indian "meals" joints dotted around the market to the opulent *Lalita Mahal Palace*, where you can work up an appetite for a gourmet meal by swimming a few lengths of the pool. To sample the celebrated Mysore *pak*, a sweet, rich, crumbly mixture made of ghee and maize flour, queue at *Guru Sweet Mart*, a small stall at KR Circle, Savaji Rao Road, which is considered the best sweet shop in the city. Another speciality from this part of the world is *malligi iddli*, a delicate light fluffy *iddli* usually served in the mornings and at lunchtime at several of the downtown "meals" restaurants.

Bombay Indra Bhavan Savaji Rao Rd. Comfortable and popular veg restaurant that serves both South and North Indian cuisine and a range of sweets and ice cream. Their other branch on Dhanavantri Road is equally popular and also has an a/c section.

Dynasty *Palace Plaza* hotel, Sri Harsha Rd. Dark but appealingly decorated restaurant/bar serving Indian, Chinese and Western veg and non-veg dishes. The same menu is also available at the roof garden restaurant in the evening.

Lalitha Mahal Palace T Narasipur Rd. Sample the charms of this palatial five-star with an expensive hot drink in the atmospheric tea lounge, or an à la carte lunch in the grand dining hall, accompanied by live sitar music. The old-style bar also boasts a full-size billiards table.

Le Olive Garden Near the bottom of Chamundi Hill, 2km southeast of the city. A large, leafy garden restaurant serving tandoori, Chinese and Western dishes. Occasional live entertainment. Moderately expensive.

Moving on from Mysore

If you're contemplating a long journey from Mysore, the best way to travel is by **train**, usually with a change at **Bengaluru**. Six or seven express services and six passenger trains leave Mysore each day for the Karnatakan capital. The fastest of these, the a/c Shatabdi Express (#2008; daily except Tues 2.20pm; 1hr 55min), continues on to Chennai (7hr 10min); most of the others terminate in Bengaluru, where you can pick up long-distance connections to a wide range of Indian cities (see box, p276). **Reservations** can be made at Mysore's computerized booking hall inside the station (Mon–Sat 8am–2pm & 2.15–8pm, Sun 8am–2pm). The daily Mysore–Dharwad Express passes through **Hassan** (#6201; 8.40pm; 2hr) as does the Mysore–Dadar Express (#1036; Thurs 6.50am; 1hr 55min).

With the completion of the four-lane Mysore–Bangalore highway the journey to **Bengaluru** (every 10min; 3hr) is fairly comfortable. Most destinations within a day's ride of Mysore can only be reached by road. Long-distance services operate out of Central Bus Stand, where you can book computerized tickets up to three days in advance. English timetables are posted on the wall inside the entrance hall, and there's a helpful enquiries counter in the corner of the compound. Regular buses leave here for **Hassan** (3–4hr), jumping-off place for the Hoysala temples at **Belur** and **Halebid**, for Channarayapatna/**Sravanabelgola** (2hr 30min–3hr) and for **Hubli** (for Hospet/**Hampi**). Heading south to **Ooty** (5hr), there's a choice of eight buses, all of which stop at **Bandipur National Park**. Direct services to several cities in Kerala, including **Kannur**, **Kozhikode** and **Kochi**, also operate from Mysore. The only way to travel direct to **Goa** is on the 4pm or 5pm overnight buses that arrive at **Panjim** at 9am and 10am respectively. Most travellers, however, break this long trip into stages, heading first to **Mangalore** (7hr), and working their way north from there, usually via **Gokarna** – which you can also reach by direct bus (14hr) – or **Jog Falls**. Mangalore-bound buses and coaches tend to pass through **Madikeri**, capital of Kodagu (Coorg), which is also served by frequent buses (every 15–30min), most of which travel through the Tibetan enclave of **Bylakuppe**. For details of services to **Somnathpur** and **Srirangapatnam**, see the relevant accounts.

Mysore's long-awaited **airport** is scheduled to open at the end of 2008 but at present the nearest one is at Bengaluru. You can confirm and book Indian Airlines flights at their office in the KSTDC *Mayura Hoysala* (Mon–Sat 10am–1.30pm & 2.15–5pm; ☏0821/242 1846).

Parklane Sri Harsha Rd. Congenial courtyard restaurant-cum-beer garden, with moderately priced veg and non-veg food (meat sizzlers are a speciality). Popular with travellers and Indians alike, and there's a ladies and family balcony upstairs.

Pizza Corner BN Rd, near Harding Circle. Branch of the Bengaluru chain serving high-quality pizza in bright, plastic Western-style surrounds.

RRR Gandhi Square. A plain "meals" restaurant in front with a small but plush a/c room at the back which gets packed at lunchtimes and at weekends. Well worth the wait for its excellent set menus served on banana leaves, chicken biriyani and fried fish.

Shanghai 1487 Shivrampet. Fine Oriental food served in an elongated dining room. *Teppanyaki* dishes feature among the favourites.

Shilpashri Gandhi Square. Quality North Indian-style food, with particularly tasty tandoori (great chicken tikka) plus plenty of good veg options, including lots of dhals and curd rice. Serves alcohol.

Siddharth Guest House Rd. Very popular place serving great South Indian food, including lunchtime thalis. The adjacent a/c section (*Om Shanthi*) serves excellent North Indian cuisine with a range of tasty paneer dishes.

Around Mysore

Mysore is a jumping-off point for some of Karnataka's most popular destinations. At **Srirangapatnam**, the fort, palace and mausoleum date from the era of Tipu Sultan, the "Tiger of Mysore", a perennial thorn in the side of the British. To the southeast, the superb **Hoysala temple** of **Somnathpur** is an architectural masterpiece, while the little-visited hilltop Jain shrine at **Gomatagiri** is a veritable oasis of tranquillity northwest of the city.

If you're heading south towards Ooty, **Bandipur National Park**'s forests and hill scenery offer another escape from the city, although your chances of spotting any rare animals are quite slim. The same is true of **Nagarhole National Park**, three hours southwest of Mysore towards the Kerala border.

Srirangapatnam and around

The tiny island of **Srirangapatnam**, in the Kaveri (Cauvery) River, 14km north of Mysore, measures only 5km by 1km. Long a site of Hindu pilgrimage, it is named after its tenth-century Sriranganathaswamy Vishnu temple, which in 1133 served as a refuge for the philosopher Ramanuja, a staunch Vaishnavite, from the Shaivite Cholas in Tamil Nadu. The Vijayanagars built a fort here in 1454, and in 1616 it became the capital of the Mysore Wadiyar rajas. However, Srirangapatnam is more famously associated with Haider Ali, who deposed the Wadiyars in 1761, and even more so with his son, **Tipu Sultan**. During Tipu's seventeen-year reign – which ended with his death in 1799, when the future Duke of Wellington took the fort at the bloody battle of Seringapatnam – he posed a greater threat than any other Indian ruler to British plans to dominate India.

Tipu Sultan and his father were responsible for transforming the small state of Mysore into a major Muslim power. Born in 1750, of a Hindu mother, Tipu Sultan inherited Haider Ali's considerable military skills. However, unlike his illiterate father, he was an educated, cultured man who introduced radical agricultural reforms. His burning, life-long desire to rid India of the hated British invaders naturally brought him an ally in the French. He obsessively embraced his popular name of the **Tiger of Mysore**, surrounding himself with symbols and images of tigers; much of his memorabilia is decorated with the animal or its stripes, and, like the Romans, he is said to have kept tigers for the punishment of criminals.

The site

Tipu Sultan's Srirangapatnam was largely destroyed by the British, but parts of the **fort** area in the northwest survive, including gates, ramparts, arsenals, the grim dungeons (where chained British prisoners were allegedly forced to stand neck-deep in water) and the domed and minareted Jami Masjid mosque. At the heart of the fortress, the great temple of **Sri Ranganathaswamy** (daily 6am–2pm & 4–8.30pm) still stands proud and virtually untouched by the turbulent history that has flowed around it, and remains, for many devotees, the prime draw. Built at the end of the ninth century in Dravidian style and further developed by the succeeding Hoysala and Vijayanagar dynasties, the temple consists of three distinctive sanctuaries and is entered via an impressive five-storey gateway and a hall built by Haider Ali. The innermost sanctum contains an image of Vishnu, reclining on Adisesha, the seven-headed serpent, with the Goddess Cauvery at his feet, complete with lotus flower.

The former summer palace, the **Daria Daulat Bagh** (daily 9am–5pm; $2 [Rs5]), literally meaning "wealth of the sea", is situated 1km east of the fort and was used to entertain Tipu Sultan's guests. At first sight, this low, wooden colonnaded building set in an attractive formal garden fails to impress because most of it is obscured by sunscreens. However, the superbly preserved interior, displaying ornamental arches, tiger-striped columns and floral decoration on every inch of the teak walls and ceiling, is remarkable. A much-repainted mural on the west wall relishes every detail of Haider Ali's victory over the British at Pollilore in 1780. Upstairs, a small collection of Tipu Sultan memorabilia, European paintings, Persian manuscripts on handmade paper and a model of Srirangapatnam are on show.

An avenue of cypress trees leads from an intricately carved gateway to the **Gumbaz mausoleum** (daily 10am–5pm; free), 3km east of the palace. Built by Tipu Sultan in 1784 to commemorate Haider Ali, and to serve as his own resting place, the lower half of the grey-granite edifice is crowned by a dome of whitewashed brick and plaster. Ivory-inlaid rosewood doors lead to the tombs of Haider Ali and Tipu Sultan, each covered by a pall (tiger stripes for Tipu), while a tablet in Urdu records Tipu Sultan's martyrdom. The interior walls are also painted in striking tiger colours.

Practicalities

Frequent **buses** from Mysore City Bus Stand (including #313 and #316) and **trains** (on the Mysore–Bengaluru line) pull in near the temple and fort. Srirangapatnam is a small island, but places of interest are quite spread out; tongas, auto-rickshaws and bicycles are available on the main road near the bus stand. There are a couple of **accommodation** options should you wish to stop over. The KSTDC hotel and restaurant, *Mayura River View* (☎08236/252114; ➍), occupies a pleasant spot beside the Cauvery, 3km from the bus stand, while the smart and elegant *Fort View Resorts* (☎08236/252777, ⓦwww.fortviewresorts.com; ➏), set in its own grounds, is not far from the fort entrance.

Brindavan Gardens

Fifteen kilometres north of Mysore and 8km northwest of Srirangapatnam, the beautifully landscaped **Brindavan Gardens** (10am–10pm; Rs20) are a very popular excursion for domestic tourists. They are at their best in the evening (take mosquito repellent) when illuminated and the park's fountains are accompanied by music. There is also a small lake for boating. The gardens are sited next to the Krishnaraja Sagar dam, which was built across the sacred river Cauvery in 1932, creating a 130 square-kilometre reservoir. Taxis (around Rs450 return) and auto-rickshaws ply the route from Mysore, as does the city bus #365, or you can visit as part of the KSTDC tour (see p.278).

Gomatagiri

Eighteen kilometres to the northwest of the city near the small town of Bettadoor is the hill of **Gomatagiri**, where a monolithic five-metre-high statue of **Gomateshvara** stands gazing serenely over the surrounding countryside from atop a rocky granite outcrop. Small shrines litter the base of the outcrop and house footprints of the 24 Jain *tirthankaras*, from which steps hewn out of rock lead up the hill to the temple and eleventh-century statue. Also known as Bahubali, the son of the first Jain *tirthankara*, Gomateshvara is shown here, as he is in sites all over southern Karnataka, naked and in a state of deep meditation, with his arms limp by his sides. From the top there are views of Brindavan Gardens and the Krishnaraja Sagar dam in the distance. An idyllic spot among eucalyptus groves, Gomatagiri sees very few tourists except during the **Mastakabhisheka ceremony** around September, when the statue is anointed with a nectar of milk. The only other building here besides the hilltop temple is the Jain guesthouse where the welcoming caretaker-cum-priest lives; he will gladly open the temple for you.

Accommodation is limited to the very basic rooms of the guesthouse (❶), none of which have beds, so bring a mat if you're planning to stay. Bus #264 from Mysore's City Bus Stand gets you close to Gomatagiri. There are just five services a day (1hr) – the first at 6.30am and the last at 6.30pm. The bus terminates at a nearby village then after a short break heads back to Mysore.

Somnathpur ✓

Built in 1268 AD, the exquisite **Keshava Vishnu temple** ✓ (daily 9am–5pm; $2 [Rs5]), in the sleepy hamlet of **SOMNATHPUR**, was the last important temple to be constructed by the Hoysalas; it is also the most complete and, in

△ Hoysala temple sculpture, Somnathpur

many respects, the finest example of this singular style (see box, p296). Somnathpur itself is little more than a few neat tracks and some attractive simple houses with pillared verandas.

Like other Hoysala temples, the Keshava is built on a star-shaped plan, but, as a triple shrine, it represents a mature development from the earlier constructions. Staff can show you around and also give you permission to clamber up onto the enclosure walls to get a marvellous bird's-eye view of the modestly proportioned structure. It's best to do this as early in the day as possible, as the stone gets very hot to walk on in bare feet.

The temple is in the style of a *trikutachala* or "three-peaked hill", with a tower on each shrine – a configuration also seen in certain Chalukya temples and in the three temples on Hemakuta Hill at Vijayanagar (Hampi; see p.335).

Each shrine, sharing a common hallway, is dedicated to a different form of Vishnu. In order of importance they are Keshava in the central shrine, Venugopala to the right and Jagannath to the left. The Keshava shrine features a very unusual *chandrasila* ("moonstone") step at its entrance and, diverging from the usual semicircular Hoysala style, has two pointed projections.

The Keshava's high plinth (*jagati*) provides an upper ambulatory, which on its outer edge reproduces the almost crenellated shape of the structure and allows visitors to approach the upper sections of the profusely decorated walls. Among the many superb images here are an unusually high proportion of Shaivite figures for a Vishnu temple. As at Halebid (see p.295), a lively frieze details countless episodes from the Ramayana, Bhagavata Purana and Mahabharata. Intended to accompany circumambulation, the panels should be viewed in a clockwise direction. Unusually, the temple is autographed; all its sculpture was the work of one man, named Malitamba.

Outside the temple stands a *dvajastambha* (flag pillar) column, which may originally have been surmounted by a figure of Vishnu's bird-vehicle Garuda. The wide ground-level ambulatory that circles the whole building is edged with numerous, now empty, shrines.

Practicalities

There are no direct **buses** from Mysore to Somnathpur. Buses from the Private Bus Stand run to **Tirumakudal Narasipur** (every 30min; first bus 6am), from where there are regular buses to Somnathpur (20min). The road is terrible, and though it's only 35km, the journey takes two hours; you might consider taking a taxi or joining KSTDC's guided tour instead (see p.278). There's nowhere to stay near the temple and no restaurants – just a few stalls selling chai, biscuits and bananas. However there are a few cheap "meals" hotels at Tiramakudal Narasipur.

Tucked in the backwaters of a dammed section of the Cauvery, a further 25km southeast, the exquisite *Talakadu Jaladhama* **resort** (book through Bengaluru office ℡080/6565 3333, ✉priya@greynium.com; ⑨) offers secluded cottages, some with rooftop hot tubs and herb garden. Full board costs Rs2000 per person, plus tax, and yoga, meditation, sports activities and boating are available. The resort can be reached by direct bus from Mysore.

National parks around Mysore

Mysore lies within striking distance of three major wildlife sanctuaries: **Bandipur**, **Nagarhole** and Mudumalai, across the border in Tamil Nadu (see p.640) – all of which are part of the vast **Nilgiri Biosphere Reserve**, one of India's most extensive tracts of protected forest. The parks are once again fully open for tourism, now that the threat from Veerappan (see p.641), the infamous smuggler and bandit, has subsided since his death in 2004. A few upmarket private "resorts" on the edge of the parks and one or two tourist lodges give visitors the opportunity to experience the delights of an area renowned for its **elephants**. Forest Department accommodation at Bandipur (see p.291) and Nagarhole (see p.292) must be booked as far in advance as possible.

Bandipur National Park

Situated among the broken foothills of the Western Ghats, **Bandipur National Park**, 80km south of Mysore, covers 880 square kilometres of dry deciduous forest south of the River Kabini. Created in the 1930s from the local maharaja's hunting lands and expanded in 1941, Bandipur has a good

Wildlife sanctuaries around Mysore

In addition to Bandipur and Nagarhole (see p.289 & p.291), two lesser wildlife sanctuaries lie within striking distance of Mysore. The closer, some 2km southwest of Srirangapatnam, is the **Ranganathittu Bird Sanctuary** (daily 8.30am–6pm; Rs60 [Rs20]). It's a must for ornithologists, especially during October and November, when the lake, fed by the Cauvery River, attracts huge flocks of migrating birds. At other times it's a tranquil spot to escape the city, with boat rides (Rs25) available through the backwaters to look for crocodiles, otters and dozens of species of resident waders, wildfowl and forest birds. The easiest way to get there is by **rickshaw** from Srirangapatnam.

The **Biligiri Rangaswamy Temple Wildlife Sanctuary**, 90km to the southeast of Mysore and also easily accessible from Coimbatore in Tamil Nadu, lies in an unspoiled corner of the state inhabited by the Soliga tribe. Covering an area of 525 square kilometres, the deciduous forests spread over the picturesque Biligiri Rangaswamy Hills harbour wildlife including elephant, panther, tiger, wild dog, sloth bear and several species of deer. Despite the thick cover, the sanctuary is a bird-watcher's dream, with over 270 species, including the majestic crested hawk eagle. Accessible by bus via Nanjangod and Chamarajnagar, the sanctuary is being promoted by Jungle Lodges & Resorts, Bengaluru (see p.266). Their luxurious *K Gudi* wilderness camp at the sanctuary charges Indian visitors Rs1000 per person per night and foreigners US$65 for an all-inclusive stay, including elephant ride and forest walks. An interesting alternative is the *Attikan Fig Forest Ecolodge* (book via www.dreamcatcher.co.in; including meals), which offers a combination of colonial heritage, coffee plantation and wildlife viewing. Located on a ridge providing superb views, this long-established coffee plantation is a scenic two-hour jungle drive from the forest gate at Pulinjur. There are four large en-suite double rooms in two atmospheric, colonial-era cottages decorated with old photographs and complete with log fires; excellent fresh coffee is served. Advance bookings only are accepted, and transport can be arranged.

range of accommodation and well-maintained Jeep tracks. It is also one of the few reserves in India where you stand a very good chance of sighting wild **elephants**, particularly in the wet season, when water and forage are plentiful and the animals evenly scattered. Later in the monsoon, huge herds congregate on the banks of the River Kabini, in the far north of the park, where you can see the remnants of an old stockade used by one particularly zealous nineteenth-century British hunter as an elephant trap. You should also catch glimpses of *gaur* (Indian bison), spotted deer and langurs, though the park's small number of tigers and leopards are rarely sighted outside the core area, which is off-limits. Bandipur also boasts some fine scenery: Gopalswamy Betta, the highest peak in the region (1455m), is situated just 12km from the park reception centre and there are a series of well-marked trails inside the park, ranging from 6km to 26km in length, including a trek along the slopes of the Moyar Gorge.

Some visitors find the park disappointing as a place to view wildlife, however: the noisy vehicles laid on by the Forest Department to transport tourists around the accessible areas of the park don't really encourage the wildlife to hang around the tracks.

Practicalities

The **best time to visit** is during the rainy season (June–Sept); unlike neighbouring parks, Bandipur's roads do not get washed out by the annual deluge. By

November/December, however, most of the larger animals have migrated across the state border into Mudumalai, where water is more plentiful in the dry season. Avoid weekends, as the park attracts busloads of noisy day-trippers.

Getting to Bandipur by bus is easy; all regular KSRTC services to Ooty from Mysore's Central Bus Stand (14 daily; 2hr 30min) pass through the reserve (the last one back to Mysore leaves at 5pm), stopping outside the Forest Department's reception centre (daily 7am–5pm). There's a Rs150 [Rs50] **entrance fee**, plus Rs20 per camera.

The Forest Department's **bungalows** (❸–❹) can be booked through their offices at Aranya Bhavan, Ashokapuram (☎0821/248 0901), 6km south of Mysore, on bus #61 from the City Bus Stand or at Aranya Bhavan, 18th Cross, Malleswaram, Bengaluru (☎080/2334 1993); accommodation bookings can be confirmed at the Forest Department's reception centre in the sanctuary. Comfort varies from beds in large, institutional dorms to the "VIP" *Gajendra Cottages*, which have en-suite bathrooms and verandas. Up a notch or two from the Forest Deparment accommodation, upmarket options include: *Tusker Trails*, a resort run by members of the royal family of Mysore, at Mangala village, 3km from Bandipur (bookable through their office at Hospital Cottage, Bangalore Palace, Bangalore; ☎080/2353 0748, Ⓕ2334 2862; ❾), which has cottages, a swimming pool and a tennis court and organizes trips into the forest; and Jungle Lodges & Resorts' *Bandipur Safari Lodge* (☎080/2559 7021, ⓦwww .junglelodges.com; ❼–❽), which has twelve comfortable en-suite rooms with panoramic views of the surrounding hills (including Gopalaswamy Betta), a multi-cuisine restaurant and bar.

Unless you have your own vehicle or are booked on an upmarket hotel tour, the only **transport around the park** is the hopeless Forest Department bus, which makes two tours daily (6–9am & 4–6pm; Rs25). You may see a deer or two, but nothing more, on the half-hour **elephant ride** (Rs50) around the reception compound. **Car rental** is available at Gundlupet, 13km from the park entrance, but operators will try and charge a lot more than the official Rs500. You must exit the park before nightfall.

Nagarhole National Park ✓ Kabini River Lodge.

Bandipur's northern neighbour, **Nagarhole** ("Snake River") **National Park**, extends 640 square kilometres north from the River Kabini, dammed to form a picturesque artificial lake. During the dry season (Feb–June) the muddy riverbanks and grassy swamps, or *hadlus*, offer better chances of sighting gaur (Indian bison), elephant, *dhole* (wild dog), deer, boar, and even the odd tiger or leopard, than any of the neighbouring sanctuaries. The forest here is of the moist deciduous type – thick jungle with a thirty-metre-high canopy – and more impressive than Bandipur's drier scrub.

However, disaster struck Nagarhole in 1992, when friction between local pastoralist "tribals" and the park wardens over grazing rights and poaching erupted into a spate of arson attacks during which thousands of acres of forest were burned to the ground. The trees have grown back in places, but it will be decades before animal numbers completely recover.

Practicalities

Nagarhole is open year-round, but avoid the monsoons, when floods wash out most of its dirt tracks and leeches make hiking impossible; the best time to visit is at the peak of the dry season, between April and early June. To get here from Mysore, catch one of the two daily **buses** from the Central Bus Stand to **Hunsur** (3hr), 10km from the park's north gate, where you can pick up

Since colonial days when many rivers and lakes were stocked with trout to satisfy the needs of the angling fraternity, fishing has been a hugely popular pastime in India. And the biggest prize, found in many of the country's rivers, is the world's greatest freshwater game fish, the mighty **mahseer** – the largest caught of which weighed in at 55kg and measured 2m in length. Known as the "tiger of the river" and long revered for its beauty, strength and magnificence, the fish is named after Matsya, Vishnu's first fish incarnation, who according to legend rescued humanity during ancient floods through his great strength. It's not surprising therefore to find mahseer depicted on family crests.

Karnataka is home to India's prime mahseer stretches, and it is the sacred **River Cauvery** (Kaveri) that breeds the biggest specimens. Should you be interested in a world-record mahseer haul, contact Jungle Lodges & Resorts in Bengaluru (see p.266), who organize inclusive packages based at their "Fishing and Nature Camps" at Bheemeshwari and Galibore, midway between Mysore and Bangalore ($65 per day per person, plus $65 per day to fish. Cheaper packages ($40 per day) are available at *Doddamakali Camp*, 6km from Bheemeshwari, which is also run by Jungle Lodges. Alternatively you could try *Bush Betta Wildlife Adventure Resort* (book through their office at 3 President Chambers, 8 Richmond Rd, Bengaluru ☎080/5112 5220, ✉bushbetta@vsnl.com), situated off the main Mysore highway at the confluence of the Cauvery and Arkravathi rivers. Accommodation, in comfortable cottages, costs an all-inclusive Rs2400 per person per day.

transport to the Forest Department's two **rest houses** (❷–❺). These have to be booked well in advance through the Forest Department offices in Mysore or Bengaluru (see Bandipur, p.291). Turn up on spec, and you'll be told that accommodation isn't available. It's also essential to arrive at the park gates well before dusk, as the road through the reserve to the lodges closes at 6pm and is prone to "elephant blocks". The Nagarhole **visitor centre** charges a Rs150 [Rs50] entrance fee plus Rs20 per camera. They organize elephant rides (Rs50) and schedule bus tours round the sanctuary (6–9am & 3.30–6pm; Rs50).

Other **accommodation** around Nagarhole includes the highly acclaimed and luxurious *Kabini River Lodge* (book through Jungle Lodges & Resorts in Bengaluru; ☎080/2559 7021, ⓦwww.junglelodges.com; ❾), approached via the village of Kharapur, 3km from the park's south entrance. Set in its own leafy compound on the lakeside, this former maharaja's hunting lodge costs a hefty $120 package per person per night, but includes meals and transport around the park accompanied by expert guides, with a coracle trip and elephant ride thrown in. It's impossible to reach by public transport, so you'll need your own transport, and you'll also have to book well in advance. Another upmarket option, though not quite in the same league, is the *Jungle Inn* at Veerana Hosahalli (☎08222/252781; ❾; bookable through their Bengaluru office ☎080/2224 3172), which is close to the park entrance and arranges wildlife safaris, though there is a very hefty surcharge for foreign visitors. Some tour groups prefer the luxury of *Orange County* (see p.308), near the town of Siddapura in Kodagu 75km to the north, despite the long drive.

Hassan and around

Unprepossessing **HASSAN**, 118km northwest of Mysore, is visited in disproportionately large numbers because of its proximity to the Hoysala temples at

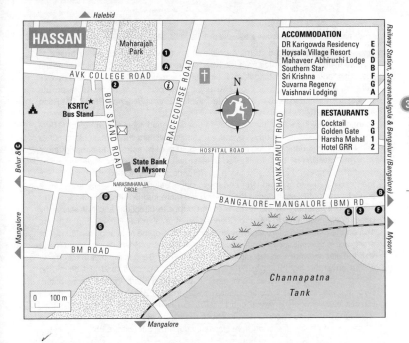

Map labels:

HASSAN

Halebid

Maharajah Park

AVK COLLEGE ROAD

KSRTC Bus Stand

Belur & ●

Mangalore

RACECOURSE ROAD

BUS STAND ROAD

State Bank of Mysore

NARASIMHARAJA CIRCLE

HOSPITAL ROAD

SHANKARMUTT ROAD

BANGALORE–MANGALORE (BM) RD

BM ROAD

Channapatna Tank

0   100 m

Mangalore

Mysore

Railway Station, Sravanabelgola & Bengaluru (Bangalore)

ACCOMMODATION

DR Karigowda Residency	E
Hoysala Village Resort	C
Mahaveer Abhiruchi Lodge	D
Southern Star	B
Sri Krishna	F
Suvarna Regency	G
Vaishnavi Lodging	A

RESTAURANTS

Cocktail	3
Golden Gate	G
Harsha Mahal	1
Hotel GRR	2

3

KARNATAKA | Hassan and around

Belur and Halebid, both northwest of the town, and the Jain pilgrimage site of Sravanabelgola to the southeast. It's a bustling little town with few attractions of its own but its reasonable accommodation options make it an ideal place from which to explore the nearby sights.

Practicalities

Hassan's **KSRTC bus stand** is in the centre of town, at the northern end of Bus Stand Road, which runs south past the post office to **Narsimharaja Circle**. Here you'll find most of the town's accommodation and also the State Bank of Mysore, which has an ATM and exchange counter. Local auto-rickshaws operate without meters and charge a minimum of Rs10. The friendly and informative **tourist office** (Mon–Sat 10am–5.30pm; ☎08172/268862) is on AVK College Road, less than five minutes' walk from the bus stand. The **railway station**, served by one express and three slow passenger trains a day from Mysore, is a further 2km down the road. The long-awaited route from Hassan across the Ghats to Mangalore on the coast is still closed due to the long-standing engineering work (long-standing-still, some locals might comment).

Accommodation

Considering the number of tourists that pass through, Hassan is certainly not awash with hotels. However there are a few decent mid-range options and one or two good budget places; most of the latter options are within walking distance of the bus stand, around Narsimharaja Circle. Wherever you intend to stay it's worth calling in advance as most hotels tend to fill up by early evening.

Hassan is well connected to most points in southwest Karnataka, with **buses** to Mysore every fifteen minutes from the KSRTC bus stand. Hassan lies midway on the main bus route between Mangalore (180km) and Bangalore (187km), serviced by very frequent KSRTC buses, occasional luxury buses, plus more comfortable private buses, such as those run by Vijayananda Travels, *Suvarna Regency*, PB 97, BM Road (☎08172/265807), which runs the private VRL service.

Apart from taking a tour, the only way to see Sravanabelgola (53km), Belur (37km) and Halebid (30km) in one day is by car, which some visitors share; most of the hotels can fix this up (around Rs1000 per day or Rs5.50 per kilometre up to a maximum of 250km). Travelling by bus, you'll need at least two days. **Belur** and **Halebid** can be comfortably covered in one day, along good roads; it's best to take the first (6am) of the hourly buses to Halebid (1hr) and move on to Belur (30min; 16km), from where services back to Hassan during the evening are more frequent (6.30am–6.15pm; 1hr 10min). **Sravanabelgola**, however, is in the opposite direction, and not served by direct buses; you have to head to Channarayapatna (aka "CR Patna"; from 6.30am; 1hr) on the main Bengaluru highway and pick up one of the regular buses (30min) or any number of minibuses from there. If you want to get to Sravanabelgola in time to visit the site and move on the same day (to Mysore or Bengaluru), aim to catch one of the private luxury buses to Bengaluru that leave from the road just below the *Vaishnavi Lodge* before dawn (5.30–6am); they all stop briefly in Channarayapatna. Bear in mind, too, that there are places to stay in both Belur and Halebid; arrive in Hassan early enough, and you can travel on to the temple towns before nightfall, although you should phone ahead to check rooms are available.

For more on public transport from Hassan, see "Travel details", p.362.

DR Karigowda Residency BM Rd, 1km from the railway station ☎08172/264506. Immaculate budget hotel – friendly, comfortable and great value. Some a/c rooms, and single occupancy rates. ②–③

Hoysala Village Resort Belur Rd, 8km northwest of the centre ☎08172/256764, ⓦwww.trailsindia.com. Luxury cottages in a peaceful rural setting run by Orange County Resorts. It also has a fine multi-cuisine restaurant and the only pool in the area open to non-residents (Rs100 per hr). ⑧

Mahaveer Abhiruchi Lodge BM Rd, near Narsim-haraja Circle ☎08172/268885. Reasonable budget rooms (most with TVs and mosquito nets) and a veg restaurant, *Abhiruchi*. ②

Southern Star BM Rd, 500m from train station ☎08172/251816, ⓦwww.ushalexushotels.com. The smartest place in town, recently renovated to three-star status with all mod cons, plus a restaurant and massage parlour. Busking resident magician Babu is well worth a few minutes of your time. ⑤–⑦

Sri Krishna BM Rd ☎08172/263240. Large, moderately new hotel with some a/c rooms, though the spacious non-a/c rooms are a particularly good deal. The restaurant downstairs produces excellent South Indian cooking. ④–⑦

Suvarna Regency PB 97, BM Rd ☎08172/264006, ⓦwww.hotelsuvarnaregency.com. Swish, great-value place with a shiny marble lobby, comfortable rooms (some a/c), pool and health club and a garden restaurant. ④–⑥

Vaishnavi Lodging Harsha Mahal Rd ☎08172/263885. Hassan's best budget lodge, with big clean rooms (all with phone and TV) and a veg restaurant next door. Reservations essential. Turn left out of the bus stand, right onto AVK College Rd and it's on the corner of the first left turn. ②

Eating

Most of the **hotels** listed above have commendable restaurants, or you can take your pick from the string of cheap snack bars and thali joints outside the bus stand.

Cocktail BM Rd near Krishna. Quite new, multi-storey place with a ground-floor bar and terrace restaurant offering cheap veg and non-veg meals and a range of alcoholic drinks.

Golden Gate *Suvarna Regency*, PB 97, BM Rd. Plush restaurant and bar with a garden extension, and the best food Hassan has to offer, though the varied menu – including Indian, Chinese and Western dishes – is not cheap.
Harsha Mahal Below the *Harsha Mahal Lodge*, Harsha Mahal Rd. Simple veg canteen just 5min from the bus stand serving freshly cooked *iddli* and *dosa* breakfasts from 7.30am.
Hotel GRR Opposite the bus stand. Traditional, tasty and filling "mini-meals" served on plantain leaves, with a wide choice of non-veg dishes and some ice creams.

Halebid

Now little more than a scruffy hamlet of brick houses and chai stalls, **HALEBID**, 32km northwest of Hassan, was once the capital of the powerful Hoysala dynasty, which held sway over south Karnataka from the eleventh until the early fourteenth centuries. Once known as **Dora Samudra**, the city's name was changed to Hale-bidu, or "Dead City", in 1311 when Delhi Sultanate forces under the command of Ala-ud-Din-Khilji swept through and reduced it to rubble. Despite the sacking, several large Hoysala temples survive, two of which, the Hoysaleshvara and Kedareshvara, are covered in exquisite carvings. A small **archeological museum** (daily except Fri 10am–5pm; free) next to the Hoysaleshvara temple houses a collection of Hoysala art and other finds from the area.

The Hoysaleshvara temple

The **Hoysaleshvara** temple (daily sunrise–sunset; free) was started in 1141, and after some forty years of work was left unfinished, which possibly accounts for the absence of the type of towers that feature at Somnathpur. It is no longer known which deities were originally worshipped here, though the double shrine is thought to have been devoted at one time to Shiva and his consort. In any event, both shrines contain *shivalingams* and are adjoined by two linked, partly enclosed *mandapa* hallways in which stand Nandi bulls.

Like other Hoysala temples, the Hoysaleshvara is raised on a high plinth (*jagati*) which follows the star-shaped plan and provides an upper ambulatory; the *mandapas* are approached by flights of steps flanked by small, free-standing, towered shrines. Inside, the lower portions of the black polished stone pillars were lathe-turned, though the upper levels appear to have been hand-carved to reproduce the effect of turning.

Hoysaleshvara also features many Vaishnavite images. The **sculptures**, which have a fluid quality lacking in earlier work at Belur, include: Brahma aboard his swan-vehicle, Hansa; Krishna holding up Mount Govardhana; Krishna playing the flute; and Vishnu (Trivikrama) bestriding the world in three steps. One of the most remarkable images is of the demon king **Ravana** shaking Shiva's mountain abode, Mount Kailash. The mountain is populated by numerous animals and figures, and Shiva is seated atop with Parvati. Secular themes, among them dancers and musicians, occupy the same register as the gods, and you'll come across the odd erotic tableau featuring voluptuous, heavily bejewelled maidens. A narrative frieze, on the sixth register from the bottom, follows the length of the Nandi *mandapas* and illustrates scenes from the Bhagavata Gita, Vishnu Puranas, Mahabharata and Ramayana.

The Jain bastis and the Kedareshvara temple

About 600m south of the Hoysaleshvara, a group of Jain *bastis* (temples) stands virtually unadorned; the only sculptural decoration consists of ceiling friezes inside the *mandapas* and elephants at the entrance steps, where there's an impressive donatory plaque. The thirteenth-century temple of **Adi Parshwanatha**,

Hoysala temples

The **Hoysala** dynasty ruled southwestern Karnataka between the eleventh and thirteenth centuries. From the twelfth century, after the accession of King Vishnu Vardhana, they built a series of distinctive temples centred primarily at three sites: Belur and Halebid, close to modern Hassan, and **Somnathpur**, near Mysore.

At first sight, and from a distance, Hoysala temples appear to be modest structures, compact and even squat. On closer inspection, however, their profusion of fabulously detailed and sensuous sculpture, covering every inch of the exterior, is astonishing. Detractors are prone to class Hoysala art as decadent and overly fussy, but anyone with an eye for craftsmanship is likely to marvel at these jewels of Karnatakan art.

The intricacy of the carvings was made possible by the material used in construction: a soft stearite soapstone that on oxidization hardens to a glassy, highly polished surface. The level of detail, similar to that seen in sandalwood and ivory work, became increasingly freer and more fluid as the style developed, and reached its highest point at Somnathpur. Beautiful bracket figures, often delicate portrayals of voluptuous female subjects, were placed under the eaves, fixed by pegs top and bottom. A later addition (except possibly in the Somnathpur temple), these serve no structural function.

Another technique more usually associated with wood is the unusual treatment of the massive stone **pillars**: lathe-turned, they resemble those of the wooden temples of Kerala. They were probably turned on a horizontal plane, pinned at each end, and rotated with the use of a rope. It may be no coincidence that, to this day, wood turning is still a local speciality. Only the central shaft of each pillar seems to have been turned; in the base and capitals, a less precise, presumably handworked imitation of turning is evident.

The architectural style of the Hoysala temples is commonly referred to as **vesara**, or "hybrid" (literally "mule"), rather than belonging to either the northern, *nagari*, or southern Dravidian styles. However, they show great affinity with *nagari* temples of western India and represent another fruit of contact, like music, painting and literature, facilitated by the trade routes between the north and the south. All Hoysala temples share a star-shaped plan, built on high plinths (*jagati*) that follow the shape of the sanctuaries and *mandapas* to provide a raised surrounding platform. Such northern features may have been introduced by the designer and artists of the earliest temple at Belur, who were imported by Vishnu Vardhana from further north in Andhra Pradesh. Also characteristic of the Hoysala style is the use of ashlar masonry, without mortar. Some pieces of stones are joined by pegs of iron or bronze, or mortice and tenon joints. Ceilings inside the *mandapas* are made up of corbelled domes, looking similar to those of the Jain temples of Rajasthan and Gujarat; in the Hoysala style they are only visible from inside.

marked by a large entrance *mandapa*, is dedicated to the 23rd *tirthankara*, while the newer **Vijayanatha**, built in the sixteenth century and easily recognized by its predominant *manasasthamba* pillar in front, is dedicated to the *tirthankara* Shantinatha. The *chowkidar* at the Parshwanatha temple will demonstrate various tricks made possible by the carved pillars' highly polished surfaces; some are so finely turned they sound metallic when struck.

A further 400m east, there's a smaller Shiva temple, **Kedareshvara** (1217–21), also built on a stellate plan. Many fine images decorate the exterior, including an unusual stone Krishna dancing on the serpent demon Kaliya – more commonly seen in bronze and painting. The interior is closed due to structural instability.

Practicalities

Frequent **buses** run between Halebid (the last at 8.30pm) and Hassan. From Halebid you can also continue to Belur, from where there are more services back to Hassan (the last at 8pm). The private **minibuses** that leave from the crossroads outside the Hoysaleshvara temple take a lot longer and only leave when crammed to bursting.

The monuments lie within easy walking distance of each other, but if you fancy exploring the surrounding countryside, rent a **bicycle** from the stalls by the bus stand (Rs3 per hour). The road running south past the temples leads through some beautiful scenery, with possible side-hikes to hilltop shrines, while the road to Belur (16km) makes for another pleasant bicycle ride. **Accommodation** in the village is limited to the four–roomed KSTDC *Mayura Shantala* (☎08177/273224; ➋), opposite the main temple, which has comfortable doubles with verandas, and a four-bedded room – all should be booked in advance. Food is available here and at the vegetarian *Shree Nandi* near the temple entrance, and there are also a few chai/snack stalls.

Belur ✓

BELUR, 37km northwest of Hassan, on the banks of the Yagachi, was the Hoysala capital – prior to Halebid – during the eleventh and twelfth centuries. Still in use, the **Chennakeshava temple** (7.30am–8.30pm) is a fine and early example of the singular Hoysala style (see opposite). The temple was built by King Vishnuvardhana in 1117 to celebrate his conversion from Jainism, victory over Chola forces at Talakad and independence from the Chalukyas. Today, its grey-stone *gopura* soars above a small, bustling market town – a popular pilgrimage site from October to December, when busloads of Ayappan devotees stream through en route to Sabarimala (see p.437). The **car festival** held around March or April takes place over twelve days and has a pastoral feel, attracting farmers from the surrounding countryside, who conduct a bullock-cart procession through the streets to the temple. If you have time to linger, Belur, with marginally better facilities than those found at Halebid, is a far better place to base yourself in order to explore the Hoysala region.

Built on a star-shaped plan, Chennakeshava stands in a huge walled courtyard, surrounded by smaller shrines and columned *mandapa* hallways. Lacking any form of superstructure, and terminating at the first floor, it has the appearance of having a flat roof. If it ever had a tower, it would have disappeared by the Vijayanagar period (sixteenth century); above the cornice, a plain parapet, presumably added at the same time as the east entrance *gopura*, shows a typically Vijayanagar Islamic influence. Both the sanctuary and *mandapa* are raised on the usual plinth (*jagati*). Double flights of steps, flanked by minor towered shrines, afford entry to the *mandapa* on three sides; this hallway was originally open, but in the 1200s pierced stone screens carved with geometric designs and scenes from the Puranas were inserted between the lathe-turned pillars. The main shrine opens four times a day for worship (8.30–10am, 11am–1pm, 2.30–5pm & 6.30–8.30pm) and it's worth considering using one of the guides who offer their services at the gates (around Rs 50) to explain the intricacies of the carvings.

The quantity of **sculptural decoration**, if less mature than in later Hoysala temples, is staggering. Carvings on the plinth and lower walls, in successive and continuous bands, start at the bottom with depictions of elephants, followed by garlands and arches with lion heads. As you progress, the carvings portray stylized plants with dancing figures, and then birds and animals with pearl garlands. Projecting niches contain male and female figures and seated *yakshas*, or spirits; miniature pillars are sculpted with female figures dressing or dancing; and the miniature temple towers are interspersed with dancers. Above the screens, a series of 42 figures, added later, shows celestial nymphs hunting, playing music, dancing and beautifying themselves.

Columns inside, each unique, feature extraordinarily detailed carving, with more than a hundred deities on the central **Narasimha pillar**. The inner sanctum contains a black image of Chennakeshava, a form of Krishna who holds a conch (*shankha*, in the upper right hand), discus (*chakra*, upper left), lotus (*padma*, lower right) and mace (*gada*, lower left). He is flanked by consorts Shri Devi and Bhudevi. Within the same enclosure, the **Kappe Channigaraya temple** has some finely carved niche images and a depiction of Narasimha (Vishnu as man-lion) killing the demon Hiranyakashipu. Further west, fine sculptures in the smaller **Viranarayana** shrine include a scene from the Mahabharata of Bhima killing the demon Bhaga.

Practicalities

Buses from Hassan and Halebid pull into the small bus stand in the middle of town, ten-minutes' walk along the main street from the temple; some through buses don't bother to pull into the bus stand but stop on the highway next to it. There are auto-rickshaws available, but a good way to explore the area, including Halebid, is to rent a **bicycle** (Rs3 per hour) from one of the stalls by the bus stand. The **tourist office** (Mon–Sat 10am–5.30pm), located within the KSTDC *Mayuri Velapuri* compound near the temple, has all the bus times and other useful local information.

The KSTDC *Mayuri Velapuri* (☎08177/222209; ❸) is the best **place to stay**, with clean, airy, good-sized rooms in its new block. The two dorms are rarely occupied (Rs75 per bed), other than between March and May, when the hotel tends to be block-booked by pilgrims. A couple of minutes' walk towards the temple, the *Sumukha Residency* (☎08177/222181; ❸–❹) has clean rooms and a pure veg restaurant, while the *Vishnu Residency* (☎08177/223011; ❹), 150m from Kempe Gowda Circle, offers spacious rooms, both a/c and non-a/c, and also offers decent pure veg food. Around the bus stand, the *Vishnu Lodge* (☎08177/222263; ❶–❷), 100m down the Halebid road above a restaurant and sweet shop, is the best bet, with spacious rooms (some with TV), though the en-suite bathrooms are tiny and hot water is only available in the mornings. Basic budget accommodation is available at *Sri Raghavendra* (❶), 50m to the right of the temple entrance. The rooms are grubby but room 1 has a small balcony overlooking the temple and all the action.

A good **place to eat** is at KSTDC *Mayuri Velapuri*'s spacious and airy restaurant, but the menu is fairly limited, though there are a few other options, mainly located beneath hotels strung along the main road. There are a few other restaurants along the main road belonging to the hotels; the *Vishnu Residency* restaurant serves fine masala dosas and is a good place for breakfast. If you have a weakness for Indian sweets, the adjacent *Poonam's* can sort you out.

Sravanabelgola

The sacred Jain site of **SRAVANABELGOLA**, 49km southeast of Hassan and 93km north of Mysore, consists of two hills and a large tank. On one of the hills, **Indragiri** (also known as Vindhyagiri), stands an extraordinary eighteen-metre-high monolithic statue of a naked male figure, **Gomateshvara**. Said to be the largest free-standing sculpture in India, this tenth-century colossus, visible for miles around, as well as the nearby *bastis* (Jain temples), make Sravanabelgola a key pilgrimage centre, though surprisingly few Western travellers find their way out here. Spend a night or two in the village, however, and you can climb Indragiri Hill before dawn to enjoy the serene spectacle of the sun rising over the sugar-cane fields and outcrops of lumpy granite that litter the surrounding plains – an unforgettable sight.

Sravanabelgola is linked in tradition with the Mauryan emperor Chandra-gupta, who is said to have starved himself to death on the second hill in around 300 BC, in accordance with a Jain practice. The hill was renamed **Chandragiri**, marking the arrival of Jainism in southern India. At the same time, a controversy regarding the doctrines of Mahavira, the last of the 24 Jain **tirthankaras** (literally "crossing-makers", who assist the aspirant to cross the "ocean of rebirth"), split Jainism into two separate branches. *Svetambara*, "white-clad" Jains, are more common in North India, while *digambara*, "sky-clad", are usually associated with the south. Truly ascetic *digambara* devotees go naked, though few do so away from sacred sites.

All the *tirthankaras* are represented as naked figures, differentiated only by their individual attributes: animals, inanimate objects (such as a conch shell), or symbols (such as the swastika). Each of the 24 is also attached to a particular *yaksha* (male) or *yakshi* (female) spirit; such spirits are also evident in Mahayana Buddhism, suggesting a strand of belief with extremely ancient origins. *Tirthankaras* are represented either sitting cross-legged in meditation – resembling images of the Buddha, save for their nakedness – or *kayotsarga*, "body upright", where the figure stands impassive; here Gomateshvara stands in the latter, more usual, posture.

The monuments at Sravanabelgola probably date from no earlier than the tenth century, when a General Chamundaraya is said to have visited Chandragiri in

Gomateshvara and Mahamastakabhisheka

Gomateshvara, or Bahubali, who was the son of the legendary King Rishabdev of Ayodhya (better known as Adinath, the first *tirthankara*), had a row with his elder brother, Bharat, over their inheritance. After a fierce fight, he lifted his brother above his head, and was about to throw him to the ground when he was gripped by remorse. Gently setting Bharat down, Gomateshvara resolved to reject the world of greed, jealousy and violence by meditating until he achieved *moksha*, release from attachment and rebirth. This he succeeded in doing, even before his father.

As a *kevalin*, Gomateshvara had achieved **kevalajnana**, or "sole knowledge", acquired through solitude, austerity and meditation. While engaged in this non-activity, he stood "body upright" in a forest. So motionless was he that ants built their nest at his feet, snakes coiled happily around his ankles, and creepers began to grow up his legs.

Every twelve years, at an auspicious astrological conjunction of certain planets, the Gomateshvara statue is ritually anointed in the **Mahamastakabhisheka ceremony** – this last took place in late 2005, and the next ceremony will be in 2017. The process lasts for several days, culminating on the final morning when 1008 *kalashas* (pots) of "liberation water", each with a coconut and mango leaves tied together by coloured thread, are arranged before the statue in a sacred diagram (*mandala*), on ground strewn with fresh paddy. A few priests climb scaffolding, erected around Gomateshvara, to bathe him in milk and ghee. After this first bath, prayers are offered. Then, to the accompaniment of temple musicians and the chanting of sacred texts, a thousand priests climb the scaffold to bathe the image in auspicious unguents, including the water of holy rivers, sandalwood paste, cane juice, saffron and milk, along with flowers and jewels.

search of a Mauryan statue of Gomateshvara. Failing to find it, he decided to have one made. From the top of Chandragiri he fired an arrow across to Indragiri Hill; where the arrow landed, he had a new Gomateshvara sculpted from a single rock.

Indragiri Hill

Gomateshvara is approached from the tank between the two hills by 620 steps, cut into the granite of **Indragiri Hill**, which pass numerous rock inscriptions on the way up to a walled enclosure. Shoes must be deposited at the stall to the left of the steps, and you can leave bags at the site office nearby. Anyone unable to climb the steps can be carried up by a chair known as a *dholi*. Take plenty of water, especially on a hot day, as there is none available on the hill. Entered through a small wagon-vaulted *gopura*, the **temple** is of the type known as *betta*, which, instead of the usual *garbha griha* sanctuary, consists of an open courtyard enclosing the massive sculpture. Figures and shrines of all the *yaksha* and *yakshi* spirits stand inside the crenellated wall, but the towering figure of Gomateshvara dominates. With his elongated arms and exaggeratedly wide shoulders, his proportions are decidedly non-naturalistic. The sensuously smooth surface of the white granite "trap" rock is finely carved, particularly the hands, hair and serene face. As in legend (see box, p.299), anthills and snakes sit at his feet and creepers appear to grow on his limbs.

Bhandari Basti and monastery (math)

The road east from the foot of the steps at Chandragiri leads to two interesting Jain buildings in town. To the right, the **Bhandari Basti** (1159), housing a shrine with images of the 24 *tirthankaras*, was built by Hullamaya, treasurer of the Hoysala Raja Narasimha. A high wall encloses the temple, forming a plain ambulatory which contains a well. Two *mandapa* hallways, where naked *digambara* Jains may sometimes be seen discoursing with devotees clad in white, lead to the shrine at the back. Pillars in the outer *mandapa* feature carvings of female musicians, while mythical beasts adorn the entrance to the inner, *navaranga*, hallway.

At the end of the street, the **math** (monastery) was the residence of Sravanabelgola's senior *acharya*, or guru. Thirty male and female monks, who also "go wandering in every direction", are attached to the *math*; normally a member of staff will be happy to show you around. Among the rare palm-leaf manuscripts in the library, some more than a millennium old, are works on mathematics and geography, and the *Mahapurana*, hagiographies of the *tirthankaras*. Next door, a covered, walled courtyard contains a number of shrines; the entrance is elaborately decorated with embossed brass designs of *yali* mythical beasts, elephants, a two-headed eagle and an image of Parshvanath, the 23rd *tirthankara*, shown here as Padmavati. Inside, the courtyard is edged by a high platform on three sides, on which a chair is placed for the *acharya*. A collection of tenth-century bronze *tirthankara* images is housed here, and vibrant murals detail the various lives of Parshvanath. The hills where the *tirthankaras* stood to gain *moksha* are represented in a model, somewhat resembling a jelly mould, with tacked-on footprints.

Chandragiri Hill

Leaving your shoes with the keeper at the bottom, take the rock-cut steps to the top of the smaller **Chandragiri Hill**. Miraculously, the sound of radios and rickshaws down below soon disappears. Fine views stretch south to Indragiri and, from the north on the far side, across to a river, paddy and sugar-cane fields, palms and the village of **Jinanathapura**, where there's another ornate Hoysala temple, the Shantishvara *basti*.

Rather than a single large shrine, as at Indragiri, Chandragiri holds a group of *bastis* in late Chalukya Dravidian style, within a walled enclosure. Caretakers will take you around and open up the closed shrines. Save for pilasters and elaborate parapets, all the temples have plain exteriors. Named after its patron, the tenth-century **Chamundaraya temple** is the largest of the group, dedicated to Parshvanath. Inside the twelfth-century **Chandragupta temple**, superb carved panels in a small shrine tell the story of Chandragupta and his teacher Bhadrabahu. Traces of painted geometric designs survive and the pillars feature detailed carving. Elsewhere in the enclosure stands a 24-metre-high *manast-ambha*, or "pillar of fame", decorated with images of spirits, *yakshis* and a *yaksha*. No fewer than 576 inscriptions, dating from the sixth to the nineteenth centuries, are dotted around the site, on pillars and on the rock itself.

Practicalities

Sravanabelgola, along with Belur and Halebid, features on **tours** from Bengaluru and Mysore (see box, p266 & p.278). However, if you want to look around at a civilized pace, it's best to come independently (see box, p294). The **tourist office** (Mon–Sat 10am–5.30pm; ☎08176/657254), at the bottom of the steps, has little to offer and the management committee office next door only serves to collect donations and hand out tickets for the *dholis*.

For **accommodation**, head for the numerous *dharamshalas*, situated in a large compound with pleasant gardens and courtyards, and all managed by the temple. To get there, turn left out of the bus stand and walk past the clock tower; the compound is on your left. Make for the 24-hour accommodation office (☎08176/657258), which is located 100m down the drive on the left. You will be allocated one of their simple, scrupulously clean rooms, most of which have their own bathrooms and sit-outs (❷; there are also three- and six-bed rooms). *Hotel Raghu*, opposite the main tank, near the foot of the hill is the best of the many small local **restaurants**.

Crisscrossed by winding back roads, the idyllic (and mostly flat) countryside around Sravanabelgola is perfect cycling terrain. **Bicycles** can be hired at Saleem Cycle Shop (9am–7pm; Rs4 per hour), on Masjid Road, opposite the northeast corner of the tank or stalls on the main road. If you're returning to Hassan, you'll have to head to **Channarayapatna**, aka "CR Patna", by bus or in one of the shared vans that regularly ply the route and depart only when bursting; change at CR Patna for a bus to Hassan.

Kodagu (Coorg)

The hill region of **Kodagu**, formerly known as **Coorg**, lies 100km west of Mysore in the Western Ghats, its eastern fringes merging with the Mysore Plateau. Comprising rugged mountain terrain interspersed with cardamom jungle, coffee plantations and acres of lush rice paddy, it's one of South India's most beautiful areas. Little has changed since Dervla Murphy spent a few months here with her daughter in the 1970s (the subject of her classic travel-ogue, *On a Shoestring to Coorg*), and was entranced by the landscape and people, with their distinctive customs, language and appearance.

Today tourism is still very low-key, and the few travellers who pass through rarely venture beyond **Madikeri** (Mercara), Kodagu's homely capital. However,

The Kodavas

Theories abound as to the origins of the **Kodavas**, or **Coorgis**. Fair-skinned and with their own language and customs, they are thought to have migrated to southern India from Kurdistan, Kashmir and Rajasthan, though no one knows exactly why or when. One popular belief holds that this staunchly martial people, who since Independence have produced some of India's leading military brains, are descended from Roman mercenaries who fled here following the collapse of the Pandyan dynasty in the eighth century; some even claim connections with Alexander the Great's invading army. Another theory is that the Kodavas were originally from Arabia, having been pushed out by the early Muslims and made to flee into exile.

Whatever their origins, the Kodavas have maintained their unique cultural identity, quite distinct from the freed plantation slaves, Moplah Muslim traders and other immigrants who have settled here. More akin to Tamil than Kannada, their language is Dravidian, yet their religious practices, based on ancestor veneration and the worship of nature spirits, differ markedly from those of mainstream Hinduism. Land tenure in Kodagu is also quite distinctive, with taxation based on type of land and, unlike in some other traditional societies, women have a right to inheritance and ownership; they are also allowed to remarry. Kodava martial traditions are grounded in the family where, according to custom, one son was raised to work the land while another joined the army. Even today, they are allowed to carry weapons without licence.

Spiritual and social life for traditional Kodavas revolves around the **Ain Mane**, or ancestral homestead. Built on raised platforms to overlook the family land, these large, detached houses, with their beautiful carved wood doors and beaten-earth floors, generally have four wings and courtyards to accommodate various branches of the extended family, as well as shrine rooms, or **Karona Kalas**, dedicated to the clan's most important forebears. Key religious rituals and rites of passage are always conducted in the Ain Mane, rather than the local temple. However, you could easily travel through Kodagu without ever seeing one, as they are invariably away from roads and shrouded in thick forest.

You're more likely to come across traditional Kodava **costume**, which is donned for all auspicious occasions, such as marriages, funerals, harvest celebrations and clan get-togethers. The men wear dapper knee-length coats called *kupyas*, bound at the waist with a scarlet and gold cummerbund, and daggers (*peechekathis*) with ivory handles. Most distinctive of all, though, is the unique flat-bottomed turban; sadly, the art of tying these is dying, and most men wear ready-made versions (which you can buy in Madikeri bazaar). Kodava women's garb is even more stunning, comprising long, richly coloured silk saris, pleated at the back and with a *pallav* draped over their shoulders, enlivened by heaps of heavy gold and silver jewellery, along with precious stones. Women also wear headscarves, in the fields as well as for important events, tying the corners behind the head, Kashmiri style.

if you plan to cross the Ghats between Mysore and the coast, the route through Kodagu, swathed in lush **coffee plantations**, is definitely worth considering. Some coffee-plantation owners open their doors to visitors; to find out more contact the Kodagu Planters Association, Mysore Road, Madikeri (℡08272/229873). A good time to visit is during the festival season in early December or during the **Blossom Showers** around March and April, when the coffee plants bloom with white flowers, although some find the strong scent overpowering.

Though Kodagu is relatively undeveloped and "sights" are few, the surrounding countryside is idyllic and the climate is refreshingly cool, even in summer. An increasing number of visitors now come to Kodagu to **trek** through the unspoilt forest tracts that fringe the district (see box, p.305).

△ Kodava harvest celebration

The Kodava **diet** is heavily carnivorous, their favourite meat being pork: an important dish at festive occasions where it is often served as a dryish but rich and spicy dish known as *pandi curry*, but sometimes substituted by *nooputtakoli curry* made with chicken, and usually accompanied with a rice preparation, *tumbuttu pandi*. Their traditional breakfast, *akki otti* (rice chapatis made from a dough of cooked rice and rice flour), served with honey and *pajji*, a chutney, is far lighter, and the sweet *tambittu* should appeal to vegetarians.

Like all traditional Indian cultures, this one is on the decline, not least because young Kodavas, predominantly from well-off land-owning families, tend to be highly educated and move away from home to find work, weakening the kinship ties that have for centuries played such a central role in the life of the region. Today, they comprise less than one-sixth of the hill region's population. However, in recent years there has been a rekindling of Kodava pride, with calls for a state separate from Karnataka.

Futhermore, on the eastern borders of Kodagu on the Mysore Plateau, large **Tibetan settlements** around Kushalnagar have transformed a once barren countryside into fertile farmland dotted with busy monasteries, some of which house thousands of monks.

Some history

Oblique references to Kodagu crop up in ancient Tamil and Sanskrit scriptures, but the first concrete evidence of the kingdom dates from the eighth century, when it prospered from the salt trade passing between the coast and the cities on the Deccan Plateau. Under the Hindu **Haleri Rajas**, the state repelled invasions by its more powerful neighbours, including Haider Ali and his son Tipu Sultan, the infamous Tiger of Mysore. A combination of hilly terrain,

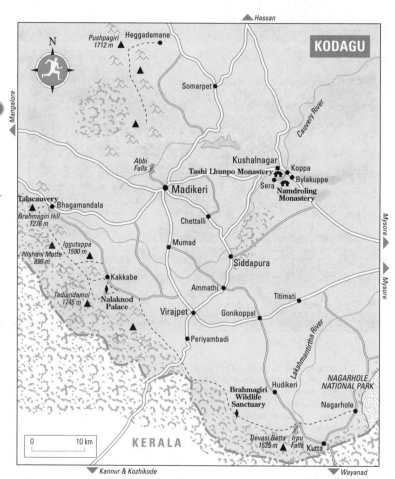

absence of roads (a deliberate policy on the part of defence-conscious Kodagu kings) and the tenacity of its highly trained army ensured that Kodagu was the only Indian kingdom never to be conquered.

Peace and prosperity prevailed through the 1700s, when the state was ruled by a line of eccentric rajas, among them the paranoid Dodda Vira (1780–1809), who reputedly murdered most of his relatives, friends, ministers and palace guards. The monarchy was more accountable during the reign of his son, Chickavirarajah Rajendra, known as **Vira Raja**, but eventually lapsed into decadence and corruption. Emulating his father's brutal example, Vira Raja imprisoned or assassinated his rivals and indulged his passion for women and spending. The king's ministers eventually appealed to the British Resident in Mysore for help to depose the despot. Plagued by threats from Vira Raja, the colonial administration was eager for an excuse to intervene; they got it in 1834 when the unruly raja killed his cousin's infant son. Accusing him of maladministration, the British massed troops on the border and forced a short siege, at the end of which Vira Raja (and what remained of his family) fled into exile.

Trekking in Kodagu

The finest of Kodagu's **treks** lie to the south of the region along the Keralan border, where an ancient path snakes through forests and across mountain ridges linking **Nagarhole National Park** to the sacred site of **Talacauvery** in the southwest; it takes about a week. From the entrance to Nagarhole, the trail passes by the Shri Ramneshwarna Temple, with a side-trip through forest to the Irpu Falls. It then runs to Nalaknod Palace, an old hunting lodge now used as a camp and for bee-keeping, and continues to the hill temple atop Nishani Motte before arriving at Brahmagiri Hill and Talacauvery (see p.310). From **Kakkabe**, a small town 50km to the southwest of Madikeri, near the Nalaknod Palace, there are two alternative routes to Talacauvery that join the main trail – one takes a more gentle, lower route while the other tackles challenging high ground over Kodagu's highest peak, **Tadiandamol** (1745m), and the peak of **Iggutappa** (1590m), where there are a couple of old temples. You are best advised to take a guide to help avoid elephants, and for finding the route through sometimes difficult terrain. Kakkabe is a good base, with excellent **accommodation** and food at the *Palace Estate* (T08272/238446;), where Mr A.P. Poonamma will assist in planning treks and negotiating guides. Several direct buses leave Madikeri for Kakkabe every morning from 6.30am.

Other possible treks in Kodagu include a climb to the hill of **Devasi Betta**, close to Irpu Falls, through the **Brahmagiri Wildlife Sanctuary**, for which you will need permission from the sanctuary office. Elsewhere, connecting trails from Talacauvery can be taken to the top of Kodagu's second highest peak, **Pushpagiri** (1712m), to the north of the region. Pushpagiri can also be climbed via the village of Heggademane to the north of Madikeri, and is accessible by bus.

Walking routes are best explored with the help of the handful of **specialist agencies**, some working out of Madikeri, such as Ganesh Aiyanna at the *Hotel Cauvery* (T08272/225492), or Coorg Travels, next to the *Rajdarshan Lodge* (T08272/225817). If you want to try to arrange your own itinerary, approach the Conservator of Forests, Deputy Commissioner's Office, at the fort (T08272/225708), for permission to enter the forests and to stay at their forest bungalows, and for a (mandatory) guide (Rs150–300 per day). Even if you intend to do it yourself, it's well worth talking to Ganesh Aiyanna and to the helpful Kodagu Wildlife Society, Chain Gate Road (T08272/223505), 2km east of the centre. Further afield, Clipper Holidays (W www.clipperholidays.com), with offices in Bengaluru (T080/2559 9032) and Cochin (T0484/236 4443), have been organizing forest treks in Kodagu for years, while Woody Adventures, based in Bengaluru (T080/2225 9159) specialize in a variety of outdoor sports, including trekking in Kodagu.

The best **season** to trek in the area is between October and March; April and May aren't quite as hot as some other parts of Karnataka, but avoid the monsoons between June and September, when the trails can get muddy and the leeches are rampant.

Thereafter, Kodagu became a princely state with nominal independence, which it retained until the creation of Karnataka in 1956. During the Raj, **coffee** was introduced and, despite plummeting prices on the international market, this continues to be the linchpin of the local economy, along with pepper and cardamom. Nowadays Kodagu is Karnataka's wealthiest region and provides the highest level of revenue to the state. However it does not reap the rewards, a fact which – coupled with the distinct identity and fiercely independent nature of the Kodavas – has given spark to the Kodagu freedom movement, known as **Kodagu Rajya Mukti Morcha**, which seeks its own statehood. Methods used by the KRMM include occasional strikes, known as *bandhs*, designed to close down all commercial activity in protest, as well as spreading the word through cultural programmes.

Madikeri (Mercara) and around

Nestling beside a curved stretch of craggy hills, **MADIKERI** (**Mercara**), capital of Kodagu, undulates around 1300m up in the Western Ghats, roughly midway between Mysore and the coastal city of Mangalore. It's a pleasant enough town, with red-tiled buildings and undulating roads that converge on a bustling bazaar, and is gradually attracting an increasing number of foreigners.

The **Omkareshwara Shiva** temple, built in 1820, features an unusual combination of red-tiled roofs, Keralan Hindu architecture, Gothic elements and Islamic-influenced domes. The fort and palace, worked over by Tipu Sultan in 1781 and rebuilt in the nineteenth century, now serve as offices and a prison. Also worth checking out are the huge square **tombs of the Rajas** which, with their Islamic-style gilded domes and minarets, dominate the town's skyline. **St Mark's Church** holds a small **museum** (Tues–Sun 9am–5pm, closed second Sat of the month; free) of British memorabilia, Jain, Hindu and village deity figures and weapons. At the western edge of town, **Raja's Seat**, next to KSTDC *Mayura Valley View*, is a belvedere, said to be the Kodagu kings' favoured place to watch the sunset.

Madikeri is the centre of the lucrative coffee trade, and although autorickshaws will take you there and back for around Rs200, a walk up through the forest and plantations along the road to **Abbi Falls** (8km) is a good introduction to coffee-growing country. From the car park at the end of the road, a

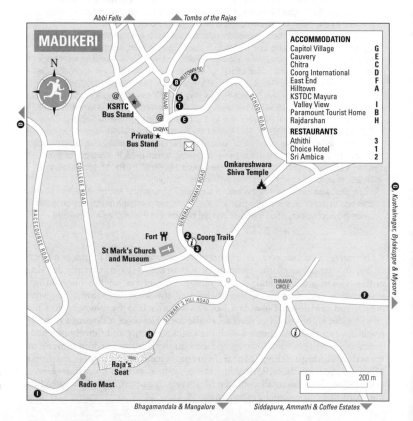

Abbi Falls ▲   ▲ Tombs of the Rajas

MADIKERI

N

ACCOMMODATION
Capitol Village	G
Cauvery	E
Chitra	C
Coorg International	D
East End	F
Hilltown	A
KSTDC Mayura Valley View	I
Paramount Tourist Home	B
Rajdarshan	H

RESTAURANTS
Athithi	3
Choice Hotel	1
Sri Ambica	2

KSRTC Bus Stand

Private Bus Stand

CHOWK

BAZAAR

HILLTOWN RD

SCHOOL ROAD

Omkareshwara Shiva Temple

GENERAL THIMAYA ROAD

COLLEGE ROAD

RACECOURSE ROAD

Fort
St Mark's Church and Museum

Coorg Trails

THIMAYA CIRCLE

STEWART'S HILL ROAD

Raja's Seat

Radio Mast

0   200 m

Bhagamandala & Mangalore ▼   Siddapura, Ammathi & Coffee Estates ▼

Kushalnagar, Bylakuppe & Mysore

gate leads through a private coffee plantation sprinkled with cardamom sprays and pepper vines to the bottom of the large stepped falls – most impressive during and straight after the monsoons.

Practicalities

You can only reach Madikeri by road, a scenic three-hour **bus** ride from Mysore, 120km southeast via Kushalnagar (some services go via Siddapura, which take at least an hour longer). Regular services, including deluxe buses, also connect Madikeri with Mangalore, 135km northwest. The KSRTC state **bus stand** is at the lower end of town, below the main bazaar; the private bus stand, for local village services, is 150m away, just up on the main street.

There are a few small local **information offices** including: Coorg Trails, next to *Athithi* restaurant on General Thimaya Road, who can organize homestays, trekking, plantation tours and bike rental (☎m93426 32813); Coorg Tourist Information Centre, opposite the Union Bank on the second floor of the Chetan Complex, Chowk (☎08272/223545, ✉coorgtrekking@yahoo.com), who provide similar services; and a small office just below Thimaya Circle next to the *PWD Travellers Bungalow* (☎08272/228580). See the box on p.305 for agencies that specialize in trekking. **Internet** access is available at Paramount Cyber Zone, near Chowk in the heart of the bazaar, and Cyber Land, opposite the bus stand; both cost Rs20 per hour.

Accommodation

Accommodation in Madikeri isn't usually hard to come by, except occasionally at the budget end of the spectrum. Most cheaper places are concentrated around the bazaar and bus stand.

Capitol Village ☎08272/225975. Six kilometres east of Madikeri, this is the best place to stay in the area, but you'll need your own transport. The "village" consists of a cottage complex surrounded by splendid flowerbeds on the edge of a coffee plantation. It's quiet, secluded and excellent value, with a lakeside dorm (Rs400). ❺

Cauvery School Rd ☎08272/225492, ☎225735. Below the private bus stand, this large and friendly place is almost hidden behind their excellent *Capitol* restaurant. ❸

Chitra School Rd ☎08272/225372. Best value in town, with neat, well-kept rooms, the slightly pricier ones with cable TV. There's an excellent non-veg restaurant-cum-bar downstairs. ❸–❹

Coorg International Convent Rd ☎08272/229390, ⓦwww.coorginternational.com. Ten minutes by rickshaw west of the centre, this is one of the few upmarket options in Madikeri, with comfortable Western-style rooms, a multi-cuisine restaurant, pool, ayurvedic centre, exchange facilities and shops. ❽–❾

East End General Thimaya Rd (aka Mysore Rd) ☎08272/229996. A large, plain, tiled-roof colonial bungalow turned into a hotel with a hint of character, but more renowned for its popular bar and restaurant. ❹

Hilltown Hilltown Rd ☎08272/223801, ✉hilltown@rediffmail.com. Decent-sized doubles and a few good-value singles, with a good restaurant on the ground floor serving Kodagu specialities, a pleasant garden and parking for guests across the road. ❹–❻

KSTDC Mayura Valley View ☎08272/228387, ⓦkstdc.nic.in. Well away from the main road, past Raja's Seat, this place has huge rooms, a restaurant serving beer and excellent views. Hail a rickshaw to get there, as it's a stiff twenty-minute uphill walk from the bus stand. ❹–❺

Paramount Tourist Home School Rd ☎08272/221880. Simple but neat rooms, marginally cheaper than most other places round the bazaar. ❸

Rajdarshan Stewart's Hill Rd ☎08272/229142. Modern and salubrious place just below Raja's Seat, with a landscaped garden, valley views from some rooms, and a good restaurant and bar. ❹–❻

Eating

The better-class hotels (and a few of the budget places) listed above generally have **restaurants**, and some also have bars. In addition to the places above, the

Choice Hotel on School Road serves breakfast items and a decent range of veg and non-veg dishes while up near the Fort, *Sri Ambica* serves wholesome veg snacks and meals.

Siddapura and around

The sleepy coffee town of **SIDDAPURA**, on the banks of the River Cauvery (Kaveri), lies 32km to the south of Madikeri in the heart of coffee country, and offers the chance to stay on a plantation – a delightful, if pricey, experience. Across the river, the **Dubare Reserve Forest** offers good short treks with the chance of seeing wildlife, including the occasional elephant; contact the Conservator of Forests in Madikeri (see box, p305) for more information and take a guide. Frequent local buses connect Madikeri and Siddapura.

The *Orange County* resort (T08274/258481, bookings via the Bangalore office T080/4191 1000, W www.trailsindia.com; 9), at Karadigodu, 4km from Siddapura, is the most luxurious place to stay in the whole of Kodagu. The resort lies at the edge of a wealthy estate and is approached by a small road that winds through lush plantations. Accommodation is in mock-Tudor cottages and villas, and there are three restaurants – vegetarian, multi-cuisine and a third serving some local Kodava specialities. There's a pleasant pool for residents only, and the priciest villas also have their own private pools. Activities on offer include treks and horse-riding and the resort also provides a base for visiting Nagarhole National Park. Book in advance as it's very popular with affluent Indians and foreign tour groups. Five kilometres from Siddapura, the *School Estate* (T08274/258358, W www.travelcoorg.com; 9) is another plantation homestay. Run by the Aiyapa family, this eighty-year-old plantation has just two rooms available for guests, and is set in extensive and beautiful lakeside gardens.

Other plantation options around Siddapura include two homely and friendly places just outside the small town of **Ammathi**. 🍴 *Sand Banks*, on the Polyacad Estate (T08274/252130, W www.sand-banks.com; advance booking only; 6), just 2.5km from town, has two cottages available. Each has two spacious high-ceilinged rooms, and all rooms have fireplaces; one cottage is made from coffee wood and features beautiful coffee-wood furniture. Next door, the slightly bigger *Alath Cad Estate* (T08274/252190, W www.alathcadcoorg.com; advance booking only; 6) has accommodation in two five-room buildings and a separate cottage; meals cost an extra Rs350 per person per day. Both estates offer a laid-back ambience, plantation walks and good home-cooked food. Regular buses run from Madikeri to Ammathi, via either Siddapura or Virajpet.

Tibetan settlements around Kushalnagar

Madikeri provides an excellent base from which to explore the **Tibetan settlements** that straddle the district border to the east. Co-operatives line the Madikeri–Mysore highway, and maroon-clad monks ride tractors to work the fields around the small but bustling market town of **Kushalnagar**, 30km from Madikeri, and the Tibetan villages, known as "camps", scattered around **Bylakuppe**, 6km away across the district border. Although the term "camp" suggests a sense of transition, the Tibetans who first settled here as refugees in the 1960s make up one of the largest settlements outside their homeland and have adapted remarkably well to a starkly different environment. There are now around eight thousand monks out of a total Tibetan population in the area of over eighteen thousand, mostly in the vicinity of **SERA**, 5km to the south of the main highway. Life here is certainly tough, and the settlements are clearly poor. The monastic tradition remains strong, however, and the magnificence of the monastic buildings is testament to the resilience and character of the many Tibetans who have been forced to make their home here. All four of the major Tibetan monastic traditions have a presence in the area, and the area's isolation makes it an ideal place for some students to do long-term Tibetan Buddhism practice.

Chief amongst the numerous monasteries that punctuate the landscape is the great *gompa* of **Sera**, a huge complex that acts as a university for the monks. At the centre of Sera is a large main hall built on three floors, designed to accommodate the vast congregation that gathers here for instruction and ceremony. Despite the colossal image of the Buddha Shakyamuni at the head of the hall, there's nothing especially attractive about the rather functional monastery, although the village has a buzz and the monks are welcoming. Another important monastery, **Tashi Lhunpo**, is closer to the settlement of Koppa, and lies 1km or so off the main road. Although much smaller than Sera it is significant as the seat of the Panchen Lama, Tibet's second most revered spiritual leader.

Halfway towards Sera from the main road is the Nyingmapa monastery of **Namdroling**, with its magnificent Golden Temple, situated in the middle of the peaceful monastery grounds. This huge and colourful prayer hall is decorated by two startling dragon columns and houses three enormous gilt Buddhas. Namdroling is very popular with domestic tourist groups and has become firmly established on the South Indian pilgrimage trail.

Practicalities

Kushalnagar is well connected by state and luxury **buses** to Mangalore (via Madikeri), Bengaluru, Mysore and Hassan, as well as to several destinations in Kerala. Bus times are posted in English. The only transport to the settlements from the Madikeri–Mysore highway is on the **auto-rickshaws** that regularly ply the route. Auto-rickshaws are available at the bus stand in Kushalnagar; the fare to Koppa is Rs30–40, or you can share one for Rs10 per head. Coming from Mysore by bus you need to alight in Bylakuppe, recognizable by the Tibetan farm cooperatives strung out along the main road, for Tashi Lhunpo (turn left off the main road just past the police station), or at Koppa, midway between Bylakuppe and Kushalnagar, for Namdroling and Sera.

The only **places to stay** around Bylakuppe are the monastery guesthouses. However, the whole area has recently been declared a "protected place" by the Indian government, which means that foreigners now officially require a **protected area permit (PAP)** to enter the area. While daytime visits are not always monitored, you are supposed to have one to stay overnight. Permits are free but can take up to eight weeks to process; download the application form from Ⓦwww.tibet.net/home/eng/pap. It's worth checking the current PAP situation by phoning ahead. If you do get one, in Sera try the friendly *Theckchen Khangsar Guest House* (Ⓣ08223/258135; ❶), *Sakya Guest House* (Ⓣ08223/252155, Ⓔsakyamonastery@yahoo.com; ❷) or *Tashi Lhunpo Guest House* (Ⓣ08223/254282; ❶). At Namdroling, the newish *Paljor Dhargey Ling Guest House* (Ⓣ08223/258686; ❷–❸) on the first floor of the shopping plaza near the Golden Temple is a clean, spacious and central option. The *Olive Restaurant* and *Dawa's*, just beyond Namdroling monastery on the Sera road, serves Tibetan **food** including *thukpa* (noodle soup), *momos* (stuffed dumplings) and fried rice. There are one or two fairly basic "meals" joints on the main highway at Bylakuppe, such as the *Green Land Hotel*; otherwise, head down the road to Kushalnagar.

There's plenty of accommodation in **Kushalnagar**, situated on the main highway and outside the PAP zone. The most comfortable of the **hotels** is the

Kannika International (☎08276/274728, ✆kannika@rediffmail.com; ④-⑤), set back from the main road near the bus stand, with its own garden, restaurant and bar, and airy rooms with satellite TV. The *Geetha Residency* (☎08276/274272; ④-⑤), on the main road, and the *Maharaja Lodge* (☎08276/273075; ④-⑤), near the River Cauvery at the eastern edge of town, are both new hotels with good, clean rooms. A cheaper option is the quiet *Mahalaxmi Lodge* (☎08276/274622; ②), down the lane alongside the bus station and just past the communications tower. Aside from the hotels, the pure-veg *Athithi* **restaurant** on the main road east of the bus stand does a range of excellent South Indian dishes, and there are meals places and snack stalls around the bus station.

Bhagamandala and Talacauvery

Another pleasant excursion from Madikeri is to the quiet village of **BHAGAMANDALA** (40km west), and from there to the sacred site of Talacauvery, the source of the holy River Cauvery. The hill scenery is superb, and you can opt to walk part of the way on blissfully quiet country roads. The 6.30am bus from Madikeri's private stand arrives in Bhagamandala at around 8am, giving you enough time to grab a good breakfast of *parathas* and local honey at one of the tea shops before the Talacauvery bus departs at 8.30am for the final 8km. If you stick around for a bit longer in Bhagamandala, you can visit the **Bhagandeshwara Temple**, situated where the Cauvery merges with two streams, the Kanike and the Sujyothi. It's a fine example of Keralan-style architecture, with tiled roofs and courtyards. Accommodation is available in Bhagamandala at the KSTDC *Hotel Mayura Cauvery* (☎08272/243145; ③) offering good-value doubles and a dormitory (Rs70 per head).

At **Talacauvery**, the bus stops on the slopes of Brahmagiri Hill by the entrance to the sacred tank and **temple**. During **Cauvery Shankrama** in October, thousands of pilgrims come here to witness a spring – thought to be the goddess Cauvery, known locally as Lopamudra, the patron deity of the area – suddenly spurting into a small well. To bathe in the tank at this auspicious time is considered especially efficacious for absolving sins. The belief is that if the spring dries up, all the rivers of southern India will dry up too. Whenever you come, you're likely to find wild-haired *sadhus* and bathing pilgrims, and the surrounding walls swathed in drying *dhotis* and saris. Two small shrines stand at the head of the tank, one containing an image of Ganesh and the other a metal *lingam* with a *naga* snake canopy. Steep granite steps to the right lead up to the peak of **Brahmagiri Hill**, which affords superb 360-degree views over Kodagu.

Mangalore and around

MANGALORE is one of the region's main transport hubs, with good links to Madikeri and the Kodagu (Coorg) hills to the southeast, the Hoysala and Jain monuments near Hassan, 172km east, and to Goa and Kerala along the coastal route. Many visitors simply pass through, but if you have some time it's worth exploring its Christian legacy and nearby beaches and temples.

Mangalore's strong Christian legacy dates back to the arrival of St Thomas on these shores in the first century AD. Its location at the confluence of two rivers, the Gurupur and Netravathi, and the presence of a long protective spit of land, made it an ideal natural harbour and consequently one of the most important ports of South India. Since the sixth century it has been known as

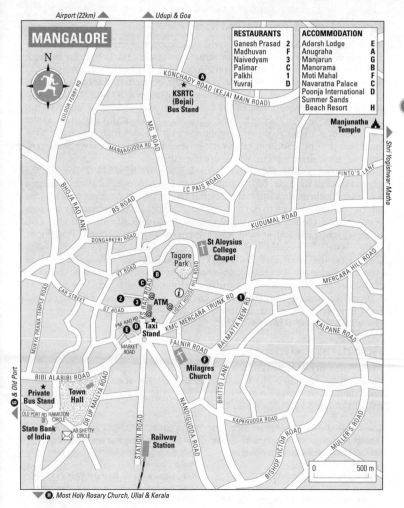

Airport (22km) ▲   ▲ Udupi & Goa

MANGALORE

N

RESTAURANTS
Ganesh Prasad	2
Madhuvan	F
Naivedyam	3
Palimar	C
Palkhi	1
Yuvraj	D

ACCOMMODATION
Adarsh Lodge	E
Anugraha	A
Manjarun	G
Manorama	B
Moti Mahal	F
Navaratna Palace	C
Poonja International	D
Summer Sands Beach Resort	H

KONCHADY ROAD (KEJAI MAIN ROAD)
★ KSRTC (Bejai) Bus Stand Ⓐ

KULOOR FERRY RD
MG. ROAD
MANNAGUDDA RD
BHOJA RAO LANE
BS ROAD
LC PAIS ROAD
KUDUMAL ROAD
DONGARKERI ROAD
VT ROAD
CAR STREET
GT ROAD
MULKY PRANA TEMPLE ROAD
PM. RAO RD
KS. RAO RD
LIGHT HOUSE HILL ROAD
KMC MERCARA TRUNK RD
BALMATTA NEW RD
MERCARA HILL ROAD
KALPANE ROAD
FALNIR ROAD
BRITTO LANE
MARKET ROAD
BIBI ALABIBI ROAD
OLD PORT RD
HAMILTON CIRCLE
AB SHETTY CIRCLE
STATION ROAD
NANDIGUDDA ROAD
KAPRIGUDDA ROAD
BISHOP VICTOR ROAD
MULLER'S ROAD
PINTO'S LANE

Manjunatha Temple

Shri Yogishwar Matha

Tagore Park
† St Aloysius College Chapel
Ⓑ Ⓒ ⓘ
Ⓐ ATM ⓘ ①
② ③ ⓐ @ATM@
Ⓔ Ⓓ Taxi Stand
★ Milagres Church Ⓕ

★ Private Bus Stand
Town Hall
State Bank of India ✉
Railway Station

Ⓖ & Old Port

0   500 m

▼ Ⓗ, Most Holy Rosary Church, Ullal & Kerala

KARNATAKA | Mangalore and around

3

a major source of pepper; the fourteenth-century Muslim writer Ibn Battuta noted its trade in pepper and ginger and the presence of merchants from Persia and the Yemen. In the mid-1400s, the Persian ambassador Abdu'r-Razzaq saw Mangalore as the "frontier town" of the Vijayanagar empire, which was why the Portuguese captured it in the sixteenth century. In Haider Ali's time, during the eighteenth century, the city became a shipbuilding centre. Nowadays, the modern port, 10km north of the city proper, is principally known for the export of coffee and cocoa (much of which comes from Kodagu), and cashew nuts from Kerala and Karnataka, as well as granite; the city itself is renowned for the production of *beedi* cigarettes. Mangalore's heady ethnic mix lives more or less in harmony, although in 1998 there were communal riots as sections of the city's large Christian community were attacked by right-wing Hindu fundamentalists.

Arrival and information

Mangalore's busy **KSRTC Bus Stand** (also known as the Bejai bus stand) is 2km north of the town centre, at the bottom of Kadri Hill. Private buses arrive at the much more central stand near the Town Hall. **Bajpe airport** (☎0824/225 4253) is 22km north of the city; to get into the centre take the Indian Airlines city bus, buses #47, 47B, 22 or 22A, or a taxi (around Rs400). The **railway station** is on the south side of the city centre; auto-rickshaws and taxis are available outside or it's about a ten-minute walk to Hampankatta, close to the amenities of KS Rao Road and Lighthouse Hill Road, which acts as the city's main transport hub. You can catch **city buses** and **auto-rickshaws** from here, although their drivers prefer not to use their meters.

The **tourist office** (Mon–Sat 10am–5.30pm; ☎0824/244 2926), on the ground floor of the *Hotel Nalapad* building on Light House Hill Road, is helpful for general information and bus times, but carries no information on trains, for which you'll need to go to the railway station. You can **change money** at Trade Wings, Light House Hill Road (Mon–Sat 9.30am–5.30pm), who also cash traveller's cheques, and at Wall Street Interchange (same hours), First Floor, Utility Royal Towers, KS Rao Road. The State Bank of India, on Hamilton Circle near the Town Hall, has an **ATM**, as does the CorpBank on KS Rao Road, opposite the *Mangalore International* hotel; there's also one at the *Hotel Poonja* complex. Mangalore's **post office** (Mon–Sat 10am–7pm, Sun 10.30am–1.30pm) is near both Hamilton Circle and AB Shetty Circle on PM Rao Road. For **Internet** access, try Access Browsing on Light House Hill Road or Cyber Drive Inn, KS Rao Road (Rs20/hr).

Accommodation

Mangalore's **accommodation** standards are forever improving; it even has a modern five-star hotel. The main area for hotels, **KS Rao Road**, runs south from the bus stand and has an ample choice to suit most pockets. You can also stay out of town by the beach in **Ullal**.

Adarsh Lodge Market Rd ☎0824/244 0878. Compact, reasonably clean en-suite rooms in a tall block, and fairly convenient for the Private Bus Stand. ②

Anugraha Konchady Rd, opposite KRSTC bus station ☎0824/221 5775. Clean, good-sized rooms in a large concrete block and very handy for the station. ③

Manjarun Old Port Rd, 2km west of the railway station ☎0824/666 0420, ⓦ www.tajhotels.com. Modern business hotel belonging to the Taj group. Some rooms have sea views, and all have a/c. Facilities include a travel desk, currency exchange, pool, bar, two classy restaurants and a 24hr coffee shop. ⑦–⑨

Manorama KS Rao Rd ☎0824/244 0306, ⓕ241 0887. A 65-room concrete block with large and very clean, if spartan, rooms (some a/c). Good value, though there are better central options. ③–④

Moti Mahal Falnir Rd ☎0824/244 1411, ⓦwww .motimahalmangalore.com. Large hotel with some a/c rooms, 24hr room service, pool and health club,

shops, currency exchange, travel desk, coffee shop and bar. The *Mangala* (non-veg) and *Madhuvan* (veg) restaurants serve Indian, Chinese and Western food. ④–⑥

Navaratna Palace KS Rao Rd ☎0824/244 1104. Preferable to its adjacent older sister, *Navaratna*, with better rooms (some a/c) for not much extra, plus two good a/c restaurants. ③–④

Poonja International KS Rao Rd ☎0824/244 0171, ⓦwww.hotelpoonjainternational.com. Comfortable rooms in a smart, mostly a/c, high-rise hotel with all facilities. Great views across the city from the upper floors. South Indian breakfast buffet is included and the *Yuvraj* restaurant is recommended. ④–⑧

Summer Sands Beach Resort Chota Mangalore, Ullal, 13km south of the city ☎0824/246 7690, ⓦwww.summer-sands.com. This excellent resort has a range of spacious cottages (some a/c) near the beach, a pool and a bar-restaurant serving local specialities, plus other Indian and Chinese food. Currency exchange for guests. Take bus #44A from town. ④–⑧

The colonial legacy

Throughout history, South Indians have displayed an uncommon genius for absorbing outside influences and adapting them to their own needs. New trade goods, politics, games, gods, technologies and – most discernibly – the English language, have all been introduced by colonizing powers, only to emerge from the Subcontinental masala mix with a distinctly Indian flavour. The other great South Indian talent is for preserving ways of life long after they may have disappeared from the places they originated. Coming across these quirky vestiges, preserved in the aspic of Indian tradition, is one of the great pleasures of travelling in the region: whether narrow-gauge trains chugging through the Nilgiri's tea gardens, cricketers in their whites on the maidans of central Mumbai or the gendarme-style képis worn by policemen in Pondicherry (Puducherry).

Forts and ports

▲ Portuguese church, Kochi

South India has been a centre of urban civilization for thousands of years, but the greatest of its modern port cities – Mumbai (Bombay), Chennai (Madras) and Kochi (Cochin) – were all founded as colonial trading posts. Fragments of the old forts that formed their original nuclei survive and, though half-buried under more modern accretions, still evoke the spirit of the early colonial period.

In Kochi, some of Fort Cochin's sixteenth-century stone-vaulted *palacios* and churches were standing when Vasco da Gama was a resident. Grander still are the Portuguese basilicas and cathedrals soaring above the palm canopy of Old Goa, further north. The vast European city that once enveloped them has dissolved without trace into the jungle, but streams of fervent Catholic pilgrims still flock to these churches – testament to the enduring legacy of the Jesuit missionaries who evangelized India's southwest coast almost half a millennium ago.

The main contributions of the British Raj to Indian architecture were not so much religious as military, municipal and commercial. Fort St George, whose sloping eighteenth-century walls preside over the beachfront in Chennai, encloses some of the oldest examples: stalwart Neoclassical mansions fronted by lawns and a very sober Anglican church, where a depressed young Robert Clive – one of the founding fathers of the Raj – once attempted to commit suicide. By comparison, the hybrid behemoths of Victorian Bombay (now Mumbai), built more than a century later, appear bursting with confidence. None better epitomizes the grandiloquence of empire than Victoria Terminus (now Chhatrapati Shivaji Terminus), still used by tens of thousands of railway travellers daily.

▼ Chhatrapati Shivaji Terminus (fomerly Victoria Terminus), Mumbai

Sahibs and snobbery

British exploration of the Western Ghat mountains was driven by the search for suitable land on which to plant tea and coffee. But it had the happy side-effect for those sweltering at sea level of revealing ideal places to escape the intense tropical weather. Up in the cool, fresh air of the mountains, homesick burra- and memsahibs could ride, hunt, ramble and sketch without fear of collapsing from the heat. Bungalows were built as hot-season boltholes, and swathed in rose bushes and ivy. Railway lines, racecourses and that most British of institutions, the Members' Club, followed in their wake, eventually coalescing into the hotbed of snobbery and sexual intrigue that would become the "Hill Station".

High up in the Nilgiris, **Ootacamund**, or "Snooty Ooty" as it was dubbed, became the archetypal hot-season capital of the South Indian Raj. These days, the town's former stiff-upper-lipped gentility is barely discernible under the brouhaha of modern holiday culture, though it's worth visiting for a ride on the Blue Mountain steam railway, whose ageing locomotives puff and wheeze their way up there from the Tamil

▲ Tea-pickers near Munnar

Nadu plains. For a taste of the empire's prewar twilight, you're better off crossing the border to **Munnar**, in neighbouring Kerala, where rolling tea estates are dotted with pretty little planters' bungalows, many of them converted into guesthouses with neatly clipped lawns falling away to valley views. Further north, within a few hours' train ride of downtown Mumbai, leafy **Matheran** is perhaps the loveliest hill station of all in the south, not least because it's the only one to have remained car-free.

▼ *The Verandah in the Forest*, Matheran

Cuisine

The exquisitely rich and varied flavours of Indian cuisine are appreciated across the West. Less well understood, however, is the European culinary influence on South India. Many of the region's best-loved foods were introduced by the Portuguese, including papaya, pineapple, cashews, guava, potatoes, tomatoes, pumpkin and – perhaps most significant – chillies. And in Goa, you

▲ Chouriço sausages, Goa

can still trace the connections between dishes eaten by the local population and those of their former colonizers. Freed from Hindu and Muslim dietary taboos, Goan Catholics love to eat both beef and pork – the latter in the form of spicy *chouriço* sausages, which are fried and stuffed into fluffy white Portuguese-style bread rolls, or *pao*. Vindaloo is another speciality of Indo-Portuguese origin, first prepared using the marinade of wine- (*vinho*) vinegar and garlic (*alho*) in which European sailors used to preserve meat on long voyages.

Predictably, the British contribution to South Indian cuisine is somewhat less distinguished. One dish however still finds favour, at least in the kitchens of Mumbai's dwindling, Anglophile Zoroastrian population: good old-fashioned custard.

The perfect brew

The most pervasive of all the British Raj's bequests to its former colony is without doubt tea. India is responsible for just over one third of global production, and around a quarter

▼ Chai-wallah

of that comes from plantations in the Nilgiri Hills in the south, which churn out between 180 and 200 million kilograms per year. Since the demise of the traditional export market in the former USSR in the 1990s, the bulk of it goes to domestic consumption in the form of CTC ("crush, tear and curled") – a lumpy black powder yielding a dark, flavoursome chai. South Indians like it brewed milky and sweet. Filling glasses from kettles raised to arm's height, chai-wallahs pop up wherever, and whenever, anyone might conceivably need a pick-me-up.

At the opposite end of the scale, the Rani of South Indian teas, reserved almost exclusively for export, is **Orange Pekoe**. Grown only in the highest estates of the Nilgiris, it comes in various grades, ranging from regular "OP" to the pricer "FOP ("Flowery Orange Pekoe") and, most expensive of all, "Super Fine Tippy Golden Flowery Orange Pekoe". At a tea auction in Las Vegas in 2006, a particularly desirable SFTGFOP sold for $600 per kilogram.

The city and beaches

Mangalore boasts an impressive array of churches, the origins of which date back to Portuguese times. The earliest, the **Most Holy Rosary Church**, south of Hamilton Circle and close to the old port, was founded in 1568, although the present building dates only from 1910. It houses an ornate wooden pulpit and a royal stone bearing the insignia of the Portuguese king. The grand **Milagres Church** on Falnir Road dates from 1680 and was built by Bishop Thomas de Castro. Boasting a fine facade, it contains a large shrine devoted to St Anthony of Padua and is believed to be imbued with miraculous powers. Romanesque **St Aloysius College Chapel** on Lighthouse Hill Road, built in 1885, has some fine frescoes depicting the life of St Thomas and Biblical scenes – the work of an Italian priest and artist, Antonio Moscheni. The chapel also houses some restored oil on canvas paintings.

At the foot of Kadri Hill, 3km north and served by numerous city buses, Mangalore's tenth-century **Manjunatha Temple** is an important centre of the Shaivite and Tantric Natha-Pantha cult, thought to be an outgrowth of Vajrayana Buddhism. Enshrined in the sanctuary are a number of superb **bronzes**, including a 1.5-metre-high seated Lokeshvara (Matsyendranatha), made in 958 AD and considered the finest southern bronze outside Tamil Nadu. To see it close up you'll have to visit at *darshan* times (6am–1pm & 4–8pm), although the bronzes can be glimpsed through the wooden slats on the side of the sanctuary. If possible, time your visit to coincide with **mahapooja** at 8am, noon or 8pm, when the priests give a fire blessing to the accompaniment of raucous music. Manjunatha's square and towered sanctuary, containing an unusual *lingam*, is surrounded by two tiled and gabled colonnades with louvred windows, showing strong affinity with the temple complexes further south in Kerala. Nine water tanks adjoin the temple. Opposite the east entrance, steps lead via a laterite path to a curious group of minor shrines. Beyond this complex stands the **Shri Yogishwar Math**, a hermitage of Tantric *sadhus* set round two courtyards, one of which contains shrines to Kala Bhairava (a form of Dakshinamurti, the southern aspect of Shiva and deity of death), Durga and the god of fire, Agni. Nearby, cut into the side of the hill, a tiny unadorned **cave** is credited with being one of the "night halts" for the Pandava brothers from the Mahabharata.

Ullal

If you're looking to escape the city for a few hours, head out to the village of **ULLAL**, 12km south. Around 700m from the main bus stand is the *dargah* (burial shrine) of **Seyyid Mohammad Shareeful Madani**, a sixteenth-century Sufi saint who is said to have come from Medina in Arabia and floated across the sea on a handkerchief. The extraordinary nineteenth-century building with garish onion-domes houses the saint's tomb, which is one of the most important Sufi shrines in southern India. Visitors are advised to follow custom and cover their heads and limbs and wash their feet before entering.

Most people visit Ullal however for its long sandy **beach**, backed by wispy fir trees and stretching for miles in both directions. It's a deservedly popular place for a stroll, particularly in the evening when families and courting couples come out to watch the sunset, but a strong undertow makes swimming difficult, and at times unsafe. You're better off using the pool at the excellent *Summer Sands Beach Resort* (see opposite), immediately behind the beach (Rs100 for non-residents). A further 2km past the *Summer Sands*, a banyan-lined road leads to the Shiva temple of **Someshwar**, built in Keralan style, overlooking a rocky promontory, and another popular beach which is subject to gangs of gawking youths.

Mangalore is a major crossroads for tourist traffic heading along the Konkan coast between Goa and Kerala, and from Mysore to the coast. The city is also connected **by air** to **Mumbai**, **Bengaluru** and **Chennai**. The Indian Airlines office is at Airlines House, Hat Hill Rd, Lalbagh (☎0824/245 1046) and the Jet Airways office at DS Ram Bhavan Complex, Navabharath Circle, Kodiabail (☎0824/244 1181). Air Deccan can be contacted at the airport (☎0824/225 4389), and Kingfisher through agents such as Four Wings (☎0824/244 0531).

By train

Services run north to Goa and Mumbai along the **Konkan Railway**. The daily *Matsya-gandha Express* (#2620) departs at 2.40pm, stopping in **Udupi** (1hr 45min), Madgaon in **Goa** (6hr 5min) and terminating at Kurla (LTT) Station in **Mumbai** (15hr 55min). However, there's a better choice of northbound train connections on the Konkan Railway from **Kankanadi**, around 10km north of Mangalore, as some trains to and from Chennai, Bengaluru and Hassan also pass through.

Heading south from Mangalore the service is quicker and more relaxing than the bus. Three to four services leave Mangalore station every day for **Thiruvanan-thapuram** via **Kozhikode**, **Ernakulam/Kochi**, **Kottayam** and **Kollam**. The fastest is the thrice-weekly *Maveli Express* (#6603; Mon, Wed, Fri), departing at 11pm and arriving at 12.30pm the next day. The most convenient however is the daily overnight *Malabar Express* (#6330), which leaves at 6pm, arriving in Thiruvananthapuram at 9.05am. Early birds may prefer the *Parasuram Express* (#6350), which leaves daily at 4.15am and arrives at 6.25pm.

For journeys inland to Tamil Nadu, the *Mangalore–Chennai Mail* (#2602) departs daily at 1.15pm travelling via **Palakaad** and Erode and arrives at **Chennai** at 5.25am, while the daily *Trichy Express* (#6868) departs at 6.40am and terminates at **Tiruchirapalli Junction** at 9.30pm. Conversion work on the line inland to Hassan for Mysore and Bengaluru is expected to resume at some point in 2007 after lengthy engineering works.

By bus

The coastal **bus** route from Mangalore up to **Goa** is increasingly being usurped by the Konkan Railway. There are now only two buses that leave the KSRTC Bejai stand daily, taking around 10 hours to reach Panjim. You can jump off at Chaudi (for Palolem) en route. Tickets should be booked in advance (preferably the day before) at KSRTC's well-organized computer booking hall (daily 7am–8pm), or at the Kadamba office on the main concourse. KSRTC also has a central office (daily 8.30am–8.30pm) on the ground floor of Utility Royal Towers, KS Rao Road. The Goa buses are also good for **Gokarna**; hop off at **Kumta** on the main highway, and catch an onward service from there. The only direct bus to Gokarna leaves Mangalore at 1.30pm. There are plenty of state buses heading north to **Udupi** and south along the coast towards **Kerala**, though it's easier to pick up the more numerous private services to those places.

For Mysore, Bengaluru and Hassan, you're restricted to the bus until the railway line reopens, but there are plenty of services, both state and private. All the **Mysore** buses (every 15min) go via **Madikeri**. KSRTC buses to **Hassan** leave hourly and take around 4 hours. KSRTC services to **Bengaluru** leave every 30 minutes or so or you can choose from a plethora of private companies on Konchady Road opposite the KSRTC bus stand. One of the best is VRL, whose distinctive yellow luxury coaches can be booked through Vijayananda Travels, PVS Centenary Building, Kodiyalbail, KS Rao Road (☎0824/249 3536). Agents along Falnir Road include Anand Travels (☎0824/244 6737) and Ideal Travels (☎0824/242 4899), who also run luxury buses to Bengaluru (8hr) and two buses to **Ernakulam** (8pm & 9pm; 9–10hr).

Bus #44A runs from the junction at the south end of KS Rao Road direct to Ullal, or you can take any bus to Thokkottu on the main coastal highway, from where it's a 2km walk. As you cross the Netravathi River en route, look out for the brick chimneystacks clustered on the banks at the mouth of the estuary. Using quality clay shipped downriver from the hills, these factories manufacture the famous terracotta red **Mangalorean roof tiles**, which you see all over southern India.

Eating

The best **places to eat** are in the bigger hotels. If you're on a tight budget, try one of the inexpensive café-restaurants opposite the bus stand, or the excellent canteen inside the bus stand itself, which serves great *dosas* and other South Indian snacks.

Ganesh Prasad Down a lane off KS Rao Rd. Small but very popular place serving cheap, tasty thalis and South Indian food.

Madhuvan *Moti Mahal* hotel, Falnir Rd. Reputable canteen-style restaurant which does a wide range of excellent thalis and other dishes. The hotel also has a good multi-cuisine restaurant (*Mangala*) serving non-veg dishes.

Naivedyam *Mangalore International* hotel, KS Rao Rd. Pure-veg cuisine in one of the best hotel restaurants, with both plush a/c and comfortable non-a/c sections.

Palimar *Navaratna Palace Hotel*. KS Rao Rd. Quality, reasonably priced pure-veg restaurant. The *Heera Panna* in the same hotel serves a range of non-veg food.

Palkhi Mercara Trunk Rd. Airy, rooftop family restaurant with a wide range of South Indian food.

Yuvraj *Poonja International* hotel, KS Rao Rd. Pleasant ambience and a wide menu including good Mughlai cuisine as well as veg, Western and Chinese food.

Around Mangalore

Although the most famous of all the **Jain bastis** (temples) is at Sravanabelgola 49km southeast of Hassan (see p.298), the greatest concentration of these shrines lies to the east and northeast of Mangalore. The *bastis* of **Mudabidri**, **Karkala** and **Dharamastala**, some of which date back to the ninth century, continue to form part of a pilgrimage circuit attracting Jains from all over India, and can be taken in on day-trips from Mangalore. Of the Hindu pilgrimage centres near Mangalore, the great *matha* at **Sringeri**, to the east, is the most important.

Regular buses from the KSRTC Bus Stand in Mangalore run to Dharmastala, Mudabidri and Karkala; the latter can also be approached directly from Udupi to the northwest. Several buses continue on to Sringeri, but you can also change at Karkala. The road between Karkala and Sringeri is particularly beautiful, as it passes through a lush belt of forest on its way up the Western Ghats.

Mudabidri

The most extensive of the *bastis* can be found in the small and quiet town of **MUDABIDRI**, 35km north of Mangalore. According to legend, a Jain ascetic settled here in the eighth century when he saw a tiger playing with a cow. Most of the eighteen *bastis* and several *mathas* (monasteries) at Mudabidri were built during the fifteenth and sixteenth centuries. The most impressive, close to the town centre, is the **Chandranatha Basti**, completed in 1430 AD and known more commonly as the "thousand-pillar hall". Approached by an imposing entrance gate and fronted by a tall, multistorey stone lamp, the main temple consists of two large interconnected columned halls. The surrounding veranda has stone columns supporting a sloping stone roof that is, in turn, crowned by a roof coated with copper tiles supported by carved wooden angle brackets.

Karkala

An eighteen-kilometre bus ride north of Mudabidri, the small town of **KARKALA** is famous for the thirteen-metre high statue of **Gomateshvara**, which stands placid and naked atop a rocky granite outcrop 1km from the town centre. Steps hewn out of rock lead up to the dramatic freestanding image, which was built in 1432 by Veerapandyadeva, a local ruler, and inspired by the monolith at Sravanabelgola. At the bottom of the hill lies the **Chaturmukha Basti**, built in 1586 and so called because of its identical four (*chatur*) faces (*mukha*) or directions. The main object of the symmetry is the columned hall where four doors punctuate the porch, each with a view of three deities within the inner sanctum. By circumambulating the sanctuary, the devotee is thus able to take in twelve *tirthankaras* in all.

Dharmastala and around

A popular Hindu pilgrimage town set against a pleasant backdrop of paddy fields, wooded hills and plantations, **DHARMASTALA**, 75km east of Mangalore, has another monolithic stone image of **Gomateshvara**, completed in 1973 by the artist Ranjal Gopal Shenoy. Although impressive, the fourteen-metre-high statue, which borrows heavily from its predecessors and took five years to create, lacks the refinement of those at Karkala and Sravanabelgola. It stands on a hill, above the frenetically busy **Manjunatha Temple** (daily 6.30am–2pm & 6.30–8.30pm; no bags or cameras), where both Hindus and Jains worship. An important Shaivite shrine, managed by Vaishnava priests, the temple was founded in 1780 by the influential Heggades, a renowned Jain family whose lineage stretches back to the sixteenth century and who still oversee the running of the complex. They also arranged transportation of the 170-tonne Gomateshvara statue from Karkala, 64km away, where it was carved. According to custom, pilgrims to Dharmastala bathe in the **Netravati River**, 3km away.

A further 5km from Dharmastala stands the **Shree Rama Kshetra**, a modern temple built entirely out of Rajasthani marble in a mix of North and South Indian styles. The slightly kitsch exterior belies an immaculate interior, complete with 21 images of the Hindu pantheon.

Rooms in Dharmastala can be reserved at the temple office close to the temple entrance (☎08256/277123).

Sringeri

On the banks of the River Tunga, the scenic village of **SRINGERI**, on the edge of coffee plantations 100km northeast of Mangalore, is notable for its ancient *matha*, established in the ninth century by the great Hindu reformer and theologian Sri Sankaracharya, who is said to have spent twelve years of his life here. The village has been a renowned place of pilgrimage for centuries and held strong influence over the Vijayanagar empire. During the festival of Navaratri, held each September/October, which commemorates the goddess Sharada's triumph over evil, it swells with the influx of pilgrims.

Sringeri's modern **Sharada temple**, devoted to a form of the goddess Saraswati, receives a steady stream of pilgrims. More interesting architecturally is the sixteenth-century **Vidyashankara temple**, a short distance to the south of the Sharada temple, in a picturesque riverside location. Built on a high plinth decorated with friezes of animals, figures and gods, the temple enshrines a *lingam* that is considered to be the *samadhi* (memorial) to Shankara. The twelve pillars of the *mandapa* support a set of heavy ceiling-slabs and feature lavish details including riders on mythical beasts, representing each of the twelve signs of the zodiac. The walls of the temple are richly adorned with carvings depicting the gods, while the niches hold various aspects of Shiva and the incarnations of Vishnu, including Krishna playing the flute. Steps lead down to the river, where devotees congregate to feed the sacred fish.

Sringeri has **room reservation offices** near the temple entrance, which will assign you temple-run rooms (❶). These are usually excellent value and can range from very basic rooms with shared bathrooms to comfortable doubles with attached baths. Private accommodation is also available at *Shubhodaya Lodge* (☎08265/251167; ❸), at the end of town opposite the petrol station.

North of Mangalore: coastal and western Karnataka

Whether you travel the **Karnatakan (Karavali) coast** on the Konkan Railway or along the busy NH-14, the route between Mangalore and Goa is among the most scenic anywhere in the country. Crossing countless palm- and mangrove-fringed estuaries, the recently upgraded road, dubbed by the local tourist board as "The Sapphire Route", scales several spurs of the Western Ghats, which in places creep to within a stone's throw of the sea, with stunning views over long, empty beaches and deep blue bays. Highlights include the pilgrim town of **Udupi**, site of a famous Krishna temple, and **Gokarna**, a bustling village which provides access to exquisite beaches. A couple of bumpy back roads wind inland through the mountains to **Jog Falls**, India's highest waterfall. Infrequent buses crawl from the coast through rugged jungle scenery to this spectacular spot, but you'll enjoy the trip more by motorbike; it's possible to rent one in Goa and

Kambla

If you're anywhere between Mangalore and Bhatkal from October to April and come across a crowd gathering around a water-logged paddy field, pull over and spend a day at the races – Karnatakan style. Few Westerners ever experience it, but the unique and spectacular rural sport of **kambla**, or **bull racing**, played in the southern-most district of coastal Karnataka (known as Dakshina Kannada), is well worth seeking out.

Two contestants, usually local rice-farmers, take part in each race, riding on a wooden plough-board attached to a pair of prize bullocks. The object is to reach the opposite end of the field first, but points are also awarded for style, and riders gain extra marks – and roars of approval from the crowd – if the muddy spray kicked up from the plough-board splashes the special white banners, or *thoranam*, strung across the course at a height of 6 to 8m.

Generally, race days are organized by wealthy landowners on fields specially set aside for the purpose. Villagers flock in from all over the region, as much for the fair, or *shendi*, as the races themselves: men huddle in groups to watch cock fights (*korikatta*), women haggle with bangle sellers and kids roam around sucking sticky *kathambdi goolay*, the local bon-bons. It is considered highly prestigious to be able to throw such a party, especially if your bulls win any events or, better still, come away as champions. Known as *yeru* in Kannada, racing bulls are thoroughbreds who are rarely, if ever, put to work. Pampered by their doting owners, they are massaged, oiled and blessed by priests before big events, during which large sums of money are often won and lost.

ride down the coast from there, stopping off at secluded beaches, falls and viewpoints en route.

Just across the Ghats from the coast are several places worth visiting. The temple towns of **Sirsi**, with its unique Kavi art, and ancient **Banvasi** both offer quiet escapes from the main tourist trail, while **Dandeli Wildlife Sanctuary** is renowned for its population of black panthers. **Hubli**, the region's main commercial centre and transport hub, provides a convenient base for exploring the large Tibetan settlement of **Mundgod** and the ancient temple compound in **Gadag**.

Udupi and around

UDUPI (also spelt Udipi), 60km north of Mangalore, is one of South India's holiest Vaishnavite centres. The Hindu saint **Madhva** (1238–1317) was born here, and the **Krishna temple** and *mathas* he founded are visited by lakhs of pilgrims each year. The largest numbers congregate during the late winter, when the town hosts a series of spectacular **car festivals** and gigantic, bulbous-domed chariots are hauled through the streets around the temple. Even if your visit doesn't coincide with a festival, Udupi is a good place to break the journey along the Karavali coast. Thronging with *pujaris* and pilgrims, its small sacred enclave is wonderfully atmospheric, and you can take a boat from the nearby fishing village at **Malpé beach** to **St Mary's Island**, the deserted outcrop of hexagonal basalt where Vasco da Gama erected a crucifix prior to his first landfall in India.

Incidentally, Udupi also lays proud claim to being the birthplace of the nation-ally popular **masala dosa**; these crispy stuffed pancakes, made from fermented rice flour, were first prepared and made famous by the Udupi brahmin hotels.

Arrival, information and accommodation

Udupi's three **bus stands** are dotted around the amorphous square in the centre of town: the KSRTC and private stands form a practically indistinguish-able gathering spot for the numerous services to Mangalore (every 5min; 1hr 30min), Mysore, Bengaluru, Gokarna, Jog Falls, and other towns between northern Kerala and Goa. The City Bus Stand, down some steps to the north, handles private services to nearby villages, including Malpé. Udupi's **railway station** is at Indrali on Manipal Road 3km from the centre; there are at least five trains in each direction daily.

The modest **tourist office** is near the temple in the Krishna Building, Car Street (Mon–Sat 10am–5.30pm; ☎0820/252 9718). Gayathri Tours and Travels (☎0820/253 4095), in the Anugraha Complex, Corp Bank Road, can arrange tours and **car hire**. Several banks have **ATMs** in town, and you can **change money** at the KM Dutt branch of Canara Bank on the main road just south of the bus stands. There are a number of **Internet** outlets (both Rs20/hr), including Netpoint on the central square and Cyber Inn, opposite the *Sriram*.

Udupi has a good choice of **places to stay** to suit all budgets, most within a few minutes' walk of the temple and city centre.

Durga International Just west of City Bus Stand ☎0820/253 6971. Airy and efficient lodge with a variety of en-suite rooms with TV, some a/c, on the upper storeys of a modern block. ❸–❹

Sharada International 2km out of town on the NH-17 ☎0820/252 2910. Mid-range place with light, airy, good-value rooms, some a/c, and a few singles. There are also veg and non-veg restau-rants and a bar. ❸–❹

Sriram Residency Opposite the Head Post Office ☎0820/253 0761, ✉sriramresidency@indiatimes .com. Plushest place in the centre, with a smart lobby, comfortable a/c rooms, two restaurants (see p.320) and a bar. ❸–❹

Sri Vidyasamudra Chatra Opposite Krishna temple ☏0820/252 0820. Basically for pilgrims, but foreigners are welcome. It's ultra-basic, but the front rooms overlooking the temple and bathing tank are incredibly atmospheric ➊

Vyavahar Lodge Kankads Rd ☏0820/252 2568. Basic but friendly and clean lodge between the bus stands and temple. ➋–➍

The Krishna temple and mathas

Udupi's **Krishna temple** lies five minutes' walk east of the main street, surrounded by the eight **mathas** founded by Madhva in the thirteenth century. Legend has it that the idol enshrined within was discovered by the saint himself after he prevented a shipwreck. The grateful captain of the vessel concerned offered Madhva his precious cargo as a reward, but the holy man asked instead for a block of ballast, which he broke open to expose a perfectly formed image of Krishna. Believed to contain the essence (*sannidhya*) of the god, this deity draws a steady stream of pilgrims and is the focus of almost constant ritual activity. It is cared for by the *acharyas*, or priests, of the *mathas*, who are the only people allowed to touch the idol. They perform puja (5.30am–8.45pm), accompanied by a cacophony of clanging bells and clouds of incense smoke. The temple is open to non-Hindus but all men must enter the main shrine bare-chested.

A stone tank adjacent to the temple, known as the **Madhva Sarovara**, is the focus of a huge festival every two years (usually January 17–18), when a new head priest is appointed. Preparations for the **Paryaya Mahotsava** begin thirteen months in advance, and culminate with the grand entry of the new *acharya* into the town at the head of a huge procession. Outside in the street, a window in the wall affords a view of the deity; according to legend, this is the spot where a Harijan, or "untouchable" devotee, denied entry due to his caste, was worshipping Krishna from outside when the deity turned to face him. A statue of the devotee stands opposite. Nearby, there's a magnificent gold-painted wooden temple chariot (*rath*), carved in the distinctive Karnatakan style, its onion-shaped tower decked with thousands of pieces of coloured paper, cloth and tinsel.

Staff at the **Regional Resources Centre for the Performing Arts** in the MGM College, towards the railway line on Manipal Road, can tell you about local festivals and events that are well off the tourist trail; the centre's collection includes film, video and audio archives. The pamphlet *Udupi: an Introduction*, on sale in the stalls around the sacred enclave, is another rich source of background detail on the temple and its complex rituals.

Malpé, Thottam and St Mary's Island

Udupi's popular weekend picnic spot, **Malpé beach**, 5km north of the centre, is disappointing, marred by a forgotten concrete structure that was planned to be a government-run hotel. However, after wandering around the fish market at the harbour, you can haggle to arrange a boat (around Rs800) to take you out to **St Mary's Island**, an extraordinary rock face of hexagonal basalt. Vasco da Gama is said to have placed a cross here in the 1400s, prior to his historic landing at Kozhikode in Kerala. From a distance, the sandy beach at **Thottam**, 1km north of Malpé and visible from the island, looks tempting; in reality it's an open sewer.

Eating

As you might expect of the birthplace of the masala dosa, there are many simple but excellent **restaurants** serving South Indian food. To sample Udupi cooking (see Basics, p.52), head for the busy little pilgrim places around the temple square, though you may have to wait for a place to sit. For North Indian as well as South Indian options, head to *Woodlands*, a basement restaurant at the end of a lane off the southwest corner of the square. Several of the hotel restaurants also serve decent food, such as the *Adarsha*, below the *Janardhan*, where you can sample a range of good vegetarian dishes. Moving slightly upmarket, the *Achinta* at the *Sriram* also does quality veg options while the hotel's other restaurant, the *Pisces*, specializes in seafood and is one of the few places in town that serves alcohol.

Jog Falls

Hidden in a remote, thickly forested corner of the Western Ghats, **Jog Falls** (Rs2; rate varies for vehicles), 240km northeast of Mangalore, are the highest **waterfalls** in India. These days, they are rarely as spectacular as they were before the construction of a large dam upriver, which impedes the flow of the River Sharavati over the sheer red-brown sandstone cliffs. However, on public holidays the dam is often opened to cater for the crowds of camera-wielding domestic tourists who flock here to pose in Bollywood style before descending the 1700 steps to the plunge pool for a dive and a splash. Allow around half an hour to get down and an hour for the climb back up.

The whole area opposite the falls has now been landscaped, with appealing viewing platforms and an impressive entrance gate. Regardless of the water levels, the surrounding scenery is spectacular at any time, with dense scrub and jungle carpeting the sparsely populated mountainous terrain. Although the volume of water is much greater during the monsoons, visibility is affected by mist and rain clouds, the paths become slippery and the abundance of leeches makes the **hike** to the valley floor a misery. The best time to visit is between October and January.

Practicalities

Getting to Jog Falls by **bus** is now a lot easier thanks to the completion of the NH-206 across the Ghats. There are buses to the falls from Honavar (5 daily; 2hr 30min), which is on the Konkan Railway; from Kumta (3 daily; 3hr), reachable by bus from Gokarna; from Udupi and Mangalore (both 2 daily; 5hr 30min/7hr); from Shimoga (every 30min; 3hr), which is accessible by bus from Hospet and Hampi; from Panaji (1 daily; 7hr); from Bengaluru (1 daily; 10hr); and from Mysore (4 nightly; 10hr). Better onward connections to Shimoga, Udupi, Mysore, Hassan and Bangalore can be found at Sagar, 30km (1hr) away, to which buses run every 30 minutes. With a **car or motorbike**, you can approach the falls from the coast along one of several scenic routes through the Ghats. The **tourist office** (Mon–Sat 10am–1.30pm & 2.30–5pm), upstairs at the new reception centre, opens rather erratically but can supply info on transport and vehicle hire.

Accommodation includes the KSTDC *Mayura Sharavathi* (☎08186/244732; ❸), which has ten vast rooms with fading plaster and rickety plumbing (but good views), the humbler KSTDC *Tunga Tourist Home*, nearer the reception centre, with cheaper, basic en-suite doubles (☎08186/244464; ❸), and the Shimoga District *PWD Inspection Bungalow* (☎08186/244333; ❸), situated on a hillock about 400m west of the falls' reception centre, with comfortable, very good value rooms. The youth hostel (☎08186/244375; ❶), ten minutes' walk down the Shimoga road, has ridiculously cheap, simple rooms and a pleasant garden. The *PWD Inspection Bungalow*, on the north side of the gorge, has great views from its spacious, comfortable rooms but it has to be booked in advance through the Assistant Engineer's office in Siddapur (☏08389/230134; ②) and is usually full.

Apart from the KSTDC canteen next to the *Tunga Tourist Home*, which offers adequate but uninspiring fare, the only **food** options are the enclave of small chai stalls and shops at the reception centre.

Gokarna

GOKARNA (also spelt Gokarn), a seven-hour bus ride north of Mangalore, is one of South India's most important pilgrimage sites. Set behind a broad white-sand beach, with the forest-covered foothills of the Western Ghats forming a blue-green backdrop, it's been a Shaivite centre for more than two millennia. Yet this compact little coastal town remained largely undiscovered by Western tourists until the early 1990s, when it began to attract dreadlocked and didgeridoo-toting travellers fleeing the commercialization of Goa. Now, with a rash of luxury ayurvedic spas mushrooming on the surrounding hillsides and **beaches**, Gokarna is firmly on the tourist map, although the Hindu pilgrims pouring through still far outnumber the foreigners that flock here in winter.

Even if you're not tempted to while away weeks on its isolated beaches, Gokarna is well worth a short detour from the coastal highway. Like Udupi, it's an ancient pilgrimage centre with a markedly traditional feel: shaven-headed brahmins sit cross-legged on their verandas chanting Sanskrit *shlokas* (vedic verses), while Hindu pilgrims file through a bazaar crammed with religious paraphernalia to the sea for a holy dip.

Arrival and information

The **KSRTC bus stand**, 300m from Car Street, is within easy walking distance of all Gokarna's accommodation. However you may well find that

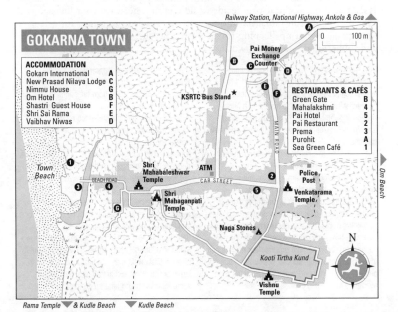

Railway Station, National Highway, Ankola & Goa

GOKARNA TOWN

0   100 m

ACCOMMODATION
Gokarn International	A
New Prasad Nilaya Lodge	C
Nimmu House	G
Om Hotel	B
Shastri Guest House	F
Shri Sai Rama	E
Vaibhav Niwas	D

Pai Money Exchange Counter

KSRTC Bus Stand

RESTAURANTS & CAFÉS
Green Gate	B
Mahalakshmi	4
Pai Hotel	5
Pai Restaurant	2
Prema	3
Purohit	A
Sea Green Café	1

Town Beach

BEACH ROAD

Shri Mahabaleshwar Temple

ATM

CAR STREET

Police Post

Venkatarama Temple

Om Beach

Shri Mahaganpati Temple

MAIN ROAD

Naga Stones

Kooti Tirtha Kund

N

Rama Temple & Kudle Beach   Kudle Beach

Vishnu Temple

your bus, especially if coming from major tourist points like Goa and Hampi, deposits you at the police checkpost on the edge of town, where you have to register. Alternatively you jump off either at Ankola, or at the Gokarna junction on the main highway, from where private minibuses and *tempos* run into town. Gokarna Road **railway station** is 9km inland; minibuses (Rs50 per head) and a couple of beaten-up taxis (Rs300–400) are available at the station to take you into town, or there are regular buses from the main highway, 1km away. There are more services to **Ankola**, 25km away, from which hourly buses (45min) run to Gokarna.

You can **change money** at the *Om Hotel* near the KRSTC bus stand but the Pai STD booth (on the main road into town before the bus stand), one of several licensed dealers, usually gives better rates. The Karnataka Bank subsidiary just off Car Street has an ATM. There are several tiny **Internet** places dotted around (Rs30/hr), though none has very reliable connections. **Bicycles** are available for rent from a stall next to the *Pai Restaurant* (Rs3/hr or Rs30/day). English-speaking Dr Shastri (☎08386/256220), based next to *Shastri Guest House*, is highly recommended for anyone requiring **medical** attention.

Accommodation

Gokarna has a reasonable selection of small, independent **hotels** and simple, family-run **guesthouses** but during peak times such as New Year it can be very difficult to find anything. As a last resort, you may be able to get a bed in one of the pilgrims' hostels, or *dharamshalas*, dotted around town. With dorms, bare, cell-like rooms and basic washing facilities, these are intended mainly for Hindu visitors, but Western tourists are welcome if there are vacancies: try the *Prasad Nilaya*, just down the lane from *Om Hotel*.

After staying in the village for a couple of days, however, many visitors strike out for the **beaches** where – in addition to the new **luxury resorts** appearing on the hillsides – there are dozens of rough-and-ready palm huts. Lumpy coir mattresses and shared toilets are the norm in these places, which typically charge Rs125–250 per night; if you decide to hole up in one, leave your luggage and valuables behind in Gokarna (most guesthouses will store things for a fee). A few travellers end up sleeping rough on the beaches, but nights can be chilly and robberies are not unknown.

CGH Earth Resort Close to Om beach; book through their office in Kochi ☎0484/301 1711, ⓦwww.cghearth.com. Beautifully designed "ethnic" villas spread over terraces on a hillside overlooking the bay. There's a pool, yoga dome, and ayurvedic treatment centre, all set in extensive gardens. ⑥

Gokarn International On the main road into town ☎08386/256622, ⓦwww .geocities.com/hotelgokarn. Popular mid-scale place in a four-storey block on the edge of Gokarna, offering good value, differently priced rooms – from no-frills singles to deluxe a/c doubles with coir carpets, TVs and baths. The better ones also have balconies overlooking the palmtops. In addition to a poky bar, the ground floor hosts a pair of budget restaurants, popular with visiting bus parties – the pure-veg *Purohit* serves better than average South Indian breakfasts. ②–④

Gokarn International Beach Resort Kudle Beach; book through the *Gokarn International* in town (see left). Set back from the sands in its own small garden, this compact, newly constructed hotel offers comfortable mid-price rooms with small kitchenettes and verandas, some of them sea-facing. ⑤

Namaste Om Beach ☎08386/257141. Best of the budget guesthouses out on the beaches. Its rooms are well built, with attached shower-toilets. Each has a different theme: in one, everything is round (including the bed); another resembles a rustic log cabin; and there's a thatched cottage option. Phone and Internet connection on site. ①–③

New Prasad Nilaya Lodge Near the KRSTC Bus Stand ☎08386/257135. A friendly, well-run guesthouse a 5min walk from the bazaar. Its rooms are large for the price, and are all attached, though some face south and heat up during the day.

There's also a railway booking office here, to save the trek to the station. **2–3**

🏃 **Nimmu House** A minute's walk from the temples towards Gokarna beach ☎08386/256730, ✉nimmuhouse@yahoo.com. The first choice of most foreign backpackers, run by the friendly and helpful woman whose name it bears. Double rooms in the modern concrete block are well maintained and have decent mattresses, but avoid the grungier old wing, with its lumpy coir beds and grubby walls. The family offers a reliable left-luggage facility and Internet access, and there's a peaceful yard to sit in. **2–4**

Om Beach Resort 1.5km east of town ☎0944/857 9395, ⓦwww.ombeachresorts.com. Despite the name, this campus of a dozen, newly built colonial-style chalets, is actually near Gokarna town – high on a sun-blasted hilltop, a good 45-minute (shadeless) walk from the beaches. It was conceived primarily as an ayurvedic health spa, so there are qualified doctors on site, along with

masseurs from the acclaimed Keralan Ayurveda outfit, Kairali. Rates from $100–150 (Rs4450–6700) per night (full board); details of spa packages appear on their website. **7**

Om Hotel Just north of the KRSTC Bus Stand ☎08386/256445. Dowdy economy hotel pitched at budget-conscious middle-class Indian visitors, with plain, good-sized en-suite doubles and some overpriced a/c rooms. The bar on the ground floor is gloomy and male-dominated. **2–5**

Seabird Resort 1.5km east of town, just across the road from the Om Resort ☎08386/257689. Marooned on the hilltop above Gokarna town, but a good value option, with choice of modern a/c or non a/c, all opening on to private sitouts. The views over the scrubby slopes are great and there's a multicuisine restaurant and small pool. **5–6**

Shastri Guest House 100m east of the KRSTC Bus Stand ☎08386/256220. Tucked behind the Shastri Clinic on the main road, this quiet place

▲ **A**, **B**, National Highway, Railway Station, Ankola & Goa

GOKARNA: BEACHES

Town Beach
Shri Mahabaleshwar
Gokarna Town
Shri Mahaganpati
Kooti Tirtha Kund
Vishnu Temple
See Gokarna Town Map
Rama Temple & Spring

ACCOMMODATION
CGH Earth Resort	D
Gokarn International Beach Resort	C
Namaste	E
Om Beach Resort	B
Seabird Resort	A

0   500 m

N

Kudle Beach
C

D
E

Om Beach

Half Moon Beach

Paradise Beach

offers some en-suite rooms and rock-bottom single rates. ❶–❷

Shri Sai Rama Main road, near bus stand ☎08386/257775. Brand-new place with clean rooms and a (separate) ayurvedic centre on the ground floor. ❹

Vaibhav Nivas Off the main road, less than five minutes from the bus stand ☎08386/256714. Friendly, cheap and justifiably popular guesthouse pitched at foreigners, with a rooftop café-restaurant; all rooms en suite. Internet and left-luggage facilities available. ❶–❸

The Town

Gokarna **town**, a hotchpotch of wood-fronted houses and red terracotta roofs, is clustered around a long L-shaped bazaar, its broad main road – known as **Car Street** – running west to the town beach, a sacred site in its own right. Hindu mythology identifies it as the place where Rudra (an early name for Shiva) was reborn through the ear of a cow from the underworld after a period of penance. Gokarna is also the home of one of India's most powerful *shivalingam* – the **pranalingam**, which came to rest here after being carried off by Ravana, the evil king of Lanka, from Shiva's home on Mount Kailash in the Himalayas. Sent by the gods to reclaim the sacred object, Ganesh, with the help of Vishnu, tricked Ravana into letting him look after the *lingam* while he prayed, knowing that if it touched the ground it would take root and never be moved. When Ravana returned from his meditation, he tried to pick the *lingam* up, but couldn't, because the gods had filled it with "the weight of three worlds".

The *pranalingam* resides in Gokarna to this day, enshrined in the medieval **Shri Mahabaleshwar Temple**, at the far west end of the bazaar. It is regarded as so auspicious that a mere glimpse of it will absolve a hundred sins, even the murder of a brahmin. Local Hindu lore also asserts that you can maximize the *lingam*'s purifying power by shaving your head, fasting and taking a holy dip in the sea before *darshan*, or ritual viewing of the deity. For this reason, pilgrims traditionally begin their tour of Gokarna with a walk to the beach. They are aided and instructed by their personal *pujari* – one of the bare-chested priests you see around town, wearing sacred caste threads and with single tufts of hair sprouting from their shaven heads – whose job it is to guide the pilgrims. Next, they visit the **Shri Mahaganpati Temple**, a stone's throw east of Shri Mahabaleshwar, to propitiate the elephant-headed god Ganesh. Sadly, owing to some ugly incidents involving insensitive behaviour by a minority of foreigners (Israeli girls dressed in party clothes), tourists are now banned from the temples, though you can still get a good view of proceedings in the Shri Mahaganpati from the entrance. En route, check out the splendid **rath**, or chariot, that stands at the end of the bazaar next to the Mahaganpati temple. During important festivals, notably Shiva's "birthday", **Shivratri** (Feb), deities are installed inside this colossal carved-wood cart and hauled by hand along the main street, accompanied by drum bands and watched by huge crowds.

East of the main Car Street and bazaar, **Kooti Tirtha Kund** is a large, rectangular water tank surrounded by sacred *ghats* where pilgrims perform ritual ablutions. It is believed to have been created by Vishnu's mount, the winged-gryphon Garuda. Vishnu performed penance here after he'd vanquished the thousand-armed demon Banasura. Early in the morning, pilgrims come to the tank to bathe, wash their clothes and carry out funerary rituals for recently deceased relatives, consigning sandalwood ash and *pinda* (balls of barley, ghee and coconut) to the water. On the south side of the tank, a white-painted **temple** is the most important *vaishnava* shrine in Gokarna, and a prominent call on the pilgrims' circuit. Also worth a look is the collection of carved *naga* worship stones stacked under the peepal tree on the opposite, northwestern corner of Kooti Tirtha. Liberally dusted with turmeric powder and red *kumkum*,

△ Pilgrims performing funerary rites at Kooti Tirtha Kund, Gokarna

ancient cobra deities such as these are a common feature of popular South Indian worship, and are associated with female ritual activities.

The beaches

Notwithstanding Gokarna's numerous temples, shrines and tanks, most Western tourists come here for the beautiful **beaches** situated south of the more crowded town beach, beyond the lumpy laterite headland that overlooks the town. You can reach them either on foot, or by jumping in one of the **fishing boats** that leave periodically through the day from the main town beach – prices range from Rs50–150 per head, depending on the number of passengers and how well you can haggle.

To pick up the footpath, head along the narrow alley opposite the south entrance to the Mahaganpati temple, and follow the path uphill from the south end of the town beach, past the Rama temple and spring. After twenty minutes, you drop down from a rocky plateau to **Kudle beach** – a wonderful kilometre-long sweep of golden-white sand sheltered by a pair of steep-sided promontories. The palm-leaf chai stalls and seasonal cafés that spring up here during the winter offer some respite from the heat of the midday sun, and very basic accommodation in bamboo shacks.

It takes around twenty minutes to hike over the headland from Kudle to the exquisite **Om beach**, so named because its distinctive twin crescent-shaped bays resemble the auspicious Om symbol. The advent of a dirt road from town means the coves are now frequented by a more diverse crowd than the hardcore hippy fringe whose exclusive preserve it used to be. For the time being, hammocks, palm-leaf huts and chai stalls still dominate the palm groves behind, though they're fast being overshadowed by the luxury "eco" resorts sprouting on the hillsides above Om Beach. Set up to emulate Keralan-style Ayurveda spas, these places compete for the custom of wealthy health-conscious tourists with their Panchakarma clinics, yoga *shalas* and obligatory thatched roofs (hiding decidedly un-eco-friendly constructions).

It's unlikely the concrete mixers will – at least in the next few years – reach Gokarna's two most remote beaches, which lie another twenty- to forty-minute walk over the hill. **Half Moon** and **Paradise** beaches are, despite the presence of one or two simple bamboo-hut guesthouses and cafés, mainly for intrepid sun-lovers happy to pack their own supplies. If you're looking for near-total isolation, these are your best bet.

Eating and drinking

Gokarna town offers a good choice of **places to eat**, with a string of busy joints along Car Street and the main road. Beer is freely available and fairly cheap, both in town and on the beaches. Look out for the local sweet speciality *gadbad* – several layers of different ice creams mixed with chopped nuts and chewy dried fruit.

There are also plenty of simple shack cafés out on the beaches, serving the usual traveller-oriented grub. Be warned, however, that incidents of food poisoning from some of these places are all too common among foreigners.

Green Gate *Om Hotel*, near the KRSTC bus stand. The *Om Hotel's* pleasant upstairs courtyard restaurant offers a range of Mexican, Italian and Israeli dishes, as well as fish and sizzlers. The snack bar downstairs is a male-dominated, dimly lit drinking den, though it serves spicy chicken tikka and other North Indian-style non-veg food. Most mains Rs125–150.

Mahalakshmi Beach Rd. Delicious, carefully prepared veg food – Indian, Western and Chinese – served on a snug rooftop terrace close to the beach. Long waits, but the cooking's worth it. Try their marvellous home-made pesto and pasta, or creamy *malai kofta*. Most mains under Rs100.

Pai Hotel Car St. A favourite meeting spot for travellers, this tiny joint has excellent, inexpensive veg snacks and delicious milky coffee.

Pai Restaurant Main Rd. Top-notch local Udupi place close to the market. Its filling rice-and-veg thalis, served daily from 11.30am, are the best budget meals in Gokarna, and they do crispy masala dosas, *iddli-vadai-sambar*, and teas and coffees at all hours. Open until late.

Prema Beach Rd. Standard traveller-friendly menu of pasta, sandwiches and bland Indian food, plus the biggest *gadbad* in town.

Purohit *Gokarn International* hotel. Fresh, cheap and very good food, especially recommended for its South Indian breakfasts.

Sea Green Café Just behind the main town beach. Tibetan and Nepali food in a breezy courtyard – a good place to enjoy the sunset over a beer. Mains Rs 50–80.

Moving on from Gokarna

Gokarna is well connected by direct daily **bus** to Madgaon in Goa (4hr) and several towns in Karnataka, including Bangalore (13hr), Hospet (9hr) for Hampi and Mysore (13hr) via Udupi (6hr) and Mangalore (7hr). Although there are only three direct buses north along the coast to Karwar (2hr), close to the border with Goa, you can change at Ankola on the main highway for more services. For more buses to Hospet and Hampi and the best connections to Jog Falls, change at Kumta; **tempos** regularly ply the route between Gokarna and Kumta (32km), as well as Ankola. The KSRTC counter at the bus stand is helpful for information about current bus timings.

Gokarna Road railway station now has at least two daily stopping **trains** in each direction. Heading up to Goa, #KR002 Up departs at 10.44am, arriving in Chaudi (Canacona) at 11.46am and Margao at 1pm; the southbound service leaves for Mangalore at 3.29pm (#KR001). Alternatively, the *Matsyagandha Express* runs north to Goa and Mumbai at 6.15pm (#2620) and south to Mangalore (#2619) at the inconvenient time of 1.45am. A couple of weekly expresses also stop here, but you'll get better connections to Goa, Mangalore, Udupi and Kerala by heading first to either Kumta or Ankola. As well as at the railway station, tickets can be booked in Gokarna town at the *New Prasad Nilaya Lodge* (see p.332), though at a hefty commission.

Sirsi and around

The large, bustling administrative centre of **SIRSI**, 83km east of Gokarna, sees few visitors but provides a good stop on long journeys to and from the coast. The main point of interest in the town itself is the striking **Marikamba temple**, but the chief reason for stopping here is to visit the fascinating temple complex at nearby **Banvasi**.

The Marikamba Temple

Marikamba temple, 500m from the bus stand, sees a steady stream of devotees coming to propitiate Durga, the ferocious multi-armed goddess who, as usual, is depicted astride a tiger and slaying a demon. The temple is at its most frenetic in the evenings, but is best seen during the day when it's easiest to appreciate the remarkable murals, some of the finest surviving examples of **Kavi art**. A rare form of wall-art once prevalent throughout the coastal Konkan region of west Karnataka but now practically extinct, Kavi art uses an unusual technique whereby a top layer of plaster, dyed with a blood-red pigment, is etched away to create detail revealed by the white layer of plaster beneath.

An imposing nineteenth-century facade, finished in red, leads into a grand courtyard with the temple at its centre; the cloisters are lavishly decorated with gods and goddesses. Parts of the inner sanctum, which houses an image of Durga, date back to the sixteenth century, but numerous additions hide any traces of the original structure. Marikamba's **rath festival**, during which the deity is placed on a *rath* (chariot) and paraded through the town, is held here once every other year in February and is one of the grandest in Karnataka. The next festival here will be held in 2009.

Practicalities

Buses connect Sirsi to numerous destinations, including Gokarna (via Kumta) and Karwar to the west, Hospet to the east, Jog Falls to the south, and Hubli and the Tibetan settlements of Mundgod to the north. The **KSRTC bus stand** is over 1km north of the centre; private companies operate deluxe buses from nearby to destinations such as Hubli and Bangalore. The best way of getting around town is an **auto-rickshaw**; **taxis** are available near the old bus stand, although you may find it cheaper to book through a hotel.

Accommodation in Sirsi is good value. Ignore the dives around the bus stand and head 2km out to College Road, where you'll find a handful of good options, including the *Madhuvana* (℡08384/237496, ℮hotelmadhuvana@ hotmail.com; ❷–❸), a large, clean and well-run hotel with excellent-value suites and a very good veg restaurant. The *Samrat*, next door (℡08384/236278; ❷), has simple, slightly faded rooms, including some sleeping up to five. The poshest of Sirsi's hotels, the *Panchavati* (℡08384/236755, ℉238301; ❸–❺), is 4km from the centre on Yellapur Road at the edge of town, but it's well worth the ride. Set in large, pleasant grounds, it offers good facilities, including a restaurant and some a/c rooms. Of the dingy bars serving non-veg **food** in the vicinity of College Road, the *Parijata*, just round the corner towards the bus stand in Hospet Road, is the most salubrious.

Banvasi

The ancient town of **BANVASI**, 22km southeast of Sirsi, dates back to the third century BC when it was a centre of Buddhist learning. Little remains from that period, however, and the brick stupas that once graced the banks of the River Varada have all but disappeared. From the fourth century onwards, under the Kadambas, a dynasty that ruled the region for around two hundred years,

Banvasi became the capital of Kannada, the forerunner of modern Karnataka, and is still held in high esteem as the home of the Kannada script.

The **Madhukeshvara Temple**, at the far end of Banvasi's winding Car Street, 1.5km from the bus stand, is still in use today. It dates back to the Kadamba period, although most of the major additions are attributed to the late Chalukya period of the twelfth century. The inner sanctum of the main temple – dedicated to Shiva as the lord (*ishvara*) of the bees (*madhuka*), who is represented here with a honey-coloured *lingam* – is said to date back to the fourth century, and the adjoining pillared stone hall to the sixth century. To the right of the inner sanctum stands a marble image of Datatreya, a three-headed combination representing the Hindu trinity of Brahma the creator, Vishnu the preserver and Shiva the destroyer. A most imposing Nandi, Shiva's bull and vehicle, sits outside in ever-faithful attendance facing the *lingam*.

The entrance hall (*mukhamandapa*) has numerous pillars, all unique in style except for the four highly polished reflective granite pillars that surround the stone dance circle, now no longer in use. In the middle chamber, a stone throne with lavishly carved pillars, built in 1628, is still used to hold idols during special occasions such as Vasant Utsava, the summer festival held around April every year. Immediately to the right of the main temple is a temple dedicated to Parvati, built in the late twelfth century. The extensive courtyard has an interesting collection of stone images, including gods known as the Ashtadigpalakas (the guardians of the eight directions), each with his own animal vehicle. The Ashtadigpalakas, who date back to the Vedic period, include Indra (east) on his elephant; Agni (southeast) on his ram; Yama, the god of death (south) on his buffalo; Niraruti (southwest), whose vehicle is a man; Varuna (west) on a crocodile; Yayu (northwest) on a deer; Kubera (north) on a horse, and Ishana, one of the prototypes of Shiva (northeast), on his bull. Each of the gods is also shown with his consort. At one side of the courtyard stands a small temple dedicated to Ganesh.

A small **museum** by the main gates holds a collection of sculpture from around Banvasi, including a striking fifteenth-century image of the Jain Gomateshvara and Buddhist plaques from the second century. Outside the main temple stands the majestic temple *rath*, built in 1608 and used to transport the gods during Vasant Utsava. A path opposite the temple entrance leads down between some shacks to the river and is a favourite picnic spot for visiting pilgrims.

Buses run several times a day from Sirsi to Banvasi, though services stop after 6pm. There is no accommodation in Banvasi.

Dandeli Wildlife Sanctuary

Lying between Hubli 75km to the east and Panjim 145km to the west, the scruffy town of **DANDELI**, on the banks of the River Kali in Uttar Kanada (Northern Karnataka), provides access to the **Dandeli Wildlife Sanctuary** (best time to visit Dec–April, closed June–Sept; Rs150 [Rs50]), an extensive, unspoiled forest on the edge of the Deccan Plateau. Despite its close proximity to Goa and its situation at a major crossroads on the route to Hampi via Hubli, the sanctuary sees few visitors except for occasional jeeploads from nearby Maharashtra, and remains a low-key and undeveloped wildlife destination.

Spread across 834 square kilometres, the large, mixed-deciduous forest, famed for its teak, spills over the lip of the Deccan where it gives way to the hills, ravines and deep river valleys of the Western Ghats. At the heart of the forest, 22km from the entrance gate, the 100-metre-high **Cyntheri Rock** rises out of the **River Kanari**. The river provides an excellent vantage point for observing animals. The sanctuary is famous for its black panthers, but sightings are rare, especially with the deep cover; you stand a better chance of seeing sambar deer, spotted deer, flying squirrels, wild boar and Indian bison – distinguishable by the white bands across their legs. Dandeli also shelters elephants, sloth bears and a handful of tigers, while its rivers, including the **Kali**, which sweeps past the town of Dandeli, are home to mugger crocodiles. **Sunset Point**, 6km from the gate, and remote **Sykes Point** provide sweeping views of the jungle-covered ridges of the Western Ghats.

The main Hubli–Karwar highway, which passes by Dandeli, is one of the most beautiful in Karnataka as it descends through the verdant **Anasi National Forest**, which forms part of the same forest belt as the Dandeli Wildlife Sanctuary. Travelling through the area you may notice the striking features of the **Siddhis**, a group of African descent who live in the region and maintain their own customs and language; they were brought over in the nineteenth century by a local raja to act as bodyguards.

Practicalities

Dandeli's **KSRTC Bus Stand**, in the centre of town, has hourly services to Hubli, four daily services to Karwar, and half-hourly buses to Ramnagar, from which you catch a bus to Panjim, 45km away. The forest checkpost, at the gate of the wildlife sanctuary, is around 12km from town so you will need to arrange your own vehicle, either privately or through the Forest Department in Dandeli (☎08284/220128), which is on the main Karwar road, near the Kali River. You'll also need to contact their office if you want to stay at any of their **resthouses** (❷–❸) in the sanctuary. Their *Nature Camp* (☎08284/231585), at the forest gates next to the interpretation centre has doubles or dorm beds for Rs50.

Cheap, simple accommodation in Dandeli town is available around the bus stand, the best of which is the *State Lodge* (☎08284/231920; ❷–❸), right opposite, which has large rooms (some a/c) and a roof terrace. They can arrange jungle treks, Jeep safaris (Rs600 [Rs350 for Indians] for 4hr) and white-water rafting ($35 [Rs1100] for 4hr). The nearby *PWD Guest House* (☎08284/231299; ❷) also has clean, reasonable rooms. Across the River Kali from Dandeli lies Jungle Lodges & Resorts' *Kali Adventure Camp* (☎08284/233360, book through their Bengaluru office ☎080/2559 7021, ⓦwww.junglelodges.com; ❸), with ten spacious rooms in the main concrete building and twelve luxurious tents with attached bath along the river. Bring mosquito repellent and be aware that as a foreigner you'll be paying an inflated price of $65 per person per night, though the package does include accommodation, entrance fees, Jeep safari and a coracle ride along the River Kali. Both food, served in an open thatched restaurant, and their safaris, are excellent. Finally, the *Bison River Resort* (☎08383/246539, ⓦwww.indianadventures.com/bisonriverresort.htm; ❸), on the other side of the sanctuary at Bangur Nagar, has luxury cabins, which are offered at half-price during the off-season, when the park is closed – fine for a pampered break, though of course you can't go wildlife spotting.

Hubli and around

Karnataka's second most industrialized city, **HUBLI**, 418km northwest of Bengaluru, has little to offer tourists except for its transport connections to Mumbai, Goa, the coast of Uttar Kanada (Northern Karnataka), Hampi and other points in the interior. It does, however, make a convenient base from which to explore the various sites in the area.

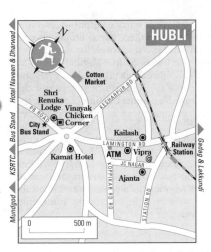

Practicalities

Hubli's **railway station**, close to the town centre and within walking distance of several of the hotels, is well connected to Bengaluru, Mumbai, Pune and Hospet (see box, p332). Hubli's efficient **KSRTC Bus Stand** is 2km south of town, and can be reached by bus from the chaotic City Bus Stand, about 1km west of the railway station, and from outside the station itself. The best way of getting around the city is by **auto-rickshaw**; these have meters, but there's also an efficient pre-paid booth outside the railway station. ICICI Bank has an **ATM** at the railway station and another one halfway along to the City Bus Stand. For **Internet** access, head to JC Nagar, where both I-way, almost opposite the *Ajanta*, and the Cybercafé in the Sri Naradmuni Complex, offer a rate of Rs20 per hour.

Accommodation around the railway station includes the huge *Hotel Ajanta* on JC Nagar (☏0836/236 2216; ❶–❸), which has a range of rooms, including very cheap singles with shared bathroom, and rickety plumbing. Opposite the City Bus Stand, the large and well-organized *Shri Renuka Lodge* (☏0836/225 3615; ❷–❹) offers a good range of reasonable rooms, some with a/c, and has its own vegetarian restaurant. There are a few hotels between the railway station and the bus stand on Lamington Road, including the pleasant *Kailash* (☏0836/235 2732, ⓦwww.hotelkailash.com; ❷–❹), an efficient business hotel with good-value a/c rooms and a decent restaurant, and the *Vipra*, opposite, which is cheaper but still has a range of simple rooms (☏0836/236 2336, ⓔvipratravels@satyam.net.in; ❶–❷). The *Naveen* (☏0836/237 2283, ⓦwww.nivalink.com/hotelnaveen; ❼–❾), 6km west of the centre at Unkal, is the most comfortable option, and (once you're past the concrete frontage) is quite attractive, with pleasant lakeside cottages and a swimming pool. Transport can be laid on from the railway station or bus stand by prior arrangement.

Most hotels have their own **restaurants** – the *Shri Renuka*, for example, has two sections, one serving South Indian veg food and the other Chinese and North Indian cuisine. The best of the independent restaurants is the *Kamat Hotel*, part of the ever-reliable vegetarian chain, by the traffic island at the bus stand end of Lamington Road: the downstairs restaurant serves excellent South Indian food, while the plush restaurant upstairs serves vegetarian North Indian and Chinese dishes; there's another branch opposite the railway station. *Vinayak Chicken Corner*, opposite the City Bus Stand, is a good spot for inexpensive non-veg and beer.

Dharwad

Some 10km to the west of Hubli, the leafy university town of **DHARWAD** is nationally renowned for its Hindustani classical music connections, being home to several famous musicians and vocalists. In musical terms, this region marks the watershed between the Carnatic classical music of South India, and the

Hindustani music of North India (see Contexts, p.776). The main concert season is in the winter, and performances are held at various venues around Dharwad and Hubli; check local papers for listings.

Frequent **buses** run to Dharwad from the KSRTC stand in Hubli. Comfortable, mid-range **accommodation** is available at the smart *Central Park* (☎0836/244 0797; ❸–❹) on PB Road, and the similar but slightly more expensive *Hoysala* (☎0836/244 5627; ❸–❹), next door.

Drepung

Though rarely visited, the busy Tibetan monastery of **Drepung**, 48km south of Hubli on the outskirts of the town of **Mundgod**, is one of the most important Tibetan monasteries in India. Home to several hundred monks, it continues the traditions of the famous scholastic monastery of Drepung that once flourished outside Lhasa. The environs of the monastery, as around Bylakuppe (see p.308), have been settled by Tibetan refugees, who have industriously farmed the once barren land since the 1960s. Visitors are welcome and cheap, clean accommodation is available at *Drepung Lachi* and *Drepung Gomang Khangsar* guesthouses (❶). In theory a PAP (see p.309) is required to visit the settlements but they are more remote than at Bylakuppe and there are no checkposts.

The easiest way to get to Drepung is to hire a car for the day from Hubli. Alternatively, wander down to *Modern Lodge* in Hubli, where the Tibetan community congregates, and squeeze into one of the shared Jeeps that ply the route. A cheaper option is take a Sirsi–bound bus from the KSRTC Bus Stand in Hubli (every 15min), and jump off in Mundgod, from where you can get onward transport. And finally, for a more scenic route, hop on any bus for Yellapur and alight in Kalghatgi, 28km from the town. From here small local buses, tractors, and rickshaws cover the 20km road – a bumpy but memorable journey – deep into rural Karnataka.

Gadag and Lakkundi

The cotton town of **GADAG**, 53km east of Hubli and 90km west of Hospet, is a useful stop-off on the main Goa–Chennai railway line, and if the long-awaited metre-gauge to broad-gauge conversion ever happens, will become an important junction for connections north to Badami, Pattadakal, Aihole and Bijapur. During the cotton season (Feb–June), the town is a hive of activity, but at other times returns to its quiet ways. Few travellers stop here, but for those with the time and inclination, Gadag and its environs make a good diversion from the well-travelled route to and from Hampi, with a handful of rarely visited Chalukya temples dating back to the eleventh century. The best of the Gadag monuments are the **Trikuteshwara** and **Saraswati temples**, which share a compound in the southern part of the town. The inner sanctum of the Trikuteshwara temple houses a triple *lingam*; the adjoining Saraswati temple shares the same hall and boasts a porch with impressive carvings. If the complex is locked, you can get the key from one of the temple's priests.

Gadag's other temples are in a terrible state of repair, and travelling to the village of **LAKKUNDI**, a further 11km east along the Hospet highway, is more rewarding. Less threatened by urban growth, Lakkundi's Chalukya temples, from the same period as those in Gadag, include a **Jain** *basti*, dominating the north of the village, with an impressive tower and sanctuary walls. A short distance away, the **Kashi Vishwanatha Temple**, dedicated to Shiva as lord of Kashi (Varanasi), consists of two temples facing each other and sharing the same plinth. Unfortunately, the connecting porch has collapsed, but the animal and flower friezes along the plinth are impressive, as are the carvings along the

By bus

Hubli has regular services linking the city with coastal Karnataka, Badami, Bijapur, Mumbai and Bengaluru, leaving from the KSRTC Bus Stand; most long-distance services are overnight. Buses for Hospet leave every hour – far more frequently than trains plying the same route; for Dandeli, they leave every two hours. **Private operators** can be found across the main road from the KSRTC Bus Stand: Vijay-ananda Travels (℡0836/223 7629), distinguishable by their yellow-and-black signs, is perhaps the most reputable of the private outfits, and operates luxury buses to Mumbai, Pune, Gulbarga, Bijapur, Sirsi and Bengaluru; Janata Travel (℡0836/222 8031) also operates services to Mumbai and Pune.

By train

The services listed below are the **most convenient** and/or the **fastest**. This list is by no means exhaustive and there are numerous slower trains which are often more convenient for smaller destinations – see p.362. The line to Goa has now been converted but the train service is irregular, so bus remains the most dependable option.

Destination	Train	Number	Departs	Total Time
Bangalore	Hubli–Bangalore Siddhaganga Intercity Express	#2726	Daily 6.20am	7hr 30min
Hospet	Hubli–Bangalore Hampi Express	#6591	Daily 5pm	2hr 55min
Mumbai	Bangalore–Mumbai Chalukya Express	#1018	Daily except 4pm Thurs	15hr 20min*
	Mysore–Mumbai Sharavathi Express	#1036	Thurs 4pm	15hr 20min*
Mysore	Dharwad–Mysore Express	#6202	Daily 9pm	9hr

* Stops in Pune

doorways and pillars. Close to the bus stand, a square stepped bathing tank with a columned bridge halfway through was designed to provide privacy for women bathers.

Practicalities

Gadag lies on the main road between Hubli and Hospet – buses ply the route hourly; Lakkundi is linked to both Gadag and Hospet. **Accommodation** in Gadag includes the *Vishwa Lodge* (℡08372/236072; ❷–❹), with comfortable, cheap, en-suite rooms and an excellent pure-veg restaurant (try the pulao rice), located at the eastern edge of town near the new bus station, and the *Shivani Inn* (℡08372/235277; ❷–❹), a huge, brand-new hotel with congenial doubles and good-value singles right next to the bus stand.

Hospet

HOSPET, a busy, dusty market town around 120km east of Hubli, is of little interest except as a springboard for the ruined city of Vijayanagar (Hampi), 13km northeast. If you want somewhere fairly comfortable to sleep, it makes sense to stay here and catch a bus or taxi out to the ruins the following morning.

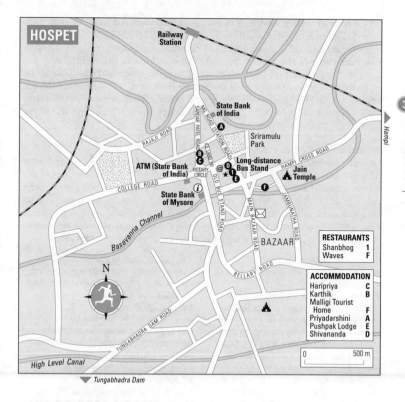

HOSPET

Railway Station

State Bank of India

Sriramulu Park

MG ROAD (STATION ROAD)

SARDAR PATEL ROAD

RAJAJI ROAD

ICE FACTORY

ATM (State Bank of India)

ROTARY CIRCLE

Long-distance Bus Stand

HAMPI CROSS ROAD

Jain Temple

OLD BUS STAND ROAD

COLLEGE ROAD

State Bank of Mysore

Basavanna Channel

MAIN BAZAAR ROAD

JAMBUNATHA ROAD

BAZAAR

BELLARY ROAD

N

TUNGABHADRA DAM ROAD

High Level Canal

▼ Tungabhadra Dam

Hampi

KARNATAKA | Hospet

RESTAURANTS	
Shanbhog	1
Waves	F

ACCOMMODATION	
Haripriya	C
Karthik	B
Malligi Tourist Home	F
Priyadarshini	A E
Pushpak Lodge	E
Shivananda	D

0   500 m

Otherwise, find a room in Hampi itself, where the setting more than compensates for the basic facilities.

Practicalities

Hospet's **railway station**, 1.5km north of the centre, is served by the overnight Hampi Express (#6592) from Bengaluru and services from Hyderabad, via Guntakal Junction. The line continues west to Hubli for connections to the coast and Goa. From Goa, the Vasco–Howrah Express (#2848) departs every Tuesday, Thursday, Friday and Sunday at 8.15am, arriving just over six hours later. For Badami, travel to Gadag and either change onto the slow metre-gauge track to Bagalkot or continue by bus. From Bagalkot there is a broad-gauge line up to Bijapur. From the station, auto-rickshaws are plentiful or you can get into town by cycle rickshaw (Rs10). The **long-distance bus stand** is in the centre, just off MG (Station) Road, which runs south from the railway station. The most frequent services are from Bangalore and Hubli, and there are daily arrivals from Mysore, Gokarna (via Kumta) and Goa. For a summary of services see Travel details on p.362. Bookings for long-distance routes can be made at the ticket office on the bus stand concourse (daily 8am–noon & 3–6pm), where there's also a left luggage facility. Private **luxury buses** to Goa are operated by Paulo Travels (☎08394/225867, ⓦwww.paulotravels.com), next to the *Hotel Priyadarshini*, with a/c or non-ac sleeper berths or non-a/c-only regular push-back seats available. Another reliable private bus company is Vijayanand (☎08394/220701), based on Shanbagh Circle.

The **tourist office**, at the Rotary Circle (daily except Sun: April & May 8am–1.30pm; June–March 10am–5.30pm; ℡08394/228537), offers limited information and sells tickets for KSTDC tours (see below). You can **change** traveller's cheques and cash at the State Bank of Mysore (Mon–Fri 10.30am–2.30pm, Sat 10.30am–12.30pm), next to the tourist office, and cash only at the State Bank of India (same hours) on Station Road. Full exchange facilities are available at the *Malligi Tourist Home*, whose Hamsa Travel Service (in the foyer) has a ticketing and tours service. There's **Internet** access at Cybernet (Rs40 per hour), next to the *Shivananda* hotel.

Accommodation and eating

Hospet may not be the most inspiring place to spend the night, but its **hotels** offer more comfort than Hampi's guesthouses, while its restaurants are, on the whole, considerably more hygienic. Most tourists end up whiling away their evenings at 🎋 *Waves*, a terrace restaurant owned by the *Malligi* hotel, serving tandoori and chilled beer from 7pm to 11pm (bring lots of mosquito repellent). *Shanbhog*, an excellent little South Indian Udupi restaurant next to the bus station, is a perfect pit stop before heading to Hampi and opens early for breakfast.

Haripriya Ice Land Road ℡08394/224622. Brand new guesthouse with clean, excellent-value non-a/c rooms. ②

Karthik Pampa Villa, off MG Station Rd ℡08394/220038. Characterless block featuring unremarkable rooms, although more comfortable "deluxe" options were being added on the top storey when we last checked. To the rear, there's an extraordinary nineteenth-century stone villa housing a pair of huge, fading suites. ④–⑤

🎋 **Malligi Tourist Home** 6/143 Jambunatha Rd, 2min walk east of MG Rd (look for the signs) and the bus stand ℡08394/228101, ⓦwww.malligihotels.com. This well-managed hotel is by far the most comfortable place to stay in Hospet, with something to suit most pockets. Options include clean economy rooms in an old block and two new wings with luxurious a/c rooms across immaculate lawns. There's also a good

sized pool (Rs25/hour for non-residents), an ayurvedic massage centre and the popular *Waves* complex, which boasts two quality multi-cuisine restaurants – one al fresco, the other in an a/c dining hall. ③–⑧

Priyadarshini MG Rd, 5min from the bus stand, towards the railway station. ℡08394/228838. Large hotel with comfortable a/c rooms and TVs – some have balconies. Also two good restaurants, the veg *Naivedyam* and the non-veg *Manasa* bar and beer garden. ⑤–⑥

Pushpak Lodge Near the bus stand, MG Rd ℡08394/221380. The best of the budget options, with 24 basic but clean en-suite rooms. Next door to the *Shanbhog* restaurant (see above). ①–②

Shivananda Next to the KSRTC bus stand ℡08394/220700, ⓕ08394/220030. Well-maintained hotel with spotless rooms, all en suite with cable TV. Some a/c. Good value. ④

Getting to Hampi

By far the most ostentatious way to arrive in Hampi is on KSTDC's daily six-seater **helicopter** flight from Bengaluru, which includes a guided local tour by taxi, breakfast, lunch and "high tea" at Hampi ($3990). KSTDC's humbler guided **tour** by bus (daily; Rs 140) stops at just three of Hampi's sites and spends an inordinate amount of time at the far less interesting Tungabhadra Dam. Even so, it could be worthwhile if you're short of time. Book through the KSTDC Transport Wing (℡08394/221008).

Frequent **buses to Hampi** run from Hospet's bus stand between 6.30am and 7.30pm; the journey takes thirty minutes. If you arrive late, either stay in Hospet, or take a taxi (Rs120–150) or one of the rickshaws (Rs60–80) that gather outside the railway station. It's also possible to catch a bus to **Kamalapuram**, at the south side of the site, and explore the ruins from there, catching a bus back to Hospet from Hampi Bazaar at the end of the day. **Bicycles** are available for rent at several stalls along the main street, but the trip to, around, and back from the site is a long one in the heat. **Auto-rickshaws**, best arranged through hotels such as the *Malligi* or *Priyadarshini*, will also take you to Hampi and back and charge around Rs50–60 per hour, but the road is horrendously pot-holed, making the trip preferable by bus. For the adventurous, Bullet **motorbikes** are available to rent (or buy) from Bharat Motors (☏08394/224704) near *Rama Talkies*. Finally, some hotels can arrange **guides** to meet you in Hampi; ask at the *Malligi* or *Priyadarshini*.

Hampi (Vijayanagar)

The city of Bidjanagar [Vijayanagar] is such that the pupil of the eye has never seen a place like it, and the ear of intelligence has never been informed that there existed anything to equal it in the world... The bazaars are extremely long and broad... Roses are sold everywhere. These people could not live without roses, and they look upon them as quite as necessary as food... Each class of men belonging to each profession has shops contiguous the one to the other; the jewellers sell publicly in the bazaars pearls, rubies, emeralds and diamonds. In this agreeable locality, as well as in the king's palace, one sees numerous running streams and canals formed of chiselled stone, polished and smooth... This empire contains so great a population that it would be impossible to give an idea of it without entering into extensive details.

Abdu'r-Razzaq, the Persian ambassador who visited Vijayanagar in 1443

The ruined city of **Vijayanagar** (City of Victory) – better known as **HAMPI**, the name of the main local village – spills from the south bank of the River Tungabhadra, littered among a surreal landscape of golden-brown granite boulders and leafy banana fields. According to Hindu mythology, the settlement began its days as Kishkinda, the monkey kingdom of the Ramayana, ruled by the monkey kings Bali and Sugriva, and their ambassador, Hanuman; the weird rocks – some balanced in perilous arches, others heaped in colossal, hill-sized piles – are said to have been flung down by their armies in a show of strength.

Between the fourteenth and sixteenth centuries, this was the most powerful Hindu capital in the Deccan. Travellers such as the Portuguese chronicler Domingo Paez, who stayed for two years after 1520, were astonished by its size and wealth, telling tales of markets full of silk and precious gems, beautiful, bejewelled courtesans, ornate palaces and joyous festivities. However, in the second half of the sixteenth century, the dazzling city was devastated by a six-month Muslim siege. Only stone, brick and stucco structures survived the ensuing sack – monolithic deities, crumbling houses and abandoned temples dominated by towering *gopuras* – as well as the sophisticated irrigation system that channelled water to huge tanks and temples.

Thanks to the Muslim onslaught, most of Hampi's monuments are in disappointingly poor shape, appearing a lot older than their four or five hundred years. Yet the serene riverine setting and air of magic that lingers over the site, sacred for centuries before a city was ever founded here, make it one of India's most extraordinary locations. Mainstream tourism has thus far made little impact: along with streams of Hindu pilgrims and tatty-haired *sadhus* who hole up in the more isolated rock crevices and shrines, most visitors are budget travellers straight from Goa. Many find it difficult to leave, and spend weeks chilling out in cafés, wandering to whitewashed hilltop temples and gazing at the spectacular sunsets.

The **best time to come** to Hampi, weather-wise, is from late October to early March, when daytime temperatures are low enough to allow long forays on foot through the ruins. The village starts to get busy over Christmas and New Year, however, and for a month or so from early January the site is swamped by an exodus of travellers from Goa. If you want to enjoy Hampi at its best, come outside peak season.

Some history

This was an area of minor political importance under the Chalukyas, but the rise of the **Vijayanagar empire** seems to have been a direct response, in the first half of the fourteenth century, to the expansionist aims of Muslims from the north, most notably Malik Kafur and Muhammad-bin-Tughluq. Two Hindu brothers from Andhra Pradesh, **Harihara** and **Bukka**, who had been employed as treasury officers in Kampila, 19km east of Hampi, were captured by the Tughluqs and taken to Delhi, where they supposedly converted to Islam. Assuming them to be suitably tamed, the Delhi sultan despatched them to quell civil disorder in Kampila, which they duly did, only to abandon both Islam and allegiance to Delhi shortly afterwards, preferring to establish their own independent Hindu kingdom. Within a few years, they controlled vast tracts of land from coast to coast. In 1343, their new capital, Vijayanagar, was founded on the southern banks of the River Tungabhadra, a location long considered sacred by Hindus. The city's most glorious period was under the reign of **Krishna Deva Raya** (1509–29), when it enjoyed a near monopoly on the lucrative trade in Arabian horses and Indian spices passing through the coastal ports.

With its natural features and massive fortifications, Vijayanagar was virtually impregnable. In 1565, however, following his interference in the affairs of local Muslim sultanates, the regent Rama Raya was drawn into a battle with a confederacy of Muslim forces, 100km away to the north, which left the city open to attack. At first, fortune appeared to be on the side of the Hindu forces, but there were as many as ten thousand Muslims in their number, and loyalties may well have been divided. When two Vijayanagar Muslim generals suddenly deserted, the army fell into disarray. Defeat came swiftly; although members of his family fled with untold hoards of gold and jewels, Rama Raya was captured and suffered a grisly death at the hands of the sultan of Ahmadnagar. Vijayanagar then fell victim to a series of destructive raids, and its days of splendour were brought to an abrupt end.

Practicalities

Buses from Hospet terminate close to where the road joins the main street in Hampi Bazaar, halfway along its dusty length. On the main bazaar, a little further towards the Virupaksha Temple, the **tourist office** (daily except Fri 10am–5.30pm; ☏08394/241339) can put you in touch with a **guide** (Rs500 per day) but not much else. Most visitors coming from Hospet organize a guide from there (see p.335).

Rented **bicycles**, available from stalls near the lodges, cost Rs5 per hour or Rs30–40 for a 24-hour period. They can be hard work on the bumpy roads, so consider a **motorbike** or **scooter**, which can be rented for Rs150–200 per day from the Raju stall, round the corner from the tourist office. Be warned, however, that the condition of some machines may not be all that safe.

The Canara Bank (Mon, Tues, Thurs & Fri 11am–2pm, Sat 11am–12.30pm) on Main Bazaar can **change money** and offers the best rates though they operate limited hours. Sneha Travels, whose main office is at D131/11 Hampi Bazaar (daily 9am–9pm; ☏08394/241590), can change money (at low-ish

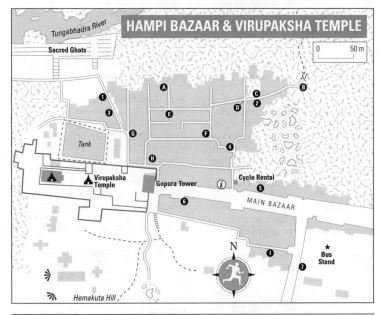

ACCOMMODATION				RESTAURANTS & CAFÉS			
Archana Guest House	A	Shanti Guest House	G	Geeta	5	Sri Sangameshwara	6
Garden Paradise	B	Shri Hari Krishna	F	New Shanti	3	Suresh	1
Gopi Guest House	E	Shri Rama Guest House	H	Ravi's Rose	2	Trishul	4
Rahul Guest House	I	Sudha Guest House	C	Shanthi	7		
		Vikky	D				

rates), advance cash on credit cards and book airline and train tickets as well as luxury buses to Bengaluru and sleeper coaches to Goa and Gokarna (although the buses drop people off right in Hampi Bazaar, you have to pick them up from Hospet, due to pressure from the local taxi/rickshaw mafia). Also, whatever you may have been told, Paulo Travels' Gokarna bus involves a transfer at Ankola in the small hours (often with a long wait for a connecting service, and/or the option of rickshaws to complete the journey, as the service continues to Goa. You may prefer the local KSTDC buses from Hospet, which do go all the way into Gokarna town. There are at least a dozen **Internet** outlets around town, which have fixed a rate of Rs60/hr.

Run by Shri Swamy Sadashiva Yogi, the **Shivananda Yoga Ashram** overlooking the river, past the site of the new footbridge and coracle crossing, offers courses in **yoga and meditation**. The **Amcart Ayurvedic Centre** (daily 10.30am–6pm), near the *Mango Tree* café, has eight consultant doctors and offers a wide range of treatments and courses.

Accommodation

If you're happy to make do with basic amenities, Hampi is a far more enjoyable place to stay than Hospet, with around fifty congenial **guesthouses** and plenty of cafés to hang out in after a long day in the heat. Staying in the village also means you can be up and out early enough to catch the sunrise over the ruins – a mesmerizing spectacle. Some travellers shun Hampi Bazaar for fast-growing **Virupapuragadda** across the river, favoured by Israeli travellers. Outside **high** season, which lasts for six weeks starting around Christmas, you may well get a substantial discount on the room rates quoted below. Note there is generally a 10am checkout.

Places under the Hampi Bazaar heading appear on the Hampi Bazaar and Virupaksha Temple map (p.337); those under the Virupapuragadda and Kamalapuram heading appear on the main Hampi/Vijayanagar map (p.340).

Hampi Bazaar

Archana Guest House River View, Janata Plot ☎08394/241547. Friendly place comprising an old and new block. All the rooms are clean and have hot water, plus there's a rooftop terrace affording river and temple views. No restaurant, but hot and cold drinks available. ❸

Garden Paradise Eastern edge of village ☎m94496 80314. Four cute but cramped huts (shared bathrooms) and five en suite, in a prime riverside location with a relaxing restaurant. ❸–❹

Gopi Guest House A short walk down the lanes behind *Shanti* ☎08394/241695, ✉gopiguesthouse93@yahoo.co.in. Ten en-suite rooms and a pleasant rooftop café with temple view. ❸

Rahul Guest House South of Main St, near the bus stand ☎08394/241648. Tiny place offering just two rooms – clean and friendly. Mosquito nets provided. ❹

Shanti Guest House Just north of the Virupaksha temple ☎08394/241568. An enduring favourite, comprising a dozen or so twin-bedded cells ranged on two storeys around a leafy inner courtyard. It's basic (showers and toilets are shared) but spotless, and all rooms have fans and windows. ❷–❸

Shri Hari Krishna Janata Plot ☎m94480 03672. The most appealing of the many small backpackers' guesthouses crammed into the narrow lanes north of the main bazaar, run by a friendly brother and sister, Champa and Ranjeet. The pink-painted rooms, opening on to a central corridor on the ground floor, are immaculate and all have mosquito nets, quiet fans, windows and well-maintained tiled bathrooms (a rarity for this area). ❷–❸

Shri Rama Guest House Next to the Virupaksha temple ☎08394/241219, ✉venkannaj@yahoo.com. Rock-bottom en-suite rooms. Also has a rooftop restaurant. ❷

Sudha Guest House At the east end of the village ☎08394/241451. Very welcoming, attractively situated family operation. The en-suite rooms downstairs are cooler; those on the upper floor are smaller with shared facilities. Mosquito nets provided. Good value. ❶–❸

Vikky Just beyond *Trishul Restaurant* ☎08394/241694. Welcoming place with small clean en-suite rooms (mosquito nets provided) and a popular rooftop restaurant. ❸

Virupapuragadda and Kamalapuram

Goan Corner 600m northeast from the coracle crossing ☎m94487 718951. Large complex tucked away in the paddy fields near the rocky outcrop, with a lively restaurant and a range of rooms and huts, some offering attached bathrooms. ❶–❷

KSTDC Mayura Bhuvaneshwari Kamalapuram, 4km from Hampi Bazaar ☎08394/241574, ✆08394/241474. The only remotely upmarket place to stay within reach of the ruins: clean en-suite rooms and inexpensive a/c options. Fixed government rates mean that there are no peak season price hikes. In addition, there's a pleasant garden, restaurant and a bar serving cold beers, but it feels detached from Hampi Bazaar and Kamalapuram itself lacks charm. ❸–❻

Sai Plaza ☎08533/287066, ✉vir_hampi@yahoo.com. Attractive en-suite huts, dotted around a pleasant landscaped garden, with swing beds outside. ❷

Sunny Guest House ☎08533/324000. A row of compact rooms and somewhat roomier huts set in nicely landscaped garden. ❷

Umashankar Lodge ☎08533/287067. One of the better places to stay across the river. Small but clean en-suite rooms (the upstairs ones have hot showers) grouped round a leafy courtyard. ❷–❸

The site

Although spread over 26 square kilometres, the ruins of Vijayanagar are mostly concentrated in two distinct groups: the first lies in and around **Hampi Bazaar** and the nearby riverside area, encompassing the city's most sacred enclave of temples and *ghats*; the second centres on the **royal enclosure** – 3km south of the river, just northwest of **Kamalapuram** village – which holds the remains of palaces, pavilions, elephant stables, guardhouses and temples.

Festivals in Hampi

Vijayanagar's main **festivals** include, at the Virupaksha Temple, a **car festival** with street processions each April, and, in December, the marriage ceremony of the deities, accompanied by drummers and dances. The **Hampi Festival** (Nov 3–5), organized by the tourist department, features classical music and dance from both Carnatic and Hindustani (North Indian) traditions performed on temple stages and at Anegondi. The festival, which is beginning to attract well-known musicians and dancers, has been growing in size and prestige, and hotels in the area can get booked up well in advance. The national **Shivaratri** festival in February or March also draws thousands of pilgrims to the Virupaksha Temple.

Between the two stretches a long boulder-choked hill and a number of banana plantations, fed by ancient irrigation canals.

Frequent buses run from Hospet to Hampi Bazaar and Kamalapuram, and you can start your tour from either; most visitors prefer to set out on foot or bicycle from the former. After a look around the soaring **Virupaksha Temple**, work your way east along the main street, Hampi Bazaar, and riverbank to the beautiful **Vitthala Temple**, and then back via the **Achutharaya** complex at the foot of Matanga Hill. From here, a dirt path leads south to the royal enclosure, but it's easier to return to the bazaar and pick up the tarred road, calling in at **Hemakuta Hill**, a group of pre-Vijayanagar temples, en route.

On KSTDC's whistle-stop **guided tour**, it's possible to see most of the highlights in a day. If you can, however, set aside at least two or three days to explore the site and its environs, crossing the river by **coracle** to **Anegondi** village, with a couple of side hikes to hilltop viewpoints: the west side of Hemakuta Hill, overlooking Hampi Bazaar, is best for sunsets, while **Matanga Hill** offers what has to be one of the world's most exotic sunrise vistas.

Hampi Bazaar, the Virupaksha Temple and around

Along Hampi's long, straight main street, **Hampi Bazaar**, which runs east from the eastern entrance of the Virupaksha Temple, you can still make out the remains of Vijayanagar's ruined, columned bazaar, partly inhabited by today's lively market. Landless labourers live in many of the crumbling 500-year-old buildings.

Dedicated to a local form of Shiva known as Virupaksha or Pampapati, the still-functioning **Virupaksha Temple** (daily 6.30am–12.30pm & 2–8.30pm; Rs2; camera Rs50, video Rs500) dominates the village, drawing a steady flow of

Admission charges

Admission to some of the best preserved of Hampi's archeological sites – namely the Vitthala Temple and Lotus Mahal – is by **ticket**. Issued by the ASI at the entrances between 8am and 4pm and valid for one day only, the pass gains you entry to both sites, as well as the Royal Enclosure and Zenana complex surrounding the Lotus Mahal, and officially costs US$5 – or its rupee equivalent – for foreigners, and Rs10 for Indians. You'll probably be approached by characters outside the gates offering significantly reduced rates; they're local guides who've got together with the Survey ticket-wallahs to run a nice little scam which gets you in for less (a lot less if you haggle hard) and allows them to pocket the fee.

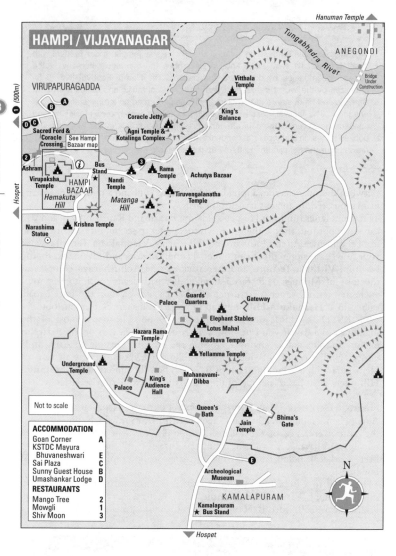

HAMPI / VIJAYANAGAR

Hanuman Temple

Tungabhadra River

ANEGONDI

Bridge Under Construction

VIRUPAPURAGADDA

Ⓐ

Ⓑ

Vitthala Temple

King's Balance

Ⓞ Ⓒ

Sacred Ford & Coracle Crossing

See Hampi Bazaar map

Coracle Jetty

Agni Temple & Kotalinga Complex

Ⓞ Ashram

Bus Stand

ⓘ

Ⓞ

Rama Temple

Achutya Bazaar

Virupaksha Temple

HAMPI BAZAAR

Nandi Temple

Tiruvengalanatha Temple

Hemakuta Hill

Matanga Hill

Narashima Statue

Krishna Temple

Palace

Guards' Quarters

Gateway

Elephant Stables

Hazara Rama Temple

Lotus Mahal

Madhava Temple

Yellamma Temple

Underground Temple

Palace

King's Audience Hall

Mahanavami-Dibba

Queen's Bath

Bhima's Gate

Jain Temple

Not to scale

Ⓔ

Archeological Museum

N

KAMALAPURAM

Kamalapuram Bus Stand

Hospet

ACCOMMODATION

Goan Corner	A
KSTDC Mayura Bhuvaneshwari	E
Sai Plaza	C
Sunny Guest House	B
Umashankar Lodge	D

RESTAURANTS

Mango Tree	2
Mowgli	1
Shiv Moon	3

pilgrims from all over southern India. Also known as **Sri Virupaksha Swami**, the temple is free for all who come for *arati* (worship; daily 6.30–8am & 6.30–8pm), when the temple is at its most atmospheric. The complex consists of two courts, each entered through a *gopura*. The larger gateway, on the east, is approximately 56m high, topped by a single wagon-vault and *kalasha*, a pot-shaped finial. In the southwest corner, a water channel runs along a large columned *mandapa*.

A colonnade surrounds the inner court, usually filled with pilgrims dozing and singing religious songs. On entering, if the temple elephant is around, you can get her to bless you by placing a rupee in her trunk. In the middle, the principal temple is approached through a *mandapa* hallway whose carved

△ Coracle crossing, Hampi

columns feature rearing animals. Rare Vijayanagar-era paintings on the *mandapa* ceiling show aspects of Shiva, a procession with the sage Vidyaranya, the ten incarnations of Vishnu and scenes from the Mahabharata; the style of the figures is reminiscent of local shadow puppets. Faced by a brass image of Nandi, a *shivalingam* is housed in the small sanctuary, its entrance decorated with painted *makaras*, semi-aquatic mythical animals whose bodies end with foliage instead of a tail. Blue water spouts from their mouths, while above them flicker yellow flames. Just outside the main temple's wall, immediately to the north, is a small earlier temple, thought to have been the "ancestor" of the Virupaksha.

The sacred **ford** in the river is reached from the Virupaksha's north *gopura*; you can also get there by following the lane around the impressive temple **tank**. A *mandapa* overlooks the steps that originally led to the river, now some distance away. **Coracles** ply from this part of the bank, just as they did five centuries ago, ferrying villagers to the fields and tourists to the increasingly popular enclave of **Virupapuragadda** on the other side. The path through the village eventually winds to an impressive ruined bridge, and on to the hilltop Hanuman shrine – a recommended round walk described on p.343.

Matanga Hill

The place to head for sunrise is the boulder hill immediately east of Hampi Bazaar. From the end of the main street, an ancient paved pathway winds up a rise, at the top of which the magnificent **Tiruvengalanatha Temple** is revealed. The views improve as you progress up **Matanga Hill**, at whose summit a small stone temple provides an extraordinary vantage point. It's a good idea to go in a small group and remain vigilant, as muggings have been known early in the morning along this path.

The riverside path

To reach the Vitthala Temple, walk east from the Virupaksha along the length of Hampi Bazaar, at the end of which a monolithic **Nandi** statue gazes from afar at the main temple from its shrine. You can also nip into the Cauvery Crafts Shop and small photo gallery on the left-hand side of the colonnade here. Fifty metres or so before the end of the bazaar, a path on the left, staffed at regular intervals by conch-blowing *sadhus* and an assortment of other ragged mendicants, follows the river past a couple of cafés and numerous shrines, including a **Rama temple** – home to hordes of fearless monkeys. Beyond at least four Vishnu shrines, the paved and colonnaded **Achutya Bazaar** leads due south to the **Tiruvengalanatha Temple**, whose beautiful stone carvings – among them some of Hampi's famed erotica – are being restored by the ASI. Back on the main path again, make a short detour across the rocks leading to the river to see the little-visited waterside **Agni Temple**; next to it, the **Kotalinga** complex consists of 108 (an auspicious number) tiny *lingas*, carved on a flat rock. As you approach the Vitthala Temple, to the south is an archway known as the **King's Balance**, where the rajas were weighed against gold, silver and jewels to be distributed to the city's priests.

Vitthala Temple

Although the area of the **Vitthala Temple** (daily 6am–6pm; $5 [Rs10]; ticket also valid for the Lotus Mahal on the same day) does not show the same evidence of early cult worship as Virupaksha, the ruined bridge to the west probably dates from before Vijayanagar times. The bathing *ghat* may be from the Chalukya or Ganga period, but as the temple has fallen into disuse it seems that the river crossing (*tirtha*) here has not had the same sacred significance as the Virupaksha site. Now designated a World Heritage Monument by UNESCO, the Vitthala Temple was built for Vishnu, who according to legend was too embarrassed by its ostentation to live there. The tower of the principal Vishnu shrine is made of brick – unusual for South India – capped with a hemispherical roof; in front is an enclosed *mandapa* with carved columns, the ceiling of which has partly collapsed. Two doorways lead to a dark passageway surrounding the sanctuary.

The open *mandapa* features slender monolithic granite **musical pillars**, which were constructed so as to sound the notes of the scale when struck. Today, due to vandalism and erosion from being repeatedly beaten, heavy security makes sure that no one is allowed to touch them. Guides, however, will happily demonstrate the musical resonance of other pillars on an adjacent structure. Outer columns sport characteristic Vijayanagar rearing horses, while friezes of lions, elephants and horses on the moulded basement display sculptural trickery – you can transform one beast into another simply by masking one portion of the image.

In front of the temple, to the east, a stone representation of a wooden processional **rath**, or chariot, houses an image of Garuda, Vishnu's bird vehicle. Now cemented, at one time the chariot's wheels revolved. The three *gopura* entrances, made of granite at the base with brick and stucco multistorey towers, are now badly damaged.

Anegondi and beyond

With more time, and a sense of adventure, you can head across the Tungabhadra to **ANEGONDI**, a fortress town predating Vijayanagar and the city's fourteenth-century headquarters. The most pleasant way to go is by **putti**, a circular rush-basket coracle, from the ford 1500m east of the Vitthala temple; the *puttis*, which are today reinforced with plastic sheets, also carry bicycles. Work on a new road bridge, which would almost certainly put the coracle crossing out of business, had been temporarily abandoned due to a political dispute at the time of writing.

Forgotten temples and fortifications litter Anegondi village and its quiet surroundings. The ruined **Huchchappa-matha Temple**, near the river gateway, is worth a look for its black stone lathe-turned pillars and fine panels of dancers. **Aramani**, a ruined palace in the centre, stands opposite the home of the descendants of the royal family; also in the centre, the **Ranganatha temple** is still active.

A huge wooden temple chariot stands in the village square. To complete a five-kilometre loop back to Hampi from here (best attempted by bicycle), head left (west) along the road, winding through sugar-cane fields towards the sacred **Pampla Sarovar**, signposted down a dirt lane to the left. The small temple above this square bathing tank, tended by a *swami* who will proudly show you photos of his pilgrimage to Mount Kailash, is dedicated to the goddess Lakshmi and holds a cave containing a footprint of Vishnu. If you are staying around Anegondi, this quiet and atmospheric spot is best visited early in the evening during *arati* (worship).

Another worthwhile detour from the road is the hike up to the tiny white-washed **Hanuman Temple**, perched on a rocky hilltop north of the river, from where you can enjoy superb views over Hampi, especially at sunrise or sunset. The steep climb up to it takes around half an hour. Keep following the road west for another 3km and you'll eventually arrive at an impressive old **stone bridge** dating from Vijayanagar times. The bridge no longer spans the river, but just beyond it to the west, another coracle crossing returns you to a point about halfway between the Vitthala Temple and Hampi bazaar. This rewarding round walk can, of course, be completed in reverse, beginning at the sacred ford. With a bike, it takes around three hours, including the side trips outlined above; allow most of the day if you attempt it on foot, and take plenty of water.

Hemakuta Hill and around

Directly above Hampi Bazaar, **Hemakuta Hill** is dotted with pre-Vijayanagar temples that probably date from between the ninth and eleventh centuries (late Chalukya or Ganga). Three are of the *trikutachala* (three-peaked hills) type, with three shrines facing into a common centre. Aside from the architecture, the main reason to clamber up here is to admire the **views** of the ruins and surrounding countryside. Looking across the boulder-covered terrain and banana plantations, the sheer western edge of the hill is Hampi's number-one sunset spot, attracting a crowd of blissed-out tourists most evenings, along with a couple of entrepreneurial chai-wallahs and little boys posing for photos in Hanuman costumes.

A couple of interesting monuments lie on the road leading south towards the main, southern group of ruins. The first of these, a walled **Krishna temple complex** to the west of the road, dates from 1513. Although dilapidated in parts, it features some fine carving and shrines.

Hampi's most-photographed monument stands just south of the Krishna temple in its own enclosure. Depicting Vishnu in his incarnation (*avatar*) as the Man-Lion, the monolithic **Narashima** statue, with its bulging eyes and crossed legs strapped into yogic pose, is one of Vijayanagar's greatest treasures.

The southern and royal monuments

The most impressive remains of Vijayanagar, the city's **royal monuments**, lie some 3km south of Hampi Bazaar, spread over a large expanse of open ground. Before tackling the ruins proper, it's a good idea to get your bearings with a visit to the small **Archeological Museum** (daily except Fri 10am–5pm; free) at Kamalapuram, which can be reached by bus from Hospet or Hampi. Turn right out of the Kamalapuram bus stand, take the first turning on the right, and the museum is on the left after two minutes' walk. Among the sculpture, weapons, palm-leaf manuscripts and painting from Vijayanagar and Anegondi, the highlight is a superb scale model of the city, giving an excellent bird's-eye view of the entire site.

To walk into the city from the museum, go back to the main road and take the nearby turning marked "Hampi 4km". After 200m or so you reach the partly ruined massive **inner city wall**, made from granite slabs, which runs 32km around the city, in places as high as 10m. The outer wall was almost twice as long. At one time, there were said to have been seven city walls; coupled with areas of impenetrable forest and the river to the north, they made the city virtually impregnable.

Just beyond the wall, the **citadel area** was once enclosed by another wall and gates, of which only traces remain. To the east, the small *ganigitti* ("oil-woman's") fourteenth-century **Jain temple** features a simple, stepped pyramidal tower of undecorated horizontal slabs. Beyond it is **Bhima's Gate**, once one of the principal entrances to the city, named after the Titan-like Pandava prince and hero of the Mahabharata. Like many of the gates, it is "bent", a form of defence that meant anyone trying to get in had to make two ninety-degree turns. Bas-reliefs depict such episodes as Bhima avenging the attempted rape of his wife, Draupadi, by killing the general Kichaka. Draupadi vowed she would not dress her hair until Kichaka was dead; one panel shows her tying up her locks, the vow fulfilled.

Back on the path, to the west, the plain facade of the fifteen-metre-square **Queen's Bath** belies its glorious interior, open to the sky and surrounded by corridors with 24 different domes. Eight projecting balconies overlook where once was water; traces of Islamic-influenced stucco decoration survive. Women from the royal household would bathe here and umbrellas were placed in shafts in the tank floor to protect them from the sun. The water supply channel can be seen outside.

Continuing northwest brings you to **Mahanavami-Dibba**, or "House of Victory", built to commemorate a successful campaign in Orissa. A twelve-metre pyramidal structure with a square base, it is said to have been where the king gave and received honours and gifts. From here he watched the magnificent parades, music and dance performances, martial arts displays, elephant fights and animal sacrifices that celebrated the ten-day Dussehra festival famed throughout the land (the tradition of spectacular Dussehra festivals is continued at Mysore; see box on p.282). Carved reliefs of dancers, elephant fights, animals and figures decorate the sides of the platform. Two huge monolithic doors on the ground nearby may have once been part of a building atop the platform, of which no signs remain. To the west, another platform – the largest at Vijayanagar – is thought to be the basement of the **King's Audience Hall**. Stone bases of a hundred pillars remain, in an arrangement that causes speculation as to how the building could have been used; there are no passageways or open areas.

The two-storey **Lotus Mahal** (daily 6am–6pm; $5 [Rs10]; ticket also valid for the Vitthala Temple on the same day), a little further north and part of the **Zenana enclosure** (women's quarters), was designed for the pleasure of Krishna Deva Raya's queen: a place where she could relax, particularly in summer. Displaying a strong Indo-Islamic influence, the pavilion is open on the ground floor, whereas the upper level (no longer accessible by stairs) contains windows and balcony seats. A moat surrounding the building is thought to have provided water-cooled air via tubes.

Beyond the Lotus Mahal, the **elephant stables**, a series of high-ceilinged, domed chambers entered through arches, are the most substantial surviving secular buildings at Vijayanagar – a reflection of the high status accorded to elephants, both ceremonial and in battle. An upper level, with a pillared hall, is capped with a tower at the centre; it may have been used by the musicians who accompanied the royal elephant processions. There are usually tender coconuts on sale under the shade of a nearby tree.

Walking west of the Lotus Mahal, you pass two temples before reaching the road to Hemakuta Hill. The rectangular enclosure wall of the small **Hazara Rama** ("One thousand Ramas") **Temple**, thought to have been the private palace shrine, features a series of medallion figures and bands of detailed friezes showing scenes from the Ramayana. The inner of two *mandapas* contains four finely carved polished black columns. Many of the ruins here are said to have been part of the Hazara Rama Bazaar, which ran northeast from the temple. Much of the so-called **Underground Temple**, or Prasanna Virupaksha, lies below ground level and is filled with rainwater for part of the year. Turning north (right) onto the road that runs west of the Underground Temple will take you back to Hampi Bazaar, via Hemakuta Hill.

Eating

Hampi has a plethora of traveller-oriented chai stalls and **restaurants** – many of the most popular are attached to guesthouses, such as *Rahul, Gopi, Vikky* and *Sudha*, all around the bazaar, or in the growing row of joints in Virupapuragadda. As a holy site, the whole village is supposed to be strictly vegetarian and alcohol-free, but one or two places bend the rules for inveterate carnivores and even more are happy to supply a surreptitious beer or two.

Geeta On the main bazaar. Old favourite not far from the bus stand, serving wholesome Western snacks, Indian veg, *momos* and ravioli.

Mango Tree 300m beyond the sacred ford. A relaxed hangout with a terraced garden overlooking the river that does a wide range of vegetarian dishes including good thalis and delicious salads. A great place to linger, with a terrace garden overlooking the river.

Mowgli Virupapuragadda. At the west end of the strip, this popular lodge-restaurant has plenty of space to lounge on mattresses beside the rice paddies bordering the river, though the food – Indian, Israeli and Western – is mostly bland.

New Shanti On the path from the Virupaksha Temple down to the river. Best known for its delicious cakes and breads, but also does standard Indian and continental dishes.

Ravi's Rose East end of the village. Rooftop restaurant that (unlike many tourist places) can actually make spicy dishes. Good music system and lassis.

Shanthi Bus stand. Delicious breakfast *parathas* and spicy Tamil-style dishes served up at this small stall at the end of the row.

Shiv Moon On the riverside path east of the village. A pleasant place to break the journey to Vitthala Temple, serving pasta and curries, and with lovely views.

Sri Sangameshwara On the main bazaar. One of the more authentically Indian meals joints on the main street, boasting the best thalis and masala dosas in the village.

Suresh On the path from the Virupaksha Temple down to the river. Established rooftop restaurant specializing in tuna, Goan dishes and *momos*.

Trishul On the lane beside the tourist office. One of the widest menus in the village, including chicken, tuna, lasagne, pizza and desserts such as apple crumble.

Badami and around

Now quiet villages, **Badami**, **Aihole** and **Pattadakal** in northwest Karnataka were once the capital cities of the **Chalukyas**, who ruled much of the Deccan between the fourth and eighth centuries. The astonishing profusion of **temples** in the area defies belief, and it is hard to imagine a society imbued with such artistry and devotion. Badami and Aihole's cave temples are some of the most important of their type. The many freestanding temples include some of the earliest in India and, uniquely, it is possible to see both northern (Nagari) and southern (Dravidian) architectural styles side by side. Several other temples in the area fit into neither style (classified by art historians as "undifferentiated"), thus providing evidence of the experimentation and creativity of the stonemasons of this era.

The earliest cave and structural temples around Badami and Aihole are assigned to the period of the Chalukyas' rise to power in the mid-sixth century and are predominantly **Hindu**, although there is also evidence of Jain and Buddhist influence. The first important Chalukyan king was Pulakeshin I (535–66), but it was Pulakeshin II (610–42) who captured the Pallava capital of Kanchipuram in Tamil Nadu and extended the empire to include Maharashtra to the north, the Konkan coast on the west and the whole of Karnataka. Although the Pallavas subsequently briefly took most of his territory, including the capital Badami, at the end of his reign, Pulakeshin's son Vikramaditya I (655–81) later recovered it, and the Chalukyas continued to reign until the mid-eighth century. Some suggest that the incursion of the Pallavas accounts for the southern elements seen in the structural temples.

Badami has the best accommodation and eating options so most visitors use it as their base for the whole area: as well as the remains at Aihole and Pattadakal, there are more temples to explore in the villages of **Mahakuta** and **Banashankari**, on the outskirts of town. The **best time to visit** is from October to early March, between the monsoons and the scorching summers. In April and May much of northwest Karnataka becomes unbearably hot and government offices only open between 8am and 1pm.

Badami

Surrounded by a yawning expanse of flat farmland, **BADAMI**, capital of the Chalukyas from 543 AD to 757 AD, extends east into a gorge between two red sandstone hills, topped by two ancient fort complexes. The south is riddled with cave temples, while to the north stand early structural temples. Beyond Badami, to the east, is an artificial lake, **Agastya**, said to date from the fifth century. The whole Badami area is also home to numerous troupes of **monkeys**, especially around the monuments, and you're likely to find yourself surrounded if you're unwise enough to produce any comestibles.

Practicalities

Badami **bus stand** – in the centre of the village on Main (Station) Road – sees frequent daily services to Gadag (2hr), Hospet (5hr), Hubli (3hr), Bijapur (4hr) and Kolhapur, and local buses to Aihole and Pattadakal. The **railway station** is 5km north, along a road lined with *neem* trees; tongas (Rs30 or Rs5 per head shared), buses and auto-rickshaws are available for the journey into town. The slow metre-gauge line connects Badami to Gadag to the south and Bagalkot to the north, from where a broad-gauge line runs to Bijapur and beyond. The conversion to bring Badami onto the broad-gauge network is still awaited.

The friendly **tourist office** (Mon–Sat: April & May 8am–1pm; June–March 10am–5.30pm; ☎08357/220414), off Ramdurg Road next to the KSTDC *Hotel Mayura Chalukya*, can put you in touch with a **guide**. The Syndicate Bank, opposite the bus station in the Rajsangam Complex, can **change traveller's cheques** and there is also a State Bank of India **ATM** there. The *Hotel Badami Court* has exchange facilities as well.

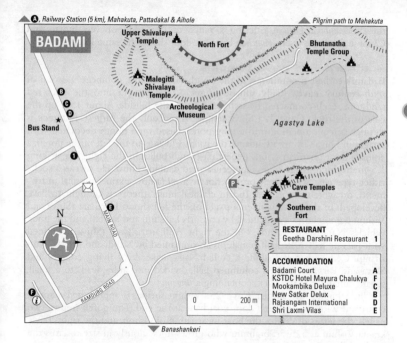

BADAMI

Upper Shivalaya
Temple
North Fort

Bhutanatha
Temple Group

Ⓑ
Ⓒ
Ⓓ

Malegitti
Shivalaya
Temple

Archeological
Museum

Agastya Lake

Bus Stand

Ⓕ

N

Cave Temples

Southern
Fort

RESTAURANT
Geetha Darshini Restaurant   1

ACCOMMODATION
Badami Court   A
KSTDC Hotel Mayura Chalukya   F
Mookambika Deluxe   C
New Satkar Delux   B
Rajsangam International   D
Shri Laxmi Vilas   E

MAIN ROAD

RAMDURG ROAD

Ⓕ
ⓘ

0   200 m

▼ Banashankeri

Ambika Tours & Travels (☎08357/220067) at *Hotel Mookambika* run **tours** in Ambassador taxis taking in Badami, Mahakuta, Aihole and Pattadakal (Rs700 for a fairly full day). One of the best ways of exploring the closer sites, including Mahakuta and the temple village of Banashankari, is to rent a **bicycle** (Rs3 per hr) from stalls in front of the bus stand. Cycling to Aihole and Pattadakal is a challenge though.

Accommodation and eating

Of Badami's handful of **places to stay**, the most comfortable is the *Hotel Badami Court* (☎08357/220230, ✉rafiqmht@blr.vsnl.net.in; ⓪–⑧), 2km north of town towards the railway station, which has 27 en-suite, plain but spacious rooms on two storeys ranged around a garden. Meals and expensive beer are available, and their swimming pool is open to non-residents for Rs80 per hour. The friendly ⚚ *Rajsangam International* (☎08357/221991, ⓦwww .hotelrajsangam.com; ④–⑦), opposite the bus stand, is by far the best option in the centre of town, with very good, clean rooms, a small rooftop pool, two restaurants (see below) and a bar. Next door, the *Mookambika Deluxe* (☎08357/220067, ⑤220106; ③–⑤) has slightly dingy doubles on the ground floor and better a/c rooms upstairs. The KSTDC *Hotel Mayura Chalukya* (☎08357/220046; ②), on the south side of town just off Ramdurg Road, has fairly basic rooms with decrepit plumbing and peeling plaster but, despite fearless scavenging monkeys, the gardens are pleasant and there's a restaurant. Renovations planned for 2007 include a/c rooms.

The *Rajsangam* has two good **restaurants**: the *Banashree* serves pure-veg food at the front of the complex, while the *Shubashree* at the rear is non-veg and has a bar. A hundred metres south of the bus stand, good *iddlis*, *vadas* and *dosas* can be had at the *Geetha Darshini*. Alternatively, there's a plain restaurant upstairs at the *Mookambika Deluxe*, offering a range of veg and non-veg Indian and Chinese food; the lively *Kanchan* bar next door shares the same kitchen.

Southern Fort cave temples

Badami's earliest monuments, in the Southern Fort area, comprise a group of sixth-century **caves** (daily sunrise–sunset; $2 [Rs5]) cut into the hill's red sandstone, each connected by steps leading up the hillside. About 15m up the face of the rock, **Cave 1**, a Shiva temple, is probably the earliest. Entrance is through a triple opening into a long porch raised on a plinth decorated with images of Shiva's dwarf attendants, the *ganas*. Outside, to the left of the porch, a *dvarpala* door guardian stands beneath a Nandi bull. On the right is a striking 1.5-metre-high image of an eighteen-armed dancing Shiva. He carries a stick-zither-type *vina*, which may or may not be a *yal* (a now-extinct musical instrument), on which the earliest Indian classical music theory is thought to have developed. In the antechamber, a panel on the left shows Harihara (Shiva and Vishnu combined), accompanied by consorts Lakshmi and Parvati and the gods' vehicles Nandi and Garuda. On the right, Ardhanarishvara (Shiva combined with Parvati; half-male, half-female) is accompanied by Nandi and the skeleton Bringi. Ceiling panels include a coiled Naga snake deity, flying couples and Shiva and Parvati. Inside, a columned hall, divided into aisles, leads to a small, square sanctuary at the back, containing a *lingam*.

A little higher, the similar **Cave 2**, a Vishnu shrine, is approached across a courtyard with two *dvarpala* door guardians at the end. The porch houses two panels; the left is of Varaha, the boar incarnation of Vishnu, and the right, Trivi-krama, Vishnu as a dwarf brahmin who grows miraculously in size to cross the earth in three steps. On the ceiling nearby, Vishnu is shown riding his vehicle, Garuda. The central square of the ceiling features a lotus encircled by sixteen fish; other decoration includes swastika designs and flying couples. Traces of paintwork hint at how colourful the caves originally were.

Steps lead upward, past a natural cave containing a smashed image of the Buddhist *bodhisattva*, Padmapani (he who holds the lotus). On the right, a cleft

△ Cave temple, Badami

in the rock leads up to the fort. **Cave 3** (578 AD) stands beneath a thirty-metre-high perpendicular bluff. The largest of the group, with a facade measuring 21m from north to south, it is also considered the finest on account of the quality of its sculptural decoration. Eleven steps lead up to the plinth decorated with dwarf *ganas*. The stonework on the pillars is extremely elaborate, featuring male and female figures, lotus motifs and medallions portraying amorous couples.

Cave 4, a Jain temple, overlooks Agastya Lake and the town. This simpler shrine, carved from striped rock, dates from the sixth century. Seated and standing figures of the 24 *tirthankaras*, most without their identifying emblems, line the walls.

After seeing the caves, you can climb up to the **Southern Fort** and continue round the cliff before descending to the **Bhutanatha temples** at the lakeside. Look out for the rock carvings of Vishnu both reclining on the serpent Adisesha and in his ten incarnations.

North Fort

North of **Lake Agastya** lie a number of structural temples and the small **Archeological Museum** (daily except Fri 10am–5pm; Rs2), which contains sculpture from the region. Close to the museum is the start of the pilgrim's path to Mahakuta (see below). Although now dilapidated, the **Upper Shivalaya Temple** is one of the earliest Chalukyan buildings here. Scenes from the life of Krishna decorate the base and various images of him can be seen between pilasters on the walls. Only the sanctuary and tower of the **Lower Shivalaya** survive. Perched on a rock, the **Malegitti Shivalaya** (late seventh century) is the finest southern-style early Chalukyan temple. Its shrine is adjoined by a pillared hallway with small windows hewn out of stone and a single image on each side: Vishnu on the north and Shiva on the south. A path leads down to a small **Hanuman shrine** behind the fort, from which you can see the broad, well-defined path to Mahakuta.

Banashankari

A pleasant excursion by foot, bicycle or rickshaw is to the temple village of **BANASHANKARI**, 5km to the northwest of Badami; it is believed to date back to the sixth century, although much of it was built during the Maratha period of the eighteenth century. Banashankari is worth a visit more for its peaceful atmosphere than for its architectural interest. Dedicated to Shiva's consort Parvati, the shrine, with a large bathing tank, is the most important living temple of the region and attracts a steady stream of devotees throughout the year. During the *rath* (chariot) festival (held either in January or February), when the deity is led through the streets in procession, the usually quiet village is transformed into a noisy, chaotic, bustling fair, complete with tacky stalls, circus acts and live music.

Mahakuta

Another crop of seventh-century Chalukyan temples lies 15km out of Badami en route to Pattadakal at **MAHAKUTA**, a temple village which attracts local devotees, pilgrims and a sprinkling of *sadhus* – it may only be a minor league Chalukyan architectural sight, but it does have a timeless atmosphere, enhanced by its brooding banyan trees. Four buses a day and the occasional shared tempo run to the site, but the most interesting way to get here is to walk along the ancient **pilgrim trail** from Badami, a well-defined, paved, five-kilometre path, which will take you around two hours to complete. It can get very hot, so take plenty of water and an umbrella for shade.

The path starts a short way beyond the Archeological Museum, where it winds uphill past a series of crumbling shrines, gateways and old watercourses before levelling out on the plateau. The turning down to Mahakuta is easy to miss: look for a stone marker-post that reads "RP", which leads you to a steep, roughly paved stairway. At the bottom, the main temple complex is ranged around a crystal-clear spring-fed tank, popular with bathers (it's open to all) and offering an enjoyable spot for a dip at the end of your walk. On a rise above the tank, next to a shady courtyard dominated by a huge banyan tree, stands the whitewashed **Mahakutesvara Temple** with its silver-crowned *lingam*. Carved around the base of the temple are fine stone friezes, including an impressive detail on the southwest corner of Shiva and Parvati with Ravana, the demon king of Lanka. More carvings adorn the entrance and ceilings of the **Mallikar-juna Temple** on the opposite side of the tank, while in the clearing outside the nearby **Sangameshwar Temple** stands a gigantic stone-wheeled chariot used during the annual festival in May.

There are a couple of teashops but no official guesthouse; if you want **to stay**, you may be able to negotiate to use one of the very basic rooms outside the temple gates.

Aihole

No fewer than 125 temples, dating from the Chalukyan and the later Rashtra-kuta periods (sixth to twelfth centuries) can be found in the tiny village of **AIHOLE** (Aivalli), near the banks of the River Malaprabha. Lying in clusters within the village, in surrounding fields and on rocky outcrops, many of the temples are remarkably well preserved; most are abandoned but some have been converted into houses and cattle sheds. Reflecting both its geographical position and spirit of architectural experimentation, Aihole boasts northern (Nagari) and southern (Dravidian) temples, as well as variants which failed to survive subse-quent stylistic developments.

Two of the temples are rock-hewn caves dating from the sixth century. The Hindu **Ravanaphadigudi**, northeast of the centre, a Shiva shrine with a triple entrance, contains fine sculptures of Mahishasuramardini, a ten-armed Nateshan (the precursor of Shiva Nataraja) dancing with Parvati, Ganesh and the Sapta Matrikas (Seven Mothers). A central lotus design, surrounded by mythical beasts, figures and foliate decoration, adorns the ceiling. Near the entrance is Gangadhara (Shiva with the River Ganga in his hair), accompanied by Parvati and the skeleton Bringi. A two-storey cave, plain save for decoration at the entrances and a panel image of Buddha in its upper veranda, can be found part way up the hill to the southeast, overlooking the village. At the top of that hill, the Jain **Meguti Temple**, which may never have been completed, bears an inscription on an outer wall dating it to 634 AD. The porch, *mandapa* hallway and upper storey above the sanctuary, which contains a seated Jain image, are later additions. You can climb up to the first floor for fine views of Aihole and surrounding country.

The late seventh-to early eighth-century **Durga Temple** (daily 6am–6pm; $2 [Rs5]), one of the most unusual, elaborate and largest in Aihole, stands close to others on open ground in the Archeological Survey compound, near the centre of the village. It derives its name not from the goddess Durga, but from the Kannada *durgadagudi*, meaning "temple near the fort". Its apsidal-ended sanctuary shows influence from earlier Buddhist *chaitya* halls; another example of this curved feature, rare in Hindu monuments, can be seen in one of the *rathas* at Mamallapuram in Tamil Nadu. Here the "northern"-style tower is probably a later addition, and is incongruously square-backed. The temple is raised on a plinth featuring bands of carved decoration. A series of pillars – many featuring amorous couples – forms an open ambulatory that continues from the porch around the whole building. Other sculptural highlights include the decoration on the entrance to the *mandapa* hallway and niche images on the outer walls of the now empty semicircular sanctum. To the south there are remains of a small and early *gopura* gateway. Nearby, the small **Archeological Museum** (daily except Fri 10am–5pm; free) displays early Chalukyan sculpture and sells *Glorious Aihole*, a booklet describing the monuments.

Further south, beyond several other temples, the **Ladh Khan** (the name of a Muslim who made it his home) is perhaps the best known of all at Aihole. Now thought to have been constructed at some point between the end of the sixth century and the eighth, it was dated at one time to the mid-fifth century and was seen as one of the country's temple prototypes. The basic plan is square, with a large adjoining rectangular pillared porch. Inside, twelve pillars support a raised clerestory and enclose a further four pillars; at the centre stands a Nandi bull. A small sanctuary containing a *shivalingam* is next to the back wall. Both the *lingam* and Nandi may have been later additions, with the original inner sanctum located at the centre.

Practicalities

Five daily **buses** run to Aihole from Badami (1hr 30min) via Pattadakal (45min) from 7am to 9pm; the last bus returns around 6pm. The only **place to stay** in Aihole is the small, clean and Spartan KSTDC *Mayura Yatri Niwas* (☎08351/284541; ❷), a five-minute walk up the main road north out of the village, next to the ASI offices. The new wing has en-suite rooms, which are slightly smarter and more expensive than those in the old wing; dorm beds are also available (Rs75). Simple, tasty food is available by arrangement – and by candlelight during the frequent power cuts – though the whole place lacks atmosphere. The *Kiran Bar* on the same road, but in the village, serves beer and spirits and has a restaurant.

Pattadakal

The village of **PATTADAKAL**, on a bend in the River Malaprabha 22km from Badami, served as the site of Chalukyan coronations in the seventh and eighth centuries; in fact, it may only have been used for such ceremonials. Like Badami and Aihole, Pattadakal boasts fine Chalukyan architecture, with particularly large and mature examples, and, as at Aihole, both northern and southern styles can be seen. Pattadakal's main group of monuments (daily 6am–6pm; $5 [Rs10]) stands in a well-maintained compound next to the village, and has recently been declared a World Heritage Site.

Earliest among the temples, the **Sangameshvara**, also known as **Shri Vijayeshvara**, a reference to its builder, Vijayaditya Satyashraya (696–733), shows typical southern features, such as the parapet lined with barrel-vaulted miniature roof forms and walls divided into niches flanked by pilasters. To the south, both the **Mallikarjuna** and the enormous **Virupaksha**, side by side, are in the southern style, built by two sisters who were successively the queens of Vikramaditya II (733–46). The temples were inspired by the Pallava Kailashanatha temple at Kanchipuram in Tamil Nadu, complete with enclosure wall with shrines and small *gopura* entranceway. Along with the Kanchi Temple, the Virupaksha was probably one of the largest and most elaborate in India at the time. Interior pillars are carved with scenes from the Ramayana and

Mahabharata, while in the Mallikarjuna the stories are from the life of Krishna. Both temples have open Nandi *mandapa* hallways and sanctuaries housing black polished stone *lingams*.

The largest northern-style temple, the **Papanatha**, further south, was probably built after the Virupaksha in the eighth century. It features two long pillared *mandapa* hallways adjoining a small sanctuary with a narrow internal ambulatory. The outside walls feature reliefs (some of which, unusually, bear the sculptors' signatures) depicting scenes from the Ramayana, including Hanuman's monkey army.

About 1km south of the village, a fine **Rashtrakuta** (ninth–tenth-century) **Jain temple** is fronted by a porch and two *mandapa* hallways with twin carved elephants at the entrance. Inexplicably, the sanctuary contains a *lingam*. In the first *mandapa*, on the right, a stone staircase leads up to the roof where there's a second, empty sanctuary. The porch is lined with bench seats interspersed with eight pillars; the doorway is elaborately decorated with mythical beasts.

Pattadakal is connected by regular state **buses** and hourly private buses to Badami (45min) and Aihole (22km; 45min). Apart from the few stalls selling chai, coconuts and soft drinks, there are no facilities. At the end of January, Pattadakal hosts an annual three-day **dance festival** featuring dancers from all over the country.

Bijapur and the north

Boasting some of the Deccan's finest Muslim monuments, **BIJAPUR** is often billed as "The Agra of the South". The comparison is partly justified: for more than three hundred years, this was the capital of a succession of powerful rulers whose domed mausoleums, mosques, colossal civic buildings and fortifications recall a lost golden age of unrivalled prosperity and artistic refinement. Yet there the similarities between the two cities end. A provincial market town of just 220,000 inhabitants, modern Bijapur is a world away from the urban frenzy of Agra. With the exception of the mighty **Golgumbaz**, which attracts bus loads of day-trippers, its historic sites see only a slow trickle of tourists. And though the town centre is noisy, grubby and chaotic, respite can be found in the peaceful green spaces and colonnaded mosque courtyards dotted around the town. The best **time to come** here is between November and early March; in summer, Bijapur gets unbearably hot, and in April and May offices shut at 1pm. On February 6 and 7, Bijapur hosts an annual **music festival**, which attracts well-known musicians from both the Carnatic (South Indian) and the Hindustani (North Indian) classical music traditions.

Some history

Bijapur began life in the tenth century as **Vijayapura**, the Chalukyas' "City of Victory". Taken by the Vijayanagars, it passed into Muslim hands for the first time in the thirteenth century with the arrival of the Sultans of Delhi. The Bahmanis administered the area for a time, but it was only after the local rulers, the **Adil Shahis**, won independence from Bidar by expelling the Bahmani garrison and declaring this their capital that Bijapur's rise to prominence began.

Burying their differences for a brief period in the late sixteenth century, the five Muslim dynasties that issued from the breakdown of Bahmani rule – based at Golconda, Ahmadnagar, Bidar and Gulbarga – formed a military alliance to defeat the Vijayanagars. The spoils of this campaign, which saw the total destruction of

Vijayanagar (Hampi), funded a two-hundred-year building boom in Bijapur, during which the city acquired its most impressive monuments. However, old enmities between rival Muslim sultanates on the Deccan soon resurfaced, and the Adil Shahis' royal coffers were gradually squandered on fruitless and protracted wars. By the time the British arrived on the scene in the eighteenth century, the Adil Shahis were a spent force, locked into a decline from which they and their capital never recovered.

Arrival, information and city transport

State and interstate **buses** from as far afield as Mumbai and Hyderabad pull into the somewhat acrid KSRTC bus stand on the southwest edge of the town centre; ask at the enquiries desk for exact timings, as the timetables are all in Kannada. For a full rundown of destinations, see Travel details, p.362. Auto-rickshaws and legions of horse-drawn tongas await your custom and charge around the same price for journeys around the town. The **railway station**, outside the city walls and 3km northeast of the bus stand, is a more inspiring point of arrival – it's a stone's throw away from the Golgumbaz and convenient for the hotels along Station Road. Tongas and auto-rickshaws wait outside.

Besides the usual literature, the **tourist office** (Mon–Sat 10am–5.30pm; ☏08352/250359), behind the *Hotel Mayura Adil Shahi Annexe* on Station Road, can help with arranging itineraries and guides. If you need to **change money** (or traveller's cheques), the most reliable service is at Girikand Tours and Travels (☏08352/220510) on the first floor at Nishant Plaza, Rama Mandir Road; for an **ATM** head to the State Bank of India below the *Pearl* hotel. **Internet** access is available at Friends Cyber Zone and the adjacent Cyber Park (both Rs25/hr), on the second floor of the building opposite the **post office**.

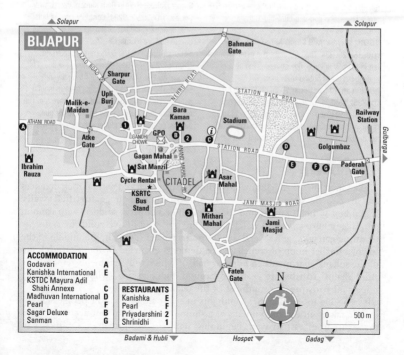

Bijapur is flat, relatively uncongested, and generally easy to negotiate by **bicycle**; rickety Heros are available for rent from several stalls outside the bus stand for Rs3 per hour. **Auto–rickshaws** don't have meters and charge a minimum of Rs10; most of Bijapur is covered by a fare of Rs30. However, you'll find them an expensive way of getting around the monuments, as prices rocket to around Rs200 for a four-hour tour. **Taxis**, available from near the bus stand, charge Rs5.50 per kilometre.

Accommodation and eating

Accommodation standards have improved in recent years in Bijapur and finding a room is rarely a problem. The hotels are fairly widely spread across town, so it's not a bad idea to decide where you want to stay in advance. **Restaurant** options are largely confined to the hotels – the *Kanishka*'s basement restaurant serves good non-veg food and serves alcohol, while the *Pearl*'s restaurant is excellent. The few independent eating establishments are invariably pure veg unless you brave one of the dingy drinking dens; the *Shrinidhi Hotel* on Gandhi Chowk serves good South Indian vegetarian food, as does the *Priyadarshini*, across the main road from the Gagan Mahal.

Godavari Athani Rd ☎08352/270827, ℗256225. Close to the Ibrahim Rouza complex, this recently renovated monolith has very large rooms with bold colour combinations. Pleasant but pricey. ⑥–⑦

Kanishka International Station Rd ☎08352/223788. Comfy rooms with huge double beds at good-value rates. There's also a health club, and two good restaurants – veg on the ground floor and non-veg-cum-bar in the basement. ③–④

KSTDC Mayura Adil Shahi Annexe Station Rd ☎08352/250934. The only state-run establishment left in town with large, dowdy rooms (some a/c) and sit-out areas but no restaurant. ③–④

Madhuvan International 100m off Station Rd ☎08352/255571, ⓦwww.hotelmadhuvan.com. The smartest place in town, with a variety of rooms ranging from ordinary doubles to more comfortable a/c deluxe options. There's a restaurant that serves good-value thalis at lunchtime, a small garden and money-changing facilities for guests. ⑤

Pearl Station Rd ☎08352/256002, ℗243606. Bright modern hotel with clean, sizeable rooms. The front ones have balconies and those at the top give views of Golgumbaz, as does the roof terrace. Better value than the *Madhuvan*, and with an excellent restaurant too. ④

Sagar Deluxe Next to Bara Kaman, Busreshwar Chowk ☎08352/259234. Centrally located hotel with unremarkable but cheap doubles and some deluxe and a/c rooms. ②–④

Sanman Opposite the Golgumbaz, Station Rd ☎08352/252977. Best value among the budget places, and fairly well placed for the railway station. The good-sized rooms all have mosquito nets and clean bathrooms, and some have a/c. The restaurant next door is used as a stop for bus parties, so their South Indian snacks are all freshly cooked. ②–④

The Town

Unlike most medieval Muslim strongholds, Bijapur lacked natural rock defences and had to be strengthened by the Adil Shahis with huge **fortified walls**. Extending some 10km around the town, these ramparts, studded with cannon emplacements (*burjes*) and watchtowers, are breached in five points by *darwazas*, or strong gateways, and several smaller postern gates (*didis*). In the middle of the town, a further hoop of crenellated battlements encircled Bijapur's **citadel**, site of the sultans' apartments and durbar hall, of which only fragments remain. The Adil Shahis' **tombs** are scattered around the outskirts, while most of the important **mosques** lie southeast of the citadel.

It's possible to see Bijapur's highlights in a day, although most people stay for longer, taking in the monuments at a more leisurely pace. Our account covers the sights from east to west, beginning with the **Golgumbaz** – which you should aim to visit at around 6am, before the bus parties descend – and ending with the exquisite **Ibrahim Rauza**, an atmospheric spot to enjoy the sunset.

The Golgumbaz

The vast **Golgumbaz** mausoleum (daily 6am–6pm; $2 [Rs5]), Bijapur's most famous building, soars above the town's east walls, visible for miles in every direction. Built towards the end of the Adil Shahis' reign, the Golgumbaz is a fitting monument to a dynasty in its twilight years – pompous, decadent and ill proportioned, but conceived on an irresistibly awesome scale.

The cubic tomb, enclosing a 170-square-metre hall, is crowned with a single hemispherical **dome**, only 5m narrower than St Peter's in Rome. Spiral stair-cases wind up the four seven-storey octagonal towers that buttress the building to the famous **Whispering Gallery**, a three-metre-wide passage encircling the interior base of the dome from where, looking carefully down, you can get a real feel of the sheer size of the building. Get here just after opening time and you can experiment with the extraordinary acoustics; by 7am, though, the cacophony generated by bus-loads of whooping and clapping tourists means you can't hear yourself think, let alone make out whispering 38m away. A good antidote to the din is the superb **view** from the mausoleum's ramparts, which overlook the town and its monuments to the dark-soiled Deccan countryside beyond, scattered with minor tombs and ruins.

Set on a plinth in the centre of the hall below are the gravestones of the ruler who built the Golgumbaz, **Muhammed Adil Shahi**, along with those of his wife, daughter, grandson and favourite courtesan, Rambha. At one corner of the grounds stands a simple white shrine to **Hashim Pir**, a sufi saint of the Adil Shahi period. In February it becomes the focus of *qawwalis* (singers of devotional *qawwali* music) at the annual three-day *urs*.

The Jami Masjid

A little under 1km southwest of the Golgumbaz, the **Jami Masjid** (Friday Mosque) presides over the quarter that formed the centre of the city during Bijapur's nineteenth-century nadir under the Nizam of Hyderabad. Widely regarded as one of the finest mosques in India, it was commissioned by Ali Adil Shahi, the ruler credited with constructing the city walls and complex water-supply system, as a monument to his victory over the Vijayanagars at the Battle of Talikota in 1565. As it is still in use, you should cover your head and limbs when entering.

Approached via a square *hauz* (ablutions tank), the main **prayer hall** is surmounted by an elegantly proportioned central dome, with 33 smaller shallow domes ranged around it. Simplicity and restraint are the essence of the colonnaded hall below, divided by gently curving arches and rows of thick plaster-covered pillars. Aside from the odd geometric design and trace of yellow, blue and green tile-work, the only ornamentation is found in the mihrab, or Mecca-facing prayer niche, which is smothered in gold leaf and elaborate calligraphy. The marble floor of the hall features a grid of 2500 rectangles, known as *musallahs* (after the *musallah* prayer mats brought to mosques by worshippers). These were added by the Mughal emperor Aurangzeb, allegedly as recompense for making off with the velvet carpets, long golden chain and other valuables that originally filled the prayer hall.

The Mithari and Asar Mahals

Continuing west from the Jami Masjid, the first monument of note is a small, ornately carved gatehouse on the south side of the road. Although of modest size, the delicate three-storey structure, known as the **Mithari Mahal**, is one of Bijapur's most beautiful buildings, with ornate projecting windows and minarets crowning its corners. It too was built by Ali Adil Shahi, as was the mosque behind, using gifts presented to him during a state visit to Vijayanagar. The Hindu rajas' generosity, however, did not pay off. Only a couple of years later, Adil Shahi and his four Muslim allies sacked their city, plundering its wealth and murdering most of its inhabitants.

The lane running north from opposite the Mithari Mahal leads to the dilapidated **Asar Mahal**, a large open-fronted hall propped up by four green-painted pillars and fronted by a large stagnant step-well. Built in 1646 by Muhammed Adil Shahi as a Hall of Justice, it was later chosen to house hairs from the Prophet's beard, thereby earning the title **Asar-i-Sharif** (place of illustrious relics). In theory, women are not permitted inside to see the upper storey, where fifteen niches are decorated with mediocre, Persian-style pot-and-foliage murals, but, for a little *baksheesh*, one of the girls who hang around the site will unlock the doors for you.

The citadel

Bijapur's **citadel** stands in the middle of town, hemmed in on all but its north side by battlements. Most of the buildings inside have collapsed, or have been converted into government offices, but enough remains to give a sense of how imposing this royal enclave must once have been.

The best-preserved monuments lie on or near the citadel's main north–south artery, Anand Mahal Road and can be reached by skirting the southeast wall from the Asar Mahal, or from the north side via the road running past the defunct KSTDC *Mayura Adil Shahi Hotel*. The latter route brings you first to the remnants of **Gagan Mahal**. Originally Ali Adil Shahi's "Heavenly Palace", it served as a durbar hall for the sultans, who would sit in state on the platform at the open-fronted north side, watched by crowds gathered in the grounds opposite. West off Anand Mahal Road, the five-storey **Sat Manzil** was the pleasure palace of the courtesan Rambha, entombed with Muhammed Adil Shahi and his family in the Golgumbaz. In front stands an ornately carved water pavilion, the **Jal Mandir**, now left high and dry in an empty tank.

Bara Kaman

Just north of the citadel on the far side of the main road, a quiet lane leads to one of Bijapur's less-visited sights, the peaceful **Bara Kaman**. Begun in 1658, this mausoleum for Ali Rauza was still incomplete at the time of his death in 1673. Chunky stone columns and linking arches surround the central courtyard with the single central tomb, set upon a huge square plinth, rising high above the tranquil landscaped gardens.

Malik-i-Maidan and Upli Burj

Guarding the principal western entrance to the city is the **Burj-i-Sherza** (Lion Gate), one of several bastions (*burje*) that punctuate Bijapur's battlements. It sports a colossal cannon, known as the **Malik-i-Maidan**, literally "Lord of the Plains", which was brought here as war booty in the sixteenth century. Four hundred bullocks, ten elephants and an entire battalion were needed to haul it up the steps to its emplacement. An inscription reveals that the cannon, whose muzzle features a relief of a monster swallowing an elephant, was cast in Ahmadnagar in 1551.

A couple more discarded cannons lie atop the watchtower a short walk northwest. Steps wind around the outside of the oval-shaped **Upli Burj**

Moving on from Bijapur

Moving on from Bijapur is getting easier with several efficient private companies operating luxury **bus** services from just outside the bus stand. VRL, with their distinctive yellow-and-black luxury coaches, have services daily to Bengaluru (4 buses between 6pm and 9.45pm), Mumbai (8.30pm and 9pm) and Mangalore, via Udupi (4pm). Seats on VRL services can be booked through Vijayanand Travel, Terrace floor, Shastri Market, Gandhi Circle (T 08352/251000) or at their other branch just south of the bus stand. KSRTC also run deluxe buses to Bengaluru, Hubli, Hospet, Mumbai and Hyderabad (via Solapur). There are three direct services to Badami, or you can change in Bagalkot, to which there are half-hourly services.

Express **trains** run three times a week to Bengaluru (Yeshwanthpur; 17hr 40min), as do passenger trains to Mumbai; there is also a daily service for Hyderabad. Four trains a day run north to Solapur (2hr 15min), from which there are much better connections, including express trains to Mumbai, Chennai, Bengaluru, Kochi and Thiruvananthapuram. The broad-gauge line south goes only as far as Bagalkot, from where a metre-gauge line, long overdue for conversion, continues down to Gadag. For more on public transport from Bijapur, see Travel details, p.362.

(Upper Bastion), to a gun emplacement that affords unimpeded views over the city and plains.

The Ibrahim Rauza

Set in its own walled compound just under 1km west of the ramparts, the **Ibrahim Rauza** represents the zenith of Bijapuri architecture (daily 6am–6pm; $2 [Rs5]). Whereas the Golgumbaz impresses primarily by its scale, the appeal of this tomb complex lies in its grace and simplicity. It's also a haven of peace, with cool colonnaded verandas and flocks of iridescent parakeets careering between the mildewed domes, minarets and gleaming golden finials.

Opinions differ over whether the tomb was commissioned by Ibrahim Adil Shah (1580–1626), or his favourite wife, Taj Sultana, but the former was the first to be interred here, in a gloomy chamber whose only light enters via a series of exquisite pierced-stone (*jali*) windows. The elaborate Koranic inscriptions that bedeck them are the finest examples of their kind in India. More amazing stonework decorates the exterior of the mausoleum and the equally beautiful **mosque** opposite, the cornice of whose facade features a stone chain carved from a single block. These two buildings, bristling with minarets and domed cupolas, face each other across a rectangular raised plinth, divided by a small reservoir and fountains. Viewed from the walls that enclose the complex, you can see why the architect – Malik Sandal – added a self-congratulatory inscription in his native Persian over the tomb's south doorway, modestly describing his masterpiece as "A beauty of which Paradise stood amazed".

Gulbarga

GULBARGA, 165km northeast of Bijapur, was the founding capital of the Bahmani dynasty and the region's principal city before the court moved to Bidar in 1424. It has remained a staunchly Muslim town, its bulbous onion-domes and mosque minarets still soaring prominently above its ramshackle concrete-box skyline. Gulbarga is also famous as the birthplace of the *chisti*, or saint, Hazrat Bandah Nawaz Gesu Daraz (1320–1422), whose tomb, situated next to one of India's foremost Islamic theological colleges, is a major shrine.

The tomb complex, known as the **Dargah**, is on the northeast edge of town, and approached via a broad bazaar. The marble-lined enclosure, plastered in mildew-streaked limewash, centres on the tomb of Hazrat Gesu Daraz, affectionately known to his devotees as **Bandah Nawaz**, or "the long-haired one who brings comfort to others". The saint was spiritual mentor to the Bahmani rulers, and it was they who erected his beautiful double-storey mausoleum, now visited by hundreds of thousands of Muslim pilgrims each year. Men can enter the tomb, which is surrounded by a wooden screen inlaid with mother-of-pearl and draped with green silk, to admire the elaborate mirror-mosaic ceiling. Women however must make do with peering at the tomb through the pierced-stone windows. The same gender bar applies to the neighbouring tomb, whose interior has retained its exquisite Persian paintings.

The Dargah's other important building is the **madrasa**, or theological college, founded by Bandah Nawaz and enlarged during the two centuries after his death. The curriculum here is dominated by the Qur'an but the saint's own works on Sufi mysticism and ethics are also still studied. The *madrasa* is open to both sexes.

Practicalities

Daily KSRTC **buses** from Bijapur, Bidar and Hospet pull in to the state bus stand on the southwest edge of town. It's not worth taking one of the Bidar-bound private minibuses from the roadside opposite as they only run as far as Humnabad, 40km short, where you'll be stranded. Gulbarga's main-line **railway station**, with services to and from Mumbai, Pune, Hyderabad, Bengaluru and Chennai, lies 1.5km east of the bus stand, along Mill Road. The town's other main artery, Station Road, runs due north of here past the lake, to the busy Chowk crossroads at the heart of the bazaar.

Gulbarga's main sights are well spread out, so you'll need to get around by **auto-rickshaw**; fix fares in advance. There is a Syndicate Bank **ATM** on Station Road.

Accommodation and eating

Gulbarga is well provided with good-value **accommodation**, and even travellers on tight budgets should be able to afford a clean room with a small balcony. All the hotels listed below have **restaurants**, mostly pure-veg places with a no-alcohol rule. *Kamat*, the chain restaurant, has several branches in Gulbarga, including a pleasant one at Station Chowk, specializing in vegetarian "meals" as well as *iddlis* and *dosas*; try *joleata roti*, a local bread cooked either hard and crisp or soft like a chapati. Several hole-in-the-wall spots on the road up from the station sell freshly fried chicken and fish.

Aditya 2-244 Station Rd, opposite public gardens ☎08472/224040, ⓕ235661. Upmarket a/c rooms plus non-a/c ones for almost the same price. Their impeccably clean pure-veg Udupi restaurant, *Pooja*, on the ground floor, does great thalis and snacks. ❹

Prashant First lane on right leaving the station ☎08472/221456. Decent rooms of varying size and amenities, and surprisingly quiet. ❷–❹

Preetam Lodge Mill Rd ☎08472/221673. Head and shoulders above the rest of the places in the vicinity of the bus stand, with clean, spacious rooms in a newish block. ❸–❹

Raj Rajeshwari Vasant Nagar, Mill Rd ☎08472/225881. A five-minute walk from the bus stand, this place is friendly and has large en-suite rooms with balconies. There's also a reasonable veg restaurant, but strictly no alcohol. ❸–❹

Southern Star Near the Fort, Super Market ☎08472/224093. Comfortable place with two restaurants, a bar and some a/c rooms. ❷–❹

Bidar

In 1424, following the break-up of the Bahmani dynasty into five rival factions, Ahmad Shah I shifted his court from Gulbarga to a less constricted site at **BIDAR**, spurred, it is said, by grief at the death of his beloved spiritual mentor, Bandah Nawaz Gesu Daraz (see p.357). Revamping the town with a new fort, splendid palaces, mosques and ornamental gardens, the Bahmanis ruled from here until 1487, when the Barid Shahis took control. They were succeeded by the Adil Shahis from Bijapur, and later the Mughals under Aurangzeb, who annexed the region in 1656, before the Nizam of Hyderabad finally acquired the territory in the early eighteenth century.

Lost in the far northwest of Karnataka, Bidar, 284km northwest of Bijapur, is nowadays a provincial backwater, better known for its fighter-pilot training base than the monuments gently decaying in and around its medieval walls. Yet the town, half of whose 140,000 population are still Muslim, has a gritty charm, with narrow red-dirt streets ending at arched gates, which provide vistas across the plains. Littered with tile-fronted tombs, rambling fortifications and old mosques, it merits a visit if you're travelling between Hyderabad (150km east) and Bijapur, although expect little in the way of Western comforts, and more than the usual amount of curious approaches from locals. Lone women travellers, especially, may find the attention more hassle than it's worth.

Arrival, information and accommodation

Bidar lies on a branch line of the main Mumbai–Secunderabad–Chennai rail route, and can only be reached by slow passenger **train**. The few visitors that come here invariably arrive **by bus**, at the KSRTC bus stand on the far north-western edge of town, which has hourly direct services to Hyderabad (3hr 30min) and Gulbarga (3hr), and several a day to Bijapur (7hr) and Bengaluru (12hr). There is no tourist office or currency exchange facilities, although there are several **Internet** outlets, such as *Swamy's Cyber Café* (9am–10pm; Rs40/hr), 100m southeast of the bus stand on Udgir Road.

Bidar's sights are too spread out to be comfortably explored on foot. Auto-rickshaws tend to be thin on the ground away from the main streets, however, and are reluctant to wait while you look around the monuments, so it's a good idea to rent a **bicycle** for the day from Rouf's, 50m east of the bus stand next to the excellent *Karnatak Juice Centre*.

Bidri

Bidar is celebrated as the home of a unique damascene metalwork technique known as **bidri**, developed by the Persian silversmiths who came to the area with the Bahmani court in the fifteenth century. These highly skilled artisans engraved and inlaid their traditional Iranian designs onto a metal alloy composed of lead, copper, zinc and tin, which they blackened and polished. The resulting effect – swirling silver floral motifs framed by geometric patterns and set against black backgrounds – has since become the hallmark of Muslim metalwork in India.

Bidri objets d'art are displayed in museums and galleries all over the country. If you want to see pukka bidri-wallahs at work, take a walk down Bidar's **Siddiq Talim Road**, which cuts across the south side of the old town, where skull-capped artisans tap and burnish vases, goblets, plates, spice boxes, betel-nut tins and ornamental hookah pipes, as well as less traditional objects – coasters, ashtrays and bangles – that crop up (at vastly inflated prices) in silver emporiums across the country.

Most **places to stay** are an auto-rickshaw ride away in the centre, so it makes sense to opt for the new *Hotel Mayura* (☎08482/228142; ❷–❸), opposite the bus stand, which has large rooms with optional a/c and its own non-veg restaurant. The *Ashoka* (☎08482/227621; ❶–❸), 1.5km from the bus stand past Dr Ambedkar Chowk, is the *Mayura*'s older sister; it has comfortable, good-value deluxe rooms, some with a/c. The *Kailash* (☎08482/227727; ❷–❸), near the old bus stand on Udgir Road in the centre of town, looks a little tired but has clean rooms.

The old town

The heart of Bidar is its medieval **old town**, encircled by crenellated ramparts and eight imposing gateways (*darwazas*). This predominantly Muslim quarter holds many Bahmani-era mosques, *havelis* and *khanqahs* – "monasteries" set up by the local rulers for Muslim cleric-mystics and their disciples – but its real highlight is the impressive ruin of **Mahmud Gawan's Madrasa**, or theological college, whose single minaret soars high above the city centre. Gawan, a scholar and Persian exile, was the *wazir*, or prime minister, of the Bahmani state under Muhammed Bahmani III (1463–82). A talented linguist, mathematician and inspired military strategist, he oversaw the dynasty's expansion into Karnataka and Goa, bequeathing this college as a thank-you gift to his adoptive kingdom in 1472. The distinctively Persian-style building, originally surmounted by large bulbous domes, once housed a world-famous library. However, this burnt down after being struck by lightning in 1696, while several of the walls and domes were blown away when gunpowder stored here by Aurangzeb's occupying army caught fire and exploded. Today, the *madrasa* is little more than a shell, although its elegant arched facade has retained large patches of the vibrant Persian glazed tile-work that once covered most of the exterior surfaces. This includes a beautiful band of Koranic calligraphy, and striking multicoloured zigzags wrapped around the base of the one remaining *minar*, or minaret.

The fort

Presiding over the dark-soiled plains from atop a sheer-faced red laterite escarpment, Bidar's **fort**, at the far north end of the street running past the *madrasa*, was founded by the Hindu Chalukyas and strengthened by the Bahmanis in the early fifteenth century. Despite repeated sieges, it remains largely intact, encircled by 10km of ramparts that drop away in the north and west to three-hundred-metre cliffs. The main southern entrance is protected by equally imposing man-made defences: gigantic fortified gates and a triple moat formerly crossed by a series of drawbridges. Once inside, the first building of note (on the left after the third and final gateway) is the exquisite **Rangin Mahal**. Mahmud Shah built this modest "Coloured Palace" after an unsuccessful uprising of Abyssinian slaves in 1487 forced him to relocate to a safer site inside the citadel. The palace's relatively modest proportions reflect the Bahmanis' declining fortunes, but its interior comprises some of the finest surviving Islamic art in the Deccan, with superb wood-carving above the door arches and Persian-style mother-of-pearl inlay on polished black granite surfaces. If the doors to the palace are locked, ask for the keys at the nearby ASI **museum** (daily 8am–1pm & 2–5pm; free), which houses a missable collection of Hindu temple sculpture, weapons and Stone Age artefacts.

Opposite the museum, an expanse of gravel is all that remains of the royal gardens. This is overlooked by the austere **Solah Khamb** mosque (1327), Bidar's oldest Muslim monument, whose most outstanding feature is the intricate pierced-stone *jali* calligraphy around its central dome. From here, continue west through the ruins of the former royal enclosure – a rambling complex of half-collapsed palaces, baths, *zenanas* (women's quarters) and assembly halls – to the fort's west walls. You can complete the round of the **ramparts** in ninety minutes, taking time out to enjoy the views over the red cliffs and across the plains.

Ashtur: the Bahmani tombs

As you look from the fort's east walls, a cluster of eight bulbous white domes floats alluringly above the trees in the distance. Dating from the fifteenth century, the mausoleums at **Ashtur**, 3km east of Bidar (leave the old town via Dulhan Darwaza gate), are the final resting places of the Bahmani sultans and their families, including the son of the ruler who first decamped from Gulbarga, Alauddin Shah I. His remains by far the most impressive **tomb**, with patches of coloured glazed tiles on its arched facade and a large dome whose interior surfaces writhe with sumptuous Persian paintings. Reflecting sunlight onto the ceiling with a small pocket mirror, the *chowkidar* picks out the highlights, among them a diamond, barely visible among the bat droppings.

The tomb of Alauddin's father, the ninth and most illustrious Bahmani sultan, Ahmad Shah I, stands beside that of his son, decorated with Persian inscriptions. Beyond this are two more minor mausoleums, followed by the partially collapsed tomb of Humayun the Cruel (1458–61), cracked open by a bolt of lightning. Continuing along the line, you can chart the gradual decline of the Bahmanis as the mausoleums diminish in size, ending with a sad handful erected in the early sixteenth century, when the sultans were no more than puppet rulers of the Barid Shahis.

Crowning a low hillock halfway between Ashtur and Bidar, on the north side of the road, the **Chaukhandi of Hazrat Khalil Ullah** is a beautiful octagonal-shaped tomb built by Alauddin Shah for his chief spiritual adviser. Most of the tiles have dropped off the facade, but the surviving stonework and calligraphy above the arched doorway, along with the views from the tomb's plinth, deserve a quick detour from the road.

The Badri Shahi tombs

The **tombs of the Shahi** rulers, who succeeded the Bahmanis at the start of the sixteenth century, stand on the western edge of town on the Udgir road, 200m beyond – and visible from – the bus stand. Although not as impressive as those of their predecessors, the mausoleums, mounted on raised plinths, occupy an attractive site. Randomly spaced rather than set in a chronological row, they are surrounded by lawns maintained by the ASI. The most interesting is the tomb of **Ali Barid** (1542–79), whose Mecca-facing wall was left open to the elements. A short distance southwest lies a mass grave platform for his 67 concubines, who were sent as tribute gifts by vassals of the Deccan overlord from all across the kingdom. The compound is only officially open for afternoon promenading (daily 4.30–7.30pm; $2 [Rs5]), but the gateman may let you in earlier if he's around.

Eating

Finding somewhere good to **eat** is not a problem in Bidar, thanks to the restaurants at the *Mayura* and *Ashoka*, which both offer a varied selection of North Indian veg and meat dishes (try the *Mayura*'s pepper chicken) and cold beer. Also recommended, and much cheaper, is the popular *Udupi Krishna* restaurant, overlooking the *chowk*, which serves up unlimited pure-veg thalis for lunch; they have a "family room" for women, too, and open early (around 7.30am) for piping hot South Indian breakfasts. The *Jyothi Udupi*, opposite the KRSTC bus stand, is another classic South Indian joint.

Travel details

Trains

Bengaluru (Bangalore) to: Chennai (5–7 daily; 5hr 5min–7hr 35min); Gulbarga (3 daily; 10hr 30min–12hr 45min); Hospet (1–2 daily; 8hr 40min–9hr 30min); Hubli (3–5 daily; 7–13hr); Hyderabad (Secunderabad; 1–3 daily; 10hr 25min–15hr 15min); Kochi (Ernakulam; 1–3 daily; 11hr 5min–12hr 15min); Mumbai (2–3 daily; 23hr 15min–24hr); Mysore (6–7 daily; 2hr–3hr 25min); Pune (2–3 daily; 18hr 15min–25hr 30min); Thiruvananthapuram (1–2 daily; 17hr–17hr 20min).
Hassan to: Mysore (3–4 daily; 2hr–2hr 55min).
Hospet to: Bengaluru (1–2 daily; 10hr–10hr 40min); Gadag (3–5 daily; 1hr 30min–1hr 50min); Hubli (3–5 daily; 3hr–3hr 15min).
Mangalore to: Chennai (2–3 daily; 16hr–17hr 45min); Goa (Madgaon; 2 daily; 6hr 5min); Gokarna (2 daily; 3hr 5min–3hr 50min); Kochi (Ernakulam; 3–4 daily; 9hr 10min–9hr 40min); Kollam (3–4 daily; 12hr 10min–12hr 55min); Mumbai (1 daily; 15hr 55min); Thiruvananthapuram (3–4 daily; 13hr 30min–15hr 5min).
Mysore to: Bengaluru (6–7 daily; 1hr 55min–3hr 25min); Chennai (1–2 daily; 7hr 10min–11hr 15min); Hassan (2–3 daily; 1hr 55min–2hr 25min).

Buses

Bengaluru (Bangalore) to: Bidar (1 daily; 16hr); Bijapur (4 daily; 13hr); Chennai (hourly; 8hr); Coimbatore (7 daily; 9hr); Goa (3 daily; 14hr); Gokarna (2 daily; 13hr); Gulbarga (8 daily; 15hr); Hassan (every 15min; 4hr); Hospet (every 30min; 8hr); Hubli (every 30min; 9hr); Hyderabad (10 daily; 16hr); Jog Falls (1 daily; 10hr); Karwar (3 daily; 13hr); Kochi (Ernakulam; 6 daily; 12–13hr); Kodaikanal (1 nightly; 13hr); Madikeri (every 30min; 6hr); Madurai (2 daily; 12hr); Mangalore (every 30min; 10hr); Mumbai (2 daily; 24hr); Mysore (every 10min; 3hr); Ooty (7 daily; 7hr 30min); Pondicherry (Puducherry) (2 daily; 9–10hr).
Bijapur to: Badami (3 daily; 3hr); Bengaluru (5 daily; 12hr); Bidar (4 daily; 6hr); Gulbarga (every 30min; 4hr); Hospet (12 daily; 5hr); Hubli (every 30min; 5hr); Hyderabad (4 daily; 11hr); Mumbai (8 daily; 12hr); Pune (8 daily; 8hr).
Hassan to: Channarayapatna (for Sravanabelgola; hourly; 1hr); Halebid (hourly; 1hr); Hospet (1 daily;

10hr); Mangalore (hourly; 4hr); Mysore (every 15min; 3hr).
Hospet to: Badami (2 daily; 6hr); Bengaluru (every 30min–1hr; 8hr); Bidar (2 daily; 10hr); Gokarna (2 nightly; 9–10hr); Hampi (every 30min; 20min); Hubli (hourly; 4hr); Hyderabad (4 daily; 12hr); Goa (Madgaon; 4 daily; 9hr); Mysore (2 daily; 10–11hr); Panjim (4 daily; 10hr).
Hubli to: Badami (6 daily; 4hr); Bengaluru (hourly; 9hr); Bijapur (every 30min; 6hr); Dandeli (every 2hr; 3hr); Gokarna (4 daily; 5hr); Hospet (hourly; 4hr); Mumbai (12 daily; 12hr).
Mangalore to: Bengaluru (every 30min–1hr; 8hr); Bijapur (1 daily; 16hr); Gokarna (1 daily; 7hr); Kannur (hourly; 3hr); Kasargode (every 30min–1hr; 1hr); Kochi (Ernakulam; 1 daily; 9hr); Madikeri (every 15min; 3hr 30min); Mysore (every 15min; 7hr); Panjim (2 daily; 10–11hr 30min); Udupi (every 5min; 1hr 30min).
Mysore to: Bengaluru (every 10min; 3hr); Channarayapatna (for Sravanabelgola; every 30min; 2hr); Hassan (every 15min; 3hr); Jog Falls (via Shimoga; hourly; 7hr); Kannur (8 daily; 7hr); Kochi (6 daily; 12hr); Kozhikode (6 daily; 5hr); Madikeri (every 15min; 3hr); Mangalore (hourly; 7hr); Ooty (8 daily; 5hr); Srirangapatnam (every 30min; 20min).

Flights

For a list of airline addresses, see p.274; for travel agents, see p.275; and for airline websites, see p.38. In the listings below IA is Indian Airlines, AI Air India, JA Jet Airways, KF Kingfisher, SA Sahara Airlines, AD Air Deccan, GO Go Air, IG IndiGo Airlines, and SJ SpiceJet.
Bengaluru (Bangalore) to: Chennai (IA, JA, KA, AD 15 daily; 45min–1hr); Coimbatore (JA, AD 3 daily; 45min); Goa (IA, JA, KA, AD 6 daily; 1hr–2hr 55min); Hyderabad (IA, JA, KA, AD, SA 13 daily; 1hr–1hr 30min); Kochi (Ernakulam; IA, JA, KA, AD 7 daily; 55min–1hr 20min); Mangalore (JA, KA, AD 3 daily; 45min–1hr 5min); Mumbai (IA, JA, KA, AD, SA 21 daily; 1hr 30min–2hr 15min); Pune (IA, JA, KA, SA 5 daily; 1hr 20min); Thiruvanthapuram (IA, JA, AD 5 daily; 1hr 20min–2hr 5min).
Mangalore to: Bengaluru (JA, KA, AD 3 daily; 45min–1hr 5min); Chennai (KA 1 daily; 1hr 40min); Mumbai (IA, JA, KA 4 daily; 1hr 15min).

4

Kerala

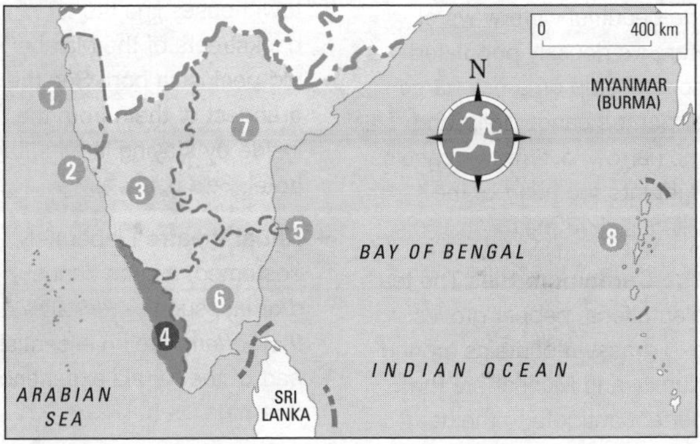
0
400 km
N
MYANMAR (BURMA)
BAY OF BENGAL
INDIAN OCEAN
ARABIAN SEA
SRI LANKA
1
2
3
4
5
6
7
8

CHAPTER 4

Highlights

✳ **Temple festivals** Parades of extravagantly decorated elephants, backed by drummers and firework displays, form the focal point of Kerala's Hindu festivals. See p.369

✳ **Varkala** Chill out in a cliff-top café, sunbathe on the beach or soak up the atmosphere around the town's busy temple tank. See p.398

✳ **The backwaters** Explore the beautiful waterways of Kerala's densely populated coastal strip on a rice barge or punted canoe, following the narrow, overgrown canals right into the heart of the villages. See p.416

✳ **The Cardamom Hills** The tea plantations, pepper groves and grassy mountains around Kumily and Munnar are the perfect antidote to the heat and humidity of the coast. See p.430 & p.438

✳ **Wildlife** The sanctuaries of Periyar, Eravikulam and Wayanad offer plenty of opportunities to spot elephants, buffalo, boar, deer and – if you're extremely lucky – the elusive tiger. See p.430, p.444 & p.488

✳ **Fort Cochin** Dutch, Portuguese, British and traditional Keralan townhouses line the backstreets of the Malabar's old peninsula port. See the grandest of them from the inside by staying in a heritage hotel. See p.453

✳ **Ritual theatre** Elaborately costumed, arcane dance dramas, such as *kathakali* and *theyyattam*, are an essential part of the Kerala experience. See p.457 & p.472

△ A boat on the backwaters

Kerala

A sliver of dense greenery sandwiched between the Arabian Sea and the forested Western Ghat mountains, the state of **KERALA** stretches for 550km along India's southwest coast, and is just 120km wide at its broadest point. It's blessed with unique geographical features, and the lush tropical landscape, fed by two annual monsoons, intoxicates every newcomer. Equally, Kerala's arcane rituals and spectacular festivals stimulate even the most jaded imagination.

Better educated, more literate and more politically savvy than any other in India, the state's 32-million-strong population has also embraced the globalized economy with great enthusiasm. Remittance dollars sent home by expatriate workers in the Gulf account for nearly a quarter of domestic income, while Kerala's sophisticated, go-ahead tourism industry is the envy of other less entrepreneurial states.

The most popular destination for visitors is undoubtedly the great port of **Kochi** (formerly Cochin), where Kerala's extensive history of peaceful foreign contact is evident in the atmospheric old quarters of Mattancherry and Fort Cochin – hubs of a still-thriving tea and spice trade. The capital, **Thiruvananthapuram** (aka Trivandrum), almost as far south as you can go, and a gateway to the nearby palm-fringed beaches of **Kovalam**, provides various opportunities to sample Kerala's rich cultural and artistic life. More physical pleasures are the reason travellers flock to **Varkala**, just over an hour north of the capital, where Hindu pilgrims share the beach with ranks of sun worshippers and yoga buffs, against a spectacular backdrop of red laterite cliffs.

More than anywhere else in India, the great joy of exploring Kerala is in the travelling itself, especially by **boat**. Ferries, cruisers, wooden longboats and houseboats ply the **backwaters**, slowly meandering through the spellbinding **Kuttanad** region near historic **Kollam** (Quilon) and **Alappuzha** (Alleppey), on the southern tip of the huge **Vembanad Lake**. Drifting between swathes of palm trees and past tiny villages in the humid heat, you cannot fail to be lulled by the unhurried pace of life.

The only way to escape the humidity of the lowlands is to head for the **hills**. Roads wind through landscapes dotted with churches and temples and past spice, tea, coffee and rubber plantations, as well as natural forest, en route to wildlife reserves such as **Tholpetty** and **Periyar**, where sightings of wild elephants are virtually guaranteed. Further highland options include the former British hill station of **Munnar**, surrounded by endlessly rolling tea estates, the spice plantations of **Palakkad**, and the beautiful forested district of **Wayanad**, with its indigenous tribal population.

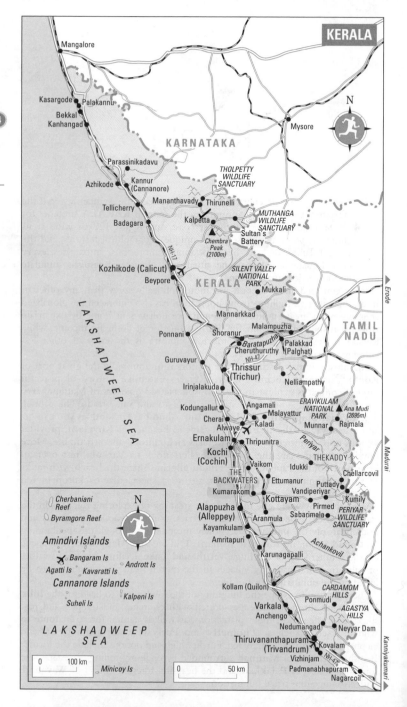

KERALA

KERALA

N

Erode

Madurai

Kanniyakumari

Mangalore

Kasargode Palakannu
Bekkal
Kanhangad

KARNATAKA

Mysore

Parassinikadavu

Kannur
Azhikode (Cannanore)

*THOLPETTY
WILDLIFE
SANCTUARY*

Tellicherry Mananthavady Thirunelli
Badagara Kalpetta

*MUTHANGA
WILDLIFE
SANCTUARY*

▲ *Chembra
Peak
(2100m)* Sultan's
Battery

Kozhikode (Calicut) ✈
Beypore **KERALA**

*SILENT VALLEY
NATIONAL
PARK*

Mukkali

Mannarkkad

Ponnani Shoranur Malampuzha
Baratapuzha Palakkad
Cheruthuruthy (Palghat)

**TAMIL
NADU**

Guruvayur NH-47
Thrissur
(Trichur) Nelliampathy

Irinjalakuda

Kodungallur Angamali
Cherai Malayattur
Alwaye Kaladi

*ERAVIKULAM
NATIONAL
PARK* ▲ *Ana Mudi
(2695m)*

Munnar Rajmala

Ernakulam ✈ Thripunitra
Kochi
(Cochin) Vaikom *Periyar* **THEKADDY**

*THE
BACKWATERS* Idukki
Ettumanur Chellarcovil
Kumarakom Puttady
Kottayam Vandiperiyar Kumily
Alappuzha Pirmed *PERIYAR
WILDLIFE
SANCTUARY*
(Alleppey) Aranmula
Kayamkulam Sabarimala

Amritapuri

Achankovil

Karunagapalli

*CARDAMOM
HILLS*

Kollam (Quilon)
Ponmudi *AGASTYA
HILLS*
Varkala
Anchengo
Nedumangad Neyyar Dam
Thiruvananthapuram ✈
(Trivandrum) Kovalam
Vizhinjam
Padmanabhapuram
Nagarcoil

L A K S H A D W E E P   S E A

*Cherbaniani
Reef*
Byramgore Reef

Amindivi Islands

N

✈ *Bangaram Is*
Agatti Is *Andrott Is*
Kavaratti Is
Cannanore Islands
Kalpeni Is
Suheli Is

**L A K S H A D W E E P
S E A**

0   100 km *Minicoy Is*

0   50 km

Kerala is short on the historic monuments prevalen
the ancient temples that do remain are still in use, an
Hindus. Following an unwritten law, few buildings in
houses or temples, are higher than the trees, often creati
green cities. Typical features of both domestic and temp
pillared verandas and long, sloping tiled and gabled roof
from both rain and sunshine. The definitive example is **}
Palace**, just over the border in Tamil Nadu, and
Thiruvananthapuram.

Phenomenal amounts of money are lavished upon the ma
all-night **entertainments** based in Kerala's temples. Fire   ..u sky,
while processions of gold-bedecked elephants are accompani\u by some of the
loudest (and deftest) drum orchestras in the world. The famous **Puram** festival
in Thrissur is the most extravagant, but smaller events take place throughout
the state.

Theatre and **dance** styles abound; not only the region's own female classical
form, **mohinyattam** (dance of the enchantress), but also the martial-art-influ-
enced **kathakali** dance-drama (see p.457), which has brought gods and demons
from the Mahabharata and Ramayana to Keralan villages for four centuries. Its
2000-year-old predecessor, the Sanskrit drama **kutiyattam**, is still performed by
a handful of artists, while localized rituals known as **theyyam**, in which dancers
wearing tall masks become "possessed" by temple deities, continue to be a
potent ingredient of village life in the northern part of the state. Few visitors
ever witness these extraordinary all-night performances, but between November
and May it is possible to spend weeks travelling between colourful festivals,
experiencing a way of life that has altered little in centuries.

Travelling around is relatively easy as the state is so compact. There are
efficient rail services from the main coastal towns to the rest of the country,
but local passenger trains are not necessarily the best mode of transport within
the state itself. Most visitors use a combination of local ferries, buses and the
odd taxi.

The **best time to visit** Kerala is in January and February, when the skies are
generally clear and humidity at its least debilitating. From March onwards, the
weather becomes progressively more oppressive in the pre-monsoon build up,
with the heat peaking in May. The rains usually hit the following month, in
early June. This is considered the auspicious time to begin a course in Ayurvedic
treatment if you want to really experience the benefits, but a beach holiday is
out as the sand often disappears under the high tides and crashing waves. The

Malayalam

Malayalam, the **official state language** of Kerala, is spoken by an estimated 37
million people worldwide. It's closely related to Tamil, from which it diverged around
the fifth century AD, but boasts its own script, recently boiled down from a bewildering 900 characters to a more keyboard-friendly 51 (including 16 separate vowels).
Reflecting the region's complex cultural history, lots of Romance, Hebrew, Arabic,
Portuguese, Dutch and English words have their place the Malayali lexicon, although
only three words – teak, coir and copra – have travelled in the opposite direction and
entered English. The first Malayalam/English dictionary was written in 1872, by the
German missionary Herman Gunder (grandfather of the novelist Herman Hesse). As
any India trivia lover will tell you, Malayalam is also the longest English palindrome in
everyday use in the country.

… "retreating") monsoon that sweeps through Tamil Nadu from … December leaves Kerala overcast.

… history

The god **Parasurama**, or "Rama with the battleaxe", the sixth incarnation of Vishnu, is credited with creating Kerala. Born a brahmin, he set out to re-establish the supremacy of the priestly class, whose position had been usurped by arrogant *kshatryas*, the martial aristocracy. Brahmins were forbidden to engage in warfare, but Parasurama embarked upon a campaign of carnage which only ended when Varuna, the all-seeing god of the sea, gave him the chance to create a new land from the ocean, where brahmins could live in peace. Its limits were defined by the distance Parashurama could throw his axe; the waves duly receded up to the point where it fell. Fossil evidence suggests that the sea once extended to the Southern Ghats, so the legend reflects a geological truth.

Ancient Kerala is mentioned as the land of the Cheras in a third-century BC Ashokan edict, and also in the Ramayana (the monkey king Sugriva sent emissaries here in search of Sita) and the Mahabharata (in which a Chera king sent soldiers to the Kurukshetra war). The Tamil epic poem *Silappadikaram* ("The Jewelled Anklet") was composed here and provides a valuable picture of life around the time of Christ. Early foreign accounts, such as those by Pliny and Ptolemy, testify to thriving trade between the ancient port of Muziris (now known as Kodungallur) and the Roman Empire.

Little is known about the early history of the **Cheras**; their dominion covered a large area, but their capital, Vanji, has not been identified. Other contemporary rulers included the Nannanas in the north and the Ay chieftains in the south, who battled with the Pandyas from Tamil Nadu in the eighth century. At the start of the ninth century, the Chera king Kulashekhara Alvar – a poet-saint of the Vaishnavite *bhakti* movement known as the *alvars* – established his own dynasty. His son and successor, Rajashekharavarman, is thought to have been a saint of the parallel Shaivite movement, the *nayannars*. Eventually, the prosperity acquired by the Cheras through trade with China and the Arab world proved too much of a temptation for the neighbouring **Chola** empire; at the end of the tenth century, they embarked on a hundred years of sporadic warfare with the Cheras. Around 1100, the Cheras lost their capital at Mahodayapuram in the north, and shifted south to establish a new capital at Kollam (Quilon).

When the **Portuguese** ambassador and general Vasco da Gama and his fleet first arrived in India in 1498, people were as much astounded by their reckless-ness in sailing so close to the Malabar Coast during the monsoons as by their physical and sartorial strangeness. Crowds filled the streets of Calicut to see them, and a Moroccan found a way to communicate with them. Eager to meet the king – whom they believed to be a Christian – the Portuguese were escorted in torrential rain to his palace. However, Vasco da Gama soon estab-lished that the gifts he had brought from the king of Portugal had not made the good impression he had hoped for. The *zamorin,* as the ruler of Calicut was known, wanted silver and gold, not a few silk clothes and a sack of sugar.

Da Gama, after such diplomatic initiatives as the kidnapping, mutilation and murder of assorted locals, came to an agreement with the *zamorin*, after which he demanded exclusive rights to the **spice trade**. He was determined to squeeze out the Keralan Muslim (Moppila) traders who for centuries had been a respected section of the community – acting as middlemen between local producers and traders in the Middle East. Exploiting an existing enmity between the royal families of Cochin and Calicut, da Gama turned to

The festivals of Kerala

Kerala's extraordinary temple festivals, known as **utsavam** in Malayalam, present some of the most arresting spectacles the Subcontinent has to offer. Held mainly in the winter months, between November and March, they invariably have as their centrepiece a grand **elephant procession** in which the shrine's presiding deity (or a portable replica of it) is paraded around the temple compound, accompanied by ranks of ear-shattering *chenda melam* drummers, trumpet fanfares, fireworks and rapt crowds of onlookers. A sumptuous **kudamattom** ritual, when colourful parasols, yak-tail hair whisks and peacock feather fans are brandished in synchronized moves by young men standing on the backs of the elephants, forms the highlight of the parade.

The number of animals involved can vary according to the size and wealth of the temple and the prominence of its deity: seven is a respectable number, but 25 or more isn't uncommon, while the state's biggest celebration, **Puram** (see p.470), in the central Keralan town of Thrissur, features over a hundred caparisoned (decorated) elephants massed in long rows – a sight of incomparable splendour.

Tracking down such events is usually a simple matter of asking around: hoardings and posters advertising elephant processions pop up on roadsides and in newspapers, and the local tourist office will also be able to point you in the right direction. Failing that, telephone the private tourist desk at Ernakulam boat jetty (see p.449), who are festival experts and keep a monthly list of what's on where across the state.

Another event worth trying to catch is the annual **elephant race**, held at Guruvayur in February/March. Although the temple itself is off-limits to non-Hindus, the public part of the festivities showcases over forty galloping pachyderms. **Onam**, the annual harvest festival found throughout Kerala (Aug/Sept), also hosts elephant processions and water carnivals – one of the best of them at **Aranmula**, near the town of Kottayam, which holds a **snake boat race** involving long, elegantly curved boats propelled by two lines of rowers – another of Kerala's hallmark spectacles. The most dramatic of all, the **Nehru Trophy Boat Race**, is staged at Alappuzha in August and, unlike its more light-hearted counterpart in Aranmula, is seriously competitive.

Many Keralan festivals also stage **classical music** and **dance** recitals, and provide an excellent opportunity to catch a **kathakali** performance in an authentic setting. The **Shri Purnatrayisa** temple, in the small town of Thripunitra near Kochi, runs an all-night *kathakali* show during its annual festival (Oct/Nov), while the royal family of Travancore are great patrons of the arts and hold a yearly **Carnatic music** festival at the Puttan Malika Palace in Thiruvananthapuram. Probably the best place to experience one of the numerous performing art forms of Kerala and other regions of South India, however, is at the Kalamandalam Academy in **Cheruthuruthy**, near Thrissur, where an annual performing arts festival is held every year towards the end of December.

For a full rundown of the many events held across Kerala, pick up the free leaflet *Fairs and Festivals of Kerala*, available from all KTDC and India government tourist offices.

Cochin, which became the site of India's first Portuguese fortress in 1503. The city's strategic position enabled the Portuguese to break the Middle Eastern monopoly of trade with western India. They introduced new agricultural products such as cashew and tobacco, and turned coconut into a cash crop, having recognized the value of its by-products: coir (coconut fibre) rope and matting.

The rivalry between Cochin and Calicut allowed other colonial powers to move in: both the **Dutch**, who forcibly expelled the Portuguese from their forts, and the **British**, in the shape of the East India Company, firmly established

No smoking

In 2003 Kerala became the first state in India to **ban smoking** from all public places, including streets, parks and beaches. Unlike such laws in the West, though, the ban doesn't include restaurants or bars, where it remains at the owner's discretion. There's a Rs200 on-the-spot fine for offenders, though the law seems to be more strictly enforced in larger cities than rural areas. Of course, you won't receive a ticket if fined, so it's a handy extra source of *baksheesh* for the Keralan police.

themselves early in the seventeenth century. During the 1700s, first Raja Marthanda Varma, then Tipu Sultan of Mysore, carved out independent territories, but the defeat of Tipu Sultan by the British in 1792 left them in control right up until Independence.

Kerala today can claim some of the most startling **radical** credentials in India. In 1957 it was the first state in the world to democratically elect a communist government, and still regularly returns communist parties in elections (the present chief minister, V.S. Achuthanandan, is a communist party leader). Due to uncompromising reforms made during the 1960s and 1970s, Kerala currently has the most equitable land distribution of any Indian state. Poverty is not absent, but it appears far less acute than in other parts of the country, with rates of life expectancy and per capita income well above the national averages.

Kerala is also justly proud of its reputation for healthcare and education, with **literacy** rates that stand, officially at least, at 91 percent for men and 88 percent for women. Industrial development is negligible, however: potential investors from outside tend to fight shy of dealing with such a politicized workforce. Many Keralans now work in the Gulf and the resultant influx of **remittance-dollars** has led to greater wealth and spending power for the migrant workers and their families (money sent home by relatives accounts for around 20 percent of the region's GDP). As you explore the state, you'll see ostentatious mansions erected by Gulf returners on the outskirts of every village – but you'll also see plenty of red hammer-and-sickle flags flying from street corners.

Thiruvananthapuram

Kerala's capital, the coastal city of **THIRUVANANTHAPURAM** (still widely and more commonly known as **Trivandrum**), is set on seven low hills, 87km from the southern tip of India. Despite its administrative importance – demonstrated by wide roads, multi-storey office blocks and gleaming white colonial buildings – it's a decidedly easy-going city, with a mix of narrow backstreets and traditional red-tiled gabled houses, and palm trees and parks breaking up the bustle of its modern concrete centre.

Although it has few monuments as such, Thiruvananthapuram holds enough of interest to fill a day or two. The oldest and most interesting part of town is the **Fort** area in the south, around the **Shri Padmanabhaswamy temple** and **Puttan Malika Palace**, while the **Sri Chitra Art Gallery** and **Napier Museum**, showcases for painting, crafts and sculpture, stand together in a park in the north. In addition, schools specializing in the martial art *kalarippayattu* and the dance/theatre forms of *kathakali* and *kutiyattam* offer visitors an insight into the Keralan obsession with physical training and skill.

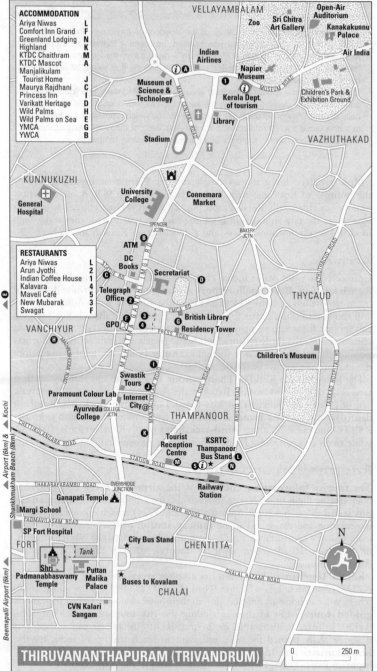

▲ Kollam, Kochi & NH-47

VELLAYAMBALAM

Open-Air
Auditorium

Zoo | Sri Chitra
Art Gallery | Kanakakunnu
Palace

Air India

ACCOMMODATION
Ariya Niwas — L
Comfort Inn Grand — F
Greenland Lodging — N
Highland — K
KTDC Chaithram — M
KTDC Mascot — A
Manjalikulam
 Tourist Home — J
Maurya Rajdhani — C
Princess Inn — I
Varikatt Heritage — D
Wild Palms — H
Wild Palms on Sea — E
YMCA — G
YWCA — B

Indian
Airlines

Napier
Museum

Museum of
Science &
Technology

Kerala Dept.
of tourism

Children's Park &
Exhibition Ground

Library

Stadium

VAZHUTHAKAD

KUNNUKUZHI

University
College

Connemara
Market

General
Hospital

SPENCER
JCTN

BAKERY
JCTN

ATM

DC
Books

Secretariat

THYCAUD

RESTAURANTS
Ariya Niwas — L
Arun Jyothi — 2
Indian Coffee House — 1
Kalavara — 4
Maveli Café — 5
New Mubarak — 3
Swagat — F

Telegraph
Office

GPO

British Library

Residency Tower

VANCHIYUR

PRESS ROAD

Children's Museum

Swastik
Tours

Paramount Colour Lab

Ayurveda
College

COLLEGE
JCTN

Internet
City@

THAMPANOOR

Tourist
Reception
Centre

KSRTC
Thampanoor
Bus Stand

STATION ROAD

Railway
Station

THAKARAPARAMBU ROAD

OVERBRIDGE
JUNCTION

Ganapati Temple

POWER HOUSE ROAD

Margi School

SP Fort Hospital

FORT

City Bus Stand

CHENTITTA

Shri
Padmanabhaswamy
Temple

Puttan
Malika
Palace

Tank

Buses to Kovalam

CHALAI BAZAAR ROAD

N

CVN Kalari
Sangam

CHALAI

Airport (6km) &
Kochi

Chettikulangara Road

Shankhumukham Beach (8km)

Beemapalli Airport (6km)

THIRUVANANTHAPURAM (TRIVANDRUM)

0   250 m

▼ Kovalam & Kanyakumari

The city of the snake Anantha

Thiruvananthapuram was the capital of the kingdom of Travancore from 1750 until 1956, when the state of Kerala was created. Its name – formally re-adopted to replace the anglicized version of "Trivandrum" – derives from *thiru-anantha-puram*, or "the holy city of Anantha", the **coiled snake** on which the god Vishnu reclines in the midst of the cosmic ocean.

Vishnu is given a special name for this non-activity – Padma-nabha (lotus-navel) – and is invariably depicted lying on the sacred snake with a lotus growing from his belly button. The god Brahma sits inside the flower, which represents the beginning of a new world era. Padmanabha is the principal deity of the royal family of Travancore and of Thiruvananthapuram's Shri Padmanabhaswamy temple.

Most travellers choose to pass straight through Thiruvananthapuram, lured by the promise of Kovalam's palm-fringed beaches (see p.383). A mere twenty-minute bus ride south, Kerala's most popular resort is close enough to use as a base to see the city, although its booming package tourist trade means sky-high food and accommodation prices, and a decidedly un-Keralan atmosphere.

Arrival

Connected to most major Indian cities, as well as Sri Lanka, the Maldives and the Middle East, **Beemapalli airport** is 6km southwest of town and serviced by an airport bus and bus #14 to and from the City bus stand. Auto-rickshaws will run you into the centre for around Rs75 and there's also a handy pre-paid taxi service, for which you pay a set fee before departure of Rs175 for the train station, and Rs375 for Kovalam's Lighthouse Beach. A Kerala Tourism information booth and Thomas Cook foreign exchange facility are located just before the exit of the arrivals concourse.

The long-distance KSRTC **Thampanoor bus stand** and **railway station** face each other across Station Road in the southeast of the city, a short walk east of Overbridge Junction on MG Road. **Local buses** (including Kovalam) depart from **City bus stand**, in East Fort, ten minutes' walk south from the KSRTC and railway stations. **Auto-rickshaws** run to Kovalam for Rs100–150, while **taxis** charge around Rs250 – but beware of overcharging scams.

Information and tours

The **tourist information counters** at the **airport** (☎0471/250 1085) are open during flight times. Kerala Tourism also has a booth at the **Thampanoor bus stand** (Mon–Sat 10am–5pm; ☎0471/232 7224), which is good for general information and maps, and at the **railway station** (☎0471/233 4470). Their main visitor ("tourist facilitation") centre is 150m south of the Napier Museum on Museum Road (open 24hr in theory); ☎0471/232 1132, ⓦwww .keralatourism.org).

Kerala Tourism (KTDC) also has a visitor reception centre, next to their *KTDC Chaitram* hotel on Station Road (☎0471/233 0031, ⓦwww.ktdc.com), where you can book accommodation in their hotel chain and tickets for various **guided tours**. Most of these, including the city tours (daily: 8.30am–7pm, Rs130; half-day 8.30am–1pm or 2–7pm, Rs70/80), are far too rushed, but if you're really pushed for time and want to reach the tip of India, try the **Kanyakumari** tour (daily 7.30am–9pm; Rs250), which takes in Padmanabhapuram Palace (except Mon), Suchindram temple and Kanyakumari.

Accommodation

Accommodation in all categories is a lot easier on the pocket in Thiruvananthapuram than at nearby Kovalam beach. That said, this is one city where budget travellers, in particular, should consider spending a couple of hundred rupees more than they might usually; with the exception of the YWCAs and *Greenland Lodging*, there's nowhere really worth bothering with for under Rs300, whereas in the Rs450–500 bracket you're spoilt for choice.

Close on a hundred **hotels** and lodges lie within ten-minutes' walk of the railway and bus stations, in the district known as **Thampanoor** – the best of them up Manjalikulam Road, which runs due north from the main road outside the stations. As ever with state capitals and other large cities, it pays to book ahead, and reconfirm the day before checking in.

Inexpensive

Greenland Lodging Aristo Rd, Thampanoor ☎0471/232 8114. Large and efficient lodge with spotless attached rooms for Rs270. The best low-cost option in the vicinity of the bus stand and railway station. Book ahead or arrive before noon. ➋

Manjalikulam Tourist Home Manjalikulam Rd, Thampanoor ☎0471/233 0776. Don't be fooled by the shining glass and marble ground floor – above lurks a basic budget place offering variously priced rooms, all of them clean and with good, comfy mattresses. ➍

Princess Inn Manjalikulam Rd, Thampanoor ☎0471/233 9150, ✉princess.inn@yahoo.com. Well-scrubbed, respectable cheapie close to the stations. One of the more welcoming and better value small hotels in this busy enclave, though it's a bit more of a plod up the lane from Station Rd than some. ➌

YMCA YMCA Rd, near the Secretariat ☎0471/233 0059, ✉ymcatvm @sancharnet.in. Neat, smartly furnished rooms at bargain rates for the levels of comfort. The "luxury" options (Rs500) are enormous and have high ceilings, quiet fans, TVs and spacious bathrooms; singles from Rs200; some a/c. Amazing value, though you'll probably need to book at least 2 weeks in advance. ➌–➍

YWCA Spencer Junction ☎0471/247 7308. Spotless attached doubles (from Rs350) on the fourth floor of a grubby, rundown office block. Friendly, safe and central, with some non-a/c rooms, but the place is locked at 10.30pm sharp. Primarily for women, although couples and men are welcome. ➌–➍

Mid-range and luxury

Ariya Niwas Aristo Rd, Thampanoor ☎0471/233 0789. Large, spotlessly clean, well-aired rooms with comfy beds and city views from upper floors. The best value in this bracket (Rs625–800; plus Rs500 for a/c) and only 2min walk from the railway station. A wonderful mural from Guruvayur is on display in the lobby, and the best "meals" restaurant in the state stands on the ground floor (see Eating, p.381). ➍–➎

Comfort Inn Grand opposite the Secretariat, MG Rd ☎0471/247 1286, ⊛www.comfortinngrand.in. Smart new business hotel in the city centre, completely refurbished in 2005. The "standard" rooms are on the small side for two, but cool and quiet. The "executive" deluxe options on the top storey are larger and more plush, and have the best views. There's also a quality a/c veg restaurant on site. ➏–➐

Highland Manjalikulam Rd ☎0471/233 3200, ⊛www.highland-hotels.com. The rooms in this dependable lower mid-range option fail to live up to the promise of the six-storey concrete and tinted-glass facade, but it's well managed, only a short walk from the stations, and easy to find. The "economy" non-a/c options are dowdy, but large enough for two. If it's full, try the *Highland Park* (☎0471/233 8800), a little further up the same street. ➍–➎

KTDC Chaithram Station Rd ☎0471/233 0977, ⊛www.ktdc.com. Big government-run tower-block hotel very close to the railway station and Thampanoor bus stand, holding a range of differently priced, spacious rooms (some a/c), restaurants, travel agent, car rental, beauty parlour, cybercafé, bookshop and bar. ➍–➏

KTDC Mascot Mascot Junction, near Indian Airlines office ☎0471/231 8990, ⊛www.ktdc.com. The city's only five-star, at the north end of town near the museums, is a state-run luxury hotel, patronized mainly by government flunkies (the Kerala State Legislature is close by). Opening onto long polished marble corridors lined with hardwood panels, the fancier "executive" and "suite" rooms occupy a wing built to house British officers in World War I; the "standard" ones are in a less attractive modern block. There's an open-air pool, bar and a/c restaurant. ➑–➒

Maurya Rajdhani General Hospital Rd, ☎0471/246 9469, ⓦwww.rajadhanihotels.com. Gleaming new, state-of-the-art business hotel, tucked away off MG Rd in a quiet backstreet, currently riding high after starring in the Bollywood hit movie *Fouj Mein Mauj*. It offers all the comforts you'd expect from a modern four-star – though there's no pool. **❼–❽**

Varikatt Heritage Poonen Rd, near Cantonment Police Station, behind the Secretariat (look for the brown gates) ☎0471/233 6057, ⓦwww.varikattheritage.com. Thiruvananthapuram's only heritage homestay, run by the affable Col. K.K. Kuncheria (Gurkha Rifles, Rtd), is a real gem. It occupies a gorgeous 1830s Indo-Sarcenic-style bungalow originally built by a lovesick British spinster, Miss Blanket, who followed a teaplanter out to India after the two had met on holiday in Yorkshire. Romance bloomed, but didn't last, and the house was

eventually sold to a prominent local lawyer, in whose family it has remained ever since. The three front-side suites ($125), opening onto a high-ceilinged veranda where you can enjoy a *chota peg* under the hunting trophies after supper, retain their original rosewood furniture – and more period atmosphere than the much less appealing rear-side doubles ($95). **❾**

Wild Palms Mathrubhoomi Rd ☎0471/247 1175, ⓦwww.wildpalmsonsea.com. Plush guesthouse in a modern suburban house, 10min walk from MG Rd. Owners Hilda and Justin Pereira lived in the UK for years, and this is as much a labour of love as a homestay, though the place is large enough to afford a degree of privacy, and the attached rooms (Rs1100–2000) are very large for the price. They also run *Wild Palms on Sea* (☎0471/275 6781, ⓦwww.wildpalmsonsea.com), a set of poolside cottages 20km west of town, in a palm grove by the beach. **❺–❼**

The City

Thiruvananthapuram's centre can be explored easily on foot, though you might be glad of a rickshaw ride back from the museums and parks, close to the top end of MG Road. The historical and spiritual heart of town is the **Fort area**, at the southern end of **MG Road**, which encloses the Shri Padmanabhaswamy Vishnu temple. En route between the two you pass through the main shopping district, which is busy all day, and especially choked when one of the frequent, but generally orderly, political demonstrations converges on the grand colonial **Secretariat** building halfway along.

The Shri Padmanabhaswamy Temple

A Neoclassical gateway leads from the Fort and City bus stands to the serene **Shri Padmanabhaswamy Temple**, which is still controlled by the Travancore royal family. Unusually for Kerala, it's built in the Dravidian style of Tamil Nadu, with a tall, seven-tiered *gopura* gateway and high fortress-like walls. Non-Hindus are not permitted inside.

Most of Padmanabhaswamy's buildings date from the eighteenth century, added by Raja Marthanda Varma (1729–58) to the much older shrine within. According to legend, the temple was founded after Vishnu – disguised as a beautiful child – merged into a huge tree in the forest, which immediately crashed to the ground. There it transformed into an image of the reclining Vishnu, a full 13km long. Divakara, a sage who witnessed this, was frustrated by his limited human vision, and prayed to Vishnu to assume a form that he could view in its entirety. Vishnu complied, and the temple appeared.

The **deity** in the central sanctum is composed of 12,008 sacred stones, or *salagrams*, brought by elephant from the bed of the Gandhaki River in Nepal. A rare form of stucco known as *katusarkara yogam*, made according to an ancient Ayurvedic recipe, forms the outer surfaces. To make offerings and receive *darshan*, or ritual viewing of the god, worshippers have to mount special stone platforms from which they can peer at different parts of the reclining Vishnu – feet, navel and face – through three openings in the floor, known as *vaayils*.

△ Shri Padmanabhaswamy Temple, Thiruvananthapuram

The main approach road to Shri Padmanabhaswamy, where devotees bathe in a huge tank, is lined with stalls selling religious souvenirs such as shell necklaces, puja offerings, jasmine and marigolds. It's an atmospheric area for a stroll – particularly in the early morning and at dusk, when devotees make their way to and from prayers (a closed iron gate bars the northern side, but everybody climbs through the gap). As recently as the turn of the last century, this was a "no go" area for members of low-caste communities – possibly on pain of death.

Puttan Malika Palace

The **Puttan Malika Palace** (Tues–Sun 8.30am–12.30pm & 3–5.30pm; Rs20, camera Rs15) immediately southeast of the temple, became the seat of the Travancore rajas after they left Padmanabhapuram at the end of the nineteenth century. It was originally commissioned by Raja Ravi Thirunal Varma, who died at the tender age of 30, only a year after the palace was completed. To generate funds for much-needed restoration, the Travancore royal family opened the palace to the public a decade ago – for the first time in more than two centuries. Although much of it remains off-limits, palace guides show you around some of the most impressive wings, which have been converted into a **museum**. The cool chambers, with highly polished plaster floors and delicately carved wooden screens, house a crop of dusty Travancore heirlooms. Among the array of portraits, royal regalia and weapons are some genuine treasures, such as a solid crystal throne – a gift from the Dutch – and some fine murals. The real highlight, however, is the elegant Keralan architecture itself. Beneath sloping red-tiled roofs, hundreds of wooden pillars, carved into the forms of rampant horses (*puttan malika* translates as "horse palace"), prop up the eaves, and airy verandas project onto the surrounding lawns.

The royal family have always been keen patrons of the arts, and the open-air **Swathi Sangeetotsavam festival**, held in the grounds during the festival of

The annual **Nishangandi Dance and Music festival** is held in the grounds of the **Kanakakunnu Palace**, just to the east of the public gardens, in mid-January. Originally built as a cultural venue for the maharajas of Thiruvananthapuram, the large, open-air amphitheatre where the event is staged makes an ideal venue for evening performances of classical dances and music. Over the past few years, the festival has gained in stature and now hosts some of India's best known artists. A lively food and crafts fair springs up below it; and in the Children's Park on the opposite side of Museum Road, a popular flower festival attracts large crowds. Ask at a KTDC tourist office for details.

The **Arattu** festival, centred around the Shri Padmanabhaswamy temple, takes place biannually, in Meenam (March/April) and Thulam (Oct/Nov). Each time, ten days of festivities inside the temple (open to Hindus only) culminate in a procession through the streets of the city, taking the deity, Padmanabhaswamy, to the sea for ritual immersion. Five caparisoned elephants, armed guards, a *nagaswaram* (double-reed wind instrument) and *tavil* drum group are led by the maharaja of Travancore, in his symbolic role as *kshatrya*, the servant of the god. Instead of the richly apparelled figure that might be expected, the maharaja (whose rank is no longer officially recognized) wears a simple white *dhoti*, with his chest bare save for the sacred thread and, rather than riding, he walks the whole way, bearing a sword. To the accompaniment of a 21-gun salute and music, the procession sets off from the east gate of the temple at around 5pm, moving at a brisk pace to reach Shankhumukham Beach at sunset, about an hour later. The route is lined with devotees, many of whom honour both the god and the maharaja. After the seashore ceremonies, the cavalcade returns to the temple at about 9pm, to be greeted by another gun salute. An extremely loud firework display rounds off the day.

For ten days in March/April, Muslims celebrate **Chandanakuda Mahotsavam** at the Beemapalli Dargah Shareef tomb, 5km southwest of the city on the coastal road towards the airport. The Hindu-influenced festival commemorates the anniversary of the death of Bee Umma (aka "Beema Beevi"), a female descendant of the Prophet Mohammed revered for her piety and spiritual powers. On its first, most important, day, pilgrims converge on the mosque inside the complex carrying earthenware pots, or *chandana-kuddam*, covered in sandalwood paste and flowers, and containing money offerings. Activities such as traditional story-telling (*kathaprasangam*) and sword play (*daharamuttu*) take place inside the mosque, while outside there is dance and music. In the early hours of the morning, a flag is brought out from Beema Beevi's tomb and taken on a procession, accompanied by a *panchavadyam* drum and horn orchestra and two caparisoned elephants, practices normally associated with Hindu festivals. Once more, the rest of the night is lit up with fireworks.

The great Keralan festival of **Onam** (late Aug or Sept) takes place during late-monsoon harvest period, when Keralans remember the reign of King Mahabali, a legendary figure who, it is believed, achieved an ideal balance of harmony, wealth and justice during his tenure. Unfortunately, the gods became upset and envious at Mahabali's success and Vishnu packed him off to another world. However, once a year the king was allowed to return to his people for ten days, and Onam is a joyful celebration of the royal visit. Families display their wealth, feasts and boat races are held and, in Thiruvananthapuram, there's a week-long cultural festival of dance and music culminating in a colourful street carnival in which thousands of local women prepare *payasam* (Keralan rice pudding) in earthen pots in the street – the greatest gathering forms on the road leading to the Shri Padmanabhaswamy temple. Again, the best source of precise dates are any of the KTDC offices dotted around the city.

Navaratri (Oct/Nov), continues the tradition. Performers sit on the palace's raised porch, flanked by the main facade, with the spectators seated on the lawn. Songs composed by Raja Swathi Thirunal (1813–1846), known as the "musician king", dominate the programme. For details, ask at the KTDC tourist office.

CVN Kalari and Chalai Bazaar

Around 500m southeast of the temple in East Fort, the red-brick **CVN Kalari Sangam** ranks among Kerala's top **kalarippayattu** gymnasiums (see box below). It was founded in 1956 by C.V. Narayanan Nair, one of the legendary figures credited for the martial art's revival, and attracts students from across the world. From 6.30am to 8am (Mon–Sat) you can watch fighting exercises in the sunken *kalari* pit that forms the heart of the complex. Foreigners may join courses, arranged through the head teacher, or *Gurukkal*, although prior experience of martial arts and/or dance is a prerequisite. You can also join the queues of locals who come here for a traditional **Ayurvedic massage**, and to consult the gym's expert Ayurvedic doctors (Mon–Sat 10am–1pm & 5–7.30pm, Sun 10am–1pm).

The Margi Theatre School

Thiruvananthapuram has for centuries been a crucible for Keralan classical arts, and the **Margi Theatre School** (℡0471/247 8806, ⓦwww.margitheatre.org),

Kalarippayattu

Practised in special earth-floored gyms and pits across the state, **kalarippayattu** is Kerala's unique martial art – a distinctive brand of acrobatic combat drawing heavily on yoga and ancient Indian knowledge of the human body. Its techniques of hand-to-hand fighting, weapon skills and healing were first formalized in the twelfth century by the bodyguards of medieval warlords and chieftains, though plenty of evidence exists to suggest the form derives from practices two or more thousand years old. Under guidance from their gurus, young boys (and sometimes girls) would be trained for years as specialist fighters, who in time would be employed to wage duels and settle disputes on behalf of landowners and chiefs. In the eighteenth century, *kalarippayattu* was banned by the British, but it has since made a strong comeback and now has dozens of followers – Hindus, Christians and Muslims alike.

Two distinct **schools** survive – the southern and northern systems. Both, however, follow a similar progression. Once initiated, students are taught a complex set of strenuous exercises designed to render their bodies strong and flexible: kicks, jumps, animal postures, spins, step sequences and vigorous stretches, joined in increasingly long and complicated sequences. Sesame oil massages, given with the feet and hands by teachers holding onto ropes suspended from the gym's rafters, are another essential part of the training. When the set moves have been mastered, students are eventually introduced to combat with weapons: the *udaval* (sword), *paricha* (shield), *kadaras* (dagger), *kuntham* (spear), *gadha* (mace) and *urumi* (a long flexible sword). The final stage, **verum kaythari**, focuses on barehanded combat against an armed enemy and is for advanced practitioners only.

Staged at gyms and tourist resorts across Kerala, *kalarippayattu* demonstrations are never dull, and injuries, although rare, do happen. As part of their advanced training, masters, known as *gurukkal*, are initiated into a system of physical therapy combining oil massage and Ayurvedic herbal medicine, which is why famous *kalarippayattu* gyms, such as CVN Kalari in Thiruvananthapuram, double as traditional out-patient clinics. For details of places to learn *kalarippayattu*, see above and p.379.

at the western corner of the Fort area, keeps the flame of the region's ritual theatre traditions burning brightly. **Kathakali** dance drama and the more rarely performed **kutiyattam** theatre form (see Contexts p.790) dominate the curriculum. By prior arrangement you can watch students being put through their paces. Foreigners are also welcome to attend introductory courses (Mon–Sat 10am–noon, Rs3000 for 20 days). However, the reason most visitors venture out here is to watch one of the authentic *kathakali* or *kutiyattam* performances staged in its small theatre, details of which are posted on the school's website.

To reach Margi, head to the SP Fort hospital on the western edge of Fort, and then continue 200m north; the school is set back from the west side of the main road in a large red-tiled and tin-roofed building, behind the High School (the sign is in Malayalam).

MG Road: markets and shopping

An assortment of **craft shops** along MG Road, north of Station Road, sell sandalwood, brass and Keralan bell-metal oil lamps (see box, p.475). The Gandhian Khadi Gramodyog, between Pazhavangadi and Overbridge junctions, stocks handloom cloth (dig around for the best stuff), plus radios and cassette machines manufactured by the Women's Federation. Natesan's Antique Arts, further up, is part of a chain that specializes in paintings, temple woodcarvings and so forth.

At first glance most of the **bookstores** in the area seem largely intended for exam entrants, but some stock a good choice of titles in English – mostly relating to India – and a fair selection of fiction too. DC Books, on Statue Road, on the first floor of a building above Statue Junction, stocks the city's best selection, with a separate area devoted to Kerala.

Almost at the top of MG Road, on the right-hand side, **Connemara Market** is the place to pick up odds and ends, such as dried and fresh fish, fruit, vegetables, coconut scrapers, crude wooden toys, coir, woven winnowing baskets and Christmas decorations.

Connemara also contains several tailors' workshops, but the main source of **textiles** in the city is **Chalai Bazaar**, the big market area centred on the road running east of from Fort district, slicing past the bus stand. Jammed with little shops selling bolts of cloth, flowers, incense, spices, bell-metal lamps and fireworks, it's a great area for aimless browsing.

The Napier Museum, Zoo and Sri Chitra Art Gallery

A minute's walk east from the north end of MG Road, opposite Kerala Tourism's information office, brings you to the entrance to Thiruvananthapuram's **public gardens**. As well as serving as a welcome refuge from the noise of the city – its lawns are usually filled with courting couples, students and picnicking families – the park holds the city's best museums. Give the dusty and uninformative Natural History Museum a miss and head instead for the more engaging **Napier Museum** of arts and crafts (Tues–Sun 10am–5pm; Rs5). Designed at the end of the nineteenth century by architect Robert Fellowes Chisolm (1840–1915), it was an early experiment in what became known as the "Indo-Saracenic" style, with tiled, gabled roofs, garish red-, black- and salmon-patterned brickwork, and, above the main entrance, a series of pilasters forming Islamic arches. The spectacular interior boasts stained-glass windows, a wooden ceiling and loud turquoise, pink, red and yellow stripes on the walls. Chisolm set out to incorporate Keralan elements into colonial architecture; the museum was named after his employer, Lord Napier, the governor of the Madras Presidency. Highlights of the collection include fifteenth-century Keralan woodcarvings from Kulathupuzha, minutely detailed ivory work, a carved temple chariot (*rath*), wooden models of Guruvayur temple and an oval temple theatre (*kuttambalam*), plus twelfth-century Chola and fourteenth-century Vijayanagar bronzes.

North of the museum, the spectacular trees of the former royal botanical gardens shade the city's famous **Zoo** (Tues–Sun 10am–5pm; Rs6), one of largest and best equipped in India. Its collection of animals, covering 75 species from the Subcontinent and beyond, are housed in a mixture of modern, open-style enclosures and an extraordinary campus of quirky Raj-era structures, little-changed since they were built in the 1850s: Grecian friezes of gorillas adorn the ape area, the giraffes inhabit an elegant Chinese pagoda and the barking deer shelter beneath a roof of Mangalorean tiles. Founded by the Maharaja of Travancore, the zoo must be one of the few in the world to have earned a place in literary history, as the place novelist Yann Martel claimed inspired him to write his 2002 Booker-prize winning *Life of Pi* (the claim was later challenged after striking similarities were found between his book and Brazilian author Moacyr Scliar's *Max and the Cats*).

You have to pass through the main ticket booth for the zoo to reach the excellent **Sri Chitra Art Gallery** (Tues–Sun 10am–5pm; Rs50), which shows paintings from the Rajput, Moghul and Tanjore schools, along with pieces from China, Tibet and Japan. The meat of the collection, however, is made up of works by the celebrated Keralan artist, **Raja Ravi Varma** (1848–1906), who is credited with introducing oil painting to India. Varma's style was much criticized for its sentimentality and for showing strong Western influence, but his treatment of Hindu mythological themes is both dramatic and beautiful. Also on view are a couple of minor Tagores, and some striking oils by the Russian artist-philosopher and mystic, **Nicholas Roerich**, who arrived in India at the turn of the twentieth century. His spiritually oriented, strongly coloured Himalayan landscapes reflect his love of the region. Roerich lived out his latter years in Nagar (in the Kulu valley), where he died in 1947.

Away from the centre

The **Chachu Nehru Children's Museum** (Tues–Sun 10am–5pm; free), in Thycaud in the east of the city, serves as a rather dusty testament to the enthusiasm of an anonymous collector back in the 1960s. One room contains ritual masks, probably from Bengal, Rajasthan and Orissa, while the rest of the place is taken up with stamps, health-education displays and over two thousand dolls featuring figures in Indian costume, American presidents, Disney characters and British Beefeaters.

Also on the eastern side of town, visitors can, by arrangement, watch classes in the martial art of *kalarippayattu* (see box, p.377), at the PS Balachandran Nair Kalari **martial arts gymnasium**, Kalariyil, TC 15/854, Cotton Hill, Vazhuthakad (daily 6–8am & 6–7.30pm). Built of stone in 1992 along traditional lines, the *kalari* fighting pit is overlooked from a height of 4m by a viewing gallery. Students (some as young as eight) train both in unarmed combat and in the use of weapons. The school arranges short courses in *kalarippayattu*, and can also provide guides for forest trekking.

On Sunday evenings, half the city migrates to **Shankhumukham Beach**, 8km west of the centre, to stroll along the sand and watch the sunset. Fried food stalls spring up on the roadside, and the *Indian Coffee House* does a roaring trade at its popular seafront branch. It occupies a building that once belonged to the royal family, where the Raja of Travancore used to preside over executions. A macabre painting displayed in the Puttan Malika Palace shows the cage of tigers used for this purpose: huge crowds would gather to gawp at the condemned criminals being torn limb from limb. These days, the main attraction, aside from the surf, is a huge sculpture of a curvaceous mermaid reclining on landscaped ground behind the *Indian Coffee House* – a work by the renowned Keralan artist Canai Kunuram.

Shankhumukham draws the biggest crowds of all during the biannual **Arattu** festival, when the Padmanabhaswamy deity is brought, amid much pomp, from the temple to be ritually immersed in the sea here (see p.376).

Eating

In common with most South Indian cities, Thiruvananthapuram has busy, hygenic places to eat on seemingly every street corner, serving freshly cooked *dosas*, *iddli-vada-sambar* and other traditional *Udupi* snacks. Wonderful Kerala-style thali "meals" are also widely available – the best places are listed below. For a quick pit stop, the *Indian Coffee House* chain has several branches around the city, including the famous circular *Maveli Café* next to the KSRTC bus stand in Thampanoor, and another, larger cafeteria on Museum Road – handy for the

Moving on from Thiruvananthapuram

Thiruvananthapuram is the main hub for traffic travelling along the coast and across the country. Towns within a couple of hours of the capital – such as Varkala, Kollam and Kanyakumari – can be reached by both bus and train, though it's always worth aiming for limited-stop services rather than much slower "local" or "passenger" ones. For longer hauls, you're invariably better off on the **train**, as buses tend to hurtle along the coastal highway at terrifying speeds; they're also more crowded. JAICO produces an excellent monthly guide with timetables and comprehensive travel details for Kerala and beyond; it's available from bookshops, Thampanoor bus stand and the railway station. For an overview of transport from Thiruvananthapuram, see Travel details, p.495.

By air

Thiruvananthapuram's **Beemapalli airport**, 6km southwest of the city, offers international and domestic flights from a rapidly expanding list of carriers, several of whom have offices downtown (see p.382). For general advice on booking flights, see p.39. Travel details at the end of this chapter includes a full rundown of who flies where, and how often. As the roads to Beemapalli were recently upgraded, it's a comfortable enough journey by auto-rickshaw (around Rs75); taxis charge Rs175–200 from the railway station, and Rs375 from Kovalam's Lighthouse Beach.

By bus

Buses to **Kovalam** leave every 20–30min from the roadside in East Fort, just south of City bus stand (see map p.371). To reach anywhere else, you'll have to head for the grimy KSRTC **Thampanoor bus stand**. Services to **Varkala** leave from here at irregular intervals throughout the day from 7.25am – though it's worth noting that many of them are nail-bitingly slow, winding through dozens of villages and taking up to two-and-a-half hours instead of the 90min required by "super-fast" buses that follow the highway. For **Ponmudi**, there are departures at 5am and 8am. Heading **north** up the coast (to Kollam, Allepey, Ernakulam, Thrissur and Palakkad), the buses to aim for are the 6am or 5.30pm "super-deluxe a/c" specials, tickets for which – along with **tickets** for all other long-distance routes – may be purchased in advance at the reservations hatch on the main bus stand concourse (daily 6am–10pm). The Tamil Nadu bus company, TNSRTC, has its own counter on the same concourse. Numerous private bus companies also run inter-state services; many of the agents are on Aristo Road near the *Greenland Lodging*.

public gardens. They also run a breezy terrace café at Shankhumukam beach where, on Sunday evenings, something of a funfair atmosphere prevails as thousands of city folk break out of the suburbs for a sunset stroll (see p.379).

Ariya Niwas *Ariya Niwas* hotel, Aristo Junction, Thampanoor. Top-class South Indian vegetarian thalis dished up on shiny green banana leaves in a scrupulously clean dining room on the hotel's ground floor. You buy your ticket first (Rs38 per head; "No Sharing"). Hugely popular with everyone from office workers to company directors and their families, and deservedly so: there's really nowhere better to eat in the city. The usual Udupi menu, along with some North Indian and Chinese dishes, is served outside lunch hours (noon–3pm).

Arun Jyothi opposite the Secretariat on MG Rd. A delightfully old-fashioned "meals" restaurant that does unlimited red- or white-rice Keralan thalis (Rs28) from noon to 3pm, including particularly delicious *avial*, an array of a half-dozen condiments and *payasam* for desert. *Dosas*, *uttapams* and other Udupi fare are served through the rest of the day.

Kalavara Press Rd. One of the city's most popular multi-cuisine restaurants, down a sidestreet off MG Rd. You can eat in their dowdy first-floor dining room or, from 6.30pm onwards, on the more attractive rooftop terrace under a pitched-tile shelter. The furniture's plastic, but the food (mostly non-veg) is tasty and inexpensive: fish, beef, mutton and pork dominate the menu, plus they do fish curry "meals' from 12.30 to 2pm.

A full list of destinations reachable by bus from Thiruvananthapuram appears in Travel details on p.495.

By train

Kerala's capital is well connected **by train** with other towns and cities in the country, although getting seats at short notice on long-haul journeys can be a problem. **Reservations** should be made as far in advance as possible from the efficient computerized booking office at the station (Mon–Sat 8am–2pm & 2.15–8pm, Sun 8am–2pm). Sleepers are sold throughout Kerala on a first-come, first-served basis, not on local stations' quotas. The following trains are recommended as the **fastest** and/or **most convenient** from Thiruvananthapuram.

Recommended trains from Thiruvananthapuram

Destination	Name	Number	Departs	Total time
Alapuzzha	Netravati Express**	#6346	daily 10am	2hr 50min
Bengaluru (Bangalore)	Bangalore Express	#6525	daily 12.55pm	18hr
Chennai	Chennai Mail*	#2624	daily 2.30pm	16hr 30min
Ernakulam (Kochi)	Kerala Express	#2625	daily 11.30am	4hr
Kanyakumari	Kanyakumari Express	#1081	daily 9.55am	2hr
Kollam	Kerala Express	#2625	daily 11.30am	1hr 5min
Kottayam	Cape–Mumbai Express	#1082	daily 8.10am	2hr 20min
Kozhikode	Mangalore Express	#6347	daily 8.45pm	9hr 30min
Madgaon (Goa)	Netravati Express	#6346	daily 10am	19hr 50min
	Rajdhani Express	#2431	Wed & Fri 7.15pm	15hr 10min
Madurai	Anantapuri Express	#6124	daily 4.20pm	6hr 40min
	Madurai Passenger	#728	daily 8.20am	9hr
Mangalore	Mangalore Express	#6347	daily 8.45pm	14hr 30min
	Parasuram Express**	#6349	daily 6.10am	13hr 30min
Mumbai	Netravati Express**	#6346	daily 10am	30hr 40min

* via Kollam, Varkala, Kottayam, Ernakulam and Palakkad
** via Kollam, Ernakulam, Thrissur, Kozhikode, Kannur, Kasargode

Maveli Café next to the bus station on Station Rd, Thampanoor. Part of the *Indian Coffee House* chain, this bizarre red-brick, spiral-shaped café (designed by the renowned expatriate British architect, Laurie Baker) is a Trivandrum institution. Inside, waiters in the trademark ICH *pugris* serve *dosas*, *vadas*, greasy omelettes, mountainous biriyanis and china cups of the usual (weak and sugary) filter coffee. An obligatory pit stop, though a grubby one.

New Mubarak off Press Rd, Statue. Terrific little no-frills backstreet joint that's famed for its wonderful Malabari-Muslim dishes, especially seafood. In addition to the usual *masala-fry* pomfret, kingfish, seer fish and pearlspot (*avioli*), you can order huge jumbo prawns, squid and crab, served with proper tapioca (*kappa*) curry and the famous house seafood pickle – at prices undreamed of in Kovalam (most mains Rs75–150). It's tricky to find: you have to squeeze down a narrow pedestrian alleyway off Press Rd (find your way to the *Residency Tower* hotel and ask there).

Swagat *Comfort Inn Grand*, MG Rd. Fine vegetarian Indian food served by black-tie waiters in a blissfully cool a/c dining hall, with tinted windows and discrete Carnatic music in the background – just the ticket if you've had enough of the heat and humidity outside. Their Rs100 "Swagat Special" thali is one for monster appetites, featuring green plantain in coconut, ladies' finger masala and tangy *rasam*. They also do a full multi-cuisine vegetarian menu, even during lunch hours.

Listings

Airlines *Air India*, Museum Rd, Vellayambalam Circle ☎0471/231 0310 (airport ☎0471/250 0585); *Gulf Air*, Ground Floor, Saran Chambers, Vellayambalam ☎0471/272 8003 (airport ☎0471/250 1205); *Indian Airlines*, Air Centre, Mascot Junction ☎0471/231 4781 (airport ☎0471/233 1063); *IndiGo*, First Floor, Krishna Commercial Complex, Bakery Junction ☎0471/233 0227; *Jet Airways*, First Floor, Akshaya Towers, Sasthamangalam Junction ☎0471/272 8864 (airport ☎0471/250 0710); *KLM/Northwest*, c/o Spencer Travel Services, Spencer Junction, MG Rd ☎0471/246 3531; *Qatar Airways*, Bela Vista, TC 30/1403, near SBT, Nalumukku, Pettah ☎0471/391 9091 (airport ☎0471/250 2548); *SriLankan Airlines*, 1st Floor, Spencer Building, Palayam, MG Rd ☎0471/247 1815 (airport ☎0471/250 1140).

Ayurveda The best dispensary in the city, where you can also consult doctors free of charge, is the Kottakkal Aryavaidya Sala, Karamana Junction, southeast of the centre on the national highway ☎0471/246 3439.

Banks and exchange A string of big banks along MG Rd – including HDFC, the SBI, UTI and ICICI – have ATMs and change traveller's cheques and currency. Thomas Cook maintains a foreign exchange counter at the airport and at its travel agency on the ground floor of the Soundarya Building (near the big Raymond's tailoring store), MG Rd (Mon–Sat 9.30am–6pm).

Hospitals SP Fort Hospital (☎0471/245 0540), just down the road from the Margi school in West Fort, has a 24hr casualty and specialist orthopedic unit; the private Cosmopolitan Hospital, in Pattom ☎0471/244 8182 is also recommended. The Government-run General Hospital, 600m east of Statue Circle on MG Rd, is one of the busiest in the state.

Internet access Internet City on Manhalikulam Rd (see map p.371) charges Rs20/hr and is convenient if you're staying in Thampanoor. There's also a tiny, more cramped cybercafé to the rear of the *KTDC Hotel Chaitam*'s lobby, next to the bus stand (Rs30/hr).

Photography and printing The excellent Paramount Colour Lab on Ayurveda College Junction, MG Rd, has state-of-the-art digital printers, sells memory cards and will load data onto discs. In the bowels of the building below ground level there's also a counter specializing in business card printing (Rs1–2/card).

Post office The main post office, with poste restante (daily 8am–6pm), is just south of the Secretariat on MG Rd.

Yoga The Sivananda Yoga Ashram at 37/1929 Airport Rd, Palkulangara, West Fort (☎0471/245 0942 or 245 1398, ⓦwww.sivananda.org), holds daily classes at various levels. See also the box, p.397.

South of Thiruvananthapuram

Despite the fact that virtually the entire 550-kilometre length of the **Keralan coast** is lined with sandy beaches, rocky promontories and coconut palms,

Kovalam is one of the only places where swimming in the sea is not considered eccentric by locals, and which offers accommodation to suit all budgets. To experience daily life away from the exploits of the Kovalam beach scene, you can take an easy wander through the toddy groves to villages such as **Pachalloor** and **Vizhinjam**. A finely preserved example of Keralan architecture is also within easy reach of Thiruvananthapuram: 63km to the south lies the magnificent palace of **Padmanabhapuram**, former capital of the kingdom of Travancore.

Kovalam

The coastal village of **KOVALAM** may lie just 14km south of Thiruvananthapuram but, as Kerala's most developed **beach resort**, it's a world away from the rest of the state. Each year greater numbers of Western visitors – budget travellers and package tourists alike – arrive in search of sun, sea and palm-fringed beaches.

Europeans have been visiting Kovalam since the 1930s, but no hotels were built until hippies started to colonize the place some thirty years later. As the resort's popularity began to grow, more and more paddy fields were filled and the first luxury holiday complexes sprang up. These soon caught the eye of European charter companies scouting for "undiscovered" beach hideaways to supplement their Goa brochures, and since the mid-1990s plane loads of package tourists have been flying here direct from Europe. This influx has had a dramatic impact, with rocketing prices and burgeoning numbers of Ayurvedic massage centres, Kashmiri souvenir shops and pricy seafood restaurants packed into a narrow strip behind Lighthouse Beach.

Kovalam's metamorphosis has coincided with the rise, along the 20km of sandy coastline stretching south of neighbouring Vizhinjam, of a string of luxury resorts. Specializing in expensive "Ayurveda-spa" treatments, these gated, high-walled campuses inhabit a separate universe from the poor fishing communities surrounding them.

Arrival, information and transport

Buses leave from the roadside south of Thiruvananthapuram's City bus stand every 20 or 30 minutes for Kovalam, looping through the top of the village before coming to a halt outside the gates of the *Leela Kempinski*, on the promontory dividing Hawah and Kovalam beaches. If you don't intend to stay at this northern end of the resort, or at Samudra, get down a couple of hundred metres earlier, just past *Hotel Blue Sea* where the road bends – a lane branching to the left drops steeply downhill towards the top of Hawah Beach. The bus journey generally takes 30–45 minutes, but you can cover the 14km from Thiruvananthapuram more quickly by **auto-rickshaw** (Rs100–125) or **taxi** (Rs350–400).

Expect to be plagued by commission touts as you arrive; an approach via the back paths is a good way of avoiding them. The friendly **tourist office** (daily 10am–5pm, closed Sun in low season; ☎0471/248 0085, ⓦwww.keralatourism .org), just inside the *Leela Kempinski* gates, close to where the buses pull in, stocks the usual range of glossy leaflets on Kerala and can offer up-to-date advice about cultural events in the area.

There are plenty of places to **change money** in Kovalam, but private exchange rates can vary so it's best to check beforehand. The Central Bank of India has a branch at the *Kovalam Beach Resort* and the Andhra Bank at KTDC *Samudra*; but for an **ATM**, you'll have to travel up to **Kovalam Junction**, 3km

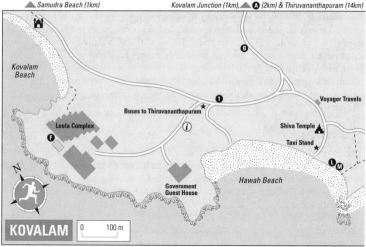

Kovalam Beach

Ⓑ

Voyager Travels

Buses to Thiruvananthapuram

ⓘ

Leela Complex

Shiva Temple

Ⓕ

Taxi Stand

ⓁⓂ

Hawah Beach

Government Guest House

N

KOVALAM   0   100 m

inland, on the national highway (Rs80–100 return in an auto-rickshaw; see map above).

Western Travels (daily 8am–8pm; ☏0471/248 1334) near the bus stand is a reliable agent for flight confirmations and ticketing, and can arrange **car rental**. Voyager Travels (☏0471/2481993), on the lane cutting uphill from the end of Hawah Beach, specializes in **motorbike rental**, at competitive rates: an Enfield Bullet is Rs350–500 per day; a scooter Rs250. You'll need to leave your driver's licence or passport with them as security. **Surfboards** can be rented on Light-house Beach for an extortionate Rs250 per hour, or boogie boards for Rs50. Alternatively, for around Rs300 you can take a ride on a traditional **kettu-maran** (*kettu* meaning tied; *maran* logs), which gave the catamaran its name. Widely used by the fishermen of Kovalam, the rudimentary boat consists of five logs lashed together with coir rope, and can feel disconcertingly vulnerable in even a slightly choppy sea: accept a lifejacket if it's offered.

Plenty of places offer broadband **Internet** access for Rs40/hr. Kovalam doesn't have a major **bookshop**, but many of the tailors and clothes stalls supplement their trade by dealing in the usual hit-and-miss selection of secondhand books, and there's a decent selection on offer at a stall upstairs in *Waves (German Bakery)*.

Accommodation

Although Kovalam is crammed with **accommodation**, decent rock-bottom rooms are hard to find, as all but a handful of the many budget traveller's guesthouses have been upgraded to suit the package tourists who flock here over Christmas and the New Year. This also means that hotels are often block-booked weeks in advance, so it's a good idea to make a reservation before you arrive, which also spares you from the tenacious touts who hang around the edges of the village. **Prices** are extortionate compared with the rest of Kerala, almost doubling in peak season (Dec to mid-Jan), when you'll be lucky to find a basic room for less than Rs500. At other times, haggling should bring the rate down by twenty to fifty percent, especially if you stay for more than a week. The codes below are for high-season prices.

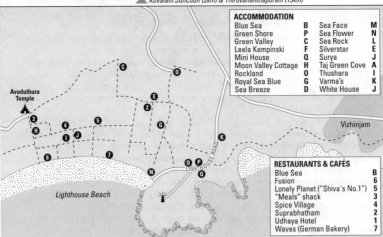

Blue Sea 100m before junction to Hawah Beach
℡0471/248 1401 ✆m94399 91992,
🌐www.hotelskerala.com/bluesea. Half-a-dozen
quirky round buildings in the rear garden of a
grand double-fronted colonial-era mansion
overlooking the main road above Hawah Beach.
Each contains three rooms, arranged on separate
storeys around a (rather shabby) central pool;
they're spacious, cool and good value, with plenty
of outside balcony space. There are also a couple
of older, more atmospheric rooms in the main
house. An established favourite, and the management is welcoming. ⑤–⑥

Green Shore Lighthouse Rd ℡0471/248 0106,
🌐www.thegreenshore.com. Eight impeccably
smart, well furnished rooms in a modern building
close to the lighthouse. It's a bit boxed in, but
the interiors are nicely done and there are big
common verandas to lounge on. A/c costs Rs600
extra. ④–⑤

Green Valley behind Lighthouse Beach
℡0471/248 0636, ✉indira_ravi@hotmail.com. Set
on the edge of the open land a couple of hundred
metres or so from the beach, this is one of
Kovalam's oldest established guesthouses. It holds
a range of differently priced rooms, from dingy
singles to spacious a/c options large enough for
three people, but the building itself is an unsightly
hotch-potch and few of the balconies offer much
privacy. ④–⑤

Leela Kempinski Hawah-Kovalam ℡0471/248
0101, 🌐www.theleela.com/kovalam. This "five-
star-deluxe" resort, set in 44 acres of mature
woodland which you navigate in golf buggies,
sweeps down the hillside to its own exclusive end
of Kovalam Beach. Wonderful views extend out to
sea and up the coast from a pair of dreamy infinity
pools. Rooms come in a range of categories, from
around $300. ⑨

Mini House Lighthouse Beach Rd ℡0471/248
0867, ✉naswara@hotmail.com. Six large, simply
furnished, sea-facing, non-a/c rooms in a prime
spot on the rocks above a small cove, just under
the lighthouse. The balconies catch uninterrupted
breezes, though even allowing for the great
location it's a bit overpriced. ⑤–⑥

Moon Valley Cottage behind Lighthouse Beach
℡94461 00291, ✉sknairkovalam@yahoo
.com. This simple budget guesthouse stands right
next to the footpath leading from the rear of Lighthouse Beach to the Avaduthura Devi temple. Its
rooms are really big for the price, have mozzie nets
and quality bedding, and are pleasantly decorated.
The best are hidden around the back of the
building, which overlooks open fields. The same
owner also offers a couple of similarly well-priced,
two-bedroomed apartments in another building
nearby. ③–④

Rockland Lighthouse Rd ℡0471/248 0588.
Rockland is one of a cluster of three co-run budget
hotels, sandwiched together just off the lane above
the south end of Lighthouse Beach. It has the edge
over its neighbours because its six comfortable
rooms – all attached and with balconies – look
straight through coconut palms to the sea. Reasonable rates given the location. ④

Royal Sea Blue Behind Lighthouse Beach
℡0471/212 7857, 🌐www.royalseablue.com.

"Health tourism" is very much a buzz phrase in Kerala these days. International-standard hospitals and dental clinics have mushroomed around resorts such as Kovalam, catering for cost-conscious patients from abroad who've travelled here expressly for treatments, while no self-respecting luxury resort is without its own money-spinning "Ayurvedic spa" or "wellness centre". Hippies who first came here to drop out are, three decades on, returning to detox and de-stress – and even for the odd hip replacement.

Synonymous with the boom in health travel is Kerala's close association with **Ayurvedic medicine**. Ayurveda, literally "science of life" (described in more detail on p.74), is an ancient system of herbal healing practised throughout India. Nowhere, however, are its Sanskrit roots so strictly adhered to as in the far southwest of the country, where the great sage **Agasthya** is said to have developed the *siddha* form of medicine from which modern Ayurveda evolved. Legend also attributes the discovery of the sacred Agashtyakooda mountain on the Tamil-Kerala border, famous as a source of medicinal herbs of unparallelled potency, to Agasthya. According to tradition, eighteen families were originally chosen by Lord Brahma to hold the secrets of Ayurveda. Over time these dwindled to eight – known as the **ashtavaidyas** – of whom only six still practise, mostly around the towns of Thrissur (see p.466) and Kozhikode (see p.482).

The Keralan approach to Ayurveda has two distinct elements: first, the body is cleansed of toxins generated by imbalances in lifestyle and diet; secondly, its equilibrium is restored using herbal medicines, mainly in the form of plant oils applied using a range of different massage techniques. A practitioner's first prescription will often be a course of **panchakarma** treatment – a five-phase therapy during which harmful impurities are purged through induced vomiting, enemas, and the application of medicinal oils poured through the nasal cavity. Other less onerous components, tailored for the individual patient, may include: *dhara*, where the oils are blended with ghee or milk and poured on to the forehead; *pizhichi*, in which a team of four masseurs apply different oils simultaneously; and, the weirdest looking of all, *sirovashti*, where the oils are poured into a tall, topless leather cap placed on the head.

Alongside these, patients are prescribed special balancing foods, and given vigorous full-body **massages**, or *abhayangam*, each day. Some practitioners may also offer **marma chikitsa** foot massage, a Keralan speciality where pressure is applied to the body with the souls of the feet; to control how much weight he or she brings to bear, the masseur grips a knotted rope suspended from the ceiling. The technique, which focuses on key connective energy "*marma*" points, was originally developed by masters of the martial art, *kalarippayattu*; part of every fighter's training routine involves a gruelling oily rub down before dawn, as does the beginning of a typical *kathakali* student's day.

Recently built three-storey block, well off the road in the palm groves. Fronted by a large garden that's big enough for kids to run around in, the rooms are sparkling, with polished marble floors, TVs, fridges and separate a/c units (Rs500 extra), and the location is very peaceful. ⑤–⑥
Sea Breeze behind Lighthouse Beach ☎0471/248 0024, ⓦwww.seabreezeayurvedicresort.com. One of Kovalam's better-value budget choices: quiet, secluded, with large and sunny communal balconies overlooking a well-tended tropical

garden. The rooms (Rs350–700) are clean and large for the price, and there's a yoga *shala* on the top floor where you can attend morning ashtanga classes. ③–④
Sea Face Hawah Beach ☎0471/248 1835, ⓦwww.seaface.com. An ugly modern block slap on the beachfront, with three-star pretensions. Looking across a raised pool and café terrace to the sea, its rooms are fronted by little walled sun decks; each has its own fridge, cable TV and good-sized bathroom. ⑧–⑨

Where to go

Kerala's tourist resorts are full of places offering Ayurvedic cures for every conceivable ailment. Few of them, however, are staffed by fully qualified practitioners, despite what the certificates displayed on their walls may suggest. Standards of both treatment and hygiene vary greatly, as do the prices – a significant factor if you sign up for a minimum three-week stint, as most places advise. Woman travellers also sometimes complain of sexual harassment at the hands of opportunistic male masseurs; cross-gender massage is forbidden in Ayurveda, though the rule is routinely ignored in small, tourist-oriented centres. Dodgy oils that can cause skin problems is another risk you might be exposed to at a backstreet clinic.

The only sure-fire way to be guaranteed bona fide treatment is to splash out on somewhere that's been approved by the government. Kerala Tourism's **accreditation scheme** divides centres into **Green Leaf** establishments – which apply the highest standards of hygiene, employ only pukka staff, never allow cross-gender massage, and use top-grade oils and medicines – and Olive Leaf ones, which offer equally dependable treatments, but in more traditionally Keralan surroundings, with massage tables carved from medicinal hardwoods, beautiful earth-walled practise rooms, yoga *shalas* and steam baths on site. This is the kind of place generally referred to as an **Ayurvedic spa** and will nearly always be attached to a posh seaside hotel or heritage resort, offering packages that include gourmet vegetarian meals, yoga lessons and cultural programmes in the evenings. We've listed many such places in this chapter, but have – with a handful of tried and tested exceptions – steered clear of smaller, less expensive clinics, whose credentials may be harder to verify.

Regardless of the claims many make, most outfits around Kovalam and Varkala - even the pricey ones - should be regarded primarily as places to seek **rejuvenation** rather than cures for **serious medical conditions**. If you've come to Kerala in search of treatment for a chronic illness of some kind, then you'd do better to explore the possibility of a spell at one of the old *Ashtavaidya* **Ayurveda hospitals** listed below, which are famous all over India for the quality of their doctors and medicines, produced on their own organic estates and in-house labs. You'll need to set aside a minimum of four weeks, and book at least nine months in advance.

Arya Vaidya Sala Kottakkal near Malappuram in northern Kerala (26km from Kozhikode airport) ℡0483/274 2216, ⓦwww.aryavaidyasala.com.

SNA Oushadhasala near Jubilee Museum, Thrissur ℡0487/242 0948, ⓦwww .thaikatmooss.com.

Vaidyaratnam Oushadhasala Thaikkattussen, 8km from Thrissur ℡0487/235 3610, ⓦwww.vaidyaratnammooss.com.

Regardless of what kind of treatment you go for, and where you go for it, bear in mind the **optimal season for Ayurveda** is said to be during the monsoons (June–Oct), when the air is free of dust and the humidity promotes detoxifying perspiration.

Sea Flower ℡0471/248 0554, ⓦwww .seaflowerbeachresort.com. You can't get closer to the sea than the orange-painted *Sea Flower*, which rises straight from the sand at the south end of Lighthouse Beach. Facing the surf, its spacious, breezy and comfortable rooms are spread over two storeys – the upper ones cost Rs350 extra, but are worth it for the views. ④

Sea Rock Hawah Beach ℡0471/248 0422. One of Kovalam's oldest hotels, right on the seafront and with a popular terrace restaurant. At identical prices to the *Sea Face* next door, the a/c rooms are perfectly aligned for the sunset views over the beach. It's a popular choice, requiring at least a fortnight's advance booking, despite the high tariffs and busy location. ⑧

Silverstar behind Lighthouse Beach ℡0471/248 2883, ℡m98956 73443, ⓦwww.silverstar -kovalam.com. Owned by a welcoming German-Keralan couple, the *Silverstar* is a relative newcomer hidden away in the palm groves a couple of hundred metres inland from the beach.

Centred on a well shaded, beaten-earth courtyard, the location is tranquil by Kovalam standards, leafy and cool, and the rooms very large, with verandas or terraces out front, and new mozzie nets inside. **❼**

Surya Lighthouse Beach ☎0471/248 1012, ✉kovsurya@yahoo.co.in. Professionally run guesthouse down a narrow lane from the seafront. Secure and quiet, with pleasant rooms for the price (a/c and non-a/c); some of the verandas look straight onto adjacent buildings, but there's lots of space inside. One of the better budget options. If it's full, try the equally spruce *White House* (☎0471/248 3388; **❹**) next door. **❹**

Taj Green Cove GV Raja Ratapara Rd, Samudra ☎0471/248 7733, ⓦwww.tajhotels.com. Taj Group's new luxury resort is spread over a lush, wooded hillside a kilometre back from Kovalam and Samudra beaches (over the headland from Hawah). Clad with local grey granite and elephant-grass thatch, its faux-rustique chalets open onto lovely sea-facing verandas smothered in greenery.

Golf buggies ("club cars") whisk guests from the lobby area, with its open-kitchen *Jasmine* restaurant, infinity pool and bar billiards table, to a private fishing lagoon and sunbathing area next to the sea. Rooms from $340 per night. **❾**

Thushara Behind Lighthouse Beach ☎0471/248 1694, ⓦwww.hotelthushara.net. Small but slick hotel in the thick of the action, mostly given over to charter tourists. The rooms are large and comfortable, and have private balconies overlooking a central, well-maintained swimming pool. Rates include continental breakfast. **❻**

Varma's Lighthouse Beach Rd ☎0471/248 0478, ✉varmabeach@hotmail.com. One of the few places in Kovalam that's tried to incorporate traditional Keralan architecture into its design (despite being Goan-owned). The result is an attractive blend of modern comforts and old-style Malabari wood and brass décor. All 12 rooms are sea-facing, tastefully fitted with block-printed textiles, and open onto secluded balconies. It's also well placed for the less frequented cove south of Lighthouse Beach. **❽**

The beaches

Kovalam consists of four fairly small stretches of sand; the southernmost, known for obvious reasons as **Lighthouse Beach**, is where most visitors spend their time. It takes about ten minutes to walk from end to end, either along the sand or on the concrete pathway (patrolled by lots of touts) which fronts a long strip of resorts, guesthouses and restaurants. You can rent surfboards, venture out to sea in wooden outriggers or rent beach chairs and parasols for the day.

The red-and-white-striped **lighthouse**, on the promontory at the southern end of the beach, is the area's most prominent landmark. It opens for two hours each afternoon (daily 3–5pm; Rs5), when you can scale the 142 spiral steps and twelve ladder rungs to the observation platform: on clear days, views extend over the beach as far as Beemapally mosque in one direction, and south to Poovar in the other.

South of the lighthouse, a tiny white-sand cove opens into a much larger beach, overlooked by a scattering of upmarket hotels, which you can reach by following the lane that peels off Lighthouse Road, before *Varma's Beach Resort* (see map, p.385). Lots of tourists mistakenly believe this is a private area, but it isn't.

Ayurvedic centres

Kovalam is crammed with places offering all manner of Ayurvedic treatments, ranging from grubby massage shacks in the palm grove behind Lighthouse Beach to fully accredited Olive Leaf clinics in the nearby five-star resorts complete with their own teak-lined steam rooms and beachside yoga *shalas*. See our box on Ayurveda in Kerala (pp.386–387) for general advice on finding a reputable place.

One thoroughly dependable mid-scale centre worth singling out, both for the standard of its practitioners and overall ambience, is *Amruthamgamaya* (☎94478 56461), tucked away on the edge of Venganoor village, 4km inland from Kovalam. Equipped with traditional palm-thatch, mud-walled huts, as well as an

Warning: swimming safety

Due to unpredictable rip currents and a strong undertow, especially during the monsoons, **swimming** from Kovalam's beaches is not always safe. The introduction of blue-shirted lifeguards has reduced the annual death toll, but at least a couple of tourists still drown here each year, and many more get into difficulties. Follow the warnings of the safety flags at all times and keep a close eye on children. There's a first-aid post midway along Lighthouse Beach.

open-sided yoga hall where clients may attend free classes, it offers the full gamut of Ayurvedic treatments at fair prices. Phone ahead for directions, as not even the local rickshaw-wallahs know where the find it.

Heading in the opposite direction (northwards) from Lighthouse Beach, you round a small rocky headland to reach **Hawah Beach** – almost a mirror image of its busier neighbour, although it is backed for most of its length by empty palm groves. In the morning before the sunworshippers arrive, it functions primarily as a base for local fishermen, who hand-haul their massive nets through the shallows, singing and chanting as they coil the endless piles of rope.

North of the next headland, **Kovalam Beach** is dominated by the angular chalets of the five-star *Leela* above it. Home to a small mosque, it's shared by guests of the luxury resort and by local fishermen in roughly equal measure; to get there, follow the road downhill past the bus terminus.

Only a short walk further north, **Samudra Beach** is very small, especially at high tide, and is backed by a cluster of package-tour resorts surrounding a tiny temple. It holds little to recommend it during the day, but comes alive at night, when rows of restaurant tables spring up along the seawall.

To escape the beach scene altogether, head into the cool and shaded **coconut groves** behind Lighthouse Beach's hotel strip. Here, ladies gossip in shrill Malayalam while they wash both clothes and children in the village tank, sewing machines whirr as tailors run up cheap cotton clothes for the tourists and children play innovative versions of cricket with coconut shells and sticks. Bear in mind that although the sight of Westerners in skimpy bathing suits on the beach has become relatively normal for locals, it's polite to dress in a respectful manner when walking in the palm groves or near Kovalam Beach's mosque.

Eating, drinking and nightlife

Lighthouse Beach is lined with identikit cafés and restaurants specializing in **seafood**: you pick from displays of fresh fish such as blue marlin, sea salmon, barracuda and delicious seer fish, as well as lobster, tiger prawns, crab and mussels. They are then weighed, grilled over a charcoal fire or cooked in a tandoor (traditional clay oven), and served with rice, salad or chips. Meals are **pricey** by Indian standards – typically around Rs175–350 per head for fresh fish, and double that for lobster or prawns – and service is often painfully slow, but the food is generally very good and the ambience of the beachfront terraces convivial.

For **breakfast** you can choose from any number of cafés offering the usual brown bread, fruit salad and pancakes, or try a traditional Keralan breakfast at one of the local teashops near the bus stand. Freshly cooked, delicious Keralan *appams* and egg masala are also on offer at a makeshift shelter on the side of the pathway leading from Lighthouse Beach to the Avaduthura temple. Further along the same path, on the right next to where it meets the surfaced lane, the locals enjoy tasty rice-plate thali "**meals**" for around Rs20 at a nameless, dingy shack. It's a rough and ready place, and you'll have to squeeze on to narrow tables to eat, but the food is delicious and probably more hygienic than most of the stuff served on the beach.

Nightlife in Kovalam is pretty laid-back, and revolves around the beach, where Westerners chill when the restaurants close. Beer and spirits are served in most cafés, albeit in discrete china teapots from under the table due to tight liquor restrictions. One or two places also run **movie nights**, screening pirate copies of just-released hits.

During your stay in Kovalam you may be offered marijuana, but bear in mind that cannabis is illegal in Kerala, as everywhere else in India, and that the local police occasionally conduct raids.

Blue Sea Above Hawah Beach ☏0471/248 1401, ☏m93499 91992. Mouthwatering garlic prawns (Rs250) and tandoori chicken are the two specialities of this slightly off-beat restaurant at the top of the village. Meals are served at poolside tables in a quiet rear garden. Phone ahead, preferably in the morning, to book and pre-order.

Fusion Lighthouse Beach. Along with *Waves*, the funkiest place on Lighthouse Beach, with three innovative menus (Eastern, Western and fusion) served on a first-floor terrace overlooking the bay. Try the fish creole in orange vinaigrette with cumin potatoes, one of the Keralan seafood specialities, or home-made tagliatelle and chilli pesto. They also have a fine selection of drinks, a hefty sound system playing Indo-Western music, and a toilet that has to be seen to be believed. Most mains Rs180.

Lonely Planet ("Shiva's No.1") behind Lighthouse Beach. Flanked by a pond that's alive with croaking frogs, the covered terrace of this large, family-run budget travellers' place is one of the most enduringly popular restaurants in the village, and a relaxed spot to while away an evening. Its menu of North and South Indian vegetarian standards is nothing to write home about, though inexpensive for Kovalam (most mains Rs50–80) and the food is well-tempered for the sensitive Western palate. Wed evenings host a cultural show with all-you-can-eat buffet (7.30–9pm; Rs150; book in advance).

Spice Village Behind Lighthouse Beach. In much the same mould as the nearby *Lonely Planet*, though smaller and run by a posse of local lads in snazzy shirts rather than a family, and it also serves cold Kingfishers.

Suprabhatham near the *Silverstar*. Simple, popular vegetarian café-restaurant in a well-shaded garden setting, where you can order inexpensive Indian breakfasts, fresh juices, lassis and shakes, as well as an extensive multi-cuisine menu: the "Bengali aubergine" and "chunky avocado salad" are popular specials. Evenings tend to end with the staff downing stiff whisky-and-soda slammers around 10.30pm, after which the service and cooking degenerate rapidly.

Udhaya Hotel near the bus terminus. Hidden away behind a tiny general store, this local teashop serves the best Keralan breakfasts for miles, in a narrow, blue-walled cafeteria lined with Hindu, Muslim and Christian religious pictures. Huge trays of steaming *iddiappam* (rice-flour vermicelli), *puttu* (rice rolls) and *appam* (steamed pancakes made from fermented rice batter) are brought at regular intervals down the wooden staircase from the kitchen on banana leaves, and served with tin plates of egg masala, spicy *sambar* and more-ish chickpea *chana wada*. The chai's delicious too. You'll be hard pushed to spend more than Rs25 per head here.

Waves (German Bakery) Lighthouse Beach. This rooftop terrace, shaded by a high tiled canopy, functions as a laid-back café during the daytime, where you can order light meals, snacks, German cakes and delicious, freshly ground coffee. After sunset, its atmospheric designer lighting makes a great backdrop for more sophisticated cooking: Thai and Kerala seafood curries, lobster in vodka, fish steaks with sesame and coriander crust, or steamed prawns with chilli and coconut milk. For desert, go for the malabar fruit flambée. Most mains Rs175–200.

North of Kovalam: Pozhikkara and Pachalloor

If you need a break from the rampant commercialism of Kovalam, keep plodding north along Samudra Beach for around 4km, past a string of fishing hamlets, until you arrive at a point where the sea merges with the backwaters to form a salt-water lagoon.

Although only thirty or forty minutes' walk away, the sliver of white sand known as **Pozhikkara Beach** is a world away from the holiday culture of Kovalam. Here, the sands are used primarily for landing fish and fixing nets. **PACHALLOOR**, a quiet village sandwiched behind the lagoon and nearby highway, makes a good alternative base for the area, with two appealing places to stay. The British-run *Lagoona Davina* (☎0471/238 0049, ⓦwww .lagoonadavina.com; ⑨), a small, exclusive boutique hotel overlooking the river mouth, is the pricier of the pair, patronized mainly by well-to-do Brits. Costing around $160/Rs7000 per night in season, its rooms are small, but individually styled with carved wood four-posters, Indian textiles and animal paintings. They open onto a terrace where staff wearing cummerbunds and gold-edged saris serve a mixture of indifferent Keralan dishes and low-fat European cuisine (Rs700 for three courses).

The other guesthouse at Pachalloor, the ⅍ *Beach and Lake Resort* (☎0471/238 2086, ⓦwww.beachandlakeresort.com; Rs3500), lies across the water from *Lagoona Davina* (you'll have to hail a boatman to reach it). It's an altogether more down-to-earth affair, with less inspired interiors, but an even better location closer to the surf and fishing beach. Opening onto a relaxing waterside terrace, the rooms are spacious, with correspondingly large bathrooms, and at around Rs3500 per night in season cost half of what you pay in *Lagoona*.

Both guesthouses organize guided **backwater trips** and offer Ayurvedic massages and yoga classes. If you book in advance, both send drivers to meet you at the airport; otherwise take a taxi 6km along the highway towards Kovalam, and bear right along the "bypass" where the road forks, just after the Thiruvallam bridge. After another 1km or so, signboards on the right-hand side of the road point through the trees to the guesthouses.

South of Kovalam: Vizhinjam to Poovar

A tightly packed cluster of tiled fishers' huts, **VIZHINJAM** (pronounced "Virinyam"), on the opposite (south) side of the headland from Lighthouse Beach, was once the capital of the Ay kings, the earliest dynasty in south Kerala. During the ninth century the Pandyans fought to control it, and it was the scene of major Chola–Chera battles in the eleventh century. A number of simple small shrines survive from those times, and can be made the focus of a pleasant afternoon's stroll through coconut groves, best approached from the centre of the village rather than the coast road – brace yourself for the sharp contrast between hedonistic tourist resort and workaday fishing village.

A strikingly modern pink **mosque** on the promontory overlooks the Muslim quarter, home to around 3000 fishermen; the Christian area,

△ Vizhinjam

with a population of around 7000, lies on the opposite side of the bay, beneath a large church. Tension between the two has frequently erupted into riots, and the village remains something of a communal flashpoint, a situation not helped any by ongoing disputes over proposals to upgrade Vizhinjam harbour into a massive container port. The plan was recently shelved in favour of a rival site in Tamil Nadu, but the recriminations rumble on.

On the far side of the fishing bay in the village centre, fifty metres down a road opposite the police station, a small unfinished eighth-century **rock shrine** features a carved figure of Shiva with a weapon. The **Tali Shiva** temple nearby, reached by a narrow path from behind the government primary school, may mark the original centre of Vizhinjam. The simple shrine is accompanied by a group of *naga* snake statues, a reminder of Kerala's continuing cult of snake worship, a survivor from pre-brahminical times.

Toward the sea, ten minutes' walk from the village's main road along Hidyatnagara Road, the grove known as **Kovil Kadu** ("temple forest") holds a square Shiva shrine and a rectangular one dedicated to the goddess **Bhagavati**. Thought to date from the ninth century, these are probably the earliest structural temples in Kerala, although the Bhagavati shrine has been renovated.

Nellinkunnu, Pulinkudi, Chowara and Poovar

Golden-sand beaches fringe the shore stretching southwards from Vizhinjam, interrupted only by the occasional rock outcrop and tidal estuary. This dramatic coastline, with its backdrop of thick coconut plantations, can appear peaceful compared with Kovalam, but it's actually one of the most densely populated – and intensely political – corners of the state. Fishing villages, dominated by out-size churches and garishly painted Hindu temples, line the entire 25km of road that winds south along the shoreline. As in Vizhinjam, communal tensions often run high, and the sand remains primarily somewhere to defecate and work rather than swim off (the undertow can be treacherous) – not that this has in the least deterred the developers. Over the past decade, virtually every metre of land backing the prettiest stretches of coast has been bought up and built on. Five kilometres south of Kovalam, at **Nellinkunnu** and neighbouring **Pulinkudi**, low, terraced cliffs enfold a sequence of beautiful palm-backed coves, each overlooked by its own luxury resort complex. Nearly all of them follow the same formula, focusing on Ayurvedic *panchakarma* treatments (see p.386), with accommodation provided in individual thatched, a/c "cottages" or antique wooden houses relocated from Keralan villages.

It's worth renting a scooter and exploring the back lanes and secluded beaches of this distinctive area – a sometimes surreal mix of undeveloped Malayali fishing villages and sumptuous wellness retreats. One of the region's most memorable views can be enjoyed just north of **Chowara** village, 8km south of Kovalam, where an oddly proportioned kneeling Christ statue surveys the sands from atop a rocky bluff. Beyond it, an endless sandy beach yawns south to the horizon, scattered with literally hundreds of wooden boats.

Chowara beach peters out twelve kilometres further south at **Poovar**, where the Neyyar River flows into the sea. Before some cataclysmic event threw up a sandbar here, a harbour used to overlook the river mouth, which some historians claim may have been the port Orphyr – famous in the ancient world as a source of spices, slaves and gemstones. The backwaters behind the sandbar today shelter a cluster of luxury hideaways, only reachable by boat, and these make comfortable bases for forays beyond the tourist belt at the southern tip of

Kerala. Non-guests may travel out to them, but will have to pay for the transfer (usually around Rs250).

Accommodation south of Kovalam

The twenty-kilometre stretch of coast between Kovalam and Poovar harbours more than thirty luxury resorts and Ayurvedic spas, in addition to a handful of more homely guesthouses. The following, divided into areas, are the pick of the crop.

Nellinkunnu and Pulinkudi

Bethsaida Hermitage Pulinkudi ☎0471/226 7554, ⓦwww.bethsaida-c.org. An "eco-friendly Ayurvedic beach resort" with a difference. The comforts – huge, well-furnished rooms in brick cottages or an imposing new block, with a pool, à la carte restaurant and prime location right next to a beautiful cove – are standard for the area, but the profits support a Church-run orphanage for 1700 boys and girls – a great initiative that's been doing a fine job for more than a decade; and at $126 per night, it's cheaper than most of the competition. ⑨

Karikkathi Beach House Pulinkudi ☎0471/240 0956, ⓦwww.karikkathibeachhouse.com. Simplicity is the essence of this exquisite little bolthole, nestled amid the palm trees above a quiet cove, only a stone's throw from the surf. You pay more for the location than luxury, though the house – encircled by a low wall with two attached rooms opening on to a common, sea-facing veranda – has its own understated style: white walls, traditional terracotta tiles, wood furniture and window shutters set the tone. Staff are on hand to provide drinks and meals. One of the most desirable places to stay in South India, though such exclusivity comes at a price ($266 per double room, or $535 if you book the whole house – recommended for privacy). ⑨

Surya Samudra Pulinkudi ☎0471/248 0413, ⓦwww.suryasamudra.com. The dreamiest of all the "heritage resorts" on this strip. An army of Keralan woodworkers and stone sculptors from Mamallapuram were drafted in to reconstruct its antique, gabled villas, scattered across a 21-acre promontory between a pair of quiet beaches. The stone carvings, oiled rosewood and bowls of floating hibiscus and marigolds glow to magical effect in the evening sunlight, and the pool, adapted from a former stone quarry, features underwater sculptures. $185–530 per night. ⑨

Thapovan Nellinkunnu, Mullor PO ☎0471/248 0453, ⓦwww.thapovan.com. This German-run heritage resort comprises two separate parts: one in a grove next to the sea shore, and another higher up the hillside, on a cliff. The latter's elevated position ion and views across the palm canopy to Vizhinjam give it the edge, and the traditional teak chalets, set amid well-tended gardens, are lovely. Indian classical concerts are a regular feature, plus the usual Ayurvedic and yoga facilities are on site. Doubles from $115 per night. ⑨

Chowara

Dr Franklin's Chowara ☎0471/248 0870, ⓦwww.dr-franklin.com. Dr Franklin was among the first Keralan physicians to spot the tourism potential of Ayurvedic medicine, and though his resort may not be as easy on the eye as some in this area, the *panchakarma* treatments it provides are of the highest quality. Accommodation comes in the form of "special" or larger "deluxe" rooms with tiled floors and patios, thatched mud huts (fully attached) and swish new Western-style rooms. ⑥–⑦

Somatheeram ☎0471/226 6501, ⓦwww.somatheeram.org. *Somatheeram* established the model which countless ayurvedic health resorts have followed, packaging high-quality herbal therapies with accommodation in traditional-style Keralan houses fitted with a/c and other mod cons. When you're not being doused with medicinal oils, you can relax in a range of rooms, all stacked on terraces overlooking the beach. Sister concern *Manaltheeram* (☎0471/226 6222, ⓦwww.manaltheeram.com), next door, offers more of the same, plus a pool (open for guests of *Somatheeram*). Doubles $100–250. ⑨

Travancore Heritage ☎0471/226 7828, ⓦwww.thetravancoreheritage.com. The centre-piece of this extravagant complex is a splendid 150-year-old mansion (serving now as the hotel reception), fronted by a kidney-shaped pool and sun terrace. Below it are set 60 relocated antique bungalows, some boasting alfresco garden bathrooms and their own plunge pools. At beach level, reached via a lift, there's a rather less inspiring modern block on two storeys, also with a big pool in front. Rooms $115–300. ⑨

Poovar Island

Estuary Island ☎0471/221 4355, ⓦwww
.estuaryisland.com. Formerly the *Poorvar Island
Resort*, this is the largest complex in the area,
and the one with the least character. Its 46 luxury
a/c rooms occupy a building inspired by the
Brunton Boatyard in Fort Cochin, but lacking the
same elegance. A row of bizarre floating wood
rooms is its only distinguishing feature. Rooms
$134–200. ⑨

Friday's Place ☎0471/293 3392,
ⓦwww.kukimedia.com/fridaysplace. One of
Kerala's more eccentric homestays: four beautifully
made teak and mahogany "eco-cottages", set in an
acre of palm and acacia gardens deep in the
backwaters. Each has its own veranda, solar
electricity supply and comfy rubber-mattress beds
and attractive hand-loom textile decor. You're well
cut off from the mainland (the river's not so much

nearby as actually flowing through the plot via a
network of little canals), but British-Sri Lankan
owners Mark and Sujeewa are sociable hosts,
offering fine organic South Indian cuisine, yoga
tuition, and use of an 8-inch telescope for
stargazing. Doubles $200 per night. ⑨

Isola di Cocco ☎0471/221 0008, ⓦwww
.isoladicocco.com. Yet another large-scale "heritage
resort", offering a/c rooms, antique Keralan
cottages and suites spread over 30 acres, but with
the distinction of being surrounded on all sides by
water. Facilities include a big pool, billiards room
and library. ⑨

Poovar House ☎0471/213 3533, ☎m99954
60368. British-owned homestay offering fully
attached rooms (a/c or non-a/c) in a grand modern
house with its own pool and Jacuzzi. Free Internet
access and three-hour backwater excursions
(Rs300) available on request. ⑦

Padmanabhapuram

Although now officially in Tamil Nadu, **PADMANABHAPURAM**, 63km
southeast of Thiruvananthapuram, was the capital of Travancore between 1550
and 1750, and maintains its historic links with Kerala, from where it is still
administered. For anyone with even a minor interest in Keralan architecture,
the small **Padmanabhapuram Palace** (Tues–Sun 9am–1pm & 2–4.30pm;
Rs50 [Rs20], cameras Rs20), whose design represents the high point of
regional building, is an irresistible attraction. It lies a pleasant ten- to fifteen-
minute walk from the bus station: cross the main road outside the station, turn
left and follow the road on the right. Once through the paddy fields, you'll
emerge at a village that clusters around the imposing walls of the royal
compound. It's worth avoiding weekends, when the complex is overrun with
bus parties.

Set in neat, gravelled grounds against a backdrop of steep-sided hills, the
palace's predominantly wooden exterior displays a perfect combination of clean
lines and gentle angles, the sloping tiled roofs of its buildings broken by triangular projecting gables that enclose delicately carved screens.

In the **entrance hall** (a veranda), a brass oil lamp hangs from an ornate teak,
rosewood and mahogany ceiling and is carved with ninety different lotus
flowers. Beautifully ornamented, the revolving lamp inexplicably keeps the
position in which it is left, seeming to defy gravity. The raja rested from the
summer heat on the cool, polished-granite bed in the corner. On the wall hangs
a collection of *onamvillu* (ceremonial bows) decorated with images of
Padmanabha – the reclining form of Vishnu – which local chieftains would
present to him during the Onam festival.

Directly above the entrance hall, on the first floor, the **mantrasala** (council
chamber) is gently illuminated by light that filters through panes of coloured
mica. Herbs soaking in water were put into the boxed bench seats along the
front wall as a natural air-cooling system. The highly polished black floor is
made from a now-lost technique using burnt coconut, sticky sugar-cane extract,
egg whites, lime and sand.

The oldest part of the complex is the **Ekandamandapam**, or "lonely place".
Built in 1550, it was used for rituals for the goddess Durga and typically

employed elaborate floor paintings known as *kalam ezhuttu*. A loose ring attached to a column is a tour de force of the carpenter's art: both ring and column are carved from a single piece of jackwood. Nearby is a *nalekettu*, a four-sided courtyard found in many Keralan houses, open to the sky and surrounded by a pillared walkway. A trapdoor once served as the entrance to a secret passageway leading to another palace, since destroyed.

The Pandya-style stone-columned **dance hall** stands directly in front of a shrine to the goddess of learning, Saraswati. The women of the royal household had to watch performances through screens on the side, and the staff through holes in the wall from the gallery above. Typical of old country houses, steep, wooden ladder-like steps, ending in trapdoors, connect the floors. Belgian mirrors and Tanjore miniatures of Krishna adorn the chamber, forming part of the **women's quarters**, where a swing hangs on plaited iron ropes, while a four-poster bed, made from sixteen kinds of medicinal wood, dominates the **raja's bedroom**. Its elaborate carvings depict a mass of vegetation, human figures, birds and, as the central motif, the snake symbol of medicine, associated with the Greek physician deity Asclepius. The **murals** for which the palace is famous – alive with detail, colour, graceful form and religious fervour – adorn the walls of the **meditation room** directly above the bedroom, which was used by the raja and the heirs apparent. Unfortunately, this is now closed to preserve the murals, which have already been damaged by generations of hands trailing along the walls.

Further points of interest in the palace include a **dining hall** intended for the free feeding of up to two thousand brahmins, and a 38-kilo stone which, it is said, every new recruit to the raja's army had to raise above his head 101 times.

Practicalities

Frequent **buses** run to Padmanabhapuram from Thiruvananthapuram's Thampanoor station; hop on any service heading south towards Nagercoil or Kanyakumari and get off at **Thakkaly** (sometimes written Thuckalai). You can flag the same buses down from the side of the highway at Kovalam Junction (3km inland from the beaches). To see Padmanabhapuram and Kanyakumari (see p.617) in one day, aim to leave early, arriving when the palace opens at 9am. Heading back, two express buses leave Thakkaly at 2.30pm and 3.30pm for Thiruvananthapuram. Alternatively, sign up for KTDC's Kanyakumari tour from Thiruvananthapuram (daily 7.30am–9pm; Rs250), which calls at the palace en route.

The small stalls inside the outer walls of the palace are the best place to get **snacks** and **drinks**, as the area around the bus station is noisy and dirty.

North of Thiruvananthapuram

When it gets too hot at sea level, **Ponmudi** and the **Peppara Wildlife Sanctuary**, just northeast of Thiruvananthapuram, make a refreshing overnight break: in a couple of hours you can be walking through rubber and cardamom plantations and endless slopes of green tea bushes in cool air. Alternatively, the richly forested **Agastya Hills** lie 25km northeast of Thiruvananthapuram. Accessible as a day-trip, they form a beautiful backdrop to the **Neyyar Dam**, on the banks of which stands the world-famous **Sivananda Yoga Centre**. Just before you turn off to the Agastya Hills, it's well worth pausing to visit **Koikkal Kottaram palace** at Nedumangod – as fine an example of traditional Keralan architecture as you'll find anywhere in the state, with the added attraction of an excellent little museum devoted to local archaeology, history and coinage.

If you want to stick to the coastline, head for **Varkala**, Kerala's number two resort and an important Hindu pilgrimage site. A little further north, the busy town of **Kollam** serves as the main departure point for boat trips through the unforgettable Keralan **backwaters**.

Koikkal Kottaram

The beautiful palace of **Koikkal Kottaram** (Tues–Sun 10am–5pm; Rs3, cameras Rs10), 18km northeast of Thiruvananthapuram, sits on the outskirts of **Nedumangad**, a busy market town near the turning to the Neyyar Dam and Agastya Hills. Considering its proximity to Kovalam and the capital, the monument sees surprisingly few visitors, yet it represents one of the highpoints of regional architecture, and its museum outstrips any other in the state. The Archaeological Survey of India maintain the building, providing knowledgeable (and obligatory) guides to show visitors around the collections and exhibits; their services are free but a tip is always appreciated.

The palace was originally constructed for Umyamma Rani, a local queen who reigned from 1677 until 1684. It retains all the distinctive features of traditional Keralan architecture: a bowed, triangular-gabled roof made of terracotta tiles, intricately carved teak features, cool stone floors and dark rooms that open onto a private central courtyard for the ladies. In common with other royal buildings in Travancore, it was cooled by a wonderfully effective natural air-conditioning system using sloping wooden slats. There is also a secret passage, leading out from the courtyard, that the queen could use as an escape when her enemies laid siege to the palace, a common military tactic in seventeenth-century Kerala.

The **ground-floor** rooms contain a vast coin collection – one of India's finest – which charts the development of international trade along the Malabar coastline. Most of the coins were discovered during archaeological excavations in the area, and include Roman finds, punch-marked pieces issued by local rajas and silver rupees from the Victorian period. Other rooms around the courtyard contain Keralan household and farming implements dating from the eighteenth and nineteenth centuries, as well as three ornamental palanquins for carrying the royal ladies.

Upstairs, the make-up and costumes for *kathakali*, *ottan thullal* and *theyyattam* dance performances are displayed on ferocious-looking models, and there is an exquisite *kettuvialaku* (platform) for the goddess Durga, which is carried around town during local spring festivities. Also displayed are the musical instruments and implements used in temple rituals, such as iron weaponry representing aspects of deities and the elaborate jewellery worn by priests.

Practicalities

Regular **buses** run to Nedumangad from Thiruvananthapuram's Thampanoor stand, taking around 45mins. If you want to refuel before heading back or onwards to the hills, try the air-conditioned *Ponmudi* **restaurant** inside the swish *Hotel Surya* on Surya Road, which serves sumptuous Keralan meals at lunch time (Rs100) in addition to a full multi-cuisine menu.

Agastya Hills and Neyyar Dam

Within easy distance of Kovalam, 25km to the northeast and feasible as a day-trip, the jagged, forested **Agastya Hills** form a verdant backdrop to the **Neyyar Dam**, which interrupts the flow of three major rivers to form a large reservoir.

Sivananda Yoga Vedanta Dhanwantari

Located amid the hills and tropical forests of the **Neyyar Dam**, 28km east of Thiru-vananthapuram, the **Sivananda Yoga Vedanta Dhanwantari** (@ www.sivananda.org) was founded by Swami Sivananda – dubbed the "Flying Guru" because he used to pilot light aircraft over war-stricken areas of the world, scattering flowers and leaflets calling for peace – as a centre for meditation, yoga and traditional Keralan martial arts and medicine. Sivananda was a renowned exponent of Advaitya Vedanta, the philosophy of non-duality, as espoused by the Upanishads and promoted later by Shankara in the eleventh century.

Aside from training teachers in advanced raja and hatha yoga, the ashram offers **introductory courses** for beginners. These comprise four hours of intensive tuition per day (starting at 5.30am), with background lectures. During the course, you have to stay at the ashram and comply with a regime that some Western students find fairly strict (no sex, drugs, rock'n'roll or smoking, pure-veg diet and early morning starts), as well as join in Hindu devotional worship. Some people have also noted strained relations with the local villagers, whom ashramites are discouraged from mixing with or even buying goods from. For more details, contact the ashram itself (☏0471/229 0493), or their branch in Thiruvananthapuram at 37/1929 Airport Rd, West Fort (☏0471/245 0942).

Standing on its banks is the world famous **Sivananda Yoga Vedanta Dhanwanthari Ashram**, one of the country's leading yoga centres (see box above). Among locals, however, the spot is better known as a picnic destination: streams of bus parties pour through on weekends to stroll around the ornamental gardens at the water's edge, dotted with garishly painted plaster images of gods and heroes, and get a glimpse of the lions at the tiny **safari park.** Buses depart from the Wildlife Interpretation Centre for the half-hour trip (Rs20) around the site, home to a pride of seven rare Asian lions. You can also hire boats from the centre for excursions to an island in the reservoir said to be inhabited by elephants, bison and deer – though few are ever spotted. Sightings of crocodile, by contrast, are guaranteed, thanks to the presence of a small **Crocodile Breeding Park** near the Interpretation Centre.

The only way to enter the 12,000-hectare **Neyyar Dam Wildlife Sanctuary** proper, however, is through the Forest Department, who will, on request, organize a boat and an obligatory guide. To **trek** in the park, you'll need a guide and prior permission from the Forest Department offices at **Vazhuthakad** in Thiruvananthapuram. The local Forest Department range officer at the Neyyar Dam also issues permits, if approached through the manager at the tourist bungalow, KTDC *Agastya House* (see below).

Practicalities

Buses from the KSRTC Thampanoor bus stand in Thiruvananthapuram depart every hour or so for the Neyyar Dam. The only **accommodation** worthy of note is the KTDC *Agastya House* (☏0471/227 2160; ●), which has huge rooms and verandas (with views), and a decent restaurant serving excellent South Indian meals and snacks. During the weekend, avoid the rooms upstairs as the popular beer bar below gets noisy.

Ponmudi and Peppara Wildlife Sanctuary

The hill station of **PONMUDI** lies in the tea-growing region of the **Cardamom** (or Ponmudi) **Hills**, about 60km northeast of Thiruvananthapuram and 77km from Kovalam. Located 1066m above sea level, on the top of a hill commanding breathtaking views out across the range as far as the sea, it comprises a range of cottages, rooms and a restaurant. The main reason to come up here is that Ponmudi serves as the only practical base for visits to the 53 square kilometres of forest set aside as the **Peppara Wildlife Sanctuary**, which protects elephants, *sambhar*, lion-tailed macaques, leopards and other assorted wildlife. Although Peppara is theoretically open all year, the main season is from January until May.

The beautiful drive up, via the small towns of Nedumangad and Vithura, runs along very narrow roads past areca nut, clove, rubber and cashew plantations, with first the River Kavakulam and then the River Kallar close at hand. The bridge at **Kallar Junction** marks the start of the real climb. Twenty-two hairpin bends (numbered at the roadside) lead slowly up, starting in the foothills, heading past great outcrops of black rock and thick clumps of bamboo (*iramula*), then through the Kallar teak forest. Finally you wind into the tea plantations; the temperature is noticeably cooler and, once out of the forest, the views across the hills and the plains below become truly spectacular – on a clear day you can see as far as the coast. There really is very little to do up here, but the high ridges and tea estates make good rambling country.

Practicalities

Six daily **buses** run from Thiruvananthapuram to Ponmudi, via Vithura, the first at 5.30am and the last at 3.30pm. The nearest **tourist office** is currently in Thiruvananthapuram, where information on Ponmudi is readily available. The *Government Guesthouse* (☎0472/289 0230; ❸–❺) has 24 rooms and seven cottages, all with attached bathrooms and hot water. Simple and inexpensive but delicious meals have to be ordered a couple of hours in advance; otherwise the cold drinks and snack shop is open daily until 4pm, or you can walk down the road to the teashop on the bend (400m from the hotel). The main building, which originally belonged to the raja of Travancore, has lost any charm it may once have possessed, but the views across the hills and misty valleys from the terrace make up for it. Weekends get lively (to say the least), thanks to the beer parlour (daily 10am–6pm).

If your budget can stretch to it, the best place to sidestep Ponmudi's noisy day-trippers, and make the most of its beautiful woodland, is ⚜ *Duke's Forest Lodge* (☎0472/285 9273, ⓦwww.dukesforest.com; ❾) at Anapara, 51km from Thiruvanathampuram. Situated on the edge of a 130-acre rubber plantation, this family-run resort has five beautiful pool villas, designed in traditional Keralan style with high, pitched-tiled roofs and deep verandas that look straight into the trees, set in landscaped gardens. Each stands on stone pillars, and spiral staircases wind from the upper floors to secluded Jacuzzi terraces below, screened by roll-down cane blinds. There's also a big, sunny main pool, and a restaurant area in front of which recitals of music, dance and ritual theatre (including *theyyattam*) are held. Rates range from $100 to $150.

Varkala

Long renowned by Hindus as a place of pilgrimage, **VARKALA**, 54km northwest of Thiruvananthapuram, with its spectacular sands and red cliffs, is these days a considerably more appealing beach destination than Kovalam. Centred on a clifftop row of budget guesthouses and palm-thatch cafés, the tourist scene is still relatively low-key, although the arrival in recent years of the first charter groups and luxury hotels may well be the harbinger of full-scale

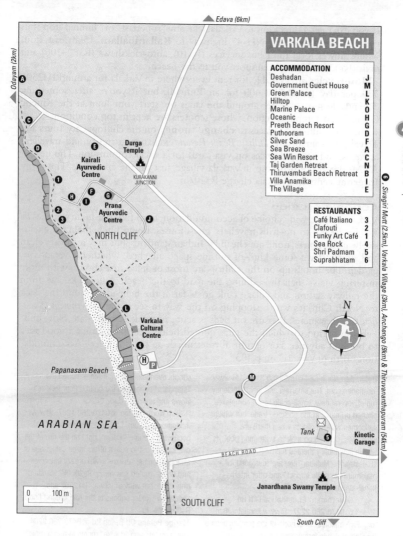

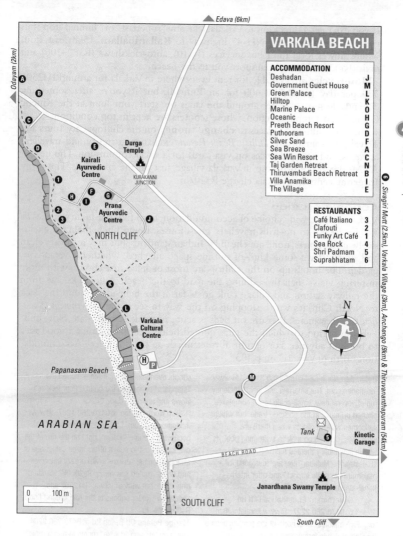
Edava (6km)

VARKALA BEACH

Odayam (2km)

ACCOMMODATION
Deshadan	J
Government Guest House	M
Green Palace	L
Hilltop	K
Marine Palace	O
Oceanic	H
Preeth Beach Resort	G
Puthooram	D
Silver Sand	F
Sea Breeze	A
Sea Win Resort	C
Taj Garden Retreat	N
Thiruvambadi Beach Retreat	B
Villa Anamika	I
The Village	E

RESTAURANTS
Café Italiano	3
Clafouti	2
Funky Art Café	1
Sea Rock	4
Shri Padmam	5
Suprabhatam	6

Durga Temple

Kairali Ayurvedic Centre

KURAKANNI JUNCTION

Prana Ayurvedic Centre

NORTH CLIFF

Varkala Cultural Centre

Papanasam Beach

ARABIAN SEA

N

Tank

Kinetic Garage

BEACH ROAD

Janardhana Swamy Temple

SOUTH CLIFF

0   100 m

South Cliff

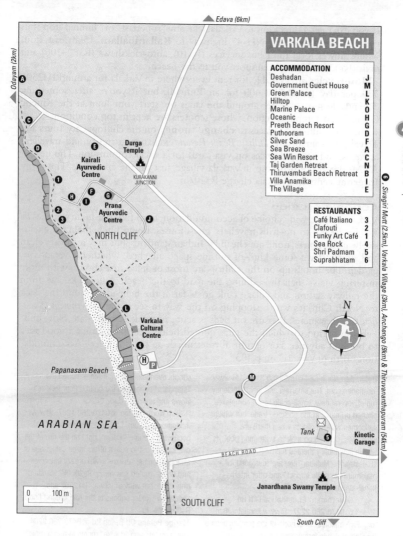

Sivagiri Mutt (2.5km), Varkala Village (3km), Anchengo (9km) & Thiruvananthapuram (54km)

4

KERALA | North of Thiruvananthapuram

development: building inland and at both ends of the beach is already proceeding apace.

Arrival and information

Varkala beach lies 4km of west of Varkala village proper, which is grouped around a busy market crossroads. The village's mainline railway station, served by express and passenger **trains** from Thiruvananthapuram, Kollam and most other Keralan towns, stands 500m north of this central junction. While some **buses** from Thiruvananthapuram's Thampanoor stand, and from Kollam to the north, continue on to within walking distance of the beach and clifftop area, most terminate in Varkala village, where you'll have to pick up an auto-rickshaw for the remaining five-minute ride (around Rs40–50) to the seashore.

If you can't get a direct bus to Varkala, take any "superfast" or "limited stop" bus running along the main NH-47 highway to **Kallamballam**, 15km east, from where slower local mini-bus services (Rs10), auto-rickshaws (Rs80–100) and taxis (Rs150–175) will transport you to the beach.

Motorcycles are available for rent everywhere in Varkala for around Rs250–300 per day (or Rs350–400 for an Enfield), but if you're after something dependable just to potter around the lanes on, start your hunt at the Kinetic Garage, near temple junction, whose scooters are kept in top condition.

There are numerous places to **change money** on the clifftop: City Tours and Travels, in front of the *Hilltop Beach Resort*, exchange currency and traveller's cheques, and offer advances on visa cards for a small commission. The nearest **ATMs** are at the banks up in Varkala village, just off the crossroads. The many **Internet** centres in Varkala charge Rs40/hr.

Accommodation

Varkala offers a wide choice of accommodation, from five-star luxury at the *Taj Garden Retreat* to no-frills travellers' guesthouses. Being pitched almost exclusively at foreigners, none are cheap by Indian standards, but they're always clean and usually have some kind of outside space attached, whether a veranda or garden. The hotels up on the clifftop are most people's first choice, with more inspiring views than those lining the road to the beach. Auto-rickshaws from the railway station and village tank go as far as the helipad or round the back to North Cliff; it's worth stopping on the way to see if the *Government Guesthouse* has vacancies. Pressure on beds is acute in **peak season** (late Nov–mid-Feb, the period to which the rates quoted below refer), when it's a good idea to book in advance. For options further north up the coast, see "Accommodation north of Varkala" on p.403.

Deshadan North Cliff ☏ m98460 31005, ⓦ www .deshadan.com. The smartest and most efficiently run of several new, small-scale resort complexes, pitched primarily at the package trade, but which welcomes walk-in clients when there are vacancies. Centred on a clean swimming pool, its twelve individually themed rooms ("Assam", "Rajasthan", "Malabar" etc) are "designed for maximum aesthetic impact" and offer international-standard comforts. ⑧

🏃 **Government Guesthouse** Cliff Rd ☏ 0470/260 2227, ⓦ www.keralatourism .org. Five minutes' walk north of the temple, behind the *Taj* hotel, this former maharajah's holiday palace has been converted into a charming guesthouse. The two attached rooms in the original building are enormous and fantastic value; the others (all attached) occupy a modern block in the same grounds and are much less inspiring. Meals available on request. ②–③

Green Palace North Cliff ☏ 0470/261 0055, ⓦ www.greenpalacevarkala.com. Currently the swishest place on the clifftop: a double-storey block built in 2006, buffered from the main path by a lawn where you can lounge in the shade. Its dozen sea-facing rooms (seven with a/c) have shiny marble floors, TVs, quality beds and individual sitouts overlooking the garden – though the "standard" options on the ground floor lack sea views and are quite dark. ⑥–⑧

Hilltop North Clifftop ☏ 0470/260 1237, ⓦ www .hilltopvarkala.com. Long-established hotel occupying a prime location, right on the rim of the cliff looking out to sea. It offers three categories of attached rooms: "deluxe" (with breezy balconies and uninterrupted sea views; Rs2000); "standard" (the same, but without views; Rs1200); and "economy" (older options to the rear ground floor; Rs800). ④–⑥

Marine Palace Off Beach Rd ☏ 0470/260 3204. The "regular" and "deluxe" rooms in this complex close to the beachfront are way overpriced and poorly maintained, but the brand new Keralan-style apartments (Rs3000 per night) are some of the nicest places to stay in Varkala, with huge wood-lined bedrooms, self-catering kitchenettes and verandas with sea views. ⑦–⑧

Oceanic North Cliff ☏ 0470/229 0373, ⓔ oceanicresidence@yahoo.co.im. Very pleasant rooms, with flowering climbers trailing from the balconies, close to the thick of things on the clifftop. Café noise is sometimes a problem at night, but this ranks among the better run, better value budget options close to the strip. ④–⑤

Preeth Beach Resort North Clifftop area, off Cliff Rd ☎0470/260 0942, ⓦwww.preethbeachresort .com. Large, well-maintained two-star complex set 5mins back from the cliff in a shady palm grove. Grouped around a kidney-shaped pool and sun terrace, its accommodation ranges from no-frills economy rooms to spacious a/c cottages with generous verandas. An additional attraction is the top-notch "Prana" Ayurvedic clinic – one of the few in Varkala with a fully qualified doctor. ❹–❼

Puthooram North Cliff ☎0470/320 2007, ☎m98952 32209. Snug chalet-cottages made entirely of polished wood, some with traditional Keralan railings and thatched roofs, opening onto a trim little garden, right on the cliff edge. Their published rates are high, but you can usually haggle hefty discounts later in the day. Courteous management, and there's a quality in-house Ayurvedic centre ("Santhigiri"). ❹–❼

Sea Breeze North Cliff ☎0470/260 3257, ☎m98460 04243. Set back in a coconut grove behind a small tidal beach, this rather grand new building is currently the northern-most guesthouse in Varkala proper – only 5mins walk from the bright lights of the clifftop area, but in a peaceful position. Its rooms are large for the price, opening onto a big common veranda that's strung with hammocks and catches the breezes straight off the surf. ❺–❼

🏃 **Sea Win Resort** North Cliff ☎0470/260 1084, ☎m98950 83950. One of several swanky modern buildings to have sprung up recently at the end of the cliff on the back of Saudi riyals. The colour-schemes are a bit off-beat, but the rooms themselves are enormous, with quality double and twin beds, fridges, a spacious common veranda on one side and large private sitouts on the other where you can crash out on cane furniture and watch the sea only a stone's throw away. ❹–❺

🏃 **Silver Sand** North Cliff ☎m98468 26144 or ☎m98464 78432. This budget guest-house, 200m back from the cliff edge behind the *Funky Art Café*, offers unbeatable value: its eight marble-clad, simply furnished rooms are large and comfortable for the price, with thick mattresses and doors opening onto a sociable common veranda. ❹

Taj Garden Retreat Cliff Rd ☎0470/260 3000, ⓦwww.tajhotels.com. Not the most alluring of Taj Group's five-star hotels (the architecture owes more to the Costas than Kerala) but the most luxurious option in Varkala: thirty plush a/c rooms and suites (sea- or garden-facing), opening onto private balconies and lawns, with direct access to a large curvi-form pool. Tariffs (from $250 per night) include breakfast and dinner buffets in the *Cape Comorin* restaurant. ❾

Thiruvambadi Beach Retreat North Clifftop ☎0470/260 1028, ⓦwww.thiruvambadihotel.com. This idiosyncratic, family-run guesthouse at the far (quiet) end of the cliff has fifteen rooms, the best of them split-level a/c suites boasting big, sea-facing balconies and over-the-top Mughal-kitsch décor (cusped Islamic arches and elaborately carved wooden doors). The rooftop restaurant is a great place to relax, looking straight out to sea. ❻–❽

🏃 **Villa Anamika** North Cliff ☎0470/260 0095, ⓦwww.villaanamika.com. A welcoming homestay, 200m from the cliff, run by a Keralan artist and her German husband. Their five variously priced rooms are all light, airy, cool and attractively furnished, with block-printed bedspreads and paintings by the hostess. Guests get the run of a beautiful rear garden, and break-fasts feature home-made German bread and jams. Best of all, the plot opposite serves as a grazing ground for one of Varkala's resident elephants. ❹–❺

The Village North Cliff, ☎m99471 55442. Three newly built, handsomely furnished octagonal cottages set back from the road in a small garden; each has its own private sitout and kitchenette. A good choice for families, as the rooms are especially large and can accommodate extra beds for kids. ❻–❼

The beach and village

Known in Malayalam as Papa Nashini ("sin destroyer"), Varkala's beautiful white-sand **Papanasam Beach** has long been associated with ancestor worship. Devotees come here after praying at the **Janardhana Swamy Temple** (said to be over 2000 years old), to bring the ashes of departed relatives for their "final rest". Non-Hindus are not permitted to enter the inner sanctum of the shrine but are welcome in the grounds.

Backed by sheer red laterite cliffs and drenched by rolling waves off the Arabian Sea, the coastline is imposingly scenic and the beach relatively relaxing – although its religious associations do ensure that attitudes to public nudity (especially female) are markedly less liberal than other coastal resorts in India. Western sun-worshippers are thus supposed to keep to the northern end of the beach (away from the main puja area reserved for the funerary rites) where they are serviced by a non-stop parade of local "hallo-pineapple-coconut?" vendors. Whistle-happy lifeguards ensure the safety of swimmers by enforcing the no-swim zones beyond the flags: be warned that the undercurrent is often strong, claiming lives every year. Dolphins are often seen swimming quite close to the coast, and, if you're lucky, you may be able to swim with them by arranging a ride with a fishing boat. Sea otters can also occasionally be spotted playing on the cliffs by the sea.

Few of Varkala's Hindu pilgrims make it as far as the **clifftop area**, the focus of a homespun but well-established tourist scene that's grown steadily over the past ten or twelve years, and now accommodates fortnighting winter sun-seekers as well as long-haul travellers. Bamboo and palm-thatch cafes, restaurants and souvenir shops jostle for space close to the edge of the mighty escarpments, which plunge vertically to the beach below in a dramatic arc, most beautiful at sunset, when their laterite tint glows molten red. Several steep flights of steps cut into the rock provide fast routes from the sand, and you can also get there via the gentler path that starts behind the *Marine Palace* restaurant, or along the metalled road winding its way up from the village, built to service the helipad in advance of Indira Gandhi's visit in 1983. She came here to inaugurate a small government "nature cure" hospital, set up to take advantage of the sea air and three natural springs whose healing waters still bubble out of the rocks.

Countless private **Ayurvedic centres** and **yoga schools** have followed in its wake, benefiting from the same salubrious location and a constant turnover through the winter months of well-off foreigners. As in Kovalam, many non-qualified practitioners have jumped on the bandwagon, so it's wise to look around, and get other travellers' recommendations before going for a treatment (see p.386). Two clinics that stand out are *Kairali*, near the *Silver Star* guesthouse behind the *Funky Art Café* (℡0470/329 4660, ⓦwww.kala.com) and *Prana*, in the *Preeth Beach Resort* (℡0470/260 0942). For yoga, one teacher receiving consistently high praise from readers is Vasu, who works from the north end of the clifftop, behind *Papaya* restaurant. You can pick up medicinal oils and other health-oriented produce, such as herbs and handmade soaps, as well as books on yoga, meditation and massage, at the Prakrithi Stores on the clifftop.

Nearby, and aimed unashamedly at the tourist market, the **Varkala Cultural Centre** (℡0470/608793), behind the *Sunrise* restaurant on North Clifftop, holds daily **kathakali** and *bharatanatyam* dance performances (make-up 5–6.45pm; performance 6.45–8.15pm; Rs150). Using live musicians instead of a recorded soundtrack, it's a pleasant and authentic-enough introduction to the two types of dance, especially if you're not going to make it to Kochi (see p.446). For anyone with a more serious interest in the classical arts, the centre also offers short courses on *kathakali* make-up and dance, *bharatanatyam*, devotional song (*bhajan*) and Carnatic percussion (*mridamgan*).

Eating

Seafood lovers will enjoy Varkala's crop of clifftop **café-restaurants**, which specialize in locally caught seafood – seer fish, shark, marlin, kingfish and prawns – prepared in a variety of styles: tandoori, masala-fried or simmered Keralan-style in spicy coconut-based gravies. You'll also find plenty of pasta and pizza, and German baked treats. Prices are fairly high: expect to pay Rs75 or more for a simple veggie curry, Rs100–150 for pizza or pasta, and Rs100–200 for a fresh fish dish. Service can be very slow, but the superb location more than compensates, especially in the evenings, when the sea twinkles with the lights of distant fishing boats.

Due to Kerala's antiquated licensing laws, which involve huge amounts of tax, a lot of cafés choose to serve **beer** discreetly; a teapot-full costs Rs80–100.

Café Italiano North Clifftop. Authentic Italian menu featuring pizza and pasta dishes in a variety of sauces (Rs120–200) – the house speciality *frutti di mare* is hard to beat.

Clafouti North Clifftop. Nepali-run restaurant serving, somewhat disappointingly given the Gallic promise of the name, the usual generic German-bakery cakes, in addition to fresh seafood dishes, Mexican and Thai specials, a crowd-pleasing steak Chateaubriand – and delicious expresso. It's right on the cliff edge, and has great sea views.

Funky Art Café North Clifftop. The naffest name but still the hippest spot on the cliff, with full tables from sunset until the small hours. It serves a predictable traveller-oriented menu, but most people come here to lounge, drink, smoke and socialize over the gut-thumping sound system.

Sea Rock Clifftop, next to the helipad. As well as fairly standard range of Indian and Continental food, this place serves tasty South Indian *iddli-vada*

breakfasts and masala dosas from 8.30am–3pm. In the evenings, fresh local fish takes over, followed by DVD screenings.

Shri Padmam Temple junction. This dingy-looking café on the temple crossroads serves freshly made, cheap and tasty South Indian veg food (including Rs25 "meals" and lunchtime). You can walk through the front dining room to a large rear terrace affording prime views of the tank – particularly atmospheric at breakfast time.

Suprabhatam Varkala village, 4km east of the beach. The cheapest and best pure-veg joint in Varkala, situated just off the main crossroads in a dining hall lined with coir mats and grubby pink walls. Their *dosas* and other fried snacks aren't up to much, but the lunchtime "unlimited" rice-plate "meals" (noon–3pm; Rs20), featuring the usual *thoran, avial, dal, rasam,* buttermilk, curd, papaddum and red or white rice, pull in streams of locals and foreigners alike.

Around Varkala

Head along the coast in either direction from Varkala and the tourist scene soon starts to feel a world away. With a scooter, motorbike or taxi, one feasible target for a short foray **south** is the former British outpost of **Anchengo Fort**, 9km south of Varkala. Anchengo was once a flourishing spice port, second only to Bombay. After a trading dispute with the local population, it was besieged for six months in 1721, but the East India Company held out – a victory that earned Anchengo's merchants a full monopoly over the region's lucrative pepper trade. Despite its pivotal role in colonial history, the citadel is now a forlorn ruin, its bleached, sloping walls enclosing a half-hearted garden and a few cannons.

North of Varkala the shoreline is a lot less densely populated, though more ostentatiously wealthy, with many out-size Gulf returners' houses dotted around its hinterland of leafy lanes and palm groves. You can comfortably walk the 2km from the north end of Varkala cliff to **Odayam**, a mixed Hindu and Muslim village where a cluster of modest guesthouses has sprung up to service the small black-sand beach. Beyond, a paved walkway winds for another three or four kilometres over low cliffs to the next settlement, **Edava**, a busier place cut through by the main train line, whose fringes hold a couple of idyllic, empty coves and more low-key accommodation (reviewed on p.404). Shimmering north from there, one vast, unbroken, white-sand beach arcs almost to the horizon, backed by a lagoon and totally empty save for the odd fishing boat.

Accommodation north of Varkala

If you're happy to watch the bright lights of Varkala's clifftop from a distance, the coast further north has a lot to recommend it, offering better value **accommodation** and access to a wild and windy shoreline where tourism has, thus far, made very little impact.

Ashthamay 10/107 East Odayam ☎0470/266 3613, ⊛www.asthamay.com. Half-a-dozen attractive semi-detached bungalows, with red-tiled roofs and pink walls, set in a garden only a few metres

from the waves. It's an efficient place, and open year round – a great spot to be during a monsoon storm. The restaurant's recommended for sunny breakfasts of fresh bread and coffee on the terrace, but not for evening meals, which are overpriced. ⑤

Kadaltheeram Edava ⓣ0470/266 4218, ⓣm94951 688574, ⓦwww.kadaltheeram.com. Friendly new 12-room resort and Ayurvedic spa, in neo-Keralan style, situated next to a lovely little beach that's deserted most of the time. It offers three types of rooms, all neat, clean and spacious, with good-sized balconies looking over the hotel's well-tended gardens to the sea. If it's free, book #107. ⑦–⑧

🏃 **Kattil Beach Resort** Odayam ⓣ0470/266 2226, ⓣm98955 82740. The best value economy option in this area, offering a choice of attached rooms in three different wings, all on high ground above the beach, with pleasant views from private or common verandas. The ones in the block called *Sona* are the pick of the crop, looking through the palm groves to the nearby stream gully and beach. ③–④

Munna Edava ⓣm98955 28150, ⓔedavasasheer @yahoo.com. This no-frills budget guesthouse, situated on a palm-shaded terrace that's open to the sea breezes on one side, is the northernmost mark of tourism in the Varkala area, and an absolute steal, with rooms from only Rs400. If you're happy with simple amenities and can sort out transport (Edava's a bit cut off), you'll probably end up staying for weeks. ③

Royal Palm Odayam ⓣ0470/266 0750 or ⓣm98958 83884, ⓔroyalpalm_beachresort @yahoo.com. Big, new, white-painted rooms (all non a/c and attached) at a breezy spot on a bluff looking out to sea. Edged by turned-wood railings, its large sitouts make the most of the idyllic views. The same owner also has cheaper budget rooms just below in a beige-coloured block called *Crystal Palace* (ⓣm99951 06089; ③). ④

Kollam (Quilon)

One of the Malabar coast's oldest harbours, **KOLLAM** (pronounced "Koillam", and previously known as Quilon), 74km northwest of Thiruvananthapuram and 85km south of Alappuzha, was once at the centre of the international spice trade. The port flourished from the very earliest times, trading with the Phoenicians, Arabs, Greeks, Romans and Chinese. It finds mention in the Persian *Book of Routes and Kingdoms* compiled by Ibn Khurdadhibh in 844–48, and again in the fourteenth century journals of the Moroccan traveller, Ibn Battuta, who saw Chinese junks loading pepper here in the 1330s. Two hundred years later, the Portuguese writer Duarte Barbossa described Quilon as a "very great city with a right good haven" visited by "Moors, Heathen and Christians in great numbers".

Nowadays, Kollam is chiefly of interest as one of the entry or exit points to the **backwaters of Kerala** (see box, pp.416-417), and most travellers simply stay overnight en route to or from Alappuzha.

Arrival and information

Kollam's busy mainline **railway station** lies east of the clocktower which marks the centre of town. Numerous daily trains run from Ernakulam and Thiruvananthapuram and beyond. The helpful **District Tourism Promotion Council** (DTPC) have a tourist office across town (daily 9am–6pm; ⓣ0474/274 5625, ⓦwww.dtpckollam.com) at the **boat jetty** on the edge of Ashtamudi Lake, where you can book tickets for the daily tourist backwater cruises (see p.416); they'll also help arrange taxis for trips around the area, and can advise on local ferry transport. The local **Alapuzha Tourism Development Council** office (ATDC; daily 7am–9pm; ⓣ0474/276 7440), on the opposite side of the road, offers comparable services.

The jetty and KSRTC **bus stand** are close together on the edge of Ashtamudi Lake. Bookable express **buses** leave for Thiruvananthapuram (1hr 45min) and Kochi (3hr) via Alappuzha (2hr) every fifteen minutes or so; as ever, the express

KOLLAM

Alappuzha, Monroe Island & Ⓐ

RESTAURANTS & CAFÉS

All Spice	3
Guruprasad	5
Indian Coffee House	4
New Mysore Café	1
Sun Moon	2

ACCOMMODATION

ATDC Beach Retreat	I
Government Guest House	B
Karthika	F
KTDC Yatri Niwas	C
Palm Lagoon	H
Shah International	E
Sudarsan	D
Summerhouse	G
Valiyavila Family Estate	A

Ashtamudi Lake

Old British Residency
Ⓑ

ASHRAMAM

Ⓒ

ALAPPUZHA ROAD

ATDC ⓘ
Boat Jetty
ⓘ DTPC
★ KSRTC Bus Stand

CHINNAKKADA ROAD

UTI Bank & ATM
Ⓔ

Ⓓ

@ ②
Bishop Jerome
Nagar Mall

④
⑤
③
Clocktower

MAIN BAZAAR ROAD

Fruit & Veg
Market

Shri Uma-
Maheswara

Ⓕ
@

Jama Masjid

Railway
Station

Ernakulam (158km)

Varkala (35km) & Thiruvananthapuram (72km)

Thankasseri (1km), Ⓖ (1km) & Ⓗ (18km)

BEACH ROAD

Fishing
Quarter

BEACH ROAD

ARABIAN
SEA

N

0   100 m

Ⓘ

services are much better than the "limited stop" buses. Note that most Thiru-vananthapuram-bound **trains** do not stop in Varkala.

Useful **facilities** such as exchange bureaux, ATMs and Internet outlets can be found in the smart Bishop Jerome Nagar shopping mall, just south of the main road between the jetty and the clocktower. The efficient UTI bank also has a dependable and secure ATM north of the clocktower near the *Shah International Hotel*; and there's another convenient, cheap Internet place, Cyber.Com, just south of the clocktower on the first floor of Yeskay Towers, charging just Rs20/hr.

Accommodation

Considering the numbers of foreign tourists that pour through during the season, accommodation is in surprisingly short supply in Kollam – book in advance if you're arriving late in the day. Reservations, however, cannot be made in the place that should be the first choice of any traveller interested in Kerala's colonial history: in the converted British Residency on the edge of town, Kollam's *Government Guesthouse* offers a unique chance to stay in one of the Raj's first, and grandest, civic buildings, at prices comparable with the grungy lodges opposite the station.

The one place to avoid unless you're desperate is the KTDC *Yatri Niwas*, close to the *Government Guesthouse* on the shores of Ashtamudi Lake: as with most in the chain, it's lapsed into an awful state of disrepair and no longer merits its rates.

ATDC Beach Retreat 3km south of centre
☎0474/275 276 3793, ⓦwww.atdcalleppey.com.
Typical government-run place with smudged walls and average-sized rooms (some a/c), situated directly across the road from the beach, and good value. It's also quiet in the evenings, has a rooftop restaurant with sea views, and an untypically enthusiastic and helpful young staff. Station pick up (Rs50) on request. ❸–❹

🚶 **Government Guesthouse** Ashtamudi Lake, 2km northeast ☎0474/274 3620. Sleeping in this grand 250-year-old building, the former British Residency (see opposite), feels like overnighting in a museum. Full of original furniture and fixtures, the rooms are gigantic for the price (go for an a/c one on the first floor if it's offered), but, as with most Government Guest Houses, you'll have to try for a vacancy on spec as they rarely accept advance bookings. Breakfast and dinner available. ❷–❸
Karthika Off Main Rd, near the Jama Masjid mosque ☎0474/275 1821. Large and popular budget hotel in a central location offering a range of acceptably clean, plain rooms (some a/c) ranged around a courtyard in which the centrepiece is, rather unexpectedly, three huge nude figures. ❷
Palm Lagoon Vellimon West ☎0474/254 8974, ⓦwww.palmlagoon.com. Traditional Keralan-style bungalows, with tiled roofs and painted pillared verandas, in a lush 6-acre plot on Ashtamudi Lake, 18km from town. There's a pool, plus a swimming enclosure in the lake itself. Good Ayurvedic treatment facilities are available, and they can arrange bike, boat and fishing trips in the surrounding backwaters. One of the few affordable resorts of this kind in Kerala, with rooms from only Rs1800, plus Rs375 for full board. ❻
Shah International Chinnakkada Rd ☎0474/274 2362, ⓔhotelshah@hotmail.com. A modern tower block hotel close to the centre of town, holding differently priced rooms, from large, clean economy doubles to full a/c suites with plasma-screen TVs and views over the town. Hardly the most atmospheric choice, but a dependably comfortable one. ❸–❻
Sudarsan Parameswar Nagar ☎0474/274 4322, ⓦwww.hotelsudarshan.com. Central and popular, though definitely not as palatial as the posh foyer would lead you to believe. Describing itself (somewhat ominously) as a "hospitalized zone that will charm your brain", the building has a range of rooms: all are the same size, but the a/c ones are cleaner, more recently refurbished and lie on the quiet side of the building. In addition to a standard multi-cuisine restaurant and bar, they've a themed diner, "Night Flight", decked out like the interior of an aircraft, where the waiters all wear camp flight-crew gear. ❹–❺

🚶 **Summerhouse** Thirumallawaram and Thankasseri ☎0474/279 4518, ☎m98956 62839, ⓔcontactsummerhouse@hotmail.com. Run by the amiable Mr Shashi, this trio of suburban homestays offers simple, characterful accommodation on the northwestern edge of town near, or next to, the sea. Pick of the bunch is "No.3", a cosy wood cabin with only two rooms (book both for privacy), opening onto a wonderful veranda enfolded by palm trees, slap on the sea wall. "No.1" is an older structure, also next to the waves, but more spartan. "No.2" is a former family house, large enough for a group, with its own garden, 5mins walk from the shore in a leafy residential area. **④**

Valiyavila Family Estate Panamukkom, Kureepzha, Ashtamudi Lake ⑦0474/270 1546, ⓦwww.kollamlakeviewresort.com. The local tourist offices tend to plug this place but it's a dud. The location, on a wooded *presqu'île* that you can only reach by boat, is certainly romantic, but the garishly coloured rooms are not all that well-maintained and ridiculously overpriced. **⑥–⑦**

The Town

Kollam **town** itself, sandwiched between the sea and Ashtamudi ("eight inlets") Lake, is less exciting than its history might suggest. It's a typically sprawling Keralan market hub, with a central bazaar of old tiled wooden houses and winding backstreets, kept busy by the local trade in coir, cashew nuts (a good local buy), pottery, aluminium and fish.

The one monument worth going out of your way to see is the former **British Residency**, a magnificent 250-year-old mansion on the shores of the lake, now used as a *Government Guesthouse* (see review opposite). Overlooking the balding expanse of the old *maidan* (parade ground) it's one of only a handful of monuments surviving from the early days of the Raj, and perfectly epitomizes the openness to indigenous influences that characterized the era, with typically Keralan gable roofs surmounting British pillared verandas. Inside, palatial rooms retain their original early Georgian furniture, giant Chinese pickle jars and floor-to-ceiling shuttered windows, while the walls sport antique East India Company lithographs of Wellesley storming "Seringatnam". Much of the structure is literally falling apart, but you're welcome to visit: there are no set hours – just turn up and ask the manager if you can have a look around.

A few kilometres southwest of the centre, on the seaward side of town, the district of **Thankasseri** holds fading remnants of other eras, when the bay it overlooked would have been filled with ships bound for Europe, Southeast Asia and China. Encircling the modern, red-and-white-striped lighthouse are the partly collapsed walls of an early sixteenth-century **Portuguese fort**, while the **Church of St Thomas**, now a pile of rubble inside, may well have been one in which the St Francis Xavier (see p.200) attended mass during his evangelical mission to the Malabar coast in the 1540s. Other buildings in the area surviving from the Portuguese period include the **Church of Infant Jesus**, and the chapel attached to the **Bishop of Quilon's palace** – both five minutes' walk north of the old fort. Throughout the British period, Thankasseri was a primarily Anglo-Indian district, but after Independence most of its elegant old bungalows were sold off as residents emigrated to the UK and Canada. Many now lie empty and in states of evocative dereliction, languishing in overgrown gardens.

To the east of Thankasseri lies one of the town's two main fishing quarters, lined by hundreds of painted boats (the other is due south of the centre; see map, p.405). They're scattered over what must, four or five centuries ago, have been Kollam's fabled harbour. As ever, if you walk on the beach, remember it's used as a public toilet in the mornings.

Backwater cruises from Kollam

DTPC and ATDC's popular **cruises from Kollam to Alappuzha** (Rs300) operate on alternate days, departing at 10.30am and taking eight hours, with stops for lunch and tea. Tickets for both can be bought on the day from the tourist offices at the boat jetty on Ashtamudi Lake (see map, p.405), and at some of the hotels. DTPC and ATDC also offer exclusive overnight *kettu vallam* cruises (see box on p.417 for details), while the DTPC runs half-day trips to nearby **Monroe Island** (9am–1pm & 2–6.30pm; Rs300), which provide a fascinating glimpse of village life in this unique – and very scenic – waterlogged region.

Tourist cruises are a real money spinner for the local tourist offices, but you may find that you get a far better impression of backwater life by hopping between villages on the very cheap **local ferries**, tickets for which are sold on the boats themselves. Consult DTPC or ATDC for timetable and route information.

Eating

All of the hotels, resorts and guesthouses listed above provide meals, but if you'd prefer to eat out, try one of the following dependable options in and around the centre of town.

All Spice near the main bazaar. This determinedly Western, brightly lit fast food joint, above a bakery, is where the town's middle classes come for family evenings out, and where foreign tourists come to escape the heat – and get away from Indian food. The a/c certainly hits the spot, but the burgers, pizzas and fried chicken turn out to be less appealing than the main North Indian and Chinese dishes (Rs100–150).

Guruprasad Main Bazaar. Cramped and sweaty, but wonderfully old-school "meals" on the market's main street: blue walls, framed ancestral photos and Hindu devotional art provide the typical backdrop for pukka pure-veg rice plates and Udupi-style snacks.

Indian Coffee House Main Bazaar. Typical ICH fare – limp *dosas*, oily biriyanis, toast, omelettes, pot-chai and filter coffee – served on regulation chipped china by waiters wearing ice-cream-fan *pugris*.

New Mysore Café boat jetty, opposite KSRTC bus stand. This is the most popular of the "meals" joints clustered around the bus stand and boat jetty area, serving delicious "all-you-can-eat" rice plates for only Rs19 at lunchtime, then the usual Udupi snacks through the rest of the day. A convenient option if you've time to kill before catching onward transport.

Sun Moon Top Floor, Bishop Jerome Nagar Mall ☏ 0474/301 3000, ⓦ www.zeez.info. Traditional Keralan cooking – *meen polichattu* (white fish steamed in banana leaf) and masala-fried calamari, as well as continental dishes and a big multi-cuisine buffet – served in a blissfully cool, a/c rooftop restaurant, against a backdrop of carved stone temple brackets and woodwork. The food's the best in town, and so are the panoramic views. Count on Rs300 for three courses.

Between Kollam and Alappuzha

Most visitors travelling north between Kollam and Alappuzha, or southwards in the opposite direction, do so by **boat** – either local tourist office cruisers or privately chartered *kettu vallam* rice barges. But if you're pushed for time and opt to cover this backwater stretch by the somewhat less scenic **NH-47** or its adjacent **railway** line, you've the option of pausing at several landmarks along the way.

Karunagapalli

In **KARUNAGAPALLI**, 23km north of Kollam on NH-47, it's possible to see traditional **kettu vallam**, or "tied boats", being built and repaired. These long cargo vessels, a familiar sight on the backwaters, are built entirely without nails. Each jackwood plank is sewn to the next with coir rope, and then the whole is coated with a caustic black resin made from boiled cashew kernels. With careful maintenance they last for generations. If you want to buy a *vallam* you'll need between ten and twenty *lakh* (one or two million) rupees; a far cheaper alternative is to rent the boats (see p.417).

Regular **buses** pass through Karunagapalli on the way to Alappuzha. One daytime **train**, #6525, leaves Kollam at 2.15pm, arriving in Karunagapalli half an hour later. On reaching the bus stand or railway station, take an autorickshaw 1km north along the national highway, then turn left into a lane for 4km to the riverside village of **Alumkattaru**, and the boatyard of the *vallam asharis*, the boat carpenters, who are generally friendly and happy to let visitors watch them work. In the shade of palm trees at the edge of the water, some weave palm leaves, others twist coir strands into rope and craftsmen repair the boats. Soaking in the shallows nearby are palm leaves, used for thatch, and coconut husks for coir rope.

The Mata Amritanandamayi Math

The **Mata Amritanandamayi ("MA") Math**, or Amritapuri as it's more familiarly known, is the home ashram of Kerala's most famous living spiritual figure, "Amma". It stands in the village of **VALLIKKAVU**, 10km northwest of Karunagapalli – a striking vision of pink tower blocks, capped with concrete domed cupolas, rising incongruously above the palm canopy on a sliver of land between the sea and the backwaters. Thousands of visitors and residents may be here at any given time, but numbers swell considerably when Amma herself is in residence – January to April and August to mid-November are the best times to catch her.

Amma offers her famous hugs to visitors during *darshan* sessions, held on Wednesdays, Thursdays and Fridays from noon, and from 10am on weekends. After 5pm, *bhajans*, or devotional songs, precede a more formal *bhava darshan* ritual, in which Amma dons the garb of Krishna and Devi (Goddess) and removes successive layers to reveal "a glimpse of the Divine beneath". Quite how this squares with Amma's repeated assertions that she does not wish to be seen as a Goddess is a matter that frequently gets debated in the Indian media, but it's a popular event for her devotees. Other more low-key activities visitors are welcome to attend include various ceremonial chants, meditation sessions, spiritual discussions and scripture classes facilitated by senior ashramites throughout the day and evening.

For those wishing to stay, **accommodation** is available in simple rooms (visitors are expected to put in a couple of hours' voluntary service). Free vegetarian meals are served three times daily. A few house rules apply: celibacy, modest dress and soft speech are mandatory; and drugs, alcohol and non-vegetarian food are forbidden.

Kayamkulam

KAYAMKULAM, served by local buses from Kollam and Alappuzha, was once the centre of its own small kingdom, which after a battle in 1746 came under the control of Travancore's king Marthanda Varma. In the eighteenth century, the area was famous for its spices, particularly pepper and cinnamon. The French Renaissance social reformer and traveller Abbé Reynal claimed that the Dutch exported some two million pounds of pepper each year, one-fifth of it from Kayamkulam. These days, NH-47's endless through traffic dominates the town's ailing economy, together with the local backwater coir and fishing industries. One vestige of Kayamkulam's former glory, however, survives.

The Hugging Saint

Mata Amritanandamayi ("Mother of Immortal Bliss") – or just plain "Amma" ("Mum") to her devotees – is one of India's all-time spiritual megastars. To call her a guru would be both an understatement and distortion, for although Amma does occasionally speak to her followers she's regarded less as a teacher than an "embodiment of pure, selfless Love" – which she imparts primarily, and most famously, though the simple act of a hug.

Born in 1953 to a low-caste fishing family, "Sudhamani", as she was first called, showed signs of being special from an early age. While still a child she would spend hours in deep meditation, composing emotionally charged *bhajans* to Krishna, having strange visions and caring for elderly or sick neighbours.

After her twenty-first birthday she left her family to escape an unwanted arranged marriage and made a vow of celibacy. Gradually, devotees began to gather around her; in May 1981, a small ashram was founded in the Kuttanad backwaters, in her home village of Parayakadavu. Thereafter, Amma's fame rapidly spread far beyond Kerala, inspiring a mass following in Europe and the States. In the process, her ashram, the **Mata Amritanandamayi** ("MA") Math, expanded into a huge complex of sugary-pink skyscrapers, with a permanent population of 1800 and a transient one of many times more.

When she's not receiving visitors at home, Amma is out on the road, taking her trademark embrace on tour to the organization's 33 centres worldwide. Over the past few decades it's been estimated that she's hugged a staggering thirty million individuals, which explains why her rate has speeded up from one to five people per minute in recent years. Yet most of those who experience an Amma hug claim to be filled with a vivid, powerful feeling of love, as if she's somehow managed to tap into their own emotional core. The years of hugging, backed up by some well-focused marketing and merchandizing in the US and Europe, have made Amma and her aides very wealthy indeed. No one can say for sure how much money the MA trust turns over, but the ashram spends vast sums on charitable works, including a pledge of $25 million to help tsunami victims in 2003. The district in which her ashram is located was badly hit by the Boxing Day waves, and the MA trust was quick to respond, providing disaster relief in Kerala, Tamil Nadu and the Andaman Islands.

Her much publicized generosity has seen a massive upsurge in Amma's popularity of late. You'll see her smile shining from roadside hoardings, taxi dashboards and hotel receptions all over Kerala, especially in the backwaters area. But Amma has her detractors, too, principally among Kerala's Christian and Muslim minorities, who accuse her of peddling a form of Hinduism with links to right-wing political groups.

Whether such claims are based on communal paranoia or actual fact, it's undeniable that Amma, who lives a modest existence in a one-bedroom flat in her ashram, has created an effective form of wealth redistribution, channelling huge amounts of cash from her wealthy supporters to the needy across India.

For more on visiting her ashram, the MA Math, see p.409.

Set in a tranquil garden on the outskirts of town, just off the main highway, the eighteenth-century **Krishnapuram Palace** (Tues–Sat 10am–4.30pm; Rs5, camera Rs15) is imbued with Keralan grace, constructed largely of wood with gabled roofs and rooms opening out onto shady internal courtyards. Inside, a small museum displays coins, puja ceremony utensils and oil lamps, some of which are arranged in an arc known as a *prabhu*, placed behind a temple deity to provide a halo of light. Fine miniature *panchaloha* ("five-metal" bronze alloy, with gold as one ingredient) figures include the water god Varuna, several Vishnus and a minuscule worshipping devotee. Small stone columns carved with serpent deities were recovered from local houses.

The prize exhibit, however, is a huge **mural** of the classical Keralan school, in muted ochre-reds and blue-greens, which covers more than fourteen square metres. It depicts **Gajendra Moksha** – the salvation of Gajendra, king of the elephants. In the tenth-century Sanskrit *Bhagavata Purana*, the story is told of a Pandyan king, Indrayumna, a devotee of Vishnu cursed by the sage Agastya to be born again as an elephant. One day, while sporting with his wives at the edge of a lake, his leg was seized by a crocodile whose grip was so tight that Gajendra was held captive for years. Finally, in desperation, the elephant called upon his chosen deity Vishnu, who immediately appeared, riding his celestial bird-man vehicle, Garuda, and destroyed the crocodile. The centre of the painting is dominated by a dynamic portrayal of Garuda about to land, with huge spread wings and a facial expression denoting *raudra* (fury), in stark contrast to the compassionate features of the multi-armed Vishnu. Smaller figures of Gajendra in mid-trumpet, and of his assailant, are shown to the right. As with all paintings in the Keralan style, every inch is packed with detail. Bearded sages, animals, mythical beasts and forest plants surround the main figures. The outer edges are decorated with floriate borders, which at the bottom form a separate triptych-like panel showing Balakrishna, the child Krishna, attended by adoring females.

Alappuzha (Alleppey)

Roughly midway between Kollam (85km south) and Kochi (64km north), **ALAPPUZHA** once ranked among the wealthiest ports along the Malabar Coast, acting as a clearing house for spices, coffee, tea, cashews, coir and other produce shipped from the backwaters. Unlike its rivals elsewhere in the region, however, the town – known in colonial times, and still commonly referred to, as "Alleppey" – didn't see its heyday until the mid-1800s, by which time the main canal scything through its heart, linking the waterways with the Arabian Sea, was lined with factories and warehouses. Alappuzha prospered to such an extent that the successful British traders who had settled here during the Raj were loath to leave at Independence. A sizeable community of expats remained after 1947, but their luck ran out ten years later, when the newly elected communist government clamped down on private businesses and they were forced to return to Britain.

With its trading history and interconnecting **canals**, tourist literature is fond of referring to Alappuzha as the "Venice of the East". Don't expect too much of a resemblance, though: cut through by the main national highway, the busy centre is as ramshackle and chaotic as any mid-sized Keralan town, although it does boast some quiet and leafy suburbs sporting rows of old colonial-era wharfs and bungalows.

The town is still a major hub in the coir industry, which accounts for much of the water-borne traffic chugging to and from the nearby lakes. However, the big bucks these days are being made from **houseboat cruises**. Around 500 *kettu vallam* barges operate in the Kuttanad area – 400 of them out of Alappuzha itself. The resulting congestion has proved a major challenge for the ecosystem of the backwaters (see box, p.416). It's possible to explore the area ethically, however, and Alappuzha provides plenty of scope for day-trips into the network of narrow canals around the town, which you can cover on environmentally friendly man-powered punts or

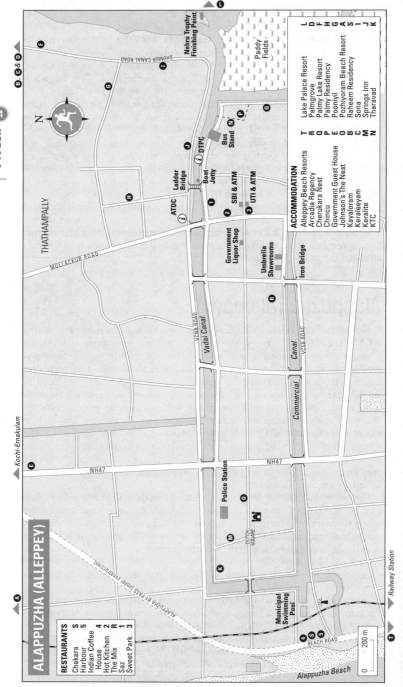

ALAPPUZHA (ALLEPPEY)

RESTAURANTS

Chakara	S
Harbour	5
Indian Coffee House	4
Hot Kitchen	2
The Mix	R
Saz	1
Sweet Park	3

ACCOMMODATION

Alleppey Beach Resorts	T	Lake Palace Resort	L
Arcadia Regency	R	Palmgrove	D
Cherukara Nest	Q	Palmy Lake Resort	F
Chincu	P	Palmy Residency	H
Government Guest House	E	Pooniyil	G
Johnson's The Nest	O	Pozhiyoram Beach Resort	A
Kayaloram	B	Raheem Residency	S
Keraleeyam	C	Sona	I
Keralite	M	Springs Inn	J
KTC	N	Tharavad	K

canoes, as well as offering some of the state's best-value accommodation – much of it in characterful homestays.

Arrival and information

The KSRTC **bus stand**, served by regular buses to and from Kollam, Kottayam, Thiruvananthapuram, Ernakulam and most other major Keralan towns, stands at the northeast edge of town. Close to its north exit, the main boat jetty on **Vadai Canal** is where the daily tourist ferry to and from Kollam, and local boat connections with Kottayam, arrive and depart. The **railway station,** on the main Thiruvananthapuram–Ernakulam line, lies 3km southwest, on the far side of Alappuzha's main waterway, **Commercial Canal**.

The town has several rival **tourist departments**, all of them eager to offer advice and book you onto their respective houseboat tours. The most conveniently situated – at the jetty itself on VCSB (Vadai Canal South Bank) Road – are the DTPC tourist reception centre (daily 7.30am–9pm; ☎0477/225 1796) and adjacent Kerala Tourism office (Mon–Sat 10am–5pm; ☎0477/226 0722, ⓦwww.keralatourism.org). On the opposite side of the canal on the corner of Mullackal and Vadai Canal North Bank (VCNB) Road, ATDC's main information office (daily 8am–8pm; ☎0477/224 346 or "Shambhu" ☎m98950 10833, ⓦwww.atdcalleppey.com) is more tucked away, on the second floor of the Municipal Shopping Complex. Both ATDC and DTPC sell tickets for their ferries, backwater cruises and charter boats, and can help you fathom the intricacies of local ferry timetables.

You can **change money** at the efficient UTI bank on Mullackal Road (Mon–Sat 9.30am–4.30pm). Both it and the State Bank of India directly opposite have reliable ATMs. **Internet** access is widely available for Rs30–40 per hour, with several outlets along the road facing the boat jetty; Mailbox on VCSB Road, five minutes' walk west of Mullackal Road, boasts the town's fastest connection.

△ Street life, Alappuzha

Accommodation

The choice of **places to stay** in the town centre is fairly uninspiring, but there are some great possibilities in all brackets if you are willing to travel to the outskirts and pay a little more. In the suburb of **Thathampally**, on the fringes of the Punnamada Lake, a string of ultra-luxurious resorts soak up the tour group and honeymoon custom in campuses of re-assembled Keralan wooden houses, located on the water's edge.

Nearly everywhere, whatever its bracket, has some kind of tie-in with a houseboat operator: good-natured encouragement tends to be the order of the day rather hard-sell tactics, but you may be able to negotiate a reduction on your room tariff if you do end up booking a backwater trip. In Alappuzha, as elsewhere in the state, rates tend to increase by 25–30 percent between mid-December and mid-January. Whenever you come, and wherever you chose to stay, though, brace yourself for clouds of **mosquitoes**.

See also "Around Alappuzha" on pp.421–423.

Budget

Chincu near KSRTC bus stand ☎0477/223 6687, ☎m9895 106817, ☜www.arcadiaregency.com. Three impeccably clean attached rooms in a converted portion of a small family home, hidden down a narrow alleyway close to (but beyond earshot of) the bus stand. If it's booked up, the slightly less appealing, but cheaper *KTC* (☎0477/225 4275, ☎m98461 15553; ❷–❸) is up the same lane. ❸

Government Guesthouse next door to KTDC *Yatri Niwas*, on NH-47 ☎0477/224 6504. Like its namesakes in other Keralan towns, this place is basically set up for the benefit of visiting officials, but they'll accommodate tourists if there are vacancies (though you'll probably have to call in person on the day). Ranged on two floors above a central courtyard, the rooms are plain and a touch institutional, but fantastic for the price (Rs220 non-a/c or Rs450 for much nicer a/c), with big, clean bathrooms. ❷–❸

Johnson's The Nest Lalbagh, Convent Square, 2km west of the centre ☎m0996 1466399, ☜www.johnsonskerala.com. Friendly, sociable homestay on a quiet suburban street, popular mainly with young backpackers. Its six individually themed attached rooms are large, with Barbie-pink mosquito nets, and most have funky little sitouts fitted with cane swings. Money exchange, laundry and meals available – and they offer enjoyable day-trips to a quiet beach north of Alappuzha. ❷–❹

🏃 **Keralite** Vadakekalam House, north of Dutch Square ☎0477/224 3569, ☜alice_t@rediffmail.com. Opening onto a broad sand courtyard filled with pot plants, the heart of this delightful 100-year-old house is a high-ceilinged salon where hostess Alice Thomas serves traditional Syrian-Christian meals under the watchful eye of ancestral portraits. Comfortable antique beds furnish the guest rooms, which have lots of period atmosphere; the only catch is that some lack attached bathrooms – hence the bargain rates. ❸–❹

Palmy Residency North of DTPC tourist office, beyond Ladder Bridge ☎0477/223 5938, ☎m94476 67888, ☜www.palmyresort.com. Up a side street 5mins walk from Main Canal, this well-run guesthouse (an off-shoot of the excellent *Palmy Resort*) is situated in a quiet neighbourhood. It has six rooms in total – the two cheaper ones around the back of the building are great no-frills budget options, with mozzie nets and attached bathrooms; an extra Rs250 buys you more space and a TV. ❸–❹

Pooniyil Thathampally, 1km north of the boat jetty ☎0477/223 2593, ☎m9847 109074. Annexe of three simple rooms, plus a curious palm-leaf and wood "cottage" (worth the Rs100 extra), in a sandy compound off the Punnamada Rd; they're a bit spartan and not all that big, but impeccably clean, and there's a long north-facing veranda to laze on. Comfortable and pretty good value, with some of the cheapest a/c options in Alappuzha. ❸–❹

Mid-range

Alleppey Beach Resorts Beach Rd ☎0477/226 3408, ☜www.thealleppeybeachresorts.com. Eccentric, slightly Fawlty-Towers-esque hotel offering Alappuzha's only beachside rooms. Opening onto common verandas with great sea views, they're huge (the non-a/c "deluxe" on the first floor are vast) and a bit overpriced, but many will consider the relaxing, breezy location worth the extra. Moreover, the food gets rave reviews from guests. ❻–❼

Arcadia Regency Near the Iron Bridge ☎0477/223 0414, ☜www.arcadiaregency.com.

A gleaming, multi-storey tower block clad in white-painted concrete and tinted windows. Hardly the most sympathetic addition to the town's historic centre in recent years, but it offers good-value three-star accommodation: modern rooms, a multi-cuisine restaurant, 24hr coffee shop and splendid rooftop pool. ⑤

Cherukara Nest 9/774 Cherukara Bldgs ☏0477/225 1509, ☏m9947 059628. Nineteenth-century "heritage" home, run by the welcoming Mr Tony John, on a quiet canal road only a short walk around the corner from the KSRTC bus stand. The cheaper of his four rooms are light with high ceilings; those to the rear, in converted teak-lined granaries, are gloomier but possess more Keralan character. Breakfast is served in an old courtyard. Eco-friendly houseboat cruises are a sideline. ④–⑤

Palmgrove Punnamada Kayal, 3.5km north of boat jetty ☏0477/223 5004, ☏m9847 430434, ⓦwww.palmgrovelakeresort.com. Situated at a tranquil spot close to where the canal meets Punnamada Lake, this relaxed resort actually overlooks the water – a perfect spot from which to watch the snake boat races. Shaded by areca and coconut palms, its quaint bamboo cottages have gabled tile roofs, private outdoor showers and sitouts opening onto the garden. *Palm Grove* isn't in the same league as the luxury places up the lane, but is a lot more affordable. Rates increase the closer you get to the water. ⑤–⑥

Palmy Lake Resort Thathampally, 2km north of boat jetty ☏0477/223 5938, ☏m9447 667888, ⓦwww.palmyresort.com. Spacious, neatly painted red-tiled "cottages" (a/c and non-a/c), grouped behind a modern family home on the northeastern limits of town. Despite the name, it isn't actually on the lake, but offers exceptional value for money. You get loads of space for the price: all rooms have private pillared verandas opening onto a restful garden. Owners Biggi and Mercy Matthews are smiling hosts, providing delicious home-cooked Keralan meals. Phone ahead for free pick up. ④–⑤

Pozhiyoram Beach Resort 5km north of Alappuzha town ☏0477/325 6238, ☏m9387 827235, ⓦwww.pozhiyorambeachresort .com. Only a 10min drive up the coast road, but a world away from the bustle of Alappuzha town, on the edge of a small lagoon and white sand beach. Its accommodation comprises four simple "beach view" rooms, with sea-facing sitouts right next to the sand, and more comfort-able, pricier "Kerala cottages" further back in the palm grove, sporting gabled roofs and little verandas. Traditional Kuttanad meals are served

in a little restaurant overlooking the waterfront, featuring seafood straight off the nearby fishing boats. ⑥–⑦

Sona Shomur Canal Rd, Thathampally ☏0477/223 5211, ⓦwww.sonahome.com. Elegant old Keralan home, with a graceful gabled roof, set back from the road to the lake. The four rooms in the original house, run by a elderly owner who loves to share his knowledge of the town and its backwaters, are far more attractive (and cheaper) than the three cheekily squeezed-in new ones in the garden. This place gets mixed reviews, but ranks among the least expensive heritage homestays within easy reach of the jetty. Meals, houseboat rental and Ayurvedic treat-ments available. ④–⑤

Tharavad West of North Police Station, Sea View Ward ☏0477/224 4599, ⓦwww .tharavadheritageresort.com. Few of Alappuzha's heritage properties retain as pukka a feel as this former doctor's mansion, which rests in the shade of an old mango tree on the quiet west side of town. Entered via a typically colonial-era veranda, its interior holds polished eggshell and teak floors, carved rosewood furniture and antique bell-metal curios collected by successive generations. The differently priced rooms (ranging from singles to family suites) are all large and well-aired, the only concessions to the modern era being their bathrooms. Meals available. ④–⑦

Luxury

Kayaloram Punnamada Kayal ☏0477/223 2040, ⓦwww.kayaloram.com. Twelve antique Keralan wood *tharavadu*, complete with luxurious interiors and private "open-to-sky" bathrooms, dotted around an immaculate palm garden running right to the lakeside. The location is sublime, offering uninterrupted views across the water, and there's a good-sized pool and open-sided restaurant if you tire of relaxing on your own terrace. *Kayaloram* claims to have been the first resort to make use of relocated period houses, and it's still one of the most congenial of its type. Rates include boat transfer from the Nehru Trophy jetty. From \$235. ⑨

Keraleeyam Nehru Trophy Rd, Thathampally ☏0477/223 1468, ⓦwww.keraleeyam.com. This small-scale backwater resort, run by a famous Ayurveda outfit, is centred on one of the most beautiful period houses in the Alappuzha area, facing the Punnamada canal close to where it runs into the lake, near the start of the Snake Boat race. Capped with a picture-postcard twin-gabled roof, the old building has a

One of the most memorable experiences for travellers in India is the opportunity to take a boat journey on the **backwaters of Kerala**. The area known as **Kuttanad** stretches for 75km from Kollam in the south to Kochi in the north, sandwiched between the sea and the hills. This bewildering labyrinth of shimmering waterways, composed of lakes, canals, rivers and rivulets, is lined with dense tropical greenery and preserves rural Keralan lifestyles that are completely hidden from the road.

Views constantly change, from narrow canals and dense vegetation to open vistas and dazzling green paddy fields. Homes, farms, churches, mosques and temples can be glimpsed among the trees, and every so often you might catch the blue flash of a kingfisher, or the green of a parakeet. Pallas fishing eagles cruise above the water looking for prey and cormorants perch on logs to dry their wings. If you're lucky enough to be in a boat without a motor, at times the only sounds are birds chattering and occasional film songs drifting across from distant radios. Some families live on tiny pockets of land, with just enough room for a simple house, yard and boat. They bathe and wash their clothes – sometimes their buffaloes, too, muddy from ploughing the fields – at the water's edge. Traditional Keralan longboats, *kettu vallam*, glide along, powered by gondolier-like boatmen with poles, the water often lapping perilously close to the edge. Fishermen work from tiny dugout canoes and long rowing boats, and operate massive Chinese nets on the shore.

Coconut trees at improbable angles form shady canopies, and occasionally you pass under simple curved bridges. Poles sticking out of the water indicate dangerous shallows. Here and there basic drawbridges can be raised on ropes, but major bridges are few and far between; most people rely on boatmen to ferry them across the water to connect with roads and bus services, resulting in a constant criss-crossing of the waters from dawn until dusk – a way of life beautifully represented in the visually stunning film *Piravi*, by Keralan director Shaji.

Threats to the ecosystem

The **African moss** that often carpets the surface of the narrower waterways may look attractive, but it is actually a menace to small craft and starves underwater life of light. It is also a symptom of the many serious **ecological problems** currently affecting the region, whose population density ranges from between two and four times that of other coastal areas in southwest India. This has put growing pressure on land, and hence a greater reliance on fertilizers, which eventually work their way into the water causing the build-up of moss. Illegal land reclamation, however, poses the single greatest threat to this fragile ecosystem. In a little over a century, the total area of water in Kuttanad has been reduced by two-thirds, while mangrove swamps and fish stocks have been decimated by pollution and the spread of towns and villages around the edges of the backwater region. Tourism is now adding to the problem, as the film of oil from motorized ferries and houseboats spreads through the waters, killing yet more fish, which has in turn led to a reduction of over fifty percent in the number of bird species found in the region. Some of the tourist agencies are trying to lessen the impact of visitors by introducing more eco-friendly vessels (see opposite).

Tourist cruises

The most popular excursion of all in the Kuttanad region is the full-day journey between **Kollam** and **Alappuzha**. All sorts of private hustlers offer their services, but the principal boats are run on alternate days by the Alleppey Tourism Development Co-op (ATDC) and the District Tourism Promotion Council (DTPC) – see p.413 for contact details. The double-decker boats leave from both Kollam and Alappuzha daily, departing at 10.30am (10am check-in); tickets cost Rs300 and can be bought in advance or on the day at the ATDC/DTPC counters, other agents and some hotels. Both companies make three stops during the eight-hour journey, including one for lunch, and another at the **Mata Amritanandamayi Math** at Amritapuri (see p. around three hours north of Kollam.

Although it is by far the main backwater route, many tourists find Alappuzha–Kollam too long, with crowded decks and intense sun. There's also something faintly embarrassing about being cooped up with a crowd of fellow tourists, madly photographing any signs of life on the water or canal banks, while gangs of kids scamper alongside the boat screaming "one pen, one pen".

One alternative is to charter a four- or six-seater motorboat, which you can do through DTPC and ATDC for around Rs300/hr. Slower, more cumbersome double-decker country boats are also available for hire from Rs250/hr.

Village tours and canoes

Quite apart from their significant **environmental impact**, most houseboats are too wide to squeeze into the narrower inlets connecting small villages. To reach these more idyllic, remote areas, therefore, you'll need to charter a punted **canoe** (see p.419). The slower pace means less distance gets covered in an hour, but the experience of being so close to the water, and those who live on it, tends to be correspondingly more rewarding. Individual guides have their own favourite itineraries. You'll also find more formal "**village tours**" advertised across the Kuttanad area, tying together trips to watch coir makers, rice farmers and boat builders in action with the opportunity to dine in a traditional Keralan village setting.

Kettu vallam (houseboats)

Whoever dreamed up the idea of showing tourists around the backwaters in old rice barges, or **kettu vallam**, could never have imagined that, two decades on, five hundred or more of them would be chugging around Kuttanad waterways. These **houseboats**, made of dark, oiled jackwood with canopies of plaited palm thatch and coir, are big business, and almost every mid- and upmarket hotel, guesthouse and "heritage homestay" seems to have one. An estimated four hundred work out of Alappuzha alone, the flashiest fitted with a/c rooms, silk cushions on their teak sun decks, imported wine in their fridges and Jacuzzis that bubble away through the night. One grand juggernaut (called the *Vaikundan*, based near Amma's ashram in Kollam district) holds ten separate bedrooms and won't slip its lines for less than Rs25,000 ($580). At the opposite end of the scale are rough-and-ready transport barges with gut-thumping diesel engines, cramped bedrooms and minimal washing facilities.

What you end up paying for your cruise will depend on a number of variables: the **size** and **quality** of the boat and its fittings; the number and standard of the **bedrooms** (a/c will bump up the price by around 50–75 percent); and, crucially, the **time of year**. Rates double over Christmas and New Year, and halve off-season during the monsoons. In practice, however, Rs4500–8000 is the usual bracket for a trip on a two-bedroom, non-a/c boat with a proper bathroom (or Rs11,000–14,000 for a/c), including three meals, in early December or mid-January. The cruise should last a minimum of 22 hours, though don't expect to spend all of that on the move: running times are carefully calculated to spare gas. From sunset onwards you'll be moored at a riverbank, probably on the outskirts of the town where the trip started.

You'll save quite a lot of cash, and be doing the fragile ecosystem a big favour, by opting for a more environmentally friendly **punted** *kettu vallam*. This was how rice barges were traditionally propelled, and though it means you travel at a more leisurely pace, the experience is silent (great for wildlife spotting) and altogether more relaxing.

Houseboat operators work out of **Kollam**, **Karunagapalli** and **Kumbakonam**, but most are in **Alappuzha**, where you'll find the lowest prices – but also the worst congestion on more scenic routes. Spend a day shopping around for a deal (your

owner will be a good first port of call) and always check the boat
's also a good idea to get the deal fixed on paper before setting
d a final payment until the end of the cruise in case of arguments.

ay offer the most comfortable way of cruising the backwaters, but
ch more vivid experience of what life is actually like in the region by
ju...,   one of the local ferries that serve its towns and villages. Particularly
recommended is the trip from Alappuzha to Kottayam (5 daily; 2hr 30min; Rs12),
which winds across open lagoons and narrow canals, through coconut groves and
islands. The first ferry leaves at 7.30am; arrive early to get a good place with uninterrupted views.

There are also numerous other local routes that you can jump on and off, though
working your way through the complexities of the timetables and Malayalam names
can be difficult without the help of the tourist office. Good places to aim for from
Alappuzha include Neerettupuram, Kidagara, and Chambakulam; all three are served
by regular daily ferries, but you may have to change boats once or twice along the
way, killing time in local cafés and toddy shops (all of which adds to the fun, of
course). Whatever service you opt for, take a sun hat and plenty of water.

---

few rooms; the palm-leaf huts in the garden, which open straight onto the water's edge and are perfectly placed to watch the houseboats chug past, are much better value. **⑦–⑧**
Lake Palace Resort 4km across Vembanad Lake ☎0477/223 9701, ⓦwww.lakepalaceresort.com. Owned by a local politician, the *Lake Palace* is the most recent, and ostentatiously grand, of Alappuzha's upscale resort complexes, though it lacks the traditional style of smaller places closer to town. The 50-acre site is centred on a private lagoon and offers three types of accommodation, the flashiest of them "Jumbo-Sized Water Villas" on stilts. Access is by boat transfer from a jetty near the KSRTC bus stand. Rates start at Rs10,5000/$250. **⑨**

Raheem Residency Beach Rd ☎0477/223 9767, ⓦwww.raheemresidency.com. The glossiest of Alappuzha's heritage hotels occupies a 140-year-old mansion on the beachfront. Sumptuously restored from near dereliction by its Indian-Irish owners, the building encloses half-a-dozen spacious, richly furnished a/c rooms, equipped with carved four-posters (some of which you need a step to climb into) and original wood and glass window shutters. For outside lounging space, you've a gorgeous imported French swimming pool, hammocks on a roof terrace and a breezy open-sided restaurant. $200–300 per night. **⑨**

The town, lakes and beach

Alappuzha tends to be eclipsed by the backwaters that unfold from its eastern flank, but it's definitely worth setting aside an afternoon to sample the town's own idiosyncratic charms. Thanks to recent efforts by the local council to clean up the canals, some of the older sidestreets, with their colonial-era factories and warehouses, are a lot more pleasant than they used to be. The best way of **getting around** them is to rent a bicycle. There's usually someone in front of the DTPC tourist office with a couple of rattly old Heros to spare: if not, ask inside and they help you find one.

Because of the intense traffic pouring through it, you're more likely to want to browse the main bazaar, **Mullackal Road**, on foot. It's crammed with a typically Keralan assortment of shops, from gold jewellery emporia to bell-metal and fishing hardware suppliers. Beyond its southern side (on the north bank of the canal; see map on p.412), is another quintessentially South Indian sight: a row of snazzy a/c **umbrella showrooms**, stocking every conceivable colour and size of brolly, whether smart monsoon-grade ones with laquered handles or the faintly ridiculous plastic parasols backwater canoeists strap on their heads.

You might well want to invest in a sunshade for trips out to **Alappuzha's lakes**: Punnamada and Vembanad. Reaching them from town is most straightforward by water. For short cruises, it's possible to charter diesel-powered **motorboats** (Rs250/hr) or more sedate, twin-decked **country boats** (Rs300/hr) from ATDC/DTPC. Better still, dispense with engines altogether and opt for a guided **village tour** in a hand-paddled canoe. Aside from being more "green", these allow you to penetrate narrow waterways beyond the range of the other tourist boats. DTPC offer their own punted tours, carrying two people for Rs150/hr. One commendable private operator who's been ferrying tourists around Alappuzha's off-track backwaters for years is Mr K.D. Prasenan (☎m93888 44712), based at the *Palm Grove Lake Resort* on the Punnamada Kayal, 3.5km north of the boat jetty. In a slender 10-metre boat, he offers five-and nine-hour trips (Rs1250/2200 respectively, for two people) via routes connecting the Holy Padma River and Punnamada Lake – both get consistently glowing reviews from readers.

In the opposite direction, on the west side of town, you pass through Alappuzha's formerly affluent, colonial-era suburbs, which gradually open out as you approach the town **beach**. Although unsuitable for swimming and sunbathing, the wide, gleaming white sands stretch out of sight in both directions and provide a welcome blast of fresh air. A British-built **pier** extends a kilometre into the surf from its centre. Dating from 1862, the jetty once supported three separate railway lines that fanned out to wharfs around the town. These days, however, its stark silhouette receives scant attention, except during Kerala Tourism's annual **beach festival** in late-December, during which it serves as a surreal backdrop for various cultural events and a procession of fifty caparisoned elephants.

The snake boat races

Alappuzha really comes alive on the second Saturday of August, in the middle of the monsoon, when it serves as the venue for one of Kerala's major spectacles – the **Nehru Trophy snake boat race**. This event, first held in 1952, is based on the traditional Keralan enthusiasm for racing magnificently decorated longboats, with raised rears designed to resemble the hood of a cobra. Each boat carries 25 singers, and 100–130 enthusiastic oarsmen power the craft along, all rowing to the rhythmic *Vanchipattu* ("song of the boatman"). There are a number of prize categories, including one for the women's race; sixteen boats compete for each prize in knock-out rounds. Similar races can be seen at Aranmula (p.427), and at Champakulam, 16km by ferry from Alappuzha. The ATDC information office (see p.413) will be able to tell you the dates of these other events, which change every year.

Eating

Aside from the **restaurants** listed on p.420, most of Alappuzha's homestays and guesthouses provide meals for guests, usually delicious, home-cooked Keralan cooking that's tailored for sensitive Western tastes. Many of them also serve cold beers, albeit discreetly, in little china pots. For **take-outs**, you can join the scrum that forms each evening outside the government "beverages" shop, just off Mullackal Road in the main bazaar.

Moving on from Alappuzha

As Alappuzha isn't on the main railway network, but on a branch line, the choice of **trains** servicing the town is limited. There are, however, train connections to Thiruvananthapuram and Kollam in the south, and to Kochi/Ernakulam, Thrissur, Palakkad and other points in the north. **Bus** connections are adequate, especially to Kochi/Ernakulam, where there is a greater choice of trains to northern destinations and Tamil Nadu. Although buses travel to Kollam, **boats** offers a more scenic, leisurely way of getting there. Regular ferry services connect Alappuzha to Kottayam, from where you can catch buses to Periyar, as well as several destinations along the coastal highway. For more on public transport from Alappuzha, see Travel details, p.495.

By bus

The filthy KSRTC bus stand, on the east side of town and a minute's walk from the boat jetty, is served by regular buses to **Kollam** (2hr), **Kottayam** (1hr 30min), **Thiruvananthapuram** (3hr–3hr 30min) and **Kochi/Ernakulam** (1hr 30min). For Fort Cochin, catch any of the fast Ernakulam services along the main highway and get down at **Thoppumpady** (7km south of the city), from where local buses run the rest of the way.

By boat

Tourist boats travel regularly to **Kollam**, with the ATDC and DTPC boats operating a similar schedule, departing at 10.30am and arriving in Kollam at 6.30pm. From the jetty just outside the KSRTC bus stand, much cheaper local **ferries** travel to **Kottayam** (service P380; 2hr 30min; Rs12), with five departures between 7.30am and 2pm, and a constellation of satellite villages in the backwaters. Regular services run to Champakulam, where you pick up less frequent boats to Neerettupuram and Kidangara, and back to Alappuzha again. This round route ranks among Kuttanad's

Chakara *Raheem Residency*, Beach Rd ☎0477/223 0767. "Chakara" means "bumper catch of fish" in Malayalam, and the accent in this, Alappuzha's classiest restaurant, is firmly on seafood, with specialities ranging from local-style fish curry (their signature dish) to seer fish simmered in flavoursome *moillie* coconut gravy, and crunchy masala-fried prawns to calamari – all fresh off the boats and prepared with minimal oil. They also have plenty of tempting, healthy continental alternatives, courteously served on a raised terrace looking across the beach. Count on Rs650 for a fixed four-course menu; or a bit more à la carte.

Harbour Beach Rd. All the food served in this gleaming little seafront restaurant is prepared in the kitchens of the classy *Raheem Residency* next door, so quality and freshness are assured. You can order grilled prawns, Alappuzha-style chicken curry, Kuttanadi fish, chilli chicken or a range of light continental meals, snacks and sandwiches, dished up in a dining hall with bare laterite walls under an old-style tiled roof. For dessert, there's fruit salad with ice cream and coconut. Most mains are under Rs100.

Hot Kitchen Mullackal Rd. The most reputed pure-veg South Indian "meals" restaurant in town, run by a Tamil family that has been here for generations. The masala dosas, *vadas* and other fried snacks aren't so great, and the dining hall's seen better days, but the lunch-time thalis (also available in the evening) are deservedly popular.

Indian Coffee House Beach Rd. The usual smudged cotton uniforms and insipid ICH menu of Udupi snacks and rice-based meals, but under a traditional pagoda-shaped shelter on the beach front. The food may not be up to much, but the coffee is okay and the location pleasantly breezy in the afternoons.

The Mix *Arcadia Regency*, near Iron Bridge, NH-47 ☎0477/223 0414. Modern multi-cuisine restaurant in Alappuzha's only Western-style business hotel, noteworthy as much for its strident red décor as good value, "all-you-can-eat" buffets (Rs125), featuring a huge range of Chinese and North Indian, as well as Keralan specialities.

Saz VCSB Rd, near Ladder Bridge. This no-frills non-veg place on Vadai Canal does a roaring trade at lunchtime with its fish-curry rice plate "meals" (Rs30), while in the evenings half the tourist classic trips, but you'll need some help from one or other of the tourist offices to make sense of the timetables.

By train

As the backwaters prevent trains from continuing directly south beyond Alappuzha, only a few major daily services and a handful of passenger trains depart from the railway station, 3km southwest of the jetty. For points further north along the coast, take the Jan Shatabdi Express and change at Ernakulam, as the afternoon Alleppey–Cannanore Express (#6307), which runs as far as **Kozhikode** and **Kannur**, arrives at those destinations rather late at night. It is, however, a good service if you only intend to travel as far as Thrissur.

The following trains are recommended as the **fastest** and/or **most convenient** from Alappuzha.

Recommended trains from Alappuzha

Destination	Name	Number	Departs	Total time
Chennai	*Alleppey–Chennai Express	#6042	daily 4.10pm	14hr
Ernakulam/ Kochi	Jan Shatabdi Express	#2076	daily 8.40am	1hr 10min
	*Alleppey–Chennai Express	#6042	daily 4.10pm	1hr 20min
Thiruvanan-thapuram	Ernakulam–Trivandrum Express	#6341	daily 7.20am	3hr 5min
	Jan Shatabdi Express	#2075	daily 6.33pm	2hr 50min
Thrissur	*Alleppey–Chennai Express	#6042	daily 4.10pm	3hr

* this train also travels to Irinjalakuda and Palakkad

population of Alappuzha pours in for the succulent flame-grilled barbeque and tandoori chicken, served at a brisk pace by black-tie waiters. They also have a full-on kebab counter outside, and offer a range of typical Kuttanadi "specials", chalked on a board on the wall. It's bit grubby, but hygienic enough and cheap, with most mains Rs80–130.

Sweet Park next to UTI Bank, Mullackal Rd. The perfect pit stop in the main bazaar, serving freshly baked macaroons, chilli and cashew cookies, samosas, veg cutlets and flaky prawn patties, with hot coffees and teas, in an open-sided café overlooking one of the main crossroads in the market area.

Around Alappuzha

With so much congenial accommodation on offer in Alappuzha, you might be tempted to stay in the town for a couple of extra days, making short trips to outlying areas by boat, taxi or bus. The following accounts cover some of the more obvious destinations, but there are dozens of similar sites scattered around the Kuttanad area, best explored by means of local ferries from the boat jetty near the DTPC tourist office, which can help with route planning (see p.413).

South of Alappuzha

CHAMPAKULAM, 14km southeast of Alappuzha in the middle of the backwaters, is home to the **Church of St Mary's,** erected in 1579 by the Portuguese on the remains of a chapel believed to have been one of the seven founded by St Thomas the Apostle. Now a centre of Syrian-Christian worship, it boasts an extravagantly decorated Rococo interior, dripping with gold leaf and elaborate murals – some fusing elements of Hindu and Christian iconography. The church rises from the bank of a broad river where, each year in the Hindu month of Midhunam (June–July), the Champakulam boat race attracts large crowds. The village's own crew recently won the big Nehru Trophy race three years in succession, and the magnificent 40-metre-long **snake boat** they competed in is stored at a shed on the outskirts, ten minutes' walk from St Mary's. Head to the riverbank behind the church, turn right and follow the lane for 400m past the bazaar and boat jetty until you reach a stepped footbridge; instead of crossing it, keep going straight on until the next bridge and cross that, following the path as it skirts some houses, by which time you'll have the boat in your sights. If you get lost, ask for the *vallam* and someone will wave you in the right direction. Champakulam is connected to Alappuzha by regular **ferries** (every 30min; 30min).

The curved sterns of Kerala's traditional racing boats are said to imitate the unfurled hood of a cobra, and at **MANNARSALA**, near the village of **Haripad**, 25km south of Alappuzha on NH-47, 30,000 carved stones of rearing snakes were inspired by the same form. Dusted in tumeric and vermillion powder, they litter a leafy forest glade attached to the state's principal **Nagaraja temple**, dedicated to the "God of Serpents". Uniquely in Kerala, the shrine is officiated over by an elderly female Naboordiri priestess, "Valliamma", who leads processions and pujas from her adjacent house each morning and evening. It is particularly popular with childless couples: on Sundays, many come to propitiate the deity with offerings of tumeric and salt, holding a brass urn (*uruli*) upside down if they've just made their petition, or carrying it right-side up if their wish has been fulfilled.

Accommodation south of Alappuzha

Emerald Isle Kanjooparambil–Manimalathara ☏0477/270 3899, ☏m9447 077555, ⓦwww.emeraldislekerala.com. For once, the real deal: an authentic, 150-year-old *tharavad*, still occupied by the owners and in its original location deep in the backwaters, sandwiched between a river and acres of rice paddy. Under an exquisite traditional Kuttanadi roof, four teak rooms have been converted for use by guests, with antique doors, lustrous carved-wood furniture and private outdoor bathrooms. Cookery lessons, fishing and canoeing trips are all on offer, and there's a beautiful garden to the rear. *Emerald Isle* is, however, fiendishly hard to find. Head east down the Kottayam highway for 13km to Neddumaddy junction, turn left and keep going until you hit the backwater, where

boatman Babu will be waiting with his dugout. Tariffs (Rs4000–48000) include all meals. ⓭

VJ's Rice Garden Pallathurthy, 6km from Alappuzha ☏0477/270 2566, ☏m9194 4611 8931, ⓦwww.ricegardenkerala .com. If you'd like to be marooned in the backwaters but can't afford any of the heritage resorts, give this quirky little guesthouse a try. Its rooms – a couple of simply furnished doubles and a larger "bamboo cottage" – hold less appeal than the romantic location, on a slither of riverbank backed by miles of rice fields. You can reach it by boat, or by taking an auto-rickshaw along the Kottayam road for 5km as far as a big concrete bridge (with a KTDC hotel below it); cross over to the other side and turn immediately right, keeping to the footpath along the bank for another 1km, where you'll be met by a boatman who'll paddle you across. ⓸

North of Alappuzha

Some of Kerala's most bijou resorts occupy prime spots on the western shores of **Vembanad Lake** – a vast, 200-square-kilometre expanse of shimmering lagoon that reaches its widest point at the village of **MUHAMMA** (you can get there either via NH-47, turning off at **Kanjikudi**, or via the more scenic backroad closer to the lake shore). For reviews of accommodation in the area, see opposite.

West of Muhamma, the wedge of densely populated coconut plantation dividing Vembanad from the sea comes to an abrupt end at **MARARIKULAM**,

on whose fringes a string of small resort hotels has sprung
palm trees behind an endless golden-sand beach strewn w
the time being, villagers far outnumber tourists along th
coast, and if you can afford the high tariffs, these places o
on the journey between Alappuzha and the Keralan capita
lies less than a couple of hours' drive north on NH-47).

The one noteworthy sight is **St Andrew's Forane**
known as **St Sebastian's**) at **ARTHUNGAL**, 4km no
Catholics who have recovered from serious illness or
pilgrimage here, hobbling on their knees from to the altar
path lined with crosses and candle stands. Curiously, it's also a popular stop on
the Sabarimala trail (see p.437), and during the season hundreds of Hindu men
in black *lunghis* pour through to pay their respects. Behind the main 19th-
century Gothic church a much older chapel built in the 1590s by Portuguese
Jesuits stands virtually forgotten. The best time to visit Arthungal is on Sunday
evenings (around sunset), when a congregation of hundreds spills into the main
square for Mass.

Accommodation north of Alappuzha

Arakal Heritage Mararikulam-North, 3km
north of *Marari Beach Resort* ☏0478/286
5545, ☏m9847 268661, ⓦwww.arakal.com This
is one of those rare homestays that manages to
provide all the comforts you could wish for of a
beachside hideaway while retaining an authentic
Keralan village atmosphere. Dotted around a sandy
plot close to the sea, the five 200-year-old houses
come complete with beautiful gabled roofs, traditional railings and original antique furniture. All
have shady verandas and hidden outdoor
bathrooms – "Mango" even has a tree growing
through the middle of it. Hosts Abi and Mini can
help arrange bicycle, elephant and boat rides in the
area, as well as cookery lessons and Ayurvedic
treatments. One of the loveliest places to stay in
the state, and well worth splashing out on for a
night or two if it's above your normal budget. From
Rs3500 (plus Rs800 for a/c). ❽

Casa del Fauno Muhamma ☏0478/286
0862, ⓦwww.casadelfauno.com. If Fellini
had ever made a film in Kerala, its set might have
looked like this dream villa on the shores of Lake
Vembanad, created by Italian designer Maria
Angela Fernhof. The fusion architecture blends
polished marble and fragments of old Tamil stone
sculpture to stunning effect (you approach the

house via a mock acropolis of temple brackets),
and the guest rooms inside are light, cool and
exquisitely furnished. Authentic Italian (and
Vietnamese) meals are served alfresco in a
secluded inner courtyard, on shabby-chic granite
tables. ❽

Marari Beach Resort Mararikulam-North
☏0478/286 3801, ⓦwww.cgearth.com. Gated
resort complex, enclosing 52 a/c thatched "fisherman's huts", each with a low raised veranda and a
little tap to wash the sand off your feet. The 25-
acre plot also boasts a large curvy pool, starred
restaurant and lotus ponds with ducks splashing
around. Security guards are, of course, on hand to
prevent the real fisherman from wandering through
and spoiling the idyll. ❾

Motty's Beach Houses Marari Beach
☏0477/224 3535, ☏m9847 032836.
Kerala has very few attractive small houses to
rent as close to the beach as this, and the traditional architecture of the relocated wooden
dwellings is as beautiful as the setting, amid the
palms of a busy fishing community. From their
verandas, cusped arches and lathe-turned pillars
frame views through the trees to the sea. Not all
of the houses are of the same standard (or price),
however, nor as nicely situated or private (one is
divided in two by a thin wall). Full details available
on booking.

Kottayam

Some 76km southeast of Kochi and 37km northeast of Alappuzha, **KOTTAYAM**
is a compact, busy Keralan town strategically located between the backwaters
to the west and the forests and mountains of the Western Ghats to the east. Most

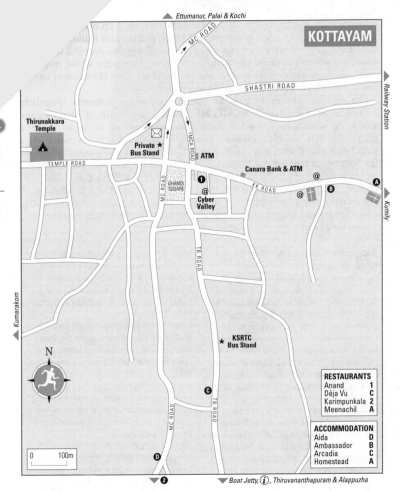

Kottayam

▲ Ettumanur, Palai & Kochi

MC ROAD

SHASTRI ROAD

Railway Station ▶

Thirunakkara Temple

Private ★
Bus Stand

MC ROAD

YMCA ROAD

✉

ATM

GHANDI SQUARE

TEMPLE ROAD

Canara Bank & ATM

@

@ ✝

❶ @
Cyber
Valley

KK ROAD

B

A ▶

Kumily ▶

◀ Kumarakom

TB ROAD

KSRTC
Bus Stand ★

MC ROAD

TB ROAD

N

C

0   100m

D

❷ ▼

▼ Boat Jetty, ⓘ, Thiruvananthapuram & Alappuzha

RESTAURANTS
Anand	1
Déja Vu	C
Karimpunkala	2
Meenachil	A

ACCOMMODATION
Aida	D
Ambassador	B
Arcadia	C
Homestead	A

visitors come here on their way somewhere else – foreigners take short boat trips to nearby Vembanad Lake or Alappuzha, or set off to Periyar Wildlife Sanctuary, while Ayappa devotees pass through en route to the forest temple at Sabarimala (see p.438).

For Keralans, the town is synonymous with **money**, both old and new. The many **rubber plantations** around it, first introduced by British missionaries in the 1820s, have for more than a century formed the bedrock of a booming local economy, most of it controlled by landed **Syrian Christians**, for whom Kottayam is something of a heartland. Younger sons and their families not in line for a slice of the estate have tended for generations to leave home and seek their fortunes abroad, and signs of the resulting remittance wealth are everywhere, from adverts for foreign banks to the huge hoardings erected by gold merchants.

Aside from rubber and its famously well-educated workforce (this was the first town in India to achieve 100 percent literacy), Kottayam's other main export is the state's number-one newspaper, the *Malayala Monorama*, which is the largest of five dailies edited in the town. Boasting a readership of 1.5 million, the *Manorama* (literally "Entertainer") has been in circulation since 1890 and has had a chequered history. Fearing the rise of its Christian-minority backers, the Raja of Travancore once closed the paper down, and its owners have been embroiled in several major financial controversies since, most recently in 2006 after the collapse of a banking firm with which the *Manorama* was connected. These days, however, it's going stronger than ever: check out the English edition at ⓦ www.manoramaonline.com.

Kottayam's long history of Syrian-Christian settlement is reflected by the presence of two thirteenth-century churches on a hill 5km northwest of the centre, which you can get to by rickshaw. Two eighth-century Nestorian stone crosses with Palavi and Syriac inscriptions, on either side of the elaborately decorated altar of the **Valliapalli** ("big") church, are among the earliest solid traces of Christianity in India. The visitors' book contains entries from as far back as the 1890s, including one by the Ethiopian king, Haile Selassie, and a British viceroy. The interior of the nearby **Cheriapalli** ("small") church is covered with lively paintings, thought to have been executed by a Portuguese artist in the sixteenth century. If the doors are locked, ask for the key at the church office (9am–1pm & 2–5pm).

Practicalities

Kottayam's KSRTC **bus stand**, 500m south of the centre on TB Road (not to be confused with the private stand for local buses on MC Road), is an important stop on routes to and from major towns in South India. Four of the frequent buses to Kumily/Periyar (3–4hr) continue daily on to Madurai in Tamil Nadu (7hr), and there are regular services to Thiruvananthapuram, Kollam and Ernakulam. The **railway station**, 2km north of the centre, sees a constant flow of traffic between Thiruvananthapuram and points north, while **ferries** from Alappuzha and elsewhere dock at the weed-clogged jetty, 2km south of town. For details of backwater trips from Kottayam, see p.418.

DTPC maintain a tiny **tourist office** at the jetty (daily 9am–5pm; ⓣ 0481/256 0479). The best place to **change money** is the Canara Bank on KK Rd, which also has one of several **ATMs** around the main square. **Internet** facilities are available at Intimacy (Rs30/hr), also on KK Rd, just north of the KSRTC bus stand.

Accommodation

Accommodation in Kottayam is very limited for a town of its size. Those travellers that do pause here tend to do so in one of the resorts or homestays in the surrounding area (see p.426), although the following places in the town centre are fine for a night.

Aida TB Junction, MC Rd ⓣ 0481/256 8391, ⓦ www.hotelaidakerala.com. Large 1980s hotel on the south side of town with a wide range of dowdy, brown rooms, including some with a/c (only Rs150 extra), plus reasonably priced singles. There's a quiet restaurant (not recommended) and bar. ❹

Ambassador KK Rd ⓣ 0481/256 3293, ⓦ www .fhrai.com. Solid, old-fashioned economy place on the northeast side of town that's worn around the edges but well scrubbed. A/c costs only Rs50 extra, but the air coolers are noisy. ❷–❹

Arcadia TB Rd ⓣ 0481/256 9999, ⓦ www .arcadiahotels.net. The town's top hotel, occupying its tallest building – a towering, white, angular monster block just south of the centre. Its rooms look much nicer from the inside, however, and are very good value (especially the "standard doubles"); there's also a fantastic rooftop pool on the 14th floor, as well as a restaurant (*Déja Vu*; see p.426) and bar (*Fahrenheit*). ❻–❼

Homestead KK Rd ⓣ 0481/256 0467. The best mid-price option: "your key to a soft pillow" goes their slogan, though the beds in the economy rooms are rock hard and it's well worth shelling out an additional Rs130 for a "deluxe" with more space, better furniture and thicker mattresses. ❸–❻

Eating

Kottayam many not be a particularly alluring destination in itself, but it has a handful of very good **places to eat**.

Anand *Anand Lodge*, KK Rd, just off the main square. If you're only passing through and want a delicious, freshly cooked pure-veg thali, look no further than here. Of its two adjacent wings, the a/c family hall is the more relaxing (the meals only cost Rs10 more and it's blissfully cool inside). In addition to traditional "keep-it-coming" rice plates (Rs30) with three or four vegetables, *rasam*, buttermilk and all the trimmings, they also do excellent Udupi snacks, including embarrassingly large paper-roast *dosas* over a metre in length.

Déja Vu *Hotel Arcadia*, TB Rd. Swish rooftop restaurant on the 14th floor of a business-oriented three-star. In a smart dining hall with polished marble floors, starched white napkins and wonderful panoramic views over the town, you can order from an exhaustive multi-cuisine menu (North and South India, Continental and Chinese); most mains Rs85–150.

Karimpunkala 6km south on the MC Rd, at Nattakom-Palam. This roadside place, which you'll need to catch an auto-rickshaw or taxi to reach if you don't have your own transport, is legendary in Kottayam for its sumptuous, village-style seafood *sadhyas*, featuring *karimeen pollichadu* (spiced *karimeen* fish steamed in a banana leaf), *kakairachi* (oysters) and proper *kappa* (tapioca), as well as moreish, crusty-edged *appam*. Count on Rs100–150 for the works.

Meenachil *Homestead Hotel*, KK Rd. Quality non-veg Keralan food – Kuttanadi chicken curry, *karimeen pollichadu* – plus Punjabi-style tandoori and Chinese duck dishes, served in a popular little hotel restaurant close to the centre. It's a/c, the service is speedy and the rates restrained (with most mains Rs75–100). They also do set Keralan "meals" (Rs45 for veg; Rs58 non-veg).

Around Kottayam

Some of Kerala's most attractive backwater scenery lies within easy reach of Kottayam. Probably the ideal destination for a day-trip – although it also has some wonderful accommodation – the beautiful **Kumarakom Bird Sanctuary** lies on the shore of Vembanad Lake to the west. **Aranmula**, to the south, is one of the last villages still making *kannadi* metal mirrors, and has a Krishna temple which organizes a ritual "non-competitive" boat race. The Mahadeva temple at **Ettumanur**, a short way north of Kottayam, is known to devotees as the home of a dangerous and wrathful Shiva and to art lovers as a sublime example of temple architecture, adorned with wood-carvings and murals (some of which, for once, are viewable by non-Hindus). Frescoes of a very different kind, dating from the eighteenth-century, adorn one of the region's oldest churches at **Palai**, a fifteen-minute drive northeast of Ettumanur in an area that sees very few visitors.

Kumarakom

KUMARAKOM, 10km west of Kottayam, is spread over a cluster of islands on Vembanad Lake, surrounded by a tangle of lush tropical waterways and low-lying paddy fields. It was here that the British missionary **Henry Baker** chose to reclaim land to make a small rubber and fruit farm in the 1820s, which was subsequently expanded by his descendants into a full-blown plantation. After Independence, the estate and its main house was ceded to the government, who designated the core area abutting the lakeside as a nature reserve. Due to its easy accessibility by road from Kottayam, this has since become the focus of a boom in backwater tourism, with a row of large luxury resorts lined up along the water's edge. Baker, meanwhile, became immortalized as the "Kari Saippu" (Black Sahib) of Arundhati Roy's *The God of Small Things* – the author grew up in a nearby village – while his house, featured as the ghostly "History House" in the novel, has been converted into a luxury hotel by Taj Group.

Kumarakom can be reached quite easily by bus (every 20–30min) from Kottayam, which lies 15km to the east. The best time to visit the **Bird Sanctuary** (daily dawn–dusk; Rs45), occupying the westernmost island of Baker's former estate, is between November and March, when it serves as a winter home for many migratory birds, some from as far away as Siberia. Species include the darter or snake bird, little cormorant, night heron, golden-backed woodpecker, crow pheasant, white-breasted water hen and tree pie. Dawn is the quietest and best time for viewing. Although the island is quite small, a guide is useful; you can arrange one through any of the hotels.

Birds, or representations of them, feature prominently in the area's most bizarre visitor attraction, the **Bay Island Driftwood Museum** (daily 10am–6pm; Rs50; W www.bay-island-museum.com), just off the main road on the outskirts of Kumarakom. While out on rambles along the shoreline of the distant Andaman Islands (see p.679), schoolteacher Raji Punnoose used to collect lumps of driftwood, twisted and worn into shapes resembling animals, birds, fish and people. Once finishing touches had been applied with a chisel and varnish, these were shipped home to form the basis of a curious exhibition. Raji guides visitors through the highlights with a breathless commentary that's as idiosyncratic and entertaining as the pieces themselves. Allow at least an hour for the full tour.

Aranmula

The village of **ARANMULA** offers another appealing day-trip from Kottayam (start early), 30km to the south. Its ancient temple is dedicated to Parthasarathy, the divine name under which Krishna acted as Arjuna's charioteer during the bloody Kurekshetra war (recorded in the Mahabharata; see p.810), and the guise in which he expounded the Bhagavad Gita. About 1800 years old, the temple is a major site on the Vishnaivite pilgrimage trail in Kerala, and, as Vishnu is represented here in the form of Annadanaprabhu ("One Who Gives Food"), it is said that no pilgrim worshipping at the temple will go hungry. Each year, towards the end of the Onam festival (Aug/Sept), a **Snake Boat Regatta** is celebrated as part of the temple rituals, and crowds line the banks of the Pampa River to cheer on the thrusting longboats (similar to those seen at Alappuzha; see p.411).

Aranmula is also known for the manufacture of extraordinary *kannadi* **metal mirrors** (called Aranmula *valkannadi*), produced using the "lost wax" technique (see p.761) with an alloy of copper, silver, brass, white lead and bronze. Once a prerequisite of royal households, these ornamental mirrors are now exceedingly rare; only a handful of master craftsmen and their families still make them. The most modest models cost around Rs300–400, while custom-made mirrors can cost Rs50,000 or more.

The **Vijana Kala Vedi Cultural Centre** in Aranmula offers ways of "experiencing traditional India through the study of art and village life". Set up in 1977 by a French scholar, Louba Schild, it stages daily classes in *kathakali*, *mohiniyattam* and *bharatanatyam* dance, wood-carving, mural painting, cooking, *kalarippayattu*, Ayurvedic medicine and several Indian languages. Courses (five hours each day) cost US$230 per week, decreasing on a sliding scale the longer you stay (to $430 per month for a course of seven months or more). They also do shorter intensives on yoga, Ayurveda and *kathakali*. For further details, go to: W www.vijnanakalavedi.org.

Ettumanur

The magnificent Mahadeva temple at **ETTUMANUR**, 12km north of Kottayam on the road to Ernakulam, features a circular shrine, fine woodcarving and one of the earliest (sixteenth-century) and most celebrated of Keralan **murals**. The deity is Shiva in one of his most terrible aspects, described as *vaddikasula vada*, "one who takes his dues with interest" and is "difficult to please". His predominant mood is *raudra* (fury). Although the shrine is open only to Hindus, foreigners can see the courtyard murals, which may be photographed after obtaining a camera ticket (Rs20; video Rs50) from the counter on the left of the main entrance gateway (the priests may try to charge you considerably more, but if you insist on seeing a printed tariff will drop the price to the official one).

The murals are spread over two four-metre panels flanking the rear side of the main doorway. The most spectacular depicts Nataraja – Shiva – executing a cosmic *tandava* dance, trampling evil underfoot in the form of a demon. Swathed in cobras, he stands on one leg in a wheel of gold, with his matted locks fanning out amid a mass of flowers and snakes, while devotees gather round. Musical accompaniment is provided by Krishna on flute, three-headed Brahma on cymbals and, playing the ancient sacred Keralan *mizhavu* drum, Shiva's special rhythm expert Nandikesvara. Another noteworthy feature of the Ettumanur temple is its *valia vilakku*, a giant oil lamp at the entrance to the main shrine. Fed by constant streams of sesame oil donated by worshippers, it is supposed to have remained lit for over 450 years.

Ettumanur's ten-day **annual festival** (Feb/March) reflects the wealth of the temple, with elaborate celebrations including music. On the most important days, the eighth and tenth, priests bring out the temple's golden elephants – seven large specimens, each fashioned from 95 kilos of gold, and a smaller one half the weight – which were presented in the eighteenth century by Marthanda Varma, the raja of Travancore.

Palai

The small town of **PALAI**, 30km northeast of Kottayam, is home to the **Church of St Thomas**, renowned for its beautiful eighteenth-century **frescoes**. Buses from Kottayam and Kochi pull in frequently at the KSRTC **bus stand** next to the bell tower in the centre of town. From here, the church is a two-kilometre walk or auto-rickshaw ride east along the main road and over a small bridge; turn right into a lane which leads to St Thomas's.

Rebuilt several times (most recently in the eighteenth century), the church has a Portuguese-style white ornamental facade, with a squat spire and nave. Inside, a bizarre spiral pulpit carved from a single piece of teak stands under ceilings richly painted with gold leaf. The *pièce de résistance*, however, lies hidden behind the altar – you'll need to ask the resident caretaker for a candle. Extraordinarily well preserved in the darkness, a wall of exquisite frescoes rendered in earthy vegetable pigments depicts the life of St Thomas and Jesus as the Lamb of God.

The larger, more modern **church** alongside was built in 1981. A finger-bone relic of St Thomas is kept here and brought out for public viewing once a year on the Feast of the Magi (mid-Oct).

Accommodation around Kottayam

With a couple of exceptions, Kumarakom's **resort complexes** are resolutely upscale and exclusive, screened by the waters of Vembanad Lake on one side and by high walls and uniformed Gurkhas on the other. However, smaller, authentic **homestays** are also starting to mushroom in the backwaters and rubber plantations further from the lakeside, the majority of them in landed Syrian-Christian households.

Akkara Mariathuruthu ⓉO481/251 6951, Ⓦwwwakkara.in. Set on a bend in the Meenachil River, 5km northwest of Kottayam, this homestay is a model backwater B&B, offering an idyllic, typically Keralan setting, traditional architecture, comfortable rooms full of 1930s–50s period furniture, wonderful Syrian-Christian cuisine and an easygoing atmosphere. Hostess Mrs Shanta Kurian provides warm hospitality while giving her guests plenty of space to enjoy the peace and quiet. Phone ahead for directions; access is by dugout canoe. ➐

Coconut Lagoon Kumarakom ⓉO481/252 4491, Ⓦwww.cghearth.com. The original, and still the most stylish of the grand-scale luxury resorts in this area, reached by boat from Kavaratikara jetty, just north of the *Taj* (see below). The launch glides right into the heart of the complex: a miniature village of red-tiled "heritage bungalows" grouped around a transplanted 1860s mansion on the lakeshore. Although fitted with mod cons, the rooms have a traditional feel, with old wood, open-roofed bathrooms and some antique fixtures. A beautiful Ayurvedic centre, *kalari* pit and butterfly garden complete the picture. From around $300. ➒

GK's Riverview Thekkakarayil, Kottaparambil, near Pulikkuttssery, 4km by water from Kumarakom ⓉO481/259 7527, Ⓜm9447 197527, Ⓦwww.gkhomestay-kumarakom.com. Award-winning homestay, buried deep in the watery wilds between Kottayam and Kumarakom. The accommodation comprises four comfortable guest rooms in a separate block behind a family home, overlooking paddy fields. There's a garden and hammocks to lounge in, and host George Kutty takes visitors out in a canoe to look at the local snake boat and other sights. Delicious home-cooked food is also available. Phone ahead from Kottayam to be picked up (free if you stay two or more nights). ➎

Illikkalam Lake Resort Karottukayal, Kumarakom ⓉO481/0252 3282, Ⓦwww.kumarakomtourism.org. A nice little mid-price option: eight simple, spacious chalets (a/c or non-a/c) right on the waterside with waves lapping against the garden walls. Each has its own lake-facing sitout (with great views), and extra room to the rear side for children. The owner, a lawyer from Kottayam, stays on site, but this is more anonymous than a homestay, which some will prefer; meals available. ➏–➐

Kumarakom Lake Resort Kumarakom ⓉO481/252 4900 Ⓦwww.klresort.com. One of India's top spa resorts, built on a similarly opulent scale to *Coconut Lagoon*, with re-located "heritage villas" ranged around a huge pool and network of

canals, right on the lakeside – though it feels very artificial. Rates $300–1000. ➒

Lakeside Homestay Kumarakom ⓉO481/316 3332. A single cottage, recently built in traditional style with gabled roof and verandas, right on the lakeshore at an idyllic, breezy spot: all you can hear are the lapping waves and rustle of palms. A much more congenial option than many of the nearby resorts, at a fraction of the price (Rs1500 per double). Meals on request. The only catch is it's hard to find: turn off 4km before the *Taj*, when you see the *Shree Chitra Tourist Home* next to a small bridge. Advance booking is essential as there are only two rooms. ➏

Philip Kutty's Pallivathukal, near Ambika Market, Vechoor, 20km northwest of Kottayam ⓉO4829/276529, Ⓜm9895 075130, Ⓦwww.philipkuttysfarm.com. Luxury homestay on a working island farm, 40min drive from Kottayam in the remote backwaters of Vembanad Lake. Five beautifully-furnished villas, built in traditional style with whitewashed walls, tiled roofs, antique doors and open-plan interiors, offer private hideaways set back from the main farmhouse but close to the water's edge. Owner Anu, her son Philip and mother-in-law Aniamma create a welcoming family atmosphere, leading cookery classes and walking tours of the 50-acre plot where nutmeg, bananas, cocoa and pepper are grown organically. $230–280 in season. ➒

Serenity at Kanam Estate 20km east of Kottayam on the Kumily/Periyar (KK) Rd at Payikad, near Vazhoor ⓉO481/245 6353, Ⓦwww.malabarescapes.com. If your budget can stretch to it, this stylish boutique hotel, part of the German-run Malabar Escapes chain, makes the perfect stopover en route to the hills. Situated on a hilltop deep in a belt of rubber plantations and spice gardens, the dreamy 1920s bungalow holds six rooms, designed in eclectic style blending antique furniture with chic original art; all have sitouts or verandas. Facilities include a pool surrounded by cocoa trees, gym, yoga *shala*, Ayurvedic spa and mountain bikes. You're also invited to spend a day with the resident elephant. From $240 per double. ➒

Taj Garden Retreat Kumarakom ⓉO481/252 4377 Ⓦwww.tajhotels.com. The Baker family's Edwardian mansion – the "History House" of Arundhati Roy's *The God of Small Things* – stands as the nucleus of this five-star resort. Its old wooden floors, high ceilings and verandas have been extensively refurbished but retain much period character, though the plush a/c villas and cottages dotted around the grounds, with their pool and private lagoon, possess much less charm. From around $325. ➒

Periyar and around

One of the largest and most visited wildlife reserves in India, the **Periyar Wildlife Sanctuary** occupies 777 square kilometres of the Cardamom hills region of the Western Ghats. The majority of its visitors come in the hope of seeing **tigers** and **leopards** – and most leave disappointed, as the few that remain very wisely keep their distance, and there's only a slight chance of a glimpse even at the height of the dry season in April and May, when water shortages force the animals to congregate around the lakeshore. However, plenty of other animals survive in healthier numbers: elephant, *sambar*, Malabar giant squirrel, gaur, stripe-necked mongoose, wild boar and over 323 species of birds, including Nilgiri wood pigeon, purple-headed parakeet, tree pie and flycatchers. See Contexts p.765 for more on wildlife.

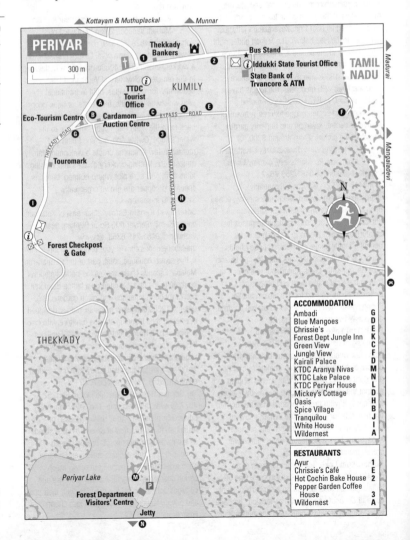

Located close to the Kerala–Tamil Nadu border, only a few kilometres off the national highway, Periyar makes a convenient place to break the long journey across the Ghats between Madurai and the coast. It's also a good base for day-trips into the Cardamom hills, with a couple of tea factories, spice plantations, the trailhead for the Sabarimala pilgrimage (see p.437), and numerous viewpoints and forest waterfalls within striking distance.

In addition, the park has a particularly enlightened conservation policy. Instead of earning their livelihoods through poaching and illegal sandalwood extraction, local Manna people in the Periyar area are employed by the Forest Department to protect vulnerable parts of the sanctuary. **Eco-tourism** initiatives such as the "Border Hiking", "Tiger Trail" and "Jungle Patrol" tours, in which visitors accompany the tribal wardens on their duties, both serve to promote community welfare and generate income for conservation work. Indigenous villagers also act as guides for forest walks and bullock cart rides.

Getting to Periyar

The base for exploring Periyar is the village of **Kumily**, a kilometre or so north of the main park entrance (known as **Thekkady**). The road that winds up through the undulating hills from Ernakulam and Kottayam makes for a slow drive but provides wonderful views across the Ghats. The route is dotted with churches and roadside shrines to St Francis, St George and the Virgin Mary – a charming Keralan blend of ancient and modern. Once you've climbed through the rubber-tree plantations into Idukki District, the mountains become truly spectacular, and the wide-floored valleys are carpeted with lush tea and cardamom plantations.

Buses from Kottayam (every 30min; 4hr), Ernakulam (10 daily; 6hr) and Madurai in Tamil Nadu (at least hourly; 5hr 30min) pull in to the scruffy bus stand east of Kumily's bazaar. **Auto-rickshaws** will run you from the bus stand to the visitor centre inside the park for around Rs40–50, stopping at the park entrance at Thekkady for you to pay the fee. The gates close at 6pm, after which you will have to show proof of an accommodation booking before they will let you in. If you are staying at the KTDC *Lake Palace*, the last boat is officially at 4pm but the hotel will arrange one during daylight hours.

Kumily

As beds inside the sanctuary are in short supply, most visitors stay in nearby **KUMILY**, a typical High Range town centred on a busy roadside bazaar. In recent years, hotels and Kashmiri handicrafts emporia have spread south from the market area to within a stone's throw of the park, and tourism now rivals the spice trade as the area's main source of income. That said, you'll still see plenty of little shops selling local herbs, essential oils and cooking spices, while in the busy **cardamom sorting yard** behind the *Spice Village* resort, rows of Manna women sift through heaps of fragrant green pods using heart-shaped baskets.

Idduki State **tourist office** (Mon–Sat 10am–5pm; ☏04869/222620) is just south of the bus stand. Besides offering information on the district itself, they organize tours, including a "spice valley" trip (6.30am–9.30pm; Rs250), which takes in Munnar and several spice plantations. To book any of the Periyar Tiger Reserve's own **eco-tourism tours** (see above), you'll have to walk down the Thekkady Road to the Eco-Tourism Centre on Ambadi Junction (daily 8am–6pm, last tickets sold at 5.30pm; ☏04869/224571).

Both the State Bank of Travancore, near the bus stand, and the Thekkady Bankers in the main bazaar can **change currency and traveller's cheques**; there's an ATM at the former. **Internet** facilities are available around Thekkady Junction for about Rs40 per hour.

Tours and treks around Kumily

As well as the attraction of the wildlife sanctuary, **tea factory** and **spice plantation tours** are offered by almost every hotel and tourist agency in Kumily. Unfortunately, many places have become heavily commercialized, so it's worth shopping around; often the best way to organize a tour is to ask at your hotel – most of the staff will have a relative who has a good plantation. The only certified organic spice garden in the area is the Aroma at Muthuplackal, 2km west of Kumily on the Kottayam road; for more details, contact the owner, Mr Sebastian, on ☏94953 67837. Most of the plantations charge around Rs300–500 per person for a three-hour tour with guide and vehicle.

A popular excursion for families is to **Elephant Junction** (daily 9am–6pm; ☏04869/320474), on the outskirts of Kumily just off the Murikkady road, where you can enjoy elephant rides, help with feeding and washing sessions in the river, and watch timber-dragging demonstrations. In addition, most winters see at least one baby tusker added to the resident herd – a child-friendly photo opportunity.

The windy, grassy ridgetops and forests around Periyar afford many fine **trekking** possibilities, with superb views over the High Range guaranteed. Ex-park wardens and other local people made redundant by the recent Eco-Tourism initiative (which reserved jobs for Manna tribal people) offer their services as guides through guesthouses, hotels and restaurants, and it can be worth employing someone for a day or more to show you the paths to the best viewpoints; check out their letters of recommendation and follow up tips from fellow visitors. One half-day route that's straightforward to attempt on your own is the ninety-minute hike up **Kurusamalai**, the prominent peak towering to the northwest of Kumily, whose summit is crowned with a Holy Cross. Follow the Kottayam road out of the main bazaar for just over fifteen minutes, until you see a turning to the left (just before the *Holiday Homestay*). From here, a track leads uphill through a string of small Manna villages to the peak, steepening the higher you climb. The owner of the *Green View* homestay in Kumily (see opposite) hands out photocopies of a roughly drawn map that will help with route finding.

Although hilly, this area is also good **cycling** territory; **bicycle rental** is available from several stalls in the market. For more physical trips into the mountains, Touromark (☏04869/224332, ⓦwww.touromark.com), midway between Kumily and Thekkady, have imported 21-speed **mountain bikes** for rent. They also offer guided trips, ranging from four-hour/fifteen-kilometre hacks through local spice gardens, coffee plantations and woodlands to longer expeditions, such as the three-night/four-day ride across the Cardamom Hills from Periyar to Munnar.

From the Eco-Tourism Centre at Ambadi Junction, the Forest Department run **village tours** (6am–2.30pm; Rs750) to a remote tribal settlement on the Tamil Nadu side of the mountains bordering Periyar. You're transported 10km by taxi to the start of the route, which is covered by **bullock cart** and **coracle** through a variety of different habitats and farmland. Profits go the development of the local community.

Accommodation

Kumily has **accommodation** to suit all pockets, offering particularly good value in lower price brackets, thanks to the recent proliferation of small homestay guesthouses on the fringes of the village. At the opposite end of the scale are some truly gorgeous colonial-era hideaways deep in the mountains which you'll need a car and driver to reach, but which provide atmospheric bases for explorations of lesser-visited corners of the High Range. For accommodation is the sanctuary itself, see p.436

Budget

Blue Mangoes Bypass Rd ☏ 04869/224603, ☏ m98951 87789. Simple attached rooms (with sitouts and balconies) in an impeccably clean modern block. Rock-bottom rates, but good bedding and a quiet location. Owner Bobby speaks excellent English. ❷–❸

Green View Bypass Rd ☏ 04869/211015, ☏ m94474 32008. One of Kumily's most popular homestays, in a newish house just off the Thekkady road. Offers 17 differently priced rooms, from basic Rs200 options with bucket hot water to large attached ones equipped with solar-heated showers and balconies looking across the valley to Kurusmalai mountain. A lovely rear garden attracts lots of wild birds. If it's full, try the identically priced *Rose Garden* next door (☏ 04869/223146). ❸–❺

Jungle View on the eastern edge of town ☏ 04869/223582, ☏ m94461 36407. The best-value budget homestay in Kumily, a 10min plod (or Rs15-auto-rickshaw ride) from the bus stand – literally on the Tamil Nadu–Kerala border. The clean, bright, attached bedrooms are all comfortably furnished; those on the upper storey are larger, opening onto a deep, marble-floored veranda only metres away from jungle. Nocturnal wildlife spotting walks into the adjacent forest are offered as a complimentary extra. ❹–❺

Kairali Palace Bypass Rd ☏ 04869/224604, ☏ m98951 87789. Outstandingly attractive homestay in a fusion building that blends traditional and modern styles, with gabled roofs, and wooden railings wrapped around the airy first-floor terrace. Its attached rooms are all well furnished for the price. ❸–❺

Mickey's Cottage Bypass Rd ☏ 04869/222196, ☏ m94472 84160. One of the oldest guesthouses in Kumily, whose smiling owner, Sujata, offers a range of differently priced rooms and cottages, all with balconies or sitouts littered with relaxing cane furniture. The more expensive ones are larger and come with more outside space. ❸–❹

Oasis Thamarakandam Rd ☏ 04869/223544, ☏ m94479 07890, ✉ oasisthekkady@yahoo.com. Large, new rooms sharing common verandas that look out across the treetops on the village's eastern fringes. Meals are served on the ground floor in a sunken lounge area, next to a kitchen which guests are welcome to use for self-catering. Clean, quiet, secure and good value. ❸–❹

Tranquilou Thamarakandam Rd ☏ 04869/223269, ☏ m94476 12149. Sunny south-facing budget rooms, or shadier, more snugly furnished "deluxe" ones with wood ceilings, in a modern house right on the edge of the forest. Comforts include piped hot water and cane swings to lounge on. ❸–❹

White House Thekkady Rd ☏ 04869/222987. A mixed but very good-value bag of bamboo huts, tree houses and rooms, handily placed for the park gates and run in a very welcoming fashion by owner Mrs Lily Joseph. Pick of the bunch are her two rear-side doubles, whose balconies have lovely green views into the sanctuary. ❷–❸

Mid-range

Ambadi Ambadi Junction, Thekkady Rd ☏ 04869/222193, ⊛ www.hotelambadi.com. Wood and red bricks dominate the architecture of this hotel, packed higgledy-piggledy onto the side of the road to the park. It offers three categories of rooms, all excellent value and with lots of Keralan character. Best are the "duplexes", which have beds on mezzanine floors and balconies sporting old-style pillars overlooking woodland. The location's busy during the day, but quiet in the evenings. ❺–❻

Chrissie's Bypass Rd ☏ 04869/224155, ☏ m94476 01304, ⊛ www.chrissies.in. Smart new four-storey hotel below the bazaar, run by expats Chrissie (from the UK) and Adel (from Egypt). It's pricier than most homestays in the area, but you get more privacy and better views, and relaxing, homely interiors featuring throws in warm colours, beds carved from local wood and watercolours of Dorset hanging on the walls. There's also a great yoga *shala* on the rooftop, and popular little café-restaurant on the ground floor (see p.434 for review). ❺–❻

Wildernest Thekkady Rd ☏ 04869/224030, ⊛ www .wildernest-kerala.com. *Wildernest's* ten quirkily designed rooms are the most appealing option in this bracket, despite their proximity to the main road. With high, slanted ceilings, red oxide floors and white walls, they're more like little maisonettes: wood staircases wind up to terraces overlooking the central courtyard, and French windows open on to secluded, private gardens. Rates include generous breakfasts. **❼**

Luxury

Green Mansions Gavi ☎04869/224571. Deep in the tropical forest lining the state border, this remote, Forest Department-run eco-lodge stands on a low hillock overlooking Gavi Lake. Its bungalow accommodation, reached via a bone-jarring 30km Jeep ride from Kumily, is simple, bordering on institutional, but perfectly comfortable and well placed for jungle trekking and wildlife-spotting trips. Tariffs (from $100 per person) include obligatory full board. Book through the Eco-Tourism Centre in Kumily. **❾**

Shalimar Spice Garden Murikaddy, 6km from Kumily ☎04869/222132, ⓦwww.shalimarkerala.net. Teak huts in traditional Keralan style, on the edge of an old cardamom and pepper estate, with elephant-grass roofs, whitewashed walls, chic interiors and verandas looking straight onto forest. Facilities include a beautiful Ayurveda centre, an outdoor pool set amid the trees and an open-sided restaurant where you can fine dine off rough-hewn granite tables. Rates $180–220. **❾**

Spice Village Thekkady Rd ☎04869/222514, ⓦwww.cghearth.com. Part of the green-conscious CGH Earth chain, this campus of mock-tribal huts is the first choice of most luxury tour groups. Its wooden thatched cottages (from $275) are dotted around substantial landscaped gardens planted with spices and flowering trees. There's also a smart restaurant, a pool, and a special wildlife resource centre where guests can attend daily lectures on Periyar's flora and fauna. **❾**

Eating

You're more likely to take meals at your guesthouse or hotel than eat out in Kumily, but for a change of scene the following are the best options within walking distance of the bazaar.

Ayur west side of the main bazaar. Quality South Indian thali "meals" (Rs50), freshly made each day and served on banana leaves from a buffet. It's more hygienic (and less manic) than the competition further down the main street. *Ginger*, upstairs, is a swisher a/c alternative offering an exhaustive Indian-Chinese-Continental menu.

Chrissie's Café Bypass Rd. This relaxing expat-run café, on the ground floor of a hotel of the same name, pulls in a steady stream of foreigners throughout the day and evening for its delicious pizzas and pasta bakes (Rs120–160), made with Kodai mozzarella; check out the specials board. They also do healthy breakfasts of muesli with fresh fruit, crunchy cereal, toast with home-made bread and cakes, with proper coffee. Count on Rs250 per head.

Hot Cochin Bake House main bazaar. The best of a pretty unimpressive batch of "meals" places on the east side of the main street, close to the bus stand. Most people come at lunchtimes for the tasty fish curry thali, with optional *avioli* (pearlspot) masala fry, served on china plates instead of the usual tin trays or leaves.

Pepper Garden Coffee House Thamarkandam Rd. In a garden filled with cardamom bushes behind a prettily painted blue-and-green house, a former park guide and his wife whip up tempting travellers' breakfasts (date and raisin pancakes, porridge with jungle honey, fresh coffee and Nilgiri tea), in addition to home-cooked lunches of veg fried rice, curry and dhal, using mostly local organic produce. Mains Rs20–75.

Wildernest Thekkady Rd. Filling continental buffet breakfasts (fruit, juices, cereals, eggs, toast, peanut butter, home-made jams and freshly ground coffee; Rs100) served on polished wood tables in the ground floor café of a stylish small hotel. In the afternoons they also do tea and cakes (including a particularly delicious, very British warm plum cake).

The Sanctuary

Centred on a vast artificial **lake** created by the British in 1895 to supply water to the drier parts of neighbouring Tamil Nadu, the Periyar Wildlife Sanctuary lies at altitudes of between 900m and 1800m, and is correspondingly cool: temperatures range from 15°C to 30°C. The royal family of Travancore, anxious to preserve favourite hunting grounds from the encroachment of tea plantations, declared it a forest reserve, and built the Edapalayam Lake Palace to accommodate their guests in 1899. It expanded as a wildlife reserve in

1933, and once again when it became part of **Project Tiger** in 1979 (see Contexts, p.769).

Seventy percent of the protected area, which is divided into core, buffer and tourist zones, is covered with evergreen and semi-evergreen forest. The **tourist zone** – logically enough, the part accessible to casual visitors – surrounds the lake, and consists mostly of semi-evergreen and deciduous woodland interspersed with grassland, both on hilltops and in the valleys. Although excursions on the lake (either by diesel-powered launch or paddle-powered bamboo raft) are the standard ways to experience the park, you can get much more out of a visit by **walking** with a local guide in a small group away from the crowd. However, avoid the period immediately after the monsoons, when **leeches** make hiking virtually impossible.

The **best time to visit** is from December until April, when the dry weather draws animals from the forest to drink at the lakeside.

Park practicalities

The **entrance fee** is Rs150 for foreigners [Rs12] for the first day, and Rs50 on subsequent days. If you're staying inside the park you must buy a new pass for each day you stay, either from the entrance gate or from the Forest Information Centre by the jetty. KTDC's hectic and uncomfortable **weekend tours** to Periyar from Kochi, calling at Kadamattom and Idukki Dam en route (Sat 7.30am–Sun 8pm), are not recommended unless you're really pushed for time.

Boat trips

KTDC's **boat trips** on the lake (daily at 7am, 9.30am, 11.30am, 2pm & 4pm; 2hr; Rs45 for the lower deck, Rs100 for the upper deck, which is less cramped and has a better view) are in large double-decker launches with noisy engines. The Forest Department also runs its own boats (9.30am, 11.30am, 2pm and 4pm; Rs35); they're smaller and shabbier, but can get closer to the banks of the lake (and thus the wildlife). Tickets for both services are sold through the Forest Department hatch just above the main **visitor centre** (daily 7am–6pm; ☏04869/222027) at the end of the road into the park.

It's unusual to see many animals from the boats – engine noise and the presence of a hundred other people make sure of that – but if you're lucky you might spot a group of elephants, wild boar and *sambar* grazing by the water's edge. To maximize your chances of wildlife sightings, take the 7am service (wear warm clothing) and try for a ticket on the upper deck if there are any left (most tend to be block-booked by the luxury hotels).

Better still, sign up for one of the Forest Department's excellent **bamboo rafting trips**, which start with a short hike from the boat jetty at 8am and return at 5pm, with a minimum of three hours spent on the water. The rafts carry four or five people and, because they're paddled rather than motordriven, can approach the lakeshore in silence, allowing you to get closer to the grazing animals and birds. Tickets cost Rs1000 per person and may be booked in advance from the Eco-Tourism Centre on Ambadi Junction.

Walks and treks

Although you can – leeches permitting – trek freely around the fringes of Periyar, access to the Sanctuary itself on foot is strictly controlled by the Forest Department. Their community-based Eco-Tourism Programme offers a variety of structured **walking tours**, ranging from short rambles to three-day expeditions, all guided by local Manna tribal wardens. Tickets should be booked in advance from the Eco-Tourism Centre on Ambadi Junction, where you can also pick up brochures and leaflets on the trips.

The **Nature Walk** (7am, 11am & 2pm; Rs100 per person) is the least demanding option, covering 4–5km of level evergreen and moist deciduous forest. Groups of up to five people are led by a single guide who identifies trees, plants and wildlife. You can also do a similar walk at night: the **Jungle Patrol** (7–10pm & 10pm–1am; Rs500) is loaded with atmosphere and the sounds of the forest, though you probably won't get to see much more than the odd pair of eyes picked out in a torch beam. For scenery, a better option is the full-day **Border Hiking** tour (8am–5pm; Rs1000 per person), which takes you into grassland and thick jungle at altitudes of between 900 and 1300m. Finally, the **Periyar Tiger Trail** (Rs3000–5000) is the one for committed trekkers. Guided by former poachers, the itinerary lasts for one night and two days, or two nights and three days. Armed guards equipped with walkie-talkies accompany the group, trekking through 35km of hill country, thick forest and grassland to top wildlife-spotting sites in the Periyar Sanctuary, sleeping outdoors in tent camps and eating vegetarian food prepared on kerosene stoves and open fires.

Accommodation and eating in the sanctuary

For the *Lake Palace*, *Periyar House* and the *Aranya Nivas* you should book in advance at the KTDC offices in Thiruvananthapuram or Ernakulam – essential if you plan to come on a weekend, a public holiday, or during **peak season** (Dec–March), when rooms are often in short supply.

Forest Department Jungle Inn 3km east of Kumily at Kokkara, off the Mangaladevi Temple Road. Located an hour's walk (3km) into the park, this simple "forest cottage" sits in a glade frequented by langur monkeys and giant tree squirrels. It's cramped and overpriced, though the location is serene and does allow you to be in position early for the wildlife. Tariffs include half-board; check-out is 9am. Book through the Eco-Tourism Centre at Ambadi Junction. ❼

KTDC Aranya Nivas Near the boat jetty, Thekkady ☎04869/222282, ⓦwww.ktdc.com. Plusher than *Periyar House*, this colonial manor has some huge rooms ($100–150), a pleasant garden and pool, multi-cuisine restaurant, bar and plenty of marauding wild monkeys to keep you entertained. Full board and upper-deck tickets for two boat trips are included in the tariff. ❽–❾

KTDC Lake Palace Across the lake from the visitor centre ☎04869/222023, ⓦwww.ktdc.com. The sanctuary's most luxurious hotel, with six suites in a converted maharajah's game lodge surrounded by forest. Wonderful views extend from the charmingly old-fashioned rooms and lawns – this has to be one of the few places in India where you stand a chance of spotting tiger and wild elephant while sipping tea on your own veranda. Full-board only at $210 per double room. ❾

KTDC Periyar House Midway between the park gates and the boat jetty, Thekkady ☎04869/9222026, ⓦwww.ktdc.com. Close to the lake, with a restaurant, bar and balcony overlooking the monkey-filled woods leading down to the waterside. Not as nice a location as the neighbouring *Aranya Nivas*, but a lot cheaper. Ask for a lake-facing room. ❺–❼

Around Periyar and Kumily: the Cardamom Hills

Periyar and Kumily are convenient springboards from which to explore Kerala's beautiful **Cardamom Hills**. Guides will approach you at Thekkady with offers of trips by Jeep; if you can get a group together, these can be good value. Among the more popular destinations is the **Mangaladevi temple**,

14km east. The rough road to this ancient ruin deep in the forest is sometimes closed due to flood damage, but when it is open the round trip takes about five hours. With a guide, you can also reach remote waterfalls and mountain viewpoints offering panoramic views of the Tamil Nadu plains. Rates vary according to the season, but expect to pay around Rs500–600 for a Jeep-taxi, and an additional Rs200 for a guide. An easy day-trip by bus (or as part of a local plantation tour) from Kumily, the grand viewpoint of **Chellarkovil** is right on the edge of the mountains, with the endless green plains of Tamil Nadu falling away below. To get here, take a bus or Jeep to the village of Anakkara, 15km north of Kumily, and jump on a rickshaw for the last 4km through the paddy fields to Chellarkovil; hang onto your driver if you don't want to walk back to the bus.

The Ayappa cult

During December and January, Kerala is packed with huge crowds of men wearing black or blue *dhotis*; you'll see them milling about train stations, driving in overcrowded and gaily decorated Jeeps and cooking a quick meal on the roadside by their tour bus. These men are all pilgrims on their way to the Shri Ayappa forest temple (also known as Hariharaputra or Shasta) at **Sabarimala**, in the Western Ghat mountains, around 200km from both Thiruvananthapuram and Kochi. The **Ayappa devotees** can seem disconcertingly ebullient, chanting "*Swamiyee Sharanam Ayappan*" ("give us protection, god Ayappa") in a call and response style reminiscent of English football fans.

Ayappa – the offspring of a union between Shiva and Mohini, Vishnu's beautiful female form – is primarily a Keralan deity, but his appeal has spread phenomenally in the last thirty years across South India, to the extent that this is said to be **the second largest pilgrimage in the world**, with as many as a million devotees each year. Pilgrims are required to remain celibate, abstain from intoxicants, and keep to a strict vegetarian diet for a period of 41 days prior to setting out on the four-day walk through the forest from the village of **Erumeli** (61km, as the crow flies, northwest) to the shrine at Sabarimala. Less keen devotees take the bus to the village of Pampa, and join the five-kilometre queue. When they arrive at the modern temple complex, pilgrims who have performed the necessary penances may ascend the famous eighteen **gold steps** to the inner shrine. There they worship the deity, throwing donations down a chute that opens onto a subterranean conveyor belt, where the money is counted and bagged.

The pilgrimage reaches a climax during the festival of **Makara Sankranti**, when massive crowds of over 1.5 million congregate at Sabarimala. On January 14, 1999, 51 devotees were buried alive when part of a hill crumbled under the crush of a stampede. The devotees had gathered at dusk to catch a glimpse of the final sunset of *makara jyoti* ("celestial light") on the distant hill of Ponnambalamedu.

Although **males** of any age and even of any religion can take part in the pilgrimage, **females** between the ages of nine and fifty are barred. This rule, still vigorously enforced by the draconian temple oligarchy, was contested in 1995 by a bizarre court case. Following complaints to local government that facilities and hygiene at Sabarimala were substandard, the local Collector, a 42-year-old woman, insisted she be allowed to inspect the site. The temple authorities duly refused, citing the centuries-old ban on women of menstrual age, but the High Court, who earlier upheld the gender bar, was obliged to overrule the priests' decision. The collector's triumphant arrival at Sabarimala soon after made headline news, but she was still not allowed to enter the shrine proper.

For advice on how to visit Sabarimala, via a back route beginning at Kumily near the Periyar Wildlife Sanctuary, see p.438.

Sabarimala

The other possible day-trip from Kumily, though one that should not be under-taken lightly (or, according to Hindu lore, by pre-menopausal women), is to the Sri Ayappan forest shrine at **Sabarimala** (see p.437). This remote and sacred site can be reached in a long day-trip, but you should leave with a pack of provi-sions, as much water as you can carry and plenty of warm clothes in case you get stranded. Jeep-taxis wait outside Kumily bus stand to transport pilgrims to the less frequented of Sabarimala's two main access points at a windswept mountaintop 13km above the temple (2hr; Rs50 per person if the Jeep is carrying ten passengers). Peeling off the main Kumily–Kottayam road at **Vandiperiyar**, the route takes you through tea estates to the start of an appall-ingly rutted forest track. After a long and spectacular climb, this emerges at a grass-covered plateau where the Jeeps stop. You proceed on foot, following a well-worn path through superb old-growth jungle, complete with hanging creepers and monkeys crashing through the high canopy, to the temple complex at the foot of the valley – a surreal spread of concrete sheds and walkways in the middle of the jungle. Allow at least two hours for the descent, and an hour or two more for the climb back up to the roadhead, for which you'll need plenty of drinking water – the cars wait till sunset. The alternative route from Kumily to Sabarimala involves a Jeep ride on a forest road to **Uppupara** (42km), with a final walk of 6km through undulating country. Given the very real risks involved with missing the last Jeep back to Kumily (the mountaintop is prime elephant and tiger country), it's advisable to get a group together and rent a 4WD for the day (about Rs900 including waiting time).

Munnar and around

MUNNAR, 130km east of Kochi and 110km north (four-and-a-half hours by bus) of the Periyar Wildlife Sanctuary, is the centre of Kerala's principal tea-growing region. A scruffy agglomeration of corrugated iron-roofed cottages and tea factories, its centre on the valley floor fails to live up to its tourist-office billing as "hill station", but there's plenty to enthuse about in the surrounding mountains, whose lower slopes are carpeted with lush tea gardens and dotted with quaint old colonial bungalows. Above them, the grassy ridges and crags of the High Range – including peninsular India's highest peak, **Ana Mudi** (2695m) – offer superla-tive trekking routes, many of which can be tackled in day-trips from the town.

It's easy to see why the pioneering Scottish planters who developed this hidden valley in the 1870s and 1880s felt so at home here. At an altitude of around 1600m, Munnar enjoys a refreshing climate, with crisp mornings and sunny blue skies in the winter – though as with all of Kerala, torrential rains descend during the monsoons. When the mists clear, the mountain summits form a wild backdrop to the carefully manicured tea plantations below.

Munnar's greenery and cool air draws streams of well-heeled honeymooners and weekenders from the metropolitan cities of South India. However, increasing numbers of foreign travellers are stopping here for a few days too, enticed by the superbly scenic bus ride from Periyar, which takes you across the high ridges and lush tropical forests of the Cardamom Hills, or for the equally spectacular climb across the Ghats from Madurai. Recent seasons have also seen the emergence of some wonderful **heritage** and **homestay accommoda-tion,** much of it in restored British bungalows, where you can sip High Range tea on lawns against vistas of rolling estates and mountains.

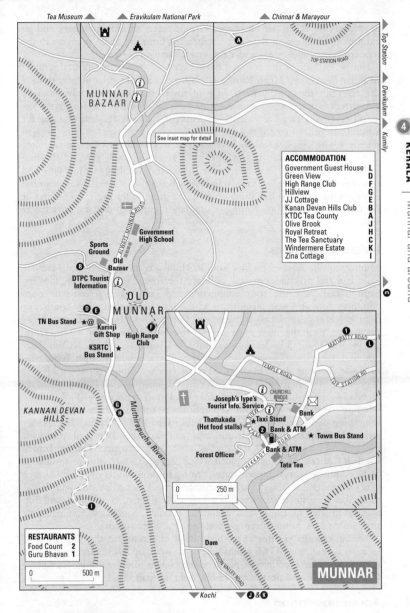

TOP STATION ROAD

Ⓐ

MUNNAR
BAZAAR

ⓘ
ⓘ

See inset map for detail

ACCOMMODATION

Government Guest House	L
Green View	D
High Range Club	F
Hillview	G
JJ Cottage	E
Kanan Devan Hills Club	B
KTDC Tea County	A
Olive Brook	J
Royal Retreat	H
The Tea Sanctuary	C
Windermere Estate	K
Zina Cottage	I

ALWAYE MUNNAR ROAD

Government
High School

Sports
Ground

Ⓑ

Old
Bazaar

DTPC Tourist
Information ⓘ

OLD
MUNNAR

Ⓓ Ⓔ

TN Bus Stand ★@

Kurinji
Gift Shop

High Range
Club Ⓕ

KSRTC
Bus Stand ★

KANNAN DEVAN
HILLS

Ⓖ
Ⓗ

Muthirapuzha River

Ⓘ

MATUPATTY ROAD

Ⓘ

Ⓛ

TEMPLE ROAD

TOP STATION RD

ⓘ CHURCHILL
BRIDGE

Joseph's Iype's
Tourist Info. Service ⓘ

†

Thattukada
(Hot food stalls)

★ Taxi Stand

Ⓑ Bank & ATM

Bank & ATM

Forest Officer

Bank

★ Town Bus Stand

THEKKADY ROAD

Tata Tea

0   250 m

Ⓖ

RESTAURANTS

Food Count	2
Guru Bhavan	1

0   500 m

Dam

BISON VALLEY ROAD

MUNNAR

The Town

Clustered around the confluence of three mountain streams, Munnar town is a typical hill bazaar of haphazard buildings and congested market streets, which you'll probably want to escape at the first opportunity. The one sight of note is the **Tea Museum** (Tues–Sun 9am–4pm; Rs50), 2km northwest of the centre on Nallathany Road, which houses various pieces of old machinery and an exhibition of photos of the area's tea industry, from the 1880s pioneers to the modern Kanan-Devan era under the Tata tea conglomerate.

The social hub of the colonial period, and an important cultural icon in Munnar, the famous **High Range Club** is perched on a balcony overlooking the river on the southeastern edge of town. Indians were only officially permitted to enter the premises as recently as 1948, but these days non-members of any race are welcome to visit the typically Raj-era building for a round of golf, or to enjoy a gin and tonic served on the lawns by liveried retainers. The clock seems to have stopped ticking somewhere in the late-1940s at the men-only bar, whose walls are hung with rows of hunting trophies and topees. The old hats were signed and dated by planters who had survived thirty years of service in the High Range tea estates. Aside from the ban on women in the bar, stiff-upper-lipped dress codes apply: no t-shirts or sandals, and after 7pm on Saturdays, men are required to don a dinner jacket and tie.

Practicalities

Munnar can be reached by **bus** from Kochi, Kottayam, Kumily and Madurai. State-run and private services all pull into the Town bus stand in the modern main bazaar, near the river confluence and Tata headquarters; state ones continue through town, terminating at the bus stands nearly 3km south. For most hotels you should ask to be dropped off at **Old Munnar**, 2km south of the centre, near the ineffectual DTPC **tourist office** (daily 8.30am–7pm; ☎04865/231516). A better source of **information** on transport, accommodation and day-trips, including to Eravikulam, is the helpful **Joseph Iype**, who runs the **Tourist Information Service** (no set hours; ☎04865/231136, ☎m94471 90954) from a small office in the main bazaar. Immortalized in Dervla Murphy's *On a Shoestring to Coorg* and more recently by Booker-Prize winning Arundhati Roy, this self-appointed tourist officer has become something of a legend. He has some useful **maps** and newspaper articles, can arrange **transport** for excursions, and will doubtless bombard you with background on the area. A few metres north is the **Munnar Tourist Information Centre** (daily 10am–8pm; ☎04865/230552), a government-sponsored body whose primary concern appears to be to promote its own guided tour (daily 9am–5pm; Rs250). Designed mainly for Indian tourists, the whistlestop tour takes in a spice plantation, boating, a dairy farm, view points and Top Station in the morning, and Rajmalai Wildlife Sanctuary, waterfalls, an amusement park in the afternoon and sunset at a viewpoint.

You can **change money** at the State Bank of Travancore, the State Bank of India or at numerous ATMs around the town (see map, p.439). **Internet** access is available from a couple of places around town, such as Alpha Computer Centre (Rs50/hour), next to the Tamil Nadu bus stand.

Accommodation

The cost of Munnar's **accommodation** is significantly higher than elsewhere in the High Range region, reflecting the pressure on beds caused by the town's popularity with middle-class tourists from the big cities. Rooms at the low end of the scale are in particularly short supply; the few we found were blighted by constant racket from the bus stand and bazaar, and are thus not listed below. On the plus side, the hill station does possess a couple of wonderfully genteel Raj-era places to stay, still redolent of the

Empire in its twilight days, while further afield in the hills around Munnar, the tea plantations and cardamom groves harbour several beautiful heritage bungalows and homestays overlooking some of the most magnificent mountain scenery in south India.

Budget

Green View Shri Parvati Amman Kovil St, near the KSRTC bus stand ☎04865/230189, ☎m94478 25447, ⊛www.greenviewmunnar .com. Clean and friendly budget guesthouse on the valley floor, down a side road just off the main drag, with rooms of various sizes – the best of them #402, a tiny double on the rooftop that has big windows and hill views. Pitched squarely at foreign backpackers, it's run by an enthusiastic, competent young crew who do a sideline in guided day treks. ❶–❸

JJ Cottage Shri Parvati Amman Kovil St, near the KSRTC bus stand ☎04865/230104. Next door to *Green View*, and very much in the same mould, though it's been open longer, charges higher rates and tends to get booked up earlier in the day. Like its neighbour, the nicest of its clean, differently sized rooms is the one at the top (front side), which has wood panel walls and fine views. ❸–❹

Kanan Devan Hills Club Kanan Devan Hills Rd ☎04865/230252, ☎kdhclub@rediffmail.com. The budget traveller's answer to the High Range Club: a typical colonial bungalow, actually built in 1983 but in Raj style with corrugated roofs, wooden verandas and coir carpets; the attached rooms are good value for Munnar. ❹

Zina Cottage Kad ☎04865/230349, ☎m94471 90954. Gorgeous British-era stone bungalow, nestled amid tea gardens high on the hillside above Munnar. Its flower-filled front terrace has magnificent views across the town to Ana Mudi, and host Joseph Iype (see opposite) will fill you in on local walks over flasks of hot tea in his sitting room. The rooms themselves lack outlook and are basic and gloomy, and you'll probably need a pile of blankets at night, but all have their own entrances and bathrooms. This is somewhere you'd stay more for the atmosphere than creature comforts, and it has plenty of it. ❹

Mid-range

Government Guest House Mattupatty Rd ☎04865/230385. On the far side of the river, around the hillside from the main bazaar, this former British bungalow stands in its own grounds looking across the valley. It has just six rooms, lined up in an annexe just above the main reception and dining room area. They're large and dowdy, and lack outside space, but have big bathrooms. Meals by arrangement. ❺

High Range Club Kanan Devan Hills ☎04865/230253, ☎hrcmunnar@sify.com. This old Raj-era club, founded by local British planters in 1909, must have been a nightmare of stuffiness and racism in its heyday. But now the faded colonial ambience, with turbaned bearers politely greeting guests in lounges filled with 1940s furniture and moth-eaten hunting trophies, feels undeniably quaint. Knock back a *chota-peg* of gin in the ("Men-Only") bar, play billiards and tennis, enjoy a round of golf on the nine-hole course, or just laze with a book on the immaculate lawns. The club's guest wing holds three kinds of rooms and cottages, varying in size and comfort. Rates include obligatory full board. ❼–❽

Hillview Kanan Devan Hills ☎04865/230567, ☎m94477 40883, ⊛www.hillviewhotel.com. A big red block on the southern edge of town. It's not much to look at from the outside, but the interiors boast stripped wood floors and traditional carved wall panels. Some rooms are much darker than others. A dependable mid-range choice, despite its rough edges. ❻–❼

Olive Brook PO Box 62, Pothamedu ☎04865/230588, ⊛www.olivebrookmunnar.com. Delightfully old-fashioned homestay, run by a schoolteacher in the thick of a cardamom estate on a hillside overlooking the southern end of Munnar. The five rooms, spread over two blocks, all have wonderful views, and the home-cooked food is excellent. Rates include full board, cookery classes, trekking, evening barbecues and campfires. ❽

Royal Retreat Kanan Devan Hills ☎04865/230240, ⊛www.royalretreat.co.in. Pleasant, efficiently run motel on the roadside at the south end of town. Go for one of its "super-deluxe" rooms if there are any free: they're south-facing, have brick fireplaces and cane furniture, and are fronted by a cheerful little flower garden. ❻

Luxury

KTDC Tea County Off Mattupathy Rd ☎04865/230460, ⊛www.ktdc.com. The poshest address in Munnar town is a rather anodyne, government-run "four-star deluxe" resort offering a range of luxurious chalet style rooms and suites ($120–150) stacked along a hilltop. There's a good multi-cuisine restaurant and beer parlour. ❾

The Tea Sanctuary KDHP House ☎04865/230141, ⓦwww.theteasanctuary .com. A selection of five former planters' bungalows, scattered across the Kanan Devan Hill Plantations Company's 240 square kilometres of tea gardens. Situated on prime viewpoints amid well-tended gardens, each has been sensitively restored to its original state – with ivy-covered exteriors and cosy open fireplaces indoors – and is staffed by a liveried *chowkidar* and cook. If you're hoping to experience the pre-war gentility of the High Range, book a couple of nights in "Chockanad

East", 4km beyond the High Range Club. $130/night for two, including full board. ⑨

Windermere Estate PO Box 21, Pothamedu ☎04865/230512, ⓦwww .windermeremunnar.com. Alpine-style chalet lodges, perched high on a hilltop above the town in cardamom and tea groves, with glorious views over the Chithirapuram Valley. Accommodation is offered in a converted farmhouse, plantation home and various garden cottages, all beautifully furnished and decorated with natural wood and stone and warm-coloured textiles. ⑨

Eating

If your hotel, homestay or guesthouse package doesn't include meals, your best option will either be one of the popular local places reviewed below, or the **thattukada** (hot food stall market) just south of the main bazaar, opposite the taxi stand. This place gets into its stride around 7.30pm and runs through the night, serving delicious, piping hot Keralan food – *dosas, parottas, iddiappam,* green–bean curry, egg masala – ladled onto tin plates and eaten on rough wood tables in the street. As with all *thattukadas,* taxi drivers and single Malayali men working away from home make up most of the clientele, as the food is homely and cheap (you'd be hard pushed to spend Rs30).

Food Count Ground Floor of the *Munnar Inn,* main bazaar. Shiny, glass-sided café serving samosas, veg cutlets, sandwiches and light meals. The most hygienic option down in the main bazaar.
Guru Bhavan Mutapatty Rd, Ikka Nagar. The most dependable of Munnar's local South Indian "meals"

joints. It's a 10min plod north of the main bazaar, but worth the walk, with a menu of delicious Keralan vegetarian dishes that changes daily, in addition to hot *parottas,* stupendously crunchy paper *dosas* and other Udupi snacks. Recommended for local breakfasts, too.

Around Munnar

Munnar bazaar may not be the most inspiring spot in the High Range, but it serves as a useful hub for explorations of the spectacular mountain region surrounding it. Several of the summits towering above the town may be reached on day **treks** through the tea gardens, and buses wind their way up to the aptly named **Top Station**, a hamlet famed for its views and meadows of **Neelaku-runji plants**, and to the more distant nature sanctuaries of **Eravikulam** and **Chinnar**, where you can spot Nilgiri tahr, elephant and many other wild animals. To reach the most remote attractions hereabouts, however, you might want to hire a taxi for the day (easily done through your hotel, Joseph Iype, or at the taxi stand in the bazaar. Rates are a standard Rs6–7/km).

Walks and treks

Given the stupendous scenery rearing on all sides of Munnar, the **hiking** scene is surprisingly undeveloped. You can ramble at leisure through the tea estates, watching local Muthuvan pluckers at work (contact Joseph Iype at his office in the bazaar for route suggestions; see p.440). For anything more ambitious, it makes sense to employ the services of a guide. A good first stop is the *Green View* guesthouse, on the south side of town (see map, p.439), whose owner, Deepak (☎m9447 825447), heads up a team of enthusiastic young guides who've devised a menu of interesting hiking trails in the area. Drop by at the

△ Tea plantation, Munnar

guesthouse to see a computer slideshow of their scenic highlights. Trips cost Rs600–800 per person per day (or Rs100/hour), with transport to and from the trailheads included.

For the **ascent of Anna Mudi**, south India's highest peak, you'll need to obtain a permit from the Forest Officer in Munnar, Mr Roy P. Thomas (⊤m94479 79093) at his office (Mon–Fri 10am–1pm & 2–5pm) just above the taxi stand. He'll arrange all the necessary paperwork and guides. With a pre-dawn start, the climb can be accomplished in a long day. Permits are not, however, granted during the mating season of the tahr in late January and February.

Top Station and Kolukkamalai

One of the most popular excursions from Munnar is the 34-kilometre climb through some of the Subcontinent's highest tea estates to **TOP STATION**, a tiny hamlet on the Kerala–Tamil Nadu border which, at 1600m, is the highest point on the interstate road. Pack ponies still labour up the endless switchbacks to the site, which takes its name from the old aerial **ropeway** that used to connect it with the valley floor, the ruins of which can still be seen in places. Apart from the marvellous views over the Tamil plains, Top Station is renowned for the very rare **Neelakurunji plant** (*Strobilatanthes*), which grows in profusion on the mountainsides but only flowers once every twelve years, when huge crowds climb up here to admire the cascades of violet blossom spilling down the slopes (the next flowering is due in October–November 2018). Top Station is accessible by **bus** from Munnar (10 daily starting at 5.30am; 1hr 30min), and Jeep-taxis do the return trip for Rs850. To catch the best views, try to get here before the mist builds up at 9am.

Top Station sees streams of visitors during the season, but you can sidestep the crowds completely, and see even more awesome scenery, at the remote **Kolukkumalai estate**, 23km out of Munnar. At an altitude of 2400m, it's officially India's highest tea plantation, producing leaves prized for their delicate flavour. The only way to reach it is by Jeep, via the **Chinnakkanal Suryanelly Estate**. An old bridleway drops down the east flank of the mountain from here to the Tamil plains, visible in the distance – a popular local trekking route.

Eravikulam National Park and Chinnar Wildlife Sanctuary

Encompassing 100 square kilometres of moist evergreen forest and grassy hilltops in the Western Ghats, the **Eravikulam National Park** (daily 7am– 6pm; Rs200 [Rs15]; ⓦwww.eravikulam.org), 13km northeast of Munnar, is the last stronghold of one of the world's rarest mountain goats, the **Nilgiri tahr**. Its innate friendliness made the tahr pathetically easy prey during the hunting frenzy of the colonial era. On a break in his campaign against Tipu Sultan in the late 1790s, the future Duke of Wellington reported that his soldiers were able to shoot the unsuspecting goats as they wandered through his camp. By Independence the tahr was virtually extinct; today, however, numbers are healthy, and the animals have regained their tameness, largely thanks to the efforts of the American biologist Clifford Rice, who studied them here in the early 1980s. Unable to get close enough to observe the creatures properly, Rice followed the advice of locals and attracted them using salt, and soon entire herds were congregating around his camp. The tahrs' salt addiction also explains why so many hang around the park gates at **Vaguvarai**, where visitors – despite advice from rangers – slip them salty snacks.

Although it borders Eravikulam, the **Chinnar Wildlife Sanctuary** (daily 6am–7pm; Rs100 [Rs10]; ⓦwww.chinnar.org) is much less visited, not least because its entrance lies a two-hour drive from Munnar along 58km of winding mountain roads. The reserve, in the rain shadow of the High Range and thus much drier than its neighbour, is one of the best spots in the state for bird watching, with 225 species recorded to date. But the real star attractions are the resident **grizzled giant squirrels**, who scamper in healthy numbers around the thorny scrub here, and the near-mythical "**white bison of Manjampatti**", thought to be an albino Indian gaur. Supported **treks** through the reserve are run by the excellent Wild Kerala Tour Company (Ⓣ0484/236 9121, ⓦwww .wildkeralatours.com), based in Kochi.

To reach Chinnar you have to pass through the small bazaar town of **MARAYOOR**, 42km east of Munnar, where it's worth stopping to admire Kerala's only **sandalwood forest**. The 92-square-kilometre reserve, a couple of kilometres out of town, holds an estimated 60,000 trees, whose wood currently sells for $1000–1500 per kilo on the international market. Wardens are on hand to shepherd visitors around the heavily protected zone which, despite its high fences and the death in 2004 of arch-smuggler Veerapan (see p.641), continues to haemorrhage illegally felled sandalwood; they'll also show you **prehistoric rock-art** sites for which this area is famous. A collection of stone-capped **burial chambers**, known locally as the Munniozens, litter the land around the old Thenkasinathan Temple at the hamlet of **Kovilkadavu**, on the banks of the River Pambar.

Thattekkad Bird Sanctuary

Kerala's number-one bird sanctuary, **THATTEKKAD**, occupies a 25-square-kilometre wedge of former rubber plantation between two branches of the Periyar River. Lying just off the highway between Munnar and Kochi, it offers a tranquil stopover on the journey from the mountains and the coast. When the world-renowned ornithologist Salim Ali visited the site in the 1930s, he described it as the "richest bird habitat in peninsular India". Since then much of the area's forest has been felled, but what remains gives you some idea of the phenomenal avian diversity that once characterized the Keralan lowlands. A total of 275 species have been sighted here, most of them endemics. On an average day, visitors can expect to see between 80 and 100, including rarities such as the crimson-throated barbet, grey-headed fishing eagle and Malabar grey hornbill. other animals, from flying lizards to elephants, also put in occasional appearances.

Practicalities

National Highway NH-49 runs to within 15km of Thattekkad; the turning off the main road is at the town of **Kothamangalam**, connected by infrequent buses to Ernakulam (55km; 2hr) and Munnar (120km; 3hr 30min). If you find yourself faced with a long wait for a service, catch one of the more frequent buses to **Muvattapuzha**, to the southwest, and change there. Once you're in Kothamangalam, you shouldn't have any problem findng a local bus for the remaining half-hour leg to the sanctuary. Pending the completion of a new road bridge (under construction at the time of writing), the crossing of the Periyar River to reach Thattekkad is achieved by means of an extraordinary *jangar* ferry, consisting of three dugouts lashed together; the bus drives onto a wooden platform on top of them – a white-knuckle affair if you happen to be stuck inside a vehicle. The nearest railway station is inconveniently situated 48km away at Aluva.

Private boat operators are also on hand to ferry birders to the sanctuary and day-trippers to Boothathanketu lake further upriver – though don't expect international safety standards. In February 2007, fifteen school children and three of their teachers died when the boat they were travelling in on an excursion capsized.

The sanctuary itself is open daily from 9am to 5pm; admission costs Rs20. Early morning, between 6 and 7.30am, is the best time for bird-watching.

Accommodation

With the exception of the *Hornbill Inspection Bungalow*, accommodation within range of Thattekkad tends to be pitched at well-heeled foreign bird-watchers, and correspondingly pricey, set on plantations or close to the riverside for early safari departures. The only place to stay inside the sanctuary itself is a three-storey, double-bedded **watchtower** on stilts (④) surrounded by a 360-degree open window and, at ground level, an electric fence (solar powered) to keep out the elephants. You can book it through the Assistant Wildlife Officer in Koothamangalam (see review for *Hornbill Inspection Bungalow*, p.446, for contact details).

🏃 **Haritha Farms ("The Pimenta")**
Kadalikad, off the Muvattupuzha–Thodu-puzha Rd, 38km southwest of Thattekkad ☎04865/260216, ⓦ www.harithafarms.com. This homestay, on a mixed organic farm hidden in the central lowlands 14km east of Muvattupuzha, was one of Kerala's eco-tourism pioneers when it opened its doors to guests in the early 1990s. Thanks to its magical setting and the warm hospi-tality of the Mathew family, it's still going strong,

with four self-contained cottages for rent. When you tire of lazing on the veranda watching the birds and butterlies flit past, host Jacob can arrange visits to local places of interest (including a truck-painting centre and elephant-training camp). Delicious organic home-cooked food is included in the rates, and cooking classes are available. ❽

Hornbill Camp book through Kalypso Eco-Lodges and Camps, G-307 Panampilly Nagar, Kochi ☎0484/209 2280, ⓦ www.thehornbillcamp.com.

Luxury camp, at a beautiful site slap on the banks of the Periyar River opposite the sanctuary. Each of the tents is furnished with comfy twin beds, a toilet and wash basin; shower facilities are in a common block. Home-cooked Keralan meals are served in a high thatched gazebo, and as well as arranging birding tours they also lay on kayaking trips in the area. From Rs3000 per day, full board. ❽

Hornbill Inspection Bungalow Book through the Assistant Wildlife Warden, Nyayapilly PO, Kothamangalam ☎0485/258 8302. No-frills government inspection bungalow close to the sanctuary gates, with simple, attached double rooms. It's a bit cheerless, and decidedly overpriced (at Rs950 per person), but still cheaper than the alternatives this close to the reserve. Book as far in advance as possible as it's popular. ❻

Mundackal Estate Pindimana PO, Kothamangalam ☎0485/257 0717, ☎m93886 20399, ⓦwww.mundackalhomestay.com. Swish

homestay in the imposing Western-style home of welcoming local aristos Jose and Daisy Mundackal, on their working rubber, coconut and pepper plantation. It's within easy range of the sanctuary and Kothamangalam bus stand, 7km southwest. The Keralan-Christian cooking gets rave reviews (Daisy runs courses by prior arrangement). Doubles from $125. ❾

Periyar River Lodge Book through 31/1027-A Friends Avenue, Vyttila Kochin ☎0484/2207173, ☎m94477 07173, ⓦwww.periyarriverlodge.com. This handsome teak-built lodge sits on the riverbank next to the Thattekkad Sanctuary, centred on a traditional *nalukettu* sunken courtyard. A spacious lounge separates its two attached bedrooms, also wood-lined and tastefully furnished, and the entire building is surrounded by a veranda on which you can enjoy the river views from a cane swing chair. Rates (Rs3200 per double or Rs5200 for the whole house) include full board. ❻

Kochi (Cochin) and around

The venerable city of **KOCHI** (long known as Cochin) is Kerala's prime tourist destination, spreading across islands and promontories in a stunning location between the Arabian Sea and the backwaters. Its main sections – modern **Ernakulam** and the old peninsular districts of **Mattancherry** and **Fort Cochin** to the west – are linked by a complex system of ferries, and distinctly less romantic bridges. Although some visitors opt to stay in the more convenient Ernakulam, the overwhelming majority base themselves in Fort Cochin itself, where the city's complex history is reflected in an assortment of architectural styles. Spice markets, Chinese fishing nets, a synagogue, a Portuguese palace, India's first European church and seventeenth-century Dutch homes can all be found within an easy walk. Kochi is also one of the few places in Kerala where you are guaranteed **kathakali** dance performances, both in authentic and abridged tourist versions. Around Kochi, a 12km auto-rickshaw or bus ride southeast of Ernakulam, the colonial-style hill palace at **Thripunitra** is now an eclectic museum, staging a music and dance festival in October or November.

Kochi sprang into being in 1341, when a flood created a natural safe port which swiftly replaced Muziris (now Kodungallur, 50km north) as the chief harbour on the Malabar Coast. The royal family moved here from Muziris in 1405, after which the city grew rapidly, attracting Christian, Arab and Jewish settlers from the Middle East. The name probably derives from *kocchazhi*, meaning the new, or small, harbour. The history of **European** involvement in Kochi from the early 1500s onwards is dominated by the aggression of the Portuguese, Dutch and British, who successively competed to control the port and its lucrative spice trade. In 1800, the state of Cochin became part of the British Madras Presidency, and from 1812 until Independence in 1947 it was administered by a succession of *diwans*, or finance ministers. In the 1920s, the British expanded the port to accommodate modern ocean-going ships, and Willingdon Island, between Ernakulam and Fort Cochin, was created by extensive dredging.

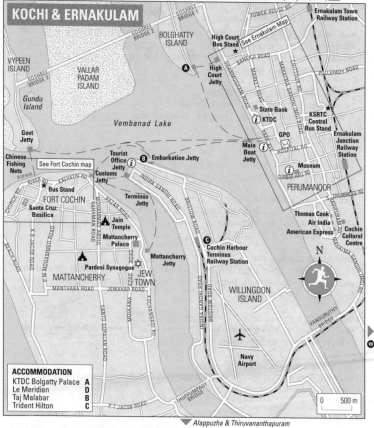

KOCHI & ERNAKULAM

Nedumbassery Airport (26km)

POWER HOUSE RD

Ernakulam Town
Railway Station

GOSHREE
BRIDGE 1

GOSHREE
BRIDGE 2

BOLGHATTY
ISLAND

High Court
Bus Stand

See Ernakulam Map

BANERJI ROAD

VYPEEN
ISLAND

VALLAR
PADAM
ISLAND

GOSHREE
BRIDGE 3

High
Court
Jetty

PULLEPADY ROAD

Gundu
Island

Vembanad Lake

State Bank

KTDC

KSRTC
Central
Bus Stand

Ernakulam
Junction
Railway
Station

Govt
Jetty

GPO

Chinese
Fishing
Nets

See Fort Cochin map

Tourist
Office

Embarkation Jetty

Customs
Jetty

Main
Boat
Jetty

HOSPITAL RD

Museum

DURBAR HALL RD

PERUMANOOR

RIVER RD

KALVATHI RD

Bus Stand

Terminus
Jetty

INDIRA GANDHI ROAD

FORT COCHIN

Santa Cruz
Basilica

BAZAR ROAD

Jain
Temple

BRISTOW ROAD

OVERBRIDGE RD

Thomas Cook
Air India
American Express

Cochin
Cultural
Centre

BEACH ROAD

K B JACOB ROAD

MOHAMMED ABDUL
RAHAMAN ROAD

Mattancherry
Palace

Pardesi Synagogue

MATTANCHERRY

MANTHARA ROAD

Mattancherry
Jetty

JEW
TOWN

JEWAHAR ROAD

Cochin Harbour
Terminus
Railway Station

WILLINGDON
ISLAND

N

VANDURUTHY
BRIDGE

SATIS GOPALAN ROAD

MULLAY

KOCHANGADI RD

Navy
Airport

MAHATMA GANDHI ROAD

P T JACOB ROAD

THOPPUMPADY
BRIDGE

0   500 m

ACCOMMODATION

KTDC Bolgatty Palace	A
Le Meridien	D
Taj Malabar	B
Trident Hilton	C

Alappuzha & Thiruvananthapuram

Arrival and local transport

Kochi's **international airport** (Ⓦwww.cochinairport.com) – one of India's most modern and efficient – is at Nedumbassery, near Alwaye (aka Alua), 26km to the north of Ernakulam. A prepaid taxi into town costs around Rs400 and takes 30–40min, traffic permitting – travelling by bus is more trouble than it's worth. There are two main **railway stations**, Ernakulam Junction, near the centre, and Ernakulam Town, 2km further north. No trains run to Fort Cochin or Mattancherry, while the Cochin Harbour Terminus, on Willingdon Island, serves the island's luxury hotels.

The KSRTC **Central bus stand** (☎0484/237 2033), beside the railway line east of MG Road and north of Ernakulam Junction, is for state-run long-distance services. There are also two stands for private services (see box, p.462): the **Kaloor Stand** (rural destinations to the south and east) is across the bridge from Ernakulam Town railway station on the Alwaye Road; while the **High Court Stand** (buses to Kumily, for Periyar Wildlife Reserve, and north to Thrissur, Guruvayur and Kodungallur) is opposite the High Court ferry jetty. The **Fort Cochin bus terminus** serves tourist buses and local services to Ernakulam.

Kochi by ferry

Half the fun of visiting Kochi is getting about on the cheap **local ferries**, which depart from the four jetties marked on the map on p.447. A pamphlet giving exact ferry times is available from the ticket hatches by the jetties and from the helpful tourist desk at the Main Boat Jetty in Ernakulam.

Ernakulam to Bolghatty Island
From Ernakulam (High Court Jetty); six per day 6.30am–9pm; journey time 10min. There are also speedboat taxis (only for guests of the *Bolgatty Palace* hotel).

Ernakulam to Fort Cochin
From Ernakulam (Main Jetty) to Fort Cochin (Customs Jetty). Every 20–55min; 5.55am–9.30pm; journey time 15min. A less frequent express service runs from Ernakulam's High Court Jetty to Government Jetty in Fort Cochin.

Ernakulam to Mattancherry
From Ernakulam (Main Jetty) via Fort Cochin (Customs Jetty) and Willingdon Island (Terminus Jetty) to Mattancherry (Mattancherry Jetty). Every 1hr 30min; 5am–5.45pm.

Ernakulam to Vypeen
From Ernakulam (Main Jetty). This service has two routes: one to Willingdon Island (Embarkation Jetty; 25min), and a fast one to Vypeen (Government Jetty; 15min). Every 30min–1hr; 7am–9.30pm.

Fort Cochin to Vypeen
From Fort Cochin (Government Jetty) to Vypeen (Government Jetty). Every 10min; 6.30am–9pm; journey time 10min.

Willingdon Island to Fort Cochin
From the Tourist Office Jetty (Willingdon Island) to Customs Jetty (Fort Cochin). Every 30min; 6.30am–6.15pm; journey time 10min.

Although **auto-rickshaws** are plentiful and reliable in Ernakulam, expect to pay well over the odds across the water in Mattancherry and Fort Cochin. Kochi's excellent **ferry system** (see box above) provides a relaxing way to reach the various parts of town. **Bicycles** can be rented from many of the hotels and guesthouses in Fort Cochin (see p.451).

Tours and backwater trips
KTDC's half-day **Kochi boat cruise** (daily 9am–12.30pm & 2–5.30pm; Rs100) is a good way to orient yourself but doesn't stop for long in either Mattancherry or Fort Cochin, so give it a miss unless you're pushed for time. Departing from the Sealord Jetty on Shanmugham Road, Ernakulam, it calls at Willingdon Island, the synagogue, Mattancherry Dutch Palace, St Francis Church, the Chinese fishing nets and Bolghatty Island. Book at the KTDC Reception Centre on Shanmugham Road (T 0484/235 3234).

The KTDC tourist office and a couple of private companies also operate popular all-day **backwater trips** out of Kochi. Taking in a handful of coir-making villages north of the city, these offer a leisurely and enjoyable way to experience rural Kerala from small hand-punted canoes. KTDC's daily tours cost Rs350, including the car or bus trip to the departure point, 30km north, and a knowledgeable guide. Better value, however, are the trips run by the private **tourist desk** (see below) at the Main Boat Jetty in Ernakulam (daily 8.30am–5pm; Rs550), which include hotel pick-up, transfer, a morning cruise (in a motorized boat) on the open backwaters, a village tour, a Keralan lunch buffet on board the *kettu vallam* and an afternoon trip through narrow waterways in a much smaller punted canoe.

Information

India Tourism's main office, providing reliable information and qualified guides for visitors, is situated on Willingdon Island (Mon–Fri 9am–5.30pm, Sat 9am–noon; ☎0484/266 8352, ⓦwww.india-tourism.com), between the *Taj Malabar Hotel* and Tourist Office Jetty; they also have a desk at the airport. KTDC's **reception centre**, on Shanmugham Road, Ernakulam (daily 8am–7pm; ☎0484/235 3234, ⓦwww.ktdc.com) reserves accommodation in their hotel chain and organizes sightseeing and backwater tours (see p.416); they too have a counter at the airport. For general advice, the two most convenient sources are the **Kerala Department of Tourism's office** next to the Government Jetty in Fort Cochin (Mon–Sat 10.15am 5pm; no phone, ⓦwww.keralatourism.com), and the tiny, independently-run **Tourist Desk** (daily 8am–6.30pm; ☎0484/237 1761, Ⓔtouristdesk@satyam.net.in) at the entrance to the Main Boat Jetty in Ernakulam. Both hand out maps of the town and backwaters, but you'll probably find the latter more helpful when it comes to checking ferry and bus times. The Tourist Desk, located directly opposite the improbably named "Livingston Tea Stall" (named after the controversial Mayor of London), is also *the* place to obtain information on ritual theatre and temple festival dates around the state. In addition, they arrange daily boat tours and accommodation on houseboats, and take bookings for two excellent guesthouses in northern Kerala (one near Kannur and the other in Wayanad). Over in Fort Cochin, you can call at their subsidiary office on Tower Road (same hours; ☎0484/221 6129).

A useful local **publication** is the monthly *Jaico Timetable* (Rs10), which lists comprehensive details of bus, train, ferry and flight times. Both KTDC and the Tourist Desk publish free walking tour maps and guides to Fort Cochin.

Accommodation

Most foreign visitors opt to stay in **Fort Cochin**, which, with its uncongested backstreets and charming colonial-era architecture, holds considerably more appeal than the mayhem of modern Ernakulam. Dozens of period buildings have been turned over to heritage hotels and homestays in recent years. There are, however, drawbacks: room rates are grossly inflated (especially over the Christmas and New Year period), with few options at the budget end of the scale, and there is a disconcertingly high concentration of tourists. **Ernakulam** may lack historic ambience, but it's far more convenient for travel connections, and offers lots of choice in all categories and far better value for money; however, its hotels do tend to fill up early in the day, so book well in advance – particularly if you're planning to be here on a weekend, when vacancies are like gold dust. Another alternative to Fort Cochin are the luxury and heritage places on **Bolghatty and Willingdon Islands**, which range from the three-star, government-run *Bolghatty Palace*, housed in a wonderful old Dutch mansion, to more formulaic five stars.

Places to stay in Ernakulam and Fort Cochin are marked on their respective maps (p.459 & p.454); those on Willingdon and Bolghatty islands appear on t' main Kochi/Ernakulam map (p.447).

Ernakulam

Budget

Biju's Tourist Home Corner of Cannonshed and Market roads ☎0484/238 1881, ⓦwww.bijustouristhome.com. The pick of the budget bunch: a friendly, efficiently run block only 2min walk from the boat jetty, with thirty spotless, well-aired and generously sized rooms ranged over four storeys. It has its own clean water supply and offers a cheap same-day laundry service. All in all, unbeatable value. For telephone reservations, ask to speak in person to the manager, Mr Thomas Panakkal. ④

Broadway Tower TD West Rd ☎0484/236 1645, ⓦwww.broadwaytowers.com. Situated in the thick of Ernakulam's busy textile bazaar, this recently built, well-scrubbed little economy hotel occupies the second and third storey of a modern block. Its rooms offer great value for money (including the cheapest a/c rooms in town); there's even a dorm (Rs75), and a nice little veg "meals" place on the ground floor. ③–④

Cochin Tourist Home Chavar Rd ☎0484/237 7577. Cleanest of the cheap hotels lined up outside Ernakulam Junction station, but often full of noisy families and pilgrim groups. The basement holds a dingy organic vegetarian restaurant. ③

Maple Guest House XL/271 Cannonshed Rd ☎0484/235 5156. Best of the few rock-bottom options in the streets immediately east of the boat jetty, with cheap, clean non-a/c rooms close to the city centre – though it's not nearly as pleasant as *Biju's*. ②–③

Modern Guest House XL/6067 Market Rd ☎0484/235 2130. Popular economy lodge in the main bazaar. The rooms are pretty standard, but inexpensive and clean for the price. If it's full, ask if they have vacancies in either of their two (slightly less appealing) sister hotels nearby. ②–③

Saas Tower Cannonshed Rd ☎0484/236 5319, ⓦwww.saastower.com. Since its refit, this tower-block hotel, with 72 well furnished rooms, has begun to rival nearby *Biju's* for quality and price at the upper end of the budget category. Singles from Rs300, and also some a/c options. ③–④

Mid-range & luxury

Excellency Nettipadam Rd, Jos Junction ☎0484/237 8251, ⓦwww.hotelexcellency.com. Smart, modern mid-range place, offering better value than most options in the city centre. The majority of its 49 rooms are a/c, and there's a 24hr coffee shop and quality multi-cuisine restaurant. ④–⑤

Government Guest House Marine Drive ☎0484/236 0502. The maharaja of Kerala's great value Government Guest Houses, in a shiny new eight-storey tower overlooking the harbour. Centred on a vast atrium lobby, with acres of brass hand rails and polished marble, its rooms offer comfort comparable to a four-star business-class hotel, only at amazingly low rates (and they do single occupancy). Advance reservation, as with all Kerala state guesthouses, can be hit-and-miss, with priority given to government officials; if they have any free, ask for a sea-facing room at the top of the building. ⑤

Grand MG Rd ☎0484/238 2061. This is the most classically glamorous place to stay in central Ernakulam. Spread over three floors of a 1960s building, its relaxing a/c rooms are done out in retro-colonial style, with varnished wood floors and split-cane blinds. Surprisingly low tariffs given the level of comfort and location. ⑥–⑧

Le Meridien Maradu ☎0484/270 5777 (See main "Kochi and Ernakulam" map, p.447). Luxury five-star on the southern outskirts of the city centre, popular mainly with business clients, flight crews and tour groups. In addition to 223 rooms overlooking the backwaters, the complex holds glitzy shopping arcades, an Ayurveda spa and a wide choice of food and beverage outlets. Charmless by comparison with places across the water, but efficient. From $240–850. ⑨

Sealord Shanmugham Rd ☎0484/238 2472, ⓦwww.sealordhotels.com. The high-rise *Sealord*, near the High Court Jetty, has been an institution in the city for four decades and, with its handsome new interiors, offers excellent value for money. Their "standard" rooms are the best deal (ask for one on the top floor), and there's a relaxing rooftop terrace restaurant (see p.460) and bar. ⑤–⑥

Taj Residency Marine Drive ☎0484/237 1471, ⓦwww.tajhotels.com. Ernakulam's most established business hotel, in a prime location overlooking the harbour, with luxury a/c rooms, an impressive green-house-like café (see "Eating", p.460) and several quality restaurants, but no pool. $135–270. ⑨

Yuvarani Residency Jos Junction, MG Rd ☎0484/237 7040, ⓦwww.yuvaraniresidency.com. Comfortable, central and well-managed three-star hotel with a choice of carpeted or tiled rooms – and especially good showers in their bathrooms. The popular Keralan seafood restaurant hosts live music recitals daily (except Tues); plus there's a bar and a coffee shop. ⑤–⑦

Budget

Adam's Old Inn 1/430 Burgher St ☎0484/221 7595. Ropey old budget travellers' lodge that's been here for years but recently came under new management. Plans are afoot to upgrade the hard coir mattresses and phase out the rooftop dorm (①), but for the time being this is still one Fort Cochin's few rock-bottom cheapies. ❹

Leelu Queiros St ☎0484/221 5377, ☎m98460 55377, ⓦwww.leeluhomestay.com. A very welcoming little homestay, tucked away down a quiet lane in a former family home that's been completely modernized. Its cheerfully decorated guest rooms are spacious, with squashy mattresses, huge bathrooms and optional a/c (Rs500 extra). Landlady Mrs Leelu Roy also offers popular daily cookery classes (non-guests welcome). Especially recommended for women travellers. ❹–❺

Orion 926 KL Bernard Rd ☎0484/321 9312, ☎m98955 24797, ✉mail@orionhomestay.com. Impeccable little homestay in a new house on the quiet south side of town. Rates vary according to size of rooms, which don't all have balconies, but are all kept shining and neat. ❹–❺

Santa Cruz Peter Celli St ☎0484/221 6250, ☎m98475 18598. Half of the rooms in this small guesthouse behind St Francis' Church have windows opening onto an enclosed corridor, but the others are well ventilated – and they're all impeccably clean, neatly tiled and freshly painted throughout, with new beds. Good value. ❸–❹

Mid-range

Ballard Bungalow River Rd ☎0484/221 5854, ⓦwww.cochinballard.com. Eighteenth-century Dutch mansion, later used as the residence of the British collector of Cochin, now converted into a good value mid-range hotel run by the local Diocese. With their garish 1980s-style bedroom furniture, the ecclesiastical owners haven't quite grasped the heritage concept, but the original wood floors have come through the renovation unscathed and the place retains plenty of period atmosphere. Friendly, helpful staff. ❺–❼

Bernard Bungalow 1/297 Parade Rd ☎0484/221 6162, ☎m98474 2799, ⓦwww.bernardbungalow .com. Half-a-dozen large, airy attached rooms, some with lovely new teak floors, in a 300-year-old Dutch house run by a welcoming couple. Despite some heavy-handed renovation, lots of historic atmosphere remains, and the accommodation is comfortable for the price. ❺–❻

Chiramel Residency 1/296 Lilly St ☎0484/221 7310, ⓦwww.chiramelhomestay.com. A great seventeenth-century heritage homestay, with welcoming owners and five lofty and carefully restored non-a/c rooms set around a fancily furnished communal sitting room. All have big wooden beds, teak floors and modern bathrooms. ❻

Delight Ridsdale Rd, opposite the Parade Ground ☎0484/221 7658, ⓦwww.delightfulhomestay .com. Occupying an annexe tacked onto a splendid 300-year-old Portuguese mansion, David and Flowery's homestay holds seven spacious, comfortable and well-aired rooms, all equipped with new bathrooms and quiet ceiling fans; some open onto a lovely courtyard garden; another has a long veranda overlooking the parade ground; and there's a high-ceilinged salon with original teak floors to lounge in. Breakfast available. ❹–❼

Fort House 2/6A Calvathy Rd ☎0484/221 7103, ⓦwww.forthousecochin.com. Stylishly simple rooms ranged along the sides of a sandy courtyard littered with pot plants and votive terracotta statues, cooled by breezes blowing straight off the waterfront. Those in the much preferable original block (#1–5) have white walls and red-oxide floors, comfy king-sized beds and good showers in their chic little wet-room bathrooms – though the a/c units can be noisy. Avoid the attached "bamboo huts" (#6–9): they're well set up but have embarrassingly thin walls. Rates include breakfast; good waterside restaurant on site (see "Eating" p.460). ❻

Napier House Napier Lane, off Napier St ☎0484/221 5715, ☎m98953 33622, ⓦwww .napierhouse.com. Relaxing, low-key guesthouse in a 120-year-old Dutch house. The interiors have been done in a somewhat anodyne Western style, but they're comfortable and some have bathtubs. The one outstanding room is the suite, which has preserved its original teak floorboards and opens onto a private balcony overlooking the street. Breakfasts (included in the rates) are served on a pleasant common terrace. ❻–❽

The Old Courtyard 1/371–2 Princess St ☎0484/2216302 ⓦwww.oldcourtyard.com. A gem of heritage hotel, whose eight rooms flank a photogenic seventeenth-century courtyard framed by elegant Portuguese arches and bands of original *azulejos* tiles. For once the decor and antique furnishings (including romantic four-posters) are in keeping with the building – though some may find them dark and lacking modern refinements. Ask for one on the upper storey as it's less disturbed by noise from the courtyard restaurant (see "Eating", p.461). ⑧–⑨

Raintree 1/618 Peter Celli St ☏0484/325 1489, ☏m98470 29000, Ⓦwww.fortcochin.com. Five outstandingly smart rooms furnished in modern style (two of them with tiny balconies) in a cosy guesthouse that's within easy walking distance of the sights, but still tucked away. The really nice thing about this place is its plant-filled roof terrace, which has panoramic views over the Basilica and old Portuguese and Dutch houses of the neighbourhood. ⑥

Spencer Home 1/298 Parade Rd ☏0484/221 5049. Warm-toned wood pillars and gleaming ceramic tiled floors line the verandas fronting this Portuguese-era house's eleven immaculate rooms, which open onto a painstakingly kept garden. Peaceful and good value for the area. A/c costs Rs600 extra. ⑤

Walton's Homestay Princess St ☏0484/221 5309,☏m92497 21935, Ⓔcewalton @rediffmail.com. Among Cochin's most characterful homestays, run by philosopher and local historian Mr Christopher Edward Walton, in a centuries-old Dutch house. Try to book the "garden cottage", which opens on to a delightful garden busy with birdlife. Facilities include a book-swap library and in-house yoga classes; breakfast (not included in tariff) is served on a communal terrace. ⑤–⑥

Luxury

Brunton Boatyard Bellar Rd, next to Fort Cochin Jetty ☏0484/221 8221, Ⓦwww.cghearth.com. Luxury chain hotel, built on the site of an eighteenth-century boatyard. The architecture and furnishings set out to replicate the feel of the British era, with antique *punkah* fans dangling from the lobby ceiling, portraits of old worthies and Dutch charts on the walls, and a billiards table set against Keralan carved wood and whitewash. Three types of room are offered, all of them overlooking the harbour (you get sea views from your bathtub) – though avoid the ones on the jetty side of the complex, which are plagued by traffic noise, at all costs. Facilities include three speciality restaurants

(see p.460), an Ayurveda centre and a waterside pool. $225–325. ⑨

Koder House Tower Rd ☏0484/221 8485. Ⓦwww.koderhouse.com. One of the Fort's newest boutique hotels, in a converted 200-year-old house that originally belonged to a prominent Jewish merchant (poets, painters and visiting dignitaries used to attend the Koder family's legendary Sabbath suppers in the early 1900s). The imposing red, double-fronted facade is less alluring than its interiors, with their long, dark wood floors, original art and antique furniture. Six sumptuous suites are on offer, from around $300; and there's a restaurant and Ayurvedic spa. ⑨

Malabar House 1/268 Parade Rd ☏0484/221 6666, Ⓦwww.malabarhouse.com. Fort Cochin's original and most stylish boutique hotel is set in a historic eighteenth-century mansion at the bottom of the Parade Ground. Crammed with antiques and contemporary Keralan art, the German-designed interiors present a mix of traditional charm and European chic, centred on a serene temple-style courtyard pool. Tariffs ($270–460) include breakfast. They have an even swankier wing, *Trinity House*, across the square – the last word in designer boutique chic. For a review of *Malabar House*'s restaurant, see p.461. ⑨

🏃 **The Old Harbour** 1/328, Tower Road ☏0484/221 8006, ☏m98470 29000, Ⓦwww.oldharbourhotel.com. This 300-year-old former Portuguese hospice, later occupied by a firm of British tea brokers, was recently restored under the direction of German architect Karl Damschen (of *Brunton Boatyard* and *Surya Samudra* fame). A storehouse of graceful Lusitanian arches, lathe-turned wood pillars and teak floors, it now accommodates one of Kerala's top heritage hotels, at a prime location close to the Chinese fishing nets. The thirteen individually-styled rooms either have private balconies facing an internal courtyard or open onto the garden and large pool, and there are also a handful of separate "cottages" in the grounds, each with roofless bathrooms and verandas. $115–230. ⑨

Willingdon and Bolghatty islands

KTDC Bolgatty Palace Bolghatty Island ☏0484/275 0500, Ⓦwww.ktdc.com. Extensively renovated palace in a beautiful location, a short hop from High Court Jetty. The main building, built by the Dutch in 1744 and later home of the British Resident, is now a three-star hotel with twenty deluxe rooms; there are also six "honeymoon"

cottages on stilts right at the water's edge. Reserve through any KTDC tourist office and come armed with mosquito repellent. At weekends, the adjacent KTDC canteen and bar is noisy with day-trippers. $125–240. ⑧–⑨

Taj Malabar Willingdon Island, by Tourist Office Jetty ☏0484/266 6811, Ⓦwww.tajhotels.com.

Pink-orange tower block in a superb location on the tip of the island with sweeping views of the bay; the old "heritage" wing, waterfront gardens and pool have been extensively refurbished, and the whole place oozes *Taj* style and quality. $220–275. ⑨
Trident Hilton Bristow Rd, Willingdon Island ☎0484/266 9595, ⓦwww.trident-hilton.com.

Despite the bleak dockyard environs, this is the most intimate of the five-stars around the island port, with interesting displays of Keralan tribal and household artefacts, a pool in a tropical oasis, a restaurant, a bar and a range of luxurious rooms. Officially $120–170, but discounts are often available online. ⑨

Old Kochi

Old Kochi, the thumb-shaped peninsula whose northern tip presides over the entrance to the city's harbour, formed the focus of European trading activities from the sixteenth century onwards. With high-rise development restricted to Ernakulam across the water, its twin districts of **Fort Cochin**, in the west, and **Mantancherry**, on the headland's eastern side, have preserved an extraordinary wealth of early-colonial architecture, spanning the Portuguese, Dutch and British eras – a crop unparalleled in India. Approaching by ferry, the waterfront, with its sloping red-tiled roofs and ranks of peeling, pastel-coloured *godoowns* (warehouses), offers a view that can have changed little in centuries.

Closer up, however, Old Kochi's historic patina has started to show some ugly cracks. The spice trade that fuelled the town's original rise is still very much in evidence: scores of shops lining the narrow streets of Mantancherry enjoy a brisk turnover of Malabari cardamom, chillies, tumeric and ginger, while the famous Pepper Exchange has boomed since it went online a couple of years back. But over the past decade, an extraordinary rise in visitor numbers has had a major impact on the town. Thousands of free-spending foreign tourists pour through daily during the winter, and with no planning or preservation authority to take control, the resulting rash of new building threatens to destroy the very atmosphere people come here to experience. Whereas old Portuguese arches and Dutch wood verandas used to dominate the streets of Fort Cochin, now garish signboards and the glass fronts of air-conditioned Kashmiri handicraft emporia are more likely to draw the eye. That said, tourism has also brought some benefits to the area, inspiring renovation work to buildings that would otherwise have been left to rot. Quite a few splendid old mansions across the town have been restored to accommodate high-end **heritage hotels**, where you can savour the 300-year-old architecture from the comfort of an antique four-poster or courtyard plunge pool.

Fort Cochin

The district where tourism has made its most discernable impact is **Fort Cochin**, the grid of venerable old streets at the northwest tip of the peninsula, where the Portuguese erected their first walled citadel, Fort Immanuel. Only a few fragments of the former battlements remain, crumbling into the sea beside Cochin's iconic Chinese fishing nets. But dozens of other evocative Lusitanian, Dutch and British monuments survive, ranging from stately tea brokers' bungalows to Bishops' palaces, spice traders' mansions and the gabled facade of the oldest Church in Asia.

A good way to get to grips with Fort Cochin's many-layered history is to pick up the free **walking tour maps** produced by both Kerala Tourism and the privately run Tourist Desk, available from their respective offices and counters (see p.449). The routes outlined in them lead you around some of the district's more significant landmarks, including the early-eighteenth-

FORT COCHIN

Customs Jetty

State Bank of India

Al Bayan Mosque

Rhythms Centre (Greenix)

Jama Masjid

KALVATHI ROAD

ASPINWALL JUNCTION

RIVER ROAD

P M MOHAMMED ROAD

PULLUPALAM RD

Government Boat Jetty

Bus Terminus

Taxi Stand ★

Tourist Desk

Childrens Park

TOWER ROAD

RIVER ROAD

Chinese Fishing Nets

N

Riverside Beach

Cochin Club

Vasco da Gama's House

Idiom Bookshop

BURGHER STREET

PRINCESS STREET

ROSE STREET

BASTION STREET

QUIROS STREET

Café de Net

Santa Cruz Basilica

Football Pitch

San Mike Tours (Motorcycle Rental)

Syrian Orthodox Church

P M MOHAMMED ROAD

FOSSE ROAD

KUNNUMPURAM JUNCTION

KUNNUMPURAM ROAD

PULLUPALAM ROAD

YMCA ROAD

ICICI Bank & ATM

Federal Bank & ATM

P M MOHAMMED ROAD

RIDSDALE BRANCH ROAD

K B JACOB ROAD

K B BERNARD ROAD

SANTA CRUZ ROAD

RIDSDALE ROAD

PETER CELLI STREET

Church of St Francis

Parade Ground

Dutch Cemetery

NAPIER STREET

LILY STREET

PARADE ROAD

CHURCH ROAD

BURGHER STREET

ELPHINSTONE ROAD

PATTALAM ROAD

Indo-Portuguese Museum (Bishop's Palace)

BEACH ROAD

Seaside Beach

100 m
0   100 m

RESTAURANTS & CAFÉS

Addy's	9
Brighton Café	2
Chariot Beach	3
Elite Bakery	6
Fort House	1
The History	A
Kashi Art Café	4
Malabar House	M
The Old Courtyard	F
The Old Harbour	D
Salt 'n' Pepper	2
Teapot Café	8
Upstairs	7
Vasco Café	5

ACCOMMODATION

Adam's Old Inn	H
Ballard Bungalow	C
Bernard Bungalow	N
Brunton Boatyard	A
Chiramel Residency	P
Delight	L
Fort House	B
Koder House	E
Leelu	J
Malabar House	M
Napier House	Q
The Old Courtyard	F
The Old Harbour	D
Orion	R
Raintree	K
Santa Cruz	I
Spencer Home	O
Walton's Homestay	G

century Dutch Cemetery, Vasco da Gama's supposed house and several traders' residences.

Fort Cochin also has a small but active **arts scene** based around the popular *Kashi Art Café* (daily 8.30am–7.30pm) on Burgher Street (reviewed on p.461). For **kathakali** and other traditional forms of ritual dance and drama, you've a choice of venues staging daily tourist shows (see box, p.457). The Fort's pair of **beaches**, on the northwest edge of the peninsula, are certainly not places you'd wish to swim from or sunbathe on, with slicks of dubious coloured pollution washing over them periodically – although Riverside Beach (the northernmost of the two) is a good spot for viewing the Chinese Fishing nets. The nearest decent seaside destination is Cherai Beach, 35km north (see p.466).

Chinese fishing nets

The huge, elegant **Chinese fishing nets** lining the northern shore of Fort Cochin add grace to the waterfront view, and are probably the single most familiar photographic image of Kerala. Traders from the court of Kublai Khan are said to have introduced them to the Malabar region. Known in Malayalam as *cheena vala*, they can also be seen throughout the backwaters further south. The nets, which are suspended from arced poles and operated by levers and weights, require at least four men to control them. You can buy fresh fish from the tiny market here and have it grilled with sea salt, garlic and lemon at one of the ramshackle stalls nearby.

St Francis Church and around

South of the Chinese fishing nets on Church Road (the continuation of River Road) is the large, typically English **Parade Ground**, where generations of colonial troops were drilled in the merciless heat, and on which local lads now brush up their cricketing skills after school.

Overlooking it is the **Church of St Francis**, (daily 8.30am–6.30pm) the first built by Europeans in India. Its exact age is not known, though the stone structure is thought to date back to the early sixteenth century; the land was a gift of the local raja, and the title deeds, written on palm leaf, are still kept inside. The facade, meanwhile, with its multi-curved sides, became the model for most Christian churches in India. Vasco da Gama was buried here in 1524, but his body was later removed to Portugal. Under the Dutch, the church was renovated and became Protestant in 1663, then Anglican with the advent of the British in 1795; since 1949 it has been attached to the Church of South India. Inside, various tombstone inscriptions have been placed in the walls, the earliest of which is from 1562. One hangover from British days is the continued use of *punkahs,* large swinging cloth fans on frames suspended above the congregation, operated by a *punkah-wallah*.

East of St Francis church, the interior of the twentieth-century **Santa Cruz Basilica** will delight fans of colourful, gaudy Indo-Romano-Rococo style of decoration. The building dates from 1887, and was constructed on the site of much older Portuguese one demolished by the British a century earlier.

The Indo-Portuguese museum

At the southern end of Ridsdale Road, the grand Bishop House of 1557 has been converted into the **Indo-Portuguese Museum** (Tues–Sun 9am–1pm & 2–6pm; Rs25 [Rs10]), hosting a none-too-impressive assortment of Catholic relics, altarpieces and other religious paraphernalia. Some minimal ruins of the fort's foundations can be seen in the basement.

Mantancherry, the old district of red-tiled riverfront wharves and houses occupying the northeastern tip of the headland, was once the colonial capital's main market area – the epicentre of the Malabar's spice trade, and home to its wealthiest Jewish and Jain merchants. Like Fort Cochin, its once grand buildings have lapsed into advanced states of disrepair, with most of their original owners working overseas. When Mattancherry's Jews emigrated en masse to Israel in the 1940s, their furniture and other un-portable hierlooms ended up in the **antique shops** for which the area is now renowned – though these days genuine pieces are few and far between. Kashmiris have taken over the majority of them, selling handicrafts and curios at inflated prices to the tour groups and cruise-ship visitors who stream through daily during the winter.

The sight at the top of most visitors' itineraries is **Mattancherry Palace** (daily except Fri 10am–5pm; Rs2), on the roadside a short walk from the Mattancherry Jetty, a kilometre or so southeast of Fort Cochin. Known locally as the Dutch Palace, the two-storey building was actually erected by the Portuguese, as a gift to the raja of Cochin, Vira Keralavarma (1537–61) – though the Dutch did add to the complex. While its squat exterior is not particularly striking, the interior is captivating.

The **murals** that adorn some of its rooms are among the finest examples of Kerala's underrated school of painting. Friezes illustrating stories from the Ramayana, on the first floor, date from the sixteenth century. Packed with detail and gloriously rich colour, the style is never strictly naturalistic; the treatment of facial features is pared down to the simplest of lines for the mouths and characteristically aquiline noses. Downstairs, the women's bedchamber holds several less complex paintings, possibly dating from the 1700s. One shows Shiva dallying with Vishnu's female form, the enchantress Mohini; a second portrays Krishna holding aloft Mount Govardhana; another features a reclining Krishna surrounded by *gopis*, or cowgirls. His languid pose belies the activity of his six hands and two feet, intimately caressing adoring admirers. While the paintings are undoubtedly the highlight of the palace, the collection also includes interesting Dutch maps of old Cochin, coronation robes belonging to past maharajas, royal palanquins, weapons and furniture. Without permission from the Archaeological Survey of India, **photography** is strictly prohibited.

A few hundred metres west of the palace, on Gujarati Road, lies the peaceful **Jain temple**, boasting a pair of airy marble sanctuaries with some delicate carving. The temple's serene atmosphere is broken daily at noon when one devotee rings a bell loudly to announce the feeding of the local pigeons. At this point the courtyard turns into a mini-Trafalgar Square, and anyone around is encouraged to help dish out grain to the hungry birds.

Jew Town

The road heading south from Mattancherry Jetty leads into the district known as **Jew Town**, where N. X. Jacob's tailor shop and the offices of J.E. Cohen, advocate and tax consultant, serve as reminders of a once-thriving Jewish community. The area is now dominated by Kashmiri shopkeepers selling mostly fake antiques, Hindu and Christian wood-carvings, oil lamps, masks, spice boxes and other bric-a-brac, plus some tempting coffee-table books; one showroom even houses a full-size snake boat.

In the heart of Jew Town, the **Kochi International Pepper Exchange** once housed a noisy trading floor, packed with dealers shouting out the latest prices and clinching deals by means of arcane sign language. Recently, however, the market was superseded by the India Pepper and Spice Trade Association (IPSTA) and converted to online trading (@www.ipsta.com), since when the building has seen fewer sacks of actual pepper pass through its doors than do the majority of spice shops further north in the main bazaar, where trucks and handcarts loaded with jute sacks of the Malabar's "black gold" routinely block the narrow lanes.

A right turn at the old pepper exchange brings you into Synagogue Lane, at the end of which stands the famous **Pardesi (White Jew) Synagogue** (daily except Sat 10am–noon & 3–5pm; Rs2). Founded in 1568 and rebuilt in 1664, the building is best known for its interior, an attractive, if incongruous hotch-potch paved with hand-painted eighteenth-century blue and white tiles from Canton. Each of the tiles is unique, depicting a love affair between a mandarin's daughter and a commoner. The nineteenth-century glass oil-burning chandeliers suspended from the ceiling were imported from Belgium. Above the entrance, a gallery supported by slender gilt columns was reserved for female members of the congregation. Opposite, an elaborately carved Ark houses four

Kathakali in Kochi

Kochi is the only city in the state where you are guaranteed the chance to see live **kathakali**, Kerala's unique form of ritualized theatre (see p.787). Whether in its authentic setting, in temple festivals held during the winter, or at the shorter tourist-oriented shows that take place year-round, these mesmerizing dance dramas – depicting the struggles of gods and demons – are an unmissable feature of Kochi's cultural life.

Four venues in the city (listed below) hold daily shows, each preceeded by an introductory talk at around 6.30pm. You can watch the dancers being made up if you arrive an hour or so beforehand, and keen photographers should turn up well before the start to ensure a front-row seat. Tickets, costing Rs100–150, can be bought at the door.

Most visitors only attend one performance, but you'll gain a much better sense of what *kathakali* is all about if you take in at least a couple. The next step is an all-night recital at a temple festival, or one of the performances given by the top-notch **Ernakulam Kathakali Club**, which stages night-long plays once each month, either at the TDM Hall in Ernakulam (see map, p.459) or at the Ernakulathappan Hall in the city's main Shiva temple. For further details contact the tourist desk at the Main Boat Jetty, Ernakulam. The four principal venues are listed below.

Art Kerala Kannanthodathu Lane, Valanjambalam ☎0484/237 5238 ©art_kerala @satyam.net.in. Next door to the See India Foundation, the *kathakali* performances here have proved popular with large tour groups, so expect a crowd. Make-up starts at 6pm, the performance at 7pm.

Dr Devan's Kathakali See India Foundation, Kalathiparambil Cross Rd, near Ernakulam railway station ☎0484/236 6471. The oldest-established tourist show in the city, introduced by the inimitable Dr Devan, who starts the show with a lengthy discourse on Indian philosophy and mythology. From 6.45pm to 8pm (make up at 6pm).

Kerala Kathakali Centre opposite *Brunton Boatyard*, Fort Cochin. Popular performances by a company of graduates of the renowned Kalamandalam Academy. You usually get to see three characters, and the music is live.

Rhythms Theatre (Greenix) opposite *Fort House*, Fort Cochin. Costing Rs450, this is the priciest show, but combines excerpts from *kathakali* plays with displays of *mohiniyattam* dance, *kalaripayattu* martial art and, on Sundays, *theyyattam*, set against a combination of live and pre-recorded music. Performances aren't of the highest standard, but the evening is more likely to appeal to kids as costumes and acts change in quick succession.

scrolls of the Torah (the first five books of the Old Testament), encased in silver and gold, on which sit gold crowns presented by the maharajas of Travancore and Cochin, testifying to good relations with the Jewish community. The synagogue's oldest artefact is a fourth-century copperplate inscription from the raja of Cochin.

An attendant is usually available to show visitors around and answer questions; his introductory talk features as part of the KTDC guided tour (see p.448). Outside, the streets surrounding the synagogue are crammed with **antique emporia**, run by Kashmiris to relieve wealthy cruise-ship passengers of their spending money.

Ernakulam and south of the centre

ERNAKULAM presents the modern face of Kerala, with more of a big-city feel than Thiruvananthapuram. Other than the contemporary art on display at the small **Durbar Hall Art Gallery** (daily 11am–7pm; free) on Durbar Hall Road, there's little in the way of sights. Along the busy, long, straight **Mahatma Gandhi (MG) Road**, which more or less divides Ernakulam in half, the main activities are shopping, eating and movie-going. Here you can catch up on your emails and phone calls, and choose from an assortment of great places to eat Keralan food. This area is particularly good for cloth, with an impressive selection of colours; whatever the current trend in *lunghis* or wedding saris this year, you'll get it on MG Road.

An eight-day annual **festival** (Jan/Feb) at the Shiva temple, on Durbar Hall Road, features elephant processions and *panchavadyam* (drum and trumpet groups) out in the street. The festival usually includes night-time performances of **kathakali**, and the temple is decorated with an amazing array of electric lights.

The village of **Netoor**, 10km southeast of the centre, is home to the ENS Kalari school of **kalarippayattu** (☎0484/270 0810, ✉enskalari@eth.net), one of the leading centres of the Keralan martial art form (see box, p.377). The well-organized centre, established in 1954, is unusual in that it blends both the northern and the southern systems of *kalarippayattu*. Twice-daily training sessions start early at 4am; visitors are welcome to attend demonstrations (6–7pm) and the open session on Sundays (3–7pm). Alternatively, you can enrol on one of their *kalarippayattu* certificate courses, which run from one week to one year and are tailored to the needs of the student. The centre also offers lessons in the unique **Uzhichil massage** – a treatment derived from Ayurvedic medicine, designed as a cure to *kalari*-related injuries, which concentrates on the lymph glands to improve tone and circulation. To get to the school take a bus from the KSRTC or the Kaloor bus stands to the Netoor INTUC bus stand, and walk down the road for half a kilometre; the school is opposite the Mahadevar Temple.

Eating

Kochi offers an outstanding choice of places to eat, from the rustic fish-fry stalls next to the Chinese nets to fine dining with harbour views. As with accommodation, restaurants in Ernakulam tend to be cheaper but less atmospheric than those in Fort Cochin. If you're dining across the water from your hotel, make sure you are familiar with the ferry timings back (see box, p.448).

Unless otherwise stated, restaurants under the "Ernakulam" and "Fort Cochin" headings are marked on their relevant maps (see p.459 & p.454).

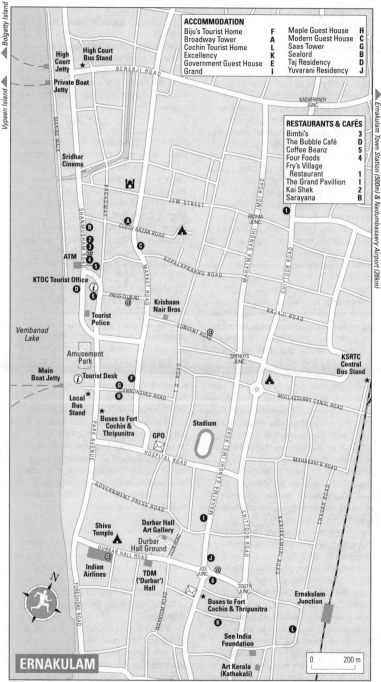

Bolgatty Island

Vypeen Island

ACCOMMODATION

Biju's Tourist Home	**F**
Broadway Tower	**A**
Cochin Tourist Home	**L**
Excellency	**K**
Government Guest House	**E**
Grand	**I**

Maple Guest House	**H**
Modern Guest House	**C**
Saas Tower	**G**
Sealord	**B**
Taj Residency	**D**
Yuvarani Residency	**J**

KACHERIPADY
JUNC.

RESTAURANTS & CAFÉS

Bimbi's	**3**
The Bubble Café	**D**
Coffee Beanz	**5**
Four Foods	**4**
Fry's Village Restaurant	
The Grand Pavillion	**1**
Kai Shek	**2**
Sarayana	**B**

BENERJI ROAD

High Court
Jetty

High Court
Bus Stand

Private Boat
Jetty

MARINE WALK

Sridhar
Cinema

BROADWAY

JEW STREET

CLOTH BAZAR ROAD

IMGI ROAD

MAHATMA GANDHI

PADMA
JUNC.

A

B

2
3
4
A
5

ATM

SHANMUGHAM ROAD

GOPALAPRABHU ROAD

C

MARKET ROAD

CHITTOOR ROAD

RAJAJI ROAD

KTDC Tourist Office

D

i
E

PRESS CLUB RD

@

Krishnan
Nair Bros

Tourist
Police

CONVENT ROAD

@

Vembanad
Lake

Amusement
Park

SHENOYS
JUNC.

**KSRTC
Central
Bus Stand**

Main
Boat Jetty

i Tourist Desk

F

G

H

CANNONSHED ROAD

MULLASSERRY CANAL ROAD

Local
Bus
Stand

Buses to Fort
Cochin &
Thripunitra

GPO

Stadium

MAHATMA GANDHI IMGI ROAD

CHITTOOR ROAD

MAHAKAVI G ROAD

KARIKKAMUR ROAD

CHAVAR ROAD

PARK AVENUE

HOSPITAL ROAD

GOVERNMENT PRESS ROAD

Shiva
Temple

**Durbar Hall
Art Gallery**

Durbar
Hall Ground

I

@

Indian
Airlines

DURBAR HALL ROAD

**TDM
('Durbar')
Hall**

J
@
6

JOS
JUNC.

SOUTH
JUNC.

**Ernakulam
Junction**

FORESHORE ROAD

Buses to Fort
Cochin & Thripunitra

K

L

N

See India
Foundation

ERNAKULAM

Art Kerala
(Kathakali)

0   200 m

Cochin Cultural Centre

Ernakulam

Bimbi's Shanmugham Rd. This modern South Indian fast-food joint, in midtown near the Sealord Boat Jetty, is hugely popular locally for its inexpensive Udupi, North Indian and Chinese snacks and meals. Their *vada-sambars* are the tangiest in town, and there's an exhaustive range of cooling ice cream and shakes to round your meal off.

The Bubble Café *Taj Residency*, Marine Drive. Luxury coffee shop in a vast, a/c glass-roofed conservatory close to the waterfront, serving pricey chilled snacks (such as prawns with papaya and mint timbale), multi-cuisine main courses and a particularly good range of Western cakes (Dundee, plum, palmettes and fudge).

Coffee Beanz Shanmugham Rd. Trendy a/c cappuccino bar, patronized mainly by well-heeled students shrieking into their mobiles over a full-on MTV soundtrack. The din notwithstanding, it's a good spot to beat the heat and grab a quick meal (burgers, fries, grilled sandwiches, *dosas*, fish curries, *appams* and samosas). The coffee's freshly ground and delicious, though the service is far less snappy than the fast-food uniforms.

Four Foods Shanmugham Rd. Busy, clean and popular roadside restaurant serving veg and non-veg meals, including generous thalis, fish dishes and a good-value "dish of the day". For dessert, try their Mumbai-style *faloodas*, vermicelli steeped in syrup with dried fruits and ice cream.

Fry's Village Restaurant Chittoor Rd, next to Mymoor Cinema. *Fry's* was the first place in the city to offer the kind of proper Keralan meals people would eat in their home towns and villages. It's busiest at lunchtimes, when workers pour in for the excellent-value thalis (veg Rs35; non-veg Rs40). You can also order mountainous Moppila-Muslim-style biriyanis (veg, prawn, mutton or chicken; Rs30–40), steaks of deliciously fresh masala-fried kingfish and the full range of traditional Keralan steamed rice cakes: *iddiappam*, *puttoo* etc. A comfortable, hygienic and cheap place to sample quality local cooking.

The Grand Pavillion MG Rd ☎0484/238 2061. An Ernakulam institution, famous for its gourmet Keralan dishes, especially the *karimeen pollichadu* with *appam*, which draws crowds on Sun evenings. They also do a huge range of Far Eastern, North Indian and Continental options, served on white table cloths by a legion of brisk waiters wearing black ties and waistcoats. The prices are restrained, too: count on Rs500–600 for three courses. Reservation recommended.

Kai Shek Penda Shopping Mall, Shanmugham Rd. Dimly-lit Chinese, with a much brighter, family a/c floor upstairs. Specialities include ginger chicken, chilli prawns and roast duck – though there are plenty of fried rice options for veggies. Mains from Rs80–120.

Sarayana *Sealord* hotel, Shanmugham Rd. Reasonably priced rooftop restaurant serving good Chinese, Indian and sizzlers. The harbour view is not what it was since the shopping centre opposite was built, but it's still a pleasant enough spot for a cold beer.

Fort Cochin

Addy's 1/286 Elphinstone Rd. Ramshackle, atmospheric and friendly, this family-run place near the Indo-Portuguese Museum occupies the ground floor of a late-eighteenth-century Dutch house. In a dining room with peeling pink plaster walls, you can enjoy homely Keralan dishes, the most tempting of them local seafood specialities steamed in banana leaves or pan-fried over a low flame on a proper *thava* griddle iron. Try the squid *chootu porachathu*, grilled seer fish with garlic and black pepper sauce or chicken *molee*. Most mains Rs165–210.

Chariot Beach Princess St. Unassuming terrace café-restaurant on one of the Fort's main crossroads, which really comes into its own in the evenings – it's one of only a handful of places serving beer (Prohibition-style from little china jugs), and stays open until midnight. The menu's a standard multi-cuisine, foreigner-oriented mix, with lots of seafood and Chinese options, and a tandoori churns out hot naan breads to go with the tasty flame-grilled chicken kebabs.

Elite Bakery Ground Floor, *Elite Lodge*, Princess St. One of very few bona fide locals' cafés left in Fort Cochin, and a dependable option if you're travelling on a budget. They serve Keralan and Western breakfasts, filling, freshly prepared veg and non-veg thalis at lunchtime, and Anglo-Indian snacks such as flaky pastry puffs (veg, beef or egg), fried potato cutlets, spring rolls and patties throughout the day and evening.

Fort House *Fort House Hotel*, 2/6A Calvathy Rd. One of the fort's hidden gems: carefully prepared Keralan specialities – including delicious *meen pollichathu* or grilled fish steak – served on a romantic, candle-lit jetty jutting into the harbour. The food is consistently good, and not too pricey (most mains Rs175–245); and the location's perfect for watching the ships chugging in and out of the docks.

The History *Brunton Boatyard*, Bellar Rd, next to Fort Cochin's Government Jetty. Renowned Keralan chef Jerry Matthew delved into the culinary traditions of Fort Cochin to devise *The History*'s eclectic menu. Served on a breezy raised terrace looking across the water to Vypeen Island, favourites include the Anglo-Indian "First-Class Railway Lamb Curry", Portuguese "Fernandes roast pork" and Syrian-Christian "Kuttanandi *tharavu* roast duck". Count on Rs750–850 for three courses, or more if you hit the (Indian) wine list.

Kashi Art Café Burgher St. Chi chi art gallery café, patronized almost exclusively by Westerners, and with a menu to match. Fragrant, freshly ground expresso coffee is the big draw, along with the *Kashi*'s famous house cakes (their chocolate gateau is legendary among travellers), but they also do a selection of light meals and savoury snacks through the day: check out the specials board.

Malabar House *Malabar House Hotel*, 1/268 Parade Rd, ☎0484/221 6666, ⓦwww .malabarhouse.com. Gourmet fusion cuisine, made from market-fresh ingredients and served on a chic garden dining terrace in one of Kerala's most stylish boutique hotels. Their signature dish is the seafood platter (Rs980), featuring juicy local lobster, tiger prawns, calamari and choice cuts of fish from the lagoon, but they offer a range of more sensibly priced Italian and South Indian alternatives, both veg and non-veg (Rs250–450). For dessert, try the chocolate samosas. The menu can be viewed online.

The Old Courtyard 1/371–2 Princess St. Few places capture the feel of old-world Cochin as vividly as this courtyard restaurant, where candlelit tables are laid out beneath Portuguese vaulted arches. The food is as fine as the location (hallmark dishes include baked seafood spaghetti and grilled fish with coriander butter) – and the *patronne-chef* is a dessert wizard. Most mains Rs200–275.

Salt 'n' Pepper/Brighton Café Tower Rd. This pair of terrace cafés, spread under the rain trees along the north side of Tower Rd, fill up after sunset and stay open until the small hours during the season. Both serve simple snacks, but the main attraction is the beer – surreptitiously poured out of china pots to rows of bored foreign budget tourists.

Teapot Café Peter Celli St. With its massive collection of teapots from around the world, shabby-chic colour-washed wood floors, tea-chest tables and funky little mezzanine floor, this backstreet tearoom has been giving the *Kashi* some much-needed

△ *Kashi Art Café*, Kochi

competition over the past few seasons. Quality teas and coffees are its mainstay, but there's also a selection of light meals and delicious home-made cakes on offer (including a stupendous "death by chocolate").

Upstairs Santa Cruz Rd. Currently the backpacker's favourite: a hip little trattoria run by a young Indian-Italian couple in a quirky, blue-and-white-painted first-floor dining room opposite the Basilica. The food's simple, fresh and authentically Italian, down to the imported olive oil and Parmesan: green leaf salad (Rs70); tasty bruschettas (Rs130); crisp-edged pizzas (Rs160–220); fresh pasta bakes and *lasagna al forno* (Rs260); and for dessert, rum-soaked pears or melt-in-the-mouth *zuccotto* (moist sponge filled with home-made ice cream).

Vasco Café Bastion St. Tiny budget travellers' breakfast joint in the heart of the tourist enclave, with relaxing wood tables and a huge bell-metal bowl in its barred window. The food – toasties, omelettes, muesli, fruit salad with curd, pancakes juices and the like – is prepared to order, tasty and inexpensive.

Listings

Airlines, domestic *Air Sahara*, airport ☎0484/261 1340; *Indian Airlines*, Durbar Hall Rd ☎0484/237114, airport ☎0484/2610101; *Go Air*, c/o UAE Travel Services, Chettupuzha Towers, PT

Usha Rd Junction ☎0484/235 5522; *Jet Airways*, 39/4158, Elmar Square Bldg, MG Rd, ☎0484/235 9212, airport ☎2610037; *Kingfisher Airlines*, K.B Oxford Business Centre, 39/4013, Free Kandath Rd,

MG Rd ☎0484/235 1144; *Paramount Airways*, airport ☎0484/2610404

Airlines, international Air Arabia XXVII/3202-A Kunnalekat Building, Atlantis Junction, MG Rd ☎484/235 9601; *Air India*, Collis Estate, MG Rd, ☎0484/235 1295, airport ☎0484/261 0040; *Air India* Express Collis Estate, MG Rd ☎0484/238 1885, airport ☎0484/261 0050; *Emirates*, Plot No. 696-A, opposite *Wyte Fort Hotel*, NH-47 Bypass, Maradu ☎0484/238 9999, airport ☎0484/261 1194; *Gulf Air*, c/o Jet Air, Atlantic Junction, MG Rd ☎0484/235 9242, airport ☎0484/261 1346; *Kuwait Airways*, 39/6823 Polachirackal Mansions, Ravipuram, MG Rd, airport ☎0484/261 0252; *Qatar Airways*, *Hotel Le Meridien*, Mezzanine Floor, Maradu ☎0484/3017350, airport ☎0484/261 1302; *Saudi Arabian Airlines*, airport ☎0484/261 1286; *Silk Air*, Aisha Manzil, Ravipuram, MG Rd ☎0484/ 236 1666, airport ☎0484/261 0157;

SriLankan Airlines, Trans Lanka Ltd, MG Rd ☎0484/236 1215, airport ☎0484/261 1313.

Banks Branches on MG Rd in Ernakulam include: ANZ Grindlays; State Bank of India (which also has a branch opposite the KTDC Tourist Reception Centre); and Andhra Bank. To exchange traveller's cheques, the best place is Thomas Cook (Mon–Sat 9.30am–6pm), near the Air India Building at Palal Towers, MG Rd; they also have a branch at the airport. ATMs can be found all over the centre of Ernakulam. In Fort Cochin, the Canara Bank has an ATM on Kanumpuram Junction (see map p.454). The Wilson Info Centre and Destinations, both on Princess St (open daily 9am–9pm) change cash and traveller's cheques at rates slightly above Thomas Cook, but are much more conveniently located.

Bookshops The two branches of Idiom (opposite the Dutch Palace, Jew Town, Mattancherry; and on Bastion St near Princess St, Fort Cochin) are

Moving on from Kochi/Ernakulam

For an overview of travel services to and from Kochi/Ernakulam, see Travel details, on p.495.

By air

The international airport (☎484/261 0113, ⌨www.cochinairport.com) at **Nedumbassery**, near Alwaye (aka Alua), is 26km north of Ernakulam and serves as Kerala's main gateway to and from the Gulf. A full list of domestic airlines appears on p.461 while destinations they fly to are covered in Travel details on p.495. For flights to the **Lakshadweep Islands** contact *Casino Hotel*, Willingdon Island (see p.465). A list of recommended travel agents is on p.464.

By bus

Buses leave Ernakulam's KSRTC Central bus stand for virtually every town in Kerala, and some beyond; most, but not all, are bookable in advance at the bus station. A full list appears in Travel details at the end of this chapter on p.495. However, for destinations further afield in Karnataka and Tamil Nadu, you're generally much better off on the train.

By train

Kochi lies on Kerala's main broad-gauge line and sees frequent trains down the coast to Thiruvananthapuram via Kottayam, Kollam and Varkala. Heading north, there are plenty of services to Thrissur, and thence northeast across Tamil Nadu to Chennai, but only a couple run direct to Mangalore. Since the opening of the Konkan Railway, a few express trains travel along the coast all the way to Goa and Mumbai, stopping close to Mangalore.

Although most long-distance express and mail trains depart from **Ernakulam Junction**, a couple of key services leave from **Ernakulam Town**. To confuse matters further, a few also start at Cochin Harbour station, so be sure to check the departure point when you book your ticket. The main reservation office, good for trains leaving all three stations, is at Ernakulam Junction; availability, fares and timetables can be checked online at ⌨www.indianrail.gov.in.

The trains listed opposite are recommended as the fastest and/or most convenient services from Kochi. If you're heading to **Alappuzha** for the backwater trip wonderful places to browse for books on travel, Indian and Keralan culture, flora and fauna, religion and art; they also have an excellent range of non-fiction.

Cinemas Sridhar Theatre (☎0484/235 2529), Shanmugham Rd, near the *Hotel Sealord*, screens English-language movies daily; check the listings pages of the *Indian Express* or *Hindu* (Kerala edition) to find out what's on. For the latest Malayalam and Hindi releases, head for the comfortable a/c Mymoon Cinema (☎0484/235 1869) at the north end of Chitoor Rd, or the Saritha Savitha Sangeetha (☎0484/ 236 6183), at the top of Market Rd.

Dentist The Emmanuel Dental Centre, Noble Square, Kadavanthara (☎0484/220 7544, ⓦwww.cosmeticdentalcentre.com) is an international-standard practice that does routine dental procedures as well as more advanced cosmetic work.

Hospitals The 600-bed Medical Trust Hospital on MG Rd (☎0484/235 8001, ⓦwww .medicaltrusthospital.com) is one of the state's most advanced private hospitals and has a 24hr casualty unit and ambulance service. Also recommended is the Ernakulam Medical Centre, NH Bypass, Paalarivattomj (☎0484/280 7101, ⓦwww.emccochin.com).

Internet access Café de Net on Bastion Rd, Fort Cochin, has nine machines and charges Rs30/hr; if it's full, try any of the smaller places off the bottom of Princess St nearby. In Ernakulam, convenient options include Net Park on Convent Rd and Mathsons on Durbar Hall Rd (both Rs30/hr).

Music stores Sargam, XL/6816 GSS Complex, Convent Rd, opposite the Public Library, stocks the best range of music tapes in the state, mostly Indian (Hindi films and lots of Keralan devotional music), with a couple of shelves of Western rock

to Kollam, take the bus, as the only train that can get you there in time invariably arrives late.

Recommended trains from Kochi/Ernakulam

Destination	Name	Number	Station	Departs	Total time
Bengaluru (Bangalore)	Kanyakumari–Bangalore Express	#6525	ET	daily 6.05pm	13hr
Chennai	Trivandrum–Chennai Mail	#2624	ET	daily 7.15pm	11hr 45min
Kozhikode (Calicut)	Netravati Express	#6346	EJ	daily 2.15pm	4hr 45min
Madgaon/ Margao (Goa)	Rajdhani Express*	#2431	EJ	Tues & Thurs 10.35pm	12hr
	Mangala–Lakshadweep Express	#2617	EJ	daily 12.45pm	14hr 30min
Madurai	Guruvayur–Chennai Express	#2617	EJ	daily 11.30pm	11hr 30min
Mangalore	Malabar Express	#6329	ET	daily 11.45pm	10hr 25min
	Parasuram Express	#6349	ET	daily 11.05am	9hr 15min
Mumbai	Netravati Express	#6346	EJ	daily 2.15pm	26hr 25min
Thiruvananthapuram	Parasuram Express	#6350	ET	daily 1.30pm	5hr 5min
Varkala	Parasuram Express	#6350	ET	daily 1.30pm	3hr 50min

EJ = Ernakulam Junction
ET = Ernakulam Town
* = a/c only, meals included

and pop. Music World, MKV Building, near Shenoy's Theatre on MG Rd is Kochi's answer to a music superstore, with Western pop, classical, compilations, world music and Indian *filmi* music. Sound of Melody, DH Rd, near the Ernakulam Junction station, has a good selection of traditional South Indian and contemporary Western music.

Musical instruments Manuel Industries, Banerji Rd, Kacheripady Junction, is the best for Indian classical and Western instruments. For traditional Keralan drums, ask at Thripunitra bazaar (see oppsoite).

Police The city's tourist police have a counter at the railway station. There is also a counter next to the KTDC Tourist Office at the southern end of Shanmugham Rd.

Post office The GPO is on Hospital Rd, not far from the Main Jetty; the city's poste restante is at the post office behind St Francis Church in Fort Cochin.

Tour and travel agents For air tickets, Kapitan Air Travel and Tours at 1/430 Burgher St in Fort Cochin (on the ground floor of *Adam's Old Inn*) is the fort's only IATA-bonded agent. Wild Kerala Tours, at VI/480 KVA Bldgs on Bazaar Rd, Mantancherry (☎0484/309 9520, ☎m98461 62157, ☜www.wildkeralatours .com) is recommended for wildlife and adventure safaris to some of Kerala's wildest corners, guided by local experts. If you'd like to book shorter backwater cruises by motorboats and canoes in the area ask at the Tourist Desk at Main Jetty in Ernakulam (☎0484/237 1761), who book accommodation for small hotels in beautiful locations in northern Kerala.

Around Kochi and Ernakulam

Within easy distance of Kochi and Ernakulam are **Thripunitra**, a small suburban town and former royal seat, and a three-kilometre stretch of sand called **Cherai**

The Lakshadweep Islands

Visitors to Kerala in search of an exclusive tropical paradise may well find it in **LAKSHADWEEP** (☜www.lakshadweep.nic.in), the "one hundred thousand islands" which lie between 200km and 400km offshore in the deep blue of the Arabian Sea. The smallest Union Territory in India, Lakshadweep's 27 tiny, coconut-palm-covered **coral islands** are the archetypal tropical hideaway, edged with pristine white sands and surrounded by calm lagoons where average water temperature stays around 26°C all year. Beyond the lagoons lie the coral **reefs**, home to sea turtles, dolphins, eagle rays, lionfish, parrotfish, octopus, barracudas and sharks. Devoid of animal and bird life, only ten of the islands are inhabited, with a total population of just over 50,000, the majority of whom are Malayalam-speaking Sunni Muslims said to be descended from seventh-century Keralan Hindus who converted to Islam.

The main sources of income are fishing and coconuts. Fruit, vegetables and pulses are cultivated in small quantities but staples such as rice have always had to be imported. The Portuguese, who discovered the value of **coir rope**, spun from coconut husk, controlled Lakshadweep during the sixteenth century; when they imposed an import tax on rice, locals retaliated by poisoning some of the forty-strong Portuguese garrison, and terrible reprisals followed. As Muslims, the islanders enjoyed friendly relations with Tipu Sultan of Mysore, which naturally aroused the ire of the British, who moved in at the end of the eighteenth century and remained until Independence, when Lakshadweep became a Union Territory.

Visiting Lakshadweep

Concerted attempts are being made to minimize the ecological impact of tourism in Lakshadweep. At present, accommodation is available for **non-Indians** on only two of the islands – Bangaram and Kadmat. Indian tourists are also allowed to visit the neighbouring islands of Kavaratti and Minicoy (both closed to foreigners).

All visits to **Kadmat** must be arranged in Kochi through the Society for Promotion of Recreational Tourism and Sports (SPORTS) on IG Road, Willingdon Island (☎0484/266 8387, ☜www.lakshadweeptourism.com). They offer a five–day package **cruise** to Kavaratti, Kalpeni and Minicoy islands ($225–375 per person) on one of their ships. Meals are included, and permits taken care of.

Beach, which offers a taste of both beach- and backwater-life. Visitors to Kochi and Ernakulam who really want to get away from it all, however, and have time and a lot of money to spare, could do no better than to head from here to **Lakshadweep** (see box below), the "one hundred thousand islands", which lie between 200km and 400km offshore, in the deep blue of the Arabian Sea.

Thripunitra

Some 12km southeast of Ernakulam and a short bus or auto-rickshaw ride from the bus stand just south of Jos Junction on MG Road, the small suburban town of **THRIPUNITRA** is worth a visit for its dilapidated colonial-style **Hill Palace** (Tues–Sun 9am–5pm; Rs10), now an eclectic museum. The royal family of Cochin at one time maintained around forty palaces – this one was confiscated by the state government after Independence, and has slipped into dusty decline over the past decade.

One of the museum's finest exhibits is an early seventeenth-century wooden *mandapa* (hall) removed from a temple in Pathanamthitta, featuring excellent carvings of themes from the Ramayana, including the coronation of the monkey king Sugriva. Of interest too are the silver filigree jewel boxes, gold and silver ornaments, and ritual objects associated with grand ceremonies. The **epigraphy gallery** contains an eighth-century Jewish Torah, Keralan stone and copperplate

The uninhabited, teardrop-shaped half-square-kilometre islet of **Bangaram** welcomes a limited number of foreign tourists at any one time, and expects them to pay handsomely for the privilege. CGH Earth's *Bangaram Island Resort* (❺www .cghearth.com; ❾), bookable through a Kochi travel agent (see above), accommodates up to thirty couples in thatched cottage rooms, each with a veranda. Cane tables and chairs sit outside the restaurant on the beach, and a few hammocks are strung up between the palms. There's no a/c, TV, radio, telephone, newspapers or shops, let alone discos. Facilities include scuba diving (again expensive at $85 per day plus $40 per dive, or $70 for two), glass-bottomed boat trips to neighbouring uninhabited islands, and deep-sea fishing (Oct to mid-May; $65–90). Kayaks, catamarans and a sailing boat are available free, and it's possible to take a day-trip to Kadmat.

A British-run diving firm based in Goa also operates diving holidays in Lakshadweep; a full rundown of prices and booking conditions appears online at ❺www.goadiving.com.

Getting to the islands

At present, the only way for foreigners to reach Bangaram is the expensive flights on small 12-seater aircraft run by Indian Airlines out of Kochi (one daily except Sun; 1hr 35min), Foreigners pay around $300 for the return trip, which takes an hour and a half. Flights arrive in Lakshadweep at the island of **Agatti**, 8km southwest of Bangaram; the connecting boat journey to Bangaram takes two hours, picking its way through the shallows to avoid corals. During the monsoon (May 16–Sept 15) helicopters are used to protect the fragile coral reefs that lie just under the surface. All arrangements, including flights, accommodation and the necessary entry permit, are handled by the *Casino Hotel*, Willingdon Island, Kochi (☎0484/266 8221, ✉casino@vsnl.net). Some foreign tour operators, however, offer all-in packages combining Lakshadweep with another destination, usually Goa.

Theoretically, it's possible to visit Lakshadweep all year round; the hottest time is April and May, when the temperature can reach 33°C; the **monsoon** (May–Sept) attracts approximately half the rainfall seen in the rest of Kerala, in the form of passing showers rather than a deluge, although the seas are rough.

inscriptions. Sculpture, ornaments and weapons in the **bronze gallery** include a *kingini katti* knife, whose decorative bells belie the fact that it was used for beheading, and a body-shaped cage in which condemned prisoners would be hanged while birds pecked them to death. Providing the place isn't crowded with noisy school groups, you could check out the nearby **deer park**; there are peaceful spots to picnic beneath the cashew trees in the garden behind the palace.

Performances of theatre, classical music and dance, including consecutive all-night **kathakali** performances, are held over a period of several days during the annual festival (Oct/Nov) at the **Shri Purnatrayisa Temple** on the way to the palace. Inside the temple compound, both in the morning and at night, massed drum orchestras perform *chenda melam* in procession with fifteen caparisoned elephants. At night, the outside walls of the sanctuary are covered with thousands of tiny oil lamps. The temple is normally closed to non-Hindus, but admittance to appropriately dressed visitors is usually allowed at this time.

Cherai Beach

The closest decent beach to Kochi is **Cherai**, 35km to the north. It shelters a backwater and supports an active fishing community, some of whom use Chinese fishing nets (see p.455). The **Sri Goureeswara Temple**, closed to non-Hindus, is dedicated to the deity Sri Subramanya Swami and holds its annual nine-day festival (*utsavam*) in January or February every year. The *utsavam* is a great time to see traditional dance, including *kathakali* performances, but the highlight of the festival is on the seventh day, when eighteen caparisoned elephants take to the streets in a spectacular procession.

To get there, you can either jump on the ferry across to Vypeen Island from Fort Cochin and transfer onto the hourly bus, or catch one of the more frequent buses from opposite the High Court Jetty in Ernakulam.

Thrissur

THRISSUR (Trichur), a bustling market hub and temple town roughly midway between Kochi (74km south) and Palakkad (79km northeast) on the NH-47, is a convenient base for exploring the cultural riches of central Kerala. Close to the Palghat (Palakkad) Gap – an opening in the natural border made by the Western Ghat mountains – it presided over the main trade route into the region from Tamil Nadu and Karnataka. For years Thrissur was the capital of Cochin State, controlled at various times by both the *zamorin* of Kozhikode and Tipu Sultan of Mysore.

The modern town dates from the eighteenth century, when Raja Rama Varma, the ruler of Travancore, developed the city, laying out roads and establishing markets with which Christian merchants were invited to trade. Although a Hindu himself, the raja helped further ensure the welfare of the Christian communities by establishing enclaves for them to the east and south of the city centre.

Today, Thrissur derives most of its income from remittance cheques sent by expatriates in the Gulf – hence the predominance of ostentatious modern houses in the surrounding villages. As the home of several influential art institutions, the town also prides itself on being the cultural capital of Kerala. The state's largest temple, **Vaddukanatha**, is here too, at the centre of a huge circular *maidan* that hosts all kinds of public gatherings, not least Kerala's most extravagant, noisy and sumptuous festival, **Puram**.

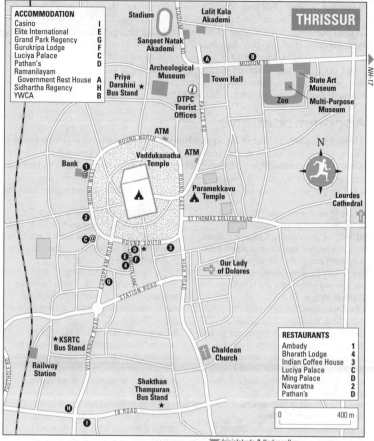

Arrival and information

The principal point of orientation in Thrissur is the **Round**, a road (subdivided into North, South, East and West) which circles the Vaddukanatha temple complex and *maidan* in the town centre. On the mainline to Chennai and other points in Tamil Nadu, and with good connections to Kochi and Thiruvananthapuram, the **railway station** is 1km southwest, opposite the **KSRTC long-distance bus stand**. **Priya Darshini bus stand** (also known as "North", "Shoranur" and "Wadakkancheri" stand), close to Round North, serves Shoranur (for the Kalamanadalam Academy). The **Shakthan Thampuran bus stand**, on TB Road, just over 1km from Round South, serves local destinations south such as Irinjalakuda, Kodungallur and Guruvayur.

The DTPC **tourist office** (Mon–Sat 10am–5pm; ☎0487/232 0800) is on Palace Road, opposite the Town Hall (five minutes' walk off Round East). Run by volunteers, its primary purpose is to promote the Puram elephant festival, but staff also give out maps of Thrissur. The best place to **change money** and traveller's cheques is the UTI Bank in the City Centre Shopping building

(Mon–Fri 9.30am–3.30pm, Sat 9.30am–1.30pm) on Round West. The UAE Exchange & Financial Services (Mon–Sat 9.30am–6pm, Sun 9.30am–1.30pm) in the basement of the *Casino Hotel* building also changes currency and travel-ler's cheques. Both of the above, and a dozen or so other banks around the centre, have ATMs. The **GPO** is on the southern edge of town, near the *Casino Hotel*, off TB Road. **Internet** facilities are available at Hugues Net on the top floor of the City Centre Shopping building and SS Consultants next to the *Luciya Palace* hotel; rates are around Rs20/hr.

Accommodation

Thrissur has a fair number of mid-price **hotels**, but only a couple of decent budget places – the best of them the splendid *Ramanilayam Government Guest House*. Almost everywhere follows a 24hr checkout policy. If you're planning to be here during **Puram**, book well in advance and bear in mind that room rates soar – some of the more upmarket hotels charge up to ten times their normal prices.

Casino TB Rd, near the railway station ☎0487/242 4699, ⓦwww.casinotels.com. Formerly the town's poshest hotel, now in decline; the rooms (non-a/c and a/c) are all attached and presentable enough, if a little rough around the edges. There's a multi-cuisine restaurant, cocktail bar, lawn and kiddies' park, and foreign exchange (residents only). ④–⑤

Elite International Chembottil Lane, off Round South ☎0487/242 1033, ⓔmail @hoteleliteinternational.com. Pronounced "Ee-light", this mid-range place in the centre of town has rooms opening onto corridors, some with balconies overlooking the green. The staff are very friendly and helpful, and there's a good restaurant and relaxing garden. Rates include breakfast. ④–⑥

Grand Park Regency Mullassery Tower, Kuruppam Road ☎0487/242 8247, ⓦwww .grandparkregency.com. Gleaming, efficient business hotel in a pink-coloured multi-storey block bang in the town centre, close to the bus stand, railway station and temple green. Its rooms are modern and centrally air-conditioned. Facilities include a fitness centre and roof garden. ⑤–⑥

Gurukripa Lodge Chembottil Lane ☎0487/242 1895. Run with great efficiency by the venerable Mr Venugopal, the *Gurukripa*, just off Round South, offers a variety of simple attached rooms (including several great-value singles) ranged around a long, pleasant inner courtyard. Some a/c. ②–③

🏃 **Kadappuram Beach Resort** Nattika Beach, 30km southwest ☎0487/239 7588, ⓦwww.kadappurambeachresorts.com. Exclusive, eco-friendly wellness resort located on a tranquil stretch of Nattika beach. Scattered under a shady palm grove criss-crossed by narrow tidal canals, its ten bamboo and coconut-leaf cottages are panelled with aromatic herbs; each has two double rooms and attached bathrooms, and there's a top-notch

Green Leaf Ayurveda centre, *Chikilsalayam*. The whole 4-acre site is blissfully quiet (no TVs or telephones in the huts) and the beach is only 200m away. From $130 for a double room per night (including obligatory full board). ⑨

Luciya Palace Marar Rd ☎0487/242 4731, ⓔluciyapalace@hotmail.com. Slightly overpriced mid-range option, with uninspiring doubles and suites, whose redeeming feature is a secluded rear garden. ④–⑥

Pathans Round South ☎0487/242 5620. Its basement entrance is none too promising, but the good-sized rooms in this conveniently central hotel, with its lavishly carved teak and rosewood furniture, have an appealing colonial feel and are good value. ③–④

🏃 **Ramanilayam Government Rest House** Palace Rd ☎0471/233 2016. Star-hotel comfort at economy lodge rates, in palatial suites with balconies, or smaller doubles (some a/c), set in manicured gardens on the northeast side of town near the zoo and museum. As with all Government Guest Houses, officials get priority (even at the last minute), which can make a mockery of advance bookings. ②–③

Sidhartha Regency Veliyannur Rd, Kokkalai ☎0487/242 4773, ⓦwww.hotelsidartharegency .com. In the southwestern corner of town near the railway station, this good-value, modern three-star ranks among the most welcoming and comfortable options within walking distance of the centre. The seven-storey block holds a swimming pool (set in lawns to the rear), multi-gym, health club, multi-cuisine restaurant, bar and gardens. ⑤–⑥

YWCA Museum Rd, Chembukabu ☎0487/232 2528. Women-only hostel opposite the town zoo and museum, popular mainly with long-staying students (both young and not so young). Its clean attached doubles (non-a/c) are a bargain. ②

The Town

At the centre of the Round, the **Vaddukanatha Temple** (closed to non-Hindus) is a walled complex of fifteen shrines, dating from the twelfth century or earlier, the principal of which is dedicated to Shiva. Inside, the grassy compound is surprisingly quiet and spacious, with a striking apsidal shrine dedicated to Ayappa (see box, p.437). Once an essential ingredient of the temple's cultural life, but now under-used and neglected, the long, sloping-roofed **Kuttambalam Theatre** (closed to non-Hindus), with carved panels and lathe-turned wooden pillars, serves as a venue for the ancient Sanskrit performance forms of *chakyar kuttu* and *kutiyattam*.

The **State Art Museum** (Tues–Sun 9am–6.30pm; Rs8) stands on Museum Road, ten minutes' walk from the Round in the northeast of town. Collections of faded local bronzes, jewellery, fine woodcarvings of fanged temple guardians and a profusion of bell-metal oil lamps make up the bulk of its collection. Next door, the **zoo** (same hours as museum; free) is a predictably sad, rundown affair. In the same compound, the **Multi-Purpose Museum** (same hours; free) is home to an odd hoard of skeletons, stuffed animals, minerals, weapons and costumes.

A five-minute rickshaw ride away, opposite the Priya Darshini bus stand, the **Archeological Museum** (Tues–Sun 9.30am–1pm & 2–4.30pm; Rs10) occupies the 200-year-old Shaktan Thampuran Palace, the former residence of the Kochi Royal Family. Beautifully decorated throughout with intricate wood- and tile-work, the building is centred on a colonnaded patio. Exhibits include fifteenth- and eighteenth-century hero stones, a fearsome selection of beheading axes, and a massive iron-studded treasury box still in its original place (presumably because no-one has ever managed to shift its 1500kg dead weight). The real highlight, however, is the royal *palliyara*, or bedchamber, boasting a traditional carved wood four-poster and vibrant ceramic tiles. Visits wind up at the **Heritage Garden**, where you can cool off in the shade next to a delightful lily pond, with exotic birds and butterflies flitting through the greenery.

Also on the northern side of the centre, on Stadium Road, the **Sangeet Natak Akademi** (℡0487/233 2134, ⓦwww.sangeetnatak.org) features a large auditorium that hosts occasional music and dance concerts as well as contemporary Keralan theatre, which has an enthusiastic following and tends to be heavily political. Around the corner stands the **Lalit Kala Akademi** (Mon–Fri 11am–7pm; ℡0487/233 3773, ⓦwww.lalitkala.gov.in), where you can see exhibitions of international artists as well as contemporary Indian art.

One of the most important churches for Thrissur's large Christian population is the Syrian-Catholic **Lourdes Cathedral**, along St Thomas College Road, 1km east of the Round, where daily Masses serve a regular congregation of nine hundred. Like many of Kerala's Indo-Gothic churches, the exterior of dome and spires is more impressive than the interior, with its unadorned metal rafters and corrugated-iron ceiling. Steps lead down from the altar to the crypt, a rather dilapidated copy of the grotto in Lourdes. The 80-metre **Bell Tower** is also open to visitors (Tues–Fri 10am–1pm & 2–6pm; Sat & Sun 10am–1pm & 2–7.30pm; Rs15); you can climb the 350 steps or take the lift to the top, from where views extend across the palms to the foothills of the distant Ghats. Those who walk can pause for breath at the permanent exhibition of artwork depicting the life of Jesus which lines the tower staircase, ranging from beautifully detailed stained-glass windows to garish frescoes and wood carvings.

Our Lady of Dolores, just south of the Round, is another important Catholic shrine, boasting neo-Gothic spires and the largest interior of any church in South India. Slightly further south, the **Chaldean Church** (services Mon–Sat 7am–9am, Sun 7.30am–9.30am), dedicated to Mary, is the most ancient of all Keralan Christian centres and the focal point of the **Nestorian Syrian** community, which also runs a school here. Not much of the original structure remains, as the church was extensively renovated in the nineteenth century. Owing to this renovation, the gabled facade is the most remarkable part of what remains of the original structure.

Shopping

Thrissur is a good place to pick up Keralan **crafts**, and its main shopping area is on the Round. On Round West, the **Kerala State Handicraft Emporium** specializes in wood; a one-minute walk from Round East at the top of Palace Road, **Co-optex** sells a good range of hand-loom cloth. At **Chemmanur's** on Round South, near the *Elite Hotel*, you'll find the usual carved wooden-elephant-type souvenirs, and, on the ground floor, a high-kitsch Aladdin's Cave of nodding dogs, Jesus clocks, Mecca table ornaments and parabolic nail-and-string art. **Alter Media** at Utility Building, Nehru Bazaar, Nayarangadi is a small but interesting bookshop devoted to women's studies, while **Cosmos**, on Round West, is a treasure-trove of novels, academic tomes and books on art, drama and culture.

For an eclectic selection of Indian music, try **Melody Corner**, at the junction of Round South and Kuruppam Road. Its shelves are stacked with classical resolutely and precisely keep the tempo, essential to the cumulative effect of the music. Over an extended period, the *melam* passes through four phases, each twice as fast as the last, from a grand and graceful dead slow through to a frenetic pace.

At the arrival of the fastest tempo, those astride the elephants stand, manipulating their feather fans and hair whisks in coordinated sequence, while behind, unfurled umbrellas are twirled in flashes of dazzling colour, their pendants glinting silver in the sun. The cymbals crash furiously, often raised above the head, requiring extraordinary stamina (and causing nasty weals on the hands). The master drummers play at their loudest and fastest, frequently intensified by surges of energy emanating from single players, one after another; a chorus of trumpets, in ragged unison, accompanies the cacophony, creating a sound that has altered little since the festival's origins.

All this is greeted by tremendous firework explosions and roars from the crowd; many people punch the air, while others are clearly *talam branthans*, rhythm "madmen", who follow every nuance of the structure. When the fastest speed is played out, the slowest tempo returns and the procession edges forward, the *mahouts* leading the elephants by the tusk. Stopping again, the whole cycle is repeated. At night, the Vaddukanatha temple entrances are a blaze of coloured lights and a spectacular firework display takes place in the early hours of the morning.

If you venture to Thrissur for Puram, be prepared for packed buses and trains. Needless to say, accommodation should be booked well in advance. An umbrella or hat is recommended for protection from the sun. Unfortunately, Puram has become an excuse for groups of Indian men to get very drunk; women are advised to dress conservatively and only to go in the morning, or to watch with a group of Indian women.

Similar but much smaller events take place in town, generally from September onwards, with most during the summer (April and May). Enquire at a tourist office or your hotel, or ask someone to check a local edition of the newspaper, *Mathrabhumi*, for local performances of *chenda melam*, and other drum orchestras such as *panchavadyam* and *tyambaka*.

Hindustani and Carnatic albums, devotional and *Panchavadyam* (Keralan temple festival music) compilations and Hindi and Malayalam film songs.

Kuruppam Road, which leads south towards the railway station from the western end of Round South, is one of the best spots in Kerala to buy **bell-metal** products, particularly oil lamps made in the village of Nadavaramba, near Irinjalakuda (see p.475). The friendly **Nadavaramba Krishna & Sons** is a good place to start browsing. Continuing south on Kuruppam Road to the next junction with Station Road, cheap Christian, Muslim and Hindu devotional pictures etched on metal are the main stock in trade, along with festival accessories such as medallion-fringed umbrellas similar to those used for Puram (see box above).

Eating and drinking

With so many hotels and busy "meals" joints lining the Round, there's no shortage of dependable places to eat in Thrissur. From 8.30pm onwards, you can also join the auto-rickshaw-wallahs, hospital visitors, itinerant mendicants, Ayyappa devotees and student revellers who congregate at the popular **thattu-kada** hot-food market on the corner of Round South and Round East, opposite the Medical College Hospital. The rustic Keralan cooking – omelettes, *dosas*, *parottas*, *iddiappam*, bean curries and egg masala – is always freshly prepared, delicious and unbelievably cheap.

Ambady Round West. Down a lane and away from the Round traffic noise. Good selection of Keralan staples as well as lunchtime thalis and dozens of milkshakes and ice creams.

Bharath Lodge Chembottil Lane, 50m down the road from the *Elite Hotel*. Piping hot South Indian *vada-sambar* and *iddli* breakfasts, as well as "all you can eat" Keralan meals (Rs24–35) at lunchtime.

Indian Coffee House Round South. The usual cheap and popular *ICH* range of South Indian snacks, as well as strong chai and weak coffee, served by waiters whose serious demeanour is undermined by their old-school ice-cream fan turbans and curry-stained tunics.

Luciya Palace Marar Rd, just off the southwest corner of the Round. Hotel restaurant serving Indian and Chinese dishes in a pleasant garden illuminated by fairy lights.

Ming Palace Pathan Building, Round South. Inexpensive "Chindian" with dim lighting, cheesy muzak and a menu of chop suey, noodles and lots of chicken and veg dishes.

Navaratna Round West. Inexpensive Keralan and North Indian veg and non-veg menus as well as Chinese noodles and fish soup. With a hefty a/c system, it's a great spot to cool down, and the compartment-style layout allows for greater privacy than most places.

Pathan's Round South. Deservedly popular veg restaurant, with a cosy a/c family annexe and a large canteen-like dining hall. Generous portions and plenty of choice, including *koftas*, kormas and lots of tandoori options, as well as Keralan thalis and wonderful Kashmiri naan.

Around Thrissur

The chief attraction of the area **around Thrissur** is the opportunity to get to grips with Kerala's cultural heritage. Countless festivals, at their peak before the monsoon hits in May, enable visitors to catch some of the best drummers in the world, **kathakali** dance-drama and **kutiyattam**, the world's oldest surviving theatre form.

Irinjalakuda

The village of **IRINJALAKUDA**, 20km south of Thrissur, is the site of the unique **Koodal Manikiyam Temple**, dedicated to **Bharata**, the brother of Rama. It boasts a superbly elegant tiled *kuttambalam* **theatre** within its outer courtyard, built to afford an unimpeded view for the maximum number of spectators (drawn from the highest castes), and known for its excellent acoustics. A profusion of painted woodcarvings of mythological animals and stories from the epics decorate the interior. On the low stage, enclosed by painted wooden columns and friezes of female dancers, stand two large copper *mizhavu* drums for use in the Sanskrit drama **kutiyattam** (see Contexts, p.790), permanently

---

Chembuthra Puram

If you're in the area in late-January or early-February, it's well worth checking the precise dates of the spectacular **Chembuthra Puram** temple festival, held in the nearby village of **CHEMBUTHRA**, 13km north of Thrissur. Second only in its scale and extravagance to Thrissur's own annual Puram, the event features no less than **46 elephants**, each with flaming firebrands attached to their trunks, and accompanied in their slow marches by the usual cacophony of drum orchestras and fireworks. Processions reach their climax as they converge on the village *maidan*, watched by ecstatic and noisy crowds.

Buses to Chembuthra leave from Thrissur's Priya Darshini stand, dropping passengers at the junction on the NH-17, a kilometre's pleasant walk from the temple.

△ Preparing for a *kathakali* performance

installed in wooden frames into which a drummer climbs to play. Traditionally, *mizhavus* were considered sacred objects; Nandikeshvara, Shiva's rhythm-man, was said to reside in them. The drama for which they provided music was a holy ritual, and traditionally the instrument was never allowed to leave the temple and was only played by members of a special caste, the Nambyars. Since then, outsiders have learned the art of *mizhavu* playing, although the orthodox authorities do not allow them to play inside.

Around 500m from the Bharata temple (turn left as you leave), **Natana Kairali** (Mon–Sat 11am–1pm & 3–7pm) is an important cultural centre dedicated to the documentation and performance of Kerala's lesser-known theatre arts, including *kutiyattam*, *nangiar koothu* (female mono-acting), shadow and puppet theatres. The centre is based in the home of one of Kerala's most illustrious acting families, Ammanur Chakyar Madhom (say this name when you ask for directions). Natana Kairali's director, Shri G. Venu (☎0488/282 5559; ✉venuji@satyam.net.in), is a mine of information about Keralan arts, and can advise on forthcoming performances. In addition, his wife Nirmala Paniker, also an acclaimed scholar, founded **Natana Kaisiki**, a research centre on the same site dedicated to the preservation of traditional dance and theatre traditions of Keralan women: *mohiniyattam*, *nangiarkoothu* and *thiruvathirakali*. A selection of books on the region's performing arts, by Dr Venu, Nirmala Panker and other academics, is sold inside.

Irinjalakuda is best reached by **bus** from the Shakthan Thampuran stand in Thrissur rather than by train, as the railway station is an inconvenient 8km east of town. If you need to stay, the *Udupi Woodlands Hotel* (☎0488/282 0149; ❸–❹), near the bus stand on the Bharata temple road, has clean, spacious double rooms – most of them with marble floors and powerful fans.

Kodungallur

Virtually an island surrounded by backwaters and the sea, **KODUNGALLUR** (Cranganore), 35km south of Thrissur, is rich in Keralan history. The relative obscurity of the unexceptional modern town contrasts with tales of its illustrious past. Kodungallur has been identified as the site of the ancient cities of **Vanji** (one-time capital of the Chera kingdom), and **Muziris**, described in the first century AD by the Roman traveller Pliny as "*primum emporium Indiae*", the most important port in India. Other accounts describe the harbour as crowded with great ships, warehouses, palaces, temples and *yavanas* (a generic term for foreigners) who brought gold and left with spices, sandalwood, teak, gems and silks. The Romans are said to have built a temple in Kodungallur, and while nothing remains, their presence has been shown through finds of coins, the majority of which date between the reigns of Augustus to Nero (27 BC–68 AD). Its life as a great port was curtailed in 1341 by floods that silted up the harbour, leading to the development of Kochi (Cochin). Today, travellers will find that most of Kodungallur's sights require some imagination to appreciate. The town is best visited in a day-trip by **bus** from Thrissur's Shakthan Thampuran stand (1hr 30min), or on a combined visit to Irinjalakuda, only 7km away.

Standing on a large piece of open ground at the centre of Kodungallur, the ancient and typically Keralan **Kurumba Bhagavati Temple** is the site of an extraordinary annual event that some residents would prefer didn't happen at all. The **Bharani festival**, held during the Malayalam month of Meenom (March/April), attracts droves of devotees, both male and female, mainly from low-caste communities previously excluded from the temple. Their devotions consist in part of drinking copious amounts of alcohol and taking to the streets to sing Bharani *pattu*, sexually explicit songs about, and addressed to, the goddess Bhagavati, which are considered obscene and highly offensive by many other Keralans. On Kavuthindal, the first day, the pilgrims run en masse around the perimeters of the temple three times at breakneck speed, beating its walls with sticks. Until the mid-1950s, chickens were sacrificed in front of the temple; today, a simple red cloth symbolizes the bloody ritual. An important section of the devotees are the crimson-clad village oracles, wielding scythe-like swords with which they sometimes beat themselves on the head in ecstatic fervour, often drawing blood. Despite widespread disapproval, the festival draws plenty of spectators.

Cheraman Juma Masjid, 1.5km south of Kodungallur centre on NH-17, is thought to be the oldest mosque in India, founded in the seventh century by **Cheraman Perumal**, the legendary Keralan king who converted to Islam, abdicated and emigrated to Mecca. The supposed site of his palace, Cheraman Parambu, is today nothing more than a few broken columns on open ground. The present building, which dates from the sixteenth century, was predominantly made of wood, in a style usually associated with Keralan Hindu temples. Unfortunately, due to weather damage, it has been partly rebuilt, and the facade, at least, is now rather mundane, with concrete minarets. The wooden interior remains intact, however, with a large Keralan oil lamp in the centre. Introduced five centuries ago for group study of the Qur'an, the lamp has taken on great significance to other communities, and Muslims, Christians and Hindus alike bring oil on the auspicious occasion of major family events. In an anteroom, a small mausoleum is said to be the burial place of Habib Bin Malik, an envoy sent from Mecca by Cheraman Perumal. Women are not allowed into the mosque at any time, but interested male visitors should contact the assistant *mukhari* (imam, or priest), K. M. Saidumohamed, who lives directly opposite and will show you around.

Less than 500m south from the Cheraman Juma Masjid, past a bend in the main highway (NH-17), a wide avenue leads past tall lamps to the **Thiruvanchikkulam Mahadeva Temple**, dedicated to Shiva. Located in a peaceful setting with a

Nadavaramba bell-metal oil lamps

Keralan nights are made more enchanting by the use of **oil lamps**. The most common type, seen everywhere, is a slim, free-standing metal column topped by a spike that rises from a circular receptacle for coconut oil, with cloth or banana plant fibre wicks. Every classical theatre performance keeps a large lamp burning centre-stage all night. The special atmosphere of temples is also enhanced by innumerable lamps, some hanging from chains; others, *deepa stambham*, are multi-tiered and stand metres high.

The village of **Nadavaramba**, 5km from Irinjalakuda on the Kodungallur road, is an important centre for the manufacture of oil lamps and large cooking vessels, known as *uruli* and *varppu*. **Bell-metal** alloys are made from copper and tin – unlike brass, which is a blend of copper and zinc – and give a sonorous chime when struck. One of the best places to buy is the Bellwics Handicrafts Cooperative, just north of Nadavaramba Church, where you can watch the various stages of the casting process, from the making of sand and wax moulds to the pouring of molten metal, labour-intensive filing and polishing. The largest independent manufacturer in Kerala, Bellwics produce an array of bell metal utensils: fourteen different kinds of lamp, Ayurvedic treatment utensils, cooking vessels of every conceivable size and temple decorations. Prices depend on the weight of the object, starting at Rs600 per kilogram.

backdrop of tall coconut trees, it's a fine example of traditional Keralan temple architecture. Access to the outer courtyard is via a majestic gateway with a sloping roof and carvings of elephants, gods and goddesses. Inside the enclosure, past a large multi-tiered metal lamp, a porch with carvings dedicated to the heroes of the great Hindu epic, the Ramayana, marks the furthest point non-Hindus are allowed. Within the restricted enclosure, an impressive columned hall shelters Shiva's ever faithful bull Nandi, while the inner sanctum houses a plain stone *lingam*. Despite the restriction, low retaining walls allow a good view of the extensive complex, which is well worth the short detour.

The **Mar Thoma Pontifical Shrine**, fronted by a crescent of Neoclassical colonnades at Azhikode (pronounced "Arikode") Jetty (6km), marks the place where the Apostle Thomas is said to have arrived in India in 52 AD. Situated on the backwaters, it's a tranquil spot with a promenade and stalls selling religious paraphernalia, but hardly warrants a detour unless you're desperate to see the shard of the saint's wrist bone enshrined within the church (daily 9am-6pm). Frequent buses from Kodungallur stop at Azhikode Jetty, at the end of the promenade past the fishing boats.

If you want **to stay**, the *Hotel Indraprestham*, close to the town centre (T0480/280 2678; ❸–❹), has standard non-a/c and a/c rooms as well as a cheap "meals" restaurant, an a/c "family" restaurant and bar.

Guruvayur

Kerala's most important Krishna shrine, the high-walled temple of **GURUVAYUR** (3am–1pm & 4.30–10pm; closed to non-Hindus), 29km northwest of Thrissur, attracts a constant flow of devotees, second only in volume to Ayyappa's pilgrimage at Sabarimala (see box, p.437). Its deity, **Guruvayurappan**, has inspired numerous paeans from Keralan poets, most notably Narayana Bhattatiri, who wrote the *Narayaniyam* in the sixteenth century, when the temple, whose origins are legendary, seems to have first risen to prominence.

Guruvayur is one of the richest temples in Kerala and is constantly awash with **pilgrims**, dressed in their best white and gold-trim clothes. The market outside is noisy and intense, with stalls full of glitter and trinkets and a palpable air of excitement, particularly when events inside spill out into the streets. A temple committee stall outside the main gates auctions off the donations, including bell-metal lamps, received at the shrine – according to superstition, if you buy any of these items they must be returned to the temple as gifts.

Of the temple's 24 annual **festivals**, the most important are Ekadashi and Ulsavam. The eighteen days of Ekadashi, in the month of Vrischikam (Nov/Dec), are marked by processions of caparisoned elephants outside the temple, while the exterior of the building is decorated with the tiny flames of innumerable oil lamps from sunset onwards. Performances staged in front of the temple (check dates with a KTDC office) attract the cream of South Indian classical music artists.

During Ulsavam, in the month of Kumbham (Feb/March), tantric rituals are conducted inside, an **elephant race** is run outside on the first day, and elephant processions take place during the ensuing six days. On the ninth day, the Palivetta, or "hunt" occurs; the deity, mounted on an elephant, circumnavigates the temple accompanied by men dressed as animals, representing human weaknesses such as greed and anger, and are vanquished by the god. The next night sees the image of the god taken out for ritual immersion in the temple tank; devotees greet the procession with oil lamps and throw rice. It is considered highly auspicious to bathe in the tank at the same time as the god.

When not involved in races and arcane temple rituals, Guruvayur's tuskers are chained at the **Punnathur Kotta Elephant Sanctuary** (daily 8am–6pm; Rs5, cameras Rs25), 4km north of town. Around fifty elephants, aged from 8 to 95, live here, munching for most of the day on specially imported piles of fodder and cared for by their three personal *mahouts*, who wash and scrub them several times a week in the sanctuary pond. Only approach an elephant if a *mahout* allows you, as they can be unpredictable and dangerous.

The animals are considered the personal possessions of Lord Guruvayur, given to the temple by wealthy donors from as far afield as Bihar and Assam. All them – apart from the most elderly, who are allowed an honourable retirement – are gainfully employed appearing at temple festivals. The standard daily charge is Rs3500 per elephant, but the prettiest pachyderms are often the subject of heated auctions, with rival villages bidding up to Rs75,000 for a single animal.

Practicalities

Buses from Thrissur (40min) arrive at the main **bus stand** at the end of East Nada Street, five minutes' walk from the temple, and the home of most of the **accommodation**. The town is crammed with strictly vegetarian **restaurants**, and there's an *Indian Coffee House* on the southern side of East Nada Street.

KTDC Mangalya near the entrance of the Krishna temple, by Devaswom Book Stall ☏ 0487/255 4061. Large, acceptably clean attached rooms for up to six people, plus a rock-bottom six-bed dorm. There's also a popular vegetarian restaurant on the ground floor. ①

KTDC Nandanam near the railway station, ☏ 0487/255 6266. Massive terracotta-coloured block surrounded by tall palm trees. It's been recently refurbished but retains a pleasantly old-fashioned look. The bright and airy rooms are terrific value and the staff helpful. ③–④

Sopanam Heritage 500m west of railway station on East Nada ☏ 0487/255 5244, ⓦ www.sopanamguruvayoor.com. Business hotel made of shining tinted glass and concrete, holding 72 smart, centrally a/c rooms on five storeys. A bit bland, but secure, efficient and good value for the level of comfort. Their a/c multi-cuisine restaurants – *Agarsala* (veg) and *Rasoi* (non-veg) – are the swankiest in town, and there's a bar serving Indian liquors and cocktails. ④–⑥

Cheruthuruthy

The village of **CHERUTHURUTHY** is internationally famous as the home of **Kerala Kalamandalam**, the state's flagship training school for *kathakali* and other indigenous Keralan performing arts. Some 32km north of Thrissur, and within range of an easy day-trip, it stands close to the banks of Kerala's longest river, the **Bharatapuzha** (pronounced "bharatapura"), considered holy by Hindus, but sadly depleted by dams recently built around its headwaters in the Ghats. Although of little consolation to locals, the demise of the once mighty river, now a shimmering expanse of pale yellow-brown sand, has produced a landscape of incomparable beauty.

The academy was founded in 1927 by the revered Keralan poet Vallathol (1878–1957). At first patronized by the raja of Cochin, the school has benefited from funding by both state and national governments and has been instrumental in the large-scale revival of interest in unique Keralan art forms. Despite conservative opposition, it followed an open-door recruitment policy, based on artistic merit, which produced "scheduled caste" Muslim and Christian graduates along with the usual Hindu castes, something that was previously unimaginable. Kalamandalam artists perform in the great theatres of the world, many sharing their extraordinary skills with outsiders, including luminaries of modern theatre such as Jerzy Grotowski and Peter Brook. Nonetheless, many of these trained artists are still excluded from entering – let alone performing in – temples, a popular venue for Hindu art forms, especially music.

Non-Hindus are welcome to attend performances of *kathakali*, *kutiyattam* and *mohiniyattam* performed in the school's wonderful **theatre**, which replicates the style of the wooden, sloping-roofed traditional *kuttambalam* auditoria found in Keralan temples. You can also sit in on classes, watch demonstrations of mural painting, and visit exhibitions of costumes by signing up for the fascinating "**a day with the masters**" cultural programme (Mon–Sat 9.30am–1.30pm; $20 per person, including lunch). Try to coincide your visit with the annual, week-long **Thauryathrikam festival** in January. Held at the *Koothambalam* auditorium and at Kalamandalam's original riverside campus amongst the trees, the event presents all the art forms taught at the academy and is free. A short walk past the old school building leads to a small but exquisite **Shiva temple** in classic Keralan style. The exterior is lit by candles during the early evening puja, a particularly rewarding time to visit.

A handful of foreigners also come to the Kalamandalam academy each year to study full-time **courses**: one-month introductions, three- to six- month intensives, and full vocational training from four to six years. Applications may be made from abroad (full details on the website), but it's a good idea to visit before committing yourself, as the training is rigorous. For information contact the school office (☎04884/262418) or check out the Kalamandalam website, Ⓦ www.kalamandalam.com.

Note that photography is not allowed anywhere in the Kalamandalam site without prior purchase of a **photography permit**, which will set you back Rs500 (for ten images only). This does not affect participants of the "a day with the masters" tour, whose cost includes the photo fee.

Practicalities

Cheruthuruthy's **accommodation** is limited, with some students staying as guests in private accommodation or in the school hostel near the main campus at Vallathol Nagar (☎04884/262418 for details). For a touch of a/c luxury, head for the *River Retreat Heritage Ayurvedic Resort* (☎04884/262244,

@www.riverretreat.in; ⑦–⑧), 2km from Kalamandalan. The former palace of the Maharaja of Cochin, the three-star heritage hotel and Ayurvedic spa occupies an idyllic position on the banks of the Bharatapuzha River on Palace Road. Despite some heavy-handed renovation work, its rooms are elegantly furnished with fine teak furniture; some have private terraces facing the river. In the lawned garden, a crystalline pool, partly shaded by coconut palms, also looks across to the Bharatapuzha. Other than the *River Retreat*, the only places to **eat** here are the simple *dhabas* in the centre of village, such as the vegetarian *Mahatma*.

Buses heading to Shoranur from Thrissur's Priya Darshini (aka "Wadakkancheri") stand pass through Cheruthuruthy; the nearest mainline **railway station** is Shoranur Junction, 3km south, served by express trains to and from Mangalore, Chennai and Kochi.

Palakkad and around

Surrounded by paddy fields, **PALAKKAD** (Palghat) lies on NH-47 between Thrissur (79km) and Coimbatore in Tamil Nadu (54km), and on the railway line from Karnataka and Tamil Nadu. Due to the natural twenty-kilometre-wide gap through the Western Ghats here, this area has always been an important entry point into the Malabar region. The town itself doesn't particularly warrant a stop in itself, other than to break a journey, though its beautiful environs do harbour some of Kerala's most appealing heritage homestays and Ayurvedic resorts. Further north, the **Silent Valley National Park** and the hill station of **Nelliampathy** are off-track destinations you might have to pick up transport here to reach.

With its imposing ramparts and moat, Palakkad's square **fort** (daily 8am–6pm; free), the best-preserved in Kerala, is the town's main sight. It was built by Haider Ali of Mysore in 1766, and witnessed a bloody skirmish a couple of decades later when the British stormed it on behalf of their ally, the *zamorin* of Calicut. These days, it's besieged every weekend by streams of local school groups and picnickers. Just outside the citadel, **Vatika Gardens** are another favourite family destination (daily 11am–8pm; Rs5), second only in popularity to the amusement park at **Malampuzha**, 10km north (daily 11am–9pm; Rs80, includes all rides), renowned locally for its cable car or "ropeway" and fantasy rock garden created by the artist Nek Chand of Chandigarh fame; on Saturday and Sunday nights the site is illuminated (although it still closes at 9pm).

Many travellers in search of **kathakali** performances also find themselves directed to Palakkad as, in April and May particularly, hundreds of one-off events take place in the area. The local Government Carnatic Music College has an excellent reputation, and a small open-air amphitheatre next to the fort often hosts first-class music and dance performances. Ask at the tourist office (see below) for details.

Practicalities

Palakkad is well connected to the rest of Kerala and most of the express trains travelling through to Chennai, Bengaluru (Bangalore) and points further north stop at the mainline **railway station**, 6km to the northeast. The KSRTC **bus stand** is right in the middle of town.

DTPC's helpful **tourist office**, around the corner from the *Hotel Indraprastha* (see opposite) at Fort Maidan (Mon–Sat 9.30am–5pm; ☎0491/253 8996), is a good source of advice on local festivals and cultural events. Both the *Indraprastha* and the *Fort Palace* have residents-only foreign exchange facilities, and you can **change money** and traveller's cheques at the State Bank of India, next door to the *Indraprastha*, where there's also a 24hr ATM.

Accommodation and eating

Palakkad's small but adequate crop of **hotels** is pitched primarily at business clients passing through. Further afield, a handful of more upscale, foreigner-oriented heritage **homestays** and Ayurvedic **spas** are desirable destinations in their own right, with lots of traditional Keralan character and potential for trips into the less-frequented rural corners of the state.

For an inexpensive pit stop in the town centre, look no further than the pure-veg *Kapilavasthu*, next to the KSRTC bus stand, which does fresh fruit juices and cool shakes in addition to the usual selection of South Indian snacks and rice-based meals – though you'll need to bring your own bottled water. A slicker, slightly pricier alternative is the *Hotel Omega,* near the *Ammbadi Hotel,* which serves good-value pan-Indian veg and non-veg dishes.

Ammbadi TB Rd ☎0491/253 1244. Plain, clean and comfortable rooms opposite the town bus stand, with a restaurant attached serving Chinese and Indian food. ❹

Ayurveda Manna Peringode, Kootanadu, Palakkad District ☎0466/237 0660, ⓦwww.ayurvedamana.com. One of the state's top Ayurvedic resorts, set in the ancestral home of a famous Namboodiri brahmin family long associated with Keralan healing sciences. Fronted by a long pillared veranda, their "heritage rooms" in a nineteenth-century palace are handsomely furnished, with original tiled floors, Keralan mural paintings on the walls and large windows. Most people come for expert medical treatments and *kalarippayattu* training, with packages ranging from a full-board single day stay with one massage ($85) to courses of a month or more (from $135 per day). ❾

Fort Palace 1km from bus stand on West Fort Road ☎0491/253 4621, ⓦwww.fortpalace.com. Situated opposite the fort, this mid-range hotel, built in humorous mock-citadel style complete with crenellations and coloured flags flying from its walls, offers a choice of polished, very good-value a/c and non-a/c rooms, all attached, as well as a bar and huge garden restaurant. ❸–❹

Indraprastha English Church Road ☎0491/253 4641, ⓦwww.hotelindraprastha.com. Palakkad town's poshest hotel is a well-managed place with spacious, modern, centrally a/c rooms. There's a lovely lawn and a dim but blissfully cool multi-cuisine restaurant, a well-stocked bar and a 24hr vegetarian coffee shop built in traditional Keralan style. The rooms are often block-booked by visiting government honchos, so reserve in advance. ❺–❼

Kalari Kovilakom 20km south of Palakkad at Kollengode ⓦwww.kalarikovilakom.com. Occupying the former residence of the Vengunad dynasty, *Kalari Kovilakom* is part palace hotel and part Ayurvedic spa, and quite simply one of the most exquisite places to stay in South India. Accommodation is offered either in a 1920s "guest wing", with its typically British furnishings and decor, or the more traditionally Keralan, *zenana*-style "palace wing". Guests are encouraged not to leave the premises during their stay, which is no great chore as the whole place, set in substantial grounds, is an architectural feast: colonnaded walkways lead to open *nadumuttam* courtyards, hidden bathing pools and wood-lined interiors, lit by louvred windows and slatted screens. The food served in the strictly vegetarian restaurant is tailored to fit individual treatment regimes; alcohol and tobacco are forbidden. Prices start at hefty $8500 full-board for two sharing for a 14-day stay. ❾

Kandath Tharavad Thenkurussi ☎04922/284124, ⓦwww.tharavad.info. Idyllic heritage homestay, in a 200-year-old ancestral seat set on the edge of a sleepy village 10km south from Palakkad. Surrounded by rice paddy, the mansion's most striking feature is the raised, colonnaded *purathalum* veranda at the front, whose bulbous pillars are capped by carvings of elephants, snakes and dragons. Host Mr Bhagwaldas and his offspring, the fifth and sixth generations to live here, offer six simply furnished guest rooms, and activities ranging from guided birding and trekking to bullock cart and cycle rides, cookery classes and even toddy-tapping trips. From $100 per night (includes full-board). ❽

Olappamanna Mana Vellinezhi, 43km northwest ☎0466/2285797, ☎m98477 64532, ⓦwww .olappamannamana.com. This stately Naboordiri *mana* (feudal mansion), resting on sandstone embankments in a clearing at the heart of a palm grove, possesses a certain mystique. Its owners were renowned patrons of local arts, particularly Carnatic music and Sanskrit literature, and during your stay here you can take short "orientation courses" in *kathakali* (Vellinezhi was one of the cradles of the dance form and retains an extraordinary 300-year-old temple-theatre, which guests are welcome to visit). The family also regularly perform *kalam ezhuttu* powder pattern rituals in the house. Strictly brahmin-vegetarian food; no alcohol. Doubles from $100, full-board. ⑧

④ The Silent Valley National Park

High up in the watershed of Western Ghats, the **Silent Valley National Park**, 75km by road northwest from Palakkad on the Tamil border, may not be Kerala's best-known nature reserve, but its 90 square kilometres of rainforest ranks among the most pristine in the Subcontinent. Some 966 species of flowering plant (including 100 different orchids) were recently identified in its moist evergreen woodlands, along with 211 different kinds of birds and 128 types of butterfly. Its enigmatic name derives from the apparent absence of cicadas remarked upon by British engineers when they explored the valley in the 1840s. The calls of plenty of other creatures resound through the tree cover, however, not least that of the rare **lion-tailed macaque**; Silent Valley holds one of the last viable breeding populations of this highly endangered primate, in addition to gaur, sloth bears, three species of jungle cats and vestigial numbers of tigers.

Barely 7km from east to west, and 12km from north to south, the park is drained by **Kunthipuzha River**, one of only two major streams in these mountains, rising and flowing through totally uninhabited, unpolluted regions. In 1973 it became the subject of a fierce environmental controversy when the Indian government announced plans to erect a dam across it. Faced with international pressure, Indira Gandhi dropped the project, and the whole zone was declared a national park in 1986. However, Silent Valley is still not entirely out of the woods. A second hydro scheme proposed in 2001 continues to be debated, with strong support from the current chief minister of Kerala, V. S. Achuthanandan. Another threat to the forest hereabouts is posed by illegal **ganja cultivation**. Under the auspices of local mafia groups, the indigenous minorities who live in the area abutting the park – the Irula and Mudugar – are the prime source of Kerala's famed grass, for which land is illegally cleared each year.

Park practicalities

The **best season** to visit Silent Valley is between December and March; in April and May the park may be closed due to forest fires. **Access** is strictly controlled by the Forest Department. You first have to obtain a **permit** from the main Silent Valley National Park office in **Mannarkkad** (☎04924/222056, ⓔwlwsvnpmkd@sancharnet.in), 32km short of the main entrance and served by regular buses from Palakkad. Private vehicles can press on another 9km as far as **Mukkali** (reachable by local bus from Mannarkkad) but from there on only authorized Jeeps are allowed. These should be booked at the office of the Assistant Wildlife Warden, currently Mr Kunjumou (☎04924/253225), in Mukkali. Return trips depart from 8am to noon, last for five hours and cost Rs600 per vehicle; visitors must report back to the office by 6pm. The entrance fee is Rs210 per person – plus an extra Rs25 per camera and Rs250 per group for the compulsory guide. The only **accommodation** option in Mukkali is the basic National Park guesthouse (book through the Assistant Wildlife Warden; ④), 100m beyond the ticket office, where beds cost Rs800 per person; meals are also available on request.

At the time of writing, a new paved road was nearing completion from Mukkali to the Silent Valley Visitors Centre at **Sairandhri**, 23 winding kilometres further north, where there's an observation tower giving a panoramic view over the park. With a standard day pass, you're permitted to follow a two-kilometre trail down the steep side of the valley to the Kunthipuzha River, spanned by a suspension bridge, but not press on any further.

Some 80km of superb **trekking** trails also radiate out of Sairandhri, served by a chain of five camps; to follow any of them you'll need to obtain permission and arrange guides through the warden at Mukkali or forest office in Mannarkkad, who'll also be able to fill you in with route options. Trekking permits cost a stiff Rs900 per day, plus the Rs250 per day guide fee and a nominal amount for meals. If you'd like a dependable firm of experts to make all the necessary arrangements on your behalf, contact the Wild Kerala Tour Company, at VI/480 KVA Buldings, Mantancherry, Kochi (☎0484/309 9520, ⓦwww.wildkeralatours.com).

Nelliampathy

Surrounded by teak forests and estates where tea, coffee, cardamom and oranges grow profusely, the tiny hill station of **NELLIAMPATHY**, 75km south of Palakkad, is often dubbed "the poor man's Ooty" – a comparison that does justice neither to its grandiose scenery nor the small scale of its tourist development. That said, the settlement, spread over undulating terrain at an altitude of a little above 1500m, has finally started to capitalize on its refreshingly cool climate and landscape with a scattering of plantation homestays and resorts from which you can explore the surrounding hills.

Sporadic KSRTC **buses** run to Nelliampathy from Palakkad, although you'll probably get there quicker by jumping on one of the more frequent services from Palakkad town bus stand to **Nemmara**, from where shared Jeeps cover the onward 26-kilometre leg. Skirting the Pothundi reservoir and dam before it begins its vertiginous ascent via a series of ten hairpin bends to the hill station, the road is scenic from start to finish.

After the spectacular climb, buses terminate at Nelliampathy's **Kaikatty** crossroads, where there's a small NTPC **tourist office** (daily 9am–5pm; ☎m94951 36463) and a fleet of local **Jeeps** waiting to ferry arrivals to their respective hotels and guesthouses. Prices depend on the number of people and whim of the driver; expect to pay around Rs10–20/km.

Accommodation

If the following established **places to stay** are fully booked, try the NTPC tourist office at Kaikatty for details of newly opened homestays in the area – though given the long slog up here, you'd be ill-advised to arrive without some reservation in the bag. As with all hill stations, rooms tend to be in shorter supply on weekends.

🏃 **Ciscilia Heritage** Ranimedu Estate, 6km from Kaikatty ☎04923/206283, ⓦwww .cisciliaheritage.com. An affordable option in a secluded, remote setting high up on the hills behind Kaikatty. Its rooms come in the form of quaint wooden huts overlooking tea gardens, with teak linings and solar-powered hot water. Your alfresco dinners will be accompanied by a cacophony of exotic animal noises emanating from the pristine *shola* forest just behind the resort which, due to its far-flung location, tends to have vacancies when places nearer Kaikatty are full. ❹ **Green Land Farmhouse** 9km from Kaikatty in Palapagandi ☎04923/246245. At a superbly isolated position amid mature coffee plantations, this simple farmstay offers great views and value-for-money. Optional full board only costs Rs200 extra. ❹ **ITL Holiday Resorts** Kaikatty ☎04923/246357, ⓔpgt_ilt@sancharnet.in. A well-set-up budget lodge close to Kaikatty, and one of the cheapest options in the area, with dorm beds (Rs225) in addition to attached non-a/c rooms. Reserve well in advance as tour groups frequently block-book the whole place. ❹–❺

Tropical Hill Resorts 4km from Kaikatty in Padagiri ☎04923/246238. Accommodation to suit all pockets – from dorm beds and tents for budget travellers to luxurious, cosy British-era bungalows with fireplaces and wood verandas – on a 2.5-square-kilometre, picture-postcard

coffee estate. Closed at the time of writing for renovation work, but scheduled to re-open in early 2008. ❸–❼

Whistling Thrush Bungalow 6km from Kaikatty on the Poothundu Plantation, Padagiri ☎04923/324 6235, ☎m94471 44921, ⓦwww.nelliampathy. com. Three smartly furnished guest rooms in a modern bungalow, surrounded on three sides by reserve forest, and on the other by a working tea, cardamom, coffee and vanilla plantation. Rates include obligatory full board. ❽

Kozhikode (Calicut)

Formerly one of Asia's most prosperous trading capitals, the busy coastal city of **KOZHIKODE** (Calicut), 225km north of Kochi, occupies an extremely important place in Keralan legend and history. It's also significant in the chronicles of European involvement on the Subcontinent, as Vasco da Gama landed nearby in 1498. Nowadays, with the exception of a crop of splendid **Moppila mosques**, precious few remnants survive of the city's illustrious past, and the few foreigners that find their way here tend only to be breaking longer journeys to somewhere else. Even so, it's a strikingly upbeat, prosperous place, riding high on a tide of remittance cheques from the Gulf and expanding rapidly in all directions: the city and its surrounding district receives more income per capita from abroad than any other in the state, hence the striking number of huge gold emporia and silk shops in its bazaars.

Kozhikode's roots are shrouded in myth. According to Keralan tradition, the powerful king Cheraman Perumal is said to have converted from Hinduism to Islam in the eighth century and left for Mecca "to save his soul", never to return. Before he set sail he divided Kerala between his relatives, all of whom had to submit to his nephew, who was given the kingdom of Kozhikode and the title *zamorin*, equivalent to emperor. The city prospered and, perhaps because of the story of the convert king, became the preferred port of Muslim traders from the Middle East in search of spices, particularly pepper. During the Raj, it was an important centre for the export of printed Indian cotton, hence the term "calico", an English corruption of the name Calicut – itself an anglicized version of the city's original Malayalam name, now reinstated.

Arrival and information

The **railway station** (☎0495/270 1234), close to the centre of town, is served by coastal expresses, slower passenger trains, and superfast express trains from Delhi, Mumbai, Kochi and Thiruvananthapuram. There are three **bus stands**. All government-run services, from destinations as far afield as Bengaluru (Bangalore), Mysore, Ooty, Madurai, Coimbatore and Mangalore, pull in at the **KSRTC bus stand**, on Mavoor Road (aka Indira Gandhi Road). Private long-distance - mainly overnight - buses stop at the **New Mofussil private stand**, 500m away on the other side of Mavoor Road – there's a row of agents for booking tickets on these along MM Ali Road. The **Palayam bus stand**, off MM Ali Road, just serves the city.

Kozhikode's **airport**, at Karippur, 23km south of the city, is primarily a gateway for emigrant workers flying to and from the Gulf, but also has flights

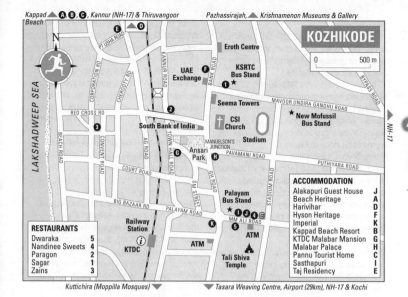

KOZHIKODE

ACCOMMODATION

Alakapuri Guest House	J
Beach Heritage	A
Harivihar	D
Hyson Heritage	F
Imperial	K
Kappad Beach Resort	B
KTDC Malabar Mansion	G
Malabar Palace	H
Pannu Tourist Home	C
Sasthapuri	I
Taj Residency	E

RESTAURANTS

Dwaraka	5
Nandinee Sweets	4
Paragon	2
Sagar	1
Zains	3

to Mumbai, Coimbatore, Chennai and several other South Indian cities (a full rundown of which appears in Travel details on p.495). A taxi from the airport into town will cost around Rs300, but you can save a few rupees by taking an **auto-rickshaw** to the Kozhikode–Palakkad highway and then catching a bus. Flight tickets can be bought through PL Worldways, on the 3rd Floor of Seema Towers, Bank Road, just north of the CSI Church. Indian Airlines (Mon–Sat 10am-1pm & 1.45–5.30pm; ☎0495/276 6243) and Air India (Mon–Sat 9.30am–5.30pm; ☎0495/276 0715) are both at the Eroth Centre, opposite Hyson Heritage on Bank Road. The rest of the carriers (listed on p.495) all have counters at the airport.

KTDC's **tourist information** booth (officially daily 9am–7.30pm; ☎0495/270 0097) at the railway station has info on travel connections and sites around Kozhikode, but opening hours are erratic. The main KTDC tourist office (☎0495/272 2391), in the *Malabar Mansion* hotel at the corner of SM Street, can supply only limited information about the town and area. With so much Gulf money floating around, you shouldn't have any difficulty **changing currency** in Kozhikode. Recommended places for exchanging cash or travel-ler's cheques are PL Worldways (see above) and the spanking new UAE Exchange on Bank Road, next to Hyson Heritage (Mon–Sat 9.30am–1.30pm & 2-6pm, Sun 9.30am–1.30pm). The Union Bank of India and the State Bank of India, opposite each other on MM Ali Road, are two of many large branches with ATMs. **Internet** access is available at the Hub, on the first floor of the block to the right of *Nandhinee Sweets*, MM Ali Road, and at Internet Zone, near *KTDC Malabar Mansion* (both Rs30/hr).

Accommodation

Kozhikode's reasonably priced city-centre **hotels**, most of which operate a 24hr check-out, often fill up by noon; the beach area and Kappad, 16km north, offer quieter alternatives.

Budget

Imperial Kallai Rd ☎0495/270 1291. Large budget lodge built around a courtyard with basic, very cheap rooms and a branch of *India Coffee House* on the ground floor. ❷

KTDC Malabar Mansion SM St ☎0495/272 2391, Ⓦwww.ktdc.com. A favourite with backpackers, although the stuffy rooms and occasional dodgy "guides" hanging around reception add little to its appeal. On the plus side, there's a beer parlour and a good South Indian restaurant. ❸

Pannu Tourist Home 16km north at Kappad Beach ☎0496/268 8634. Set back only 100m from the seafront (look for the signboard opposite the rock temple), this simple guesthouse offers quiet, simple attached rooms with large balconies looking onto a palm plantation. Not in the same league as the nearby *Beach Resort*, but correspondingly less pricey. ❸–❹

Sasthapuri MM Ali Rd ☎0495/272 3281, Ⓦwww.sasthapuri.com. Compact budget place, close to the Palayam bus stand and market, with well-maintained, nicely furnished rooms (including some of the city's cheapest a/c options), a funky little roof garden restaurant sporting ersatz tribal murals, and a bar. Very good value. ❶–❹

Mid-range and luxury

Alakapuri Guest House MM Ali Rd, near the railway station, 1km from KSRTC bus stand ☎0495/272 3451. Built around a courtyard, the a/c rooms in this dependable mid-range place have huge bathtubs, polished wood and easy chairs; the cheaper, non-a/c options are rather Spartan. There's a bar, restaurant and a relaxing lawn, and single rates are available. ❹–❺

🏃 **Beach Heritage** 3km north of the centre on Beach Rd ☎0495/236 5363, Ⓦwww.beachheritage.com. Dating from 1890, the premises of the colonial-era Malabar English Club, with its closely cropped lawns and high-pitched tiled roofs, now house a delightfully eccentric heritage hotel, whose white walls, dark-wood furniture and original tiled floors retain plenty of period feel. It's the kind of place you'd expect to see Somerset Maugham sipping a gin sling on the veranda – which indeed he did; Chester Bowles and Jawaharlal Nehru also stayed here in the 1950s. There are only six rooms and two suites, all with a/c, balconies or private patios, ceiling fans, and mod cons such as TVs and CD players. Best of

all, the tariffs are amazingly restrained by Keralan standards. ❹–❺

🏃 **Harivihar** 4km north of the centre in the suburb of Bilathikulam ☎0495/276 5865, Ⓦwww.harivihar.com. Ancestral home of the Kadathanadu royal family, converted into a particularly wonderful heritage homestay. Set in beautiful gardens landscaped with herb beds, lotus ponds and an original laterite-lined bathing tank (which guests are welcome to use), the mansion is a model of traditional Keralan refinement: white-washed, high-ceilinged rooms filled with antique furniture open on to pillared walkways inside, where you can follow short courses in yoga, astrology, cookery and Indian mythology. There's also a top-grade Green Leaf-accredited Ayurvedic treatment centre on the premises. ❽

Hyson Heritage Bank Rd, near the KSRTC bus stand ☎0495/276 6423, Ⓦwww.hysonheritage.com. Another gleaming, blissfully cool a/c business hotel close to the centre. Their "budget" non-a/c rooms are especially good value. For a review of their multi-cuisine restaurant, see "Eating" p.487. ❹–❺

Kappad Beach Resort 17km north of the railway station ☎0496/268 8777, Ⓦwww.renaissancekappadbeach.com. If you can face the 45min trip and afford its high rates, this former government place, now run by the Kochi-based Renaissance chain, is Kappad's most appealing option. Situated slap on the beach, the site holds four separate cottages, each with four rooms (two on the upper, and two on the lower floors) – the best of them have breezy rear balconies with uninterrupted sea views. There's a swimming pool, multi-cuisine restaurant with garden terrace and small Ayurveda centre. ❼–❽

Malabar Palace Manuelsons Jn ☎0495/272 1511, Ⓦwww.malabarpalacecalicut.com. Ritzy four-star bang in the city centre. Ranged over six storeys, its rooms are lavishly furnished with luxurious beds, thick burgundy carpets and polished wood writing desks; those to the rear have great views over the palm grove. There is also a quality restaurant, offering Rs125 buffet lunches. ❻–❽

Taj Residency PT Usha Rd ☎0495/276 5354, Ⓦwww.tajhotels.com. The swankiest hotel in the city, northwest of the centre close to the seafront, though it lacks the usual *Taj* grandeur. There's a pool, coffee shop, multi-cuisine restaurant, and health and Ayurvedic centre. From $150. ❾

The City

Few traces remain of the model fourteenth-century city, which followed a Hindu grid formula based on a sacred diagram containing the image of the cosmic man, Purusha. The axis and energy centre of the diagram was dictated by the position of the ancient **Tali Shiva temple** (closed to non-Hindus), just south of MM Ali Road, which survives to this day. Everything, and everybody, had a place. The district around the port in the northwest was reserved for foreigners: the Chinese community lived in and around Chinese Street (now Silk Street) and the Portuguese, Dutch and British later occupied the area. Keralan Muslims (Moppilas) lived in the southwest. The northeast of the city was a commercial quarter, while the southeast housed the Tali temple, a palace and fort; all the military *kalaris* (martial art gymnasia) that stood around the perimeter have now gone.

Kozhikode beach and Palayam market

Locals enjoy walking along the **city beach,** 3km west of the centre, in the late afternoon and early evening, especially on weekends. Although not suitable for swimming, it's a relaxing place, where you can munch on freshly roasted peanuts while scanning the sea for dolphins. The northern end towards the pier is distinctly more attractive than the southern stretch, which doubles as a lorry park. After dark it's difficult to find an auto-rickshaw to take you back into town, but there are regular buses.

Another good place for an aimless wander – if you can get there during the coolest, busiest time of day from 7am to 9am – is the fresh produce market in **Palayam**, next to the Palayam bus stand. Spilling into the backstreets around the Mohiudeen Masjid, it's a typically hectic north Keralan fruit and veg bazaar, with porters scurrying around balancing impossibly heavy loads of bananas, breadfruit, coconuts and watermelons on their heads.

The Kuttichira mosques

Prior to the arrival of the Portuguese, the Malabar's maritime trade lay largely under the control of a class of wealthy Muslim merchants, originally descended from Arabian and Middle Eastern emigrants whom successive *zamorins*, in return for the weapons and horses they supplied to their armies, afforded protection. The city's current economic dependence on the Gulf is a legacy of this centuries-old connection, and some remnants survive of the original Muslim golden age in the form of a handful of splendid old mosques, tucked away in the Moppila quarter of the city. Unlike most of their counterparts elsewhere in the state – and in spite of da Gama's repeated bombardments in the fifteenth and sixteenth centuries – these have retained their multi-tiered roofs, distinguished by gracefully angled teak beams, slatted screens and typically Keralan carved gables. Few foreigners ever set eyes on them, but they rank among some of the most handsome antique buildings in southern India.

The three most impressive specimens lie off a backroad running through the **Kuttichira** quarter of **Thekkepuram**, 2km southwest of the *maidan* (all the auto-rickshaw-wallahs will know how to find them). Start at the 1100-year-old **Macchandipalli Masjid**, at the southern end of the lane leading from Francis Road to Kuttichira Tank, whose ceilings are covered in beautiful polychrome stucco and intricate Qur'anic script. An engraved stone inside recounting the history of the thirteenth-century *zamorin* rulers provided a valuable chronology for the region's historians. A couple of hundred metres further north, the **Juma Masjid**'s main prayer hall, large enough for a congregation of 1200 worshippers, dates from the eleventh century and holds another elaborately carved ceiling. The most magnificent of this trio of mosques, however, is the **Mithqalpalli** (aka **Jama'atpalli**)

Masjid, at the northern end of the lane, hidden behind Kuttichira tank. Resting on 24 wooden pillars, its four-tier roof and turquoise walls were built over 700 years ago. Opposite the eastern wall is a small information centre where you can obtain a leaflet about the neighbourhood and its main mosques.

The museum and art gallery

The **Pazhassirajah and Krishnamenon Museum and Art Gallery** (Museum Tues–Sun 9am–4.30pm, Rs10; Art Gallery 10am–5pm, free) stand together 5km north of the centre on East Hill, fringed by palm groves and lawned gardens that provide a breezy, shaded escape from the heat of the day. Copies of murals, coins, bronzes and models of the umbrella-shaped stone megalithic remains peculiar to Kerala dominate the museum's collection. The Art Gallery displays memorabilia associated with the left-wing Keralan politician V. K. Krishnamenon, along with works by Indian artists.

CVN Kalari

Calicut district is renowned for its **kalarippayattu** gymnasiums, the most illustrious of which, CVN Kalari Sangan (☎0495/276 9114, ⓦwww .cvnkalarikerala.com), stands in the suburb of Nadakkavu, 2km north of the city centre. Established over 50 years ago by the father of the current Master, the centre enjoys an international reputation, with members regularly performing in Europe, the Middle and Far East. CVN Kalari's great claim to fame, however, is that it choreographed the combat scenes for the film *The Myth*, starring martial arts supremo Jackie Chan. Visitors are welcome to watch demonstrations and lessons (details posted on the CVN website), though you'll have to get up at the crack of dawn to catch the more worthwhile of the two daily training sessions, held in the morning from 6 to 9am; evening sessions are for beginners and children. The centre also offers three- and six-month residential courses for those interested in learning the basics of the martial art and *marma chikitsa*, the specialist Ayurveda massage technique used for *kalari* practitioners.

Kappad

Kappad beach, also known locally as Kappakadavu, a long stretch of golden sand and crashing surf 16km north of Kozhikode, is where – on May 27, 1498 – Vasco da Gama and his 170-strong crew made their first landfall in India after discovering the sea route around the Cape of Good Hope. This momentous event in the history of the Subcontinent is commemorated by a small plaque. Its historic associations aside, Kappad's refreshing breezes offer a welcome respite from the traffic and mayhem of the city, and it's only a 45-minute journey away. **Buses** leave from the new Mofussil stand (platforms #8 or #9); you have to jump on one bound for Badagam, and get down at **Pookkal**, where local services and auto-rickshaws are on hand for the remaining 2km. The beach itself sees more fishermen than bathers, but it's safe for swimming and as yet relatively undeveloped, with only a handful of modest guesthouses and resorts providing food and accommodation to the few visitors (reviewed on p.484).

Shopping

What Kozhikode lacks in monuments it more than makes up for in **shops** – a consequence of the vast number of Gulf *riyals* and *dinars* flowing through the town. Around SM Street, many fabric and ready-made clothes shops sell locally produced cotton *lunghis*, many of them in unbelievably jazzy styles and shades. You cannot fail to be dazzled by the sheer number of gold jewellery emporia, full of ladies spending lavishly ahead of family weddings. This district is also a good place to try the local *halwa* sweets, especially popular with the large Moppila community. The **Kerala State Handicrafts** on MM Ali Road, next to the *Alakapuri Guest House*, stocks the usual collection of ordinary brass, bell-metal and wood carvings.

A more promising source of souvenirs is the **Tasara Creative Weaving Centre** in Beypore North, 7km south of Kozhikode, just off the Kozhikode–Beypore Road. In a compound full of tropical flowers and plants, rugs, bedspreads and wall hangings are hand-woven in vibrant, contemporary designs that are refreshingly different from the traditional patterns found elsewhere in Kerala. Finely spun, "non-violent" silks (produced without killing the worm) are another speciality. Visitors are welcome to watch the artists at work, to view the art gallery (daily 9am–6pm; free) and buy the finished goods – prices range from $15 to $1000. You can study handloom techniques here, and try your hand at dyeing, batik and printing, under the tutelage of Mr Vasudevan Balakrishanan (☎0495/241 4832, ⓦwww.tasaraindia.com). Short "Weaver Bird" courses last for five nights and four days, and cost $275; or you can stay for a month as an "artist in residence" for $1100. Prices include all meals, and accommodation in a stylish designer guesthouse with open-plan stairs and simple, high-ceilinged rooms off a central atrium.

Eating

Kozhikode is famous for its **Moppila cusine**, which has its roots in the culinary traditions of the city's former Arab traders. Fragrant chicken biriyanis and seafood curries with distinctive Malabari blends of spices crop up on most non-veg restaurant menus, but to sample the definitive versions you should aim to have a least one meal in *Paragon* or *Zains* (or preferably both). **Mussels** are also big news here; deep-fried in crunchy, spicy millet coatings, they're served everywhere during the season, from October to December (if you order them at any other time, they'll have been imported and won't be as fresh). A great place to sample them, and other local snacks, is the *thattukada* market on Beach Road, a row of gaslit Keralan fast-food stalls that whip up cheap meals through the night from 9pm until 4am. Finally, no Kozhikode feast is considered complete without a serving of the city's legendary **halwa**: a sticky Malabari sweet made from rice flour, coconut, *jaggery* (sugar cane) and ghee. It comes in dazzling variety of Day-Gloa colours and flavours. The place to try it has always been Mithai Theruvu, or **SM ("Sweet Market") Street**, near the Palayam bus stand – though the survival of this atmospheric bazaar was in doubt after a devastating fire destroyed most of its businesses in April 2007; if the area's still not up and running, try *Nandhinee Sweets*, reviewed below.

Dwaraka opposite *Sasthapuri Hotel*. A busy, down-to-earth non-veg diner where you can order inexpensive fresh mussels as well as masala-fried fish and local seafood curries.

Nandinee Sweets MM Ali Rd. This is a hygienic place to sample the joys of Malabari *halwa*, nuts and savoury snacks; they also do great fresh fruit cocktails, *badam* milk and *falooda* shakes.

Paragon off the Kannur Rd. A short auto-rickshaw ride from the *maidan*, *Paragon* has been a city institution since it opened in 1939. Don't be put off by the uninspiring setting beneath a flyover or the somewhat hectic atmosphere: both are well worth enduring for the superb Malabari cooking. In a high-ceilinged dining hall with cast-iron columns, you can tuck into steaming plates of tamarind-tinged fish *moilee* or *the* house special, fish *kombathu*, mopped up with deliciously light *appams*, *porotta* and crumbly *puttoo*. They also do plenty of veg options. Most mains Rs70–125.

Sagar next to the KSRTC stand, Mavoor Rd. Another old favourite of Calicut's middle classes, buried amid the high-rises and traffic mayhem of Mavoor Rd. Ignore the generic North Indian-Chinese multi-cuisine menu; everyone orders proper Malabari dishes such as egg roast, fish *korma* and, best of all, the flavour-packed chicken *porichathu* –

boneless chicken pieces marinated in ginger, garlic, green chillies and curry-leaves, and then crisp fried.

Zains Convent Cross Rd. An unassuming, faded, pink-coloured family house in the west end of town is hardly what you'd expect the Holy Grail of Moppila cooking to look like, but the food served here is second to none. For the benefit of the uninitiated, the dishes of the day are displayed on a central table. There's generally a choice of biriyanis (fish, chicken or mutton), various fiery seafood curries, and a range of different *pathiris* – the definite Malabari rice-flour bread, which can be steam-cooked, and flavoured with fish, shallow fried, dipped in egg or layered with coconut. Most mains Rs100–125.

Wayanad

[handwritten annotation: Kalpetta → tree house ✓]

The hill district of **Wayanad**, situated 70km inland from Kozhikode at the southern limits of the Deccan Plateau, is one of the most beautiful regions of Kerala. Spread over altitudes of between 750m and 2100m, its landscapes vary from lush riverine rice paddy to semi-tropical savannah grasslands, and from spice, tea and coffee plantations to steep mountainsides smothered in jungle. What few towns there are tend to be typically ramshackle Indian hill bazaars, which serve widely scattered satellite villages whose 200,000 or so inhabitants are mainly *adivasi* tribal peoples, dependent on low-paid seasonal crop picking, smallholding and wild food gathering. Due to the relative isolation and lack of decent roads, these minority communities – who include the Kurumbas, Adiyas, and Paniyas – have so far managed to preserve their traditional identities, despite the gradual intrusion of modernization.

The region's only formal visitor attraction is the **Wayanad Wildlife Sanctuary** – a park split into two separate zones, **Muthanga** and **Tholpetty**, both of which hug the Tamil border and form part of the sprawling Nilgiri Biosphere. For those with time on their hands, Wayanad makes an alternative and rewarding route between coastal Kerala and Mysore in neighbouring Karnataka, or Ooty in Tamil Nadu. Travelling the 70km east from Kozhikode, a beautiful but tortuous road climbs a series of hairpin bends up the Southern Ghats through unspoiled forests, where macaques forage along the roadside, impervious to the groaning, diesel-belching trucks and buses going past. As the road arrives at the lip of the great plateau there are sweeping views back towards the coast of lush, green cover, and you can glimpse the sea in the hazy distance. On the highway to Mysore and Ooty, **Kalpetta**, the district headquarters, makes a good base from which to discover most of Wayanad, but **Mananthavady**, 27km from Kalpetta, is more convenient for exploring the northern jungles.

Kalpetta and around

Surrounded by plantations and rolling hills, the district's capital, **KALPETTA**, 72km east of Kozhikode, is a quiet market town with little to commend it except its pleasant location on the edge of the Muthanga Wildlife Sanctuary. Along with the settlement of **Vythiri**, 12km to the southwest, Kalpetta provides ample amenities and excellent walking country, including the spectacular **Chembra Peak** (2100m), the highest mountain in Wayanad.

The state **bus stand** in the centre of Kalpetta has connections to Kozhikode (72km; 2hr), Ooty (115km; 3hr 30min), Mysore (125km; 4hr) and Mananthavady (27km; 1hr). **Auto-rickshaws** and **Jeeps** are available for local destinations. **Internet access** is available at Net World (Rs25/hr) next to the *Udupi Restaurant*. The **Kerala Tourism Office** (Mon–Sat 10am–5pm, closed second Sat of each month; ☏04936/204441) is in Kalpetta North, 1km from the bus stand, in a building sharing space with the local DTPC information desk. The staff are extremely helpful and can assist with hiring **forest guides** (Rs50/day), and Jeeps (Rs8/km plus the Rs100 vehicle entrance fee) for those going to the wildlife sanctuary independently. The Mysore bus passes the **entrance** to Muthanga Sanctuary, near the scruffy town of **Sultan's Battery**.

The Muthanga Wildlife Sanctuary

The southern portion of the Wayanad reserve, located 40km east of Kalpetta, is known as the **Muthanga Wildlife Sanctuary** (daily 6–10am & 3–5pm; Rs100, camera Rs25). Like neighbouring Bandipur National Park, the reserve, with its dry deciduous forests, is noted for elephants and also shelters deer, wild boar, bear and tiger. **Trekking** in the sanctuary is only allowed during the morning slot; hiring a (mandatory) guide for the 3hr official route costs Rs150. If you opt for the two-hour-long, 22-kilometre Jeep trip, you'll still have to pay for a guide (Rs100) as well as the Jeep rental (Rs250) and the vehicle's entry fee (Rs100).

The highway from Kalpetta to Mysore and Ooty (via **Sultan's Battery**) passes through part of the sanctuary, and provides an opportunity, if you're lucky, to see wild elephants crossing the road on ancient migratory trails. **Buses** bound for Mysore and Bengaluru (Bangalore) run past the park gates, as do local services heading in the direction of Ponkuzhy.

Tholpetty Wildlife Sanctuary

Forming the northern sector of the Wayanad reserve, **Tholpetty Wildlife Sanctuary**, 25km northeast of Mananthavady, is one of the best parks in South India to see elephants, as well as plentiful bison, boar, *sambar*, spotted deer, macaques and langurs; tigers also inhabit the park, though they are rarely spotted. The forest department lays on two-hour **Jeep safaris** (daily 7–9am & 3–5pm), costing Rs300 for up to five people, with an additional Rs200 for the obligatory guide. You can also join guided treks (daily 8am–1pm; Rs750 for up to four people). Taxis charge Rs300 for the trip from Mananthavady to Tholpetty, or you can save a few rupees by taking one of the frequent KSRTC buses to Kutta, which will drop you off at the sanctuary entrance. Buses back to Mananthavady run until 8.45pm.

Accommodation is available just outside the park at *Pachyderm Palace* (book through the tourist desk in Kochi on ☏0484/237 1761; ❼), a traditional Keralan bungalow with five comfortable rooms rented on an all-inclusive basis; the authentic Keralan cuisine is delicious, and a friendly welcome guaranteed.

Chembra Peak

At 2100m, **Chembra Peak** is the highest point in the Wayanad region, dominating the landscape for miles around. Carpeted on one side by soaring ridges and grasslands and on the other by dense tropical forests, the massif can be tackled in around ten hours – a stiff physical challenge given the heat and humidity, but one that's amply rewarded with a stupendous view over Wayanad and, on clear days, out to the distant coast. The springboard for the climb is the small town of **Meppadi**, 18km south of Kalpetta and reachable on southbound buses passing through the main KSRTC stand (30min). Permission for the trek has to be applied for in advance at the Forest Range Office, 1km west of Meppadi. The permit is free, but you have to pay Rs10 to access the trailhead, situated on the Chembra Tea Estate, 7km away along a paved road, and arrange for one of the two forest rangers to accompany you (Rs200). Auto-rickshaws will do the trip to the trailhead for about Rs75–100. The recommended start time is 6am and all necessary arrangements should ideally be made a couple of days in advance.

Accommodation and eating

Kalpetta and the nearby villages of **Vythiri** and **Lakkidi**, on the Kozhikode road, are fast emerging as low-key hill **retreats** in their own right, with a clutch of mostly upscale resorts and plantation stays catering for well-heeled metropolitan Indians and foreigners eager for a break from the sticky heat of the coastal cities. Picking up on a trend that's paying dividends elsewhere in the mountains of the South, most are avowedly "green", though their much-touted eco-credentials don't always bear much scrutiny.

All of them provide quality regional **cuisine** along with accommodation, but if you're just passing through Kalpetta and in search of a pit stop, the *Indian Coffee House*, opposite the tourist office, serves the usual South Indian snacks, rice-based meals and so-so filter coffee. The *Hotel New Palace*, south of the bus stand with its kitchen open to the street, is a favourite among Kalpetti families for its mainly non-veg North Indian dishes, vegetable biriyanis, and delicious ghee rice; they also do rich Malabari-style curries made with local quail (*kada*).

Edakkal Hermitage near Edakkal Caves, Ambalavayal ☎04936/221860, ⓦwww.edakkal.com. Half-a-dozen pleasantly furnished cottages, with old floorboards and quality bathrooms, well spaced on small rock platforms overlooking a lawned garden to the valley, with breathtaking views down to the plains. An even more amazing panorama is to be had from their tree house, accessed via a rickety bamboo ladder, which literally sways in the wind as you sleep – an adventure in itself. The candle-lit restaurant occupies a man-made cave. ⓼

Green Gates TB Rd, Kalpetta North ☎04936/202001, ⓦwww.greengateshotel.com. Modern three-star hotel, tucked away in its own lush grounds 300m north of tourist office, offering variously sized, differently priced rooms in the main multi-storey block, or more private cottages to its rear. There's a pool, plenty of chill-out space in the gardens, and an Ayurveda centre. ⓻–⓼

Green Magic Vythiri book through ☎0495/652 1163, ⓦwww.jungleparkresorts.com. Kerala's ultimate eco-resort, on a 500-acre site deep in the forest that's only accessible by 4WD (with the final 1.5km on foot). Dotted around the woods are various cottages and "villa rooms", but the benchmark accommodation is in luxury treehouses (from $250) nestled 20m off

the ground under a lush rainforest canopy – you're winched to them on counterweight-pulley lifts. Energy sources include solar power and *gobar* (cow-dung) gas, and meals (included in the rates) are prepared from organically grown vegetables. Several forest trails lead out from the resort offering plenty of opportunities for guided walks; tours of the sanctuaries can also be arranged. ⓽

Harita Giri Emily Rd ☎04936/203145, ⓦwww.hotelharitagiri.com. A conventional hotel offering six different grades of room (including singles), from budget to deluxe a/c suites; also on site is a garden, restaurant, bar, rooftop terrace and good-sized pool. Rooms nearer the staircase tend to be noisier, particularly during weekends. ⓹–⓻

Rain Country Resort Lakkidi, 22km from Kalpetta ☎04936/251 1997, ☎m9447 004369, ⓦwww.raincountryresort.com. A 3km track takes you from the main road to a secluded pocket of greenery overlooking the Lakkidi valley, where eight beautifully reconstructed antique Keralan *tharavads*, culled from locations around the state, are scattered over a clearing in the forest. In front of them, pillared verandas equipped with cane furniture face a spring-fed pond, though the views are restricted by a natural balcony. There are plenty

of walks in the immediate surroundings – staff are happy to accompany you. ⑧
Vythiri Resort booking at Kochi office ☎0484/4055250, ⓦ www.vythiriresort.com. Set in a lovely seven-acre woodland plot with three boulder-strewn mountain streams flowing through it, *Vythiri Resort* feels like a small jungle-hill village, down to the terracotta roofs, wood pillars and cable suspension bridge. Accommodation comes in three forms: cottages with private sitouts; beautifully refurbished plantation-workers'

rooms, with stone-lined plunge pools; and deluxe rooms in little double-floored blocks. Guided walks and visits to a nearby tea factory number among the complimentary extras; and there's a pool. Rates include full board. ⑧–⑨
Woodlands Kalpetta ☎04936/202547, ⓦ www .thewoodlandshotel.com. Comfortable, modern rooms (some a/c) at reasonable tariffs in a smart roadside hotel, conveniently located just north of the bus stand. Courteous staff, ample off-road parking and separate veg and non-veg restaurants. ⑤–⑦

The far north

The beautiful coast **north of Kozhikode** is a seemingly endless stretch of coconut palms, wooded hills and virtually deserted beaches. The towns hold little of interest for visitors, most of whom bypass the area completely – missing out on the chance to see **theyyam**, the extraordinary masked trance dances and oracle readings that take place in villages throughout the region between November and May.

Kannur (Cannanore)

KANNUR (Cannanore), a small, run-of-the-mill market town 92km north of Kozhikode, was for many centuries the capital of the Kolathiri rajas, who prospered from the thriving maritime spice trade through its port. India's first Portuguese Viceroy, Francisco de Almeida, took the stronghold in 1505, leaving in his wake an imposing triangular bastion, **St Angelo's Fort**. This was taken in the seventeenth century by the Dutch, who sold it a hundred or so years later to the Arakkal Rajas, Kerala's only ruling Muslim dynasty. They in turn were ousted by General Abercrombie's East India Company troops, who besieged the citadel in 1790, forcing the Arakkals' female ruler, Ali Raja Beebi, to capitulate. You can still clamber up the ramparts, littered with British cannon, for views over the town's Norwegian-funded fishing anchorage, Mapila Bay. A gentle thirty-minute walk around the headland to the northwest brings you to quiet **Baby Beach**, behind the *Government Guest House* in the army's cantonment area (daily access 9am–5pm), where a leafy seaside promenade (Rs2) leads to a lighthouse (daily 3–5pm; Rs5), with fine views of the rocky coastlines and distant beaches. However, the most popular destination among local people for a stroll and splash in the surf is **Payyambalam beach**, a long stretch of white sand 4km north of town. You can bypass the crowds that converge here on evenings and weekends by walking further north: the empty sands come to an end after 4km at a headland, on the far side of which lies grim **Meankunnu beach**.

The unexploited beaches around Kannur are spectacular enough, but most visitors come to the town to search out **theyyam** (also known loosely as *theyy-attam*, meaning "performance of *theyyam*"): dramatic spirit-possession rituals held in scores of villages across the region (see Contexts, p.791). There are over 400 different manifestations of this arcane traditional art form. The best way to find them is to ask at the local tourist office, or stay at *Costa Malabari* (see p.492). Throughout the *theyyam* season, the *Malayala Manorama* daily newspaper lists forthcoming performances at the top left of the second page, though you will have to ask someone to translate it for you. For anyone short of time, the daily rituals at **Parassinikadavu** (see below), or the Sree Muthappam temple next to the railway station (daily 4pm), are worthwhile alternatives.

Practicalities

Straddling the main coastal transport artery between Mangalore and Kochi/Thiruvananthapuram, Kannur is well connected by **bus** and **train** to most major towns and cities in Kerala, as well as Mangalore in Karnataka. In addition, buses from here travel to Mysore, turning inland at Thalassery (aka Tellycherry) and climbing the beautiful wooded Ghats to Virajpet in Kodagu. The **railway station** is just over five minutes' walk southwest of the bus stand. The State Bank of India on Fort Road will **change money** and traveller's cheques, as will UAE Exchange in the City Centre Shopping complex (Mon–Sat 9.30am–1.30pm & 2–6pm), 500m east of the bus stand. There's a **tourist information centre** at the railway station (Mon–Sat 10am–5pm; ☏0497/270 3121). **Internet** access is widely available; try the a/c Padinharakandy (Mon–Sun 9am–9.30pm; Rs30/hr), 150m south of the pink City Centre Shopping building on Fort Road, or MetroNet, opposite in the Metro Hypermarket centre (daily 9am–9pm; Rs20/hr).

For inexpensive **food** there's an *Indian Coffee House* in Fort Road, 50m south of City Centre Shopping. Just behind the City Centre Shopping building, the trendy *Can Café* has a good selection of biriyanis as well as other inexpensive Malabari chicken and fish dishes. The *Hot Stone*, above the Meridian Palace (see below), enjoys a good reputation amongst the locals. Kannur is not short of **sweet shops**, where you can try the local *kinnathappam* and *kalathappam* cakes, made with rice flour and *jaggery*. Station Road is lined with them.

Accommodation

Costa Malabari 10km south near Tottada village; book through the tourist desk in Kochi (☏0484/237 1761, ⓦwww.costamalabari.com. Hidden deep in cashew and coconut groves, this welcoming guesthouse, run by one of the region's most knowledgeable *theyyam* afficionados, has five airy and comfortable rooms. Five pristine beaches lie within ten minutes' walk, and guests are plied with huge portions of excellent Keralan food (included in the rate). They also run good off-track backwater and wildlife trips in the region. Pick up from Kannur (Rs150) by prior arrangement. ⑤

Government Guest House Cantonment area ☏0497/270 6426. Superb-value government-run place on a clifftop at the edge of town, with huge, simple a/c and non-a/c rooms whose huge balconies have uninterrupted sea views; it's primarily for visiting VIPs but usually has a few vacancies. Advance booking can be a problem; ring ahead when you arrive. Inexpensive vegetarian meals on request. ②–④

Malabar Residency Thavakkara Rd ☏0497/276 5456. Smart, central hotel with comfortable attached a/c rooms, two restaurants, including the multi-cuisine *Grand Plaza*, and a 24hr coffee shop. ⑤

Mascot Beach Resort 300m before Baby Beach ☏0497/270 8445, ⓦwww.mascotresort.com. Perched on the rocky shoreline, offering large a/c rooms and cottages with views across the cove to the lighthouse. Facilities include a swimming pool, foreign exchange and a good restaurant – but no bar. ⑤–⑦

Meridian Palace Bellard Rd ☏0497/270 1676, ⓦwww.hotelmeridianpalace.com. Only two blocks from the station, this compact hotel has a wide range of comfy, clean rooms and a popular little restaurant serving veg and local seafood meals. ②–⑤

Sweety International 200m north of railway station, near Munisheeran Kovil ☏0497/270 8283. Standard economy high-rise with ordinary, "executive" and a/c rooms, all pretty decent value. ②–③

Parassinikadavu

The only place you can be almost guaranteed a glimpse of *theyyam* is the village of **PARASSINIKADAVU**, 20km north of Kannur, beside the River Valapatanam, where the head priest, or *madayan*, of the **Parassini Madammpura**

△ A *theyyam* ritual, near Kannur

temple performs twice a day during winter (6.30–8.30am & 5.45–8.30pm) before assembled worshippers. Elaborately dressed and accompanied by a traditional drum group, he becomes possessed by the temple's presiding deity – Lord Muthappan, Shiva, in the form of a *kiratha*, or hunter – and enacts a series of complex offerings. The two-hour ceremony culminates when the priest/deity dances forward to bless individual members of the congregation. Even by Keralan standards, it is an extraordinary spectacle, and well worth taking time out of a journey along the coast for.

Regular local **buses** leave Kannur for Parassinikadavu from around 7am, dropping passengers at the top of the village. If you want to get there in time for the dawn *theyyam*, however, you'll have to splash out on one of the Ambassador taxis that line up outside Kannur bus stand (around Rs400 return trip). Cabbies sleep in their cars, so you can arrange the trip on the spot by waking one up; taxis may also be arranged through most hotels. Either way, you'll have to leave around 4.30am. Alternatively, stay in the conveniently located *Thai Resort* (☎0497/278 4242; ❺–❻) 80m from the temple (to the left as you face the entrance). Shaded by coconut trees, seven circular stone cottages are dotted around a well-kept garden, with cool, comfortable rooms.

If you've come for the morning performance and have a few hours to spare afterwards, one possibility for an excursion is to take a bus from Parassinikadavu to **Trichambaram temple**, a magnificent piece of traditional architecture dedicated to Krishna, with tiered clay roofs and slatted wooden walls. A smaller temple nearby, no more than a puja room surrounded by a water moat, is devoted to Durga Devi. Buses from Parassinikadavu take 15min, and drop you at a junction 800m from the temple complex.

Bekal

Just 7km north of the town of Kanhangad, **BEKAL** is popular amongst Indians as a destination for weekend day-trips, with a **fort** (daily 8am–5pm; Rs100) standing on a promontory between two long, classically beautiful palm-fringed **beaches** (swimming is safe, but dress in suitably modest gear to avoid causing offence). Although this is one of the largest fortresses in Kerala and has been under the control of various powers including Vijayanagar, Tipu Sultan and the British, it's nothing to get excited about. Heat haze permitting, the bay views from the bastion are impressive enough, but the vast *maidan* inside the walls is a hot and dry wasteland – hardly deserving of the stiff admission fee.

A short walk beyond the main entrance to the fort, you'll find the friendly *Bekal Resorts Development Corporation (BRDC)* **tourist office** (Mon–Sat 9.30am–5pm; ☎0944/779 3815), which can point visitors in the direction of local *theyyam* performances and houseboat rentals in the nearby backwater area.

The only commendable place to stay hereabouts is the *Gitanjali Heritage* (☎0467/223 4159, ⓦwww.gitanjaliheritage.com; $100 per person full-board, ❾), a lovely heritage homestay 7km inland (to the southeast) from Bekal in the sleepy village of Panayal. Tucked away in a coconut grove near the 2000-year-old Shiva temple, the 70-year-old house has three simple rooms, furnished in traditional Keralan style, with bent-cane chairs, wooden ceilings and slatted windows. The organic vegetable garden supplies owner Mr Jaganath's kitchen with fresh produce year-round. This is also a good place from which to explore the area's *theyyam* rituals.

Travel details

For details of ferry services on the backwaters – primarily between Alappuzha and Kollam – see p.416.

Trains

Kochi/Ernakulam to: Alappuzha (5–7 daily; 1hr 10min–1hr 40min); Bengaluru (Bangalore) (1–2 daily; 13hr); Chennai (5–7 daily; 11hr 45min–16hr 20min); Kanyakumari (2–3 daily; 7hr 25min–10hr); Kollam (Quilon) (12–15 daily; 2hr 50min–4hr 25min); Kottayam (9–11 daily; 1hr–1hr 20min); Kozhikode (4–6 daily; 4hr 45min–5hr 30min); Mumbai (2–3 daily; 26hr 25min–37hr 35min); Thiruvananthapuram (11–15 daily; 5hr–5hr 35min); Thrissur (15–18 daily; 1hr 15min–2hr 30min).

Kozhikode to: Kannur (9–11 daily; 1hr 55min–2hr 25min); Kochi/Ernakulam (7–9 daily; 4hr 15min–5hr 15min); Mangalore (6–9 daily; Madgaon; 25hr 55min); 4hr 40min–5hr 30min); Mumbai (2 daily via Thiruvananthapuram (4–6 daily; 9hr 40min–10hr 15min); Thrissur (6–9 daily; 2hr 30min–3hr 25min).

Thiruvananthapuram to: Alappuzha (3–5 daily; 2hr 40min–3hr 15min); Bengaluru (Bangalore) (1 daily; 18hr); Chennai (4–5 daily; 16hr 30min–18hr 45min); Kanyakumari (2 daily; 2hr); Kochi/Ernakulam (12–16 daily; 4hr–5hr 20min); Kollam (13–16 daily; 55min–1hr 30min); Kottayam (9–10 daily; 2hr–2hr 45min); Kozhikode (3–5 daily; 9hr–10hr 30min); Madgaon (1–3 daily; 15hr 10min–20hr 20min); Madurai (3 daily; 6hr 40min–9hr); Mumbai (2–3 daily; 30hr 40min–42hr 20min); Thrissur (10–12 daily; 5hr 45min–7hr); Varkala (12–13 daily; 45–55min).

Thrissur to: Chennai (3–4 daily; 10hr 25min–11hr 45min); Kochi/Ernakulam (15–17 daily; 1hr 30min–2hr 10min); Thiruvananthapuram (10–12 daily; 5hr 55min–7hr 10min).

Buses

Alappuzha (Alleppey) to: Ernakulam (every 30min; 1hr 30min); Kollam (every 45min; 2hr); Kottayam (every 30min; 1hr 30min–2hr); Kumily (1 daily; 6hr); Thiruvananthapuram (5 daily; 3hr–4hr).

Kochi/Ernakulam to: Alappuzha (every 30min; 1hr 30min); Kanyakumari (6 daily; 9hr); Kollam (every 30min; 3hr); Kottayam (every 30min; 1hr 30min–2hr); Kozhikode (hourly; 5hr); Kumily (10 daily; 6hr); Munnar (6 daily; 4hr 30min–5hr); Periyar, see "Kumily"; Thiruvananthapuram (every 2hr; 5–6hr); Thrissur (every 30min; 2hr).

Kozhikode to: Kannur (every 30min; 2–2hr 30min); Kochi/Ernakulam (hourly; 5hr); Mysore (2 daily; 9–10hr); Ooty (4 daily; 6–7hr); Thiruvananthapuram (12–15 daily; 11–12hr); Thrissur (hourly; 3hr 30min–4hr).

Kumily to: Alappuzha (1 daily; 6hr); Kochi/Ernakulam (10 daily; 6hr); Kottayam (every 30min; 4hr); Madurai (10 daily; 5hr 30min); Munnar (4 daily; 4hr); Thiruvananthapuram (6 daily; 8–9hr).

Munnar to: Kochi/Ernakulam (6 daily; 4hr 30min–5hr); Kottayam (5 daily; 5hr); Kumily (4 daily; 4hr); Madurai (6 daily; 5hr); Thiruvananthapuram (5 daily; 8–9hr).

Thiruvananthapuram to: Alappuzha (5 daily; 4hr); Chennai (4 daily; 18hr); Kanyakumari (9 daily; 2hr 30min); Kochi/Ernakulam (every 2hr; 5–6hr); Kollam (every 2hr; 1hr 30min–2hr); Kottayam (every 30min; 4hr); Kozhikode (8 daily; 11–12hr); Kumily (1 daily; 9hr); Madurai (5 daily; 7–8hr); Mangalore (1 daily; 16hr); Munnar (3 daily; 9–10hr); Nedumangad (hourly; 45min–1hr); Neyyar Dam (hourly; 1hr 15min); Ponmudi (6 daily; 2hr–2hr 30min); Thrissur (hourly; 8–9hr); Varkala (10 daily; 1hr 30min–2hr 30min).

Thrissur to: Chennai (4 daily; 12–14hr); Guruvayur (10 daily; 40min); Kochi/Ernakulam (every 10min; 2hr); Kozhikode (every 30min; 2hr 30min); Mysore (5 daily; 8hr); Palakkad (every 20min; 2hr); Thiruvananthapuram (every 20min; 7–8hr).

Flights

For a list of airline websites, see Basics p.38. In the listings below, IA is Indian Airlines, AI Air India, AIE Air India Express, JA Jet Airways, SA Sahara Airlines, AD Air Deccan, KF Kingfisher, IG IndiGo, GO Go Air, SJ SpiceJet and PA Paramount Airways.

Kochi/Ernakulam to: Bengaluru (Bangalore) (AD, SA, KF, JA, GO, IA 8–10 daily; 1hr 15min–2hr 15min); Chennai (DA, PA, KF, JA 6–7 daily; 1hr 30); Coimbatore (AD 1 daily; 30min); Goa (AI, KF 1–2 daily; 1hr 10min); Hyderabad (AD, SA 2 daily; 1hr 30min); Kozhikode (Calicut; AIE 1 daily; 35min); Lakshadweep (IA 6 weekly; 1hr 35min); Mumbai (AD, AIE, IA, GO, KF, JA 9–12 daily; 1hr 45min–2hr 30min); Thiruvananthapuram (AD, AIE, AS, IA 4 daily; 30min).

Kozhikode to: Bengaluru (Bangalore) (IA 3 weekly; 1hr 10min); Chennai (IA 7 weekly; 1hr–2hr 25min); Goa (IA 3 weekly; 1hr 5min); Kochi/Ernakulam (IA 1–2 daily; 30min); Mumbai (JA, IA, AI 3–4 daily; 1hr 40min–3hr); Tiruchirapalli (IA 2 weekly; 55min); Thiruvananthapuram (IA 2 weekly; 50min).

Thiruvananthapuram to: Bengaluru (Bangalore) (AD, IA, KF, JA 6 daily; 1hr); Chennai (JA, DA, IA 11–14 daily; 1hr–1hr 40min); Coimbatore (DA 1 daily; 45min); Kochi (DA 1 daily; 30min); Mumbai (IA, JA, DA, 5–6 daily; 2hr); Tiruchirapalli (IA 4 weekly; 1hr).

KERALA | Travel details

5

Chennai

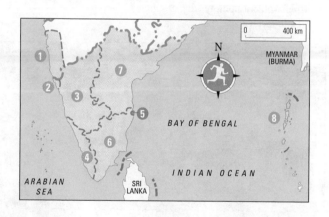

CHAPTER 5 # Highlights

✱ **Fort St George** The centre of the Madras Presidency during the Raj, this eighteenth-century fort now houses an excellent museum documenting the British occupation. See p.509

✱ **Kapalishvara temple** Chennai's most famous temple, complete with soaring *gopura*, a colourful array of shops selling devotional items and a water-lily tank. See p.516

✱ **Theosophical Society Headquarters** Visit the sprawling gardens, which include a vast banyan tree, and the fascinating library where Krishnamurti sought to understand divine truth. See p.517

✱ **Shopping** Chennai is a major commercial centre, offering plenty of shopping possibilities from the bazaars of George Town to the modern glitz of Spencer's Plaza, South India's prime mall. See p.523

△ Chennai market

Chennai

ucked into the northeastern corner of Tamil Nadu on the Bay of Bengal, **CHENNAI** (still commonly referred to by its former British name, **Madras**) is India's fourth largest city, with a population of well over six million. A hot, frenetic and congested metropolis, it is the major transportation hub of the far south and the eastern coastline, with excellent road, rail and flight connections to the rest of the Subcontinent. The major international airport here makes a marginally less stressful entry point to India than Mumbai or Delhi – but most travellers stay just long enough to book a ticket for somewhere else. The attractions of the city itself are sparse, though it does boast some fine specimens of Raj architecture, Christian pilgrimage sites connected with the apostle "Doubting Thomas", superb Chola bronzes at its state museum, and plenty of classical music and dance performances.

Chennai is capital of Tamil Nadu and, like Mumbai and Kolkata, is a relatively modern creation. It was founded by the British East India Company in 1639, on a five-kilometre strip of land between the Cooum and Adyar rivers, a few kilometres north of the ancient Tamil port of **Mylapore** and the Portuguese settlement of **San Thome**, which had been established in 1522. The site had no natural harbour and was selected by **Francis Day**, the East India Company agent, in part because he enjoyed good relations with the local Nayak governor Dharmala Ayyappa, who was able to intercede with the Vijayanagar Raja of Chandragiri, to whom the territory belonged. In addition, the land was protected by water on the east, south and west; cotton could be bought here twenty percent cheaper than elsewhere; and, apparently, Day had a mistress in San Thome.

A fortified trading post, completed on St George's Day in 1640, was named **Fort St George**. By 1700, the British had acquired neighbouring territory including **Triplicane** and **Egmore**, while over the course of the next century, as capital of the **Madras Presidency**, which covered most of South India, the city mushroomed to include many surrounding villages. The French, who had settled a little way down the coastline in Pondicherry, repeatedly challenged the British, and finally managed to destroy most of the city and bring it under their control in 1746. **Robert Clive** ("Clive of India"), then a clerk, was taken prisoner, an experience said to have inspired him to become a military campaigner. Clive was among the first to re-enter Madras when it was retaken by the British three years later, and continued to use it as his base. Following this, fortifications were strengthened and the British survived a year-long French siege in 1759, completing the work in 1783. By this time, however, Calcutta was in the ascendancy and Madras lost its national importance.

CHENNAI

BAY
OF
BENGAL

N

Enfield Factory ▲

Mofussil Bus Stand & Kanchipuram ▲

Directorate
of Shipping

Chennai Beach

GPO

RAJAJI SALAI-NORTH BEACH RD

Parry's
Corner

NSC BOSE RD

PRAKASAM RD

(POPHAM'S BROADWAY)

GEORGE TOWN

High
Court

Express
Bus Stand ★

Broadway
Bus Stand ★

Fort
St George

Fort House
& Museum

St Mary's
Church

KAMARAJAR SALAI

Anna Park
MGR Samadhi

Senate House

SOUTH BEACH ROAD

FLAG STAFF RD

The Island

River Cooum

ANNA SALAI

PALLAVAN SALAI
BODY GUARD RD

TRIPLICANE

PYCROFTS RD

BESANT RD

QUAIDE MILLETH SALAI

TTDC ℹ

WALAJAH RD

BHARATHI SALAI

WESTCOTT ROAD

VOC ROAD

WALL TAX ROAD

Chennai
Central

U Rent

St Andrew's
Kirk

Head
Post Office

ARUNACHALA NAICKEN ST

India
Tourism ℹ

WOODS RD

WHITES RD

PETERS RD

ANNA SALAI

St George's
Cathedral ✚ ❸

GREAMS RD

BUCKINGHAM CANAL

ELEPHANT GATE
BRIDGE

VEPERY

STRAHAM'S RD

PERAMBUR BARRACKS RD

RITHERDON RD

HUNTERS RD

PURASAWALKAM HIGH RD

PURASAWALKAM

Egmore

See Egmore, Anna Salai
and Triplicane map for detail

POONAMALLEE HIGH RD

EGMORE

PANTHEON RD

Government
Museum

COLLEGE RD

UK High
Commission

Foreigners'
Registration
Office

UTTAMAR GANDHI RD

DR GURUSWAMY-MCNICHOLS RD

VALLUVAR KOTTAM RD

MGR SALAI

Valluvar
Kottam ❷

KONNUR HIGH RD

NEW AVADI RD

KILPAUK GARDEN RD

DR GURUSWAMY
BRIDGE

CHETPUT

STERLING RD

River Cooum

NEW AVADI RD

2ND AVE

EVR PERIYAR HIGH RD

NELSON MANICKA MUSTALLAR RD

NSK ROAD (ARCOT RD)

NUNGAMBAKKAM

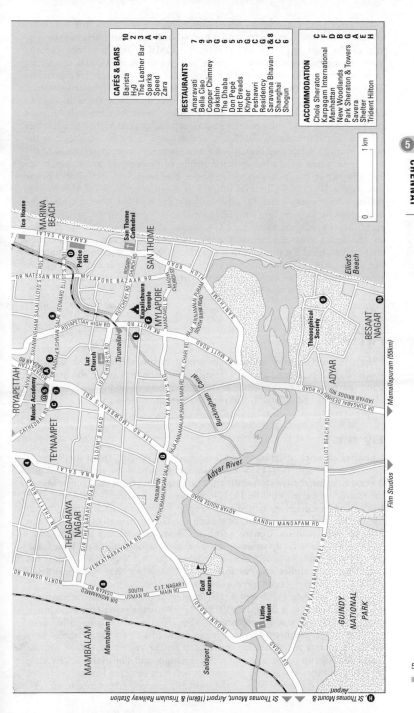

CAFÉS & BARS

Barista	10
H₂0	2
The Leather Bar	3
Sparks	4
Speed	A
Zara	5

RESTAURANTS

Amaravati	7
Bella Ciao	9
Copper Chimney	G
Dakshin	6
The Dhaba	5
Don Pepé	5
Hot Breads	G
Khyber	C
Peshawri	G
Residency	C
Saravana Bhavan	1 & 8
Shanghai	C
Shogun	6

ACCOMMODATION

Chola Sheraton	C
Karpagam International	F
Manhattan	D
New Woodlands	B
Park Sheraton & Towers	A
Savera	E
Shelter	H
Trident Hilton	G

0   1 km

The city's renaissance began after Independence, when it became the centre of the Tamil **movie industry**, and a hotbed of **Dravidian nationalism**. The rise of the two pro-Dravidian parties, the **DMK** – which ousted Nehru's Congress government from the state in 1967 – and the **AIADMK** owed a lot to their influence in the major film studios in Chennai. Marudur Gopalamenon Ramachandran (popularly known as **MGR**), Tamil Nadu's revered film-star chief minister, exploited the mistrust of central rule from New Delhi throughout his eleven-year rule in the Seventies and Eighties. Power since the early Nineties has passed back and forth between ex-actress Jayalalitha (AIADMK) and former screenwriter Karunanidhi (DMK), who was voted in for his fifth spell in the top post in 2006 (see box on p.514 for more details). These days, cutouts of the chubby lady and be-shaded gent and strings of pennants in party colours are still ubiquitous, but industry and commerce have taken over as the city's prime *raison d'être*. Renamed **Chennai** in 1997 to assert its pre-colonial identity (the fishing village upon which the city was built was named Chennaipatnam), the metropolis has boomed since the Indian economy opened up to foreign investment under prime ministers Rajiv Ghandi and Rao in the 1990s. The flip side of this rapid economic growth is that Chennai's infrastructure has been stretched to breaking point, with a reported 5000 new private cars adding to the traffic chaos every month. Consequently, oppressive heat and pollution are more likely to be your lasting impressions than the conspicuous affluence of the city's modern marble shopping malls.

Arrival

Chennai's main **railway stations** are central, but its **airport** lies a long slog south of the city, around an hour from the hotel districts, while the main **bus** stand is 10km west of the centre. If you're on a budget, finding an inexpensive place to stay can be difficult late at night, so hunt around for a vacancy by phone before arriving.

By air

Chennai airport, at Trisulam in Meenambakkam district, 16km southwest of the city centre on NH-45, is comprehensively served by international and domestic flights; the two terminals are a minute's walk from each other. Out in the main concourse, you'll find a 24-hour post office, Thomas Cook and State Bank of India foreign-exchange counters and a couple of snack bars. It's by no means certain that anyone will be staffing the **Government of Tamil Nadu Tourist Information Centre** booth at the arrivals exit, but if you're lucky you may be able to fix up accommodation from here, or at the "Free Fone" desk nearby. If you plan to leave Chennai by train, note that Southern Railways has a computerized **ticket reservation** counter (Mon–Sat 8am–8pm; Sun 8am–2pm), immediately outside the domestic terminal exit.

There are pre-paid minibus and taxi counters at the exit in the international arrivals hall. **Taxis** cost around Rs300 for the 35-minute ride to the main hotels or railway stations; rickshaws charge Rs150–200, but you'll have to lug your gear out to the main road as they're not allowed to park inside the airport forecourt. A taxi to **Mamallapuram** costs in the region of Rs900. Shuttle **buses** (Rs50) run to Egmore and Central stations and Thiruvalluvar (Express) bus stand, but they call at several upmarket hotels en route, and are certainly not "Express". The quickest, cheapest and most efficient way to get into town is by

Chennai or Madras?

The city's former name of **Madras** was changed to **Chennai** (the abbreviated form of the original settlement) at the behest of pro-Dravidian politicians back in the 1990s. Since then several major roads in the city have also been renamed as part of an ongoing attempt to "**Dravidify**" the Tamil capital (most of the new names immortalize former nationalist politicians). Thus Mount Road, the main shopping road through the centre of town, is now **Anna Salai**; to the east, Triplicane High Road, near *Broadlands Hotel*, has become **Quaide Milleth Salai**; Poonamallee High Road, running east–west across the north of the city, is **EVR Periyar High Road**; North Beach Road, along the eastern edge of George Town is known as **Rajaji Salai**; South Beach Road, the southern stretch of the coastal road, is **Kamarajar Salai**; C-in-C Road, is now **Ethiraj Salai**; south of the centre, Mowbray's Road is also known as **TTK Road** and Edward Elliot's Road has been renamed **Dr Radhakrishnan Salai**; and Nungambakkam High Road **Uttamar Gandhi Salai**.

However, far from all of Chennai's inhabitants are in favour of the recent changes, while some (notably a large contingent of auto-rickshaw-wallahs) seem completely oblivious to them. The confusing result of this is that both old and new names remain in use. We have used the new ones throughout the chapter, but many of the old ones are still more commonly understood, and using them won't cause offence – unless, of course, you happen to be talking to a pro-Dravidian activist.

suburban **train** (around Rs10). Services run every ten to fifteen minutes (4.30am–11pm) from **Trisulam station**, 500m from the airport on the far side of the road, to Park, Egmore and North Beach stations, taking 30–40 minutes. If you want to leave Chennai straight away by bus, catch local bus #70 or #70a to the new Mofussil bus stand (see below).

By train

Arriving in Chennai by train, you come in at one of two **long-distance railway stations**, 1.5km apart on EVR Periyar High Road, towards the north of the city. **Egmore Station**, in the heart of the busy commercial district of the same name, is the arrival point for most trains from Tamil Nadu and Kerala. Other services pull in at **Central Station**, further east, on the edge of George Town, which has a 24-hour left-luggage office and an excellent Internet centre (also open 24hr) in the concourse. Both stations have poorly staffed, badly equipped information offices, and are served by plenty of metered taxis and auto-rickshaws; Central has a pre-paid auto-rickshaw booth.

By bus

Long-distance buses arrive at the huge new **Mofussil** bus stand (☎044/2479 4705), inconveniently situated in the suburb of Koyambedu, over 10km west of central Chennai – the chaotic old **Express** and **Broadway** bus stands in the city centre have been amalgamated and are only used for local services. Mofussil is linked to these and other parts of Chennai by a host of city buses from the well-organized platforms outside the main terminal: buses #15b, #15f, #17e and #27 go to the Egmore/Central area and Parry's Corner; bus #27b also goes on to Triplicane, while buses #70 and #70a link the bus stand to the airport. Note that most buses from Mamallapuram, Pondicherry (Puducherry) and other towns to the south of Chennai stop at Guindy suburban railway station on their way in; you'll save a lot of time by catching a train into the city from here.

Health warning

Chennai boasts some of India's most sophisticated medical facilities, which is just as well, because it is officially one of the unhealthiest places in the world. Exponential, unplanned economic growth, coupled with inadequate investment in the municipal infrastructure, has resulted in chronic pollution problems. Exhaust emissions are the prime cause of **poor air quality**. Over the last decade the number of vehicles clogging Chennai's roads has more than quadrupled, and 75 percent of them are dirty, two-stroke two-wheelers. As a result, carbon monoxide levels are double the permitted maximum, while the amount of "suspended particulate matter" in the air is more than seven times the World Health Organization's prescribed limits. If you suffer from asthma or any other respiratory disorders, don't aim to spend long here.

Although efforts have been made to improve the city's **water quality** in recent years, there are still some question marks about its purity and there is even more concern about the quantity available for supply: water tables have been very low of late and it is unlikely the current reservoirs will be able to meet demand, which is why hundreds of crores of rupees are being poured into desalination projects. So bear this in mind and use water even more sparingly here than elsewhere. Also exercise more caution than usual regarding drinking water and the treatment of food.

Another concern is the incidence of mosquito-borne diseases. Chennai alone accounts for around half of the total number of reported **malaria** cases in Tamil Nadu, with a sixty percent increase over recent years of the number of patients developing the deadly falciparum strain (which can develop into cerebral malaria). There has also been an upsurge in less common diseases such as dengue fever and Japanese encephalitis. So take extra malaria precautions while you're in Chennai – always sleep under a net and cover yourself with repellent – especially during, and immediately after, the monsoons.

Information

The highly efficient and very helpful **India Tourism Office**, at 154 Anna Salai (Mon–Fri 9am–6pm, Sat 9am–1pm; ☎044/2846 0285), has maps and leaflets, and can arrange accommodation. They also have lists of reliable tour agents for car rental and of approved **guides**.

The **Tamil Nadu Tourism Development Corporation** (TTDC) is based in a smart new complex on Wallajah Road, near Anna Park in Triplicane (Mon–Sat 10am–5.30pm; ☎044/2538 3333, ☺www.tamilnadutourism.com), which is where you'll also find the tourist offices of many other states (including that for Kerala ☎044/2536 9789). The TTDC can book you tours or accommodation in their own hotels across the state. The **India Tourist Development Corporation** (ITDC) office at 29 Dr PV Cherian Crescent, Ethiraj Salai (Mon–Fri 10am–5.30pm; ☎044/2827 8884, ☺theashokgroup.com) handles advance bookings for ITDC hotels across the country, and can also arrange tours of the city, state and country.

The long-established *Hallo! Madras* (monthly; Rs10) has useful listings of all the city's services, plus full moon dates (useful for estimating temple festivals), a tourist guide to Tamil Nadu, exhaustive flight and train details, and an outline of Chennai bus timetables. Alternatively, the even more comprehensive quarterly directory *Madura Welcome Tamil Nadu* (Rs100) contains even fuller transport, accommodation and tourist information details for Chennai and the rest of Tamil Nadu. Both are available at all book and stationery shops. Unfortunately, neither have a "What's On" section, so for forthcoming music and dance performances, look out for *Chennai: This Fortnight*, available free from all the city's smarter hotels, or check online at Ⓦ www.explocity.com/chennai.asp or Ⓦ www.chennaionline.com.

City transport

The offices, sights, railway stations and bus stands of Chennai are spread over such a wide area that it's impossible to get around without using some form of **public transport**. Most visitors jump in auto-rickshaws, but outside rush hours you can travel around comfortably by **bus** or suburban **train**.

Incidentally, the city's drastic dry-season water shortage explains the **water carriers** trundling along its congested streets. Watch out for unofficial ones as you cross the road; tractors pull tankers so heavy that they can either topple over or fail to stop when brakes are applied, causing fatal accidents.

Buses

Compared to other parts of India, **buses** in Chennai are regular, inexpensive, and only get cramped during rush hours. On Anna Salai and other major thoroughfares, buses have dedicated stops, but on smaller streets you'll have to flag them down or wait with an obvious crowd of other would-be passengers. Buses in Egmore leave from various sides of the railway station, so it's best to ask a local where to find the one to your destination. The numbers of services to specific places of interest in the city are listed in the relevant accounts; buses to and from the new Mofussil bus stand are listed on p.503.

Trains

If you want to travel south from central Chennai to Guindy (Deer Park), St Thomas Mount or the airport, the easiest way to go is by **train**. Services run every fifteen minutes (on average) between 4.30am and 11pm, prices are minimal, and you can guarantee a seat at any time except rush hour (around 9am & 5pm). First-class carriages have padded seats rather than wooden slatted benches and are a little cleaner; there's always a carriage reserved for ladies, too, which is usually clearly signed. Buy a ticket before boarding.

City trains travel between the following stations: Beach (opposite the GPO), Fort, Park (for Central), Egmore, Nungambakkam, Kodambakkam, Mambalam (for T Nagar and silk shops), Saidapet (for Little Mount Church), Guindy (for buses to Mamallapuram and Pondicherry), St Thomas Mount and Trisulam (for the airport).

Taxis and rickshaws

Chennai's yellow-top Ambassador **taxis** gather outside Egmore and Central railway stations and at the airport. All have meters, but drivers often prefer to fix a price before leaving, and invariably charge a return fare whatever the destination, meaning that they're practically pricing themselves out of business – the trip from Central Station to Triplicane, for instance, costs around Rs150. More reliable and economical **radio taxis** are therefore becoming increasingly popular; try Bharati Call Taxi (☎ 044/2814 2233).

Flocks of auto- and cycle-rickshaws wait patiently outside tourist hotels, and not so patiently outside railway stations. **Auto-rickshaw** drivers in Chennai are notorious for demanding high fares from locals and tourists alike. A rickshaw from Triplicane to either of the bus stations, plus Egmore and Central railway

Tours and day-trips

One good way to get around the sights of Chennai is on a TTDC **bus tour** (book at their office; see p.504). The tours are good value, if rushed, and the guides can be very helpful. The TTDC **half-day tour** (daily 8am–1pm or 1.30–6.30pm; Rs120 non a/c, Rs170 a/c) starts at their office on EVR Periyar High Road and takes in Fort St George, the Government Museum, the Snake Park, Kapalishvara Temple, Elliot's Beach and Marina Beach (on Friday, the Government Museum is closed, so the tour goes to the Birla Planetarium instead). TTDC also offers good-value **day-trips** to Mamallapuram (including Kanchipuram; daily 6.30am–7pm, non-a/c Rs330, a/c Rs470) and Pondicherry/Auroville (Sat & Sun 6.30am–9pm, non-a/c Rs400, a/c Rs600); meals are included in the price in both tours.

stations should cost no more than Rs50. All rickshaws have meters; a few drivers use them if asked, but in many cases you'll save a lot of frustrating bargaining by offering a small sub above the meter-reading (a driver may offer you a rate of "meter plus 5", meaning Rs5 above the final reading). If you need to get to the airport or station early in the morning, book a rickshaw and negotiate the price the night before (the driver may well sleep in his vehicle outside your hotel). Only take **cycle rickshaws** on smaller roads; riding amid Chennai traffic on a fragile seat can be hair-raising.

Car and motorcycle rental

Car rental with driver is available at many of the city's upmarket hotels or through private agents such as Welcome Tours & Travels at 150 Anna Salai (☎044/2846 0908, ☺www.allindiatours.com). An ambassador car with driver costs around Rs1000–1200 per/day (or Rs1600–1900 for a/c) – rates may be negotiable.

Mopeds and **motorcycles** can be rented at U-Rent Services, 1 1st Main Rd, Gandhinagar, Adyar (Mon–Sat 8am–7pm, Sun 9am–6pm; ☎044/2491 0838). Prices range from Rs200 to Rs400 per/day, plus a flat Rs200 annual membership fee regardless of how long you rent a bike for.

Accommodation

Finding a **place to stay** in Chennai can be a problem, as hotels sometimes fill up early in the day and only a couple of places have anything for less than Rs250 (though at least standards in the cheapies are better than in other cities). If you're on a budget, it's advisable to phone and book in advance, at least from the railway station or airport.

Most of the city's mid-range and inexpensive hotels are located around the **railway stations**. Other popular areas include **Anna Salai**, which tends to be more expensive, and **Triplicane**, an atmospheric Muslim area boasting some of the city's best budget guesthouses. The bulk of the top hotels are in the south of the city, along Nungambakkam, Dr Radha Krishnan Salai and Cathedral roads; several offer courtesy buses to and from the airport. Almost all hotels have at least one South Indian/multi-cuisine restaurant attached.

Egmore

The following places are marked on the map on p.509.

Chandra Park 55 Gandhi Irwin Rd ☎044/2819 1177, ☺www .hotelchandrapark.com. Newly refurbished business hotel with central a/c, foreign exchange, 24hr coffee shop, bar and rooftop restaurant. The spacious, light and well-furnished standard rooms are an especially good deal. ④–⑥

Howrah 17 EVR Periyar High Rd (reception on 1st floor) ☎044/2536 7445. Clean attched rooms close to Central station, slightly cheaper than the adjacent *Central Tower*. ④

Impala Continental 12 Gandhi Irwin Rd ☎044/2819 1423. Run-of-the-mill lodge, but with clean non-a/c and a/c attched rooms, all with TV and phones. Good value, so often full. ③–④

Imperial Supreme 6 Gandhi Irwin Rd ☎044/2819 3954, ⓕ4214 7375. The best of three sister hotels set in their own enclosed courtyard opposite the station. Has a range of attched rooms, including a/c suites, all with TV and phones, and there's also a restaurant and travel service. ③–④

Masa 15/1 Kennet Lane ☎044/2819 3344, ⓕ2819 1261. Variously priced rooms with attached bathrooms in a clean, modern building, close to the station. The *Regal*, tacked onto the back, is of a similar standard and price; both hotels are popular with foreigners and Indians. ②–④

Nest Inn 55/31 Gandhi Irwin Rd ☎044/2819 2919, ⓦwww.hotelnestinn.com. Renovated and renamed business hotel, now with central a/c, and the poshest establishment in the immediate Egmore area. The rooms are small but comfortable and pleasantly decorated; there's also a multi-cuisine restaurant and bar. ⑥

New Victoria 3 Kennet Lane ☎044/2819 3638, ⓦwww.empeehotels.com. One of Egmore's more upmarket options: all rooms have a/c and hot showers, and rates include breakfast, but it's still a little overpriced. ⑤–⑦

Pandian 15 Kennet Lane ☎044/2819 1010, ⓦwww.hotelpandian.com. Pleasant, clean and modern mid-scale place within walking distance of the railway station – ask for a room on the Church Park side of the building for green views. There are exorbitant extra charges for a/c. ④

Regent 11 Kennet Lane ☎044/2819 1347. Quiet lodge set around a peaceful courtyard with non-a/c rooms – it's a bit shabby, though the bathrooms are spotless. ③

Royal Regency 26–27 EVR Periyar High Rd ☎044/2561 1777, ⓦwww.royalregency.co.in. Smart and comfortable business hotel with central a/c, equidistant to the two main railway stations. WiFi connection, multi-cuisine restaurant, 24hr coffee shop and gymnasium/yoga facilities. ⑦

Salvation Army Red Shield Guest House 15/31 Ritherdon Rd ☎044/2532 1821, ⓔredshield @hotmail.com. Tucked away in a leafy backstreet behind the station, this Sally Army lodge has

friendly and helpful staff and extremely basic accommodation in either dorms (Rs80) or attched doubles (some with a/c). ③–④

Tourist Home 43–45 Gandhi Irwin Rd ☎044/2819 4679, ⓔtourist@md3.vsnl.net.in. Popular hotel directly opposite the railway station. Rooms (some a/c) have showers, TV, phones, clean sheets and towels but could do with a spring-clean; the back rooms suffer less from early morning noise. Also has a three- and a six-bed room. ③–④

YWCA 1086 EVR Periyar High Rd ☎044/2532 4234, ⓦwww.ywcachennai.com. Attractive and friendly hotel in quiet gardens behind Egmore Station. Rooms are spotless and spacious, and there's a safe-deposit and a good restaurant. Book in advance. Rates include a buffet breakfast. ④–⑤

Anna Salai and Triplicane

The following places are marked on the map on p.509.

Ambassador Pallava 30 Montieth Rd ☎044/2855 4476, ⓦwww.ambassadorindia.com. Colossal four-star, close to Anna Salai, full of cool white marble and gold-plated mirrors, and with great views from its upper storeys. Also has a sports complex with a pool and health club. Suites go up to $200. ⑧–⑨

Broadlands 18 Vallabha Agraham St, Triplicane ☎044/2854 5573, ⓔbroadlandshotel@yahoo.com. An old whitewashed house, with crumbling stucco and stained glass, ranged around a leafy courtyard – the kind of budget travellers' enclave you either love or loathe. It has a large roof terrace and clean rooms, a few with attached bathrooms, private balconies and views of the mosque. ②

Comfort 22 Vallabha Agraham St, Triplicane ☎044/2858 7661, ⓦwww.hotelcomfortonline .com. The corridors are long and dimly lit, but the rooms are all attched and clean, albeit on the small side. ③–④

Cristal 34 CNK Rd, Triplicane ☎044/2858 5605. Friendly place, run by a team of brothers, in a modern building off Quaide Milleth Salai. Rooms are tiled and tidy, and all have attached showers; those with TVs cost Rs25 extra. As cheap as it gets in Chennai. ①

Himalaya 54 Quaide Milleth Salai, Triplicane ☎044/2854 7522, ⓔhtl_himalaya@yahoo.com. Clean, spacious rooms (some a/c) with cable TV, hot showers and balconies. Service is efficient, and there's a good restaurant and 24hr Internet access (open to non-residents). ③–④

Kanchi 28 Ethiraj Salai ☎044/2827 1100, ⓦwww.hotelkanchi.com. Soulless skyscraper with dingy corridors but with great views from its spacious balconied rooms, plus two restaurants (one rooftop) and a bar. ④

Paradise 17/1 Vallabha Agraham St, Triplicane ☏044/2859 4252, ✉paradisegh @hotmail.com. Very friendly and a dependable choice, offering inexpensive rooms (including some triples) with attached bathroom (choice of Western or Indian loos) and TV. Also has a large roof terrace. ❷–❹

Taj Connemara Binny Rd, just off Anna Salai, ☏044/5500 0000, ⓦwww.tajhotels.com. Dating from the Raj era, this whitewashed Art Deco five-star is a Chennai institution. The large "heritage" rooms are the best, with Victorian decor, dressing rooms and verandas overlooking the pool. The "standard" rooms, by contrast, are modern and a little overpriced. There's a very pleasant poolside area and two excellent restaurants, including the atmospheric alfresco *Rain Tree* with live music and dance every evening, plus a 24hr coffee shop and a bar. Doubles from $190, suites from $350. ❾

Outside the centre

The following places are marked on the map on p.500.

Chola Sheraton 10 Cathedral Rd ☏044/2811 0101, ⓦwww.sheraton.com. Palatial five-star in the city centre with all the trimmings, including a pool. The hefty $200–300 plus per night room tariff includes a buffet breakfast and a "cocktail hour". ❾

Karpagam International 41 South Mada St, Mylapore ☏044/2495 9984, Ⓕ2464 2299. Fairly ordinary hotel, with reasonable double rooms; the main attraction is the excellent location overlooking the Kapalishvara temple, and it's also on the right side of the city for the airport, 12km away. Also has some cheap but slightly dingy singles. ❸–❹

Manhattan 1 Dr Radhakrishnan Salai ☏044/2844 4546, ⓦwww.thehotelmanhattan.com. Only a few minutes' walk from Marina Beach, this comfortable modern hotel with central a/c offers decent rooms and a seaview from the rooftop terrace restaurant. ❻

New Woodlands 72–75 Dr Radhakrishnan Salai ☏044/2811 3111, ⓦwww.newwoodlands .com. Sprawling complex of clean, reasonably sized rooms and more spacious, self-contained apartments (called "cottages"), plus two restaurants and a swimming pool. Rooms ❺, cottages ❻–❼

Park Sheraton & Towers 132 TTK Rd ☏044/2499 4101, ✉writeme@parksheraton.com. Luxury hotel with bow-tied valets and all mod cons including swimming pool, health club, a decent business centre, three excellent restaurants and a 24hr coffee shop. Rooms from $190. ❾

Savera 146 Dr Radhakrishnan Salai ☏044/2811 4700, ⓦwww.saverahotels .com. Upmarket hotel boasting full facilities, including a pool, good pastry shop, three bars, a fine South Indian restaurant, plus a rooftop restaurant with great views and *Sparks* nightclub. Has a dash more local flavour than the international chains. ❽–❾

Shelter 19–21 Venkatesa Agraharam St, Mylapore ☏044/2495 1919, ⓦwww.hotelshelter.com. A stone's throw from the Kapalishvara temple, this sparklingly clean luxury hotel is better value than most upmarket places. ❼

Trident Hilton 1/24 GST Rd ☏044/2234 4747, ⓦwww.trident-hilton.com. Comfortable five-star hotel in lovely gardens with luxurious rooms and swimming pool. Near the airport (3km), but a long (12km), albeit complimentary, drive into town. Doubles start around $200. Good multi-cuisine and Indian restaurants. ❾

The City

Chennai divides into three main areas: north, central and south. The northern district, separated from the rest by the River Cooum, is the site of the first British outpost in India, **Fort St George**, and the commercial centre, **George Town**, which developed during British occupation. At the southern end of Rajaji Salai is **Parry's Corner**, George Town's principal landmark – look for the tall grey building labelled *Parry's* – and a major bus stop.

Sandwiched between the Cooum and Adyar rivers and crossed diagonally by the city's main thoroughfare, Anna Salai, **central Chennai** is the modern, commercial heart of the metropolis. To the east, this gives way to the atmospheric old Muslim quarters of **Triplicane** and a long straight **Marina** where fishermen mend nets and set small boats out to sea, and hordes of Indian tourists hitch up saris and trousers for a quick paddle. South of here, near the coast, **Mylapore**, inhabited in the 1500s by the Portuguese, boasts

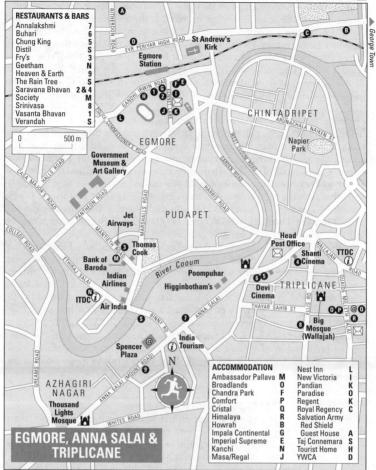

RESTAURANTS & BARS

Annalakshmi	7
Buhari	6
Chung King	5
Distil	S
Fry's	3
Geetham	N
Heaven & Earth	9
The Rain Tree	S
Saravana Bhavan	2 & 4
Society	M
Srinivasa	8
Vasanta Bhavan	1
Verandah	S

0   500 m

Chennai Central Station

George Town

St Andrew's Kirk

EVR PERIYAR HIGH ROAD

Egmore Station

RITHERDON ROAD

SANDHI IRWIN ROAD

KENNET LANE

CHINTADRIPET

ARUNACHALA NAIKEN ST

POLICE COMMISSIONER'S ROAD

EGMORE

Napier Park

WEST COOUM ROAD

Government Museum & Art Gallery

GARDEN ROAD

HALLS ROAD

CASA MAJOR'S ROAD

PANTHEON ROAD

HARRIS ROAD

Jet Airways

PUDAPET

MARSHALLS ROAD

COLLEGE ROAD

MANTIETH ROAD

Thomas Cook

Head Post Office

Shanti Cinema

TTDC

WALLAJAH ROAD

Bank of Baroda

Indian Airlines

River Cooum

Poompuhar

Higginbotham's

Devi Cinema

TRIPLICANE

ETHIRAJ SALAI

ITDC

Air India

BINNY RD

ANNA SALAI

THAYAR SAHIB ST

ELLIS RD

QUAIDE MILLETH SALAI

Big Mosque (Wallajah)

Spencer Plaza

India Tourism

N

GREAMS ROAD

AZHAGIRI NAGAR

ANNA SALAI (MOUNT ROAD)

Thousand Lights Mosque

WHITES ROAD

EGMORE, ANNA SALAI & TRIPLICANE

ACCOMMODATION

Ambassador Pallava	M	Nest Inn	L
Broadlands	O	New Victoria	I
Chandra Park	F	Pandian	K
Comfort	P	Paradise	O
Cristal	Q	Regent	K
Himalaya	R	Royal Regency	C
Howrah	B	Salvation Army	
Impala Continental	G	Red Shield	
Imperial Supreme	E	Guest House	A
Kanchi	N	Taj Connemara	S
Masa/Regal	J	Tourist Home	H
		YWCA	D

Kapalishvara temple and San Thome Cathedral, both tourist attractions and places of pilgrimage. Further out, south of the Adyar river, is the Portuguese church on St Thomas Mount.

Fort St George

Quite unlike any other fort in India, **Fort St George** stands amid state offices facing the sea in the east of the city, just south of George Town on Kamaraj Salai. It looks more like a complex of well-maintained colonial mansions than a fort; indeed many of its buildings are used today as offices, a hive of activity during the week as politicians and peons (attendants) rush between the Secretariat and State Legislature. There is also an army recruitment centre and its compounds.

The fort was the first structure of Madras town and the first territorial possession of the British in India. Construction began in 1640, but most of the original buildings were replaced later that century after being damaged during French sieges. The most imposing structure is the eighteenth-century colonnaded **Fort House**, coated in grey and white paint. Next door, in the more modestly proportioned **Exchange Building** – site of Madras's first bank – is the excellent **Fort Museum** (daily except Fri 10am–5pm; Rs100 [Rs5]; video camera Rs25). The collection inside faithfully records the central events of the British occupation of Madras with portraits, regimental flags, weapons, coins minted by the East India Company, medals, stamps and thick woollen uniforms that make you wonder how the Raj survived as long as it did. Some of the most evocative mementos are letters written by figures such as Robert Clive, reporting on life in the colony. The squat wooden cage on the ground floor was brought to Madras from China, where for five months in 1841 it was used as a particularly sadistic form of imprisonment for a British captain. The first floor, once the public exchange hall where merchants met to gossip and trade, is now an **art gallery**, where portraits of prim officials and their wives sit side by side with fine sketches of the British embarking at Chennai in aristocratic finery, attended by Indians in loincloths. Also on display are etchings by the famous artist **Thomas Daniells**, whose work largely defined British perceptions of India at the end of the eighteenth century.

South of the museum, past the State Legislature, stands the oldest surviving Anglican church in Asia, **St Mary's Church** (daily 9am–5pm), built in 1678 and partly renovated after a battle with the French in 1759. Built with thick walls and a strong vaulted roof to withstand the city's many sieges, the church served as a store and shelter in times of war. It's distinctly English in style, crammed with plaques and statues in memory of British soldiers, politicians and their wives. The grandest plaque, made of pure silver, was presented by Elihu Yale, former governor of Fort St George (1687–96) and founder of Yale University in the USA. A collection of photographs of visiting dignitaries, including Queen Elizabeth II, is on display in the entrance porch. Nearby, **Robert Clive's house** is in a rather sorry state, and is currently used by the Archeological Survey of India as offices.

George Town

North of Fort St George, the former British trading centre of **George Town** (reached on bus #18 from Anna Salai) remains the focal area for banks, offices and shipping companies. This well-ordered grid of streets harbours a fascinating medley of architecture: eighteenth- and nineteenth-century churches, Hindu and Jain temples, and a scattering of mosques, interspersed with grand mansions. However, despite its potential charm, this is Chennai's most chaotic and crowded area, a dirty and uninviting warren clogged by particularly persistent hawkers and thick traffic. Probably the best way to appreciate the area is from its edges. In the east, on Rajaji Salai, the **General Post Office** (GPO) occupies a robust earth-red Indo-Saracenic building (combining Muslim, Hindu, Jain and Western influences), constructed in 1884. George Town's southern extent is marked by the bulbous white domes and sandstone towers of the **High Court**, and the even more opulent towers of the **Law College**, both showing strong Islamic influence.

It can be fun to take a quick rummage around George Town's **bazaars**, lines of rickety stalls selling clothes, bags, umbrellas, watches, shoes and perfume, concentrated along Rajaji Salai and NSC Bose Road.

Government Museum

Unfortunately the Chennai **Government Museum** (daily except Fri 9am–5pm; Rs250 [Rs15], camera Rs200, video Rs500) has joined the ASI sites in substantially overcharging foreigners, which may put off all but the most ardent archeology buffs. The museum houses stone sculptures from many of Tamil Nadu's most famous temples, plus an excellent collection of Chola bronzes, although the (much cheaper) museum in Thanjavur also houses a very fine collection. If you do decide to visit, hop on bus #11H from Anna Salai for Pantheon Road, south of Egmore railway station.

△ Ganesh sculpture, Government Museum

The deep-red, circular **main building**, fronted by Italian-style pillars and built in 1851, stands opposite the entrance and ticket office. The archeology and geology gallery displays tools, pots, jewellery and weapons from the Stone and Iron Ages, and maps of principal excavations. Later exhibits include a substantial assortment of dismantled panels, railings and statues from the second century AD stupa complex at **Amaravati**, Andhra Pradesh (see p.668). Depicting episodes from the Buddha's life and scenes from the *Jataka* stories from ancient Hinayana Buddhist texts, these sensuously carved marble reliefs are widely regarded as the finest achievements of early Indian art, outshining even the Sanchi *toranas*. The **ethnology gallery** shows clothes and weapons, along with photographs of long-gone local tribal societies, while a fascinating display of wind and string instruments, drums and percussion includes the large predecessor of today's sitar and several very old tablas. Wooden doors and window frames from Chettinad, a region near Madurai, exquisitely carved with floral and geometric designs much like those found in Gujarati *havelis*, are also on display.

The museum's real treasure, however, is the world's most complete and impressive selection of **Chola bronzes** (see Context p.761). Large statues of Shiva, Vishnu and Parvati can be seen, along with smaller figurines, including several sculptures of Shiva as **Nataraja**, the Lord of the Dance, encircled by a ring of fire and standing with his arms and legs elegantly poised. One of the finest models is **Ardhanarishvara**, the androgynous form of Shiva (united with Shakti in transcendence of duality); the left side of the body is female and the right male, and the intimacy of detail is astounding. A rounded breast, a delicate hand and a tender bejewelled foot counterpoint the harsher sinewy limbs and torso on the male side of the figure, where the (half) head is also crowned with a mass of matted hair and serpents.

A **children's museum** demonstrates the principles of electricity and irrigation with moderately diverting, semi-functional models, while the magnificent Indo-Saracenic **art gallery** houses old British portraits of figures such as Clive and Hastings, plus Rajput and Moghul miniatures, and a small display of ivory carvings.

St Andrew's Kirk

Just north-east of Egmore station, off EVR Periyar High Road, **St Andrew's Kirk**, consecrated in 1821, is a fine example of Georgian architecture. Loosely modelled on London's St Martin-in-the-Fields, it's one of only three churches in India to have a circular seating plan, laid out beneath a huge dome painted blue with gold stars and supported by a sweep of Corinthian columns. Marble plaques around the church give a fascinating insight into the kind of people who left Britain to work for the imperial and Christian cause. A staircase leads onto the flat roof, surrounding the dome, from where you can climb further up into the steeple past the massive bell to a tiny balcony affording excellent views of the city.

Valluvar Kottam

In the south of the Nungambakkam district, just off Village Road, the **Valluvar Kottam** is an intriguing construction, built in classical style in 1976 as a memorial to the first-century Tamil poet Thiruvalluvar. The most impressive feature is the 34-metre-high stone chariot, carved from just three blocks of granite into a likeness of the great temple car of Thiruvarur. Adjoining this juggernaut is a vast public auditorium, one of the largest in Asia, with a capacity of four thousand. A stroll along the auditorium roof past shallow rectangular ponds brings you to a large statue of the poet-saint, within a shrine carved into the upper reaches of the chariot. Among the many reliefs around the monument, look out for the cat in human pose, reminiscent of the figure at Arjuna's Penance in Mamallapuram (see p.540).

Marina Beach

One of the longest city beaches in the world, the **Marina** (Kamaraj Salai) stretches 5km from the harbour at the southeastern corner of George Town all the way to San Thome Cathedral. The impulse to transform Chennai's beach into an attractive and sociable esplanade was conceived by Mountstuart Elphinstone Grant-Duff, governor of Madras from 1881 to 1886, and numerous buildings have sprung up over the years, along with surreal modern memorials to Tamil Nadu's chief political heroes and freedom fighters.

Today the **beach** itself is a sociable place, peopled by idle paddlers, picnickers and pony-riders; every afternoon crowds gather around the beach market. However, it suffers miserably from being just a little downstream from the port, which belches out waste and smelly fumes, as well as being the local toilet around the areas where the fishermen hang out. Unsurprisingly, swimming and sunbathing are neither recommended nor approved; nor is it advisable to take your shoes off on the beach, as the sand is full of bits of broken glass and rusty bottle tops. Tragically, around two hundred people were killed on Marina Beach by the **tsunami** on the morning of December 26, 2004, including many children who had come here to play cricket. Although the death toll in Chennai was lower than along other stretches of the coast – and much of the city was protected by the sheer scale of Marina beach – the youth of the victims added to the sense of bereavement.

At the northern end of the beach, the **Anna Park** and **MGR Samadhi** park attract droves of Tamil tourists intent on paying their respects at the shrine of

The Ice House

Over the years, Chennai has seen its fair share of world-shaping moments, but few can have been met with the wonder and unanimous approval that greeted the arrival of an American clipper in the early 1830s. Its cargo, rolled in pine sawdust and steered through the surf in small *masula* boats, had never been seen in peninsular India before, and one can only imagine the amazement of the local coolies when they first felt the weight and burning cold of melting **ice** on their shoulders.

In a little over four months, the ship, the *Tuscany*, had sailed halfway around the world with its precious load, harvested from frozen ponds around Boston. Little technology was required to gather the ice: grappling hooks, lengths of blocks and tackle, a few horse-drawn sleds and one hundred Irish labourers. The real break-through that made the trade possible was the discovery, by one Frederic Nathaniel Jarvis, that fresh pine sawdust would insulate ice, even from high tropical tempera-tures. A few years earlier, his friend, Frederick Tudor Boston, had tried to transport $10,000 dollars worth of New English ice to Martinique in the Caribbean, only to watch the entire cargo melt en route. However, Jarvis's bright idea enabled Boston's **Tudor Ice Company** to export 180 tons of ice to Calcutta in 1833. From that initial shipment enough profit was generated to build warehouses in Bombay and Madras, and thereafter the trade continued to boom for nearly forty years, until the invention of steam-powered ice-making machines put the company out of business.

Overlooking Chennai's sun-scorched Marina Beach, the building erected by the Tudor Ice Company in the 1840s to store their stock stands as an evocative reminder of this brief but extraordinary episode in the city's mercantile history. It was sold to a rich lawyer when the bottom fell out of the trade, and it was with him that the famous Indian philosopher, **Vivekananda**, stayed after his return from the US in 1897, when crowds would gather on the steps outside to hear the sage speak. In memory of this event, the local municipality has rechristened the building "Vivekananda Museum" (see below), but to everyone else in Chennai, the stalwart old pile, with its peeling yellow-painted walls and distinctive twin circular tiered facade, is still known simply as **"The Ice House"**.

the state's most illustrious movie actor and chief minister, **MGR** (see box, p.514). Nearby is one of the oldest of the city's university buildings, the **Senate House** (1879), an uncharacteristically Byzantine-influenced design by Robert Fellowes Chisholm (1840–1915), one of the British leaders in developing the hybrid Indo-Saracenic style.

Continuing south, past the Indo-Saracenic **Presidency College** (1865–71), a number of stolid Victorian university buildings include the **Lady Willingdon Teacher Training College**. Next door, the nineteenth-century Madras depot of the Tudor Ice Company (see box above) has been converted into the inter-esting **Vivekananda Museum** (10am–noon & 3–7pm, closed Wed; free). The grand old building contains fully narrated photo-displays of the peripatetic Hindu master's life, including his study under Ramakrishna, his attendance at the Chicago Conference on World Religions and his later teaching missions. His frequent quotes are at once enlightening and uplifting.

Mylapore

Long before Madras came into existence, **Mylapore**, south of the Marina (reached by buses #4, #5 or #21 from the LIC building on Anna Salai), was a major settlement; the Greek geographer Ptolemy mentioned it in the second century AD as a thriving port, and during the Pallava period (fifth to ninth

Bollywood may be better known, but the film studios of Chennai churn out more movies than any other city in the world – around 900 each year. The movies feature the usual Indian masala mix of fast action, wide-eyed melodrama, romance (with just the hint of a kiss), punch-ups, shoot-outs and, of course, hip-grinding song and dance sequences with as many costume changes as camera angles. They cater for the largely illiterate rural population of Tamil Nadu, although the biggest blockbusters also get dubbed into Hindi and exported north.

One notable difference between the Chennai movie industry and its counterpart in Mumbai (see p.143) is the influence of **politics** on Tamil films – an overlap that dates from the earliest days of regional cinema, when stories, stock themes and characters were derived from traditional folk ballads about low-caste heroes vanquishing high-caste villains. Already familiar to millions, such Robin Hood-style stereotypes were perfect propaganda vehicles for the nascent Tamil nationalist movement, the Dravida Munnetra Kazhagam, or **DMK**, in the decades following Independence. It is no coincidence that the party's founding father, **C.N. Annadurai**, was a top screenplay- and script-writer. Like prominent Tamil Congress leaders and movie-makers of the 1930s and 1940s, he and his colleagues used both popular film genres of the time – "mythologicals" (movie versions of the Hindu epics) and "socials" (dramas set around caste conflicts) – to convey their political ideas to the masses. Audiences were actively encouraged by party workers to boo the villains and cheer each time the proletarian hero, or DMK icons and colours (red and black), appeared on the screen. From this tradition were born the fan clubs, or *rasigar manrams*, that played such a key role in mobilizing support for the nationalist parties in elections.

The most influential fan club of all time was set up to support the superstar actor Marudur Gopalamenon Ramachandran, known to millions simply as **"MGR"**. By carefully cultivating a political image which mirrored the folk-hero roles he played in films, the maverick matinee idol generated fanatical grass-roots support in the state, especially among women, and rose to become chief minister in 1977. His eleven-year rule is still regarded by liberals as a dark age in the state's history, as chronic corruption, police brutality, political purges and rising organized crime were all rife during the period. Even the fact that his bungled economic policies penalized precisely the rural poor who voted for him never dented MGR's mass appeal. When he suffered a paralytic stroke in October 1984, 22 people cut off limbs, toes and fingers as offerings to pray for his recovery, while more than a hundred followers attempted to burn themselves to death. For the next three years MGR was barely able to speak let alone govern effectively, yet the party faithful and fan club members still did not lose faith in his leadership. When he died in 1988, two million people attended his funeral, and 31 grief-stricken devotees committed ritual suicide. Even today, MGR's statue, sporting trademark sunglasses and lamb's-wool hat, is revered at tens of thousands of wayside shrines across Tamil Nadu.

MGR's political protégé, and eventual successor, was a teenage screen starlet called **Jayalalitha**, a convent-educated brahmin's daughter he spotted at a school

centuries) it was second only to Mamallapuram (see p.536), a little way down the coastline. The three most worthwhile sites to visit are all religious ones: San Thome Cathedral, the Kapalishvara temple and the Ramakrishna Mutt.

San Thome Cathedral

An important stop – with Little Mount and St Thomas Mount – on the St Thomas pilgrimage trail, the **San Thome Cathedral** (daily 6am–8pm) lies close to the sea at the southern end of Marina Beach, and marks the eastern boundary of Mylapore. St Thomas is credited as the first to bring Christianity dance and, despite an age difference of more than thirty years, recruited to be both his leading lady and mistress. The couple would star opposite each other in 25 hit films, and when MGR eventually moved into politics, Jayalalitha followed him, becoming leader of the AIADMK (the party MGR set up after being expelled from the DMK in 1972) after a much publicized power struggle with his widow. Larger-than-life in voluminous silver ponchos and heavy gold jewellery, the now portly Puratchi Thalavi ("Revolutionary Leader") has taken her personality cult to extremes brazen even by Indian standards. On her 46th birthday in 1994, Rs50,000 of public money was spent on giant cardboard cutouts depicting her in academic and religious robes, while 46 of her more fervent admirers rolled bare-chested along the length of Anna Salai. Jayalalitha's spell as chief minister, however, was brought to an ignominious end at the 1996 elections, after allegations of fraud and corruption on an appropriately monumental scale. Despite being found guilty by the High Court, she still managed to bring down the national government and force a general election in 1999 by withdrawing AIADMK support from Prime Minister Vajpayee's shaky, BJP-led coalition, and later ousted her arch rival, **M.K. Karunanidhi**, leader of the DMK, to regain her old job as chief minister of Tamil Nadu. One of her first acts was to exact revenge on Karunanidhi, throwing him and one thousand of his supporters into prison on corruption charges. However, she lost a large percentage of her following in the 2004 elections, as voters showed their increasing dissatisfaction with her vindictive and unpopular policies and Karunanidhi was duly returned to power in 2006. Now in his eighties, the indefatigable politician, known to most simply as MK, has always been a populist and has achieved his five terms in office by a careful balancing act. His Tamil tub-thumping appeals to all, including enough of the elite, while his social justice measures, such as supporting job and academic quota systems, makes him especially popular with the lower castes.

Working as an extra

If you've a fervent interest in the Chennai movie industry, you can rub shoulders with today's Tamil movie stars by appearing as an extra in a film at MGR or one of the other major studios on the outskirts of Chennai. Scouts regularly trawl the tourist spots downtown (notably the *Maharaja Restaurant* around the corner from *Broadlands Hotel* in Triplicane) for foreigners to spice up crowd and party scenes. People with long blond hair stand a better chance of getting picked, but being in the right place at the right time is more important. If you're really keen, though, do the rounds of the studios yourself (details available from the Government of India tourist office). If someone does approach you with an offer of work as a movie extra, be sure to check their credentials (scouts always carry laminated cards from the studio with their photos on; you can also ask to see their business card), and the conditions of the job (approximately Rs300 per day, plus meals and transport to and from your hotel are standard). For obvious reasons, it's also advisable to refuse any work offered to one person only, especially if you're female.

to the Subcontinent, in the first century AD. Although the present neo-Gothic structure dates from 1896, San Thome stands on the site of two earlier churches (the first possibly erected by Nestorian Christians from Persia during the tenth century), built over the tomb of St Thomas. His relics are kept in a casket under the nave and are the object of great reverence and worship. They can be accessed via an underground passage that descends from the a small **museum** (Mon–Sat 10am–5pm; free) behind the cathedral. The museum itself houses stones inscribed in Tamil, Sanskrit (twelfth-century Chola) and early Portuguese, and a map of India, dated 1519.

Kapalishvara temple

The large **Kapalishvara temple**, less than 1km west of the San Thome Cathedral, is the most famous in Chennai. Its principal shrine is dedicated to Shiva, and its soaring *gopuras* stand out proudly from the prosaic neighbourhood that surrounds it. Seventh-century Tamil poet-saints sang the temple's praises, but the present structure probably dates from the sixteenth century. Before then, it is thought to have occupied a site on the shore; sea erosion or demolition at the hands of the Portuguese led it to be rebuilt inland. The huge (40m) towered gateway above the main east entrance, plastered in stucco figures, was added in 1906. Surrounding an assortment of busy shrines, where priests offer blessings for devotees and non-Hindus alike, the atmospheric **courtyard** features an old tree where a small shrine to Shiva's consort, Parvati, shows her in the form of a peahen (*mayil*) worshipping a *lingam*. This commemorates the legend that she was momentarily distracted from concentrating on her lord by the enchanting dance of a peacock. Shiva, miffed at this dereliction of wifely duty, cursed her, whereupon she turned into a peahen. To expiate the sin, Parvati took off to a place called Kapalinagar, and embarked upon rigorous austerities. In honour of her success, the town was named Mayilapore or **Mylapore**. The oldest artefacts in the Kapalishvara temple are the movable bronze images of deities and the 63 Shaivite Nayanmar poet-saints, two of whom came from Mylapore. Unusually, the main shrine faces west, towards a space dominated by an eighteenth-century water-lily tank, which appears vast in this cramped suburban district.

Important **festivals** held at Kapalishvara include **Thaipusam** (February; see p.616), when the bronze images of Shiva and Parvati are pulled around the temple tank in a decorated boat to the accompaniment of music. **Brahmotsava** (March/April) celebrates the marriage of Shiva and Parvati; in the afternoon of the eighth day, all 63 bronze images of the Nayanmar saints are clothed, garlanded and taken out in palanquins along the streets to meet the bejewelled images of Shiva and Parvati. **Vasantha** (May/June), the summer festival, is marked by concerts.

In the busy **market streets** that surround the temple, amid stalls selling pots and pans, flowers, religious paraphernalia and vegetables, glittering shops spill over with gold wedding-jewellery. Exquisite saris are unfolded for scrutiny in silk emporia; the finest quality garments come from Kanchi and are delicately embroidered with gold and silver thread. Saris of this distinction can add as much as Rs30,000 to the cost of a wedding.

A little further west, before you come to TTK Road, the **Luz Church**, on Luz Church Road, is thought to be the earliest Christian building still standing in Chennai, built by the Portuguese in the sixteenth century. Its founding is associated with a miracle; Portuguese sailors in difficulties at sea were once guided to land and safety by a light which, when they tried to find its source, disappeared. The church, dedicated to Our Lady of Light, was erected where the light left them.

Ramakrishna Mutt

Under a kilometre south of the Kapalishvara temple, on RK Dutt Rd, lie the peaceful and extensive grounds of the **Ramakrishna Mutt**, an active place of study for devotees wishing to follow the teachings of the famous nineteenth-century master. The focus of interest for the casual visitor is the **Universal Temple of Sri Ramakrishna** (daily 5.30am–1.30pm & 3.30–8.30pm; free), an elegant construction combining architectural motifs from Hindu, Buddhist and Jain temples, as well as European churches, while the manicured forecourt echoes the Islamic themes of the Mughals. The impressive decorative gateway to the complex is aligned with the shrine and frames it exquisitely, when viewed from the road. Within the temple itself are a series of prayer halls, approached by steps, and the inner sanctum contains a solid marble statue of Ramakrishna seated on a lotus.

Little Mount Caves

St Thomas is said to have sought refuge from persecution in the **Little Mount Caves**, 8km south of the city centre (bus #18A, #18B, or #52C from Anna Salai), 200m off GST Road towards Guindy National Park. Entrance to the caves is beside steps leading to a statue of Our Lady of Good Health. Inside, next to a small natural window in the rock, are impressions of what are believed to be St Thomas' handprints, created when he made an escape through the tiny opening.

Behind the new circular church of Our Lady of Good Health, with its brightly painted replicas of the *Pietà* and Holy Sepulchre, is a natural **spring**, said to have been created when Thomas struck the rock so that the crowds that came to hear him preach could quench their thirst. Even today, when Chennai is hit by drought the water level of the well remains unaffected. Samples of its holy water are on sale.

St Thomas Mount

Tradition has it that St Thomas was speared to death (another version has him struck by a hunter's arrow) while praying before a stone cross on **St Thomas Mount**, 11km south of the city centre, close to the airport (take a suburban train to Guindy railway station, and walk from there). **Our Lady of Expectation Church** (1523), at the summit of the Mount, can be reached by 134 granite steps marked with the fourteen stations of the Cross, or by a road which curls its way to the top. At the top of the steps, a huge old banyan tree provides shade for devotees who come to fast, pray and sing. Inside the church, St Thomas's cross is rumoured to have bled in 1558, while the altar is said to mark the exact spot of the apostle's death; the painting above the altar of the Madonna and Child is attributed to St Luke. Cold drinks are available in the adjacent Holy Apostle's Convent.

The Theosophical Society Headquarters

The **Theosophical Society** was established in New York in 1875 by American Civil War veteran Colonel Henry S. Olcott, a failed farmer and journalist, and the eccentric Russian aristocrat Madame Helena Petrovna Blavatsky, who claimed occult powers and telepathic links with "Mahatmas" ("great souls") in Tibet. Based on a fundamental belief in the equality and truth of all religions, the Society in fact propagated a modern form of Hinduism, praising all things Indian and shunning Christian missionaries. Needless to say, its two founders were greeted enthusiastically when they transferred their operations to Madras in 1882, establishing their headquarters near Elliot's Beach in Adyar (buses #5, #5C or #23C from George Town/Anna Salai). Even after Madame Blavatsky's psychic powers were proved to be bogus, the society continued to attract Hindus and Western visitors, and its buildings still stand today, sheltering several shrines and the excellent **Adyar library** (Tues–Sun 9.30–4pm, free but see p.519) of books on religion and philosophy. The collection, begun by Olcott in 1886, comprises 165,000 volumes and nearly 200,000 palm-leaf manuscripts from all over the world. A selection is housed in an exhibition room on the ground floor. This includes 800-year-old scroll pictures of the Buddha, a seventeenth-century treatise on embalming bodies from London, rare Tibetan manuscripts written on bark paper, exquisitely illuminated Qur'ans, a giant copy of Martin Luther's *Biblia* printed in Nuremberg three hundred years ago,

The reluctant guru

For a spiritual organization based on principles of inclusiveness and harmony, the Theosophical Society has suffered some acrimonious schisms over the years, particularly after the deaths of its founders Olcott and Blavatsky, when its most prominent personalities clashed in an unseemly power struggle. The most infamous rift of all, though, was one between the Society's mandarins and the young man they identified in 1905 as the "Buddha to Be", **Jiddu Krishnamurti**, a Telegu-speaking brahmin boy brought to Adyar by his father after his mother died. He was first "discovered" by Charles Webster Leadbeater, a leading light in the Theosophical Society who claimed clairvoyant powers. Among the central tenets of the movement was a belief that Lord Krishna and Christ were about to be reborn as a "World Teacher", and from the moment Leadbeater saw the ten-year-old Krishnamurti playing football on the beach at Adyar he knew he had found the "Enlightened One". Jiddu, however, did not initially look the part. Wild, malnourished and sickly, with "crooked teeth . . . and a vacant, almost moronic expression", he seemed more like a street kid than a messiah in the making.

Informed that the "Vehicle" had been identified, **Annie Besant** – the then-President of the Theosophical Society – was quick to take the boy under her wing. Over the coming years, Krishnamurti, with the support of the TS and its benefactors, was to receive the best education that money could buy, with places at famous colleges in England and California. Spiritual instruction, meanwhile, came from Leadbeater's own guru, a mystical Buddhist lama who lived in a remote Tibetan ravine and delivered his teachings on the "astral plane".

Not surprisingly, Krishnamurti's father resented Besant's adoption of his son and initiated custody proceedings to prevent the TS from taking him abroad. The High Court of Madras found in Krishnamurti senior's favour, but its decision was overturned after Besant took the case to London (in spite of allegations of "unnatural practices" levelled against Leadbeater). By the time the legal battle had run its course, Krishnamurti was legally an adult and already teaching. He'd also matured into an exceedingly handsome, suave young man, with a trademark sweep of jet black hair and a taste for fashionable clothes.

While his teachings were being received with growing enthusiasm, both within India and the US, the fledgling guru was showing definite signs of resenting the role thrust upon him by the Theosophists. Soon, this found expression in criticism of the ritual, mysticism and self-aggrandizing "wise men" that had become features of the Society's new leadership, some of whom then began to turn against their charismatic detractor, claiming he had been "possessed by black forces". The conflict came to a head when Krishnamurti, addressing a Theosophy camp in the US, formally renounced his position as head for the OSE (Order of the Star in the East), originally formed to promote his teachings. He resigned from the TS soon afterwards, with the famous pronouncement that "Truth is a pathless land . . . you cannot approach it by any path whatsoever, by any religion, by any sect."

For the rest of his life, Krishnamurti – or "K" as he preferred to be known – wandered the world as a individual, lecturing, writing and setting up **educational institutions** where young people could, as he said, "flower as human beings, without fear, without confusion, with great integrity". When he died in 1986, aged 91, he was one of the most famous philosophers of his generation, but always resisted the label of guru; "mediators", he said, "must inevitably step down the Truth, and hence betray it."

and a thumbnail-sized Bible in seven languages. Anybody is welcome to look around but to gain full use of the library you have to register as a member (Rs30 per year plus Rs200 deposit).

The 270 acres of woodland and gardens surrounding the society's headquarters make a serene place to sit and restore spirits away from the noise and heat of the city streets. In the middle of the grounds, a vast 400-year-old **banyan tree**, said to be the second largest in the world, provides shade for up to 3000 people at a time. J. Krishnamurti and Maria Montessori have both given talks under its tangle of pillar-like root stems, whose growth Theosophists see as symbolizing the spread of the Society itself.

Nearby **Elliot's Beach**, in the adjacent area of Besant Nagar (named after theosophist Annie Besant – see box opposite), makes another fine escape from the hubbub of the city. It only really comes to life in the evening, so during the day its relative quietness and the comparative cleanliness of the sea make it a far better place to relax and take a dip than Marina Beach.

The Enfield factory

India's most stylish home-made motorcycle, the **Enfield Bullet**, is manufactured at a plant on Thiruvottiyur Road in the outskirts of Chennai, 18km north of Anna Salai (bus #1 from LIC Building or Parry's Corner). With its elegant tear-drop tank and thumping 350cc single-cylinder engine, the Bullet has become a contemporary classic – in spite of its propensity to leak oil and break down. Bike enthusiasts should definitely brave the long haul north of town to see the **factory**, which is as much a period piece as the machines it turns out. Guided tours, which last around ninety minutes (Mon–Fri 9.30am–5.30pm; Rs500; ☎044/4204 3300, ⓦwww.royalenfield.com), have to be arranged in advance by phone or through the website, which also contains a cyber factory visit.

△ An Enfield Bullet

Eating and drinking

Chennai runs on inexpensive Indian fast-food **restaurants** and "meals" (thali) joints, in particular the legendary *Saravana Bhavan* chain, which serves superb South Indian food for a fraction of the cost of a coffee at one of the five-stars. That said, a minor splurge at *Annalakshmi* on Anna Salai or the *Park Sheraton* on TTK Road is well worth considering. The city does, however, lag well behind Mumbai and Bengaluru (Bangalore) when it comes to places for bright young things to unwind – most of those that do exist are established hotel bars and discos, while there's a smattering of trendy coffee houses.

Egmore, Anna Salai and Triplicane

The following places are marked on the map on p.509.

Restaurants, bars and cafés

Annalakshmi 804 Anna Salai. A non-profitmaking venture run voluntarily by devotees of Swami Shivenanda, where you can enjoy a well-prepared, leisurely and expensive meal in beautiful surroundings. You choose one of several set menus (each with different Ayurvedic properties), and the profits go to charitable works in the community.

Buhari 83 Anna Salai. Idiosyncratic 1950s-style dining hall overlooking the main street. For some reason, Russian chicken dishes are the house speciality (à la Moscow, Kiev or Leningrad), but they also offer a full tandoori menu, cold beers and freshly baked cakes.

Chung King Anna Salai, down an alleyway on the left of *Buhari* restaurant. A wide range of delicious Chinese cuisine prepared by a pukka Chinese chef.

Distil *Taj Connemara* hotel, Binny Rd. Flashy disco with the pick of the local DJs and occasional live bands. Specializes in fruit-based cocktails.

Fry's Opposite the *Ambassador Pallava* hotel, 30 Montieth Rd. Good, cheap, authentic Keralan food – try the fish in coconut sauce.

Geetham *Kanchi Hotel*, 28 Ethiraj Salai. Circular, glass-sided restaurant on the rooftop of a nine-storey tower block. The multi-cuisine menu is surprisingly inexpensive, and the views are superb.

Heaven & Earth Anna Salai, opposite Spencer's Plaza. Mainly vegetarian Chinese restaurant with some meat and seafood dishes. The Malaysian chef adds a few Pan-Asian touches to the varied menu, which offers high quality at very reasonable prices.

The Rain Tree *Taj Connemara* hotel, Binny Rd ☎044/5500 0000. This excellent and very popular place does superb Chettinad (South Indian) specialities accompanied by live Carnatic music and dance in the evenings. A three-course meal will cost around Rs500–800 (veg/non-veg). Book in advance.

Saravana Bhavan Shanti cinema forecourt, 44 Anna Salai with another branch on Kenet Lane, Egmore. This famous South Indian fast-food chain is an institution among the Chennai middle class, with several branches. Try their delicious *rawa iddlis* or one of the range of thalis, rounded off with some freshly made *ladoo* or *barfi* from the sweets counter outside.

Society *Ambassador Pallava* hotel, 30 Montieth Rd ☎044/2855 4476. Worth a visit for the excellent all-you-can-eat lunchtime buffet (around Rs350), with a choice of over twenty veg and non-veg dishes plus an array of sweets.

Srinivasa Ellis Rd, Triplicane. Excellent South Indian breakfasts – try their *kitchadi* and *vada pongal* – for next to nothing, and the coffee is genuine Coorg. Open the rest of the day for very cheap meals and snacks. There's a separate area for women and families.

Vasanta Bhavan 20 Gandhi Irwin Rd. Easily the best "meals" joint among many around Egmore station, with ranks of attentive waiters and delicious pure veg food – just Rs30 for an unlimited thali. It's busy, spotlessly clean, and their coffee and sweets are delicious too. There are two other branches opposite Egmore station, one specializing in ice cream.

Veranda *Taj Connemara* hotel, Binny Rd ☎044/5500 0000. The ideal venue for a posh Sunday morning breakfast buffet, with crisp newspapers and fresh coffee served in silver pots. The blow-out lunchtime buffets (around Rs400) are also recommended, and à la carte Italian food is on offer in the evening.

Outside the centre

The following places are marked on the map on p.500.

Restaurants

Amaravati Corner of Cathedral and TTK roads. Good option tucked in a complex of regional speciality restaurants, south of the downtown area. This one does excellent Andhran food, including particularly tasty biriyanis.

Bella Ciao 4 Sree Krishna Enclave, near the Theosophical Headquarters ☎044/2451 1130. Tiny Italian restaurant, under Italian ownership, serving authentic pizza, as well as fresh gnocchi with blue cheese and mushrooms, lamb in red wine, pork chops and eighteen different organic salads (mains cost about Rs200). Add a little tiramisu and Pavarotti to complete the evening. Officially there's no alcohol, although beer can be arranged. Book in advance. Closed Mon.

Copper Chimney 74 Cathedral Rd ☎044/827 5770. Franchise of the famous Mumbai restaurant, offering quality tandoori cuisine, opulent decor and a/c comfort. The meat-eater's equivalent of *Annalakshmi*. Count on Rs200–250 per head.

🏃 **Dakshin/Khyber/Residency** *Park Sheraton* hotel, 132 TTK Rd ☎044/299 4101. Excellent upmarket hotel restaurants – the *Residency* serves Indian, Western and Chinese, and the *Khyber* offers a meaty poolside barbecue, but best of all is the *Dakshin*, one of the country's top South Indian restaurants. It dishes up a wide choice of unusual dishes from the four southern states, including seafood in marinated spices, Karnataka mutton biriyani, and piping-hot *iddiappam* and *appam* made on the spot, and has live Carnatic music in the evenings. Expect to pay around Rs600 for a meal with drinks and beer at any of the three.

Don Pepé 1st floor, above *Hot Breads*, 73 Cathedral Rd. Swish a/c Tex-Mex joint serving a predictable menu of fajitas, enchiladas, tortillas and burritos, plus so-so pasta dishes (dubbed "Euro-Mex"). Main courses are about Rs120.

Hot Breads 73 Cathedral Rd. Wholewheat breads, baguettes, fresh quiches and an impressive range of cakes, biscuits and pastries. Decent espresso coffee, too. Eat in or take away.

Peshawri & Shanghai *Chola Sheraton* hotel, 10 Cathedral Rd ☎044/2828 0101. Two good restaurants sit in this upmarket hotel; the *Peshawri* serves lavish (and expensive) northwestern frontier food, while the excellent rooftop *Shanghai* specializes in Chinese dishes.

🏃 **Saravana Bhavan** Thanigai Murugan Rathinavel Hall, 77 Usman Rd, Theagaraya Nagar. Other branches of this chain stand opposite the bus stand in George Town and on Anna Salai, see opposite.

Shogun/The Dhaba 84 Dr Radhakrishnan Salai. Upmarket complex featuring the nicely decorated Chinese *Shogun* and fancy Punjabi *The Dhaba*; the food is good and the ambience pleasant.

Bars and cafés

Barista Elliot's Beach Rd, Besant Nagar. The seafront location makes this branch of the developing chain a very pleasant one. Serves Italian coffee, sandwiches and pastries.

H₂O *Harrison's* hotel, 315 Valluvar Kottam Rd. Basement nightclub with eerie blue and white lighting and the usual dance mix.

The Leather Bar *Park* hotel, 601 Anna Salai. Don't be fooled by the name: the leather floors and suede walls at this disco attract some poseurs but no genuine fetishists, while the music is certainly more Bee Gees than Velvet Underground.

Sparks *Savera* hotel, 146 Dr Radhakrishnan Salai. Fairly wacky Indian take on what a pub should be, with karaoke to break the monotony of the bog-standard DJs.

🏃 **Speed** *Grand Orient* hotel, 693 Anna Salai. This joint offers a more eclectic mixture of rock, R'n'B, hip-hop and house; popular with the college crowd as it's cheaper than most bars.

Zara 74 Cathedral Rd. In the same building as *Copper Chimney*, this claims to be India's first genuine tapas bar and also features excellent cocktails and regular live music.

Culture and entertainment

Chennai is the deep south's prime location for culture and the performance arts, with regular events throughout the year, culminating in the prestigious **Chennai Festival** (see box p.522) in December. Outside the festival period, to find out about performances of music and dance, ask at the government tourist office on Anna Salai, consult the listings pages of local papers such as *The Hindu*, or have a look in *Chennai: This Fortnight* (see p.504). The most renowned performance spaces are:

Kalashetra Academy Besant Nagar ☏044/2452 0836. Frequent performances of Bharat Natyam and other leading dance forms.
The Music Academy 306 TTK Rd ☏044/2811 5162. The number one spot for classical Indian

music and dance, this is also the main host of the Chennai Festival.
Museum Theatre Pantheon Rd ☏044/2819 3238. The city's premier location for theatrical performances, from old classics to the avant-garde.

The Chennai Festival and the sabhas

The **sabhas** of Chennai – the city's arts societies and venues, of which the most illustrious is the Chennai Music Academy – stage regular public performances of Carnatic classical music and *Bharatanatyam* dance. Here, ambitious artists have to undergo the scrutiny of an often fanatical audience and a less-than-generous bevy of newspaper critics, whose reviews can make or break a career. Musicians are expected to correctly interpret the subtleties of any given composition, *raga* or *tala*. The sets of notes that make up a *raga* occupy a place midway between melody and scale; they must at once be imaginatively improvised and played in strict sequences and with correct emphasis. The worst crime, the sign of an amateur, is to slip accidentally into a different *raga* that might share the same scale. *Tala*, the rhythmic cycle and bedrock of the music, will often be demonstrated by someone on stage, and consists of a series of claps and waves. A relatively subtle part of the performance in North India, this element is overt in the South and the audience delights in clapping along to the often-complex time signatures. The pleasure is heightened during percussion improvisations on the barrel-shaped *mridangam* drum or *ghatam* clay pot that accompany many performances.

The **Chennai Festival** is an annual event held from December 15 until January 1, during which up to five hundred events are staged, primarily at the **Music Academy** (see above) on TTK Road. It's a real orgy of classical music and dance recitals, in which many of India's greatest artistes, from all over the country, can be seen at work. Top names to look out for include **female vocalists** Mani Krishnaswamy, Charumathi Ramachandran, Sudha Raghunathan and Bombay Jayashree; **male singers** K.V. Narayanaswamy, B. Rajam Iyer; **younger artists** Thrissur Ramachandran and T.N. Seshagopalan; and **duos** such as the Bombay and Hyderabad Sisters. Among the best of the **instrumentalists** are E. Gayatri and Rama Varma on the gentle, melodic *vina*, a stringed instrument unique to the South; N. Ramani on flute; violinists such as T.N. Krishnan and D. Ananda Raman; and N. Ravikiran on gottuvadyam, a rare member of the *vina* family, laid flat on the floor and played much like a slide guitar. Carnatic music's answer to John Coltrane is Kadri Gopalnath, whose soaring saxophone and flamboyant dress have made him one of the most distinctive figures on the circuit. Former child prodigy U. Sriniwas is a maestro on the electric mandolin. Cassettes and CDs of all the above artistes are available at Music World in Spencer Plaza. For addresses of good musical instrument shops in the city, see p.524.

The predominant **dance** style is *Bharatanatyam*, as performed by stars such as the Dhananjayans and Alarmail Valli. Dance-dramas are also staged by the **Kalakshetra Academy** (see above), a school of dance and music set in a beautiful hundred-acre compound near the sea in Tiruvanmiyur, on the southern outskirts of the city. You might also like to pay a visit to the **Sangita Vadyalaya**, behind the HDFC Bank on Anna Salai (Mon–Fri 9.15am–5.45pm; free), which displays an impressive array of Indian musical instruments. The centre, recently shifted to this new ground-floor building in the centre of town, was set up to preserve and restore antique pieces, but resident artisans also revive rare instruments which are no longer commonly played. You can try your hand at a few of them yourself, and experiment with an amazing hoard of old percussion pieces.

Mylapore Fine Arts 16 Musiri Subramaniam Salai ☎044/2499 7755. This auditorium specializes in South Indian music, including the Carnatic style.
Narada Gaba Sabha 314 TTK Rd ☎044/2499 3201. Almost next door to the Music Academy, this smaller location also hosts regular dance performances.
Rasika Ranjani Sabha 1 Sundareswarar St, Mylapore ☎044/2494 1767. One of the city's oldest sabha's, this holds classes, as well as monthly programmes of music and dance.

As you might expect for a city with such a huge film industry, there is no shortage of **cinemas**, where you can enjoy the full experience of the screen idols playing to a Tamil home crowd. The best place for this is the Shanti, at the top of Anna Salai, which boasts Chennai's biggest screen and most state-of-the-art sound system. The nearby Devi tends to show more of the latest Bollywood blockbusters. Further down Anna Salai, you can catch up with reasonably new English-language releases at either the Abhirami or Lakshmi.

Shopping

As befits a major city, Chennai offers a pretty wide selection of **shopping** possibilities. From the crowded and noisy traditional **bazaars** of George Town to the equally busy new **malls** of the southern suburbs, where the stores gleam, the customers drip jewellery and and the ambient noise consists of people bellowing into mobile phones, you are likely to find most of the items you might require. Although the city is not particularly renowned for any special local products, if you discount Enfield motorcycles (see p.519), it is an important merchandise hub and quality goods are plentiful, whether you're looking for souvenirs, clothing, books or music.

Souvenirs and handicrafts

Apart from the tourist knick-knacks available in malls like Spencer's Plaza, the three-storey Victoria Technical Institute (VTI), a little further down at 180 Anna Salai, offers a fine range of **crafts** and most of its profits go to charity. Still on the same side of Anna Salai but back in the other direction, Poompuhar, the official Tamil Nadu state emporium, also offers a decent selection of goods at fixed prices. On the opposite side of the road, amidst a row of tourist shops, including the official outlets of Kashmir and Karnataka, the Indian Arts Emporium, 152 Anna Salai, has handicrafts, furniture and metalwork. Among the items to look out for here are copies of Tanjore paintings (see p.763) and mock Chola bronzes (see p.761). New Age items (as well as wholefoods) can be found at hipper establishments such as the Naturally Auroville Boutique, 30 Khader Nawaz Khan Rd.

Clothing and jewellery

Chennai is especially strong on **clothing** and **textile** shops. Two of the best places for various handwoven fabrics, made with traditional craftsmanship, are Fabindia, 3 Woods Rd, and Shilpa, 29 CP Ramaswamy Rd, Alwarpet, which specializes in hand-spun silk saris. Prices are a little higher than elsewhere but you have the consolation that the villagers who made the garments get a fair price for their work. Two other recommended clothing and fabric shops, both in T Nagar, are Nalli, 9 Nageswaram Rd, and Naidu Hall, 56 Pondy Bazaar; both have extremely helpful assistants who will advise you on how much material you need to have the item you envisage made.

Apart from the outlets in snazzy new malls such as Chennai Citi Centre (a misnomer, as it's quite far out) on Dr Radhakrishnan Salai, some of the most popular places for **gold**, **silver** and **precious stones** are Dhanalakshmi Jewellery, 59 Usman Rd, T Nagar, Kuber, 43 Cathedral Rd, and the highly rated Amethyst, housed in a converted cottage down in Gopalapuram. If you are interested in the gaudy but distinctively Tamil **dance jewellery** worn by Bharat Natyam performers, then the vicinity of the Kapalishvarar temple in Mylapore is also a prime place to hunt after it. Made from gold-coated silver, studded with artificial rubies, the most striking items are the headpiece, or *thalasaman*, the *adigay*, a long chain worn around the neck with a large floral or peacock-shaped pendant known as a *padakkam* and the heavy ornamental belt, or *odyanan*.

Books

Higginbothams, on Anna Salai, is Chennai's oldest **bookshop**, with a vast assortment of Indian and Western titles, and a few maps at rupee rates. Landmark, upstairs at Spencer Plaza on Anna Salai, has a huge selection of books, stationery and music. The hole-in-the-wall Giggles in the *Taj Connemara* hotel grounds, meanwhile, is piled precariously high with novels, academic tomes on the region and coffee-table books. Unlike other bookstores in the city, this one takes credit cards and will post purchases abroad for you for a nominal charge. For a more personalized and fascinating browse, check out V.R.J Prabalan's stunning collection of books on alternative culture and political activism at Oasis Books, 17 Kutchery Rd, Mylapore.

Music

Musee Musical, 67 Anna Salai, stocks sitars, percussion instruments, flutes and the usual shoddy selection of Hofner/Gibson-copy guitars. The musical instrument shops of Chennai are a good hunting ground for **Carnatic instruments**. These include the *mridangam*, the double-headed drum that gives South Indian music its distinctive rhythms; the *vinas*, the southern cousin of the sitar; and the *nadasvaram*, a kind of over-sized oboe used in temple rituals. For the best range of concert-quality instruments, check out Saptaswara Music Store, on Raipetha Rd, Mylapore. Casio Musical Instruments on 206 TTK Rd also has a reasonable range. Music World, upstairs at Spencer Plaza, has the best selection of contemporary Indian and Western music **CDs** in the city.

Listings

Airlines, domestic *Air Deccan*, Deshabandu Plaza, 47 Whites Rd ☎044/3297 8596; *Go Air* ☎1800/222 111; *Indian Airlines*, 19 Rukhmani Lakshmipathy Rd ☎044/2855 5201 or 1800/180 1407; *IndiGo Airlines*, Malavika Centre, 144–145 KH Rd ☎044/6527 2272; *Jet Airways*, Thaper House, 43–44 Montieth Rd ☎044/3987 2222; *Kingfisher Airlines*, Spencer Travel Services Ltd, 124 Marshalls Rd ☎044/2858 4366; *Paramount Airways*, 2nd Floor, Alexander Square, Guindy ☎044/4390 9050; *Sahara*, Deshabandu Plaza, 47 Whites Rd ☎044/5208 7070; *SpiceJet* ☎1600180 3333.

Airlines, international *Air Canada*, Travel Pack, 101 Eldams Rd, Teynampet ☎044/6571 3413; *Air France*, Thaper House, 40–44 Montieth Rd ☎044/2855 4916; *Air India*, 19 Rukmani Lakshmipathy Rd ☎044/2855 4477, airport ☎044/2256 0747; *Alitalia*, Ajantha Travels, 634 Anna Salai ☎044/2434 9822; *American Airlines*, G-1 Prince Centre, 248 Pathari Rd ☎044/3988 7300; *British Airways*, 10–11 Dr Radhakrishnan Salai ☎9840 377470; *Gulf Air*, Thappar House, 43–44 Montieth Rd ☎044/2855 4417; *KLM/Northwest*, Spencer Travel Services Ltd, 124 Marshalls Rd ☎044/2852 4427; *Lufthansa*, 167 Anna Salai ☎044/2854

3500; *Malaysian Airlines*, Arihant Nico Park, 90 Dr R.K. Salai ☎044/4219 9999; *Qantas*, Eldorado Building, 112 Nungambakkam High Rd ☎044/2827 8680; *Singapore Airlines*, 108 Dr Radhakrishnan Salai ☎044/2847 3995; *SriLankan Airlines*, Vijaya Towers, Kodambakkam High Rd ☎044/4392 1100; *Swissair*, Hamid Building, 191 Anna Salai ☎044/2852 4783; *Thai Airways*, 31 Haddows Rd, Nungambakkam ☎044/4217 3311. Most offices are open Mon–Fri 10am–5pm, Sat 10am–1pm.

Banks and currency exchange You should have few difficulties changing money in Chennai: there are plenty of banks, and the major hotels offer exchange facilities (usually residents only). A conveniently central option is American Express, G-17, Spencer Plaza, 769 Anna Salai (Mon–Fri 9.30am–5.30pm, Sat 9.30am–2.30pm). Thomas Cook (Mon–Sat 9am–6pm) has offices at the Ceebros Centre, 45 Montieth Rd, Egmore, at the G-4 Eldorado Building, 112 Uttamar Gandhi Salai, and also at the airport (open to meet flights). For cash advances on Visa cards, go to Bobcards, next door to the Bank of Baroda on Montieth Rd. There's also an increasing number of 24hr ATMs popping up around town, such as at Citibank, 766 Anna Salai, as well as machines at the airport and both major railway stations.

Consulates *Australia*, TT Services, Omega Wing, 113–124 Anna Salai ☎044/4210 5111; *Canada*, VFS India Ltd, 3 College Lane, Nungambakkam ☎044/3295 7730; *New Zealand*, 132 Cathedral Rd ☎044/2811 2472; *Sri Lanka*, 196 TTK Rd ☎044/2498 7896; *Thailand*, VFS India Ltd, 560–562 Anna Salai ☎044/3298 6690; *UK*, 20 Anderson Rd, Nungambakkam ☎044/2825 7422; *USA*, 220 Anna Salai ☎044/2811 2000.

Hospitals Chennai's best-equipped private hospital is the Apollo, 21/22 Greams Rd ☎044/2829 3333. For an ambulance, try ☎102, but it's usually quicker to jump in a taxi.

Internet Internet access is widely available in cyber-cafés for around Rs20/hour, or for a bit more in hotel business centres. The snazziest option is the pricier-than-average Net Café at 101/1 Kanakasri Nagar, down an alleyway off Cathedral Rd – look for the neon @ sign. SRIS Netsurfing Café on the first floor of Spencer Plaza is a cheaper, though smaller, alternative. Gee Gee Net in Triplicane, next door to the *Hotel Comfort*, is open 24hr. Egmore options include the 24hr service at the *Pandian* hotel.

Photographic equipment Dozens of stores around town offer film and developing services on modern machines (Konica studios are particularly reliable), but the only Kodak-approved Q-Lab in the city (recommended for transparency processing) is Image Park, GEE Plaza, 1 Craft Rd. Nungambakkam. Reliance Opticals, at 136 Anna Salai, stocks Fuji Provia and Sensia II. For camera repairs, try Camera Crafts, 325/8A Quaide Milleth Salai, Triplicane, near *Broadlands Hotel*. Delhi Photo Stores, in an arcade directly behind the big Konica shop on Wallajah Rd, is crammed with spare parts and other useful Indian-made bits and bobs for cameras.

Postal services Chennai's main post office is opposite the Shanti Theatre on Anna Salai (Mon–Sat 8am–8pm, Sun 10am–5pm). If you're using it for poste restante, make sure that anyone writing to you marks the envelope "Head Post Office, Anna Salai", or your letters could well end up across town at the GPO, north of Parry's Corner on Rajaji Salai (same hours). The post office on Quaide Milleth Salai, in Triplicane (Mon–Sat 7am–3pm) is convenient if you're staying at *Broadlands*.

Tax clearance To get a tax clearance certificate (see Basics, p.87) take exchange documents and your passport to 121 Uttamar Gandhi Rd, and allow for 3–4hr of tedious form-filling.

Travel agents Reliable travel agents include American Express, 5th Floor, Phase 2, Spencer Plaza, 768–769 Anna Salai ☎044/2852 3592, ⓦwww.americanexpress.com; Surya Travels, F-14 1st Floor, Spencer Plaza ☎044/2852 3937; Thomas Cook, Eldorado Building, 112 Nungambakkam High Rd ☎044/2827 5052, ⓦwww.thomascook.com; Welcome Tours and Travels, 150 Anna Salai ☎044/2846 0908, ⓦwww.allindiatours.com.

Yoga Chennai may seem like an insalubrious place to study yoga, but some of South India's most renowned schools are based here. The following offer short courses: Adyar Yoga Centre, 6 2nd Cross St, Kasturba Nagar, Adyar, near the Theosophical Society Headquarters (☎044/2441 3399); The Art of Living, 132 Usman Rd, T Nagar (☎044/2489 8867); Kriya Yoga Initiation, 44 1st Main Rd, Indira Nagar (☎044/5528 3911); Yoga Nilayam, 1 Venkata Narayana Rd, T Nagar (☎044/2434 7669).

Moving on from Chennai

Transport connections between Chennai and the rest of India are summarized on p.527. If you're short of time, consider employing one of the **travel agents** listed on p.525 to book your plane, train or bus ticket for you. This doesn't apply to boat tickets for the Andaman Islands, which have to be booked in person (see below).

By air

Chennai's domestic airport is next to the international terminal, 16km southwest of the centre at Trisulam in **Meenambakkam** district. The easiest way to get there is by taxi or auto-rickshaw, but if you're not too weighed down with luggage you can save money by jumping on a suburban train to **Trisulam station**, 500m from the airport.

Including Air India's internal routes, the ten domestic airlines serve over twenty destinations between them, with particularly frequent flights to the other major cities of Mumbai, Bengaluru (Bangalore) and Hyderabad.

By train

Trains to Tiruchirapalli (Trichy), Thanjavur, Pudukottai, Kodaikanal Road, Madurai, and most other destinations in south Tamil Nadu leave from **Egmore Station**, with the occasional service departing from the suburban **Tambaram** station. All other trains leave from **Chennai Central** where, left of the main building on the first floor of the Moore Market Complex, the efficient **tourist reservation counter** (Mon–Sat 8am–8pm, Sun 8am–2pm; no phone) sells "tourist quota" tickets for trains from either station, which you can pay for in dollars, sterling, traveller's cheques or rupees (providing you have a recent encashment certificate). The booking office at Egmore, up the stairs left of the main entrance (same hours), also handles bookings for both stations, but has no tourist counter.

If you're arriving in Chennai by plane, note that Southern Railways also has a **reservation counter** (daily 10am–5pm) outside the domestic terminal at the airport.

By boat

Boats leave Chennai every five to ten days for **Port Blair**, capital of the **Andaman Islands**. However, getting a ticket can be a rigmarole, even though the schedule is now more regular. The first thing you'll need to do is head up to the Chennai Port Trust, next to the Directorate of Shipping on Rajaji (North Beach) Salai, George Town, where a small hut houses the Andaman Administration Office. A chalkboard on the wall advertises details of the next sailing, and you buy a ticket from the hatch around the corner, at the front of the main building. There are no ticket sales on the day of sailing. You no longer have to get a **permit** on the mainland, as they are available on arrival in Port Blair. For more details, see the Andaman Islands chapter, p.686.

By bus

All long-distance buses leave from the new **Mofussil bus stand**, the largest bus stand in South Asia. The stand is clean and well organized, although it's also rather inconveniently located 10km west of the centre in the suburb of Koyambedu – local buses (see Arrival, p.502) and auto-rickshaws ply the route. From Mofussil there are frequent services to destinations throughout Tamil Nadu and neighbouring states. The first stop beyond Chennai for many people is **Mamallapuram**, for which the fastest services are #188, #188A and

Recommended trains from Chennai

Destination	Name	No.	From	Departs	Total time
Bengaluru	Shatabdi Express*	#2007	Central	6am**	4hr 50min
(Bangalore)	Bangalore Express	#6523	Central	11.30pm	6hr 25min
Coimbatore	Kovai Express	#2675	Central	6.15am	7hr 40min
	Cheran Express	#2673	Central	10.10pm	8hr
Hyderabad	Charminar Express	#2759	Central	6.10pm	13hr 50min
Kanyakumari	Kanyakumari Express	#2633	Egmore	5.25pm	13hr 5min
Kochi/	Alleppey Express	#6041	Central	8.15pm	11hr 45min
Ernakulam	Trivandrum Mail	#2623	Central	8pm	10hr 55min
Kodaikanal Road	Pandyan Express	#2637	Egmore	9.30pm	7hr 36min
Madurai	Vaigai Express	#2635	Egmore	12.25pm	7hr 45min
Mettuppalayam (for Ooty)	Nilgiri Express	#2671	Central	9pm	9hr 15min
Mumbai	Mumbai Express	#6012	Central	11.45am	26hr
	Dadar Express	#2164	Central	7am	23hr
Mysore	Shatabdi Express*	#2007	Central	6am**	7hr
	Mysore Express	#6222	Central	9.30pm	10hr 35min
Thanjavur	Rock Fort Express	#6177	Egmore	10.30pm	7hr 45min
Thiruvanantha-puram	Trivandrum Mail	#2623	Central	8pm	15hr 40min
Tirupati	Sapthagiri Express	#6057	Central	6.25am	3hr 5min

*A/c only
**Except Tues

anything marked "ECR" (every 15–30min; less than 2hr); #19A, #19C, #119 and #119A all take rather longer, and the 108B (via the airport and Chengalpattu) much longer.

Travel details

Trains

Services leave from Central Station unless marked with on asterisk. Trains fom Egmore are marked*, from Egmore and Tambaram **, and from Egmore and Central ***.
Chennai to: Bengaluru (Bangalore) (7 daily; 4hr 50min–8hr 30min); Chengalpattu (9–10 daily**; 1hr–1hr 20min); Coimbatore (3 daily; 7hr 40min–8hr); Hyderabad (2 daily; 13hr 50min–14hr 30min); Kanyakumari (1–2 daily; 13hr 5min–16hr 55min); Kochi (Ernakulam: 2–3 daily; 10hr 55min–14hr 15min); Kodaikanal Road (3–4 daily*; 7hr 35min–8hr 30min); Kumbakonam (2 daily**; 7hr 45min–8hr 30min); Madurai (6–8 daily*; 7hr 45min–10hr 30min); Mettuppalayam (1 daily; 9hr 15min);

Mumbai (3 daily; 23hr –28hr 25min); Mysore (1–2 daily; 7hr–10hr 35min); Pune (3 daily; 19hr–24hr 15min); Thanjavur (1 daily*; 7hr 45min); Thiruvananthapuram (2–3 daily***; 15hr 40min–18hr 20min); Tiruchirapalli (9–10 daily*; 5hr 10min–6hr 45min); Tirupati (3 daily; 3hr 5min–3hr 35min); Vijayawada (10–11 daily; 6hr 35min–8hr 30).

Buses

Chennai to: Bengaluru (Bangalore) (every 15–30min; 8–11hr); Chengalpattu (every 5–10min; 1hr 30min–2hr); Chidambaram (20 daily; 5–7hr); Coimbatore (every 30min; 11–13hr); Kanchipuram (every 20min; 1hr 30min–2hr); Kanyakumari (10 daily; 16–18hr); Kodaikanal (1 daily; 14–15hr); Kumbakonam (every 30min; 7–8hr); Madurai (every

20–30min; 10hr); Mamallapuram (every 15–30min; 2–3hr); Pondicherry (Puducherry; every 15–30min; 4–5hr); Rameshwaram (3 daily; 14hr); Thanjavur (20 daily; 8hr 30min); Thiruvananthapuram (6 daily; 20hr); Tiruchirapalli (every 15–30min; 8–9hr); Tirupati (every 30min–1hr; 4–5hr); Tiruvannamalai (every 20–30min; 4–5hr); Udhagamandalam (Ooty) (2 daily; 15hr).

Flights

For a list of airline addresses, see p.524; for websites, see p.38; and for travel agents, see p.525. In the listings below, IA is Indian Airlines, IG IndiGo, JA Jet Airways, SA Sahara Airlines, AD Deccan Air, KF Kingfisher, GO Go Air, PA Paramount Airways, SJ SpiceJet.

Chennai to: Bengaluru (Bangalore) (IA, JA, SA, AD, KF, PA, SJ 20 daily; 50min–1hr); Coimbatore (IA, JA, AD, PA 7 daily; 55min–1hr 55min); Hyderabad (IA, JA, AD, KF, IG, PA, SJ 18 daily; 1hr); Kochi (IA, AD, KF, PA 6–7 daily; 1hr–2hr 15min); Madurai (IA, JA, AD, PA 7 daily; 55min–1hr 20min); Mumbai (IA, JA, AD, KF, GO, SJ 22–23 daily; 1hr 45min–3hr 40min); Port Blair (IA, JA, AD daily; 2hr); Thiruvananthapuram (IA, JA, AD, PA 2 daily; 1hr 10min); Tiruchirapalli (IA, AD 1–3 daily; 50min).

6

Tamil Nadu

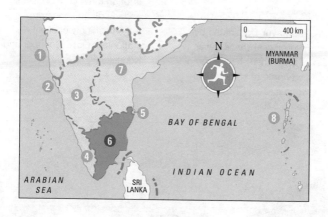

CHAPTER 6

Highlights

✳ **Mamallapuram** Stone-carvers' workshops, a long sandy beach and a bumper hoard of Pallava monuments have made Mamallapuram the state's principal tourist attraction. See p.536

✳ **Pondicherry (Puducherry)** A former French colony which has retained the ambience of a Gallic seaside town: croissants, a promenade and gendarmes wearing *képis*. See p.558

✳ **Thanjavur** Dominated by the colossal shrine tower of the Brihadishwara Temple and home to some of the world's finest Chola bronzes. See p.578

✳ **Madurai** This major temple, the love-nest of Shiva and his consort Meenakshi, hosts a constant round of festivals. See p.595

✳ **Kanyakumari** Sacred meeting point, at the Subcontinent's southern tip, of the Bay of Bengal, Indian Ocean and Arabian Sea. See p.617

✳ **The Ghats** The spine of southern India, with trekking through forested mountains and tea plantations from the refreshingly cool hill stations of Ooty, Coonoor and Kodaikanal. See p.621

△ Brihadishwara Temple, Thanjavur

6

Tamil Nadu

When Indians refer to "the South", it's usually **TAMIL NADU** they're talking about. While Karnataka and Andhra Pradesh are essentially cultural transition zones buffering the Hindi-speaking north, and Kerala and Goa maintain their own distinctively idiosyncratic identities, the peninsula's massive Tamil-speaking state is India's Dravidian Hindu heartland. Traditionally protected by distance and the military might of the southern Deccan kingdoms, the region has, over the centuries, been less exposed to northern influences than its neighbours. As a result, the three powerful dynasties dominating the South – the Cholas, the Pallavas and the Pandyas – were able, over a period of more than a thousand years, to develop their own unique religious and political institutions, largely unmolested by marauding Muslims. The most visible legacy of this protracted cultural flowering is a crop of astounding **temples**, whose gigantic gateway towers, or *gopuras*, still soar above just about every town large enough to merit a railway station, and some villages that aren't. It is the image of these colossal wedge-shaped pyramids, covered with garishly painted gods, goddesses and mythological creatures – described by Edward Lear as "stupendous and beyond belief" – that lingers longest in the memory of most travellers.

The great Tamil temples are merely the largest landmarks in a vast network of **sacred sites** – shrines, bathing places, holy trees, rocks and rivers – interconnected by a web of ancient pilgrims' routes. Tamil Nadu harbours 274 of India's holiest Shiva temples, and 108 of its most sacred Vishnu temples. In addition, five shrines devoted to the five Vedic elements (Earth, Wind, Fire, Water and Ether) are to be found here, along with eight to the planets, as well as other places revered by Christians and Muslims. These sites were celebrated in the hymns of the Tamil saints, composed between one and two thousand years ago, and so little has changed since then that the same devotional songs are still widely sung and understood in the region today.

The Tamils' living connection with their ancient Dravidian past has given rise to a strong **nationalist movement**. With a few fleeting lapses, one or other of the pro-Dravidian parties have been in power here since the 1950s, spreading their anti-brahmin, anti-Hindi proletarian message to the masses, principally through the medium of movies (indeed, since Independence, the majority of Tamil Nadu's political leaders have been drawn from the state's prolific **cinema** industry – see pp.514 & 535). Indians from elsewhere in the country love to caricature their southern cousins as "reactionary rice growers" led by "fanatical film stars". While such stereotypes should be taken with a pinch of salt, it is undeniable that the Tamil way of life, which has evolved along a distinctive and unbroken path since prehistoric times, sets it apart

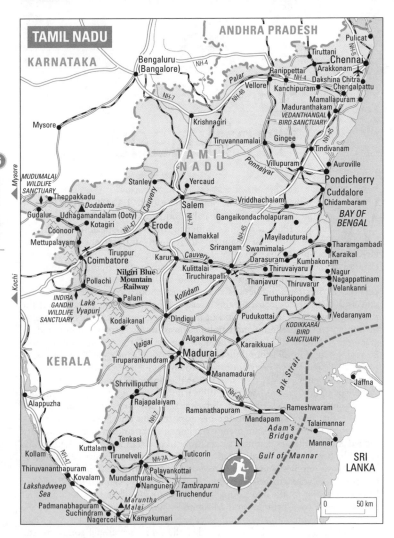

from the rest of the Subcontinent. This remains, after all, one of the last places in the world where a classical culture has survived into the present – "India's Holy Land", described by Marco Polo as "the most splendid province in the world".

Visiting Tamil Nadu

Despite its seafront fort, grand mansions and excellence as a centre for the performing arts, the state capital **Chennai** (covered in the previous chapter) is probably its least appealing destination: a scruffy, dusty, noisy city that still carries faint echoes of the Raj. Much the best place to start a temple tour is nearby **Mamallapuram** (also known as **Mahabalipuram**), a seaside village which boasts exquisite Pallava rock–cut architecture (fifth to ninth centuries) and a long stretch of white-sand beach. Inland, the pilgrimage town of **Kanchipuram** is filled with reminders of an illustrious past under successive dynastic rulers, the lake at **Vedanthangal** brims with bird life, and the holy town of **Tiruvannamalai** sits proudly under the red mountain of Arunachala. Further down the coast is one of India's rare French colonial possessions, **Pondicherry** (now Puducherry) and the "New Age" centre of **Auroville**. The road south from Puducherry puts you back on the temple trail, leading to the tenth-century Chola kingdom and the extraordinary architecture of **Chidambaram**, **Gangaikondacholapuram**, **Kumbakonam** and **Darasuram**. For the best Chola bronzes, however, and a glimpse of the magnificent paintings that flourished under Maratha rajas in the eighteenth century, travellers should head for **Thanjavur**. Chola capital for four centuries, the city boasts almost a hundred temples and was the birthplace of *Bharatanatyam* dance, famous throughout Tamil Nadu. Back on the Bay of Bengal, the Danish fort of **Tharamgambadi**, Muslim shrine at **Nagur** and Catholic pilgrimage centre of **Velankanni** are highlights of the central coast. Along here, areas of wetland provide perfect resting places for migratory birds, whose numbers soar during the winter monsoon and are best viewed at **Kodikkarai** (Point Calimere).

In the very centre of Tamil Nadu, just northwest of Thanjavur, the commercial town of **Tiruchirapalli** held some interest for the Cholas but reached its heyday under later dynasties, when the temple complex in neighbouring **Srirangam** became South India's largest. Among its patrons were the Nayaks of **Madurai**, whose erstwhile capital further south, bustling with pilgrims, priests, peddlers, tailors and tourists, is an unforgettable destination. Further south are two of the region's main pilgrimage centres: **Rameshwaram**, situated on the long spit of land stretching towards Sri Lanka, and **Kanyakumari**, at India's southern tip and the auspicious meeting place of the Bay of Bengal, Indian Ocean and Arabian Sea, where cool breezes and sea vistas are added attractions.

While Tamil Nadu's temples are undeniably its major attraction, it would take months to see them all, and there are plenty of other distractions for even the most ardent architecture buff. In the west of the state the hill stations of **Kodaikanal** and **Udhagamandalam** (Ootacamund or Ooty) are the premier attractions, set amidst verdant hills offering mountain views and a network of trails winding through forests and tea and coffee plantations. Nearby, the **Mudumalai Wildlife Sanctuary** and **Indira Gandhi (Anamalai) Sanctuary**, both fully reopened after closures for security, offer the chance of wildlife spotting.

Temperatures in Tamil Nadu usually hover around 30°C and peak in May and June, when they often soar above 40°, and the overpowering heat makes anything but sitting in a well-ventilated café exhausting. The state is barely affected by the southwest monsoon that pounds much of India from June to September: it receives most of its **rain** between October and January. Cooler, rainy days bring their own problems; wide-scale flooding can disrupt road and rail links and imbue everything with an all-pervasive dampness.

Accommodation prospects are good as all but the smallest towns and villages have something for every budget. Most hotels have their own dining halls which, together with local restaurants, sometimes serve sumptuous thalis (known simply as "meals"), tinged with tamarind and presented on banana leaves. **Indigenous cuisine** is almost exclusively vegetarian, though fish and seafood dishes can be excellent along the coast, most notably in Mamallapuram. For North Indian or Western alternatives, head for the larger hotels or more upmarket city restaurants.

Some history

Since the fourth century BC, Tamil Nadu has been shaped by its majority **Dravidian** population, a people of uncertain origins and physically quite different from North Indians. Their language developed separately, as did their social organization; the difference between high-caste brahmins and low-caste workers has always been more pronounced here than in the North, and caste divisions continue to dominate the state's political life. The influence of the powerful *janapadas*, the small republics and monarchies established in the North by the fourth and third centuries BC, extended as far south as the Deccan, but they made few incursions into **Dravidadesa** (Tamil country). Incorporating what are now Kerala and Tamil Nadu, Dravidadesa was ruled by three dynasties: the **Cheras**, who held sway over much of the Malabar coast (Kerala), the **Pandyas** in the far south, and the **Cholas**, whose realm stretched along the Coromandel Coast in the east. Indo–Roman trade in spices, precious stones and metals flourished at the start of the Christian era, when **St Thomas** arrived in the South, but dwindled when trade links began with Southeast Asia.

The prosperity of the early kingdoms having faded by the fourth century AD, the way was clear for the **Pallavas**, who emerged in the sixth century as leaders of a kingdom centred around Kanchipuram. By the seventh century, the successors of the first Pallava king, Simhavishnu, were engaged in battles with the southern Pandyas and the forces of the **Chalukyas**, based further west in Karnataka. This was also an era of social development: **brahmins** became the dominant community, responsible for lands and riches donated to temples. The emergence of *bhakti*, devotional worship, placed temples firmly at the centre of religious life, and the inspirational *sangam* literature of saint-poets fostered a tradition of dance and music that has become Tamil Nadu's cultural hallmark.

In the tenth and eleventh centuries, the Cholas experienced a period of profound expansion and revival; they soon held sway over much of Tamil Nadu, Andhra Pradesh, and even made inroads into Karnataka and Orissa. In the spirit of such glorious victories and power, the Cholas ploughed their new wealth into the construction of splendid and imposing temples, such as those at Gangaikondacholapuram, Kumbakonam and Thanjavur.

The **Vijayanagars**, who gained a firm footing in Hampi (Karnataka) in the fourteenth century, resisted Muslim incursions from the north and spread to cover most of South India by the sixteenth century. This prompted a new phase of architectural development in the building of new temples, the expansion of older ones and the introduction of colossal *gopuras*, or towers. In Madurai, the Vijayanagar governors, the **Nayaks**, set up an independent kingdom whose impact spread as far as Tiruchirapalli.

Simultaneously, the South experienced its first significant wave of **Europeans**. First came the Portuguese, who landed in Kerala and monopolized Indian trade for about a century before being joined by the British, Dutch and French. Though mostly on cordial terms with the Indians, the Western powers soon found themselves engaged in territorial disputes. The most marked were between the French, based in **Pondicherry**, and the British, whose stronghold since 1640 had been Fort St George in **Madras** (Chennai). After battles at sea and on land, the French were confined to Pondicherry, while British ambitions stepped up a gear in the eighteenth century, when the East India Company occupied Bengal (1757) and made firm its bases in Bombay and Madras.

As well as rebellions against colonial rule, Tamil Nadu also saw anti-brahmin protests, in particular those led by the Justice Party in the 1920s and 1930s. **Independence** in 1947 signalled the need for state boundaries to be reorganized, and by 1956 they had been demarcated on a linguistic basis. Andhra

Pradesh and Kerala were formed, along with Mysore state (later Karnataka) and the **Madras Presidency**, a slightly smaller area than that governed from Madras by the British, where Tamil was the predominant language. In 1965 Madras Presidency became **Tamil Nadu**, the latter part of its name coming from the Chola agrarian administrative units known as *nadus*.

Since Independence, Tamil Nadu's industrial sector has mushroomed. The state was a Congress stronghold until 1967, when the **DMK** (Dravida Munnetra Kazhagam), championing the lower castes and reasserting Tamil identity, won a landslide victory. The DMK flourished until the film star "**MGR**" (M.G. Ramachandran) broke away to form the **AIADMK** (All India Anna Dravida Munnetra Kazagam) in 1972, and won an easy victory in the 1977 elections. Virtually deified by his supporters, MGR remained in power until his death in 1987, when the Tamil government fell back into the hands of the DMK. Soon after, the AIADMK were back in power and control see-sawed between the two parties. A bitter and intense personal rivalry between AIADMK leader **Sri Jayalalitha Jayaram**, an ex-film star and dancer closely associated with MGR (see box, p.514), and DMK chief, former film producer **Karunanidhi**, has continued since the early 1990s, each holding the post of Chief Minister several times. Karunanidhi last wrestled control of the state from Jayalalitha in 2006. Despite their continual fight for control, both have pursued similar policies, targeting particularly economic growth. Their recent tenures have seen the state attract massive interest from big multinational companies, and it is now the recipient of nearly ten percent of all India's foreign investment. The concomitant effect of an increase in the upwardly mobile middle class has begun to spread out from Chennai and is now noticeable in the state's smaller cities.

The northeast

Fazed by the fierce heat and air pollution of Chennai, most visitors escape as fast as they can, and head south down the Coromandel coast, now cluttered with garish seaside restaurants and theme parks designed to appeal to the city's nouveau riche. The first major stop is India's stone-carving capital, **Mamallapuram**, whose ancient monuments include the famous Shore Temple and a batch of extraordinary rock sculptures, though en route it's well worth jumping off the bus at the artists' village of **Cholamandal**, just beyond the official city limits, and at **Dakshina Chitra**, a superb folk museum 30km south of Chennai, where traditional buildings from across South India have been beautifully reconstructed. Inland from Mamallapuram, **Kanchipuram** is an important pilgrimage and silk-sari-weaving town, from where you can loop southwest, taking in the tranquil bird sanctuary at **Vendanthangal** on the way to **Tiruvannamalai**, a wonderfully atmospheric temple town clustered at the base of the sacred mountain, Arunachala. The sprawling ruins of **Gingee** fort stand midway between here and the coast, where you can breakfast on croissants and espresso coffee in the former French colony of **Pondicherry** (Puducherry). A short way north, **Auroville**, the utopian settlement founded by followers of the Sri Aurobindo Ghose's spiritual successor, The Mother, provides a New Age haven for soul-searching Westerners and an economy for the local population.

Both Mamallapuram and Puducherry are well connected to Chennai by nail-bitingly fast bus services along the smooth coastal highway. Take care to use state buses where possible; their safety record is far better than the private ones. You can also get to Puducherry by train, but this usually involves a change at the junction town of **Villupuram**, from where services are slow and relatively infrequent.

⑥ Mamallapuram (Mahabalipuram)

Scattered around the base of a colossal mound of boulders on the Bay of Bengal, **MAMALLAPURAM** (aka Mahabalipuram), 58km south of Chennai, is dominated less by the sea, as you might expect, than by the smooth volcanic rocks that surround the town. From dawn till dusk, the rhythms of chisels chipping granite resound through its dusty lanes – evidence of a stone-carving tradition that has endured since this was a major port of the Pallava dynasty, between the fifth and ninth centuries. Little is known about life in the ancient city, and it is only possible to speculate about the purpose of much of the boulder sculpture, which includes one of India's most photographed monuments, the **Shore Temple**. It does appear, however, that the friezes and shrines were not made for worship at all, but rather as a permanent showcase for the talents of local artists. Due in no small part to the maritime activities of the Pallavas, their style of art and architecture had wide-ranging influence, spreading from South India as far north as the Ellora, the extraordinary rock caves in Maharashtra, as well as to Southeast Asia. This international cultural importance was recognized in 1995 when Mamallapuram was granted World Heritage Site status by UNESCO.

Given the location of so many stunning archeological remains right next to a long white-sand **beach**, it was almost inevitable that Mamallapuram would become a major destination for Western travellers. Over the past two decades, the village has oriented its economy to the needs of tourists, with the inevitable Kashmiri trinket sellers, bus-loads of city dwellers at the weekends, massage-wallahs and hawkers on the beach, and lots of backpacker-style budget hotels

The upside of the sea's anger

There was precious little good that came out of the devastation wreaked by the terrible tsunami of December 26, 2004 across a great swathe of South and Southeast Asia. However, in Mamallapuram, there was one surprising and positive result: two **ancient sites**, which had long been suspected to exist but had not been excavated owing to a lack of permission or funds from the ASI, were unearthed by the colossal waves as they receded into the deep. In the clear-up, under the technical pretext of debris clearance, permits were at last granted, and excavation on the sites – one just south of the Shore Temple, the other just north of the Tiger Cave – began. Though still in their initial phases, there have been some interesting developments: excavations in the former site have revealed the foundations of another shore temple, while the latter appears to have been the location of a 2300-year-old temple to Murugan (son of Shiva); findings there include terracotta figures and bronze lamps. None of the discoveries are on display yet but you can easily watch proceedings from the perimeter cordons of the respective digs.

and little fish restaurants. The Shore Temple, now protected from the corrosive effects of the salt spray by a wall of fir trees and stone blocks, is a shadow of the exotic spectacle it used to be when the waves lapped its base. However, the atmosphere generated by the busy fishermen on the beach, the steady hammering of the stone carvers and the mesmerizing ancient rock-art backdrop is unique in India. Mamallapuram is worth at least a couple of days if you're heading to or from Chennai; many people actually prefer to stay here and travel into the city for the day to book tickets or pick up mail.

Mamallapuram was badly hit by the **tsunami** of December 26, 2004, though fortunately the death-toll here was very low compared to other stretches of the Tamil Nadu coastline. Beachfront businesses have not only reopened but increased in number, although they are infringing a state law prohibiting permanent structures within 500m of the high tide mark, which was why most owners affected by the tsunami were not eligible for compensation.

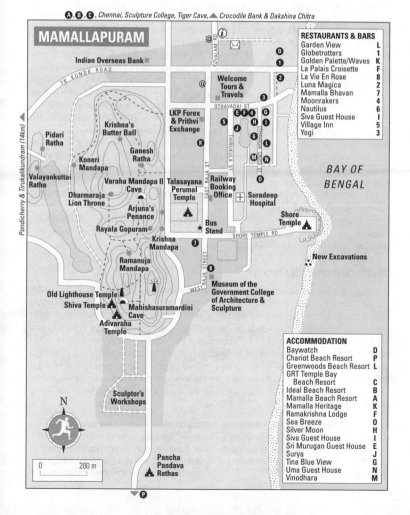

A, B, C, Chennai, Sculpture College, Tiger Cave, ▲ Crocodile Bank & Dakshina Chitra

MAMALLAPURAM

Indian Overseas Bank

TK KUNDA ROAD

KOVALAM RD

Welcome Tours & Travels

OTHAVADAI ST

LKP Forex & Prithvi Exchange

Krishna's Butter Ball

Ganesh Ratha

Koneri Mandapa

Varaha Mandapa II Cave

Talasayana Perumal Temple

Railway Booking Office

Suradeep Hospital

Dharmaraja Lion Throne

Arjuna's Penance

Rayala Gopuram

Krishna Mandapa

Ramanuja Mandapa

Old Lighthouse Temple

Shiva Temple

Mahishasuramardini Cave

Adivaraha Temple

Sculptor's Workshops

Pidari Ratha

Valayankuttai Ratha

THIRUKULA ST

EAST RAJA ST

THAVADAI CROSS ST

BAY OF BENGAL

Shore Temple

New Excavations

Bus Stand

SHORE TEMPLE RD

Museum of the Government College of Architecture & Sculpture

WEST RAJA STREET

Pondicherry & Tirukalikundram (14km)

Pancha Pandava Rathas

N

0   200 m

RESTAURANTS & BARS
Garden View	L
Globetrotters	1
Golden Palette/Waves	K
La Palais Croisette	F
La Vie En Rose	8
Luna Magica	2
Mamalla Bhavan	7
Moonrakers	4
Nautilus	6
Siva Guest House	5
Village Inn	5
Yogi	3

ACCOMMODATION
Baywatch	D
Chariot Beach Resort	P
Greenwoods Beach Resort	L
GRT Temple Bay Beach Resort	C
Ideal Beach Resort	B
Mamalla Beach Resort	A
Mamalla Heritage	K
Ramakrishna Lodge	F
Sea Breeze	O
Silver Moon	H
Siva Guest House	I
Sri Murugan Guest House	E
Surya	J
Tina Blue View	G
Uma Guest House	N
Vinodhara	M

Arrival, information and getting around

Mamallapuram is served by numerous daily **buses** from Chennai, Tiruvan-namalai, Kanchipuram and Puducherry, which pull in at the bus stand in the centre of the village. The nearest **railway station**, at Chengalpattu (Chingleput), 29km northwest on the bus route to Kanchipuram, is on the main north–south line, but not really a convenient access point. A **taxi** from Chennai costs around Rs1000 (or Rs700–800 from the airport); book through the tourist office here or in Chennai, or the pre-paid taxi booth at Chennai airport. If you're travelling to Mamallapuram by night in a taxi, make sure the price is clearly agreed before setting off. There have been recent reports of the driver stopping short of the village and demanding more money, or claiming that the fare was per person, rather than per vehicle, as it should be.

The **Government of Tamil Nadu tourist office** on Kovalam Road (Mon–Fri 10am–5.45pm; ☎044/2744 2232) is one of the first buildings you come to in the village; it's on your left as you arrive from Chennai and is a good place to find out about local festivals, hotels and bus times. Unless you're staying at one of the upmarket hotels, there are only two official places to **change money** in the village: the Indian Overseas Bank, on TK Kunda Road, or the more efficient LKP Forex and Prithvi Exchange on East Raja Street, a few metres down from Othavadai Street. The most reputable **travel agents** in the village are Welcome Tourrs and Travels (☎044/2846 0908) on Othavadai Street, Hi-Tours (☎044/2744 3260) and RJK Travels (☎044/2744 2285), both on East Raja Street. There is also a **railway booking office** on East Raja Street.

Mamallapuram itself comprises little more than a few roads and the sights are all within easy strolling distance. You can rent **bicycles** from shops on East Raja Street and the M.K. Cycle Centre, 28 Othavadai Street, for around Rs40 per day. **Scooters** and Enfield **motorcycles** are also available for Rs200–300 a day from Poornima Travels, next to *Moonrakers* restaurant, and through some guest-houses. **Net facilities** in the village have mushroomed; rates hover around Rs30–40 per hour, though connection speed and reliability may vary somewhat. The air-conditioned Cyber Café underneath the *Ramakrishna Lodge* is quiet, with a good broadband connection; the iWay branch on Kovalam Road has NetPhone. If you need **medical treatment**, visit the Suradeep Hospital, 15 Thirukula St (☎044/2744 2390).

Accommodation

Mamallapuram is not short of **accommodation**, and bargaining is the order of the day. The bulk of cheap and mid-range lodges are within the village, a short stroll from the beach, which is the preserve of the more expensive options. Checkout time tends to be noon at most places. Large resort hotels of varying standards sit side by side along the six-kilometre stretch of coast north of the village; they tend to be booked out by tour groups, so reserve a room well in advance. Without a taxi or bike, getting to these can prove a bit of a hassle; it's easy enough to take a rickshaw out there from the village, but not in the other direction – though the walk back into Mamallapuram along the beach is pleasant.

Baywatch Fishermens Colony ☎m98402 97152, ✉ hotelbaywatch@yahoo.co.in. New beachside place with smart breezy rooms, the seafront ones being more expensive, and a congenial restaurant serving grilled fish and curries. ❸–❹

Chariot Beach Resort 69 Five Rathas Rd ☎044/2498 6364, ✉ chariotbeachresort@dataone .in. Brand new resort, arranged round a 57-metre swimming pool, with unobstructed sea views, only 5min walk from Five Rathas. Beautifully furnished

You will notice that almost every hotel advertises an "in-house" **masseur** – although some women have reported that the massage experience was not at all relaxing. If you want to avoid any potentially problematic situations, make for an established practice: B. Kamaraj at *Hotel Daphne*, 17 Othavadai Cross St (☎044/2744 2811) has a good reputation, while professional Ayurvedic massage is also offered at the *Sea Breeze Hotel* (☎044/2744 3035) at the end of the street. Mr M. Kumar and his wife at 7/A Thirukula St (☎044/2744 2112) are also highly recommended, as is G Krishnakumar at *Greenwoods Beach Resort* (☎m94436 07658, ✉ayurkrishna2005@yahoo.com). All are fully qualified in Ayurveda and a range of massage techniques, and there's the option of a steam bath at the end of their sessions; full body massages cost around Rs350–400. It is a good idea to book sessions in advance and going in person beforehand will give you a feel for the place.

spacious rooms ($185) and even more luxurious cottages ($230). ❾

🏃 **Greenwoods Beach Resort** Othavadi Cross St ☎044/2744 3318, ✉greenwoods_resort@yahoo.com. A very friendly family-run place set in a lush garden, lovingly tended by the numerous ladies of the house. There are a/c and non-a/c rooms a stone's throw from the beach, some with private balcony, plus a good restaurant (see p.544) and Ayurvedic centre. Extremely good value. ❷–❺

GRT Temple Bay Beach Resort ☎044/2744 3636, ⓦwww.grttemplebay.com. Great location on the beach near the village, with views of the Shore Temple. The thatched, beachside cottages have sea-facing balconies, and there are also huge rooms in the main building, plus a swimming pool and pricey restaurant. Rates start around $160. ❾

Ideal Beach Resort 5km from town, Kovalam Rd ☎044/2744 2240, ⓦwww.idealresort.com. Comfortable cottages near the Tiger Cave, and a large pool and pleasant alfresco restaurant on site. Popular with overland tour groups, so book well ahead during the high season. ❻–❽

Mamalla Beach Resort 108 Kovalam Rd, 2.5km north the village ☎044/2744 2375, ✉mbresort @vsnl.net. Good-value resort with spacious, well-decorated chalets with attached bathrooms and verandas. There's a choice of a/c and non a/c rooms, plus a decent restaurant and games area, but no pool. ❹–❺

Mamalla Heritage 104 East Raja St ☎044/2744 2060, ⓦwww.nivalink.com/mamallaheritage. Efficient modern hotel on the main drag through the village, with spotless and comfortable a/c rooms (with fridge and TV). There's also a pool and very good restaurant (see p.544). ❺

Ramakrishna Lodge 8 Othavadai St ☎044/2744 2331, ✉hotelramakrishna@gmail.com. Clean,

well-maintained rooms in the heart of the village, all with bathrooms and a few with a/c, set round a courtyard filled with pot plants; the newest ones are on the top storey and have sea views. Sometimes has vacancies when other popular places are full, and there's a good restaurant (see p.544). ❶–❹

🏃 **Sea Breeze** Othavadai Cross St ☎044/2744 3035, ✉seabreezehotel @hotmail.com. The only bona fide beach resort in the village, featuring comfy and spacious a/c rooms (singles are particularly good value), a smart pool (open to non-residents for Rs200) and an Ayurveda centre. ❻–❽

Silver Moon 2/A Othavadai Cross St ☎044/2744 3644, ✉silver_moonguesthouse@yahoo.co.in. Very clean and friendly lodge with cosy attached rooms and a small leafy courtyard. ❶–❹

Siva Guest House 2 Othavadai Cross Rd ☎044/2744 3234, ✉sivaguesthouse@hotmail .com. Clean, tidy and good-value rooms in one of the newer guesthouses, with choice of a/c and non-a/c. ❷–❹

Sri Murugan Guest House 42 Othavadai St ☎044/2744 2552. Peaceful mid-sized place, with courteous service, clean non-a/c rooms and a rooftop restaurant. One of the nicest options in the area and therefore a little pricier than most budget places nearby. ❸–❹

Surya Thirukula St ☎044/2744 2292, 🖷242492. Lakeside hotel set in a leafy compound next to a sculpture school and gallery. There's a range of rooms, some with a/c and balconies, and all with mosquito nets. Also a small pool (non-guests Rs100). ❸–❹

Tina Blue View Othavadai St ☎044/2744 2319, ✉stevesan@yahoo.com. Established family guest-house with simple turquoise and whitewashed rooms, all attached, with mosquito nets, and a reasonable rooftop restaurant. ❷

Uma Guest House 11 Othavadai Cross St ☎044/2744 2697. Quiet and immaculate hotel with a choice of good-value a/c and non-a/c rooms. Some have sea views, and the pricier ones come with breezy private balconies and swing chairs (but no sea view). ❷–❹

Vinodhara 4 Othavadai Cross St ☎044/2744 2694, ✉vinodhara@yahoo.com. Medium-sized guesthouse with a range of immaculately tiled, good-value rooms (some with a/c) cooled by sea breezes. You can see the Shore Temple from the top floor. ❷–❺

The monuments

Mamallapuram's monuments divide into four categories: open-air **bas-reliefs**, **temples**, man-made **caves** and **rathas** ("chariots", carved in situ from single boulders to resemble temples or the chariots used in temple processions). The beautiful **Shore Temple** presides over the beachfront, while the famous bas-reliefs, **Arjuna's Penance** and the **Krishna Mandapa**, adorn massive rocks close to the centre of the village. Sixteen man-made caves in different stages of completion are scattered through the area; the most complete of the nine *rathas* are in a group, named after the five Pandava brothers of the Mahabharata.

The **entrance fee** for the Shore Temple and the Pancha Pandava Rathas is Rs250 [Rs10], payable at the ticket booth outside either monument. The ticket is valid for one day only, and will give you access to both sites (6.30am–6pm). Alternatively, you can peek through the wire-mesh fence at both sites, and the bas-reliefs are free.

The Shore Temple

East of the village, a distinctive silhouette above the crashing ocean, Mamallapuram's **Shore Temple** (see above for entrance details) dates from the early eighth century and is considered to be the earliest stone-built temple in South India. The design of its two finely carved towers was profoundly influential: it was exported across South India and eventually abroad to Southeast Asia. Today, due to the combined forces of wind, salt and sand, much of the detailed carving has eroded, giving the whole temple a soft, rounded appearance.

The taller of the towers is raised above a cell that faces out to sea – don't be surprised to see mischievous monkeys crouching inside. Approached from the west through two low-walled enclosures lined with small Nandi (bull) figures, the temple comprises two *lingam* shrines (one facing east, the other west), and a third shrine between them housing an image of the reclining Vishnu. Excavations, revealing a tank containing a structured stone column thought to have been a lantern, and a large Varaha (boar incarnation of Vishnu) aligned with the Vishnu shrine, suggest that the area was sacred long before the Pallavas chose it as a temple site.

The Krishna Mandapa and Arjuna's Penance

A little to the west of the village centre, off Shore Temple Road, the enormous bas-relief known as the **Krishna Mandapa** shows Krishna raising Mount Govardhana aloft in one hand. The sculptor's original intention must have been for the rock above Krishna to represent the mountain, but the seventeenth-century Vijayanagar addition of a columned *mandapa*, or entrance hall, prevents a clear view of the carving. Krishna is also depicted seated milking a cow, and standing playing the flute. Other figures are *gopas* and *gopis*, the cowboys and girls of his pastoral youth. Lions sit to the left – one with a human face – and above them is a bull.

Another bas-relief, **Arjuna's Penance** (also referred to as the "Descent of the Ganges") is a few metres north, opposite the modern Talasayana Perumal Temple. The surface of this rock erupts with detailed carving, most notably the endearing and naturalistic renditions of animals. A family of elephants dominates the right side, with tiny offspring asleep beneath a great tusker. Further still to the right, separate from the great rock, is a freestanding sculpture of an adult monkey grooming its young. The monument is also used as a dramatic backdrop for the annual Dance Festival (mid-Dec to late Jan), which attracts top performers from all over South India.

On the left-hand side, Arjuna, one of the Pandava brothers and a consummate archer, is shown standing on one leg. He is looking at the midday sun through a prism formed by his hands, meditating on Shiva, who is represented by a nearby statue, fashioned by Arjuna himself. The *Shiva Purana* tells that Arjuna made the journey to a forest on the banks of the Ganges to do penance, in the hope that Shiva would part with his favourite weapon, the *pashupatashastra*, a magic staff or arrow. Shiva eventually materialized in the guise of Kirata, a wild forest-dweller, and picked a fight with Arjuna over a boar they both claimed to have shot. Arjuna only realized he was dealing with the deity after his attempts to drub the wild man proved futile; narrowly escaping death at the playful hand of Shiva, he was finally rewarded with the weapon. Not far away, mimicking Arjuna's devout pose, an emaciated (presumably ascetic) cat stands on its hind legs, surrounded by mice.

To the right of Arjuna, a natural cleft represents the **Ganges**, complete with *nagas* – water spirits in the form of cobras. Near the bottom, a fault in the rock that broke a *naga* received a quick fix of cement in the 1920s. Evidence of a cistern and channels remain at the top, which at one time must have carried water to flow down the cleft, simulating the great river. It's not known if there was some ritual purpose to all this, or whether it was simply an elaborate spectacle to impress visitors. You may see sudden movements among the carved animals: lazing goats often join the permanent features.

Ganesh Ratha and Varaha Cave

Just north of Arjuna's Penance a path leads west to a single monolith, the **Ganesh Ratha** – some say that its image of Ganesh was installed at the instigation of England's King George V. The sculpture at one end, of a protecting demon with a tricorn headdress, is reminiscent of the Indus Valley civilization's 4000-year-old horned figure known as the "proto-Shiva".

Behind Arjuna's Penance, southwest of the Ganesh Ratha, is the **Varaha Mandapa II Cave**, whose entrance hall has two pillars with horned lion-bases and a cell flanked by two *dvarpalas*, or guardians. One of four **panels** shows the boar-incarnation of Vishnu, who stands with one foot resting on the *naga* snake-king as he lifts a diminutive Prithvi – the earth – from the primordial ocean. Another is of Gajalakshmi, the goddess Lakshmi seated on a lotus being bathed by a pair of elephants. Trivikrama, the dwarf brahmin who becomes huge and bestrides the world in three steps to defeat the demon king Bali, is shown in another panel, and finally a four-armed Durga is depicted in another.

A little way north of Arjuna's Penance, precipitously balanced on the top of a ridge, is a massive, natural, almost spherical boulder called **Krishna's Butter Ball**. Picnickers and goats often rest in its perilous-looking shade.

The lighthouses and the Mahishasuramardini Cave

South of Arjuna's Penance at the highest point in an area of steep paths, unfinished temples, ruins, scampering monkeys and massive rocks, the **New Lighthouse** affords fine views east to the Shore Temple and west across paddy fields and flat lands littered with rocks. Next to it, the **Olakanesvara** ("flame-eyed" Shiva), or **Old Lighthouse Temple**, used as a lighthouse until the beginning of the twentieth century, dates from the Rajasimha period (674–800 AD) and contains no image.

Nestling between the two lighthouses is the **Mahishasuramardini Cave**, whose central image portrays Shiva and Parvati with the child Murugan seated on Parvati's lap. Shiva's right foot rests on the back of the bull Nandi, and Parvati sits casually, leaning on her left hand. On the left wall, beyond an empty cell, a panel depicts Vishnu reclining on the serpent, his attitude of repose contrasted with the weapon-brandishing demons, Madhu and Kaithaba. Other figures seek Vishnu's permission to chase them. Opposite, in one of the most celebrated sculptures in Indian art, an intricately carved panel shows the eight-armed goddess Durga as Mahishasuramardini, the "crusher" of the buffalo demon Mahishasura. The story goes that Mahishasura became so powerful that he took possession of heaven, causing great misery to its inhabitants. To deal with such a dangerous foe, Vishnu and Shiva hit upon the idea of combining all the gods' powers into a single entity. This done, fiery jets appeared, from which emerged the terrifying "mother of the universe", Durga. In the ensuing battle, Durga caught Mahishasura with a noose, and he changed into a lion; she beheaded the lion, and he transformed into a human wielding a sword. Then she fired off a flight of arrows, only to see him turn into a huge trumpeting elephant; she cut off his trunk, whereupon the buffalo returned. Now furious, Durga partook of her favourite beverage: blood, "the supreme wine". Climbing on top of the buffalo, she kicked him about the neck and stabbed him with her trident. The impact of her foot forced him halfway out of his own mouth, only to be beheaded by his own sword, at which point he fell. The panel shows Durga riding a lion, in the midst of the struggle. Accompanied by dwarf *ganas* (attendants of Shiva), she wields a bow and other weapons; Mahishasura, equipped with a club, can be seen to the right, in flight with fellow demons.

The tiny **Museum of the Government College of Architecture and Sculpture** (Mon–Sat 10am–5pm; Rs2, camera Rs10) on West Raja Street, near the lighthouse, has a rather motley collection of unlabelled Pallava sculpture found in and around Mamallapuram.

Pancha Pandava Rathas (Five Rathas)

In a sandy compound 1.5km south of the village centre stands the stunning group of monoliths known – for no historical reason – as the **Pancha Pandava rathas** (see p.540 for entrance details), the five chariots of the Pandavas. Dating from the period of Narasimhavarman I (c.630–670 AD), the *rathas* consist of five separate freestanding sculptures built in imitation of traditional temples, set alongside some beautifully carved life-size animals.

The "architecture" of the *rathas* reflects the variety of styles employed in temple building of the time, and stands almost as a model for much subsequent development in the **Dravida**, or southern, style. The Arjuna, Bhima and Dharmaraja *rathas* show strong affinities with the Dravidian temples at Pattadakal in Karnataka. Carving was always executed from top to bottom, enabling the artists to work on the upper parts with no fear of damaging anything below. Any unfinished elements there may be are always in the lower areas. Intriguingly, it's thought that the *rathas* were never used for worship. A Hindu temple is only complete when the essential pot-shaped finial, the *kalasha*, is put in place – which would have presented a physical impossibility for the artisans, as the *kalasha* would have had to have been sculpted first. *Kalashas* can be seen next to two of the *rathas* (Dharmaraja and Arjuna), but as part of the base, as if it was intended to put them in place at a later date.

The southernmost and tallest of the *rathas*, named after the eldest of the Pandavas, is the pyramidal **Dharmaraja**. Set on a square base, the upper part comprises a series of diminishing storeys, each with a row of pavilions. Four

Shopping in Mamallapuram

Not surprisingly, the number-one souvenir tourists bring home from Mamallapuram is a **stone carving** from one of the town's many workshops. These vary in size from tiny Ganesh figures measuring a few centimetres and costing under Rs50 to life-size images of Shiva that will set you back hundreds of dollars, and more to ship. Price is also determined by the quality of the stone, which falls into three categories: soft grey stone is the cheapest, followed by the harder black stuff; top of the range is the smooth and alluring green stone. As ever, your bargaining skills will determine the final price and you will be better off dealing directly with the workshops, especially those towards the Five Rathas, than the tourist shops in the village.

Apart from the famous stone objects, many of the usual clothes, bags, rugs, jewellery and other knick-knacks popular with foreigners are available, mainly from the many **Kashmiri emporia** dotted around the village. By far the most honest, hassle-free place to try for such goods, however, is **Sky Blue Handicrafts** on Othavadai Street, below the *Ramakrishna Lodge*.

corner blocks, each with two panels and standing figures, are broken up by two pillars and pilasters supported by squatting lions. Figures on the panels include Ardhanarishvara (Shiva and female consort in one figure), Brahma, the king Narasimhavarman I, and Harihara (Shiva and Vishnu combined). The central tier includes sculptures of Shiva Gangadhara holding a rosary with the adoring river goddess Ganga by his side and one of the earliest representations in Tamil Nadu of the dancing Shiva, Nataraja, who became all-important in the region. Alongside, the **Bhima** *ratha*, the largest of the group, is the least complete, with tooling marks all over its surface. Devoid of carved figures, the upper storeys, as in the Dharmaraja, feature false windows and repeated pavilion-shaped ornamentation. Its oblong base is very rare for a shrine.

The Arjuna and Draupadi *rathas* share a base. Behind the **Arjuna**, the most complete of the entire group and very similar to the Dharmaraja, stands a superb unfinished sculpture of Shiva's bull Nandi. **Draupadi** is unique in terms of rock-cut architecture, with a roof that appears to be based on a straw thatched hut (a design later copied at Chidambaram; see p.567). There's an image of Durga inside, but the figure of her lion vehicle outside is aligned side-on and not facing the image, a convincing reason to suppose this was not a real temple. To the west, close to a life-size carving of an elephant, the *ratha* named after the twin brothers **Nakula** and **Sahadeva** is, unusually, apsidal ended. The elephant may be a visual pun on this, as the Sanskrit technical name for a curved-ended building is *gajaprstika*, "elephant's backside".

The road out to the *rathas* resounds with incessant hammering and chiselling from **sculptors' workshops**. Much of their work is excellent, and well worth a browse – the sculptors produce statues for temples all over the world and are used to shipping large-scale pieces. Some of the artists are very young; children often do the donkey-work on large pieces, which are then completed by master craftsmen.

Eating and drinking

Mamallapuram is crammed with small restaurants, most of which specialize in **seafood** – tiger prawns, pomfret, tuna, shark and lobster – usually served marinated and grilled with chips and salad. The upmarket hotels charge a lot more for the same variety of dishes, and lack the atmosphere of the village. Wherever you eat, establish exactly how much your fish, or lobster, is to cost in advance – the price quoted is often just the cost per kilo.

As this is a travellers' hangout, there also are numerous places offering the usual array of pasta, pancakes, brown bread and bland Indian dishes. If you want to enjoy real Indian food – including full-on fiery fish curry – head over to the bus stand where there are some good joints serving excellent, spicy thalis and *dosas*. Likewise, for breakfast you can get a plate of steaming *iddlis* from the stalls at the station for less than Rs10.

Beer is widely available, but it's on the pricey side (Rs90–100). The only places that regularly stay open for the night owls are the bar-restaurant above the *Siva Guest House*, which usually shows English football when it's on, and the *Globetrotters* bar at the northern end of the village section of beach.

Garden View Greenwoods Beach Resort, Othavada Cross St. Friendly first-floor terrace restaurant which serves delicious sizzlers, seafood and curries – they'll actually make proper hot ones if you ask. There's a choice of views – the relaxed garden or busier street-life.

Golden Palette *Mamalla Heritage Hotel*, 104 East Raja St. Blissfully cool spot with a/c and tinted windows, serving possibly the best veg food in the village – thalis at lunchtime, North Indian tandoori in the courtyard in the evenings, and wonderful ice-cream sundaes. The new rooftop *Waves* restaurant does fish and seafood too.

La Palais Croisette *Ramakrishna Hotel*, 8 Othavadai St. A popular rooftop restaurant with variations on noodles, salads and seafood, plus a range of pancakes. At its best when the itinerant Nepali cooks are in charge, so check.

La Vie En Rose West Raja St, next to the sculpture museum at the south end of the village. Pleasant garden location offering a Western-oriented menu, such as pasta dishes (the spaghetti's great) and chicken specialities, plus a few unusual salads.

Luna Magica On the beach, 100m north of Othavadai St. Top-notch seafood, including tiger prawns and lobster which are kept alive in a tank before being served up in a rich tomato, butter and

garlic sauce. There are also plenty of less expensive dishes – including a good fish curry and "sizzlers" – plus cold beer and a passable sangria made with sweet Chennai red wine.

Mamalla Bhavan Shore Temple Rd, opposite the bus stand. The village's original pure-veg joint, and usually very busy. Equally good for *dosa or iddli-wada* breakfasts and evening snacks, and there are also unlimited lunchtime thalis for around Rs30.

Moonrakers Othavadai St. Cool jazz and blues sounds, great fresh seafood, chess sets and slick service ensure this place is filled year round with foreign tourists.

Nautilus Othavadai Cross St. High-quality but reasonably priced eatery, run by an amiable French chef who turns out fine soups, meat, seafood and veg dishes, grilled or with an array of sauces, plus the usual travellers' favourites. Also does a good espresso.

Village Inn Thirukula Street. This tiny thatched eatery (with a couple of outdoor tables) serves grilled seafood and a superb butter-fried chicken in a tomato-garlic sauce.

Yogi Othavadai St. Run by a French/Indian couple, this welcoming and relaxed place is a good spot to sit and chill, with good coffee, lassis, salads and a small range of main courses.

Around Mamallapuram

The sandy hinterland and flat estuarine paddy fields around Mamallapuram harbour a handful of worthwhile sights. A short way north along the main highway, the **Government College of Sculpture** and elaborately carved **Tiger Cave** can easily be reached by bicycle. The **Crocodile Bank**, where rare reptiles from across South Asia are bred for release into the wild, and **Dakshina Chitra**, a museum devoted to South Indian architecture and crafts, are a bus ride away, or you could rent a moped for the day. Further north still, the **Chola-mandal Artists' Village** is a showcase for less traditional arts that's best visited en route to or from Chennai. Finally, a good target for a day-trip inland is the hilltop temple at **Tirukalikundram**, west of Mamallapuram across a swathe of unspoilt farmland.

△ Tiger Cave, Mamallapuram

Government College of Sculpture and the Tiger Cave

A visit to the **Government College of Sculpture**, 1km north of Mamallapuram on the Kovalam (Covelong) Road (Mon–Fri 10am–4pm; free; ☏044/2744 2261) gives a fascinating insight into the processes of sculpture training. You can watch anything from preliminary drawing, with its strict rules regarding proportion and iconography, through to the execution of sculpture, both in wood and stone, in the classical Hindu tradition. Contact the college office to make an appointment.

A further 3km north along Kovalam Road from the college, set amid trees close to the sea, the extraordinary **Tiger Cave** (sunrise–sunset; free) contains a shrine to Durga, approached by a flight of steps that passes two subsidiary cells. Following the line of an irregularly shaped rock, the cave is remarkable for its elaborate exterior, which features multiple lion heads surrounding the entrance to the main cell. If you sit and look for long enough, the section on the left with seated figures in niches above two elephants begins to resemble an enormous owl.

Crocodile Bank

The **Crocodile Bank** (Tues–Sun 8am–6pm; Rs20, camera Rs10, video Rs75) at Vadanemmeli, 14km north of Mamallapuram on the road to Chennai, was set up in 1976 by the American zoologist Romulus Whittaker to protect and breed indigenous crocodiles. The bank has been so successful (expanding from fifteen crocs to five thousand in the first fifteen years) that its remit now extends to saving endangered species, such as turtles and lizards, from around the world.

Low-walled enclosures in its garden compound house hundreds of inscrutable crocodiles, soaking in ponds or sunning themselves on the banks. Breeds include the fish-eating, knobbly-nosed gharial, and the world's largest species, the saltwater Australian *Crocodylus porosus*, which can grow to 8m in length. You can watch feeding time at about 4.30pm on Monday or Thursday or have your own brief feeding session anytime for a fee of Rs20. The temptation to take photos is tempered by the sight of those hungry saurians clambering over each other to snap up the chopped flesh, within inches of the top of the wall.

Another important field of work is conducted with the collaboration of local Irula people, whose traditional expertise is with snakes. Cobras are brought to the bank for **venom collection**, to be used in the treatment of snakebites. Elsewhere, snakes are repeatedly "milked" until they die, but here at the bank only a limited amount is taken from each snake, enabling them to return to the wild. This section costs an extra Rs5.

Coastal route buses #117 and #118 stop at the entrance.

Dakshina Chitra

Occupying a patch of sun-baked sand dunes midway between Chennai and Mamallapuram, **Dakshina Chitra** (daily except Tues 10am–6pm; Rs175 [Rs50]; ⓦwww.dakshinachitra.net), literally "Vision of the South", is one of India's best-conceived folk museums, devoted to the rich architectural and artistic heritage of Kerala, Karnataka, Andhra Pradesh and Tamil Nadu. The museum was set up by the Chennai Craft Foundation with support from local government and American sponsors. Apart from giving you the chance to look around some immaculately restored old buildings, a permanent display exposes visitors to many disappearing traditions of the region, from tribal fertility cults and *Ayyannar* field deities to pottery and leather shadow puppets (see box below).

Visits kick off with a short introductory video, followed by a **guided tour** of the campus, where a selection of traditional buildings from across India have been painstakingly reconstructed using authentic materials. Highlights include an airy Tamil brahmins' dwelling; a Chettinad merchant's mansion filled with Burmese furniture and Chinese lacquerware; a Syrian Christian home from the backwaters of Kerala with a fragrant jackwood interior; and a north Keralan house with separate rooms for the women – a unique feature reflecting the area's strongly matrilineal society. Exhibitions attached to the various structures convey the environmental and cultural diversity of the South, most graphically expressed in a wonderful textile collection featuring antique silk and cotton saris from various castes and regions. There is also a pottery demonstration,

Shadow puppetry

On sale in miniature scale as souvenirs at most government emporia across Tamil Nadu, **shadow puppetry** (*tolu bommalaatam* in Tamil) is a traditional South Indian way of amusing and instructing kids. Made of translucent leather, dyed and decorated with geometric perforations, the puppets are manipulated with bamboo sticks by teams of puppeteers seated behind a back-lit cloth screen – a technique that was exported by medieval Tamil traders and which has subsequently taken root in parts of Indonesia, including Bali. Music and percussion accompanies the performances of mythological epics such as the Ramayana and Mahabharata. Squeezed out by cinema, puppetry is sadly a dying art in South India these days, but you can still see performances at the Dakshina Chitra folk museum.

where you can try your hand at throwing clay on a Tamil wheel, and a memorable slapstick shadow-puppet display, as well as a separate restaurant with fixed-price meals.

Cholamandal Artists' Village

Tucked away on the scruffy southern edge of Chennai, the **Cholamandal Artists' Village** (daily 10am–7pm; free; Ⓦwww.cholamandalartvillage.com) was established in the mid-1960s to encourage contemporary Indian art. In a country where visual culture is so comprehensively dominated by convention, fostering innovation and artistic experimentation proved no easy feat. Despite an initially hostile response from the Madrasi establishment (who allegedly regarded the tropical storm that destroyed the artists' first settlement as an act of nemesis), the village has prospered. Today, Cholamandal's thirty-strong community has several studios and a large gallery filled with paintings, sketches, sculpture and metalwork, and a shop selling work produced here. For those with more than a passing interest in the village, there's also a small **guesthouse** (Ⓣ044/2492 6092; ❸).

Tirukalikundram

The village of **TIRUKALIKUNDRAM**, 16km west of Mamallapuram on the road to Kanchipuram, is famous for its hilltop Shiva temple, known locally as the "Eagle Temple". Rather than eagles, it was actually a pair of white Egyptian vultures (*Neophron percnopterus*), believed to be reincarnated saints on their way between Varanasi and Rameshwaram, that used to swoop down at noon to be fed by the temple priests. The vultures stopped coming in 1994 (a consequence probably of their exposure to the drug diclofenac – see also p.132). Their absence, however, was taken as a bad omen and the explanation for the massive cyclones that ravaged the Tamil Nadu coast that year.

Four hundred hot stone steps need to be scaled to reach the top, but don't let that – or the effort required to disabuse various individuals, including the priests, of the impression that you need their multifarious services and paid company – deter you. Once on the hilltop, the views are sublime, especially at sunset. The temple is closed between 1pm and 4pm.

Regular **buses** run to Tirukalikundram from Mamallapuram, en route to Kanchipuram, but it's more fun to rent a moped or motorcycle for the trip (see p.538). You could conceivably pedal out here, too (the route is flat all the way), but you'll need to start out early in the day to avoid the worst of the heat.

Kanchipuram

Flanked on the south by the Vegavathi River, the temple town of **Kanchipuram** (aka "Kanchi") lies 70km southwest of Chennai and about the same distance from the coast. Ask any Tamil what the town is famous for, and they'll probably say silk saris, shrines and saints – in that order. A dynastic capital throughout the medieval era, it remains one of the seven holiest cities in the Subcontinent, sacred to both Shaivites and Vaishnavites, and among the few surviving centres of goddess worship in the south. Year round, pilgrims pass through for a quick puja stop on the Tirupati tour circuit and, if they can afford it, a spot of shopping in the sari emporia. For non-Hindu visitors, however, Kanchipuram holds less appeal. Although the temples are undeniably

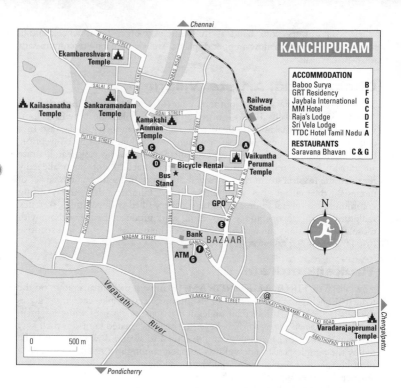

impressive – and there is some reasonable accommodation if you choose to stay – the town itself is unremittingly hot and dusty. Alternatively, it's possible to visit as a rather long **day-trip** from either Chennai or Mamallapuram, both a two-hour bus ride east.

Arrival and information

Buses from Chennai, Mamallapuram and Chengalpattu stop at the stand in the town centre just off Kosa Street. The sleepy **railway station** in the northeast of town sees just four daily passenger services from Chengalpattu (three of them originating in Chennai) and two from Arakkonam, to the north.

As most of the main roads are wide and traffic rarely unmanageable, the best way to **get around** Kanchi is by **bicycle** – available for minimal rates (Rs3/hr) at stalls west and northeast of the bus stand. The town's vegetable markets, hotels, restaurants and bazaars are concentrated in the centre of town, near the bus stand. There is an **ATM** on Gandhi Road, though the nearest official foreign exchange places are in Chennai and Mamallapuram. Fast **Internet** connection is available at Net4U at the town end of TK Road.

Accommodation

There's not a great choice of **accommodation** in Kanchipuram, though the recent addition of a couple of mid-range places has improved matters. Most places are reasonably clean and comfortable and some have their own restaurants, almost exclusively vegetarian.

Baboo Surya 85 East Raja St ☎044/2722 2556, ⓦwww.hotelbaboosoorya.com. One of Kanchi's best hotels: large and modern with immaculate a/c and non-a/c rooms, a glass lift, a good veg/tandoori restaurant and a chill a/c bar. Ask for a room with temple view. ❸–❹

GRT Residency 487 Gandhi Rd ☎044/2722 5250, ⓦwww.grtregency.com. Totally refurbished hotel with central a/c and clean, decent-sized rooms. The *Royal Spice* restaurant is the only non-veg place in town. Credit cards accepted. ❺–❻

Jaybala International 504 Gandhi Rd (just off the road at the end of a short narrow drive), ☎044/2722 4348, ⓦwww.hoteljaybala.com. Slightly more old-fashioned than the *Baboo Surya*, with large, clean rooms (some with a/c) and lower tariffs. They also offer good-value single rates, and the excellent *Saravana Bhavan* restaurant is downstairs. ❸–❹

MM Hotel 65/66 Nellukkara St ☎044/2723 7250, ⓦwww.mmhotels.com. New, very clean mid-range option, with reasonably large, good-value rooms. It's also right above a branch of the *Saravana Bhavan* restaurant, which provides room-service food. Credit cards accepted. ❸–❹

Raja's Lodge 20B Nellukkara St ☎044/2722 2603. Modern, simple but spotlessly clean lodge, easily the best at the bottom end of the price range, with some a/c rooms. ❶–❸

Sri Vela Lodge Railway Station Rd ☎044/2722 1504. Cheap but slightly grubby lodge offering larger-than-average rooms with attached shower-toilets and fans, though still airless. Busy "meals" restaurant downstairs. ❶–❷

TTDC Hotel Tamil Nadu Railway Station Rd ☎044/2722 2553, ✉ttdc@md3.vsnl.net.in. Friendly state-run hotel with large rooms, the a/c ones being especially good value, although the place is looking slightly shabby and the restaurant is dingy. ❸

The Town and temples

Established by the **Pallava** kings in the fourth century AD, Kanchipuram served as their capital for five hundred years, and continued to flourish throughout the Chola, Pandya and Vijayanagar eras. Under the Pallavas, it was an important scholastic forum, and a meeting point for Jain, Buddhist and Hindu cultures. Its **temples** dramatically reflect this enduring political prominence, spanning the years from the peak of Pallava construction to the seventeenth century, when the ornamentation of the *gopuras* and pillared halls was at its most elaborate (for more on Tamil Nadu's temples, see Contexts p.757).

All the temples have the same opening times (daily 6am–noon & 4pm–8pm) and can be easily reached by foot, bike or rickshaw. You'll be offered a panoply of services – from sanctuary priests, shoe bearers, guides, women giving out food for fish in the temple tanks, and well-trained temple elephants that bless you with their trunks – so go prepared with a pocketful of change but also with the resolve to draw the line if asked unreasonable amounts for unwanted services. Always animated, the temples really come alive during major festivals such as the **Car Festival** (May) and **Navaratri** (Oct/Nov).

Ekambareshvara Temple and around

Kanchipuram's largest temple and most important Shiva shrine, the **Ekambareshvara Temple** (camera Rs10, video Rs20) – also known as Ekambaranatha – on the north side of town, is easily identified by its colossal whitewashed *gopuras*, which rise to almost 60m. The main temple contains some Pallava work, but was mostly constructed in the sixteenth and seventeenth centuries, and stands within a vast walled enclosure beside some smaller shrines and a large fish-filled water tank.

The entrance is through a high-arched passageway beneath an elaborate *gopura* in the south wall. It leads to an open courtyard and a majestic "thousand-pillared hall" (*kalyan mandapa*), whose slightly decaying grey stone columns are modelled as nubile maidens, animals and deities. This hall faces the tank to the north and a sanctuary to the west protecting an "earth" *lingam* (one of five types of *lingam* in Tamil Nadu that represent the elements), the emblem of Shiva here in his form as **Kameshvara**, or "Lord of Desire". Legend connects it with the goddess **Kamakshi** (Shiva's consort, "Wanton-Eyed"), who angered Shiva by playfully covering his eyes and plunging the world into darkness. Shiva reprimanded her by sending her to fashion a *lingam* from the earth in his honour; once it was completed, Kamakshi found she could not move it. Local myths tell of a great flood that swept over Kanchipuram and destroyed the temples, but did not move the *lingam*, to which Kamakshi clung so fiercely that marks of her breasts and bangles were imprinted upon it.

Behind the sanctum, accessible from the covered hallway around it, an eerie bare hall lies beneath a profusely carved *gopura*, and in the courtyard a venerable **mango tree** represents the tree under which Shiva and Kamakshi were married. This union is celebrated during a festival each April, when many couples are married in the *kalyan mandapa*. The four branches of the tree are supposed to yield different-tasting fruit, believed to symbolize the four Vedas, which are collected by the temple priests and given to women coming here to petition for fertility. For Rs50 you can perform a special problem-solving puja: walk three times around the tree to sort out financial difficulties or to find a husband for your daughter. Finally, don't miss the temple's other "thousand-pillared" *mandapa*, beneath the *gopura* on the west wall, which houses the extraordinary **Pictorial Depication of Historical Episodes in Sound and Light by Electronic Meriods** (sic), a collection of bizarre gizmos elucidating the basic tenets of Hinduism. One involves thrusting your head into a contraption to hear electronically triggered excerpts from the Vedas.

The somewhat neglected twelfth-century **Jvaraheshvari Temple**, in leafy gardens to the south, is the only Chola (tenth–twelfth centuries) structure in Kanchipuram not to have been modified and overshadowed by later buildings. Unlike the Pallava constructions, it is built of hard grey stone and its sculpted pyramidal roof is an early form of the *gopuras* used extensively by the Pandyas.

Sankaramandam

Kanchipuram is the seat of a line of holy men bearing the title **Acharya**, whose lineage dates back to the saint Adi Sankaracharya. The 68th Acharya, the highly revered Sri Chandrasekharendra Sarasvati Swami, who died in 1994 at the age of 101, is buried in the sitting position, as is the custom for great Hindu sages. His mortal remains are enshrined in a *samadhi* at the **Sankaramandam**, a *math*

Sankara shenanigans

One of the biggest scandals to hit South India in recent years was the arrest of the current **Adi Sankaracharya** (see above), Jayendra Saraswati, and his deputy on charges of murder in November 2004: they stood accused of unceremoniously hacking the Varadarajaperumal Temple manager, Sankararaman, to death within the temple precincts two months earlier. It was the culmination of a number of allegations concerning improper sexual behaviour and violence over the preceding years. The pair spent a couple of months in jail before being released on bail.

The case, which has obvious religious and political ramifications, took on further dramatic colour in January the following year when the chief investigator offered prayers to Vishnu at the scene of the crime, before laying the 1873-page charge sheet at the deity's feet. Since then, however, the sluggish cogs of the Indian legal system have left the case in limbo and a trial is still awaited. Public debate remains rife on the topic, with secularists citing it as an example of favourable treatment of a holy man (as bail was granted) and devout followers defending their guru's innocence. These arguments will no doubt continue to rage until well after the final court verdict is given.

(monastery for Hindu renunciates) down the road from the Ekambareshvara Temple. The present incumbent, the 69th Acharya, has his quarters on the opposite side of a marble meditation hall to the shrine, and gives *darshan* to the public during the morning and early evening, when the *math*'s two huge elephants are given offerings. Lined with old photographs from the life of the former swami, with young brahmin students chanting Sanskrit verses in the background, it's a typically Tamil blend of simple sanctity and garish modern glitz.

Kailasanatha Temple

The **Kailasanatha Temple**, the oldest structure in Kanchipuram and the finest example of Pallava architecture in South India, is situated among several low-roofed houses just over 1km west of the town centre. Built by the Pallava king Rajasimha early in the eighth century, its intimate size and simple carving distinguish it from the town's later temples. Usually quieter than its neighbours, the shrine becomes the focus of vigorous celebrations during the **Mahashivar-atri festival** each March. Like its contemporary, the Shore Temple at Mamal-lapuram, it is built of soft sandstone, but its relatively sheltered position inland has spared it from wind and sand erosion, and it remains remarkably intact, despite some rather clumsy recent renovation work.

Topped with a modest pyramidal spire, the small temple stands within a rectangular courtyard, enclosed by a wall inlaid with tiny meditation chambers and sculpted with images of Shiva, Parvati and their sons, as well as rearing mythical lions (*yalis*). On the south side of the spire Shiva is depicted as a begging ascetic (Bhikshatana); on the north he's in the pose of the dance of destruction (Samhara-Tandava). Walls in the dim interior bear traces of frescoes, and the ceilings are etched with religious verses written in Pali. The sanctum, inaccessible to non-Hindus, shelters a sturdy sixteen-sided black *lingam,* guarded by elephant-headed Ganesh and Shiva's other son, Skanda, the god of war, with whom Rajasimha was closely associated. Double walls were built round the sanctuary to support the weighty tower above; the passage between them is used as a circumambulatory path as part of the ritual worship of Shiva.

Kamakshi Amman Temple

Built during Pallava supremacy and modified in the fourteenth and seventeenth centuries, the **Kamakshi Amman Temple** combines several styles, with an ancient central shrine, gates from the Vijayanagar period, and high, heavily sculpted creamy *gopuras* set above the gateways in a later period. To the right of the central shrine, inaccessible to non-Hindus, a raised *mandapa* is now an art gallery, housing many pictures of the recent **Acharyas** (see opposite). This is one of India's three holiest shrines to Shakti, Shiva's cosmic energy depicted in female form, usually as his consort. The goddess Kamakshi, a local form of Parvati, shown with a sugar-cane bow and arrows of flowers, is honoured as having lured Shiva to Kanchipuram, where they were married, and thus having forged the connection between the local community and the god. Inside the gate a couple of temple elephants bestow gentle blessings with their trunks upon the bowed heads of pilgrims in exchange for donations to the *mahout*.

In February or March, deities are wheeled to the temple in huge wooden "cars", decked with robed statues and swaying plantain leaves – the intricately carved "cars" are kept behind bars on Gandhi Road during the rest of the year.

Vaikuntha Perumal Temple

Built shortly after the Kailasanatha Temple at the end of the eighth century, the smaller **Vaikuntha Perumal Temple**, a few hundred metres south of the railway station, is dedicated to Vishnu. Its lofty carved *vimana* (towered sanctuary) crowns three shrines containing images of Vishnu, stacked one on top of the other. Unusual scenes carved in the walls enclosing the temple yard depict events central to Pallava history, among them coronations, court gatherings and battles with the Chalukyas who ruled the regions to the northwest. The temple's pillared entrance hall was added by Vijayanagar rulers five centuries later, and is very different in style, with far more ornate sculpting.

Varadarajaperumal Temple

The Vaishnavite **Varadarajaperumal Temple** stands within a huge walled complex in the far southeast of town, guarded by high gates topped with *gopuras*. The inner sanctuary boasts superb carving and well-preserved paintings, but non-Hindus only have access to the outer courtyards and the elaborate sixteenth-century pillared hall close to the western entrance gate. The outer columns of this *mandapa* are sculpted as lions and warriors on rearing horses, to celebrate the military vigour of the Vijayanagars, who believed their prowess was inspired by the power of Shakti.

Eating

The best **place to eat** in town is *Saravana Bhavan* (daily 6am–10pm), part of the famous Chennai chain of pure veg restaurants. There are branches on Gandhi Road and Nellukkara Street, both of which offer superb Rs30 "meals" at lunch time, a long list of delicious South Indian snacks and good Coorg coffee the rest of the day; they're also marginally less bedlam-like than the other "meals" joints in the centre, which tend to get swamped by shaven-headed pilgrims from Tirupati.

Vedanthangal Bird Sanctuary

One of India's most spectacular bird sanctuaries lies roughly 1km east of the village of **VEDANTHANGAL**, a cluster of squat, brown houses set in a patchwork of paddy fields 30km from the east coast and 86km southwest of Chennai. Bisected by one road, it's a tiny, relaxed place, with just two chai stalls.

The **sanctuary** (daily dawn–dusk; Rs5), a low-lying area less than half a kilometre square, is at its fullest between December and February, when it's totally flooded. The rains of the northeast monsoon, sweeping through in October or November, bring indigenous water birds here to nest and settle until the dry season (usually April), when they leave for wetter areas. Abundant trees on mounds above water level provide perfect nesting spots, alive by January with fledglings. Visitors can watch the avian action from a path at the water's edge, or from a watchtower, although it's best to bring a pair of binoculars with you as the stall that rents them is not always open. Try to come at sunset, when the birds return from feeding. Common Indian species to look out for are openbill storks, spoonbills, pelicans, black cormorants and herons of several types. You may also see ibises, grey pelicans, migrant cuckoos, sandpipers, egrets, which paddle in the rice fields, and tiny, darting bee-eaters. Some migrant birds pass through and rest on their way between more permanent sites; swallows, terns and redshanks are common, while peregrine falcons, pigeons and doves are less frequently spotted.

Practicalities

Getting to Vedanthangal can present a few problems. The nearest town is **Maduranthakam**, 8km east on NH-45 between Chengalpattu and Tindivanam, from which hourly buses run to the sanctuary. Services also run every hour or two from Chengalpattu. Taxis make the journey from Maduranthakam for Rs300–350, but cannot be booked from Vedanthangal.

Vedanthangal's only accommodation is the four-room **forest lodge** (❸–❹), near the bus stand, school and chai stall. The spacious, comfortable rooms with attached bath (a/c or non-a/c) should be booked through the Wildlife Warden in Chennai (☎044/2432 1471 or ☎m95415 20006). It often gets full, especially at weekends, in December and January.

Tiruvannamalai

Synonymous with the fifth Hindu element of fire, **TIRUVANNAMALAI**, 100km south of Kanchipuram, ranks, along with Madurai, Kanchipuram, Chidambaram and Tiruchirapalli, as one of the five holiest towns in Tamil Nadu. Its name, meaning "Red Mountain", derives from the spectacular extinct volcano, **Arunachala**, that rises behind it, and which glows an unearthly crimson at dawn. This awesome natural backdrop, combined with the presence in the centre of town of the colossal **Arunchaleshvara Temple**, make Tiruvannamalai one of the region's most memorable destinations, and far removed from the tourist trail, it's a perfect place to get to grips with life in small-town Tamil Nadu. For those searching for the spiritual South, the countless shrines, sacred tanks, ashrams and paved pilgrim paths scattered around the sacred mountain (not to mention the legions of dreadlocked *babas* who line up for alms outside the main sites) will keep anyone interested in Hinduism absorbed for weeks.

Mythology identifies Arunachala as the place where Shiva asserted his power over Brahma and Vishnu by manifesting himself as a *lingam* of fire, or **agnilingam**. The two lesser gods had been disputing their respective strengths when Shiva pulled this primordial pyro-stunt, challenging his adversaries to locate the top and bottom of his blazing column. They couldn't (although Vishnu is said to have

---

Pradakshana

During the annual **Karttigai festival**, Hindu pilgrims are supposed to perform an auspicious circumambulation of Arunachala, known as the **Pradakshana** (*pra* signifies the removal of all sins, *da* the fulfilment of desires, *kshi* freedom from the cycle of rebirth and *na* spiritual liberation). Along the way, offerings are made at a string of shrines, tanks, temples, *lingams*, pillared meditation halls, sacred rocks, springs, trees and caves related to the Tiruvannamalai legends. Although hectic during the festival, the paved path linking them all together is quiet for most of the year and makes a wonderful day-hike, affording fine views of the town and its environs.

An even more inspiring prospect is the **ascent of Arunachala** itself, which can be completed in two to three hours if you're fit and can cope with the heat (if you can't, don't attempt this hike). The path is less easy to follow than the Pradakshana, and you may feel like employing one of the guides who offer their services at the trailhead, just above the Shri Ramanashramam ashram. At the summit you can see remnants of the annual Deepam blaze, which lights the mountain up for many miles around.

faked finding the head) and collapsed on their knees in a gesture of supreme submission. The event is commemorated each year at the rising of the full moon in November/December, when the **Deepam ceremony**, bringing to an end the ten-day **Karttigai festival** (see box, p.563), culminates with the illumination of gallons of camphor in the temple courtyard. This acts as a signal for brahmins stationed on the summit of Arunachala to light a vast vat of ghee and paraffin, which blazes for days and can be seen from a radius of more than 20km. It represents the fulfilment of Shiva's promise to reappear each year to vanquish the forces of darkness and ignorance with firelight. The massive *agnilingam* attracts tens of thousands of pilgrims, who rush from the temple below to the summit in time to fuel the inferno with their own offerings. The whole event, best enjoyed from the relative safety of a rooftop in town, is one of the great spectacles of sacred India. The latest incarnation of a prehistoric fire-worshipping cult, it has probably been performed here in some form or another, without interruption, for four thousand years.

The alleged regenerative and healing powers of the sacred Red Mountain also explain why the famous twentieth-century saint **Shri Ramana Maharishi** chose this as the site for his 23-year meditation retreat in a cave on the side of the hill. Shri Ramana's subsequent teachings formed the basis of a worldwide movement, and his former ashram on the edge of Tiruvannamalai attracts a stream of Western devotees. A crop of other smaller ashrams have mushroomed alongside it, some of them more authentic than others, and the ranks of white-cotton-clad

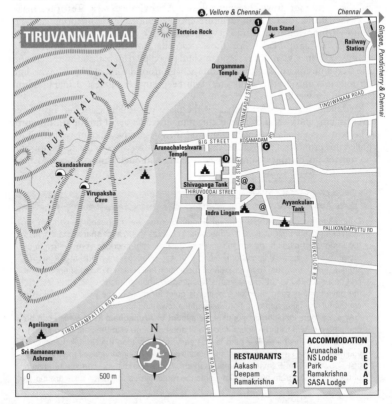

foreigners floating between them have become a defining feature of the area south of town.

Arrival, information and accommodation

Tiruvannamalai is served by regular **buses** from Vellore and Puducherry. Coming from the coast, it's easiest to make your way there on one of the numerous buses from Tindivanam. The town **bus stand** is just over 1km north of the temple on the main road to Gingee. Half a kilometre east of there is the **railway station**, which is on the Tirupati–Madurai line, with a daily service in each direction. There's **Internet access** at the Image Computer Centre, 52 Car St and at Sri Sai, 14A Kadambarayam St.

For such an important pilgrimage place, Tiruvannamalai has surprisingly few **hotels** and those there are all fall into the budget to lower mid-range categories.

Arunachala 5 Vada Sannathi St ☏ 04175/228300. Large, clean and comfortable hotel, right outside the main temple entrance. Not the quietest place to stay but certainly atmospheric. ❸–❹
NS Lodge 47 Thiruvoodai St ☏ 04175/225388. Facing the Arunachaleshvara Temple's south entrance, this good-value place has clean rooms with attached bath, some with a/c and all with cable TV; there's also a great view of the temple towers from the roof. ❷–❹
Park 26 Kosamadam St, two minutes' walk northeast of the main temple enhance ☏ 04175/222471. Another reliable option; all rooms are non-a/c and basic but clean, with

singles costing only Rs70. There's a busy vegetarian canteen on the ground floor. ❶
Ramakrishna 34-F Polur Rd ☏ 04175/250005, ✉ info@hotelramakrishna.com. One of the best places in town, with large rooms with attached bath (a/c or non-a/c) and a decent restaurant. It's a 5min walk north of the bus stand: follow Chinnakadai St north and take the left fork; the hotel is 200m along on the right ❶–❹
SASA Lodge Chinnakadai St, almost opposite the bus stand ☏ 04175/253431. One of the best budget lodges, painted bright blue and white, with decent enough rooms, some of which are a/c. ❶–❸

The Town

The town sprawls in a leisurely fashion in all directions from its centrepiece, the lively **Arunachaleshvara Temple**. Away from its buzzing precincts, the pace is slow, and everywhere you go the presence of the holy mountain of Arunachala, looming majestically to the west, makes itself felt. On its slopes a couple of **caves** where the famous saint Shri Ramana Maharishi lived can be visited; back in town is a large **ashram** dedicated to him.

Arunachaleshvara Temple

Known to Hindus as the "Temple of the Eternal Sunrise", the enormous **Arunachaleshvara Temple**, built over a period of almost a thousand years and incorporating several distinct styles, consists of three concentric courtyards whose gateways are topped by tapering *gopuras*, the largest of which cover the east and north gates. The best spot from which to view the precinct, a breathtaking spectacle against the sprawling plains and lumpy, granite Shevaroy hills, is the path up to Sri Ramana Maharishi's meditation cave, Virupaksha (see p.556), on the lower slopes of Arunachala. To enter the temple, however, head for the huge eastern gateway, which leads through the thick outer wall carved with images of deities, local saints and teachers, to a paved inner courtyard. The large stepped Shivaganga Tank to the left originally lay outside the temple precincts; on the right stands a vast "thousand-pillared" *mandapa*, where the temple elephant lives when not taking part in rituals. In the basement of a raised hall to the right before entering the next courtyard is the Parthala *lingam*, where

Shri Ramana Maharishi is said to have sat in a state of Supreme Awareness while ants devoured his flesh.

The second enclosure, built a couple of centuries earlier, in the 1200s, is much smaller, with a large Nandi bull facing the sanctuary and a shrine to the goddess (Shiva's consort) on its northern edge. In the temple kitchens in its southeastern corner, food is prepared for the gods. A nineteenth-century roof shelters the central courtyard, surveyed by numerous deities etched into its outer walls, among them Shiva, Parvati, Venugopala (Krishna), Lakshmi, Ganesh and Subrahmanya. In the dim interior, arcaded cloisters supported by magnificently carved columns lead to the main shrine dedicated to Shiva (and accessible to non-Hindus): a *lingam* raised on a platform bearing tenth-century inscriptions. This is the location of six daily puja, when the *lingam* is bathed, clothed and strewn with flower garlands amid the heady smell of incense and camphor and the sound of bells and steady chanting. Queues to get into the inner sanctum can be quite daunting but the worst of them can be avoided by paying Rs20 for "special" *darshan*.

In one of the outer courtyards on the north side, devotees – mostly women, drenched having bathed in the nearby tank – circumambulate an ancient hybrid *neem* and *bodhi* tree, draping it with offerings for the health of offspring and the success of married life.

Virupaksha and Skandashram caves

Opposite the western entrance of the temple complex, a path leads up a holy hill (15min) to the **Virupaksha cave**, where Shri Ramana Maharishi stayed between 1899 and 1916. He personally built the bench outside and the hill-shaped *lingam* and platform inside, where all are welcome to meditate in peace. When this cave became too small, constantly crowded with relatives and devotees, Ramana shifted to another, hidden away in a clump of trees a few minutes further up the hill. He named this one, and the small house built onto it, **Skandashram**, and lived there between 1916 and 1922. The inner cave here is also set aside for meditation, and the front patio affords splendid views across the temple, town and surrounding plains.

Sri Ramanashramam Ashram

The caves can also be reached via the pilgrims' path winding uphill from the **Sri Ramanashramam Ashram** (office daily 8–11am & 2–5pm; ☎04175/237292), 2km south of the temple along the main road. This simple complex is where the sage lived after returning from his retreat on Arunachala, and where his body is today enshrined (Hindus customarily bury saints in the sitting position rather than cremate their bodies). The *samadhi* has become a popular place for Sri Ramana's devotees on pilgrimage, but interested visitors are welcome to stay in the dorms here. There's also an excellent **bookshop** stocking a huge range of titles on the life and teachings of the guru.

Eating

There are plenty of typical South Indian "meals" joints in town. One of the best is the food-only *Aakaash Hotel*, almost opposite the bus stand, which also does very filling *dosas*. Another commendable restaurant in town is the *Deepam*, on Car Street opposite the temple's east entrance, which boasts a cooler "deluxe" wing next door where you can order ice creams and milkshakes; both parts serve excellent *parathas*. Finally, the restaurant at the *Ramakrishna* hotel serves a range of North (and South) Indian food in the evenings, as well as decent lunchtime thalis.

Gingee

An epic landscape of huge boulder hills, interspersed by lush splashes of rice paddy and banana plantations, stretches east of Tiruvannamalai towards the coast. The scenery peaks at **GINGEE** (pronounced "*Shinjee*" and also spelt Senji), 37km east of the Red Mountain, where the ruins of Tamil Nadu's most spectacular **fort** (whole complex, including palace: daily 9am–5pm; Rs100 [Rs5]) sprawl over a vast swathe of sun-scorched granite. If this were anywhere except India, you wouldn't be able to move for interpretative panels and audioguides, but here the miles of crumbling ramparts and temple masonry have been left to the mercy of the weeds and tropical weather. Only on weekends, when bus parties pour around the most accessible monuments, does the site receive more than a trickle of visitors. Come here in the week, and you may well have the place to yourself, save for the odd troupe of monkeys and inquisitive tree squirrels.

Bisected by the main Tiruvannamalai–Puducherry road, Gingee fort comprises three separate citadels, crowning the summits of three dramatic hills: Krishnagiri to the north, Rajagiri to the west and Chandrayandurg to the southeast. Connecting them to form an enormous triangle, 1.5km from north to south, are twenty-metre-thick walls, punctuated by bastions and gateways giving access to the protected zones at the heart of the complex. It's hard to imagine such defences ever being overrun, but they were on numerous occasions following the fort's foundation by the Vijayanagars in the fifteenth century. The Muslim Adil Shahis from Bijapur, Shivaji's Maharatas and the Mughals all conquered Gingee, using it to consolidate the vulnerable southern reaches of their respective empires. The French also took it in 1750, but were ousted by the British after a bloody five-week siege eleven years later.

A network of raised, paved paths links the site's principal landmarks. From the road, head south to the main **east gate**, where a snaking passage emerges, after no fewer than four changes of direction, inside the **palace** enclave. Of the many structures unearthed by archeologists here, the most distinctive is the square seven-storey **Kalyana Mahal tower**, focal point of the former governor's residence; featuring an ingenious hydraulic system that carried water to the uppermost levels, it is crowned by a tapering pyramidal tower. Continue west through a gateway, and you'll pick up the path to **Rajagiri**, Gingee's loftiest citadel; at 165m above the surrounding plain it's a very stiff climb in the heat, but the views are well worth the effort.

The other ruins worth exploring lie a short way beyond the east gate. Typifying Gingee's position at the interface between the warring powers of North and South India is the **mosque of Sadat Ullah Khan I**, built in the early years of the eighteenth century. It stands a stone's throw from the sixteenth-century **Venkatarama temple**, dedicated to an aspect of Vishnu known as "Lord of the Venkata Hills". A dilapidated seven-storey *gopura* caps the east entrance, its passageway carved with scenes from the Ramayana.

Practicalities

Gingee is easily accessible by **bus** from Tiruvannamalai, 37km west, and Puducherry, 68km southeast. You can either alight at the site itself, 2km west of Gingee town, or, if you intend to spend the night there, dump your bags at the hotel and continue to the ruins by auto-rickshaw (Rs50–60 for the return trip; you'll have to settle an additional fee for waiting time). The only **accommodation** to speak of (and the only dependable place to leave luggage while you visit the fort) is the *Shivasand* hotel, on MG Road, opposite the main bus stand (☎04145/222218; ❷–❹), whose *Vasantham* South Indian restaurant is Gingee's classiest place to eat. Note that there are no refreshments, not even drinking water, available at the site, so take your own, or wander 500m back down the road towards town to the small roadside chai stall.

Pondicherry (Puducherry) and Auroville

First impressions of **PONDICHERRY**, the former capital of French India, now officially renamed **Puducherry**, can be unpromising. Instead of the leafy boulevards and *pétanque* pitches you might expect, its messy outer suburbs and bus stand are as cluttered and chaotic as any typical Tamil town. Closer to the seafront, however, the atmosphere grows tangibly more Gallic as the bazaars give way to rows of houses whose shuttered windows and colourwashed facades wouldn't look out of place in Montpellier. For anyone familiar with the British colonial imprint, it can induce culture shock to see richly ornamented Catholic churches, French road names and policemen in de Gaulle-style *képis*. Even today, it is possible to hear French spoken in the street and to see elderly men playing a late afternoon game of *pétanque* in the dusty squares around Ambour Salai and Gingee Salai.

Known to Greek and Roman geographers as "Poduke", Pondicherry was an important staging post on the second-century maritime trade route between Rome and the Far East (a Roman amphitheatre has been unearthed at nearby Arikamedu). When the Roman empire declined, the local Pallava and Chola kings took control, followed by a succession of colonial powers, from the Portuguese in the sixteenth century to the French, Danes and British. The enclave was exchanged several times between them during the various battles and treaties of the Carnatic Wars in the early eighteenth century, finally leaving the small territory in the hands of the French. Finally left in peace, Pondicherry's

△ A game of pétanque, Pondicherry (Puducherry)

heyday dates from the arrival of **Dupleix**, who accepted the governorship in 1742 and immediately set about rebuilding a town decimated by its former British occupants. It was he who instituted the street plan of a central grid encircled by a broad oblong boulevard, bisected north to south by a canal dividing the "Ville Blanche", to the east, from the "Ville Noire", to the west.

Although relinquished by the French in 1954 – when the town became the headquarters of the **Union Territory of Pondicherry**, administering the

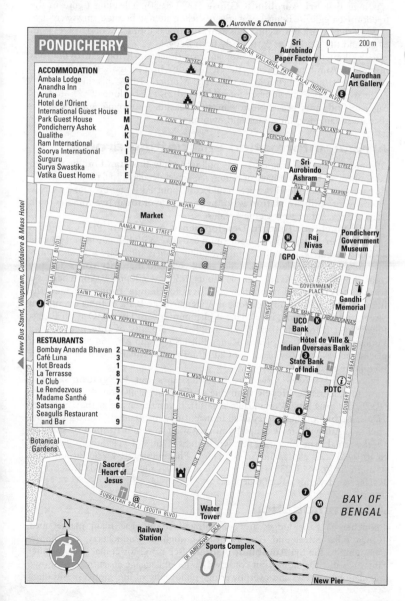

three other former colonial enclaves scattered across South India – Pondicherry's split personality still prevails. West of the canal stretches a bustling Indian market town, while to the east, towards the sea, the streets are emptier, cleaner and decidedly European. The seaside promenade, **Goubert Salai** (formerly Beach Road), has the forlorn look of an out-of-season French resort, complete with its own white Hôtel de Ville. Tanned sun-worshippers share space with grave Europeans in white Indian costume, busy about their spiritual quest. It was here that **Sri Aurobindo Ghose** (1872–1950), a leading figure in the freedom struggle in Bengal, was given shelter after it became unwise to live close to the British in Calcutta. His **ashram** attracts thousands of devotees from all around the world, but particularly from Bengal.

Ten kilometres north, the utopian experiment-in-living **Auroville** was inspired by Aurobindo's disciple, the charismatic Mirra Alfassa, a Parisian painter, musician and mystic better known as "The Mother". Today this slightly surreal place is populated by numbers of expats and visited by long-stay Europeans eager to find inner peace. Nearby are two beaches – Auroville and Serenity – that are suitable for sunbathing and swimming.

Arrival, information and getting around

All buses – local and long distance – pull into **New bus stand** on the western edge of town; for a summary of routes, see Travel details on p.642. From here, a ride into the main hotel district should cost about Rs40–50 by auto-rickshaw. Puducherry's **railway station** is on the south side of town, five minutes' walk from the sea – though it sees few trains.

The **Puducherry Tourism Development Corporation** (PDTC) office is at 40 Goubert Salai (daily 8.45am–5pm; ☎0413/233 9497, ⓦtourism.pon.nic .in). The staff are extremely helpful, providing leaflets and a city map, and information about Auroville; they can also book you onto their **city tours** (full-day tours 9.30am–6pm, Rs110; half-day tours 1.30pm–5.30pm, Rs90). There is a wealth of **ATMs**, and recommended places to **change money** include: the Indian Overseas Bank, in the Hôtel de Ville; the State Bank of India on Surcouf Street; and UCO Bank, Rue Mahe de Labourdonnais. The **GPO** is on Ranga Pillai Street (Mon–Sat 10am–7.30pm). There are plenty of **Internet** joints in Puducherry along Rue Nehru, Ranga Pillai Street and Mission Street. Several places, such as the iWay branch at Club Internet, 36 Nidarajapayar St, also offer Netphone facilities.

Puducherry is well served by auto-rickshaws, but for **getting around** most tourists rent a **bicycle** from one of the many stalls dotted around town (Rs25/day plus Rs200 refundable deposit). If you're staying at the *Park Guest House*, use one of theirs (they're all immaculately maintained). For trips further afield (to Auroville, for example) you may want to rent a **moped** or **scooter**. Of the rental firms operating in town, both Sri Ganesh Cycle Store, 39 Mission St (☎0413/222 2801), and Sri Sri Durga Pharameshwari Cycle Stores, 106B Mission St (☎0413/233 4101), have new models such as Honda Kinetics for Rs100 per day, plus a Rs500 deposit.

Accommodation

Puducherry's basic lodges are concentrated around the main market area, Ranga Pillai Street and Rue Nehru. Throughout Puducherry, guesthouses belonging to the **Sri Aurobindo Ashram** (see p.562 for contact details) offer fantastic value for money, but come with a lot of baggage apart from your own (regulations, curfews and overpowering "philosophy of life" notices). Although supposedly open to all, they are not keen on advertising, or catering to those simply indulging in "spiritual tourism".

Ambala Lodge 92 Ranga Pillai St ☎0413/233 8910. One of the best and most central cheapies. The rooms, some with common bathrooms, are a little poky but clean enough. ❶

Anandha Inn 154 Sardar Vallabhai Patel Salai ☎0413/233 0711, ⓦwww.anandhainn.com. Centrally a/c hotel with seventy luxurious rooms, two restaurants and a cocktail lounge in a gleaming white building. Good value and popular with tour groups, so book well in advance. ❼–❽

Aruna 3 Zamindar Garden, off Sardar Vallabhai Patel Salai ☎0413/233 7756. Situated on a quiet side street, with clean attached doubles of varying sizes. There is a/c and TV in some, and all have balconies. ❷–❹

🕴 **Hotel de l'Orient** 17 Rue Romain Rolland ☎0413/234 3067, ⓦwww.neemranahotels .com. A beautiful, UNESCO heritage-listed French house with sixteen rooms, individually decorated with French antiques, tiled balconies and long shuttered windows overlooking a leafy courtyard restaurant. Wonderfully romantic. ❼–❾

International Guest House 47 Gingee Salai, near the GPO ☎0413/233 6699, ⓔingh@vsnl.net. The largest Aurobindo establishment, with dozens of very large, clean rooms, some with a/c. One of the best budget options in town, and safe for single women. ❷–❸

Park Guest House Goubert Salai ☎0413/223 4412, ⓔparkgh@sriaurobindoashram.org. A Sri Aurobindo Society pad, with strict rules (no alcohol or TVs) and a 10.30pm curfew. Rooms are spotless and very comfortable, however, and are right on the seafront, with new mozzie nets and sit outs overlooking a well-watered garden. There's also bike rental, laundry and restaurant. ❸

Pondicherry Ashok Chinnakalapet, 12km from Puducherry on the old coastal road to Mamal-lapuram, near Auroville ☎0413/265 5160,

ⓦwww.theashokgroup.com. Comfortable rooms in a quiet, breezy location on the seashore. There's a children's park, restaurant, barbecue and bar, plus generous discounts for stays of three days or more. ❼–❽

Qualithe 3 Rue Mahe de Labourdonnais ☎0413/233 4325, ⓔrajarathnam@engineer.com. Pondy's most characterful budget lodge, in a slightly rickety old French building. Upstairs, big, spotless rooms that fit four lead off a pleasant balcony with wicker chairs and great views over Government Place. Just one cheap single. ❸

Ram International 398 Anna Salai ☎ & ⓕ0413/233 7230. Very good-value, efficient, modern place on the western edge of town. Advance booking recommended. ❸–❹

Soorya International 55 Ranga Pillai St ☎0413/233 6856, ⓔhotelsooryainternational @hotmail.com. Central hotel with very large, immaculate rooms. Prices are reasonable, despite the ostentatious exterior. ❹–❺

Surguru 104 Sardar Vallabhai Patel Salai ☎0413/233 9022. A decent-value, mid-range option, with spruce, spacious rooms, brisk service and most mod cons, including an excellent veg restaurant. ❹–❺

Surya Swastika 11 ID Koil St ☎0413/234 3092, ⓔsuryaswastika@sify.com. Traditional guesthouse in a quiet corner of town, with nine basic rooms around a central courtyard that doubles as a pilgrims' canteen at lunchtime. Incredibly cheap, and cleaner than most of the bazaar lodges. ❶–❸

🕴 **Vatika Guest Home** 67 François Martin St ☎0413/233 3980, ⓦwww .vatikaguesthome.com. Spanking new mid-range place near the sea. in the quiet north end of the old town, with classy rooms bedecked with paintings and a couple of kitchenettes, plus a boutique in reception. Great value. ❹

The Town

Puducherry's beachside promenade, **Goubert Salai**, is a favourite place for a stroll, with cafés and bars to idle in and cooling breezes blowing in off the sea. There's little to do, other than watch the world go by, but the Hôtel de Ville, today housing the municipal offices, is still an impressive spectacle, and a four-metre-high Gandhi memorial, surrounded by ancient columns, dominates the northern end of the promenade. Nearby, a French memorial commemorates Indian soldiers from French territories who lost their lives in World War I.

Just north of the Hôtel de Ville, a couple of streets back from the promenade, is the leafy old French-provincial-style square now named **Government Place**. A fountain stands at the centre, while among the square's paths and lawns are a number of sculptures carved in nearby Gingee. On its northern side, guarded by policemen in red *képis*, the impressive, gleaming white **Raj Nivas**, official home to the present lieutenant governor of Puducherry Territory, was built late in the eighteenth century for Joseph Francis Dupleix, who became governor of French India. Unfortunately, the home of Ananda Ranga Pillai (1709–61), *dubash*, or close adviser, of Dupleix – once one of the highlights of a visit to Puducherry – is now closed to the public.

The **Pondicherry Government Museum** (Tues–Sun 10am–5pm; Rs2), on Ranga Pillai Street opposite Government Place, has an archeological collection comprising Neolithic and 2000-year-old remains from Arikamedu, a few Pallava (sixth–eighth centuries) and Buddhist (tenth century) stone sculptures, bronzes, weapons and paintings. Alongside these are displayed a bizarre collection of French salon furniture and bric-a-brac from local houses, including a velvet S-shaped "conversation seat".

The **Sri Aurobindo Ashram**, 300m north of Government Place on Rue de la Marine (daily 8am–noon & 2–6pm; no children under 3; @www .sriaurobindosociety.org.in), is one of the best known and wealthiest ashrams in India, founded in 1926 by the Bengali philosopher-guru Aurobindo Ghose and his chief disciple, personal manager and mouthpiece, "The Mother". It now serves as the headquarters of the Sri Aurobindo Society (or SAS), which today owns most of the valuable property and real estate in Puducherry, and wields what many consider to be a disproportionate influence over the town. A beautifully maintained small rockery, cactus and flower garden greet you as you enter the compound. The **samadhi**, or mausoleum, of Sri Aurobindo and "The Mother" is covered daily with flowers and usually surrounded by supplicants with their hands and heads placed on the tomb. Inside the main building is an incongruous and very bourgeois-looking Western-style room, complete with three-piece suite, where "The Mother" and Sri Aurobindo used to chill out. Avoid treading on the Persian carpet, as devotees prostrate themselves here. The **bookshop** next door has Aurobindo literature and details of the various cultural programmes put on in the building opposite.

The **Aurodhan Art Gallery**, at 11 Thillai Nattar St, just off SV Patel Salai (Mon–Sat 9.30am–7pm; free), is a peaceful sanctuary dedicated to contemporary Indian art. The permanent exhibition showcases the talent of local artists, with pictures and sculptures lining the rooms and corridors of both floors. Many of the exhibits reflect the influence of Sri Aurobindo or the environment of Auroville, and there are some excellent portraits. Five minutes' walk away is the **Sri Aurobindo Paper Factory**, on SV Patel Salai (Mon–Sat 8.30am–noon & 1.30–5pm; free), where you can watch the fascinating and laborious process of making the handmade paper that is sold in tourist spots all over India.

In the southwest of town, near the railway station, is the huge cream and brown **Sacred Heart of Jesus**, one of Puducherry's finest Catholic churches, built by French missionaries in the 1700s. Nearby, the shady **Botanical Gardens** (daily 9.30am–6pm; free), established in 1826, offer many quiet paths to wander. The French planted nine hundred species of imported trees, shrubs and flowers here, experimenting to see how they would fare in Indian conditions; one, the *Khaya senegalensis*, has grown to a height of 25m.

Eating

If you've been on the road for a while and are hankering for healthy salads, fresh coffee, crusty bread, cakes and real pastry, you'll be spoilt for choice in Puducherry. Unlike the traveller-oriented German-Bakery-style places elsewhere in the country, the Western **restaurants** here cater for a predominantly expatriate clientele with discerning palettes and fat euro pay cheques. Cheap **beer** is available just about everywhere except the SAS-owned establishments, and indeed some travellers maintain that this is the only reason to visit Pondy – the ubiquitous presence of the restaurant-cum-bar and predominance of male drinkers can be off-putting to some female travellers. Many mid-range hotels have their own bars, which may feel less seamy than some of the downtown joints.

Bombay Ananda Bhavan 199 Mission St. Good, quiet and very hygienic South Indian veg joint, serving particularly fine masala dosas.

Café Luna Rue Suffren, near the State Bank of India. A little hole in the wall where old men gather to drink coffee and pass the time of day. The coffee is prepared with great pomp and style, and the ultra-cheap lunch-time plate of lemon rice and *vada* is absolutely superb.

Hot Breads 42 Ambour Salai. Crusty croissants, fresh baguettes, and delicious savoury pastry snacks, served in a squeaky-clean French *boulangerie*-café full of French expats.

La Terrasse 5 Subbaiyah Salai. The most popular French restaurant amongst European backpackers, who hang out here to devour croissants and cappuccino alfresco. Excellent prawn dishes start at Rs80, pizzas go for Rs70–175, and there's also a range of Indian, Chinese and French food. Closed Wed.

Le Club 33 Dumas St. One of the best-known eateries, and not quite as expensive as you might expect. The predominantly French menu features their famous coq au vin, steak au poivre, plenty of seafood options (each at around Rs200) and a full wine list, plus cocktails (Rs150). There's also a bistro downstairs that is great for Sunday brunch. It's closed Mon but there is also a Vietnamese and Southeast Asian restaurant in the same complex that's open daily.

Le Rendezvous 30 Rue Suffren. Filling seafood sizzlers, fantastic pizza and tandoori brochettes are specialities of this popular expat-oriented restaurant. They also serve fresh croissants and espresso for breakfast. Dine indoors or up on the more romantic rooftop, where you can relax to eclectic sounds in the evenings. Most main dishes Rs120–250.

Madame Santhé's Romain Rolland St. Friendly, attractively designed and atmospheric roof terrace serving a mixture of extremely tasty French, Indian and Chinese dishes for Rs100–150. Their steak in mushroom sauce is a delight. More laid back and better value than the established quality restaurants.

Satsanga 30 Rue La Bourdonnais. The menu, devised by the French patron, in this converted colonial mansion is carefully prepared: organic salads with fresh herbs, tzatziki and garlic bread, sauté potatoes, tagliatelle alla carbonara and mouthwatering pizzas, washed down with chilled beer. Check their *plat du jour* for fresh fish dishes. Around Rs400 per head for three courses, with drinks.

Seagulls Restaurant and Bar Dumas St. Reasonably priced, open-air rooftop restaurant in a breezy spot right next to the sea, new pier and cargo harbour. Huge, inexpensive menu, with veg dishes, meat, seafood, Indian, Chinese and even some Italian (pizza and spaghetti).

Auroville

The most New Age place anywhere in India must surely be **AUROVILLE**, the planned "City of Dawn", 10km north of Puducherry, which covers an area of some fifty or so square kilometres just outside the Union Territory in Tamil Nadu. Founded in 1968, Auroville was inspired by "The Mother", the spiritual successor to Sri Aurobindo. Around 1350 people live in communes here (two-thirds of them non-Indians), with names such as Fertile, Certitude, Sincerity, Revelation and Transformation, in what it is hoped will eventually be a city with a population of 50,000 people. Architecturally experimental buildings, combining modern Western and traditional Indian elements, are set in a rural landscape of narrow lanes, deep red earth and lush greenery. Income is derived from ecofriendly agriculture, handicrafts and home-made foodstuffs, alternative technology, educational and development projects and Aurolec, a computer software company. The entire complex is run on natural

Trouble in Paradise

The avowed aim of the Auroville commune is harmony, leading a life made meaningful through hard physical work backed up by a spiritual discipline of inner consciousness, rather than dogma, rule or ritual behaviour. Nonetheless, the place has had its ups and downs, not least of which have been the **disputes** between the community and the Sri Aurobindo Society (SAS) over ownership since the death of "The Mother" in 1973. Rejecting the Aurovillians' calls for self-determination, the SAS cut off funds to the community, forcing its members to become financially self-sufficient. The power struggle intensified in the mid-1970s, erupting into full-blown violence on a couple of occasions before the police were called in. At one stage, the war of attrition got so tough that some Western countries had to provide aid to the Aurovillians. Eventually, however, the High Court ruled in their favour, and in 1988 the Auroville Foundations Act was passed, placing responsibility for the administration of the settlement in the hands of a seven-member council, with representatives from the state government, the SAS and Auroville itself.

One of the accusations levelled at the settlers around the time of the Act was that, although Auroville was supposedly an egalitarian community, most of the Indians involved were being relegated to the status of labourers. Aurovillians countered these attacks by pointing to the numerous ways they had worked to improve the lives of low-caste Tamils in the surrounding villages, many of whom had been given full-time jobs manufacturing textiles, software and non-polluting unbaked bricks. Although some efforts have been made to integrate the locals more into the community, there's still a sense of New Age colonialism about the place. One very positive development, however, has been the school for local Tamil children started by a retired policeman from Essex in England.

energy generated by solar panels and windmills, and water is drawn using wind turbines.

Despite all this, there is in fact very little to see here, and Auroville attracts a disproportionately large number of day-trippers – much to the chagrin of its inhabitants, who rightly point out that you can only get a sense of what the settlement is all about if you stay a while. However, interested visitors are welcomed as paying guests in most of the communes, where you can work alongside permanent residents (see opposite).

The Matri Mandir

Auroville has seen its fair share of conflict (see box above), but there is one thing that unites the whole community: the **Matri Mandir**, or "dwelling place of The Mother", a gigantic hi-tech meditation hall at the heart of the site, 36m in diameter. Begun in 1970, the space-age structure was conceived as "a symbol of the Divine's answer to man's inspiration for perfection". Soil from 126 countries was symbolically placed in an urn, and is kept in a concrete cone in the amphitheatre adjacent to Matri Mandir, from where a speaker can address an audience of 3000 without amplification. In accordance with the instructions of "The Mother", this is open to all, although the Aurovillians' reluctance to admit outsiders is palpable. After obtaining tickets (9am–noon & 2–4pm; free) from the visitor centre (see opposite), you have to watch an orientation video giving strict instructions on how to behave while inside. Then, after sometimes lengthy queues, visitors are ushered in silence to the Matri Mandir's ramped entrance. You are allowed a fleeting glimpse of the seventy-centimetre crystal ball that forms its focal point, made by the German optical company, Carl Zeiss, which is believed to be the largest of its kind in the world. Contrary to the intentions of the architects, the whole experience can leave a bad taste in your mouth: the Aurovillians clearly hate having to herd day-trippers through what most of them regard as the soul of their community. You are likely to get a different reaction if you arrange to stay longer in the community, whereby you will be allowed longer access to the Matri Mandir. Only then, Aurovillians claim, will you appreciate the real significance of the place.

Practicalities

You can reach Auroville from Puducherry either on the main Chennai road or via the new coastal highway, turning off at the village of Chinna Mudaliarcha-vadi. **Bus** services are frequent along both routes but – as Auroville is so spread out – it's best to come with your own transport, at the very least a bike. Most people rent a scooter or **motorcycle** from Puducherry and ride up. Alternatively, there are PTDC's daily **tours**, bookable at the Pondy office (see p.560).

For a pre-visit primer, call in at the **visitor centre** (daily 9am–5.30pm; ☎0413/262 2239), bang in the middle of the site. Nearby is the **Bharat Niwas**, which holds a permanent exhibition on the history and philosophies of the settlement. Apart from getting tickets to visit the Matri Mandir, you can also pick up some inexpensive literature on Auroville in the adjacent bookshop and check out a notice board for details of **activities** in which visitors may participate (these typically include yoga, reiki and Vipassana meditation, costing around Rs100 per session). In addition, there are a couple of quality handicraft outlets and several pleasant little vegetarian cafés serving snacks, meals and cold drinks.

The information desk at the visitor centre (see above) is the place to enquire about **paying guest accommodation** in Auroville's thirty or so communes. Officially there's no lower limit on the time you have to stay, but visitors are encouraged to stick around for at least a week, helping out on communal projects; tariffs range from Rs100 to Rs500 per day, depending on levels of comfort. Alternatively, you can arrange to stay in one of the four guesthouses, which offer a/c rooms for Rs1500. It's advisable to book well in advance (☎0413/262 2704, ✉avguests@auroville.org.in), especially during the peak periods from December to March and from July to August, as accommodation is in short supply. Otherwise, the best of the very limited options nearby is the *Satsanga Guest House* (☎0413/222 5867, ✉pierre_satsanga@yahoo.com; ❷–❸), only 500m from the beach, which has a choice of attached or non-attached rooms and a two-bedroom flat (❹). For **food**, you won't do better than the excellent vegetarian meals served in Auroville itself.

Central Tamil Nadu

To be on the banks of the Cauvery listening to the strains of Carnatic music is to have a taste of eternal bliss

Tamil proverb

Continuing south of Puducherry along the Coromandel coast you enter the flat landscape of the **Cauvery** (aka Kaveri) **Delta**, an intensely green world of paddy fields cut by thirty major rivers, canals, dams, dykes and rivulets that has been intensively farmed since ancient times. Only a hundred miles in diameter, it forms the rice bowl of Tamil Nadu. The **Cauvery** is the largest river, known in Tamil as Ponni, "The Lady of Gold" (a form of the Mother Goddess), and is revered as a conduit of liquid *shakti*, the primordial female energy that nurtures the millions of farmers who live on her banks and tributaries. Three bumper crops each year are coaxed from the giant patchwork of paddy, which Colonel Fullarton in his *View of English Interests in India* (1785) described as "teeming with an industrious race expert in agriculture". Amid the stifling heat of mid-July, on the eighteenth day of the solar month Adi, villagers have for hundreds, possibly thousands, of years gathered in vast numbers to mark the rising of the river. During the festival, money, cloth, jewellery, food, tools and household utensils are thrown into the river as offerings, so that the goddess will have all she needs for the coming year. From October until December the delta is washed with the powerful second annual monsoon, bringing a rich harvest of rainwater for the paddy. This is one of the most beautiful periods of the year, as diagonal swathes of rain sweep across the endless green fields between bursts of dazzling sunshine, and the sunrise is pure and clear after stormy nights.

This mighty delta formed the heartland of the **Chola** empire, which reached its apogee between the ninth and thirteenth centuries, an era often compared to classical Greece and Renaissance Italy both for its cultural richness and the sheer scale and profusion of its architectural creations. Much as the Cholas originally intended, every visitor is immediately in awe of their huge temples, not only in cities such as **Chidambaram**, **Kumbakonam**, **Thanjavur** and **Thiruvarur**, but also out in the countryside at places like **Gangaikonda-cholapuram**, where the magnificent temple is all that remains of a once-great city. Exploring the area for a few days will bring you into contact with the more delicate side of Chola artistic expression, such as the magnificent **bronzes** of Thanjavur, and the incantatory **saints' hymns** of the *sangam* and *Tevaram* – bodies of oral poetry that emerged in the delta more than a thousand years ago. Its composers were wandering poets who travelled the length and breadth of the South, singing, dancing and spreading a new devotional brand of Hinduism known as **bhakti**. Phrased in classical Tamil and with a richness rarely equalled since, their verses praise the beauty of the delta's natural landscape and recall the significance of the countless shrines and sacred sites (more than half of the 274 holy Shaivite places in Tamil Nadu are found here). Considering many were not set down in Sanskrit until centuries after they were composed, it's a miracle that the hymns have survived at all. But today they form the basis of a thriving oral tradition, sung in temples, *maths* (religious institutions), pilgrims' buses and homes wherever Tamil is the lingua franca. The poems have also provided the raw material for many a hit mythological movie, and you'll hear modern versions of the better-known ones, jazzed up with electric guitars and synthe-sizers, blaring out of CD and audio-cassette stores.

Nowhere else in the world has a classical civilization survived till the twenty-first century, and the knowledge that the ancient culture of the Cholas endures here alongside their awesome monuments lends a unique resonance to any journey across the Cauvery Delta.

Away from the ancient cities, the region has some further attractions to explore. On the quiet central coast itself, the old Danish colony of **Tharam-gambadi** boasts some splendid colonial architecture and an imposing fort. Further south, on either side of the busy port of Nagapattinam, the important Muslim and Catholic pilgrimage centres of **Nagur** and **Velankanni** attract large numbers of devotees to the *dargah* and church respectively. This stretch of coast comes to an end in the sleepy wetlands of the bird sanctuary at

Kodikkarai (Point Calimere). Back inland and to the southwest of Thanjavur, **Tiruchirapalli** (Trichy) is a large and bustling commercial hub, well worth a stop for the massive temple complex of Srirangam, just across the river from the city centre. Some other outlying temples and ashrams also surround the city.

Chidambaram

CHIDAMBARAM, 58km south of Puducherry, is so steeped in myth that its history is hard to unravel. As the site of the *tandava*, the cosmic dance of Shiva as **Nataraja**, King of the Dance, it is one of the holiest Hindu sites in South India, and a visit to the **Sabhanayaka Nataraja temple** affords a fascinating glimpse into ancient Tamil religious practice and belief. The legendary king **Hiranyavarman** is said to have made a pilgrimage here from Kashmir, seeking to rid himself of leprosy by bathing in the temple's Shivaganga tank. In thanks for a successful cure, he enlarged the temple and brought in 3000 brahmins of the Dikshitar caste. Their descendants, distinguishable by top-knots of hair at the front of their heads, are the ritual specialists of the temple to this day.

Few of the fifty *maths*, or monasteries, that once stood here remain, but the temple itself is still a hive of activity and hosts numerous **festivals**. The two most important are ten-day affairs, building up to spectacular finales: on the ninth day of each, temple chariots process through the four Car streets in the **Car festival**, while on the tenth day, **abhishekham**, the principal deities in the Raja Sabha (thousand-pillared hall) are anointed. For exact dates (one is in May/June, the other in Dec/Jan), contact any TTDC tourist office and plan well ahead, as they are very popular. Other local festivals include fire-walking and *kavadi* folk dance (dancing with decorated wooden frames on the head)

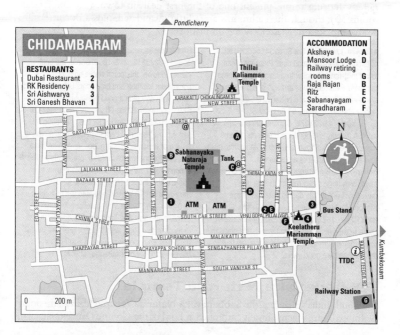

at the Thillai Kaliamman Kali (April/May) and Keelatheru Mariamman (July/Aug) temples.

The town also has a hectic market and a large student population, based at Annamalai University's centre of Tamil studies in the east. Among the simple thatched huts in the flat, sparsely populated surrounding countryside, which becomes very dry and dusty in summer, the only solid-looking structures are the small roadside temples, most of which are devoted to Aiyannar, the village deity who protects borders, and whose shrines are flanked with *kudirais*, brightly painted terracotta or wooden figures of horses.

Arrival, information and accommodation

Chidambaram revolves around the Sabhanayaka Temple and the busy market area that surrounds it, along North, East, South and West Car streets. Though little more than a country halt, the **railway station**, just over 1km southeast of the centre, has good connections both north and south, and boasts retiring rooms and, on platform 1, a **post office** (Mon–Sat 9am–1pm & 1.30–5pm). Frequent buses from Chennai, Thanjavur, Mamallapuram and Madurai pull in at the **bus stand**, also in the southeast, but nearer the centre, about 500m from the temple.

Staff at the TTDC **tourist office** (Mon–Fri 10am–5.30pm; ☏04144/238739), next to the *Vandayar Gateway Inn* hotel on Railway Feeder Road, are charming and helpful, but only have a small pamphlet to give visitors. None of the **banks** in Chidambaram change money, although the *Saradharam* hotel, near the bus stand, will change cash; there are ATMs in the hotel forecourt and a couple more on South Car Street. **Internet** is also available at the *Saradharam*, as well as at I-Castle, by the east entrance to the temple.

Chidambaram abounds in budget **accommodation** aimed at the influx of tourists and pilgrims, but there are also a few decent mid-range options. The railway retiring rooms present one of the best deals in town, with huge clean rooms (❶); though the bathrooms are a little dilapidated, plus a dorm (Rs50). Ask at the Station Master's office on platform 1.

Akshaya 17/18 East Car St ☏04144/220192, ⓔakshayahotel@hotmail.com. Pleasant, clean, lower mid-range hotel with a lawn backing onto the temple wall. There is a range of a/c and non-a/c, though the latter are better value. ❸–❹

Mansoor Lodge 91 East Car St ☏04144/221072, ⓔmansoorlodge@hotmail.com. A friendly and good-value cheapie. Rooms have spotless tiled floors and clean bathrooms, all freshly painted, and TVs are available. ❶

Railway retiring rooms One of the best deals in town, with huge clean rooms, though the bathrooms are a little dilapidated. Ask at the Station Master's Office on platform 1. ❷

Raja Rajan 162 West Car St ☏04144/222690. Close to the west gate of the temple, this place has clean rooms with tiled bathrooms and low tariffs; the a/c ones are good value. ❶–❸

Ritz 2 VGP St, near the bus stand ☏04114/223312, ⓕ221098. One of the best places in town, this comfortable hotel boasts a convenient location and big rooms (all with TV, and some with a/c) plus a good restaurant. ❸–❹

Sabanayagam 22 East Sannathi St, off East Car St ☏04144/220896. Despite its flashy exterior, this is just a run-of-the-mill budget place. Rooms have a choice of Indian or Western loos, and some have a/c; ask for one with a window, preferably on the second floor overlooking the temple entrance. There's also a good veg restaurant. ❷–❹

Saradharam 19 VGP St, opposite the bus stand ☏04144/221336, ⓦwww.hotelsaradharam.com. Large, clean and well-kept rooms (some with a/c) in modern buildings, with three decent restaurants (including one non-veg), a small garden, bar, laundry and foreign exchange. ❸–❹

Sabhanayaka Nataraja Temple

For South India's Shaivites, the **Sabhanayaka Nataraja Temple** (daily 4am–noon & 4pm–10pm), where Shiva is enthroned as Lord of the Cosmic Dance (Nataraja),

△ Detail from the Sabhanayaka Nataraja Temple, Chidambaram

is the holiest of holies. Its huge *gopuras*, whose lights are used as landmarks by sailors far out to sea in the Bay of Bengal, soar above a 55-acre complex, divided by four concentric walls. The oldest parts now standing were built under the Cholas, who adopted Nataraja as their chosen deity and crowned several kings here. Four gates on each side of the rectangular outermost wall afford entry, so if you have the time the best way to tackle the complex is to work slowly inwards from the third enclosure in clockwise circles. **Guides** are readily available but tend to shepherd visitors towards the central shrine too quickly. Frequent devotional (puja) **ceremonies** take place at the innermost sanctum, the most popular being at noon and 6pm, when a fire is lit, great gongs are struck and devotees rush forward to catch a last glimpse of the *lingam* before the doors are shut. On Friday nights before the temple closes, during a particularly elaborate puja, Nataraja is carried on a palanquin accompanied by music and attendants carrying flaming torches and tridents. At other times, you'll hear ancient devotional hymns from the *Tevaram*.

Unlike most major temples in Tamil Nadu, which are funded by the state, Chidambaram is a privately owned and dependent solely upon pilgrims' donations. This has at times led to tourists being **hassled** by aggressive members of the Dikshitar brahmin families who own and maintain the temple for unreasonable donations. Recently, however, the Dikshitars seem to have been behaving in a more godly fashion and, as long as you avoid being lured into signing the guest book within the temple's second enclosure, you should not be held to ransom.

The third enclosure

Four gigantic *gopura* towers rise out of the irregular third wall, each with a granite base and a brick-built superstructure of diminishing storeys covered in a profusion of carved figures. The western *gopura* is the most popular entrance, as well as being the most elaborately carved and probably the oldest (c.1150 AD). Turning north (left) from here, you come to the colonnaded **Shivaganga tank**, the site of seven natural springs. From the broken pillar at the tank's edge, all four *gopuras* are visible.

Shiva and Kali's dance

The image of **Shiva** dancing in the wheel of fire is now known throughout the world, though far fewer people are familiar with its mythological origins in Chidambaram. The thousand-headed cosmic serpent, **Adisesha**, upon whose coiled body Vishnu reclines in the primordial ocean, once expressed a wish to see Shiva's famed dance. Having arranged time off from his normal duties with Vishnu, Adisesha prayed to Shiva, who was so impressed by the serpent's entreaties that he promised to dance in the forest of Tillai (the site of Chidambaram). Adisesha was reborn as the human sage **Patanjali** (represented as half-man, half-snake) and made straight for Tillai. There he met another sage who shared his wish to see Shiva dance, **Vyaghrapada** – "Tiger Feet", who had been granted the claws of a tiger to help him climb trees and pluck the best flowers to offer Shiva. Together, they worshipped a *svayambhulingam*, a *shivalingam* that had "self-manifested" in the forest, now housed in the Mulasthana shrine of Sabhanayaka temple. However, the guardian of the forest, who turned out to be the goddess **Kali**, refused to allow Shiva to dance when he arrived. In response, he challenged her to a **dance competition** for possession of the forest. Kali agreed but, perhaps due to modesty, she could not match a pose of Shiva's – it involved raising the right foot above the head. Defeated, Kali was forced to move off a little way north, where a temple now stands in her honour.

Facing the tank, on the left side, is the **Shivakamasundari Temple**, devoted to Parvati, consort of Shiva. Step inside to see the Nayak (sixteenth-century) ceiling paintings arranged in cartoon-like frames in muted reds and yellows. On the right as you enter, the story of the leper king Hiranyavarman is illustrated and, at the back, frames form a map of the temple complex. Next door, in the northwest corner, a shrine to Subrahmanya, the son of Shiva, is adorned with paintings illustrating stories from the *Skanda Purana*. Beyond this, in front of the northern *gopura*, stands a small shrine to the Navagraha (nine planets).

In the northeast corner, the largest building in the complex, the **Raja Sabha** (fourteenth to fifteenth century) is also known as "the thousand-pillared hall"; tradition holds that there are only nine hundred and ninety-nine actual pillars, the thousandth being Shiva's leg. During festivals the deities Nataraja and Shivakamasundari are brought here and mounted on a dais for the anointing ceremony, *abhishekha*.

The importance of **dance** at Chidambaram is underlined by the reliefs of dancing figures inside the east *gopura* demonstrating 108 *karanas* (a similar set is to be found in the west *gopura*). A *karana* (or *adavu* in Tamil) is a specific point in a phase of movement prescribed by the extraordinarily comprehensive Sanskrit treatise on the performing arts, the *Natya Shastra* (c.200 BC–200 AD) – the basis of all classical dance, music and theatre in India. A caption from the *Natya Shastra* surmounts each *karana* niche. Four other niches are filled with images of patrons and *stahapatis* – the sculptors and designers responsible for the iconography and positioning of deities.

A pavilion at the south *gopura* houses an image of Nandi, Shiva's bull. Although not accessible from here, the central Nataraja shrine faces south; as with all Shiva temples, Nandi sits opposite the god. In the southwest corner, a shrine contains one of the largest images in India of the elephant-headed son of Shiva, Ganapati (Ganesh). If you stand inside the entrance (*mandapa*), with your back to Ganapati, you'll see carvings of the two important devotees of Nataraja (see box above) at the base of the two pillars nearest the shrine. To the right is the sage Patanjali, with a snake's body, and on the left Vyaghrapada, with a human body and tiger's feet.

The second enclosure

To get into the square **second enclosure**, head for its western entrance (just north of the west *gopura* in the third wall) which leads into a circumambulatory passageway. Once beyond this second wall it's easy to become disorientated, as the roofed inner enclosures see little light and are supported by a maze of colonnades. The atmosphere is immediately more charged, reaching its peak at the very centre.

On the north side, the **Mulasthana** houses the *svayambhulingam* (see box opposite) worshipped by Patanjali and Vyaghrapada. The **Deva Sabha**, or "hall of the gods", on the east, shelters as many as a hundred bronze images used in processions and is a meeting place for the Dikshitars. Beyond it lies the other, eastern, entrance to the second enclosure.

The **Nritta Sabha**, or "dance hall", stands on the site where Shiva outdanced Kali (see box opposite), now the southwest corner of the second enclosure. Probably the oldest surviving structure of the two inner areas, its raised platform was fashioned in stone to resemble a wooden temple chariot, or *ratha*. Before they were inexplicably concreted over in the mid-1950s, the east and west sides of the base were each adorned with a wheel and a horse; all that can be seen now are fragments.

The innermost enclosure

Passing through the southern entrance (marked by a gold flagstaff) to the **innermost enclosure** brings you immediately into a hallway which leads west to the nearby **Govindaraja shrine**, dedicated to Vishnu – a surprise in this most Shaivite of environments. The deity is attended by non-Dikshitar brahmins, who, it is said, don't always get along with the Dikshitars. From outside the shrine, non-Hindus can see through to the most sacred part of the temple, the **Kanaka Sabha** and the **Chit Sabha**, adjoining raised structures, roofed with copper and gold plate and linked by a hallway. Two huge bells and extremely loud *nagaswarams* (double-reed wind instruments), *tavils* (drums) and *nattuvangams* (cymbals) call worshippers for ceremonies. The only entrance – closed to non-Hindus – is up five silver-plated steps into the Chit Sabha, guarded by the devotees Vyaghrapada and Patanjali and lit by an arc of flickering oil lamps.

The Chit Sabha houses bronze images of Nataraja and his consort Shivakamasundari. Behind and to the left of Nataraja, a curtain, sacred to Shiva and strung with rows of leaves from the *bilva* tree, demarcates the most potent area of all. Within it lies the **Akashalingam**, known as the *rahasya*, or "secret", of Chidambaram; made of the most subtle of the elements, Ether (*akasha*) – from which Air, Fire, Water and Earth are born – the *lingam* is invisible. This is said to signify that God is nowhere, only in the human heart.

A crystal *lingam*, said to have emanated from the light of the crescent moon on Shiva's brow, and a small ruby Nataraja are worshipped in the Kanaka Sabha. They are ritually bathed in the flames of the priests' camphor fire or oil lamps six times a day. This inner area is where you're most likely to hear **oduvars**, hereditary singers from the middle, non-brahmin castes, intoning verses of ancient Tamil poetry. The songs with which they regale the deities at puja time, drawn from compilations such the *Tevaram* or earlier *Sangam*, are believed to be more than a thousand years old.

Eating

There are plenty of basic, wholesome "meals" places on and around the Car streets – the *Sri Ganesh Bhavan*, on West Car Street, gets the locals' vote. East of the Sabhanayaka temple, the *Sri Aishwarya*, by the clocktower near the bus stand, is a clean, modern South Indian and Chinese veg restaurant, or, close by, there's the airy rooftop restaurant at the *RK Residency*, which serves non-veg, both Indian and Chinese. Alternatively, on Venu Gopal Pillai (VGP) Street is the Middle Eastern *Dubai Restaurant*, a tiny hole in the wall serving tasty kebabs, fish and other non-veg fare.

Gangaikondacholapuram

Devised as the centrepiece of a city built by the Chola king Rajendra I (1014–42 AD) to celebrate his conquests, the magnificent **Brihadishwara temple** stands in the tiny village of **GANGAIKONDACHOLAPURAM**, in Trichy District, 35km north of Kumbakonam. The tongue-twisting name means "the town of the Chola who took the Ganges". Under Rajendra I, the Chola empire did indeed stretch as far as the great river of the north, an unprecedented achievement for a southern dynasty. Aside from the temple and the rubble remains of Rajendra's palace, 2km east at Tamalikaimedu, nothing of the city remains. Nonetheless, this is among the most extraordinary archeological sites of South India, outshone only by Thanjavur, and devoid of visitors most of the time, which gives it a memorably forlorn feel.

Buses run here from Kumbakonam every five minutes (1hr–1hr 30min), and Gangaikondacholapuram is also served by some between Trichy and Chidambaram; to move on, buses back to Kumbakonam pass through the village every ten minutes. Be sure not to get stuck here between noon and 4pm when the temple is closed. Parts of the interior are extremely dark, and a torch is useful. Facilities in the surrounding village are minimal beyond a couple of chai shops.

Brihadishwara Temple

Dominating the village landscape, the **Brihadishwara Temple** (daily 6am–noon & 4–8pm; free) is enclosed by a rectangular wall; visitors enter through a gateway to the north, separated from the main road by a car park. You must remove your shoes and leave them at the hut in the corner of the car park, to the right of the main gateway entrance. From the gateway, you arrive at a well-maintained, grassy courtyard, flanked by a closed hallway (*mandapa*). Over the sanctuary, to the right, a massive pyramidal tower (*vimana*) rises 55m in nine diminishing storeys. Though smaller than the one at Thanjavur, the tower's graceful curve gives it an impressive refinement. At the entrance you're likely to meet an ASI caretaker, who can act as a guide to all the deities sculpted on the temple; you will also be shown the lovingly tended gardens.

Turning right (north) inside the courtyard, before you reach a small shrine to the goddess **Durga**, containing an image of Mahishasuramardini (the slaying of the buffalo demon), you come across a small well guarded by a lion statue known as Simha-kinaru and made from plastered brickwork. King Rajendra is said to have had Ganges water placed in the well to be used for the ritual anointing of the *lingam* in the main temple. The lion, representing Chola kingly power, bows to the huge Nandi respectfully seated before the eastern entrance of the temple, in line with the *shivalingam* contained within.

Directly in front of the eastern entrance to the temple stands a small altar for offerings. Two parallel flights of stairs ascend to a porch, the *mukhamandapa*, where a large pair of guardian deities flank the entrance to the long pillared hallway.

Immediately inside the temple a guide can show you the way to the tower, up steep steps. On either side of the temple doorway, sculptures of Shiva in his various benevolent (*anugraha*) manifestations include him blessing Vishnu, Devi, Ravana and the saint Chandesha. In the northeast corner an unusual square stone block features carvings of the nine planets (*navagraha*). A number of **Chola bronzes** (see p.761) stand on the platform; the figure of Karttikeya, the war god, carrying a club and a shield, is thought to have had particular significance.

The base of the main temple sanctuary is decorated with lions and scrollwork. Above this decoration, running from the southern to the northern entrance of the *ardhamandapa*, a series of sculpted figures in plastered niches, portray different images of Shiva. The most famous is at the northern entrance, showing Shiva and Parvati garlanding the saint Chandesha, who here is sometimes identified as Rajendra I.

Two minutes' walk northeast along the main road (turn right from the car park), the tiny **Archeological Museum** (daily except Fri 10am–1pm & 2–5.45pm; free) contains locally discovered Chola odds and ends including terracotta lamps, coins, weapons, tiles, bronze, bangle pieces, palm-leaf manuscripts and an old Chinese pot.

Kumbakonam and around

Sandwiched between the Cauvery (Kaveri) and Arasalar rivers is the busy town **KUMBAKONAM**, 74km southwest of Chidambaram and 38km northeast of Thanjavur. Kumbakonam is believed by Hindus to be the place where the water pot (*kumba*) of *amrita*, the ambrosial beverage of immortality, was washed up by a great deluge from atop sacred Mount Meru in the Himalayas. Shiva, who just happened to be passing the pot in the guise of a wild forest-dwelling hunter, for some reason fired an arrow at the pot, causing it to break. From the shards, he made the *lingam* that is now enshrined in the **Kumbareshwara Temple**, whose *gopuras* tower over the town, along with those of some seventeen other major shrines. A former capital of the Cholas, who are said to have kept a high-security treasury here, Kumbakonam is today the chief commercial centre for the Thanjavur region. The main bazaar, **TSR Big Street**, is especially renowned for its quality costume jewellery.

The main reason to stop in Kumbakonam is to admire the exquisite sculpture of the **Nageshwara Swami Shiva Temple**, which contains the most refined Chola stone carving still in situ. The town also lies within easy reach of the magnificent **Darasuram** temple, a spectacular ancient monument that sees very few visitors. In addition, the village of **Swamimalai**, only a bike ride away, is the state's principal centre for traditional **bronze-casting**. As is usually the case, all the temples close soon after noon and reopen around 4pm.

Arrival and information

Kumbakonam's small **railway station**, in the southeast part of town, 2km from the main bazaar, is well served by trains from both north and south, and has a left-luggage office (24hr) and decent **retiring rooms** (Rs125, a/c Rs250). The hectic **Moffussil** (local) and **Aringannar** (long-distance) bus stands are opposite each other in the southeast of town, five minutes' walk from the railway station. All the timetables are in Tamil, but there's a 24-hour enquiry office with English-speaking staff. Buses leave for Gangaikondacholapuram, Puducherry and

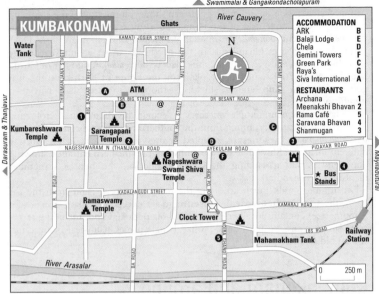

KUMBAKONAM

Ghats

River Cauvery

Swamimalai & Gangaikondacholapuram

ACCOMMODATION
ARK	B
Balaji Lodge	E
Chela	D
Gemini Towers	F
Green Park	C
Raya's	G
Siva International	A

RESTAURANTS
Archana	1
Meenakshi Bhavan	2
Rama Café	5
Saravana Bhavan	4
Shanmugan	3

Thanjavur every few minutes, many via Darasuram. Frequent services run to Chennai and Trichy, and several daily to Bengaluru (Bangalore). There are a few small **Internet** places on TSR Big Street and Ayekulam Street, plus a handful of ATMs, including an ICICI machine, 100m east of the *Siva International*.

Accommodation

Kumbakonam is not a major tourist location, and has limited **accommodation**, with only one upper-range hotel in the whole vicinity, nearly 10km southeast of town on the outskirts of Swamimalai village (see p.577). The good news for budget travellers is that most of the inexpensive places are clean and well maintained.

ARK 21 TSR Big St ☎0435/242 1234. Fifty large, clean rooms (some a/c) on five floors, all with windows, and TVs on request. Bland, but comfortable enough, with an a/c bar serving snacks. ❸–❹

Balaji Lodge 64 Nageshwaram N St ☎0435/243 0546. Good-value budget lodge, with clean rooms, all attached with TV, though they are a little dark. ❶

Chela 9 Ayekulam Rd ☎0435/243 0336, ⓕ243 1592. Large mid-range place between the bus stand and centre, distinguished by its horrendous mock-classical facade. Soap, fresh towels and TVs are offered as standard, and there are also two restaurants and a bar. ❸–❹

Gemini Towers 18 Ayekulam Rd ☎0435/243 1559. Across the road from the *Chela*; a grand name for a very run-of-the-mill budget lodge, but it's welcoming and all the rooms are tidy and good value (though non-a/c). ❶–❷

Green Park 10 Lakshmi Vilai St ☎0435/240 3912, ⓔhotelgreenpark@dataone.in. Excellent-value business-oriented hotel with spotless doubles, all with TV, and some with a/c. There's also a coffee shop. ❹

Raya's 18 Head Post Office Rd ☎0435/242 3170, ⓔhotelrayas@yahoo.co.in. A well-maintained hotel near the sights with clean and comfortable, albeit smallish, rooms, the a/c being better value; there's also a pricier new annexe opposite. ❹

Siva International 101/3 TSR Big St ☎0435/242 4013, ⓔhotelsiva@rediff.com. After the temple *gopuras*, this huge hotel complex is the tallest building in town. Their standard non-a/c is a bargain (ask for #301, which has great views on two sides) and all the spacious, airy doubles are decent value. You can climb up on the roof for incredible views of sunset and dawn behind the *gopuras*. ❷–❹

The Town

Surmounted by a multicoloured *gopura*, the eastern entrance of Kumbakonam's seventeenth-century **Kumbareshwara Temple**, home of the famous *lingam* from which the town derived its name, is approached via a covered market selling a huge assortment of cooking pots (a local speciality), as well as the usual glass bangles and trinkets. As you enter you'll pass the temple elephant, Manganal, with painted forehead and necklace of bells. Beyond the flagstaff, a *mandapa* houses a fine collection of silver *vahanas* (vehicles of the deities, used in festivals) and *pancha loham* (compound of silver, gold, brass, iron and tin) figures of the 63 Nayanmar poet-saints (see Contexts p.715).

The principal and largest of the Vishnu temples in Kumbakonam is the thirteenth-century **Sarangapani Temple**, entered through a ten-storey pyramidal *gopura* gate more than 45m high. The **central shrine** (Rs2) dates from the late Chola period, with many later accretions. Its entrance, within the innermost court, is guarded by huge *dvarpalas*, identical to Vishnu whom they protect. Between them are carved stone *jali* screens, each different, while in front of them stands the sacred, square *homam* fireplace. During the day, rays of light from tiny ceiling windows penetrate the darkness around the sanctum, designed to resemble a chariot with reliefs of horses, elephants and wheels. A painted cupboard contains a mirror for Vishnu to see himself when he leaves the inner sanctum.

The small **Nageshwara Swami Shiva Temple**, in the centre of town, is Kumbakonam's oldest temple, founded in 886 AD and completed a few years into the reign of Parantaka I (907–c.940 AD). First impressions are unpromising, as much of the original building has been hemmed in by later Disney-coloured accretions, but beyond the main courtyard, occupied by a large columned *mandapa*, a small *gopura*-topped gateway leads to an inner enclosure where the earliest Chola shrine stands. Framed in the main niches around its sanctum wall are a series of exquisite stone figures, regarded as the finest surviving pieces of **ancient sculpture** in South India. With their languid stance and mesmeric, half-smiling facial expressions, these modest-sized masterpieces far outshine the more monumental art of Thanjavur and Gangaikondacholapuram. The figures show Dakshinamurti (Shiva as a teacher, on the south wall), Durga and a three-headed Brahma (north wall), and Ardanari, half-man, half-woman (west wall). Joining them are near-life-size voluptuous maidens believed to be queens or princesses of King Aditya's court.

The most famous and revered of many sacred **water tanks** in Kumbakonam, the **Mahamakham** in the southeast of town, is said to have filled with ambrosia (*amrit*) collected from the pot broken by Shiva. Every twelve years, when Jupiter passes the constellation of Leo, it is believed that water from the Ganges and eight other holy rivers flows into the tank, thus according it the status of *tirtha*, or sacred river crossing. At this auspicious time, as many as four million pilgrims come here for an absolving bathe. On February 18, 1992, these pilgrims included Jayalalitha Jayaraman (see box, p.514). As Jayalalitha was being showered with sacred water in a specially reserved corner of the tank, the crowds pressed forward to get a closer look, provoking a *lathi* charge from her police bodyguard. In the ensuing stampede, 48 pilgrims were crushed to death. The most recent gathering, in 2004, passed without incident.

Eating

There's nothing very exciting about **eating out** in Kumbakonam, and most visitors stick to their hotel restaurant. For a change of scene, though, a few places stand out.

Archana Big Bazaar St. Right in the thick of the market, and popular among shoppers for its good-value South Indian "meals" and great *uttapams*, although it can get hot and stuffy inside. Foreigners cause quite a stir here, but are made very welcome.

Meenakshi Bhavan Nageshwaram N St. Excellent, clean South Indian veg joint, which serves some rarer snacks like *adai*, a form of spicy ricecake.

Rama Café Indira Shanti Rd. Simple and wholesome veg "meals" and snacks restaurant, in a great setting by the Mahamakham tank.

Saravana Bhavan Just east of bus stand. South Indian veg restaurant serving *iddlis*, vegetable dishes, lunchtime thalis with chai and coffee, and early breakfasts.

Shanmugan Pidayar Rd, opposite the mosque. One of the few places serving non-veg dishes, such as tasty chilli chicken and chicken fried rice.

Around Kumbakonam

The delta lands around Kumbakonam are scattered with evocative vestiges of the Cholas' golden age, but the most spectacular has to be the crumbling Airavateshwara temple at **Darasuram**, 6km southwest. Across the fields to the north, the bronze-casters of **Swamimalai** embody a direct, living link with the culture that raised this extraordinary edifice, using traditional "lost wax" techniques, unchanged since the time when Darasuram was a thriving medieval town, to create graceful Hindu deities. You can combine the two sights in an easy half-day trip from Kumbakonam. The route is flat enough to cycle, although you should keep your wits about you when pedalling the main Thanjavur highway, which sees heavy traffic. To reach Swamimalai from Darasuram, return to the main road from the temple and ask for directions in the bazaar. Swamimalai is only 3km north, but travelling between the two involves several turnings, so expect to have to ask someone to wave you in the right direction at regular intervals. From Kumbakonam, the route is more straightforward; cross the Cauvery at the top of Town Hall Street (north of the centre), turn left and follow the main road west through a ribbon of villages.

Darasuram

Built by King Rajaraja II (c.1146–73 AD), the superb if little-visited **Airavateshwara Temple**, in the village of **DARASURAM**, ranks alongside those at Thanjavur and Gangaikondacholapuram. But while the others are grandiose, emphasizing heroism and conquest, this temple is far smaller, exquisite in proportion and detail and said to have been decorated with *nitya-vinoda*, "perpetual entertainment", in mind. Shiva is here known as Airavateshwara, because he was worshipped here by Airavata, the white elephant belonging to the king of the gods, Indra.

The entrance is through a large *gopura* gateway a metre below ground level in the main wall, which is topped with small reclining bull figures. Inside, the main building is set in a spacious courtyard. Next to the inner sanctuary, fronted by an open porch, the steps of the closed *mandapa* feature elegant, curled balustrades decorated with elephants and *makaras* (mythical crocodiles with floriate tails). At the corners, rearing horses and wheels make the whole into a chariot. Elsewhere, clever sculptural puns include the head of an elephant merging with that of a bull.

Darasuram's finest pieces of sculpture are the Chola black basalt images adorning wall niches in the *mandapa* and inner shrine. These include images of Nagaraja, the snake-king, with a hood of cobras, and Dakshinamurti, the "south-facing" Shiva as teacher, expounding under a banyan tree. One rare image shows Shiva as Sharabha, part man, beast and bird, destroying the man-lion incarnation of Vishnu, Narasimha – indicative of the animosity between the Shaivite and Vaishnavite cults.

Outside, a unique series of somewhat gruesome panels, hard to see without climbing onto the base, form a band along the top of the basement of the closed *mandapa* and the sanctum sanctorum. They illustrate scenes from Sekkilar's *Periya Purana*, one of the great works of Tamil literature. The poem tells the stories of the Tamil Shaivite saints, the Nayanmars, and was commissioned by King Kulottunga II, after the poet criticized him for a preoccupation with erotic, albeit religious, literature. Sekkilar is said to have composed it in the Raja Sabha at Chidambaram; when it was completed the king sat every day for a year to hear him recite it.

Each panel illustrates the lengths to which the saints were prepared to go to demonstrate devotion to Shiva. The boy Chandesha, for example, whose job it was to tend the village cows, discovered one day that they were involuntarily producing milk. He decided to bathe a *lingam* with the milk as part of his daily worship. Appalled by this apparent waste, the villagers complained to his father, who went to the field, cursed the boy, and kicked the *lingam* over. At this affront to Shiva, Chandesha cut off his father's leg with an axe; he is shown at the feet of Shiva and Parvati, who have garlanded him. Another panel shows a man who frequently gave food to Shiva devotees. When his wife was reluctant to welcome and wash the feet of a mendicant who had previously been their servant, he cut off her hands. Elsewhere, a Pallava queen has her nose cut off for inadvertently smelling a flower, rendering it useless as an offering to Shiva. The last panel shows the saint **Sundara** who sang a hymn to Shiva, in return for which Shiva rescued a child who had been swallowed by a crocodile.

Swamimalai

SWAMIMALAI, 8km west of Kumbakonam, is revered as one of the six sacred abodes of Lord Murugan, Shiva's son, whom Hindu mythology records became his father's religious teacher (*swami*) on a hill (*malai*) here. The site of this epic role reversal now hosts one of the Tamils' holiest shrines, the **Swaminatha Temple**, crowning the hilltop of the centre of the village, but of more interest to non-Hindus are the hereditary **bronze-casters'** workshops dotted around the bazaar and the outlying hamlets.

Known as **sthapathis**, Swamimalai's casters still employ the "lost wax" process (*madhuchchishtavidhana* in Sanskrit) perfected by the Cholas to make the most sought-after temple idols in South India. Their finished products are displayed in numerous showrooms along the main street, from where they are exported worldwide, but it can be more memorable to watch the *sthapathis* in action, fashioning the original figures from beeswax and breaking open the moulds to expose the mystical finished metalwork inside. One of most welcoming workshops lies 2km south of the village, sheltered under a coconut coppice along the main road to Darasuram (look out for it on the right if you're coming from this direction). At any one time, you can see most stages of the manufacturing process, and they keep a modest selection of souvenir pieces for sale. For more on Tamil bronze-casting, see Contexts p.761.

The nearby hamlet of **Thimmakkudy**, 2km back towards Kumbakonam, is home to the area's grandest **hotel**, the ⚜ *Sterling Swamimalai* (☎0435/248 0044, ⓦwww.sterlingswamimalai.net; rooms from around \$120; ⓪), a beautifully restored nineteenth-century brahmins' mansion surrounded by lush gardens, full of sculptures. As well as lavishly furnished rooms, it also offers freshly prepared South Indian food, a resident yoga teacher, an Ayurvedic massage room, and lively culture shows in the evenings.

Thanjavur

One of the busiest commercial towns of the Cauvery delta, **THANJAVUR** (aka "Tanjore"), situated 55km east of Tiruchirapalli and 35km southwest of Kumbakonam, is often overlooked by travellers in their rush to Madurai. However, its history and treasures – among them the breathtaking **Brihadishwara Temple**, Tamil Nadu's most awesome Chola monument – give it a crucial significance to South Indian culture. The home of the world's finest Chola bronze collection, it holds enough of interest to keep you enthralled for at least a couple of days, and is the most obvious base for trips to nearby Gangaikondacholapuram, Darasuram and Swamimalai.

Thanjavur is roughly split in two by the east–west **Grand Anicut Canal**. North of the canal and once entirely enclosed by a fortified wall, the **old town** was, between the ninth and the end of the thirteenth centuries, chosen as the capital of their extensive empire by all the Chola kings save one. None of their secular buildings survives, but you can still see as many as ninety temples, of which the Brihadishwara most eloquently epitomizes the power and patronage of Rajaraja I (985–1014), whose military campaigns spread Hinduism to the Maldives, Sri Lanka and Java. Under the Cholas, as well as the later Nayaks and Marathas, literature, painting, sculpture, Carnatic classical music and *Bharatanatyam* dance all thrived here. Quite apart from its own intrinsic interest, the Nayak **Royal Palace Compound** houses an important library and museums including the aforesaid collection of bronzes.

Of major local **festivals**, the most lavish celebrations at the Brihadishwara Temple are associated with the birthday of King Rajaraja, in October. An eight-day celebration of **Carnatic classical music** is also held each January at the Panchanateshwara temple at **Thiruvaiyaru**, 13km away, to honour the great Carnatic composer-saint, Thyagaraja.

Arrival and information

Buses from Chennai pull in at the long-distance State bus stand, opposite the City Bus Stand just south of the walled old town. Most other services, including buses from Madurai, Tiruchirapalli and Kumbakonam, stop at the New bus stand, inconveniently located 4km southwest of the centre in the middle of nowhere. Rickshaws into town from here cost Rs40–50, or you can jump on one of the very frequent shuttle buses #74 or a tempo for a few rupees. The **railway station** is just south of the centre and has connections to all major destinations in the region and further afield.

The **GPO** and most of the hotels and restaurants lie on or around **Gandhiji Road** (aka Train Station Road), which crosses the canal and leads to the railway station in the south. The **TTDC tourist office** (Mon–Fri 10am–5.45pm; ☏04362/230984) is next to the *TTDC Tamil Nadu* hotel, set back from Gandhiji Road; there is also a separate tourist information office, which keeps longer hours (daily 8am–8pm), outside the TTDC complex. You can **change money** at Canara Bank on South Main Street and there are a few ATMs around town, including one at the railway station. The government **hospital** is on Hospital Road, and there are plenty of pharmacies on Gandhiji Road. For **Internet** access, head for Gemini Soft, on the first floor of the *Oriental Towers* hotel, Srinivasam Pillai Road.

Accommodation

Most of Thanjavur's **hotels** are concentrated in the area between the railway station and bus stands. They tend to be more expensive than elsewhere in the

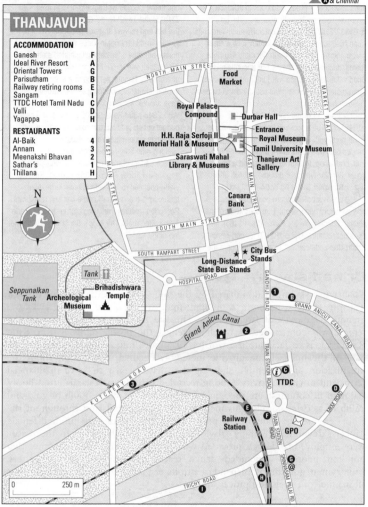

THANJAVUR

ACCOMMODATION

Ganesh	F
Ideal River Resort	A
Oriental Towers	G
Parisutham	B
Railway retiring rooms	E
Sangam	I
TTDC Hotel Tamil Nadu	C
Valli	D
Yagappa	H

RESTAURANTS

Al-Baik	4
Annam	3
Meenakshi Bhavan	2
Sathar's	1
Thillana	H

NORTH MAIN STREET

MARKET ROAD

Food Market

Royal Palace Compound

Durbar Hall

H.H. Raja Serfoji II Memorial Hall & Museum

Entrance
Royal Museum
Tamil University Museum

Saraswati Mahal Library & Museums

Thanjavur Art Gallery

WEST MAIN STREET

EAST MAIN STREET

Canara Bank

SOUTH MAIN STREET

SOUTH RAMPART STREET

City Bus Stands

Long-Distance State Bus Stands

HOSPITAL ROAD

GANDHIJI ROAD

Tank

Brihadishwara Temple

Seppunalkan Tank

Archeological Museum

Grand Anicut Canal

GRAND ANICUT CANAL ROAD

TRAIN STATION ROAD

KUTCHERY ROAD

TTDC

MKM ROAD

Railway Station

TRAIN STATION ROAD

GPO

SRINIWASAM PILLAI RD

TRICHY ROAD

N

0   250 m

New Bus Stand, Rajaraja Cholan Museum & Tiruchirapalli

state, and there's very little choice at the bottom of the market; if you're travelling on a tight budget, this may be somewhere to consider treating yourself to an upgrade. The railway retiring rooms are good value, however, seven big, clean doubles, a couple of them a/c (non-a/c Rs125, a/c Rs250). opening out onto a communal veranda overlooking the station approach.

Ganesh 314 Srinivasam Pillai Rd ☏04362/231113, ⓔhotel_ganesh2004@hotmail.com. Very close to the railway station, but also on a very noisy road. The rooms (some with a/c) are clean, however, and there's a good veg restaurant. ❷–❹

Ideal River Resort Vennar Bank, Palli Agrharam

☏04362/250833, ⓦwww.idealresort.com. Self-contained resort 7km from the centre in a very pleasant riverside location. The chalet-style rooms are luxurious, and the complex is complete with a swimming pool and very good restaurant. Free drop-offs and pick-ups from town for guests. It's popular with tour groups, so book in advance. ❽

Oriental Towers 2889 Srinivasam Pillai Rd ☎04362/230724, ⓦ www.hotelorientaltowers.com. Huge hotel-cum-shopping complex with a small swimming pool on the fourth floor and luxurious rooms, decorated in a flashy but unsubtle style. Good value for the price, with Internet access and three restaurants serving the usual Indian/Chinese/ Western fare. ❻

Parisutham 55 Grand Anicut Canal Rd ☎04362/231801, ⓦ www.hotelparisutham.com. Plush hotel with spacious a/c rooms, a large palm-fringed pool (residents only), multi-cuisine restaurant, craft shop, foreign exchange and a travel agent. Popular with tour groups, so book ahead. ❽

🏃 **Sangam** Trichy Rd ☎04362/234151, ⓦ www.hotelsangam.com. Thanjavur's newest luxury hotel, about 1km southwest of the station. Comfortable a/c rooms (from $165), an excellent restaurant, pool (Rs150 for non-residents), health club and beautiful Tanjore paintings – the one in the lobby is worth a trip here in itself. ❾

TTDC Hotel Tamil Nadu Gandhiji Rd, 10min from the bus and railway stations ☎04362/231325, ⓔ ttdc@md3.vsnl.net.in. Once the raja's guest-house, but now a typically dilapidated state-run hotel, albeit with more character than modern alternatives. Rooms, set around a leafy enclosed garden, are large, comfortable and carpeted; some have a/c. ❷–❹

Valli 2948 MKM Rd ☎04362/231580. The best budget option in town, this exceptionally friendly place has super-clean rooms (some with a/c) opening onto bright green corridors, plus a roof terrace and a popular restaurant downstairs. ❷–❹

Yagappa 1 Trichy Rd ☎04362/230421. Spacious, well-appointed rooms with sitouts, large, tiled bathrooms, friendly staff and a bar and restaurant. Reception features intriguing picture frames made from coffee roots. The *King's Bar* is friendly and not too dingy. ❸–❹

Brihadishwara Temple

Thanjavur's skyline is dominated by the huge tower of the **Brihadishwara Temple** (daily 6am–noon & 4–8pm; free), which for all its size lacks the grandiose excesses of later periods. The site has no great significance; the temple was constructed as much to reflect the power of its patron, King Rajaraja I, as to facilitate the worship of Shiva. Profuse **inscriptions** on the base of the main shrine provide incredibly detailed information about the organization of the temple, showing it to have been rich, both in financial terms and in ritual activity. Among recorded **gifts** from Rajaraja, from booty acquired in conquest, are the equivalent of 600lb of silver, 500lb of gold and 250lb of assorted jewels, plus income from agricultural land throughout the Chola empire, set aside for the purpose. No fewer than four hundred female dancers, **devadasis** (literally "slaves to the gods", married off to the deity), were employed, and each provided with a house. Other staff – another two hundred people – included dance teachers, musicians, tailors, potters, laundrymen, goldsmiths, carpenters, astrologers, accountants and attendants for all manner of rituals and processions.

The gopuras

Entrance to the complex is on the east, through two **gopura** gateways some way apart. Although the outer one is the larger, both are of the same pattern: massive rectangular bases topped by pyramidal towers with carved figures and vaulted roofs. At the core of each is a monolithic sandstone lintel, said to have been brought from Tiruchirapalli, over 50km away. The outer facade of the inner *gopura* features mighty fanged *dvarpala* door guardians, mirror images of each other, and thought to be the largest monolithic sculptures in any Indian temple. Panels illustrating scenes from the *Skanda Purana* decorate the base, including the marriage of Shiva and Parvati.

Inside the complex

Once inside, the gigantic **courtyard** gives plenty of space to appreciate the buildings. A sixteenth-century pavilion, fronted by a tall lamp column and facing the main temple, holds the third largest Nandi (Shiva's bull-vehicle) in India. The **main temple**, constructed of granite, consists of a long pillared *mandapa* hallway, followed by the *ardhamandapa*, or "half-hall", which in turn leads to the inner sanctum, the *garbha griha*. The plinth of the central shrine measures 46 square metres; above it, the pyramidal *vimana* tower (at just under 61m high, the largest and tallest in India when it was built in 1010) rises in thirteen diminishing storeys, the apex being exactly one-third of the size of the base. Such a design is quite different from later temples, where the *vimanas* become smaller as the *gopura* entranceways increasingly dominate – a desire to protect the sanctum sanctorum from the polluting gaze of outsiders. The long pillared *mandapa* from the Vijayanagar period (sixteenth century) has been roughly adjoined to the *ardhamandapa*; you can see the mouldings do not match. Inside, the walls are decorated with eighteenth-century Maratha portraits. The *vimana* is an example of a "structured monolith", a stage removed from the earlier rock-cut architecture of the Pallavas, in which blocks of stone are assembled and then carved. The profusion of carvings, aside from the inscriptions, include the *dvarpala* door guardians, Shiva, Vishnu, Durga, Ganapati (Ganesh), Bhu-devi (the female goddess Earth) and Lakshmi, arranged on three sides in two rows. As the stone that surmounts the *vimana* is said to weigh eighty tonnes, there is considerable speculation as to how it got up there; the most popular theory is that the rock was hauled up a six-kilometre-long ramp. Others have suggested the use of a method comparable to the Sumer Ziggurat style of building, in which logs were placed in gaps in the masonry and the stone raised by leverage. The simplest answer, of course, is that perhaps it's not a single stone at all.

Over 3.5m high, the black *shivalingam* in the **inner sanctum** is called Adavallan, "the one who can dance well" – a reference to Shiva as Nataraja, the King of the Dance, who resides at Chidambaram and was the *ishtadevata*, chosen deity, of the king. The *lingam* is not always on view, but during certain puja ceremonies (8 & 11am, noon & 7.30pm) a curtain is pulled, revealing the god to the devotees.

Surrounding the *garbha griha*, an **ambulatory passage** contains some of South India's greatest art treasures, including a frieze of beautiful **frescoes** dating from the reign of Rajaraja I, though unfortunately the passage is closed to the public to protect the paintings. These were only recovered in the 1930s, having remained hidden for nearly one thousand years behind layers of inferior murals from the seventeenth century. Featuring uncannily lifelike portraits of the royals, deities, celestials and dancing girls – naked save for their jewellery and ornate hairstyles – the frieze is a swirl of rich pigments made from lapis lazuli, yellow and red ochre, lime and lamp soot. In the upper ambulatory, also kept under lock and key, a sculpted series of reliefs showing the 108 classical dance poses predates the famous sets at Chidambaram (see p.570).

The courtyard and Archeological Museum

Outside, the walls of the courtyard are lined with **colonnaded passageways** – the one along the northern wall is said to be the longest in India. The one on the west, behind the temple, contains 108 *lingams* from Varanasi and (heavily graffitied) panels from the Maratha period. At the centre stands a small shrine to Varuna (the Vedic god associated with water and the sea), next to an image of the goddess Durga, usually kept clothed.

Other **shrines** in the enclosure include one behind the main temple to a devotee-saint, Karuvurar, supposedly able to cure barrenness. To the northwest, a seventeenth-century temple to Subrahmanya (a son of Shiva) has a base finely decorated with sculptures of dancers and musicians. Close to the figure of Nandi is a thirteenth-century Devi shrine; in the northeast corner, a *mandapa* houses images of Nataraja, his consort and a devotee, and is also used for decorating icons prior to processions. A **path** leads from between the two *gopuras* the length of the main wall where, behind the temple, the manicured lawn lined with benches is a haven of quiet. The temple water tank lies just beyond, next to the northwest corner.

In the southwest corner of the courtyard, the small **Archeological Museum** (daily 9am–1pm & 4–6pm; free) houses an interesting collection of sculpture, including an extremely tubby, damaged Ganesh, and displays about the Cholas. You can also buy the excellent ASI booklet, *Chola Temples*, which gives detailed accounts of Brihadishwara and the temples at Gangaikondacholapuram and Darasuram.

The Royal Palace Compound and around

Members of the erstwhile royal family still reside at the **Royal Palace Compound** (all sites daily 9am–6pm) on East Main Street (a continuation of Gandhiji Road), 2km northeast of Brihadishwara Temple. Work on the palace began in the mid-sixteenth century under Sevappa Nayak, the founder of the Nayak kingdom of Thanjavur; other sections were added by the Marathas from the end of the seventeenth century onwards. Today, the palace buildings are in something of a sorry state. Dotted around the compound are several reminders of Thanjavur's past under the Nayaks and the Marathas, including an exhibition of Oriental manuscripts and a superlative museum of **Chola bronzes**.

Durbar Hall and courtyard

Remodelled by Shaji II in 1684, the **Durbar Hall** (Rs50 [Rs10], camera Rs30, video Rs100) or audience hall, houses a throne canopy decorated with the mirrored glass distinctive of Thanjavur. Although damaged, the ceiling and walls are elaborately painted. Five domes are striped red, green and yellow, while the wall friezes showing leaf and pineapple designs, plus trumpeting angels in a night sky, show European influence. Wall niches house sculptures of deities, including the figure of Shiva devotee Patanjali (see box, p.570) with a snake winding around his leg, and an Englishman said to be in the unlikely position of learning classical dance from a young woman, to whom he is presenting a gift. Visible on the left wall, as you face the throne, are traces of a Nayak mural of deer in a forest. Next to this, two holes in the floor, once entrances to a secret passageway, are allegedly home to cobras and not recommended for exploration. Some of the later paintings portray the fighters, circus performers and wrestlers who, as recently as the 1960s, performed in the now overgrown square outside.

The **courtyard** outside the Durbar Hall was the setting for one of the more poignant moments in Thanjavur's turbulent history when, in 1683, the last of the Nayak kings gave himself up to the king of Madurai, whose forces were swarming through the city after a long siege. Legend has it that the attackers gained the upper hand after the Raja of Madurai's chief guru-magician filled the Cauvery with rotten pumpkins, casting a spell to ensure that whoever drunk its water would defect to their side. Finding himself deserted by his troops, the Nayak king is said to have donned his ceremonial gem-studded robes, pinned his bushy eyebrows back with gold wires and marched to his death intoning Vaishnavite verses. As he did so, a massive explosion behind him signalled the destruction of the palace harem, along with all its inhabitants, whose honourable deaths the king had ensured by packing the ground floor with gunpowder.

Saraswati Mahal Library and Museum

The **Saraswati Mahal Library**, one of the most important Oriental manuscript collections in India, is closed to the public, but used by scholars from all over the world. Over eighty percent of its 44,000 manuscripts are in Sanskrit, many on palm-leaves, and some are very rare or even unique. The Tamil works include treatises on medicine and commentaries on works from the *sangam* period, the earliest literature of the South. A small **museum** (daily except Wed 10am–1pm & 2–5pm; free) displays a bizarre array of books and pictures from the collection. Among the palm-leaf manuscripts is a calligrapher's *tour de force* in the form of a visual mantra, where each letter in the inscription "Shiva" comprises the god's name repeated in microscopically small handwriting. Most of the Maratha manuscripts, produced from the end of the seventeenth century, are on paper; they include a superbly illustrated edition of the Mahabharata. Sadists will be delighted to see that the library managed to hang onto its copy of the explicitly illustrated *Punishments in China*, published in 1804. Next to it, full rein is given to the imagination of French artist, **Charles Le Brun** (1619–90), in a series of pictures on the subject of physiognomy. Animals such as the horse, bullock, wolf, bear, rabbit and camel are drawn in painstaking care above a series of human faces which bear an uncanny, if unlikely, resemblance to them. You can buy postcards of this and exhibits from the other palace museums in the **shop** next door.

Thanjavur Art Gallery

A magnificent collection of **Chola bronzes** – the finest of them from the Tiruvengadu hoard unearthed in the 1950s – fills the **Thanjavur Art Gallery** (daily 9am–1pm & 3–6pm; Rs20 [Rs5], camera/video Rs30), a high-ceilinged audience hall with massive pillars, dating from 1600. The elegance of the figures and delicacy of detail are unsurpassed. A tenth-century statue of Kannappa Nayannar (#174), a hunter-devotee, shows minutiae right down to his embroidered clothing, fingernails and the fine lines on his fingers. The oldest bronze, four cases left of the main doorway (#58), shows Vinadhra Dakshinamurti ("south-facing Shiva") who, with a deer on one left hand, would have originally been playing the *vina* – though the musical instrument has long since gone. However, the undisputed masterpiece of the collection shows Shiva as Lord of the Animals (#86), sensuously depicted in a skimpy loin-cloth, with a turban made of snakes. Next to him stands an equally stunning Parvati, his consort (#87), but the cream of the female figures, a seated, half-reclining Parvati (#97), is displayed on the opposite side of the hall.

Other Royal Compound museums

Just north of the Art Gallery, the dusty and run-down **Tamil University Museum** contains coins and musical instruments, while near the entrance to the complex the rambling **Royal Museum** (Rs1) houses a modest collection of costumes, portraits, musical instruments, weapons, manuscripts and courtly accessories. Just after the ticket office for the Royal Museum, in a damp upper room of the palace, is a new collection, the **H.H. Raja Serfoji II Memorial Hall and Museum** (Rs2, camera Rs30, video Rs150). In the eighteenth century, the youthful Serfoji II was a victim of a violent feud between two regional ruling families, the Pandyas and Hoysalas, and ended up in a pitch-black prison cell for years. Despite several attempts to suffocate him by burning

In an old house in the suburb of Karanthattangudi, ten minutes by auto-rickshaw from the centre of Thanjavur, V.R. Govindarajan's **shop** at 31 Kuthirakkatti St contains an amazing array of antiques, including brass pots, betel nut boxes, oil lamps, coins and **Tanjore paintings**. Small, modern and simple examples of Tanjore paintings cost around Rs500, while large, recently made pictures with 24-carat gold decoration may cost as much as Rs20,000, and for a fine hundred-year-old painting you can expect to part with Rs80,000 or more. Upstairs, seven artists work amid a chaotic collection of clocks and bric-a-brac, and you can watch the various stages in the painting process.

Back in town, the **Chola Art Galerie**, two minutes' walk south of the palace entrance at 78/79 East Main St, opposite the Sharja Building, has a good selection of handicrafts including some excellent bronzes and woodwork. The owner of the **Parisutham hotel craft shop** is very knowledgeable about local craftsmen, Tanjore paintings, copper "art plates" and musical instruments such as the classical *vina*. A branch of the government chain, **Poompuhar Handicrafts**, on Gandhiji Road (next to the *TTDC Tamil Nadu Hotel*), stocks copper Thanjavur "art plates", brass oil lamps and sandalwood carvings, and there's also a **cooperative handicrafts shop** above the Sangeeta Mahal concert hall in the Royal Palace compound.

For more background on Tanjore paintings, see Contexts, p.763.

red chillies in his cell, Serfoji survived and was eventually rescued by a Danish missionary in 1789. He then accepted his rightful position as Maharajah of Thanjavur, and never forgot his debt to the missionary, who remained a close adviser and taught the ruler about Christianity, a religion he grew to hold in great respect. The museum's collection is the outcome of a lifetime investigation into the turbulent life and reign of Serfoji II by his grandson, though sadly it doesn't do much to illuminate his life. The permanent exhibition comprises a clutter of ivory desk sets, silverware, newspaper cut-outs, royal portraits and decaying royal finery.

Rajaraja Cholan Museum

The **Rajaraja Cholan Museum** (daily 10am–1pm & 2–5.30pm; Rs2), in the basement of the modern Mandimandapam, about 2km southwest of town on the Trichy Road, houses Chola stone sculpture and small objects excavated at Gangaikondacholapuram (see p.572) such as tiny marbles, games boards, bangles and terracotta pieces. Two illuminated maps show the remarkable extent of the Chola empire under the great kings Rajaraja I and his son, Rajendra I, but otherwise the rest of the collection is rather uninspiring and poorly labelled, with practically no English at all.

Eating and drinking

For **food**, there's the usual crop of busy and cheap "meals" canteens dotted around town. Of Thanjavur's dingy bars, *King's* in the *Yagappa* hotel is the best choice for a quiet beer.

Al-Baik Trichy Rd. Small Muslim restaurant serving tasty Indian and Chinese dishes, with a predominance of non-veg options such as tandoori chicken. **Annam** *Pandiyar Residency* hotel, 14 Kutchery Rd. Small, inexpensive and impeccably clean veg restaurant that's recommended for its cut-above-the-competition lunchtime thalis (Rs25) and evening South Indian snacks (especially the delicious cashew *uttapams*).

Moving on from Thanjavur

The best **train** service for Chennai is the Rockfort Express #6178 (departs 8.30pm; 8hr 45min), which also calls at Trichy (1hr) and Chengalpattu (7hr 10min) before terminating at Egmore Station. The handy Mayiladuturai–Mysore Express #6231 (departs 7.15pm) stops in Bengaluru (Bangalore) (11hr 15min) en route to Mysore (14hr 15min). To other places in Tamil Nadu there are more frequent connections from Trichy and Thiruvarur, both a one-hour journey from Thanjavur by **bus**. To Trichy and Kumbakonam (both 1hr), they leave the New bus stand roughly every 10 minutes; to Thiruvarur they leave every 15–30 minutes and to Madurai (4–5hr) every For more on public transport from Thanjavur see Travel details at the end of theis chapter.

Meenakshi Bhavan Corner of Gandhiji Rd and Kutchery Rd. Spotless new restaurant serving excellent *dosas* and other, less common South Indian vegetarian snacks.
Sathar's Gandhiji Rd. This is the town's most popular non-veg restaurant (mains Rs60–80), and a pretty safe place to eat chicken, thanks to the constant turnover. Seating is downstairs or on a covered terrace.

Thillana *Sangam*, Trichy Rd. Swish multi-cuisine restaurant that's renowned for its superb South Indian thalis at lunchtime (around Rs100), while evenings feature an extensive à la carte menu, including superb *chettinad* specialities. Worth a splurge just for the live Carnatic music (*vina*, flute and vocals on alternate days). Count on around Rs300–400 per head.

Thiruvarur

Often bypassed by visitors travelling between Thanjavur and the coast, **THIRUVARUR**, 55km east of Thanjavur, is famed as the birthplace of the musical saint **Thyagaraja**, to whom the town's huge temple is dedicated. According to Hindu myth, the first temple was built on this spot after Shiva and Parvati, at rest in a garden at the foot of Mount Kailash, were disturbed by a handful of *bilva* leaves scattered over them by a playful monkey. Shiva, delighted, blessed the beast, who was reincarnated as the kindly King Muchukunda of the Manu dynasty. The king built many temples but later got involved in a fight with the demon Vala, who was finally killed by the god Indra. Muchukunda was offering puja in thanks for his salvation when Shiva appeared and instructed him to build a temple at Thiruvarur.

The current **Thyagarajaswamy Temple**, on the north side of town, dates mainly from the fourteenth and fifteenth centuries. Its three successive enclosed courtyards contain a number of shrines, including one to Thyagaraja with an unusual line of the nine *navagrahas* (planet deities) peering in at the saint's image. The outer walls and ceilings are brightly painted with vivid images of Shiva and accompanying deities, while the inner sanctum houses a bronze *lingam* crowned with a seven-headed cobra. On the west side there is a huge and calm bathing tank, and just inside the west temple entrance the modest **Government Museum** (daily except Fri 9.30am–5pm, closed second Sat of the month; Rs5), which just has a few bronzes, stone sculptures and pieces of devotional art on display.

In March the town hosts the **Arulmigu Thyagarajaswamy car festival**, when for ten days animated crowds pull and push the great temple car (the largest in Tamil Nadu) and its smaller companions on a laborious path around the surrounding streets. Ask at regional tourist offices for specific dates.

Practicalities

Frequent **buses** run to Thiruvarur from Thanjavur and Nagappattinam; rail services are currently suspended, pending gauge conversion. The railway station and bus stand are five minutes' walk apart in the south of town. To reach the temple, cross the bridge just north of the bus stand, and carry straight on for ten minutes or so.

It's not difficult to find **accommodation**, even during the car festival. Several adequate lodges are situated close to the bus stand on Thanjavur Road: try the *President* (T04366/222748, F224942; ②–③) or *VPK* (T04366/222309; ②–③), which is next to the large roundabout. If you're not on a rock-bottom budget, the best option by far, though, is the *Royal Park Hotel*, just over 1km out of the centre on By-Pass Road (T04366/221020, F251024; ③–④), which has a choice of a/c and non-a/c rooms, and two decent **restaurants** serving South and North Indian cuisine. Other basic meals and snack joints abound in the vicinity of the temple.

The central coast

Relatively little visited by foreign tourists, the peaceful and relatively sparsely populated central coast of Tamil Nadu is centred around the ugly town of **Nagapattinam**, the region's transport hub and once the Chola's most important port but with little left to recommend it these days. There are, however, several places of historical, religious and ecological significance that reward any detour from the temple trail inland. The northernmost of these is the peaceful Danish ex-colony of **Tharamgambadi**, which boasts a splendid fort. Further south, on either side of Nagapattinam, are the pilgrimage centres of **Nagur**, an Islamic holy site, and **Velankanni**, which draws thousands of Catholics for healing. Down at the tip of this bulge in the coast lie the swampy wetlands of the **Kodikkarai Bird Sanctuary**, across the Palk Strait from Sri Lanka.

Tragically, this was one of the worst affected areas in the **tsunami** of December 2004, with thousands of lives lost and dwellings swept away. As you travel along the coastal road, you will see numerous signs pointing towards rehabilitation projects. Note that all train routes to the coast are currently suspended for gauge conversion until at least 2008, so the only way to travel is by bus or taxi.

Tharamgambadi

The village of **THARAMGAMBADI**, formerly known as Travancore, occupies a strategic position on the coast, 48km north of Nagapattinam. This explains why the Danes, led by Ove Gjedde, set up their first trading post here in 1620. After making a treaty with the Nayaks, who ruled the area from Thanjavur, and buying the land for Rs3111, they were allowed to build the fortress, which still stands today. It remained a Danish enclave until it was sold on to the British East India Company in 1845.

Entering the old town through the imposing arched stone gate, it's a five-minute walk past serene rows of ochre and white colonial buildings to a wide open patch of land, beside which stands the **fort** (daily except Fri 10am–5.45pm; Rs50 [Rs5]), proudly overlooking the sea. The fort consists of two levels: the rooms adjoining the squat ramparts were used as a *godown*, prison and barracks, while the upper level was the residence of the governor and the priests. The other structure of note, apart from the attractive Zion and Lutheran **churches**, is the dilapidated **Masilamaninathar Temple**, whose remains lie to the north of the fort broken on the rocks above the sea. If you fancy a swim, the splendid golden strand to the fort's south is a good bet; the north side is home to a fisherman's colony.

Practicalities

Frequent **buses** ply up and down the coast road from Nagapattinam to Tharamgambadi via the Union Territory of Karaikal. If you are coming from the north, there are hourly buses from Mayiladuturai, which is on the main road and rail route between Chidambaram and Kumbakonam, taking about an hour. The finest place **to stay** and **eat** is the beautifully restored colonial ⚱ *Bungalow on the Beach* (☎04364/288065, ⓦwww.neemranahotels.com; ⑨) at 24 King St, right opposite the fort; it has huge, lavishly furnished rooms, a spacious wraparound balcony, and a quality restaurant. The only other option is the plain, institutional *TTDC Hotel Tamil Nadu* (same contact as *Bungalow on the Beach*; ④) just behind it, which has five rather overpriced doubles and a Rs300 dorm. Apart from the restaurant at the *Bungalow on the Beach*, the only places for food are a couple of basic stalls back by the main coastal road.

Nagur

For 28 years until his death in 1558, the village of **NAGUR** (also known as Nagore), 10km north of Nagapattinam, was home to the Muslim saint Hazrat Meeran Sahib. The 450-year-old **dargah** dedicated to him, around 300m from where buses drop off, comprises five golden-domed mosques in a warren of patios, open courtyards and hallways that teem with pilgrims. Elaborate embossed silver steps adorn the shrines, while the walls and pathways are covered in white tiles with patterned friezes. Only men can enter the main shrine, which houses the saint's relics, and you should be politely firm if asked to donate more than you feel comfortable giving. At the back of the *dargah*, the devout bathe in the **Pirkulam Tank** in the hope that it will bring them good health, while in a little shelter at the water's edge, barbers busily shave pilgrims – donating hair is a form of penance. Stalls throughout the lively complex sell the blue, black and gold hats worn by many male pilgrims, as well as pictures decorated with Qur'anic texts, offerings of sweets for the shrine and other religious paraphernalia.

Practicalities

Nagur is connected with Nagapattinam by frequent buses, and there are also some services direct from Thanjavur, Trichy and Chennai. From Nagapattinam a taxi or auto-rickshaw should cost well under Rs100. One of the best of the many simple **lodges** is *AKB Guest House* (☎04365/250711; ①–③), 300m south of the *dargah* at 50 Syed Palli St; it has cleans rooms, some with a/c. The area around the *dargah* is full of snack stalls and simple *dhabas*.

Velankanni

At **VELANKANNI** (often spelt Vailankani), 11km south of Nagapattinam, a strong atmosphere of devotion pervades the brilliant white, spired Roman Catholic basilica of **Our Lady of Good Health**, South India's very own Lourdes. Although the imposing structure took centuries to expand and reach its current form, it originates as a place of worship from the sixteenth century, when Our Lady is said to have appeared to a young Hindu boy and performed a miracle.

The interior, with its vast vaulted ceilings and limited display of paintings and statues, has an air of austerity about it. Families hold lighted candles, which measure up to 1m, in front of the altar, while officials wave their bags of offerings in front of the image of the Virgin. Rows of display cases in the **museum** (daily 6.30am–8pm; free) contain silver and gold models of various parts of the human body, as well as objects such as cows, cars and houses. Each is accompanied by a testimonial and photograph of someone helped by Our Lady through some crisis, alongside hundreds of thank-you notes from, for example, couples who have received assistance in conceiving and students after passing their exams. Rows of stalls selling various trinkets descend from the church down to the sea; it was here that hundreds of devotees drowned, while paddling or hunting souvenirs, when the 2004 tsunami hit.

Practicalities

Velankanni is served by frequent **buses** back and forth from Nagapattinam, as well as by some longer distance services. Just a little inland from the church, the Church Rooms office (8am–8pm) rents out nearly a thousand Spartan but spotless rooms for a mere Rs100, but they can only be arranged in person on the day itself. Of the many private **hotels**, *ABR Lodge* on Beach Road (☎m98424 64474; ❸) is a cut above the average, with modern attached rooms. Beach Road is lined with small **restaurants** and stalls.

Kodikkarai Bird Sanctuary

On a small knob of land, known as Point Calimere, which juts out into the sea, 65km south of Nagapattinam and 80km southeast of Thanjavur, **Kodikkarai Bird Sanctuary** plays host to as many as 250 avian species in a mix of dry evergreen forest and swampland. On the way to the sanctuary, you pass through fifty thousand acres of salt marshes around **Vedaranyam**, the nearest town, 11km north. Traditionally the mainstay of the local economy, vast salt fields line the road, the salt drying in thatched mounds. During the struggle for Independence this was an important site for demonstrations in sympathy with Gandhi's famous salt protest. Over the last few years, however, salt has been pushed into second place by prawn cultivation, which brings in a good income but has necessitated widespread forest clearance, reducing the numbers of birds visiting Kodikkarai.

The **best time** to visit the sanctuary is between November and February, when migratory birds arrive, mostly from Iran, Russia and Poland, to spend the winter. The rarest species include black bittern, barheaded goose, ruddy shelduck, Indian black-crested baza and eastern steppe eagle. The deep forest is also the home of one of the most colourful birds in the world, the Indian pitta (*Pitta brachyura*). During December and January the swamps host spotted billed pelicans and around ten thousand flamingoes, who live on tiny shrimps (the source of the lurid pink colouring of their plumage); their numbers have dropped drastically from the 30,000 that wintered here in the days before prawn production took off.

Practicalities

Regular **buses** run to Kodikkarai via Vedaranyam, which is connected by bus to Nagapattinam, Thanjavur, Trichy, Chennai and Ramanathapuram (for Rameshwaram). Chennai buses can be booked in advance in a house next door to Shitharthan Medical Stores on Vedaranyam's East Main Street (over the road from the bus stand). The nearest railway station is 30km away at Tiruthuraipondi (and services are currently suspended).

The only **accommodation** in the area is at the extremely basic *Thambuswamy Lodge* (☎04365/252724; ❶), near the lighthouse, which can also be reserved through the wildlife warden in Nagapattinam (☎04365/253092). The lodge is often full during January, but at other times it's possible to turn up without a reservation. **Food** is limited to a couple of chai shops outside the gate of the sanctuary, although staff can bring meals in if asked. If you need to eat in Vedaranyam, the simple *Karaivani*, near the bus station in the main bazaar on Melai Street, serves vegetarian banana-leaf meals.

Tiruchirapalli (Trichy) and around

TIRUCHIRAPALLI – usually referred to as **Trichy** – stands in the plains between the Shevaroy and Palani hills, just under 100km north of Madurai. Dominated by the dramatic Rock Fort, it's a sprawling commercial centre with a modern feel; the town itself holds little attraction, but pilgrims flock through en route to the spectacular **Ranganathaswamy Temple** in **Srirangam**, 6km north, the work of the Chola kings who gained supremacy here in the eleventh century. In the twelfth century, the Cholas were ousted by the Vijayanagar kings of Hampi, who then stood up against Muslim invasions until 1565, when they succumbed to the might of the sultans of the Deccan. Less than fifty years later the Nayaks of Madurai came to power, constructing the fort and establishing Trichy as a trading city. After almost a century of struggle against the French and British, who both sought lands in southeast Tamil Nadu, the town came under British control, during which time Robert Clive lived here and had his office near the Rock Fort. On Independence it was declared part of Tamil Nadu state.

Arrival and information

Trichy's **airport** is 8km south of the centre; the journey into town by taxi (Rs200) or bus (#7, #28, #59, #63 and #K1) takes less than. For bookings go to Indian Airlines, 4A Dindigul Rd (☎0431/248 0233) or to any agent for Air Deccan.

Trichy's main railway station, **Trichy Junction** – which has given its name to the southern district of town – provides frequent rail links with Chennai, Madurai and the eastern coastline. From here you're within easy reach of most hotels, restaurants and banks, as well as the **bus stands**. There are two stands – **Central** and **State Express** – but no fixed rules about where a particular bus will depart from, though **private buses** mainly use the Central stand. State Express buses run frequently to major towns such as Madurai, Kodaikanal and Puducherry right around the clock. The efficient local city service (#1) that leaves from the platform on Rockins Road, opposite the *Shree Krishna* restaurant, is the most convenient way of getting to the Rock Fort, the temples and Srirangam. **Auto-rickshaws** are also widely available.

The **tourist office** (Mon–Fri 10am–5.45pm; ☎0431/246 0136) is opposite the Central Bus Stand, just outside the *Tamil Nadu* hotel, and offers helpful travel information. The **State Bank of India** on Dindigul Road exchanges American Express and Thomas Cook traveller's cheques, although the Highway Forex office (Mon–Sat 10am–6pm) in the plush Jenney Plaza is more efficient. There are several ATMs in the vicinity of the bus stands. Netpark, also in Jenney

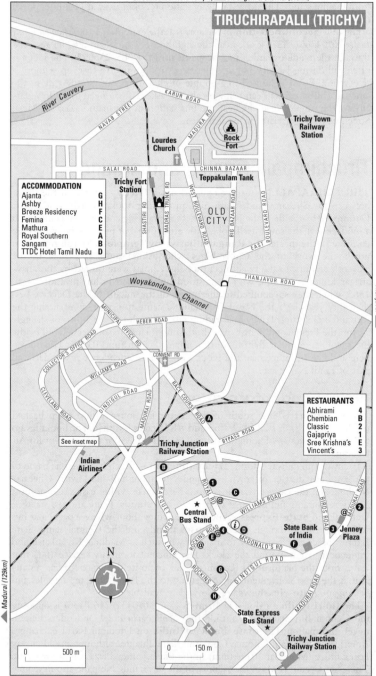

Sri Jambukeshwara Temple, ▲ Srirangam & Chennai (315km)

TIRUCHIRAPALLI (TRICHY)

River Cauvery

NAVAB STREET

KARUR ROAD

MADURA RD

Rock Fort

Trichy Town Railway Station

Lourdes Church

SALAI ROAD

CHINNA BAZAAR

Teppakulam Tank

Trichy Fort Station

SHASTIRI RD

MADRAS TRUNK RD

WEST BOULEVARD ROAD

BIG BAZAAR ROAD

EAST BOULEVARD ROAD

BOULEVARD ROAD

OLD CITY

ACCOMMODATION
Ajanta	G
Ashby	H
Breeze Residency	F
Femina	C
Mathura	E
Royal Southern	A
Sangam	B
TTDC Hotel Tamil Nadu	D

THANJAVUR ROAD

Woyakondan Channel

Thanjavur ▶

MUNICIPAL OFFICE ROAD

HEBER ROAD

COLLECTOR'S OFFICE ROAD

CONVENT RD

WILLIAMS ROAD

CLEVELAND ROAD

DINDIGUL ROAD

MADURAI ROAD

RACE COURSE ROAD

BYPASS ROAD

Ⓐ

See inset map

Indian Airlines

Trichy Junction Railway Station

RESTAURANTS
Abhirami	4
Chembian	B
Classic	2
Gajapriya	1
Sree Krishna's	E
Vincent's	3

Ⓑ

Ⓘ

Ⓒ

WILLIAMS ROAD

ROYAL ROAD

BIRDS ROAD

MADURAI ROAD

@

Ⓐ@

Ⓒ

Central Bus Stand

Ⓔ@ 4 ⓘ Ⓓ

McDONALD'S RD

State Bank of India

Ⓕ

Ⓑ

Ⓔ

3

Jenney Plaza

2

@

RACQUET COURT LANE

ROCKINS ROAD

@

DINDIGUL ROAD

Ⓖ

ROCKINS RD

Ⓗ

MADURAI ROAD

Madurai (129km) ▲

N

State Express Bus Stand

Trichy Junction Railway Station

0   500 m

0   150 m

Airport (6km) ▼

Plaza, offers **Internet** and there are several other places to get online opposite the Central bus stand.

Accommodation

Trichy has no shortage of **hotels** to accommodate the thousands of pilgrims who visit the town; dozens of places cluster around the bus stands offering cheap basic rooms, though they are pretty characterless. There are also a few more comfortable upmarket hotels, though in all categories traffic noise is a real problem in this area, so ask for a room at the back of any hotel you check into.

Ajanta Rockins Rd ⓉD 0431/241 5501. A huge, 85-room complex centred on its own Vijayanagar shrine, and with an opulent Tirupati deity in reception. Popular with middle-class pilgrims; rooms (the singles are particularly good value) are plain and clean, and some have a/c. ❷–❹

Ashby 17A Rockins Rd ⓉD 0431/246 0652, ⓌD www.ashbyhotel.com. This atmospheric Raj-era place is great value, and is most foreign tourists' first choice. The rooms are large and impeccably clean, with fresh towels, soap, cable TV and mozzie coils. There's a decent bar and a little courtyard restaurant. Great value. ❸–❹

Breeze Residency 3/14 McDonald's Rd ⓉD 0431/241 4414, ⓌD www.breezehotel.com. Renovated and now under new management, this large, central, a/c hotel boasts comfortably furnished rooms, a nicely painted foyer and a swimming pool (non-residents Rs100). ❼

Femina 109 Williams Rd ⓉD 0431/241 4501, ⓔ feminahotel@yahoo.com. Well-maintained place east of the State Express bus stand with a sprawling block of rooms and suites, some with balconies looking towards the Rock Fort. Also has plush restaurants, a pool, fitness centre, travel services, shops and a 24hr coffee bar. ❹–❻

Mathura 1 Rockins Rd ⓉD 0431/241 4737, ⓌD www.hotelmathura.com. Large, modern hotel opposite the bus stand with big a/c rooms and a veg restaurant – though it also suffers from traffic noise, so ask for a room at the back. ❸–❹

Royal Southern Race Course Rd, 1km from the centre ⓉD 0431/242 1303, ⓔ royalsouthern@eth .net. Set in five acres of grounds, and with its own pool, this places has spacious a/c rooms in a peaceful setting, plus Internet access and a very good restaurant. ❺–❻

Sangam Collector's Office Rd ⓉD 0431/241 4700, ⓌD www.hotelsangam.com. Trichy's top hotel boasts all the facilities of a four-star, including an excellent pool (Rs100 for non-residents) and the top-notch *Chembian* multi-cuisine restaurant. The spacious and comfortably furnished rooms cost $165. ❾

TTDC Hotel Tamil Nadu McDonald's Rd ⓉD 0431/241 4346, ⓔ ttdc@md3.vsnl.net.in. One of TTDC's better hotels, and just far enough from the bus stand to escape the din. Best value are the non-a/c doubles, though even these are dowdier than most of the competition. There are also a/c rooms with cable TV. ❷–❹

The Town

Although Trichy conducts most of its business in **Trichy Junction**, the southern district, the main sights are at least 4km north. The **bazaars** immediately north of the Junction heave with locally made cigars, textiles and fake diamonds made into inexpensive jewellery and used for dance costumes. Thanks to the town's frequent, cheap air connection with Sri Lanka, you'll also come across boxes of smuggled Scotch and photographic film. Head north along Big Bazaar Road (a continuation of Dindigul Road) and you're confronted by the dramatic profile of the **Rock Fort**, topped by the seventeenth-century Vinayaka (Ganesh) Temple.

North of the fort, the River Cauvery marks a wide boundary between Trichy's crowded streets and its more serene temples; the **Ranganathaswamy Temple** is so large it holds much of the village of Srirangam within its courtyards. Also north of the Cauvery is the elaborate **Sri Jambukeshwara Temple**, while several British **churches** dotted around town make for an interesting contrast. The **Shantivanam Ashram**, a bus ride away, is open to visitors year round.

△ Rock Fort, Tiruchirapalli

The Rock Fort

Looming incongruously above the bazaars in the north of town, Trichy's **Rock Fort** (daily 6am–8pm; Rs1, camera Rs10, video Rs50) is best reached by bus (#1) from outside Trichy Junction railway station or from Dindigul Road; auto-rickshaws will try to charge you Rs50 or more for the five-minute ride.

The massive sand-coloured rock on which the fort rests towers to a height of more than 80m, its irregular sides smoothed by wind and rain. The Pallavas were the first to cut into it, but it was the Nayaks who grasped the site's potential as a fort, adding a few walls and bastions as fortifications. From the entrance, at the north end of Chinna Bazaar, a long flight of red-and-white painted steps cuts steeply uphill, past a series of Pallava and Pandya rock-cut temples (closed to non-Hindus), to the **Ganesh Temple** crowning the hilltop. The views from its terrace are spectacular, taking in the Ranganathaswamy and Jambukeshwara temples to the north, their *gopuras* rising from a sea of palm trees, and the cubic concrete sprawl of central Trichy to the south.

Shri Jambukeshwara Temple

By the side of the Chennai-bound road north out of Trichy, the **Shri Jambuke-shwara Temple**, dedicated to Shiva, is smaller and dates from a later period than the Ranganathaswamy Temple. Much of it is closed to non-Hindus, but the sculptures that adorn the walls in its outer courts, of an extravagance typical of the seventeenth-century Nayak architects, are worth the short detour.

Srirangam: Ranganathaswamy Temple

The **Ranganathaswamy Temple** at **Srirangam**, 6km north of Trichy, is among the most revered Vishnu shrines in South India, and also one of the largest and liveliest, engulfing homes, shops and markets within its outer walls. Enclosed by seven rectangular walled courtyards, and covering more than 120 acres, it stands on an island defined by a tributary of the Cauvery river. This location symbolizes the transcendence of Vishnu, housed in the sanctuary reclining on the coils of the snake Adisesha, who in legend formed an island for the god, resting on the primordial Ocean of Chaos. Frequent **buses** from Trichy pull in and leave from outside the southern gate; bus #1 from the Central bus stand in Trichy is the most regular. The temple is approached from the south. A gateway topped with an immense and heavily carved *gopura*, plastered and painted in bright pinks, blues and yellows, and completed as recently as twenty years ago, leads to the outermost courtyard, the latest of seven built between the fifth and seventeenth centuries. Most of the present structure dates from the late fourteenth century, when the temple was renovated and enlarged after a disastrous sacking by the Delhi armies in 1313. The **outer three courtyards**, or *prakaras*, form the hub of the temple community, housing ascetics, priests and musicians, and the streets are lined with food stalls and shops selling souvenirs, ritual offerings and fresh flower garlands to be presented to Vishnu in the inner sanctuary. You can people-watch for hours here as the narrow streets are filled with pilgrims and locals going about their daily business and devotional activities.

Visitors remove footwear and, if desired, purchase camera and video tickets (Rs50 and Rs100) at the **entrance** to the temple proper, which is at the wall enclosing the **fourth courtyard**. You then pass through a high gateway, topped by a magnificent *gopura* and lined with small shrines to teachers, hymn-singers and sages. In earlier days, this fourth *prakara* would have formed the outermost limit of the temple, and was the closest that members of the lowest castes could get to the sanctuary. It contains some of the finest and oldest buildings of the complex, including a temple to the goddess **Ranganayaki** in the northwest corner, where devotees worship before approaching Vishnu's shrine. On the eastern side of the *prakara*, the heavily carved "thousand pillared" *kalyan mandapa*, or hall, was constructed in the late Chola period. During the month of Margali (Dec/Jan), Tamil hymns are recited from its southern steps as part of the Vaikuntha Ekadasi festival. South of the *kalyan mandapa*, the pillars of the outstanding **Sheshagiriraya Mandapa** are decorated with rearing steeds and hunters armed with spears. These are splendid examples of **Vijayanagar** style, which depicts chivalry defending the temple against Muslim invaders, and represents the triumph of good over evil. On the southern side of the *prakara*, the Venugopala shrine, dedicated to Krishna, probably dates from the Nayak period (late sixteenth century).

To the right of the gateway into the fourth courtyard, a small **museum** (daily 10am–noon & 3–5pm; free) houses a modest collection of stone and bronze sculptures, and some delicate ivory plaques. For Rs10, you can climb to the roof of the fourth wall from beside the museum and take in the view over the temple rooftops and *gopuras*, which increase in size from the centre outwards. The central tower, crowning the holy sanctuary, is coated in gold and carved with images of Vishnu's incarnations, on each of its four sides.

Inside the gate to the **fifth courtyard** – the final section of the temple open to non-Hindus – is a pillared hall, the **Garuda Mandapa**, carved throughout in typical Nayak style. Maidens, courtly donors and Nayak rulers feature on the pillars that surround the central shrine to Garuda, the man-eagle vehicle of Vishnu. Other buildings in the third courtyard include the vast kitchens, which emanate delicious smells as *dosas* and *vadas* are prepared for the deity, while devotees ritually bathe in the tanks of the moon and the sun in the northeast and southeast corners.

The dimly lit **sixth** (and innermost) **courtyard**, the most sacred part of the temple, shelters the image of Vishnu in his aspect of Ranganatha, reclining on the serpent Adisesha. The shrine is usually entered from the south, but for one day each year, during the **Vaikuntha Ekadasi festival**, the north portal is opened; those who pass through this "doorway to heaven" can anticipate great merit. Most of the temple's daily festivals take place in this enclosure, beginning each morning with *vina*-playing and hymn-singing, as Vishnu is awakened in the presence of a cow and an elephant, and ending just after 9pm with similar ceremonies.

Eating

To **eat** well in Trichy, you won't have to stray far from the bus stand, where the town's most popular "meals" joints do a roaring trade throughout the day.

Abhirami 10 Rockins Rd, opposite the bus stand. Trichy's best-known South Indian restaurant serves up unbeatable-value lunchtime "meals" (Rs20), along with the standard range of snacks during the rest of the day. They also have a fast food counter where you can get *dosas* and *uttapams* at any time. It opens early for piping hot *wada-pongal* breakfasts.

Chembian Hotel Sangam, Collector's Office Rd. Excellent restaurant offering a range of delicious Indian dishes, as well as unusually good Western and Chinese cuisine, in an atmospheric, beautifully decorated dining hall. Main dishes around Rs200. Live Carnatic music at weekends.

Classic 4 Madurai Rd, down the road from Jenney's Plaza. This bakery-cum-snack bar is *the* place to buy fresh bread, cream cakes, biscuits, cinnamon rolls and filled sandwiches. You can choose from a seemingly limitless variety of ice-cream sundaes, served up by a gaggle of giggling girls.

Gajapriya Royal Rd, on the ground floor of the *Gajapriya* hotel. Non-veg North Indian and noodle dishes are specialities of this small but blissfully cool and clean a/c restaurant. A good place to chill out over coffee.

Sree Krishna's 1 Rockins Rd, opposite the bus stand. Delicious and very filling "American" or South Indian "set breakfasts", plus specialities from all over the South in the evening, and unlimited Rs35 banana leaf thalis served at lunchtime.

Vincent's Dindigul Rd. An "Oriental" theme restaurant, set back from the road on its own terrace, with mock pagodas, concrete bamboo, a multi-cuisine menu that includes tasty chicken tikka and other tandoori dishes. A bit shabby now, but it's an escape from the hectic bus stand area. No alcohol.

Shantivanam Ashram

Situated on the banks of the sacred River Cauvery, the peaceful **Shantivanam Ashram** (☎04323/222262, ⓔsaccidananda@hotmail.com) is located in the small village of **THANNEEPALLI**, forty minutes northwest of Trichy by bus (towards Kullithalai). Its Sanskrit name literally means "Forest of Peace", an appropriate title for this small haven of ecumenical study. Founded by a Benedictine monk, the late Father Bede Griffiths (who is buried in the ashram grounds), the ashram is based on a fusion of Christianity and Hinduism – lines from the bhagavad Gita and *Om* symbols share space in the chapel with crosses and biblical verses. Visitors can participate in as much or as little of the ashram's programme as they wish, and are free to make use of the extensive library. **Accommodation** in rooms and dorms is available (suggested donation Rs200 daily, including all food), and visitors are expected to share in simple chores such as food preparation. Note that the ashram is usually full during Christian celebrations. See ⓦwww.bedegriffiths.com for more information.

The far south

The **far south** of Tamil Nadu comprises the broad sweep of the Vaigai plains, enfolded in the west by the bare brown Alagar Hills, which arch south from the edge of the Cauvery Delta to the tip of peninsular India. Studded with massive outcrops of pink and pale-brown granite, the region is rich in ancient myths:

daredevil Shiva is said to have turned evil elephants into stone boulders, and rivers were formed to quench the thirst of giant pot-bellied dwarfs. Many of these stories probably predate the earliest traces of human settlement, but most were set down when this was the heartland of the mighty **Pandyas**, the southernmost of South India's three great warring dynasties. Their former capital, **Madurai**, is today the state's second city and, as the site of the famous Meenakshi-Sundareshwarar temple, the region's spiritual root, often dubbed "The Varanasi of the South". Further east, **Rameshwaram**, occupying a narrow spit that fractures into dozens of islets as it nears the north coast of neighbouring Sri Lanka, is equally sacred to Hindus. It forms the eastern point of a sacred triangle whose apex, at **Kanyakumari**, combines the heady intensity of an age-old pilgrimage place with all the gimcrackery you'd expect from India's own Land's End.

Madurai and around

... a city gay with flags, waving over homes and shops selling food and drinks; the streets are broad rivers of people, folk of every race, buying and selling in the bazaars, or singing to the music of wandering bands and musicians ... amid the perfume of ghee and incense [are stalls] selling sweet cakes, garlands of flowers, scented powder and betel paan ... [while nearby are] men making bangles of conch shells, goldsmiths, cloth dealers, tailors making up clothes, coppersmiths, flower sellers, vendors of sandalwood, painters and weavers.

The Garland of Madurai, traditional Tamil poem, second century AD

One of the oldest cities in south Asia, **MADURAI**, on the banks of the River Vaigai, has been an important centre of worship and commerce for as long as there has been civilization in South India – indeed, it has long been described as "the Athens of the East". Not surprisingly, then, when the Greek ambassador Megasthenes came here in 302 BC, he wrote of its splendour, and described its queen, Pandai, as "a daughter of Herakles". Meanwhile, the Roman geographer Strabo complained that the city's silk, pearls and spices were draining the imperial coffers of Rome. It was this lucrative trade, meticulously detailed in the Alexandrian mariner's manual *The Periplus of the Erythraean Sea*, dating from the first century AD, that enabled the **Pandyan** dynasty to erect the mighty **Sri Meenakshi-Sundareshwarar Temple**. Although today surrounded by a sea of modern concrete cubes, the massive *gopuras* of this vast complex, writhing with multicoloured mythological figures and crowned by golden finials, remain the greatest man-made spectacle of the south. Any day of the week no less than 15,000 people pass through its gates; increasing to over 25,000 on Friday (sacred to the goddess Meenakshi), while the temple's ritual life spills out into the streets in an almost ceaseless round of festivals and processions. The chance to experience sacred ceremonies that have persisted largely unchanged since the time of the ancient Egyptians is one that few travellers pass up.

Madurai is the subject of an extraordinary number of **myths**. Its origins stem from a *sthala* (a holy site where legendary events have taken place) where Indra, the king of the gods, bathed in a holy tank and worshipped Shiva. Hearing of this, the Pandyan king Kulashekhara built a temple on the site and installed a *shivalingam*, around which the city grew. The name Madurai is popularly derived from the Tamil word *madhuram*, meaning "sweetness"; according to legend, Shiva shook his matted locks over the city, coating it with a fine sprinkling of *amrita*, the nectar of immortality.

Madurai's urban and suburban sprawl creates traffic jams to rival India's very worst. Chaos on the narrow, potholed streets is exacerbated by political demonstrations and religious processions, wandering cows – demanding right of way with a peremptory nudge of the haunch – and put-upon pedestrians forced onto the road by ever-increasing numbers of street traders. Open-air kitchens extend from chai-shops, where competing *paratha*-wallahs literally drum up custom for their delicious fresh breads with a tattoo of spoon-on-skillet signals. Given the traffic problems, it's just as well that Madurai, with its profusion of markets and intriguing corners, is an utterly absorbing city to walk around.

Some history

Although invariably interwoven with myth, the recorded history of Madurai stretches back well over 2000 years. Numerous natural **caves** in local hills and boulders, often modified by the addition of simple rock-cut beds, were used both in prehistoric times and by ascetics, such as the Ajivikas and Jains, who practised withdrawal and penance. Madurai appears to have been the capital of the **Pandya empire** without interruption for at least a thousand years. It became a major commercial city, trading with Greece, Rome and China through the Pandyan seaports along the Tamil coastline. Some *yavanas* (a generic term for foreigners) were employed in Madurai as palace guards and policemen; the Tamil epics describe them walking around town with their eyes and mouths wide open with amazement, much as foreign tourists still do when they first arrive. Under the Pandyan dynasty, Madurai also became an established seat of Tamil culture, credited with being the site of three **sangams**, "literary academies", said to have lasted 10,000 years and to have supported some 8000 poets; despite this fanciful reckoning, the most recent of these academies does

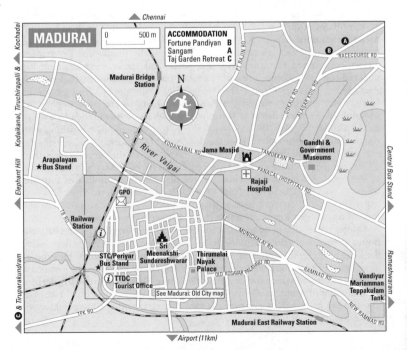

have a historical basis. The "*sangam* period" is generally taken to mean the first three to four centuries of the Christian era.

The Pandyas' capital finally fell in the tenth century, when the **Chola** king Parantaka took the city. In the thirteenth century, the Pandyas briefly regained power until the early 1300s, when the notorious **Malik Kafur**, the Delhi Sultanate's "favourite slave", made an unprovoked attack during a plunder-and-desecration tour of the South and destroyed much of the city. Forewarned of the raid, the Pandya king, Sundara, fled with his immediate family and treasure, leaving his uncle and rival, Vikrama Pandya, to repel Kafur. Nevertheless, the latter returned to Delhi with booty said to consist of "six hundred and twelve elephants, ninety-six thousand *mans* of gold, several boxes of jewels and pearls and twenty thousand horses".

Shortly after this raid Madurai became an independent sultanate; in 1364, it joined the Hindu **Vijayanagar** empire, ruled from Vijayanagar/Hampi (see p.335) and administered by governors, the **Nayaks**. In 1565, the Nayaks asserted their own independence. Under their supervision and patronage, Madurai enjoyed a renaissance, being rebuilt on the pattern of a lotus centring on the Meenakshi Temple. Part of the palace of the most illustrious of the Nayaks, **Thirumalai** (1623–55), survives today. The city remained under Nayak control until the mid-eighteenth century when the **British** gradually took over. A hundred years later the British de-fortified Madurai, filling its moat to create the four Veli streets that today mark the boundary of the old city.

Arrival

Madurai's small domestic **airport** (☎0452/269 0433), 12km south of the city, is served by flights to and from Chennai, Mumbai and Bengaluru (Bangalore). Theoretically you should be able to get information at the **Government of Tamil Nadu tourist information centre** booth by the exit, but it's not always open to meet flights. There's also a bookshop and a branch of Indian Bank, which changes traveller's cheques only. **Taxis** charge fixed rates of around Rs200 for journeys within the city. **City Bus** #10A leaves frequently from near the exit and will drop you at Periyar bus stand in town.

Arriving in Madurai by **bus**, you come in at one of two stands. The new **Central bus stand** is 7km east from the centre, to which it's connected by among others, city bus #700 and #75. This stand is the arrival point for all services except those from towns in the west, including Kodaikanal and Coimbatore, and Kerala, which terminate at the **Arapalayam bus stand** in the northwest corner of town, about 2km from the railway station. In the centre, local city buses operate from either the **STC bus stand**, or **Periyar stand** next door. Both are on West Veli Street in the west of the old city, and are very close to the railway station and most accommodation.

Madurai's clean and well-maintained **railway station** is just west of the centre off West Veli Street. You can leave your luggage at the 24hr cloakroom in the main hall, where you'll also find a very helpful branch of the **Tourism Department information centre** (daily 6.30am–8.30pm). The **reservations office** is in a new building to the left of the main station hall. There's a small veg **canteen** on Platform 1 and a **pre-paid auto–rickshaw** and **taxi booth** outside the main entrance, which opens to coincide with train arrivals.

Information

The **TTDC** tourist office, on West Veli Street (Mon–Fri 10am–5.45pm, plus Sat during festivals 10am–1pm; ☎0452/233 4757), is useful for general information and maps, and can provide details of **car rental**. If you want to rent a **taxi** to see the outlying sights, head to the rank at the main railway station, which abides by government set rates; a five-hour city tour will cost Rs600–700.

Madurai's **GPO** is at the corner of West Veli and North Veli Streets. For postal services, enter on the Scott Road side (Mon–Sat 8am–7.30pm, Sun 9am–4.30pm; Speedpost 10am–7pm). **Internet access** is offered at many places around town – try: Net Tower, 13/8 Kaka Thoppu St, beside the *Hotel International*; Friends, just around the corner; or the two branches of iWay on West Perumal Maistry Street, which both have Netphone connections.

The best place to **change money** is Tradewings at 168 North Veli St, almost opposite the post office (Mon–Sat 9am–6.30pm). The State Bank of India is at 6 West Veli St. There are several 24hr ATMs in town, including those at the Canara Bank on West Perumal Maistry Street and the UTI Bank on Station Road. Cheap **bike rental** is available at SV, West Chitrai Street, near the west entrance to the temple, or at the stall on West Veli Street, opposite the *Tamil Nadu* hotel.

Accommodation

Madurai has a wide range of **accommodation** to cater for the flocks of pilgrims and tourists, from rock-bottom lodges to good, clean mid-range places, with a cluster of hotels on **West Perumal Maistry Street**. The railway retiring rooms, on the first floor of the station, are huge and cleanish (non-a/c Rs225, a/c Rs350), though they often get booked up. To reach them, turn right from the main entrance hall and head up the stairway on platform 1. More upmarket options lie a few kilometres out of the town centre, north of the Vaigai. Unless otherwise stated, the hotels listed below are marked on the Old City map (see opposite).

Aarathy 9 Perumal Kovil, West Mada St ☎0452/233 1571, ℻233 6343. Great location overlooking the Kundalagar Temple. All rooms have TV, and some have a/c and a balcony, though ask to see your room before checking in – not all of them are up to standard. The restaurants – both a/c and out in the courtyard – are good (see p.606). Usually full of foreigners so book ahead. ❸–❹

Duke 6 North Veli St, close to the junction with West Veli St ☎0452/234 1154, ℻262 6773. Good-value modern hotel with its own rooftop restaurant and larger-than-average non-a/c rooms (plus smaller a/c rooms); ask for one with a window. ❷–❹

Fortune Pandiyan Racecourse Rd, north of the river (see main Madurai map, p.596) ☎0452/253 7090, ⊛www.fortunepandiyanhotel.com. Smart, centrally a/c hotel with large comfortable rooms. It's quiet and relaxed, if a little way out of town, and there's a good restaurant, bar, exchange facilities and a travel agency. ❽

International 46/80 West Perumal Maistry St ☎0452/234 1552. Recently renovated lodge with laid-back service, but the rooms (some a/c) are decent and all have cable TV. ❷–❹

Neethi Deluxe 89 West Perumal Maistry St ☎0452/234 3666. Basic but clean lodge, close to the central transport hubs, with a Rs60 dorm and very cheap rooms, some with TV. ❶

New College House 2 Town Hall Rd ☎0452/234 2971, ℮info@newcollegehouse.com. This huge, maze-like place has more than 200 rooms (a few with a/c), and one of the town's best "meals" canteens on the ground floor (see p.606). The very cheapest rooms are grubby, but there are likely to be vacancies here when everywhere else is full. ❷–❹

Padmam 1 Perumal Tank West St ☎0452/234 0702, ℮hotelpadmam@hotmail.com. Modern, clean, comfortable, centrally a/c hotel, with a small rooftop restaurant – although it's popular with the foreign crowd, so book in advance. The views from the front rooms, overlooking the ruined Perumal tank, are worth paying extra for. ❹

Prem Nivas 102 West Perumal Maistry St ☎0452/234 2532, ℮hotelpremnivas@sify.com. From the outside this place looks a lot swankier than it is, but the spacious rooms are among the best deals in the city, especially the singles. ❸–❹

Rathna Residency 109 West Perumal Maistry St ☎0452/537 4444, ⊛www.hotelrathnaresidency .com. Decent, clean a/c and non-a/c rooms (the latter are better value), plus two restaurants, one on the rooftop. ❸–❹

Sangam Alagar Koil Rd (see main Madurai map, p.596) ☎0452/253 7531, ⊛www.hotelsangam .com. Situated in its own grounds on the northern outskirts of town, this plush, centrally a/c hotel has very comfortable rooms from $165), 24hr room service, bar, currency exchange, swimming pool and pleasant gardens. ⑨

Sree Devi 20 West Avani Moola St ☎0452/234 7431. Always filled with foreigners thanks to its good-value, spotless non-a/c doubles right next to the temple. The deluxe a/c rooftop room has matchless views over the western *gopura*. No restaurant, but they will order in food and beer for you. ①–④

Supreme 110 West Perumal Maistry St ☎0452/234 3151, ⓦwww.supremehotels.com. A large, swish and centrally located hotel, with amply sized rooms with modern furniture, a great rooftop restaurant for sundowners and bar (see p.606) as well as a 24hr Forex desk, Internet facilities and travel counter. Book in advance. ④–⑤

Taj Garden Retreat 40 TPK RD, Pasumalai Hills, 6km from town (see main Madurai map, p.596) ☎0452/237 1601, ⓦwww.tajhotels.com. Madurai's most exclusive hotel, occupying a beautifully refurbished colonial house set in 63 acres of landscaped grounds in the hills overlooking Madurai. There are three kinds of rooms, starting around $150 on special deals: standard rooms in the new block, superior period rooms, and modern deluxe cottages dotted around the delightful gardens with great views over the Vaigai plain. Facilities include a gourmet restaurant, pool, bar and tennis court. ⑨

TTDC Hotel Tamil Nadu I West Veli St ☎0452/233 7471, Ⓔttdc@md3.vsnl.net.in. Set somewhat out on a limb, away from the temples and bazaar, but therefore pleasantly quiet, with spacious rooms overlooking a leafy courtyard. The smaller non-a/c rooms are especially good value. ②–④

The City

Although considerably enlarged and extended over the years, the overall layout of Madurai's **old city**, south of the River Vaigai, has remained largely unchanged

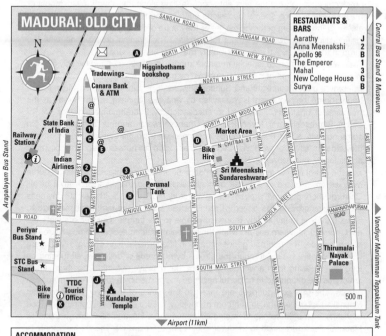

Date	Name	No. of days
Jan/Feb	Teppam	12
Feb/March	Machi Mantala	10
March/April	Kotaivasanta	9
April/May	Chittirai	12
May/June	Vasanta	10
June/July	Unchal	10
July/Aug	Ati Mulaikkottu	10
Aug/Sept	Avani Moola	12
Sept/Oct	Navaratri	9
Oct/Nov	Kolatta	6
Nov/Dec	Tirukkarttikai	10
Dec/Jan	Ennai Kappu	9

The date of each of the Madurai temple's **annual festivals** varies each year; check with a tourist office when you plan your visit. The principal and most exciting component of most of them is the **procession** (*purappatu*, or "setting forth"), held on the morning and evening of every day. Each procession is accompanied by officiating brahmins, temple employees bearing royal insignia, umbrellas, silver staffs and, at night, flaming torches. The entourage is invariably preceded by the penetrating orchestra of *tavil* (barrel drum), hand cymbals and the distinctive *nagaswaram*, a double-reeded, oboe-like wind instrument for which the Madurai area is particularly famous.

Processions circumambulate clockwise inside the temple, and many leave its precincts, starting from the east entrance, passing along the Chitrai, Avani Moola or Masi streets and, on special occasions such as the floating festival (days ten and eleven of the Teppam ceremonies), leave the centre of the city altogether. Locals and visiting pilgrims crowd the streets for *darshan*. The evening processions, weaving through the starlit night, are undoubtedly the most atmospheric.

Icons from the temple, special movable images, are taken out and lavishly clothed in silk and ornaments of rubies, sapphires, pearls, silver and gold. When the festival celebrates both Meenakshi and Sundareshwarar (Shiva in his form as Meenakshi's bridegroom), the contingent is usually led by Vinayaka (Ganesh, son of Shiva), as the "remover of obstacles", followed in succession by Subrahmanya (another son of Shiva), Sundareshwarar, Meenakshi and Chandeshwarar (another form of Shiva). On some occasions, the deities may be enshrined on a simple canopy, but on others, they ride on silver or gold vehicles (*vahanas*) such as horses, elephants or, most auspiciously, huge silver bulls.

At the **Avani Moola** festival, the coronation of Shiva is celebrated and his Maduran miracles are enacted in a series of plays (*lilas*). During the greatest festival of all, **Chittirai**, more plays are staged, telling the story of Meenakshi. The eighth day sees the goddess crowned as queen of the Pandyas and, on the tenth, her marriage to Shiva draws as many as fifty thousand people to the temple. Out in the streets the next morning, mayhem ensues when the most elaborate transport is brought into use for procession. The god and goddess travel in fifteen-metre-high **chariots**, with giant wooden wheels, hauled through the streets by hundreds of devotees, all tugging on long ropes. Rising from a wooden platform, the massive pyramidal bamboo superstructures are decorated in colourful appliqué and fronted by a row of rearing wooden horses. The god and goddess are taken to the banks of the River Vaigai to meet Meenakshi's brother who, in southern mythology, is Lord Kallalagar (Vishnu). The icon of Vishnu is brought from the forested hilltop temple at Alagarkovil, 20km northeast of Madurai. Vishnu travelled to Madurai to give his sister away at the wedding, only to find on reaching the river that the ceremony had already occurred. Because of this, to appease the deity, the festivities always take place on the northern bank of the river.

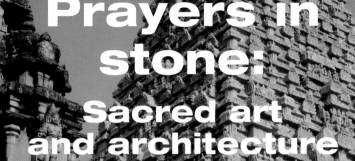

Prayers in stone:

Sacred art and architecture

South India bursts with sublime examples of man's ability to glorify the divine, made even more remarkable by the fact that, at many of the region's holy places, the vibrant traditions that created them still survive. In the enormous Meenakshi-Sundareshwara temple complex in Madurai, for example, pilgrims still perform millennia-old rituals at shrines virtually unchanged since the days of ancient Greece. Whether gazing to the heavens from the train as a towering gopura looms into view at Thanjavur, blinking at the gleaming white minarets and domes of a Mughal tomb in Mumbai or admiring the delicate beauty of a Nataraj Shiva bronze statue in Chidambaram, you will find yourself awe-struck by a living gallery of sacred art and architecture.

▲ Arjuna's Penance bas-relief, Mamallapuram

Early dynasties: the Pallavas and Chalukyas

Some of the most ancient surviving Hindu art dates back to the era of the **Pallava** and **Chalukya** dynasties, who ruled at opposite ends of the region between the sixth and eighth centuries. The Pallavas' extraordinary skill can be admired most readily in Mamallapuram in Tamil Nadu, where the famous Shore Temple stands like a sentinel beside the Bay of Bengal, alongside intricately carved and wonderfully lifelike bas-reliefs and *rathas* (chariots). Almost 1500 years on, the town remains a centre for masonry, and the resounding tap of chisel upon stone that echoes through many of its sandy lanes makes a visit all the more evocative. For the finest work of the Chalukyas, head to the peaceful town of Badami, Karnataka, high above which is perched an astonishing profusion of atmospheric cave temples; the nearby villages of Aihole and Pattadakal reveal yet more temple clusters, which blend local architectural styles with those of the north.

The majesty of the Cholas

The ingenuity of the powerful **Chola** dynasty, who held sway over most of Southeastern India at the turn of the first millennium, is evident in the temples of the Tamil Nadu heartlands. Their architecture reached its zenith at Gangaikondacholapuram, where a vast, stunning Nandi keeps guard over the peaceful Brihadishwara Temple. Equally dramatic is the namesake temple to the south at Thanjavur, dominated by its splendid tiered *vimana*, which stands like a silent watchtower high above the Grand Anicut Canal. Perhaps the most celebrated legacy of the Cholas, however, is their magnificent bronze-work, in particular the iconic image of the Nataraj – Shiva dancing in the cosmic wheel of fire – which finds its spiritual home at the great Sabhanayaka Nataraja Temple at Chidambaram, near Pondicherry (Puducherry).

▼ Sabhanayaka Nataraja Temple, Chidambaram

The South's rich palette

As well as architectural treasures, other art forms have flourished at different times in South India. Bold, dynamic and complex, **Keralan murals**, mostly dating from the sixteenth century onwards, were created by the method of fresco-secco, in which paint is applied to dry or moistened plaster; Mattancherry Palace in Old Kochi is one of the best places to appreciate them. The famous technique of **Tanjore painting** was developed in the court at Thanjavur in the eighteenth century; it is remarkable for its use of various materials, such as glass, stones and ivory, to create three-dimensional artworks. One art form that is still very much alive all over Kerala is **kalam ezhuttu**, whereby religious designs are laid down on the ground using powder – almost psychedelic in its range of colour – only to be destroyed on completion. The custom is echoed in the more common painted versions seen in temple courtyards and outside houses all over the South.

The Hoysala and Vijayanagar empires

In the first part of the second millennium, two more great Hindu dynasties left their mark on the South Indian landscape. First came the **Hoysalas**, who ruled for two centuries in southwestern Karnataka. Their black-stone temples, centred on the now sleepy environs of Belur, Halebid and Somnathpur, are covered in sensuous sculpture, boasting an astoundingly intricate level of detail. Then between the thirteenth and fifteenth centuries, the **Vijayanagars** took control of almost the whole southern half of the Subcontinent, leaving exquisite temples that feature soaring *gopuras*, thousand-pillared *mandapas* and even musical pillars, which play the notes of a scale when struck. Nowhere summons up the majesty of their creations more evocatively than their erstwhile capital, Hampi, where the magnificent Virupaksha Temple still draws pilgrims from across the South to its daily rituals and spectacular festivals.

▼ Hoysala temple detail, Belur

Footprints of other faiths

▲ Gateway, Tomb of Haji Ali, Mumbai

Non-Hindu artists have also embellished the South Indian landscape with their creations. In the north of the region, the **Muslim** Deccan Sultanate left imposing mosques, mausolea and other structures in centres of Islamic dominance such as Bijapur, Bidar and Hyderabad. There are traces of **Buddhist** *stupas* and sculpture at Amaravati and in the Kanheri caves near Mumbai, while at Sravanabelgola the huge **Jain** statue of Mahavira towers over the dry plateau of Karnataka. Finally, of course, wonderful **churches** of differing styles and denominations are the legacy of the various colonial powers, the crumbling Portuguese structures of Old Goa being perhaps the most famous examples.

Ten wonders of the South

Hampi, Karnataka A living museum of sacred architecture, its overgrown temples set against a backdrop of otherworldly rocky outcrops.

Hyderabad, Andhra Pradesh Southern India's principal Muslim city boasts a wonderful mosque, the Charminar gateway and Golconda Fort.

Mamallapuram, Tamil Nadu The site of some of the Pallavas' most sophisticated creations and still a thriving centre of stone sculpture.

▼ Church of the Immaculate Conception, Panjim

Kochi, Kerala Mattancherry Palace is one of the best places to admire delicate Keralan murals.

Bijapur, Karnataka An array of grand Islamic edifices, crowned by the mighty Golgumbaz mausoleum.

Goa The atmospheric Catholic churches provide a direct link with the Portuguese colonial past.

Thanjavur, Tamil Nadu The imperious main temple is a lively place of worship and the palace complex contains a wealth of bronzes.

Badami, Karnataka A centre of Chalukyan cave art, though you may find yourself vying with monkeys for the best viewing spot.

Mumbai, Maharashtra India's business capital also offers a vast range of art, from impressive museums to sculpted caves.

Somnathpur, Karnataka The deep rural setting adds to the mystique of the finest of the three famous Hoysala temples.

since the first centuries AD. It comprises a series of concentric squares, centred on the massive **Sri Meenakshi-Sundareshwarar Temple** and aligned with the cardinal points. The intention of the ancient architects was clearly to follow the dimensions of an auspicious mandala, or sacred diagram, set down in canonical texts known as the *Vastu Shastras*. These provided the blueprints for the now-lost cities of the Vedic age, 3000 years ago, and were believed to represent the laws governing the universe; they are also abstract depictions of the Hindu creator god, Brahma, in the form of the primeval being, Parusha. Whereas rectangular grid plans symbolize temporal or royal power, squares are used by Hindus to indicate the Absolute, which is why the streets boxed around Madurai's temple, each named after the different Tamil months, are of even lengths. The reason many of the city's mass rituals involve circuits of these streets in a strictly clockwise direction is because circumambulation of a powerful shrine, such as the Meenakshi Temple, is believed to activate the sacred properties of the giant mandala. The other main place of interest to visit on the edge of the old city is the **Thirumalai Nayak Palace**, southeast of the temple.

North of the river, Madurai becomes markedly more mundane and irregular. You're only likely to cross the Vaigai to reach the city's more expensive hotels or the Gandhi Museum.

Sri Meenakshi-Sundareshwara Temple

Enclosed by a roughly rectangular six-metre-high wall, in the manner of a fortified palace, the **Sri Meenakshi–Sundareshwara Temple** (daily 5.30am–12.30pm & 4–9.30pm; camera permit Rs30) is one of the largest temple complexes in India. Much of it was constructed during the Nayak period between the sixteenth and eighteenth centuries, but certain parts are very much older. The principal shrines (closed to non-Hindus) are those to Sundareshwarar (Shiva) and his consort Meenakshi (a form of Parvati); unusually, the goddess takes precedence and is always worshipped first.

For the first-time visitor, confronted with a confusing maze of shrines, sculptures and colonnades, and unaware of the logic employed in their arrangement, it's very easy to get disorientated. However, if you're not in a hurry, this should not deter you. Quite apart from the estimated thirty-three million sculptures to arrest your attention, the life of the temple is absolutely absorbing, and many visitors find themselves drawn back at several different times of the day. There's always plenty of activity: endless rounds of puja ceremonies; loud *nagaswaram* and *tavil* music; weddings; brahmin boys being instructed in the Vedas; devotees prostrating themselves; glittering market stalls inside the east entrance; and the occasional festival procession. All this makes it one of the most compelling places in Tamil Nadu.

Approximately fifty priests work in the temple, and live in houses close to the north entrance. They are easily identified – each wears a white *dhoti* (*veshti* in Tamil) tied between the legs, on top of which, around the waist, is a second, coloured cloth, usually of silk. Folded into the cloth, a small bag contains holy white ash. The bare-chested priests invariably carry a small towel over the shoulder. Most wear earrings and necklaces including *rudraksha* beads, sacred to Shiva. As Shaivite priests, they place three horizontal stripes of white ash on the forehead, arms, shoulders and chest and a red powder dot, sacred to the goddess, above the bridge of the nose. Most also wear their long hair tied into a knot, with the forehead shaved. Inside the temple they also carry brass trays holding offerings of camphor and ash.

The Meenakshi Temple takes the **gopura**, so prominent in other southern temples, to its ultimate extreme. The entire complex has no fewer than twelve

Meenakshi the fish-eyed goddess

The goddess **Meenakshi** of Madurai emerged from the flames of a sacrificial fire as a three-year-old child, in answer to the Pandyan king Malayadvaja's prayer for a son. The king, not only surprised to see a female, was also horrified that she had three breasts. In every other respect, she was beautiful, as her name, Meenakshi ("fish-eyed"), suggests – fish-shaped eyes are classic images of desirability in Indian love poetry. Dispelling his concern, a mysterious voice told the king that Meenakshi would lose the third breast on meeting her future husband.

In the absence of a son, the adult Meenakshi succeeded her father as Pandyan monarch. With the aim of world domination, she then embarked on a series of successful battles, culminating in the defeat of Shiva's armies at the god's Himalayan abode, Mount Kailash. Shiva then appeared at the battlefield; on seeing him, Meenakshi immediately lost her third breast. Fulfilling the prophecy, Shiva and Meenakshi travelled to Madurai, where they were married. The two then assumed a dual role, firstly as king and queen of the Pandya kingdom, with Shiva assuming the title Sundara Pandya ("King Shiva"), and secondly as the presiding deities of the Madurai temple, into which they subsequently disappeared.

Their shrines in Madurai are today the focal point of a hugely popular fertility cult, centred on the gods' coupling, which temple priests maintain ensures the preservation and regeneration of the universe. Each night, the pair are placed together in Sundareshwarar's bedchamber, but not before Meenakshi's nose ring has been carefully removed so that it won't cut her husband in the heat of passion. Their celestial lovemaking is consistently earth-moving enough to ensure that Sundareshwarar remains completely faithful to his consort (exceptional for the notoriously promiscuous Shiva). Nevertheless, this fidelity is never taken for granted, and has to be ritually tested each year when the beautiful goddess Cellattamman is brought to Sundareshwarar "to have her powers renewed". After she is spurned, she flies into a fury that can only be placated with the sacrifice of a buffalo – one among the dozens of arcane ceremonies that make up Madurai's round of temple rituals.

such towers; set into the outer walls, the four largest reach a height of around 46m, and are visible for miles outside the city. Each is covered with a profusion of gaily painted stucco gods and demons, with the occasional live monkey scampering and chattering among the divine images. After a referendum in the 1950s, the *gopuras*, which had become monochrome and dilapidated, were repainted in the vivid greens, blues and bright reds you can see today; they have to be completely redone every ten years or so. It is sometimes possible, for a small fee, to climb the southern, and tallest, tower to enjoy superb views over the town; for permission, enquire with the guards at one of the gateways.

The outer corridors

The most popular entrance to the temple is on the eastern side and leads directly to an auspicious Shiva shrine. Another entrance nearby, parallel to this, leads through a towerless gate to the Meenakshi shrine deep inside. In the **Ashta Shakti Mandapa** ("Eight Goddesses Hallway"), a market sells puja offerings and souvenirs, from fat garlands of flowers to rough-hewn, sky-blue plaster deities. Sculpted pillars illustrate different aspects of the goddess Shakti, and Shiva's 64 miracles at Madurai. Behind this hall, to the south, are stables for the temple elephants and camels.

If you continue straight on from here and go through the seven-storey **Chitrai gopura**, you enter a passageway leading to the eastern end of the **Pottamarai Kulam** ("Tank of Golden Lotuses"), where Indra bathed before worshipping the *shivalingam*. From the east side of the tank you can see the glistening gold of the Meenakshi and Sundareshwarar *vimana* towers. Steps lead down to the water from the surrounding colonnades, and in the centre stands a brass lamp column. People take a ritually cleansing bath here, prior to entering the inner shrines, or just sit, gossip and rest on the steps.

The ceiling paintings in the open corridors are modern, but Nayak murals around the tank illustrate scenes from the *Gurur Vilayadal Puranam*, which describe Shiva's Madurai miracles. Of the two figures located halfway towards the Meenakshi shrine on the north side, one is the eighth-century king Kulashekhara Pandyan, said to have founded the temple; opposite him is a wealthy merchant patron.

Around the Meenakshi shrine

On the western side of the tank is the entrance to the **Meenakshi shrine** (closed to non-Hindus), popularly known as **Amman Kovil**, literally the "mother temple". The immoveable green stone image of the goddess is contained within two further enclosures forming two ambulatories. Facing Meenakshi, just past the first entrance and in front of the sanctum sanctorum, stands Shiva's bull-vehicle, Nandi. At around 9pm, the moveable images of the god and goddess are carried to the **bed chamber**. Here the final puja ceremony of the day, the **lalipuja**, is performed, when for thirty minutes or so the priests sing lullabies (*lali*), before closing the temple for the night.

The corridor outside Meenakshi's shrine is known as the **Kilikkutu Mandapa** ("Parrot Cage Hallway"), after the parrots which are kept here as offerings to Meenakshi. Sundareshwarar and Meenakshi are brought every Friday (6–7pm) to the sixteenth-century **Oonjal Mandapa** further along, where they are placed on a swing (*oonjal*) and serenaded by members of a special caste, the Oduvars. The black-and-gold, almost fairground-like decoration of the *mandapa* dates from 1985.

Across the corridor, the small **Rani Mangammal Mandapa**, next to the tank, has a detailed eighteenth-century ceiling painting of the marriage of Meenakshi and Sundareshwarar, surrounded by lions and elephants, against a blue background. Sculptures in the hallway portray characters such as the warring monkey kings from the Ramayana, the brothers Sugriva (Sukreeva) and Bali (Vahli), and the indomitable Pandava prince, Bhima, from the Mahabharata, who was so strong that he uprooted a tree to use as a club.

Around the Sundareshwarar shrine

Walking back north past the Meenakshi shrine, through a towered entrance, leads you to the area around the **Sundareshwarar shrine**. Just inside is the huge monolithic figure of Ganesh, **Mukkuruni Vinayaka**, believed to have been found during the excavation of the Vandiyur Mariamman Teppakulam tank (see p.604). Chubby Ganesh is well known for his love of sweets, and during his annual **Vinayaka Chaturthi festival** (Sept) a special *prasad* is concocted from ingredients including 300 kilos of rice, 10 kilos of sugar and 110 coconuts. Around a corner, a small image of the monkey god **Hanuman**, covered with ghee and red powder, stands on a pillar. Devotees take a little with their finger for a *tilak*, to mark the forehead. A figure of Nandi and two gold-plated copper flagstaffs face the entrance to the **Sundareshwarar shrine** (closed to non-Hindus). From here, outsiders can just about see the *shivalingam* beyond the blue-and-red neon "Om" sign (in Tamil).

North of the flagstaffs are figures of Shiva and Kali in the throes of a dance competition. A stall nearby sells tiny **butter balls** from a bowl of water, which visitors throw at the god and goddess "to cool them down". If you leave through the gateway here, on the east, you'll find in the northeast corner the fifteenth-century **Ayirakkal Mandapa**, or thousand-pillared hall, now transformed into the temple's **Art Museum** (daily 10am–5.30pm; Rs5, camera Rs25) – disappointingly, screens and dusty educational displays now prevent visitors getting a clear view of this gigantic hall. However, there's a fine, if rather dishevelled, collection of wood, copper, bronze and stone sculpture, and an old nine-metre-high teak temple door. Throughout the hall, large sculptures of guardians and cosmic deities rear out at you from the broad stone pillars; many of these columns, when tapped, produce different, and startlingly metallic, musical tones.

Vandiyur Mariamman Teppakulam Tank

At one time, the huge **Vandiyur Mariamman Teppakulam Tank** in the southeast of town (bus #4 or #4A; 15min) was full with a constant supply of water, flowing via underground channels from the Vaigai. Nowadays, however, it is only filled during the spectacular Teppam **Floating Festival** (Jan/Feb), when pilgrims take boats out to the goddess shrine in the centre. Before their marriage ceremony, images of Shiva and Meenakshi are brought in procession to the tank, where they are floated on a raft decorated with lights, which devotees pull by ropes three times, encircling the shrine. The boat trip is believed to be the overture to a seduction that reaches its passionate conclusion later that night in the temple. This traditionally makes the Teppam the most auspicious time of year to get married.

During the rest of the year the tank and the central shrine remain empty. Accessible by steps, the tank is most often used as an impromptu cricket green, and the shade of the nearby trees makes a popular gathering place. Tradition states that the huge image of Ganesh, Mukkuruni Vinayaka, in the Meenakshi Temple, was uncovered here when the area was originally excavated to provide bricks for the Thirumalai Nayak Palace.

Thirumalai Nayak Palace

Only a quarter of the seventeenth-century **Thirumalai Nayak Palace** (daily 9am–1pm & 2–5pm; Rs50 [Rs10], includes Palace Museum), 1.5km southeast of the Meenakshi Temple, now survives. Much of it was dismantled by Thirumalai's grandson, Chockkanatha Nayak, and the materials used for a new palace at Tiruchirapalli. What stands here today is a result of the restoration and renovation in 1858 by the governor of Chennai, Lord Napier, and of further work done in 1971. The palace originally consisted of two residential sections, plus a theatre, private temple, harem, bandstand, armoury and gardens.

The remaining building, the **Swargavilasa** ("Heavenly Pavilion"), is a rectangular courtyard, flanked by eighteen-metre-tall colonnades. As well as occasional live performances of music and dance, the Tourism Department arranges a nightly **Sound and Light Show** (in English 6.45pm; 45min; Rs10), which relates the story of the Tamil epic, *Shilipaddikaram*, and the history of the Nayaks. Some find the spectacle edifying, and others soporific. In an adjoining hall, the **Palace Museum** (same hours as the palace) includes unlabelled Pandyan, Jain and Buddhist sculpture, terracottas and an eighteenth-century print showing the palace in a dilapidated state.

Tamukkam Palace: the Gandhi Library and Government Museum

Across the Vaigai, 5km northeast of the centre near the Central Telegraph Office, stands **Tamukkam** (bus #1, #2, #11, #17 or #24; 20min), the seventeenth-century palace of Queen Rani Mangammal. Built to accommo-date regal entertainments such as elephant fights, Tamukkam was taken over by the British and used as a courthouse and collector's office, and in 1955 became home to the Gandhi and Government museums. The **Gandhi Memorial Museum** (daily 10am–1pm & 2–5.30pm; free), far better organized than most of the species, charts the history of India since the landing of the first Europeans, viewed in terms of the freedom struggle. Generally the perspective is national but, where appropriate, reference is made to the role played by Tamils. It is wholeheartedly critical of the British, quoting the Englishman John Sullivan: "We have denied to the people of the country all that could raise them in society, all that could elevate them as men; we have insulted their caste; we have abrogated their laws of inheritance; we have seized the possessions of their native princes and confiscated the estates of their nobles; we have unsettled the country by our exactions, and collected the revenue by means of torture." One chilling artefact, kept in a room painted black, is the bloodstained *dhoti* the Mahatma was wearing when he was assassinated. Next door to the museum, the **Gandhi Memorial Museum Library** (daily except Wed 10am–1pm & 2–5.30pm; free) houses a reference collection, open to all, of 15,000 books, periodicals, letters and microfilms of material by and about Gandhi.

Shopping and markets in Madurai

Old Madurai is crowded with **textile and tailors' shops**, particularly in West Veli, Avani Moola and Chitrai streets and Town Hall Road. If you're looking to have some tailoring done, the locally produced textiles are generally good value, and the tailors pride themselves on turning out faithful copies of favourite clothes in a matter of hours. Unfortunately, most of the **souvenir shops** in the vicinity of the temple employ touts who invite tourists to "come and enjoy temple view free of charge only looking". It's worth doing once as the views are impressive, but getting back down to street level without making a purchase at hugely inflated prices is quite a challenge.

South Avani Moola Street is packed with **jewellery**, particularly gold shops, while at 10 North Avani Moola St, you can plan for the future at the Life & Lucky Number Numerology Centre. Madurai is also a great place to pick up South Indian **crafts**. Among the best outlets are All India Handicrafts Emporium, 39–41 Town Hall Road; Co-optex, West Tower Street, and Pandiyan Co-op Supermarket, Palace Road, for handwoven textiles; and Surabhi, West Veli Street, for Keralan handicrafts. For souvenirs such as sandalwood, temple models, carved boxes and oil lamps head for Poompuhar, 12 West Veli St, or Tamilnad Gandhi Smarak Nidhi Khadi Gramodyog Bhavan, West Veli Street, opposite the railway station, which sells crafts, oil lamps, Meenakshi sculptures and *khadi* cloth and shirts.

The old purpose-built, wooden-pillared **fruit and vegetable market**, between North Chitrai and North Avani Moola streets, provides a slice of Madurai life that can't have changed for centuries. Beyond it, on the first floor of the concrete building at the back, the **flower market** (24hr) is a riot of colour and fragrance; weighing scales spill over with tiny white petals and plump pink garlands hang in rows. Varieties such as orange, yellow or white marigolds (*samandi*), pink jasmine (*arelli*), tiny purple spherical *vanameli* and holy *tulsi* plants come from hill areas such as Kodaikanal and Kumily. These are bought in bulk and distributed for use in temples or to wear in the hair; some are made into elaborate wedding garlands (*kalyanam mala*). The very friendly traders will show you each and every flower, and if you've got a camera will more than likely expect to be recorded for posterity. It's a nice idea to offer to send them a copy of any photograph you take.

Opposite, the small **Government Museum** (daily 9am–5pm; Rs100 [Rs5]) displays stone and bronze sculptures, musical instruments, paintings (including examples of Tanjore and Kangra styles) and folk art such as painted terracotta animals, festival costumes and hobbyhorses. There's also a fine collection of shadow puppets said to have originated in the Thanjavur area and probably exported to Southeast Asia during the Chola period – though the admission price will deter all but the most ardent aficionados. A small house in which **Gandhi** once lived stands in a garden within the compound.

Kochadai Aiyannar Temple

The village of **Kochadai**, a northwestern suburb of Madurai, has a beautifully maintained temple dedicated to **Aiyannar**, the Tamil village deity and guardian of borders. Travelling through Tamil Nadu, you often see such shrines from the road, but it may not always be possible, or appropriate, to investigate them. Here, however, they are accustomed to visitors. Flanked by two huge garish *dvarpalas*, the entrance opens directly onto two sculptures of gigantic horses with riders and furious-looking armed attendants. The shrine on the left houses the god Rama and his brother Lakshmana, while facing the entrance is the shrine to Aiyannar. To the right, the *alamaram* tree, also a shrine, apparently houses a **cobra**, fed with eggs and milk; according to the priests, it only comes out during full moon. During a big **festival** in the Tamil month of Panguni (March/April), Aiyannar is taken around the village to the accompaniment of music and fireworks.

Kochadai is served by frequent buses (#68 or #54) en route to Solavandan.

Eating and drinking

As with accommodation, the range of **places to eat** in Madurai is gratifyingly wide, and standards are generally high whether you're eating at one of the many utilitarian-looking "meals" places around the temple, or in an upscale hotel – though to make the most of Madurai's exotic skyline you'll have to seek out a **rooftop restaurant** – another of the modern city's specialities. When the afternoon heat gets too much, head for one of the **juice bars** dotted around the centre, where you can order freshly squeezed pomegranate, pineapple, carrot or orange juice for around Rs15 per glass.

Restaurants

Aarathy *Aarathy Hotel*, 9 Perumal Kovil, West Mada St. Tasty tiffin (*dosas*, *iddlis* and hot *wada sambar*), served on low tables in a hotel forecourt, where the temple elephant turns up at various times of day. The blissfully cool a/c restaurant is very popular with locals and serves excellent food including great lunchtime thalis for just Rs40.

Anna Meenakshi West Perumal Maistry St. Arguably the most hygienic and best-value food in the centre, this upmarket branch of *New College House's* more traditional canteen (see opposite) serves top tiffin to a discerning, strictly vegetarian clientele. Absolutely delicious coconut or lemon "rice meals" and cheap banana-leaf thalis are served daily.

The Emperor *Chentoor Hotel*, 106 West Perumal Maistry St. Not quite such a stunning view as at the *Surya* but the multi-cuisine food is better and includes some non-veg dishes, such as delicous sizzlers.

Mahal 21 Town Hall Rd. Nicely decorated street level restaurant serving small but tasty portions of fish and chips, plus tandoori items and South Indian veg snacks.

New College House 2 Town Hall Rd. Huge meals-cum-tiffin hall in old-style hotel. Lunchtime, when huge piles of pure veg food are served on banana leaves to long rows of locals, is a real deep-South experience; and the coffee's pure Coorg.

Surya *Supreme Hotel*, 110 West Perumal Maistry St. One of Madurai's most popular rooftop restaurants, with sweeping views of the city and temple. Although the pure veg food is average and service is a little lax, it's still a fine venue for a sundowner.

By air

Indian Airlines' city office is at 7a West Veli St, near the post office (☎0452/234 1234) and is efficient and helpful. Jet Airways (☎0452/269 0771), Air Deccan and Paramount Airways (both national number only) all have offices at the airport. There are regular flights to **Chennai**, with one Indian Airlines service daily going on to **Mumbai** and another with Paramount Airways flying on to **Bengaluru** (Bangalore). To get to the airport, catch a taxi (around Rs200), or take city bus #10A from the Periyar bus stand.

By bus

Services to Chennai, Bengaluru (Bangalore), Mysore, Chengalpattu, Chidambaram, Tirupati, Thanjavur, Tiruchirapalli, Kumbakonam, Rameshwaram, Kanyakumari and Thiruvananthapuram (in Kerala) all leave from the **Central bus stand**. From the **Arapalayam stand**, buses depart to Coimbatore, Kodaikanal, Kumily (for Periyar Wildlife Sanctuary), and Ernakulam/Kochi via Kottayam. There are no direct services from Madurai to Ooty; change in Coimbatore.

By train

Madurai is well connected by train to most major towns and cities in South India. For **timetable** details, ask the Tourism Department information centre, to the right of the ticket counters.

It's possible to reach the railhead for **Kodaikanal** (Kodaikkanal Road) by train but the journey is much faster by express bus. The quickest way to get to **Thiruvananthapuram, Kochi** (Ernakulam), **Kollam** and **Mettupalayam**, departure point for the Nilgiri Blue Mountain Railway (see p.633), is to change in **Coimbatore** (see p.629). The daily Chennai–Kanyakumari Express #2633 passes through Madurai at the rather unsociable hour of 2.10am while the #2663/2665 Howrah–Kanyakumari Express departs at the friendlier time of 6.30am on Sunday, Monday and Thursday. At the time of writing, the line to Rameshwaram was undergoing gauge conversion and was not due to open until some time in 2008.

For more on transport out of Madurai, see Travel details, p.642.

Recommended trains from Madurai

Destination	Name	No.	Departs	Total time
Bengaluru (Bangalore)	Tuticorin–Mysore Express	#6731	8.05pm	10hr 35min
Chennai	Vaigai Express	#2636	6.45am	7hr 55min
	Pandiyan Express	#2638	8.45pm	9hr
Coimbatore (Ooty)	Madurai–Coimbatore Express	#6716	10.50pm	6hr 10min
			6.30am	
Tiruchirapalli	Vaigai Express	#2636	6.45am	2hr 20min

Bar

Apollo 96 *Supreme Hotel*, 110 West Perumal Maistry St. Boasting 75,000 flashing diodes and a punchy sound system, Tamil Nadu's most hi-tech bar looks like the set from a low-budget 1970s sci-fi movie – an altogether surreal experience.

Around Madurai: Tiruparankundram

Stretching west towards the blue haze of the Alagar Hills, the Vaigai plains around Madurai are broken by colossal outcrops of granite, some of them weathered into weird forms like petrified monsters. Each occupies a place in the mythological landscape of the Pandyan heartland. To the northeast of the city is **Elephant Hill**, said to have been created by Shiva to punish a rampaging pachyderm. The holiest rock hereabouts, however, looms over the southwest fringes of the city, where the Muslim conquerors of the early fourteenth century consolidated their fleeting colonization of the far south by founding a capital at the foot of an ancient Hindu site. Referred to by Islamic historians as "City of Ma'bar", the orderly grid-planned town served as the headquarters of the **Madurai Sultanate**, whose origins remain obscure. The sultanate endured for eight generations until the army of the mighty Hindu Vijayanagar empire swept south to mop up the remnants of Muslim rule left after Malik Kafir's bloody sack of 1311. The last sultan, **Sikander Shah**, allegedly died defending the town, and his tomb crowns the top of the 365-metre monolith, known to Muslim pilgrims throughout India as **Sikandermalai**, "Hill of Sikander", at the village of **TIRUPARANKUNDRAM**, 8km southwest of Madurai (buses #4A and #32 from the STC bus stand).

For Hindus, however, the sheer-sided rock is revered as one of the six abodes of Shiva's son and the Tamils' favourite god, Lord Murugan. Identified in mythology as the site of Murugan's marriage to Indra's daughter, Deivani, it is one of the most sacred shrines in Tamil Nadu. At the auspicious time of Murugan's wedding anniversary in early February, thousands of newly-weds come here to be blessed. In the summer, the god's birthday is celebrated with displays of fire-walking and body-piercing, along with other acts of ostentatious masochism, such as devotees dragging ox carts along with chains embedded in the flesh of their shoulders. Outside festival time, however, Tiruparankundram is a peaceful spot offering a welcome respite from the frenzy of Madurai.

The temple

Tirparankundram's **temple**, built around an eighth-century shrine cut into the rock 35m above the town's rooftops, comprises a series of huge terraces and halls, interconnected by stone staircases. At ground level, the main colonnaded *mandapa*, adorned with brightly painted horses and *yalis*, served as a field hospital for British soldiers in the 1760s, when the temple was badly defaced (one local priest allegedly burned himself to death in protest at the British vandalism). Perhaps as a consequence of this, non-Hindus are not always allowed to visit the upper levels (if you're refused entry, seek permission at the temple office). It's definitely worth making the climb to see the ancient rock-carvings in, around and below the walls of the central shrine, where Murugan's vehicle (*vahana*) the peacock, features prominently; these are some of the best surviving examples of Pallava rock art in the South.

The Dargah

Crowning the windswept summit of the hill, amid gnarled old umbrella trees that cling to the bare rock, the **Dargah of Sikander Shah** is the region's holiest Muslim shrine. The ruler – whose heroic death on this spot failed to save his capital from the Vijayanagar reconquest – is today revered as a saint. His tomb complex, made up of a domed mosque and covered colonnade dating from the fifteenth century, attracts pilgrims from across the country. Sikander's reputation for piety, however, doesn't square with the account of the Madurai Sultanate featured in the chronicles of Shams Siraj of Delhi, in which Sikander is accused of having succumbed to the decadence of neighbouring Madurai:

He began to perform acts of indecency in public . . . when he held court in the audience hall he wore women's ornaments on his wrists and ankles, and his neck and fingers were adorned with feminine decorations. His indecent acts with pederasts were performed openly . . . (and) the people of Ma'bar were utterly and completely weary and out of patience with him and his behaviour.

Given the paucity of other historical sources relating to this brief period of Muslim supremacy in South India, it's hard to know which version of the story – Sikander as valiant sage or as sybaritic sultan – is the more apocryphal. The **views** of Madurai and the surrounding plains from the tomb, however, are unambiguously impressive.

Rameshwaram and around

The sacred island of **RAMESHWARAM** – 163km southeast of Madurai and less than 20km from Sri Lanka across the Gulf of Mannar – is, along with Madurai, South India's most important pilgrimage site. Hindus tend to be followers of either Vishnu or Shiva, but Rameshwaram brings them together, being the place where the god Rama, an incarnation of Vishnu, worshipped Shiva in the Ramayana. The **Ramalingeshwara Temple** complex, with its magnificent pillared walkways, is the most famous on the island, but there are several other small temples of interest, such as the **Gandhamadana Parvatam**, sheltering Rama's footprints, and the **Nambunayagi Amman Kali Temple**, frequented for its curative properties. **Dhanushkodi**, "Rama's bow", at the eastern end of the peninsula, is where Rama is said to have bathed, and the string of tiny islands and sandbanks known as Adam's Bridge, peppering the sea between here and Sri Lanka are believed to be the stepping stones used by Hanuman in his search for Rama's wife, Sita, after her abduction by Ravana, the demon king of Lanka.

Rameshwaram, whose streets radiate out from the vast block enclosing the Ramalingeshwara, is always crowded with day-trippers, and ragged mendicants who camp outside the Ramalingeshwara and the **Ujainimahamariamman**, the small goddess shore temple. An important part of their pilgrimage is to

Sethusamudram Shipping Canal project

Originally conceived in 1860 under British rule, the project to dredge a deep canal across the Palk Straits through the island chain of Adam's Bridge to the Gulf of Mannar, a patch of water also known as Sethusamudram, in order to enable large vessels to avoid sailing around Sri Lanka, was finally given the go ahead by the government of Manmohan Singh in June 2005. Opposition has been very vocal from environmental groups, fearful of the disturbance to marine life and the increase in pollution, and fishing groups, particularly concerned that the dredging could release toxins buried in the sea bed. The project has also met resistance from Hindu fundamentalist groups (championed by the BJP), who regard it as sacrilegious to plough through such a holy and mythologically significant spot as Adam's Bridge. The project has been dogged by bad luck in its initial stages – some interpret the sinking of both the "Cutter-Sucker-Dredger" *Aquarius* and the crane that was sent out to retrieve it as a sign from God. Whatever the case may be, it seems that it is set to remain a bone of contention and possible embarrasment to the government for some time to come.

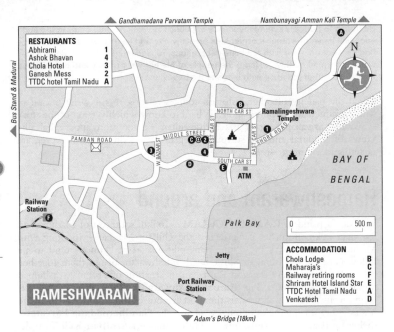

Gandhamadana Parvatam Temple   Nambunayagi Amman Kali Temple

RESTAURANTS
Abhirami	1
Ashok Bhavan	4
Chola Hotel	3
Ganesh Mess	2
TTDC hotel Tamil Nadu	A

BAY OF
BENGAL

Palk Bay

0   500 m

ACCOMMODATION
Chola Lodge	B
Maharaja's	C
Railway retiring rooms	F
Shriram Hotel Island Star	E
TTDC Hotel Tamil Nadu	A
Venkatesh	D

RAMESHWARAM

Adam's Bridge (18km)

bathe in the main temple's sacred tanks and in the sea; the narrow strip of beach is shared by groups of bathers, relaxing cows and mantra-reciting *swamis* sitting next to sand *lingams*. As well as fishing – prawns and lobsters for packaging and export – the coastal villages make a lot of money selling shells to pilgrims – a symbol that they have been to Rameshwaram and worshipped Vishnu (he is always portrayed as holding a conch).

Arrival and information

The NH-49, the main road from Madurai, connects Rameshwaram with Mandapam on the mainland via the impressive two-kilometre-long Indira Gandhi Bridge, originally built by the British in 1914 as a railway link. **Buses** from Madurai (via Ramanathapuram), Trichy, Thanjavur, Kanyakumari and Chennai pull in at the bus stand, 2km west of the centre. Private buses pull up around the temple; travel agents nearby run fast and comfortable services all round South India. The railway station, 1km southwest of the centre, is the end of the line for trains from Chennai, Madurai and further afield but services are suspended until at least 2008, while the gauge is converted.

Yellow-and-green city bus #1 runs every ten minutes from the bus stand to the main temple; otherwise, **local transport** consists of unmetered cycle- and auto-rickshaws that gather outside the bus stand. Jeeps are available for rent near the railway station, and bicycles from shops in the four Car streets around the temple.

The main TTDC **tourist office** at the bus stand (daily 10am–5.45pm; ☏04573/221371) gives out information about guides, accommodation and boat trips but does not always keep its official times. The **post office** is on Pamban Road, and there are a couple of **Internet** places near the west entrance to the temple.

Accommodation

Most of the **accommodation** in Rameshwaram is restricted to basic lodges in and around the Car streets around the temple. The temple itself has a range of rooms for pilgrims; ask at the Devasthanam Office, East Car Street (☎04573/221223). Railway retiring rooms are still open despite the suspension of the railway line, and offer six large doubles plus a dorm (❶), which are generally cleaner and quieter than those in the town lodges.

Chola Lodge North Car St ☎04573/221307. Basic but adequate pilgrim place in the quietest of the Car streets, with a couple of more expensive a/c rooms, and some with TV. Very welcoming. ❶–❹
Maharaja's 7 Middle St ☎04573/221271, ⓔhotelmaharajas@sancharnet.com. Located next to the temple's west gate, this place has good clean and comfortable rooms with attached bathrooms and TV (some also have a/c), plus temple views from balconies. ❷–❹
Shriram Hotel Island Star 41a South Car St ☎04573/221472, ⓕ239332. Large, clean hotel with pleasantly appointed a/c and non-a/c rooms, most with sea views. The non-a/c rooms are

particularly good value, but the most expensive a/c ones are a little overpriced. ❷–❹
🏃 **TTDC Hotel Tamil Nadu** Near the beach, 700m northeast of main temple ☎04573/221277, ⓔttdc@md3.vsnl.net.in. The best place in Rameshwaram, in a pleasant location and with a bar, restaurant and comfortable sea-facing rooms (some a/c); the best are actually the cheaper ones in the new block, with pleasant sit-outs. ❸–❺
Venkatesh South Car St ☎04573/221296. Functional modern three-storey hotel with clean, decent-sized rooms, most with TV and some with a/c. ❷–❹

Ramalingeshwara Temple

The core of the **Ramalingeshwara** (or Ramanathaswamy) **Temple** was built by the Cholas in the twelfth century to house two much venerated **shivalingams** associated with the Ramayana. After rescuing his wife Sita from the clutches of the demon Ravana, Rama was advised to atone for the killing of the demon king – a brahmin – by worshipping Shiva. Rama's monkey lieutenant, Hanuman, was despatched to the Himalayas to fetch a *shivalingam*, but when he failed to return by the appointed day, Sita fashioned a *lingam* from sand (the *Ramanathalingam*) so the ceremony could proceed. Hanuman eventually showed up with his *lingam* and in order to assuage the monkey's guilt Rama decreed that in future, of the two, Hanuman's should be worshipped first. The *lingams* are now housed in the inner section of the Ramalingeshwara, not usually open to non-Hindus. Much of what can be visited dates from the 1600s, when the temple received generous endowments from the Sethupathi rajas of Ramanathapuram.

△ Ramalingeshwara Temple colonnade, Rameshwaram

The Ramalingeshwara is enclosed by high rectangular walls with a huge pyramidal *gopura* entrance on each side. The gateways lead to a spacious closed ambulatory, flanked to either side by continuous platforms with massive pillars set on their edges. These **corridors** are the most famous attribute of the temple, their extreme length – 205m, with 1212 pillars on the north and south sides – giving a remarkable impression of receding perspective. Delicate scrollwork and brackets of pendant lotuses supported by *yalis*, mythical lion-like beasts, adorn the pillars.

Before entering the inner sections, pilgrims are expected to take a ritual bathe in water from each of the 22 **tirthas** (tanks) in the temple. The groups of dripping-wet pilgrims, most of them fully clothed, make their way from one tank to the next to be doused in a bucket of water by a temple attendant. Each tank is said to have special benefits: the Rama Vimosana Tirtha provides relief from debt, the Sukreeva Tirtha gives "complete wisdom" and the attainment of *Surya Loka*, the realm of the Sun, and the Draupadi Tirtha ensures long life for women and "the love of their spouses".

Monday is Rama's auspicious day, when the Padilingam puja takes place. **Festivals** of particular importance at the temple include Mahashivaratri (ten days during Feb/March), Brahmotsavam (ten days during March/April) and Thirukalyanam (July/Aug), celebrating the marriage of Shiva to Parvati.

Minor temples

On a hill 2km north of Rameshwaram town centre, the **Gandhamadana Parvatam** (daily 6–11am & 3.30–6.30pm) is a venerable shrine housing Rama's footprints. On some days, ceremonies are conducted here after the 5.30am puja at the Ramalingeshwara temple, encouraging pilgrims to climb the hill to continue their devotions. From the roof, fine views extend over the surrounding country – on clear nights you can see the lights of Jaffna.

Three kilometres east of town towards the old fishing village of **Dhanush-kodi**, the small **Nambunayagi Amman Kali Temple**, set in a quiet sandy grove 200m off the main road, attracts people in search of cures for illnesses. Inside a banyan tree next to it is a shrine dedicated to the spirit Retatalai, "the two-headed". A pair of wooden sandals with spikes, said to belong to the spirit, is left in the shrine and locals say they can hear them clip-clopping at night when Retatalai chooses to wander. Pieces of cloth are tied to the branches of the tree to mark thanks for such boons as pregnancy after barrenness and the healing of family feuds. The bus terminates at **Dhanushkodi**, from where you can walk along the ever-narrowing spit of sand until the sea finally closes in and the island peters out, tantalizingly short of Adam's Bridge.

Eating

Eating in Rameshwaram is more about survival than delighting the taste buds. Most places serve up fairly unexciting "meals" for Rs30–50.

Abhirami Shore Rd, near the east entrance to the temple. Reasonably clean South Indian veg joint with street views en route to the seashore.

Ashok Bhavan West Car St. Basic place offering cheap regional varieties of thalis.

Chola Hotel West Bazaar St. Food-only joint, a good choice for carnivores, with biriyanis and other dishes including chicken, mutton, liver and "head curry".

Ganesh Mess Middle St. One of the better "meals" joints, which also does classic South Indian snacks at other times of day.

TTDC Hotel Tamil Nadu Near the beach. Gigantic, noisy, high-ceilinged glass building near the sea, serving good South Indian snacks and "meals", plus chicken and sometimes fish dishes. There is also a bar in the main hotel building.

RAMANATHAPURAM (aka Ramnad), 36km west of Rameshwaram, offers a possible break on the bus or train journey down from Madurai, 120km northwest. It's worth stopping here to see the neglected but atmospheric **Ramalinga Vilasam**, palace of the Sethupati rajas, who by tradition were guardians of the mythical Sethu bridge built by Rama to cross to Lanka. The entrance to the **palace** (daily except Fri 9am–1pm & 2–5pm; Rs50 [Rs5]), 2km from the bus stand, takes you into the big and dusty **Durbar Hall**, whose central aisle is hung with oil portraits of the rajas of the last few hundred years. Throughout the building, ceilings and walls are decorated with early eighteenth-century murals, depicting subjects such as business meetings with the English, battles with the Maratha king Sarabhoji, and scenes from the epics; one battle scene shows soldiers fighting with boomerangs, and there's a real Indian boomerang on display. Also on show are palm-leaf manuscripts, a Ravi Varma painting (see p.379) with appliquéd brocade and sculptures of Vishnu from the eighth and thirteenth centuries.

From the **throne room**, a secret passageway once gave an escape route to a local temple. The raja's throne, supported on carved elephant legs, is decorated with a coat of arms, given by the British, featuring a lion and unicorn. As further proof of the royal family's compliance with the foreign power, the raja, at the end of the eighteenth century, allowed them to use the bedchambers upstairs – decorated with erotic murals – as a meeting hall. This cosy relationship did not find unanimous approval among his subjects. Influential local landowners showed their contempt for the British by responding to tax demands with bags of stones, and in 1798 and 1801 rebellions took place, sometimes dubbed the "South Indian War of Independence". In 1803, at the request of the British, the Ramnad raja was obliged to accept the lesser rank of *zamindar* (feudatory chieftain). On the roof is a stone bed on which the raja would lounge in the evenings to enjoy panoramic views of the town and surrounding country. The buildings immediately below were royal guesthouses; a descendant of the rajas now lives in one of them.

Tirunelveli and around

Separated by the only perennial river in the far south, the Tambraparni, **TIRUNELVELI** and its modern counterpart **PALAYANKOTTAI** together form the largest conurbation in the densely populated red-soil region south of Madurai. Aside from the huge **Nellaiyappa temple**, built by the Pandyas in the thirteenth century with a towering pyramidal *gopura*, situated 2km west of the river, neither holds much of specific interest. However, you may want to use Tirunelveli as a base for day-trips to nearby **Thiruppudaimarudur**, 25km west, whose old riverside temple is famed for its wood-carvings, or further west to **Kuttalam**, in the foothills of the Ghats, where a series of dramatic waterfalls attract streams of day-trippers. An hour or so east on the Coromandel Coast, the traditional Tamil pilgrimage town of **Tiruchendur** has the region's most spectacular shore temple, dominating an appropriately impressive sweep of surf-lashed beach. The sea between the Coromandel coast and Sri Lanka is rich enough to support a string of fishing settlements, but the most lucrative harvest yielded by the Gulf of Mannar are the pearls gathered by divers from the port of **Tuticorin**, an hour north of Tiruchendur. The Portuguese founded one of their first colonies in India here.

Tirunelveli's **bus stand**, in the town centre just across the river from Palayankottai, has services to and from Madurai (3hr), Tuticorin (1hr), Tiruchendur (1hr) and Kollam (5hr). For Kuttalam, you have to change in Tenkasi (1hr 30min; see below). **Trains** from Chennai, Madurai and Kollam pull in at the main-line station, five minutes' walk west on the opposite side of Madurai Road.

Most of the **accommodation** in town is lined up outside the bus stand, on Madurai Road. Pick of the bunch is the *Sri Jankiran* (☎0462/233 1941, ⓔsjh_tvl@sancharnet.in; ❷–❹), which has some a/c rooms, a cosy **restaurant** and roof terrace. Next door, the *Barani* (☎0462/233 3234; ❷–❹) is marginally cheaper and dependably clean, as is the extremely good-value *Balaji Mansion* (☎0462/233 3302; ❶–❷), just off Madurai Road near the station, whose rooms have TVs.

Thiruppudaimarudur

THIRUPPUDAIMARUDUR, a small riverside village 25km west of Tirunelveli, is the site of a **temple** renowned throughout the region for its splendid medieval wood-carvings and murals. The best-preserved of these murals line the interior of the temple's east tower, which you can scale via flights of precariously steep wooden steps. Pillars and brackets propping up a succession of ceilings have been sumptuously decorated, while the walls (which you'll need a flashlight to see clearly) are covered with vibrant paintings, depicting scenes from the Ramayana, Vishnu's various incarnations and mythical battles.

Buses to Thiruppudaimarudur leave more or less hourly from Tirunelveli, and take fifty minutes. The village doesn't have any hotels or guesthouses.

Kuttalam

An image familiar to collectors of exotic prints and engravings in Victorian Britain was that of the great waterfalls at **KUTTALAM** (Courtalam), 136km northwest of Kanyakumari, where the River Chittar plunges down a sheer cliff on the very edge of the Western Ghats. A couple of centuries ago, when the famous Raj-era artist Thomas Daniells came to sketch the falls, this was still a remote spot, overgrown with vegetation and frequented only by wandering *sadhus* and the odd party of sickly Brits. A hydro project upstream has somewhat diminished the falls' splendour, and the barrage of film music and hoardings in the modern concrete village that has sprung up at their feet does little to enhance the overall atmosphere, but it's still worth coming here for an invigorating bathe. Bussing in from all over the state, thousands of Tamils do just that each day, especially at weekends and between July and late September, when water levels are at their highest. From late January until May, the falls can dry up completely.

In all, nine major cascades are dotted around Kuttalam, but only one, known for obvious reasons as **Main Falls**, is located in the village proper. This is where the largest crowds congregate – with ladies to the left, fully dressed in soaking saris; old folk and kids to the right; and men, in regulation voluminous underpants, taking the full force of the central flow. It's worth pointing out that few foreigners come to Kuttalam, so expect to create a bit of a stir if you strip off; for a little more privacy, try jumping onto one of the minibuses that run throughout the day to smaller waterfalls around Kuttalam.

To reach Kuttalam by bus, you first have to head for **Tenkasi**, which is well connected to Tirunelveli (1hr 30min) and Madurai (3hr), from where local buses run the final twenty minutes to the falls. The limited **sleeping** and **eating** options in Kuttalam include the *TTDC Hotel Tamil Nadu I,* opposite Parasakthi Women's College (☎04633/221 0003; ❷–❸), with overpriced and uniformly shabby double rooms, some with a/c; next door, the *TTDC Hotel Tamil Nadu II* (☎04633/232 2263; ❷–❸) has the same rates for a similar range of rather dilapidated a/c and non-a/c rooms, which include some triples.

Tuticorin

TUTICORIN (also known as Thootukudi), 51km east of Tirunelveli on the NH-7 or 130km northeast of Kanyakumari, developed as a flourishing Portuguese colony in the sixteenth century and later expanded under the Dutch and British. Eclipsed by Madras in the late 1700s, it is nowadays the state's second port and would be an entirely forgettable, gritty Tamil town were it not for the prodigious quantities of **pearl**-bearing saltwater molluscs, *Pinctada martensi,* that grow in the shark-infested shallows offshore. These are harvested for one month each year (normally in March–April) by divers equipped with little more than antiquated face masks. The pearls they collect are said to rank among the finest in the world, on a par with those found in the Persian Gulf, which is presumably why you won't easily find any for sale in the bazaar; all but a tiny proportion are exported.

Tuticorin is largely industrial and not a particularly appealing place to stay, but if you find yourself in need of a **hotel**, head for VE Road, a short rickshaw ride from the centre of town. The business-traveller-orientated *Jony International* (☎0461/232 8640; ❹–❺) has decent rooms with a/c and cable TV; nearby, the *Sugam* (☎0461/232 8172; ❷–❹) is a clean and dependable budget option.

Tiruchendur

TIRUCHENDUR, some 60km southeast of Tirunelveli, means "beautiful holy town" in Tamil, and for once the epithet fits, thanks to the awesome presence on its shoreline of the mighty **Subrahmanya Temple**. The shrine – one of the six sacred abodes of the Tamils' favourite god, **Lord Murugan** (Shiva's son, Subrahmanya), here in the form of the Ascetic ("renouncer of the transitory and illusory"), presides over a spectacular sandy beach, with breakers crashing in off the Gulf of Mannar. Corrosive salt winds have taken their toll on the original building erected by the Pallavas in the ninth century, and large sections of what you see today are modern, dating from 1941. However, references to the deity inside occur in some of the Tamils' oldest scriptures, while archeological digs conducted in the 1890s on the banks of the River Tambraparni nearby yielded evidence of a three-thousand-year-old religious cult focused on a spear-wielding deity very similar to Murugan. More extraordinary still were the prehistoric mouth locks that came to light at the same time, identical to those worn by more fervent devotees at Murugan festivals in Tamil Nadu today.

The Subrahmanya Temple is approached via a long colonnaded walkway, running 700m through a sacred precinct lined with shops selling puja paraphernalia and pilgrims' souvenirs. Non-Hindus are permitted to enter the central shrine on payment of a small donation. The deity inside is among the most revered in South India, attracting crowds of more than a million during the temple's annual **Thaipusam festival**, just before the monsoon, when 108 different herbs and auspicious preparations are offered to the god, symbolizing the renewal of the earth. The ritual is accompanied by the chanting of some of the oldest Sanskrit verses surviving in India. In his travelogue *The Smile of Murugan*, the British historian Michael Wood speculates that these may even predate human speech; scholars have shown their nearest analogue is birdsong,

During the month of *Thai* (February) in the Tamil calendar, the usual intensity of the devotional activities among the thousands of Shaivite pilgrims trailing around Tamil Nadu reaches a fanatical peak on the occasion of **Thaipusam**, the full-moon festival in honour of Lord Murugan (aka Lord Subrahmanya), son of Shiva and Parvati, who represents the triumph of good over evil. Thaipusam recalls the day that Parvati gave Murugan the *vel*, a magical weapon that destroys all wickedness, sins and banishes negativity from the soul.

The archaic rituals seen today are rooted in myth and legend. The most popular version is that there was a devotee, Idumban, who, on the night of the full moon in the month of *Thai*, was instructed in a dream to go to Shivagiri hill to worship Lord Murugan. Idumban dutifully set off, taking with him two pots of milk as an offering, and along the way he sang devotional hymns.

Today, the practice continues as **Shaivite pilgrims** from all over India congregate to venerate Lord Murugan; there are temples dedicated to him throughout Tamil Nadu, and a few in Kerala. Each pilgrim has to take an offering, called a **kavadi**, meaning "sacrifice at each step", to remind them of their previous sin and their personal vow to Lord Murugan. In accordance with the tradition set by Idumban, most devotees carry a milk *kavadi* (a pot filled with milk), which is covered in fruit and flowers and carried on the head in a long and winding procession; up to 20,000 people may gather at a shrine to offer their milk *kavadis* on *Thaipusam*. The pilgrims sing hymns as they wander from temple to temple to do puja.

A *kavadi*, however, can also be a huge metal or wooden structure. These are strung with razor-sharp hooks and lavishly decorated with flowers, bells and peacock feathers. In an extreme act of personal penance and homage to Murugan, a devotee may volunteer to be hooked up to one of these frames. Before they can be pierced, they have to undergo a whole month of inner cleansing, with a strict vegetarian diet, celibacy and spiritual nourishment to give them strength. On the day of *Thaipusam*, with the help of the frantic drumming and the chanting by the crowds, the devotee enters a deep trance to make the pain disappear, then spears and hooks are pushed through the flesh. Alternatively, a devotee may pull a wagon or chariot by a set of hooks pierced in the skin of their back.

The most famous Murugan temples are at Palani (see p.627) and Tiruchendur (see p.615), which can see crowds of over a million during the festival; ask at a TTDC tourist office to find out exact places and dates (which change each year). The act of piercing is now officially prohibited in India, although the practice may still be witnessed on extremely rare occasions in the very rural areas. Piercing continues unabated in those countries, such as Thailand, Sri Lanka, Singapore and Malaysia, where there are significant populations of Tamil Hindus.

lending credence to the theory that ritual came before verbal language in human evolution.

Tiruchendur is well connected by **bus** to Tirunelveli (1hr), Madurai's Arapalayam bus stand (4hr) and Tuticorin (40min), and there are four daily **trains** to and from Tirunelveli. The best **accommodation** in town is the *TTDC Hotel Tamil Nadu* (☏04639/242268; ❷–❹), a typically lacklustre government-run place, with a/c and non-a/c options, five minutes' walk northeast of the temple, in a pleasant setting by the sea. Nearer the temple, on Kovil Street, there's a cluster of small but adequate hotels including the *Rathina Lodge* (☏04639/242383; ❶–❸), also with a choice of a/c and non-a/c. The *Ashoka Bhavan* on Kovil Street is the best of the cheap snacks and "meals" joints, and caters for a constant stream of pilgrims.

Kanyakumari and around

KANYAKUMARI, at the southernmost extremity of India, is almost as compelling for Hindus as Rameshwaram. It's significant not only for its association with a virgin goddess, Kanya Devi, but also as the meeting point of the Bay of Bengal, Indian Ocean and Arabian Sea. Watching the sun rise and set from here is the big attraction, especially on full moon day in April, when it's possible to see both the setting sun and rising moon on the same horizon. Although Kanyakumari is in the state of Tamil Nadu, most foreign visitors arrive on daytrips from Thiruvananthapuram (Trivandrum), the capital of Kerala, 86km northwest. While the place is of enduring appeal to pilgrims, other visitors may find it bereft of atmosphere, its magic obliterated by ugly concrete buildings and hawkers selling shells and trinkets – although anyone with completist tendencies will regard it as *de rigueur* to visit India's own "Land's End". Those with a little more time on their hands may also choose to visit the temple at **Suchindram** of go for a hike up **Maruntha Malai** in the Travancore Hills.

Kanyakumari was seriously affected by the **tsunami** of December 26, 2004. The town's seafront and jetty were devastated and around a thousand people were killed, many of them pilgrims on tours of Tamil Nadu's sacred places. In one of the tsunami's most dramatic rescue operation, more than five hundred people were airlifted to safety after being stranded on the Vivekananda

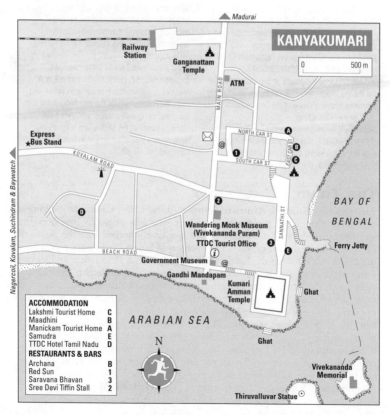

Nagercoil, Kovalam, Suchindram & Baywatch

KANYAKUMARI

▲ Madurai

Railway Station
Ganganattam Temple
Main Road
ATM
Express ★Bus Stand
KOVALAM ROAD
North Car St
A
B
C
South Car St
East Car St
Sannathi St
BAY OF BENGAL
Wandering Monk Museum (Vivekananda Puram)
TTDC Tourist Office
Ferry Jetty
BEACH ROAD
Government Museum
Gandhi Mandapam
Kumari Amman Temple
Ghat
ARABIAN SEA
Ghat
N
Vivekananda Memorial
Thiruvalluvar Statue

ACCOMMODATION
Lakshmi Tourist Home   C
Maadhini   B
Manickam Tourist Home   A
Samudra   E
TTDC Hotel Tamil Nadu   D
RESTAURANTS & BARS
Archana   B
Red Sun   1
Saravana Bhavan   3
Sree Devi Tiffin Stall   2

0   500 m

Memorial for around ten hours. The enormous statue on its tiny rocky isle was sufficiently distant from the shore to escape the ferocity of the breaking waves.

Arrival and information

Trains from Thiruvananthapuram, Mumbai and Bengaluru (Bangalore) (and even Jammu – at 86hr the longest rail journey in India) stop at the **railway station** in the north of town, 2km from the seafront. **From Madurai** the best train service is the fast passenger train which leaves at 3pm and takes just over four hours. You can leave **luggage** in the generator room behind the ticket office.

The well-organized **Express bus stand**, near the lighthouse on the west side of town, is served by regular buses from Thiruvananthapuram, Kovalam, Madurai, Rameshwaram and Chennai. Auto-rickshaws and taxis provide **local transport**.

The main **tourist office** is on Main Road (Mon–Fri 10am–5.30pm); there's **Internet** access further up Main Road, as well as just around the corner on Beach Road.

Accommodation

As Kanyakumari is a "must-see" for Indian tourists and pilgrims, **hotels** can fill up early. However, recent developments have raised standards and relieved the pressure on space.

Lakshmi Tourist Home East Car St ☎04652/246203, ⓕ 246627. Smart rooms, some sea-facing with swish a/c, though the best views are from the non-a/c (especially room #408). Also has an excellent non-veg restaurant. ❷–❹

Maadhini East Car St ☎04652/246787, ⓕ 246657. Large hotel right on the seafront above the fishing village, with fine sea views, comfortably furnished rooms and one of the best restaurants in town (see p.620). ❹–❺

Manickam Tourist Home North Car St ☎04652/246387. Spacious and modern rooms with sea views facing the sunrise and the Vivekananda rock. Good value. ❷–❹

Samudra Sannathi St ☎04652/246162, ⓕ 246627. Smart hotel near the temple entrance, with well-furnished deluxe rooms facing the sunrise and satellite TV, plus a veg restaurant. ❹–❺

TTDC Hotel Tamil Nadu On the seafront ☎04652/346257, ⓔ ttdc@md3.vsnl.net.in. A range of accommodation in cottages (some a/c) and clean rooms (a/c on the first floor), most with sea view, along with cheaper and very basic "mini" doubles at the back and a dorm (Rs50). Good square meals are served in functional surroundings. ❸–❺

The Town

The seashore **Kumari Amman Temple** (daily 4.30–11.30am & 4–8pm) is dedicated to the virgin goddess **Kanya Devi**, who may originally have been the local guardian deity of the shoreline, but was later absorbed into the figure of Devi, or Parvati, consort of Shiva. One version of Kanya Devi's story relates how she did penance to win the hand of Shiva. The god was all in favour and set out from Suchindram for the wedding, due to take place at midnight. The celestial *devas*, however, wanted Kanya Devi to remain a virgin, so that she could retain her full quota of *shakti*, or divine power, and hatched a plot. Narada the sage assumed the form of a cock and crowed; on hearing this, Shiva, thinking that it was dawn and that he had missed the auspicious time for the ceremony, went home. The image of Kanya Devi inside the temple wears a diamond nose-stud of such brilliance that it's said to be visible from the sea. Male visitors must be shirtless and wear a *dhoti* before entering the temple; non-Hindus are not allowed in the inner sanctum. It is especially auspicious for pilgrims to wash at the bathing *ghat* here.

Resembling a prewar British cinema, the **Gandhi Mandapam** (daily 7am–7pm; free), 300m northwest of the Kumari Amman Temple, was actually

△ Pilgrims, Kanyakumari

conceived as a modern imitation of an Orissan temple. It was designed so that the sun strikes the auspicious spot where the ashes of Mahatma Gandhi were laid, prior to their immersion in the sea, at noon on his birthday, October 2. South of here, the small **Government Museum** (daily except Fri & 2nd Sat of the month; 9.30am–5pm; Rs100 [Rs5]) has a motley collection of sculptures.

Possibly the original sacred focus of Kanyakumari are two **rocks**, about 60m apart, half-submerged in the sea 500m off the coast, which can be reached by the Poompuhar ferry service from the jetty on the east side of town (every 30min; daily 7am–4pm; Rs20). In 1892 they attracted the attention of the Hindu reformer Vivekananda (1862–1902), who swam out to the rocks to meditate on the syncretistic teachings of his recently dead guru, Ramakrishna Paramahamsa. Incorporating elements of architecture from around the country, the 1970 **Vivekananda Memorial** (daily 7am–4pm; Rs10) on the eastern rock houses a statue of the saint. What are said to be the footprints of Kanya Devi can also be seen here, at the spot where she performed her penance. The boat then visits the second rock, which features an imposing forty-metre-high statue of the ancient Tamil saint **Thiruvalluvar**.

For more on the life and teachings of Vivekananda, visit the **Wandering Monk Museum** (or **Vivekananda Puram**), just north of the tourist office at the bottom of town (daily 8am–noon & 4–8pm; Rs2). A sequence of 41 panels (in English, Tamil and Hindi) provide a meticulously detailed account of the *swami*'s odyssey around the Subcontinent at the end of the nineteenth century. In his philosophy, he countered the traditional Hindu dogma that the universe is a delusion beyond the sole reality of Brahma, and attempted to replace it with a proactive ethos based on social work and reform – a kind of early Indian *engagement* without Jean-Paul Sartre's baggy suits and strong coffee.

Kanyikumari's newest attraction, aimed primarily at domestic tourists, is the **Baywatch** theme park (daily 10am–7pm; Rs50). Apart from rides, which do not rival their Western counterparts, the big draw is what claims to be India's first **wax museum** (daily 10am–9.30pm; Rs40). The facsimiles are exclusively of well-known Indian political, sporting and cinematographic figures, so don't go expecting to see Pamela Anderson.

Eating and drinking

Aside from the usual "meals" places and hotel dining rooms, there are a few popular veg and non-veg **restaurants** in the centre of town, most attached to one of the hotels. The ✦ *Archana*, at the *Maadhini Hotel* on East Car Street, has an extensive veg and non-veg multi-cuisine menu, served either inside a well-ventilated dining hall or alfresco in a courtyard (evenings only). They also have the town's widest selection of ice cream. *Saravana Bhavan*, north of the Kumari Amman Temple, on the main bazaar, is arguably Kanyakumari's best "meals" restaurant, serving all the usual snacks, cold drinks, and huge Tamil thalis at lunchtime to hordes of hungry pilgrims. Their coffee is good, too. Also look out for the excellent fried fish and chicken on sale for around Rs25 at small joints on and around Main Road, such as the *Sree Devi Tiffin Stall*. For a drink, the most salubrious of the **bars** around town is the seriously a/c *Red Sun* on South Car Street.

Around Kanyakumari

The most interesting side-trip from Kanyakumari is to **Suchindram**, whose splendid temple is the oldest in the region. There are also several interesting walks into the Travancore Hills, including the strenuous hike up **Maruntha Malai**.

Suchindram

At **SUCHINDRAM**, 12km northwest of Kanyakumari, stands the **Stanunathaswami Temple**, construction of which extended over a period of at least six hundred years: parts date back as far as the ninth or tenth century, others are from the fifteenth, and a huge seven-storey pyramidal *gopura* was erected during the sixteenth. The temple's oldest and most remarkable feature, however, is a series of beautifully preserved **epigraphs** carved on a huge boulder in the main *mandapa*. Some are in the ancient Pali language, dating from the third century BC when this was the most southerly outpost of the Mauryan empire, while later inscriptions in classical Tamil are the first known references to the three traditional dynasties of the South – the Cholas, the Pandyas and the Pallavas.

Dedicated jointly to Brahma, Vishnu and Shiva – surprising as its main sanctuary houses a *shivalingam* – the temple has some other notable features, including its **musical pillars**, which emit a chime when struck, and an extraordinary three-metre-high figure of Hanuman. A special puja takes place at sunset (around 6pm) every Friday, with music and a procession. The temple is open to non-Hindus and all castes, although male visitors must remove their shirts before entering.

Local buses run from Kanyakumari to Suchindram.

Maruntha Malai

As you head along the NH-47 towards Kerala, the spectacular crags of the **Travancore Hills** encroach upon the flats of iridescent rice paddy lining the coastal strip, completely dominating the landscape to Thiruvananthapuram. The most prominent peak in the area is the pyramidal **Maruntha Malai** (aka "Maruval Malai"), 13km from Kanyakumari, which is renowned among Tamils as "Medicine Mountain". During the monsoon, its steep green slopes sprout a profusion of medicinal herbs, a fact which local healers must have been aware of for thousands of years, since the hill crops up time and again in Hindu mythology, most famously in the Ramayana. According to the epic, Hanuman had been dispatched to Mount Kailash in the Himalayas to look for herbs for Laxmana, who had been wounded by a poisoned arrow during the battle with the evil demon Ravana's army in Lanka. Instead of picking the plants, however, Hanuman ripped up the whole mountain to keep them fresh. On his way back to Rama, Hanuman dropped a piece of Mount Kailash at this spot on his way. Today, the Maruntha Malai remains an important source of curative herbs used in the preparation of Ayurvedic medicines. It's also home to a scattering of *sadhus* who, when they aren't away wandering, live in a string of caves that dot the pilgrim path to the *shivalingam* crowning the summit. Taking around six hours, the **hike** to it is especially popular with pilgrims who have walked to Kanyakumari in fulfilment of a vow. It should not be attempted without a guide as the route is hard to follow; the best place to find one is in the village of **Pothayadi**, near the trailhead.

The Southern Ghats

Sixty or more million years ago, what we know today as peninsular India was a separate land mass drifting northwest across the ocean towards central Asia. Current geological thinking has it that this mass must originally have broken off the African continent along a fault line that is today discernible as a north–south ridge of volcanic mountains, stretching 1400km down the west coast of India, known as the **Southern Ghats**. The range rises to a height of around 2500m, making it India's second-highest mountain chain after the Himalayas.

Forming a natural barrier between the Tamil plains and coastal Kerala and Karnataka, the Ghats (literally "steps") soak up the bulk of the southwest monsoon, which drains east to the Bay of Bengal via the mighty Cauvery and Krishna river systems. The massive amount of rain that falls here between June and October (around 2.5m) allows for an incredible **biodiversity**. Nearly one-third of all of India's flowering plants can be found in the dense evergreen and mixed deciduous forests cloaking the Ghats, while the woodland undergrowth supports the Subcontinent's richest array of wildlife, from jungle civets, muntjac and the rare tahr antelope to gaur (Indian bison), herds of wild Asian elephant and tigers.

It was this abundance of game, and the cooler temperatures of the range's high valleys and grasslands, that first attracted the sun-sick British, who were quick to see the economic potential of the temperate climate, fecund soil and plentiful rainfall. As the forests were felled to make way for tea plantations, and the region's many tribal groups – among them the Todas – were forced deeper into the mountains, permanent **hill stations** were established. Today, as in the days of the Raj, these continue to provide welcome escapes from the fierce summer heat for the middle-class Tamils who can afford the break, and foreign tourists.

Much the best known of the hill resorts – in fact better known and more visited than it deserves – is **Udhagamandalam** (formerly **Ootacamund**, and usually known just as "**Ooty**"), in the **Nilgiris** (from *nila-giri*, "blue mountains"– named after the profusion of blue gum trees). The ride up to Ooty, on the **miniature railway** via Coonoor, is fun, and the views breathtaking, but in general (unless you have the means to stay in the best hotels), the grey and concrete centre of town comes as a rude shock. The other main hill station, founded by American missionaries, is leafy and quiet **Kodaikanal**, further south near Madurai. In between these two popular destinations, the temple town of **Palani** is attracting a growing number of visitors for trekking in its surrounding hills.

Accessed via the hill stations, the forest areas lining the state border harbour Tamil Nadu's principal wildlife sanctuaries, **Indira Gandhi** (**Anamalai**) and **Mudumalai**, which, along with Wayanad in Kerala and Nagarhole and Bandipur in Karnataka, form the vast **Nilgiri Biosphere Reserve**, the country's most extensive tract of protected forest. Road building, illegal felling, hydroelectric projects and overgrazing have gradually whittled away large tracts of this huge wilderness area over the past two decades but what is left still constitutes home to an array of wildlife. Even if you don't visit the parks, the main route between Mysore and the cities of the Tamil plains wriggles through the Nilgiris, so you may well find yourself pausing for a night or two along the way, if only to enjoy the cold air and serene landscape of the tea terraces. Whichever direction you're travelling in, a brief stopover at the dull and congested textile-producing city of **Coimbatore** is hard to avoid.

The **best time to visit** the Ghats is between late November and early March. At other times, either the weather is too cloudy and wet, or the hill stations are swarming with hordes of summer tourists. Winter is also the optimum period for **trekking** in the Nilgiris, which allows you to visit some of the region's most unspoilt forest areas, the traditional homeland of the Todas.

Kodaikanal

After a while in the South Indian plains, a retreat to the cool heights of **KODAIKANAL** (also known as Kodai), perched on top of the Palani range around 120km northwest of Madurai, is more than welcome. The town owes its perennial popularity to its hilltop situation, which at an altitude of more than 2000m affords breathtaking views over the blue-green reaches of the Vaigai plain. Raj-era bungalows and flower-filled gardens add atmosphere, while short walks out of the centre lead to rocky outcrops, waterfalls and dense shola forest. Kodai's outstandingly scenic hinterland also offers some of South India's best **trekking** terrain. Even if you're not tempted by the prospect of the open trail and cool air, the jaw-dropping **bus ride** up here from the plains makes the detour into this easternmost spur of the Ghats an essential one.

Despite Kodai's attractions, in the height of summer (June–Aug), when temperatures compete with those in the lowlands, it's not worth the trip – nor is it a good idea to come during the monsoon (Oct–Dec), when the town is shrouded in mists and drenched by heavy downpours. In late February and early March the nights are chilly; the **peak tourist season**, therefore, is from April to June, when prices soar.

Arrival and information

Buses pull in at the **bus stand** in the centre of town. Unless you're coming from as far as Chennai or Tiruchirapalli, the bus is much more convenient than the train: the nearest **railhead**, Kodaikanal Road – also connected to Dindigul (30min), where you may need to change bus if coming from Kerala, and

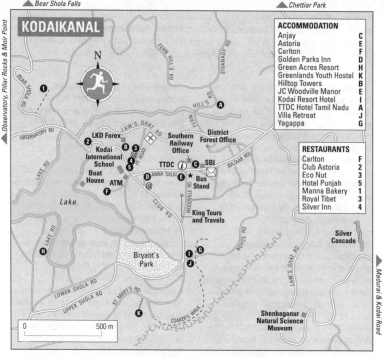

▲ Bear Shola Falls ▲ Chettiar Park

KODAIKANAL

◄ Observatory, Pillar Rocks & Moir Point

ACCOMMODATION

Anjay	C
Astoria	E
Carlton	F
Golden Parks Inn	D
Green Acres Resort	H
Greenlands Youth Hostel	K
Hilltop Towers	B
JC Woodville Manor	E
Kodai Resort Hotel	I
TTDC Hotel Tamil Nadu	A
Villa Retreat	J
Yagappa	G

RESTAURANTS

Carlton	F
Club Astoria	2
Eco Nut	3
Hotel Punjab	5
Manna Bakery	1
Royal Tibet	3
Silver Inn	4

TAMIL NADU | Kodaikanal

▶ Madurai & Kodai Road

Madurai (50min) – is three hours away by bus. There are two roads to Kodaikanal: the lesser-used route from Palani is by far the more spectacular approach, and during the monsoon is the only one open.

Tickets for onward rail journeys from Kodaikanal Road can be booked at the Southern Railway office, down a lane beside the *Anjay* hotel (Mon–Sat 8am–noon & 2.30–5pm, Sun 8am–noon). King Tours and Travels (☎04542/240047, ⓔkingtours@sancharnet.in) on Woodville Road can reserve seats on trains, buses and planes across South India. The **TTDC tourist office** (Mon–Fri 10am–5.45pm; ☎04542/241675) on Anna Salai (Bazaar Road) can arrange **treks** (5hr with a guide costs Rs300/group); longer routes such as the three-day trek to Munnar in Kerala can also be negotiated (around Rs1700/day, including basic accommodation). For **Internet** access, try Q Internet on Club Road, or the slower Flashnet, next to the *Royal Tibet* restaurant on PT Road.

Taxis line Anna Salai in the centre of town, offering sightseeing at high fixed rates. Most tourists, however, prefer to amble around at their own pace. Kodaikanal is best explored on foot, or by **bicycle**, which you can rent for around Rs10 per hour/Rs75 per day from numerous stalls around the lake. If you need to **change money**, head for the State Bank of India or the Canara Bank, both on Anna Salai near the *Anjay* hotel, or LKP Forex, next to the *Hilltop Towers*; there is also a State Bank of India ATM near the *Carlton Hotel*.

Accommodation

Kodaikanal's inexpensive **lodges** are grouped at the lower end of Anna Salai; many are dim and poky, however, so hunt around. Always ask whether blankets and hot water are provided (this should be free in the moderate to expensive places, but you may be charged in budget hotels). **Mid–range hotels** are usually good value, especially if you get a room with a view, but they hike their prices drastically during high season (April–June). The codes below reflect rates outside these months.

Anjay Anna Salai ☎04542/241089, ⓕ242636. Simple budget lodge slap in the centre. Rooms are smarter than you'd expect from the outside, and many have views, although those at the front suffer some traffic noise. If they're full, check out the similarly good-value *Jaya* behind. ❸–❹

Astoria Anna Salai ☎04542/240524, ⓔastoria1@eth.net. Well-kept hotel opposite the bus stand, with homely rooms and a good, mid-priced restaurant, though no views. ❹–❺

Carlton Off Lake Rd ☎04542/240056, ⓦwww.krahejahospitality.com. The most luxurious hotel in Kodaikanal, set in a spacious, tastefully renovated and well-maintained colonial house overlooking the lake, with a bar and comfortable lounge. Rooms in the house start around $100, and pricier accommodation is available in cottages within the grounds – attractive if a little overpriced; all rates include meals. ❽–❾

Goldan Parks Inn Anna Salai ☎04542/246181, ⓔgoldanparksinn@sify.com. This friendly and central hotel has sixty clean and spacious carpeted rooms with TVs, though it lacks character. There's a decent veg restaurant attached, plus an Ayurvedic massage service. ❺–❼

Green Acres Resort 11/213 Lake Road ☎04542/242384, ⓦwww.greenacresresort.biz. Spiffing new resort in a great setting in a quiet corner of the lake, with rooms and suites of varying sizes dotted around carefully manicured grounds. ❺–❽

Greenlands Youth Hostel St Mary's Rd ☎04542/240879, ⓔgreenlandsyh@rediffmail.com. Attractive old stone house offering unrivalled views and sunsets from its deep verandas. The rooms are basic, with wooden beds, open fireplaces (wood Rs50) and attached bathrooms. Book ahead. Dorm beds Rs100, rooms ❷–❹

Hilltop Towers Club Rd ☎04542/240413, ⓔhttowers@sancharnet.in. Block very near the lake and school, with comfortable modern rooms, three restaurants and attentive service. ❹–❺

JC Woodville Manor Woodville Rd ☎04542/240456, ⓔjcwoodvillemanor @yahoo.co.in. Small comfy rooms in a compact modern block by the bus stand, all with TV and tiny balconies, but no real views. Rs70 for a dorm bed. ❸

Kodai Resort Hotel Noyce Rd ☎04542/241301, ⓦwww.kodairesorthotel.com. Large complex of fifty incongruous-looking but very pleasant chalets situated at the top of the hill, with good views of the town, a health club and a rather dull restaurant. ❺–❻

TTDC Hotel Tamil Nadu Fern Hill's Rd ☎04542/241336. Large government-run hotel block northwest of town, primarily aimed at Indian family groups. Various types of rooms and cottages are available. There's also a restaurant, bar and large child-friendly gardens with swings and slides. Good off-season discounts. ❸–❹

Villa Retreat Coaker's Walk, off Club Rd ☎04542/240940, ⓦwww.villaretreat.com. Comfortable and characterful old stone house, set in lovely gardens with superb views. All rooms have attached hot-water bathrooms, and wood and electric heaters are available on request. There's a range of rooms of various sizes and prices – a touch overpriced, but compensated for by the sunrise views. ❹–❻

Yagappa Noyce Rd ☎04542/241235. The best budget deal in town, this small, clean lodge is set in old buildings ranged around a lawn-cum-courtyard and has good views. Rooms are modest but clean, and there's a great little bar with wicker chairs and a tiny whitewashed restaurant serving veg meals and breakfasts. ❷

The Town

Kodai's focal point is its **lake**, sprawling like a giant amoeba over a full 24 hectares just west of the town centre. This is a popular place for strolls, or bike rides along the five-kilometre path that fringes the water's edge. Pedal or rowing **boats** can be rented from the Boat House on the eastern shore (Rs30–100/30min, plus Rs25 if you require an oarsman), and you can go **horse riding** – it costs Rs50 to be led along the lakeside for 500m, or Rs200 for an hour's ride.

Shops, restaurants and hotels are concentrated in a somewhat congested area of brick, wood and corrugated iron buildings east and downhill from the lake.

Kodaikanal has become something of a low-key **trekking** centre in recent years. As you wander around town, **guides** continually approach offering their services on day hikes to local view points and beauty spots, or for longer trips involving night halts in villages. Scrutinize their recommendation books for comments by other tourists, and before you employ anyone go for a coffee to discuss possible routes, costs and the nature of the walks they're offering. While most are relatively straightforward, some tackle unstable paths and steep climbs for which you'll need sturdy footwear. You should also clarify accommodation and food arrangements, transport costs and also their fees, in advance.

Generally, simple meals and tiffin are available at villages along the routes of longer hikes, so you don't need to carry much more than a sleeping bag, water, emergency food supplies and warm clothes for the evening. **Maps** of the area tend to be hopelessly inaccurate, but the one featured in the booklet *Beauty in Wilderness* (Rs10), available from the DFO (District Forest Office; ☏04542/240287) near the *Hotel Tamil Nadu*, gives you a rough idea of distances, if not the lie of the land. While at the DFO, get a free permit to enter the area and to stay in the **Forest Rest Houses**, which provide rudimentary accommodation for around Rs25–50 per night; most have fireplaces, but bear in mind that any wood you might burn contributes to the overall **deforestation** of the Palanis. Local environmental groups are concerned about the potential long-term impact of trekking on the economy and ecology of the range, and as a result encourage walkers to carry all rubbish, bury their faeces where toilets are not available and use purification tablets rather than bottled water.

For more information on environmentally friendly trekking in the Kodai area, contact the **Palani Hills Conservation Council (PHCC)** at Amarville House on Lower Shola Road (☏04542/240711). This excellent environmental organization also welcomes foreign volunteer workers to help with their various campaigns and grassroots projects in the Palanis.

A recommended hike

If you'd prefer to hike without a guide, the following route is worth considering; most of it follows forest roads, and there are settlements at regular intervals, many of them connected to Kodai by daily bus services. You don't get to explore the wild tops of the range, but the views and countryside throughout are beautiful, with patches of indigenous shola forest accessible at various points.

First head out of town on the **Pillar Rocks** road towards Berijam; if you can hitch a ride, you'll avoid the horn beeping that otherwise accompanies your progress as far as the end of the road at **Moir Point**. Berijam (23km), a picturesque lake surrounded by dense pine and acacia forest, is little more than an outpost for forest wardens. From here, however, you can follow quiet country roads, taking local herders' and wood gatherers' paths that cut between the bends, to **Kavunji**, which is served by six daily buses to Kodai – handy if you're short of time. This sleepy Palani village is the home of a small NGO that promotes children's health projects, run by S.A. Iruthyaraj (look for the house with a white chicken painted on the wall), who is highly knowledgeable about local shola forests and off-track routes in the area. Further along the trail at **Polur** (8km) are some spectacular **waterfalls**. The locals say it is impossible to get close to them, but you can, by scrambling down the hillside via a muddy overgrown cattle path – and it's well worth it for the refreshing shower.

The only monuments to Kodai's colonial past are the neat **British bungalows** that overlook the lake and Law's Ghat Road on the eastern edge of town. The British first moved here in 1845, to be joined later by members of the American Mission, who set up schools for European children. One remains as the **Kodai**

International School; despite the name, almost all its students are Indian. The school occasionally holds concerts on the green just east of the lake.

To the south of the centre is **Bryant's Park** (daily 8.30am–6.30pm, last entry 6pm; Rs5, camera Rs25, video Rs500), with tiered flowerbeds against a backdrop of pine, eucalyptus, rhododendron and wattle, which stretches southwards to Shola Road, less than 1km from the point where the hill drops abruptly to the plains. A path, known as **Coaker's Walk** (Rs2, camera Rs5) skirts the hill, winding from the *Villa Retreat* to *Greenland's Youth Hostel* (10min), offering remarkable views, which on a clear day stretch as far as Madurai, and fantastic sunsets.

One of Kodai's most popular natural attractions is **Pillar Rocks**, 7km south of town, where a series of granite cliffs rise more than 100m above the hillside. To get there, follow the westbound Observatory Road from the northernmost point of the lake (a steep climb) until you come to a crossroads. The road heading south from here passes the gentle **Fairy Falls** on the way to Pillar Rocks, while Observatory Road continues west to the **Astrophysical Observatory**, perched at Kodai's highest point (2347m), although it's closed to visitors. Closer to the north shore of the lake, **Bear Shola Falls** are at their strongest early in the year, just after the second annual monsoon.

Southeast of the town centre, about 3km down Law's Ghat Road (towards the plains), the **Shenbaganur Natural Science Museum** (Mon–Sat 9am–5pm; Rs5) has a far from inviting collection of stuffed animals. However, the orchid house is spectacular, and well worth a look on the way to **Silver Cascade** waterfalls, a further 2km along the road.

Chettiar Park, on the very northeast edge of town, around 3km from the lake at the end of a winding uphill road, flourishes with trees and flowers all year round, and every twelve years is flushed with a haze of pale-blue **Kurinji blossoms** (unfortunately, the next flowering will not be until 2018). These unusual flowers are associated with the god Murugan, the Tamil form of Karttikeya (Shiva's second son), and god of Kurinji, one of five ancient divisions of the Tamil country. A temple in his honour stands just outside the park.

Eating

If you choose not to eat in any of the hotel **restaurants**, head for the food stalls along PT Road, a five-minute walk from the bus stand. Menus include Indian, Chinese, Western and Tibetan dishes, and some places cater specifically for vegetarians. Look out, too, for the **bakeries**, with their wonderful, fresh, warm bread and cakes each morning.

Carlton *Carlton Hotel*, off Lake Rd. Splash out on a buffet spread (Rs330) at Kodai's top hotel, rounded off with a *chhota* peg of IMFL scotch in the bar.

Club Astoria Lake Rd. Bright and breezy multi-cuisine restaurant with a large terrace overlooking the lake. Better to come for a snack or drink and the view than a main meal, though.

Eco Nut J's Heritage Complex, PT Rd. One of South India's few bona fide Western-style wholefood shops and a great place to stock up on trekking supplies: muesli, home-made jams, breads, pickles and muffins, high-calorie "nutri-balls" and delicious cheeses from Auroville.

Hotel Punjab PT Rd. Top North Indian cuisine and reasonably priced tandoori specialities; try their great butter chicken and hot naan.

Manna Bakery Bear Shola Rd, 15–20min by foot from the centre. The fried breakfasts, pizzas and home-baked brown bread and cakes served in this eccentric, self-consciously ecofriendly café-restaurant are great, though the bare concrete dining hall is a bit dingy.

Royal Tibet PT Rd. One of three small Tibetan joints in town, with dishes ranging from thick home-made bread to particularly tasty *momos* and noodles, and some Indian and Chinese options.

Silver Inn PT Rd. Western favourites like porridge, lasagne, mashed potato and apple crumble are all adequately served at this hole-in-the-wall place. Two pavement tables allow you to get some fresh air as you eat.

Palani

Few sacred sites in South India enjoy as dramatic a location as **PALANI**, just over 100km northwest of Madurai. Crowning a smooth-sided, perfectly dome-shaped outcrop of granite, the town's principal shrine overlooks a vast lake, **Vyapuri**, enfolded by the pale yellow crags of the Palani Hills, rising sheer to the south. During the monsoons, the tortuous road that scales the mountains from here provides the only dependable access to Kodaikanal; at other times, relatively few travellers are aware of its existence. The views, however, outstrip those from the busier southern approach to the hill station, while Palani itself, a busy little Tamil pilgrimage town, warrants at least a day-trip or stopover between Kodai and Ooty.

The Malaikovil Temple

Praised for over two thousand years in the songs of the wandering Tamil saints, Palani's red-and-white-striped **Malaikovil Temple** attracts thousands of Hindu pilgrims each day. Each visitor is expected to perform two important rituals. The first involves an auspicious circuit of the base of the hill, via a two-kilometre-long sandy path known as the **Giri-Veedhi**, which is punctuated with shrines and stone-carved peacocks (Murugan's *vahana*, or vehicle). The second is an ascent of the sacred walkway via its 704 steps, illuminated from dusk onwards with tiny camphor lamps left by the devotees (and interrupted by more prosaic billboards advertising the names of the temple's corporate sponsors), to the hilltop shrine itself. During Palani's main festival in April/May, thousands of devotees – mostly male and clad in black *dhotis* – pour up the winding flight to worship the image, said to be formed from an aggregate of poisonous minerals, that, if mixed with coconut milk, fruits and flowers, produces medicinal herbs. Some carry pails of milk on yokes as offerings for Lord Murugan, while the more fervent among them perform austerities (cheek-piercing with metal leaf-shaped skewers is a

△ Pilgrims at Malaikovil Temple, Palani

favourite). Those unable to climb the steps can ascend in a carriage pulled slowly up the steep incline by electric winch (Rs10). It can take a lot of queuing to get on but you can fast-track yourself by paying Rs50. The summit **views** across Vyapuri lake and the Vaigai plain to the distant Ghats are unforgettable.

Practicalities

Buses to Palani from Kodaikanal (every 1hr 30min; 3hr) often fill up, but it's possible to book some services the day before. The town is also well connected by train and bus to Coimbatore, via Pollachi (for the Indira Gandhi Wildlife Sanctuary), and Madurai via Dindigul.

Apart from the numerous simple *choultries* – pilgrims' hostels owned by various caste associations from all over South India – Palani has a few proper **hotels**. The *TTDC Tamil Nadu* on West Giri Street, opposite the winch station (☏04545/241156; ❷–❸), has decent a/c and non-a/c doubles with attached bathrooms and hot water, as does the smart *Subam Hotel*, 7 North Giri St near the main temple entrance (☏04545/242672, Ⓦwww .hotelsubam.com; ❷–❹). Of the few hotels near the bus stand, the *Deepam* (☏04545/242834; ❷–❹), on Dindigul Road, is a decent choice, with basic but clean rooms. There is a cluster of small veg and non-veg **restaurants** on (and just off) Dindigul Road.

Indira Gandhi (Anamalai) Wildlife Sanctuary

Indira Gandhi (Anamalai) Wildlife Sanctuary is a 958-square-kilometre tract of forest on the southern reaches of the Cardamom Hills, 37km southwest of the busy junction town of **Pollachi**. Vegetation ranges from dry deciduous to tropical evergreen, and the sanctuary is home to lion-tailed macaques (black-maned monkeys), wild elephants, crocodiles, *sambar*, spotted and barking deer, as well as a handful of tigers. Sadly, the government has been developing some major hydroelectric and irrigation projects in the area, and there have been several water and land rights disputes with local tribal people. The good news is that the park is now fully open again following the death of Veerappan (see p.641). A Forestry Department van conducts **safari tours** on request (Rs655 for the van), and **treks** of varying lengths and strenuousness can be attempted with the aid of a guide; they can be hired from the Forestry Department office. Local highlights include Ambuli watch-tower and Mount Stuart.

Practicalities

Pollachi has good bus connections to Palani and Coimbatore. From the town there are only three buses a day (7am, 11am & 3pm) up to the park's reception centre at **Top Slip**. These run via the official entrance at the **Sethumadai** checkpost, where you pay the Rs50 entry fee. The Forestry Department runs four **rest houses** (❶–❸), including one atmospheric tree house. These have to be booked in advance through the Wildlife warden at Pollachi (☏04253/225356). Apart from a couple of basic chai stalls, there is no food available, so it is wise to take your own provisions.

Coimbatore

Visitors tend only to use the busy industrial city of **COIMBATORE** as a stopover on the way to Ooty, 90km northwest. Once you've climbed up to your hotel rooftop to admire the blue, cloud-capped haze of the Nilgiris in the west, there's little to do here other than kill time wandering through the nuts-and-bolts bazaars, lined with lookalike textile showrooms, "General Traders" and shops selling motor parts.

Coimbatore earned its reputation as the "Manchester of South India" in the 1930s, when the nearby **Pykara Falls** dam was built to provide cheap power for its huge **textile mills** and spin-off industries. Since then, the city has never looked back. If you arrive here from more traditional corners of Karnataka or the deep south, you'll find it distinctly prosperous, modern and orderly: new office buildings and business hotels dominate the skyline, while in the street, trousers far outnumber *lunghis* and virtually every man sports a pen in his shirt pocket.

Practicalities

Coimbatore has four main **bus stands**, three of which are fairly near each other in the northern part of town, a couple of kilometres north of the railway station. The Thiruvalluvar bus stand is the main

Ukkadam Bus Stand, Pollachi, Kodaikanal & Palan

state and interstate station; buses from Ooty, Coonoor and Mettupalayam come into the Central bus stand, while the busy Town bus stand is sandwiched in between. The fourth bus stand, Ukkadam, in the south of town, serves Palani, Pollachi, Madurai and towns in northern Kerala. The **railway station** is in the southern part of town. Local buses ply between bus and train stations. Coimbatore's **airport** is 12km northeast of town and served by buses to and from Town bus stand; a taxi will charge around Rs200.

You can **change money** at the State Bank of India and Bank of Baroda, near the railway station, or at the American Express Foreign Exchange on Avanashi Road, a five-minute auto-rickshaw ride northeast of the railway station; there are plenty of ATMs. **Internet** access is available all over Coimbatore; options include Globalnet, on the first floor of Krishna Towers,

---

Map: COIMBATORE

CROSS CUT ROAD (P. GOUNDER STREET)
Blazenet
NEHRU STREET
SASTRI ROAD
SATHYAMANGALAM ROAD
Thiruvalluvar Bus Stand
BHARATHIYAR ROAD
Town Bus Stand
Globalnet
RAMAKROVIL STREET
KALINGARAYAR STREET
Central Bus Stand
SIVASWAMY ROAD
DR NANJAPPA ROAD
Ooty
N
Nehru Stadium
Airport (12km)
AVANASHI ROAD
Immanuel Church
BANK ROAD
RAILWAY FEEDER STREET
GPO
State Bank of India ATM
GEETHA HALL ROAD
State Bank of India
Net Hut
Bank of Baroda
TTDC Tourist Office
Railway Station
TRICHY ROAD
BIG BAZAR ST
Valan Kulam
Tiruchirapalli
0   500 m

ACCOMMODATION

Blue Star	A
CAG Pride	B
City Tower	F
Heritage Inn	G
KK Residency	C
New Vijaya Lodge	I
Park Inn	H
Sri Raja Lodge	D
TTDC Tamil Nadu	E

RESTAURANTS

Cloud 9	E
Gayathri Bhavan	1
KR	2
Malabar	C

For more information on moving on from Coimbatore, see Travel details at the end of this chapter.

By air

There are daily flights to Bengaluru (Bangalore), Chennai, Hyderabad, Kochi, Kozhikode and Mumbai. The Indian Airlines office is 2km east of the railway station on Trichy Road (☏0422/239 9833); Jet Airways is 4km along the same road (☏0422/221 2034). Air Deccan, Go Air and Paramount Airways do not have dedicated offices but you can book their flights at any travel agent.

By train

Coimbatore is well connected to major southern destinations by train. To catch the Nilgiri Blue Mountain Railway (see p.633) to **Ooty**, join the #2671 Nilgiri Express from Chennai, which leaves Coimbatore at 5.15am, and change onto the Blue Mountain Railway line at **Mettupalayam** (1hr), from where the one daily train departs at 7.10am. Should you get stuck in Mettupalayam, try the *EMS Maruya Hotel* at 212 Coimbatore Rd (☏04254/227 936; ❸), which has a/c doubles with attached bath. Overnight services from Coimbatore to **Chennai** include the Cheran Express #2674 (daily 10.15pm; 8hr 20min) and the Nilgiri Express #2672 (daily 8.55pm; 8hr 15min). For **Kochi**, catch the daily #2626 New Delhi–Trivandrum Kerala Express to Ernakulam (daily at 5.15am; 4hr 20min); the train terminates in Thiruvananthapurum (9hr 5min).

By bus

Buses leave for Ooty every fifteen minutes from Central bus stand. There are frequent services to Chennai, Pondicherry, Tiruchirapalli, Bengaluru (Bangalore) and Mysore from Thiruvalluvar bus stand, though they may also leave from Central. At both Central and Thiruvalluvar you can book tickets in advance at the **reservation office** (9am–noon & 1–8pm). Ukkadam bus stand, in the southwest of the city next to the lake, serves Madurai, local towns such as Pollachi and Palani, and destinations in northern Kerala, such as Palakkad and Thrissur.

---

on Sathyamangalam Road, just north of the Central bus stand; the smaller Blazenet, on Nehru Street next to the *Blue Star* hotel; and Net Hut, on Geetha Hall Road near the *Park Inn*.

Accommodation

Most of Coimbatore's **accommodation** is concentrated around the bus stands. The cheapest places line Nehru Street and Sastri Road, but whatever you do avoid the rock-bottom places facing the Central bus stand, which are plagued with traffic noise from around 4am onwards. Close to the railway station, there's a whole street of hotels along Geetha Hall Road.

Blue Star 369 Nehru St ☏0422/223 0635, ℱ223 3096. The best mid-price place in this area, with impeccably clean rooms, some with balconies, quiet fans and bathrooms, in a modern multistorey building five minutes' walk from the bus stands. ❸–❹
CAG Pride 312 Bharathiyar Rd ☏0422/252 7777, ⓦwww.cagpride.com. One of the best hotels in town, fully a/c with comfortable rooms, health club, garden restaurant, cocktail bar, foreign exchange and and even WiFi Internet access. ❻–❽

City Tower Sivasamy Rd, just off Dr Nanjappa Rd, a two-minute walk south of the Central bus stand ☏0422/223 0681, ⓦwww.hotelcitytower.com. Smart a/c city centre hotel with decent-sized rooms with modern interiors (heavy on leatherette and vinyls) and marble flooring; the "Executive" rooms are slightly more luxurious. The rooftop restaurant is first class (see opposite). ❺–❻
Heritage Inn 38 Sivasamy Rd ☏0422/223 1451, ⓔheritageinn@vsnl.com. Another smart business

hotel, with very comfortable a/c rooms, a couple of quality restaurants (veg and non-veg) and foreign exchange. **6**

KK Residency 7 Sastri Rd ℡0422/223 2433, ℗437 8111. Large tower-block hotel with very clean rooms and a couple of good restaurants (see below). **3–4**

New Vijaya Lodge 8/24 Geetha Hall Rd ℡0422/230 1794. Simple but adequate place with compact, clean rooms, very close to the railway station. **2–3**

Park Inn 37 Geetha Hall Rd ℡0422/230 1284, ℮parkinn_cbe@sify.com. The smartest option on this street – immaculate, quiet and good value (especially the non-a/c rooms). Rates include breakfast. **4–5**

Sri Raja Lodge 242 Sastri Rd ℡0422/223 5641. Extremely basic but clean enough lodge, conveniently located a minute away from the Central bus stand. **1**

TTDC Hotel Tamil Nadu 2 Dr Nanjappa Rd ℡0422/230 2176. Opposite the Central bus stand, this convenient, clean and reliable place, set a little back from the road, is one of the TTDC's better hotels, with a choice a/c or non-a/c rooms. **3–4**

Eating

For food, your best bets are the bigger hotels such as the *City Tower*, whose excellent rooftop restaurant, *Cloud 9*, serves a top-notch multi-cuisine menu to a predominantly business clientele; mains are around Rs100. The *Malabar*, on the first floor of the *KK Residency*, is a less pricey option, popular with visitors from across the Ghats for its quality non-veg Keralan cuisine. Meat-eaters will also enjoy the crispy fried chicken at *KR*, opposite the railway station, which has a good bakery as well. For vegetarian South Indian food, however, you won't do better than the ultramodern *Gayathri Bhavan*, opposite the *Blue Star* hotel on Nehru Street, which has a squeaky clean "meals" restaurant, open-air terrace, and an excellent little juice bar.

Coonoor and Kotagiri

At an altitude of 1858m, **COONOOR**, a scruffy bazaar and tea-planters' town on the Nilgiri Blue Mountain Railway (see box, p.633), lies at the head of the Hulikal ravine, on the southeastern side of the Dodabetta mountains, 27km north of Mettupalayam and 19km south of Ooty. Often considered second best to its more famous neighbour, Coonoor has luckily avoided Ooty's over-commercialization, and can make a pleasant place for a short stop. In addition to an atmospheric little hill market specializing in leaf tea and fragrant essential oils, there are also plenty of rejuvenating strolls to be taken in the outlying hills and valleys.

Coonoor loosely divides into two sections, with the bus stand (regular services to Mettupalayam, Coimbatore and elsewhere in the Nilgiris), railway station and market huddled together in **Lower Coonoor**. In **Upper Coonoor**, **Sim's Park** is a fine botanical garden on the slopes of a ravine, with hundreds of rose varieties (daily 8am–6.30pm; Rs5).

Visible from miles away as tiny orange or red dots amid the green vegetation, **tea-pickers** work the slopes around Coonoor, carrying wicker baskets of fresh leaves and bamboo rods that they use like rulers to ensure that each plant is evenly plucked. Once the leaves reach the factory, they're processed within a day, producing seven grades of tea. **Orange Pekoe** is the best and most expensive; the seventh and lowest grade, a dry dust of stalks and leaf swept up at the end of the process, is used to make the tea "dust" used in chai. To visit a tea or coffee plantation, contact UPASI (United Planters' Association of Southern India; ⓦwww.upasi.org), "Glenview", Coonoor.

Around the town, rolling hills and valleys, carpeted with spongy green tea bushes and stands of eucalyptus and silver oak, offer some of the most beautiful scenery in the Nilgiris, immortalized in many a Hindi movie dance sequence. Cinema fans from across the South flock here to visit key locations from their favourite blockbusters, among them **Lamb's Rock** (5km) and **Dolphin's Nose** (9km), former British picnicking spots with paved pathways and dramatic views of the Mettupalayam plains. Buses to both from Coonoor leave every two hours, but it's a good idea to catch the first one at 7am, which gets you to Dolphin's Nose before the mist starts to build up. It's possible to walk the 9km back into town via Lamb's Rock – an enjoyable amble that takes you through tea estates and dense forest.

Practicalities

There isn't much choice of places to **stay** or eat in Coonoor, and it's not a good idea to leave looking for a room until too late in the day. By and large the more appealing hotels are dotted around Upper Coonoor, within 3km of the station; you'll need an auto-rickshaw to find most of them. As ever, ignore any rickshaw-wallahs who tell you the hotel you want to go to is "full" or "closed". The fare from the bus stand to Bedford Circle or the *YWCA* is around Rs30–40.

If you're staying at the *YWCA* or one of the upmarket hotels your best bet is to eat there. In the bazaar, the only commendable **restaurants** are *Hotel Tamizhamgam* (pronounced "Tamirangum"), on Mount Road near the bus stand, which is Coonoor's most popular vegetarian "meals"-cum-tiffin joint. For good-value non-veg North Indian tandoori and Chinese food, try the *Greenland* hotel, up the road, while at Bedford Circle, the *Dragon* serves up even more authentic and tasty Chines dishes.

The Travancore Bank, on Church Road in Upper Ooty, near Bedford Circle, **changes currency**, but not always traveller's cheques. Otherwise, you'll have to go to Ooty (see p.635).

Accommodation

The tariffs included here are for the low season. High-season prices may increase by anywhere between twenty and a hundred percent, depending on the tourist influx.

La Barrier Inn Coonoor Club Rd ☏ 0423/223 2561. Comfortable mid-range option located way up above the bazaar, with great views of surrounding hills. The rooms are spotless, very large and open onto flower-filled balconies. ④–⑤

Sree Venkateshwara Lodge Cash Bazaar ☏ 0423/220 6309. The best option in Lower Coonoor, right by the railway station. Clean, average-sized attached rooms with TV. ②

Taj Garden Retreat Church Road, Upper Coonoor ☏ 0423/223 0021, ⓦ www.tajhotels.com. This luxurious but very overpriced colonial-era hotel offers cottage accommodation, a tea-garden, lawns and spectacular views, plus a good range of sports and activities, including freshwater fishing. The restaurant serves spectacular lunchtime buffets (around Rs300). Rooms from $150. ⑨

Velan (aka Ritz) Ritz Rd, 10min walk from Bedford Circle ☏ 0423/223 0784, ⓦ www.velanhotels.com. Recently refurbished, this luxury hotel is in a great location on the outskirts of town. Very spacious carpeted rooms with deep balconies and fine views – much better value than the *Taj Garden Retreat* but lacking its charm. ⑤

Vivek Tourist Home Figure of Eight Rd, nr Bedford Circle ☏ 0423/223 0658. Clean rooms (some with tiny balconies overlooking the tea terraces) in a rather starchy, institutional atmosphere. Beware of the monkeys. ②–③

YWCA Guest House Near the hospital, Upper Coonoor ☏ 0423/223 4426. Five double rooms and two singles in a characterful Victorian-era house on a bluff overlooking town, with flower garden, tea terraces and fine views from relaxing verandas. There are also superb home-cooked meals at very reasonable rates, which should be ordered in advance. ③

Kotagiri

The only other major settlement hereabouts, **KOTAGIRI**, lies a winding one-hour bus ride from Coonoor at an altitude of just under 2000m. High on the cloudy hilltops, it's even more given over to tea planting than Coonoor, and has little else going on. The one reason you might want to venture up here is to shop at the **Women's Cooperative** off Ramchand Square, which stocks the region's best selection of locally made handicrafts, including traditional red-and-black **Toda embroidery** (see box, p.638). Hand-woven woollen shawls are the most expensive items on offer, but they also keep smaller souvenir items such as spectacle cases and wallets, all at very fair fixed prices. Income from the shop is used to fund women's development projects in the area, principally among the Todas; they've an interesting frieze of photos on the wall showing where the money goes.

Kotagiri is connected to Coonoor (every 15min; 1hr) and Mettupalayam (every 30min; 2hr) by regular and reliable **bus** services. You can also get here from Ooty, 28km west (hourly; 2hr), via one of the highest motorable roads in the Nilgiris.

Udhagamandalam (Ootacamund) and around

British *burra-sahib* John Sullivan is credited with "discovering" **UDHAGA-MANDALAM**, still more commonly referred to as **Ooty**, a shortened version of its anglicized name, **Ootacamund**. When he first clambered into this corner of the Nilgiris through the Hulikal ravine in the early nineteenth

The Nilgiri Blue Mountain Railway

The famous narrow-gauge **Nilgiri Blue Mountain Railway** climbs up from Mettupalayam on the plains, via Hillgrove (17km) and Coonoor (27km) to Udhagamandalam, a journey of 46km passing through sixteen tunnels, eleven stations and nineteen bridges. It's a slow haul of four-and-a-half hours or more – sometimes the train moves little faster than walking pace, and always takes at least twice as long as the bus – but the **views** are absolutely magnificent, especially along the steepest sections in the Hulikal ravine.

The line was built between 1890 and 1908, paid for by tea-planters and other British inhabitants of the Nilgiris. It differs from India's two comparable narrow-gauge lines, to Darjeeling and Shimla, in that it uses the so-called **Swiss rack system**, by means of which the tiny locomotives are able to climb gradients of up to 1: 12.5. Special bars were set between the track rails to form a ladder, which cogs of teeth (connected to the train's driving wheels) engage like a zip mechanism. Because of this novel design, only the original locomotives can still run the steepest stretches of line, which is why the section between Mettupalayam and Coonoor has remained one of South Asia's last functioning **steam routes**. The chuffing and screeching whistles of the tiny train, echoing across the valleys as it pushes its blue-and-cream carriages up to Coonoor (where a diesel locomotive takes over) rank among the most romantic sounds of South India, and evoke the determined gentility of the Raj era even more strongly than Ooty's faded colonial monuments.

Timetable details for the line appear in the account of Coimbatore (see p.630) and in the "Moving on from Ooty" box, p.640.

century, the territory was the traditional homeland of the pastoralist **Toda** hill tribe. Until then, the Todas had lived in almost total isolation from the cities of the surrounding plains and Deccan plateau lands. Sullivan quickly realized the agricultural potential of the area, acquired tracts of land for Rs1 per acre from the Todas, and set about planting flax, barley and hemp, as well as potatoes, soft fruit and, most significantly, **tea**, which all flourished in the mild climate. Within twenty years, the former East India Company clerk had made himself a fortune and drawn the attention of British residents sweating it out on the southern plains. Sullivan and his business cronies planned and founded Ootacamund, a town complete with artificial lake, churches and stone houses that wouldn't have looked out of place in Surrey or the Scottish Highlands. Ootacamund quickly become the most popular hill retreat in peninsular India, known fondly by the *burra-* and *memsahibs* of the south as "Ooty", the "Queen of Hill Stations".

Of the Todas, little further note was made beyond a couple of anthropological monographs, references to their *munds*, or settlements, in the *Madras Gazette*, and the financial transactions that deprived them of the traditional lands. Christianized by missionaries and uprooted by tea-planters and forest clearance, they retreated with their buffalo into the surrounding hills and wooded valleys where, in spite of hugely diminished numbers, they continued to preserve a more or less traditional way of life (see box, p.638).

By a stroke of delicious irony, the Todas outlived the colonists whose cash crops originally displaced them – but only just. Until the mid-1970s, "Snooty Ooty" (as the notoriously snobby town became known) was home to some of the Subcontinent's last British inhabitants, those who chose to "stay on" after Independence, living out their last days on tiny pensions that only here allowed them to continue living in their accustomed style. Over the past three decades, travellers have continued to be attracted by Ooty's cool climate and peaceful green hills, forest and grassland. However, if you come in the hope of finding quaint vestiges of the Raj, you're likely to be disappointed; what with indiscriminate development and a deluge of holiday-makers, they're few and far between.

The **best time to come** is between January and March, thereby avoiding the high-season crowds (April–June & Sept–Oct). In May, the summer festival brings huge numbers of people and a barrage of amplified noise; worlds away from the peaceful retreat envisaged by the *sahibs*. From June to September, and during November, it'll be raining and misty, which appeals to some. The skies are clear between October or November until February, when it can get really cold at night – but it's pleasantly warm in the midday sunshine.

Arrival, information and local transport

Most visitors arrive in Ooty either by bus from Mysore in Karnataka (the more scenic, if steeper, route goes via Masinagudi), or on the miniature **Nilgiri Blue Mountain Railway** (see p.633) from Coonoor and Mettupalayam. The **bus stand** and **railway station** are fairly close together, at the western end of Big Bazaar and racecourse. **Local transport** consists of auto-rickshaws and taxis, which meet incoming trains and gather outside the bus stand and on Commercial Road around Charing Cross. You can **rent bikes**, but the steep hills make cycling very hard work, as they are all non-gear Heros.

The **TTDC tourist office** (Mon–Sat 10am–5.45pm; ☎0423/244 3977), at the *TTDC Hotel Tamil Nadu II*, is eager to help, but their information is not always reliable. You can book tours here, among them one that takes in Ooty,

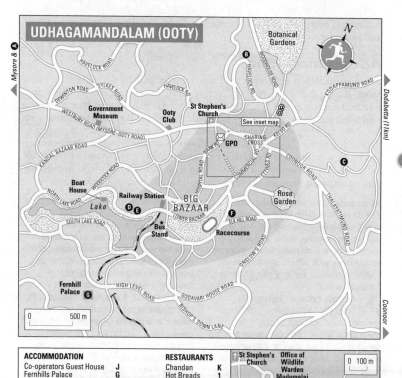

UDHAGAMANDALAM (OOTY)

Botanical Gardens

N

HAVELOCK ROAD

DEWNTON ROAD

SYLKES ROAD

HAVELOCK RD

HAVELOCK RD

WOODHOUSE ROAD

KODAPPAMUND ROAD

WESTBURY ROAD (MYSORE–OOTY ROAD)

Government Museum

Ooty Club

St Stephen's Church

See inset map

GPO

CHARING CROSS

KELSO RD

KANDAL BAZAAR ROAD

BANK RD

HOSPITAL ROAD

COMMERCIAL RD

ETTINES RD

COONOOR ROAD

C

Boat House

WOODCOCK ROAD

Railway Station

NORTH LAKE ROAD

Lake

D E

BIG BAZAAR

LOWER BAZAAR

Rose Garden

THALAYATTMUND ROAD

SOUTH LAKE ROAD

★ Bus Stand

F

ELK HILL ROAD

Racecourse

ONSLOW'S ROAD

Fernhill Palace G

HIGH LEVEL ROAD

GODAVARI HOUSE ROAD

BISHOP'S DOWN LANE

0   500 m

ACCOMMODATION		RESTAURANTS	
Co-operators Guest House	J	Chandan	K
Fernhills Palace	G	Hot Breads	1
Glyngarth Villa	A	Irani	3
Green Valley	E	Preethi Palace	4
Hills Palace	L	Shinkows	2
King's Cliff	B	Sidewalk Café	K
Nahar	K	Willy's	5
Reflections Guest House	D		
Regency Villas	G		
Sherlock	C		
TTDC Hotel Tamil Nadu	H & I		
YWCA Anandagiri	F		

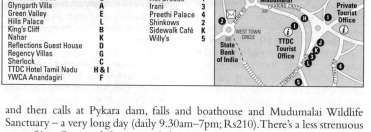

St Stephen's Church

Office of Wildlife Warden Madumalai

CHARING CROSS

Private Tourist Office

BACK RD

WEST TOWN CIRCLE

State Bank of India

TTDC Tourist Office

COMMERCIAL RD

ETTINES RD

0   100 m

and then calls at Pykara dam, falls and boathouse and Mudumalai Wildlife
Sanctuary – a very long day (daily 9.30am–7pm; Rs210). There's a less strenuous
tour of just Ooty and Coonoor (daily 9.30am–5.30pm; Rs130), which goes to
the local Sim's Park, the Botanical Gardens, the lake, Dodabetta Peak, Lamb's
Rock and Dolphin's Nose (see p.632). The private **tourist information
centre** (daily 10am–7pm, ☎m94433 45258), in the clocktower building on
Charing Cross, is very helpful and more reliable for hotels, restaurants, sightseeing and trekking.

Ooty's **post office** is northwest of Charing Cross at West Town Circle, near
St Stephen's Church. **Internet access** is widely available, especially around
Charing Cross. The only **bank** in Ooty that changes traveller's cheques and
currency is the very pukka State Bank of India, on West Town Circle; there
are also ATMs. While you're waiting for your cash, check out the photos in
the hallway connecting the old and new blocks, dating from the era when
this was the "Imperial Bank of India": stalwart, stiff-backed *burra-sahibs* pose
with pipes, wives and mandatory Scottish terriers in front of the old bank

building. There is an SBI ATM near the *Hotel Nahar* on Commercial Road, and numerous others.

Accommodation

Accommodation in Ooty is a lot more expensive than many places in South India; during April and May the prices given below can rise by thirty to a hundred percent. It also gets very crowded, so you may have to hunt around to find what you want. The best by far are the grand old Raj-era places (one such favourite, the *Nilgiri Woodlands*, is closed for renovation but should reopen in 2008); otherwise, the choice is largely down to average hotels at above-average prices. In **winter** (Nov–Feb), when it can get pretty cold, most hotels provide extra blankets and buckets of hot water on request, but a few sharks may quietly add a charge for these services onto your final bill, so check beforehand.

Co-operators Guest House Charing Cross ☎0423/244 4046. Cheap and central guest house in an L-shaped Raj-era building with clean rooms and turquoise balconies looking down to a courtyard; it's set slightly back from the main road so is relatively quiet. Unfortunately the place has become somewhat cramped by a large concrete *Nahar* next door. ❷

🏃 **Fernhills Palace** off High Level Rd ☎0423/244 3097, ⓦwww .welcomheritagehotels.com. Occupying the Maharajah of Mysore's palace, this luxury hotel has been fully refurbished, adding modern bathrooms complete with Jacuzzis whilst maintaining its old-world charm. The rooms are huge, with fireplaces and central heating, and prices range from around $120 to $300. ❾

Glyngarth Villa Golf Club Rd, 4.5km out of town on the Mysore Rd ☎0423/ 244 5754, ⓦwww .glyngarthvilla.com. A 150-year-old colonial villa set in four acres of greenery. The five double rooms, comfortable and with wooden interiors, give the place a charming atmosphere, and there are great valley views. Rates include breakfast. ❻

Green Valley North Lake Rd ☎0423/244 4219. A little grubby but friendly and a good fallback if *Reflections* next door is full. Sizeable rooms with attached bath, some with lake views, all with TV and all painted in wild colours. ❷–❸

Hills Palace Commercial Rd, Charing Cross ☎0423/244 6483, ⓔhillspalace@sify.com. Modern place that's just below the main bazaar, but secluded, quiet and spotlessly clean inside. Great value in low season. ❸

King's Cliff Havelock Rd ☎0423/245 2888, ⓦwww.kingscliff-ooty.com. Imposing ancestral mansion with four grades of lavishly furnished rooms, each with a Shakespearian theme; great value. There's also a stylish dining room and lounge, with terrific food and a resident singer/ guitarist. ❹–❻

Nahar Commercial Rd, Charing Cross ☎0423/244 2173, ⓔnahar@mds.vsnl.net.in. One of Ooty's smartest hotels, offering spacious, well-furnished rooms (the best are in the modern building at the back), two veg restaurants and an excellent café (see p.638). A favourite with large Indian family holiday parties, so book ahead. ❻–❾

Reflections Guest House North Lake Rd ☎0423/244 3834, ⓔreflectionsin@yahoo.co.in. Homely, relaxing guesthouse by the lake, five minutes' walk from the railway station, with rooms opening onto a small terrace. Easily the best budget option in Ooty, but it's small and fills up quickly, so book in advance. ❸

Regency Villas off High Level Rd ☎0423/244 3097, ⓦwww.welcomheritagehotels.com. Somewhat cheaper than *Fernhills*, the Maharajah's converted guesthouse, in the same grounds, is run by the same group.

🏃 **Sherlock** 2.5km southeast of Charing Cross ☎0423/244 1641, ⓦwww.littlearth.in /sherlock. Beautifully landscaped Victorian mansion with a Conan Doyle theme and stunning views from the grassy terrace. All rooms are tastefully furnished and the deluxe ones have sitouts. Friendly service and quality food too. ❺

TTDC Hotel Tamil Nadu, Unit I & II Unit I is in the northwest corner of the complex above Charing Cross, reached by a flight of stairs, and Unit II is just across the road ☎0423/244 4370, ⓔttdc @md3.vsnl.net.in. Two large, characterless complexes near the centre of town, but with good-value restaurants, a bar and billiards rooms. ❷–❹

YWCA Anandagiri Ettines Rd ☎0423/244 2218. Charming 1920s building, set in spacious grounds near the racecourse. Seven varieties of rooms and chalets are on offer, all immaculate, with bucket hot water and bathrooms, plus a dorm (Rs110). There is a dining room and you can while away the evening in the cosy "English parlour" or by the piano. Excellent value. Book ahead. ❷–❹

The Town

Ooty sprawls over a large area of winding roads and steep climbs. The obvious focal point is **Charing Cross**, a busy road junction on dusty **Commercial Road**, the main, relatively flat, shopping street that runs south to the Big Bazaar and municipal **vegetable market**. Goods on sale range from fat plastic bags of cardamom and Orange Pekoe tea to presentation packs of essential oils (among them natural mosquito repellent citronella). A little way northeast of Charing Cross, the **Botanical Gardens** (daily 8.30am–6.30pm; Rs10, camera Rs30, video Rs500), laid out in 1847 by gardeners from London's Kew Gardens, consist of forty acres of immaculate lawns, lily ponds and beds, with more than a thousand varieties of shrubs, flowers and trees. There's a refreshment stand inside, shops outside selling snacks and souvenirs, and a small Tibetan market.

Northwest of Charing Cross, the small Gothic-style **St Stephen's Church** was one of Ooty's first colonial structures, built in the 1820s on the site of a Toda temple; timber for its bowed teak roof was taken from Tipu Sultan's palace at Srirangapatnam and hauled up here by elephant. The area around the church gives some idea of what the hill station must have looked like in the days of the Raj. To the right of the church is the rambling and rather dilapidated **Spencer's store**, which opened in 1909 and sold everything a British home in the colonies could ever need; it's now a computer college.

South of here, in the same compound as the post office, gowned lawyers buzz around the red-brick **Civil Court**, a quasi-Gothic structure with leaded diamond-shaped windows, corrugated iron roofs and a clocktower capped with a weather vane. Over the next hill (west) is the snootiest of Ooty's institutions, the **Club**, which dates from 1830. Originally the house of Sir William Rumbold, it became a club in 1843 and expanded thereafter. Its one claim to fame is that the rules for snooker were first set down here (although the members of Jabalpur Club in Madhya Pradesh are supposed to have originated the game in the first place). Entry is strictly restricted to members and their guests, or members of affiliated clubs. Further along Mysore Road, the modest **Government Museum** (daily except Fri & second Sat of month 10am–5.30pm; free) houses a few paltry tribal objects, sculptures and crafts.

West of the railway station and racecourse (races mid-April to mid-June), the **lake**, constructed in the early 1800s, is one of Ooty's main tourist attractions, despite being heavily polluted (most of the town's raw sewage gets dumped here – worth bearing in mind if you're tempted to venture out on it). Boats are available for rent (daily 9am–6pm; paddle boats Rs60–100, rowing boats Rs80–110, charter motor boats seating 8–15 people Rs250–450), and you can also go horse riding here for Rs150 per hour.

Not far from the southeast end of the lake lies **Fernhills Palace**, once the summer residence of the Maharaja of Mysore and now a smart hotel (see opposite). It's an extraordinary place, built in the fullest expression of Ooty's characteristic Swiss-chalet style, with carved wooden bargeboards and ornamental cast-iron balustrades. *Regency Villas*, the Maharajah's guesthouse, located just behind the palace, is also a hotel and well worth a stop for a cup of tea on the lawn.

Eating

Many of the mid-range hotels serve up good South Indian food, but Ooty has yet to offer a gourmet **restaurant**, unless you want to take a taxi out to *Fernhill Palace* or *King's Cliff*. For an inexpensive Udupi breakfast, just head for one of the "meals" restaurants around Charing Cross serving *iddli-dosa* and filter coffee.

Until the arrival of the British, the **Todas** of the Nilgiri Hills maintained their own language and customs in villages (*munds*) of wagon-shaped huts made from bamboo, thatch and reeds. Today the Toda tribal community still exists, albeit in depleted numbers: just under two thousand Todas at the last count (of whom a quarter are Christian). Some wear traditional costume: plain white waistcloths under thick white woven shawls (*puthikuzhi*) striped with red and black. Once, all adult women had their upper body tattooed and their hair oiled and curled into long ringlets at the front – feminine beauty is judged by the narrowness of the feet and facial hair is admired. Men keep their hair and beards long.

Toda culture centres around the **buffalo**, which is held sacred; the only product the Todas use is its milk, consuming it in vast quantities – Toda temples are dairies, off-limits to everyone save the officiating priests. The community is divided into fourteen patriarchal clans, though its polyandrous social system is fast breaking down. "Marriages" were arranged at birth with partners from another clan; at the age of fifteen the female moved in with the husband's family and automatically became the wife of his younger brothers too. She could also seek further partners from other families, with the permission of her principal partner, who would generally assume the paternal role for any resultant offspring. Traditionally, the Todas lived in interdependence with four other tribal groups, based on a barter system under which their main responsibility was to supply the others with dairy products. Of these, the **Irulus** – Vishnu-worshipping tool-makers and ritual specialists who are regarded by the Todas as caste inferiors – are today the most numerous, with a population of around seven thousand. Fears of caste pollution also determine relations between the Todas and the **Kotas**, ironsmiths and potters who provide music for rituals. The jungle-dwelling **Kurumbas**, known for their aptitude in magic, gathered honey and wood, while the **Badagas**, who arrived in the fourteenth century after being displaced by Muslim invasions, kept the others supplied with grain and beans.

Due to high infant mortality and the introduction of life-threatening diseases by the British, their population had dwindled to little more than six hundred by the 1940s. This alarming situation was dramatically reversed, however, largely through the efforts of an exceptional Toda woman, **Evam Piljain-Wiedemann**, who trained as a nurse in England and succeeded in winning the confidence of other Todas to take advantage of a mobile medical clinic. She continues to work to secure rights for the Todas, and to protect the natural environment.

Blame for the threat to the survival of the Nilgiris cannot simply be laid at the door of colonial exploitation, though the story does begin with the arrival of the British in

Chandan *Nahar Hotel*, Commercial Rd, Charing Cross. Inexpensive, carefully prepared North Indian specialities (their *paneer kofta* is particularly good), and a small selection of tandoori vegetarian dishes, served inside a posh restaurant or on a lawnside terrace. They also do a full range of lassis and milkshakes.

Hot Breads Charing Cross. French-established franchise selling the usual range of quality pastries, cheesy and plain breads and savouries from a bakery outlet downstairs, as well as pizzas and other tasty snacks in a rather dull first-floor café.

Iranis Commercial Rd. A gloomy old-style Persian joint run by Bahá'ís. Uncompromisingly non-veg (the menu's heavy on mutton, liver and brains), but an atmospheric coffee stop, and a popular hangout for both men and women.

Preethi Palace Ettines Rd. Excellent lunchtime thalis (North and South Indian) and a range of superb pure-veg food in the evenings.

Shinkows 42 Commissioners Rd. Authentic Chinese restaurant serving up good-sized portions on the spicy side. It's more expensive than the downtown restaurants but still good value – main meat courses cost around Rs120–150, veg dishes are cheaper (Rs50–80).

Sidewalk Café *Nahar Hotel,* Commercial Rd. Bright, modern café offering soups, sandwiches, pizza, cakes and fresh fruit juices.

1821. Despite the British penchant for hunting (panther, tiger and deer) and fishing, they were aware, within the vision of the time, of protecting the natural landscape. The most destructive period came after Independence. From 1952, a series of five-year plans were implemented involving the widespread planting of exotic trees, principally eucalyptus, wattle and pine – they provided a generous income for the government, but had far-reaching effects on local ecology. A synthetic fibre industry, established in the foothills, requires huge amounts of pulp to make fibre. Despite local fears and protests, including a *satyagraha*-style public fast, land is still being cleared in order to feed factories.

Traditional shola forest, once destroyed, takes thousands of years to replace, and newly planted eucalyptus trees draw water from miles around – for the first time in its history, this once swampy region suffers from **water shortages**. The Todas can no longer get enough thatching grass to build houses and temples, and their traditional homes are being replaced by concrete. Nothing grows under eucalyptus and pine, and the sacred buffalo have nowhere to graze. Many Todas have been forced to sell their stock, and barely enough are left to perform the ceremonies at the heart of Toda life.

Visiting the Todas

In recent years, the Todas have become something of a tourist curiosity, and numerous trekking agencies and guides offer day-trips, or longer treks, to their settlements from Ooty. Although nothing on the scale of Thailand's Hill Tribe tourist circuit, the experience has to be a hollow one, consisting of a brief visit, and possibly a meal, followed up with the inevitable photo session. There is the additional problem that the influx of tourist dollars largely gets poured down the male population's necks in the form of alcohol. This helps to explain why the Todas in the more commonly visited villages do little to discourage foreigners from coming; on the contrary, they are only too happy to pose in traditional costume for the pre-arranged fee handed over to them by the tour leaders. You might want to ponder whether a visit ultimately benefits them though.

If you do decide to go, a recommended **guide** for trips to Toda settlements around Ooty is Johnson (T m98435 11458), who can often be found at the official guides' office on the corner between the bus stand and railway station. Count on around Rs300–400 per day for his fee, and additional costs for meals and transport. You'll probably learn just as much, however, if not more, about the Todas' way of life by reading Anthony Walker's definitive anthropological study, *The Todas of South India: A New Approach*, researched in the 1970s.

Willy's KRC Arcade, Walsham Rd. First-floor café, popular with students for its modern, buzzy vibe, tasty Western savouries and cakes, and range of gourmet coffees.

Around Ooty

Regular local bus services to outlying villages and plantations allow you to reach the less developed regions **around Ooty**. The most popular destination for a day-trip is the Nilgiris' second highest mountain, **Dodabetta** (2623m), 10km east along the Kotagiri road. Sheltering Coonoor from the southwest monsoon (and, conversely, Ooty from the reach of the northwest monsoon of October and November), the peak is the region's most prominent landmark. It's also easily accessible by road: buses run every couple of hours from Ooty (10am–3.30pm) to the summit, where a viewing platform and telescope make the most of a stunning panorama. To enjoy it, however, you'll have to get here before the daily deluge of bus parties.

Ooty **railway station** has a booking office (6.30am–7pm), where you can buy tickets for the Nilgiri Blue Mountain Railway (see p.633), and a reservation counter (daily 8am–12.30pm & 2.30–4.30pm) for booking onward services to most other destinations in the South. Four trains daily (9.15am, 12.15pm, 3pm & 6pm) pootle down the narrow-gauge line to Coonoor, but only one (3pm) continues down to Mettupalayam, which is on the main broad-gauge network. If you're heading to Chennai, the 3pm train should get you to Mettupayalam to connect with the daily #2672 Nilgiri Express (depart 7.45pm; 9hr 25min).

You can also book **buses** in advance, at the reservation offices for both state buses (daily 9am–12.30pm & 1.30–5.30pm) and the local company, Cheran Transport (daily 9am–1pm & 1.30–5.30pm), at the bus stand. A combination of stop-start local and express "super-deluxe" state buses serve Bengaluru (Bangalore) and Mysore (every thirty minutes), Kodaikanal, Thanjavur, Thiruvananthapuram and Kanyakumari, as well as Kotagiri, Coonoor and Coimbatore. Mysore- and Bengaluru (Bangalore)-bound buses both pass through Theppakkadu, for Mudumalai, but note that if you want to go to the Masinagudi side of the sanctuary, you have to get the dedicated hourly minibus from the southeast corner of the bus stand. **Private buses** to Mysore, Bengaluru (Bangalore) and Kodaikanal can be booked at hotels, or agents in Charing Cross; even when advertised as "super-deluxe", many turn out to be cramped minibuses.

There are many **trekking** possibilities in the Ooty region, apart from to the Toda villages (see box p.638). Many involve trips to tracts of privately owned jungle, such as **Secret Valley**, 17km north, which commands spectacular views across Mudumalai. The best person to contact is lifelong local British resident Mike Dawson (☏m94864 50100), who knows the region and its wildlife inside out and charges Rs400 per person for a local guided tour (Rs550 if the trip requires a Jeep). Another good trekking area is **Red Hills**, 20km southwest of Ooty. There is a sporadic bus service to the area, or you can opt for the swish **farmstay** near the village of **Emerald** at *Destiny* (booked through Little Earth in Ooty; ☏0423/244 5322, ⓦwww.littlearth.in/destiny; ⑤–⑥), which has spacious rustic rooms in a splendid hilltop location above a lake.

Mudumalai Wildlife Sanctuary

Set 1140m up in the Nilgiri Hills, the **MUDUMALAI WILDLIFE SANCTUARY** covers 322 square kilometres of deciduous forest, split by the main road from Ooty (64km to the southeast) to Mysore (97km to the northwest). Occupying the thickly wooded lower northern reaches of the Nilgiri mountains, it boasts one of the largest populations of elephants in India, along with wild dogs, gaur (Indian bison), common and Nilgiri langur and bonnet macaques (monkeys), jackal, hyena and sloth bear, and even a few tigers and leopards. Of the wealth of local flora, the dazzling red flowers of the flame of the forest, stand among the most noticeable. Now that the park is fully operational again, you can explore by vehicle or on foot. Generally speaking, the best time to visit is during and after monsoon.

The main route from Ooty to Mudumalai, taken by most Mysore- and Bengaluru (Bangalore)-bound buses, goes via Gudalur and takes 2 hours 30 minutes to reach **Theppakkadu**, the main access point to the sanctuary. The alternative route is a tortuous journey of very steep gradients and hairpin bends,

Veerappan and sandalwood smuggling

The delicate scent of **sandalwood** – *chandan* in Hindi – is one of the quintessential fragrances of South India, particularly around Mysore in Karnataka, where specialist craftsmen carve combs, beads, elephants and gods and use its oil to make incense and soap. Mashed into a paste, the valuable heartwood of the tree is regarded as a powerful antiseptic capable of curing migraine and skin ailments. Vaishnavites also smear their foreheads with sandalwood powder before performing puja, a practice recorded in the Ramayana, as well as the poetry of the sage Kalidasa, dating from the third century BC.

Sandalwood may be an essential element in traditional Indian culture, but it is fast becoming a rare commodity due to demand from foreign markets, which has forced the price skywards in recent years (a kilo of sandalwood oil will now fetch around US$1000–1500 at wholesale prices). The largest importer is the US, whose perfume industry uses vast quantities of the oil as a base and fixative, followed by the Gulf states, where sandalwood (along with myrrh, jasmine and amber) ranks among the few fragrances permitted by Islamic law.

The vast bulk of India's sandalwood comes from mixed, dry deciduous forests of the southern Deccan Plateau, around Bengaluru (Bangalore), where trees – if allowed to grow for at least thirty years – reach an average height of 20m. Extraction and oil-pressing are strictly controlled by the Indian government, in accordance with a law passed by the Sultan of Mysore in 1792, who declared that no individual other than himself could own a sandalwood tree, even if it grew on private land. This law is still enforced, although these days foresters receive seventy percent of the sale value if they can prove they have grown and protected the wood.

Up until recently, the Indian government failed miserably in its attempts to control sandalwood stocks. Through the 1990s and the early 2000s, the illegal trade in the precious wood was contolled by the notorious smuggler **Veerappan**, whose cartel handled an estimated seventy percent of Karnataka's total export, amounting to billions of rupees of lost revenue each year. South India's most infamous brigand, Veerappan began his career at the age of 14, when he poached his first elephant. Two thousand pachyderm carcasses later, he jacked in ivory smuggling for the sandalwood racket, was imprisoned in 1986, but escaped soon after, remaining at large until October 18, 2004, when he was tracked down and shot dead in the Dharmapuri district. Although he was always brutal in his treatment of the police, he gained something of a Robin Hood reputation among the local villagers, whom he paid generously for their compliance. He even received praise from one of his famous detainees, the Tamil actor Rajkumar, who was held to ransom by Veerappan for several months in 2000. The film star had nothing but complimentary remarks about the gentlemanly disposition of the outlaw when he was eventually released.

Veerappan and his band were the main reason given for the government closure to tourists of huge tracts of protected forest in the Western Ghats. For the best part of a decade, access to Mudumalai was restricted to the small area around the park HQ, and other sanctuaries, such as Anamalai (see p.628), were closed completely. Although it is doubtful that the smuggling of sandalwood has ceased completely (and there are rumours that corrupt forestry department officials are complicit in its continuance), the region is once again completely safe for visitors, although some areas are still off-limits, supposedly for ecological reasons.

which can only be attempted by smaller vehicles such as the Cheran transport minibuses. These take around one hour and end up at **Masinagudi**, which is closer to most of the area's accommodation.

At Theppakkadu, the main focus of interest is the **Elephant Camp** show (daily 8–9.30am & 5.30–6.30pm; free), where you can watch the sanctuary's tame pachyderms being fed and bathed. This is also the starting point for the government **safari tour** (7–9am & 4–6pm; 40min; Rs35 per person, camera Rs25, video Rs150), which is the only way of accessing the official park limits. Unfortunately, the tour is in a large minibus and the jabbering of your domestic fellow tourists is likely to frighten off the more timid animals. It is actually better to take a private **Jeep tour** or **guided trek** into some of the parts of Mudumalai that are outside the state-controlled area. These can be arranged through any guesthouse or direct at Nature Safari in Masinagudi (☎0423/252 6340, ⓔsaveelephasmaximus@yahoo.co.in).

Accommodation and eating

There is a reasonable selection of fairly luxurious jungle lodges, which invariably do pick-ups from Theppakkadu or Masinagudi, dotted around the park perimeter, plus a few budget options. Most people eat in their resorts; otherwise, there are a couple of basic "meals" joints in Masinagudi.

Casa Deep Woods Bokkapuram, 5km southwest of Masinagudi ☎0423/252 6391, ⓦwww.indian jungle.com. Classily designed bungalows, set in the forest, with well-furnished rooms. The suites boast enclosed open-air tubs. Meals included. ⑧

Jungle Retreat Bokkapuram, 6km southwest of Masinagudi ☎0423/252 6469, ⓦwww.jungleretreat.com. Mudumalai's prime resort, offering accommodation ranging from Rs400 beds in spacious dorms, through large and comfortable rooms and cottages, to a pair of elegant treehouses. Rs700 covers three sumptious buffet meals per day and unlimited tea/coffee. There's also an ecofriendly swimming pool and convivial bar with snooker table. ⑥–⑧

St Xavier's Lodge Ooty Rd, Masinagudi ☎0423/252 6371. Clean, basic lodge with small, Spartan rooms, but the best option right in the

village and one of the few budget places in the area. ②

TTDC Hotel Tamil Nadu Theppakkadu ☎0423/252 6580, ⓔttdc@md3.vsnl.net.in. Typical state-run hotel, but better than the Forest Department rest house (the only other option in Theppakkadu itself). Non-a/c rooms only, plus a Rs75 dorm. ②

Wild Haven Chadapatti, 6km south of Masinagudi ☎0423/252 6490, ⓔkarimjohn@hotmail.com. Simple but spacious concrete rooms, set in open land with great mountain views. Meals available at reasonable rates. ④

The Wilds at Northern Hay Theppakkadu ☎0423/244 9490, ⓔthewildstay@yahoo.com. Set in deep woods amongst coffee plantations, this relaxing place has pleasant outdoor seating areas and offers a choice of characterful rooms or a treehouse. Breakfast included. ⑥

Travel details

Trains

Coimbatore to: Bengaluru (Bangalore) (2–3 daily; 6hr 45min–9hr); Chennai (5–6 daily; 7hr 50min–8hr 55min); Ernakulam, for Kochi (7–8 daily; 4hr 20min–5hr 30min); Hyderabad (1 daily; 21hr 20min); Kanyakumari (1 daily; 11hr 45min); Madurai (1–2 daily; 6hr 15min–6hr 35min); Mettupalayam, for Ooty (1 daily; 1hr); Mumbai (2 daily; 31hr 15min–32hr 40min); Thiruvananthapuram (4–5 daily; 9hr 5min–10hr 25min); Tiruchirapalli (2 daily; 5hr 15min–5hr 45min).
Kanyakumari to: Bengaluru (Bangalore) (1 daily; 19hr 30min); Chennai (2–3 daily; 13hr 15min–15hr 25min); Coimbatore (1 daily; 11hr 55min); Kochi

(2 daily; 6hr 15min–6hr 30min); Madurai (1–2 daily; 4hr 20min–5hr 15min); Mumbai (1 daily; 47hr 20min); Thiruvananthapuram (2 daily; 1hr 35min–2hr); Tiruchirapalli (1–2 daily; 7hr 15min–8hr 15min).
Madurai to: Bengaluru (Bangalore) (1 daily; 10hr 30min); Chengalpattu (6–7 daily; 6hr 55min–9hr); Chennai (7–9 daily; 7hr 55min–10hr 30min); Coimbatore (1–2 daily; 6hr 15min); Kanyakumari (1–2 daily; 4hr–5hr 50min); Kodaikanal Road (2–4 daily; 33–45min); Tiruchirapalli (7–8 daily; 2hr 15min–3hr 10min); Tirupati (3 weekly; 11hr 30min).
Tiruchirapalli to: Bengaluru (Bangalore) (1 daily; 8hr 55min); Chengalpattu (6–7 daily; 4hr–5hr

20min); Chennai (7–9 daily; 5hr 20min–7hr);
Coimbatore (2 daily; 4hr 55min–5hr 10min);
Kanyakumari (1–2 daily; 7hr 30min–9hr); Kochi
(1 daily; 9hr 30min); Kodaikanal Road (2–4 daily;
1hr 50min–2hr 15min); Madurai (8–9 daily;
2hr 45min–3hr 30min); Thanjavur (2 daily; 1hr
10min–1hr 25min).

Buses

Chidambaram to: Chengalpattu (every 20–30min;
4hr 30min–5hr); Chennai (every 20–30min; 5–6hr);
Coimbatore (6 daily; 7hr); Kanchipuram (hourly;
7–8hr); Kanyakumari (3 daily; 10hr); Kumbakonam
(every 10min; 2hr 30min); Madurai (6 daily; 8hr);
Puducherry (every 15–20min; 2hr); Thanjavur
(every 15–20min; 4hr); Tiruchirapalli (every 30min;
5hr); Tiruvannamalai (hourly; 3hr 30min).

Coimbatore to: Bengaluru (Bangalore) (hourly;
8–9hr); Chennai (every 30min–1hr; 10–12hr);
Kodaikanal (4 daily; 6hr); Madurai (every 30min;
5–6hr); Mysore (3 daily; 6hr); Ooty (every 15min;
3hr 30min–4hr); Palakaad (hourly; 2hr); Palani
(hourly; 2hr 30min–3hr); Pollachi (every 30min;
1hr); Puducherry (10 daily; 9hr); Rameshwaram
(2 daily; 14hr); Thrissur (hourly; 5hr); Tiruchirapalli
(every 30min; 5hr).

Kanchipuram to: Chennai (every 10min; 1hr
30min–2hr); Coimbatore (3 daily; 9–10hr); Madurai
(4 daily; 10–12hr); Puducherry (10 daily; 3–4hr);
Tiruchirapalli (3 daily; 7hr); Tiruvannamalai (every
30min–1hr; 3–4hr).

Kanyakumari to: Chennai (hourly; 16–18hr);
Kovalam (10–12 daily; 2hr); Madurai (every 30min;
6hr); Puducherry (hourly; 12–13hr); Rameshwaram
(3 daily; 10hr); Thiruvananthapuram (every 30min–
1hr; 2hr 45min–3hr); Tiruchirapalli (every 30min;
10–12hr).

Madurai to: Bengaluru (Bangalore) (hourly; 8–9hr);
Chengalpattu (every 20–30min; 9hr); Chennai
(every 20–30min; 11hr); Chidambaram (6 daily;
8hr); Coimbatore (every 30min; 5–6hr);
Kanchipuram (4 daily; 10–12hr); Kanyakumari
(every 30min; 6hr); Kochi (9 daily; 10hr);

Kodaikanal (hourly; 4hr); Kumbakonam (8 daily;
6hr–6hr 30min); Kumily (hourly; 5hr); Mysore
(5 daily; 10hr); Puducherry (hourly; 9–10hr);
Rameshwaram (every 30min–1hr; 4hr); Thanjavur
(every 30min; 4–5hr); Thiruvananthapuram (hourly;
7hr); Tiruchirapalli (every 30min; 4–5hr); Tirupati
(4 daily; 15hr).

Puducherry to: Bengaluru (Bangalore) (4 daily;
10–12hr); Chennai (every 10–20min; 2hr 30min–
3hr); Chidambaram (every 20min; 2hr); Coimbatore
(10 daily; 9hr); Kanchipuram (10 daily; 3–4hr);
Kanyakumari (hourly; 12–13hr); Madurai (hourly;
9–10hr); Mamallapuram (every 10–20min; 1hr
30min–2hr); Thanjavur (hourly; 5hr); Tiruchirapalli
(every 30min; 5–6hr); Tiruvannamalai (every
20min; 2hr).

Tiruchirapalli to: Chengalpattu (every 20–30min;
7–8hr); Chennai (every 20–30min; 8hr 30min–9hr
30min); Coimbatore (every 30min; 5hr);
Kanchipuram (3 daily; 7hr); Kanyakumari (every
30min; 10–12hr); Kodaikanal (8–10 daily; 5hr);
Madurai (every 30min; 4–5hr); Puducherry (every
30min; 5–6hr); Thanjavur (every 10min; 1hr–1hr
30min); Tiruvannamalai (5 daily; 6hr).

Flights

For a list of airline websites, see p.38. In the
listings below IA is Indian Airlines, AI Air India, JA
Jet Airways, KF Kingfisher, SA Sahara Airlines, AD
Air Deccan, GO Go Air, IG IndiGo Airlines, PA
(Paramount Airways) and SJ SpiceJet.

Coimbatore to: Bengaluru (Bangalore) (AD, JA, KA;
4 daily; 40–55min); Chennai (AD, IA, JA, PA; 7–8
daily; 1hr 5min–1hr 15min); Hyderabad (JA, 1hr
20min–2hr 30min); Kochi (AD, IA; 1–2 daily; 30
min); Kozhikode (IA; 1 daily; 30min); Mumbai (AD,
IA, JA, GO; 5 daily; 1hr 45min).

Madurai to: Bengaluru (Bangalore) (AD; 1 daily;
1hr 20min); Chennai (AD, IA, JA; 7 daily; 55min–
1hr 25min); Mumbai (IA; 1 daily; 3hr 15min).

Tiruchirapalli to: Chennai (AD, IA; 1–3 daily;
50min–1hr 10min); Kozhikode (IA; 2 weekly;
55min); Thiruvananthapuram (IA; 4 weekly; 40min).

Andhra Pradesh

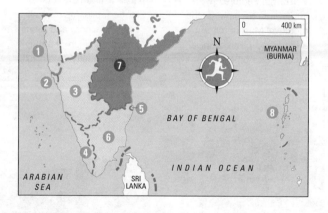

CHAPTER 7

Highlights

✳ **Hyderabad** A predominantly Islamic city offering a compelling combination of monuments, museums, lively bazaars and hi-tech wizardry. See p.649

✳ **Golconda Fort** Set in a lush landscape just west of Hyderabad, the capital of the Qutb Shahi dynasty boasts a dramatic fort. See p.659

✳ **Warangal** Features two important monuments: the medieval Muslim fort and a thousand-pillared Shiva temple. See p.665

✳ **Amaravati** Fine carvings surround the remains of a great Buddhist stupa at this village on the banks of the Krishna. See p.668

✳ **Tirumala Hill, Tirupati** The most visited pilgrimage centre in the world, Tirumala Hill is crowned by the Venkateshvara Vishnu Temple. See p.674

✳ **Puttaparthy** Sai Baba's main ashram attracts modern pilgrims from all over the world, and forms the centrepiece of a thriving community. See p.676

△ Golconda Fort

Andhra Pradesh

The largest state in South India, **ANDHRA PRADESH** occupies a great swathe of land that stretches for over 1200km along the coast from Orissa to Tamil Nadu and reaches far inland from the fertile deltas of the Godavari and Krishna rivers to the semi-arid Deccan Plateau. It is not, however, a place that receives many tourists: most foreign travellers pass through en route to its more attractive neighbours, which is understandable as places of interest are few and far between. However, the sights that Andhra Pradesh does have to offer are absorbing and well enough connected to warrant at least a few stops on a longer tour of South India.

The state capital, **Hyderabad**, which is now thriving as a hi-tech hub, dates from the late sixteenth century and remains an atmospheric city. Its endless bazaars, eclectic Salar Jung Museum and the mighty **Golconda Fort** nearby make it an enticing place to spend a day or two. **Warangal**, 150km northeast of Hyderabad, has both Muslim and Hindu remains from the twelfth and thirteenth centuries, while the region's Buddhist legacy – particularly its superb sculpture – is preserved in museums at sites such as **Nagarjunakonda**, south of Hyderabad, and **Amaravati**, the ancient Satavahana capital. In the east, the big cities of **Vishakapatnam** and **Vijayawada** have little of particular interest, though the former does boast a pleasant coastal stretch and the latter makes a convenient access point for Amaravati. The temple town of **Tirupati** in the far southeast and best reached from Chennai in Tamil Nadu, is one of India's great Hindu phenomena – a fascinating and impossibly crowded pilgrimage site, said to attract more pilgrims than either Mecca or Rome. In the southwest of the state, the small town of **Puttaparthy** draws a more international pilgrim crowd, enticed here by the prospect of *darshan* from spiritual leader Sai Baba; nearby, the ancient Hindu temple at **Lepakshi** is well worth a detour.

Although modern industries continue to boom around the capital, and shipbuilding, iron and steel are important on the coast, most people in Andhra Pradesh remain poor. Away from the Godavari and Krishna deltas, where the soil is rich enough to grow rice and sugar cane, the land is in places virtually impossible to cultivate. For further insight into the state and information on regional events, it is worth logging onto the online monthly magazine Ⓦwww.primetimeprism.com.

Some history

Earliest accounts of the region, dating back to the time of **Ashoka** (third century BC), refer to a people known as the Andhras. The **Satavahana dynasty** (second century BC to second century AD), also known as the Andhras, came to control much of central and southern India from their second capital at

Amaravati on the River Krishna. They enjoyed extensive international trade with both eastern Asia and Europe, and were great patrons of Buddhism. Subsequently, the Pallavas from Tamil Nadu, the Chalukyas from Karnataka, and the Cholas all held sway. By the thirteenth century, the Kakatiyas of Warangal were under constant threat from Muslim incursions, while later on, after the fall of their city at Hampi, the Hindu Vijayanagars transferred operations to Chandragiri near Tirupati.

The next significant development was in the mid-sixteenth century, with the rise of the Muslim **Qutb Shahi dynasty** (see box, p.660). In 1687, the son of the Mughal emperor Aurangzeb seized Golconda. Five years after Aurangzeb died in 1707, the viceroy of Hyderabad declared independence and established the Asaf Jahi dynasty of **Nizams** (see box, p.650). In return for allying with the British against Tipu Sultan of Mysore, the Nizam dynasty was allowed to retain a certain degree of autonomy even after the British had come to dominate all India.

During the struggle for Independence, harmony between Hindus and Muslims in Andhra Pradesh disintegrated, and **Partition** brought matters to a bloody climax (see box, p.650). Andhra Pradesh state was created in 1956 from Telugu-speaking regions (although Urdu is widely spoken in Hyderabad) that had previously formed part of the Madras Presidency on the east coast and the princely state of Hyderabad to the west. Today almost ninety percent of the population is Hindu, with Muslims largely concentrated in the capital. In 2004

Congress regained control of the state government from the pro-business and nationalistic Telugu Desam Party (TDP), easing lingering sectarian tensions. Meanwhile, however, the minority Telangana Rashtra Samithi (TRS) Party is pushing ever harder for northwestern Andhra Pradesh to split off as a separate state, to be named Telangana and with Warangal as its projected capital. Following a crucial and convincing by-election victory in Karimnagar in late 2006, the TRS are campaigning for Congress to quit stalling and take their demand for independence to central government, though this is strongly opposed by the TDP.

Hyderabad and Secunderabad

A melting pot of Muslim and Hindu cultures, the capital of Andhra Pradesh comprises the twin cities of **HYDERABAD** and **SECUNDERABAD**, which have a combined population of around six million. Secunderabad, of little interest to visitors, is the modern administrative city founded by the British, whereas Hyderabad, especially the old city, with its teeming **bazaars**, **Muslim monuments** and **Salar Jung Museum**, has far more character. Hyderabad went into decline after Independence, with tensions often close to the surface due to lack of funding – the old city only received 25 percent of the cities' budget despite having 45 percent of the population.

In the 1990s, however, Hyderabad began to capitalize on its good transport links and cheap land prices, and followed Bengaluru's (Bangalore's) lead in attacting investors. Now "**Cyberabad**" is the South's major hi-tech hub, and India's foremost computer and information technology centre. The growth of the local economy has far outstripped India's impressive annual growth in recent years, and property and land prices have crashed through the roof, with even moderate- sized pieces of real estate in the more desirable areas fetching millions of dollars. The noticeable increase in the number of private cars and the opening of over twenty Reliance hypermarkets around the city are other indicators of the ongoing boom.

Some history

Hyderabad was founded in 1591 by **Mohammed Quli Shah** (1562–1612). The new city was built beside the River Musi, as the fortress capital of the Golconda empire, just 8km east, had begun by that time to suffer from overcrowding and a serious lack of water. Unusually, it was laid out on a grid system, with huge arches and stone buildings that included what was to become Hyderabad's most famous monument, **Charminar**. At first the city had no walls; these were only added in 1740 as defence against the Marathas. Legend has it that it was linked with the spectacular **Golconda Fort** by a secret tunnel, which was dotted with dome-shaped structures at suitable intervals to provide the unfortunate messengers who had to use it with the opportunity to come up for fresh air.

For the three hundred years of Muslim reign, there was harmony between the predominantly Hindu population and the minority Muslims. Hyderabad was the most important focus of Muslim power in South India at this time; the princes' fabulous wealth derived primarily from the fine gems mined in the Kistna Valley at Golconda, which during the 1600s was the diamond centre of the world. The famous **Koh-i-Noor** diamond was found here – the legendary stone was tussled over and possessed by a succession of Mughal

The last Nizam

Picking your way through the sprawl of modern Hyderabad, it's hard to imagine that only sixty years ago this was the capital of a vast and powerful state, whose sumptuous palaces, mosques and ornamental gardens made it among the most splendid cities ever seen in south Asia. That the last outpost of living Mughal grandeur in the Subcontinent could be so quickly and so thoroughly reduced hints at the terrible events surrounding the demise of the state's last ruler. Direct descendants of the prophet Mohammed on one side, and the prophet's right-hand man, the Khalifa, on the other, the Asaf Shah dynasty of Hyderabad – known since the seventeenth century by its honorific Mughal title, **Nizam** – rose to pre-eminence in the twilight of Muslim rule in India. Feuds of succession nearly consumed the family, but it survived the colonial incursions of the French, British East India Company and Marathas, and by the twentieth century presided over the premier princely state in British India, home to a population of between fifteen and twenty thousand.

Marooned amid the vast ocean of Hindu India, the state capital, Hyderabad, emerged from the collapse of the Mughal empire and Deccan Sultanates as a lone outpost of courtly Muslim culture in India. Its nobles, merchants, craftsmen and artists, drawn from as far afield as Turkey, Persia and Central Asia, as well as the fading Indo-Islamic capitals of the north, lived in a splendid isolation epitomized by the extravagant lifestyles of the Nizams. Behind the high walls of the King Kothi palace, some 10,000 people – ranging from the Arab mercenaries and Abyssinian amazons who guarded the harem, to the legions of wives, courtesans and servants who attended the ruler – lived an increasingly anachronistic, introverted life, regulated by complex medieval etiquette and old-world courtly manners.

When he ascended to the throne in 1911, the tenth and last Nizam, **Mir Osman Ali**, was reputedly the richest man in the world. Memoirs of former British diplomats and local aristocrats describe his collection of 300 vintage Daimlers and Rolls-Royce cars; the famously huge, 185-carat "Jacobi" diamond, thought to be the largest ever found, which the Nizam used as a paperweight; and the trucks stacked with pearls, precious stones and gold ingots – a portable fortune that could be spirited away in the event of revolution or attack.

Taciturn, paranoid and addicted to opium, the last Nizam grew progressively more eccentric as British rule waned. The city was as rife with rumours of his extreme stinginess as of his unsurpassed wealth. Visitors, it was said, were limited to one biscuit when they called for tea, while the Nizam wore the same threadbare clothes for thirty or more years. One British resident mistook him for "a snuffly old clerk too old to be sacked". He even reputedly knitted his own socks, and ate all his meals off a tin plate on his bedroom floor, surrounded by the contents of overspilling waste-paper baskets. Perhaps the most surprising facet of the last Nizam's eccentricity, however, was his prodigious sexual appetite; he is said to have fathered more than one hundred illegitimate children. Hidden cameras installed inside the guest quarters

and Afghan rulers, including Aurangzeb, until it finally came to rest in the British crown jewels after Prime Minister Disraeli declared Victoria Empress of India in 1877.

Arrival and information

The old city of Hyderabad straddles the River Musi. Most places of interest lie south of the river, while just about all of the accommodation is to the north. **Hyderabad railway station** (also known as Nampally), 3km north of the river, is close to all amenities and offers a fairly comprehensive service to all major destinations. Some long-distance trains terminate at **Secunderabad**, to of his palaces also enabled him to compile what is thought to be India's largest collection of pornographic photographs.

When the end of the Raj finally came in 1947, Mir Osman Ali was given one year in which to make a choice: join India or throw in his lot with faraway Pakistan. In the event, much to the amazement of Prime Minister Nehru and Home Affairs Minister Patel, he chose instead to tough it out alone, declaring himself ruler of a fully autonomous Hyderabad state. The decision, symptomatic of the Nizam's introversion and bull-headed cupidity, was an act of hubris that would cost the lives of hundreds of thousands of this former subjects.

Often glossed over by historians as a bloodless formality, the ensuing **assault on Hyderabad** ordered by Nehru in 1948 – in which a fully mechanized Indian army attacked a feudal force armed with few more than 300 rifles – turned into one of the ugliest episodes in the history of Independent India. After being held at bay for four days, Nehru's troops rampaged through Hyderabad state, looting and leaving a trail of destruction in their wake. Taking advantage of the mayhem, gangs of Hindu *goondas* also ran amuck, slaughtering their Muslim neighbours and systematically raping the women. Although outwardly unruffled, Nehru was privately outraged by reports of the atrocities committed by the Indian army in **"Operation Polo"**, and commissioned an official enquiry once the dust had settled. The report, entitled *Hyderabad: After the Fall*, concluded that as many as 200,000 Muslims were massacred in the wake of the army action.

While tens of thousands of his former supporters, staff and nobles fled to escape execution and imprisonment, Nizam Mir Osman Ali was accorded the usual princely rights, along with a privy purse amounting to Rs5 million per year. He was also allowed to retain income derived from his estates and keep his treasure. Nevertheless, he died in 1967 complaining that the annexation of Hyderabad had reduced him to poverty.

Among the Nizam's surviving assets being squabbled over by his heirs is a mysterious million pounds, deposited in a London bank account shortly before the 1948 debacle. Following Partition, both the Indian and Pakistani governments laid claim to the sum, as did several of the Nizam's descendants and a princess called Tahera, who told the High Court of Andhra Pradesh that a stake of the money was owed to her as a *mehr*, or dowry given by a Muslim woman's family upon marriage which is traditionally returned in the event of divorce. So far the only beneficiary of the unending legal wrangle over the lost million has been the UK's NatWest bank. Since it was deposited in 1947, the £1,007,940 and nine shillings are estimated to have grown to anything from £25 million to £100 million. The bank insists it cannot relinquish the money until all the parties involved in the dispute are in agreement – an unlikely prospect indeed, given the perennially turbulent state of Indo–Pakistani relations, and the refusal of the various protagonists involved to recognize each other's claims.

the north, where some long-distance trains terminate, and where all through trains deposit passengers. If you do have to get off at Secunderabad, your ticket is valid for any connecting train to Hyderabad; if none is imminent, many buses, including #5, #8 and #20, ply between the two stations. The well-organized **long-distance bus stand** occupies an island in the middle of the River Musi, 3km southeast of the railway station. Hyderabad **airport**, 8km north of the city at Begumpet, is served by auto-rickshaws, taxis and buses #9M and #10, via Nampally station, and a number of routes including #45, #47 and #49 from Secunderabad.

The main **tourist office** in Hyderabad is the **AP Tourism office** (daily 8am–7pm; ☎040/2345 3110, ⓦ www.aptourism.com) on Secretariat Road just

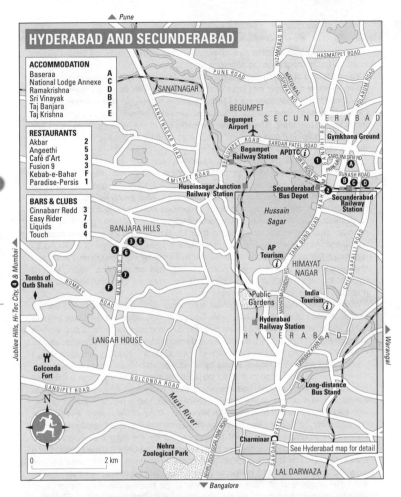

HYDERABAD AND SECUNDERABAD

ACCOMMODATION

Baseraa	A
National Lodge Annexe	C
Ramakrishna	D
Sri Vinayak	B
Taj Banjara	F
Taj Krishna	E

RESTAURANTS

Akbar	2
Angeethi	5
Café d'Art	3
Fusion 9	3
Kebab-e-Bahar	F
Paradise-Persis	1

BARS & CLUBS

Cinnabarr Redd	3
Easy Rider	7
Liquids	6
Touch	4

Guided tours

APTDC operates a number of **guided tours** (which can be booked via their two offices, see opposite). Times quoted below are for when tours set off from the Secunderabad office; pick-up time in Hyderabad is 15–20 minutes later. The better of the two APTDC **city tours** (daily 8am–5.45pm; Rs230) includes Hussain Sagar, the Birla Mandir and planetarium, Qutb Shahi tombs (not Fri), Salar Jung Museum (not Fri), Charminar and Golconda. There are also shorter morning and afternoon city tours and one to **Golconda Fort's sound and light show** (daily 2–9pm; Rs155 including entrance fee), which also stops at the Botanical Gardens and drives past Hi-Tec City. **Ramoji Film City** also has its own tour (daily 7.45am–6pm; Rs415 including entry).

APTDC's **Nagarjuna Sagar** tour (Sat & Sun 7.30am–9.30pm; Rs360, excluding entry fees) covers 360km in total, and is rather rushed, but is a convenient way to get to this fascinating area (see p.665). The longer tours to **Tirupati/Tirumala**, more conveniently reached from Chennai and further afield in South India, are not worth considering.

ANDHRA PRADESH | Hyderabad and Secunderabad

before it becomes Tank Bund Road, near the start of the flyover. The **APTDC office** next door (daily 7am–8pm; ☎040/2345 3036, ⓦwww.aptdc.in) and the other APTDC office, at Yatri Nivas, Sardar Patel Road, Secunderabad (☎040/2781 6375), are useful principally if you want to book one of their tours (see box opposite). The **India Tourism office**, 2nd floor, Netaji Bhavan, Liberty Road, Himayatnagar (Mon–Fri 9am–5pm; ☎040/2763 1360), offers a few brochures. However, the best source of local information is the monthly listings **magazine**, *Channel 6* (Rs15; ⓦwww.channel6magazine.com), available from most bookstalls. It lists airlines, hospitals, rail enquiries, as well as body-freezing boxes and eye banks.

Accommodation

The area in front of **Hyderabad railway station** (Nampally) has the cheapest accommodation, but you're unlikely to find even a basic double room for less than Rs250. The grim little enclave of five lodges with "Royal" in their name is usually full and best avoided. The real **bargains** are in the mid- to upper-range hotels, which offer better facilities for lower rates than in other big cities. Little over 1km north of Secunderabad railway station, decent mid-range places can be found on **Sarojini Devi Road**, near the Gymkhana Ground. Most hotels operate a 24-hour checkout system.

Hyderabad

The following places are marked on the map on opposite, except where noted:

Amrutha Castle 5-9-16 Saifabad, opposite the Secretariat ☎040/5663 3888, ⓦwww .amruthacastle.com. A Best Western franchise, this extraordinary hotel, designed like a fairytale castle with round turret rooms, offers international facilities at fair prices and a fine restaurant (see p.662). With its rooftop swimming pool, it's a good place to splash out. ❼–❾

Anmol Residency Next to the Ek Minar Mosque, Nampally ☎040/2460 8116. Great-value, friendly mid-range place, handily placed for the station. The deluxe corner rooms have a lot more space and windows covering two walls. ❹–❻

Ashoka 6-1-70 Lakdi-ka-Pul ☎040/2323 0105, ⒻF6651 0220. Standard mid-range hotel with a variety of clean attached rooms with cable TV. The a/c rooms are much better value at little more than the non-a/c ones. ❹

Imperial 5-8-107 Nampally Station Rd ☎040/6682 7777, ⒻF2320 9089. Reasonably well-kept lodge a three-minute walk from the station. Some of the rooms have a/c and/or TV. ❸–❹

Quality Inn Residency Nampally High Rd ☎040/3061 6161, ⓦwww.theresidency-hyd.com. Swish, modern hotel belonging to the multinational chain; the most upmarket option near the station but overcharges foreigners at $95 and up. Good veg restaurant. ❽–❾

Rajmata Nampally High Rd, opposite the railway station ☎040/5566 5555, ⒻF2320 4133. Set back from the road in the same compound as the various *Royal* lodges, with large and clean non-a/c deluxe rooms. The adjacent *Lakshmi* restaurant offers good South Indian veg food. ❹

Sai Prakash Station Rd ☎040/2461 1726, ⓦwww .hotelsaiprakash.com. A five-minute walk from the station, this modern, centrally a/c hotel has comfortable carpeted rooms, all with cable TV, plus good restaurants (see p.662) and a bar. ❺–❻

Hyderabad addresses

Hyderabadis appear to have a deep mistrust of logical, consistent road-naming, mapping and **addresses**. One road merges into another, some addresses refer to nothing more specific than a locality and others identify themselves as being opposite buildings that no longer exist. Just as confusing are those that have very specific addresses consisting of a string of hyphenated numbers referring to house and plot numbers, incomprehensible to anybody other than town surveyors, and perhaps not even them. All this is somewhat ironic in a city that is home to one of the major sections of the Survey of India.

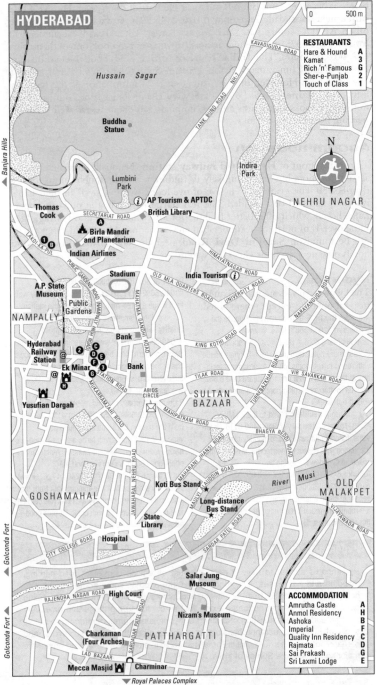

HYDERABAD

0   500 m

RESTAURANTS
Hare & Hound	A
Kamat	3
Rich 'n' Famous	G
Sher-e-Punjab	2
Touch of Class	1

N

KAVADIGUDA ROAD

Hussain Sagar

**Buddha
Statue**

TANK BUND ROAD NH-7

*Indira
Park*

NEHRU NAGAR

Banjara Hills

Lumbini
Park

i **AP Tourism & APTDC**

**Thomas
Cook**

SECRETARIAT ROAD

British Library

A

**Birla Mandir
and Planetarium**

HIMAYATNAGAR ROAD

1 B

LA-KDI-KA-PUL

Indian Airlines

PUBLIC GARDENS ROAD

Stadium

OLD MLA QUARTERS ROAD

India Tourism *i*

UNIVERSITY ROAD

NARAYANGUDA ROAD

**A.P. State
Museum**

**Public
Gardens**

MAHATMA GANDHI ROAD

NAMPALLY HIGH ROAD

NAMPALLY

Bank

KING KOTHI ROAD

**Hyderabad
Railway
Station**

@ **2** **C** **E**

D

Ek Minar **F** **3**

G

STATION ROAD

Bank

TILAK ROAD

VIR SAVARKAR ROAD

TURREBAZKHAN ROAD

@ **H**

Yusufian Dargah

MUKARRAMJAHI ROAD

ABIDS
CIRCLE

**SULTAN
BAZAAR**

✉

MAHIPATRAM ROAD

BHAGYA REDDY ROAD

Golconda Fort

GOSHAMAHAL

JAWAHARLAL NEHRU ROAD

MAHARANI JHANSI ROAD

MAULVI ALAUDDIN ROAD

Koti Bus Stand

River Musi

**OLD
MALAKPET**

VIJAYWADA ROAD

**Long-distance
Bus Stand** ★

★

**State
Library**

SARDAR PATEL ROAD

Hospital

CITY COLLEGE ROAD

**Salar Jung
Museum**

Golconda Fort ◄

RAJENDRA NAGAR ROAD

High Court

SARDAR PATEL ROAD

Nizam's Museum

**Charkaman
(Four Arches)**

PATTHARGATTI

LAD BAZAAR

Mecca Masjid **Charminar**

ACCOMMODATION
Amrutha Castle	A
Anmol Residency	H
Ashoka	B
Imperial	F
Quality Inn Residency	C
Rajmata	D
Sai Prakash	G
Sri Laxmi Lodge	E

ANDHRA PRADESH 7

Sri Laxmi Lodge Gadwal Compound, Station Rd ☏040/5563 4200. Quiet place down a small lane opposite the *Sai Prakash*, with reasonably clean rooms. Good value, especially for singles. ❷

Taj Banjara Main Road No. 1, Banjara Hills, 4km from the centre ☏040/6666 9999, ⓦwww .tajhotels.com. See map on p.652. In a pleasant location behind a small lake, with all the usual top-notch facilities including three restaurants (see p.662) and a 24hr coffee shop. Internet specials are often lower than the official rates, which start at $255. ❾

Taj Krishna Main Road No. 1, Banjara Hills, 4km from the centre ☏040/6666 4242, ⓦwww .tajhotels.com. See map on p.652. Just up the road from the *Taj Banjara*, the most palatial of the three Taj Group hotels in Banjara Hills. Official rates start at $375 and there's a presidential suite with its own pool for a cool $1200, as well as half a dozen quality eateries and bars. ❾

Secunderabad

The following places are marked on the map on p.652.

Baseraa Sarojini Devi Rd ☏040/2770 3200, ⓦwww.baseraa.com. The plushest hotel within fifteen minutes' walk of the station, with 77 modern rooms and suites boasting all mod cons. ❼–❾

National Lodge Annexe Opposite Secunderabad railway station ☏040/2770 5572. No-frills lodge amongst the motley cluster of hotels opposite the railway station. ❷

Ramakrishna St John's Rd ☏040/2783 4567, ⓕ2782 9033. Comfy mid-range option with some a/c rooms in a large concrete block opposite the railway reservation complex 400m from station. ❹–❺

Sri Vinayak Off Regimental Bazaar ☏040/2771 0146, ⓕ2780 2146. Decent lower mid-range lodge tucked away in a quiet lane behind a large white Sikh *gurudwara*, only a few minutes from the station. All rooms have attached bath; some have a/c. ❹–❺

The City

Hyderabad has three fairly distinct sectors: **Hyderabad**, divided between the old city and newer areas towards Hi-Tec City; **Secunderabad**, the modern city (originally called Hussain Shah Pura); and **Golconda**, the old fort. The two cities are basically one big sprawl, separated by a lake, **Hussain Sagar**.

The most interesting area, south of the River Musi, holds the **bazaars**, **Charminar** and the **Salar Jung Museum**. The river itself is just a trickle, even after the rains, and most of the riverside is grassed over and planted with palms and rice. It is bordered by two striking palatial buildings with attractive onion-shaped cupolas to the north and south, which are in fact the General Hospital and High Court respectively, both endowed by the last Nizam. North of the river, the city's more established shopping malls are found around **Abids Circle** and the **Sultan Bazaar** (ready-made clothes, fruit, veg and silk), ten minutes' walk east of the railway station. Abids Circle is connected to MG Road, which runs north to join Tank Bund Road at Hussain Sagar and continues to Secunderabad, while to the south it metamorphoses into Nehru Road. Four kilometres west of Hyderabad railway station, trendy new shops, restaurants and bars are also springing up in the posh **Banjara Hills** district, and around the exclusive residential area of **Jubilee Hills**.

Salar Jung Museum

The unmissable **Salar Jung Museum** (daily except Fri 10am–5pm; Rs150 [Rs10]), on the south bank of the Musi, houses part of the huge collection of Salar Jung, one of the Nizam's prime ministers, and his ancestors. A wealthy and well-travelled man with an eye for objets d'art, he bought whatever took his fancy from both the East and West, ranging from the sublime to the ridiculous. His extraordinary hoard includes Indian jade, miniatures, furniture, lacquer-work, Mughal opaque glassware, fabrics, bronzes, Buddhist and Hindu sculpture, manuscripts and weapons. There are also good examples of *bidri*, decorated metalwork cast from an alloy of zinc, copper and tin, which originated in Bidar in northern Karnataka. Avoid visiting the museum at the weekend, when it gets very crowded.

Charminar, Lad Bazaar and the Mecca Masjid

At the heart of the old city's crowded maze of bazaars is the **Charminar** (daily 9am–5pm; $2 [Rs5]), or Four Towers, a triumphal arch built at the centre of Mohammed Quli Shah's city in 1591 to commemorate an epidemic. As its name suggests, it features four graceful minarets, each 56m high, housing spiral staircases to the upper storeys. The mosque on the roof (now defunct) was built to teach the royal children the Qur'an, and is the oldest in Hyderabad. The yellowish colour of the building is due to a special stucco made of marble powder, gram (a local pulse) and egg yolk.

Charminar marks the beginning of the fascinating **Lad Bazaar**, as old as the town itself, which leads to **Mahboob Chowk**, a market square featuring a

△ Charminar, Hyderabad

mosque and Victorian clocktower. Lad Bazaar specializes in everything you could possibly need for a Hyderabadi marriage, with old stores selling jewellery, rosewater, herbs and spices, and cloth, including *lunghis*. You'll also find silver filigree jewellery, antiques and *bidri* ware, as well as boxes, plates, hookah paraphernalia and the like, delicately inlaid with silver and brass. Hyderabad is the centre of the national trade in **pearls** – so beloved of the Nizams (see p.650) that they not only wore them but apparently liked to have them ground into powder to eat as well. Pearls can be bought, for good prices, in the markets near the Charminar. Southeast of Lad Bazaar, the complex of **Royal Palaces** includes Chaumahalla, four palaces set around a central courtyard.

The fish miracle

In a land of a-thousand-and-one holy healers, miracle cures and all-round weird phenomena, one stands out as the fishiest. Each year, around June 6–9, on "mrigasira karti", the traditional arrival of the monsoon in Andhra, more than half a million **asthmatics** wheeze their way across India to Hyderabad on a quest to solve their breathing problems. With the summer heat at its fiercest and most humid, they stand for hours in the sun clutching little plastic bags containing a small live fish. Once patients reach the head of the mile-long queue, the fish, together with a nut-sized pellet of marzipan-coloured paste, is rammed wriggling down their throats.

The secret recipe for the wonder seafood cure is jealously guarded by the three brothers of a family of Hyderabadi toddy tappers, the **Bathini Gouds**. It was revealed in 1845 to one of their ancestors, Veerana Goud, by a *rishi* (saint) returning after a pilgrimage to the Himalayas, to thank the Gouds for their hospitality and kindness. The holy man, however, insisted the fish cure would only work if administered once each year, free of charge and using the exact ingredients prescribed by him, among them "holy water" from the so-called "Milk-well" (*Doodhbaowli*) in the toddy tappers' back yard.

Over the century-and-a-half-plus since the first fish cure, the treatment's fame has grown to such an extent that the Gouds are now unable to host the annual dispensary at their home, in the cramped confines of the old bazaar, 2km from the Charminar. Instead, the local municipality has set aside the city's vast Exhibition Ground in Gandhi-nagar to accommodate the hundreds of thousands of asthmatics and their families who pour in. Indian Railways lays on several special trains from Delhi, Guwahati and Thiruvananthapuram, and extra divisions of police are drafted in to cope with the crowds.

To keep up with the ever-increasing demand, the Gouds employ a team of dozens to prepare the paste in the months leading up to the break of the monsoon. But none of the old *rishi*'s provisos are ignored. The expense of making and administering the cure – roughly Rs20,000 annually – is still met entirely by the three brothers, although patients have to buy their own fish (unless they're vegetarian, in which case bananas may be used) at a nominal price of Rs5–7 from the on-site AP Fisheries Dept stalls.

If you're tempted to take the treatment, it's a good idea to contact the Goud family in advance through their website at Ⓦwww.bathinifish.com. Get to Hyderabad a couple of days in advance, and they will issue you with a pass that will save you having to queue for hours in the heat. Bear in mind, too, that to benefit fully from the fish cure you should have the treatment three times on successive years, and stick to a special Ayurvedic diet for 45 days after each one.

Finally, watch out for the crop of soundalike Goud impostors trying to cash in on the fish cure, who prey on unsuspecting new arrivals at the railway station. Not only do these fly-by-nights charge for the treatment, but none are likely to have mastered the deft finger-down-the-throat stab required to shove the fish speedily on its wiggly way.

For a vivid account of what the fish cure actually feels like, hunt out a copy of Tahir Shah's *The Sorcerer's Apprentice* (see Books, p.795).

Just a stone's throw from the Charminar stands **Mecca Masjid**, one of the largest mosques in India. It was constructed in 1598 by the sixth king, Abdullah Qutb Shah, from locally hewn blocks of black granite and small red bricks from Mecca, which are slotted over the central arch. The mosque can hold 3000 worshippers with up to 10,000 more in the courtyard; on the left of the courtyard are the tombs of the Nizams. In May 2007, the mosque was the scene of a tragic act of terrorism by unknown perpetrators, when a "tiffin box" bomb exploded during Friday prayers, killing twelve and injuring forty worshippers.

The **Charkaman**, or "Four Arches", north of Charminar, were built in 1594 and once led to the parade ground of royal palaces to the south (now long gone). The surrounding narrow streets spill over with interesting small shops: through **Doulat-Khan-e-Ali**, the western arch, which originally led to the palace, stores sell lustrous brocade and antique saris. The arch itself is said to have been once hung with rich gold tapestries.

The **Nizam's Museum** at Purana Haveli (daily except Fri 10am–5pm; Rs65) houses the longest wardrobe in the world, with built-in changing rooms where the Nizam would consider which of his innumerable costumes to don for the day. There is also an impressive display of gold, silver, pearls, precious jewels and artefacts as well as family portraits and newspaper cuttings that chart the history of the Nizam's family and lineage.

North of the river

The **Yusufian Dargah**, with its striking bulbous yellow dome, is set in a leafy courtyard not far south of the railway station (follow the road that runs down from the Ek Minar Mosque and look for an alley on the right). It's the shrine of a seventeenth-century Sufi saint of the venerable Chisti order, and you can enter (with covered head) to view the flower-decked tomb. About a kilometre north of the station, set in Hyderabad's tranquil public gardens, the **AP State Museum** (daily except Fri and every other Sat 10.30am–5pm; Rs10) displays a modest but well-labelled collection of bronzes, prehistoric tools, copper inscription plates, weapons, household utensils and even an Egyptian mummy. There's a gallery of modern art in the extension.

The **Birla Venkateshwara Temple** (daily 7am–noon & 3–9pm) on Kalapahad ("black mountain") Hill, north of the public gardens, was constructed in Rajasthani white marble in 1976 by the Birla Trust, set up by the wealthy industrialist Birla family. Although the temple itself is not of great interest, it affords fine views over the whole city. Nearby, and built by the same organization, is the **planetarium** (shows in English daily except Thurs at 11.30am, 4pm & 6pm; Rs20) and a **science centre** (daily 10.30am–8pm; Rs17) with lots of satellite hardware and photos, machines demonstrating sensory perceptions and a small dinosaur display.

Hussain Sagar

Hussain Sagar, the large expanse of water separating Hyderabad from Secunderabad, was created in the 1500s and named after Hussain Shah Wali, who had helped Ibrahim Quli Qutb Shah recover from a serious illness. It offers a welcome area of tranquillity within the busy conurbation. People come here to stroll along Tank Bund, the road that runs around the eastern side of the lake, and to relax in the small parks dotted along the water's edge. The parks contain numerous statues of prominent local figures from the last few centuries, and comes alive with ice-cream and snack stalls, particular as sunset approaches and people gather to watch the glowing red reflections in the lake.

In the centre of the lake stands a large stone statue of the **Buddha Purnima** or "Full Moon Buddha". The huge figure measures 17m high, weighs 350 tons and took five years to build – tragically, during the first attempt to install it in 1990 the barge carrying it sank, killing eight people. After spending two years underwater it was finally placed on its plinth by a salvage company in 1992.

Boats chug out to the statue from Lumbini Park, just off Secretariat Road, every hour from 9am to 6pm; the thirty-minute round trip costs Rs30. Two luxury boats – the *Bhageerathi* and the *Bhagmati* – operated by APTDC offer hour-long **cruises** of the lake (hourly: 11am–3pm & 6–8pm; Rs60–90). Both boats can also be chartered for special functions – check with APTDC for details.

Golconda Fort and the tombs of the Qutb Shahi kings

Eleven kilometres west of old Hyderabad, **Golconda** was the capital of the seven Qutb Shahi kings who ruled from 1518 until the end of the sixteenth century, when the court moved to Hyderabad. Set on a rock outcrop that rises imposingly above the surrounding plain, the well-preserved fort is one of the most impressive in India, though large portions of its battlements are draped in grasses, lending it a soft, natural air. Its outer wall was formerly 18m high in places and the citadel boasted 87 semicircular bastions and eight mighty gates, four of which are still in use, complete with gruesome elephant-proof spikes.

To get **to the fort**, take bus #119, which runs from Nampally, or the #66G direct bus from Charminar, or the #80D from the railway station in Secunderabad, each of which stop outside the main entrance. **For the tombs**, take #123 or #142S from Charminar. From Secunderabad the #5, #5S and #5R all go to Mehdipattanam, where you can hop onto #123. Or, of course, you could take a rickshaw and spare yourself the bother; plenty of them hover about to take people back so you needn't hire one for the day. Set aside a full day to explore the fort, which covers an area of around four square kilometres; it's well worth

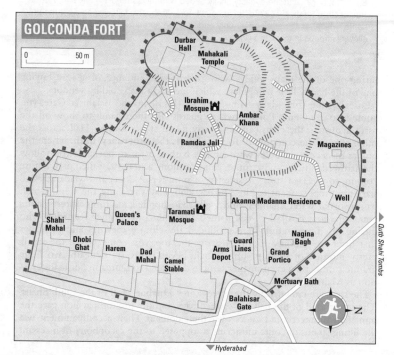

The Qutb Shahi

Quli, destined to become the first king of the Qutb Shahi dynasty, came from Persia with his uncle to sell horses to the Bahmani kingdom at Gulbarga and Bijapur. After a spell as a popular governor, he was titled **Quli Qutb Shah** by the Bahmani ruler Mamu Shbahmani who had appointed him. By 1518 the power of the Bahmanis was waning and Quli Qutb Shah raised an army and established independence for his state, ruling for 25 years and making Golconda his dynastic capital. When he was in his nineties, his eldest son Jamshed – who had briefly succeeded to the throne – attempted to have his father beheaded while praying in the mosque and his brothers exiled. However, an outraged people prevented Jamshed's coup by forcibly deposing him. Quli Qutb Shah preferred, thereafter, one of his younger sons, Ibrahim, to inherit his throne.

Ibrahim Quli Qutb Shah returned from exile to take over the kingdom at the age of eighteen. He was a learned man who wrote poetry in both Urdu and Telugu and oversaw the construction of many of Golconda's most important buildings, including the stone fort. His reign saw the dynasty reach the height of its power, despite occasional conflicts with the neighbouring states of Bijapur and Ahmadnagar. These three kingdoms later formed an alliance to defeat the powerful Vijayanagars in 1565.

The reigns of Ibrahim's only son, **Muhammad Quli Qutb Shah** (1580–1612), and grandson, **Muhammad Qutb Shah** (1612–26), both cultured men, saw the expansion of Golconda and foundation of Hyderabad once a bridge had been built over the River Musi in 1578. Despite the growing threat from the Mughals to the north, these were peaceful times, and prosperous trade was established with the European merchants on the coast, including diamonds. Rumour has it that a mine still exists in the fort, its exact location known only to the government.

Increasing pressure came from the Mughals during the long reign of **Abdullah Qutb Shah** (1626–72), and the dynasty finally ended with the surrender of his son, **Abdul Hasan Qutb Shah**, in 1687 to the forces of Aurangzeb. This followed an eight-month battle, which, as the story goes, only ended when Aurangzeb bribed a doorman to allow his troops in to secure victory.

hiring one of the many guides who gather at the entrance, or at least buying one of the handy little pamphlets, which include a map, sold by vendors.

Entering the **fort** (daily 9am–5pm; $2 [Rs5]) by the Balahisar Gate, you come into the Grand Portico, where guards clap their hands to show off the fort's acoustics; the claps can be clearly heard at the Durbar Hall across the other side of the compound. To the right is the **mortuary bath**, where the bodies of deceased nobles were ritually bathed prior to burial. If you follow the arrowed anticlockwise route, you pass along a straight, walled path before coming to the two-storey residence of ministers Akkana and Madanna, and start the proper ascent to the Durbar Hall. Halfway along the steps, which pass assorted water channels and wells that supplied the fort's water system, you come to a small, dark cell named after the court cashier **Ramdas**, who during his incarceration here produced the clumsy carvings and paintings that litter the gloomy room. Nearing the top, you come across the small, pretty mosque of Ibrahim Qutb Shah; beyond this, set beneath two huge granite stones, is an even smaller temple dedicated to Durga in her manifestation as Mahakali.

The steps are crowned by the three-storey **Durbar Hall** of the Qutb Shahs. The lower level of the hall has vaulted bays, and the rooftop pavilion gave the monarchs uninterrupted views over their domain. Their accompaniment was the lilting strains of court musicians, as opposed to the cacophony of incessant clapping heard today from far below. As you head back down to the palaces and harems, you pass the tanks that supplied the fort's water system.

The ruins of the **Queen's Palace**, once elaborately decorated with multiple domes, stand in a courtyard centred on an original copper fountain that used to be filled with rosewater. You can still see traces of the "necklace" design on one of the arches, at the top of which a lotus bud sits below an opening flower with a cavity at its centre that once contained a diamond. Petals and creeper leaves are dotted with tiny holes that formerly gleamed with rubies and diamonds; parrots, long gone, had rubies for their eyes. Today visitors can only speculate how splendid it must all have looked, especially at night, when flaming torches illuminated the glittering decorations. At the entrance to the palace itself, four chambers provided protection from intruders. Passing through two rooms, the second of which is overgrown, you come to the **Shahi Mahal**, the royal bedroom. Originally it had a domed roof and niches on the walls that sheltered candles or oil lamps. It is said that the servants used silver ladders to get up there to light them. Golconda's **sound and light show** (in English daily: March–Oct 7pm; Nov–Feb 6.30pm; Rs40) is suitably theatrical.

There are 82 **Qutb Shahi tombs** (daily except Fri 9.30am–4.30pm; Rs10) about 1km north of the outer wall. Set in peaceful gardens, they commemorate commanders, relatives of the kings, dancers, singers and royal doctors, as well as all but two of the Qutb Shahi kings. Faded today, they were once brightly coloured in turquoise and green; each has an onion dome on a block, with a decorative arcade. You can reach them by road or, more pleasantly, by picking your way across the quiet grassy verges and fields below the fort's battlements.

The western suburbs

Most of Hyderabad's new-found wealth is concentrated in the city's western suburbs. The nearest of these is the **Banjara Hills**, around 4km from Nampally, which comprises spacious residences in quiet streets surrounding the busy Main Road No. 1, a glitzy business strip that contains many of the city's trendiest shops, bars and restaurants and most luxurious hotels. The western appearance and dress, particularly of the young women who frequent the jewellery shops and coffee houses, is a startling contrast to the burkas and saris ubiquitous in the old city. Several kilometres further west you enter the even leafier and more upmarket district of **Jubilee Hills**, which is largely residential apart from the odd gleaming mall.

The upturn in Hyderabad's fortunes was driven by its becoming a hi-tech hub in the late 1990s, which earned it the nickname of Cyberabad, although it is also home to other growth industries including car manufacture. **Hi-Tec City** itself is several square kilometres of modern blocks and complexes about 10km from the city centre. Its centrepiece, Cyber Towers, was opened by Bill Clinton at the turn of the millennium and its subsequent growth encouraged by then TDP chief minister Chandrababu Naidu. Although strict security prevents casual visits by those with no business within the complexes, you can get a flavour by touring the area, which is bordered on the south and west by a large lake and beautiful rock formations, reminiscent of Hampi. Still further west, a new hi-tech area and business park is in its early stages at **Gsachibolli**, where local landowners have been relocated to make way for the prestigious International School of Business and other enterprises. A brand-new international airport is also planned for this side of the city, to provide easy access for the visiting suits. Naturally, the perennial question of whether any of all this wealth will filter down to the city's poor remains unanswered.

Ramoji Film City

Despite the greater fame of Bollywood and Tollywood (the Telugu-language film industry), it is **Ramoji Film City** (RFC; 10am–6pm; tours 10am–4.30pm; Rs250), around 25km north of Hyderabad, that is listed in the *Guinness Book of Records* as the world's largest film studio complex. Covering nearly 2000 acres, RFC offers around 500 set locations and can produce twenty international and forty Indian movies simultaneously. Although you cannot see films actually being made, you can tour this dazzling array of make-believe in a vintage bus. Given the Indian obsession with cinema, it's no surprise that over a million tourists are drawn here every year.

If you don't take APTDC's tour (see p.652), you will either have to hire a taxi for the trip (roughly Rs600–900), or take any of buses 204A, 205 or 206 from Women's College in near Koti bus stand, just north of the Long-distance bus stand.

Eating and drinking

In addition to the hotel restaurants, plenty of "meals" places around town specialize in **Hyderabadi cuisine**, such as authentic biriyanis, or the famously chilli-hot Andhra cuisine. Hyderabadi cooking is derived from Mughal court cuisine, featuring sumptuous meat dishes with northern ingredients such as cinnamon, cardamom, cloves and garlic, and traditional southern vegetarian dishes with an array of flavourings like cassia buds, peanuts, coconut, tamarind leaves, mustard seeds and red chillies.

Though not as abundant as in Bengaluru (Bangalore), **bars** welcoming to both sexes have started cropping up, mostly along Main Road No. 1 in Banjara Hills: try the plush white leather couches and Indo-Euro pop at *Liquids*, the disco theme nights at *Cinnabar Redd* (above *Fusion 9*), or the basement rock sounds at *Easy Rider*, further down the road. *Touch*, a futuristic pop and dance club above a new mall on Main Road No. 12 towards Jubilee Hills, is another trendy hangout.

Hyderabad

Angeethi Main Rd No. 1, Banjara Hills. Highly rated and rather pricey North Indian restaurant, with excellent Punjabi and tandoori dishes.

Café d'Art Main Rd No. 1, Banjara Hills. Along with the adjacent *Deli 9* takeaway, this trendy café, owned by the same people as *Fusion 9* above, serves quality baked goodies and gourmet coffee and tea.

Fusion 9 Main Rd No. 1, Banjara Hills. Expensive but quality global cuisine, from regions as diverse as Mexico, Europe, the Middle East and Southeast Asia, served in a smart modern lounge with tinted windows overlooking the street.

Hare & Hound *Amrutha Castle* hotel, Secretariat Rd, Saifabad. The hotel's multi-cuisine restaurant and bar, presided over by suits of armour, has a wide-ranging à la carte menu, while there's a great-value lunchtime buffet (12.30–3pm; Rs175) in the section outside the restaurant next to the reception and foyer.

Kamat Station Rd, opposite *Sai Prakash* hotel. Conveniently located branch of the extremely inexpensive and clean veggie chain. Their masala dosas never disappoint.

Kebab-e-Bahar Main Rd No. 1, Banjara Hills. The *Taj Banjara*'s classy lakeside patio restaurant specializes in a range of succulent kebabs and tandoori dishes but also offers delicious curries. Most main courses in the Rs200–400 range.

Rich 'n' Famous Station Rd. The posher and pricier of the *Sai Prakash* hotel's two restaurants, with comfy chairs, bamboo blinds and imaginative daily specials including crab, prawns and specialities from both Hyderabad and further afield; the veg *Sukha Sagara* downstairs serves cheaper South Indian meals and North Indian dishes.

Sher-e-Punjab Corner of Nampally High Rd and station entrance. Popular basement restaurant with good tasty North Indian veg and non-veg food at bargain prices.

Touch of Class Lakdi-ka-Pul. The *Central Court* hotel's restaurant offers good Hyderabadi non-veg cuisine, plus some veg options. It also serves barbecue kebabs, Mughlai, Western and Chinese food, and good-value lunch (Rs175) and late-night (Rs125) buffets.

See Travel details on p.678 at the end of this chapter for more information on journey frequencies and durations.

By train

Daily **train** services from **Hyderabad railway station (Nampally)** include: the Charminar Express #2760 to Chennai (6.30pm; 13hr 45min); the Hyderabad–Ernakulam Sabari Express #7230 (noon; 25hr 40min); the Hyderabad–Mumbai Express #7032 (8.40pm; 16hr 25min); the East Coast Express #8646 to Kolkata (10am; 30hr 15min), via Vijayawada, Vishakapatnam and Bhubaneswar; and the Rayasaleema Express #7429 to Tirupati (5.25pm; 15hr 20min). Almost all northeast-bound services call at Warangal and at Vijayawada. **From Secunderabad**, there are some originating services and many through trains in all directions. Useful services include the Konark Express #1020 to Mumbai (11.45am; 16hr 10min); and the Secunderabad–Bangalore Express #2785 (7.05pm; 11hr 10min).

The **railways reservations office** at Hyderabad (Mon–Sat 8am–2pm & 2.30–8pm, Sun 8am–2pm) is to the left as you enter the station. Counter #211 (next to enquiry counter) is supposedly for tourist reservations, but it's also used for group bookings and lost tickets. Foreign visitors can also make bookings at the Chief Reservation Inspector's Office on platform 1 for same-day journeys (daily 9am–5pm). The **Secunderabad reservation complex** is by the major junction with St John's Road, 400m to the right as you exit the station. Counter #34 is for foreigners.

By bus

From the Central bus stand, **regular bus services** run to Amaravati, Bengaluru (Bangalore), Bidar, Chennai, Mumbai, Nagarjuna Sagar, Tirupati, Vijayawada and Warangal. Various **deluxe and video buses** depart for Bengaluru (Bangalore), Chennai, Mumbai and other major destinations from outside Nampally station, where you'll find a cluster of private agencies, such as National Travels (☎040/2320 3614).

By air

The recent appearance of all the new competing domestic airlines means there are now at least ten **daily flights** to each of Bengaluru (Bangalore), Chennai and Mumbai. The growing network means there are also one to three flights daily to Coimbatore, Panjim in Goa, Pune, Tirupati, Vijayawada and Vishakapatnam, with new destinations appearing all the time. See Travel details for airlines and specific information on routes.

Secunderabad

Akbar 1-7-190 MG Rd, Secunderabad. A fine range of Hyderabadi dishes at moderate prices, including excellent biriyanis.

Paradise-Persis MG Rd, Secunderabad. Very popular multi-restaurant complex bashing out fine and inexpensive Hyderabadi cuisine, as well as kebabs and Chinese food.

Listings

Airlines, domestic *Air Deccan*, airport ☎m98496 77008; *Go Air*, Bollywood Tours & Travels, 176 1st floor, B block, Babukhan Estate, Basheerbagh ☎040/5546 4560; *Indian Airlines*, opposite Assembly, Hill Fort Rd, Saifabad ☎040/2343 0334; *IndiGo*, 2nd floor, 5-9-86/1 Chapel Rd ☎040/2321 1635; *Jet Airways*, 6-3-1109/1 GF Nav Bharat Chambers, Raj Bhavan Rd ☎040/3982 4444; *Kingfisher Airlines*, toll free ☎1800 180 0101;

Paramount Airways, airport ☎040/2790 4964; *Sahara*, 15 Sahara Manzil, opposite Secretariat, Saifabad ☎040/2321 2767; *SpiceJet*, toll free ☎1800 180 3333.
Airlines, international *Air France*, Gupta Estate 1st floor, Basheerbagh ☎040/2323 0947; *Air India*, 5-9-193 HACA Bhavan, opposite public garden, Saifabad ☎040/2338 9719; *British Airways*, Nijhawan Travel Services, 5-9-88/4 Ainulaman

Fateh Maidan Rd ☎040/2324 1661; *Emirates*, Floor F, Reliance Classic Bldg 3 & 4, Main Rd No. 1, Banjara Hills ☎040/2332 1111; *Gulf Air*, Jet Air, Flat 202, 5-9-58 Gupta Estate, Basheerbagh ☎040/2324 0870; *KLM*, Ashok Bhoopal Chambers, opposite Anand Talkies, SP Rd ☎040/2772 0940; *Lufthansa*, 3-5-823 Shop #B1–B3, Hyderaguda ☎040/2323 5537; *Malaysia Airlines*, 5th Floor, 502 White House, Kundanbagh ☎040/2341 0292; *Qantas*, Transworld Travels, 3A 1st floor, 5-9-93 Chapel Rd ☎040/2329 8495; *Singapore Airlines/ Swissair*, Aviation Travels, Navbharat Chambers, 6-3-1109/1 Raj Bhavan Rd ☎040/2340 2664.

Banks and exchange Surprisingly few banks do foreign exchange, two exceptions being the State Bank of Hyderabad, MG Rd, and Federal Bank, 1st floor, Orient Estate, MG Rd (both open Mon–Fri 10.30am–2.30pm, the latter also Sat 10.30am–12.30pm). It's better to head for an agency such as Thomas Cook ☎040/2329 6521 at Nasir Arcade, Secretariat Rd; or L.K.P. Forex ☎040/2321 0094 on Public Gardens Rd, only ten minutes' walk north of Nampally station; both open Mon–Sat 9.30am–5.30pm. There are an increasing number of ATMs around town, however, including at the State Bank of India on Nampally High Rd, Syndicate Bank on Station Rd, Oriental Bank at Secunderabad railway station and numerous machines on Main Rd No. 1, Banjara Hills.

Bicycle hire Bikes can be rented for Rs20 per day at the friendly stall on the right as you approach Hyderabad station from Nampally High Rd.

Bookshops A.A. Hussain & Co., 5-8-551 Arastu Trust Building, Abid Rd, Hyderabad; Akshara, 8-2-273 Pavani Estate, Road No. 2, Banjara Hills, Hyderabad; Higginbothams, 1 Lal Bahadur Stadium, Hyderabad; Gangarams, 62 DSD Rd, Secunderabad; and Kalaujal, Hill Fort Rd, opposite the public gardens, which specializes in art books.

Car rental Air Travels in Banjara Hills (☎040/2335 3099, ✉airtravels@yahoo.com) and Classic Travels in Secunderabad (☎040/2775 5645) both provide a 24hr service, with or without driver.

Crafts Lepakshi, the AP state government emporium at Gunfoundry on MG Rd, stocks a wide range of handicrafts, including *bidri* metalwork, jewellery and silks. Utkalika (Government of Orissa handicrafts), House no. 60-1-67, between the Ravindra Bharati building and *Hotel Ashoka*, has a modest selection of silver filigree jewellery, handloom cloth, *ikkat* tie-dye, Jagannath papier-mâché figures and buffalo-bone carvings. Cheneta Bhavan is a modern shopping complex a little south of the railway station, stuffed with hand-loom cloth shops from various states. For silks and saris, try Meena Bazaar, Pochampally Silks and Sarees, and Pooja Sarees, all on Tilak Rd.

Dentist Kakade's Dentistree, opposite *Taj Banjara*, Rd No. 1 ☎040/ 2330 2633.

Hospitals The government-run Gandhi Hospital is in Secunderabad ☎040/2770 2222; the private CDR Hospital is in Himayatnagar ☎040/2322 1221; and there's a Tropical Diseases Hospital in Nallakunta ☎040/2766 7843.

Internet access Internet outlets abound throughout both cities: try Modi Xerox opposite Ek Minar mosque or the CyberNet outlet within Nampally station. Net2phone facilities can be found at HK Travels on Staion Rd, close to the *Imperial* hotel, and behind the large Medwin Hospital on Nampally High Rd.

Library The British Library, Secretariat Rd (Tues–Sat 11am–7pm; ☎040/2323 0774) has a wide selection of books and recent British newspapers. Officially you must be a member or a British citizen to get in, but if you look Western you're unlikely to be asked to prove it.

Pharmacies Apollo Pharmacy ☎040/2323 1380 and Health Pharmacy ☎040/2331 0618 are both open 24hr.

Police ☎040/2323 0191. In an emergency call ☎100.

Travel agents General agents for airline and private-bus tickets include: Travel Club Forex ☎040/2323 4180, Nasir Arcade, Saifabad, close to Thomas Cook; and Kamat Travels in the *Hotel Sai Prakash* complex ☎040/2461 2096. There's a host of private-bus agents on Nampally High Rd outside Hyderabad railway station. Check prices as they vary from agent to agent.

Around Hyderabad

As you head north from Hyderabad towards the borders with Maharashtra and Madhya Pradesh, the landscape becomes greener and more hilly, sporadically punctuated by photogenic black-granite rock formations. There is little to detain visitors here except the small town of **Warangal**, situated on the main railway line, worth a stop to visit the nearby medieval fort and Shiva temple. South of the capital, vast swathes of flat farmland stretch into the centre of the state, where the Nagarjuna Sagar dam has created a major lake with the important Buddhist site of **Nagarjunakonda**, now an island, in its waters.

Warangal

WARANGAL – "one stone" – 150km northeast of Hyderabad, was the Hindu capital of the Kakatiyan empire in the twelfth and thirteenth centuries. Like other Deccan cities, it changed hands many times between the Hindus and the Muslims – something that is reflected in its architecture and the remains you see today.

Warangal's **fort** (daily 9am–5pm; $2 [Rs5]), 4km south, is famous for its two circles of fortifications: the outer made of earth, with a moat, and the inner of stone. Four roads into the centre meet at the ruined temple of **Svayambhu** (1162), dedicated to Shiva. At its southern, freestanding gateway, another Shiva temple, from the fourteenth century, is in much better shape; inside, the remains of an enormous *lingam* came originally from the Svayambhu shrine. Also inside the citadel is the eleventh-century **Shirab Khan**, or audience hall.

The largely basalt Chalukyan-style **"thousand-pillared" Shiva temple** (daily 6am–6pm; free), just off the main road, beside the slopes of Hanamkonda Hill 5km north, was constructed by King Rudra Deva in 1163. A low-roofed building on several stepped stages, it features superb carvings and shrines to Vishnu, Shiva and Surya the sun god. These lead off the *mandapa*, whose numerous finely carved columns give the temple its name. In front sits a polished Nandi bull, carved out of a single stone. A Bhadrakali temple stands at the top of the hill.

Practicalities

If you make an early start, it's just about possible to visit Warangal in a day-trip from Hyderabad on the frequent buses and trains (roughly 3hr). Warangal's **bus stand** and **railway station** are opposite each other in the southeast quadrant of town, served by local buses, auto- and cycle-rickshaws. The easiest way to cover the site is to **rent a bicycle** from one of the stalls on Station Road. To reach the fort, follow Station Road from the station and turn left just beyond the post office, under the railway bridge, and left again at the next main road. For Hanamkonda turn right onto JPN Road at the next main junction after the post office, left at the next major crossroads onto MG Road, and right at the end onto the Hanamkonda main road. The temple and hill are on the left. **Internet** facilities are available at Durga Xerox on Station Road, almost opposite the *Vijaya Lodge*.

Accommodation is limited: basic lodges on Station Road include the *Vijaya Lodge* (T0870/225 1222, F0870/244 6864; ❶–❸), which is the close to the station and best value, and *Vaibhav Lodge* (T0870/694 2895; ❷–❸), just beyond JPN Road, which has some a/c rooms. A new mid-range option even closer to the station on Station Road is *Hotel Surya* (T0870/244 1834; ❸–❹), while the marginally poshest option is *Hotel Ashoka* (T0870/285491, Wwww.hotelashoka.in; ❸–❹), not far beyond the thousand-pillared temple on Main Road, Hanamkonda, which has a/c rooms, a restaurant and bar. Several decent **eating places** line Station Road – the *Surabhi* restaurant in the *Hotel Surya* serves good quality veg and non-veg in cool, comfortable surroundings, while further along on the left, beyond the post office, the much more basic *Bharati Mess* offers help-yourself veg meals, to which you can add chicken or mutton.

Nagarjunakonda

NAGARJUNAKONDA, or "Nagarjuna's Hill", 166km south of Hyderabad and 175km west of Vijayawada, is all that now remains of the vast area, rich in archeological sites, submerged when the huge Nagarjuna Sagar dam was built across the River Krishna in 1960. Ancient settlements in the valley were first discovered in 1926, and extensive excavations carried out between 1954 and 1960 uncovered more than one hundred sites dating from the early Stone Age to late medieval times. Nagarjunakonda was once the summit of a hill, where a fort towered 200m above the valley floor; now it's just a small oblong island near the middle of Nagarjuna Sagar lake, accessible by boat from the mainland. Several Buddhist monuments have been reconstructed, in an operation reminiscent of that at Abu Simbel in Egypt, and a **museum** exhibits the more remarkable ruins of the valley. **VIJAYAPURI**, the village on the shore of the lake, overlooks the colossal dam itself, which stretches for almost 2km. Torrents of water flushed through its 26 floodgates produce electricity for the whole region and irrigate an area of almost 800 square kilometres. Many villages had to be relocated to higher ground when the valley was flooded.

The island and the museum

Boats arrive on the northeastern edge of **Nagarjunakonda island** (daily 9am–5pm), unloading passengers at what remains of one of the gates to the fort, built in the fourteenth century and renovated by the Vijayanagar kings in the mid-sixteenth century. Low, damaged, stone walls skirting the island mark the edge of the fort, and you can see ground-level remains of the Hindu temples that served its inhabitants. Well-kept gardens lie between the jetty and the museum, beyond which nine Buddhist monuments from various sites in the valley have been rebuilt. West of the jetty, there's a reconstructed bathing *ghat*, built entirely of limestone during the reigns of the Ikshvaku kings (third century AD). Boards etched into some of the slabs were probably used for dice games.

The **maha-chaitya**, or stupa, constructed at the command of King Chamtu-la's sister in the third century AD, is the earliest Buddhist structure in the area. It was raised over relics of the Buddha – said to include a tooth – and has been reassembled in the southwest of the island. Nearby, a towering **statue** of the Buddha stands draped in robes beside a ground plan of a monastery that enshrines a smaller stupa. Other **stupas** stand nearby; the brick walls of the *svastika chaitya* have been arranged in the shape of swastikas, common emblems in early Buddhist iconography.

In the **museum** ($2 [Rs5]), **Buddhist sculptures** include large stone friezes decorated with scenes from the Buddha's life: his birth; his mother's vision of an elephant and a lotus blossom; his renunciation; and his subversion of evil as he meditated and realized enlightenment under the *bodhi* tree. Twelve statues of standing Buddhas – one of which reaches 3m – show the Buddha in various postures of teaching or meditation. Many of the pillars are profusely carved with Buddha images, bowing devotees, elephants and lotus medallions.

Earlier **artefacts** include stone tools and pots from the Neolithic age (third millennium BC), and metal axe heads and knives from the first millennium BC. Among later finds are several inscribed pillars from Ikshvaku times, recording in Prakrit or Sanskrit the installation of Buddhist monasteries and statues. The final phase of art at Nagarjunakonda is represented by **sculptures**: a thirteenth-century *tirthankara* (Jain saint), a seventeenth-century Ganesh and Nandi, and a set of eighteenth-century statues of Shiva and Shakti, his female consort. Also on display is a model showing the excavated sites in the valley.

Practicalities

Organized **APTDC tours** from Hyderabad to Nagarjunakonda at weekends (see p.652) – taking in the sites and museum, the nearby Ethiopothala waterfalls (entry Rs20) and an engraved third-century Buddhist monolith known as the Pylon – can be a bit rushed; if you want to spend more time in the area you can take a bus from the Central bus stand in Hyderabad (4hr; all the regular Macherla services stop at Vijayapuri) or Vijayawada (6hr; a direct service runs daily at 11am and frequent services leave from Guntur). If you arrive independently, tickets for **boats** to the island (daily 9am & 1.30pm; 45min; Rs60) go on sale 25 minutes before departure. Each boat leaves the island ninety minutes after it arrives, which allows enough time to see the museum and walk briskly round the monuments, but if you want to take your time and soak up the atmosphere, take the morning boat and return in the afternoon. A cafeteria on the island serves drinks and occasionally biscuits, but only opens when the boat is in, so take provisions.

Accommodation at Vijayapuri is limited, and you need to decide in advance where you are going to stay to know where to get off the bus, as there are two distinct settlements 6km apart on either side of the dam. For easy access to the sites it's better to stay near the jetty on the right bank of the dam; ask the bus to leave you at the launch station. The drab-looking concrete *Nagarjuna Motel Complex* (T08642/278188; ❷–❸) has adequate rooms, some with a/c, while 500m away in the village, the *Golden Lodge* (T08642/278148; ❶) is much more basic. APTDC runs two hotels in the area, which can be booked via Wwww .tourisminap.com: the all-a/c *Punnami Vijay Vihar* (T08680/277362; ❺–❻) on the other side of the dam as you approach the lake form Hyderabad, and the *Punnami Ethipothala* (T08680/276540; ❸–❹), by the waterfalls, which has more modest a/c and non-a/c rooms.

Eastern Andhra Pradesh

One of India's least visited areas, **eastern Andhra Pradesh** is sandwiched between the Bay of Bengal in the east and the red soil and high peaks of the Eastern Ghats in the north. Its one architectural attraction is the ancient Buddhist site of **Amaravati**, near the city of **Vijayawada**, whose sprinkling of historic temples is completely overshadowed by impersonal, modern buildings. The region's other major city, the bustling port of **Vishakapatnam**, is a useful place to break the lengthy journey along the coast, with a handful of nearby attractions.

If you want to get well off the beaten track, however, there are rewarding pockets of natural beauty along the coast and in the hills of eastern Andhra Pradesh. In this sleepy landscape, little affected by modernization, bullocks amble between swaying palms and the rice fields are iridescent against rusty sands. However, unless you have the patience to endure the excruciatingly slow public transport system, your own vehicle is essential.

Vijayawada and around

Almost 450km north of Chennai, **VIJAYAWADA** is a bustling commercial centre on the banks of the Krishna delta, hemmed in by bare granite outcrops 90km from the coast. This mundane city, alleviated by the mountain backdrop and some urban greenery, is seldom visited by tourists, but does make the obvious stopoff point for visits to the third-century Buddhist site at **Amaravati**, 60km west. The city becomes a major pilgrimage destination once every twelve years, when the Krishna Pushkaram festival is held here; the next one is due in 2016.

A handful of temples in Vijayawada merit a quick look. The most important, raised on the low Indrakila Hill in the east, is dedicated to the city's patron goddess **Kanaka Durga** (also known as Vijaya). Though it is believed to be thousands of years old, what you see today, with the exception of a few pillared halls and intricate carvings, is largely renovated. Some 8km out of town across the river there's an ancient cave temple at **Undavalli**, a tiny rural village set off the main road, easily reached on any bus bound for Guntur or Amaravati or by the local #13 service. The temple is cut out of the granite hillside in typical Pallava style: simple, solid and bold. Each of its five levels contains a deep low-roofed hall, with small rock-cut shrines to Vishnu, Shiva and Parvati, and pillared verandas guarded by statues of deities, saints and lions. Views from the porches take in a sublime patchwork of rivulets, paddy fields and banana plantations.

Practicalities

The city is bisected by **Ryes Canal**, which flows through the heart of town. Vijayawada's **railway station**, on the main Chennai–Kolkata (Calcutta) line, is in the centre of town. Buses arriving from Guntur, Amaravati and as far afield as Hyderabad and Chennai pull into the **Pandit Nehru bus stand**, 1.5km further west, on the other side of the canal at the end of Elluru Road. Specific ticket offices cater for each service, while a **tourist office** (℡0866/252 3966) has details on local hotels and sights. You can **change money** at Zen Global Finance, 40-6-27 Krishna Nagar in Labbipet, or use the State Bank of India. There's an ATM at the HDFC Bank at Mahalakshmi Towers on Atchutaramaiah Street, which links the railway station to Elluru Road. You can **get online** at Madhavi's, about 100m along Elluru Road towards the bus stand from the *Hotel Swarna Palace* (see below).

Vijayawada is a major business centre, with a good selection of mid-range **hotels**, all within 1km of the railway station and bus stand. *Monika Lodge* (℡0866/257 1334; ❷), just off Elluru Road about 300m northeast of the bus stand, is one of the cheapest but a bit grubby. Two better-value places, both on Atchutaramaiah Street, are the *Hotel Narayana Swamy* (℡0866/257 1221, ℱ257 2489; ❸–❹) and the ⚹ *Sri Ram* (℡0866/257 9377, ℱ257 7721; ❸–❹), both with spotless rooms (some a/c) and cable TV; the latter also has a particularly fine restaurant serving pure South Indian veg cuisine. *Raj Towers* (℡0866/257 1311, ℱ556 1714; ❹–❻) on Elluru Road is a tall modern block with good mid-range rooms and a good restaurant. The fourth-floor *Palace Heights* restaurant at the *Hotel Swarna Palace*, where Atchutaramaiah Street meets Elluru Road, has city views and provides large portions of Indian, Chinese and continental food; it also has a bar. In addition, cheap Andhran thali joints abound.

Guntur

Another sprawling and bustling commercial city, 30km southwest of Vijayawada, **GUNTUR** has no merits of its own but makes an even more convenient jumping-off point for Amaravati than Vijayawada, especially if you are coming from Nagarjuna Sagar. Buses to Vijayawada and Amaravati leave from the old bus stand (adjacent to the main bus stand). If you decide to spend the night here, try the **lodges** opposite the bus stands. *Annapurna Lodge* (℡0863/235 6493; ❷–❹) has decent-sized clean rooms and some a/c; *Padmasri Lodge* (℡0863/222 3813; ❷–❸) also has a/c and cheaper singles.

Amaravati

AMARAVATI, a small town on the banks of the Krishna around 50km west of Vijayawada, is the site of a Buddhist settlement, formerly known as

Chintapalli (daily except Fri 10am–5pm; $2 [Rs5]), where a stupa was erected over relics of the Buddha in the third century BC, during the reign of Ashoka. The stupa no longer stands, but its size is evident from the mound that formed its base. There was a gateway at each of the cardinal points, one of which has been reconstructed in an open courtyard. Its decoration, meticulously carved and perfectly preserved, shows the themes represented on all such Buddhist monuments: the Buddha's birth, renunciation and life as an emaciated ascetic, enlightenment under the *bodhi* tree, his first sermon in the Deer Park, and *parinirvana*, or death. Several foundation stones of the monastic quarters remain on the site. A two-week **Kalachakra initiation programme** (a special form of Buddhist meditation) was conducted by the Dalai Lama here in January 2006, to commemorate 2550 years since the Buddha's birth; it is reckoned the Buddha himself held such a ceremony at the same spot. At the same time the **Dhyana Buddha** project was inaugurated about 500m towards the river from the stupa. At the time of writing this large structure, which consists of a 15-metre-tall serene Buddha figure seated above an intricately carved circular prayer hall, was nearing completion.

Exhibits at the small but fascinating **museum** (same hours as site; Rs2) range in date from the third century BC to the twelfth century AD and include Buddha statues with lotus symbols on his feet, tightly curled hair, and long ear lobes – all traditional indications of an enlightened teacher. Other stone carvings include symbols such as the chakra (wheel of dharma), a throne, a stupa, a flaming pillar, a *bodhi* tree and the lotus flower. The lotus motif is connected with a dream the Buddha's mother had shortly after conception, and represents purity. Later sculptures include limestone statues of the goddess Tara and *bodhisattva* Padmapani, both installed at the site in medieval times when the community had adopted Mahayana teachings in place of the earlier Theravada doctrines. Although some fine sculpture is on display, many of the best pieces are now in the Chennai Government Museum (see p.510) and the British Museum in London. Outside in the museum's courtyard, there is a small model of the stupa.

If you have time to spare, the town's living Amareswara Swamy Devasthanam **temple**, at the far and of the main street towards the river, is also worth a quick look for its impressive *gopura* and shrine dedicated to an aspect of Shiva.

Practicalities

Buses run at least once an hour from Vijayawada to Amaravati (1hr 45min–2hr) and more frequently from Guntur (every 15min; 45min–1hr). The excavated site and museum are under a kilometre from the bus stand. Trishaws – miniature carts attached to tricycles and brightly painted with chubby film stars – shuttle visitors around town. The APTDC *Punnami*, on the bank of the Krishna (☏08645/255332; ❹), has just four a/c rooms and a dorm (Rs100); its canteen provides basic meals and snacks. The only other place to stay is the clean and modern *Sindura Residency* (☏08645/254100; ❸–❹), halfway along the main street. For eating, there is a smattering of simple food stalls along the main street.

Vishakapatnam and around

India's fourth largest port, **VISHAKAPATNAM** (aka Vizag), 350km north of Vijayawada, is a huge and rapidly growing city, with large parts choked with the smells and dirt of a busy shipbuilding industry, an oil plant and a steel factory. Its centre is a typically bustling hub of commerce and such is its sprawl that it has merged with the neighbouring town of **Waltair**, once a health resort.

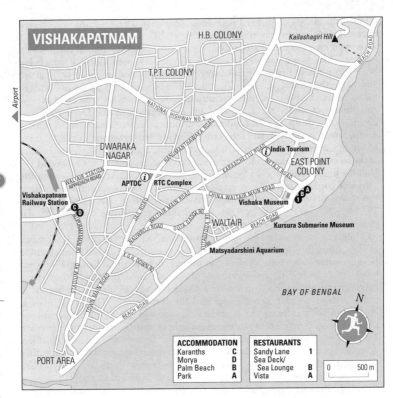

VISHAKAPATNAM

H.B. COLONY

Kailashagiri Hill

BEACH ROAD

T.P.T. COLONY

Airport

NATIONAL HIGHWAY NO 5

DWARAKA NAGAR

HANUMANTHAWAKA ROAD

i India Tourism

KARASACHETTU ROAD

NETAJI ROAD

EAST POINT COLONY

WALTAIR STATION APPROACH ROAD

APTDC *i* RTC Complex

CHINA WALTAIR MAIN ROAD

Vishakapatnam Railway Station

i B A

Vishaka Museum

C D

JAIL ROAD

WALTAIR MAIN ROAD

ODDA GADDA RD

WALTAIR

BEACH ROAD

Kursura Submarine Museum

NAUWROJI ROAD

MURAGADDA

K.C.H. DOWN RD

Matsyadarshini Aquarium

VEERANARAYAN ST

DBK RAILWAY

TOWN MAIN ROAD

BAY OF BENGAL

N

BEACH ROAD

PORT AREA

ACCOMMODATION		RESTAURANTS	
Karanths	C	Sandy Lane	1
Morya	D	Sea Deck/	
Palm Beach	B	Sea Lounge	B
Park	A	Vista	A

0   500 m

Worthwhile trips out of town include the fort of **Bheemunipatnam**, the temples at **Mukhalingam** and the **Borra caves**.

The City

The main focus of interest in Vishakapatnam is the district of Waltair, with its uncrowded tree-lined roads and attractive seafront, Beach Road, which makes for a pleasant stroll and is also home to the town's few attractions. These include the **Vishaka Museum** (Tues–Fri 11am–7pm; Rs5) on Beach Road near the *Hotel Park*, a surprisingly well-laid-out and labelled maritime museum, covering seafaring from ancient times to post-Independence, with plenty of paintings and naval equipment, though with perhaps a little too much emphasis on the military. The sea-going theme is consolidated by the opening of the **Kursura Submarine Museum** (Tues–Fri 2–9pm, Sat 2–8.30pm, Sun 10am–1.30pm & 3.30–8.30pm; Rs25), housed in a decommissioned submarine several hundred metres south in a dry dock at the back of the beach. A kilometre further south along Beach Road is the **Matsyadarshini Aquarium** (daily 9am–9pm; Rs25), with a fairly mundane array of fish and loggerhead turtles.

The beach along this stretch is far enough from the port for the sea to be reasonably clean, though the best beach for swimming is below **Kailashagiri Hill**, over a kilometre further north. Special deluxe buses, clearly labelled in English, will take you from the RTC Complex (see opposite) to the beach and all the way up to Kailashagiri's popular hilltop park, which boasts fantastic coastal and city vistas and a hilarious viewing deck in the shape of the *Titanic*'s bow, as well as the usual modest funfair paraphernalia and stalls. The park is also linked to the coast road by a **cable car** (Rs22 one way).

Practicalities

Vishakapatnam's **railway station**, on the Chennai–Kolkata (Calcutta) coastal route, is in the old town, towards the port. The **bus stand**, known as the RTC Complex, is just over 1km away in a newer area, while the beach is a further 4km on, reached by bus #28, among others. There's an **airport**, 12km west of town, from which bus #38 runs to the centre. Despite constant rumours of plans to improve the service, **ships** making the three-day crossing from here to Port Blair on the Andaman Islands are still highly irregular, usually departing no more frequently than once a month.

The **India Tourism** office (Mon–Sat 10am–5pm; ☏0891/275 4716) is situated in the Vuda complex, Sitapura, 3km east of the RTC Complex; there's also an **APTDC office** (daily 6am–10pm; ☏0891/274 6446) in the RTC complex, which is useful for booking **tours** of the city (Leisure tour daily 10am–8pm, Rs325; Heritage tour 9am–5pm, Rs245; both include lunch) and the Borra caves (daily 7am–9pm; Rs380 or Rs430 by train; includes breakfast and lunch). The Andhra Bank near the RTC complex will **change money** and there are numerous ATMs in the vicinity and other parts of town. There are also several places around the complex offering **Internet** access.

If you arrive late by bus, head for the well-maintained **retiring rooms** (❶) in the bus stand. Otherwise, most **hotels** are in the old town, near the railway station: turn right out of the station and walk for a few minutes. The best is ⚑ *Hotel Karanths*, 33-1-55 Patel Marg (☏0891/256 0347, ✆256 0416; ❷–❸), whose spotless rooms have balconies, pressed sheets, cable TV and attached bathrooms. The downstairs restaurant serves unbeatable thalis and tiffin at low prices. Just round the corner on Bondara Road (Allipuram Main Road), the larger *Hotel Morya* (☏0891/273 1112, ✉hotelmorya@yahoo.co.in; ❸–❹) comes a good second. Vishakapatnam's nicest upmarket hotel, the *Park* on Beach Road (☏0891/275 4488, �🌐www.theparkhotels.com; ❾), has luxurious rooms starting at $110, a swimming pool, a bar, the upmarket *Vista* restaurant, and access to the beach. Adjacent to the *Park* is the pleasant but far more modest *Palm Beach* (☏0891/255 4026, �🌐www.palmbeachvizag.com; ❼), which also offers good amenities, central a/c and two quality restaurants: the indoor *Sea Lounge* and outdoor *Sea Deck*. Apart from these hotel restaurants, another pleasant place to **eat** is *Sandy Lane* on Beach Road, which serves reasonably priced Indian and Chinese food in a grassy garden by the sea.

Around Vishakapatnam

Various traces of older civilizations lie within a day's journey of the city. At **Bheemunipatnam**, 30km north, you can see the remains of a Dutch fort and a peculiar cemetery with slate-grey pyramidal tombs. You'll need a car to get to **Mukhalingam**, 100km north of Bheemunipatnam, where three Shaivite temples, built between the sixth and twelfth centuries, rest in low hills. Their elaborate carvings and well-preserved towering *shikharas* display slight local variations from the otherwise standard Orissan style. There's nowhere to stay in either place.

Ninety kilometres inland on a minor road that winds through the Eastern Ghats and the Araku forest, **BORRA** boasts a set of dark and eerie limestone **caves**, pierced with age-old stalactites and stalagmites (daily 10am–12.30pm &

2–5pm; Rs25). The caves can be visited on an APTDC tour (see p.671) on a long day-trip by road or train, or you can **stay** nearby in the log huts or cottages of the ticklishly named APTDC ecotourism resort *Jungle Bells* (T0891/271 3135, Wwww.aptdc.in; ❹–❺). The resort is situated in the lush forest en route from Vishakapatnam to Borra and Araku at **TYDA**, where you should disembark the train.

Southern Andhra Pradesh

The further south you travel from the fertile lands watered by the great Krishna and Godavari rivers, the less hospitable the terrain becomes, especially in the rocky southwest of the state. For Hindus, the main attraction in southern Andhra Pradesh is the tenth-century **Shri Venkateshvara Temple**, outside **Tirupati**, the most popular Vishnu shrine in India, where thousands of pilgrims come each day to receive *darshan*. In the state's arid southwestern corner, **Puttaparthy**, the home town of the spiritual leader Sai Baba, is the only other place in the region to attract significant numbers of visitors, mostly devotees of the guru from many parts of India and the world. By contrast, the ancient Shaivite temple at nearby **Lepakshi** is a little-visited gem. Both Tirupati and Puttaparthy are closer to big cities to the south – the former to Chennai in Tamil Nadu, the latter to Bengaluru (Bangalore) in Karnataka – than to other points in Andhra Pradesh, and for many tourists constitute their only foray into the state.

Tirupati and Tirumala Hill

Set in a stunning position, surrounded by wooded hills capped by a ring of vertical red rocks, the **Shri Venkateshvara Temple** at **Tirumala Hill**, 170km northwest of Chennai, is said to be the richest and most popular place of pilgrimage in the world, drawing more devotees than either Rome or Mecca. With its many shrines and *dharamshalas*, the whole area provides a fascinating insight into contemporary Hinduism. Most practical services and accommodation are at the town of **TIRUPATI**, 11km away as the crow flies, but double that by road.

Arrival and information

The best way of **getting to Tirupati** is by train from Chennai; the trip can be done in a day if you get the earliest of the three daily services (around 3hr). Frequent express buses run from Chennai (4hr), but the train is far more comfortable. From Hyderabad it's a gruelling 11- to 15-hour journey by bus or train. There are also direct trains from Vishakapatnam and Vijayawada.

The main APTDC **tourist office** is on 2nd Floor, Sri Devi Complex, Tilak Road (daily 6.30am–9pm; T0877/225 5385), and there's also an APTDC counter (daily 8am–9pm; T0877/228 9129) at the **railway station** accessible from the entrance hall and platform 1, where there's a 24hr left-luggage office and a self-service veg refreshment room. Stands sell English copies of T.K.T. Viraraghava Charya's *History of Tirupati*, and there's a Vivekananda religious bookshop next door. Tirupati's APSRTC central **bus stand** – also with 24-hour left-luggage – is about a little under 1km east of the railway station. Beautifully decorated cycle-rickshaws and auto-rickshaws ply the city streets looking for custom.

A special section at the back of the bus stand has services every few minutes **to Tirumala** and the Venkateshvara Temple, although you can also reach the hill from a separate local bus stand outside the railway station. You shouldn't have to wait too long for a bus unless it's a weekend or festival. An easier option is to take a **taxi**, best organized through the APTDC counter at the railway station; avoid the unlicensed taxis outside the station as they could be stopped by the Tirumala police. If you're climbing the hill on foot, take any of the temple buses and alight at Alipiri where the trail starts. The tourist office runs **tours** which take in Chandragiri Fort (except Fri) and a number of temples (10am–5.30pm; Rs165 or Rs190 including Chandragiri sound & light show), but don't include the Venkateshvara Temple because of the queues.

There are a few **Internet** places in Tirupati, such as Net Hill in the shopping complex at the corner of the bus stand. The Syndicate and ICICI banks both have **ATMs** on Netaji Road, and there are even a couple up on Tirumala Hill.

Accommodation and eating

Unless you're a pilgrim seeking accommodation in the *dharamshalas* near the temple, all the decent **places to stay** are in Tirupati, near the railway station and bus stand; there's a vast array of hotels and lodges to suit all budgets. **Eating** is almost exclusively vegetarian, even in the hotels, and cheap "meals" places abound in town and on Tirumala Hill. If you're in need of meat and booze, head for the *Yalamuri* beer garden, off the traffic circle opposite the bus stand.

Annapurna 349 G Car St, opposite the railway station ☎0877/225 0666. Smart modern hotel with clean, simply furnished rooms and good stand-up snack bar on the ground floor. ❸–❹

Apsara 213 TP Area ☎0877/657 8063. Basic but clean attached rooms on the street almost opposite the bus station. ❶

Balaji Deluxe 291 Railway Station Rd ☎0877/222 5930. Not much deluxe about it, but this typical basic lodge opposite the station is adequate for a night. ❶

Bhimas Deluxe 34–38 G Car St, near the railway station ☎0877/222 5521, ⓦwww.hotelbhimas.com. Decent, comfortable rooms with central a/c; 12hr "transit rooms" available at around half price. The *Maya* veg restaurant serves North and South Indian food plus some Chinese dishes in the evenings. ❹

Durga Residency 164 TP Area ☎0877/222 9111. Spacious mid-range option with some new a/c rooms, on a quiet back street between the station and bus stand. ❸–❹

Mayura 209 TP Area ☎0877/222 5925, ⓔmayura@nettlinx.com. The most comfortable, spacious – and expensive – of a host of hotels opposite the bus station. ❹–❺

Sindhuri Park Beside the Govindarajaswamy bathing tank ☎0877/225 6430, ⓦwww.hotelsindhuri.com. The smartest place in the centre, this all-a/c hotel has excellent facilities and great views of the tank and temple. The basement *Vrinda* restaurant serves quality veg food, including a range of thalis, and has a good-value buffet on weekend evenings. ❺

Govindarajaswamy Temple

Just a five-minute walk from the railway station and with a modern grey *gopura* visible from many points in town, Govindarajaswamy is the town's main temple and the one temple in Tirupati itself which is definitely worth a visit. Begun by the Nayaks in the sixteenth century, it's an interesting complex with large open courtyards decorated with lion sculptures and some ornately carved wooden roofing. The temple's **inner sanctum** is open to non-Hindus and contains a splendid large black reclining Vishnu, coated in bronze armour and bedecked in flowers. If you visit during *darshan* (daily 10am–8.45pm; Rs5) you'll be allowed in to glimpse the deity and participate in fire blessings at the main and subsidiary shrines.

Tucked away at the side of the complex, not far from the south *gopura*, is the fine little **Venkateshvara Museum of Temple Arts** (daily 8am–8pm; Rs1). Set in a colonnaded compound, the bulk of the displays of old stone and bronze statues and more modern paintings and dolls are arranged around the perimeter of the courtyard. The shrine in the middle of the compound is supported by some beautifully carved pillars and contains cases of colourful dolls portraying scenes from mythology. The temple's impressive **bathing tank** lies 200m to the east.

Tiruchanur Padmavati Temple

Between Tirupati and Tirumala Hill, the **Tiruchanur Padmavati Temple** (no photography; a Rs20 ticket allows you to jump the queue to enter the sanctuary) is another popular pilgrimage halt. A gold *vimana* tower with lions at each corner surmounts the sanctuary, which contains a black stone image of Lakshmi with one silver eye – you can donate a sari to the goddess for Rs1200.

Tirumala Hill

There's good reason for the small shrine to Ganesh at the foot of **Tirumala Hill**. The journey up is hair-raising and it's worth saying a quick prayer when embarking on it, but at least separate routes up and down preclude head-on crashes. Overtaking is strictly forbidden, but drivers do anyway; virtually every bend is labelled "blind" and every instruction to drive slowly is blithely ignored. The fearless sit on the left for the best views.

The most devout pilgrims, of course, climb the hill **on foot**. An early start is recommended. The **trail** starts at **Alipuri**, 4km from the centre of Tirupati (all the pilgrim buses pass through) – look out for a large Garuda statue and the soaring *gopura* of the first temple. The first hour consists of a flight of knee-crunching concrete steps, covered in yellow, orange and red *tika* daubed by pilgrims as they ascend. The path then mercifully levels out before the final assault some two hours on. Allow at least four hours to the top – fitter pilgrims might do it half an hour quicker. The trail is covered over for most of the way, affording protection from the blistering sun, and there are drinks stalls all along the route. When you get to the top, you will see barbers busying themselves giving pilgrims tonsures as part of their devotions.

The Venkateshvara Temple and Kapilateertham

The **Venkateshvara Temple** (aka Sri Vari), dedicated to **Vishnu** and started in the tenth century, is surrounded by a rabbit warren of passages and waiting rooms winding their way around the complex, through which pilgrims interminably shuffle towards the inner sanctum (weekends, public holidays and festivals are even busier). Non-Hindus are permitted to enter the inner sanctum, but for everyone *darshan* is the briefest of experiences as you will be moved on in a matter of seconds by the temple officials. Unless your visit is intended to be particularly rigorous, on reaching the temple you

△ Worshippers at the Venkateshvara Temple

The **museum** (daily 10am–noon), situated up a small hill to the left after entering the main gates, is undoubtedly the most interesting place for the casual visitor. The ground floor contains a fascinating display on the world's major faiths with illustrations and quotations from their sacred texts, punctuated by Sai Baba's comments which are invariably intended to point out the underlying unity of the different belief systems. The first floor has more colourful exhibits, focusing on various places of worship, plus one dedicated to Sai Baba's predecessor, the Shirdi Sai Baba (see box opposite). Finally, the third-floor displays bring the animistic tribal religions of Africa into the universal fold, and cover the beliefs and philosophy of the ancient Greeks – it's noteworthy that the divinity of Socrates is accorded special emphasis.

Practicalities

Buses from Bengaluru (Bangalore), Hyderabad and Chennai stop at the stand outside the ashram entrance. The new **railway station**, named Sri Satya Sai Prasanti Nilayam, is 8km from town on the main north–south route, from which you should be able to get a shared auto-rickshaw to the ashram for Rs10. There are more services to and from **Dharmavaram**, 42km away, which is connected to Puttaparthy by regular buses.

Accommodation in the ashram is available in single-sex dormitories or "flats" for four people, and is strictly segregated by sex, except for families, as are meals and *darshan*. Overt socializing is discouraged and there is a strict policy of lights-out at 9pm. Costs are minimal and, though you can't book in advance, you can enquire about availability at the secretary's office (☎08555/287164 ext 211). Visitors sometimes comment on the strict security staffing and rigid rules and regulations. Space is only usually a problem around the time of Sai Baba's birthday in late November. If you do want to stay, you have to register by filling out forms and surrendering your passport at the office before being allocated a bed by the Public Relations Officer. Your passport is returned after attending the first orientation session. Outside the ashram, many of the basic **lodges** are rather overpriced, but a good cheap option is the friendly *Sai Ganesh Guest House* near the police station (☎08555/287079; ❸). The *Sri Sai Sadan* at the far end of the main street (☎08555/287507, ✉srisaisadan@yahoo.com; ❹) is also fair value; all rooms have fridges and a balcony with views of the countryside or the ashram, and there's a meditation room and rooftop restaurant. At the top end, the centrally a/c *Sai Towers* near the ashram entrance (☎0855/287270, ⓦwww.saitowers.com; ❹–❻), charges a fair bit for its rooms, but its singles are decent value and there is a good **restaurant** downstairs. The ashram also has a canteen that's open to non-residents, and there are simple snack stalls along the main street outside the ashram. Or you could try the delicious Tibetan grub at either the *Bamboo Nest* on Chitravathi Road or *Little Tibet Kitchen*, a mellow upstairs hangout just down from *Sai Towers*. As you'd expect of such a cosmopolitan place, there are plenty of exchange bureaus, **ATMs** and **Internet** joints dotted the length of the main drag.

Lepakshi

Around 50km south of Puttaparthy, set quite off the beaten track, the small village of **LEPAKSHI** is the site of the splendid **Virabhadra Swamy Temple**, built in 1538 during the period of the Vijayanagar kingdom by the merchant prince Virupanna. On the inside of the complex's surrounding compound wall is a colonnade, whose columns in the shape of bug-eyed beasts are reminiscent of the kingdom's capital at Hampi (see p.335). The central attraction is the *natya-mandapa* (dance hall), which is supported by seventy pillars, all finely sculpted with figures such as a dancing Shiva, Brahma and buxom dancing girls. There are also remnants of ceiling frescoes showing episodes from the Puranas; Virupanna with his entourage is supposedly witnessing them. The darkened inner sanctum is open for all to partake in puja ceremonies at the main shrine, dedicated to Virabhadra, a mythical warrior created by Shiva to battle with rival deities. About 200m back along the main road from the temple, there is an enclosure housing a magnificent nine-metre statue of **Nandi** in a landscaped garden.

Unless you come on one of the two daily **buses** from Bengaluru (Bangalore), getting to Lepakshi usually involves a change of bus (or onto one from the train) at Hindupur, about 12km west, which has far more frequent services. The easiest way to reach the village from Puttaparthy is to get one of the several daily buses to Kodikonda checkpoint, around 15km east, and hop on another bus from there. There was no accommodation available at the time of our research, but for **food** simple snacks can be had on the main street.

Travel details

Trains

Hyderabad/Secunderabad to: Bengaluru (Bangalore) (3–5 daily; 11hr 5min–13hr 25min); Chennai (2 daily; 13hr 45min–14hr 10min); Ernakulam, for Kochi (1 daily; 25hr 40min); Mumbai (4–5 daily; 13hr 10min–16hr 25min); Tirupati (4–6 daily; 11hr 25min–15hr 20min); Vijayawada (10–12 daily; 5hr 25min–7hr 20min); Vishakapatnam (5–6 daily; 11hr 30min–14hr 15min); Warangal (9–11 daily; 2hr 5min–3hr 30min).

Puttaparthy (Sri Satya Sai Prasanti) to: Bengaluru (Bangalore) (4 daily; 3hr 30min–4hr).

Tirupati to: Chennai (2–3 daily; 3hr 15min); Hyderabad/Secunderabad (4–6 daily; 12hr 15min–16hr 10min); Mumbai (1–2 daily; 24hr 20min–25hr 35min); Vijayawada (3–5 daily; 7hr–8hr 25min); Vishakapatnam (2–4 daily; 12hr 50min–17hr 55min).

Vijayawada to: Chennai (7–11 daily; 6hr 25min–8hr 50min); Hyderabad/Secunderabad (10–12 daily; 5hr 20min–8hr 20min); Tirupati (3–5 daily; 6hr 30min–8hr 35min); Vishakapatnam (12–15 daily; 6hr 5min–11hr 15min).

Vishakapatnam to: Chennai (5–8 daily; 12hr 20min–16hr 5min); Hyderabad/Secunderabad (5–6 daily; 11hr 50min–15hr 15min); Tirupati (2–4 daily; 13hr 15min–16hr 45min); Vijayawada (12–15 daily; 6hr 15min–11hr 20min).

Buses

Hyderabad to: Amaravati (2 daily; 7hr); Bengaluru (Bangalore) (hourly; 13hr); Bidar (1–2 hourly; 4hr); Chennai (3 daily; 16hr); Mumbai (7–10 daily; 17hr); Puttaparthy (3 daily; 10hr); Tirupati (8 daily; 12hr);

Vijayapuri (hourly; 4hr); Vijayawada (every 15min; 6hr); Warangal (every 15–30min; 3hr).

Puttaparthy to: Bengaluru (Bangalore) (7 daily; 4hr); Chennai (2 daily; 11hr); Hyderabad (3 daily; 10hr).

Tirupati to: Bengaluru (Bangalore) (hourly; 5hr); Chennai (every 15–30min; 3hr 30min–4hr); Hyderabad (8 daily; 12hr); Kanchipuram (hourly; 3hr 30min); Mamallapuram (3 daily; 5hr 30min); Puttaparthy (2 daily; 10–11hr).

Vijayawada to: Amaravati (hourly; 2hr); Guntur (every 15min; 1hr–1hr 30min); Hyderabad (every 15min; 6hr).

Flights

For a list of airline addresses, see p.663; for travel agents, see p.664; and for airline websites, see p.38. In the listings below IA is Indian Airlines, JA Jet Airways, KF Kingfisher, SA Sahara Airlines, AD Air Deccan, GO Go Air, IG IndiGo Airlines, PA Paramount Airways and SJ SpiceJet.

Hyderabad to: Bengaluru (Bangalore) (IA, JA, KF, SA, AD, SJ 12 daily; 1hr–1hr 30min); Chennai (IA, JA, KF, AD, IG, PA, SJ 10–11 daily; 1hr–1hr 30min); Coimbatore (KF, AD, PA 1–2 daily; 1hr 20min); Mumbai (IA, JA, KF, SA, AD, GO, SJ 12 daily; 1hr 15min–3hr 45min); Panjim (AD 2 daily; 1hr 35min); Pune (IA, AD 2 daily; 1hr); Tirupati (IA, AD 2 daily; 55min); Vijayawada (KF 1 daily; 2hr); Vishakapatnam (IA, KF, SA, AD 2 daily; 1hr–1hr 30min).

Tirupati to: Bengaluru (Bangalore) (AD; 1 daily; 50min); Hyderabad (IA, AD; 3 daily; 1hr 20min); Vishakapatnam (AD; 1 daily; 1hr 40min).

Vishakapatnam to: Bangalore (SA; 1 daily; 2hr 45min) Chennai (IA, KF 2–3 daily; 1hr 5min–1hr 50min); Hyderabad (IA, KF, SA 2 daily; 1hr–1hr 30min); Mumbai (IA 2–3 daily; 1hr 45min).

8

The Andaman Islands

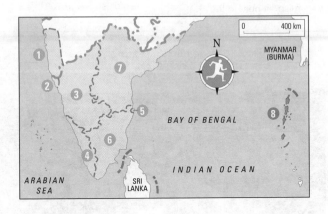

CHAPTER 8

Highlights

＊ **Port Blair** The Cellular Jail stands as a stark reminder of the Andaman capital's bleak colonial past. See p.687

＊ **Wandoor** The white sandy beach and islets of the Mahatma Gandhi National Marine Park are the archipelago's most popular day-trip destination, and a good appetizer for more remote areas. See p.694

＊ **Havelock and Neill islands** Cruise by boat to the Andamans' most popular holiday hangouts, both laid-back, friendly and great for snorkelling or diving. See p.696

＊ **Scuba diving** Plunge into the islands' beautiful coral reefs, which teem with vivid underwater life. See p.697

＊ **North Andaman** The long haul up the road from Port Blair is worth it for North Andaman's dazzling tropical beaches, set against a backdrop of thick rainforest. See p.703

△ Surgeonfish, Andaman Sea

8

The Andaman Islands

The **ANDAMAN ISLANDS** – India's most remote state – are situated over 1000km off the east coast in the middle of the Bay of Bengal, connected to the mainland by flights and ferries from Kolkata (Calcutta), Chennai and Vishakapatnam. Thickly covered by deep green tropical forest, the archipelago supports a profusion of wildlife, including some extremely rare bird species, but the principal attraction for tourists lies offshore, around the pristine reefs that ring most of the islands. Filled with colourful fish and kaleidoscopic corals, the crystal-clear waters of the Andaman Sea feature some of the world's richest and least spoilt marine reserves – perfect for **snorkelling** and **scuba diving**. After the initial tumble the burgeoning tourist scene took following the tsunami (see box, p.683), the islands have recovered remarkably well, aided by cheaper and more frequent flights from the mainland. Despite continuing concerns over the fragile ecological and ethnological balances, many foreigners see the Andamans as something between a final frontier and a lost paradise and have decided to go now – before the seemingly inevitable mass influx begins.

For administrative purposes, the Andamans are grouped with the **Nicobar Islands**, 200km further south and separated from the Andamans by the deep Ten Degree Channel. Foreign tourists are only permitted to visit certain parts of the Andaman group, while the Nicobar Islands remain strictly off-limits to non-Indians and are not covered by this guide. There are approximately 200 islands, of varying sizes, in the Andaman group and nineteen in the Nicobar. The summits of a submarine mountain range, the two chains stretch 755km from the Arakan Yoma hills in Burma (Myanmar) to the fringes of Sumatra in the south. All but the most remote of these are populated in parts by **indigenous tribes**, whose numbers fell dramatically as a result of nineteenth-century European settlement and, more recently, rampant **deforestation**. New felling is now supposed to be strictly controlled, but how closely this is adhered to is a matter for conjecture, and there is the additional problem of timber poachers from Burma and Thailand.

The point of arrival for boats and planes is **South Andaman**, where the predominantly Tamil and Bengali community in the small but busy capital, **Port Blair**, accounts for almost half the islands' total population. The most beautiful beaches and coral reefs are found on **outlying islands**, and a healthy get-up-and-go spirit is essential if you plan to explore these, as connections and transport can be erratic, are frequently uncomfortable and are limited in scope, especially on the smaller islands. Once away from the settlements, you enter a world of minimal amenities, where you'll need your own camping supplies and equipment. It's also worth pointing out that a surprising number of travellers fall sick in the Andamans.

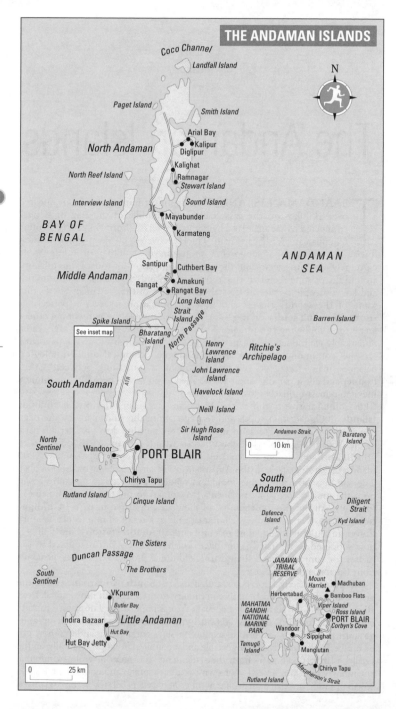

THE ANDAMAN ISLANDS

Coco Channel

Landfall Island

N

Paget Island

Smith Island

Arial Bay
● Kalipur
Diglipur

North Andaman

Kalighat
Ramnagar
Stewart Island

North Reef Island

Sound Island

Interview Island

*BAY OF
BENGAL*

Mayabunder

Karmateng

*ANDAMAN
SEA*

Santipur Cuthbert Bay

Middle Andaman

Amakunj
Rangat ● Rangat Bay
Long Island

*Strait
Island*

Barren Island

Spike Island

See inset map

Bharatang
Island

North Passage

*Henry
Lawrence
Island*

*Ritchie's
Archipelago*

*John Lawrence
Island*

South Andaman

Havelock Island

Neill Island

*Sir Hugh Rose
Island*

*North
Sentinel*

Wandoor
PORT BLAIR

Chiriya Tapu

Rutland Island *Cinque Island*

*South
Sentinel*

Duncan Passage

The Sisters

The Brothers

VKpuram
Butler Bay

Indira Bazaar *Little Andaman*
Hut Bay

Hut Bay Jetty

Inset map — South Andaman

Andaman Strait *Baratang
Island*

0   10 km

*South
Andaman*

*Diligent
Strait*

*Defence
Island*

Kyd Island

*JARAWA
TRIBAL
RESERVE*

Mount
Harriet
● Madhuban

Herbertabad
Bamboo Flats

*MAHATMA
GANDHI
NATIONAL
MARINE
PARK*

Viper Island
Ross Island
PORT BLAIR
Corbyn's Cove

Wandoor
Sippighat

*Tamugli
Island*

Manglutan

Chiriya Tapu

Rutland Island

Macpherson's Strait

0   25 km

Contrary to the half-baked rumours that emerged from the region in the days following the devastating **tsunami** of December 26, 2004, the Andamans did not suffer total destruction. After a much worse initial assessment, the official death count in the two island chains was 454, with a further 3073 declared missing, presumed dead. Almost all of these fatalities occurred in the Nicobars, which lie much closer to the earthquake's epicentre off Indonesia, especially the islands of Car Nicobar, Katchall and Great Nicobar. The only island in the Andamans to suffer extensively was **Little Andaman**. In addition, there was Rs3300 crore's worth of damage to roads, jetties, farmland and private property.

The handful of deaths and the structural damage in the Port Blair area – mainly to a few old buildings around the town and quay, and the water sports complex at Aberdeen Jetty – were caused by the **earthquake** itself rather than the ensuing tsunami. Elsewhere, the Austin Bridge connecting Middle and North Andaman also had to be closed for repairs. No foreigners suffered anything more serious than the loss of a few belongings, and the worst effect for the tourist industry was that the flow of visitors to the islands diminished almost to nothing in the months following the disaster.

Remarkably, in both the Andamans and Nicobars there was not a single reported fatality amongst those indigenous natives who are still allowed to live in the traditional way, even on islands which were badly battered. Tribal people are said to have been alerted to the impending tragedy by observing the agitation amongst the wildlife, and quickly shifted to higher ground.

The dense tree cover, marshy swamps and high rainfall combine to provide the perfect breeding ground for mosquitoes, and **malaria** is endemic in even the most remote settlements. Sandflies are ferocious in certain places and **tropical ulcer** infections from scratching the bites is another potential hazard. See Basics p.63 for more information on health and prevention.

The **climate** remains tropical throughout the year; temperatures range from 24°C to 35°C, while humidity levels never fall below seventy percent. By far the best time to visit is between January and March, before the pre-monsoon heat sets in. From mid-May to October, heavy rains flush the islands, often bringing violent cyclones that leave west-coast beaches strewn with fallen trees, while in November and December less severe rains arrive with the northeast monsoon. Despite being so far east, the islands run on Indian time, so the sun rises as early as 4.30am in summer and darkness falls soon after 5pm.

Some history

The earliest mention of the Andaman and Nicobar islands is found in **Ptolemy's** geographical treatises of the second century AD. Other records from the Chinese Buddhist monk I'Tsing some five hundred years later and Arabian travellers who passed by in the ninth century describe the inhabitants as fierce and cannibalistic. **Marco Polo** arrived in the thirteenth century and could offer no more favourable description of the natives: "The people are without a king and are idolaters no better than wild beasts. All the men of the island of Angamanian have heads like dogs . . . they are a most cruel generation, and eat everybody they catch . . ." It is unlikely, however, that the Andamanese were cannibals, as the most vivid reports of their ferocity were propagated by the Malay pirates who held sway over the surrounding seas, and needed to keep looters well away from trade ships that passed between India, China and the Far East.

Quite where the **indigenous population** of the Andaman and Nicobar islands originally came from is a puzzle that has preoccupied anthropologists since Alfred Radcliffe-Brown conducted his famous field work among the Andamanese at the beginning of the twentieth century. Asian-looking groups such as the Shompen may have migrated here from the east and north when the islands were connected to Burma, or the sea was sufficiently shallow to allow transport by canoe, but this doesn't explain the origins of the black populations, whose appearance suggests African roots. Wherever they came from, the survival of the islands' first inhabitants has been threatened by traders and colonizers, who introduced disease and destroyed their territories through widespread felling. Thousands also died from addiction to alcohol and opium, which the Chinese, Japanese and British exchanged for valuable shells. Many have had their populations decimated, while others like the Nicobarese have assimilated to modern culture, often adopting Christianity. The indigenous inhabitants of the Andamans, divided into *eramtaga* (those living in the jungle) and *ar-yuato* (those living on the coast), traditionally subsisted as hunter-gatherers, living on fish, turtles, turtle eggs, pigs, fruit, honey and roots. For more information, visit Survival International's excellent website (Ⓦ www.survival-international.org).

Although they comprised the largest group when the islands were first colonized, only around forty **Great Andamanese** now survive. In the 1860s, the Rev H. Corbyn set up a "home" for the tribe to learn English on Ross Island, insisting that they wear clothes and attend reading and writing classes. Five children and three adults from Corbyn's school were taken as curiosities to Calcutta in 1864, where they were shown around the sights. The whole experience, however, proved more fascinating for the crowds who'd come to ogle the "monkey men" than for the Andamanese themselves, who, one of the organizers of the trip ruefully remarked, ". . . never evinced astonishment or admiration at anything which they beheld, however wonderful in its novelty we might suppose it would appear to them". From the foreign settlers the Andamanese tragically contracted diseases such as syphilis, measles, mumps and influenza, and fell prey to opium addiction. Within three years almost the entire population had died. In recent years the surviving Great Andamanese were forcibly settled on Strait Island, north of South Andaman, as a "breeding centre", where they were forced to rely on the Indian authorities for food and shelter. In the aftermath of the tsunami they were relocated to Port Blair, though for how long remains uncertain.

The **Jarawas**, who were shifted from their original homes when land was cleared to build Port Blair, currently number around 270 and now live on the remote western coasts of Middle and South Andaman, hemmed in by the Andaman Trunk Road (ATR), which since the 1970s has cut them off from hunting grounds and freshwater supplies. During the 1980s and 1990s, encroachments on their land by loggers, road builders and Bengali settlers met with fierce resistance, and dozens, possibly hundreds, of people died in **skirmishes**. In one incident a party of Burmese were

During the eighteenth and nineteenth centuries, **European missionaries** and trading companies turned their attention to the islands with a view to colonization. Unsuccessful attempts to convert the Nicobarese to Christianity were made by the French, Dutch and Danish, all of whom were forced to abandon their plans in the face of hideous diseases and a severe lack of food and water. Though the missionaries themselves seldom met with any hostility, several fleets of trading ships which tried to dock on the islands were captured, and their crews murdered, by the Nicobarese. In 1777, the British Lieutenant Blair chose the South Andaman harbour now known as **Port Blair** as the site caught poaching on Jarawa land; of the eleven men involved, six limped out with horrific injuries, two were found dead, and the other three were never seen again. Most incidents occurred on or near the ATR, which is why armed escorts board buses at several points during the journey north from Port Blair to Mayabunder. Some **contact** between settlers and tribals was made for a while through gift exchanges at each full moon, when consignments of coconuts, bananas and red cloth were taken to a friendly band of Jarawas on a boat, but the initiative was later cancelled. These meetings nevertheless led to some Jarawas becoming curious about what "civilization" had to offer, and they started to hold their hands out for goodies to passing vehicles and even visiting Indian settlements near their territory. When the initially generous reception waned, their visits evolved into surreptitious raids culminating in an attack on a police outpost in March 1998. Since then the authorities have tried to minimize contact, and conflicts have ceased. The government has also increased Jarawa land by 180 square kilometres, but has dragged its feet over enforcing a 2002 Indian Supreme Court order to close the ATR which was passed following protests by international pressure groups such as Survival International. In 2007 the court order was still undergoing an official review.

Aside from a couple of violent encounters with nineteenth-century seamen, relations with the **Onge**, who call themselves the **Gaubolambe**, have been relatively peaceful. Distinguished by their white-clay and ochre body paint, they continue to live in communal shelters (*bera*) and construct temporary thatched huts (*korale*) on Little Andaman. The remaining population of around one hundred retain their traditional way of life on two small reserves. The Indian government has erected wood and tin huts for them, dispatched a teacher to instruct them in Hindi, and encouraged coconut cultivation, but to little avail. Contact with outsiders is limited to an occasional trip into town to purchase liquor, and visits from rare parties of anthropologists. The reserves are strictly off limits to foreigners, but you can learn about the Onge's traditional hunting practices, beliefs and rituals in Vishvajit Pandya's wonderful ethnography study, *Above the Forest*.

Only very limited contact is ever had with the isolated **Shompen** tribe of Great Nicobar, whose population of around 380 manage to lead a traditional hunting-and-gathering existence. The most elusive tribe of all, the **Sentinelese**, live on North Sentinel Island west of South Andaman. After the first encounter in 1967, some contact was made with them in 1990, after a team put together by the local administration left gifts on the beaches every month for two years, but subsequent visits have invariably ended in a hail of arrows. Since the early 1990s, the AAJVS, the government department charged with tribal welfare, has effectively given up trying to contact the Sentinelese, who are estimated to number anywhere between fifty and two hundred. Flying in or out of Port Blair, you pass above their island, ringed by a spectacular coral reef. It's reassuring to think that the people sitting at the bottom of the plumes of smoke drifting up from the forest canopy have for so long resisted contact with the outside world.

for a **penal colony**, based on the system of deporting of criminals that had proved successful in Sumatra, Singapore and Penang. This scheme (and a later attempt to settle the Nicobar Islands, in 1867) were thwarted by the harsh climatic conditions of the forests, but in 1858 Port Blair became a penal settlement where political activists who had fuelled the Uprising in 1857 were made to clear land and build their own prison. Out of 773 prisoners, 292 died, escaped or were hanged in the first two months. Many also lost their lives in attacks by Andamanese tribes who objected to forest clearance, but the settlement continued to fill with people from mainland India, and by 1864 the number of convicts had grown to 3000. In 1896, work began on a jail made up of hundreds of tiny solitary cells, which was used to confine political prisoners until 1945. The prison still stands and is one of Port Blair's few tourist "attractions".

In 1919, the British government in India decided to close down the penal settlement, but it was subsequently used to incarcerate a new generation of freedom fighters from India, Malabar and Burma. During World War II, the islands were occupied by the **Japanese**, who tortured and murdered hundreds of indigenous islanders suspected of collaborating with the British, and bombed the homes of the Jarawa tribe. British forces moved back in 1945, and at last abolished the penal settlement.

After **Partition**, refugees, mostly low-caste Hindus from Bangladesh and Bengal, were given land in Port Blair and North Andaman, where the forest was clear-felled to make room for rice paddy, cocoa plantations and new industries. Since 1951, the population has increased more than tenfold, swollen by repatri-ated Tamils from Sri Lanka, thousands of Bihari labourers, ex-servicemen given land grants, economic migrants from poorer Indian states and legions of government employees packed off on two-year "punishment postings". This replanted population greatly outnumbers the Andamans' indigenous people, who currently comprise around half of one percent of the total. Contact between the two societies is limited, and not always friendly. In addition, within Port Blair a clear divide exists between the relatively recent incomers and the so-called "**pre-42s**" – descendants of the released convicts and freedom fighters whose families settled here before the major influx from the mainland. This small but influential minority, based at the exclusive Browning Club, has been calling for curbs on immigration and new property rules to slow down the rate of settlement. While doubtless motivated by self-interest, their demands reflect growing concern for the future of the Andamans, where rapid and largely unplanned development has wreaked havoc on the natural environment and indigenous population.

As **tourism** continues to replace the almost defunct logging industry as the main source of revenue, the extra visitors are already starting to overtax the inadequate infrastructure, aggravating seasonal water shortages and sewage disposal problems and making inter-island boat tickets even harder to come by. Given India's track record with tourism development, it's hard to be optimistic. Mercifully, Delhi seems to be dragging its feet over giving the go-ahead to the arrival of international flights in Port Blair. If even a small percentage of the tourist traffic between Southeast Asia and India were to be diverted through the Andamans, the impact on this culturally and ecologically fragile region could be catastrophic.

Getting to the Andaman Islands

Port Blair, on South Andaman, is currently served by around three **flights** a day from Chennai on a growing number of airlines, and the new competition has driven prices for the two-hour trip down considerably (see box, p.692 for details). It's also possible to get to Port Blair by **ship**. Services to and from Chennai can be reasonably relied upon to leave in each direction every five to ten days. Those from Kolkata (departing roughly every two weeks) and Vishakapatnam (usually once a month) are still somewhat erratic. Although far cheaper than flying, the crossings are long (3–5 days), uncomfortable and often delayed by bad conditions.

However you arrive, thirty-day **permits** are obtainable on arrival in Port Blair. It is now a lot easier to extend them by fifteen days but the authorities sometimes ask to see a return ticket, which is no problem in the case of flights but not so easy when travelling by ship, as tickets only go on sale the week before departure.

South Andaman: Port Blair and around

Its tree cover now drastically thinned, **South Andaman** is the most heavily populated of the Andaman Islands – particularly around the capital, **Port Blair**. Foreign tourists can only visit the island's southern and east central reaches – including the beaches at **Corbyn's Cove** and **Chiriya Tapu**, the fine reefs on the western shores at **Wandoor**, 35km southwest of Port Blair and the area around **Madhuban** and **Mount Harriet** on the east coast across the bay from the capital. With your own transport it's easy to find your way along the narrow bumpy roads that connect small villages, weaving through forests and coconut fields, and skirting the swamps and rocky outcrops that form the coastline.

Port Blair

PORT BLAIR is a refreshingly leafy but ultimately characterless cluster of tin-roofed buildings tumbling towards the sea in the north, east and west and petering out into fields and forests in the south. There's little to see here – just the **Cellular Jail** and a few small **museums** – but as the point of arrival for the islands, and the only place with a bank (except Havelock), tourist offices and a range of hotels, it can't be avoided. The only time the place really comes alive is during the Island Tourism Festival in the second and third weeks of January, when various cultural events take place. If you plan to head off to more remote islands, the capital is the best place to stock up on supplies and buy necessary equipment.

Arrival and information

Port Blair has two jetties: **boats** from the mainland moor at **Haddo Jetty**, nearly 2km northwest of **Phoenix Jetty**, the arrival point for inter-island ferries. The Director of Shipping Services at Phoenix Jetty has the latest information on boats and ferries, but you can also check the shipping news column of the local newspaper, the *Daily Telegrams* (Rs1.50), for details of forthcoming departures. Advice on booking ferry tickets appears in the box on pp.692–693.

The smart **Veer Sarvakar airport** terminal is 4km south of town at Lamba Line. Free entry **permits** are issued to foreigners from the immigration counters as you enter the arrivals hall. **Taxis** and **auto-rickshaws** are on hand for short trips into town (Rs40–50), but if you have booked a room in any of the middle- or upper-range hotels (or do so at the counter in the airport), you should find a shuttle bus waiting outside. Local **buses** also frequently ply the route to town from the main road about 300m from the terminal building.

The **A&N Directorate of Tourism** counter at the **airport** (☏03192/232414) hands out a useful brochure, but trying to get more than basic tour and hotel info from the desk in the lobby of their **main office** (Mon–Fri 10am–5pm, Sat 10am–1pm; ☏03192/232747, ⓦwww.andaman.nic.in), situated in a modern building diagonally opposite Indian Airlines on the southern edge of the town, can be frustrating – try to talk to someone in the hierarchy upstairs. Further southwest, on Junglighat Main Road, the **India Tourism office** (Mon–Fri 8.30am–5pm; ☏03192/233006) isn't much cop either. Note that if you intend to visit Interview Island (see p.703), you must first obtain a free

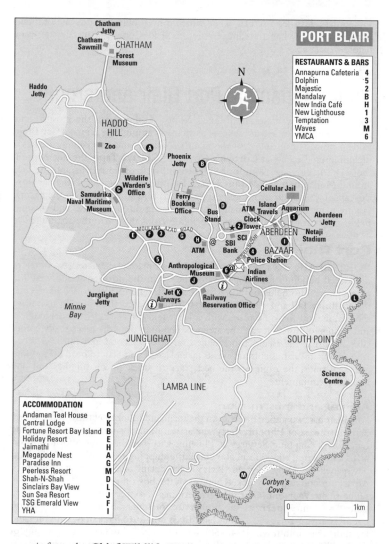

PORT BLAIR

RESTAURANTS & BARS

Annapurna Cafeteria	4
Dolphin	5
Majestic	2
Mandalay	B
New India Café	H
New Lighthouse	1
Temptation	3
Waves	M
YMCA	6

ACCOMMODATION

Andaman Teal House	C
Central Lodge	K
Fortune Resort Bay Island	B
Holiday Resort	E
Jaimathi	H
Megapode Nest	A
Paradise Inn	G
Peerless Resort	M
Shah-N-Shah	D
Sinclairs Bay View	L
Sun Sea Resort	J
TSG Emerald View	F
YHA	I

permit from the **Chief Wildlife Warden**, whose office (☎03192/233270) is next to the zoo in Haddo.

Road names are not used much in Port Blair, with most establishments addressing themselves simply by their local area. The name of the busiest and most central area is **Aberdeen Bazaar**, where you'll find the superintendent of police (for permit extensions), the State Bank of India (Mon–Fri 9am–1pm, Sat 9–11am) and most other facilities. Some hotels will change traveller's cheques, but you'll get faster service and better rates at Island Travels (Mon–Sat 9am–6pm; ☎03192/233034), which has a licence to change money, and is just down the road towards Aberdeen Jetty from the clocktower in Aberdeen Bazaar. There's an ICICI Bank **ATM** at the lower end of Moulana Azad Road and a UTI Bank ATM near Netaji Stadium. **Internet** access is available at a number of locations around town, including a couple of anonymous places between the bus stand and clock tower, at CyberNet on the other side of the bus stand and at the *Holiday Resort* (see below).

Local transport and tours

Walking is tiring and time-consuming in hilly Port Blair – even taking into account the minimal amount of sightseeing the place offers – making transport essential. Yellow-top **taxis** gather opposite the bus stand. They all have meters, but negotiating the price before leaving is usual practice. Expect to pay Rs50 for a trip from the centre of town to Corbyn's Cove. The islands' **auto-rickshaws** try to charge just as much as taxis but shouldn't cost more than Rs10–20 for a ride within town.

Local **buses** run infrequently from the bus stand in central Port Blair to Wandoor and Chiriya Tapu, and can be used for day-trips, though it's best to have your own transport to get around South Andaman. **Bicycles** can be rented from Aberdeen Bazaar, at Rs5 per hour, but the roads to the coasts are most easily covered on a **motorbike** or **scooter**, available for rent at around Rs200–250 per day from GDM Tours (☎03192/232999) on Moulana Azad Road or Karishma Tours & Travels, 22 MG Rd, Middle Point (☎m94342 74314); you'll need to show a licence and leave a Rs1000 deposit. There are petrol pumps on the crossroads west of the bus stand and on the road towards the airport. Fill up before you leave town, as petrol is hard to come by elsewhere.

Most of the ANIIDCO **tours** – cramming the island's few interesting sights together with a string of dull destinations – are a complete waste of time; you're better off renting a scooter or taxi and taking in the jail and museums at your own pace. The more worthwhile ANIIDCO **harbour cruises** (daily 3–5pm; Rs65) depart from Phoenix Jetty, for fleeting visits to the floating docks and **Viper Island** and excursions to **Ross Island** (daily 8.30 & 10.30am and 12.30pm; Rs60). They also run day-trips to **Mt Harriet** (8am; Rs157) and **Wandoor/Mahatma Gandhi National Marine Park**: the bus tour to Wandoor (8am; Rs105) connects with the 10am boat to the islands of Red Skin and Jolly Buoy (Rs300).

Accommodation

Port Blair boasts a fair selection of places to stay. Concentrated mainly in the centre of town, the bottom-range **accommodation** can be as dour as any port town on the mainland. More comfortable hotels occupy more salubrious locations on the outskirts. The abundance of places means it's only a problem finding a room during major holiday periods and the Island Tourism Festival. The prices coded below also spike sharply at these times, while they drop during the monsoon rains.

Andaman Teal House Delanipur ☎03192/234060, ⓦwww.and.nic.in. High on the hill above Haddo port, this A&N Tourism place offers great views, spacious and pleasant rooms, and is very good value, although the location can be inconvenient unless you have your own transport. ❹

Central Lodge Middle Point ☎03192/233634. Rock-bottom option occupying a ramshackle wooden building situated in a quiet and secluded corner of town. Accommodation is in either basic rooms or a dorm (Rs80), and there's also garden space for hammocks. ❷

Fortune Resort Bay Island Marine Hill ☎03192/234101, ⓦwww.fortuneparkhotels.com. Port Blair's swishest hotel is elegant and airy, with polished dark wood. All rooms have carpets and balconies overlooking Phoenix Jetty (the less expensive ones are a little cramped), and there's also a quality restaurant, gardens and an open-air sea-water swimming pool. Prices for suites with full board reach $165. ❽–❾

Holiday Resort Premnagar, a fifteen-minute walk from the centre ☎03192/230516, ⓔholidayresort88@hotmail.com. Only a little more expensive – and much better value – than most budget places with clean, spacious and airy rooms with TV, plus a bar and Internet access. ③–④

Jaimathi Moulana Azad Rd ☎03192/230836. Popular with both Westerners and Indians, this place has clean rooms of varying sizes with communal balconies. ③

Megapode Nest Haddo Hill ☎03192/232380, ⓦwww.aniidco.nic.in. ANIIDCO's upmarket option offers comfortable rooms along with pricier self-contained "cottages" ranged around a central lawn with good views. There's also a quality restaurant. ⑥–⑦

Paradise Inn Moulana Azad Rd ☎03192/245772, ⓕ233479. Compact and great-value modern lodge, offering rooms with TV and phone for the same price as a bare room in places of a similar standard. ③

Peerless Resort Corbyn's Cove ☎03192/229263, ⓦwww.peerlesshotels.com. Lovely setting amid gardens of palms, jasmine and bougainvillea opposite a white sandy beach, but the balconied a/c rooms and cottages are a bit tatty given the prices they charge. There's a bar and a mid-range restaurant with an average evening buffet. ⑧

Shah-N-Shah Mohanpura ☎03192/233696. Set between the bus stand and Phoenix Jetty, this basic but friendly place has attached rooms, as well as a quiet terrace and little-used restaurant. ③

Sinclairs Bay View On the coast road to Corbyn's Cove ☎03192/227824, ⓦwww.sinclairshotels .com. Clifftop hotel with balconies, attached bathrooms, dramatic views, bar and restaurant and airport shuttle bus. Prices may rise significantly after the promised renovations (due to be completed in 2008). ⑥

Sun Sea Resort MG Rd, Middle Point ☎03192/238330. Snazzily designed mid-range hotel with central a/c that beats most of its more expensive rivals for comfort – although it is located on a busy road. Has tastefully furnished rooms and a fine restaurant. ⑤

TSG Emerald View 25 Moulana Azad Rd ☎03192/246488, ⓦwww.andamantsghotels.com. Smart new place with spacious, colourfully furnished rooms (some a/c) boasting all mod cons. ④–⑤

YHA Opposite Netaji Stadium ☎03192/232459. Run-down and predictably institutional hostel, but dorm beds are only Rs50. Students or itinerant workers often fill the 18 beds long term. ①

The Town

Port Blair's only firm reminder of its gloomy past, the sturdy brick **Cellular Jail** (Tues–Sun 9am–noon & 2–5pm; Rs5) overlooks the sea from a small rise in the northeast of town. Built between 1896 and 1905, its tiny solitary cells were far worse than the dormitories in other prison blocks erected earlier. Only three of the seven wings that originally radiated from the central tower now remain. Visitors can peer into the cells (3m by 3.5m) and imagine the grim conditions under which the prisoners existed. Cells were dirty and ill-ventilated, drinking water was limited to two glasses per day, and the convicts were expected to wash in the rain as they worked clearing forests and building prison quarters. Food, brought from the mainland, was stored in vats where the rice and pulses became infested with worms; more than half the prison population died long before their twenty years' detention was up. Protests against conditions led to hunger strikes in 1932, 1933 and 1937, resulting in yet more deaths, and frequent executions took place at the gallows that still stand in squat wooden shelters in the courtyards, in full view of the cells. The reasonably absorbing **Sound and Light Show** (English version Mon, Wed & Fri 6.45pm; Rs20) outlines the history of the prison, and a small **museum** by the entrance gate (same hours as the jail) exhibits lists of convicts, photographs and grim torture devices.

About 300m east of the jail, near the Water Sports Complex, you can see murky tanks full of fish and coral from the islands' reefs at the disappointing **Aquarium** (daily 9am–1pm & 2–4.45pm; Rs5). Three kilometres out along the coast road towards Corbyn's Cove, Port Blair's newest attraction is the **Science Centre** (Tues–Sun 10am–5.30pm; Rs5), where you can choose to pay an extra Rs2 each to visit the main displays such as the Sky Observatory, Science Magic and other interactive exhibits.

On the south side of the centre, close to the Directorate of Tourism, the **Anthropological Museum** (Mon–Sat 9am–noon & 1–4pm; free) has exhibits on the Andaman and Nicobar tribes, including weapons, tools and rare photographs of the region's indigenous people taken in the 1960s. Among the most striking of these is a sequence featuring the Sentinelese, taken on April 26, 1967, when a party of Indian officials made the first contact with the tribe. After scaring the aborigines, the visitors marched into one of their hunting camps and made off with the bows, arrows and other artefacts now displayed in the museum. The anthropologist charged with documenting the expedition noted afterwards that "the whole atmosphere was that of conquering hordes over-running conquered territory".

Further northwest in Delanipur close to the *Andaman Teal House* hotel, the **Samudrika Naval Maritime Museum** (Tues–Sun 9am–5.30pm; Rs10) is an excellent primer if you're heading off to more remote islands, with a superlative shell collection and informative displays on various aspects of local marine biology. One of the exhibits features a cross-section of the different corals you can expect to see on the islands' reefs, followed by a rundown of the various threats these fragile plants face, from mangrove depletion and parasitic starfish to clumsy snorkellers.

Wildlife lovers are advised to steer clear of the grim little **zoo** (Tues–Sun 8am–5pm; Rs2), further down towards Haddo, whose only redeeming feature is that it has successfully bred rare crocodiles and monkeys for release into the wild. Further north, the **Chatham Sawmill** (daily 7am–2.30pm; free) is at the end of the peninsula and marks the northernmost edge of Port Blair. One of the oldest and largest wood-processing plants in Asia, it seasons and mills rare hardwoods taken from various islands – a sad testimony to the continued abuse of international guidelines on tropical timber production, although the authorities swear that only fallen trees are processed. Photography is prohibited. The nearby **Forest Museum** (Mon–Sat 8am–noon & 2–5pm; free) is another dismal spectacle, feebly attempting to justify the Indian Forest Service's wholesale destruction of the Andamans' plant life with a series of lacklustre photographs of extraction methods.

Eating and drinking

Between them, Port Blair's **restaurants** offer dishes from north and south India and a wide variety of seafood. There are a few run-of-the-mill "meals" joints in Aberdeen Bazaar: of these, the *Gagan* and *Milan* on AB Road are the best, but steer clear of the *Dhanalakshmi*'s notoriously dreadful canteen. **Alcohol** is becoming increasingly easy to come by, either in the upscale hotels or a smattering of less salubrious bars such as the one underneath the *Jaimathi* lodge.

Annapurna Caféteria Aberdeen Bazaar, towards the post office. Far and away Port Blair's best South Indian joint, serving the usual range of huge crispy *dosas*, North Indian and Chinese plate meals, delicious coffee, and wonderful *pongal* at breakfast. The lunchtime thalis are also great. Closed Sundays.

Dolphin Marthoma Church Complex, Golghar. Pleasantly decorated restaurant with cane chairs and blinds and a menu of carefully prepared dishes, mostly Indian and Chinese, but also featuring some European dishes and a few house chicken and seafood specialities.

Majestic Aberdeen Bazaar, just up from the bus stand. Simple canteen with a decent range of North and South Indian veg and non-veg dishes at very low prices.

Mandalay *Fortune Resort*, Marine Hill. Airy open restaurant with great bay views dishing up overpriced à la carte dishes and a reasonable Rs350 dinner buffet of mixed Indian, Chinese and Western food, though service can be a bit lax for its class. The adjacent *Nico Bar* is good for a drink.

New India Cafe Moulana Azad Rd. In the basement of *Jaimathi* lodge, this cheap restaurant is popular with Westerners and Indians alike. Wide menu of extremely tasty veg and meat dishes, but expect to wait if you order anything that's not already prepared.

New Lighthouse Near Aberdeen Jetty. Popular place with outdoor seating where you can catch the sea breeze while feasting on some of the cheapest lobster and other seafood in India.
Temptation Moulana Azad Rd. Located in the *Comfort Inn*, this bamboo and mock-stone grotto offers huge portions of Indian and Chinese food. Just beware of the "boneless" meat dishes.

Waves *Peerless Resort*, Corbyn's Cove. Slightly pricey but very congenial alfresco hotel restaurant under a shady palm grove, and one of the few places in town you can order a beer with your meal. Most dishes around Rs100–150.
YMCA Near Post Office. North and South Indian standards served on a pleasant covered terrace. The pure veg thalis are especially good.

Around Port Blair

At some point, you're almost certain to find yourself killing time in Port Blair, waiting for boats to show up or tickets to go on sale. Rather than wasting days in town, it's worth exploring the **coast** of South Andaman which, although far more densely populated than other islands in the archipelago, holds a handful of easily accessible beauty spots and historic sites. Among the latter, the ruined colonial

Moving on from Port Blair

Port Blair is the departure point for all flights and ferry crossings to the **Indian mainland**; it is also the hub of the Andamans' inter-island bus and ferry network. Unfortunately, booking tickets (especially back to Chennai, Kolkata or Vishakapatnam) can be time-consuming, and many travellers are obliged to come back here well before their permit expires to make reservations, before heading off to more pleasant parts again. For more information on transport, see Travel details, p.706

To the mainland

If you've travelled to the Andamans **by ship**, you'll know what a rough ride the three-day (or more) crossing can be in bunk class, and how difficult tickets are to come by (see p.688). It's also a good idea to talk to fellow travellers about current conditions, which vary from year to year and vessel to vessel. The one factor you can be sure about is that, at around Rs1300–1500, the ship offers the cheapest route back. The downside is that schedules can be erratic, and accurate information about them difficult to obtain – annoying when you only have a one-month permit. Tickets for all three mainland ports are now handled by the DSS (☎03192/245555) and go on sale, supposedly a week in advance of departure, at the allotted booths within the Computerised Reservation Centre (Mon–Fri 9am–1pm & 2–4pm and Sat 9am–noon) at Phoenix Jetty. It's wise to find out when they are going on sale and be there to join the fray ahead of time. Bear in mind, too, that if you're reading this a couple of days' journey from the capital, and with only a week or less left on your permit, that the local police can get heavy with foreigners who outstay their allotted time.

Returning to the mainland by **plane** in just two hours instead of seventy-two can save lots of time and hassle, and though still not cheap, the appearance of newer airlines such as Air Deccan has lowered ticket prices to **Chennai** and **Kolkata** to around Rs4000–6000 one way. The extra flights, currently five daily to Chennai and three or four to Kolkata, also mean it's usually possible to book a seat at short notice apart from peak times like Diwali, Christmas or the Island Tourism Festival. The Indian Airlines office (☎03192/234744) is diagonally opposite the ANIIDCO office, while Jet Airways (☎03192/236922) is on the first floor at 189 Main Road, Junglighat, next to the GITO office. Other airlines can be booked through the host of travel agents such as Island Travels (see p.688).

Travellers intending to catch onward **trains** from their port of arrival on the mainland should note that Port Blair has an efficient computerized Southern Railways reservation office near the Secretariat (Mon–Sat 8.30am–1pm & 2–4pm).

monuments on **Viper** and **Ross islands** can be reached on daily harbour cruises or regular ferries from the capital. For **beaches**, head southeast to **Corbyn's Cove**, or south to the more secluded **Chiriya Tapu**, both of which are easily accessible on day-trips if you rent a moped or taxi. By far the most rewarding way to spend a day out of town, however, is to catch the tourist boat from **Wandoor** to **Jolly Buoy** or **Red Skin islands** in the **Mahatma Gandhi National Marine Park** opposite, which boasts some of the Andamans' best snorkelling. The hilly area around **Mount Harriet** and **Madhuban** on the central part of South Andaman, across the bay from Port Blair, offers some pleasant walking routes.

Viper and Ross islands

The first stop on the harbour cruise from Port Blair (daily 3–5pm; Rs60) is generally **Viper Island** (entry Rs5), named not after the many snakes that doubtless inhabit its tangled tropical undergrowth, but a nineteenth-century merchant vessel that ran aground on it during the early years of the colony.

Inter-island services

Buses connect Port Blair with most major settlements on South and Middle Andaman, mainly via the Andaman Trunk Road. From the mildly chaotic bus stand at the bottom of town, one daily government service at 5am runs via **Rangat** (6hr) and **Mayabunder** (9hr) to **Diglipur** (11hr) and **Arial Bay**. There's another daily service to Rangat at 6am. Several private companies including Geetanjali Travels (tickets at *Tillai* teashop by the bus stand) and the cheaper Ananda (☎03192/233252) run deluxe or video coach (ear-plugs essential) services, which leave from the road outside the bus stand also at 4–5am. Ticket prices are in line with the mainland: a ticket to Rangat is around Rs150 and travelling all the way to Diglipur will cost you no more than Rs200.

Most of the islands open to foreign tourists, including **Neill**, **Havelock**, **Middle**, **North** and **Little Andaman**, are also accessible by **boat** from Phoenix Jetty. Details are posted in the shipping news columns of the local newspapers, but they only appear two days before departure. The only way to guarantee a passage is to book tickets in advance at the Inter-Island booths in the Computerised Reservation Centre at Phoenix Jetty, though any remaining tickets are issued prior to departure on the quay. Queues at the office can descend into quite a scrum, which can sometimes be avoided by paying an agent a fee to send somebody else in your place. Fares are government-subsidized and very cheap, going for as little as Rs20 for the six-hour voyage to Little Andaman, for example. Even the two-tier pricing system for islanders and non-islanders in place for more touristy destinations such as Havelock only leaves you Rs150 poorer. Schedules change regularly but during the main season you can expect two to three boats daily to Havelock, one or two daily to Neill, one daily to both Rangat and Hut Bay on Little Andaman, four a week to Long and five a week to Arial Bay (for Diglipur). If possible, try to travel on newer, faster and more comfortable vessels like the *Wandoor* or *Jolly Buoy* than on an older bucket such as the *Ramanujam*. The journeys on older boats can be a lot longer and more uncomfortable than you might expect. From 9am onwards, the heat on board is intense, with only corrugated plastic sheets for shade, while the benches are highly uncomfortable and the toilets generally dismal. You should take adequate supplies of food and water with you; only biscuits and simple snacks are sold on the boats, if that. More details of boat services to destinations outside the capital appear in the relevant accounts.

Lying a short way off Haddo Wharf, it served as an isolation zone for the main prison, where escapees and convicts (including hunger strikers) were sent to be punished. Whipping posts and crumbling walls, reached from the jetty via a winding brick path, remain as relics of a torture area, while the prominent gallows occupy the site's elevated position.

No less eerie are the decaying colonial remains on **Ross Island** (entry Rs20), at the entrance to Port Blair harbour, where the British sited their first penal settlement. Originally cleared by convicts wearing iron fetters (most of them sent here in the wake of the 1857 Uprising), Ross witnessed some of the most brutal excesses of British colonial history, and was the source of the prison's infamy as **Kalapani**, or Black Water. Of the many convicts transported here, distinguished by their branded foreheads, the majority perished from disease or torture before the clearance of the island was completed in 1860. Thereafter, it served briefly as the site of Rev Henry Corbyn's "Andaman Home" – a prison camp created with the intention of "civilizing" the local tribespeople – before becoming the headquarters of the revamped penal colony, complete with theatre hall, tennis courts, swimming pool, hospitals and grand residential bungalows. Rather ambitiously dubbed "the Paris of the East", the settlement typified the stiff-upper-lipped spirit of the Raj at its most cruel: while the *burra*- and *memsahibs* dressed for dinner and sang hymns in church, convicts languished in appalling conditions only a kilometre away. In the end, the entry of the Japanese into World War II, hot on the heels of a massive earthquake in 1941, forced the British to evacuate, and in the coming years most of the buildings were dismantled by the new overlords, who themselves founded a POW camp here. Little more than the hilltop **Anglican church**, with its weed-infested graveyard, has survived the onslaught of tropical creepers and vines, but the island makes a peaceful break from Port Blair. To get here, jump on one of the regular launches from Phoenix Jetty (daily; departing 8.30am, 10.30am & 12.30pm and returning 8.45am, 10.45am & 12.40pm; Rs60).

Corbyn's Cove and Chiriya Tapu

The best beach within easy reach of the capital lies just over 5km southeast at **Corbyn's Cove**, a small arc of smooth white sand backed by a swaying curtain of palms. There's a large hotel here (*Peerless Resort*, see p.690), but the water isn't particularly clear, and bear in mind that lying around scantily clothed may bring you considerable attention from crowds of local workers.

For more isolation, rent a moped or take a taxi 30km south to **Chiriya Tapu** ("Bird Island") – not actually an island, but a peninsula at the tip of of South Andaman. The motorable track running beyond this small fishing village leads through thick jungle overhung with twisting creepers to a large bay, where swamps give way to shell-strewn beaches. Other than at lunchtime, when it often receives a deluge of bus parties, the beach offers plenty of peace and quiet, with forest walks on the woodcutters' trails that wind inland from it and easy access to an inshore reef. However, the water here is nowhere near as clear as at some spots in the archipelago, and serious snorkellers and divers should enquire if any boats are going out from the big hotels to volcanic **Cinque Island** (see p.705), a couple of hours' further south. It's also possible to charter your own fishing boat here; ask around the bar in the village, and expect to pay around Rs3000 per boat for the return trip to Cinque.

Wandoor and the Mahatma Gandhi National Marine Park

Much the most popular excursion from Port Blair is the boat ride from **Wandoor**, 35km southwest, to one of the fifteen islets comprising the

Mahatma Gandhi National Marine Park. Although set up purely for tourists, the trip is worth considering, as it gains you access to one of the richest coral reefs in the region. The downside is that entry into the park for foreigners now costs Rs500 (Indians Rs50). Boats depart at 10am (daily except Mon; Rs300) from Wandoor, which you can reach on A&N Tourism's **tour** (Rs105) or by local bus, but it is more fun to rent a moped and ride down to meet the boat yourself.

The long white **beach** at Wandoor is littered with the dry, twisted trunks of trees torn up and flung down by annual cyclones, and fringed not with palms, but by dense forest teeming with bird life. The water's very shallow, so you should only snorkel here at high tide. From the jetty, the boats chug through broad creeks lined with dense mangrove swamps and pristine forest to either **Red Skin Island** or, more commonly, **Jolly Buoy**. The latter, an idyllic deserted island, boasts an immaculate shell-sand beach, ringed by a bank of superb coral. The catch is that the boat only stops for around an hour, which isn't nearly enough time to explore the shore and reef. Beware of **strong currents** while snorkelling off the edges of the reef.

Mount Harriet and Madhuban

The richly forested slopes of **Mount Harriet** can easily be visited as a day-trip from Port Blair. You can either take one of the passenger ferries (every 30min) from Chatham Jetty to **Bamboo Flats** or, if you want to have your own transport on the other side, there are eight daily vehicle ferries from Phoenix Jetty between 5.30am and 8.30pm, costing a few rupees. From Bamboo Flats it's a pleasant seven-kilometre stroll east along the coast and north up a path through trees hung with thick vines and creepers to the 365-metre summit, which affords fine views back across the bay. An intermittent bus service runs between Bamboo Flats and Hope Town, where the path starts, saving you 3km. Alternatively, Jeeps and taxis are available to take you all the way to the top but they charge at least Rs300. There's a charge of Rs250 (Indians Rs25; students/teachers Rs5) to enter Mount Harriet National Park, but the checkpost is on the road so you probably won't be asked to pay if you take the path. It's 2.5km from the checkpost up to the resthouse and viewing tower at the summit. If you have strong legs you can reach **Madhuban** on the coast northeast of the mountain by the sixteen-kilometre round route via Kala Patthar (Black Rock) and back via the coast. There's a decent beach at Madhuban and the area is still used for training logging **elephants**, so you stand a good chance of seeing them learning their trade.

Islands north of Port Blair

Printed on the permit card you receive on arrival in the Andamans is a list of all the other **islands** you're allowed to visit in the archipelago. Having travelled all the way to the Andamans, the vast majority of visitors make a beeline for the only two developed islands in the group, the admittedly enchanting **Neill** and **Havelock**, both of which are within easy reach of Port Blair.

To get further north, where tourism of any kind has thus far had very little impact, you can take a bus or boat from the capital or ferry from Havelock to ramshackle **Rangat**, at the south end of **Middle Andaman**, or bypass the whole east coast by catching a bus (Rs200) or boat (Rs40) from Port Blair direct to **Diglipur**'s port of Arial Bay, at the top of **North Andaman**. Either way, you'll be lucky not to be marooned from time to time in some truly grim little settlements, interspersed with a few long hard slogs up the infamous **Andaman Trunk Road** (or "ATR"). On Middle and North Andaman and their satellite islands, **accommodation** is scarce, to say the least. Aside from a handful of A&N Tourism hotels (bookable in advance in Port Blair), the only places to stay are a few basic lodges or, preferably, APWD *Rest Houses* (see box p.701). To escape the settled areas you have to be prepared to rough it, travelling on inshore fishing dugouts, sleeping on beaches and cooking your own food.

The rewards, however, are great. Backed by dense forest filled with colourful birds and insects, the beaches, bays and reefs of the outer Andamans teem with wildlife, from gargantuan crabs, pythons and turtles to dolphins, sharks, giant rays and the occasional primeval-looking dugong. Essential **kit** for off-track wanderings includes a sturdy mosquito net, mats to sleep on (or a hammock), a large plastic container for water, some strong antiseptic for cuts and bites (sand flies are a real problem on many of the beaches) and, most important of all, **water purification** tablets or a water purifier, since bottled water is virtually nonexistent. Wherever you end up, preserve the goodwill of local people by packing your rubbish out – carrying it in your backpack – or burning it, and being sensitive to scruples about dress and nudity, especially in areas settled by conservative Bengali or Tamil Hindus.

Neill

Tiny, triangular-shaped **Neill** is the most southerly inhabited island of **Ritchie's Archipelago**, and is barely two hours northeast of Port Blair on a fast ferry. The source of much of the capital's fresh fruit and vegetables, its fertile centre, ringed by a curtain of stately tropical trees, comprises vivid patches of green paddy dotted with small farmsteads and banana plantations. It's a quiet, atmospheric place, and while most of the beaches are mediocre by the Andamans' standards, is worth a day or two en route to or from Havelock. **Boats** leave Port Blair's Phoenix Jetty for Neill (1–2 daily; 2hr–3hr 30min; Rs150); all services connect with Havelock, and also run to Rangat. When you disembark, you will be asked to register your permit number with a police officer – one awaits all ferries at the jetty.

Neill boasts three **beaches**, all within easy cycling distance of the small bazaar just up the lane from the jetty (you can rent **cycles** from one of several stall-holders from Rs40–50 per day). The best place to swim is on the east coast is **Neill Kendra**, a gently curving bay of white sand that straddles the jetty and is scattered with picturesque wooden fishing boats. This blends into **Lakshmangar**, which continues for 3km north: to get there by road, head right when you reach the main road and follow it for around twenty minutes until it dwindles into a surfaced track, then turn right. Wrapped around the headland, the beach is a broad spur of white shell sand with shallow water offering good snorkelling, although entry into the water is tough except at high tide. Exposed to the open sea and thus prone to higher tides, **Sitapur** beach, 6km south at the tip of the island, is also appealing and has the advantage of a sandy bottom extending into the sea. The ride there, by hourly bus or bicycle, across Neill's central paddy land is pleasant, but there are no facilities when you get there, so stock up for the day. This will change, however, when the new venture by the owners of *Wild Orchid* on Havelock (see p.699) opens some time in 2008.

Currently, the island has four **accommodation** places. From the jetty, a two-minute walk brings you to A&N Tourism's *Hawabill Nest* (T03192/282630, Wwww.and.nic.in; ④), which has a dozen a/c rooms with sitouts ranged around a central courtyard and restaurant, best booked in advance from Port Blair; there is

The seas around the Andaman and Nicobar islands are some of the world's most unspoilt. Marine life is abundant, with an estimated 750 species of fish existing on one reef alone. Parrot, trigger and angel fish live alongside manta rays, reef sharks and loggerhead turtles. Many species of fish and coral are unique to the area and fascinating life-systems exist in ash beds and cooled lava based around the volcanic Barren Island (see p.705).

For a quick taste of marine life, you could start by **snorkelling**; most hotels can supply masks and snorkels, though some equipment is in dire need of replacement. The only way to get really close, however, and venture out into deeper waters, is to **scuba dive**. The experience of swimming with dolphins and barracudas or weaving in and out of coral beds, coming eye to eye with fish, is unforgettable.

Dive operations have come and gone more frequently than the rains in recent years and the picture is constantly changing. Apart from a new outfit operating out of Port Blair (see below), at the time of writing the most organized diving was on Havelock, with three fully certified centres up and running, but it's worth checking what the current scene is when you arrive. Prices are very similar at all three, with dives for certified divers running around Rs2000 for one tank, Rs3000 for two and Rs4000 for three; more economical packages, often including accommodation and food, are available for multiple dives and Discover Scuba introductory days go for Rs4500. Courses cost about Rs16,000 for a basic four-five day PADI open-water qualification, Rs12,000 for advanced or Rs30,000 to go all the way up to Divemaster. The current trio are the Indian-run **Andaman Dive Club** (Tm99321 74793, Wwww.andamandiveclub.com), whose premises are only about 500m from the jetty and who should by now have a smart 12-cabin sleepover boat to enable longer trips to more remote islands. Further down the coast at *Café del Mar* on beach #3, Barefoot Scuba (T03192/282181, Wwww.barefootindia.com) is manned by mainly British instructors and has the biggest – and newest – range of equipment, while **Dive India** (Tm98318 02204, Wwww.diveindia.com), a little further on at *Island Vinnie's*, is run by friendly divemasters from the Karen community (Burmese brought here by the British as a source of labour) around Mayabunder, at the northern end of Middle Andaman, where they are planning to set up another operation. The only reliable place to arrange diving in the Port Blair area is with Bhumi Divers (Tm98318 02204, Efundive3@yahoo.com), who have an erratically manned office in Aberdeen Bazaar, although legendary ex-navy diver Captain Bhart may be taking trips out from Wandoor, so ask around.

Underwater in the Andamans, it is not uncommon to come across schools of reef sharks, which rarely turn hostile, but one thing to avoid is the **black-and-white sea snake**. Though the snakes seldom attack – and, since their fangs are at the back of their mouths, they find it difficult to get a grip on any human – their bite is twenty times more deadly than that of the cobra.

Increased tourism inevitably puts pressure on the delicate marine ecosystem, and poorly funded wildlife organizations can do little to prevent damage from insensitive visitors. You can ensure that your presence in the sea around the reefs does not harm the coral by observing the following **Green Coral Code** while diving or snorkelling:

• Never touch or walk on living coral – it will die.

• Try to keep your feet away from reefs while wearing fins; the sudden sweep of water caused by a flipper kick can be enough to destroy coral.

• Always control the speed of your descent while diving; enormous damage can be caused by divers landing hard on a coral bed.

• Never break off pieces of coral from a reef, and remember that it is illegal to export dead coral from the islands, even fragments you may have found on a beach.

also a Rs150 dormitory. The three private options are all at Lakshmangar or en route to it: the best of the bunch is *Tango Beach Resort* (☏03192/282634, ✉tangobeachresort@rediffmail.com; ❶–❹), a friendly place right on the beach, with two deluxe and ten much more basic bamboo huts, as well as several cement rooms. Before *Tango*, a little over 500m from the jetty, you pass *Cocon Huts* (☏03192/282528, ✉coconhuts@yahoo.com; ❶–❸), which has a similar range of huts and nicely thatched rooms, although the bar can attract rowdy revellers and may consequently be moved closer to the village. The furthest option, 1km north of *Tango*, is *Pearl Park Hotel* (☏03192/282510, ✉pearlpark2002@yahoo.com; ❶–❺), which has some small huts and larger but somewhat overpriced a/c bungalows. Although many people stick to the **restaurants** at these three establishments, far and away the best place to eat is the delightful and welcoming ⚓ *Gyan Garden*, opposite the football pitch 500m along the road to Lakshmangar, where fresh fish and home-grown veg dishes are a speciality; there's even space for a handful of people to stay if the island's full. Of the few tiny eateries in the bazaar, *Hotel Chand* serves up the tastiest, albeit somewhat oily, food.

Havelock

Havelock is the largest island in Ritchie's Archipelago, and the most intensively cultivated, settled like many in the region by Bengali refugees after Partition.

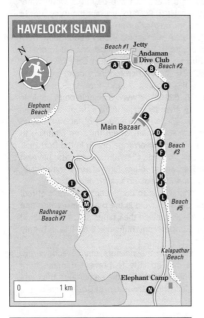

Thanks to its regular ferry connections (2–3 daily; 2hr–4hr 30min; Rs150) with the capital, it is also visited in far greater numbers than anywhere else in the Andamans. There can now be as many as five hundred tourists holed up here at any one time during peak season, which makes some parts of the island feel overwhelmed and can create accommodation shortages. The boat journey here from Neill, skirting a string of uninhabited islets with shadowy views of South Andaman to the west, is wonderful, and wildlife – both on land and in the sea – remains abundant, despite intensive settlement and deforestation.

Arrival, information and getting around
Havelock's main **jetty** is on the north side of the island, at the village known as **Beach #1**. After registering with the police as you disembark, it's best to make your own way to where you plan to stay, though if you've booked in advance, most places arrange a pick-up. There's a small tourist shop to the right of the road that

ACCOMMODATION		Emerald Gecko	L	MS Lodge	A
Barefoot at		Happy Resort	B	Pooja Paradise	N
Havelock	I	Harmony Resort	K	Pristine Beach	
Café del Mar	D	Island Camping	M	Resort	E
Dolphin Resort	J	Island Vinnie's	F	Wild Orchid	H
Eco Villa	C	Jungle View			
		Nest	G		
RESTAURANTS					
Arati	3	Blackbeard's		Red Snapper	H
Barefoot		Bistro	L	Riya Priya	2
Lounge	I	Nala's Kingdom	1		

leaves the jetty but it's neither official nor all that helpful. Five daily buses run to **Radhnagar** (aka #7 beach) but only one morning route heads down the east coast, where the bulk of the accommodation is located. Instead, you can take a Rs40–50 auto-rickshaw ride or rent a **scooter**, **motorbike** (both Rs200–250 per day) or **cycle** (Rs50 per day) for a few days. The only place to change money, the State Co-operative Bank (Mon–Fri 9am–1pm, Sat 9–11am) is at the main bazzar, 2km inland. The **Internet** arrived on the island in 2006 but the three places that have it, the jetty tourist shop and two of the guest houses listed below, charge an exorbitant Rs120 for a slow dial-up to Port Blair; the inevitable arrival of broadband will change that, however.

Accommodation

As really the only developed tourist scene in the Andamans, Havelock now has over twenty establishments to choose from, offering everything from the most basic unlockable **huts** to luxuriously furnished **cottages**, although **hotels** in the conventional sense are non-existent. Prices codes here indicate rates through most of the season. They can rise by fifty percent from mid-December to mid-January, and drop considerably between May and September.

Barefoot at Havelock Radhnagar ☎03192/220191, ⓦwww.barefootindia.com. Havelock's most luxurious resort, with fan-cooled duplex and Nicobari cottages and a/c Andaman villas. Most of these, and the large restaurant, are attractive timber and thatch structures. ❽–❾

Café del Mar Beach #3 ☎03192/282343, ⓦwww.barefootindia.com. Barefoot's budget branch and home to their dive centre. There's a choice of sturdy cottages and average-sized huts, all with attached bathrooms. ❸–❺

Dolphin Resort Beach #5 ☎03192/282411, ⓦwww.and.nic.in. A&N Tourism's smartest resort is still lacking in atmosphere, though the detached concrete cottages are spacious and comfortable. More popular with Indians than foreign tourists. ❹–❻

Eco Villa Beach #2 ☎03192/282171, ⓔandamanecovilla@yahoo.com. All huts are attached, and mostly quite small, with a couple of two-tier structures. Internet available. ❸

Emerald Gecko Beach #5 ☎03192/282170, ⓦwww.emerald-gecko.com. The nicest budget resort, with ten modest attached and non-attached huts and half a dozen superbly designed two-tier cottages. ❷–❺

Happy Resort Beach #2 ☎03192/282061, ⓔrajhavelock@yahoo.in. One of the best real cheapies, with a bunch of basic huts, all with shared bathrooms, and a vibe to match the name. ❶

Harmony Resort Radhnagar ☎03192/282120.

Under a kilometre back from the beach on the main road, these huts with shared facilities are a bit overpriced but the only cheap ones close to Beach #7. ❷

Island Camping Radhnagar. No local phone but can be booked through A&N Tourism in Port Blair. It's not for pitching your own tent – there's a range of various sizes already set up for rent. ❶

Island Vinnie's Beach #3 ☎03192/282187, ⓦwww.islandvinnie.com. Spacious and beautifully constructed Rajasthani tents, attached and not, make for a unique and comfortable stay. ❸–❺

Jungle View Nest Under 3km inland from Radhnagar ☎03192/282143. Some very basic huts and some half-concrete ones, but it's the only place in the interior and one of the last to fill up. ❶

Pooja Paradise Kala Pathar ☎m94742 10549. The most remote place to stay on the island has a mixture of simple huts and cement cottages. Another good fall-back when more popular places are full. ❶–❸

Pristine Beach Resort Beach #3 ☎03192/282344, ⓔalexpristinebeach @hotmail.com. One of the friendliest and most sociable places, with a good range of huts, mostly attached, one duplex and an Internet café. ❶–❺

Wild Orchid Beach #5 ☎03192/282472, ⓦwww.wildorchidandaman.com. Easily the best higher-end resort for its classy cottages (some a/c), splendid restaurant and lounge and laid-back atmosphere. ❼

The island

Havelock's hub of activity is not the jetty village, which just has a few stalls, a couple of dowdy lodges, the odd restaurant and the police station, but the **Main Bazaar**, which you come to if you follow the road straight ahead from the jetty for two kilometres, passing beach #2 on the way. Here you'll find a greater variety of shops and eateries, the only bank and the island's main junction. The right turn, which leads nine kilometres towards **Radhnagar,** passes paddy fields and other crops before dropping through some spectacular woodland to a two-kilometre-long arc of perfect white sand, backed by stands of giant *mowhar* trees. The water is a sublime turquoise colour and, although the coral is sparse, marine life here is diverse and plentiful, especially among the rocks around the corner from the main beach (accessible at low tide). The main drawback, which can make sunbathing uncomfortable, is a preponderance of pesky sandflies.

As the nesting site for a colony of Olive Ridley **turtles** (see box, p.231), Radhnagar is strictly protected by the Forest Department, whose wardens ensure tourists don't light fires or sleep on the beach. Elephant "jolly rides" (10am–1pm; Rs20) are available from a podium en route to the beach. A couple of kilometres before the road descends to Radhnagar, a path on the right leads over a hill and down through some scattered settlements to far wilder **Elephant Beach,** although the only trunks you are likely to spot are those of huge fallen trees. Snorkelling here is good, and coral reefs are accessible from the shore, but it can be tough to find the way unless somebody takes you; look out for the start of the path at a sharp bend in the road with a Forest Department notice board in a small clearing and then keep asking the way whenever you see a local.

If you take the left turn through the busier strip of Main Bazaar, the road leads on past beaches #3 and #5, where most of the beach huts and resorts are located. As on Neill, these east-facing beaches, though exquisitely scenic, have fairly thin strips of golden-white sand and when the sea recedes across the lumps of broken coral and rock lying offshore, swimming becomes all but impossible. After beach #5 the road continues south for several kilometres before turning slightly inland and eventually petering out **Kalapathar** beach. Here you can visit the Forest Department's elephant training camp, although the sight of the gentle giants being rather ferociously whacked with heavy sticks is hardly an edifying one. The entire southern half of Havelock consists of impenetrable forest.

△ Elephants on Radhnagar beach, Havelock

Eating and drinking

Dining options on Havelock have improved no end, with a couple of the better resorts importing proper chefs. Western travellers' favourites and bland curries are widely available at all the beach hut cafés but if you want authentic, mainly Bengali, food then it's better to head for a local restaurant in one of the settlements. Beer and basic spirits are sold at most travellers' haunts but are not cheap and supply of the former from Port Blair can be erratic.

Arati Radhnagar. The best of the row of simple shacks that line the end of the road before the beach, serving cheap, wholesome Bengali fare.

Barefoot Lounge Radhnagar. The eponymous resort's spacious restaurant specialises in continental and Indian veg and seafood dishes for around Rs200-300. There's a nice cushioned seating area with low tables, as well as a more conventional section.

Blackbeard's Bistro at *Emerald Gecko*, Beach #5. The lovely open dining area has furniture created from recycled timber and offers rare dishes such as cerviche as well as fresh fish cooked in delicious and imaginative sauces for Rs150-200. There is a friendly bar to cap it all off.

Nala's Kingdom Beach #1, Jetty. The most salubrious place in the jetty area, serving Indian, Chinese and fish dishes.

Red Snapper at *Wild Orchid*, Beach #5. Excellent upmarket seafood, meat and veg menu, served in quality surroundings. There's a sumptious weekly buffet for Rs400, usually featuring the catch of the day.

Riya Priya Main Bazaar. One of the best places to eat in the busiest part of the island. Fish, chicken and spicy local curries are all available.

Long Island

Just off the southeast coast of Middle Andaman, **Long Island** is dominated by an unsightly plywood mill, but don't let this put you off. Served by just four boats per week from the capital (4–5hr) and Rangat (1–1hr 30min), plus two daily launches from Yeratta (7am & 2pm; 1hr), around 10km from Rangat, it sees only a trickle of visitors but boasts a couple of excellent beaches, at **Marg Bay** and **Lalaji Bay**. Both are most easily reached by chartering a fisherman's dinghy from the jetty, as they are a good couple of hours' hike from where the boat docks. The **main settlement** by the jetty has the island's only facilities, including a couple of tatty lodges – try *Kaniappa* (☏03192/278529; ❶). Most foreigners head for the beaches with tents, hammocks and supplies; mercifully, plans to develop the beaches into an upscale resort have been shelved, so the Robinson Crusoe experience remains, although you may have to share the coast with belligerent sandflies.

APWD rest houses

Though theoretically set aside for government officials and engineers, travellers are often allowed to stay at **APWD rest houses**, frequently the best – and sometimes the only – accommodation in Middle and North Andaman. To stay at these rest houses it's best to get a free **letter of recommendation** from the APWD office (☏03192/232294), just up the road from the *Hotel Blair* in Port Blair, but you'll have to give specific dates. Theoretically they'll reserve a room for you, but you'll still get bumped if a pukka VIP shows up in the meantime. Just turning up at a rest house isn't guaranteed to meet with success even if rooms are free, but you'll stand a much better chance of getting in if you can provide them with photocopies of your permit and the Indian visa and personal details pages from your passport. Details of particular rest houses are given throughout the text, but all have standardized prices despite varying standards of comfort; all rooms are doubles, but costs are per bed (Rs200 for non-a/c, Rs400 for a/c).

Middle Andaman

For most travellers, **Middle Andaman** is a charmless rite of passage to be endured en route to or from the north. Of its two main settlements, the more northerly **Mayabunder**, the port for alluring **Interview Island**, is slightly more appealing than characterless **Rangat** because of its pleasant setting by the sea, but neither town gives any reason to dally for long. Elsewhere, the sinuous Andaman Trunk Road, hemmed in by walls of towering forest, winds through miles of jungle; drivers cross the strait that separates the island from its neighbour, Baratang Island, by means of rusting flat-bottomed ferry. The island's frontier feeling is heightened by the presence of armed guards on the buses, and the knowledge that the impenetrable forests west of the ATR make up the **Jarawa Tribal Reserve** (see p.684).

Rangat and around

At the southeast corner of Middle Andaman, **RANGAT** consists of a ramshackle sprawl ranged around two rows of chai shops and general stores divided by the ATR. However, as a major staging post on the journey north, it's impossible to avoid – just don't get stranded here if you can help it.

The five or six **ferries** per week to and from Port Blair (5–7hr) dock at **Rangat Bay** (aka **Nimbutala**), 7km east; all stop at Havelock Island and most at Long Island (4 weekly), and there are also two daily launches to Long Island from nearby **Yeratta**. In addition, Rangat is served by two daily government **buses** to Port Blair (6–7hr) as well as some private services, which pass through in the morning en route from further north. The APWD *Rest House* (☎03192/274237; ❸–❹), pleasantly situated up a winding hill from the bazaar with views across the valley, is the best place to stay and eat, providing good, filling fish thalis. The *RG Lodge* (☎03192/274237; ❷), just off the main road, is a decent fallback. The best places to eat are the *Hotel MK*, on the main road, which serves basic Indian and Chinese food, and the *Hotel Star*, on a nearby alley leading to the small market square, for Indian veg and non-veg.

If you do get stuck here, rather than staying put in Rangat, jump on a bus to **Amakunj beach**, about 9km north, for a swim or snorkel, or head a further 6km to Cuthbert Bay aka RRO, where you can stay at the characterless but comfortable A&N Tourism **hotel** *Hawksbill Nest* (☎03192/279159; ❸–❹), which is invariably empty. If you have an early ferry out of Rangat Bay, it is better to stay down near the jetty at the friendly *Sea Shore Lodge* (☎03192/274464; ❷). Basic meals can be had from the motley conglomeration of stalls between the lodge and the jetty.

Mayabunder

Only 70km north of Rangat by road (a bus journey of three hours or more), perched on a long promontory right at the top of the island and surrounded by mangrove swamps, **MAYABUNDER** is a springboard for the remote northern Andaman Islands. The village, home to a large minority of former Burmese **Karen** tribal people who were originally brought here as cheap logging labour by the British, is more appealing than Rangat, but again there is little to hold your interest for long.

At the brow of the hill, before it descends to the jetty, a small hexagonal wooden structure houses the **Forest Museum/Interpretation Centre** (Mon–Sat 8am–noon & 1–4pm; free), which holds a motley collection of turtle shells, snakes in formaldehyde, dead coral, a crocodile skull and precious little information. Next door, the APWD *Rest House* (☎03192/273211; ❸–❹) is large and very comfortable, with a pleasant garden and gazebo overlooking the sea, and a dining room serving good set meals. The only other reasonable accommodation nearby is back in the centre of the bazaar at the *Anmol Lodge* (T03192/262695; ❷), some of whose attached rooms have TV, and the nearby *S&S Lodge* (T03192/273449; ❶), which has clean rooms with shared bathrooms; the dilapidated and cockroach-infested *Lakshminarayan Lodge* should be avoided at all costs. Further afield at **Karmateng beach**, 14km southeast, there's another A&N Tourism hotel, the *Swiftlet Nest* (T03192/273495; ❸–❹) but nothing else. Two buses are supposed to go there daily, failing which there are taxis or auto-rickshaws.

Buses from Port Blair now continue over the new bridge to Diglipur on North Andaman at least twice a day, some bypassing Mayabunder altogether. Heading back towards the capital, there are a couple of private services, such as Geetanjali Travels, as well as one government bus, all departing very early in the morning.

Interview Island

Mayabunder is the jumping-off place for **Interview Island**, a windswept nature sanctuary off the remote northwest coast of Middle Andaman. Only opened to tourists in 1997, it's large, mainly flat and completely uninhabited save for a handful of unfortunate forest wardens, coast guards and policemen, posted here to ward off poachers. Foreigners aren't permitted to spend the night on the island, and to visit you must first obtain permission from the Chief Wildlife Warden in Port Blair. If you've come to the Andamans to watch **wildlife**, a visit here should be top of your list.

The only way to reach Interview is to charter a private fishing dinghy from Mayabunder jetty for around Rs500. Arrange one the day before and leave at first light. Approaching the island, you'll be struck by its wild appearance, particularly noticeable on the northwest, where the monsoon storms have wrecked the shoreline forest. If you can, however, get your boatman to pull up on to the **beach** at the southern tip of the island, which has a perennial fresh-water pool inside a low cave; legend has it that the well, a nesting site for white-bellied **swifts**, has no bottom. At the forest post, where you have to sign an entry ledger, ask the wardens about the movements of Interview's feral **elephants**, descendants of trained elephants deserted here by a Kolkata-based logging company after its timber operation failed in the 1950s.

When food (or potential mates) are scarce, the elephants take to the sea and swim to other islands (sometimes, it is said, all the way to Mayabunder). **Salt water crocodiles** are found on the island's eastern coastline.

North Andaman

The least populated of the region's large islands, **North Andaman** is crossed by just two roads linking its scattered Bengali settlements. Timber extraction is proceeding apace here, though the authorities claim they are sticking to new regulations, and the total absence of motorable roads into northern and western areas of the island has ensured blanket protection for a vast stretch of convoluted coastline, running from Austin Strait in the southeast to the northern tip, Cape Price. There is concern, however, that the completion of the ATR so close to this wilderness may herald the start of a new settlement influx, with the same disastrous consequences for the environment seen elsewhere.

There is no reason to spend more time either **Kalighat**, if you arrive by boat from Mayabunder, than it takes to get a bus out, or North Andaman's ugly main town of **Diglipur**, than it takes to get a connection down to **Arial Bay** for **Smith** and **Ross** islands or on to the attractive coastal area round **Kalipur**.

Kalighat and around

Although you can now proceed directly to Diglipur by road across the Austin Bridge, a small ferry still runs once daily (departs 9.30am; returns 12.30pm) from Mayabunder to **KALIGHAT**, chugging through a narrowing, mangrove-lined estuary and offering a more relaxed, if slower, point of entry. A cluttered little bazaar unfolds from the top of the slipway, hemmed in by dense mangrove swamps, and when you arrive, a bus should be standing here to take you to Diglipur. If there isn't, head for one of the village's dismal little chai stalls and dig in for a wait, or turn right to see if there's a **room** in the three-roomed APWD *Rest House* (☏03192/273360; ❸–❹) on the hill overlooking the end of the street. The only **food** is at chai stalls in the bazaar.

The one worthwhile place to visit in this area is **Ramnagar**, 10km northeast of town and served by hourly buses, where there's a beautiful sandy beach backed by unspoilt forest in which it's possible to camp. Try to rent a **cycle** from one of the stalls in Kalighat, though, as the beach is 2km from Ramnagar bazaar, the nearest source of refreshments. In principle, four **buses** per day run north from Kalighat to **Diglipur**; they get crammed full, but the trip takes only 45 minutes. Look out for logging elephants beside the road shortly after leaving Kalighat.

Diglipur, Arial Bay and around

Known in the British era as Port Cornwallis, **DIGLIPUR**, North Andaman's largest settlement, is another disappointing market settlement, useful mostly for its connections to the north. On the hill above the main road, the APWD *Rest House* (☏03192/272203; ❸–❹) offers the village's nicest **accommodation**; the *Maa Yashoda Lodge* (☏03192/272258; ❷) is a cheaper alternative. Reasonable veg and non-veg fare can be found at the central *Ganga Devi* **restaurant**, while *Ice Cube*, on the road north, serves Chinese and tandoori cuisine, and you can wet your whistle at the *Kalyani* bar. It's better, however, to head 9km on to **ARIAL BAY**, where an APWD *Rest House* (☏03192/271230; ❸–❹) stands on a hillock overlooking the settlement's tiny bazaar. The best place to while away time with a snack or beer while waiting for a boat is the Annu General Store. From Arial Bay, the **boat** that has made its way up from the capital returns direct to Port Blair overnight (5 weekly; 8–12hr).

Better still, continue another 9km to **Kalipur**, served by several daily buses, where A&N Tourism's ⚓ *Turtle Resort* (☏03192/272553; ❸–❹), occupies a perfect spot on a hilltop with superb views inland and out to sea. It's an unfeasibly large hotel for such a remote location, with spacious, clean rooms (some a/c) and a restaurant. Their only competition is *Pristine Jungle Resort* (☏03192/220681; ❶–❸), whose bamboo huts of various sizes lie on the opposite side of the road below. Just five minutes' walk down the path by the sharp bend in the road there's an excellent deserted **beach**, backed by lush forest and covered in photogenic driftwood. Swimming is best at high tide before the water recedes across rocky mudpools, unless you head left to the corner of the bay opposite a small offshore island, where there is sand at all times.

It's possible to walk from here to **Saddle Peak**, at 737m the highest mountain in the Andamans, which rises dramatically to the south, swathed in lush jungle. A permit (Rs250) to make the three- to four-hour climb must be obtained from the Range Officer at the Forest Check Post, but don't attempt it without a guide and plenty of drinking water. The staff at *Pristine* can arange a guide for Rs100 per person.

Many of the tourists who make it up here do so in order to explore the various **islands** dotted around the gulf north of Arial Bay, particularly **Smith** and **Ross** (joined to Smith by a sandbar at low tide, and not to be confused with its namesake near Port Blair), where you'll find splendid white sand bars, coral reefs and flora. Neither island is officially listed on the arrival permit, but day-trips can be sanctioned on payment of Rs500 at the Forestry Dept in Arial Bay; you will need to charter a dinghy for around Rs400 to reach the islets.

Other islands

The remaining islands open to foreign tourists in the Andaman group are all hard to get to and, with the exception of **Little Andaman** – where a vestigial population of Onge tribespeople (see box, p.684) has survived a massive influx of Indian Tamils and native Nicobarese – uninhabited. Two hours' boat ride south of Chiriya Tapu on South Andaman, **Cinque Island** offers superlative diving, outshone only by distant **Barren Island**, whose volcanic sand beds teem with marine life.

Cinque Island

Cinque Island actually comprises two islets, joined by a spectacular sand isthmus, with shallow water either side that covers it completely at high tide. The main incentive to come here is the superlative diving and snorkelling around the reefs. However, heaps of dead coral on the beach attest to damage wreaked by the Indian navy during the construction of the swish "cottages" overlooking the beach. Rumour has it that these were built for the visit of a Thai VIP in 1996, but local government officials now use them as bolt holes from Port Blair. Although there are no **ferries** to Cinque, it is possible to arrange dinghies from Chiriya Tapu village on South Andaman (see p.694). Currently, your permit only allows you to spend the day on the island; overnight stays are prohibited.

Barren Island

The furthest flung island open to tourists in the Andaman group is **Barren Island**, an eight-hour sea voyage northeast of Port Blair, though a fast boat can do it much quicker. India's only active **volcano**, the arid brown mountain blew its top in May 1991 after lying dormant for 188 years, and repeated the performance twice more in the mid-Nineties. The only living creatures on Barren are a herd of **goats**, released in 1891 by the British to provide sustenance for any shipwrecked sailors. There are no ferries to the island, but diving expeditions (see p.697) sometimes make the trip, as the seas around Barren are the richest in the region.

Little Andaman

Little Andaman is the furthest point south in the archipelago foreigners can travel to on their tourist permit. Most of the island has been set aside as a tribal reserve for the **Onge** (see p.684) and is thus off limits. It was also the only island open to foreigners to sustain extensive damage in the 2004 **tsunami**, but although a number of buildings were destroyed, and sixty-four people died, the island has recovered well. Very few tourists ever make it down here, however. Daily boats from Port Blair (Rs20–50) arrive at **Hut Bay**, the faster ones making the voyage in under six hours. The main settlement, aka **Indira Bazaar**, is two kilometres north. The only **places to stay** are here, the best being the two-storey *Sealand Tourist Home* (☎03192/284306; ❶), whose splendid bayfront location is only marred by the fact that the architect inexplicably put all the windows facing the interior. Just a little further along, the *Vvet Guest House* (☎03192/284155; ❷) has simple rooms that cost a little more but are no better, although the small garden is pleasant enough to relax in and there's an offshoot, the *Cozy Cave*, about 500m away, in the unlikely event that both places are full. Basic **meals** are available at food-only hotels such as the *Snehu* and *AG Bengali*, while the *Kurinchi Parotta Stall* offers tasty savoury and sweet snacks. Bicycles can be rented for Rs40 per day from a stall between the two guesthouses but are in very short supply.

Hut Bay curves gradually round in a majestic eight-kilometre sweep and the quality of the sand and beauty of the adjacent jungle increase the further you go. The top stretch is named **Netaji Nagar** after the village on the island's only road, which runs behind it. A couple of drink stalls constitute the only facilities. En route, you can detour a kilometre inland at the huge signpost about two and a half kilometres north of Indira Bazaar, to see the **White Surf Waterfalls** (dawn to dusk; Rs20). Made up of three ten- to fifteen-metre-high cascades, it's a relaxing spot and it's possible to clamber into the right-hand fall for a soothing shower. Crocodiles are supposed to inhabit the surrounding streams, however. Short elephant rides are available for Rs50 per person at the entrance to the falls. Over the headland at the top of Hut Bay, twelve or so kilometres from the jetty, lies the smaller but equally picturesque crescent of **Butler Bay**. There's not much to do here but swim, sunbathe or look around the slightly eerie remains of the government beach resort, which was swept away by the tsunami. That is unless you've brought your surfboard with you; Little Andaman has a cult reputation among surfers for having some of the best conditions anywhere in South Asia.

Travel details

Flights

For a list of airline websites, see Basics p.38. In the listings below IA is Indian Airlines, JA Jet Airways and AD Air Deccan.
Port Blair to: Chennai (3 daily IA, JA & AD; 2hr)

Boats

Arial Bay to: Port Blair (5 weekly; 8–12hr).
Havelock to: Long Island (4 weekly; 2–3hr); Neill Island (1–2 daily; 1hr–1hr 30min); Port Blair (2–3 daily; 2hr–4hr 30min); Rangat Bay (4 weekly; 3–5hr).
Mayabunder to: Kalighat (1 daily; 2hr 30min).
Port Blair to: Arial Bay (5 weekly; 8–12hr); Chennai (every 5–10 days; 2.5–3 days); Havelock Island (2–3 daily; 2hr–4hr 30min); Little Andaman (1 daily; 6–8hr); Long Island (4 weekly; 5–7hr); Neill Island (1–2 daily; 2hr–3hr 30min); Rangat Bay

(1 daily; 6–8hr); Vishakapatnam (1 monthly; 3–3.5 days).
Rangat Bay to: Havelock Island (4 weekly; 3–4hr); Long Island (2–3 daily; 1hr–1hr 30min); Neill Island (1–2 weekly; 4–6hr); Port Blair (1 daily; 6–8hr).

Buses

Diglipur to: Arial Bay (every 1–2hr; 20min); Kalighat (4 daily; 45min); Kalipur (every 1–2hr; 40min); Port Blair (2–3 daily; 11–12hr).
Mayabunder to: Karmateng beach (2 daily; 30min); Port Blair (2–4 daily; 9–10hr); Rangat (1 hourly; 2hr 30min–3hr).
Port Blair to: Chiriya Tapu (3 daily; 1hr 15min); Diglipur (2–3 daily; 11–12hr); Mayabunder (2–4 daily; 9–10hr); Rangat (5 daily; 6–7hr); Wandoor (4 daily; 1hr 15min).
Rangat to: Mayabunder (1 hourly; 2hr 30min–3hr); Port Blair (5 daily; 6–7hr).

Contexts

Contexts

History

S outh India – the vast triangular-shaped peninsula beyond the River Narmada – is separated from the North by the Vindhya Range, a barren band of sheer-sided table mountains. For many centuries, this geographical obstacle discouraged the movement of peoples between the two regions, and the South remained largely isolated from the changes imported by successive waves of invaders who swept across the Gangetic plains from the northwest. Tracing the progress of these newcomers, written histories of the Subcontinent have tended to focus on the impact of North upon South. Influences did traverse the Vindhyas and Deccan Plateau, but they invariably did so slowly, by a process of gradual assimilation rather than conquest, enabling the societies of the peninsula to develop in their own way. Moreover, some of India's most defining cultural traits and traditions originated in the deep Dravidian south, from where they spread northwards.

Prehistory

Compared to the extraordinary wealth of archeological finds in northwestern India, evidence of **prehistoric settlement** in the South is scant – although one of the oldest human artefacts ever unearthed in Asia was discovered at Pallavaram, near Chennai (Madras), in 1863, by British archeologist Bruce Foote, who found an oval-shaped hand-axe which he surmised must have originated in the Lower Paleolithic era. Since this initial discovery, similar tools have come to light as far south as the Cauvery River delta, indicating that the region was inhabited by **nomadic hunter-gatherers** at the same time as similar groups emerged in the distant North, between 400,000 and 10,000 years ago.

The first archeologist to establish a sequence for the various stone implements discovered in the South was **Mortimer Wheeler**, whose work on the Coromandel coast near Pondicherry (now Puducherry) in 1945 showed that metal was introduced comparatively late to the region. Fixing the date-spans of upper strata with the Roman coins he found in them, Wheeler showed how copper made its first appearance midway through the second millennium BC, by which time rudimentary **agriculture** and the **domestication of animals** were widespread along open coastal areas and river deltas.

It has never been proven, but new technologies, including metal, were probably imported into South India from the northwest, where the sophisticated urban civilizations of the Indus Valley – the region straddling the present-day India–Pakistan border – were already well established by 3000 BC. Recent paleo-botanical studies have shown that a sharp rise in rainfall occurred around this time, which probably explains why agriculture was able to flourish and cities emerge. The inhabitants of **Harappa** and **Mohenjo Daro**, large urban centres which reached their peaks between 2300 and 1800 BC, were certainly experts in the management of water. Amid the ruins of their well-organized cities, remnants of elaborate sewerage and irrigation systems have been found, along with scales and weights, metal jewellery, weapons, precious stones, seals and delicate pottery. Huge communal granaries stored the surplus grain that underpinned a flourishing foreign trade, and the existence of palaces and spacious houses show that this was a highly stratified society, with its own script and formalized religion.

After the sensational rediscovery of the Harappan ruins in the 1920s, it was long assumed that invasions from the northwest brought about the eventual demise of the Indus Valley civilizations, but it now seems more likely that prolonged drought caused the decline. The same climatic changes may also explain how **metal** technology and knowledge of **rice cultivation** first found their way south: as rainfall decreased, the corresponding drop in agricultural output impoverished the once-thriving cities of the Indus Valley, forcing its inhabitants to flee in search of more fertile land.

The Dravidians

Some historians have advanced this migration theory to account for the origins of the so-called **Dravidians**, who are believed to have colonized the South around the same time as the Indus Valley civilization went into decline in the second millennium BC. However, the most compelling evidence that the Dravidians originated in the northwest is linguistic. Kannada, Telegu, Malayalam and Tamil – the principal modern languages of South India – have a completely different root from the main languages of the North, which derive from the so-called Indo-Aryan group, and are based principally on Sanskrit. Over the years, some wild comparisons have been made between Dravidian and other Asian tongues (most notably Japanese), but the only surviving Asian language with definite Dravidian antecedents is Brahui, spoken by the nomadic people of the Baluchistan uplands on the Iran–Pakistan border. This fact suggests that the Dravidians almost certainly came from the Baluchi grasslands in the fourth or third millennium BC, via the Indus Valley, where they would have acquired the metalwork and farming techniques that subsequently allowed them to establish permanent settlements in the far south.

Although far less technologically advanced than the Indus Valley civilizations, the Dravidian tribes – based around fertile riverine lands separated by densely wooded hills and mountain ranges – forged a strong agrarian base and gradually evolved into distinct chiefdoms. Like the Harappans, their essentially agricultural economies were supplemented by trade in luxury goods such as shells, precious stones and pearls (the Old Testament records that King Solomon sent ships every three years to South India to buy silver, gold, ivory, monkeys and peacocks). This maritime trade expanded steadily over the centuries, enabling the region's chiefs to extend their rule inland and create larger settlements away from the coast.

The Aryans

For most of the twentieth century, archeologists believed the dramatic demise of the Indus Valley cities, between 1800 and 1700 BC, was precipitated by the arrival of invaders from the northwest. Recent carbon-dating techniques, however, have shown that the decline occurred between two and three centuries before the first appearance on the northern plains of a fairer-skinned nomadic people, who called themselves the *Aryas*, or **Aryans**.

The precise route of this migration remains a moot point among historians. Some argue that the newcomers travelled southeast through Persia, while others claim they came via Afghanistan. There is, however, a general consensus that they originated in a region around the Caucasus Mountains, and were part of an ancient diaspora that spread as far as Western Europe (their language, an antiquated form of Sanskrit, has astonishingly close affinities with Latin, Greek and Celtic).

The main historical source for this era is the **Rig Veda**, a vast body of 1028 hymns, epic chants, spells, songs and instructions for religious rituals equal in length to the *Iliad* and *Odyssey* combined. Phrased in 10,600 elaborate metered verses, this laboriously sophisticated work includes sections composed between 1400 and 1500 BC, transmitted orally and only set down in writing in the modern era. The Aryans' sacred scriptures contain a wealth of detail about their daily life, philosophical ideas and religious practices. Frequent references to Agni, the "God of Fire", and Indra, the "Fort Breaker", are indicative of violent encounters with the dark-skinned indigenous inhabitants of northern India, known as *Dasa* or *Dasyus*, whom the warrior bands swept aside in their slow expansion eastwards over the middle of the second millennium BC. These conquests were facilitated by the Aryans' use of horse-drawn, spoke-wheeled **chariots**, an incomparably fast and effective way of crossing the dry plains.

By the dawn of the **Iron Age** early in the first millennium BC, the dominion of the Aryans, by now a loose confederacy of tribes who fought each other as much as their indigenous enemies, stretched south as far as the Vindhya Range and the rich soils of the Deccan Plateau. Beyond lay the wild unexplored territory of **Dakshinapatha**, "the Way South", blocked by dense forests and ravine-scarred hills.

Sanskritization of the South

The Rig Veda records the reluctance of the Aryans to press south along this route, but it is clear that some of their priests (brahmins) and wandering ascetics (*rishis*) did, probably in search of patronage. Along with their sacred verses, Vedic philosophies and knowledge of iron, they took with them concepts of racial discrimination derived from centuries of war with the *Dasyus*, who by this time seem to have become a sub-class below the three existing grades in Aryan society: priests (brahmins), warriors (*kshatriyas*) and artisans (*vaishyas*). A product of the transition from nomadic to settled society, the **caste** system – based on notions of **varna**, or colour, and ritual pollution (see p.741) – seemed to have found favour among the tribal chiefs of southern India, who deployed the new ideas and scriptures of the brahmins to legitimize their rule.

The transmission of cultural influences from north to south was slow but pervasive. By the sixth century BC, brahmanical philosophies formed the religious bedrock of the many petty chiefdoms and larger principalities that had proliferated in the South, where village culture had by now firmly taken root under the tutelage of the brahmins – a way of life that would remain largely intact in the region for another two thousand years.

The Mauryan era

In the Gangetic basin, meanwhile, small tribal kingdoms (*janapadas*) were beginning to merge with others to form larger confederacies (*mahajanapadas*) governed by single rulers from fortified capitals. Two new reforming religious movements were also gaining ground in the North. The first, **Buddhism** (see p.749), arose from the teachings of a young prince from the Nepalese foothills, Siddhartha, or **Gautama Buddha** (563–483 BC). In addition, **Jainism**, founded by the prophet **Mahavira** (599–527 BC) around the same time, began to attract followers, most notably among the ruling elite of a dynasty that was destined to become the most powerful in the Subcontinent.

Stepping into the vacuum left by the departure of **Alexander the Great** from the northwest, the **Mauryans**, who ruled the region southeast of the Ganges, usurped the throne of their arch-adversaries, the Nandas, in 320 BC to make their king, **Chandragupta Maurya**, the first *de facto* emperor of India, with control of an area stretching from the Punjab to Karnataka. A strict Jain, he eventually renounced his throne and starved himself to death on a hilltop at Sravanabelgola (still an important South Indian pilgrimage centre), thereby achieving the status of a saint.

From their capital at Pataliputra (in Bihar, near present-day Patna), the Mauryans ruled over a vast swathe of the Subcontinent, greatly enlarged during the reign of Chandragupta's grandson, **Ashoka**, who defeated the mighty Kalingas on the east coast (modern Orissa). It was the bloody aftermath of that battle, in which 100,000 people were killed and 150,000 abducted, that the emperor embraced Buddhism and the path of non-violence. Edicts proclaiming the tenets of the new imperial faith were erected throughout the empire, and missionaries and ambassadors dispatched to spread the message of "right conduct", or dharma, abroad. No such edicts, however, have so far come to light further south than the goldfields around Mysore, and it seems likely that most of the Deccan and peninsular India, including all of modern Andhra Pradesh, Kerala and Tamil Nadu, remained outside Mauryan influence.

The Mauryans may never have conquered the far south, but their way of life and system of government strongly influenced developments in the region. Through trade and interaction with Jain and Buddhist monk-missionaries, concepts of statehood gradually filtered south, encouraging the dominant powers in the peninsula to expand their realms.

Dravidadesa: the early kingdoms

Inscribed on the eight rock-cut edicts that Ashoka raised on the frontiers of his empire in the third century BC are verses expressing goodwill towards his "undefeated neighbours" (*avijita*). The list includes the earliest known references to the three ancient ruling clans who dominated the far south in the final centuries of the first millennium BC: the **Cholas** of the Coromandel region and Cauvery basin; the **Pandyas**, whose capital was at Madurai; and the **Cheras**, from southwest Kerala. Collectively, the kingdoms of these three dynasties comprised a domain known to northerners as **Dravidadesa**, "Land of the Tamils".

A wealth of historical detail relating to the early kingdoms of the South has survived, most of it in a remarkable body of classical Tamil poetry known as the **Sangam**, composed between the first and third centuries AD in the literary academies (*sangam*) of Madurai. The texts, which were only rediscovered in the nineteenth century, refer to an era when the indigenous Dravidian culture of the deep south was being transformed by Sanskritic influences from the North. Nevertheless, they vividly demonstrate that some of the most distinctive characteristics of Indian civilization – including yoga, *tantra*, the cult of the god Murugan and goddess worship – were almost certainly indigenous to the South, and widespread well before the Aryans came to dominate the region completely.

The Sangam also records the stormy political relations between the three dynasties, who were frequently at war with each other, or with the rulers of neighbouring Sri Lanka. Ultimately, however, all three seem to have succumbed to an enigmatic fourth dynasty, the **Kalabhras**, about whom the Sangam poems say very little other than that they were "bad kings" (*kaliarasar*). Buddhist texts from a later period suggest the Kalabhras were originally hill tribes who swept down from the Deccan Plateau to harass the inhabitants of the river valleys and coastal areas, and later took up Jainism and Buddhism, deposing the Dravidian kings and persecuting the brahmins.

The expansion of trade

The cultural flowering of the Sangam era in the south, during the first two centuries AD, was stimulated by a rapid growth in **maritime trade** throughout the region. As well as Arab merchants, the ports of the Malabar and Coromandel coasts now began to welcome **Roman** ships. After a century of relentless civil war, peace had returned to Rome, bringing with it renewed demand in the imperial capital for luxury goods such as pearls, spices, perfumes, precious stones and silk. When Augustus conquered Egypt to open up the Red Sea, and Hippalus discovered that the monsoon winds would blow a ship from there across the Arabian Sea in around a fortnight, the means to supply this appetite for exotic Oriental merchandise was within the Romans' grasp.

A vivid picture of the boom that ensued has survived in an extraordinary mariners' manual entitled the *Periplus of the Erythraean Sea*, written by an anonymous Alexandrian merchant-adventurer. Featuring meticulous descriptions of the trade, ports and capital cities of the far south, it reveals that the region was an entrepôt for valuable foreign goods – notably Chinese silk and oil from the Gangetic basin – and that the Coromandel was gradually eclipsing the Malabar as peninsular India's principal trade platform.

This fact was borne out by Mortimer Wheeler's discovery of the Romans' main trading post at **Arikamedu**, just south of modern Puducherry (Pondicherry) in Tamil Nadu, where large brick buildings, water reservoirs, baths and a huge number of artefacts – including shards of pre-Christian ceramics from Arezzo and hoards of coins – suggest it was largely the lust for Roman gold that fuelled the ancient trade in the South. Indeed, the Roman chronicler, Strabo, famously complained that the Indian merchants were threatening to completely empty the treasuries of Rome of gold coins. Prodigious quantities of these have been unearthed in recent times, especially in the area around the ancient port of **Muziris**, near the present-day town of Kodungallur, just north of Kochi (Cochin) in Kerala.

The Satavahanas

Coupled with the advances in knowledge of state administration made by the Mauryans, the vast trade wealth pouring into South India around the turn of the millennium enabled the region's rulers to create larger and more organized kingdoms, backed by well-equipped armies. Conditions were ripe for the rise of a major power, and this came in the first century BC with the advent of the **Satavahanas**, an obscure tribal dynasty from the Deccan who, in the space of a hundred years, assumed the imperial mantle of the Mauryans. By the time Ptolemy was writing his *Geography*, midway through the second century AD, the empire, based in **Pratisthana** (near modern Paithan in Maharashtra), comprised thirty fortified cities and stretched from coast to coast. Administered by a network of noblemen, it was upheld by semi-autonomous military garrisons, with an army said by the Roman chronicler Pliny to consist of 30,000 cavalry and nine thousand war elephants.

Thanks to their control of the region's lucrative foreign trade, the Satavahanas (or Andhras, as they are referred to in some ancient texts) were also prolific patrons of the arts, responsible for the greatest monuments in India at that time and many of the most accomplished rock-cut caves of the northwest Deccan. However, the crowning glory of Andhran art was to be the Great Stupa complex at **Amaravati**, in Andhra Pradesh (see p.668), whose exquisite bas-reliefs (some of which are now housed in the Government Museum, Chennai; see p.510) are considered by many scholars to be the finest ancient Indian sculpture.

The Early Middle Ages: 600–1200 AD

The history of the early middle ages in South India, from the time of the Satavahanas' demise to the arrival of the Muslims, revolves around the rise and fall of a mosaic of **regional dynasties**. These invariably fought each other to gain supremacy for short periods, and then found their rule usurped by one or other of their adversarial neighbours. Not until the sword of Islam descended on the Deccan in the thirteenth century did the peninsula succumb to a single overlord.

Various theories have been advanced to explain this, but the most convincing is that the warring kingdoms were generally too small to exert control over large territories for long. Bringing rebellious chiefdoms to heel meant costly military expeditions, which would inevitably render the ruler's own region vulnerable to attack. Despite this, the ongoing power balance mitigated against the rise of an empire and the long-term political stability it afforded allowed for the development of distinct regional cultures. The wealth of historic monuments scattered across South India today graphically exemplifies the differences between these cultures, and the way in which they interacted over the centuries.

Chalukyas, Pallavas and Cholas

Foremost among the states of the southern Deccan were the **Chalukyas**, who had been underlings of the Kadambas (Hindu rulers of the region that later became Goa) until **Pulakeshin I** broke away and founded a capital at Vatapi (**Badami**; see p.346). Here, atop a rocky escarpment overlooking a lake, the king and his descendants erected a series of magnificent stone temples. From simple rock-cut excavations, these evolved into more sophisticated free-standing structures, embellished with elaborate iconographic sculpture, which were among the first buildings in the region to fuse indigenous architectural styles with those of Northern India. The Chalukyas' conspicuous wealth inevitably attracted the attentions of their neighbours. After fending off two invasions, they eventually succumbed in 753 AD to the **Rashtrakutas**, whose domain extended most of the way across the Deccan.

The Chalukyas' southern enemies, the **Pallavas**, emerged after defeating the Kalabhras, the "bad kings" who originally routed the region's three early dynasties. Originally Buddhists, they converted to brahmanism sometime in the fifth century and thereafter carved out a kingdom that would spread from the mouth of the River Krishna to the edge of the Cauvery basin in the South. From the outset, the Pallavas seem to have been keen seafarers, trading with Greeks, Satavahanas and Romans, whose coins have all been found amid the ruins of ancient **Mamallapuram** (see p.536), just south of Chennai. The extraordinary crop of stone temples, open-air bas-reliefs and finely carved caves dotted around this fishing and stone-carving village recall the era when it ranked among the busiest ports in Asia.

The majority of Mamallapuram's monuments were begun in the mid-seventh century, during the reign of Narasimha Varman I (aka Mamalla, "the Great Wrestler"), and completed over the following two generations. Of them all, the best known is the **Shore Temple**, overlooking the beach and thought to be the first shrine built of loose stone blocks in the Subcontinent. Surmounted by a steep pyramidal tower (*vimana*), it closely resembles the better preserved Kailasanatha temple in the Pallavas' former capital, **Kanchipuram**, where, in the mid-seventh century, the Chinese pilgrim Hsiuen-Tsang reported seeing one hundred Buddhist monasteries as well as eighty major Hindu temples.

The Shore Temple at Mamallapuram provided the main architectural inspiration for the **Cholas**, an offshoot of the ancient dynasty of the same name who asserted their independence from the Pallavas in 897 AD, when the latter had their hands full fighting off the Rashtrakutas. During their 250-year rule, the Cholas expanded out of their royal capital, **Thanjavur**, in the Cauvery basin, defeating both the Pandyas and Cheras, and later conquering Sri Lanka, the Maldives and the Andamans, in addition to enclaves in Java and Sumatra, which they captured in order to control trade with Southeast Asia.

Combined with the huge sums in plunder yielded by their military campaigns, the Cholas' trade monopoly financed an awesome building spree. The dynasty's most visionary ruler was **Rajaraja I** (985–1014), who erected the colossal Brihadishwara temple, in its day the largest in India. Decorating the walls of the shrine, beneath its soaring tower, exquisite frescoes recall the opulence and sophistication of the Chola court, where keen patronage of the arts – most famously bronze-casting, but also Carnatic music, sculpture, dance and literature – produced works that have never been surpassed since.

Bhakti and the Tamil poets

From the eighth century onwards, the devotional form of Hinduism known as **bhakti**, which first blossomed in Tamil Nadu, spread north into the rest of India to become, as it still is, the dominant strain of Hinduism throughout the country. This was essentially a popular movement which encouraged individual devotees to form a highly personal relationship with a chosen god (*ishtadevata*), an approach which revolutionized Hindu practice by offering a religious path and goal open to all castes.

The great champions of *bhakti* were the **poet–saints** of Tamil Nadu, often said to have "sung" the religions of Jainism and Buddhism out of South India. Although in practice a variety of deities was worshipped, the movement had two strands: the **Nayanmars**, devoted to Shiva, and the **Alvars**, faithful to Vishnu. Collections of their poetry, the greatest literary legacy of South India, remain popular today, and the poets themselves are almost deified, featuring in carvings in many temples.

The four most prominent of the 63 Nayanmar poet-saints were **Campantar**, who converted the king of Madurai from Jainism and had a great cult centre at Chidambaram; **Cuntarar**, a brahmin who had two low-caste wives; **Appar**, himself a convert from Jainism; and **Manikkavachakar**, whose mystical poems are still sung in homes and temples throughout Tamil Nadu. The Vaishnavite movement centred on Srirangam (near Trichy), its poets including men and women of all social classes. The most celebrated Alvar was **Nammalvar**, a *shudra* who spent his life in fasting and meditation. **Antal**, the most popular female Alvar, is said to have married Vishnu's statue at Srirangam, and was thereafter regarded as an incarnation of Vishnu's consort, Shri.

All the poems tell of the ecstatic response to intense experiences of divine favour, an emotion frequently described in terms of conjugal love, and expressed in verses of great tenderness and beauty. They stress selfless love between man and god, claiming that such love alone can lead to everlasting union with the divine. Devotees travelled the South, singing, dancing and challenging opponents to public debates.

Among the most significant consequences of the *bhakti* revolution in Hinduism was the emergence of **temple cities**. By stressing the importance of the individual's devotion to a particular god or goddess, *bhakti* inspired a massive upsurge in popular worship and, inevitably, a proliferation of shrines to accommodate worshippers. This process went hand in hand with the assimilation of important regional deities into the Hindu pantheon. Thus, trees, rocks, caves or bodies of water held sacred in a given place began to be "legitimized" through identification with Shiva or Vishnu. Notable examples include the deities of Chidambaram and Madurai, two of South India's most important religious centres, whose importance was firmly established well before the Sanskritization that associated them with Shiva in the sixth century.

In time, the same happened to lesser local gods and village deities, until innumerable cult centres across the South became bound in a complex web of interconnections. The institution of **pilgrimage**, linking local and distant deities, emerged as an essential element of Hinduism for the first time during the era of the Tamil saints, and has remained an important unifying force in India ever since. It is no coincidence that some of the most defining texts of the *bhakti* movement are the *Mahatmyas*, oral chants intoned by brahmins that elucidate the significance of individual temples and their relationship to other shrines.

Muslim incursions

At the start of the eleventh century, a new player appeared on the political map of northern India. **Mahmud**, a Turkish chieftain who had established a powerful kingdom at Ghazni, near Kabul in Afghanistan, made seventeen plundering raids into the plains of northern India between 1000 and 1027 AD. His was the first of many Muslim incursions from the northwest that would, after two hundred years of constant infighting and wars with local rulers, lead to the creation of an Islamic empire based in Delhi.

Founded in 1206 AD, the **Delhi Sultanate** made little impact on the South during its formative years. In 1309, however, the redoubtable Sultan **Allauddin Khilji** set his sights southwards. Having heard rumours of the treasures stored in the great Tamil temples (Rajaraja had not long before donated 880kg of gold to the Brihadishwara temple), he took advantage of the Cholas' decline to mount a raid. It is recorded that his general, the ruthless military genius and former Hindu slave **Malik Kafur**, returned with a thousand camels bearing booty, including the famous Koh-i-noor diamond.

This, however, was merely a prelude to the Sultanate's second expedition of 1310–11, in the course of which Allauddin's army pressed into the deep south itself. Raiding towns and desecrating the splendid Chola temples of the Cauvery Delta, it reached Madurai on April 10, 1311, and mercilessly sacked the Pandyas' capital, massacring the few of its inhabitants who had not fled. Forewarned of Kafur's approach, many temples had hidden or buried their treasures. Some, like the eighty priceless Chola bronzes that came to light in Chidambaram in the 1960s, were rediscovered; others remain lost.

Aside from the wholesale destruction of art treasures, the main legacy of Allauddin's plunder was the creation of a short-lived **Muslim Sultanate** at Tirupparakunram, near Madurai. Overlooking the town from the top of a huge sandstone outcrop, the tomb of its eighth and last Sultan, **Sikander Shah**, remains one of the far south's few bona fide Muslim shrines.

The Deccan Sultanates

The Delhi Sultanates possessed sufficient military strength to subdue most of India, but time and again showed themselves incapable of consolidating their territorial gains with strong administrations. In the end, the despot **Muhammed-bin-Tughluq**'s incessant wars, together with his crackpot plan to relocate the capital from Delhi to Daulatabad, 1000km south on the Deccan, saw the sultanates' reign degenerate into one of terror and profligacy. Forced by drought, famine and the threat of Mughal invasion to abandon Daulatabad and return to Delhi, Tughluq struggled until his death to hold onto power. By the mid-fourteenth century, his successor, **Feroz Shah**, had completely lost control of the Deccan.

In the wake of the Daulatabad debacle, one of Tughluq's former generals, **Zafar Shah**, aka **Bahman Shah**, saw his chance to found his own dynasty, which he located at a safe distance south of the old capital, at **Gulbarga** (in present-day northern Karnataka). The **Bahmanis'** rule lasted around two hundred years, and was as bloody as the old Delhi Sultanate's; Zafar Shah's son, Mohammed Shah (1358–73), is said to slaughtered half a million people in his wars with neighbouring states, which included the Vijayanagars, who founded their empire at around the same time (see below).

In the fifteenth century AD, the Bahmanis shifted their capital further northeast to **Bidar**, constructing a massive fortress that still survives. Under the careful stewardship of **Mahmud Gawan**, a talented prime minister who served several successive sultans, the dynasty flourished, but went into a dramatic decline after his death. The ensuing power struggle saw the governors of the four largest districts in the kingdom – Bijapur, Ahmadnagar, Bidar and Golconda – declare independence, with Bijapur eventually emerging as the major power by the sixteenth century. Their rule, however, was bedevilled by conflict with both Vijayanagar and the Portuguese; they lost the port of Goa to the latter in 1510.

The power balance between the Deccan kingdoms was decisively turned in the Muslims' favour after 1565 when, following years of fighting each other, the sultanates formed a pact to wage war on their common Hindu enemies, the **Vijayanagars** (see below). At the battle of Talikota that year, the alliance crushed the Hindu army and set about the most destructive sack of a city the Subcontinent had ever seen. Within 21 years, however, the Deccan sultanates had succumbed completely to the might of the Mughals.

Vijayanagar: 1346–1565

To the south of the Bahmanis' territory, the River Krishna formed the border with the mighty Hindu kingdom of **Vijayanagar**, which emerged in response to the threat of Muslim invasions. Its founders were two brothers from Andhra Pradesh, **Harihara** and **Bukka**, who were allegedly captured by Tughluq during his sack of Kampili in 1327 AD and taken as prisoners to Delhi, where they converted to Islam before being dispatched as governors to their native town to restore order after an uprising. Legend has it that the sage Vidyaranya then reconverted the brothers to Hinduism and encouraged them to defect (although some Indian historians have disputed this, claiming Harihara and Bukka were actually offshoots of the Hoysalas).

Whatever its roots, the dynasty the brothers founded on the banks of the River Tungabhadra (at modern-day Hampi; see p.335) quickly flourished. Following a series of short wars with the Hoysalas, Madurai and the Gajapatis of eastern India, the rulers of the southern kingdoms pragmatically threw in their lot with the ambitious newcomers, realizing their best chance of protection from marauding Muslims lay in a strong Hindu front to the north. This proved to be the case. At a time when the influence of Turkish, Persian and Afghan culture on northern India was most marked, the South, insulated by Vijayanagar, remained outside the sway of Islam – a fact that accounts perhaps better than anything else for the striking cultural differences that still exist between the north and the south of the Subcontinent.

Vijayanagar's golden period was during the reign of **Krishna Deva Raya** (1509–29), before its monopoly over the trade in spices and Arabian horses had been undermined by the Portuguese and other European powers. While the Bijapuris were a constant and costly source of irritation, the king's well-organized administration, together with his control of some thirty or so rich ports, ensured a steady flow of wealth.

The dynastic capital, Vijayanagar ("City of Victory") became, for an all too brief period, among the most splendid in the world. Travellers such as Domingo Paes, who stayed there between 1522 and 1524, marvelled at the opulence of its royal court, the richness of its bazaars and the sumptuousness of its festivals. Krishna Deva Raya's rule was also the period when the South acquired some of its most impressive **temple towers** (**gopuras**), erected by the king to foster loyalty among brahmins and inhabitants of distant regions over which Vijayanagar's hold was precarious.

After Krishna Deva Raya's death in 1529, internal struggles and conflicts with the Portuguese weakened the empire. However, it was the Vijayanagars' old foes, the Bijapuris, who eventually brought their glorious rule to an abrupt and bloody end. Having benefited from the Deccan Sultanates' constant feuding for more than a century, the Vijayanagars made a fatal mistake when they desecrated mosques during campaigns in the 1550s. This finally galvanized the sultans to set aside their differences and march on Vijayanagar. The armies met at Talikota in 1565. At first, the battle seemed to be going the Hindus' way, but suddenly turned against them when two of their Muslim generals defected. The Vijayanagar regent, Rama Raya, was captured and beheaded, while his brother, Tirumala, fled with what was left of the army, leaving the capital defenceless.

The ensuing sack lasted six months and reduced Asia's most illustrious city to rubble. Predictably, the Deccan sultans squabbled over the spoils and spent the next century fighting each other, leaving the region vulnerable to invasion by the Mughals.

The Portuguese

Around the same time as Vijayanagar was enjoying its period of greatest prosperity, the harbinger of a new regional power appeared on the horizon of

On May 18, 1498, three Portuguese *caravelas* dropped anchor off the coast of northern Kerala at a beach called Kappad, having sailed from Lisbon via the Cape of Good Hope in a little over ten months. Five hundred years later, to the day, groups of angry protesters gathered on the same beach to burn effigies of the explorer who had led that expedition, **Vasco da Gama**. By rounding the tip of Africa and opening up a maritime route to the spice markets of western India, da Gama would change the pattern of world history, for which he has been feted as a national hero ever since by the Portuguese public. In India, however, he is reviled as a pirate and looter who committed acts of appalling barbarism out of greed for "black gold" – the pepper of the Malabar Coast.

The essential facts of da Gama's three expeditions to India have survived thanks to the diaries of Alvaro Velho, one of his soldiers. These describe in detail how the small fleet of five ships set sail from Lisbon in July 1497, the sacred symbol of Christ billowing in their sails. Their route took them around the islands of Cabo Verde (Cape Verde) and four thousand miles southeast to round the Cape of Good Hope at the beginning of November.

At Malindi, da Gama was granted the services of an expert navigator, an Arab sea captain called **Ibn' Masjid**, who piloted the three remaining *caravelas* across the Indian Ocean to Calicut. However, news of atrocities committed by the Portuguese en route had preceded their arrival, and the local *zamorin*, Mana Vikrama, briefly imprisoned da Gama before he was allowed to fill his holds with pepper and leave – an insult the proud Portuguese admiral would never forget.

Four years later he returned to Calicut, this time bent on revenge. In addition to what he perceived as his own "contumely treatment" at the hands of the Hindu ruler, he intended to avenge the murder of 53 Portuguese killed during a previous expedition in 1500. As a prelude to the onslaught, da Gama waylaid a Muslim ship en route from Mecca and burned alive all 700 of its passengers and crew. Then he set about bombarding the city. While the cannonade decimated Calicut's temples and houses, da Gama ordered the crews of a dozen or so trade ships anchored in the harbour to be rounded up. Before killing them, he had the prisoners' hands, ears and noses hacked off and the pieces sent ashore piled in a small boat.

Violence became a hallmark of early Portuguese colonialism in Asia, as the Europeans extended their trade links up the South Indian coast to Goa. And so it was with some astonishment that, five centuries later, Goan nationalist politicians and journalists greeted Portugal's invitation to participate in the festivities marking the quincentennial of Vasco da Gama's voyage. Goan freedom fighters, who had struggled to oust the Portuguese, found it particularly absurd that they should now be expected to celebrate the start of their rule. An organization called **Deshpremi Samiti** was duly formed to campaign against the celebrations, stirring up acrimonious debate in the Goan press.

The controversy eventually came to a head with the Kerala Tourism Development Corporation's announcement that they were intending to stage a re-enactment of da Gama's landing, complete with replicas of the three *caravelas* and tourists acting the parts of Portuguese mariners. The plans provoked large protest marches in Goa, and the Delhi government was forced to issue a statement saying India would not participate in the so-called "celebrations" of 1498.

In the event, the anniversary passed peacefully, though clearly the raking over of da Gama's conduct did little to enhance relations between India and its first colonizer. Significantly, however, the controversy did serve to fix in Indian minds a parallel between the exploitation of colonial times and the activities of today's multinationals. It is no coincidence that alongside the effigies of Vasco da Gama being burned on Kappad beach were others of Coca-Cola and Pepsi bottles.

the Arabian Sea. Driven by the lust for "Christians and Spices", **Vasco da Gama**'s arrival on the Malabar Coast in 1498 (see box, p.719) blazed a trail that would, after only fifteen years, result in the creation of Europe's first bona fide colony in the East.

Formerly a Vijayanagar port, **Goa** had been taken by the Bahmanis, whom the Portuguese, under **Admiral Afonso de Albuquerque**, expelled in 1510. Thereafter, despite repeated attempts by the Muslims to regain their possession, the colony expanded at a breathless pace. At the height of its power, the city was the lynchpin of a trade network extending from the Philippines to the north Atlantic, with cathedrals to rival Rome's and a population that at one time was greater even than Lisbon's.

Yet, despite enjoying an early monopoly on maritime trade in Asia, ruthlessly enforced by their insurmountable naval supremacy, the Portuguese were unable to sustain an early lead over their European rivals. Repeated outbreaks of disease depleted the population of Goa, while the defeat in 1565 of Vijayanagar, which by that time accounted for a significant portion of the city's trade, had a disastrous effect on the whole Portuguese economy. Unable to maintain control of the sea lanes, Portugal gradually saw its trade empire whittled away, first by the Dutch, and later by the French and British. Goa actually survived as a Portuguese colony until 1961, but was effectively a spent force by the end of the seventeenth century.

The Mughal Empire

Descendants of Timur and Genghis Khan's Mongols from Samarkhand in Central Asia, the **Mughals** staked their claim to North India with Babur's defeat of the Delhi Sultan, Ibrahim Lodi, in 1526. Through the revolutionary deployment of small arms and mobile artillery, the invaders routed an army ten times their size. The victory inaugurated an empire that would, by the time of its demise two hundred years later, become the largest and most powerful since Ashoka's, eighteen centuries earlier. Keen patrons of the arts as well as fearsome military strategists, successive emperors blended Persian and Indian culture to create some of the Subcontinent's greatest treasures, including the Red Fort in Delhi and the Taj Mahal in Agra.

Aurangzeb and the Marathas

The Mughals' influence, however, had little impact on the South until the reign of **Shah Jahan** (1627–58), when the northernmost of the Deccan Sultanates, Ahmadnagar, was annexed. A hundred years after their sack of Vijayanagar, Bijapur and Golconda also succumbed, this time to the last of the Great Mughals, **Aurangzeb** (1658–1707).

The most expansionist ruler of the dynasty, Aurangzeb was also a devout Sunni, notorious for his rough treatment of Hindus, and for reinstating the much-hated *jizya* tax on non-Muslims that his great-grandfather, Akbar, had repealed. Aurangzeb's arch-adversaries in the Deccan region were a confederacy of low-caste Hindu warriors called the **Marathas**. Unlike the Mughals, they attacked not with large, formal armies, but by mounting guerrilla-style raids, retreating to the safety of impregnable fortresses perched on the top of table mountains.

Under their most audacious and gifted leader, **Shivaji**, whom Aurangzeb named "The Mountain Rat", the Marathas managed on numerous occasions to outwit the Mughal's superior forces, and over time came to dominate a large chunk of western India. The year of Shivaji's death in 1680, Aurangzeb's son, Akbar, slipped south from Delhi to form an alliance with his opposite number, with whose help he hoped to overthrow his father. But the plot ended in a heavy defeat for the usurper and his Hindu allies. Soon afterwards, Aurangzeb moved his court from Delhi to Aurangabad in order to personally supervise the subjugation of the Marathas. It was from there, too, that he mounted the victorious campaigns against Bijapur and Golconda that extended Mughal rule to its eventual high-water mark.

Aurangzeb may have pushed the empire's boundaries further south than any of his predecessors, but his policies ultimately brought about the dynasty's downfall. To win over the nobles of his new acquisitions in the Deccan, the emperor demanded lower taxes from them, which left an administrative shortfall that he subsequently made up for by over-taxing his farmers. This duly provoked **peasant uprisings**, made more deadly by the proliferation of small arms at that time, which Aurangzeb's cumbersome, elephant-based army was ill suited to quell. In addition, the burden on the shattered Deccan states of reprovisioning an army whose annual losses were calculated at 100,000 men and around 300,000 animals was enormous. In 1702–03, famine and pestilence wiped out an estimated two million people in the region.

After the last Great Mughal's death in 1707, half a century of gradual decay was presided over by a succession of eight incompetent emperors. The final blow to the Mughal dynasty came in 1779, when the Persian Nadir Shah raided Delhi and made off with a vast loot that included the Peacock Throne itself. "The streets", wrote one eyewitness, "were strewn with corpses like a garden with weeds. The city was reduced to ashes and looked like a burnt plain."

The Dutch, British and French

The Portuguese domination of the Indian Ocean was complete by the time Babur descended on Delhi, and neither he nor his Mughal successors felt in the least threatened by the presence of foreign powers on their coastal borders. In fact, they welcomed the traders as providers of silver and gold which they could use to mint money. In the course of the seventeenth and eighteenth centuries, however, the European powers would become a force to be reckoned with, eventually replacing the Mughals as India's rulers.

The first challengers of the Portuguese trade supremacy were the **Dutch**, whose cheaper and more manoeuvrable *fluyt* ships easily outsailed the more old-fashioned, ungainly *caravelas* from Lisbon. Determined not to allow Asia to be carved up by the proselytizing Roman Catholics, the Protestant Dutch East India Company – founded in 1602, only a couple of decades after Holland's victorious war of independence over Spain – systematically took control of the international spice trade, relieving the Portuguese of the strategically essential Molaccas in 1641, Ceylon in 1663 and their chief ports on the Malabar Coast soon after.

Although established two years before its Dutch counterpart, the British East India Company lagged behind initially, operating on a more modest scale with a fleet of smaller, privately run ships. Following the example of the Dutch, they set up a string of trading posts, or **factories**, around the coast, where goods – mostly **textiles** – could be stored awaiting annual shipment. Its first headquarters (from 1612), in Surat, Gujarat, was relocated to Bombay (Mumbai) in 1674, and by the mid-seventeenth century the British possessed 27 such outposts, the largest being **Fort St George** on the Coromandel coast – the forerunner of Madras (modern

Chennai). Over time, as the nature of the textile trade in India changed, the factories evolved from mere warehouses into large financial centres whose influence spread far inland. Gradually, communities of weavers settled around them, while growing numbers of recruits arrived to staff ever-expanding administrations and the military apparatus required to protect them.

The greatest threat to Britain's early Indian colonies was not local rulers, but rival Europeans. In the case of Fort St George, the **French** – whose own East India Company, started in 1664, was based further south on the Coromandel coast at **Pondicherry** (now Puducherry) – were to prove the most troublesome. Initially, agreements between the two rival companies forestalled any armed encounters. But with the outbreak of the War of the Austrian Succession in 1740, Britain and France found themselves members of opposing coalitions in a conflict which, although rooted in central Europe, proved a turning point in the history of South Asia.

The first clash between France and Britain came in 1746 when the French governor of Pondicherry, wily diplomat **Joseph François Dupleix**, captured Fort St George with the help of a French fleet commanded by **Admiral La Bourdonnais**. Among those imprisoned during the short French occupation (the fort was handed back two years later) was a young East India Company clerk whose humiliation at the hands of the French is often used to explain his sudden career change from pen-pushing to soldiering. Considered one of the founders of the British Raj, **Robert Clive** cut his military teeth in the politically unstable Carnatic region around Madras.

Dupleix had long since learned that the best way to extend French influence, and trade, was to forge alliances with whichever local ruler looked likely to emerge victorious from the furious in-fighting that wracked the South during the break-up of the Mughal empire. In this way, the British and the French were drawn into the conflicts of regional rulers, often facing each other from opposite ends of a battlefield.

In one such encounter, where the European powers pitched in to support rival sons of the Nawab of **Arcot** in 1751, Clive, then only 26 years old, distinguished himself by holding a breached and sprawling fortress for fifty days with only two hundred men against a vastly superior force of fifteen thousand French and their Indian allies. The first great triumph of British arms in the history of India, this feat made Clive a hero, a reputation he consolidated soon afterwards by marching through the monsoons to intervene decisively at the siege of **Trichinopoly**. The French lost half their army in this second battle, and saw their protégé, Chandra Sahib, captured and killed. Dupleix's reputation never recovered; he was recalled two years later and died destitute.

The British went on to defeat the French again at Wandiwash in 1760, and finally took Pondicherry after an eight-month siege, effectively bringing to an end the French bid for power in India. For Robert Clive, the Carnatic war was but a local skirmish compared to the significance of his later achievements in Bengal, where his victory at **Plassey** in 1757 laid the foundations of a British rule that would last for two hundred years. It did, however, teach him and his compatriots lessons that would serve them well in the future: not least of all, how effective a relatively small number of highly disciplined troops could be against a far larger, but undisciplined, army.

Haider Ali and Tipu Sultan of Mysore

After the heavy defeats in the Carnatic, the French were certainly down, but they were not yet quite out, thanks to the one remaining thorn in the side of

British territorial ambitions: **Haider Ali**. A former general of the Maharaja of Mysore, Haider Ali had usurped his master's throne in 1761 and within a short time ruled over virtually the entire South. The secret of his dramatic success lay in his readiness to learn from the Europeans, in particular the French, whose military tactics he emulated, and who provided him with officers to train his infantry. Between 1767 and 1769, he fought a series of battles with the British, whom he had always, unlike other Indian rulers, regarded as a threat to India as a whole, and whom he eventually coerced into a highly favourable treaty after threatening to attack Madras.

Held back by corrupt officials in both Madras and Calcutta, the British failed to provide a robust response, but rallied during the governorship of **Warren Hastings**. In 1778, they were once again at war with the French, and fending off Marathas in the west, which Haider Ali took as his cue to launch a major offensive. Assisted by the French, who landed troops by sea to join the battle, Haider again forced the British to sue for peace.

This was far from the most honourable period in the imperial history of France and Britain. During their various marches and skirmishes across the Carnatic, temples were regularly desecrated and massacres were commonplace; in all, a million Tamils were killed. On one occasion, four hundred wounded Hindu women were raped by rioting British soldiers, while in the Cauvery region, the French general, Lally, fired brahmin priests from his cannons for refusing to tell him where their temple treasure was hidden.

After Haider's death in 1782, his son **Tipu Sultan**, aka "the Tiger of Mysore", carried on his father's campaigns, but did so with diminished support from the French, who had by this time begun to wind down their Indian operations. In the end, Tipu Sultan was let down badly by his father's former allies. In 1799, they failed to dispatch troops to reinforce him when an army, led by Lord Wellesley and his brother Arthur (later the Duke of Wellington, of Waterloo fame) marched on **Srirangapatnam**. Tipu Sultan died defending a breach in his capital's walls (a story that later inspired Wilkie Collins's novel, *The Moonstone*), and Mysore was returned to the old Hindu dynasty Haider Ali had deposed. After more than a century of continual conflict between the European powers and their various allies, the struggle for control of India was finally won by the British.

British rule in the South

Following their victory at Srirangapatnam, the British, under Hastings' successor, **Lord Cornwallis**, annexed the coastal areas and interior plains that had been under Tipu Sultan's sway, settling down to a period of relatively trouble-free rule. Stretching from the Telegu-speaking region of present-day Andhra Pradesh to the Malabar Coast, the **Madras Presidency** was a notoriously "hands-off" regime, with vast administrative districts on which colonial officers could make very little impact. Life basically continued as it had before the advent of the British Raj. Unlike in the North, where the economic changes brought about by the Industrial Revolution in Britain had a huge impact, the South's output was geared towards domestic consumption; when the Lancashire mills forced the bottom out of the cotton industry in Bengal, the weavers of Madras were largely unaffected.

Nevertheless, resentment at British rule was not confined to the northern plains, where the so-called **Indian Mutiny** (re-dubbed "the First War of

Independence" by nationalist politicians, and referred to in the Guide as the 1857 uprising) broke out in Lucknow. **Uprisings** also occurred in forest regions of Andhra Pradesh, and the Moppila Muslims of the Malabar who took arms against the oppressive rule of both Hindu landowners and the British. Generally, however, opposition to the British came not from low-caste or tribal populations, but ironically from members of the English-speaking, university-educated elite in Madras, where the end of the nineteenth century saw the emergence of a nascent **nationalist movement**.

As this nationalist movement continued to grow, it found expression in the strategy of *swadeshi* ("self-sufficiency"), which involved a boycott of imported goods, in particular British textiles, and the revival of India's own production techniques. *Swadeshi* soon spread across southern India, creating economic chaos, and the arrest and imprisonment of one extremist, **Bal Tilak**, caused an uprising that brought Bombay's industry to a standstill; troops were sent on to the streets to quell it and several deaths resulted. In 1916, Tilak joined up with Annie Besant, who strongly believed in India's right to self-government, to form the Home Rule League, based at the Theosophical Society's headquarters in Adyar, Madras. The organization openly objected to the colonial regime, spreading its nationalistic message through publications such as *The Hindu* among the literate classes. Tilak's vision for distinct language-based states in the South was later borne out with the State Reorganization Act (see below). He died in 1920, and **Mahatma Gandhi** emerged from his shadow to dominate Congress. Gandhi spent much of the 1920s and 1930s in Bombay, and launched his Quit India campaign in 1942 from his Mani Bhavan home.

The South since Independence

Independence passed off relatively peacefully in South India in 1947, as the North succumbed to the horrors of Partition. With the exception of the Nizam of Hyderabad, who tried to retain his dominions and had to be ousted by the new Indian army (see box, p.650), the Princely States – namely Cochin, Travancore and Mysore – acceded gracefully to the Indian Union. Although deprived of their privy purses and most of their land, many of the former rulers used their privileged backgrounds to secure powerful roles in their new states, becoming members of parliament or industrialists.

The dissolution of British rule also generated an upsurge in regional sentiments. In the South, calls to restructure state boundaries along linguistic lines gained pace, culminating in the 1956 **State Reorganization Act**, when the region was divided into four main states: the Kannada-speaking area became Mysore (later changed to Karnataka); the Telegu zone made up Andhra Pradesh; the former Tamil region of the Madras Presidency became Madras (subsequently renamed Tamil Nadu); and Kerala was created from the Malayalam-speaking Malabar coastal zone. Goa, meanwhile, remained under Portuguese control until 1961, when India's first prime minister, **Jawaharlal Nehru**, lost his patience with the Portuguese dictator Salazar and sent in the troops.

From the start, Nehru vociferously opposed the creation of language-based states, predicting such a move would lead to fragmentation, schisms and regionalism. The political upheavals of the past fifty years have proved him right. With the rise in popularity of the pro-Dravidian **DMK** in Tamil Nadu and the **Telegu Desam** in Andhra Pradesh, the South's political scene has been completely dominated by **regional parties** in one guise or another, reflecting widespread mistrust of central government rule from Delhi. This has been most vehemently expressed in resistance to the imposition of Hindi – the most widely spoken language in northern India – as the medium of education and law. As these parties gained larger shares of the vote, state-specific issues and calls for greater regional autonomy have increasingly dominated the political agendas of all four states.

Caste and communal conflict

The period since Independence has also seen a marked rise in **caste conflict**. Caste (see p.741) has always been more firmly rooted in South Indian society than the more Muslim-influenced North, but political legislation passed over the previous two decades to encourage greater participation in government and education of low, tribal and "Other Backward Castes" (OBCs) has done little to erase these age-old social divisions. Adopted in 1950, the Constitution of India paved the way for laws to combat caste discrimination, with clauses obliging the states to implement policies of positive discrimination. "Untouchables" and OBCs were given **quotas** in educational institutions, parliament, regional assemblies and state sector jobs.

The Mandal Commission, set up in 1979 to look at the impact of quotas, came out strongly in favour of positive discrimination, and in August 1990 Prime Minister **V.P. Singh** announced that his party would implement its recommendations. Cynics accused him of trying to poach the Muslim and low-caste vote blocks from the opposition Congress Party, but the ensuing backlash was a strong contributory factor in the downfall of Singh's Janata Dal coalition in the elections of 1991.

The issue of quotas remains a contentious one in the South. "Affirmative action" policies have certainly increased the level of scheduled caste participation in government, but they have had some negative effects too. Inevitably, sought-after university places and public sector jobs are often granted to unqualified people instead of better-qualified members of higher castes, creating sectarian resentment that has increasingly spilled into violence. Clashes between brahmins and low-caste farmers have led to whole districts of Tamil Nadu being placed under martial law on several occasions.

The other harmful repercussion of positive discrimination has been the **politicization** of caste. In order to be elected or to form power-wielding coalitions, Indian politicians these days have to galvanize **vote banks** – blocks of support from specific caste or ethnic groups. In return, these vote banks look to their leaders to advance their agendas in government, a process that all too often results in national or state interests being subordinated to the demands of minority groups.

With the expansion of the quota system under Prime Minister **Narasimha Rao** in 1994 to include disadvantaged Muslims and other "ethnic" minorities, state and national politics have become increasingly dominated not only by caste, but by communal issues – precisely the kind of sectarianism that the Mandal report and India's resolutely secular constitution sought to eradicate.

The South has traditionally been spared the kind of **communal conflict** that has so often plagued the North. In recent years, however, the steady rise of communal parties, such as the far right pro-Hindu BJP, has been accompanied by violent confrontations between Hindus and Muslims, particularly in Tamil Nadu. The spiralling violence came to a head on February 14, 1998, when fifteen bombs exploded in crowded districts of Coimbatore, killing sixty people. The Home Affairs Minister and BJP leader at that time, L.K. Advani, was due to address a rally in the city, which the Islamic extremist organization **Al-Umma** decided to use as a pretext to settle communal scores for earlier attacks on Muslims in the region.

Tamil nationalism and the war in Sri Lanka

The highest profile victim of communal violence in India since the assassination of Mahatma Gandhi by Hindu extremists in 1948 was the former prime minister **Rajiv Gandhi** (son of Indira), killed while electioneering in Tamil Nadu on May 21, 1991 in reprisal for his role in the civil war in neighbouring Sri Lanka – a conflict that dominated foreign policy in the south for over twenty years and made a lasting impression on the coastal regions of Tamil Nadu.

The **ethnic conflict** between the majority (Buddhist) Sinhalese and minority Tamil populations of Sri Lanka erupted into full-scale war in 1987. Following several years of escalating clashes between Sri Lankan government forces and the Liberation Tigers of Tamil Eelam (LTTE – popularly known as the Tamil Tigers), Sri Lankan president J. R. Jayawardene sent the Sri Lankan Army in against the LTTE stronghold on the Jaffna peninsula in the north of the island. Prime Minister Rajiv Gandhi, under pressure from Indian Tamils concerned at the treatment of their fellow Tamils in Sri Lanka, began talks with the Jayawardene government, and in July 1987 the two countries signed a peace accord, part of which permitted the Indian army to intervene and disarm the LTTE. In the event, however, India became bogged down in a messy war with the LTTE, with high casualties on both sides – it was this debacle, with Indian troops fighting Tamil guerrillas, which led to Rajiv Gandhi's assassination. Millions of Tamil refugees, meanwhile, poured across the Palk Straits to settle in camps around Rameshwaram, Tamil Nadu. Though some returned to Sri Lanka following the cessation of hostilities in 2002, the upsurge of violence in 2004 led many more to seek refuge across the straits, and the number of camps in the state remains over one hundred.

India was only able to extricate itself after the defeat of Rajiv Gandhi in the 1989 elections, following which, in March 1990, the new government withdrew all troops from the island. It was during the campaign for the following elections, in May 1991, that Rajiv and sixteen others were **assassinated** by a female suicide bomber. Seven years later, an Indian court convicted 26 people for the killing – all were Sri Lankan militants or Indian allies of the LTTE conspirators.

Ripples from the war in Sri Lanka have also had a marked influence on political life in Tamil Nadu, home to an estimated sixty million Tamil speakers. Following its resounding defeat in the wake of Rajiv's assassination, when it was accused of harbouring and training **separatist guerrillas** to fight the war, the **DMK**, the then dominant (Tamil nationalist) party, has had to distance itself from the LTTE. Its increasingly high profile within central government also required it to adhere to New Delhi's "hands off" line. In the background, however, DMK ministers and parliament representatives in the capital were able to exert influence over foreign policy, keeping Indian troops out of the war and banning pro-Tiger demonstrations. Tamil Nadu's previous Chief Minister, M. Karunanidhi, had an additional reason to downplay his party's connections with the LTTE. Through the late 1990s, he made several speeches insisting that the Tigers should not be seen as the only legitimate representatives of the Tamil people, hinting that he saw himself as a potential pan-Tamil leader if and when the north of Sri Lanka ever gained independence. At the same time, Tamil

nationalist leaders such as Karunanidhi could not afford to overtly
oppose the LTTE, who command
huge popular support in Tamil
Nadu, and thus considerable
influence at election time. The other
main party to have ruled the state,
the **AIADMK**, led by the maverick
ex-film starlet **Jayalalitha** (see box,
p.514), have consistently exploited
this fact to kindle support, forming
coalitions with more openly pro-
Tiger nationalist parties and leaders.

The rise of the BJP

With the demise of the Congress
Party (and corresponding rise of the
pro-Hindu, nationalist BJP)
throughout the 1990s, politics at
national level became increasingly
fragmented. No longer dominated
by a single party, the succession of
short-lived governments in New
Delhi tended to be formed by shaky

△ Poster of Jayalalitha

coalitions brought together by political expediency. Thus regionalist parties
such as the pro-Tamil DMK and AIADMK, who had for decades enjoyed
massive support in their home state but wielded disproportionately little
influence at national level, emerged as a potent new force.

The strength of this new political element was dramatically demonstrated in
the wake of the 1998 national elections, won by a BJP-led coalition. To bring
it down, Congress – now led by Sonia Gandhi, the Italian-born widow of the
former prime minister Rajiv Gandhi – collaborated with Jayalalitha, leader of
the AIADMK. When she pulled out of the BJP-led coalition, Prime Minister
Vajpayee lost a vote of no confidence and was forced to call yet another general
election in April 1999 – the third in three years.

At the start of the campaign, Congress hopes were high that with a Gandhi
once again as party leader, it could revive the popular support lost after years of
in-fighting and corruption scandals. Moreover, to compound the BJP's
problems, Vajpayee's caretaker government was saddled with a worsening
financial deficit and a welter of domestic difficulties. Events took an unexpected
turn following a sudden and dramatic flare up in the long-standing **border war**
between India and Pakistan in Kashmir.

While the world was preoccupied with NATO's bombing of Belgrade, at
least eight hundred Pakistani fighters crept across the so-called Line of
Control (the de facto border) overlooking the Srinagar–Leh road near
Kargil. India's response was to move thousands of troops and heavy artillery
into the area, swiftly followed up with an aerial bombardment. Within days
the two countries were poised on the brink of all-out war, only months after
both had successfully tested long-range nuclear missiles. In the event the
conflict was contained, but Pakistan took a bloody nose from the encounter,
and by July 1999 the Indian army had retaken all the ground previously lost
to the militants. An estimated seven hundred Pakistani and 330 Indian

soldiers died before the Pakistani premier, Nawaz Sharif, bowed to international pressure and withdrew his forces.

The wave of patriotism that swept India after the 1998 nuclear tests and then the Kargil victory was a godsend for Vajpayee (cynics argued it may well have been the hidden policy behind the army's uncompromising response to the crisis). Riding high on the feel-good factor, his party inflicted the biggest defeat Congress had sustained since it first came to power in 1947. Vajpayee's majority was far from as large as he might have hoped, and the BJP-led **National Democratic Alliance** (**NDA**) coalition was fractured and tenuous. But those who gleefully interpreted Sonia's second election defeat as the end of dynastic politics in India were to be proved wrong in the most dramatic fashion only five years later.

Having betrayed the former BJP government, Jayalalitha, meanwhile, was thrust into something of a political wilderness, with her party soundly beaten by a BJP-led coalition that included the DMK, led by her arch-rival, the then chief minister of Tamil Nadu, **M. Karunanidhi**. No longer a minister, she lacked protection against the raft of **corruption** charges dating from the period when she was the state's chief minister (1991–96). Finally, in October 2000, the High Court in Chennai (Madras) found her guilty of accepting bribes from businessmen to permit illegal construction projects, and issued a three-year suspended prison sentence. In the riots that followed five thousand demonstrators were arrested, as Jayalalitha's supporters set fire to a bus full of students, killing three innocent women – an incident filmed and broadcast by Star TV news.

The new millennium

To rub salt in Jayalalitha's wounds, her appeal against the conviction was quashed by the High Court of Chennai in April 2001, casting doubts on whether she would be able to run in the state assembly **elections** the following month (Indian electoral law debars candidates who've been sentenced to a prison term of more than two years). However, the ruling only seems to have intensified her desire to get even with Karunanidhi, and Jayalitha announced she would run anyway, expecting that the corruption charges could be overturned at a later date. In the build-up to the election, her AIADMK-led coalition comprised the Tamil Maanila Congress, the (overtly pro-Tamil Tiger) Pattali Makkal Katchi (or PMK), two communist parties and two Muslim parties.

From the outset, the thrust of Jayalalitha's campaign was to personally target Karunanidhi, now heading a sixteen-party coalition dominated by the DMK and BJP. She even vowed that if she were re-elected she would incarcerate Karunanidhi in the same cell she'd been locked up in, and make him eat off the same tin plate. Jayalalitha's **vendetta** seemed to capture the imagination of Tamil voters, who returned her coalition with a landslide majority. The new chief minister wasted no time in settling scores with her opponents, ordering Karunanidhi's arrest on corruption charges, along with that of around one thousand of his supporters. Television audiences across the country were shocked by film footage of the then 78-year-old former chief minister being roughly pulled down the stairs of his house by police. The indignity of the arrest, followed by that of two federal cabinet ministers who tried to intervene, caused a political storm in Delhi.

Karunanidhi's release (on "humanitarian grounds") came a few days later, but the ageing former premier had to face the charges that he accepted bribes from road constructors in Chennai while in power. Violent protests accompanied the dispute. One Tamil farmer burned himself to death in protest at Karunanidhi's arrest, and a purge of Jayalalitha's political opponents followed her election. A high-ranking BJP government official, dispatched by prime minister Vajpayee from New Delhi to investigate the situation, reported that "no law of the land prevails in Tamil Nadu".

To the brink of war

Political life in early years of the new millennium may have been dominated by the power struggle between Jayalalitha and Karunanidhi, but the foreign media was at the time more enthralled by the exploits of the sandalwood bandit **Veerappan** (see p.641) who demonstrated his legendary elusiveness by kidnapping South India's most famous living matinee idol, **Rajkumar**, in 2000. Despite a massive manhunt, the luxuriantly mustachioed brigand remained at large in the forests lining the Karnatakan, Keralan and Tamil Nadu borders, and held on to his hostage for 107 days, during which time protest riots by fans brought Bangalore (now Bengaluru) to a standstill on several occasions. Following Rajkumar's release, secured in a shady deal involving payment of undisclosed sums by state politicians to the bandit, Veerappan and his band slipped back into the jungle. The hunt stepped up in December 2002, after the decomposing body of another of his hostages, a senior politician, was discovered, but the failure of the crack National Security Squad to bring him to justice only fed rumours that Veerappan had somehow managed to bribe or intimidate the state's most powerful players into protecting him. It wasn't until October 20, 2004, that police finally caught up with the bandit. By then wanted for killing 130 people and two thousand elephants, Veerappan had been suffering from acute ill health, which undercover agents who had infiltrated his gang exploited to lure him into an ambush. En route to hospital in a nearby town, he and his entourage were gunned down on a deserted jungle road – the end of a manhunt which had, by its conclusion, cost the government a stagging Rs1.5 billion (£19 million).

Meanwhile, in rural South India, the start of the third millennium was marked by catastrophic **tropical storms**, which ripped across the region during the monsoons. In 2000, record rainfalls wrought havoc in the southern state of Andhra Pradesh. An estimated twelve million were left marooned or homeless as river levels rose by as much as four metres in places. With transport and communications at a standstill for weeks, food distribution and rescue efforts all but ground to a halt. Riots broke out in camps set up by the army for **flood** victims, as supplies of food and plastic sheets ran out.

Ironically, only the previous year the chief ministers of Tamil Nadu and Karnataka had been locked in a bitter dispute about **water shortages** – a debate that has been rumbling on ever since. Karnataka had repeatedly withheld supplies of water on the River Cauvery, guaranteed by the terms of an accord forged by Prime Minister Vajpayee. Many commentators at the time regarded the fallout from the "**River Dispute**", as the Cauvery controversy has become known, as symptomatic of the **regionalism** that had long been on the rise in the South. The growth of parties such as the DMK, AIADMK and Telegu Desam has been accompanied by a marked weakening of New Delhi's grip. Incapable of forming a majority government, Atal Bihari Vajpayee's ruling BJP had to forge coalitions with, and yield concessions to, its political partners in the NDA (or National Democratic Alliance) government, which markedly increased the power of the southern states at the centre.

Domestic politics, however, took a backseat in late 2001, as India entered one of the tensest periods in its troubled **relations with Pakistan**. Following the collapse of talks on **Kashmir** at a summit in Agra, a series of major terrorist attacks brought the two countries once again to the brink of full-scale war. First, the car bombing of the State Assembly building in Srinagar provoked a furious tirade from Delhi about "Pakistani-sponsored cross-border terrorism". Then, in December 2001, three Muslim gunmen mounted an **attack on the Parliament Building** in New Delhi. Having killed several police guards they were picked off by army marksmen, but the sense of outrage grew in the days afterwards. Pakistani involvement was inevitably suspected, and Vajpayee announced he was in favour of declaring war immediately. Only after some deft US and British diplomacy, and some conciliatory remarks from Islamabad, were New Delhi's ruffled feathers temporarily smoothed.

A more heated confrontation was about to erupt, though. Its catalyst was the suicide attack by *fedayin* Islamicists on an army cantonment near Jammu in April 2002; women and children numbered among the dead. This time Vajpayee was in no mood for diplomacy. Bowing to the hawks on the right of his own party, he called for a "decisive battle", initiating a massive build up of troops on the western border. An estimated million men at arms were involved in the ensuing stand-off, which was only defused after concerted diplomacy by the US, who sent Colin Powell to lead negotiations.

Also in the spring of 2002, India was wracked by **communal tension** after 38 Hindu pilgrims returning by train from the disputed temple site of Ayodhya were brutally murdered by Muslim mobs in Godhra, Gujarat. The atrocity sparked off terrible reprisal massacres across the country, in which an estimated two thousand died, but the troubles did not spread to the South. The killings of Hindus in Kashmir and an attack by Islamist gunmen on the headquarters of a Swaminarayan sect in Gujarat further strained communal relations. Yet none of these events managed their intended aim – to derail the peace talks over Kashmir that followed.

Peace talks and the Mumbai bombings

Indo-Pak negotiations over Kashmir lasted until March 2003, but were suspended by India after Islamabad announced the successful testing of its Shaheen missile, capable of delivering nuclear warheads over a distance of 750km – as far as Delhi. The talks, however, resumed in May, when Vajpayee made a **declaration of peace**, announcing that the Delhi–Lahore bus connection would recommence and that hundreds of Pakistanis detained in Indian prisons since the Kargil war would be released. Pakistan responded with more "confidence-building measures", announcing that it would ease trade restrictions, improve travel and sporting links and, later, by declaring a ceasefire along the Line of Control.

These moves paved the way for a full-blown **summit**, eventually held in Islamabad in early 2004. Watched by the world's press, President Pervez Musharraf and Atul Bihari Vajpayee posed for a historic handshake and even managed an hour-long discussion in which plans to strengthen diplomatic ties and reopen the Kashmir Highway (between Srinagar and Muzaffarabad) were mooted. In tandem with these formal dialogues, Indian officials also held behind-the-scenes talks with Kashmiri separatist leaders. Both sides emerged optimisitic and committed to a non-violent "Road Map". Not since the start of the troubles had a rapprochement between the Subcontinent's old foes looked so likely to result in a definitive end to hostilities.

Nevertheless, relations between Hindus and Muslims in some parts of India remained at crisis point. As the first trials of suspects accused of atrocities in the wake of the Godhra massacres reached court in Ahmedabad, the Archeological Survey of India released its long-awaited **report on Ayodhya**. Since the destruction of the Babri Masjid by Hindu extremists in 1992, debate had raged as to whether there had in fact ever been a Rama temple beneath the mosque. To no one's surprise, the ASI panel of "experts" appointed by the right-wing BJP government (prominent members of which had incited the Babri Masji destruction in the first place), declared they'd found evidence to show there had been a temple, in effect condoning the tearing down of the mosque by Hindu activists.

Opening up old wounds, the ruling did little to quell post-Godhra tensions; and when, on August 25, 2003 (the day after the Ayodhya report was published) two bombs ripped through the centre of downtown **Mumbai**, commentators were quick to identify the Babri Masjid dispute as the provocation. One of the bombs exploded in a taxi next to the Gateway of India, Mumbai's main tourist hub, killing 107 people. No one claimed responsibility, but four suspects believed to have links with Islamic militant groups were arrested soon after.

The fragile balance between India's Hindu and Muslim population was shaken once more by the train bombings in Mumbai on **July 11, 2006**, when seven synchronized explosions within eleven minutes killed more than two hundred people and injured over seven hundred. Two Kashmiri groups, Lashkar-e-Tayyiba and Jaish-e-Mohammed, were immediately suspected of the attack. Initial concerns in the city were for a potential backlash and communal violence against the Muslim population, while in Delhi there were fears that talks with Pakistan might also be derailed. Talks were temporarily halted, but in September 2006, Prime Minister Manmohan Singh and President Musharraf made a joint statement that peace negotiations would resume.

The 2004 elections

With India booming as never before and peace on the horizon in Kashmir, Prime Minister Vajpayee and his BJP-led coalition decided to cash in on the perceived "feel good" factor and call a snap **election** in May 2004. "India Shining" was their slogan, but the campaign strategy boomeranged badly. True, India was experiencing a period of unparalleled economic growth, but the boom was based largely on information technology, benefiting the urban professional classes, and had had little impact on the vast majority of India's population. Congress leader Sonia Gandhi was quick to seize the initiative and appealed directly to rural, poor voters to show the government what they thought of Vajpayee's vision of the country. She also played the dynastic card, introducing her son Rahul and daughter Priyanka to the campaign, which caught the imagination of younger voters (one in two of the Indian electorate is aged under 35).

Far from increasing his majority, as he had expected, Vajpayee and his government were thrown out in the most dramatic political turnaround of recent times. Congress gained the largest share of the vote and **Sonia Gandhi** was duly invited to form a government. However, she stunned supporters by "humbly declining" the invitation and stepped down. The announcement caused clamorous scenes in parliament, provoking the worst losses ever seen in the 129-year history of India's stock market. Eventually, former finance minister, 71-year-old **Manmohan Singh**, stepped into the breach and was named as prime minister, the first Sikh to lead the country.

One of the casualties of the national elections in the South was Andhran chief minister **Chandrababu Naidu**. The darling of the World Bank, Naidu had come to power vowing to stamp out corruption, make state government more transparent and efficient and transform the region's economy, following a blueprint drawn up by international management consultants McKinsey. In "Vision 2020", **IT** was given a leading role. Up until the late 1990s, Bangalore (Bengaluru) had remained the unchallenged info-tech capital of India, but spurred on by Naidu's reforms, the Andhra capital Hyderabad soon overtook its rival as the country's

For over a decade now, a mounting agricultural crisis in South India has had a massive impact on rural populations. Hundreds of thousands of farming families have been forced off their land by debt and crop failure; many have chosen to take their own lives in protest against the government policies they feel are to blame.

The roots of the crisis lie in the so-called **Green Revolution**. From the 1960s, encouraged by Western governments and aid donors, India introduced modern farming techniques to intensify wheat and rice production. Based on the use of new high-yield varieties of seed, together with chemical fertilizers, the new methods led to a dramatic increase in agricultural output (India survived a severe drought in 1988 and even managed to contribute grain to famine-stricken farmers in the African Sahel at around the same time). Their longer-term impact, however, remains under scrutiny.

One of the major drawbacks of the Green Revolution has been a growing disparity between the wealthy land-owning farmers and their landless share-cropping tenants. Unable to afford the expensive seeds and accompanying chemicals, poor farmers and their families have been forced, by mounting debts, to leave the countryside in search of waged employment. The majority end up living on the streets, or in the vast slum encampments that have sprung up on the edges of all South Indian cities over the past two decades.

Recent global economic trends have also been felt in the South Indian countryside. The General Agreement on Tariffs and Trade, or **GATT**, is potentially the most significant of these. Signed in 1994, the treaty aims to promote free trade by defending foreign investors from economic protectionism. While popular with the business community, GATT and other policies like it have proved controversial in a country as sensitive to its colonial history as India (particularly one brought up on the Gandhian ideals of *svadeshi*, or small-scale, non-polluting self-reliance).

A component of the treaty that has come in for particular criticism in India is its promotion of **genetic patenting**. This enables the large multinationals who manufacture seed used by South Indians to patent their products, making it illegal for farmers to replant them – no matter that the seeds may have originated in developing countries such as India, where generations of peasant farmers have painstakingly experimented to create pest- and drought-resistant strains. If a company can prove that it has modified the seed in any way, it is entitled by GATT to patent it.

The issue prompted indignation in India, but little more than that until it transpired the expensive seeds didn't even produce the promised increased yields – their one redeeming feature in the eyes of small farmers. In 1993, on the anniversary of Gandhi's birthday, half a million farmers issued "Quit India" notices to the US company Cargill, whose genetically modified sunflower seeds had been used by many farmers in northern Karnataka. Angry protesters succeeded in dismantling the company's plant in Bangalore (now Bengaluru) within half an hour. The police, most of whom had family in the countryside, did not offer significant resistance.

The **Seed Satyagraha**, as this grassroots farmers' movement became known, makes explicit the connection with the anticolonial struggle by using the name chosen by Gandhi for his campaign of non-violent civil disobedience, or *satyagraha*. Replacing the spinning wheel with a seed as the movement's symbol, it has been seen by many as a second freedom struggle and its ideas have spread from Karnataka through Andhra Pradesh, Tamil Nadu and Kerala in recent years.

Government support for the Seed Satyagraha, however, did not materialize until the late 1990s, following rumours that the giant corporation Monsanto planned to unleash the new so-called "**Terminator Gene**" on the region. Designed to protect the company's patents, the new genetically modified gene produces plants that yield sterile seeds (i.e. ones that cannot be resown, and thus forces farmers to purchase new ones – and the accompanying fertilizers – each season). Moreover, it is widely feared that cross-pollination would render other crops sterile, resulting in complete dependence on foreign companies. To draw attention to this risk, a coalition of ten million Karnatakan farmers, the KRSS, mounted "**Operation Cremate Monsanto**", pulling up cotton crops at test sites and organizing mass rallies against the WTO. Its leader, the maverick **Professor Najundasmamy**, also staged a much publicized laugh-in, when six thousand farmers laughed all day outside the town hall in Bangalore (Bengaluru) at their elected representatives, for "subverting democracy". To diffuse the crisis, and the prospect of a full-scale rural uprising, the Indian government banned the technology and required all exporting countries to guarantee that seeds entering India are "terminator free". It then spent hundreds of thousands of dollars unsuccessfully fighting a US decision to grant a Texan company patents on basmati rice in 1997. Meanwhile, Monsanto, the world's largest genetically modified seed producer, was awarded patents on the wheat used for making chapatis, even though the strain had been developed over centuries of experimentation by Indian farmers.

Another change that has had serious implications for millions of Indian farmers over the past decade or so has been the government's relationship with the International Monetary Fund (IMF) and its sister organization, the World Bank. In order to qualify for a £90 billion loan in the late 1980s, India was obliged to end its programme of **subsidies** to farmers, who for years had been entitled to free or cheap electricity, diesel, fertilizers and pesticides. According to the World Trade Organization, such aid constituted "interference with the free market". Farmers were instead encouraged by a raft of incentives and publicity drives to grow **cash crops** such as cotton, which offered the additional benefit of generating foreign currency (needed to repay the IMF loans). Using specially developed high-yield seeds and chemicals, improved harvests and profits were assured, and within a couple of years, huge chunks of the country (as much as sixty percent of farm land in Andhra Pradesh) had been given over to the "White Gold".

The advertising campaigns mounted by the multinational agri-manufacturers, however, failed to warn that cotton prices might suddenly drop, that pests might develop immunities to the chemicals, that the new seeds didn't always grow, or that much greater quantities of water would be needed to cultivate them. When all these disasters struck at once, as they did in 1999–2000, millions of farmers in South India were ruined. Their only option was to borrow money from the *aarthis*, or "money lenders", who had sold them the seeds and chemicals in the first place.

In **Andhra Pradesh** alone, around five hundred farmers committed suicide by drinking the useless insecticide, lying down to die amid their failed crops. Despite such obvious drawbacks, field trials of GM cotton continued in 2001–02, with results published the following year showing an eighty percent increase in yields. The findings increased pressure on the central government to relax laws preventing the introduction of GM crops – music to the ears of the then chief minister of Andhra Pradesh, **Chandrababu Naidu**, who had long championed the GM cause in his bid to squeeze the state's rural-based economy into the more lucrative "service sector". Famous as the go-ahead leader responsible for bringing Dell and Microsoft to Hyderabad, Naidu had earlier enraged farmers (and delighted the World Bank) by slashing rice subsidies. Despite his popularity among the professional classes, he fell victim to a rural backlash in the elections of May 2004 when he and his party were wiped out. This dramatic electoral upset served notice to leaders throughout the region that they could ignore the plight of the South Indian farmers only at their peril and the subsequent government has, with the help of huge subsidies from Delhi, tried to address the crop crisis, which hit a new high with over six hundred farmer suicides in the Vidarbha region alone in 2006. Whether anything substantial is done about the root causes of the crisis remains to be seen.

Although southeast India was 2000km away from the epicentre of the Indonesian earthquake on the morning of December 26, 2004, much of its coast lay in the direct path of the **tsunamis**, and three giant waves, between nine and twelve metres high, swept ashore from the Bay of Bengal. The Nicobar Islands, at the southern end of the Andaman and Nicobar archipelago (see p.679), were much closer to the epicentre, though fatalities were relatively low. The areas of the mainland worst hit were, in order of severity, the Nagapattinam–Karaikal and Cuddalore districts of Tamil Nadu, Kanyakumari at the southern extremity of the peninsula, the coast in and around Chennai and a small stretch of coastline west of the Kollam–Alappuzha backwaters in Kerala. Official estimates placed the death toll in these areas at around seven thousand, with as many as ten times that made homeless. The real figure, however, was probably a good deal higher.

Millions of dollars in donations from around the world flooded in, Amma, the "hugging saint" (see p.410), leading the way with $23 million from her foundation. Of course, there were ample charges of **corruption** levelled at the authorities and numerous officials were accused of lining their pockets with funds intended for victims. A massive **clear-up** operation ensued nonetheless, with rehabilitation efforts focusing on the subsistence fishing communities who lost their homes and liveli-hoods in the disaster. Countless houses, boats, nets and tools had been destroyed, and few of their owners could afford replacements. Many international organisations donated boats and other equipment and their logos are clearly visible on the new vessels to be seen at beaches in the affected areas. Tent camps and programmes for longer term rehabilitation were also soon instituted and are still flourishing. Inland, vast areas of formerly fertile paddy were badly salinated; it is still unclear whether much of this land will ever be productive again, though parts have been converted into shrimp farms. Overall, the region's recovery has been impressive, though it will still be many years before some people's lives are back to normal. The ferocity of the waves will certainly never be forgotten by those who survived them.

leading software enclave. Subsidies of Rs20,000 were granted to companies for every job created in "**Cyberabad**", as the new development was nicknamed. Big players persuaded to relocate there included Microsoft and Dell, and when Bill Clinton came to see India's IT miracle in action, it was Hyderabad he chose to visit and Chandrababu Naidu who showed him around.

Naidu passionately believed that the answer to Andhra's problems was to shift its economy from a rural, agricultural base into the service sector and IT. Call centres not fields would henceforth form the basis of future prosperity in the state, and "e-Government" would make its leaders more accountable to the people. Needless to say, although the World Bank loved Naidu's revolution, it was far from popular with farmers. While Hyderabad's professional classes surged ahead, Andhra's rural poor were suffering the worst economic crisis in decades. Crop failure and debt caused primarily by the government's policies led to the suicides of thousands of farmers across the South in the 2000s. Yet in the face of what the press dubbed "the Digital Divide", Naidu continued to slash subsidies to agriculture and denied farmers the **free electricity** they'd previously been promised (see box, p.733). The 2004 elections finally gave the rural population the opportunity to express their opinion of Naidu's experi-ment: the party suffered a resounding defeat and its reforms were halted. Having pinned its colours to the BJP-led coalition in Delhi, Jayalalitha's AIADMK also crashed at the polls in Tamil Nadu after her government had cut free electricity to farmers and introduced other measures penalizing rural populations.

South India today

Trade between the UK and India is currently growing at around twenty percent a year, with Britain the third largest investor in India and India in turn the second largest investor in the UK. Within India, **technological development** continues to rise at a phenomenal rate, with Tamil Nadu leading the way: the state's economy is now the country's fifth largest, with the second highest per capita income. Some 345 IT firms arrived in Chennai in 2005, and global giants such as Nokia, Dell, Ford, Samsung and Hyundai all took root. This has all been achieved despite the fierce rivalry between the two main political parties, the DMK and AIADMK, and the constant swing from one to the other. Despite their differences, the economic stance of both Jayalalitha and the current Chief Minister M. Karunanidhi remains similar, and both have helped the state to its healthy position.

The success of the technological hubs of Bangalore (Bengaluru), Hyderabad and Chennai has sparked a **consumer revolution**, with the cities' emergent middle class benefiting from rapidly rising disposable incomes. Retail sales are currently worth around $550 billion and are predicted to grow to around $900 billion by 2015. Wal-Mart, Tesco, Marks & Spencer, Carrefour, Next and Mothercare have already gained a foothold, but whether they succeed remains to be seen – the deep cultural and religious beliefs of many may not sit comfortably with mass consumerism and there is still a residual mistrust of foreign power.

While concerns about Hindu–Muslim relations and the potential derailment of peace talks with Pakistan following the **Mumbai bombings** continued to be at the forefront of political agenda in 2006 (see p.731), the year will be remembered primarily for the huge realignment that took place between India and **the US**. Traditionally the relationship between the two countries lay somewhere between cool and frosty, with the US more closely aligned with Pakistan and India with Russia. After India conducted the Pokhran nuclear tests in 1974 the US banned all sales of **nuclear technology** – a ban that stayed in place for 32 years. In March 2006, however, Condoleeza Rice visited India and stated that the US wanted "to help India become a major power in the twenty-first century". Then, on July 18, came a landmark agreement between George Bush and Prime Minister Manmohan Singh which permanently lifted the ban. The Indian government's side of the bargain involved an agreement to separate civilian and military power plants, apply international safeguards and a promise not to conduct any more nuclear tests. In return, however, India will be able to buy limitless nuclear fuel and technology – thus shifting from its status from "nuclear pariah" to a power at the forefront of the international scene, a move that will significantly change the political jigsaw of Asia. This monumental move for India has stirred up much argument and controversy – are the advantages of nuclear development and US support worth the loss of independent policy?

Visiting India, the ironies resulting from decades of poor governance are all too evident. The country chosen by Bill Gates as the site of a new Microsoft complex, capable of launching satellites, nuclear rockets and manned-space programmes, is still unable to provide clean drinking water, adequate nutrition and basic education for millions of its citizens. As Goldman Sachs commented, India is home to "nearly a third of the world's software engineers and a quarter of the world's undernourished". Its continuing challenge is to negotiate the ever-widening gap between the emergent middle class and the rural poor. This will depend on the extent to which India's leaders can deliver stable government over the coming years and curb the self-interest that has come to dominate public life, particularly in the South.

Religions

This great and ancient nation was once the fountain of human light, the apex of human civilization, the exemplar of courage and humanity, the perfection of good government and settled society, the mother of all religions, the teacher of all wisdom and philosophy.

Shri Aurobindo (1907)

Long regarded as the bastion of Hindu values, South India boasts many of the finest, oldest and most extravagant temples in the country. The devotion displayed by the millions of pilgrims is just the most obvious aspect of the fact that Hinduism permeates every element of life here, from social structures to education and politics. The vast pantheon of Hindu deities is manifest everywhere, from soaring temple gateways to *beedi* packets and the little mobile shrines erected in houses, buses, cars and shops. The South is also home to a substantial Muslim community; since the twelfth century, Muslims have settled in the South as traders and rulers, constructing pearl-domed mosques throughout the region. today, Muslims are largely concentrated in the major cities and Kerala. Christians, believed to have been living in South India since the first century AD, have developed distinct denominations, and worship in buildings that range from simple thatched huts to the grand basilicas and churches erected by the Portuguese, French and British. Although Jains and Buddhists are now a minute fraction of the southern population, several magnificent temples stand testament to an impressive presence in the past. The once influential Keralan Jews are now a pitifully small group, originally attracted here from both the Arab world and Europe by the rich pickings of the Malabar Coast and its spice belts, but their influence can still be strongly felt in Fort Cochin (Kochi). Mumbai features a rapidly dwindling society of Zoroastrian Parsis (see p.753). Both groups continue to intermarry to preserve their unique heritage and identity.

Hinduism

Contemporary **Hindu society** – making up over 85 percent of South Indians – is the product of several thousand years of evolution and assimilation. The South has played a vital role in the development of Hinduism in the

---

Useful websites

Ⓦ**www.sacredsites.com** The India section of this website features scholarly background on India's most holy places, with quality images.

Ⓦ**www.hinduweb.org** Amazingly comprehensive site featuring diverse topics such as Hindu art, history, religion and philosophy, with links to other sites created by users.

Ⓦ**www.hindulinks.org** Portal with nearly 30,000 links to a multitude of India-related matters.

Ⓦ**www.jainnet.com** Site dedicated to Jainism, featuring a concise introduction, devotional songs and e-cards.

Subcontinent, producing reformers like **Shankara**, who travelled throughout India in the ninth century, bringing about sweeping reforms by utilizing Buddhist models to establish a Hindu monastic order that is still active today. In the thirteenth century, in the face of a Muslim onslaught on Hindu institutions, South Indian **Vaishnavas** (worshippers of Vishnu and his incarnations) were pivotal in the development of Krishna worship, establishing centres in Krishna's mythological homeland of Braj, to the south of Delhi. Ever since, Vaishnavism has been at the heart of South Indian Hindu life.

The Hindu religion boasts no founder or prophet, no single creed and no single prescribed practice or doctrine; it takes in hundreds of gods, goddesses, beliefs and practices, and widely variant cults and philosophies. Some Hindu deities are recognized by only two or three villages; others, such as Vishnu and Shiva, are popular right across the Subcontinent, with devotion tending to border on fanaticism in the South. Hindus (from the Persian word for Indians) call their beliefs and practices **dharma**, which embraces natural and moral law to define a way of living in harmony with a natural order, while achieving personal goals and meeting the requirements of society.

Early developments

In the second millennium BC, the foundations of Hinduism as a religion and way of life were laid down by the Aryans, a semi-nomadic people who probably originated from the Caucasus Mountains and had wandered into the Indus Valley in northern India. They brought a belief in gods associated with the elements, including **Agni**, the god of fire and sacrifice, **Surya**, the sun god, and **Indra**, the chief god. Most of these deities faded in importance in later times, but Indra is still regarded as the father of the gods, and Surya was widely worshipped until the medieval period.

Aryan beliefs were set out in the **Vedic** scriptures as they had been "heard" (*shruti*) by "seers" (*rishis*). Transmitted orally for centuries, they were finally written, in Sanskrit, between 1000 BC and 500 AD. The earliest were the *Samhitas*, or hymns; the *Brahmanas*, sacrificial texts, and *Aranyakas*, or "forest treatises" came later.

The earliest and most important *Samhita*, the **Rig Veda**, contains hymns to deities and *devas* (divine powers), and is supplemented by other books detailing rituals and prayers for ceremonial use. The **Brahmanas** stress correct ritual performance, drawing heavily on concepts of **purity and pollution** which persist today and concentrating on sacrificial rites. Pedantic attention to ritual soon supplanted worship of the *devas*, whose importance was further undermined by a search for a single cosmic power thought to be their source, eventually conceived of as **Brahma**, the absolute creator, personified from earlier mentions of Brahman, an impersonal principle of cosmic unity.

The **Aranyakas** focused on this all-powerful godhead, and reached their final stage in the **Upanishads**, which describe in beautiful and emotive verse the mystic experience of unity of the soul (*atman*) with Brahma, ideally attained through asceticism, renunciation of worldly values and meditation. In the *Upanishads* the concepts of **samsara**, a cyclic round of death and rebirth characterized by suffering and perpetuated by desire, and **moksha**, liberation from *samsara*, became firmly rooted. Fundamental aspects of the Hindu world view, both are accepted by all but a handful of Hindus today, along with the belief in **karma**, the belief that one's present position in society is determined by the effect of one's previous actions in this and past lives.

Vishnu

The chief function of **Vishnu**, the "pervader", is to keep the world in order. With four arms holding a conch, discus, lotus and mace, he is blue-skinned, and is often shaded by a serpent, or resting on its coils, afloat on an ocean. He is often seen alongside his vehicle, the half-man-half-eagle Garuda. **Vaishnavites**, often distinguishable by two vertical lines on their foreheads, recognize Vishnu as the supreme lord, and hold that he has manifested himself on earth nine times. These incarnations, or *avatars*, have been as fish (Matsya), tortoise (Kurma), boar (Varaha), man-lion (Narsingh), dwarf (Vamana), axe-wielding brahmin (Parasuram), Rama, Krishna and Balaram (though some say that the Buddha is the ninth *avatar*). Vishnu's future descent to earth as Kalki, the saviour who will come to restore purity and destroy the wicked, is eagerly awaited.

The most important *avatars* are Krishna and Rama, star of the epic Ramayana (see p.812). **Krishna** is the hero of the Bhagavad Gita, in which he proposes three routes to salvation (*moksha*): selfless action (*karmayoga*), knowledge (*jnana*) and devotion to God (*bhakti*), and explains that *moksha* is attainable in this life, even without asceticism and renunciation. This appealed to all castes, as it denied the necessity of ritual and offici-ating brahmin priests, and evolved into the popular *bhakti* cult that legitimized love of God as a means to *moksha*. Through *bhakti*, Krishna's role was extended, and he assumed different faces: most popularly he is the playful cowherd who seduces and dances with cowgirls (*gopis*), giving each the illusion that she is his only lover. He is also pictured as a chubby, mischievous baby, known for his butter-stealing exploits, who inspires tender motherly love in women. Like Vishnu, Krishna is blue, and is often shown dancing and playing the flute. Vishnu is worshipped especially in the form of Lord Venkateshvara at Tirumala in Andhra Pradesh, where his role as the granter of wishes leads many thousands to his shrine daily to pray for favours.

Shiva

Shaivism was also inspired by *bhakti*, requiring selfless love from devotees in a quest for divine communion, but Shiva has never been incarnate on earth. He is presented in many different aspects, such as **Nataraja**, "Lord of the Dance", **Mahadev**, "Great God", and **Maheshvar**, "Divine Lord", source of all knowledge. Though he does have several terrible forms, his role extends beyond that of destroyer, and he is revered as the source of the whole universe. Shiva is often depicted with four or five faces, holding a trident, draped with serpents, and bearing a third eye in his forehead. In temples, he is identified with the *lingam*, or phallic symbol, resting in the *yoni*, a representation of female sexuality. Whether as statue or *lingam*, Shiva is guarded by his bull-vehicle, Nandi, and often accompanied by a consort, who assumes various forms and is looked upon as the vital energy, *shakti*, that empowers him. Their erotic exploits were a favourite sculptural subject between the ninth and twelfth centuries.

Shiva is the object of popular veneration all over India; devotees are identifiable by the horizontal lines (between one and three) painted on their foreheads. In particular, Shaivite **ascetics** worship Shiva in the aspect of the terrible **Bhairav**. The ascetics renounce family and caste ties and perform extreme meditative and yogic practices. Many smoke *ganja*, Shiva's favourite herb; all see renunciation and realization of God as the key to *moksha*. Some ascetic practices enter the realm of **tantrism**, in which confrontation with all that is impure, such as alcohol, death and sex, is used to merge the sacred and the profane, and bring about the profound realization that Shiva is omnipresent.

Ganesh

Tubby and smiling, elephant-headed **Ganesh**, the first son of Shiva and Parvati, is invoked before every undertaking (except funerals). Seated on a throne or lotus, his image is often placed above temple gateways, in shops and in houses. In his four arms he holds a conch, discus, a bowl of sweets and a water lily, and he is always attended by his vehicle, a rat. Credited with writing the Mahabharata as it was dictated by the sage Vyasa, Ganesh is regarded by many as the god of learning, the lord of success, prosperity and peace. In the South he is often known as **Vinayaka** and there is a huge festival, Vinayakapuja, in his honour in late monsoon, when images of the god are immersed in the sea. The celebration in Mumbai is the most ostentatious and famous.

Other gods and goddesses

Shiva's consort, **Parvati**, or Uma, is remarkable only for her beauty and fidelity, although in another aspect, as **Durga**, she is the fiercest of the female deities, eager to slay demons. In whatever form, Shiva's consort is *shakti*, the fundamental energy that spurs him into action. Durga has many aspects, and statues show her with ten arms, holding the head of a demon, a spear and other weapons; she tramples demons underfoot, or dances upon Shiva's body. She is particularly gruesome as **Kali,** wearing a garland of skulls, her tongue dripping with blood. In all her temples, animal sacrifices are a crucial element of worship, to satisfy her thirst for blood and deter her ruthless anger.

The comely goddess **Lakshmi**, usually shown sitting or standing on a lotus flower, and sometimes called Padma (lotus), is the embodiment of loveliness, grace and charm, and the goddess of prosperity and wealth. Vishnu's consort, she appears in different aspects alongside each of his *avatars*; the most important are Sita, wife of Rama, and Radha, Krishna's favourite *gopi*. In many temples she is shown as one with Vishnu, in the form of Lakshmi Narayan.

Pictured as a triumphant youth, bedecked with flowers, images of **Murugan**, son of Shiva and his consort Parvati, are particularly common in Tamil Nadu and rural Kerala (see box, p.616). He provides protection from evil and negative actions, which makes him a popular family deity. **Karttikeya** is popularly believed to be the second son of Shiva and Parvati. Primarily a god of war, he was popular among the northern Guptas, who worshipped him as Skanda, and the southern Chalukyas, for whom he was Subrahmanya. Usually shown with six faces, standing upright with bow and arrow, Karttikeya is commonly petitioned by those wishing for male offspring. Another son of Shiva, this time from a peculiar mythological union with Vishnu (see box, p.437), **Ayappa** is also associated with the role of protection, and his shrine in northern Kerala is a huge magnet to pilgrims, making the black-clad, mostly male, devotees a familiar sight. The common depiction of Ayappa riding a tiger with an entourage of leopards denotes his victory over evil.

India's great monkey god, **Hanuman**, features in the Ramayana as Rama's chief aide in the fight against the demon king of Lanka. He wields a mace and is the deity of acrobats and wrestlers, but is also seen as Rama and Sita's greatest devotee, and an author of Sanskrit grammar. As his representatives, monkeys find sanctuary in temples across southern India. The most beautiful Hindu goddess, **Saraswati**, the wife of Brahma – with her flawless milk-white complexion – sits or stands on a water lily or peacock, playing a lute, *sitar* or *vina*. A goddess of purification and fertility, she is also revered as the inventor of writing, queen of eloquence and goddess of music. Closely linked with the planet Saturn, **Sani** is feared for his destructive powers. His image, a black statue with protruding blood-red tongue, is often found on street corners; strings of green chillies and lemon are hung in shops and houses each Saturday (*Saniwar*) to ward off his evil influences.

The sacred cow, **Khamdenu**, receives devotion through the respect shown to all cows, who are allowed to amble through streets and temples all over India. Some myths record that Brahma created cows at the same time as brahmins, to provide *ghee* (clarified butter) for use in priestly ceremonies. To this day cow dung and urine are used to purify houses (the urine keeps insects at bay), and the killing or harming of cows by any Hindu is a grave offence. The cow is often referred to as mother of the gods, and each part of its body is significant: its horns symbolize the gods, its face the sun and moon, its shoulders Agni (god of fire) and its legs the Himalayas.

Philosophical trends

The complications presented by Hinduism's view of deities, *samsara*, *atman* (the human soul) and *moksha* naturally encouraged philosophical debate, and led eventually to the formation of six schools of thought, known as the **darshanas**. Each presented a different exposition of the true nature of *moksha* and how to attain it.

Foremost among these was the **Advaita Vedanta** school of **Shankara** (c.788–850 AD), who interpreted Hinduism as pure monotheism verging on monism (the belief that all is one: in this case, one with God). Drawing on Upanishadic writings, he claimed that they identified the essence of the human soul with that of God (*tat tvam asi*, "that thou art"), and that all else – the phenomenal world and all *devas* – is an illusion (*maya*) created by God. Shankara is revered as saint-philosopher at the twelve **jyotirlingas**, the sacred Shaivite sites associated with the unbounded *lingam* of light, which as a manifestation of Shiva once persuaded both Brahma and Vishnu to acknowledge Shiva's supremacy.

Another important *darshana* centred around the age-old practice of **yoga** (literally "the action of yoking [to] another"), elucidated by **Patanjali** (second century BC) in his Yoga Sutras. Interpreting yoga as the yoking of mind and body, or the yoking of the mind with God, Patanjali detailed various practices, which used in combination may lead to an understanding of the fundamental **unity** of all things. The most common form of yoga, and the best known in the West is Hatha yoga, whereby the body and its vital energies are brought under control through physical positions and breathing methods, with results said to range from attaining a calm mind to being able to fly through the air, enter other bodies or become invisible. Other practices include Mantra yoga, the recitation of formulas and meditation on mystical diagrams (mandalas), Bhakti yoga (devotion), Jnana yoga (knowledge) and Raja yoga (royal) – the highest form of yoga when the mind is absorbed in God.

Popular deities

Alongside the Dharma Shashtras and Dharma Shutras, the most important works of the *smriti* tradition, thought to have been completed by the fourth century AD at the latest, were the **Puranas**, long mythological stories focused on the Vedic gods and their heroic actions, and Hinduism's two great epics, the **Mahabharata** and the **Ramayana** (see boxes, p.810 & p.812). Through these texts, the main gods and goddesses became firmly embedded in the Hindu religion. Alongside **Brahma**, the creator, **Vishnu** was acknowledged as the preserver, and **Shiva** ("auspicious, benign"), referred to in the Rig Veda as Rudra, was recognized for his destructive powers. The three are often depicted in a trinity, *tri-murti*, but in time Brahma's importance declined, and Shiva and Vishnu became the most popular deities. Nearly all Hindus belong to sects that actively worship Shiva or Vishnu in one form or another (see box, p.738).

Other gods and goddesses who came alive in the mythology of the Puranas – each depicted in human or semi-human form and accompanied by an animal "**vehicle**" – are still venerated across South India. River goddesses, ancestors, guardians of particular places and protectors against disease and natural disaster are as central to village life as the major deities.

Caste and social structure

The stratification of Hindu society is rooted in the **Dharma Shashtras** and **Dharma Shutras**, scriptures written from "memory" (*smriti*) at the same time as the Vedas. These defined four hierarchical classes, or **varnas**, each assigned specific religious and social duties known as **varnashradharma**, and established Aryans as the highest social class. The **Aryans** already had a class system in place before reaching the Subcontinent; their nobility was known as the *kshatra* and the ordinary tribesman as the *vish*. However, their contact with darker-skinned people known as the **Dasas** caused them concern about racial purity, resulting in a division of society based on **varna** – literally "colour" – a unique institution of **racism** that has lasted over three thousand years. In descending order the *varnas* are: **brahmins** (priests and teachers), **kshatryas** (rulers and warriors), **vaishyas** (merchants and cultivators) and **shudras** (menials). The first three classes, known as "twice-born"– initially to distinguish those born in their native place and then born again during their induction as an Aryan – are distinguished by a sacred thread worn from the ceremony of initiation, and are granted full access to religious texts and rituals. Below all four categories, groups whose jobs involve contact with dirt or death (such as undertakers, leather workers and cleaners) were classified as **Untouchables**. Though discrimination against Untouchables is now a criminal offence, in part thanks to the campaigns of Gandhi – who renamed Untouchables *Harijans*, "Children of God" – the lowest stratum of society has by no means disappeared. Today, the word "**dalit**" is the politically correct term to use when talking about this class. Children, widows and ascetics remained outside the *varna* system.

When at the end of the Vedic age new ideas threatened the absolute power of the priesthood, and religions such as Buddhism and Jainism preached equality, the brahmins responded with the manuscript **Manu-smriti** (the words of Manu, the original man, remembered). Composed by a succession of authors some time around the third century BC, Manu-smriti laid out the *varna* system in detail and defined the role and tasks of each *varna*, as well as the strict interaction between each group. The moral grounds laid out for the system of division was that one should perform every task well and with pride rather than to try and take on someone else's tasks. This argument, combined with **karma** (the result of one's deeds), and the concept of rebirth which developed from the late Vedic period onwards, proposes that you are what you are born. Through good deeds you may have the fortune of being reborn at a higher level in the next life.

These ethics also carried through to the **Bhagavad Gita**, where Aryan beliefs are protected against reformers and non-believers by singing the virtues of each

The left hand versus the right

Literature suggests that caste came late to Tamil country, in about the ninth century. As Tamil society was fundamentally agrarian, there were few families who could claim to be *kshatriyas* (warriors) and so most of the population was divided between brahmins, *shudras* and untouchables. The largest group among the Tamils, the *shudras*, divided itself into a further two groups, the **left-handed** and the **right-handed** castes – the **Idangai** and the **Valangai**. The left and right hands allude to which hand was considered pure by either group (in most of Hindu India, the right hand is the pure hand while the left is menial). These two seemingly innocuous divisions have been at odds with each other ever since their inception, leading to bitter conflict and rivalry. The left-hand group includes craftsmen, weavers, some cultivators, cowherds and leather workers; the right-hand one includes traders, most cultivators, some weavers, musicians, barbers, washermen, potters and labourers.

of the four divisions – wisdom for the brahmin, valour for the *kshatriya*, industry for the *vaishya* and service for the *shudra*. Interaction between the divisions had become clearly defined. Manu-smriti, which continues to act as the foundation of **Hindu law**, lays down the rules of purity – for example, a *shudra*'s shadow may never cross a brahmin, and if it does the brahmin will have to perform a ritual to purify himself.

Within the four *varnas*, social status is further defined by **caste**, which refers to numerous social groupings within Hindu society. When the Portuguese first came to India in the sixteenth century, they came across these divisions and referred to them as "*castas*" (tribes, clans or families), a term which led to the word "caste". Caste lays restrictions on all aspects of life, from food consumption, religious obligations and contact with other castes, to the choice of marriage partners. Those that belong to other faiths have been given a caste status to clarify their position in the general social hierarchy; Christians in Kerala have actually adopted this system of classification and developed a caste system of their own.

Within the broader caste identity, there are sub-groups known as **jati**, which classify individuals by family and precise occupation (for example, a *vaishya* may be a jewellery-seller, cloth merchant or farmer). There are almost three thousand *jatis*, and the divisions and restrictions they have enforced have become, time and time again, the substance of reform movements and the target of critics. Whereas *varna* and caste is fixed from birth to death, there is a degree of flexibility to a *jati* identity, and some have a tendency to be upwardly mobile, in which case the members try to assume the ethics, manners and ways of the *jati* group they aspire to. Their tenure at this new rung in the hierarchy depends solely on whether the other *jatis* are willing to accept their new position. Despite this, Hindus still tend to marry members of the same caste and *jati* – marrying someone of a different caste often results in ostracism from both family and caste, leaving the couple stranded in a society where caste affiliation takes primacy over all other aspects of individual identity.

Castes have distinctive patterns of intra-caste relationships within themselves while at the same time interacting with other castes along strict rules of behaviour. Although castes maintain their structural place in society through both interaction and segregation, there is an element of fraternity, especially with castes close to each other in the hierarchy. Horizontal caste relations are limited by the diversity of India's geography and culture; while *varna* has its roots in theology, caste and *jati* is able to adapt itself to its local environment. Each region has such strong ritual and linguistic traits that a brahmin in Goa is unable to relate directly to a brahmin in Tamil Nadu.

Practice

A Hindu has three aims in life: **dharma**, fulfilling one's duty to family and caste and acquiring religious merit (*punya*) through right living; **artha**, the lawful making of wealth; and **karma**, desire and satisfaction. The primary concern of most Hindus is to reduce bad *karma* and acquire merit (*punya*), by honest and charitable living within the restrictions imposed by caste and worship, in the hope of attaining a higher status in rebirth.

These goals are linked with the four traditional **stages in life**. The first is as a child and student, devoted to learning from parents and a guru. Next comes the stage of householder, expected to provide for a family and raise sons. That accomplished, he or she may then take up a life of celibacy and retreat into the forest to meditate alone, and finally renounce all possessions to become a homeless ascetic, hoping to achieve the ultimate goal of *moksha*. According to ancient custom, the life of a high-class Hindu man progressed through four distinct phases – *brahmachari* (celibate) following his initiation or "thread ceremony", *grhastha* (householder), *vanaprashta* (forest dweller) following middle age and after his children have grown up, and finally, *sanyasi* (a renunciate). However, in practice, few follow this course in life and the *vanaprashta* is no more; in general, life is meant to progress along ordered lines from initiation (for high-caste Hindus) through education, career and marriage. A small number of Hindus who follow this ideal life, including some women, assume the final stage as **sanyasis**, saffron-clad **sadhus** who wander throughout India, begging for food and retreating to isolated caves, forests and hills to meditate. They are a common feature in most Indian towns, and many stay for long periods in particular temples. Not all have raised families: some assume the life of a *sadhu* at an early age as a *chella* (pupil or disciple) to an older *sadhu*.

However, strict rules still address the dharmic principles of **purity** and **pollution**, the most obvious of them requiring high-caste Hindus to limit their contact with potentially polluting lower castes. All bodily excretions are polluting (hence the strange looks Westerners receive when they blow their noses and return the handkerchief to their pocket or request toilet paper). Above all else, **water** is the agent of purification, used in ablutions before prayer, and revered in all rivers, especially Ganga (the Ganges).

In most Hindu homes and businesses, a small shrine is set up with pictures of chosen deities, and scriptures are read. Outside the home, worship takes place in temples, and consists of **puja**, or devotion to God. This may be a simple act of prayer, but more commonly it is a complex process when the god's image is circumambulated, offered flowers, rice, sugar and incense, and anointed with water, milk or sandalwood paste (which is usually done on behalf of the devotee by the temple priest, the *pujari*). The aim in puja is **darshan** – to glimpse the god – and thus receive his or her blessing. Whether devotees simply worship the deity in prayer, or make requests – for a healthy crop, a son, good results in exams, a vigorous monsoon or a cure for illness – they always leave the temple with *prasad*, an offering of food or flowers from the holy sanctuary, given to them by the *pujaris*.

Communal worship and get-togethers en route to pilgrimage sites are celebrated with *kirtan* or *bhajan*, singing of hymns, perhaps verses in praise of Krishna taken from the Bhagavad Purana, or repetitive cries of "Jay Shankar!" (Praise to Shiva). Temple ceremonies are conducted in Sanskrit by *pujaris* who tend the image in daily rituals that symbolically wake, bathe, feed and dress the god, and finish each day by preparing the god for sleep. The most elaborate is the evening ritual, **aarti**, when lamps are lit, blessed in the sanctuary, and passed around devotees amid the clanging of drums, gongs and cymbals. In many villages, shrines to *devatas*, village deities who function as protectors and may bring disaster if neglected, are more important than temples.

Each of the great stages in life – birth, **initiation** (when boys of the three twice-born castes are invested with a sacred thread, and a mantra is whispered into their ear by their guru), marriage, death and cremation – are marked by fervent prayer, energetic celebration and feasting. The most significant event in a Hindu's life is **marriage**, which symbolizes ritual purity, and for women is so important that it takes the place of initiation. Feasting, dancing and singing among the bride and groom's families, usually lasting for a week or more before and after the marriage, are the order of the day all over India. The actual marriage is consecrated when the couple walk seven times round a sacred fire, accompanied by sacred verses read by an officiating brahmin. Relatives pour in from all over the country and abroad to witness not just the union of man and wife, but also to reaffirm the group's social standing. Today, most Hindu marriages traditionally involve the parents, who negotiate the match; love marriages are increasingly common, especially in urban areas, but still tend to depend on parental consent and collusion.

The age-old Indian tradition of giving **dowry**, a gift of money, jewellery and goods from the bride's family to the groom's, is now officially illegal, but still widely demanded and invariably given, for fear that a daughter's welfare will be in jeopardy if it is withheld. Dowry is prevalent in both Hindu and Christian communities, and is as much practised by the upper and middle classes as it is by the poor, but for the latter it can represent an endless cycle of saving and debt with each new generation. Among more wealthy and cosmopolitan families, scooters, TVs and holidays are now the essential elements of a modern dowry. As it is a "gift", dowry is undeclared income, and the groom's family can place relentless pressure on the bride's family to continue providing "gifts" long after the wedding. The abuse, torture and burning of wives whose family provides a dowry that is below expectations is still all too common, especially in rural areas where there is little female literacy and brides are not aware of their rights under the constitution. Despite active opposition by progressive women's groups, dowry is a practice that is too deeply ingrained in Indian culture to easily eradicate, and the government seems unable to put a stop to it.

As a rule, Hindu society frowns upon **divorce**, but with increasing modernization, especially among the middle classes, it has become more common. Hindu law does not recognize divorce, and the legal procedure is relatively complicated.

For Hindus, **death** is an essential process in an endless cycle of rebirth in the grand illusion (*maya*) until the individual attains enlightenment and freedom (*moksha*) from *samsara* (transmigration). Hindus cremate their dead (except for young children, whom they bury or cast into a river). The eldest son is entrusted to light the funeral pyre and the ashes are scattered, usually on a sacred river, such as the Ganges in northern India. Rites after death can be lengthy and complicated according to each Hindu community, and the role of the *purohit* (priest) is indispensable. **Widows** traditionally wear white and, according to ancient Hindu belief, are considered to be outside society.

Pilgrimage

The Hindu calendar is jam-packed with **festivals** devoted to deities, re-enacting mythological stories and commemorating holy sites. The grandest festivals are held at places made holy by association with gods, goddesses, miracles and great teachers, or at sacred rivers and mountains; throughout the year these are all important **pilgrimage** sites, visited by devotees eager to receive *darshan*, glimpse the world of the gods, and attain merit. The journey, or *yatra*, to a pilgrimage site is every bit as significant as reaching the sacred location, and bands of Hindus (particularly *sadhus*) often walk from site to site. Modern transport, however, has made things easier, and every state lays on pilgrimage tours, when buses and Jeeps full of chanting families roar from one temple to another, filling up with religious souvenirs as they go.

South India has many important sites. The Venkateshvara temple atop Tirumala Hill in Andhra Pradesh claims to draw more pilgrims than any other holy place in the world. Every year, another two million or so devotees head up to the Ayappa Forest Temple at Sabarimala in Kerala. At Kanyakumari, the southern tip of India, the waters of the Indian Ocean, the Bay of Bengal and the Arabian

Sea are thought to merge at an auspicious point. Pilgrimages here are often combined with visits to the great temples of Tamil Nadu, where Shaivite and Vaishnavite saints established cults and India's largest temples were constructed. Madurai, Thanjavur, Chidambaram and Srirangam are major pilgrimage centres, representing the pinnacle of the architectural development that began at Mamallapuram. Their festivals often involve the pulling of deities on vast wooden chariots through the streets, lively and noisy affairs that make for an unforgettable experience. As well as specific temples sacred to particular gods, historical sites, such as the former Vijayanagar capital at Hampi, remain magnets for pilgrims. More than a common ideology, it is this map of sacred geography, entwined with popular mythology, that unites hundreds of millions of Hindus, who have also been brought together in nationalistic struggles, particularly in response to Christian missionaries and Muslim and British domination.

Islam

Across South India, **Muslims** – some ten percent of the total population – form a significant presence in almost every town, city and village. In most of the southern states, the percentage is slightly lower, the exception being Kerala, where nearly a quarter of the populace are Muslims, concentrated in fishing and trading communities right along the Malabar Coast. The only major southern city with a distinctly Islamic flavour is Hyderabad in Andhra Pradesh, although Mumbai and Chennai also boast well-established Muslim quarters.

The belief in only one god, **Allah**, the condemnation of idol worship and the observance of strict dietary laws and specific festivals sets Muslims apart from their Hindu neighbours, with whom they have coexisted for centuries, although not always peaceably. Such differences have helped fuel communal tensions, most notably during Partition in 1947, and more recently in the violent wake of the destruction of the Babri Masjid in Ayodhya in Uttar Pradesh in 1992. Although most of southern India managed to avoid the worst excesses of the early 1990s, Mumbai turned into a bloodbath, an experience documented in the magnificent film *Bombay*, directed by M. Ratnam.

Origins and development

Islam, "submission to God", was founded by **Mohammed** (570–632 AD), who is regarded as the last in a succession of prophets and who transmitted God's final and perfected revelation to mankind through the writings of the divinely revealed "recitation", the **Koran** (Qur'an). The Koran is the authoritative scripture of Islam that sets down the basics of Islamic belief: that there is one god, Allah (though he has 99 other beautiful names), and that Mohammed is his prophet. The beginning of Islam is dated at 622 AD, when Mohammed and his followers, exiled from Mecca, made the **hijra**, or migration, north to Yathrib, later known as Medina, "City of the Prophet". The *hijra* marks the start of the Islamic lunar calendar; the Gregorian year 2008 is for Muslims 1429 AH (*Anno Hijra*).

From Medina, Mohammed ordered raids on caravans heading for Mecca, and led his community in battles against the Meccans, inspired by *jihad*, or "striving" on behalf of God and Islam. This concept of holy war was the driving force behind the incredible expansion of Islam – by 713 Muslims had settled as far west as Spain and as far east as the banks of the Indus. When **Mecca** surrendered peacefully to Mohammed in 630, he cleared the sacred shrine, the Ka'ba, of idols, and proclaimed it the pilgrimage centre of Islam.

Mohammed was succeeded as leader of the *umma*, the Islamic community, by Abu Bakr, the prophet's representative, or caliph, the first in a line of caliphs who led the orthodox community until the eleventh century AD. However, a schism soon emerged when the third caliph, Uthman, was assassinated by followers of Ali, Mohammed's son-in-law, in 656 AD. This new sect, calling themselves **Shi'as**, "partisans" of Ali, looked to Ali and his successors, infallible *imams*, as leaders of the *umma* until 878 AD, and thereafter replaced their religious authority with a body of scholars, the *ulema*.

By the second century after the *hijra* (ninth century AD), orthodox, or **Sunni**, Islam had assumed the form in which it survives today. A collection of traditions about the prophet, **Hadith**, became the source for ascertaining the **Sunna**, customs, of Mohammed. From the Koran and the Sunna, seven major **articles of belief** were laid down: belief in one God; in angels as his messengers; in prophets (including Jesus and Moses); in the Koran; in the doctrine of predestination by God; in the Day of Judgement; and in the bodily resurrection of all people on this day. Religious practice was also standardized under the Muslim law, **Sharia**, in the **Five Pillars of Islam**. The first "pillar" is the confession of faith, *shahada*, that "There is no god but God, and Mohammed is his messenger." The other four are: prayer (*salat*) five times daily, almsgiving (*zakat*), fasting (*saum*), especially during the month of Ramadan and, if possible, pilgrimage (*hajj*) to Mecca, the ultimate goal of every practising Muslim.

Islam in South India

The first Muslims to settle in India were traders who arrived on the south coast in the seventh century, probably in search of timber for shipbuilding. Later, in 711, Muslims entered Sind, in the northwest, to take action against Hindu pirates, and dislodged the Hindu government. Their presence, however, was short-lived. Much more significant was the invasion of North India, first under **Mahmud of Ghazni**, then under the Turkish **sultanates** from the twelfth century on. The powerful **Mughals** (see p.720) succeeded them and pushed Islam deep into central and northern India, although the South remained largely unconquered.

The Muslims of the Malabar Coast, especially Kerala, owe their roots not to migration from central Asia but to the long history of trade and interaction with the Arab world. These Muslims of the **Moplah** community have nurtured a unique heritage alongside their Hindu and Christian neighbours. More recently, returning expatriate workers from the Gulf have helped to inject new wealth into the Moplah community and provide a facelift for towns like Kozhikode.

Many of the Muslims who settled in South India intermarried with Hindus, Buddhists and Jains, and the community spread. A further factor in its growth was the arrival of the **Sufis**, whose proselytizing missions in what is now northern Karnataka intensified with the rise of the Deccani sultans in the fourteenth century. Their teachings emphasized abstinence and self-denial in service to God, and stressed the attainment of inner knowledge of God through meditation and mystical experience. Sufi teachings particularly appealed to Shaivites and Vaishnavites, who shared their passion for personal closeness to God. This similarity meant that Sufis were more easily able to adapt to the cultural landscape of medieval India – although not all groups of Sufis were benign; some took to the task of spreading the word with zeal and with the occasional use of force.

For sufis, music (particularly *qawwali* singing) and dance is a significant medium of expression, and for this reason they have always been shunned by orthodox Muslims. However, this devotional music appealed to Hindus, for whom *kirtan* (singing) has played an important role in religious practice. One *qawwali*, relating the life of the Sufi saint Waris Ali Shah, draws parallels between his early life and the childhood of Krishna – an outrage for hardline Muslims, but attractive to Hindus. Sufi shrines, or *dargahs*, all over India bridge the gap between Islam and Hinduism. The most important in the region are Hazrat Gesu Daraz in Gulbarga, northern Karnataka; the hilltop shrine of Sikander Shah near Madurai; and the Golgumbaz in Bijapur.

Practice

Muslims should pray five times daily. They may do this at home or in a **mosque**; the latter are always full at noon on Friday for communal prayer (although the Druze, an esoteric sect based in Mumbai, hold communal prayers on Thursdays). All mosques are distinguishable by their bulbous white domes and minarets, from which a *muezzin* calls the faithful to prayer, although they range in scale from the grand edifices of Hyderabad to those in rural areas of Karnataka, where the landscape is scattered with mosques that are no more than a simple wall between two minarets, standing in a field outside the village. All mosques also feature a *mihrab*, or niche indicating the direction of prayer (to Mecca), and some may also include a *mimbar* or pulpit, from which the Friday sermon is read, a source of water for ablutions, and a separate balcony for women.

The position of **women** in Islam is a subject of great debate. It is customary for women to be veiled, and in strictly orthodox communities most wear a *burqa*, usually black, that covers them from head to toe. In larger cities, however, many women do not cover their head. Like other Indian women, Muslim women take second place to men in public, but in the home, where they are often shielded from men's eyes in an inner courtyard, they wield great influence. In theory, **education** is equally available to boys and girls, but girls tend to forgo learning soon after they are 16, encouraged instead to assume the traditional role of wife and mother.

On **marriage**, a woman receives a **dowry** from her husband as financial security and a sign of respect. Contrary to popular belief, polygamy is not widespread; while it does occur, and Mohammed himself had several wives, many Muslims prefer monogamy, and several sects actually stress it as the duty of Muslims.

In Islam, **divorce** may occur through the Indian court, or according to Muslim law, but a woman can only divorce her husband if there is mutual consent.

Christianity

Around fifteen million of India's twenty two million **Christians** live in the South, practising in one or another of the largely indigenized versions of established Church denominations. There has also been a spread of alternative experiments, including ashrams in which devotees practise a synthesis of Hindu and Christian elements, following programmes of retreat and meditation not so different from those in traditional monasteries in the West.

Christianity in South India

The Christian presence in South India goes back a long way – the **Apostle Thomas** ("Doubting Thomas") is said to have arrived in Kerala in 54 AD to convert itinerant Jewish traders living in the flourishing port of Muziris. There are many tales of the miracles performed by **Mar Thoma**, as St Thomas is known in Malayalam. One legend tells of how he approached a group of Hindu brahmins of Palur (now Malabar) who were trying to appease the gods by throwing water into the air; if the gods accepted the offerings, the droplets would hang above them. St Thomas also threw water in the air, which miraculously remained suspended, leading the brahmins to convert to Christianity there and then. It is customarily believed in the South that St Thomas was martyred and buried on December 21, 72 AD, at Mylapore in Chennai, whose former name, Madras, comes from the Syriac, "*madrasa*" meaning "monastery". His tomb has since been a major place of pilgrimage and, in recognition of this, in the late nineteenth century the Portuguese built the San Thome Cathedral on the site. By oral tradition, this is the **oldest Christian denomination** in the world, but actual documentary evidence of Christian activity in the Subcontinent can only be traced back to the sixth century, when immigrant Syrian communities were granted settlement rights along the Malabar coastline by royal charter. Christianity has flourished in Kerala ever since, aided by magnanimous Hindu rulers.

Christianity then spread across the South by attracting indigenous congregations; the concept of a godhead and soul, simplicity and prayer, was not dissimilar to traditional Indian mysticism and spirituality. In the pre-colonial era, the manner in which Christianity developed was largely shaped by the local cultural environment and Indian customs, with congregations bringing their social beliefs and habits to church. The Syrian Christians, especially, developed a social hierarchy that had overtones of the Hindu caste system.

The history of **foreign domination** from the sixteenth century in India is closely affiliated to the spread of Christianity across the whole Subcontinent. **St Francis Xavier** arrived in the Portuguese trading colony of Goa in 1552 to convert and establish missions to reach out to the Hindu "untouchables"; his tomb and alleged relics are retained in the Basilica of Bom Jesus in Old Goa. In 1559, the bloody and brutal Inquisition in Goal, led by Portuguese Jesuit missionaries, at the behest of their king, marked the height of a campaign to "cleanse" the small colony of Hindu and Muslim religious practice, although it was actually set up primarily to purge the colony of Jews.

The **British** initially took the attitude that the Subcontinent was a heathen and polytheistic civilization waiting to be proselytized. By the nineteenth century, conversion to Christianity was particularly appealing to those of the lower and sub-castes, and in the South mass conversions took place in Andhra Pradesh. Later, the British realized that conversion did not necessarily incur a change in moral and educational standards; they gradually became less zealous in their missionary efforts, content to provide social welfare among the more established Christian communities and build very English-looking churches in their cantonments.

Christian society

Today, Christians in Goa and Kerala number nearly a third and a fifth of the population respectively. While most in Goa follow the **Catholicism** of their former Portuguese rulers, Kerala is home to an array of denominations, ranging from Catholic through Syrian and Malankara **Orthodox** to the Church of South India, modelled on **Anglicanism**.

As Christianity, based on the equality and brotherhood expounded by its founder Jesus Christ, is intended to be free of caste stigmas, it is attractive to those seeking social advancement and consequently there have always been conversions among disaffected tribal peoples and Untouchables. Christianity's integration with Hinduism and Islam in southern India has meant that it has largely avoided the situation in some of the northern states, where there has been a rise in tension between Christian communities and Hindu extremists.

Practice

Christian practice in South India has, over the centuries, absorbed many elements of Hindu worship. In Tamil Nadu, Christian **festivals** are highly structured along "caste" lines and, like their Hindu brethren, Tamil Christians never eat beef or pork, which are considered to be polluting. In many churches across the South, you will see devotees offering the Hindu *arati*-plate of coconut, sweets and rice, and women wearing a *tilak* dot on their forehead. Christians carry plates of food to the graves of their ancestors to honour their dead, on the anniversary of their death, in much the same manner that a Hindu family will share a feast on such a day.

In the same way that Hindus and Muslims consider the **pilgrimage** to be an integral part of life's journey, Indian Christians tend to visit churches where there is a relic, such as a shard of finger bone alleged to have belonged to St Thomas. Most churches in Kerala and Goa claim to hold at least one part of the saint's body, especially his fingers and toes. These relics are brought out on special feast days, and huge crowds will jostle to catch a rare sight of the tiny bit of yellowing bone lying in a casket.

Christians in India have never adopted the practice of giving or receiving **dowry** on the occasion of marriage, although in an arrangement similar to Hindu practice, a Christian **marriage** tends to take place between a man and woman who are members of the same denomination or sect. In most cases, the parents of the couple play a central role in the selection process, paying particular attention to the social status and education of the prospective bride or groom. If a woman becomes a **widow**, she is not socially ostracized as a Hindu woman would be, but is instead encouraged to remarry.

Buddhism

For several centuries **Buddhism** dominated India, with adherents in almost every part of the Subcontinent. However, having reached its height in the fifth century, it had been all but eclipsed by the time of the Muslim conquest. Today, Buddhists constitute a minute fraction of the population in South India, but a collection of superb monuments offer firm reminders of the previous importance of the faith, and its central role in southern India's cultural legacy.

Origins and development

The founder of Buddhism, **Siddhartha Gautama**, known as the **Buddha**, "the awakened one", was born into a wealthy *kshatrya* family in Lumbini, north of the Gangetic plain in present-day Nepal, around 566 BC. Brought up in luxury as a prince and a Hindu, he married at an early age but renounced family life when he was 30. Unsatisfied with the explanations of worldly suffering proposed by Hindu gurus, and convinced that asceticism did not lead to spiritual awakening, Siddhartha spent years in meditation, wandering through the ancient kingdom of Magadha, in northeast India. His enlightenment (*bodhi*) is said to have taken place under a *bodhi* tree in **Bodhgaya** (Bihar), after a night of contemplation during which he resisted the worldly temptations set before him by the demon, Mara. Soon afterwards he gave his first sermon in **Sarnath**, just outside Varanasi, now a major pilgrimage centre. For the rest of his life he taught, expounding **Dharma**, the true nature of the world, human life and spiritual attainment. Before his death (c.486 BC) in Kushinagara (Uttar Pradesh, North India), he established the **sangha**, a community of monks and nuns, who continued his teachings.

The Buddha's view of life incorporated the Hindu concepts of *samsara* and karma, but remodelled the ultimate goal of religion, calling it **nirvana** (literally "no wind"). Indefinable in worldly terms, *nirvana* is represented by clarity of mind, pure understanding and unimaginable bliss. Its attainment signals an end to rebirth, but no communion of a "soul" with God; neither has independent existence. The most important concept outlined by the Buddha was that all things, subject to change and dependence, are characterized by **impermanence**, and there is **no self**, no permanent ego, so **attachment** to anything (possessions, emotions, spiritual attainment and *devas*) must be renounced before impermanence can be grasped, and *nirvana* realized.

Disregarding caste and priestly dominance in ritual, the Buddha formulated a teaching open to all. His followers took refuge in the "three jewels" – the Buddha, Dharma, and Sangha – and his teachings became known as **Theravada**, or "Doctrine of the Elders". By the first century BC the **Tripitaka**, or "Three Baskets" (a Pali canon in three sections), had set out the basis for early Buddhist practice. *Dana* (selfless giving) and *sila* (precepts which aim at avoiding harm to oneself and others), were presented as the most important guidelines for all Buddhists, and the essential code of practice for the lay community.

Carried out with good intentions, *dana* and *sila* maximize the acquisition of good karma, and minimize material attachment, thus making the individual open to the more religiously oriented teachings, the **Four Noble Truths**. The first of these states that all is suffering (*dukkha*), not because every action is necessarily unpleasurable, but because nothing in the phenomenal world is permanent or reliable. The second truth states that *dukkha* arises through attachment, the third refers to *nirvana*, the cessation of suffering, and the fourth details the path to *nirvana*. Known as the **Eightfold Path** – right understanding, thought, speech, action, livelihood, effort, mindfulness and concentration – it aims at reducing attachment and ego and increasing awareness, until all four truths are thoroughly comprehended, and *nirvana* is achieved. Even this should not be clung to – those who experience it are advised by the Buddha to use their understanding to help others to achieve realization.

The Sanskrit word **bhavana**, referred to in the West as **meditation**, translates literally as "bringing into being". Traditionally meditation is divided into two categories: **Samatha**, or calm, which stills and controls the mind, and **Vipassana**, or insight, during which thought processes and the noble truths are investigated, leading ultimately to a knowledge of reality. Today, both methods are taught.

At first, Buddhist iconography represented the Buddha by symbols such as a footprint, *bodhi* tree, parasol or vase. These can be seen on stupas (domed monuments containing relics of the Buddha) built throughout India from the time of the Buddhist emperor Ashoka (see p.712), and in ancient Buddhist caves, which served as meditation retreats and *viharas* (monasteries). Though the finest examples are to be found in the North, there are interesting sites in the South, such as the stupas at Amaravati and Nagarjunakonda in Andhra Pradesh and caves at Aihole and Badami in Karnataka.

This artistic development coincided with an increase in the devotional side of Buddhism, and the recognition of **bodhisattvas** – those bound for enlightenment who delayed their self-absorption in *nirvana* to become teachers, spurred by compassion and altruism. The importance of the *bodhisattva* ideal grew as a new school, the **Mahayana**, or "Great Vehicle", emerged. By the twelfth century it had become fully established and, somewhat disparagingly, renamed the old school **Hinayana**, or "Lesser Vehicle". Mahayanists proposed emptiness (*sunyata*) as the fundamental nature of all things, taking to extremes the belief that nothing has independent existence. The **wisdom** necessary to understand *sunyata*, and the **skilful means** required to put wisdom into action in daily life and teaching, and interpret emptiness in a positive sense, became the most important qualities of Mahayana Buddhism. Before long *bodhisattvas* were joined in both scripture and art by female consorts who embodied wisdom.

Theravada Buddhism survives today in Sri Lanka, Burma, Thailand, Laos and Cambodia. Mahayana Buddhism spread from India to China, Japan, Korea and Vietnam, where it incorporated local gods and spirits into a family of *bodhisattvas*. In many places further evolution saw the adoption of magical methods, esoteric teachings and the full use of sense experience to bring about spiritual transformation, resulting in a separate school known as **Mantrayana** or **Vajrayana** based on texts called *tantras*. Mantrayana encouraged meditation on *mandalas* (symbolic diagrams representing the cosmos and internal spiritual attainment), sexual imagery and sometimes sexual practice.

Practice

For Buddhist monks and nuns, and some members of the lay community, meditation is an integral part of religious life. Most lay Buddhists concentrate on *dana* and *sila*, and on auspicious days, such as *Vesak* (marking the Buddha's birth, enlightenment and death), make **pilgrimages** to Bodhgaya, Sarnath, Lumbini and Kushinagar (all in northern India). After laying offerings before Buddha statues, devotees gather in silent meditation, or join in chants taken from early Buddhist texts.

Uposathas, full moon days, are marked by continual **chanting** through the night. Temples are lit by glimmering butter lamps, often set afloat on lotus ponds, among the flowers that represent the essential beauty and purity to be found in each person in the thick of the confusing "mud" of daily life.

Jainism

The **Jain** tradition has been tremendously influential for at least 2500 years, though there is now only a tiny Jain population in South India, with most families involved in commerce and trade. Similarities to Hindu worship, and a shared respect for nature and non-violence, have contributed to the decline of the Jain society through conversion to Hinduism, but there is no antagonism between the two faiths.

Origins and development

The Jain doctrine is based upon the teachings of **Mahavira**, or "Great Hero", the last in a succession of 24 **tirthankaras** ("crossing-makers") said to appear on earth every 300 million years. Mahavira (c.599–527 BC) was born as Vardhamana Jnatrputra into a *kshatrya* family near modern Patna, in northeast India. Like the Buddha, Mahavira rejected family life at the age of thirty, and spent years wandering as an ascetic, renouncing all possessions in an attempt to conquer attachment to worldly values. Firmly opposed to sacrificial rites and caste distinctions, after gaining complete understanding and detachment, he began teaching others, not about Vedic gods and divine heroes, but about the true nature of the world, and the means required for release, *moksha*, from an endless cycle of rebirth.

His teachings were written down in the first millennium BC, and Jainism prospered throughout India, under the patronage of kings such as Chandragupta Maurya (third century BC). Not long after, there was a schism, in part based on linguistic and geographical divisions, but mostly due to differences in monastic practice. The **Digambaras** ("sky-clad") believed that nudity was an essential part of world renunciation, and that women are incapable of achieving liberation from worldly existence. The ("white-clad") **Svetambaras**, however, disregarded the extremes of nudity, incorporated nuns into monastic communities and even acknowledged a female *tirthankara*.

In an incredibly complicated process of philosophical analysis known as **Anekanatavada** (many-sidedness), Jainism approaches all questions of existence, permanence and change from seven different viewpoints, maintaining that things can be looked at in an infinite number of valid ways. Thus it claims to remove the intellectual basis for violence, avoiding the potentially damaging result of holding a one-sided view. In this respect Jainism accepts other religious philosophies, and it has adopted, with a little reinterpretation, several Hindu festivals and practices.

Focusing on the practice of **ahimsa** (non-violence), Jains follow a rigorous discipline to avoid harm to all **jivas**, or "souls", which exist not only in animals and humans, but also in plants, water, fire, earth and air. They assert that every *jiva* is pure, omniscient and capable of achieving liberation, or *moksha*, from existence in this universe. However, *jivas* are obscured by **karma**, a form of subtle matter that clings to the soul, is born of action, and binds the *jiva* to physical existence. For the most orthodox Jain, the only way to dissociate karma from the *jiva*, and thereby escape the wheel of death and rebirth, is to follow the path of asceticism and meditation, rejecting passion, wrong view, attachment, carelessness and impure action.

Practice

Today the two Jain sects worship at different temples, but the number of naked Digambaras is minimal. Many Svetambara monks and nuns wear white masks to avoid breathing in insects, and carry a "fly-whisk", sometimes used to brush their path; none will use public transport, and they often spend days or weeks walking barefoot to a pilgrimage site. Practising Jain householders vow to avoid injury, falsehood, theft (which includes cheating in commerce), infidelity and worldly attachment.

Jain **temples** are wonderfully ornate, with pillars, brackets and spires carved into voluptuous maidens, musicians, saints and even Hindu deities; the swastika symbol commonly set into the marble floors is central to Jainism, representing the four states of rebirth as gods, humans, "hell beings", or animals and plants.

Worship in temples consists of prayer and puja before images of the *tirthankaras*; the devotee circumambulates the image, chants sacred verses and makes offerings of flowers, sandalwood paste, rice, sweets and incense. It's common to fast four times a month on *parvan* (holy) days, the eighth and fourteenth days of the moon's waxing and waning periods. While reducing attachment to the body, this emulates the fast to death (while in meditation), or *sallekhana*, accepted by Jain mendicants as a final rejection of attachment, and a relatively harmless way to end worldly life.

To enter a monastic community, lay Jains must pass through eleven *pratimas*, starting with right views, the profession of vows, fasting and continence, and culminating in the renunciation of family life. Once a monk or nun, a Jain aims to clarify understanding through meditation, hoping to extinguish passions and sever the ties of karma and attachment, entering fourteen spiritual stages (*gunas-thanas*) to emerge as a fully enlightened, omniscient being. Whether pursuing a monastic or lay lifestyle, however, Jains recognize the rarity of enlightenment, and religious practice is, for the most part, aimed at achieving a state of rebirth more conducive to spiritual attainment.

Pilgrimage sites are known as **tirthas**; the word also translates as "river crossing", sacred to Hindus because of the purificatory nature of water. One of the foremost Svetambara *tirthas* is **Shatrunjaya**, in Gujarat in northern India, where over nine hundred temples crown a single hill. There is also an important Digambara *tirtha* at **Sravanabelgola** in Karnataka, where an eighteen-metre-high image of Bahubali (recognized as the first human to attain liberation) stands at the summit of a hill, and is anointed in the huge *abhishekha* festival every twelve years.

Zoroastrianism

Of all South India's religious communities, Western visitors are least likely to come across – or recognize – **Zoroastrians**, who have no distinctive dress and few houses of worship. Most live in Mumbai, where they are known as **Parsis** (Persians) and are active in business, education and politics. Today, the most famous Parsis are the Tata family – leading industrialists who have long held an unprecedented monopoly over a vast range of commercial interests that range from trucks, cars and scooters to several major steel and chemical factories, tea plantations and even lipsticks. Economic successes aside, Zoroastrian numbers (roughly ninety thousand) are dwindling rapidly, mainly due to the strict rule of intermarriage and a sharp decline in the birth rate; Parsis are increasingly forced to marry into the wider community and their distinct identity is slowly becoming diluted.

Origins and development

The religion's founder, **Zarathustra** (Zoroaster), who lived in Iran in 6000 BC according to Zoroastrians – most modern historians place him somewhere between 1700 and 1400 BC – was the first religious prophet to expound a dualistic philosophy, based on the opposing powers of good and evil. For Zarathustra, the absolute, wholly good and wise god, **Ahura Mazda**, together with his holy spirit and six emanations present in earth, water, the sky, animals, plants and fire, is constantly at odds with an evil power, **Angra Mainyu**, who is aided by **daevas**, or evil spirits.

Mankind, whose task on earth is to further good, faces judgement after death, and depending on the proportion of good and bad words, thoughts and actions will find a place in heaven or suffer the torments of hell. Zarathustra looked forward to a day of judgement, when a saviour, **Saoshyant**, miraculously born of a seed of the prophet and a virgin maiden, will appear on earth, restoring Ahura Mazda's perfect realm and expelling all impure souls and spirits to hell.

The first Zoroastrians to enter India arrived on the Gujarati coast in the tenth century, soon after the Arabian conquest of Iran, and by the seventeenth century most had settled in Mumbai.

Practice

Zoroastrian practice is based on the responsibility of every man and woman to choose between good and evil and to respect God's creations. Five daily prayers, usually hymns (*gathas*), uttered by Zarathustra and standardized in the main Zoroastrian text, the **Avesta**, are said in the home or in a temple, before a fire, which symbolizes the realm of truth, righteousness and order. For this reason, Zoroastrians are often, incorrectly, called "fire-worshippers". **No Ruz**, or "New Day", which celebrates the creation of fire and the ultimate triumph of good over evil, is the most popular Zoroastrian festival, taking place in late March.

Members of other faiths may not enter Zoroastrian temples, but one custom that is evident to outsiders is the method of disposing of the dead. A body is laid on a high open rooftop (or isolated hill) known as *dakhma* (often referred to as a "tower of silence"), for the flesh to be eaten by vultures, and the bones cleansed by the sun and wind. Recently, some Zoroastrians, by necessity, have adopted more common methods of cremation or burial; in order not to bring impurity to fire or earth, they only use electric crematoria, and shroud coffins in concrete before laying them in the ground.

Sacred art and architecture

I t's often said that South India is the most religious place on earth, a claim given some credence by the region's vast storehouse of sacred art and architecture. For thousands of years, successive chieftains, emperors, nawabs and nizams – whether Hindu, Buddhist, Jain or Muslim – have assigned huge sums of money and human resources towards raising religious structures, as much to symbolize the power of their earthly rule as the superhuman power of the gods and natural forces. Some, like the towering temple *gopuras* of Tamil Nadu and the gigantic Golgumbaz tomb at Bijapur, were conceived on an awesome scale; others, such as the rock-cut Pallava shrines in Mamallapuram and the meticulously crafted architecture of the Hoysalas in Karnataka, were more intimate. Yet the South's religious monuments have one thing in common: nearly all of them testify to the Indians' enduring love of elaboration. Even the most austere Muslim sultans of the Deccan couldn't resist decorating their tombs and mosques with exquisite geometric shapes, while the attention to fine detail demonstrated by the sculptors of the Chola statues is astonishing when juxtaposed with the sheer size of the buildings within which they stand.

Another common feature of South Indian religious art and architecture is the extent to which the various mediums have, over the centuries, been governed by **convention**. In the same way as ritual follows precise rules passed through generations, buildings and their decor conform to the most exacting specifications, set down in ancient canonical texts. This is particularly true of **iconography** – the complex language of symbols used to represent gods, goddesses and saints, in their many and diverse forms. Even nowadays, the stone-carvers of Mamallapuram spend years learning how to render the exact size and lines of their subjects. Without such exactitude, an icon or religious building is deemed to be devoid of its essential power. If the proportions are incorrect, the all-important sequence of auspicious numbers through which the magical power of the gods become manifest is disrupted, and the essential order of the universe compromised.

Such rigorous adherence to tradition would seem to leave little scope for innovation, but somehow South Indian artists have devised an amazing variety of **regional styles**. One of the most absorbing aspects of travelling around the peninsula is comparing these. After a while, you'll begin to be able to differentiate between them and, in the process, gain a more vivid sense of the people and period that created them. The following descriptions are intended as a primer; for more in-depth explorations, hunt out some of the titles listed on p.798.

Stupas

Among the very earliest sacred structures built in India were hemispherical mounds known as **stupas**, which have been central to Buddhist worship since the sixth century BC, when the Buddha himself modelled the first prototype.

Asked by one of his disciples for a symbol to help disseminate his teachings after his death, the master took his begging bowl, teaching staff and a length of cloth – his only worldly possessions – and arranged them into the form of a stupa, using the cloth as a base, the upturned bowl as the dome and the stick as the projecting finial, or spire.

Originally, stupas were simple burial mounds of compacted earth and stone containing relics of the Buddha and his followers. As the religion spread, however, the basic components multiplied and became imbued with **symbolic significance**. The main dome, or *anda* – representing the sacred mountain, or axis, linking heaven and earth – grew larger, while the wooden railings, or *vedikas*, surrounding it were replaced by massive stone equivalents. A raised ambulatory terrace, or *medhi*, was added to the vertical sides of the drum, along with two flights of stairs and four ceremonial entrances, carefully aligned with the cardinal points. Finally, crowing the tip of the stupa, the single spike evolved into a three-tiered umbrella, or *chhattra*, representing the Three Jewels of Buddhism: the Buddha, the Law and the community of monks, or *sangam*.

The *chhattra*, usually enclosed within a low square stone railing, or *harmika* (a throwback to the days when sacred *bodhi* trees were surrounded by fences), formed the topmost point of the axis, directly above the reliquary in the heart of the stupa. Ranging from bits of bone wrapped in cloth to fine caskets of precious metals, crystal and carved stone, the reliquaries were the "seeds" and their protective mounds the "egg". Excavations on the estimated eighty-four thousand stupas scattered around the Subcontinent have shown that the solid interiors were also sometimes built as elaborate **mandalas** – symbolic patterns that exerted a beneficial influence over the stupa and those who walked around it. The ritual of **circumambulation**, or *pradakshina*, which enabled the worshipper to tap into a magical force-field and be transported from the mundane to the divine realms, was always carried out in a clockwise direction from the east, in imitation of the sun's passage across the heavens.

In South India, the **Satavahana** (or Andhra) dynasty, who ruled a vast tract of the country towards the end of the first millennium (see History, p.713), erected stupas across the region, among them the Great Stupa at **Amaravati** in Andhra Pradesh (see p.668). Little of this once-impressive monument remains in situ, but you can admire some of the outstanding sculpture that decorated its ornamental gateways (*toranas*) in the Government Museum at Chennai (see p.510). To see a stupa in action, however, you have to follow in the footsteps of the emperor Ashoka's missionaries southwards to Sri Lanka, where stupas are still revered as repositories of sacred energy.

Temples

To make sense of Hindu **temples**, you need to be able to identify their common features. Many of these conventions are recorded in the **Shilpa Shastras** – Sanskrit manuals that set out, in meticulous detail, ancient building specifications and their symbolic significance.

Unlike Christian churches or Muslim mosques, temples are not simply places of worship, but are objects of worship in themselves – recreations of the "Divine-Cosmic-Creator-Being" or the particular deity enshrined within them. For a Hindu, to move through a temple is akin to entering the very body of the god, and to glimpse the deity in the shrine-room during the moment of *darshan*, or ritual viewing, is the culmination of an act of worship. In South India, this concept also finds expression in the technical terms used in the Shastras to designate different parts of the structure: the foot, shin, torso, neck, head and so forth.

The temples of Tamil Nadu

No Indian state is more dominated by its **temples** than Tamil Nadu, whose huge temple towers dominate most towns and villages. The majority were built in honour of Shiva or Vishnu and their consorts; all are characterized not only by their design and sculptures, but by constant activity – devotion, dancing, singing, pujas, festivals and feasts. Each is tended by brahmin priests, recognizable by their *dhotis* (loincloths), a sacred thread draped over the right shoulder and marks on the forehead. One to three horizontal (usually white) lines distinguish Shaivites; vertical lines (yellow or red), often converging into a near-V shape, are common among Vaishnavites.

Dravida, the temple architecture of Tamil Nadu, first took form in the **Pallava** port of **Mamallapuram**. A step up from the cave retreats of Hindu and Jain ascetics, the earliest Pallava monuments were **mandapas**, shrines cut into rock-faces and fronted by columns. The magnificent **bas-relief** at Mamallapuram, **Arjuna's Penance**, shows the fluid carving of the Pallavas at its most exquisite. This sculptural skill was transferred to free-standing temples, **rathas**, carved out of single rocks and incorporating the essential elements of Hindu temples: the dim inner sanctuary, the *garbhagriha*, capped with a modest tapering spire featuring repetitive architectural motifs. In turn, the Shore Temple was built with three shrines, topped by a *vimana* similar to the towering roofs of the *rathas*; statues of Nandi, Shiva's bull, later to receive pride of place, surmount its low walls. In the finest structural Pallava temple, the Kailasanatha Temple at **Kanchipuram**, the sanctuary, again crowned with a pyramidal *vimana*, stands within a courtyard enclosed by high walls. The projecting and recessing bays of the walls, carved with images of Shiva, his consort and ghoulish mythical lions, *yalis*, were the prototype for later styles.

Pallava themes were developed in Karnataka by the Chalukyas and Rashtrakutas, but it was the Shaivite **Cholas** who spearheaded Tamil Nadu's next architectural phase, in the tenth century. In **Thanjavur**, Rajaraja I created the Brihadeshwara temple principally as a status symbol. Its proportions far exceed any attempted by the Pallavas. Set within a vast walled courtyard, the sanctuary, fronted by a small pillared hall (*mandapa*), stands beneath a sculpted *vimana* that soars over sixty metres high. Most sculptures once again feature Shiva, but the **gopuras**, or towers, each side of the eastern gateway to the courtyard, were an innovation, as were the lions carved into the base of the sanctuary walls, and the pavilion erected over Nandi in front of the sanctuary. The second great Chola temple was built in **Gangaikondacholapuram** by Rajendra I. Instead of a mighty *vimana*, he introduced new elements, adding subsidiary shrines and placing an extended *mandapa* in front of the central sanctuary, its pillars writhing with dancers and deities.

By the time of the thirteenth-century **Vijayanagar** kings, the temple was central to city life, the focus for civic meetings, education, dance and theatre. The Vijayanagars extended earlier structures, adding enclosing walls around a series of *prakaras*, or courtyards, and erecting free-standing *mandapas* for use as meeting halls, elephant stables, stages for music and dance, and ceremonial marriage halls. Raised on superbly decorated columns, these *mandapas* became known as **thousand-pillared halls** (*kalyan mandapas*). **Tanks** were added, doubling as water stores and washing areas, and used for festivals when deities were set afloat in boats surrounded by glimmering oil lamps.

Under the Vijayanagars, the *gopuras* were enlarged and set at the cardinal points over the high gateways to each *prakara*, to become the dominant feature. Rectangular in plan, and embellished with images of animals and local saints or rulers as well as deities, *gopuras* are periodically repainted in pinks, blues, whites and yellows, a sharp and joyous contrast with the earthy browns and greys of halls and sanctuaries below. **Madurai** is the place to check out Vijayanagar architecture, and experience the timeless temple rituals. Dimly lit halls and sun-drenched courtyards hum with murmured prayers, and regularly come alive for festivals in which Shiva and his "fish-eyed" consort (see p.738) are hauled through town on mighty wooden chariots tugged by hordes of devotees. Outside Tiruchirapalli, the temple at **Srirangam** was extended by the Vijayanagar Nayaks to become South India's largest. Unlike that in Madurai, it incorporates earlier Chola foundations. The ornamentation, with pillars formed into rearing horses, is superb.

Hoysala temples

The Hoysala dynasty ruled southwestern Karnataka between the eleventh and thirteenth centuries. From the twelfth century, after the accession of King Vishnu Vardhana, they built a series of distinctive temples centred primarily at three sites: **Belur** (see p.297) and **Halebid** (see p.295) close to modern Hassan, and **Somnathpur** (see p.288), near Mysore.

At first sight, and from a distance, Hoysala temples appear to be modest structures, compact and even squat. On closer inspection, however, their profusion of fabulously detailed and sensuous sculpture, covering every inch of the exterior, is astonishing. Detractors are prone to class Hoysala art as decadent and overly fussy, but anyone with an eye for craftsmanship is likely to marvel at these jewels of Karnatakan art.

The intricacy of the carvings was made possible by the material used in construction: a soft **steatite soapstone** which on oxidization hardens to a glassy, highly polished surface. The level of detail, similar to that seen in sandal-wood and ivory work, became increasingly freer and fluid as the style developed, and reached its highest point at Somnathpur. Beautiful bracket figures, often delicate portrayals of voluptuous female subjects, were placed under the eaves, fixed by pegs top and bottom. A later addition (except possibly in the Somnathpur temple), these serve no structural function.

Another technique more usually associated with wood is the unusual treatment of the massive stone pillars: lathe-turned, they resemble those of the wooden temples of Kerala. They were probably turned on a horizontal plane, pinned at each end, and rotated with the use of a rope. It may be no coincidence that, to this day, wood-turning is still a local speciality. Only the central shaft of each pillar seems to have been turned; in the base and capitals, a less precise, presumably handworked, imitation of turning is evident.

The architectural style of the Hoysala temples is commonly referred to as **vesara**, or "hybrid" (literally "mule"), rather than belonging to either the northern, nagari, or southern, Dravidian styles. However, they show great affinity with nagari temples of western India, and represent another fruit of contact, like music, painting and literature, facilitated by the trade routes between the North and the South. All Hoysala temples share a star-shaped plan, built on high plinths (*jagati*) which follow the shape of the sanctuaries and *mandapas* to provide a raised surrounding platform. Such northern features may have been introduced by the designer and artists of the earliest temple at Belur, who were imported by Vishnu Vardhana from further north in Andhra Pradesh. Also characteristic of the Hoysala style is the use of ashlar masonry, without mortar. Some pieces of stones are joined by pegs of iron or bronze, or mortice and tenon joints. Ceilings inside the *mandapas* are made up of corbelled domes, looking similar to those of the Jain temples of Rajasthan and Gujarat; in the Hoysala style they are only visible from inside.

Keralan temples

As you'd expect from one of India's most culturally distinct regions, **Kerala**'s temples are quite unlike those elsewhere in the South. Their most striking features are the sloping tiled roofs – built to defend against torrential downpours – that crown the sanctuaries, colonnades and gateways. In addition, the innermost shrines are invariably circular, or apsidal – perhaps in imitation of earlier indigenous styles.

In the corner of the spacious temple courtyards (which are often very broad to make room for the annual elephant processions) stands a covered hall with beautiful lathe-turned pillars and wooden panels, where performances of Kathakali and other forms of ritualized theatre are held (see p.787). In some older temples, **murals** also adorn the inner faces of the high enclosing walls (see p.762).

Keralan temples are generally closed to non-Hindus, but many make exceptions during festivals, when drum bands, tuskers and ritual dances comprise some of the most compelling spectacles in all of South India (see Thrissur Puram, p.470).

Goan temples

Stick to the former Portuguese heartland of Goa, and you'd be forgiven for thinking the state was exclusively Christian. It isn't, of course, as the innumerable brightly painted Hindu temples hidden amid the lush woodland and areca groves of the more outlying areas confirm. The oldest-established and best known lie well away from the coastal resorts, but are worth hunting out.

Goa's first stone temples date from the rule of the Kadamba dynasty, between the fifth and fifteenth century AD. From the few fragments of sculpture and masonry unearthed at the ruins of their old capital, it is clear that these were as skilfully constructed as the famous monuments of the neighbouring Deccan region. However, only one, the richly carved Mahadeva temple at **Tamdi Surla** in east Goa, has survived. The rest were systematically destroyed, first by Muslim invaders, and later by the Portuguese.

Goan temples incorporate the main elements of Hindu architecture, but boast some unusual features of their own – some developed in response to the local climate or the availability of building materials, others the result of outside influences. The impact of European-Portuguese styles (inevitable given the fact that the majority of Goan temples were built during the colonial era, but ironic considering that the Portuguese destroyed the originals) is most evident on the exterior of the buildings. Unlike conventional Hindu temple towers, which are curvilinear, Goan *shikharas*, taking their cue from St Cajetan's church in Old Goa (see p.197), consist of octagonal drums crowned by tapering copper domes. Hidden inside the top of these is generally a pot of holy water called a **poornakalash**, drawn from a sacred Hindu river or spring. The sloping roofs of the *mandapas*, with their projecting eves and terracotta tiles, are also distinctively Latin, while the glazed ceramic Chinese dragons often perched above them, originally imported from Macau, add to the colonial feel. Embellished with Baroque-style balustrades and pilasters, Islamic arches and the occasional bulbous Mughal dome, the sides of larger temples also epitomize Goan architecture's flair for fusion.

Always worth looking out for inside the main assembly halls are **wood-carvings** and panels of **sculpture** depicting mythological narratives, and the opulently embossed solid silver **doorways** around the entrance to the shrines, flanked by a pair of guardians, or **dvarpalas**. The most distinctively Goan feature of all, however, has to be the **lamp tower**, or *deepmal*, an addition introduced by the Marathas, who ruled much of Goa during the seventeenth and eighteenth centuries. Also known as *deep stambhas*, literally "pillars of light", these five- to seven-storey whitewashed pagodas generally stand opposite the main entrance. Their many ledges and windows hold tiny oil lamps that are illuminated during the *devta's* weekly promenade, when the temple priests carry the god or goddess around the courtyard on their shoulders in a silver sedan chair known as a **palkhi**.

Near the *deepmal* you'll often come across an ornamental plant pot called a **tulsi vrindavan**. The straggly sacred shrub growing inside it, tulsi, represents a former mistress of Vishnu whom his jealous consort Lakshmi turned into a plant after a fit of jealous pique.

Hindu sculpture

Hindu sculpture has traditionally been an integral part of temple architecture. Masons and stone-carvers often laboured for decades, even a whole lifetime, on the same site, settled in camps with their families, in much the same style as modern construction workers live around what they are building in India today. Each grade of artisan – from the men who cut the stone blocks or etched bands of decorative friezes to the master-artists who fashioned the main idols – was a member of a **guild** that functioned along the same lines as caste, determining marriages and social relations. Guilds also controlled the handing down of tools, specialist knowledge and techniques to successive generations, through years of rigorous apprenticeship.

Another role of the guilds was to apply the rules of iconography set in the Shilpa Shastras, still followed today. Measurement always begins with the proportions of the artist's own hand and the image's resultant face-length as the basic unit. The overall scheme is allied to the equally scientific rules applied to classical music, specifically *tala* or rhythm. Human figures total eight face-lengths, eight being the most basic of rhythmic measures. Figures of deities are *nava-tala*, nine face-lengths.

Like their counterparts in medieval Europe, South Indian sculptors remained largely anonymous. Even though the most talented artists may have been known to their peers – in some rare cases earning renown in kingdoms at opposite ends of the Subcontinent – their names have become lost over time. An explanation often advanced for this is the Shastras' insistence that the personality of an individual artist must be suppressed in order for divine inspiration to flow freely. For this reason, only a tiny number of stone sculptures in India bear inscriptions that preserve the identity of their creators.

With the entry of Indian religious sculpture into the international art market, the old conventions of anonymity are beginning to break down. A handful of sculptors at South India's stone-carving capital, **Mamallapuram** in Tamil Nadu (see p.536), have become well known, as the demand for pieces to adorn temples and shrines in the homes of expatriate Indians has increased. However, age-old guidelines governing iconographic sculpture are still applied here as rigorously as they have been for more than a thousand years, which makes it difficult to differentiate between the work of masters and less experienced apprentices.

You can watch sculptors in action, and buy their work, at innumerable workshops around Mamallapuram, while the Government Sculpture College nearby welcomes visitors, offering you the chance to see how students learn to measure out the proportions of the sculpture with their hands and memorize the extraordinary body of iconographic lore that must be fully internalized before they graduate.

Chola bronzes

Originally sacred temple objects, **Chola bronzes** are another art form from Tamil Nadu that has become highly collectable (even if their price tags are considerably higher than stone sculptures). The most memorable bronze icons are the **Natarajas**, or dancing Shivas. The image of Shiva, standing on one leg encircled by flames, with wild locks caught in mid-motion, has become almost as recognizably Indian as the Taj Mahal, and few Indian millionaires would feel their sitting rooms were complete without one.

The principal icons of a temple are usually stationary and made of stone. Frequently, however, ceremonies require an image of the god to be led in procession outside the inner sanctum, and even through the streets. According to the canonical texts known as Agamas, these moving images should be made of metal. Indian bronzes are made by the **cire perdu** ("lost-wax") process, known as *madhuchchistavidhana* in Sanskrit. Three layers of clay mixed with burned grain husks, salt and ground cotton are applied to a figure crafted in beeswax, with a stem left protruding at each end. When that is heated, the wax melts and flows out, creating a hollow mould into which molten metal – a rich five-metal alloy (*panchaloha*) of copper, silver, gold, brass and lead – can be poured through the stems. After the metal has cooled, the clay shell is destroyed, and the stems filed off, leaving a unique completed figure, which the caster-artist, or *sthapathi*, remodels to remove blemishes and add delicate detail.

Knowledge of bronze-casting in India goes back at least as far as the Indus Valley civilization (2500–1500 BC), and the famous "**Dancing Girl**" from Mohenjo Daro. The earliest produced in the South were made by the Andhras, whose techniques were continued by the Pallavas, the immediate antecedents of the Cholas. The few surviving **Pallava** bronzes show a sophisticated handling of the form; figures are characterized by broad shoulders, thick-set features and an overall simplicity that suggests all the detail was completed at the wax stage. The finest bronzes of all, however, are from the **Chola** period, from the late ninth to early eleventh centuries. As the Cholas were predominantly Shaivite, Nataraja, Shiva and his consort Parvati (frequently in a family group with son Skanda) and the 63 Nayanmar poet-saints are the most popular subjects. Chola bronzes display more detail than their predecessors. Human figures are invariably slim-waisted and elegant, with the male form robust and muscular and the female graceful and delicate. As with stone sculpture, the design, iconography and proportions of each figure are governed by the strict rules laid down in the Shilpa Shastras, which draw no real distinction between art, science and religion.

Those bronzes produced by the few artists practising today invariably follow the Chola model; the chief centre is now **Swamimalai**, 8km west of Kumbakonam (see p.577). Original Chola bronzes are kept in many Tamil temples, but as temple interiors are often dark it's not always possible to see them properly. Important **public collections** include the Nayak Durbar Hall Art Museum at Thanjavur and the Government State Museum at Chennai.

Murals

Fragments of paint indicate that **murals** adorned the walls and ceilings of India's oldest rock-cut prayer halls, dating from the third century BC. Only a couple of hundred years later, the art form reached its peak in the sumptuous Satavahana paintings at Ajanta, in the northwest Deccan, where the walls of huge caves were covered in the most exquisite images – mainly episodes from the life of the Buddha (*jatakas*) – rendered in muted reds, greens and blues. However, remnants of ancient murals in the far south are scant, limited to a few patches at **Badami** in Karnataka (see p.346), and the Kailasanatha temple at **Kanchipuram** (see p.547).

Not until the resurgence of the Tamil Cholas in the ninth and tenth centuries did mural painting flourish again in the region. The finest examples – showing sensuously detailed vignettes from life at the royal court of Rajaraja I – are those decorating the interior of the main sanctum of the Brihadishwara temple at

△ Keralan mural

Thanjavur (see p.578). Sadly, these are closed to the public, but you can still enjoy the wonderful ceiling paintings of the Nayak rulers at the Shivakamasundari temple in **Chidambaram** (see p.567), which illustrate Shaivite myths and legends.

Keralan murals

One of the best-kept secrets of South Indian art are the unique Keralan murals found at Mattancherry Palace in old Kochi (see p.456) and at around sixty other locations in the state. Most are on the walls of functioning temples; they are not marketable, transportable, or indeed even seen by many non-Hindus. Few date from before the sixteenth century, though their origins may go back to the seventh century, probably influenced by the Pallava style of Tamil Nadu, but only traces in one tenth-century cave temple survive from the earliest period. Castaneda, a traveller who accompanied Vasco da Gama on the first Portuguese landing in India, described how he strayed into a temple, supposing it to be a church, and saw "monstrous looking images with two inch fangs" painted on the walls, causing one of the party to fall to his knees exclaiming, "if this be the devil, I worship God".

Technically classified as **fresco-secco**, Kerala murals employ vegetable and mineral colours, predominantly ochre reds and yellows, white and blue-green, and are coated with a protective sheen of pine resin and oil. Their ingenious design incorporates intense detail with clarity and dynamism in the portrayal of human (and celestial) figures; subtle facial expressions are captured with the simplest of lines, while narrative elements are always bold and arresting. In common with all great Indian art, they share a complex iconography and symbolism.

Non-Hindus can see fine examples in Kochi, Padmanabhapuram (see p.394), Ettumanur (see p.427) and Kayamkulam (see p.409). Visitors interested in how they are made should head for the Mural Painting Institute at Guruvayur. A paperback book, *Murals of Kerala*, by M.G. Shashi Bhooshan serves as an excellent introduction to the field.

Tanjore (Thanjavur) painting

The name **Tanjore painting** is given to a distinctive form of southern picture-making that came to prominence in the eighteenth century, encouraged by the Maratha Raja of Thanjavur, Serfoji. The term "painting", however, is misleading, and inadequate to describe work of the Tanjore school. It is distinctive because – aside from a painted image – details such as clothing, ornaments and any (typically Baroque) architectural elements are raised in low plaster relief from the surface, which is then decorated by the sumptuous addition of glass pieces, pearls, semi-precious or precious stones and elaborate gold-leaf work. Other variations include pictures on mica, ivory and glass. Figures are delineated with simple outlines; unmixed primary colours are used in a strict symbolic code, similar to that found in the make-up used in the classical dramas of Kerala, where each colour indicates qualities of character. Other schools of painting normally show Krishna with blue-black skin; in the Tanjore style, he is white.

Traditionally, most Tanjore paintings depicted Vaishnavite deities, with the most popular single image probably being that of **Balakrishna**, the chubby baby Krishna. In the tenth-century Sanskrit Bhagavata Purana, Balakrishna was portrayed as a rascal who delighted in stealing and consuming milk, butter balls and curd. Despite his naughtiness, all women who came into contact with him were seized with an overflowing of maternal affection, to the extent that their breasts spontaneously oozed milk. Thanks to such stories, Krishna as a child became the chosen deity par excellence of mothers and grandmothers. Tanjore paintings typically show him eating, accompanied by adoring women.

Although Tanjore painting went into decline after the nineteenth century, in recent years there has been new demand for works, though intended for domestic, rather than temple, shrines. High-quality work is produced in Thanjavur (see p.578), Kumbakonam (see p.573) and Tiruchirapalli (see p.589).

Kalam ezhuttu

The tradition of **kalam ezhuttu** (pronounced "kalam-erroo-too") – detailed and beautiful ritual drawings, in coloured powder, of deities and geometric patterns (*mandalas*) – is very much alive all over **Kerala**, although few visitors to the region even know of its existence. The designs usually cover an area of around thirty square metres, often outdoors and under a *pandal* – a temporary shelter made from bamboo and palm fronds. Each colour, made from rice flour, turmeric, ground leaves and burnt paddy husk, is painstakingly applied using the thumb and forefinger as a funnel. Three communities produce *kalams*; two come from the temple servant (*amblavasi*) castes, whose rituals are associated with the god Ayappa (see p.739) or the goddess Bhagavati; the third, the *pullavans*, specialize in serpent worship. Iconographic designs emerge gradually from the initial grid lines and turn into startling figures, many of terrible aspect, with wide eyes and fangs. Noses and breasts are raised, giving the whole a three-dimensional effect. As part of the ritual, the significant moment when the powder is added for the iris or pupil, "opening" the eyes, may well be marked by the accompaniment of *chenda* drums and *elatalam* hand-cymbals.

Witnessing the often day-long ritual is an unforgettable experience. The effort expended by the artist is made all the more remarkable by the inevitable destruction of the picture shortly after its completion; this truly ephemeral art cannot be divorced from its ritual context. In some cases, the image is destroyed by a fierce-looking *vellichapad* ("light-bringer"), a village oracle who can be recognized by shoulder-length hair, red *dhoti*, heavy brass anklets and the hooked sword he brandishes either while jumping up and down on the spot (a common sight), or marching purposefully about to control the spectators. At the end of the ritual, the powder, invested with divine power, is thrown over the onlookers. *Kalam ezhuttu* rituals are not widely advertised, but check at tourist offices.

Islamic architecture

South India may be best known for its Hindu monuments, but the southern **Deccan** region – the modern states of Karnataka and western Andhra Pradesh – is littered with wonderful Muslim **mosques** and **tombs**, dating from an era when this was the buffer zone between the ancient Indian cultures of the Dravidian south and the dynasties who succeeded the Delhi sultans.

The buildings that survive from this era illustrate the extraordinary cross-fertilization that took place between indigenous art forms and Islamic styles from distant Central Asia. Thus, some of the oldest Muslim constructions at **Bidar** (see p.359) and **Gulbarga** (see p.357) look Afghan, whereas the later masterpieces of the Bahmani dynasty, such as the Ibrahim Rauza at **Bijapur** (see p.352), incorporate motifs that wouldn't have looked out of place on a temple. This fusion occurred both because of a certain stylistic tolerance on the part of later Muslim rulers in southern India, and because the craftsmen they employed were often Hindus, to whom lotus flowers and fancy floral scrollwork came more easily than Persian geometric patterns.

The most famous Muslim monument in the South is the **Golgumbaz** at **Bijapur** (see p.355) – India's largest domed structure – but there are enough superb buildings in the same town, and in the other old capitals of the former Deccan sultans, dotted along the northern border of Karnataka between Bijapur and Hyderabad, to keep enthusiasts of Islamic architecture occupied for weeks.

Wildlife

A fast-growing population and the rapid spread of industries have inflicted pressures on the rural landscape of South India, but the region still supports a wealth of distinct flora and fauna. Although many species have been hunted out over the past fifty years, enough survive to make a trip into the countryside well worthwhile. Walking on less frequented beaches or through the rice fields of the coastal plain, you'll encounter dozens of exotic birds, while the hill country of the interior supports an amazing variety of plants and trees. The majority of the peninsula's larger mammals keep to the dense woodland of the Western Ghat mountains, where a string of contiguous reserves affords them some protection from the hunters and loggers who have wrought such havoc on India's fragile forest regions over the past few decades.

Flora

Something like 3500 species of flowering plants have been identified in South India, as well as countless lower orders of grasses, ferns and brackens. In the Western Ghats, it is not uncommon to find one hundred or more different types of trees in an area of just one hectare. Many species were introduced by the Portuguese from Europe, South America, Southeast Asia and Australia, but there are also a vast number of indigenous varieties which thrive in the moist climate.

Along the coast, the rice **paddy** and **coconut** plantations predominate, forming a near-continuous band of lush foliage. Spiky **spinifex** helps bind the shifting sand dunes behind the miles of sandy beaches lining both the Malabar and Coromandel coasts, while **casuarina** bushes form striking splashes of pink and crimson during the winter months.

In towns and villages, you'll encounter dozens of beautiful **flowering trees**. The Indian **laburnum**, or cassia, throws out masses of yellow flowers and long seed pods in late February before the monsoons. This is also the period when mango and Indian **coral trees** are in full bloom; both produce bundles of stunning red flowers.

One of the region's most distinctive trees, found in both coastal and hill areas, is the stately **banyan**, which propagates by sending out roots from its lower branches. The largest specimens spread out over an area of two hundred square metres. The banyan is revered by Hindus, and you'll often find small shrines at the foot of mature trees. The same is true of the **peepal**, which has distinctive spatula-shaped leaves. Temple courtyards often enclose large peepals, which usually have strips of auspicious red cloth hanging from their lower branches.

The Western Ghats harbour a bewildering wealth of flora, from flowering trees and plants to ferns and fungi. **Shola** forests, lush patches of moist evergreen woodland which carpet the deeper mountain valleys, exhibit some of the greatest biodiversity. Sheltered by a leafy canopy, which may rise to a height of twenty metres or more, buttressed roots and giant trunks tower above a luxuriant undergrowth of brambles, creepers and bracken, interspersed by brakes of bamboo. Common tree species include the kadam, sisso or martel, kharanj and teak, while rarer sandalwood thrives on the higher, drier plateaux south of Mysore. There are dozens of representatives of the fig family, too, as

Ⓦ **www.5tigers.org** Everything you ever wanted to know about tigers.

Ⓦ **www.camacdonald.com/birding/asiaindia.htm** Exhaustive reviews of India's birdwatching hotspots, online resources and printed material, with dozens of pretty pictures and reports from recent field trips by bona fide enthusiasts.

Ⓦ **www.wpsi-india.org** The Wildlife Protection Society of India was set up to provide support in the struggle against poaching, and its site holds a wealth of information, links and news on everything connected to tigers in India.

Ⓦ **www.indianwildlifeportal.com** Portal devoted to Indian wildlife, with links you can browse by species, destination or theme.

Ⓦ **www.saveindiastigers.co.uk** UK-based tiger conservation group.

Ⓦ **www.eia-international.org** One of the best sources for up-to-date news, facts and figures on India's poaching crisis.

C

well as innumerable (and ecologically destructive) eucalyptus and rubber trees, planted as cash crops by the Forest Department.

Mammals

Although peninsular India boasts more than fifty species of wild mammals, visitors who stick to populated coastal areas are unlikely to spot anything more inspiring than a monkey or squirrel. During a field expedition to Goa in the 1970s, the eminent Indian naturalist, Salim Ali, complained that the only animal he spotted was a lone leopard cat, dead at the roadside. Most of the larger animals have been hunted to the point of extinction; the few that remain roam the dense woodland lining the Western Ghats, in the sparsely populated forest zones of the **Nilgiri Biosphere Reserve**.

The largest Indian land mammal is, of course, the Asian **elephant**, stockier and with much smaller ears than its African cousin, though no less venerable. Travelling around Kerala and Tamil Nadu, you'll regularly see elephants in temples and festivals, but for a glimpse of one in the wild, you'll have to venture into the mountains where, in spite of the huge reduction of their natural habitat, around six and a half thousand still survive. Among the best places for sightings are Periyar in Kerala (see p.430) and Nagarhole in Karnataka (see p.291). In the era when it was a maharaja's hunting reserve, the latter became infamous as the place where British hunter G.P. Sanderson devised the brutal *khedda* system for trapping elephants: herds were driven into stockades and captured or killed. Between 1890 and 1971, 1536 elephants were allegedly caught in this way, of which 225 died – a figure that probably only represents the tip of the iceberg. Today, wild elephants, which are included under the Endangered Species Protection Act, are under increasing threat from villagers: each adult animal eats roughly two hundred kilos of vegetation and drinks one hundred litres of water a day, and their search for sustenance inevitably brings them into conflict with rural communities.

Across India, local villagers displaced by wildlife reserves have often been responsible for the poaching that has reduced **tiger** populations to such fragile levels (see box, p.769). These days, sightings in South India are very rare indeed, though several kinds of big cat survive. Among the most beautiful is the **leopard**, or panther (*Panthera panthus*). Prowling the thick forests of the Ghats,

△ Indian tiger

C CONTEXTS | Wildlife

these elusive cats prey on monkeys and deer, and occasionally take domestic cattle and dogs from the fringes of villages. Their distinctive black spots make them notoriously difficult to see amongst the tropical foliage, although their mating call (reminiscent of a saw on wood) regularly pierces the night air in remote areas. The **leopard cat** (*Felis bengalensis*) is a miniature version of its namesake, and more common. Sporting a bushy tail and round spots on soft buff or grey fur, it is about the same size as a domestic cat and lives around villages, picking off chickens, birds and small mammals. Another cat with a penchant for poultry, and one which villagers occasionally keep as a pet if they can capture one, is the docile Indian **civet** (*Viverricula indica*), recognizable by its lithe body, striped tail, short legs and long pointed muzzle.

Wild cats share their territory with a range of other mammals unique to the Subcontinent. One you've a reasonable chance of seeing is the **gaur**, or Indian bison (*Bos gaurus*). These primeval-looking beasts, with their distinctive sleek black skin and knee-length white "socks", forage around bamboo thickets and shady woods. The bulls are particularly impressive, growing to an awesome height of two metres, with heavy curved horns and prominent humps.

With its long fur and white V-shaped bib, the scruffy **sloth bear** (*Melursus ursinus*) – whose Tamil name (*bhalu*) inspired that of Rudyard Kipling's character in *The Jungle Book* – ranks among the weirder-looking inhabitants of the region's forests. Sadly, it's also very rare, thanks to its predilection for raiding sugar-cane plantations, which has brought it, like the elephant, into direct conflict with man. Sloth bears can occasionally be seen shuffling along woodland trails, but you're more likely to come across evidence of their foraging activities: trashed termite mounds and chewed-up ants' nests. The same is true of both the portly Indian **porcupine** (*Hystrix indica*), or *sal*, which you see a lot less often than the mounds of earth it digs up to get at insects and cashew or teak seedlings; and the **pangolin** (*Manis crassicaudata*), or *tiryo*, a kind of armour-plated anteater whose hard, grey overlapping scales protect it from predators.

Full-moon nights and the twilight hours of dusk and dawn are the times to look out for nocturnal animals such as the **slender loris** (*Loris tardigradus*). This shy creature – a distant cousin of the lemur, with bulging round eyes, furry body and pencil-thin limbs – grows to around twenty centimetres in length. It moves as if in slow motion, except when an insect flits to within striking distance, and is a favourite pet of forest people. The **mongoose** *(Herpestes edwardsi)* is another animal sometimes kept as a pet to keep dwellings free of scorpions, mice, rats and other vermin. It will also readily take on snakes – you might see one writhing in a cloud of dust with king cobras during performances by snake charmers.

Late evening is also the best time for spotting **bats**. South India boasts four species, including the fulvous fruit bat (*Rousettus lechenaulti*), or *vagul* – so-called because it gives off a scent resembling fermenting fruit juice; Dormer's bat (*Pipistrellus dormeri*); the very rare rufous horseshoe bat; and the Malay fox vampire (*Magaderma spasma*), which feeds off the blood of live cattle. **Flying foxes** (*Pteropus giganteus*), the largest of India's bats, are also present in healthy numbers. With a wingspan of more than one metre, they fly in cacophonous groups to feed in fruit orchards, sometimes falling foul of electricity cables on the way: frazzled flying foxes dangling from live cables are a common sight in the interior.

Other species to look out for in forest areas are the Indian **giant squirrel** (*Ratufa indica*), or *shenkaro*, which has a coat of black fur and red-orange lower parts. Two and a half times larger than its European cousins, it lives in the canopy, leaping up to twenty metres between branches. The much smaller three-striped squirrel (*Funambulus palmarum*), or *khadi khar*, recognizable by the three black markings down its back, is also found in woodland. The five-striped palm squirrel (*Funambulus pennanti*) is a common sight, especially in municipal parks and villages.

Forest clearings and areas of open grassland are grazed by four species of deer. Widely regarded as the most beautiful is the **cheetal** (*Axis axis*), or spotted axis deer, which congregates in large groups around water holes and salt licks, occasionally wandering into villages to seek shelter from its predators. The plainer, buff-coloured **sambar** (*Cervus unicolor*) is also common, despite being affected by diseases spread by domestic cattle during the 1970s and 1980s. Two types of deer you're less likely to come across, but which also inhabit the border

The Indian tiger: survival or extinction?

Feared, adored, immortalized in myth and used to endorse everything from breakfast cereals to petrochemicals, few animals command such universal fascination as the **tiger**. Small populations exist in several areas, including the Russian Far East and Malaysia, but it's only in India that you have a real chance of glimpsing this magnificent beast in the wild, stalking through the teak forests and terai grass to which it is uniquely adapted. A solitary predator at the apex of the food chain, it has no natural enemies save man.

As recently as 1900 up to 100,000 tigers still roamed the Subcontinent, even though **shikar** (tiger hunting) had long been the "sport of kings". An ancient dictum held it auspicious for a ruler to notch up a tally of 109 dead tigers, and nawabs, maharajas and Mughal emperors all indulged their prerogative to devastating effect. But it was the trigger-happy British who brought tiger hunting to its most gratuitous peak. Photographs of pith-helmeted, bare-kneed *burrasahibs* posing behind mountains of striped carcasses became a hackneyed image of the Raj. Even Prince Philip (now president of the Worldwide Fund for Nature) couldn't resist bagging one during a royal visit.

In the years following Independence, **demographic pressures** nudged the Indian tiger perilously close to extinction. As the human population increased in rural districts, more and more forest was cleared for farming – thereby depriving large carnivores of their main source of game and of the cover they needed to hunt. Forced to turn on farm cattle as an alternative, tigers were drawn into direct conflict with humans; some animals, out of sheer desperation, even turned man-eater and attacked human settlements.

Poaching has taken an even greater toll. The black market has always paid high prices for live animals – a whole tiger can fetch up to $100,000 – and for the various body parts believed to hold magical or medicinal properties. The meat is used to ward off snakes, the brain to cure acne, the nose to promote the birth of a son and the fat of the kidney – applied liberally to the afflicted organ – as an antidote to male impotence.

By the time an all-India moratorium on tiger shooting was declared in the 1972 Wildlife Protection Act, numbers had plummeted to below two thousand. A dramatic response geared to fire public imagination came the following year, with the inauguration of **Project Tiger**. At the personal behest of then prime minister Indira Gandhi, nine areas of pristine forest were set aside for the last remaining tigers. Displaced farming communities were resettled and compensated, and armed rangers employed to discourage poachers. Demand for tiger parts did not end with Project Tiger, however, and the poachers remained in business, aided by organized smuggling rings. Undercover investigators repeatedly come across huge hauls of tiger bones and skins, and over the past few years the discovery of tiger carcasses rotting in several reserves indicates that poachers have been resorting to new, more random killing methods. In 2005, eight officials at Sariska National Park in Rajasthan were suspended after it emerged that virtually all of the park's 26 listed tigers had been poached. And in 2006, video footage came to light of a major festival in Chinese-occupied Tibet at which officials and even tourists were shown wearing tiger skins; its highlight was a tent made up of 108 individual pelts.

Today, even though there are 23 Project Tiger sites, numbers continue to fall. Official figures optimistically claim a **population** of up to 3750, but independent evidence is more pessimistic, putting the figure at around half of that. The population rise indicated by counts based on pug marks – thought to be like human fingerprints, unique to each individual – that gave such encouragement in the early 1990s has been declared inaccurate. Poorly equipped park wardens are still fighting a losing battle: in 1998 it was estimated that one tiger was being poached every day, and the situation is at least as bad today. The most pessimistic experts even claim that at the present rate of destruction, India's most exotic animal could face extinction within two decades.

forests, are the **barking deer** (*Muntiacus muntjak*), whose call closely resembles that of a domestic dog, and the timid **mouse deer** (*Tragulus meminna*), a speckled-grey member of the *Tragulidae* family that is India's smallest deer, growing to a mere thirty centimetres in height. Both of these are highly secretive and nocturnal; they are also the preferred snack of Goa's smaller predators: the **striped hyena** (*Hyaena hyaena*), **jackal** (*Canis aureus*), or *colo*, and **wild dog** (*Cuon alpinus*), which hunt in packs.

Long-beaked **dolphins** are regular visitors to the shallow waters of South India's more secluded bays and beaches. They are traditionally regarded as a pest by local villagers, who believe they eat scarce stocks of fish. However, this long-standing antipathy is gradually being eroded as local people realize the tourist-pulling potential of the dolphins: Palolem beach, in Goa (see p.247), is a dependable dolphin-spotting location.

Finally, no rundown of South Indian mammals would be complete without some mention of **monkeys**. The most common species is the mangy pink-bottomed **macaque** (*Macaca mulatta*), or *makad*, which hangs out anywhere scraps may be scavenged or snatched from unwary humans: temples and picnic spots are good places to watch them in action. The black-faced Hanuman **langur**, by contrast, is less audacious, retreating to the trees if threatened. It is much larger than the macaque, with pale grey fur and long limbs and tail. In forest areas, the langur's distinctive call is an effective early-warning system against big cats and other predators, which is why you often come across herds of cheetal grazing under trees inhabited by large colonies of them.

Reptiles

Reptiles are well represented in the region, with more than forty species of snakes, lizards, turtles and crocodiles recorded. The best places to spot them are not the interior forests, where dense foliage makes observation difficult, but open, cultivated areas: paddy fields and village ponds provide abundant fresh water, nesting sites and prey (frogs, insects and small birds).

Your hotel room, however, is where you are most likely to come across tropical India's most common reptile, the **gecko** (*Hemidactylus*), which clings to walls and ceilings with its widely splayed toes. Deceptively static most of the time, these small yellow-brown lizards will dash at lightning speed for cracks and holes if you try to catch one, or if an unwary mosquito, fly or cockroach scuttles within striking distance. The much rarer chameleon is even more elusive, mainly because its constantly changing camouflage makes it virtually impossible to spot. They'll have no problem seeing you, though: independently moving eyes allow them to pinpoint approaching predators, while prey is slurped up with their fast-moving forty-centimetre-long tongues. The other main lizard to look out for is the **Bengal monitor**. This giant brown speckled reptile looks like a refugee from *Jurassic Park*, growing to well over a metre in length. It used to be a common sight in coastal areas, basking on roads and rocks. However, monitors are often killed and eaten by villagers, and have become increasingly rare. Among the few places you can be sure of sighting one is South Andaman, in the Andaman archipelago.

The monsoon period is when you're most likely to encounter **turtles**. Two varieties paddle around village ponds and wells while water is plentiful: the flap-shell (*Lissemys punctata*) and black-pond (*Melanochelys trijuga*) turtles, neither of which are endangered. Numbers of Olive Ridley marine turtles (*Lepidochelys olivacea*), by contrast, have plummeted over the past few decades as a result of villagers raiding their nests when they crawl onto the beach to lay their eggs. This amazing natural spectacle occurs each year at a number of beaches in the region, notably Morgim in north Goa and Havelock Island in the Andamans (see box, p.231). Local coastguards and scientists from the Institute of Oceanography in Goa monitor the migration, patrolling the beaches to deter poachers, but the annual egg binge remains a highlight of the local gastronomic calendar, eagerly awaited by fisher families, who sell the illegal harvest in local markets. Only in Orissa, in eastern India, where a special wildlife sanctuary has been set up to protect them, have the sea turtles survived the seasonal slaughter to reproduce in healthy numbers.

An equally rare sight nowadays is the **crocodile**. Populations have dropped almost to the point of extinction, although the Cambarjua Canal near Old Goa, and more remote stretches of the Mandovi and Zuari estuaries, support vestigial colonies of saltwater crocs, which bask on mud flats and river rocks. Dubbed "salties", they occasionally take calves and goats, and will snap at the odd human if given half a chance. The more ominously named mugger crocodile, however, is harmless, inhabiting unfrequented freshwater streams and riversides. You can see all of India's indigenous crocodiles at the wonderful Crocodile Bank near Mamallapuram (see p.545).

Snakes

Twenty-three species of snake are found in South India, ranging from the gigantic **Indian python** (*Python molurus*, or *har* in Konkani) – a forest-dwelling constrictor that grows up to four metres in length – to the innocuous worm snake (*Typhlops braminus*), or *sulva*, which is tiny, completely blind and often mistaken for an earthworm.

The eight **poisonous snakes** present in the region include India's four most deadly species: the cobra, the krait, Russel's viper and the saw-scaled viper. Though these are relatively common in coastal and cultivated areas, even the most aggressive snake will slither off at the first sign of an approaching human. Nevertheless, ten thousand Indians die from snake bites each year, and if you regularly cut across paddy fields or plan to do any hiking, it makes sense to familiarize yourself with the following four or five species, just in case; their bites nearly always prove fatal if not treated immediately with anti-venom serum – available at most clinics and hospitals.

Present in most parts of the region and an important character in Hindu mythology, the Indian **cobra** (*Naja naja*), or *naga*, is the most common of the venomous species. Wheat-brown or grey in colour, it is famed for the "hood" it unfurls when confronted and whose rear side usually bears the snake's characteristic spectacle markings. Its big brother, the **king cobra** (*Naja hannah*), or *Naga raja*, is much less often encountered. Inhabiting the remote forest regions along the Karnataka border, this beautiful brown, yellow and black snake, which grows to a length of four metres or more, is very rare, although the itinerant snake charmers who perform in markets occasionally keep one. Defanged, they rear up and "dance" when provoked by the handler, or are set against mongooses in ferocious (and often fatal) fights. The king cobra is also the only snake in the world known to make its own nest.

Distinguished by their steel-blue colour and faint white cross markings, **kraits** (*Bungarus caeruleus*) are twice as deadly as the Indian cobra: even the bite of a newly hatched youngster is lethal. **Russell's viper** (*Vipera russelli*) is another one to watch out for. Identifiable by the three bands of elliptical markings that extend down its brown body, the Russell hisses at its victims before darting at them and burying its centimetre-long fangs into their flesh. The other common poisonous snake in South India is the **saw-scaled viper** (*Echis carinatus*). Grey with an arrow-shaped mark on its triangular head, it hangs around in the cracks between stone walls, feeding on scorpions, lizards, frogs, rodents and smaller snakes. They also hiss when threatened, producing the sound by rubbing together serrated scales located on the side of their head. Finally, **sea snakes** (*Enhydrina schistosa*) are common in coastal areas and potentially lethal (with a bite said to be twenty times more venomous than a cobra's), although rarely encountered by swimmers, as they lurk only in deep water off the shore.

Harmless snakes are far more numerous than their killer cousins and frequently more attractive. The beautiful **golden tree snake** (*Chrysopelea ornata*), for example, sports an exquisitely intricate geometric pattern of red, yellow and black markings, while the **green whip snake** (*Dryophis nasutus*), or *sarpatol*, is a stunning parakeet-green. The ubiquitous **Indian rat snake**, often mistaken for a cobra, also has beautiful markings, although it leaves behind a foul stench of decomposing flesh. Other common non-poisonous snakes include the wolf snake (*Lycodon aulicus*), or *kaidya*; the Russell sand boa (*Eryx conicus*), or *malun*; the kukri snake (*Oligodon taeniolatus*), or *pasko*; and the cat snake (*Boiga trigonata*), or *manjra*.

Birds

You don't have to be an aficionado to enjoy South India's abundant **birdlife**. Breathtakingly beautiful birds regularly flash between the branches of trees or appear on overhead wires at the roadside. For more information than we have space for here, see ⓦ www.binding.in.

Thanks to the internationally popular brand of Goan beer, the **kingfisher** has become that state's unofficial mascot: it's not hard to see why the brewers chose it as their logo. Three common species of kingfisher frequently crop up amid the paddy fields and wetlands of the coastal plains, where they feed on small fish and tadpoles. With its enormous bill and pale green-blue wing feathers, the stork-billed kingfisher (*Perargopis capensis*) is the largest and most distinctive member of the family, although the white-throated kingfisher (*Halcyon smyrnensis*) – which has iridescent turquoise plumage and a coral-red bill – and the common kingfisher (*Alcedo atthis*), identical to the one frequently spotted in northern Europe, are more alluring.

Other common and brightly coloured species include the green, blue and yellow **bee-eaters** (*Merops*), the stunning **golden oriole** (*Oriolus oriolus*), and the **Indian roller** (*Coracias bengalensis*), famous for its brilliant blue flight feathers and exuberant aerobatic mating displays. **Hoopoes** (*Upupa epops*), recognizable by their elegant black-and-white tipped crests, fawn plumage and distinctive "hoo…po…po" call, also flit around fields and villages, as do **purple sunbirds** (*Nectarina asiatica*) and several kinds of **bulbuls**, **babblers** and **drongos** (*Dicrurus*), including the fork-tailed **black drongo** (*Dicrurus macrocercus*) – which can often be seen perched on telegraph wires. If you're lucky, you may also catch a glimpse of the **Asian paradise flycatcher** (*Terpsiphone paradisi*), which is widespread and among the region's most exquisite birds: males of more than four years of age sport a thick black crest and long silver white streamers, while the more often seen females and young males are reddish-brown.

Paddy fields, ponds and saline mudflats usually teem with water birds. The most ubiquitous is the snowy white **cattle egret** (*Bubulcus ibis*), which can usually be seen wherever there are cows and buffalo, feeding off the grubs, insects and other parasites that live on them. The **great egret** (*Casmerodius albus*) is also pure white, although lankier and with a long yellow bill, while the **little egret** (*Egretta garzetta*), sports a short black bill. Look out too for the mud-brown Indian pond heron, or "**paddy bird**", India's most common heron. Distinguished by its pale green legs, speckled breast and hunched posture, it stands motionless for hours in water, waiting for fish or frogs.

The hunting technique of the beautiful **white-bellied sea eagle** (*Haliaetus leucogaster*), by contrast, is truly spectacular. Cruising twenty to thirty metres above the surface of the water, this black and white osprey stoops at high speed to snatch its prey – usually sea snakes and mackerel – from the waves with its fierce yellow talons. More common birds of prey such as the **brahminy kite** (*Haliastur indus*) – recognizable by its white breast and chestnut head markings – and the **black kite** (*Milvus migrans*) – a dark-brown bird with a fork tail – are widespread around towns and fishing villages, where they vie with raucous gangs of house **crows** (*Corvus splendens*) for scraps.

Other birds of prey to keep an eye open for, especially around open farmland, are the **white-eyed buzzard** (*Butastur teesa*), the **oriental honey buzzard** (*Pernis ptilorhynchus*), the **black-shouldered kite** (*Elanus caeruleus*) – famous for its blood-red eyes – and the **shikra** (*Accipiter badius*), which closely resembles the European sparrowhawk.

Forest birds

The region's forests may have lost many of their larger animals, but they still offer exciting possibilities for bird-watchers. One species every enthusiast hopes to glimpse while in the woods is the magnificent **hornbill**. The Malabar grey hornbill (*Ocyceros griseus*), with its blue-brown plumage and long curved beak, is the most common, although the Indian pied hornbill (*Anthracoceros malabaricus*), distinguished by its white wing and tail tips and the pale patch on its face, often flies into villages in search of fruit and lizards. The magnificent great hornbill (*Buceros bicornis*), however, is more elusive, limited to the most dense forest areas, where it may occasionally be spotted flitting through the canopy. Growing to 130cm in length, it has a black-and-white striped body and wings, and a huge yellow beak with a long curved casque on top.

Several species of **woodpecker** also inhabit the interior forests, among them three types of flameback woodpecker: the common black-rumped flameback (*Dinopium bengalense*) has a wide range and also ventures into gardens and hotel grounds. The Cotigao sanctuary in south Goa is one of the last remaining strongholds of the white-bellied woodpecker (*Dryocopus javensis*); in spite of its bright red head and white rump, this shy bird is more often heard than seen, making loud drumming noises on tree trunks between December and March.

A bird whose call is a regular feature of the Western Ghat forests, though you'll be lucky to catch a glimpse of one, is the wild ancestor of the domestic chicken – the **jungle fowl**. The grey or Sonnerat's jungle fowl (*Gallus sonneratii*), has dark plumage scattered with yellow spots and streaks.

Wildlife viewing

Although you can expect to come across many of the species listed above on the edge of towns and villages, a spell in one of South India's nature reserves (see box, p.774) offers the best chance of viewing wild animals. Although these reserves are a far cry from the well-organized and -maintained national parks you may be used to at home, at the larger and more easily accessible wildlife reserves – such as Periyar and Mudumalai – a reasonable infrastructure exists to transport visitors around, whether by Jeep, minibus, coach or, in the case of the former, boat. Don't, however, expect to see much if you stick to these standard excursion vehicles laid on by the park authorities. Most of the rarer animals keep well away from noisy groups of trippers. Wherever possible, try to organize **walking safaris** with a reliable, approved guide in the forest, while bearing in mind that not all guides may be as knowledgable and experienced as they claim, and that an untrained guide may even lead you into dangerous situations. Ask to see recommendation books before parting with any money.

South Indian wildlife sanctuaries and national parks

The South Indian states covered in this book harbour a total of 96 **wildlife sanctuaries and national parks**, if you include the various protected islets of the Andaman and Nicobar Islands, and the many minor reserves dotted around the region. What follows is a selection (listed in alphabetical order) of the most rewarding, both in terms of their wildlife and the natural environment.

Cotigao Wildlife Sanctuary (Goa). Tucked away in the extreme south of Goa, near Palolem beach, its extensive mixed deciduous forest and hilly backdrop make up for a relative paucity of wildlife. Best time: November to March. See p.253.

Eravikulam National Park (Kerala). Located 17km northeast of Munnar in the lap of the Western Ghats. Famous for its thriving population of Nilgiri tahr, a rare antelope that lives only here, on the high rolling grasslands. See them on the hard hike up Anamudi, South India's highest mountain. Best time: January to April. See p.444.

Indira Gandhi (Anamalai) Wildlife Sanctuary (Tamil Nadu). On the southernmost reaches of the Cardamom Hills, this park is more remote than Mudumalai, and consequently less visited, but encompasses some beautiful mountain scenery as well as abundant fauna. Best time: January to March. See p.628.

Kodikkarai (Point Calimere) (Tamil Nadu). On a promontory jutting into Palk Bay, some 250 species of bird, mostly migrants, descend on a swathe of mixed swampland and dry deciduous forest in the wake of the monsoon. Best time: November to February. See p.588.

Mahatma Gandhi National Marine Park (Andaman Islands). The islets in this reserve, encircled by vivid coral reefs, rise out of crystal-clear water that teems with tropical fish, turtles and other marine life. Can be reached by daily excursion boats, via bus links, from the capital Port Blair. Best time: January to March. See p.695.

Mudumalai Wildlife Sanctuary (Tamil Nadu). Set 1140m up in the Nilgiri Hills, Mudumalai is one of the most easily reached reserves in the South. It offers a full range of accommodation and trails and gives access to huge areas of protected forest. Best time: January to March. See p.640.

Periyar Wildlife Sanctuary (Kerala). A former Maharaja's hunting reserve, centred on an artificial lake high in the Cardamom Hills. Occasional tiger sightings, but you're much more likely to spot an elephant. Well placed for trips into the mountains and tea plantations, with good accommodation, including remote observation towers which you have to trek to. Best time: October to March. See p.430.

Vadanemmeli Crocodile Bank (Tamil Nadu). Endangered species of indigenous crocodiles, lizards and turtles are bred here, 14km north of Mamallapuram, for release into the wild. Local Irula tribes people collect venom from poisonous snakes to make serum. Open year round. See p.545.

Vedanthangal Bird Sanctuary (Tamil Nadu). A wonderful mixed sanctuary, 86km southwest of Chennai, where you can sight 250 species of migrant wetland birds, blown in by the northwest monsoon. Best time: December and February. See p.552.

Music

One who is an expert in playing the veena, well versed in shruti and other forms of musical sound, and has a deep understanding of thaalam, will attain enlightenment with ease.

Tyagaraja (1767–1847)

Hindustani music from North India may be better known internationally, but the classical music of the South – called Carnatic – is by far the more ancient. Its tenets, once passed on only orally, were codified in Vedic literature between 4000 and 1000 BC, long before Western classical music was even in its infancy. Visiting the region, you'll have ample opportunity to attend Carnatic recitals, a key feature of cultural life in major cities such as Chennai, while religious rituals in South Indian temples invariably feature some kind of musical accompaniment. Styles of music – whether secular or religious – vary greatly from state to state, but among the most singular South Indian idioms are Keralan percussion, and the heavily Portuguese-accented music of Goa, both of which convey the cultural distinctiveness of these two regions more vividly than anything else.

Carnatic instrumental music

The **Carnatic music** of South India might be labelled "classical", but it's nothing like classical music anywhere else in the world. Rather than being the province of an urbane elite, it's an explosion of colour, sound and Hindu worship. While Hindustani music developed close associations with court and palace, Carnatic music remained part of the warp and weft of South Indian culture, both religious and secular. The other major difference is that Carnatic music, lacking written notation, is taught by demonstration and learned by ear or – in the case of its highly sophisticated rhythmic system – taught by a marvellous, mathematical structure of "finger computing" which enables a percussionist to break down a complex *thaalam* (rhythmic cycle) into manageable units. Indian percussion maestros readily admit the supremacy of Carnatic concepts of rhythm, and increasing numbers of Hindustani percussionists have studied in the South.

The music and the faith which inspired Carnatic music have remained inseparable. Visitors to the vast temples of South India are much more likely to encounter music than in the North. It's usually the piercing sound of the *nagaswaram* (shawm) and the *tavil* (barrel drum). More than likely it accompanies flaming torches and a ceremonial procession of the temple deity.

While devotional and religious in origin, Carnatic music is as much a vehicle for education and entertainment as for spiritual elevation. **Kritis**, a genre of Hindu hymn, are hummed and sung as people go about their daily business. Tuneful and easily recognizable, they hold a similar position in popular culture to the Christian hymn in Western societies.

The association of music and **dance** with Hindu thought has a long heritage, beginning with Shiva himself as Nataraja, the Cosmic Dancer, whose potent image is ever present in Hindu iconography. His temple at Chidambaram, for example, is rich with sculptures of *natya* dance poses, music-making and musical instruments,

bansuri transverse bamboo flute (*venu* in Sanskrit), typically shorter than its Hindustani counterpart of the same name. The *venu* is Lord Krishna's instrument, and therefore holds a special place in Indian music.

bharatanatyam literally "Dance of India", the classical dance of South India, formerly known as *dasi attam* or the dance of the *devadasis*.

clarionet an alternative local name for the Western clarinet; its introduction into *chenda melam* (see box, p.782) is attributed to the nineteenth-century musician Madadeva Nathamuni.

devadasi female temple- or courtesan-dancers, trained in music and dance.

ghatam tuned clay pot played with the hands or, for effect, by bouncing off the belly.

jalatarangam a half-ring of water-filled china bowls tuned so the biggest vessel produces the deepest note. Musicians such as M.S. Chandrasekharian (also a renowned vina player), Krishnarajapuram Dhanam, the instrument's first female player, and Seeta Doraiswamy (featured on *An Anthology of South Indian Classical Music*) are amongst its exponents.

javali type of composition, often playfully erotic in content.

kanjira tambourine-like hand drum, lacking the Western tambourine's side jingles.

morsing Jew's harp.

mridangam double-headed barrel drum, termed the "king of percussion and the queen of melody".

mukhavina soft-toned, double-reed woodwind instrument.

tanpura four- or sometimes five-stringed drone instrument; some "modernists" substitute an electronic version called a shruti box or a sur peti.

tavil double-headed barrel drum, closely associated with *nagaswaram* ensembles and the Pillai caste.

tillana type of composition, associated with the *bharatanatyam* style of classical dance.

vina or **veena** fretted seven-string instrument, the southern equivalent of the sitar.

violin the European violin, tuned to suit Indian tastes.

and the *devadasis*, the servants of God, were traditionally temple dancers. Carnatic composers, too, are looked upon with some reverence. Indeed, the music's three great composers – **Tyagaraja** (1767–1847), **Muttuswamy Dikshitar** (1776–1835) and **Syama Sastri** (1762–1827) – are known as the *Trimurti* or "Holy Trinity" and are regarded as saint-composers. Between them, the trinity were responsible for hundreds of compositions: Tyagaraja alone is credited with some six hundred *kritis*.

Indians compare the music of the Trimurti to the grape, the coconut and the banana. Tyagaraja can be consumed and enjoyed immediately; appreciating Muttuswamy Dikshitar is like cracking open a shell to get to the contents; with Syama Sastri you have to remove the soft outer layer to get to the fruit. Their era has become known as the **Golden Period**, and their music is revered and celebrated year in, year out, at various music conferences (festivals) and on a never-ending stream of recordings.

In performance

In concert, Carnatic music often seems to lack Hindustani music's showmanship and flamboyance. But neither does it require the same sustained level of concentration from both performer and audience. A Carnatic melody, or **ragam** (raga) might be said to resemble a miniature beside a large-scale Hindustani canvas.

Carnatic musicians will distil the essence of a ragam into six to eight minutes. In part this is because a *kriti*, the base of many performances, is a fixed composition without improvisation. Carnatic musicians' creativity lies in their ability to interpret that piece faithfully while shading and colouring the composition appropriately. The words of a *kriti* affect even non-vocal compositions: instrumentalists will colour their interpretations as if a vocalist were singing along; the unvoiced lyric determines where they place an accent, a pause or melodic splash.

Improvisation has its place too, most noticeably in a sequence known as **ragam-thanam-pallavi**. This is a full-scale flowering of a Carnatic ragam and is every bit the equal of a Hindustani performance, although it is employed more sparingly, tending to be the centrepiece or climax of a Carnatic concert.

Whereas Carnatic music tends to break down into three strands: temple music, temple dance-accompaniment, and music for personal and private devotional observance, **sabha**, or paying concert performances, have somewhat blurred these distinctions. During the 1890s, the sabha associations in **Madras** (now Chennai) took an innovative path, moving from music performances to dance recitals. Chennai remains a centre of excellence and its music conferences, especially around December and January, attract devout audiences each year.

Concert-giving led to other changes, and **microphones** came into use during the 1930s. They lent soft-voiced instruments such as members of the vina family (see opposite) a new lease of life, and replaced full-tilt vocal power with greater subtlety. Nowadays, concerts will typically feature a named principal soloist (either vocal or instrumental) with melodic and rhythmic accompaniment and a *tanpura* or drone player. Percussionists of standing are often included in concert announcements and advertising as they are attractions in their own right. Female musicians involved in a principal role tend to be vocalists, vina players or violinists. Male musicians have access to a wider range of musical possibilities as well as outnumbering female principal soloists or accompanists by roughly three to one.

Traditional Carnatic instruments

The **vina** (or *veena*) is the foremost Carnatic **stringed instrument**, the southern equivalent (and ancestor) of the sitar. A hollow wooden fingerboard with 24 frets is supported by two resonating gourds at each end. The vina has seven strings, four used for the melody and the other three for rhythm and drone. Current leading players include V. Doreswamy Iyengar, Chitti Babu, S. Balachandar and Sivasakti Sivanesan. The **chitra vina** (or *gotuvadyam*) is an unfretted 21-string instrument with sets for rhythm and drone as well as sympathetic strings. It has a characteristically soft voice which, before amplification, meant it was best suited to intimate surroundings. The best-known player is the young N. Ravikiran, who has switched to a hollow cylinder of teflon for his slide.

As in the North, the transverse bamboo flute goes under the name of **bansuri** or **venu**, although it is typically shorter and higher in pitch than the Hindustani instrument. Watch out for recordings by N. Ramani and the younger S. Shashank. The **nagaswaram** (or *nadaswaram*) is a piercing double-reed shawm-like instrument. It's longer and more deep-toned than the Hindustani *shehnai*, is associated with weddings, processions and temple ceremonies and is

Compilations

An Anthology of South Indian Classical Music (Ocora, France). This substantial four-CD primer, compiled by the eminent violinist Dr L. Subramaniam, gathers many of Carnatic music's vocal and instrumental giants with detailed descriptions of the music they make and the instruments they play. M.S. Subbulakshmi (vocals), T.R. Mahalingam (flute), A.K.C. Natarajan (clarinet), Raajeshwari Padmanabhan (*vina*), N. Ravikiran (*chitra vina*), Subashchandran (*morsing*), V.V. Subrahmanyam (violin) and T.H. Vinayakram (*ghatam*) are among the virtuosos featured.

Vocal artists

M. Balamuralikrishna Born in 1930 into a musical family, Balamuralikrishna was a child prodigy. He is also credited as a composer of new ragam formulations and some four hundred classical compositions.

Vocal (Moment, US). A *kriti* in Lathangi lasting nearly an hour, followed by a spectacular *tillana* performance using four different ragams in succession to create a *tillana ragamalika* (garland of ragams). Zakir Hussain (tabla) and T.H. Vinayakram (*ghatam*) provide rhythmic support.

Sudha Ragunathan Since her debut, Ragunathan (b.1958) has proved to be one of the most illuminating female singers in Carnatic music. Although she has recorded for labels such as EMI India and Inreco, her prime work is to be found on Winston Panchacharam's New York-based Amutham label.

Kaleeya Krishna (Amutham, US). Released in 1994, this album of devotional music finds Ragunathan in the company of a full Indian orchestra conducted by Vazhuvoor R. Manikkavinayakam. The record celebrates the work of the composer Venkatasubbaiyar (1700–65), whose muse was Krishna. It's an uplifting performance, even for non-Hindus. The more intimate violin, *mridangam* and *ghatam* instrumentation on *San Marga* (Amutham, US) is also recommended.

M.S. Subbulakshmi Subbulakshmi (1916–2004) was a cultural ambassador for Indian arts on a par with Ravi Shankar, though unlike Ravi Shankar she did not support her recording career with constant touring. Even so, she was heaped with honours, and considered a national treasure.

M.S. Subbulakshmi at Carnegie Hall (Gramophone Company of India, India). This double CD captures the late Subbulakshmi in New York in October 1977 with her daughter Radha Viswanathan, the violinist Kandadevi Alagiriswami and the percussionist Guruvayur Dorai.

Instrumental artists

S. Balachander The *vina* maestro S. Balachander (1927–90) was one of the best known Carnatic instrumentalists, having been one of the influential World Pacific label's major artists with groundbreaking issues such as *Sounds of the Veena* (featuring the flute of N. Ramani) and *The Magic Music of India*. His recorded interpretations of ragams tend to be longer than average.

The Virtuoso of Veena (Denon, Japan). An interpretation of *ragam chakravaakam* forms the centrepiece of this disc. Taeko Kusano's touching notes marvellously capture the spirit of this maverick musician.

Kadri Gopalnath Gopalnath's father started on his father's instrument, the *nagaswaram*, but got turned on to the saxophone after hearing the palace band at Mysore. Pioneering the use of the saxophone in a Carnatic classical setting, his work typifies the duality of Carnatic music in playing a modern instrument in a tradition that goes back centuries.

Gem Tones: Saxophone Supreme, South Indian Style (Globestyle, UK). A fervent and thrilling collection with accompaniment by A. Kanyakumari on her low-tuned violin, sounding for all the world like a tenor sax, plus *mridangam* (M. R. Sainatha) and *morsing* (B. Rajasekhar).

Lalgudi Jayaraman Violin may only be a relatively recent South Indian import – just a few centuries old – but it is difficult to imagine Carnatic music without it and Jayaraman is one of the finest contemporary violinists.

Violin (Moment, US). An interesting North–South excursion with a *kriti*, a *bhajan* (a Hindu devotional song form) and a *tillana* (a light dance-derived form using drum syllables as well as lyrics proper). Percussion accompaniment is from Vellore Ramabhadran (*mridangam*) and Zakir Hussain (tabla).

The Karnataka College of Percussion The Karnataka College has worked with German fusionists Dissidenten on their *Germanistan* and *Jungle Book* albums, and has made a number of records in its own right. Despite the ensemble's percussive-sounding identity, KCP also features the voice of Ramamani and melody instruments such as *vina* (played by leader K. Raghavendra), violin (M.S. Govindaswamy) and flute (V.K. Raman).

River Yamuna (Music of the World, US). This 1997 album is an edited, reworked and reordered version of *Shiva Ganga*, the 1995 album produced by Dissidenten's Marlon Klein. An accessible introduction for beginners testing the heat of Carnatic water.

N. Ramani The flautist Dr N. Ramani (b. 1934) was born in Thiruvarur in Tamil Nadu, the birthplace of Tyagaraja, and by the age of 12 was accomplished enough to be appearing on All India Radio.

Classical Carnatic Flute (Nimbus, UK). A recording with a great deal of presence dating from 1990. Ramani is accompanied on the violin by T.S. Veeraraghhavan, *mridangam* by Srimushnam Rajarao and *ghatam* by E.M. Subramaniam in pieces by Tyagaraja and Ramani himself.

N. Ravikiran The magisterial Ravikiran (b. 1967), who gave his first recital at the age of 5, is the foremost exponent of the *chitra* vina, making it an instrument capable of arcane and ethereal sounds. Ravikiran is also the author of the first-rate introductory guide, *Appreciating Carnatic Music* (Ganesh & Co., Madras, 1997). Log on to Ⓦwww.ravikiranmusic.com for more information.

Young Star of Gottuvadyam (Chhanda Dhara, Germany). Mesmerizing performances, accompanied on *mridangam* by Trichur R. Mohan and on *ghatam* by T.H. Subashchandran – the nearly nineteen-minute long performance of *Shankara Bharanam* is especially good.

Shankar L. Shankar (b. 1950) played in a violin trio with his brothers L. Vaidyanathan and L. Subramaniam before embarking on a solo career, and founding the Indo-Jazz fusion group Shakti with guitarist John McLaughlin. He is renowned for creating a ten-string double violin with a startling extended range.

Raga Aberi (Music of the World, US). A spectacular *ragam-thanam-pallavi* performance growing out the growling low notes of Shankar's extraordinary violin. The performance also features spectacular vocal percussion and solos by Zakir Hussain (tabla) and Vikku Vinayakram (*ghatam*).

U. Srinivas Mandolin-player U. Srinivas (b. 1969) uses a five-string, solid body instrument, akin to a cut-down electric guitar, rather than the eight-string western mandolin, which he claims is ideally suited to the ragas of South Indian music. Like many Carnatic musicians he was a child prodigy and has excited listeners the world over, notably in the west with a successful fusion album, *Dream* (1995 – see p.778), with Michael Brook. He sometimes performs mandolin duets with his brother U. Rajesh.

Rama Sreerama (RealWorld, UK). An inspiring introduction to Srinivas's music, including pieces by Srinivas himself and Tyagaraja. Strongly devotional in character, with violin, *mridangam* and *ghatam* accompaniment.

L. Subramaniam L. Subramaniam (b. 1947) is from a dynasty of violinists (his brothers are L. Vaidyanathan and Shakti-founder L. Shankar). One of the most recorded Carnatic artists in the West, he has regularly played in non-Carnatic contexts – with Hindustani musicians, jazz-fusion groups, western orchestras and in films (including Mira Nair's *Salaam Bombay* and *Mississippi Masala*).

Electric Modes (Water Lily Acoustics, US). A two-CD set, one volume of which consists of original compositions, while the second focuses on traditional ragams. The album's title recalls Muddy Waters' album *Electric Mud*.

Fusion

Michael Brook Toronto-born composer and producer Michael Brook has had an eclectic career, with early stints in rock bands (including Martha and the Muffins) leading to ambient/minimalist-influenced soundtrack work, including the 2006 film, *An Inconvenient Truth*. But he is perhaps best known as a producer, working on albums for Peter Gabriel's Real World label with U. Srinavas and Nusrat Fateh Ali Khan amongst others.

Dream (Realworld, UK). An album that began with the idea of Brook producing Srinavas and turned into a full-blown East–West collaboration, including contributions from Canadian singer Jane Siberry.

John McLaughlin/Shakti Guitarist John McLaughlin has been a linchpin of East–West fusion since introducing Miles Davis to Indian music back in the 1960s, moving through solo work, the jazz-rock Mahavishnu Orchestra and, most impressively, the all-acoustic group Shakti, formed in 1974 with tabla player Zakir Hussain, L. Shankar (violin) and T.H. Vinayakram (*ghatam*). Shakti toured and recorded to great acclaim until 1977, when Columbia, used to massive-selling albums from McLaughlin, withdrew support. The group has since continued to perform in various permutations, including the Remember Shakti revival in 1997 with musicians such as Selvaganesh (percussion), Debashish Bhattacharya (guitar) and U. Srinivas (mandolin) in place of L. Shankar.

Remember Shakti *The Believer* (Verve, UK). In this wonderful live recording, made during a tour in 2000, McLaughlin teams up with mandolin maestro U. Srinivas and percussion virtuosos Zakir Hussain and V. Selvaganesh to rework the successful Shakti formula. The result is some of the most inspired improvisation ever captured on disc.

often paired with a drone nagaswaram or *ottu*. Besides its ceremonial functions – and it is perhaps best heard in the open air – it is sometimes employed in formal classical concert settings. Leading players include Sheik Chinnamoulana and the brothers M.P.N. Sethuraman and M.P.N. Ponnuswamy.

The Carnatic counterpart to the tabla is the **mridangam**, a double-headed, barrel-shaped drum made from a single block of jackwood. Both heads are made from layers of hide and can be tuned according to the ragam being performed. Vellore Ramabhadran and Mysore Rajappa Sainatha are two of the top players. Other percussion instruments include the **tavil**, a folk-style barrel drum commonly found in ceremonial nagaswaram ensembles, and the **ghatam**, a clay pot tuned by firing. The latter is frequently found in South Indian ensembles and, unlikely as it may seem, in the hands of a top player like T.H. "Vikku"Vinayakram it can contribute some spectacular solos. The **morsing** (or *morching*) is a Jew's harp, often part of the accompanying ensemble, although it is frequently dropped when groups tour to save on the air fare. The **jalatarangam** (or *jalatarang*) is something of a curiosity: a melodic percussion instrument comprising a semicircle of water-filled porcelain bowls. It can create a sound of extraordinary beauty as the lead melody instrument in a typical

Carnatic ensemble with violin, *mridangam* and *ghatam*. Players include Mysore's M.S. Chandrasekharian and the brothers Anayampatti S. Dhandapani and Anayampatti S. Ganesan.

New instruments

Both the Subcontinent's two classical systems give pride of place to the voice, while melodic instruments, to some degree, are played to mimic it. Nevertheless, Carnatic music makes use of a fascinating array of stringed, wind and percussion instruments, many unique to the Subcontinent.

From the nineteenth century, Carnatic music began to appropriate **Western instruments**, notably the violin and clarinet. More recent additions include the mandolin and saxophone. In the South – where the northern *sarangi* is a stranger – the **violin**'s fluidity, grace, speed and penetrative volume guaranteed it a complement of converts during the nineteenth century, most notably **Tanjore Vadivelu** of the Tanjore Quartette. Nowadays, Carnatic music without the violin is inconceivable. Credit for introducing it and adapting its Western tuning is given to **Balaswamy Dikshitar** (1786–1859), younger brother of the saintly composer Muttuswamy (see p.776) – though some traditionalist scholars claim it as a descendant of the earlier *dhanur vina*. Maestros such as Lalgudi G. Jayaraman, V.V. Subrahmanyam and L. Subramaniam are major artists, while A. Kanyakumari typifies the female violinists who are coming to the fore. In South India, the violin is played sitting on the floor with the body of the violin against the upper chest and the scroll wedged against the ankle, leaving the left hand free to slide more freely up and down the strings. **Shankar**, brother of L. Subramaniam, has devised his own electric double violin with an extended bottom range and dark tone.

The introduction of the **clarinet** (*clarionet*), in around 1860, is credited to Mahadeva Nattuvanar. Until around 1920, it was mostly used as an ensemble instrument in *cinna melam*, a dance accompaniment form. Thereafter, it was gradually established as a soloist's instrument. Balaraman of the Nadamuni Band was one of the twentieth century's first *clarionet* maestros and his work has been continued by musicians like A.K.C. Natarajan.

The **mandolin** has gained acceptance thanks to another of South India's child prodigies, **U. Srinivas**, often known as Mandolin Srinivas. He started playing the instrument aged six and has since toured worldwide and proved that the mandolin (albeit heavily modified) is highly effective at spinning gossamer webs of Tyagaraja improvisations. He is a very devout musician and his performances usually have a devotional ingredient.

The **saxophone** is another recent import, and its champion, Kadri Gopalnath, is one of South India's most popular musicians, with dozens of recordings to his credit. Gopalnath demonstrates Carnatic music's particular ability to be ancient and modern at the same time. When he plays the Carnatic ragams, the powerful sound of the saxophone echoes the ancient *nagaswaram*, but with a distinctively contemporary tone and attitude.

Ken Hunt

Goan music

With reggae and techno blaring out of so many beach bars, you'd be forgiven for thinking **Goa's music and dance scene** started with the invention of the synthesizer. However, the state boasts a vibrant musical tradition of its own: a typically syncretic blend of east and west that is as spicy and distinctive as the region's cuisine. You won't hear the calypso-like rhythms of Konkani pop or haunting Kunbi folk songs at the full-moon parties, though. Rooted in village and religious life, Goan music is primarily for domestic consumption, played at temple festivals, harvest celebrations, as an accompaniment to popular theatre and, most noticeably, on the crackly cassette machines of local buses.

Wander into almost any Hindu village on the eve of an important puja, particularly around harvest time after the monsoons, and you'll experience Goan roots music and dance at its most authentic. The torchbearers of the region's thriving **folk tradition** are the Kunbi class of landless labourers, often seen bent double in rice paddy, the women with garish coloured cotton saris tied *dhoti*-style around their legs. Agricultural work – planting, threshing and grinding grain, raking salt pans, and fixing fishing nets – provides the essential

Chenda Melam: Keralan ritual percussion

The noisiest, rowdiest and most intense phase of any Keralan temple festival is the one presided over by the local drum orchestra, or **chenda melam**, whose ear-shattering performances accompany the procession of the deity around the sacred precinct and into the shrine. As impressive for their mental arithmetic as percussion technique and showing enormous stamina in the intense heat, the musicians play an assortment of upright barrel drums (**chenda**) supported over the shoulder, bronze cymbals and wind instruments – the oboe-like **kuzhal** and the spectacular C-shaped brass trumpets (**kombu**), which emphasize and prolong the drum beating.

Performances invariably begin with an impressive "ghrr" and "dhim" produced on the drums. This is said to symbolize a lion's roar and was probably once performed in support of a lion hunt. After this mighty introduction, the drums drop the tempo and the music builds up like a pyramid. It starts slowly with long-lasting musical cycles and works up to a short, fast, powerful climax. During the performance, an elephant, musicians and the crowd process round the temple precinct – after more than two hours, the excited crowd and sweating musicians celebrate the conclusion and follow the elephant and deity into the inner temple.

The first stage broadly symbolizes the ordinary life of men, while the peak of the last stage shows the ideal human or divine aspect of reality. The music must please the god on top of the elephant and, of course, the assembled temple crowd. While the main beats are provided by hitting the underside of the *chenda*, the skilled solo *chenda* players create intricate patterns over the top. Different players may gather for each event, but they are capable of playing together perfectly with no rehearsal. The concept is more like a big jazz band than a European classical orchestra.

A typical setup for a medium-sized temple festival kicks off with a turn from the **panchavadyam** orchestra, comprising three types of drums, cymbals and the *kombu* trumpets. A conch is blown three times, symbolizing the holy syllable "Om", and the performance begins its first stage with a slow, 1792-beat rhythmic cycle. The next cycle has 896 beats, half that number, then 448, half again, then 224 and so on. The speed increases until fast 56-beat cycles round it off. Fireworks, a large crowd and elephants trumpeting support the ecstatic climax.

For the evening, performances of **tayambaka**, **keli** and **kuzhal pattu** are announced. Each is a solo performing style, with players from the *chenda melam* and *panchavadyam* orchestras. *Tayambaka* is the main attraction, an improvised *chenda* solo played with a small ensemble of accompanying treble and bass *chenda* and cymbals. The other solo styles, *keli* (with a soloist on the *maddalam*, horizontally slung barrel drum) and *kuzhal pattu* (oboe), precede the midnight performance of the last *chenda melam*.

Rolf Killius

rhythms for Konkani songs, known as **Kunbi geet**. More rehearsed performances take place during the Hindu month of Paush (late Feb), when groups of
women gather in the village square-cum-dance ground (*mannd*) to sing *dhalos*
and *fugdis*. The singing may run over seven or more nights, culminating with
outbreaks of spirit possession and trances.

The most famous Goan folk song and dance form, though, has to be the
mando. Originally, this slow and expressive dance (whose name derives from
the Sanskrit mandala, meaning circular pattern) was traditionally performed in
circles, but these days tends to be danced by men and women standing
opposite each other in parallel lines, waving fans and coloured handkerchiefs.
Mandos gather pace as they progress and are usually followed by a series of
dulpods, quick-time tunes whose lyrics are traditionally satirical, exposing
village gossip about errant housewives, lapsed priests and so on. *Dulpods*, in
turn, merge into the even jauntier rhythms of **deknis**, bringing the set dances
to a tumultuous conclusion.

The basic rhythmic cycles, or *ovis*, of Goan folk songs were exploited by early
Christian missionaries in their work. Overlaid with lyrics inspired by Bible
stories, many were eventually assimilated into the local Catholic tradition: today,
the *mando*, for example, is usually danced by Christians on church festivals and
wedding days. It also became the favourite dance of the Goan gentry who,
dressed in ball gowns and dinner suits with fans and flamboyant handkerchiefs,
used to perform it during the glittering functions held in the reception rooms
of the territory's top houses.

Fado

The most European-influenced of all the Goan folk idioms is the **fado**. Rendered
in a turgid mock operatic style, these melancholic songs epitomize the colonial
predilection for nostalgia or longing for the home country, known in Portuguese
as *saudade*. Ironically, though, few *fadistas* actually laid eyes on the fabled lights of
Lisbon or Coimbra they eulogized in their lyrics, and today the fado is a dying

△ Musicians playing the *vina*

art form. However, a couple of renowned folk singers, notably the band leader **Oslando** and singer-guitarist **Lucio Miranda**, invariably include a couple of old fado numbers on their albums. Lucio, the greatest living exponent of the form, also gives the odd performance in the five-star hotels around Panjim.

Konkani pop

Rave music aside, most of the sounds you hear around Goa these days are either *filmi* hits from the latest blockbuster Hindi movies, or a mishmash of folk tunes and calypso rhythms known as **Konkani pop**. Backed by groups of women singers and fanfaring mariachi-style brass sections, Konkani lead vocalists croon away with the reverb cranked up against a cacophony of electric guitar and keyboard accompaniment.

Konkani pop is best experienced live (the costumes tend to be as lurid as the music), but if you don't manage to get to a gig, every roadside cassette-wallah stocks a range of popular tapes. No particular artist is worth singling out – nor are many likely to find fans among Western visitors. However, world-music aficionados should definitely check out a couple of cassettes to sample the sometimes surreal blend of musical influences. Underpinning the Portuguese-style melodies are conga-driven African and Caribbean rhythms, Brazilian syncopations, and almost Polynesian-sounding harmonies. The only part of the world Konkani pop sounds like it doesn't come from is India.

Dance

Among the most magical experiences a visitor to South India can have is to see one of the dances that play such an important part in the cultural life of the region. India's most prevalent classical dance style, *bharatanatyam*, originated in the South and still fills concert halls in Tamil towns, while other types of ritualized theatre, such as **kathakali, kutti-yattam and theyyam**, remain integral to temple worship in Kerala. If you're lucky enough to catch an authentic performance in situ, you'll never forget it: the stamina of the performers and the spectacle of an audience sitting up all night to see the finale of a dance drama at dawn is utterly remarkable.

The Natya Shastra

All forms of Indian dance share certain broad characteristics and can be traced back to principles enshrined in the **Natya Shastra**, a Sanskrit treatise on dramaturgy dating from the first century BC. The text covers every aspect of the origin and function of **natya**, the art of dance-drama, which combines music, stylized speech, dance and spectacle, and characterizes theatre throughout South Asia. The spread of this art form occurred during the centuries of cultural expansion from the second century BC to the eighth century AD, when South Indian kings sent trade missions, court dancers, priests and conquering armies all over the region. Even in countries that later embraced Buddhism or Islam, dances continue to show evidence of Indian forms, and Hindu gods and goddesses still feature, mixed with indigenous heroes and deities.

Indian dance is divided into two temperaments: **tandava**, which represents the fearful male energy of Shiva, and **lasya**, representing the grace of his wife Parvati. Dances can fall into one or other category (kathakali is *tandava* and *bharatanatyam* is *lasya*), or combine the two elements. Equally, they include in differing degrees the three main components of classical dance: **nritta**, pure dance in which the music is reflected by decorative movements of the body; **natya**, which is the dramatic element of the dance and includes the portrayal of character; and **nritya**, the interpretive element, in which mood is portrayed through hand and facial gestures and the position of the feet and legs.

The term **abinaya** describes the resources at the disposal of a performer in communicating the meaning of a dance; they include costume and make-up, speech and intonation, psychological understanding and, perhaps the most distinctive and complex element, the language of gestures. Stylized gestures are prescribed for every part of the body – there are seven movements for the eyebrows, six for the nose and six for the cheeks, for example – and they can take a performer years of intensive training to perfect.

Useful websites

Ⓦ **www.artindia.net** Portal for India's performing arts. Ⓦ **www.carnaticmusic.com** Very well-organized site which explores Carnatic (South Indian) classical music. Ⓦ **www.sruti.com** The online version of a very informative and in-depth music and dance magazine devoted to India's performing arts.

Dance recitals take place throughout the winter, building up to fever pitch during April and May before pausing for the monsoon (June, July & Aug). Finding them requires a little perseverance, and a certain amount of luck, but it's well worth the effort.

Bharatanatyam is performed at concert halls in most major cities and towns in the South. In addition, it is always well represented at the annual dance festivals held at Mamallapuram (see p.541), Hampi (see p.339) and Thiruvananthapuram (see p.376). Wherever you are, it's always worth enquiring at tourist offices. If you're in Chennai, check out the Listings pages of the regional press, such as *The Hindu*, for details of forthcoming events.

In Kerala, buy a copy of the Malayalam daily paper *Mathrabhumi* and ask someone to read the listings for you. **Temple festivals**, where most of the action takes place, are invariably announced. Tourist **kathakali** is staged in Kochi (see p.457), but to find authentic performances, contact performing arts schools such as Thiruvananthapuram's Margi (see p.377) and Cheruthuruthy's Kerala Kalamandalam (see p.477). **Kutiyattam** artists work at both, as well as at Natana Kairali at Irinjalakuda (see p.472). A good source of information on more obscure Keralan rituals, festivals and dance forms is the privately run tourist desk at Main Boat Jetty, Ernakulam (see p.449).

Once complete control of the body has been mastered, a performer will have a repertoire of several thousand meanings. In combination with other movements, a single hand gesture, with the fingers extended and the thumb bent for example, can be used to express heat, rain, a crowd of men, the night, a forest, a flight of birds or a house. Similarly, up to three characters can be played by a single performer by alternating facial expressions.

Despite frequent feats of technical brilliance, performers are rarely judged by their skill in executing a particular dance, but by their success in communicating certain specific emotions, or **bhava**, to the audience. This can only be measured by the quality of **rasa**, a mood or sentiment, one for each of the nine *bhavas*, which the audience experiences during a performance.

Bharatanatyam

The best-known Indian classical dance style is *bharatanatyam*, a composite term made up of **bharata**, an acronym of "*bhava*" (expression), "*raga*" (melody) and "*tala*" (rhythm) and **natyam,** the Tamil word for 'dance'. It is a graceful form, rich in gesture, and performed only by women. A popular subject for temple sculptures throughout South India (especially Tamil Nadu), it originated in the dances of the **devadasis**, temple dancing girls who originally performed as part of their devotional duties in the great Tamil shrines. Usually "donated" to a temple by their parents, the young girls were formally "wedded" to the deity and spent the rest of their lives dancing or singing as part of their devotional duties. Later, however, the *devadasis* system became debased, and the dancers, who formerly enjoyed high status in Hindu society, became prostitutes controlled by the brahmins, whom male visitors to the temple would pay for sexual services.

In the latter half of the nineteenth century, four brothers set themselves the task of saving the dance from extinction and pieced together a reconstruction of the form through study of the Natya Shastra, the images on temple friezes and through information gleaned from former *devadasis*. Although the dance today is largely based on their findings, this was only the first step in its revival, as *bharatanatyam* continued to be confined to the temples and was danced almost exclusively by men – the only way, as the brothers saw it, of preventing its moral decline. Not until the 1930s, when **Rukmini Devi**, a member of the Theosophical Society, introduced the form to a wider middle-class audience, did *bharatanatyam* begin to achieve popularity as a secular art form.

As ward of the nineteenth-century British rebel **Annie Besant**, Devi had greater exposure to foreign arts than many women of her generation. She developed an interest in Western dance while accompanying her husband, George Arundale, former principal of the Theosophical Society's school in Adyar, Chennai, on lecture tours and had studied under Pavlova, among others. In 1929, however, after witnessing a performance of the dance she later named "*bharatanatyam*", she dedicated her life to its revival. The dance school she founded at Adyar is now known as Kalakshetra, and continues to develop some of the world's most accomplished exponents.

In her determination to make the art form socially respectable, Devi eliminated all erotic elements and was known to be rigid and authoritarian in her views about how *bharatanatyam* should be danced. Many ex-pupils have gone on to develop their own interpretations of the style, but the form continues to be seen as an essentially spiritual art. Its theme is invariably romantic love, with the dancer seen as a devotee separated from the object of her devotion. In this way, she dramatizes the idea of **sringara bhakti**, or worship through love.

As with other classical dance forms, training is rigorous. Performers are encouraged to dissolve their identity in the dance and become instruments for the expression of divine presence. The order in which the phases of the dance are performed and practised is considered to be the one best suited to this goal. A recital usually lasts about two hours and consists of the following phases: *alarippu, jatiswaram, sabdam, varnam, padams, javalis, tillana* and *mangalam*.

All performances are preceded by a *namaskaram*, a salutation to the gods, offered by the stage, musicians and audience; a floral offering is made to a statue of the presiding deity, which stands at the right of the stage. The pivotal part of the performance is **varnam**, which the preceding three phases build up to through *nritta* (pure dance based on rhythm), adding melody and then lyrics. In *varnam*, every aspect of the dancer's art is exercised through two sections, the first slow, alternating *abinhaya* with rhythmic syllables, and the second twice the pace of the first, alternating *abinhaya* with melodic syllables. In the following two phases the emphasis is on the expression of mood through mime, and in the penultimate phase, the *tillana*, the dancer reverts again to the pure rhythm which began the dance. A *mangalam*, or short prayer, marks the end of a performance.

Kathakali

Here is the tradition of the trance dancers, here is the absolute demand of the subjugation of body to spirit, here is the realization of the cosmic transformation of human into divine.

Mrinalini Sarabhai, classical dancer

The image of a **kathakali** actor in a magnificent costume with extraordinary make-up and a huge gold crown has become Kerala's trademark, seen on

anything from matchboxes to TV adverts for detergents. There are still many traditional performances, which take place on open ground outside a temple, beginning at 10pm and lasting until dawn, illuminated solely by the flickers of a large brass oil lamp centre stage. Virtually nothing about kathakali is naturalistic, because it depicts the world of gods and demons. Both male and female roles are played by men.

Standing at the back of the stage, two musicians play driving rhythms, one on a bronze gong, the other on heavy bell-metal cymbals; they also sing the dialogue. Actors appear and disappear from behind a handheld curtain and never utter a sound, save the odd strange cry. Learning the elaborate hand gestures, facial expressions and

△ Classical dance, Kerala

choreographed movements, as articulate and precise as any sign language, requires rigorous training that can begin at the age of eight and last ten years. At least two more drummers stand left of the stage; one plays the upright **chenda** with slender curved sticks, the other the **maddalam**, a horizontal barrel-shaped hand drum. When a female character is "speaking", the chenda is replaced by the hourglass-shaped **ettaka**, a "talking drum" on which melodies can be played. The drummers keep their eyes on the actors, whose every gesture is reinforced by their sound, from the gentlest embrace to the gory disembowelling of an enemy.

Although it bears the unmistakable influences of *kutiyattam* and indigenous folk rituals, kathakali, literally "story-play", is thought to have crystallized into a distinct theatre form during the seventeenth century. The plays are based on three major sources: the Mahabharata, the Ramayana and the Bhagavata Purana. While the stories are ostensibly about god-heroes such as Rama and Krishna, the most popular characters are those that give the most scope to the actors – the villainous, fanged, red-and-black-faced *katti* ("knife") anti-heroes. These types, such as the kings Ravana and Duryodhana, are dominated by lust, greed, envy and violence. David Bolland's handy paperback *Guide to Kathakali*, widely available in Kerala, gives invaluable scene-by-scene summaries of the most popular plays and explains in simple language a lot more besides.

When attending a performance, arrive early to get your bearings before it gets dark, even though the first play will not start much before 10pm. Members of the audience are welcome to visit the dressing room before and during the performance, to watch the **masks** and **make-up** being applied. The colour and design of these, which specialist artists take several hours to apply, signify the personality of each character. The principal characters fall into the following seven types.

Pacca ("green" and "pure") characters, painted bright green, are the noble heroes, including gods such as Rama and Krishna.

Katti ("knife") are evil and clever characters such as Ravana. Often the most popular with the audience, they have green faces to signify their noble birth, with upturned moustaches and white mushroom knobs on the tips of their noses.

Chokannatadi ("red beard") characters are power-drunk and vicious, and have black faces from the nostrils upwards, with blood-red beards.

Velupputadi ("white beard") represents Hanuman, monkey son of the wind god and personal servant of Rama. He always wears a grey beard and furry coat, and has a black and red face and green nose.

Karupputadi ("black beard") is a hunter or forest-dweller and carries a sword, bow and quiver. He has a coal-black face with a white flower on his nose.

Kari ("black") characters, the ogresses and witches of the drama, have black faces, marked with white patterns, and huge breasts.

Minnukku ("softly shaded") characters are women, brahmins and sages. The women have pale yellow faces sprinkled with mica and the men wear orange *dhotis*.

Once the make-up is finished, the performers are helped into their costumes – elaborate wide skirts tied to the waist, towering head-dresses and long silver talons fitted to the left hand. Women, brahmins and sages are the only characters with a different style of dress: men wear orange, and the women wear saris and cover their heads. The transformation is completed with a final prayer before the performance begins.

Visitors new to kathakali will undoubtedly get bored during such long programmes, parts of which are very slow indeed. If you're at a village performance, you may not always find accommodation, so you can't leave during the night. Be prepared to sit on the ground for hours, and bring some warm clothes. Half the fun is staying up all night to witness, just as the dawn light appears, the gruesome disembowelling of a villain or a demon *asura*.

Kuchipudi

Kuchipudi originated in Andhra Pradesh and is considered to follow the Natya Shastra more closely than any other form – though despite this it was until recently seen essentially as a folk idiom and a means of presenting scenes from mythology and the Hindu epics to relatively unsophisticated audiences. Similar in form to *bharatanatyam*, it also shares a history of decline and regeneration. Its present form is thought to date back to the seventeenth century, when a local man capsized his boat while on the way to his wedding and prayed that his life might be saved. On finding his prayers answered, he wrote, in his new incarnation as **Siddhappa Yogi**, a dance drama in praise of Krishna, and gathered a troupe of brahmin men to perform it. When presented at court in 1675, it so impressed the resident *nawab* that he granted the village of Kuchipudi to the artists so that they might pass on their art to future generations. Taking its name from the village, the dance has been practised by the same fifteen brahmin families ever since.

Traditionally performed only by groups of men, *kuchipudi* requires seven years of rigorous training, with parallel education in music, Sanskrit, the ancient scriptures and mythology. In recent years, however, there has been an increase in solo performances, as well as those by women dancing.

Like *bharatanatyam*, *kuchipudi* follows a fixed sequence of phases and uses similar techniques and costumes, but is distinguished by the important role given to dialogue and song. It also differs from other forms in that the dancers sing for themselves, usually in Telugu. Humour and spectacle are other important elements that distinguish it from the more restrained mood of *bharatanatyam*: the highlight of most performances is a scene in which one dancer carries a pot of water on her head while balancing on the edge of a brass plate.

Mohiniyattam

A semiclassical form originating in Kerala, **mohiniyattam**, like *bharatanatyam*, grew out of the temple dances of the *devadasis*. It, too, was revived through the efforts of enthusiastic individuals, first in the nineteenth century by Swati Thirunal, the king of Travancore, and again in the 1930s, after a period of disrepute, by the poet Vallathol. Mohiniyattam ("the dance of the enchantress") takes its name from the mythological maiden **Mohini**, who evoked desire and had the ability to steal the heart of the onlooker. Usually a solo dance performed by women, it is dominated by the mood of *lasya*, with graceful movements distinguished by a rhythmic swaying of the body from side to side. The central theme is one of love and devotion to god, with Vishnu or Krishna appearing most frequently as the heroes.

Dancers of *mohiniyattam* wear realistic make-up and the white, gold-bordered Kasavu sari of Kerala. The music which accompanies the dancer is classical Carnatic, with lyrics in Malayalam.

Kutiyattam

Three families of the Chakyar caste and a few outsiders perform the Sanskrit drama **kutiyattam**, the oldest continually performed theatre form in the world. Until recently, it was only performed inside temples, and then only in front of the uppermost castes. Visually, it is very similar to its offspring, kathakali, but its atmosphere is infinitely more archaic. The actors, eloquent in sign language and symbolic movement, speak in the bizarre, compelling intonation of the local brahmins' Vedic chant, unchanged since 1500 BC.

A single act of a *kutiyattam* play can require ten full nights; the entire play forty. A great actor, in full command of the subtleties of gestural expression, can take half an hour to do such a simple thing as murder a demon, berate the audience, or simply describe a leaf falling to the ground. Unlike kathakali, *kutiyattam* includes comic characters and plays. The ubiquitous Vidushaka, narrator and clown, is something of a court jester, and traditionally has held the right to criticize openly the highest in the land without fear of retribution.

Theyyattam

In northern Kerala, a wide range of ritual "performances", loosely known as **Theyyattam**, are extremely localized, even to particular families. They might include *bhuta* (spirit or hero worship), trance dances, the enactment of legendary events and oracular pronouncements. Performers are usually from low castes, but during the ritual, a brahmin will honour the deities they represent, so the status of each individual is reversed.

Although *theyyattam* can nowadays be seen in government-organized cultural festivals, the powerful effect is best experienced in the courtyard of a house or temple, in a village setting. Some figures, with painted faces and bodies, are genuinely terrifying; costumes include headgear metres high, sometimes doubling as a mask, and clothes of leaves and bark.

The only place you can be sure of seeing *theyyattam* is at **Parassinikadavu**, a small village 20km north of Kunnur, in the far north of Kerala, where the head priest of the local temple dances each day. This is an extraordinary spectacle that shouldn't be missed if you're in the area. For more typical village *theyyattam*, you have to be in the right place at the right time. First, head for Kunnur and ask the local tourist officer to point you in the right direction; after a few days' of waiting around, someone will hear you're looking for *theyyattam* and take you back to their village if a performance is planned – an experience anyone with more than a passing interest in ritual theatre and costume definitely shouldn't miss.

Vicki Maggs

C

CONTEXTS | Dance

Books

Appropriately for a part of the world with a written history dating back nearly two and a half thousand years, South India has spawned an extraordinary wealth of books – what follows is merely a small selection. Most are available in the UK and US, and frequently in India, too, where they tend to be much cheaper. Where separate editions exist in the UK and US, publishers are detailed below in the form "UK publisher/US publisher", unless the publisher is the same in both countries. Where books are published in India only, this follows the publisher's name. The abbreviation o/p signifies an out-of-print book (sometimes available through ⓦwww.amazon.com or ⓦwww.amazon.co.uk). Titles marked with a 🕱 are particularly recommended.

History

Jad Adams and Phillip Whitehead *The Dynasty: the Nehru-Gandhi Story* (Penguin). A brilliant and intriguing account of India's most famous – or infamous – family and the way its various personalities have shaped post-Independence India.

A.L. Basham *The Wonder that was India* (South Asia Books, India). A veritable encyclopedia by India's foremost authority on his country's ancient history. Every page of this masterpiece bristles with the author's erudition. A companion volume, by S.A. Rizvi, brings it up to the arrival of the British.

Larry Collins and Dominique Lapierre *Freedom at Midnight* (HarperCollins). Readable, if shallow, account of Independence, highly sympathetic to the British and, particularly, to Mountbatten, who was the authors' main source of information.

🕱 **William Dalrymple** *White Mughals* (HarperCollins). In the course of five years' research into the lives of early European colonials who adopted "native" customs and married Indian women, William Dalrymple stumbled upon the forgotten story of James Achilles Kirkpatrick, British Resident at Hyderabad at the end of the eighteenth century, who fell in love with, and subsequently married, the great niece of the Nizam's prime minister. Both it, and the author's account of how he pieced the picture together, make an extraordinary tale, told with relish, erudition and an impeccable sense of pace in a book that grips like a great nineteenth-century novel.

Charles Dellon *L'Inquisition de Goa* (Editions Chandeigne, Paris). The only surviving first-hand account of the Goan Inquisition, by a French traveller who survived it in the seventeenth century. Dellon's chilling narrative, in this French edition illustrated with the original engravings, was the *Papillon* of its day, and remains a shocking indictment of the genocide perpetrated by the colonial clergy – at least, if you can read French (its English translation is out of print and extremely rare).

Patrick French *Liberty or Death* (HarperCollins). The definitive account of the last years of the British Raj. Material from hitherto unreleased intelligence files shows how Churchill's "florid incompetence" and Attlee's "feeble incomprehension" contributed to the debacle that was Partition, which French concludes was doomed through "confusion, human frailty and neglect". All in all, a damning indictment of Britain's role that debunks many myths.

Dilip Hiro *The Rough Guide History of India* (Rough Guides; o/p). No other book crams so much background material on India into such a small format as this pocket history, which fleshes out a bare-bones time line with contextual boxes, literary extracts, potted biographies, quotations and black and white photos.

Lawrence James *Raj: the Making and Unmaking of British India* (Abacus, UK). A door-stopping 700-page history of British rule in India, drawing on recently released official papers and private memoirs. The most erudite survey of its kind, and unlikely to be bettered as a general introduction.

John Keay *India: a History* (HarperCollins). In this, the most recent of his five consistently excellent books on India, John Keay manages to coax clear, impartial and highly readable narrative from 5000 years of fragmented events. Arguably the best single-volume history currently in print.

John Keay *The Honourable East India Company* (HarperCollins). In characteristically fluent style, Keay strikes the right balance between those who regard the East India Company as a rapacious institution with malevolent intentions, and those who present its acquisition of the Indian empire as an unintended, almost accidental process.

Bhermann Kulke and Dietmar Rothermund *A History of India*

(Routledge). Among the few complete histories of India to give adequate coverage to the South (one of the authors' specialist subjects), from the Mesolithic era (100,000 BC) to the war in Sri Lanka.

Geoffrey Moorhouse *India Britannica* (HarperCollins; Academy Chicago). A balanced, lively survey of the rise and fall of the British Raj, with lots of illustrations. Recommended if this is your first foray into the period, as it's a lot more concise and readable than Lawrence James' *Raj*.

Robert Sewell *A Forgotten Empire* (reprinted in facsimile by Asian Educational Services, New Delhi). The definitive history of the Vijayanagars, supplemented with the translated chronicles of Domingo Paes and Fernao Nuniz, two Portuguese travellers who visited in the royal city at the height of its splendour. Essential reading if you want to get to grips with the history behind Hampi's ruins.

Percival Spear *History of India* Volume II (Penguin/Viking). Covers the period from the Mughal era to the death of Gandhi. Among the most readable offerings of its kind, and the most widely available.

Romila Thapar *History of India* Volume I (Penguin/Viking). Concise paperback account of early Indian history, ending with the Delhi Sultanate.

Gillian Tindall *City of Gold* (Penguin, India). Definitive, if rather dry biography of Mumbai, from colonial trading post to modern metropolis.

Society

William Dalrymple *The Age of Kali* (HarperCollins). This collection of stylish essays from ten years of journalistic assignments is rich with

insights drawn from encounters and interviews with a vast range of personalities. Madurai's Meenakshi temple and the extraordinary history of the Nizam of Hyderabad comprise the South India content. Published in India as *In the Court of the Fish-Eyed Goddess*.

Rachel Dwyer and Divia Patel *Cinema India: The Visual Culture of Hindi Film* (Reaktion). Definitive guide to the dynamic visual cinematic culture of India, charting developments from 1913 up to the present. It describes in great detail how changes in Indian society have been mirrored through the media of film. The evolution of styles and advertising trends are lavishly illustrated in both black-and-while and colour.

Edward Luce *In Spite of the Gods* (Abacus, London). "An unsentimental evaluation of contemporary India" is how this book bills itself, and in truth there's no more authoritative, penetrating account of the current state of the nation in print. Written by a former South Asia correspondent of the FT, it's packed full of sobering statistics and myth-busting facts that challenge common misconceptions about the country, yet somehow manages to remain eminently readable throughout, even witty in places. Different themes – from caste conflict to the rise of Hindu fundamentalism and relations with Pakistan – are addressed in successive chapters that could stand alone, allowing you to dip in and out.

Gita Mehta *Karma Cola: Marketing the Mystic East* (Minerva/Fawcett Books). Satirical look at the psychedelic 1970s freak scene in India, with some hilarious anecdotes, and many a wry observation on the wackier (US) excesses of spiritual tourism. Her latest book, *Snakes and Ladders* (Vintage/Fawcett Books), is a brilliant overview of contemporary urban India in the form of a pot-pourri of essays, travelogues and interviews. It covers issues from Bollywood and the sex industry to caste, gender, ecology and the contradiction between Indian poverty and the country's multi-million-dollar arms and business sectors.

V.S. Naipaul *India: a Wounded Civilisation* (Penguin). This bleak political travelogue, researched and written during and shortly after the Emergency, gained Naipaul, an Indian Trinidadian, a reputation as one of India's harshest critics. Two decades later, he returned to see what had happened to the country his parents left. The result, *A Million Mutinies Now*, is an altogether more sympathetic and rounded portrait – a superbly crafted mosaic of individual lives from around the Subcontinent, including a memorable portrait of a staunchly traditional Tamil brahmin. One of the best books on India ever written.

Christopher Pinney *Photos of the Gods* (Reaktion Books). This history of the printed image in Indian popular culture focuses on political, cultural and religious themes and traces the importance that the visual arts – in the form of posters, postcards and other printed images – have had on India's history since the 1870s. A fascinating book illustrated with 80 colour and 87 black-and-white pictures.

Mark Tully *No Full Stops in India* (Penguin/Viking). Crystallizing a lifetime's experience as the BBC's man in India, Tully's thesis – that Indians should seek inspiration for their future in their own great traditions rather than those of the West – provoked widespread scorn from the country's Westernized elite. Yet this remains among the best-informed critiques on India of its generation. Most of the ten essays in it refer to the North, but the issues tackled are equally relevant to the South. The later *India in Slow Motion* covers a similarly diverse range of subjects, from Hindu extremism, child labour and Sufi mysticism to the crisis in South Indian agriculture and the persistence of political corruption to the problem of Kashmir. Both challenge preconceptions foreigners often hold about India, and those held by Indians about their own country.

Travel

Alexander Frater *Chasing the Monsoon* (Penguin). Frater's wet-season jaunt down the west coast and across the Ganges plains took him through an India of muddy puddles and grey skies: an evocative account of the country as few visitors see it, and now something of a classic of the genre.

Justine Hardy *Bollywood Boy* (John Murray). Sassy, chick-lit-style travelogue through the larger-than-life world of the Bombay film industry, following the author's quest to interview heartthrob Hrithik Roshan at the height of his fame. Along the way, Justine brushes shoulders with a lurid cast of has-been movie stars, Grant Road prostitutes, gangsters and some formidable regulars at her local beauty salon. Much of the book's appeal lies in the fact that its author finds the glamour as seductive as she does shallow.

Suketa Mehta *Maximum City: Bombay Lost and Found* (Penguin India/Review). This extraordinary portrait of India's biggest city is destined to become the classic account of life in Mumbai. A mixture of memoir, social analysis and travelogue, it reveals in great detail both the chaos and anarchy of the metropolis and its amazing abiltiy to survive and provide structure for its millions of inhabitants. Essential reading, especially if you're planning to spend time here.

Geoffrey Moorhouse *Om* (Sceptre). Not Moorhouse's best, but nevertheless an absorbing account of his 1992 journey to South India's key spiritual centres, following the death of his daughter, with typically well informed asides on history, politics, contemporary culture and religion.

Dervla Murphy *On a Shoestring to Coorg* (Flamingo/Overlook Press). Murphy stays with her young daughter in the little-visited tropical mountains of Coorg, Karnataka. Arguably the most famous modern Indian travelogue, and a manifesto for single-parent budget travel.

François Pryard *Voyage to the East Indies, the Maldives, the Moluccas and Brazil* (Hakluyt Society, India). Goa was Pryard's first port of call after being shipwrecked in the Maldives in 1608, and Albert Gray's translation of the famous French chronicler's travelogue includes a vivid first-hand description of the Portuguese colony during its decadent heyday.

Tahir Shah *Sorcerer's Apprentice* (Weidenfeld & Nicolson). A journey through the weird underworld of occult India. Travelling as apprentice to a master conjurer and illusionist, Shah encounters hangmen, baby renters, skeleton dealers, *sadhus* and charlatans.

David Tomory *Hello Goodnight* (Lonely Planet). An upbeat account of Goa through the ages, enlivened with a seamless bricolage of anecdotes, experiences and encounters distilled from over thirty years of visiting and reading about the region. It's all in here: from Albuquerque to Wendell Rodricks and Jungle Barry to the Nine Bar, crammed into 23 chapters of poppy prose that faithfully capture Goa's essential quirkiness. Some will find it short on analysis, but the book's depiction of contemporary tourist culture, in particular, is spot on.

🏃 **Michael Wood** *The Smile of Murugan* (Viking). A supremely well-crafted and affectionate portrait of Tamil Nadu and its people in the mid-1990s, centred on a video-bus pilgrimage tour of the state's key sacred sites. Indispensable if you plan to explore the deep southeast.

Fiction

David Davidkar *The House of Blue Mangoes* (Phoenix). A beautifully written story, spanning three generations of a South Indian family. Set in the deep south of Tamil Nadu, it evokes village life with such power the reader can almost smell the fruit. As the story unfolds, the effects of social change on the strong family traditions take a toll.

🏃 **Anita Desai** *Feasting and Fasting* (Vintage). This novel by one of India's leading female authors eloquently portrays the frustration of a sensitive young woman stuck in the stifling atmosphere of home while her spoilt brother is packed off to study in America.

Clive James *The Silver Castle* (Picador/Random House). A delightful story of a street urchin's rise from the roadside slums of outer Mumbai to the bright lights of Bollywood. James succeeds in balancing his witty celebration of the Hindi film world with an earnest attempt to dissect the ironies of the Maharashtran capital.

Rohinton Mistry *A Fine Balance* (Faber/Vintage). Two friends seek promotion from their low-caste rural lives to the glitz of the big smoke. A compelling and savage triumph-of-the-human-spirit novel exposing the evils of the caste system and of Indira Gandhi's brutal policies during the Emergency years. Mistry's *Such a Long Journey* (Faber/Vintage) is a highly acclaimed account of a Mumbai Parsi's struggle to maintain personal integrity in the face of betrayals and disappointment.

R.K. Narayan *Gods, Demons and Others* (Minerva/University of Chicago Press). Many of Narayan's beautifully crafted books, full of subtly drawn characters and good-natured humour, are set in the fictional South Indian territory of Malgudi. This one tells classic Indian folktales and popular myths through the voice of a village storyteller.

🏃 **Arundhati Roy** *The God of Small Things* (Flamingo/HarperCollins). Haunting Booker Prize-winning novel about a well-to-do South Indian family caught between the snobberies of high-caste tradition, a colonial past and the diverse personal histories of its members. Seen through the eyes of two children, the assortment of scenes from Keralan life are as memorable as the characters themselves, while the comical and finally tragic turn of events says as much about Indian history as the refrain that became the novel's catchphrase: "things can change in a day."

🏃 **Salman Rushdie** *The Moor's Last Sigh* (Jonathan Cape/Pantheon). Set in Kerala and Mumbai, Rushdie's follow-up to *The Satanic Verses*, a characteristically lurid and spleen-ridden evocation of the Maharashtran capital's paradoxes, caused a stir in India, and was the subject of a defamation case brought by Shiv Sena leader Bal Thackeray.

Manohar Shetty (ed) *Ferry Crossing: Short Stories From Around Goa* (Penguin, India). This long-awaited anthology of Goan fiction, compiled by a local poet, comprises broadly-themed short stories woven around the local landscape and people. Translated from Konkani, Marathi and Portuguese, none is world-class, but they offer fresh perspectives on Goan life, particularly the impact of modernization on villages.

William Sutcliffe *Are You Experienced?* (Penguin). Easy-read send up of a "typical" backpacker trip around India.

Tarun J.Tejpal *The Alchemy of Desire* (Picador). A sensuous sojourn, set mainly in the Himalayas, focusing on two lovers and exploring the depths of human desire. A passionate, poetic and contemporary tale, which uses its characters to explore the nature of modern India.

Biography and autobiography

Charles Allen *Plain Tales from the Raj* (Abacus). First-hand accounts from erstwhile sahibs and memsahibs of British India.

James Cameron *An Indian Summer* (Penguin). Affectionate and humorous description of the veteran British journalist's visit to India in 1972, and his marriage to an Indian woman. An enduring classic.

Louis Fischer *The Life of Mahatma Gandhi* (HarperCollins). First published in 1950, this biography has been re-issued several times since, and quite rightly – veteran American journalist Louis Fischer knew his subject personally, and his book provides an engaging account of Gandhi as a man, politician and propagandist.

M.K. Gandhi *Experiments with Truth* (Penguin/Dover). Gandhi's fascinating records of his life, including the spiritual and moral quests,

changing relationship with the British Government in India, and gradual emergence into the forefront of politics.

Robert Harvey *Clive: The Life and Death of a British Emperor* (Sceptre). The most recent biography of the man often dubbed the "founding father" of the British empire. Although more famous for his role in the battle of Plassey, he pulled off some extraordinary military feats during a formative early spell in the South, based in Madras, which are recounted here in engaging style.

Gregory David Roberts *Shantaram* Whether it's really autobiographical or highly fictionalized, this riveting account of an escaped Australian convict taking refuge in India (mainly Mumbai) is superbly written. The depiction of India, her people and the soul-searching she provokes are first class.

Women

Chantal Boulanger *Saris: An Illustrated Guide to the Indian Art of Draping* (Shakti Press International). The fruit of six years' fieldwork by a French anthropologist, this astonishingly comprehensive book catalogues the numerous styles of sari tying, and their sociocultural

significance (check out their site at ⓦ www.devi.net).

Elizabeth Bumiller *May You Be the Mother of a Hundred Sons* (Fawcett Books/Penguin India). Lucid exploration of the Indian woman's lot, drawn from dozens of first-hand encounters, by an American journalist. Subjects tackled include dowries, arranged marriages, *sati*, magazines and film stars.

Shashi Deshpande *The Binding Vine* (Virago). Disturbing story of one woman's struggle for independence, and her eventual acceptance of the position of servitude traditionally assumed by an Indian wife.

Anees Jung *The Night of the New Moon* (Penguin UK/India). Revealing and poetic stories woven around interviews with Muslim women from all sectors of Indian society. Jung's *Unveiling India* is a compelling account of the life of a Muslim woman who has chosen to break free from orthodoxy.

Vrinda Nabar *Caste as Woman* (Penguin India). Conceived as an Indian counterpart to Greer's *The Female Eunuch*, this is a wry study of the pressures brought to bear during the various stages of womanhood. Drawing on scripture and popular culture, Nabar looks at issues of identity and cultural conditioning.

Viramma, Josiane Racine and Jean-Luc Racine *Viramma: Life of an Untouchable* (Verso). Unique autobiography of an untouchable woman told in her own words (transcribed by French anthropologists), over a fifteen-year period, offering frank, often humorous insights into life in rural Tamil Nadu, the universe and everything.

Development

Julia Cleves Mosse *India: Paths to Development* (Oxfam). Concise analysis of the economic, environmental and political changes affecting India, focusing on the lives of ordinary poor people and the exemplary ways some have succeeded in shaping their own future. The best country brief on the market; only available through Oxfam.

Jeremy Seabrook *Notes from Another India* (Pluto Press). Life histories and interviews – compiled over a year's travelling and skilfully

contextualized. They reveal the everyday problems faced by Indians from a variety of backgrounds, and how grassroots groups have tried to combat them. One of the soundest and most engaging overviews of Indian development issues ever written.

Paul Sainath *Everybody Loves a Good Drought* (Review). A classic report on India's poorest districts, telling the stories of individual villages that are usually lost in a maze of development statistics.

Wildlife and the environment

Grimmet & Inskipp *Birds of Southern India* (Helm, UK). The birders' bible, a beautifully organized, written and illustrated 240-page field guide listing every species known in South India. It's a tailored, region-specific version of the heftier Pocket Guide to the Birds of the Indian Subcontinent by the same authors (Helm), which lists all 1300 species spotted in south Asia.

P.V. Bole and Yogini Vaghini *Field Guide to the Common Trees of India* (OUP, UK/US; o/p). A handy-sized, indispensable tome for serious tree spotters.

Kamierczak and Van Perlo *A Field Guide to the Birds of the Indian Subcontinent* (Pica/Helm, UK). Less popular than Grimmet and Inskipp's competing guide, but just as thorough, expertly drawn and well laid out, with every species named.

Insight Guides *Indian Wildlife* (APA Publications, UK). An excellent all-round introduction to India's wildlife, with scores of superb colour photographs, features on different animals and habitats, and a thorough bibliography.

S. Prater *The Book of Indian Animals* (OUP, UK/Bombay Natural History Society). The most comprehensive single-volume reference book on the subject, although only available in India.

Romulus Whitaker *Common Indian Snakes* (Macmillan, UK). A detailed and illustrated guide to the Subcontinent's snakes.

The arts and architecture

Roy Craven *Indian Art* (Thames & Hudson). Concise general introduction to Indian art, from Harappan seals to Mughal miniatures, with lots of illustrations.

Mohan Khokar *Traditions of Indian Classical Dance* (Clarion Books, India). Detailing the religious and social roots of Indian dance, this lavishly illustrated book, with sections on regional traditions, is an excellent introduction to the subject.

George Michell *The Hindu Temple* (University of Chicago Press). The definitive primer, introducing Hindu temples, their significance, and architectural development.

George Michell and Antonio Martinelli *The Royal Palaces of India*

(Thames & Hudson). Now available in affordable paperback, this overview of India's royal architecture is a recommended coffee-table tome for serious India buffs, memorable less for its lacklustre prose than magnificent images of India's decaying architectural treasures. Photographer Antonio Martinelli's genius is his ability to frame the buildings from novel perspectives, highlighting their natural backdrops and revealing the interiors in natural light.

Bonnie C. Wade *Music in India: the Classical Traditions* (Manmohar, India). A scrupulous catalogue of Indian music, outlining the most commonly used instruments, with illustrations and musical scores.

Religion

Dorf Hartsuiker *Sadhus: Holy Men of India* (Inner Traditions International). The weird world of India's itinerant ascetics exposed in glossy colour photographs and erudite but accessible text.

J.R. Hinnelle (ed) *A Handbook of Living Religions* (Penguin). The beliefs, practices, iconography and historical roots of all India's major faiths explained in accessible language, with full bibliographies to back up each chapter. Deservedly the most popular

book of its kind in print, and an ideal introduction.

Roger Hudson *Travels through Sacred India* (o/p). Knowledgeable and accessible introduction to religious India, with a gazetteer of holy places, listings of ashrams and lively essays on temples, *sadhus*, gurus and sacred sites. Hudson derives much of his material from personal encounters, which bring the subjects to life. Includes sections on all of India's main faiths, and an excellent bibliography.

Stephen P. Huyler *Meeting God* (Yale). This acclaimed introduction provides an unrivalled overview of the beliefs and practices of contemporary Hinduism. Accompanied by text that evokes general principles by focusing on individual acts of worship, Huyler's photographs are in a class of their own, suffused with sublime colours, magical light, and an intimate sense of spirituality.

Sarah McDonald *Holy Cow* (Bantam/Broadway). Very readable account of how a young Aussie journalist grew to love India, concentrating particularly on her personal brushes with the various spiritual traditions of the country. Prone to hyberbole at times, but consistently perceptive and occasionally hilarious.

Wendy O'Flaherty (transl) *Hindu Myths* (Penguin). Translations of key myths from the original Sanskrit texts, providing an insight into the foundations of Hinduism.

Yoga

B.K.S. Iyengar *Yoga: the Path to Holistic Health* (Dorling Kindersley). The definitive guide to yoga by the world's leading teacher, and the only book of its kind recommended by practitioners from across the yoga spectrum. Some 1900 colour photos illustrate step-by-step instructions on how to achieve the postures, and there's a copious introduction giving the philosophical background and history. Too heavy to cart around India with you, but indispensable as a reference tool. A lighter (and much less expensive) version – fully endorsed by the great man, though modelled and written by three of his senior pupils – is *Yoga: the Iyengar Way*, by Silva, Mira and Shyan Mehta (also Dorling Kindersley).

Language

Language

Language

No fewer than seventeen major languages officially recognized by the constitution, numerous minor ones and over a thousand dialects are spoken across India. When Independent India was organized, the present-day states were largely created along linguistic lines, which helps the traveller at least make some sense of the complex situation. Considering the continuing prevalence of English, there is rarely any necessity to speak a local language but some theoretical knowledge of the background and having a few words of one or two can only enhance your visit.

While the main languages of northern India are all Indo-Aryan, in South India the picture changes completely: the four most widely spoken languages, Tamil (Tamil Nadu), Telugu (Andhra Pradesh), Kannada (Karnataka) and Malayalam (Kerala), all belong to the **Dravidian** family, the world's fourth largest group. These and related minor languages grew up quite separately among the non-Aryan peoples of southern India over thousands of years. The exact origins of the Dravidian group have not been established but it's possible that proto-Dravidian was spoken further north in prehistoric times before the people were driven south by the Aryan invaders.

The earliest written records of **Tamil**, the most dominant and oldest language of the family, date back to the second century AD, while **Malayalam**

Indian English

Over the period of the British Raj, Indian English developed its own characteristics, which have survived to the present day. The lilting stress and intonation patterns are the result of crossover from the Indian languages, as is the sometimes bewildering pace of delivery. Likewise, certain vowel sounds, for example the lack of distinction between the pronunciation of "cot" and "caught", and the utterance of some consonants, such as the common retroflex nature of "d", "t" and "r" with the tongue touching the soft palate, are also due to strong local linguistic features.

Indian languages have contributed a good deal of vocabulary to everyday English as well, including words like veranda, bungalow, sandal, pyjamas, shampoo, jungle, turban, caste, chariot, chilli, cardamom and yoga. The traveller to India soon becomes familiar with other terms in common usage that have not spread so widely outside the Subcontinent: *dacoit*, *dhoti*, *bandh*, *panchayat*, *lakh* and *crore* are but a few (see Glossary, p.814, for definitions).

Perhaps the most endearing aspect of Indian English is the way it has preserved forms now regarded as highly old-fashioned in Britain. Addresses such as "Good sir" and questions like "May I know your good name?" are commonplace, as are terms like "tiffin", "cantonment" or "top-hole". This type of usage reaches its apogee in the more flowery expressions of the media that regularly feature in the vast array of daily newspapers published in English. Thus headlines often appear such as "37 perish in mishap", referring to a train crash, or passages like this splendid report of a bank robbery: "The miscreants absconded with the loot in great haste. They repaired immediately to their hideaway, whereupon they divided the iniquitous spoils before vanishing into thin air."

is the most closely related to Tamil but also the newest, dating from the tenth century. In between those two in age, **Telugu** (seventh century) has the second most speakers and **Kannada** (fourth century) follows closely on the heels of Tamil in terms of both antiquity and literary tradition. The beautiful flowing **scripts**, especially the exquisite curls of Kannada, add an aesthetic quality to any tour of the South. They developed in such a way thanks to the palmyra and talipot palm leaves prevalent in the South, which were turned under a firmly held hard stylus – a technique also adopted in Southeast Asian scripts like Burmese, Thai and Khmer.

Of the non-Dravidian languages, two have a substantial number of speakers: **Konkani**, only recognized as the official language of Goa in 1992, is Indo-Aryan and closely related to Marathi; while **Dakhani**, an old form of Urdu, dates back to the fourteenth century and remains the first language in the Muslim communities of Karnataka and Andhra Pradesh, especially noticeable in Hyderabad. Of course, the trained ear may catch numerous **minor languages** or dialects while travelling in South India – indigenous peoples, such as the tribes of the Andaman Islands, all have their own languages, some of very uncertain linguistic origins.

Useful words and phrases

Tamil

Basic words

Aamaam	Yes
Illai	No
Varavaanga	Goodbye (will return again)
Koncham dhayavuseydhu	Please
Nauri	Thanks
Romba nanringa	Thank you very much
Enga	Excuse me
Mannikkavum	Pardon
Vaanaga	Come (inviting someone in)
Neruthu	Stop
Idhu	This
Adhu	That
Evaikal	These
Idhu/adhu ennaanga?	What is this/that?
Romba nallayirukkudhu	Very good
Paravaayillai	Not bad
Pareya	Big
Sarreya	Small
Athekam	Much
Kuvrairu	Little

Time

Enrru	Today
Naalai	Tomorrow
Neerru	Yesterday
Pakal/kezhamai	Day
Eravu	Night
Athekaalai	Early morning
Kaalai	Morning
Matiyam	Afternoon
Maalai	Evening
Thengal	Monday
Chavvaay	Tuesday
Buthan	Wednesday
Veyaacha	Thursday
Valle	Friday
Chane	Saturday
Gnaayetrru/ Kezhama	Sunday

Communicating

Enakku puriya-villaiye	I don't understand
Enakku puriyudhu	I understand

Enakku thamizh theriyaathunga	I don't know Tamil
Inge aangilam therinchavanga yaaraavadhu irukkiraangalaa?	Do you know someone who knows English?
Koncham methuvaa pesuveengalaa?	Could you speak slowly?
Koncham balamaa pesunga?	Could you speak loudly?
Avar enna sollugiraar?	What does he say?

Food and shopping

Enakku pasikkudhul	I am hungry
Enakku dhaga maayirukkudhu	I am thirsty
Athanudaiya vilaienna?	How much is it?
Enakku kapi maththi-ram than vendum	I only want coffee
Koncham kan-pikkireengalaa	Please show me
Kapi	Coffee
Teyneer	Tea
Paal	Milk
Sakkaray	Sugar
Neer	Water
Arese	rice
Satham	Cooked rice
Kaaykarikal	Vegetables
Kane	Cooked vegetables
Thayer	Curd/yoghurt
Thaenkaay	Coconut

Directions

Enge iruk-kuthunga...?	Where is... ?
Turam	Far
Arukkil	Near
Athu ingeyirundhu pakkam thaane?	Is it near here?
Athu ingeyirundhu evvalavu dhoora-mayirukkunga?	How far is it from here?
Enga auto enga kidaikunga?	Where can I get an auto-rickshaw?
Empaa, anga povad hukku evvalavu?	What is the charge to get there?

Vangi enge irukkuthunga?	Where is the bank?
Bas staandu enge irukki radhu?	Where is the bus stand?
Tireyn staashan enge iruk-kuthunga?	Where is the train station?
Kakkoos enge irukkudhu?	Where is the lavatory?
Visaranai enge irukki radhu?	Where is the enquiries (information) office?
... theru enge irukkiradhu?	Where is... road?
Anja lagam	Post office

Numbers

onru	1
eranndu	2
mundru	3
naangu	4
iyendhu	5
aaru	6
aezshu	7
ayttu	8
nbathu	9
patthu	10
pathenonrru	11
panereynndu	12
pathemoonrru	13
pathenaangu	14
pathenainthu	15
pathenaaru	16
pathnaezshu	17
pathenayttu	18
pathenthonbathu	19
erapathu	20
muppathu	30
naarpathu	40
iymbathu	50
arupathu	60
azhupathu	70
aennapathu	80
thonnoorru	90
noorru	100
aayeram	1000
latcham	100,000

Malayalam

Basic words

Aanaate	Yes
Alla	No
Namaste	Hello
Dayavuchetu	Please
Nanni	Thank you
Ksamikkuu	Excuse me
Etra?	How much is it?
Enikka arriyilla	I don't understand
Ninal englisha samsaarik-kumo?	Do you speak English?
Ente pero…	My name is…
Eviteyaannaa…?	Where is… ?
Etra?	How much is it?
Kaappi	Coffee
Chaaya	Tea
Paalu	Milk
Panchasara	Sugar
Marunnu	Medicine
Vellam	Water
Pachakkari	Vegetables
Meen	Fish
Tairu	Curd
Ari	Rice
Eyttappalam	Banana
Teynna	Coconut

Numbers

onnu	1
randu	2
muunu	3
naalu	4
anchu	5
aaru	6
eylu	7
ettu	8
ombatu	9
pattu	10
pationnu	11
pantrantu	12
pati-muunu	13
pati-…	14–18
pattonpattu	19
irupatu	20
irupattonnu	21
irupatti-randu	22
muppatu	30
muppati-yonnu	31
nalpatu	40
anpatu	50
arupatu	60
elapatu	70
enpatu	80
tonnuru	90
nuura	100
aayiram	1000
laksham	100,000

Telugu

Basic words

Awunu	Yes
Kaadu	No
Namaskaram	Goodbye
Dayatesi	Please
Dhanyawadalu	Thank you
Ksamiynchannddi	Excuse me
Enta?	How much is it?
Ni peru eymitti?	What is your name?
Naa peru…	My name is…
Naadu artham kaawattamleydu	I don't understand
Miku angalam vaacha?	Do you speak English?
Ekkada undi… ?	Where is… ?
… Enta duram?	How far is… ?
Pedda	Big
Tsinna	Small
Iroju	Today
Pagalu	Day
Raatri	Night

Kaafii	Coffee	tommidi	9
Tti	Tea	padi	10
Palu	Milk	pada-kondu	11
Chakkera	Sugar	pad-rendu	12
Uppu	Salt	pad-…	13–19
Nillu	Water	iruvay	20
Biyyamu	Rice	iruvay-okatti	21
Chepa	Fish	muppay	30
Kuragayalu	Vegetables	muppay-okati	31
		nalapay	40

Numbers

		yaabay	50
okatti	1	aruvay	60
renddu	2	debbay	70
muddu	3	enabay	80
naalugu	4	tombay	90
aaydu	5	nuru/wanda	100
aaru	6	renddu-wanda	200
eyddu	7	veyi	1000
enimidi	8	laksha	100,000

Kannada

Basic words

		Neeru	Water
		Akki	Rice
Havdu	Yes	Tarakari	Vegetables
Illa	No	Massali	Fish
Namaskara	Hello	Yella-neeru	Coconut water
Dayavittu	Please		

Numbers

Vandanegallu	Thank you		
Kshamisi	Excuse me	ondu	1
Nillisu	Stop	eradu	2
Eshttu?	How much is it?	mooru	3
Nimma hesaru eynu?	What is your name?	naalku	4
		aydu	5
Nanna hesaru…	My name is…	aaru	6
Ellide… ?	Where is… ?	eylu	7
Nanage artha aagalla	I don't understand	entu	8
		ombhattu	9
Neevu english mataaddtiiraa?	Do you speak English?	hattu	10
		hannondu	11
Hagalu	Day	hanneradu	12
Raatri	Night	hadi-mooru	13
Ivattu	Today	hadi-…	14–18
Kaafi	Coffee	hattombhattu	19
Tea	Tea	ippattu	20
Haalu	Milk	ippattondu	21
Sakkare	Sugar	muvattu	30

muvattondu	31	tombattu	90
naalvattu	40	tombattombattu	99
aivattu	50	nooru	100
aravattu	60	ondu saavira	1000
eppattu	70	laksha	100,000
embattu	80		

Konkani

Basic words

Hoee	Yes
Na	No
Paypadta	Hello
Miochay	Goodbye
Upkar kor	Please
Dio borem korunc	Thank you
Upkar korkhi	Excuse me
Kitlay?	How much?
Kitlay poisha lakthele?	How much does it cost?
Mhaka naka tem	I don't want it
Mhaka kay samzona na	I don't understand
Khoy aasa… ?	Where is… ?
Prayia	Beach
Rosto	Road
Kaafi	Coffee
Chai	Tea
Dudh	Milk
Shakhar	Sugar
Shakhar naka	No sugar

Tandul	Rice
Oodak	Water
Nal	Coconut
Adzar	Tender coconut

Numbers

ek	1
dohn	2
teen	3
char	4
paanch	5
soh	6
saht	7
ahrt	8
nou	9
dha	10
vees	20
tees	30
cha-ees	40
po-nas	50
chem-bor	100
ek-azaar	1000
laakh	100,000

Hindi/Urdu

(Not spoken in Tamil Nadu, Kerala, Karnataka [except in the northeast] or much of Andhra Pradesh)

Basic words and phrases

Namaste	Greetings (said with palms together at chest height as in prayer – not used for Muslims)
Aslaam alequm	Greetings (to a Muslim)
Ale qum aslaam	Greetings (in reply)
Phir milenge	We will meet again (goodbye)
Khudaa Haafiz	Goodbye (may god bless you) (to a Muslim)
Aap kaise hain?	How are you? (formal)
Kya hal hai?	How are you? (familiar)
Bhaaii/bhaayaa	Brother (a common address to a stranger)
Didi	Sister
Saaheb	Sir (Sahib)
Haan	Yes

Achhaa	OK/good	char	4
Nahiin	No	paanch	5
Kitna?	How much?	chey	6
Kharaab	Bad	saat	7
Mera nam... hai	My name is...	aatth	8
Aapka naam kya hai?	What is your name? (formal)	now	9
		das	10
Tumhara naam kya hai	What is your name? (familiar)	giara	11
		bara	12
Samaj nahin aayaa	I don't understand	tera	13
Thiik hai	It is OK	chawda	14
Kitna?	How much?	pandra	15
... Kahaan hai?	Where is the... ?	sola	16
Kitnaa duur?	How far?	satra	17
Ruko	Stop	atthara	18
Thero	Wait	unnis	19
Dawaaii	Medicine	bis	20
Dard	Pain	Tis	30
Pet	Stomach	Chaalis	40
Aankh	Eye	Pachaas	50
Naakh	Nose	Saath	60
Kaan	Ear	Sathar	70
Piit	Back	Assii	80
Paao	Foot	Nabbe	90
Numbers		saw	100
		do saw	200
ek	1	hazaar	1000
do	2	laakh	100,000
tin	3		

Literary traditions

The rich will make temples for Shiva,
What shall I, a poor man, do?
My legs are pillars, the body the shrine,
The head a cupola of gold.
Listen, O lord of the meeting rivers,
Things standing shall fall, but the moving shall stay forever

Basavanna (Kannada poet, tenth century AD)

Of South India's main languages, **Tamil** boasts a literary tradition that goes back to pre-Pallava times. According to popular belief, three literary academies or **Sangam** met at Madurai, the earliest of which was attended by the gods and is no longer in existence. The Second Sangam is supposed to have been responsible for the **Tolkappiyam** – a treatise on Tamil grammar – but on close examination this would seem to have appeared later than the **Ettutogai**, the "Eight Anthologies" ascribed to the Third Sangam. Although in archaic Tamil, and barely readable by ordinary Tamils today, the Eight Anthologies, consisting of over two thousand poems composed by around two hundred authors, and

Eight times as long as the *Iliad* and *Odyssey* combined, the **Mahabharata** is the most popular of all Hindu texts. Written around 400 AD, it tells of a feuding *kshatrya* family in upper India (Bharata) during the fourth millennium BC. Like all good epics, the *Mahabharata* recounts a gripping tale, using its characters to illustrate moral values. In essence it attempts to elucidate the position of the warrior castes, the *kshatryas*, and demonstrate that religious fulfilment is as accessible for them as it is for brahmins.

The chief character is **Arjuna**, a superb archer, who with his four brothers – Yudhishtra, Bhima, Nakula and Sahadeva – represents the **Pandava** clan, upholders of righteousness and supreme fighters. Arjuna won his wife **Draupadi** in an archery contest, but wishing to avoid jealousy she agreed to be the shared wife of all five brothers. The Pandava clan is resented by their cousins, the evil **Kauravas**, led by Duryodhana, the eldest son of Dhrtarashtra, ruler of the Kuru kingdom.

When Dhrtarashtra handed his kingdom over to the Pandavas, the Kauravas were far from happy. Duryodhana challenged Yudhishtra (known for his brawn but not his brain) to a gambling contest. The dice game was rigged; Yudhishtra gambled away not only his possessions, but also his kingdom and his shared wife. The Kauravas offered to return the kingdom to the Pandavas if they spent thirteen years in exile, together with their wife, without being recognized. Despite much scheming, the Pandavas succeeded, but on return found that the Kauravas would not fulfil their side of the bargain.

Thus ensued the great battle of the Mahabharata, told in the sixth book, the **Bhagavad Gita** – immensely popular as an independent story. Vishnu descends to earth as **Krishna**, and steps into battle as Arjuna's charioteer. The Bhagavad Gita details the fantastic struggle of the fighting cousins, using magical weapons and brute force. Arjuna is in a dilemma, unable to justify the killing of his own kin in pursuit of a rightful kingdom for himself and his brothers. Krishna consoles him, reminding him that his principal duty, his *varnashradharma*, is as a warrior. What is more, Krishna points out, each man's soul, or *atman*, is eternal, and transmigrates from body to body, so Arjuna need not grieve the death of his cousins. Krishna convinces Arjuna that by fulfilling his *dharma* he not only upholds law and order by saving the kingdom from the grasp of unrighteous rulers, he also serves God in the spirit of devotion (*bhakti*), and thus guarantees himself eternal union with the divine in the blissful state of *moksha*.

The Pandavas finally win the battle, and Yudhishtra is crowned king. Eventually Arjuna's grandson, Pariksit, inherits the throne, and the Pandavas trek to Mount Meru, the mythical centre of the universe and the abode of the gods, where Arjuna finds Krishna's promised *moksha*.

the **Pattuppattu**, or "Ten Songs", represent the greatest works of ancient Tamil literature. Even from this early stage, literature was subject to the Tamil love of classification, and the poems were divided into two main categories: *agam* (internal), dealing with love, and *puram* (external), laudatory poems in praise of the kings.

Although the Aryan influence on Tamil culture was already evident in Sangam literature, the influence of northern civilization grew and, in the sixth century, Hindu, Buddhist and Jain practices were widespread in the far south. Sanskrit left an indelible impression on Tamil literature, and the epic style of Sanskrit was emulated by long narrative poems such as **Shilappadigaram** (*The Jewelled Anklet*). Unlike the Sanskrit epics, however, Tamil poems such as the *Shilappadigaram* deal with the lives of ordinary people – in this case the hapless couple,

Kovalan and Kannagi – and provide an invaluable insight into everyday life of the time. Shortly after the *Shilappadigaram* was written, Sattan, a poet from Madurai, composed the **Manimegalai**, a sort of anthology to the *Shilappadigaram*, but with a philosophical bent and a Buddhist message. The **Shivaga Shidamani**, another great early Tamil epic, was written by the Jain author Tiruttakkadevar and emulates Sanskrit court poetry, but concerns itself with the fantastic heroics of Shivaga (aka Jivaka) who eventually embraces the faith and becomes a monk.

Perhaps the greatest of all Tamil epics is Kamban's **Ramayanam**, composed in the ninth century – not just a translation from the Sanskrit Ramayana (see p.812) but a reinterpretation, with additional story lines, and, on occasion, markedly different interpretations of the main characters. Rama is not always shown as heroic, while Ravana, the demon king, occasionally is. During this period, inspired by the Bhagavad Purana, Vaishnavism became a predominant force in Tamil literature, promoting the new-found hero and man-god, Krishna.

In terms of antiquity, **Kannada**, the language of Karnataka, comes second only to Tamil amongst the Dravidian languages, with its earliest literature dating back to the ninth century AD and evidence from inscriptions that traces the language back to the fourth century. The golden age of Kannada literature was between the tenth and the twelfth centuries, when the poet-saints of the **Virashaiva** sect composed their **Vacanas** or "sayings". Also known as the **Lingayatas**, or "those who wear the *linga*", the Virashaiva poets dedicated their lives to the god Shiva. Although the sect, distinguished by the lingam encased in a small stone casket and worn around the neck, is still in existence, and *vacanas* are still composed, the four greatest poet-saints – **Basvanna**, **Dasimayya**, **Allama** and **Mahadeviyakka** all flourished in the early medieval period. Basvanna, the most illustrious of all, epitomized the spirit of Virashaiva, with an uncompromising view of life and society and a single-minded devotion to the pursuit of truth through homage to Shiva. Basvanna and the Virashaivas rejected caste and believed the true path was open to all; they believed in the equality of women and the right of widows to remarry. They also rejected the highly structured poetic devices of classical Sanskrit poetry and composed simple free verse with a direct and universal philosophical wisdom, causing some to refer to their work as the **Kannada Upanishads**.

The Lingayatas also composed their *vacanas* in **Telugu**, the language of Andhra Pradesh and parts of northern Tamil Nadu and southeast Karnataka. Telugu literature did not really develop until the twelfth century, and not as strongly as those of Tamil and Kannada until the sixteenth century, when it was adopted at the court of the Vijayanagar empire at Hampi (see p.335). Telugu-speaking brahmins – most dedicated Vaishnavas (devotees of the god Vishnu and his incarnations) – were attracted to the court of King Krishna Deva Raya, who was also an accomplished composer of Sanskrit and Telugu verse. After the fall of Vijayanagar, the cultural centre shifted to the court of Tanjore where, despite its location in the heart of Tamil country, Telugu continued to enjoy its privileged status, partly due to the high calibre of religious poets who travelled to Tanjore and the surrounding country. In its heyday Tanjore was home to the merging of devotional literature with theatre, music and dance – nowhere better seen than in the work of the saint, poet and songwriter Tyagaraja (1767–1847), another Telugu-speaking brahmin, who was to leave an indelible impression on Carnatic music (see p.776).

Post Independence issues

With **Independence** it was decided by the government in Delhi that Hindi should become the **official language** of the newly created country. Interestingly, the idea of using Hindustani, a more recent colloquial hybrid of Hindi and Urdu, popular with Gandhi and others in an effort to encourage communal unity during the fight for freedom, was never pursued; this was due to a mixture of political reasons following Partition and the fact that the language lacked the necessary refinement. A drive to teach Hindi in all schools followed and over half the country's population is now reckoned to have a decent working knowledge of the language. However, the **Tamil-led** Dravidian South has

The Ramayana

Rama is the seventh of Vishnu's ten incarnations and the story of his life unfolds in the epic **Ramayana**. Although possibly based on a historic figure, Rama is seen rather more as a representation of the qualities of Vishnu. Rama was the oldest of four sons born to Dasaratha, King of Ayodhya, by his three wives and was heir to the throne. At the time of the coronation one of the king's wives, Kaikeya, seized the moment to ask for the two favours he had previously promised her in a moment of rash appreciation. Her first request was that her oldest son Bharata be anointed king instead of the rightful Rama. Her second request was that Rama be banished to the forest for fourteen years.

Rama, in an exemplary show of filial piety, accepted the unfortunate request and left the city together with his wife **Sita** and brother Laksmana. From their place of exile they continued their long battle against the demon forces led by **Ravana**, the evil king of Lanka. One day Ravana's sister Suparnakhi spotted Rama in the woods and immediately fell in love with him. Being a faithful and ideal husband Rama rebuffed her advances; Suparnakhi as a result tried to kill Sita, seeing her as the obstacle to Rama's heart. Laksmana intervened and cut off her nose and ears in retaliation. Suparnakhi fled to her brother, who mobilized fourteen giants to dispose of Rama. Rama destroyed them single-handedly and then similarly killed 14,000 warriors. Ravana was furious but heeded his advisers who suggested they should fight Rama no longer but just kidnap his beloved, hinting that he would then quickly die of a broken heart. Sita was thus captured and flown by chariot to one of Ravana's palaces on the island of Lanka.

Determined to find Sita, a distraught Rama enlisted the help of **Hanuman**, lord of the monkeys. Rama and Laksmana then start their search for Sita, which leads to the discovery that she is being held on the island of Lanka. Hanuman leaps across the strait and makes his way surreptitiously into Ravana's palace where he hears the evil king trying to persuade Sita to marry him instead of the squeaky clean Rama – offering her the choice of consummation or consumption – become my bride or "My cooks shall mince thy limbs with steel and serve thee for my morning meal." Hanuman reports back to Rama who gathers an army and prepares to attack. This time the monkeys form a bridge across the straits allowing the army to cross and after much fighting Sita is rescued and reunited with the victorious Rama.

During the long journey back to Ayodhya Sita's honour was brought into question. To verify her innocence she asks Laksmana to build a funeral pyre. She prays to **Agni** before stepping into the flames and asks for protection before walking through them. Agni walks her through the fire to a delighted Rama. They march into Ayodhya guided by a trail of lights put there by the local people and this enlightened homecoming has long since been celebrated as **Divali** – the festival of lights. Soon after, Rama is finally crowned as rightful king, his younger brother gladly stepping down.

always been at the forefront of a strong **resistance** to the imposition of Hindi, which has even led to riots over the issue on occasions. The practical outcome of this southern distaste for Hindi is that the vast majority of people living below the Deccan plateau have little or no knowledge of it.

This is where English, the language of the ex-colonists, becomes an important means of communication. Not surprisingly, given India's rich linguistic diversity, **English** remains a **lingua franca** for many people (see box, p.803). It's still the preferred language of law, higher education, much of commerce and the media, and to some degree political dialogue. For many educated Indians, not just those living abroad, it is actually their first language. All this explains why the Anglophone visitor can often soon feel surprisingly at home despite the huge cultural differences. It is not unusual to overhear everyday contact between Indians from different parts of the country being conducted in English, and surprisingly stimulating conversations can often be had, not only with students or business-people, but also with chai-wallahs or shoeshine boys.

Glossary

acharya religious teacher

adivasi official term for tribal person

agarbati incense

ahimsa non-violence

amrita nectar of immortality

anda literally "egg": the spherical part of a stupa

anicut irrigation dam

ankusha elephant goad

anna coin, no longer minted (sixteen annas to one rupee)

apsara heavenly nymph

arak liquor distilled from rice or coconut

arati evening temple puja of lights

asana yogic seating posture; small mat used in prayer and meditation

ashram centre for spiritual learning and religious practice

asura demon

atman soul

avatar reincarnation of Vishnu on earth, in human or animal form

ayurveda ancient system of medicine employing herbs, minerals and massage

baba grandfather; used as a term of respect for an old man

bagh garden, park

baksheesh tip, donation, alms, occasionally meaning a corrupt backhander

bandh or **bundh** a one-day general strike (literally "closed")

bandhani tie-and-dye

baniya another term for a *vaishya*; a money lender

banyan vast fig tree, used traditionally as a meeting place, or shade for teaching and meditating; also, in South India, a cotton vest

baradari summer house, pavilion

bastee slum settlement

basti Jain temple

bazaar commercial centre of town; market

beedi tobacco rolled in a leaf; the "poor man's puff"

begum Muslim princess; Muslim women of high status

betel leaf chewed in paan, with the nut of the areca tree; loosely applies to the nut

bhajan Hindu devotional song

bhakti religious devotion expressed in a personalized or emotional relationship with the deity

bhang pounded marijuana, often mixed in lassis

bhawan (also *bhavan*) palace or residence

bhumi earth, or earth goddess

bhumika storey

bidri inlaid metalwork as produced in Bidar

bindu seed, or the red dot (also *bindi*) worn by women on their foreheads as decoration

bodhi enlightenment

bodhi tree/bo tree peepal tree, associated with the Buddha's enlightenment (*Ficus religiosa*)

bodhisattva Buddhist saint

brahmin a member of the highest caste group; priest

burkha body-covering shawl worn by orthodox Muslim women

burra-sahib colonial official, boss or a man of great importance

cantonment area of town occupied by military quarters

caste social status acquired at birth

cella chamber in temple, often housing the image of a deity

cenotaph ornate tomb

chaat snack

chaddar large head-cover or shawl

chaitya Buddhist temple

chakra discus; focus of power; energy point in the body; wheel, often representing the cycle of death and rebirth

chandan sandalwood paste

chandra moon

chappal sandals or flip-flops (thongs)

charas hashish

charbagh garden divided into quadrants (Mughal style)

charpoi string bed with wooden frame

chaumukh image of four faces placed back to back

chauri fly whisk, regal symbol

chela pupil

cheruvu lake

chhatri tomb; domed temple pavilion

chillum cylindrical clay or wood pipe for smoking *charas* or *ganja*

chital spotted deer

choli short, tight-fitting blouse worn with a sari

chor robber

choultry quarters for pilgrims adjoining South Indian temples

chowgan green in the centre of a town or village

chowk crossroads or courtyard

chowkidar watchman, caretaker

coolie porter, labourer

crore ten million

cupola small delicate dome

dacoit bandit

dalit "oppressed", "out-caste"; the term, introduced by Dr Ambedkar, is preferred by so-called "untouchables" as a description of their social position

danda staff or stick

dargah sufi shrine

darshan vision of a deity or saint; receiving religious teachings

darwaza gateway, door

dawan servant

deg cauldron for food offerings, often found in *dargahs*

deva god

devadasi temple dancer

devi goddess

dhaba food hall selling local dishes

dham important religious site, or a theological college

dharamshala rest house for pilgrims

dharma sense of religious and social duty

(Hindu); the law of nature, teachings, truth (Buddhist)

dhobi man who washes clothes

dholak double-ended drum

dholi sedan chair carried by bearers to hilltop temples

dhoop thick pliable block of strong incense

dhoti white ankle-length cloth worn by males, tied around the waist, and sometimes hitched up through the legs

dhurrie woollen rug

digambara literally "sky-clad": a Jain sect, known for the habit of nudity among monks, though this is no longer commonplace

dikpalas guardians of the four directions

diwan (*dewan*) chief minister

diwan-i-am public audience hall

diwan-i-khas hall of private audience

dowry payment or gift offered in marriage

dravidian of the southern culture

dukka tank and fountain in courtyard of mosque

dupatta scarf or stole worn with a *salwar kamise*

durbar court building; government meeting

dvarpala guardian image placed at sanctuary door

eve-teasing sexual harassment of women, either physical or verbal

fakir ascetic Muslim mendicant

feni Goan spirit, distilled from coconut or cashew fruits

finial capping motif on temple pinnacle

gada mace (the weapon)

gadi throne

gandharvas Indra's heavenly musicians

ganj market

ganja marijuana buds

garbha griha temple sanctuary, literally "womb-chamber"

garh fort

gari vehicle, or car

gaur Indian bison

ghat mountain, landing platform, or steps leading to water

ghazal melancholy Urdu songs

ghee clarified butter

Owing to the very distinct languages of South India, an effective glossary of food terms is almost impossible, but the following list represents a highlight of food and the terms you are likely to come across as a visitor. For a more detailed account, see Basics, p.48.

apa de camarão	spicy prawn pie with a rice and semolina crust (Goa)		fried in the form of a flat cake (universal)
appam	wok-cooked rice pancake speckled with holes, soft in the middle; a speciality of the Malabar coast (Kerala)	**dahi rice**	a pleasant and light preparation – sometimes lightly spiced – of boiled rice with yoghurt (*dahi*)
assado	a spicy pan-cooked beef preparation (Goa)	**dhal**	lentils, pronounced "da'al" and found in one form or another throughout India; in the South often replaced by *sambar* (universal)
bagheri baingan	small aubergine cooked with peanut paste and spices (Hyderabad)	**dhansak**	meat and lentil curry, a Parsi speciality; medium-hot (Mumbai)
bebinca	custard made with *gram* (chickpea) flour, eggs and coconut juice (Goa)	**dosa**	rice pancake – should be crispy; when served with a filling it is called a masala dosa and when plain, a *sada dosa* (Andhra Pradesh, Karnataka, Tamil Nadu, universal)
biriyani	rice baked with saffron or turmeric, whole spices and meat (sometimes vegetables), and often hard-boiled egg (North India and Hyderabad)	**eshtew**	a stew, usually made with chicken, cooked with potatoes in a creamy white sauce of coconut milk (Kerala)
Bombay duck	dried bummalo fish (Mumbai)		
caldeen	fish marinated in vinegar and cooked in a spicy sauce of coconut and chillies (Goa)	**ghee**	clarified butter sometimes used for festive cooking, and often sprinkled onto food before eating (universal)
chapati	unleavened bread made of wholewheat flour and baked on a round griddle-dish called a *tawa* (universal)	**iddli**	steamed rice cake, usually served with *sambar*; *malligi* (jasmine) *iddlis* around Mysore are exceptionally fluffy and so-named because of their lightness – the scent of jasmine is said to
chop	minced meat or vegetable surrounded by breaded mashed potato (universal)		
cutlet	cutlet – often minced meat or vegetable		

jaggery unrefined sugar made from palm sap (universal)

jeera rice rice cooked with cumin seeds (*jeera*) (universal)

karhi leaf a type of laurel from which the leaf and the seeds are widely used as a spice throughout South India (universal)

keema minced meat (Hyderabad)

khichari rice cooked with lentils in various ways, from plain to aromatic and spicy (Hyderabad, universal)

kofta balls of minced vegetables or meat in a curried sauce (Hyderabad)

kokum purple berry with a sweet-sour taste, used as a digestive (Maharashtra)

korma meat braised in yoghurt sauce; mild (Hyderabad)

kulcha fried flat bread to accompany curries (Hyderabad)

molee curry with coconut, usually fish; originally Malay (hence the name); hot (Kerala)

mulligatawny curried vegetable soup, a classic Anglo-Indian dish rumoured to have come from "Mulligan Aunty" but probably South Indian; medium-strength (universal)

naan white, leavened bread kneaded with yoghurt

waft on the breeze (Andhra Pradesh, Karnataka, Kerala, Tamil Nadu, universal)

and baked in a *tandoor* (universal)

pao round Portuguese-style bread roll (Goa)

papad crisp, thin chickpea flour *poppadu* cracker (universal)

paratha wholewheat bread made with butter, rolled thin and griddle-fried; a little bit like a chewy pancake, sometimes stuffed with meat or vegetables (universal)

parota South India's answer to the North Indian paratha – a wheat-flour pancake, for which the dough is oiled and coiled into a spiral before being griddle-fried (universal)

pilau also known as *pilaf*, *pulau* or *pullao*, rice, gently spiced and pre-fried (universal)

pomfret a flatfish especially popular in Mumbai (universal)

puri crispy, puffed-up, deep-fried whole-wheat bread (universal)

rasam spicy, pepper water often drunk to accompany "meals" in the South

roti loosely used term; often just another name for *chapati*, though it should be thicker, chewier and baked in a *tandoor* (universal)

sambar soupy lentil and vegetable curry with asafoetida and tamarind; used as an accompaniment to *dosas*, *iddlis* and *vadas* (universal)

sarpotel	pork dish with liver and heart, cooked in plenty of vinegar and spices (Goa)	**vadai**	also known as *vada*, a doughnut-shaped deep-fried lentil cake, which usually has a hole in its centre
uppma	popular breakfast cereal made from semolina, spices and nuts, and served with *sambar* (Kerala, Tamil Nadu)	**vindaloo**	Goan meat – seasoned with vinegar – (sometimes fish) curry, originally pork; very hot (but not as hot as the kamikaze UK version) (Goa, universal)
uttapam	thick rice pancake often cooked with onions (Karnataka, Tamil Nadu, Kerala, universal)		

giri hill

godown warehouse

gompa Tibetan Buddhist monastery

goonda ruffian

gopi young cattle-tending maidens who feature as Krishna's playmates and lovers in popular mythology

gopura towered temple gateway, common in South India

gumbad dome on mosque or tomb

guru teacher of religion, music, dance, astrology etc

gurudwara Sikh place of worship

haj Muslim pilgrimage to Mecca

hajji Muslim engaged upon, or who has performed, the haj

hammam sunken hot bath, Persian-style

harijan title – "Children of God" – given to "untouchables" by Gandhi

hartal strike (of any length)

haveli elaborately decorated (normally wooden) mansion

hijra eunuch or transvestite

hinayana literally "lesser vehicle": the name given to the original school of Buddhism by later sects

hookah water pipe for smoking strong tobacco or marijuana

howdah bulky elephant saddle, sometimes made of pure silver, and often shaded by a canopy

idgah area laid aside in the west of town for prayers during the Muslim festival Id-ul-Zuhara

imam Muslim leader or teacher

imambara tomb of a Shi'ite saint

imfl Indian-made foreign liquor

indo-saracenic overblown Raj-era architecture that combines Muslim, Hindu, Jain and Western elements

ishwara God

iwan the main (often central) arch in a mosque

jaghidar landowner

jali lattice work in stone, or a pierced screen

jangha the body of a temple

jatakas popular tales about the Buddha's life and teachings

jati sub-caste, determined by family and occupation

jawan soldier

jhuta soiled by lips: food or drink polluted by touch

-ji suffix added to names as a term of respect

jihad striving by Muslims, through battle, to spread their faith

jina another term for the Jain *tirthankara*

johar old practice of self-immolation by women in times of war

jyotirlinga twelve sites sacred by association with Shiva's unbounded lingam of light

kabutar khana pigeon coop

kailasa or **kailash** Shiva's mountain abode

kalam school of painting

kalasha pot-like capping stone characteristic of South Indian temples

kama satisfaction

kamise women's knee-length shirt, worn with *salwar* trousers

karan wallah in Tamil

karma weight of good and bad actions that determine status of rebirth

katcha the opposite of pukka, unacceptable

kathakali traditional Keralan dance-drama

kavad small decorated box that unfolds to serve as a travelling temple

khadi home-spun cotton; Gandhi's symbol of Indian self-sufficiency

khan honorific Muslim title

khol black eyeliner, also known as *surma*

khud valley side

kirtan hymn-singing

kot fort

kothi residence

kotla citadel

kovil term for a Tamil Nadu temple

kshatrya the warrior and ruling caste

kumkum auspicious red powder applied to the forehead as a symbol of blessing and good fortune

kund tank, lake, reservoir

kurta men's long shirt worn over baggy pyjamas

lakh one hundred thousand

lama Tibetan Buddhist monk and teacher

lathi heavy stick used by police

lingam phallic symbol in places of worship representing the god Shiva

liwan cloisters in a mosque

loka realm or world, eg *devaloka*, world of the gods

lunghi male garment; long wrap-around cloth, like a *dhoti*, but usually coloured

madrasa Islamic school

maha- common prefix meaning great or large

mahadeva literally "Great God", a common epithet for Shiva

mahal palace; mansion

maharaja (Maharana, Maharao) king

maharani queen

mahatma great soul

mahayana literally "great vehicle": a Buddhist school that has spread throughout Southeast Asia

mahout elephant driver or keeper

maidan large open space or field

makara crocodile-like animal featuring on temple doorways, and symbolizing the River Ganges; also the vehicle of Varuna, the Vedic god of the sea

mala necklace, garland or rosary

mandala religious diagram

mandapa hall, often with many pillars, used for various purposes, eg *kalyan(a) mandapa* for wedding ceremonies and *nata mandapa* for dance performances

mandi market

mandir temple

mantra sacred verse or word

maqbara Muslim tomb

marg road

masjid mosque

mataji respectful way to address an old lady (literally "mother")

math Hindu or Jain monastery

maund old unit of weight (roughly 20kg)

mayur peacock

medhi terrace

mehendi henna

mela festival

memsahib respectful address to European woman

mihrab niche in the wall of a mosque indicating the direction of prayer (to Mecca); in India the *mihrab* is in the west wall

mimbar pulpit in a mosque from which the Friday sermon is read

minaret high slender tower, characteristic of mosques

mithuna sexual union, or amorous couples in Hindu and Buddhist figurative art

moksha blissful state of freedom from rebirth aspired to by Hindus and Jains

mor peacock

mudra hand gesture used in Vedic rituals, featuring in Hindu, Buddhist and Jain art and dance, and symbolizing teachings and life stages of the Buddha

muezzin man behind the voice calling Muslims to prayer from a mosque

mullah Muslim teacher and scholar

mund village

mundu male garment like *lunghi*

mutt Hindu or Jain monastery

nadi river

naga mythical serpent

nala stream gorge in the mountains

natak drama

natya (also *natyam*) dance

nautch performance by dancing girls

nawab Muslim landowner or prince

nilgai blue bull

nirvana Buddhist equivalent of *moksha*

niwas building or house

nizam title of Hyderabad rulers

nullah stream gorge in the mountains

om (aka *aum*) symbol denoting the origin of all things, and ultimate divine essence, used in meditation by Hindus and Buddhists

paan betel nut, lime, calcium and aniseed wrapped in a leaf and chewed as a digestive; it is mildly addictive

pada foot, or base, also a poetic metre

padma lotus; another name for the goddess Lakshmi

pagoda multistoreyed Buddhist monument

paise small unit of currency (100 paisa = 1 rupee)

palanquin enclosed sedan chair, shouldered by four men

pali original language of early Buddhist texts

palli old mosque or church in Kerala

panchayat village council

panda pilgrims' priest

parikrama ritual circumambulation around a temple, shrine or mountain

parsi Zoroastrian

pir Muslim holy man

pole fortified gate

pradakshina patha processional path circling a monument or sanctuary

prakara enclosure or courtyard in a South Indian temple

pranayama breath control, used in meditation

prasad food blessed in temple sanctuaries and shared among devotees

prayag auspicious confluence of two or more rivers

puja worship

pujari priest

pukka correct and acceptable, in the very English sense of "proper"

punya religious merit

Puranas Sacred texts, written in Sanskrit, which elaborate the myths and legends of the Vedas

purdah seclusion of Muslim women inside the home, and the general term for wearing a veil

purnima full moon

purohit priest

qabr Muslim grave

qawwali devotional singing popular among sufis

qila fort

raga or **raag** series of notes forming the basis of a melody

raj rule; monarchy; in particular the period of British imperial rule 1857–1947

raja king

rakshasa demon (demoness: *rakshasi*)

rangoli geometrical pattern of rice powder laid before houses and temples

rath processional temple chariot of South India

rawal chief priest (Hindu)

rishi "seer"; philosophical sage or poet

rudraksha beads used to make Shiva rosaries

Sabha assembly or – particularly in a Tamil context – musical venue

sadhu Hindu holy man with no caste or family ties

sagar lake

sahib respectful title for gentlemen; general term of address for European men

salabhanjika wood nymph

salwar kamise long shirt and baggy ankle-hugging trousers worn by Muslim women

samadhi final enlightenment; a site of death or burial of a saint

samsara cyclic process of death and rebirth

sangam sacred confluence of two or more rivers, or an academy

sangeet music

sannyasin homeless ascetic without possessions (Hindu)

sarai resting place for caravans and travellers who once followed the trade routes through Asia

sari usual dress for Indian women: a length of cloth wound around the waist and draped over one shoulder

sarovar pond or lake

sati one who sacrifices her life on her husband's funeral pyre in emulation of Shiva's wife; no longer a common practice, and officially illegal

satsang teaching given by a religious figurehead

satyagraha literally "grasping truth": Gandhi's campaign of non-violent protest

scheduled castes official name for "untouchables"

sepoy an Indian soldier in European service

seth merchant or businessman

seva voluntary service in a temple or community

shaivite Hindu recognizing Shiva as the supreme god

shankha conch, symbol of Vishnu

shastra treatise

shikar hunting

shikhara temple tower or spire

shishya pupil

shloka verse from a Sanskrit text

shri respectful prefix; another name for Lakshmi

shudra the lowest of the four castes or varnas; servant

singha lion

soma medicinal herb with hallucinogenic properties used in early Vedic and Zoroastrian rituals

stambha pillar, or flagstaff

sthala site sacred for its association with legendary events

stupa large hemispherical mound, representing the Buddha's presence, and often protecting relics of the Buddha or a Buddhist saint

surma black eyeliner, also known as *kohl*

surya the sun, or sun god

sutra (*sutta*) literally "thread": verse in Sanskrit and Pali texts

svetambara "white-clad" sect of Jainism, that accepts nuns and shuns nudity

swami title for a holy man

swaraj "self-rule"; synonym for independence, coined by Gandhi

tala rhythmic cycle in classical music; in sculpture a tala signifies one face-length; in architecture a storey

taluka district

tandava vigorous, male form of dance; the dance of Shiva Nataraja

tandoor clay oven

tapas literally "heat": physical and mental austerities

tempo three-wheeled taxi

thali combination of vegetarian dishes, chutneys, pickles, rice and bread served, especially in South India, as a single meal; the metal plate on which a meal is served

tharavad ancestral Keralan aristocratic home – often made of teak, with gabled tiled roofs, and incorporating rice granaries

theravada "Doctrine of the Elders": the original name for early Buddhism, which persists today in Sri Lanka and Thailand

tiffin light meal

tiffin carrier stainless steel set of tins used for carrying meals

tika devotional powder-mark Hindus wear on forehead, usually after puja

tilak red dot smeared on the forehead during worship, and often used cosmetically

tirtha river crossing considered sacred by Hindus, or the transition from the mundane world to heaven; a place of pilgrimage for Jains

tirthankara "ford-maker" or "crossing-maker": an enlightened Jain teacher who is deified – 24 appear every 300 million years

tola the weight of a silver rupee: 180 grains, or approximately 11.6g

tonga two-wheeled horse-drawn cart

topi cap

torana arch, or free-standing gateway of two pillars linked by an elaborate arch

trimurti the Hindu trinity

trishula Shiva's trident

tuk fortified enclosure of Jain shrines or temples

tulku reincarnated teacher of Tibetan Buddhism

untouchables members of the lowest strata of society, considered polluting to all higher castes

urs Muslim saint's day festival

vahana the "vehicle" of a deity; the bull Nandi is Shiva's vahana

vaishya member of the merchant and trading caste group

varna literally "colour": one of four hierarchical social categories – brahmins, *kshatryas, vaishyas* and *shudras*

vedas sacred texts of early Hinduism

vedika railing around a stupa

vihara Buddhist or Jain monastery

vilasa hall or palace

vimana tower over temple sanctuary

wada mansion or palace

wallah suffix implying occupation, eg dhobi-wallah, rickshaw-wallah

wazir chief minister to the king

yagna Vedic sacrificial ritual

yaksha pre-Vedic folklore figure connected with fertility and incorporated into later Hindu iconography

yakshi female *yaksha*

yali mythical lion

yantra cosmological pictogram, or model used in an observatory

yatra pilgrimage

yatri pilgrim

yogi sadhu or priestly figure possessing occult powers gained through the practice of yoga (female: *yogini*)

yoni symbol of the female sexual organ, set around the base of the lingam in temple shrines

yuga aeon: the present age is the last in a cycle of four *yugas, kali-yuga*, a "black age" of degeneration and spiritual decline

zamindar landowner

zenana women's quarters

Travel store